BMW
5 Series
(E39)

Service Manual
525i, 528i, 530i, 540i
Sedan, Sport Wagon
1997, 1998, 1999, 2000, 2001, 2002

[B] BentleyPublishers
.com

BENTLEY PUBLISHERS™ | Automotive Reference™

Bentley Publishers, a division of Robert Bentley, Inc.
1734 Massachusetts Avenue
Cambridge, MA 02138 USA
800-423-4595 / 617-547-4170

Information that makes the difference®

BentleyPublishers.com

Technical contact information

We welcome your feedback. Please submit corrections and additions to our BMW technical discussion forum at:

http://www.BentleyPublishers.com

Errata information

We will evaluate submissions and post appropriate editorial changes online as text errata or tech discussion. Appropriate errata will be incorporated with the book text in future printings. Read errata information for this book before beginning work on your vehicle. See the following web address for additional information:

http://www.BentleyPublishers.com/errata/

WARNING—important safety notice

Do not use this manual unless you are familiar with basic automotive repair procedures and safe workshop practices. This manual illustrates the workshop procedures required for most service work. It is not a substitute for full and up-to-date information from the vehicle manufacturer or for proper training as an automotive technician. Note that it is not possible for us to anticipate all of the ways or conditions under which vehicles may be serviced or to provide cautions as to all of the possible hazards that may result.

The vehicle manufacturer will continue to issue service information updates and parts retrofits after the editorial closing of this manual. Some of these updates and retrofits will apply to procedures and specifications in this manual. We regret that we cannot supply updates to purchasers of this manual.

We have endeavored to ensure the accuracy of the information in this manual. Please note, however, that considering the vast quantity and the complexity of the service information involved, we cannot warrant the accuracy or completeness of the information contained in this manual.

FOR THESE REASONS, NEITHER THE PUBLISHER NOR THE AUTHOR MAKES ANY WARRANTIES, EXPRESS OR IMPLIED, THAT THE INFORMATION IN THIS BOOK IS FREE OF ERRORS OR OMISSIONS, AND WE EXPRESSLY DISCLAIM THE IMPLIED WARRANTIES OF MERCHANTABILITY AND OF FITNESS FOR A PARTICULAR PURPOSE, EVEN IF THE PUBLISHER OR AUTHOR HAVE BEEN ADVISED OF A PARTICULAR PURPOSE, AND EVEN IF A PARTICULAR PURPOSE IS INDICATED IN THE MANUAL. THE PUBLISHER AND AUTHOR ALSO DISCLAIM ALL LIABILITY FOR DIRECT, INDIRECT, INCIDENTAL OR CONSEQUENTIAL DAMAGES THAT RESULT FROM ANY USE OF THE EXAMPLES, INSTRUCTIONS OR OTHER INFORMATION IN THIS BOOK. IN NO EVENT SHALL OUR LIABILITY WHETHER IN TORT, CONTRACT OR OTHERWISE EXCEED THE COST OF THIS MANUAL.

Your common sense and good judgment are crucial to safe and successful service work. Read procedures through before starting them. Think about whether the condition of your car, your level of mechanical skill, or your level of reading comprehension might result in or contribute in some way to an occurrence which might cause you injury, damage your car, or result in an unsafe repair. If you have doubts for these or other reasons about your ability to perform safe repair work on your car, have the work done at an authorized BMW dealer or other qualified shop.

Part numbers listed in this manual are for identification purposes only, not for ordering. Always check with your authorized BMW dealer to verify part numbers and availability before beginning service work that may require new parts.

Before attempting any work on your BMW, read the **001 General Warnings and Cautions**, and any **WARNING** or **CAUTION** that accompanies a procedure in the service manual. Review the **WARNINGS** and **CAUTIONS** each time you prepare to work on your BMW.

Special tools required to perform certain service operations are identified in the manual and are recommended for use. Use of tools other than those recommended in this service manual may be detrimental to the car's safe operation as well as the safety of the person servicing the car.

Copies of this manual may be purchased from most automotive accessories and parts dealers specializing in BMW automobiles, from selected booksellers, or directly from the publisher.

This manual was published by Robert Bentley, Inc., Publishers. BMW has not reviewed and does not vouch for the accuracy of the technical specifications and procedures described in this manual.

Library of Congress Cataloging-in-Publication Data

BMW 5 Series (E39) : service manual : 525i, 528i, 530i, 540i, sedan, sport wagon, 1997, 1998, 1999, 2000, 2001, 2002
p. cm.
Includes index.
ISBN 0-8376-0317-X (pbk)
1. BMW 5 series automobiles--Maintenance and repair--Handbooks, manuals, etc. I. Robert Bentley, Inc.
TL215.B25B623 2003
629.28'722--dc23

2003052231

Bentley Stock No. B502

Editorial closing 08/03

09 08 07 06   10 9 8 7 6 5 4 3

The paper used in this publication is acid free and meets the requirements of the National Standard for Information Sciences–Permanence of Paper for Printed Library Materials. ∞

Manufactured in the United States of America

You are now in **Volume 2**

Selected Books and Repair Information from Bentley Publishers

Driving

Alex Zanardi - My Sweetest Victory
Alex Zanardi with Gianluca Gasparini
ISBN 0-8376-1249-7

The Unfair Advantage
Mark Donohue ISBN 0-8376-0073-1(hc); 0-8376-0069-3(pb)

Going Faster! Mastering the Art of Race Driving
The Skip Barber Racing School
ISBN 0-8376-0227-0

A French Kiss With Death: Steve McQueen and the Making of *Le Mans*
Michael Keyser ISBN 0-8376-0234-3

Sports Car and Competition Driving
Paul Frère with foreword *by Phil Hill*
ISBN 0-8376-0202-5

Engineering / Reference

Supercharged! Design, Testing, and Installation of Supercharger Systems
Corky Bell ISBN 0-8376-0168-1

Maximum Boost: Designing, Testing, and Installing Turbocharger Systems
Corky Bell ISBN 0-8376-0160-6

Bosch Fuel Injection and Engine Management
Charles O. Probst, SAE ISBN 0-8376-0300-5

Race Car Aerodynamics
Joseph Katz ISBN 0-8376-0142-8

Road & Track Illustrated Automotive Dictionary
John Dinkel ISBN 0-8376-0143-6

Scientific Design of Exhaust and Intake Systems
Philip H. Smith 0-8376-0309-9

Alfa Romeo

Alfa Romeo All-Alloy Twin Cam Companion 1954–1994
Pat Braden ISBN 0-8376-0275-0

Alfa Romeo Owner's Bible™
Pat Braden ISBN 0-8376-0707-8

Audi

Audi A4 Repair Manual: 1996–2001, 1.8L turbo, 2.8L, including Avant and quattro
Bentley Publishers ISBN 0-8376-0371-4

Audi A6 Sedan 1998–2004, Avant 1999–2004, allroad quattro 2001–2005, S6 Avant 2002-2004, RS6 2003-2004 Official Factory Repair Manual on CD-ROM
Audi of America ISBN 978-0-8376-1257-7

BMW

BMW Z3 Service Manual: 1996–2002, including Z3 Roadster, Z3 Coupe, M Roadster, M Coupe
Bentley Publishers ISBN 0-8376-1250-0

BMW 3 Series (E46) Service Manual: 1999–2005, M3, 323i, 325i, 325xi, 328i, 330i, 330xi, Sedan, Coupe, Convertible, Wagon
Bentley Publishers ISBN 0-8376-1277-2

BMW 3 Series (E36) Service Manual: 1992–1998, 318i/is/iC, 323is/iC, 325i/is/iC, 328i/is/iC, M3
Bentley Publishers ISBN 0-8376-0326-9

BMW 5 Series Service Manual: 1997–2002 525i, 528i, 530i, 540i, Sedan, Sport Wagon
Bentley Publishers ISBN 0-8376-0317-X

BMW 6 Series Enthusiast's Companion™
Jeremy Walton ISBN 0-8376-0193-2

BMW 7 Series Service Manual: 1988–1994, 735i, 735iL, 740i, 740iL, 750iL
Bentley Publishers ISBN 0-8376-0328-5

Bosch

Bosch Automotive Handbook 6th Edition
Robert Bosch, GmbH ISBN 0-8376-1243-8

Bosch Handbook for Automotive Electrics and Electronics
Robert Bosch, GmbH ISBN 0-8376-1050-8

Bosch Handbook for Diesel-Engine Management
Robert Bosch, GmbH ISBN 0-8376-1051-6

Bosch Handbook for Gasoline-Engine Management
Robert Bosch, GmbH ISBN 0-8376-1052-4

Chevrolet

Corvette Illustrated Encyclopedia
Tom Benford ISBN 0-8376-0928-3

Corvette Fuel Injection & Electronic Engine Management 1982–2001:
Charles O. Probst, SAE ISBN 0-8376-0861-9

Zora Arkus-Duntov: The Legend Behind Corvette
Jerry Burton ISBN 0-8376-0858-9

Chevrolet by the Numbers 1965–1969: The Essential Chevrolet Parts Reference
Alan Colvin ISBN 0-8376-0956-9

Ford

Ford Fuel Injection and Electronic Engine Control: 1988–1993
Charles O. Probst, SAE ISBN 0-8376-0301-3

The Official Ford Mustang 5.0 Technical Reference & Performance Handbook: 1979–1993
Al Kirschenbaum ISBN 0-8376-0210-6

Jeep

Jeep CJ Rebuilder's Manual: 1972-1986
Moses Ludel ISBN 0-8376-0151-7

Jeep Owner's Bible™, Third Edition
Moses Ludel ISBN 0-8376-1117-2

Mercedes-Benz

Mercedes-Benz Technical Companion™
Bentley Publishers ISBN 0-8376-1033-8

Mercedes-Benz E-Class (W124) Owner's Bible™ : 1986–1995
Bentley Publishers ISBN 0-8376-0230-0

MINI Cooper

MINI Cooper Service Manual: 2002-2004
Bentley Publishers ISBN 0-8376-1068-0

Porsche

Porsche: Excellence Was Expected
Karl Ludvigsen ISBN 0-8376-0235-1

Porsche 911 Carrera Service Manual: 1984–1989
Bentley Publishers ISBN 0-8376-0291-2

Porsche 911 Enthusiast's Companion™
Adrian Streather ISBN 0-8376-0293-9

Porsche 911 SC Coupe, Targa, and Cabriolet Service Manual: 1978–1983
Bentley Publishers ISBN 0-8376-0290-4

Volkswagen

Battle for the Beetle
Karl Ludvigsen ISBN 0-8376-0071-5

Jetta, Golf, GTI Service Manual: 1999–2005 1.8L turbo, 1.9L TDI diesel, PD diesel, 2.0L gasoline, 2.8L VR6
Bentley Publishers ISBN 0-8376-1251-9

New Beetle Service Manual: 1998–2002 1.8L turbo, 1.9L TDI diesel, 2.0L gasoline
Bentley Publishers ISBN 0-8376-0376-5

New Beetle 1998–2005, New Beetle Convertible 2003-2005 Official Factory Repair Manual on CD-ROM
Volkswagen of America ISBN 978-0-8376-1265-2

Passat Service Manual: 1998–2004, 1.8L turbo, 2.8L V6, 4.0L W8, including wagon and 4MOTION
Bentley Publishers ISBN 0-8376-0369-2

Passat, Passat Wagon 1998–2005 Official Factory Repair Manual on CD-ROM
Volkswagen of America ISBN 978-0-8376-1267-6

Golf, GTI, Jetta 1993–1999, Cabrio 1995–2002 Official Factory Repair Manual on CD-ROM
Volkswagen of America ISBN 978-0-8376-1263-8

Jetta, Golf, GTI: 1993–1999, Cabrio: 1995-2002 Service Manual
Bentley Publishers ISBN 0-8376-0366-8

EuroVan Official Factory Repair Manual: 1992–1999
Volkswagen of America ISBN 0-8376-0335-8

BentleyPublishers™.com

Automotive Reference

Bentley Publishers has published service manuals and automobile books since 1950. Please write to us at 1734 Massachusetts Ave., Cambridge, MA 02138, visit our web site, or call 1-800-423-4595 for a free copy of our catalog.

Foreword

For the BMW owner with basic mechanical skills and for independent auto service professionals, this manual includes many of the specifications and procedures that were available in an authorized BMW dealer service department as this manual went to press. The BMW owner with no intention of working on his or her car will find that owning and referring to this manual will make it possible to be better informed and to more knowledgeably discuss repairs with a professional automotive technician.

The BMW owner intending to do maintenance and repair should have screwdrivers, a set of metric wrenches and sockets, and metric Allen and Torx wrenches, since these basic hand tools are needed for most of the work described in this manual. Many procedures will also require a torque wrench to ensure that fasteners are tightened properly and in accordance with specifications. Additional information on basic tools and other tips can be found in **010 General**. In some cases, the text refers to special tools that are recommended or required to accomplish adjustments or repairs. These tools are usually identified by their BMW special tool number and illustrated.

Disclaimer

We have endeavored to ensure the accuracy of the information in this manual. When the vast array of data presented in the manual is taken into account, however, no claim to infallibility can be made. We therefore cannot be responsible for the result of any errors that may have crept into the text. Please also read the **Important Safety Notice** on the copyright page at the beginning of this book.

Thoroughly read each procedure, **001 General Warnings and Cautions** at the front of the book and those that accompany the procedure Reading a procedure before beginning work will help you determine in advance the need for specific skills, identify hazards, prepare for appropriate capture and handling of hazardous materials, and the need for particular tools and replacement parts such as gaskets.

Bentley Publishers encourages comments from the readers of this manual with regard to errors, and/or suggestions for improvement of our product. These communications have been and will be carefully considered in the preparation of this and other manuals. If you identify inconsistencies in the manual, you may have found an error. Please contact the publisher and we will endeavor to post applicable corrections on our website. Posted corrections (errata) should be reviewed before beginning work. Please see the following web address:

`http://www.BentleyPublishers.com/errata/`

BMW offers extensive warranties, especially on components of the fuel delivery and emission control systems. Therefore, before deciding to repair a BMW that may be covered wholly or in part by any warranties issued by BMW of North America, LLC, consult your authorized BMW dealer. You may find that the dealer can make the repair either free or at minimum cost. Regardless of its age, or whether it is under warranty, your BMW is both an easy car to service and an easy car to get serviced. So if at any time a repair is needed that you feel is too difficult to do yourself, a trained BMW technician is ready to do the job for you.

Bentley Publishers

Please read these warnings and cautions before proceeding with maintenance and repair work.

WARNINGS—
See also *CAUTIONS*

- Some repairs may be beyond your capability. If you lack the skills, tools and equipment, or a suitable workplace for any procedure described in this manual, we suggest you leave such repairs to an authorized BMW dealer service department or other qualified shop.
- Do not re-use any fasteners that are worn or deformed in normal use. Many fasteners are designed to be used only once and become unreliable and may fail when used a second time. This includes, but is not limited to, nuts, bolts, washers, self-locking nuts or bolts, circlips and cotter pins. Always replace these fasteners with new parts.
- Never work under a lifted car unless it is solidly supported on stands designed for the purpose. Do not support a car on cinder blocks, hollow tiles or other props that may crumble under continuous load. Never work under a car that is supported solely by a jack. Never work under the car while the engine is running.
- If you are going to work under a car on the ground, make sure that the ground is level. Block the wheels to keep the car from rolling. Disconnect the battery negative (–) terminal (ground strap) to prevent others from starting the car while you are under it.
- Never run the engine unless the work area is well ventilated. Carbon monoxide kills.
- Rings, bracelets and other jewelry should be removed so that they cannot cause electrical shorts, get caught in running machinery, or be crushed by heavy parts.
- Tie long hair behind your head. Do not wear a necktie, a scarf, loose clothing, or a necklace when you work near machine tools or running engines. If your hair, clothing, or jewelry were to get caught in the machinery, severe injury could result.
- Do not attempt to work on your car if you do not feel well. You increase the danger of injury to yourself and others if you are tired, upset or have taken medication or any other substance that may keep you from being fully alert.
- Illuminate your work area adequately but safely. Use a portable safety light for working inside or under the car. Make sure the bulb is enclosed by a wire cage. The hot filament of an accidentally broken bulb can ignite spilled fuel, vapors or oil.
- Catch draining fuel, oil, or brake fluid in suitable containers. Do not use food or beverage containers that might mislead someone into drinking from them. Store flammable fluids away from fire hazards. Wipe up spills at once, but do not store the oily rags, which can ignite and burn spontaneously.
- Always observe good workshop practices. Wear goggles when you operate machine tools or work with battery acid. Gloves or other protective clothing should be worn whenever the job requires working with harmful substances.
- Greases, lubricants and other automotive chemicals contain toxic substances, many of which are absorbed directly through the skin. Read the manufacturer's instructions and warnings carefully. Use hand and eye protection. Avoid direct skin contact
- Disconnect the battery negative (–) terminal (ground strap) whenever you work on the fuel system or the electrical system. Do not smoke or work near heaters or other fire hazards. Keep an approved fire extinguisher handy.
- Friction materials (such as brake pads or shoes or clutch discs) contain asbestos fibers or other friction materials. Do not create dust by grinding, sanding, or by cleaning with compressed air. Avoid breathing dust. Breathing any friction material dust can lead to serious diseases and may result in death.
- Batteries give off explosive hydrogen gas during charging. Keep sparks, lighted matches and open flame away from the top of the battery. If hydrogen gas escaping from the cap vents is ignited, it will ignite gas trapped in the cells and cause the battery to explode.
- Connect and disconnect battery cables, jumper cables or a battery charger only with the ignition switched off. Do not disconnect the battery while the engine is running.
- Do not quick-charge the battery (for boost starting) for longer than one minute. Wait at least one minute before boosting the battery a second time.
- Do not allow battery charging voltage to exceed 16.5 volts. If the battery begins producing gas or boiling violently, reduce the charging rate. Boosting a sulfated battery at a high charging rate can cause an explosion.
- The air conditioning system is filled with chemical refrigerant, which is hazardous. The A/C system should be serviced only by trained technicians using approved refrigerant recovery/recycling equipment, trained in related safety precautions, and familiar with regulations governing the discharging and disposal of automotive chemical refrigerants.
- Do not expose any part of the A/C system to high temperatures such as open flame. Excessive heat will increase system pressure and may cause the system to burst.
- Some aerosol tire inflators are highly flammable. Be extremely cautious when repairing a tire that may have been inflated using an aerosol tire inflator. Keep sparks, open flame or other sources of ignition away from the tire repair area. Inflate and deflate the tire at least four times before breaking the bead from the rim. Completely remove the tire from the rim before attempting any repair.
- Cars covered by this manual are equipped with a supplemental restraint system (SRS), that automatically deploys airbags and pyrotechnic seat belt tensioners in the event of a frontal or side impact. These are explosive devices. Handled improperly or without adequate safeguards, they can be accidently activated and cause serious injury.
- The ignition system produces high voltages that can be fatal. Avoid contact with exposed terminals and use extreme care when working on a car with the engine running or the ignition switched on.
- Place jack stands only at locations specified by manufacturer. The vehicle lifting jack supplied with the vehicle is intended for tire changes only. A heavy duty floor jack should be used to lift vehicle before installing jack stands. See **010 General**.
- Battery acid (electrolyte) can cause severe burns. Flush contact area with water, seek medical attention.
- Aerosol cleaners and solvents may contain hazardous or deadly vapors and are highly flammable. Use only in a well ventilated area. Do not use on hot surfaces (engines, brakes, etc.).
- Do not remove coolant reservoir or radiator cap with the engine hot. Danger of burns and engine damage.

Continued on next page

Please read these warnings and cautions before proceeding with maintenance and repair work.

CAUTIONS—
See also *WARNINGS*

- If you lack the skills, tools and equipment, or a suitable workshop for any procedure described in this manual, we suggest you leave such repairs to an authorized BMW dealer or other qualified shop.
- BMW is constantly improving its cars and sometimes these changes, both in parts and specifications, are made applicable to earlier models. Therefore, part numbers listed in this manual are for reference only. Always check with your authorized BMW dealer parts department for the latest information.
- Before starting a job, make certain that you have all the necessary tools and parts on hand. Read all the instructions thoroughly, and do not attempt shortcuts. Use tools appropriate to the work and use only replacement parts meeting BMW specifications. Makeshift tools, parts and procedures will not make good repairs.
- Use pneumatic and electric tools only to loosen threaded parts and fasteners. Never use these tools to tighten fasteners, especially on light alloy parts. Always use a torque wrench to tighten fasteners to the tightening torque specification listed.
- Be mindful of the environment and ecology. Before you drain the crankcase, find out the proper way to dispose of the oil. Do not pour oil onto the ground, down a drain, or into a stream, pond or lake. Dispose of in accordance with Federal, State and Local laws.
- The control module for the anti-lock brake system (ABS) cannot withstand temperatures from a paint-drying booth or a heat lamp in excess of 203° F (95° C) and should not be subjected to temperatures in excess of 185° F (85° C) for more than two hours.
- Before doing any electrical welding on cars equipped with ABS, disconnect the battery negative (–) terminal (ground strap) and the ABS control module connector.
- Always make sure ignition is off before disconnecting battery.
- Label battery cables before disconnecting. On some models, battery cables are not color coded.
- Disconnecting the battery may erase fault code(s) stored in control module memory. Using special BMW diagnostic equipment, check for fault codes prior to disconnecting the battery cables. If the Malfunction Indicator Light (MIL) is illuminated, see **OBD On-Board Diagnostics**. This light is identified as the Check Engine light (1997-2000 models) or Service Engine Soon light (2001 and later models). If any other system faults have been detected (indicated by an illuminated warning light), see an authorized BMW dealer.
- If a normal or rapid charger is used to charge battery, the battery must be disconnected and removed from the vehicle in order to avoid damaging paint and upholstery.
- Do not quick-charge the battery (for boost starting) for longer than one minute. Wait at least one minute before boosting the battery a second time.
- Connect and disconnect a battery charger only with the battery charger switched off.
- Sealed or "maintenance free" batteries should be slow-charged only, at an amperage rate that is approximately 10% of the battery's ampere-hour (Ah) rating.
- Do not allow battery charging voltage to exceed 16.5 volts. If the battery begins producing gas or boiling violently, reduce the charging rate. Boosting a sulfated battery at a high charging rate can cause an explosion.

600 Electrical System - General

General

A brief description of the principal parts of the electrical system is presented here. Also covered here are basic electrical system troubleshooting tips.

See also **121 Battery, Starter, Alternator**.

Electrical test equipment

Many electrical tests described in this manual call for measuring voltage, current, or resistance using a digital multimeter. Digital meters are preferred for precise measurements and for electronics work because they are generally more accurate than analog meters. An analog meter (swing-needle) may draw enough current to damage sensitive electronic components.

An LED test light is a safe, inexpensive tool that can be used to perform many simple electrical tests that would otherwise require a digital multimeter. The LED indicates when voltage is present between any two test-points in a circuit.

The integrated safety, comfort, security and handling systems on E39 cars are designed with self-diagnostic capabilities. The quickest way to diagnose many problems is to start out with a scan tool read out of Diagnostic Trouble Codes (DTCs). See On-Board Diagnostics at rear of manual.

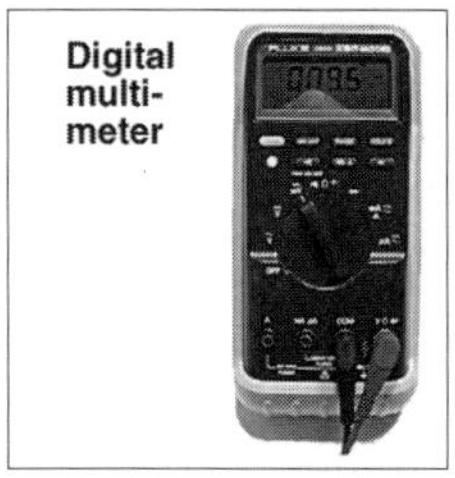

< Digital multimeter

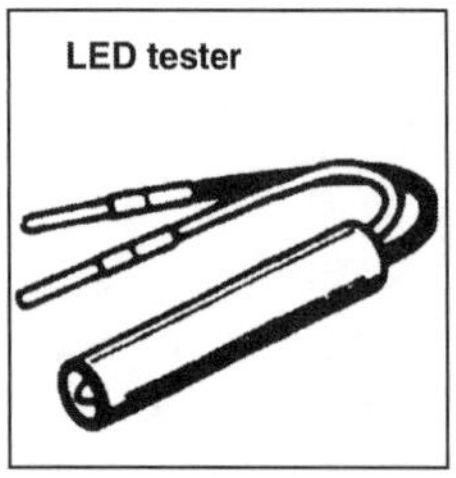

< LED tester
(Tool No. Baum Tools 1115)

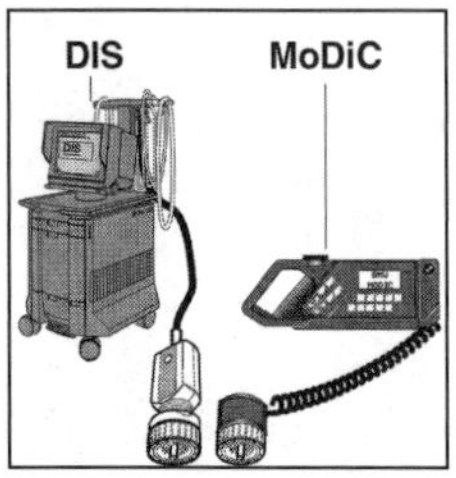

< BMW scan tools DIS and MoDiC

CS2000

Aftermarket scan tool
(Tool No. Baum Tools CS2000)

E39 Electrical System

E39 cars are electrically complex. Many vehicle systems and subsystems are interconnected or integrated. In addition, the requirements of second generation On-Board Diagnostics (OBD II) are such that there are now many more circuits and wires in the vehicle than ever before. The components must exchange large volumes of data with one another in order to perform their various functions.

The use of dedicated data lines for each link in the system has reached the limits of its capabilities. Wiring harnesses are becoming too complex to manage. In addition, the finite number of pins on conventional connectors becomes a limiting factor in electronic control module development.

The solution is to use specialized, vehicle compatible serial bus systems. A bus is a group signal line that transmits serial data in both directions. It consists of two wires (twisted pair). Electronic control modules are connected in parallel using the bus system, and the information transmitted by any module is available to all others on the same bus.

Bus information is sent in serial mode. Serial means one event at a time. In data transmission, the technique of time division is used to separate bits of sent data. Data transmitted over a bus consists of:

- Transmitter address
- Length of data
- Receiver data
- Command or information
- Detailed description of data
- Summary of transmitted information (check sum)

All of the bus-connected modules receive the data but only the unit with the correct receiver address accepts and reacts to the data.

Bus systems are divided according to groups of control modules which share common functionality and information. The commonly used busses are:

- CAN-Bus
- D-Bus
- I-Bus
- K-Bus
- P-Bus
- M-Bus

See the accompanying **E39 bus systems (V-8 models)** illustration.

E39 bus systems (V-8 models)

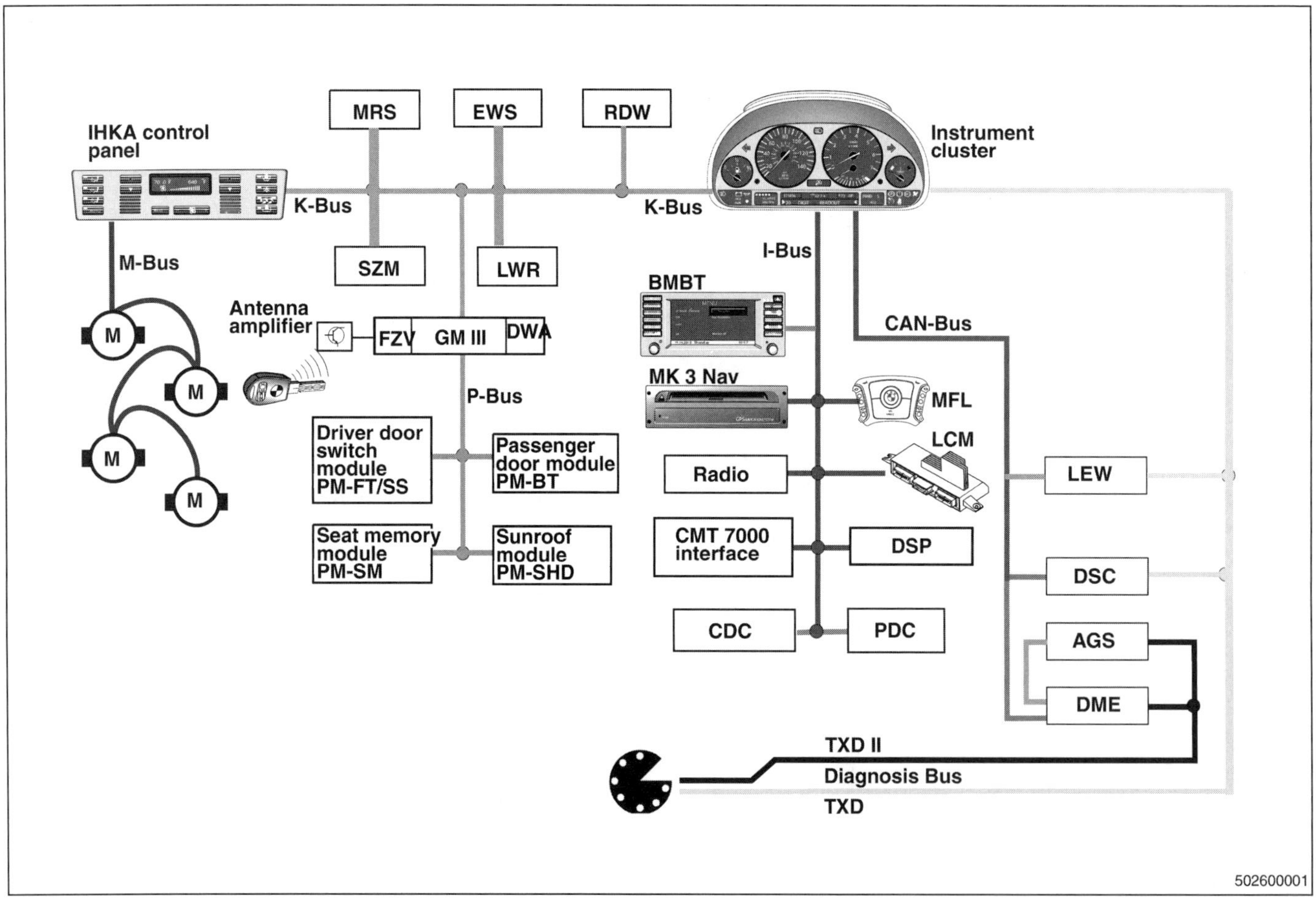

Voltage and polarity

The vehicle operates on a 12 volt direct current (DC) negative-ground system. A voltage regulator controls system voltage at approximately 12 volts. All circuits are grounded by direct or indirect connection to the negative (-) terminal of the battery. A number of ground connections throughout the car connect the wiring harness to chassis ground. These circuits are completed by the battery cable or ground strap between the body and the battery negative (-) terminal.

Wiring, fuses and relays

Electrical components connect using one of the following:

- Heavy cables with lug-type connectors (battery and starter).
- Electrical harnesses with keyed, push-on connectors that lock into place.
- Busses with modular connectors.

Most electrical power is routed from the battery through high-amperage fuses under the passenger's seat and then on through the main relay panel and fuse panel in back of the glove compartment. Fuses are color coded to indicate current capacities. Additional high current fuses are mounted in the trunk.

Relays and control modules are mounted in various places throughout the vehicle.

See **610 Electrical Component Locations**.

Electrical system safety precautions

– Please read the warnings and cautions in this section before doing any work on your electrical system

WARNING —

- *An airbag unit houses an explosive powerful charge. Making repairs without the proper knowledge and special test equipment may cause serious personal injury. See* **721 Airbag System (SRS)**.
- *The ignition system of the car operates at lethal voltages. People with pacemakers or weak hearts should not expose themselves to the ignition system electric currents. Extra caution must be taken when working on the ignition system or when servicing the engine while it is running or the key is on. See* **120 Ignition System** *for additional ignition system warnings and cautions.*
- *Keep hands, clothing and other objects clear of the electric radiator cooling fan when working on a warm engine. The fan may start at any time, even when the ignition is switched off.*

CAUTION—

- *Always turn off the engine and disconnect the negative (-) cable from the battery before removing any electrical components. Disconnecting the battery may erase fault code(s) stored in control module memory. Check for fault codes using special BMW diagnostic equipment.*
- *Prior to disconnecting the battery, read the battery disconnection cautions given in* **001 General Warnings and Cautions**.
- *Connect and disconnect ignition system wires, multiple connectors and ignition test equipment leads only while the ignition is off.*
- *Do not disconnect the battery with the engine running.*
- *Do not quick-charge the battery (for boost starting) for longer than one minute, and do not exceed 16.5 volts at the battery with the boosting cables attached. Wait at least one minute before boosting the battery a second time.*
- *Do not use an analog meter for electrical testing. An analog meter (swing-needle) or a test light with a normal incandescent bulb may draw enough current to damage sensitive electronic components. Use only a digital multimeter.*
- *Choose test equipment carefully. Use a digital multimeter with at least 10 megaohm input impedance, or an LED test light.*
- *Always switch a digital multimeter to the appropriate function and range before making test connections.*
- *Many of the solid-state modules are static sensitive. Static discharge will permanently damage them. Always handle the modules using proper static prevention equipment and techniques.*
- *To avoid damaging harness connectors or relay panel sockets, use jumper wires with flat-blade connectors that are the same size as the connector or relay terminals.*
- *Do not try to start the engine of a car which has been heated above 176°F (80°C), (for example, in a paint drying booth). Allow it to cool to normal temperature.*
- *Disconnect the battery before doing any electric welding on the car.*
- *Do not wash the engine while it is running, or any time the ignition is switched on.*
- *Do not use an ohmmeter to measure resistance on solid state components such as control units or time delay relays.*
- *Always disconnect the battery before making resistance (ohm) measurements on the circuit.*

Central Body Electronics (ZKE III)

Central body electronics (ZKE III) integrates and controls a large number of vehicle functions. Most of the ZKE III sub-systems communicate via P-Bus (peripheral bus).

The general module (GM III) is the master controller for other ZKE system modules. It serves as the gateway for data communication between modules on the P-Bus and modules on other bus systems or with BMW scan tool DIS. GM III also communicates with the remote locking module over the K-Bus for keyless entry system (FZV) operation.

In addition to the GM III, the following peripheral modules (PM) complete the ZKE III system:

- Driver and passenger door control modules (PM-FT and PM-BT) located at forward edge of each door behind trim panel.
- Driver door switch block (PM-SB) located on driver's door panel.
- Sun roof control module (PM-SHD) located on sun roof motor behind headliner.
- Seat and mirror memory control module (PM-SM) located behind driver's seat adjustment switch block.
- Keyless (remote) entry control module (FBZV) located behind left rear seat backrest.

The following functions are controlled directly by GM III:

- Power windows. See **512 Door Windows**.
- Central locking, power trunk or tailgate release, keyless entry (FZV), Car Memory/Key Memory, alarm system (DWA). See **515 Central Locking and Anti-Theft**.
- Windshield and tailgate wiper/washer system. See **611 Wipers and Washers**.
- Interior lighting. See **630 Lights**.
- Consumer sleep mode, described later in this section.

Other functions are not directly controlled by the GM III but interconnected:

- Outside rear-view mirror control and heating. See **510 Exterior Trim, Bumpers**.
- Seat memory (SM) and electrical operation. See **520 Seats**.
- Sunroof operation (SHD). See **540 Sunroof**.
- Rain sensor (AIC) and windshield washer jet heating. See **611 Wipers and Washers.**

Central body electronics (ZKE III) diagram

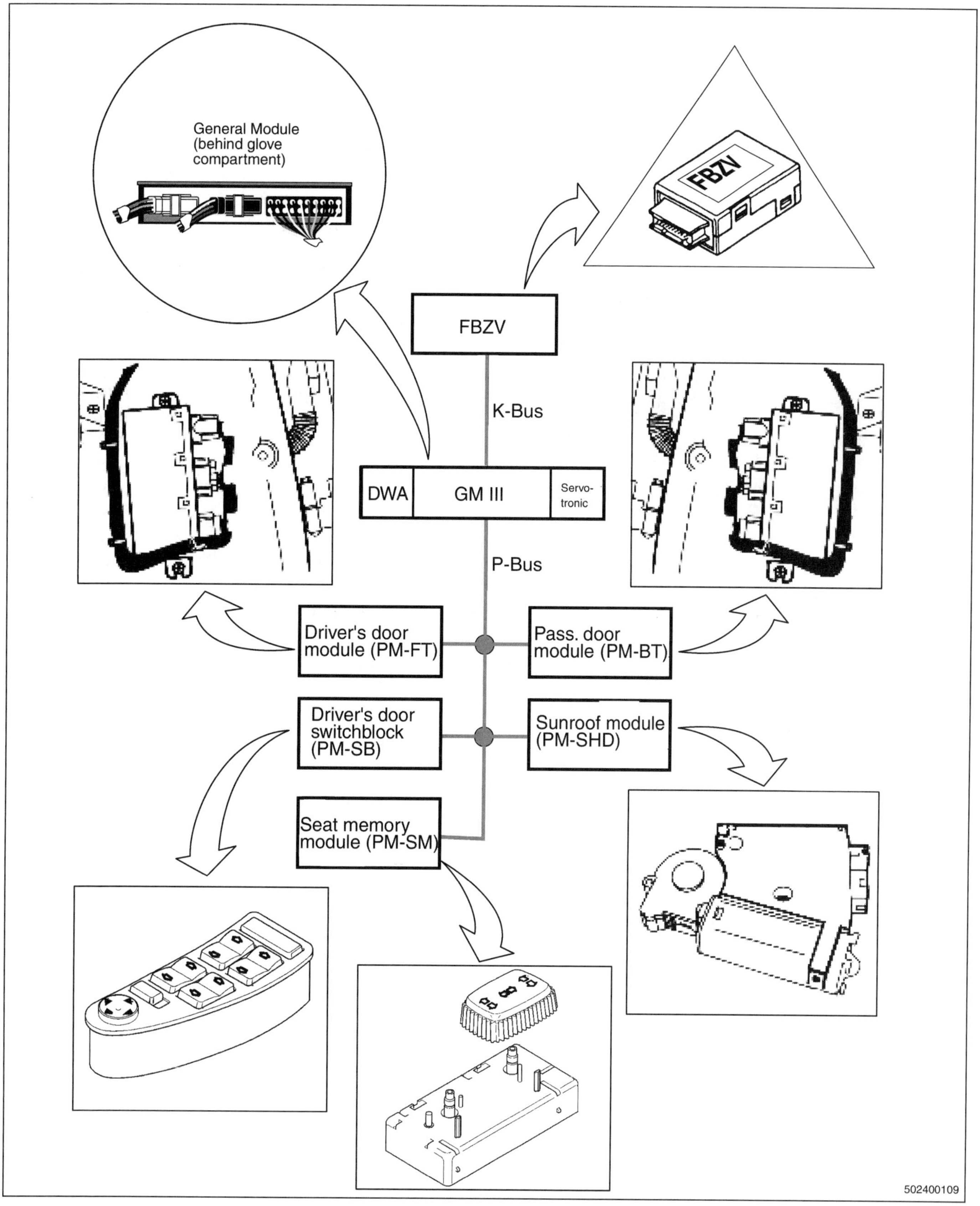
General Module
(behind glove
compartment)
FBZV
FBZV
K-Bus
DWA
GM III
Servo-
tronic
P-Bus
Driver's door
module (PM-FT)
Pass. door
module (PM-BT)
Driver's door
switchblock
(PM-SB)
Sunroof module
(PM-SHD)
Seat memory
module (PM-SM)
502400109

Car Memory/Key Memory

A number of car comfort features can be programmed customized to the driver(s) preference. The identity of the vehicle user is provided by a signal from the keyless entry system (FZV).

Car Memory and Key Memory are actually two separate functions. See **515 Central Locking and Anti-Theft** for further details.

Fault code storage

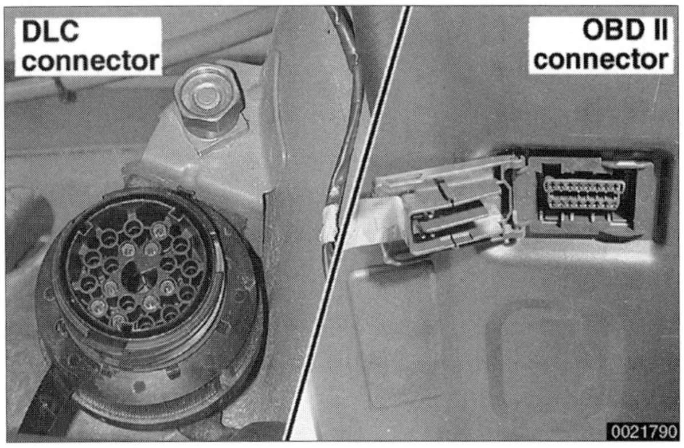

Scan tool fault codes or diagnostic trouble codes (DTCs) are stored in the general module (GM III). They are accessible electronically through the data-link connector (DLC).

NOTE —
- *Cars produced through June 2000 are equipped with the DLC socket in the rear right corner of the engine compartment.*
- *In cars produced after June 2000, the DLC socket in the engine compartment has been discontinued. All scan tool codes can now be accessed through the OBD II interface socket on the driver's side of the dashboard, left and below the instrument cluster, under a cover.*

Consumer cutoff

Consumer current cutoff interrupts battery voltage to specific circuits, preventing inadvertent battery drain if one of these consumers were to remain on after the engine is shut off.

For example, if one of the interior light control switches is left on, consumer cutoff will deactivate power (KL 30) to the interior lighting module after 16 minutes.

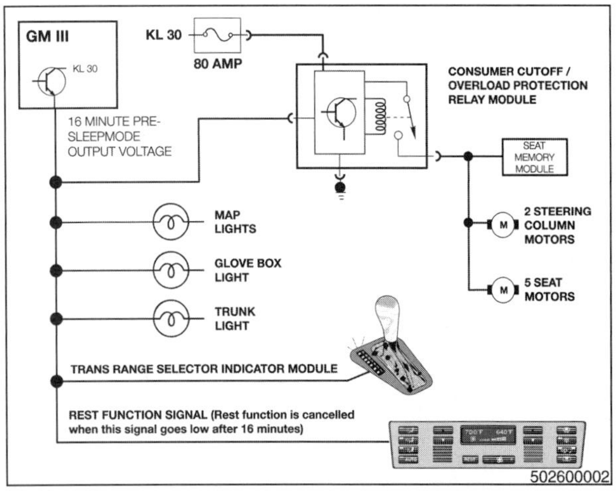

The following circuits are controlled by consumer cutoff:

- Map / reading lights
- Glove compartment / trunk lights
- Transmission range indicator light
- Overload protection relay for power seat motors
- Steering column motors

Circuits controlled by consumer cutoff will be switched off as the General Module enters into sleep mode.

Sleep mode

To lower constant battery draw when the vehicle is parked, the complete ZKE system goes into sleep mode 16 minutes after the ignition has been switched off and no further ZKE function is active.

For example, approximate E39 (528i) battery draw is:

- With Ignition switch off = approx. 750 mA
- One minute later = approx. 560 mA
- After 16 minutes (sleep mode) = approx. 18 mA

All electronic control modules in the ZKE system go into sleep mode. P-Bus, which connects the General Module with the door lock and seat control modules, remains active. However no data transfer takes place until a wake-up request is received. The General Module, door modules or keyless remote module (FZV) can wake the system up. The K-Bus is also active in sleep mode.

Overload protection

The seat and steering column motors receive operating power through the current cutoff (or overload protection) relay module, K72. The consumer cutoff signal from the General Module signals the relay to maintain operating power to consumers. If the module detects an increase in amperage (overload) the relay will open.

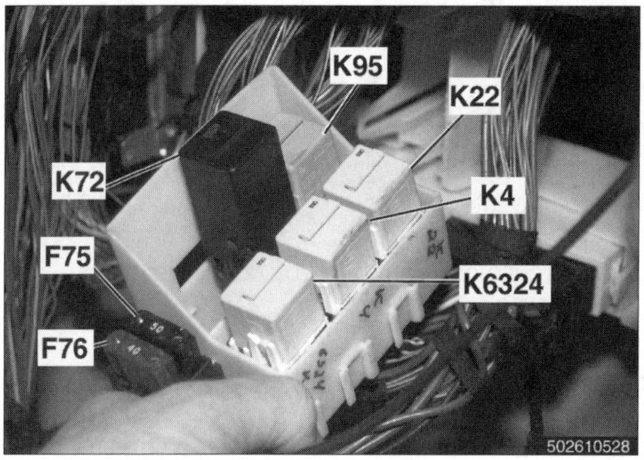

The current cutoff relay module (K72) is located in the electrical carrier behind the glove compartment.

Reset the relay by switching the ignition OFF for 16 minutes, and disconnect the relay. Alternatively, use the BMW Service Tester (DISplus, GT1 or MoDiC) to reset.

WIRING DIAGRAMS

Wiring diagrams can be found in **ELE Electrical Wiring Diagrams**.

Wiring codes and abbreviations

A lot of information is included in each wiring diagram if you know how to read them. Wire colors in the diagrams are abbreviated. Combined color codes indicate a multicolored wire. For example the code BLU/RED indicates a blue wire with a red stripe.

Many electrical components, connectors, fuses, and ground locations are identified using a unique number. Each of these numbers corresponds to a particular part in the circuit commonly found in electrical wiring diagrams.

NOTE —
Sometimes the color of an installed wire may be different from the one on the wiring diagram. In this situation, check to be sure that the wire connects to the proper terminals as confirmation.

Wiring color codes

German code	English code	Color
SW	BLK	Black
BL	BLU	Blue
BR	BRN	Brown
GN	GRN	Green
GR	GRY	Gray
RT	RED	Red
VI	VIO	Violet
WS	WHT	White
GE	YEL	Yellow

Most terminals are identified by numbers on components and harness connectors. Terminal numbers for major electrical connections are shown in the diagrams. Though many terminal numbers appear only once, several other numbers appear in numerous places throughout the electrical system and identify certain types of circuits. Some common circuit numbers are listed in the table **Terminal and circuit numbers**.

Terminal and circuit numbers

Number	Circuit description
1	Low voltage switched terminal of coil
4	High voltage center terminal of coil
+X	Originates at ignition switch. Supplies power when the ignition switch is in the PARK, RUN, or START position
15	Originates at ignition switch. Supplies power when ignition switch is in RUN or START position
30	Battery positive (+) voltage. Supplies power whenever battery is connected. (Not dependent on ignition switch position, possibly unfused.)
31	Ground, battery negative (–) terminal
50	Supplies power from battery to starter solenoid when ignition switch is in START position only
+54	Originates at ignition switch. Supplies power when ignition switch is in the RUN position only
85	Ground side (–) of relay coil
86	Power-in side (+) of relay coil
87	Relay actuated contact
D	Alternator warning light and field energizing circuit

Additional abbreviations shown in the wiring diagrams are given in the table **Common BMW abbreviations**.

Common BMW abbreviations

Abbreviation	Component or system	Abbreviation	Component or system
ABS	antilock brakes	KL 50	ignition start position, power
A/C	air conditioning	LED	light emitting diode
ADS	auxiliary throttle valve	LCM	light control module
AGS	adaptive transmission control	LDP	fuel tank leak diagnosis pump
AIC	rain sensor	LED	light emitting diode
ASC	traction control	LEV	low emissions vehicle
AUC	automatic air recirculation control	LWR	automatic headlight adjustment
BST	battery safety terminal	MAF	mass air flow sensor
CAN	controller area network (bus)	MDK	motor driven throttle
DK	throttle valve, electric	MRS	multiple restraint system
DLC	diagnostic link connector (20 pin)	MIL	malfunction indicator light
DME	digital motor electronics	NAV	navigation system
DM-TL	diagnosis module—tank leakage	NLEV	national low emissions program
DSC	dynamic stability control	NTC	negative temperature coefficient resistor
DWA	antitheft alarm	OBC	on board computer
ECM	engine control module	OBD II	second generation on-board diagnostics
ECT	engine coolant temperature (sensor)	PDC	park distance control
EDK	electronic throttle	PWG	accelerator pedal position sensor
EEPROM	flash programmable read-only memory	RAM	random access memory
EGS	electronic transmission control	RDC	tire pressure control
EPROM	erasable/programmable read-only memory	RXD	receive data line
EWS	electronic immobilizer	SHD	sunroof module
FZV	keyless entry system	SII	service interval indicator
GM	general module	SM	seat memory module
GPS	geographic positioning system	SRS	supplemental restraint system
HPS	head protection airbag	TCM	transmission control module
IAT	intake air temperature (sensor)	TDC	top dead center
IHKA	automatic heating and air conditioning system	TLEV	transitional low emissions vehicle
IHKR	regulated heating and air conditioning system	TXD	transmit data line
IKE	integrated instrument cluster module	ULEV	ultra low emissions vehicle
ITS	inflatable tubular structure (head protection airbag)	ZCS	central locking coding key
KL 15	battery positive, ignition switch on RUN, power	ZKE	central body electronics
KL 30	battery positive (B+), power		
KL 31	battery/chassis ground		

Electrical Troubleshooting

Four things are required for current to flow in any electrical circuit: a voltage source, wires or connections to transport the voltage, a load or device that uses the electricity, and a connection to ground.

Most problems can be found using a digital multimeter (volt/ohm/amp meter) to check the following:

- Voltage supply
- Breaks in the wiring (infinite resistance/no continuity)
- A path to ground that completes the circuit

Electric current is logical in its flow, always moving from the voltage source toward ground. Electrical faults can usually be located through a process of elimination. When troubleshooting a complex circuit, separate the circuit into smaller parts. General tests outlined below may be helpful in finding electrical problems. The information is most helpful when used with wiring diagrams.

Be sure to analyze the problem. Use wiring diagrams to determine the most likely cause. Get an understanding of how the circuit works by following the circuit from ground back to the power source.

When making test connections at connectors and components, use care to avoid spreading or damaging the connectors or terminals. Some tests may require jumper wires to bypass components or connections in the wiring harness. When connecting jumper wires, use blade connectors at the wire ends that match the size of the terminal being tested. The small internal contacts are easily spread apart, and this can cause intermittent or faulty connections that can lead to more problems.

Voltage and voltage drops

Wires, connectors, and switches that carry current are designed with very low resistance so that current flows with a minimum loss of voltage. A voltage drop is caused by higher than normal resistance in a circuit. This additional resistance actually decreases or stops the flow of current. A voltage drop can be noticed by problems ranging from dim headlights to sluggish wipers. Some common sources of voltage drops are corroded or dirty switches, dirty or corroded connections or contacts, and loose or corroded ground wires and ground connections.

A voltage drop test is a good test to make if current is flowing through the circuit but the circuit is not operating correctly. A voltage drop test will help to pinpoint a corroded ground strap or a faulty switch. Normally, there should be less than 1 volt drop across most wires or closed switches. A voltage drop across a connector or short cable should not exceed 0.5 volts.

NOTE —
- *A voltage drop test is generally more accurate than a simple resistance check because the resistances involved are often too small to measure with most ohmmeters. For example, a resistance as small as 0.02 ohms would results in a 3 volt drop in a typical 150 amp starter circuit. (150 amps x 0.02 ohms =3 volts).*
- *Keep in mind that voltage with the key on and voltage with the engine running are not the same. With the ignition on and the engine off (battery voltage), voltage should be approximately 12.6 volts. With the engine running (charging voltage), voltage should be approximately 14.0 volts. Measure voltage at the battery with the ignition on and then with the engine running to get exact measurements.*

Voltage, measuring

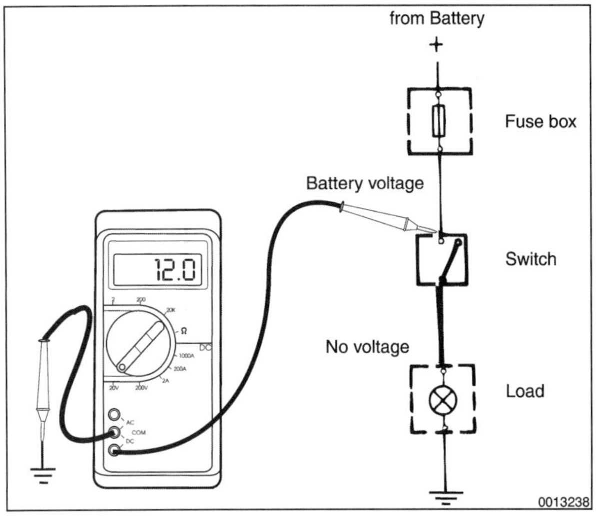

- Connect digital multimeter negative lead to a reliable ground point on car.

NOTE —
The negative (-) battery terminal is always a good ground point.

- Connect digital multimeter positive lead to point in circuit you wish to measure.

NOTE —
The voltage reading should not deviate more than 1 volt from voltage at the battery. If voltage drop is more than this, check for a corroded connector or loose ground wire.

Voltage drop, testing

Voltage drop can only be checked when there is a load on the circuit, such as when operating the starter motor or turning on the headlights. A digital multimeter should be used to ensure accurate readings.

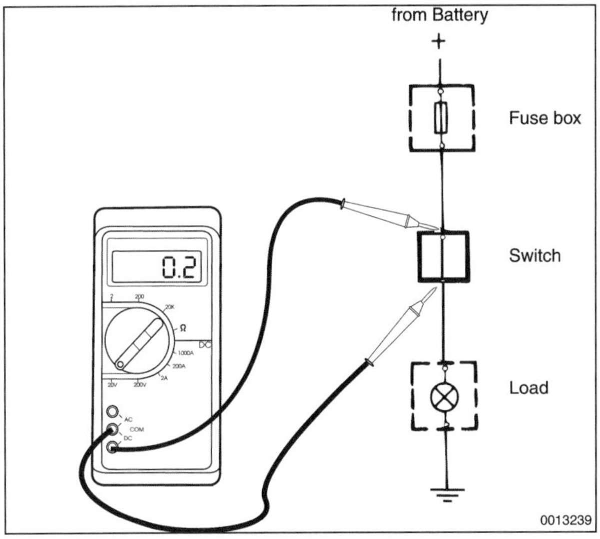

< Connect digital multimeter positive lead to positive (+) battery terminal or a positive power supply close to battery source.

– Connect digital multimeter negative lead to other end of cable or switch being tested.

– With power on and circuit working, meter shows voltage drop (difference between two points). This value should not exceed 1 volt.

NOTE—
- *The maximum voltage drop in an automotive circuit, as recommended by the Society of Automotive Engineers (SAE), is as follows:*
- *0 volts for small wire connections*
- *0.1 Volts for high current connections*
- *0.2 volts for high current cables*
- *0.3 volts for switch or solenoid contacts*
- *On longer wires or cables, the drop may be slightly higher. In any case, a voltage drop of more than 1.0 volt usually indicates a problem.*

Continuity, checking

Continuity tests can be used to check a circuit or switch. Because most automotive circuits are designed to have little or no resistance, a circuit or part of a circuit can be easily checked for faults using an ohmmeter. An open circuit or a circuit with high resistance will not allow current to flow. A circuit with little or no resistance allows current to flow easily.

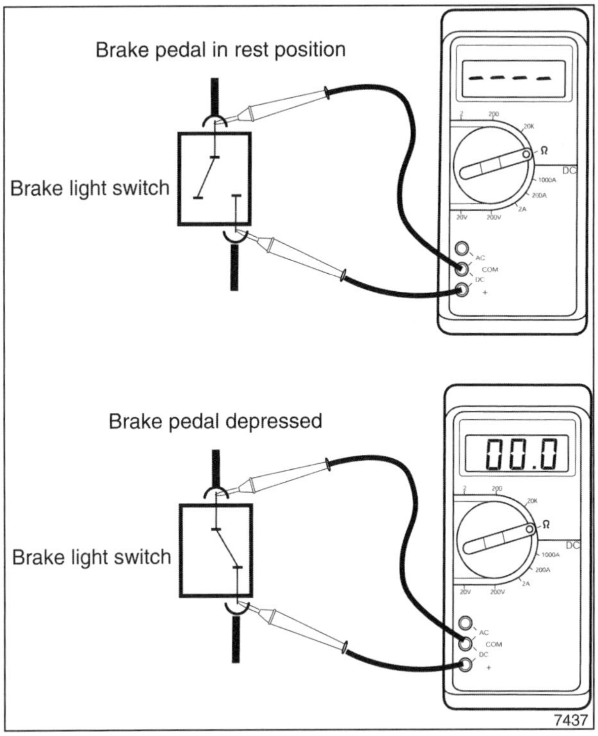

When checking continuity, the ignition should be off. On circuits that are powered at all times, the battery should be disconnected. Using the appropriate wiring diagram, a circuit can be easily tested for faulty connections, wires, switches, relays and engine sensors by checking for continuity.

< For example, to test brake light switch for continuity:
- With brake pedal in rest position (switch open) there is no continuity (infinite Ω).
- With pedal depressed (switch closed) there is continuity (0Ω).

Short circuits

Short circuits are exactly what the name implies. The circuit takes a shorter path than it was designed to take. The most common short that causes problems is a short to ground where the insulation on a positive (+) wire wears away and the metal wire is exposed. When the wire rubs against a metal part of the car or other ground source, the circuit is shorted to ground. If the exposed wire is live (positive battery voltage), a fuse will blow and the circuit may be damaged.

Shorts to ground can be located with a digital multimeter. Short circuits are often difficult to locate and may vary in nature. Short circuits can be found using a logical approach based on knowledge of the current path.

NOTE—
- *On circuits protected with high rating fuses (25 amp and greater), wires or circuit components may be damaged before the fuse blows. Always check for damage before replacing fuses of this rating.*
- *When replacing blown fuses, use only fuses having the correct rating. Always confirm by checking for the correct fuse rating printed on the fuse panel cover.*

Short circuit, testing with ohmmeter

– Remove blown fuse from circuit and disconnect cables from battery. Disconnect harness connector from circuit load or consumer.

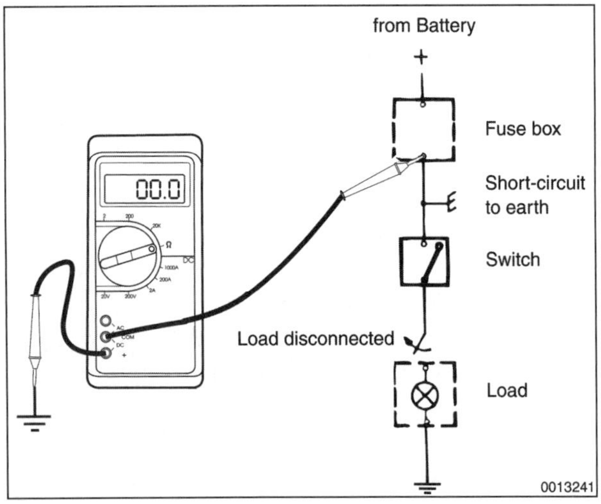

Using an ohmmeter, connect one test lead to load side of fuse terminal (terminal leading to circuit) and the other test lead to ground.

– If there is continuity to ground, there is a short to ground.

– If there is no continuity, work from wire harness nearest to fuse/relay panel and move or wiggle wires while observing meter. Continue to move down harness until meter displays a reading. This is the location of short to ground.

– Visually inspect wire harness at this point for any faults. If no faults are visible, carefully slice open harness cover or wire insulation for further inspection. Repair any faults found.

Short circuit, testing with voltmeter

– Remove blown fuse from circuit. Disconnect harness connector from circuit load or consumer.

NOTE —
Most fuses power more than one consumer. Be sure all consumers are disconnected when checking for a short circuit.

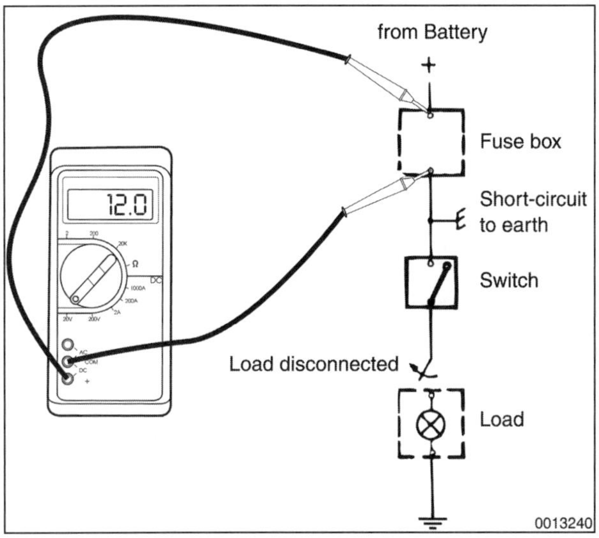

◄ Using a digital multimeter, connect test leads across fuse terminals. Make sure power is present in circuit. If necessary turn key on.

– If voltage is present at voltmeter, there is a short to ground.

– If voltage is not present, work from wire harness nearest to fuse/relay panel and move or wiggle wires while observing meter. Continue to move down harness until meter displays a reading. This is the location of short to ground.

– Visually inspect wire harness at this point for any faults. If no faults are visible, carefully slice open harness cover or wire insulation for further inspection. Repair any faults found.

610 Electrical Component Locations

General

This repair group covers fuse, relay and control module location information. Ground points and other component locations are also covered, primarily via photos or illustrations.

Keep in mind that electrical equipment and accessories installed vary depending on model and model year. Always confirm that the proper electrical component has been identified.

For additional E39 electrical system information, see:

- **600 Electrical System-General**
- **ELE Electrical Wiring Diagrams**

Special tools

Some special tools are needed to test and repair the electrical systems in the car.

◀ Automotive digital multimeter

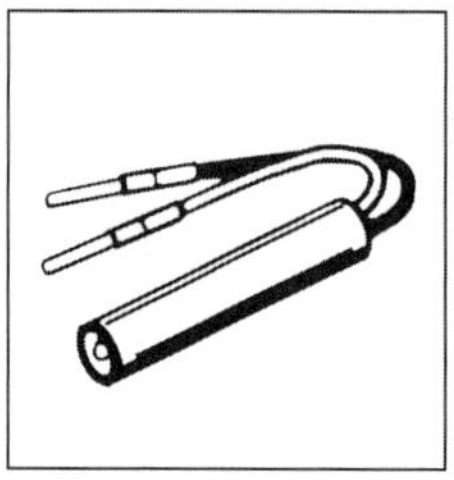

◀ LED test light
(Tool No. Baum tools 1115)

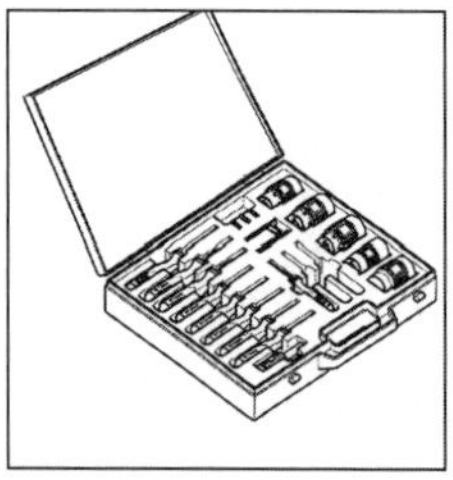

◀ Wiring harness repair kit
(Tool No. BMW 61 1 150)

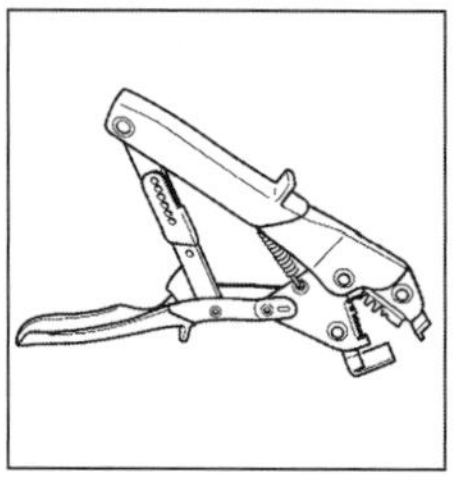

◀ Wire end crimp tool
(Tool No. BMW 61 9 041)

Electrical system safety precautions

Please read the following warnings and cautions before doing any work on your electrical system.

> ***WARNING —***
> *The battery safety terminal, pyrotechnic seat belt tensioners, and airbags utilize explosive devices and must be handled with extreme care. Refer to the warnings and cautions in* **121 Battery, Alternator, Starter**; **720 Seat Belts**; *and* **721 Airbag System (SRS)**.

> ***CAUTION—***
> - *Prior to disconnecting the battery, read the battery disconnection cautions in* **001 General Warnings and Cautions**.
> - *Relay and fuse positions are subject to change and may vary from car to car. If questions arise, an authorized BMW dealer is the best source for the most accurate and up-to-date information.*
> - *A good way to verify a relay position is to compare the wiring colors at the relay socket to the colors indicated on the wiring diagrams in* **ELE Electrical Wiring Diagrams**.
> - *Always switch the ignition off and remove the negative (-) battery cable before removing any electrical components. Connect and disconnect ignition system wires, multiple connectors, and ignition test equipment leads only while the ignition is switched off.*
> - *Only use a digital multimeter for electrical tests.*

ELECTRICAL COMPONENTS

Electrical component location table is a cross-referenced listing of electrical components in E39 vehicles. Where available, photos of components in this repair group are referred to in the fourth column.

Electrical component location table

Component	Location	Designation	Figure No.
3/2-way valve (DME running loses)	Under car, left side, ahead of fuel filter, under protective cover	Y31	92
ABS wheel speed sensor			
• Left front	Left front wheel hub	B2	
• Left rear	Left rear wheel bearing housing	B4	
• Right front	Right front wheel hub	B1	27
• Right rear	Right rear wheel bearing housing	B3	36

Component	Location	Designation	Figure No.
ABS/ASC electronic control module	Left of glove compartment	A52	
ABS/ASC hydraulic unit	Right side of engine compartment on strut tower	Y1	
ABS/ASC switch	On center console below radio		
ABS/ASC throttle valve position sensor	Left side top of engine at ASC throttle assembly	R6253	
ABS/ASC/DSC warning lights	In instrument cluster		
ABS/DSC charge pressure sensor	In ABS/DSC hydraulic unit, right rear engine compartment		
ABS/DSC electronic control module			
• 1997 — 1998	Left of glove compartment	A65	
• 1999 — 2002:	Right side of engine compartment on hydraulic unit	A65	138
ABS/DSC hydraulic unit	Right side engine compartment on strut tower	Y15	19
ABS/DSC precharge pump	Left side of engine compartment	M118	54
ABS/DSC pressure sensor			
• To 9/1998	Left side engine compartment, on ABS/DSC precharge pump	M118	54
• From 9/1998	Right side engine compartment, on ABS/DSC hydraulic unit		
ABS/DSC RPM rate (rotational rate or yaw) sensor	Under driver side carpet	B75	53
ABS/DSC steering angle sensor	Base of upper steering column	R33	104
ABS/DSC switch	On center console below radio		
ABS/DSC transverse (lateral) acceleration sensor	Under left front seat carpet	B74	52
A/C blower motor	Behind center of dash	M30	89
A/C blower final stage (resistor pack)	Right side of IHKA blower housing below glove compartment	N2	102
A/C blower motor output stage, rear compartment	Rear of center console	I01102	78
A/C blower relay	Relay panel 2 behind glove compartment	K4	8
A/C compressor	On engine, right front, lower	Y2	18
A/C compressor connector	On A/C compressor	X163	18
A/C control module	Center of dashboard, integrated into IHKA control panel	A11	138
A/C evaporator temperature sensor			
• IHKR	Right side of heater housing, behind footwell duct		
• IHKA to 3 / 2000	Left side of heater housing, behind footwell duct	B14	29
• IHKA from 3 / 2000	Right side of heater housing, behind footwell duct		
A/C footwell sensor, left	Driver's footwell	B26	
A/C footwell sensor, right	Passenger footwell	B27	
A/C high pressure switch	Right front of engine compartment	B8	55
A/C stepper motors	see Stepper motors		

Component	Location	Designation	Figure No.
Accelerator pedal sensor (PWG)			
• DME MS 42.0	Integral part of throttle housing		
• DME MS 43.0, ME 7.2	Above accelerator pedal	R10	
Acceleration sensor, right front	Right front wheel well	B41	
Acceleration sensor, right rear	Right rear wheel well	B48	
AGS	see Automatic transmission control module (AGS)		
Airbag contact slip ring	Steering column	I01031	
Airbag connector, passenger side	Right side dashboard support		
Airbag connector, steering wheel	Under steering wheel airbag		
Airbag diagnosis module (SRS)	Below center console at rear	A12	118
Airbag			
• Driver's	Steering wheel center pad	G5	65
• Left front door	Driver's door	G14	63
• Left front curtain (head area) (ITS)	Windshield pillar, driver's side	G17	
• Left rear door	Left rear door	G20	
• Left rear curtain (head area) (ITS)	Under left rear window shelf and C pillar	G22	
• Passenger	Right side dashboard	G6	
• Right front door	Passenger door	G15	
• Right front curtain (head area) (ITS)	Windshield pillar, passenger side	G18	64
• Right rear door	Right rear door	G21	
• Right rear curtain (head area) (ITS)	Under right rear window shelf and C pillar	G23	
Airbag sensor (crash sensor)			
• Left front	Under carpet beneath driver's seat	S71	113
• Right front	Under carpet beneath passenger seat	S72	114
Airbag warning light	In instrument cluster		
Air conditioner	See A/C entries		
Air distribution motors	see Stepper motors (IHKA)		
Air flow sensor	see Mass air flow sensor		
Air quality sensor (AUC) for automatic recirculation system	Lower right engine cooling fan housing	B414	38
Air suspension (EHC) compressor pump assembly	Spare tire well, under tire	I01017	73
Air suspension (EHC) compressor pump control relay	Spare tire well, under tire	I01027	73
Air suspension (EHC) control module	Right side cargo compartment		138, 140
Air suspension (EHC) level sensor	see Level sensor, rear		
Alarm control module (DWA)	In headliner		
Alarm horn (siren), antitheft (DWA)	Right rear wheel well behind inner panel	H1	67

Component	Location	Designation	Figure No.
Alarm horn battery (DWA)	Inside alarm horn, right rear wheel well behind inner panel		
Alarm indicator LED (DWA)	Attached to rear view mirror		
Alternator (generator)	Left front of cylinder block	G6524, G2023	66
Amplifier, FM lockout circuit	Right rear C-pillar	I01004	72
Amplifier, radio	see Radio amplifier		
Antenna			
• AM	Sport Wagon: Left rear window		139
• Diversity	Left rear C-pillar	I01113	79
• FM1	Sport Wagon: Rear window (vertical traces)		139
• FM2	Sport Wagon: Left rear window		139
• FZV (remote entry)	Sport Wagon: Left rear window		139
Antenna amplifier			
• FM1	Sport Wagon: Top center of tailgate		138, 139
• FM2 / FZV	Behind left C-pillar trim panel	N8	61, 138, 139, 140
Anti-slip	see ABS, ABS/ASC and ABS/DSC entries		
Antitheft	see Alarm entries		
ASC	see ABS/ASC entries		
ASC/DSC switch	Bottom of center console	S6	
Automatic air recirculation sensor (AUC)	see Air quality sensor (AUC) for automatic recirculation system		
Automatic climate control (IHKA)	see A/C entries		
Automatic transmission control module (AGS)	Right rear engine compartment in E-box	A7000 A8600	22, 138
Automatic transmission park / neutral position switch	Center console	Y19	
Automatic transmission range switch (gear position/neutral safety switch)	Left side of transmission	S8532	117
Automatic transmission selector lever position switch	Center console, right side of selector lever, under bezel	S227	
Automatic transmission Steptronic switch	Center console, right of shifter, below bezel	S224	
Auxiliary coolant pump	Left side of engine compartment, bottom	M37	
Auxiliary fan	see Engine cooling fan entries		
Auxiliary throttle position motor (ADS)	Front of left strut tower	M93	96
B+ junction cable shoe	Right side of frame rail, under car	X6404	130
Back-up light switch (automatic transmission)	see Automatic transmission range switch		
Back-up light switch (manual transmission)	On transmission housing, position varies depending on transmission installed. See **240 Automatic Transmission**.	S8524	
Battery	Right side trunk, behind trim panel	G1	62, 138

Component	Location	Designation	Figure No.
Battery safety terminal (BST)	On positive battery terminal, right side of trunk	G19	
Blower	see A/C blower motor		
Body electronics control module	see General module (GM III)		
Brake fluid level switch	Top of brake fluid reservoir, left rear engine compartment	B18	32
Brake fluid pressure sensor	see ABS/DSC pressure sensor		
Brake light switch	Above brake pedal	S29	107
Brake pad wear sensor, left front	Brake caliper, left front	B16	30
Brake pad wear sensor, right rear	Brake caliper, right rear	B17	31
Brake pad wear sensor connector, left front	In left front wheel housing		
Brake pad wear sensor connector, right rear	Ahead of right rear wheel housing		
Camshaft position sensor			
• M52, M52 TU, M54 (6–cylinder) intake camshaft	Left front of cylinder head	B6214	42
• M52 TU, M54 (6–cylinder) exhaust camshaft	Right front of cylinder head	B6224	46
• M62, M62 TU (V-8) right intake cam-shaft	Front of right cylinder head	B6219	43
• M62 TU (V-8) left intake camshaft	Front of left cylinder head	B6229	
Camshaft actuator (VANOS)	see VANOS entries		
Carbon canister valve			
CD changer	Left side of trunk	N22	
Center brake light			
• Sedan models	Center rear window shelf	H34	69
• Sport Wagon	Top of rear window		
Central body electronics (ZKE III) control module	see General module (GM III)		
Central locking switch	Center console, front	S302	
Changeover valve, LWS (M52 TU, M54, M62 TU)	Front left wheel well, at rear behind liner	Y28	
Characteristic map cooling sensor	see Thermostat, characteristic map cooling		
Charge pressure sensor	see ASC/DSC pressure sensor		
Child safety switch	In driver's door switch block		
Chime module	Dash panel above driver's footwell	H10	68
Cigarette lighter (front)	Center console, near shifter	E28	56
Closed circuit current cutoff relay	Relay panel 2, behind glove compartment	K72	8
Clutch pedal position switch (manual transmission)	On clutch pedal cluster	S32	

Component	Location	Designation	Figure No.
Coil spring	Center of steering wheel under driver airbag, between steering wheel and column switches	I01030	74
Combination (stalk) switch	On steering column		
Compensator	Luggage compartment, left side, rear	I01039	
Converter (PDC)	see Park distance control converter entries		
Coolant	see Engine coolant entries		
Coolant thermostat	see Thermostat, characteristic map cooling		
Crankshaft position sensor(6–cylinder)	Left rear of engine block, under starter motor		
Crankshaft position sensor	Lower right side of engine bell housing	B6203	40
Crash sensor	see Airbag sensor entries		
Cruise control module (Tempomat)	Driver's footwell, left, behind trim	A8	
Cruise control main switch (without multifunction steering wheel)	Steering column stalk	S28	
Cruise control, switches (steering wheel)	Steering wheel right side keypad		
Data link connector (DLC)			
• 20–pin (to 6/2000)	Right front engine compartment	D100	45
• 16–pin (OBD II)	below dashboard, driver's left	I01010	
Data link connector (20–pin DLC) component connector	Right front engine compartment (20–pin, black)	X6002	45
Defroster stepper motor	see Stepper motors (IHKA)		
Dimmer switch	Left side of dash	N3	
DME control module	see Engine control module, DME (ECM)		
DME main relay	Relay panel 1, right rear engine compartment in E-box	K6300	7
DMTL	see Fuel tank leakage diagnosis module (LDP or DMTL)		
Door access light, driver's	Bottom of driver's side front door	E88	60
Door contact switch			
• Left front	Driver's B pillar at latch	S14	
• Left rear	Left rear C pillar door jamb at latch	S16	
• Right front	Passenger B pillar door jamb at latch	S13	
• Right rear	Right rear C pillar door jamb at latch	S15	
Door lock motor (central locking)			
• Left front	In driver's door	M12	83
• Left rear	In left rear door	M15	84
• Right front	In passenger door	M13	
• Right rear	In right rear door	M14	
Door lock switch			
• Left front	In driver's door	S47	
• Right front	In passenger door	S49	

Component	Location	Designation	Figure No.
Driver's door module	Driver's door arm rest	A23	15
Driver's seatback head adjustment switch	Driver's seat base, left side	S199	
Driver's seatback recliner motor	Underside of driver's seat	M53	
Driver's seat cushion tilt motor	Underside of driver's seat	M50	
Driver's seat heating switch	Center console, front	S53	
Driver's seat height motor	Underside of driver's seat	M52	
Driver's seat lumbar support			
• Motor	Underside of driver's seat	M55	
• Pressure switch	In driver's seat back	S209	
• Switch	Driver's seat base, left side	S52	
• Valve block	In driver's seat back	Y193	
Driver's seat memory switch	On driver's door	S57	
Driver's seat movement motor	Underside of driver's seat	M51	
Driver's seat pressure sensor 1	Under driver's seat cushion cover	I01051	
Driver's seat pressure sensor 2	Under driver's seat cushion cover	I01052	
Driver's seat pump motor	Underside of driver's seat	I01049	
Driver's seat valve	Underside of driver's seat	I01050	
DSC	see ABS/DSC entries		
DWA	see Alarm entries		
Dynamic pressure stepper motor	see Stepper motors (IHKA)		
Dynamic stability control	see ABS/DSC entries		
E-box	Right rear engine compartment, under plastic cover		3
E-box cooling fan	Under E-box, engine compartment, right rear	M6506	99
E-box temperature switch	Rear of E-box	B6235	
ECT sensor	see Engine coolant temperature (ECT) sensor		
EHC	see Air suspension entries		
Electric coolant thermostat	see Thermostat, characteristic map cooling		
Electrochromic rear view mirror	In rear view mirror, top of windshield	A22	14
Electro-hydraulic converter (Servotronic)	Under left side of vehicle, front	B15	
Electronic driveaway protection	see EWS entries		
Electronic height control (EHC)	see Air suspension entries		
Electronic immobilizer	see EWS entries		
Electronic shock absorber control module	Right side of trunk	A80	23
Electronic throttle actuator	Top center of engine at front	Y6390	
Electronics box	see E-box		
Engine compartment light switch	see Engine hood contact switch		
Engine control module, DME (ECM)	Right rear of engine compartment in E-box	A6000	20

Component	Location	Designation	Figure No.
Engine control module relay, DME	Relay panel 1, right rear of engine compartment in E-box	K6300	7
Engine coolant level switch	Bottom of radiator expansion tank	S63	112
Engine coolant temperature (ECT) sensor			
• 6– cylinder M52	Below number one intake manifold runner	B6256	
• 6–cylinder M52 TU, M54	Under rear of intake manifold at rear of cylinder block	B6256	
• V-8	Front of engine on thermostat housing	B6256	
Engine coolant temperature sensor, radiator outlet	In lower radiator hose, right front of engine	I01058	
Engine cooling fan	Front of radiator	M9	95
• High speed relay	Relay panel 2, behind glove compartment	K22	8
• Normal speed relay	Engine compartment E-box	K21	7
• Stage 3 relay	Engine compartment E-box	K201	7
Engine cooling fan switch	Right side of radiator	S36	109
Engine electronics fuse pack	Engine compartment E-box, fuse panel 3		3
Engine hood contact switch	Left rear engine compartment at interior ventilation filter housing	S19	
Evaporative control valve			
Evaporator temperature sensor	see A/C evaporator temperature sensor		
EWS control module			
• To 3/1997	Behind glove compartment	A836	25
• Sedan from 3/1997	Under left side of dash	A836	
• Sport Wagon	Behind glove compartment	A836	138
EWS ring antenna (toroidal ring coil)	Around ignition switch	I01035	
EWS transceiver / receiver	to 3/1997: Under left side of dash, to right of steering column	A837	
Exhaust camshaft position sensor	see Camshaft position sensor entries		
Exhaust camshaft VANOS solenoid	see VANOS entries		
Face level vents stepper motor	see Stepper motors (IHKA)		
Final stage, blower motor	see A/C blower final stage		
FM antenna	see Antenna entries		
FM antenna amplifier	see Antenna amplifier entries		
Footwell stepper motor	see Stepper motors (IHKA)		
Footwell light, left	In left footwell top trim (pedal cluster trim)		
Footwell light, right	In right footwell top trim		
Footwell/rear compartment stepper motor	see Stepper motors (IHKA)		
Fresh air stepper motor	see Stepper motors (IHKA)		
Fuel changeover circuit valve	see 3/2–way valve		

Component	Location	Designation	Figure No.
Fuel injection valve			
• Cylinder 1	At intake manifold	Y6101	
• Cylinder 2	At intake manifold	Y6102	
• Cylinder 3	At intake manifold	Y6103	
• Cylinder 4	At intake manifold	Y6104	
• Cylinder 5	At intake manifold	Y6105	
• Cylinder 6	At intake manifold	Y6106	
• Cylinder 7	At intake manifold	Y6107	
• Cylinder 8	At intake manifold	Y6108	
Fuel injector relay (MS 43.0)	Left rear engine compartment in E-box	K6327	
Fuel injector electrical harness	Top of engine, under plastic cover		
Fuel level sensor I	Top of fuel tank, under right rear seat cushion, combined with fuel pump.		
Fuel level sensor II	Top of fuel tank, under left rear seat cushion	B25	34
Fuel pump	Under rear seat cushion, right. Combined with right fuel level sensor	M2	86
Fuel pump relay 1	Relay panel 3, right side of trunk	K96	9
Fuel tank access flap lock motor	Right side of trunk behind trim panel	M16	85
Fuel tank access flap relay	Relay panel 3, right side of trunk	K121	9
Fuel tank leakage diagnosis module (LDP or DMTL)	Back of wheel well, left rear, behind liner	I01071	75
Fuel tank leakage diagnosis pump	Back of wheel well, left rear, behind liner	M119	75
Fuel tank vent valve	see Evaporative control valve		
Fuse panel 4 cable shoe, voltage supply	At fuse panel 4, under carpet beneath passenger seat	X13020	133
Fuses			
• Panel 1, fuses F1 – F45	Above glove compartment		1
• Panel 2, fuses F46 – F66	Right rear of trunk above battery		2
• Panel 3, engine electronics, DME fuses F1 – F5	Right rear engine compartment in E-box	A8680	3
• Panel 4, fuses F107 – F114	Under passenger footwell carpet		4
• Panel 5, fuses F100 – F108	Right side of trunk on wheel well	X819	5, 136, 138
• Panel 6, fuses F75 – F76	Right side of relay panel 2, behind glove compartment		6
Fuses, engine electronics	see Engine electronics fuse pack		
FZV antenna	see Antenna entries		
Garage door opener	In head lining front center	S223	
Gas generator, airbag	see Airbag entries		
Gear position indicator light	Under shifter bezel		
Gear position/neutral safety switch	see Automatic transmission range switch		
General module (GM III)	Behind glove compartment	A1	11

Component	Location	Designation	Figure No.
Generator	see Alternator		
Glove compartment light switch	Glove box, top	S37	110
Glove compartment lock motor			
GPS antenna			
• Sedan models	Left side rear window shelf	I01002	71
• Sport Wagon	Center dashboard		138
GPS control module	Left side trunk or luggage compartment	A112	138, 140
GPS receiver module	Left side trunk or luggage compartment	I01001, N28	
Ground jumper lug	Right side engine compartment, at right strut tower		
Hazard warning switch	On center console, behind shifter	S18	
Headlight beam throw control actuator, left	Back of headlight, left	M80	
Headlight beam throw control actuator, right	Back of headlight, right	M81	
Headlight dimmer relay	In light control center (LSZ)		
Headlight flasher switch	Combination (stalk) switch on steering column		
Headlight vertical aim actuator (left)	In headlight assembly (left)	M80	
Headlight vertical aim actuator (right)	In headlight assembly (right)	M81	
Headlight vertical aim load sensor, front	Front sub frame at wheel well, right side	B64	
Headlight vertical aim load sensor, rear	Rear sub frame, left side near wheel well	B70	
Headlight washer pump	Back of right front wheel behind inner fender panel, on reservoir	M7	90
Headlight washer module	Behind glove compartment	K6	
Headlight widening control module	Behind glove compartment	A53	
Headlight widening potentiometer	Beside headlight switch	R13	103
Heater core temperature sensor(s)	see Heat exchanger temperature sensor entries		
Heater valve assembly	Left side of engine compartment, on inner fender	Y4	26
Heater blower	see A/C blower motor		
Heat exchanger temperature sensor(s)	Behind radio in center console	B11, B12	28
Heating - A/C	see A/C entries		
High beam switch	Combination (stalk) switch on steering column		
Hood switch	see Engine hood contact switch		
Horn relay	Under left side of dash, relay panel 4	K2	10
Horn, left	Left front wheel well	H2	
Horn, right	Right front wheel well	H3	

Component	Location	Designation	Figure No.
Horn switches	Steering wheel, behind impact cushion	S4	111
Hot film mass air flow sensor	see Mass air flow sensor		
Idle speed control valve • 6–cylinder • V-8	 Below center of intake manifold Under top engine cover		
Ignition switch	Right side steering column	S2	
IHKA / IHKR	see A/C entries		
Independent heating blower relay	see Parked car ventilation relay		
Individual control intake system valve	see Resonance valve, intake manifold		
Inertia fuel shutoff switch	Left side of driver's footwell	S27	
Instrument cluster control module (IKE)	see Integrated instrument cluster control module (IKE)		
Intake air temperature (IAT) sensor • 6–cylinder M52 • 6–cylinder, M52 TU, M54 • V-8	 Under intake housing behind throttle body Center top of engine, between intake manifold and cylinder head Air filter housing cover	 B6205 B6205 B6215	 44
Intake camshaft position sensor	see Camshaft position sensor entries		
Intake camshaft VANOS solenoid	see VANOS entries		
Integrated instrument cluster control module (IKE)	Back of instrument cluster	A63	21, 138
Intensive washer pump	Right side of engine compartment on front of strut tower, on reservoir	M5	
Interface	Below center console	I01040	
Intercom control unit (WSA)	Right side of spare tire, below trunk	A413	
Interference suppression capacitor (V-8, ignition coils 1–4)	Wiring loom top right cylinder head	I01100	76
Interference suppression capacitor (V-8, ignition coils 5–8)	Wiring loom top left cylinder head	I01101	77
Interior motion sensor and control module (UIS)	In headliner, center	A121	138
Interior reading light, front	Front of headliner at mirror	E34	58
Keyless entry antenna	see Antenna entries (FZV)		
Kickdown switch, automatic transmission	Under accelerator pedal	S8507	116
Knock sensors (6–cylinder)	Under intake manifold	B6240	48
Knock sensors (V-8)	Under intake manifold	B6240	49
Latent heat accumulator temperature sensor	Passenger footwell	R34	
Lateral acceleration sensor	see ABS/DSC entries (transverse acceleration sensor)		
LDP	see Fuel tank leakage diagnosis module (LDP or DMTL)		
Leakage diagnosis pump (LDP)	see Fuel tank leakage diagnosis module (LDP or DMTL)		

Component	Location	Designation	Figure No.
Level sensor, rear	Rear suspension subframe	B42, B43	39
Lift gate (Sport Wagon)	see Tailgate entries		
Light control module	Right side kick panel	A3	16, 138
Lighting, rear console box	Rear console	I01103	
Light switch assembly	Left side of dashboard		
Load reduction relay	see Unloader relay entries		
Luggage compartment	see Trunk entries		
LWR	Right side under dashboard		138
Make up mirror switch • Driver's • Passenger	 Driver's side make up mirror, sun visor Passenger side make up mirror, sun visor	 S77 S78	
Mass air flow sensor • 6–cylinder • V-8	 Left side engine compartment at intake air box outlet At intake air box outlet, front of engine compartment	 B6207 B6207	 41
Mixing actuators	see Stepper motors (IHKA)		
Mobile phone	Center console	I01043	
MRS module	see Airbag entries		
Multi-information display (MID)	Center console		138
Multifunction steering wheel (MFL) controls	Steering wheel pad	I01029	138
Multifunction steering wheel (MFL) control module	Below left side of dash	A105	
Multiple restraint system (MRS)	see Airbag entries		
Navigation	see GPS entries		
Neutral safety switch	see Automatic transmission range switch (gear position / neutral safety switch)		
OBD II connector	see Data link connector (DLC)		
Oil level sensor	Bottom of oil pan	B6254	50
Oil pressure switch • 6–cylinder • V-8	 Left front of engine on oil filter housing Left front of engine compartment on oil filter housing	 B6231 S95	 47 115
Oil temperature sensor	Left front of engine at oil filter housing	B2243	
On-board monitor	In center of dashboard	A196	
Outside air temperature sensor	Under right corner of front bumper	B21	33
Overload protection relay	see Closed circuit current cut-off relay		

Component	Location	Designation	Figure No.
Oxygen sensor, 6–cylinder			
• Sensor I, precatalyst, M52, M52 TU, M54	Top of exhaust manifold	B62101	
• Sensor II, precatalyst, M52, M52 TU, M54	Top of exhaust manifold	B62201	
• Sensor I, post-catalyst, M52	Exhaust center	B62102	
• Sensor II, post-catalyst, M52	Exhaust center	B62202	
• Sensor I, post-catalyst, M52 TU, M54	Bottom of exhaust manifold (access from below)		
• Sensor II, post catalyst, M52 TU, M54	Bottom of exhaust manifold (access from below)		
Oxygen sensor, V-8			
• Sensor I, precatalyst	Left side of transmission	B62101	
• Sensor I, post-catalyst	Exhaust center	B62102	
• Sensor II, precatalyst	Right side of transmission	B62201	
• Sensor II, post-catalyst	Exhaust center	B62202	
Park distance control converter (sensor)			
• Left center front	Under left front bumper	B31	
• Left center rear	In left center of rear bumper	B35	
• Left front	Under left front bumper	B30	
• Left rear	In left side of rear bumper	B34	
• Right center front	Under right front bumper	B32	
• Right center rear	In right center of rear bumper	B36	
• Right front	Under right front bumper	B33	
• Right rear	In right rear of rear bumper	B37	
Park distance control module	In right side trunk above battery	A81	24
Park distance control sensors	see Park distance control converter entries		
Park distance control warning speaker	Under rear parcel shelf	H40	
Parked car ventilation receiver	Behind rear seat backrest, right (6–pin, natural)	A128	
Parked car ventilation relay	Relay panel 3, right side trunk		
Parking brake switch	Under center console, rear of parking brake handle	S31	108
Park / neutral position switch	see Automatic transmission park / neutral position switch		
Passenger door module	In passenger door	A24	138
Passenger seat adjustment switch	Passenger seat base, right side	S56	
Passenger seat back head adjustment switch	Passenger seat base, right side	S211	
Passenger seat back head recliner motor	In passenger seat back	M110	
Passenger seat back recliner motor	Underside of passenger seat	M58	
Passenger seat cushion tilt motor	Underside of passenger seat	M61	
Passenger seat headrest motor	In passenger seatback	M57	

Component	Location	Designation	Figure No.
Passenger seat heating switch	Center console, front	S54	
Passenger seat height motor	Underside of passenger seat	M59	
Passenger seat lumbar support			
• Motor	Underside of passenger seat	M56	
• Pressure switch	In passenger seat back	S210	
• Switch	Passenger seat base, right side	S55	
• Valve block	In passenger seat back	Y194	
Passenger seat movement motor	Underside of passenger seat	M60	
Passenger seat pressure sensor 1	Under passenger seat cushion cover	I01055	
Passenger seat pressure sensor 2	Under passenger seat cushion cover	I01056	
Passenger seat pump motor	Underside of passenger seat	I01053	
Passenger seat thigh support motor	Underside of passenger seat	M66	
Passenger seat valve	Underside of passenger seat	I01054	
PDC	see Park distance control entries		
Pedal position sensor	see Accelerator pedal position sensor (PWG)		
Pinch protection, window	see Pressure sensitive finger guard entries		
Pneumatic speaker, left	Left rear of front bumper frame	B404	37
Pneumatic speaker, right	Right rear of front bumper frame	B417	
Power window	see Window entries		
Precharge pump	see ABS/DSC precharge pump		
Pressure sensitive finger guard			
• Left front window	In upper driver's door, across top of window frame	S200	
• Left rear window	In upper left rear door, across top of window frame	S185	106
• Right front window	In upper passenger door, across top of window frame	S201	
• Right rear window	In upper right rear door, across top of window frame	S186	
Pressure sensor	see ABS/DSC pressure sensor		
Radiator fan	see Engine cooling fan entries		
Radiator outlet temperature sensor	see Engine coolant temperature sensor, radiator outlet		
Radio			
• With GPS	In rear left side of trunk	N9	138, 140
• Without GPS	Center console below dashboard	N9	138
Radio amplifier	Left side luggage compartment behind trim panel	A18	12, 140
Radio antenna	see Antenna entries		
Radio controls (steering wheel)	On steering wheel left keypad		
Rain sensor and rain sensor control module (AIC)	Top center of interior windshield surface, directly ahead of rear view mirror	B57	
Rear compartment blower motor	In back of center console	M115, I01104	

Component	Location	Designation	Figure No.
Rear ventilation grill	Rear of center console	I01059	
Rear lid	see Trunk lid entries		
Rear power window lock-out switch	see Child safety switch		
Rear window antenna / defroster	Rear window	I01005	
Rear window defroster relay	Relay panel 3, right side of trunk	K13	9
Rear window defroster relay	Spare tire compartment, below trunk	K417	
Rear window defroster relay 2	Below right trunk trim, by battery	K556	
Rear window motor relay	Relay panel 3, right side of trunk	K90	9
Rear window, tailgate	see Tailgate entries		
Rear window washer pump	see Washer pump, rear		
Receiver, independent heating	see Parked car ventilation entries		
Recirculation flap motor	see Stepper motor entries		
Relay panel 1	Engine compartment E-box	R300	7
Relay panel 2	Behind glove compartment	R100	8
Relay panel 3	Right side of trunk	R200	9
Relay panel 4	Under driver's side of dash	R400	10
Remote entry	see FZV entries		
Resonance valve, intake manifold	Intake manifold (MS 42.0, MS 43.0)	Y6167	
Reversing light switch	see Back-up light switch entries		
Ring coil (toroidal ring antenna)	see EWS ring antenna		
Rotational rate sensor	see ABS/DSC RPM rate (rotational rate or yaw) sensor		
RPM rate sensor	see ABS/DSC RPM rate (rotational rate or yaw) sensor		
Running losses	see 3/2 valve see also Fuel tank leakage diagnosis entries		
SBE module	see Seat occupancy module (SBE)		
SBE mat	see Passenger seat pressure sensor entries		
Seat belt tensioner, driver's side	Under driver's seat	G12	
Seat belt tensioner, passenger side	Under passenger seat	G13	
Seat control module	see Seat/steering column memory control unit		
Seat heater	In front seat cushion and backrest		
Seat heater switch	Center console, below IHKA control panel		
Seat heater temperature sensor	Front of front seat cushion		
Seat load sensor	see Passenger seat pressure sensor entries		
Seat motors	see Driver's seat or Passenger seat entries		
Seat occupancy module (SBE)	Under passenger seat		
Seat occupancy sensor	see Passenger seat pressure sensor entries		
Seat/steering column memory control unit	Under driver's seat	A21	138
Secondary air injection pump	Right side engine compartment, in front of fender well	M63	

Component	Location	Designation	Figure No.
Secondary air injection pump relay	Relay panel 1, right rear of engine compartment in E-box	K6304	7
Secondary air injection pump valve	Top of engine	Y6163	93
Shift interlock cable	Under shifter bezel		
Shiftlock solenoid	Under shifter bezel		
Shutoff valve, LWS (M52 TU, M54, M62 TU)	Front left wheel well, at rear behind liner	Y28	
Side impact airbag	see Airbag entries		
Slip ring, airbag contact	see Airbag entries		
Socket, 12 volt	see 12 volt outlet		
Solar sensor	Above center defroster outlet at base of windshield	B66	51
Solenoid valve 2, park heating/ventilation	Left side of engine compartment on inner fender	Y12	
Sound system amplifier	see Radio amplifier		
Speakers			
• Left front	In driver's door	H41	
• Left front midrange	Driver's door by air duct	H55	
• Left front tweeter	In driver's door, upper front	H59	
• Right front	In passenger door	H44	
• Right front midrange	Passenger door by air duct	H54	
• Right front tweeter	In passenger door, upper front	H50	
• Sedan models subwoofer	Under rear window shelf	H66	70
• Sport Wagon subwoofer	In cargo compartment side compartments		140
Speed sensor	see ABS wheel speed sensor entries		
Spiral spring	Driver's airbag contact in steering wheel		
SRS control module	see Airbag diagnosis module		
Starter (6–cylinder)	Left rear of engine, under intake manifold	M6510	100
Starter (V-8)	Right rear of engine	M6510	101
Starter immobilization switch	On clutch pedal		
Starter relay	Relay panel 2 behind glove compartment	K6324	8
Starter terminals 30, 50 (6–cylinder)	Left rear of engine, under intake manifold		
Starter terminals 30, 50(V-8)	Right rear of engine, under intake manifold		
Steering angle sensor	see ABS/DSC steering angle sensor		
Steering column angle adjustment motor	Right side of steering column	M83	94
Steering column length adjustment motor	Left side of steering column	M82	94
Steering column position adjustment switch	Left side of steering column	S119	105
Steering wheel heater	In steering wheel rim	I01033	

Component	Location	Designation	Figure No.
Stepper motors (IHKA)			
• Defroster stepper motor	Right side of heater housing under dashboard	M35	91
• Dynamic pressure stepper motor	Right side of heater housing under dashboard	M177	
• Face level vents stepper motor	Left side of heater housing under dashboard	M154	
• Footwell stepper motor	Right side of heater housing under dashboard	M153	97
• Footwell / rear compartment stepper motor	Right side of heater housing under dashboard	M41	97
• Fresh air stepper motor	Left side of heater housing under dashboard	M36	
• Recirculation stepper motor	Heater housing, right, behind dash	M40	91
	also see **640 Heating and Air Conditioning**		
Stop light switch	see Brake light switch		
Sunblind motor	Under rear window shelf	M74	
Sunblind remote control switch	Center console front	S110	
Sunblind remote control switch	Center armrest	S226	
Sunroof control module	Behind front roof trim panel	A33	17, 138
Sunroof motor	Behind front roof trim panel		
Sunroof/sunshade switch	In center console ahead of shifter		
Supplemental restraint system (SRS)	see Airbag entries		
Switching center (1999 and later vehicles) (SZM)	Center console below radio	A169	13
Taillight assembly	Rear bulkhead	E46, E47	59
Tailgate emergency release	Inside tool kit, in tailgate, accessible from inside vehicle		141
Tailgate latch actuator	Bottom of tailgate	M17	141
Tailgate lock (central locking)	In tailgate latch	S167	
Tailgate soft close (SCA) motor	Rear cargo compartment floor		141
Tailgate unlock switch pad, exterior	Above license plate		141
Tailgate unlock switch, interior	Left kick panel	S204	
Tailgate window			
• Latch actuator	Below tailgate window	S170	141
• Servo motor	In tailgate	M96	
• Unlock switch pad	At base of rear wiper arm	S147	141
• Wiper motor / module	Below tailgate window		141
Telephone antenna	At top of rear window	I01042	
Telephone connector	Under center console		
Telephone controls (steering wheel)	Steering wheel left keypad		
Telephone speaker	In left footwell top trim		

Component	Location	Designation	Figure No.
Telephone transceiver			
• Sedan	In trunk below parcel shelf		
• Sport Wagon	Center front of cargo compartment		138, 140
Temperature switch (dual)	see Engine cooling fan switch		
Temperature switch, E-box	In left front of E-box, right rear of engine compartment	S2156	
Terminal point B+		I01048	
Thermostat, characteristic map cooling	Thermostat housing, front of engine	Y6279	122
Throttle valve actuator (MS 42.0)	Left side engine at throttle housing	R6385	
Tilt sensor	Left side of trunk behind radio amplifier	B28	35, 138
Tire pressure control switch (RDC)	On dash, right of steering wheel	S106	
Tire pressure control module (RDC)	Behind glove compartment	A85	
Tire pressure sensor (RDC)			
• Left front	On front left wheel well	B43	
• Left rear	On rear left wheel well	B45	
• Right front	On front right wheel well	B47	
• Right rear	On rear right wheel well	B44	
Toroidal coil	see EWS ring antenna (toroidal ring coil)		
Traction control	see ABS/ASC or ABS/DSC entries		
Trailer module	Right side of spare tire in trunk	A6	
Transmission control module	see Automatic transmission control module (AGS)		
Transmission range switch	see Automatic transmission range switch		
Transmission valve	Lower right side of transmission	Y8521	126
Transceiver / receiver	see EWS transceiver / receiver		
Transverse acceleration sensor	see ABS/DSC transverse (lateral) acceleration sensor		
Trunk lid hydraulic pump	By spare tire below trunk	M10	
Trunk lid lock switch	Underside of trunk lid, near license plate	S117	
Trunk lid module	Right side of trunk (15–pin, white)	A204	
Trunk lid motor relay	Relay panel 3, right side of trunk	K70	9
Trunk lid release switch (interior)	Driver's side footwell, left	S204	
Trunk lid servo motor	In trunk lid	M407	98
Trunk light	Luggage compartment in trim panel on trunk panel/hatch	E32	57
Trunk light switch	In trunk lid lock		
Turn-signal/headlight dimmer switch	Combination stalk switch on steering column		
TV amplifier, left	Left C pillar, behind trim	I01006	
TV amplifier, right	Right C pillar, behind trim	I01007	
UIS	see Interior motion sensor and control module (UIS)		
Ultrasonic sensor (motion detector)	see Interior motion sensor and control module (UIS)		

Component	Location	Designation	Figure No.
Unloader relay, terminal R	Relay panel 3, right side of trunk	K3	9
Unloader relay, terminal 15 (EDC switching center)	Relay panel 3, right side of trunk	K93	9
Unloader relay, terminal 15 (DME)	Relay panel 1, right rear of engine compartment in E-box	K6326	7
Valet position switch	On trunk lock cylinder		
VANOS control solenoid, 6–cylinder			
• Exhaust, M52 TU, M54	Right front of cylinder head		
• Intake, M52, M52 TU, M54	Left front of cylinder head	Y6275	121
VANOS control solenoid, V-8			
• Left intake (cylinders 5 – 8), M62 TU	Left front of right cylinder head	B6281	
• Right intake (cylinders 1– 4), M62 TU	Right front of left cylinder head	B6283	
Variable camshaft control	see VANOS entries		
Ventilation stepper motor	see Stepper motors (IHKA)		
Video module	Left rear trunk	A197	
Washer fluid level switch	Bottom of windshield washer tank, front of right front wheel well	S136	
Washer pump, rear	Right front of passenger front wheel well	M95	
Water valve(s)	see Heater valve assembly		
Wheel speed sensor	see ABS wheel speed sensor		
Window anti-trap strip	see Pressure sensitive finger guard		
Window heating control module	Right side of spare tire, below trunk.	A411	
Window lock-out switch	see Child safety switch		
Window motor			
• Left front	Inside driver's door	M21	88
• Left rear	Inside rear left door	M20	87
• Right front	Inside passenger door	M23	
• Right rear	Inside rear right door	M22	
Window switch			
• Left front	In left front door pull		
• Left rear	In left rear door pull	S128	
• Right front	In right front door pull	S127	
• Right rear	In right rear door pull	S129	
Windshield washer nozzle heaters	In washer nozzles		
Windshield washer pump	Back of right front wheel well behind inner fender trim panel, on reservoir	M4	90
Windshield wiper motor, front	Rear of engine compartment, behind bulkhead	M3	
Windshield wiper module / motor, rear	see Tailgate window entries		
Windshield wiper relay	Relay panel 1 in E-box	K11	7
Windshield wiper relay 1	Relay panel 1 in E-box	K36	7

Component	Location	Designation	Figure No.
Windshield wiper relay 2	Relay panel 1 in E-box	K37	7
Wiper/washer switch (stalk)	Right side steering column		
X38 Connector, light module	Passenger footwell, right side	X38	16
X46 Ground (airbag control)	Below center console	X46	118
X52 Engine cooling fan normal speed relay connector	E-box, right rear of engine compartment (9–pin, black)	X52	7
X53 Engine cooling fan high speed relay connector	Relay panel 2, behind glove compartment (9–pin, black)	X53	8
X56 Horn relay connector	Relay panel 3, right side of engine compartment (9–pin, black)	X56	9
X57 Unloader relay (terminal R) connector	Relay panel 3, right side of trunk (9–pin, black)	X57	9
X58 A/C blower relay connector	Relay panel 2, behind glove compartment	X58	8
X78 Brake light switch connector	Brake pedal at pedal cluster	X78	107
X85 Heater valve(s) connector	Left side of engine compartment on inner fender well (3–pin, black)	X85	26
X87 Electric cooling fan switch connector (dual)	Right side of radiator	X87	109
X107 Windshield washer pump connector	Right front wheel well behind inner fender panel at reservoir	X107	90
X111 Brake fluid level switch connector	Engine compartment, left rear	X111	32
X112 Engine coolant level switch connector	Radiator shroud, lower right	X112	112
X118 Brake pad sensor connector, left front	Brake caliper, front left	X118	30
X126 A/C high pressure switch connector	Engine compartment, front right	X126	55
X138 Center brake light connector	Rear window shelf	X138	69
X145 Oil pressure switch connector (V-8)	Engine compartment, front left, on oil filter housing	X145	18
X151 Ground cable shoe	Under carpet beneath driver's seat	X151	119
X163 A/C compressor connector	Engine compartment, lower front right	X163	145
X165 Ground cable shoe	Left front inner fender in engine compartment	X165	120
X166 Ground cable shoe	Right front inner fender in engine compartment	X166	123
X173 Ground cable shoe	Under left front carpet on door sill	X173	119
X181 Splice, brake light signal	Under carpet beneath driver's seat	X181	135
X183 Splice, data link (TXD)	Under carpet beneath driver's seat	X183	135
X188 Splice, speed signal	Under carpet beneath driver's seat	X188	135
X217 Ground cable shoe	Under right side dashboard	X217	
X218 Ground cable shoe	Under carpet, right side front footwell	X218	125
X219 Ground splice	Under carpet beneath passenger seat, right side	X219	
X243 Splice, engine speed signal (TD)	Under carpet beneath driver's seat	X243	135
X254 Connector, general module	Behind glove compartment	X254	11

Component	Location	Designation	Figure No.
X256 In-line connector, passenger door	In lower passenger side A pillar (passenger door to body, 6–pin, black)	X256	
X257 In-line connector, driver's door	In lower driver's side A pillar (driver's door to body, 6–pin, black)	X257	
X263 Electronic shock absorber control module (EDC) connector	Right side of trunk	X263	23
X273 In-line connector, left rear door	In lower left side B pillar (left rear door to body, 6–pin, black)	X273	
X274 In-line connector, right rear door	In lower right side B pillar (right rear door to body, 6–pin, black)	X274	
X275 Driver's seat connector	Underside of driver's seat (6–pin, black)	X275	
X279 Passenger seat connector	Underside of passenger seat (6–pin, black)	X279	
X292 Rear window defogger relay connector	Relay panel 3, right rear of engine compartment (9–pin, black)	X292	9
X293 Wiper relay 1 connector	In E-box, right rear of engine compartment (9–pin, black)	X293	7
X300 Park distance control (PDC) module connector	Right side of trunk	X300	24
X312 Fuel tank access flap motor connector	trunk, right	X312	85
X319 Tail light connector with trailer adaptor, left rear	Trunk, left rear	X319	59
X322 Radio/hi-fi connector	Left side of trunk (12–pin, black)	X322	
X325 In-line connector, radio	Right side of trunk on wheel housing (4–pin, black)	X325	
X336 Interior/reading lamp connector	In headliner, front	X336	58
X372 Alarm (anti-theft, DWA) horn connector	Rear right wheel well, behind liner	X372	67
X379 Antenna amplifier connector	Left C pillar, behind trim (1–pin, black)	X379	61
X384 Trunk light or tailgate connector	Trunk or tailgate inner panel	X384	57
X400 In-line connector, telephone	Left side of trunk (12–pin, natural)	X400	
X423 Parking brake switch connector	Below center console, rear of parking brake handle	X423	108
X437 Splice terminal 30	Behind glove compartment	X437	
X442 Splice (TXD)	Behind glove compartment	X442	
X455 Splice central locking (ZV)	Below left side of dash on steering column	X455	
X456 Splice lock motor signal	Behind glove compartment	X456	
X462 Splice central arrest (ZV)	Behind glove compartment	X462	
X490 Ground cable shoe	Under carpet beneath driver's seat, on door sill	X490	125
X492 Ground cable shoe	Under carpet beneath driver's seat, on door sill	X492	125
X494 Ground cable shoe	Bottom of right C-pillar	X494	134
X498 Ground cable shoe	Right side trunk, back	X498	127
X518 Chime module connector	Dash panel above driver's footwell	X518	68
X531 Cigarette lighter connector, front	Center console, near shift lever	X531	56
X540 Glove compartment light switch connector	Glove box, top	X540	110

Component	Location	Designation	Figure No.
X596 Splice terminal 31	Behind glove compartment	X596	
X638 Fuel pump connector (EKP I)	Under rear seat, right	X638	86
X644 Door lock motor connector, rear left	Rear left door	X644	84
X651 Starter solenoid connector (V-8)	Right rear of engine	X651	101
X660 Door lock motor connector, driver's	Driver's door	X660	83
X662 Recirculation stepper motor connector	Heater housing, right, behind dash	X662	91
X664 Defroster stepper motor connector	Heater housing, right, behind dash	X664	91
X665 Footwell/rear compartment stepper motor connector	Right side of heater housing	X665	97
X667 Footwell stepper motor connector	Heater housing, right, behind dash	X667	97
X671 A/C blower motor final stage connector	Lower right side of heater housing	X671	102
X679 Fuel level sensor II connector	Beneath rear seat left side	X679	34
X713 Brake pad sensor connector, right rear	Brake caliper, right rear	X713	31
X714 Window motor connector, left rear	Rear left door	X714	87
X748 Driver's door light connector	Driver's door, bottom	X748	60
X749 Driver's window motor connector	Driver's door	X749	88
X770 Outside air temperature sensor connector	under front of vehicle at bumper cover, right	X770	33
X771 A/C evaporator temperature sensor connector	Left side of heater housing, below floor outlet	X771	29
X772 Left heat exchanger temperature sensor connector	Behind center console	X772	28
X806 Splice light signal terminal 58g	Behind glove compartment	X806	
X816 A/C blower motor connector	Behind dash, center	X816	89
X819 B+ supply, fuse panel 5, cable shoe	At fuse panel 5	X819	136
X840 Ground splice	Underside of driver's seat	X840	
X844 Ground splice	Underside of passenger seat	X844	
X849 Ground splice	In driver's door	X849	
X854 Splice sensor IHKA	Behind center console, driver's side	X854	
X887 Driver's door module connector	Driver's door	X887	15
X891 Splice ground	In passenger front door	X891	
X908 Splice light signal terminal 58g	Below left side dash on steering column	X908	
X916 Connector, sunroof module	Behind headliner trim panel, front	X916	17
X939 Splice I/K—Bus	Behind glove compartment	X939	
X961 Ground cable shoe	Under carpet, right side front footwell	X961	128
X1001 Headlight washer pump connector	Rear of front right wheel well, behind liner (2–pin, gray)	X1001	90
X1110 Unloader relay connector	Relay panel 3, right side of trunk (9–pin, black)	X1110	9

Component	Location	Designation	Figure No.
X1019 Splice night time illumination terminal 58g	Under carpet, right footwell, right side	X1019	
X1022 Splice engine cooling fan normal speed	Behind glove compartment	X1022	
X1024 Independent heating blower motor relay connector	Relay panel 3, right side of trunk (9–pin, black)	X1024	9
X1101 Splice engine speed sensor signal	Behind glove compartment	X1101	
X1082 Wiper relay 2 connector	In E-box, right rear of engine compartment (9–pin, black)	X1082	7
X1106 Ground cable shoe	Right front of engine compartment	X1106	123
X1108 Ground cable shoe	Under carpet, driver's footwell	X1108	135
X1134 Pressure sensitive finger guard connection, left rear window	Left rear door, upper	X1134	106
X1143 Amplifier connector, FM, lockout circuit	Right lower C pillar	X1143	72
X1169 Splice back up signal (AGS)	Behind dash, left, on steering column	X1169	137
X1170 ABS/ASC control module connector	Front of right front strut tower	X1170	
X1222 Tilt sensor connector	Left side of trunk, behind radio amplifier	X1222	35
X1264 Terminal R splice	Behind left side of dash	X1264	137
X1242 Wiper relay connector (fast and slow speeds)	In E-box, right rear of engine compartment (9–pin, black)	X1242	7
X1310 In-line connector, navigation	Left side of trunk (6–pin, black)	X1310	
X1353 Splice EDC	Under carpet, right footwell, right side	X1353	
X1354 Splice EDC	Under carpet, right footwell, right side	X1354	
X1355 Splice EDC valves	Right side trunk	X1355	
X1356 Splice EDC valves	Right side trunk	X1356	
X1369 Cable shoe, battery	Luggage compartment, right	X1369	62
X1411 Splice EDC	Under carpet, right footwell, right side	X1411	
X1451 Right rear level sensor connector	Right rear wheel well	X1451	39
X1452 In-line connector, hydraulic unit	Below trunk, right side of spare tire	X1452	
X1461 Splice ground	Below dash, left side on steering column	X1461	
X1532 In-line connector, radio/hi-fi navigation	Left side of trunk (6–pin, natural)	X1532	
X1589 Central locking fuel tank access flap relay connector	Relay panel 3, right side of trunk (9–pin, black)	X1589	9
X1596 Splice reset contact, wiper park position	Behind glove compartment	X1596	
X1647 Shutoff valve connector, LWS (M52 TU, M54, M62 TU)	Front left wheel well, at rear behind liner (2–pin, natural)	X1647	
X1648 Changeover valve connector, LWS (M52 TU, M54, M62 TU)	Front left wheel well, at rear behind liner (2–pin, black)	X1648	

Component	Location	Designation	Figure No.
X1650 Splice auxiliary water pump	Behind glove compartment	X1650	
X1653 RPM rate (rotational rate or yaw) sensor connector	Under carpet beneath passenger seat	X1653	53
X1654 Pressure sensor connector	Engine compartment, left, on back of pre-charge pump	X1654	54
X1655 Transverse (lateral) acceleration sensor connector	Under carpet beneath driver's seat	X1655	52
X1658 ABS/DSC steering angle sensor connector	Steering column	X1658	104
X1659 EWS (electronic immobilization) control unit connector	Under left side dash	X1659	25
X1714 Leak diagnosis pump connector	Back of wheel housing, left rear, behind liner	X1714	75
X1732 Auxiliary fan stage 3 relay connector	E-box, right rear of engine compartment	X1732	80
X1869 Connector, switching center	Center console below radio	X1869	13
X1883 Driver's side airbag connector	Driver's door	X1883	63
X1885 Airbag sensor connector, left front	Under carpet beneath driver's seat	X1885	113
X1886 Airbag sensor connector, right front	Under carpet beneath passenger seat	X1886	114
X1966 Passenger side curtain airbag connector	Passenger A pillar, lower	X1966	64
X3143 Pneumatic speaker connector	Behind front bumper support	X3143	37
X3211 Automatic air recirculation sensor (AUC) connector	Engine cooling fan housing, lower right	X3211	38
X3250 Splice pneumatic speaker	Right side trunk	X3250	
X3251 Splice pneumatic speaker	Right side trunk	X3251	
X6002 Data link component connector	Engine compartment, right front	X6002	45
X6011 Engine connector I in-line connector	E-box, right rear of engine compartment (12–pin, black)	X6011	
X6031 Engine connector III in-line connector	E-box, right rear of engine compartment (18–pin, natural)	X6031	
X6021 Engine connector 2, in-line connector	E-box, right rear of engine compartment (26–pin, black)	X6021	
X6053 In-line connection, engine wiring harness	E-box, right rear of engine compartment (12–pin, black)	X6053	
X6163 Secondary air injection pump valve connector	Top of engine	X6163	93
X6207 Mass air flow sensor connector (V-8)	At engine air filter housing	X6207	41
X6215 Intake air temperature sensor connector (V-8)	Front of engine air filter housing	X6215	44
X6219 Camshaft position (Hall) sensor connector (V-8)	Top of right head wiring loom (3–pin, black)	X6219	41

Component	Location	Designation	Figure No.
X6224 Camshaft sensor II connector (exhaust camshaft, 6–cylinder)	Right front of engine, top	X6224	46
X6231 Oil pressure switch connector (6–cylinder)	Engine compartment, left, on oil filter housing	X6231	47
X6240 Knock sensor harness connector (V-8)	Top of cylinder heads at wiring duct	X6240	49
X6254 Oil level sensor connector	Oil pan, bottom	X6254	50
X6275 VANOS solenoid connector, intake side (6–cylinder)	Left front of cylinder head	X6275	121
X6279 Coolant thermostat connector	Thermostat housing, front of engine	X6279	122
X6300 Engine control unit main relay (DME) connector	Relay panel 1 in E-box	X6300	7
X6304 Secondary air injection pump relay connector	Relay panel 1 in E-box	X6304	7
X6324 Starter relay connector	Relay panel 2, above glove compartment (9–pin, black)	X6324	8
X6326 Unloader terminal 15 relay connector	E-box, right rear of engine compartment (9–pin, black)	X6326	7
X6404 B+ junction cable shoe	Right side of frame rail, under car	X6404	130
X6420 Splice terminal 30	E-box, right rear of engine compartment	X6420	
X6452 Ground cable shoe	Right rear of engine compartment, on outside of E-box	X6452	
X6453 Ground cable shoe	Right rear of engine compartment, on outside of E-box	X6453	
X6454 Ground cable shoe	On bulkhead, left rear engine compartment, at E-box	X6454	124
X6456 Ground cable shoe, ignition coil (V-8)	Center top of right head, between ignition coils	X6456	
X6458 Splice ground connector, power	E-box, right rear of engine compartment	X6458	
X6509 Alternator (generator) cable shoe	On alternator, left front of cylinder block	X6509	80
X6510 Starter solenoid connector (V-8)	Right rear of engine	X6510	101
X6512 Starter solenoid connector (V-8)	Right rear of engine	X6512	101
X6524 Alternator (generator) connector	Engine, lower left	X6524	66
X6820 Terminal 87 splice	Wire loom, top of cylinder head	X6820	81
X6821 Splice, terminal 87	E-box, right rear of engine compartment	X6821	82
X6822 Splice, terminal 87	E-box, right rear of engine compartment	X6822	82
X6841 Splice ground (V-8)	In cable duct on right head, at front	X6841	
X8507 Kick-down switch connector	Driver's side floor, under accelerator pedal	X8507	116
X8521 Transmission valve connector	Transmission, lower right	X8521	126
X8532 Automatic transmission range switch connector	Transmission, lower left	X8532	117
X8589 Splice transmission range switch position L2 (park/neutral)	E-box, right rear of engine compartment	X8589	
X8680 Fuse panel 3, engine electronics, connector	In E-box, right rear of engine compartment, at Fuse panel 3 (A8680)	X8680	3

Electrical Component Locations

Component	Location	Designation	Figure No.
X01021 Air suspension compressor pump control relay connector	Spare tire well, under tire	X01021	73
X01031 Airbag coil spring contact	Steering wheel	X01031	74
X01040 GPS antenna connector	Left side rear window shelf	X01040	71
X01054 Horn switch connector	Steering wheel, behind airbag	X01054	111
X01100 Blower motor output stage, rear compartment, connector	Rear of center console	X01100	78
X01158 Diversity antenna connector	Left C pillar	X01158	79
X10012 Ground cable shoe	Under carpet, right side front footwell	X10012	125
X10051 Headlight widening potentiometer connector	Left side of dash	X10051	103
X10088 In-line connector, washer nozzle heating	Right side engine compartment, at fender near strut tower	X10088	
X10094 Auxiliary throttle position motor (ADS) connector	Front of right front strut tower	X10094	96
X10116 Splice K-Bus	Behind glove compartment	X10116	
X10134 Splice P-Bus	Behind glove compartment	X10134	
X10148 Splice I-Bus (interior lights)	Under carpet, passenger footwell, right side	X10148	
X10156 Fuel pump relay 1 connector	Relay panel 3, right side of trunk (9–pin, black)	X10156	9
X10195 Driver's airbag connector	Steering wheel	X10195	65
X10669 Solar sensor connector	Above center dash vent at base of windshield	X10669	51
X13016 Ground cable shoe	Left side trunk, back	X13016	132
X13001 Closed circuit current cut-off relay connector	Relay panel 2, above glove compartment (9–pin, black)	X13001	8
X13020 Fuse panel 4, cable shoe voltage supply	Under carpet beneath passenger seat	X13020	133
X13030 Fuse panel 4 connector	Under carpet beneath passenger seat	X13030	4
X13075 Ground cable shoe	Right side of trunk, back	X13075	127
X13139 Electrochromic rear view mirror connector	In rear view mirror, top of windshield	X13139	14
X18093 Steering column position adjustment switch connector	Left side of steering column	X18093	105
X18096 Steering column angle adjustment motor connector	Steering column	X18096	94
X18097 Steering column length adjustment motor connector	Steering column	X18097	94
X18121 Splice consumer cut off signal	Under carpet, passenger footwell, right side	X18121	
X18129 Splice, terminal 30	Under rear window shelf at base of passenger C pillar, or trunk, right	X18129	131, 134
X18146 Brake pad sensor connector, right rear	Right rear wheel well	X18146	
X18193 Electric cooling fan connector	Front of radiator	X18193	95

Component	Location	Designation	Figure No.
X18344 Splice I/K-Bus (top hi-fi)	Left side of trunk	X18344	
X18722 A/C final stage unit in-line connector	Behind center console	X18722	129
X18740 Splice ground, seat	Underside of driver's seat	X18740	
X18749 Splice ground, seat	Underside of passenger seat	X18749	
X18771 Connector, amplifier	Luggage compartment, left	X18771	12
X18766 ABS pump relay connector	In E-box, right rear of engine compartment (9–pin, black)	X18766	7
X18767 ABS relay connector	Relay panel 2, above glove compartment (9–pin, black)	X18767	8
X18774 Speaker connector, subwoofer	Rear window shelf	X18774	70
X19527 OBD II plug component connector	Lower dash, driver's side, left	X19527	
X60001 Engine control module connector (DME)	In E-box, right rear of engine compartment	X60001	20
X70001 AGS transmission control module connector	In E-box, right rear of engine compartment	X70001	22
Xenon headlight	In front fender		138
Yaw sensor	see ABS/DSC RPM rate (rotational rate or yaw) sensor		
ZKE III control module	see General module (GM III)		

Fuse locations

There are 6 locations for fuses in E39 cars:

- Fuse panel 1 (fuses F1 — F45) above glove compartment
- Fuse panel 2 (fuses F46 — F66) on right side of trunk behind trim panel
- Fuse panel 3 (DME fuses F1 — F5) in E-box, right rear of engine compartment
- Fuse panel 4 (fuses F107 — F114) under carpet beneath passenger seat
- Fuse panel 5 (fuses F100 — F106 in trunk, right side
- Fuse panel 6 (fuses F75, F76) behind glove compartment

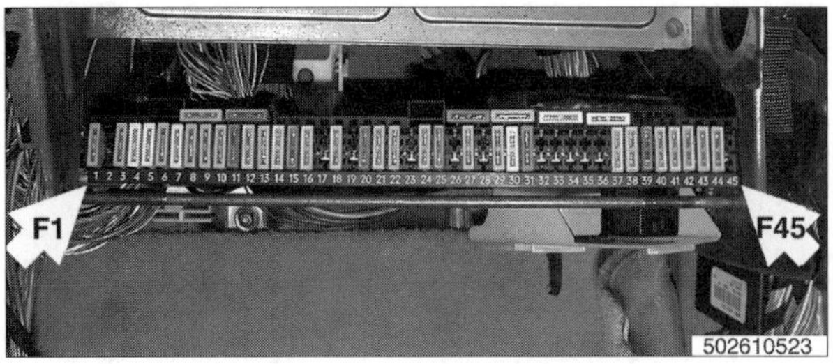

Fig. 1 Fuse panel 1 (fuses F1 — F45)

Above glove compartment. Twist white plastic retainers 90° and pull panel down from top of glove compartment. A fuse puller is located in the center, and a fuse location card is inserted below the panel.

NOTE —
- *When the fuse panel is up in the locked position, the retainers point towards each other.*
- *Vertical fuses are active; horizontal fuses are spares.*

Fuses F1 - F45, fuse panel 1, glove compartment		
Fuse	**Rating in amps**	**Protected circuit**
1	30	Wiper relay (K11)
2	30	Headlight washer module (K6)
3	15	Horn relay (K2) Horn relay (K555)
4	30	General module (A1)
5	20	Sunroof module (A33), Unloader relay (K6326)
6	30	Passenger door module (A24)
7	20	Engine cooling fan normal speed relay (K21)
8	25	ABS/ASC control module (A52)
9	15	Heating and A/C control module (A11)
10	30	Passenger seat control switch (S56) Passenger seatback head adjustment switch (S211) Passenger seat thigh support switch (S94) Passenger seat lumbar support switch (S55)
11	7.5	General module (A1)
12	5	EWS (electronic immobilizer) (A836)
13	30	Steering column angle adjustment motor (M83) Steering column length adjustment motor (M82) Driver's seat movement motors (M50, M51, M52, M53, M54, M65, M106) Seat/steering column memory control module (A21)
14	5	Engine control module, DME (ECM) (A6000)
15	7.5	Automatic transmission control module (AGS) (8532) Temperature switch (B6235) Oil level sender (B6254) Alternator (G6524)
16	5	Light module (A3)
17	10	Switching center (A169) Fuel pump relay (K96) ABS/ASC control module (A52)
18	5	Instrument cluster, Integrated instrument cluster control module
19	5	Unloader relay (K93)

Fuses F1 - F45, fuse panel 1, glove compartment		
Fuse	**Rating in amps**	**Protected circuit**
20	5	Rear window defogger (K13), Engine cooling fan stage 3 relay (K201) Heating and A/C control module (A11) RDC control module (A85)
21	5	Mirror, rear view (A22) Closed circuit current cut-off relay (K72) Garage door opener (S223) Park distance control module (A81) Cigarette lighter relay (K31)
22	30	Auxiliary fan high speed relay (K22)
23	5	Rear multi information display (MID) (A111)
24	5	Steering angle sensor (R33) Instrument cluster (A2) Integrated instrument cluster control module (A63)
25	7.5	Multi-information display (MID) (A103) OBD II plug (I01010)
26	5	Wiper relay I (K36) Wiper relay II (K37)
27	30	General module (A1)
28	30	Blower relay (K4) Transmission control module (AGS) (A7000)
29	30	Driver's door lock switch (S47) Driver's door module (A23)
30	25	Valve relay (K95)
31	10	Secondary air injection pump relay (K6304) Fuel pump relay (K96) ASC/DSC switch (S6) ABS/DSC control module (A65) 3/2–way (fuel changeover) valve circuit (Y31) Leakage diagnosis pump (M119) Steering angle sensor (R33)
32	15	Seat heater switch, left front (S53) Seat heated switch right front (S54) Switching center (A169)
33		Open
34	10	Driver's airbag slip ring (I01031)
35	5	Blower, rear compartment output stage (I01102)
36		Open
37	5	EWS (electronic immobilizer) (A836)
38	5	Horn relay (K2) General module (A1) Transmission range indicator light (E82) Rain sensor (B57) Shift lock switch (S235)

Fuses F1 - F45, fuse panel 1, glove compartment		
Fuse	**Rating in amps**	**Protected circuit**
39	7.5	Makeup mirror light left (E35) Makeup mirror light right (E36) Charging socket (X779)
40		Seat load assembly (A113), Passenger seat belt switch (S59) Airbag (crash) sensor, (S71, S72) Driver's seat belt switch (S58)
41	5	Light module (A3) Cruise control module (A8) Brake light switch (S29)
42	5	Supplemental restraint system control module (A12)
43	5	Unloader relay, terminal R (K3)
44	5	Driver's airbag slip ring (I01030) Integrated radio information system (IRIS) (A111) Multi-information display (MID) (A103)
45	7.5	Sunblind switch (S110) Switching center (A169)

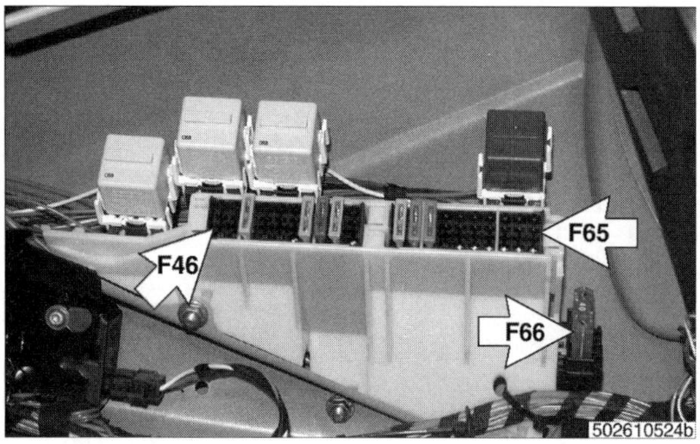

Fig. 2 Fuse panel 2 (fuses F46 — F66)

Right side of trunk behind trim panel.

Fuses F46 - F66, fuse panel 2, trunk		
Fuse	**Rating in amps**	**Protected circuit**
46	15	Blower relay (K62) Parked car ventilation (independent park/auxiliary heating) (A14) Receiver, parked car ventilation (A128)
47	15	Parked car ventilation (independent park/auxiliary heating) control module (A14) Receiver, parked car ventilation (A128)
48	5	Rear view mirror (A22) Interior motion sensor (UIS) control module (A121) Tilt sensor (B28) Anti-theft horn (H1)
49	30	Air suspension pump control relay (I01027)
50	7.5	Air suspension control unit (A118)
51	30	Air suspension pump control relay (I01027) Cigarette lighter, rear (E30)

Fuses F46 - F66, fuse panel 2, trunk		
Fuse	**Rating in amps**	**Protected circuit**
52	30	Cigarette lighter, front (E28)
53	5	FZV (remote entry) antenna amplifier (N8) Tailgate lock switch (S167) Central locking fuel tank access door (K121) Trunk lid motor relay, rear (K70) Diversity (I01113) Window motor relay (K90)
54	15	Fuel pump relay (K96)
55	20	Intermittent wiper/washer control unit, rear (A36)
56	30	On-board monitor (A196) Radio (N9) Video module (A197) CD changer (N22) Amplifier (A18) GPS control module (A112) GPS receiver (I01001) GPS receiver (N28)
57	10	Transceiver (H38) Compensator (I01039) Voice input (U422)
58	10	Unloader relay, terminal R (K3)
59	5	Trailer connector (X630)
60	15	Electronic damper control (EDC) (A80) Switching center (A169)
61	5	Park distance control module (A81) Seat heater switch, left rear (S68) Seat heater switch, right rear (S69)
62		Open
63	7.5	Radio relay (K550) Loud alarm relay (K551) Transparency relay (K554) Alarm control unit (A437)
64	30	On-board monitor (A196) Radio (N9) CD changer (N22) Amplifier (A18) GPS receiver (N28)
65	10	Transceiver (H38)
66	40	Heated rear window (K13)

Fig. 3 Fuse panel 3 (DME fuses F1–F5, engine electronics)

A fuse pack containing five fuses (**arrow**) is located in the rear of the engine compartment in the E-box. To access the E-box, remove the right interior ventilation filter housing and E-box cover. See **640 Heating and Air Conditioning**.

- X8680 Engine electronics fuse carrier connector (10–pin, black)

– To remove an individual fuse, lift out fuse pack. Slide cover off while prying gently with a pin tool to squeeze locking tabs.

– Once cover is off, fuses can fall out easily. Be sure to keep fuses in order while replacing defective fuse.

DME fuses F1 - F5, fuse panel 3, E-box		
Fuse	**Rating in amps**	**Protected circuits**
1		Open
2	30	Fuel injectors (X6101 — X6106) Engine control module (A6000)
3	20	Camshaft sensors (B6214 and B6224) Mass air flow sensor (6207) Crankshaft position sensor (B6203) Thermostat (B6279)
4	30	Heated oxygen sensors (B62101, B62201, B62102, B62202) Transmission control module (A7000)
5	30	Unloader relay (K6326)

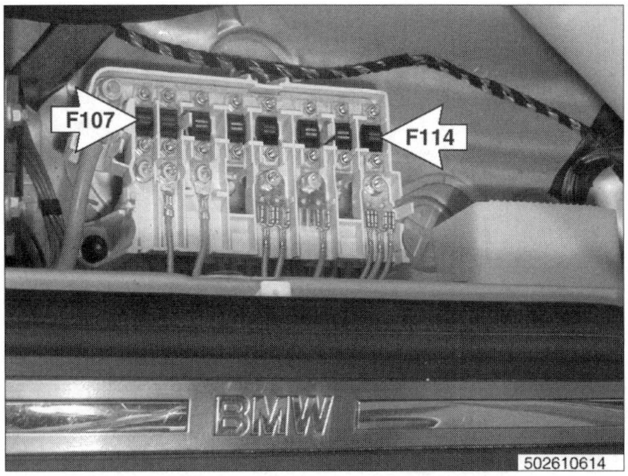

Fig. 4 Fuse panel 4 (fuses F107 — F114)

Under carpet beneath passenger seat

Fuses F107 — F114, fuse panel 4, under passenger side carpet		
Fuse	**Rating in amps**	**Protected circuits**
107	50	Secondary air injection pump relay (K6304)
108	50	Engine control relay (K94)
109	80	Fuses F4 & F5 in fuse panel 3 (engine electronics) Engine control module relay (K6300)
110	80	Power supply for fuses F1 – F12 & F22 – F26
111	50	Data link connector (D100) Ignition switch (S2)
112	80	Light module (A3)
113	80	Power supply for fuses F13 & F27 – F30 Light module (A3)
114	50	Data link connector (D100) Ignition switch (S2)

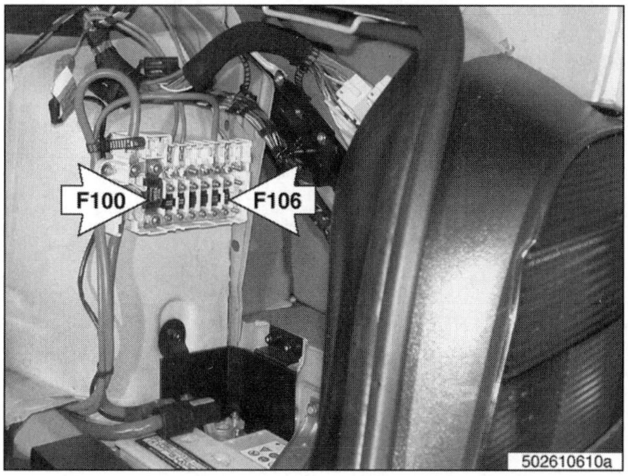

Fig. 5 Fuse panel 5 (F100 — F106)

In trunk, right side

Fuses F100 - F106, high amperage fuse panel 5, trunk		
Fuse	**Rating in amps**	**Protected circuits**
100	200	Fuse panel 4, F107 – F114
101	80	Power supply for fuses F46 – F50 and F66
102	80	Power supply for fuses F51 – F55
103	50	Open
104	50	Unloader relay terminal 15 (K93)
105	100	F75, Engine cooling fan relay stage 3 (K201)
106	80	Power supply for fuses F56 – F59

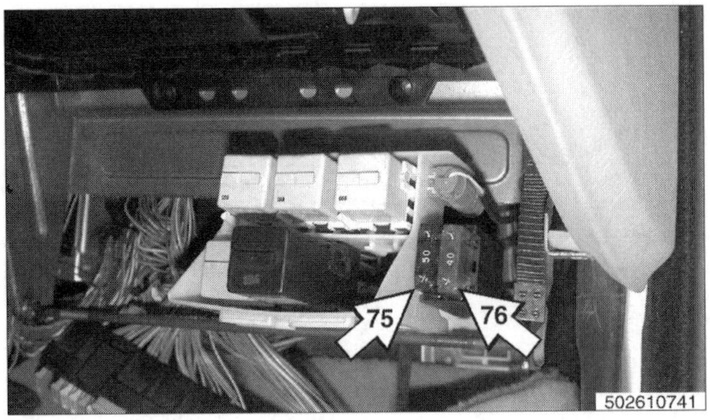

Fig. 6 Fuse panel 6 (fuses F75, F76)

Behind glove compartment. Relay panel shown in drop down position.

Fuses F75 - F76, fuse panel 6, in relay panel behind glove compartment		
Fuse	**Rating in amps**	**Protected circuits**
75	50	Engine cooling fan motor (M9)
76	40	Blower relay (K4) Final stage unit (N2)

Electrical component location photos

The following photos show the locations of major electrical components in E39 vehicles.

NOTE—
- *Every component is not installed in every car.*
- *Due to changes in production, component locations may vary from what is illustrated. Consult your BMW dealer for the latest information.*
- *The component location photos provided below are from a 1998 540i with V-8 engine and automatic transmission, unless otherwise noted.*
- *The automatic transmission range switch is also sometimes referred to as the gear-position / neutral safety switch.*
- *The EWS system is also known as the drive-away protection system or the electronic immobilization system.*

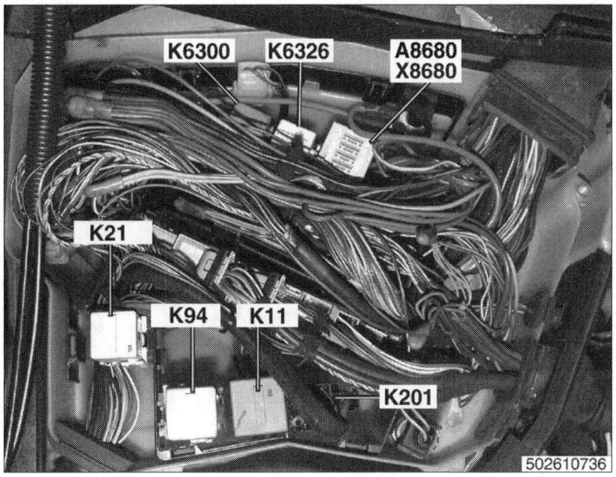

Fig. 7 E-box (electronics box)

Right rear engine compartment in E-box. To access the E-box, remove the interior ventilation filter housing. See **640 Heating and Air Conditioning**.

NOTE —
Components may be hidden by wiring harnesses. Relays are generally located at the front and back of the E-box, with control units located in the center.

- K6300 DME relay
- X6300 DME relay connector (9–pin, black)
- K6326 Unloader terminal 15 relay
- X6326 Unloader terminal 15 relay connector (9–pin, black)
- K11 Wiper relay (fast and slow speeds)
- X1242 Wiper relay connector (fast and slow speeds) (9–pin, black)
- K21 Auxiliary fan normal speed relay
- X52 Auxiliary fan normal speed relay connector (9–pin, black)
- K36 Wiper relay 1 (not shown)
- X293 Wiper relay 1 connector (not shown) (9–pin, black)
- K37 Wiper relay 2 (not shown)
- X1082 Wiper relay 2 connector (not shown) (9–pin, black)
- K94 ABS hydraulic pump relay
- X18766 ABS hydraulic pump relay connector (9–pin, black)
- K201 Auxiliary fan relay stage 3
- X1732 Auxiliary fan stage 3 relay connector (9–pin, black)
- K6304 Secondary air injection pump relay (not shown)
- A8680 Fuse carrier for engine electronics
- X8680 Fuse carrier connector, engine electronics (10–pin, black)

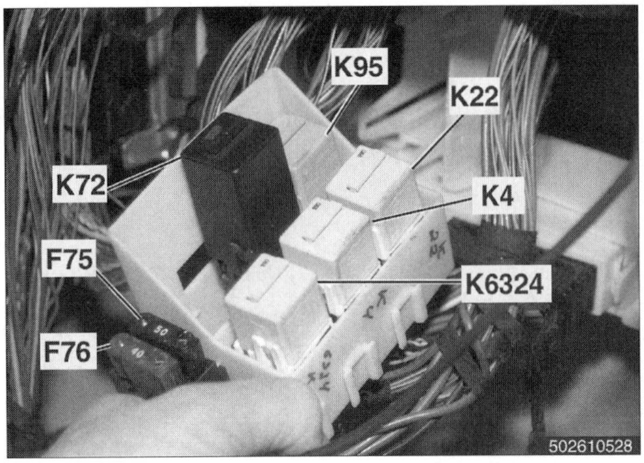

Fig. 8 Relay panel 2

Relay panel 2, located above glove compartment

- K4 A/C blower relay
- X58 A/C blower relay connector (9–pin, black)
- K22 Auxiliary fan high speed relay
- X53 Auxiliary fan high speed relay connector (9–pin, black)
- K72 Closed circuit current cut off relay (Overload protection relay)
- X13001 Closed circuit current cut off relay connector (9–pin, black)
- K95 ABS relay
- X18767 ABS relay connector (9–pin, black)
- K6324 Starter relay
- X6324 Starter relay connector (9–pin, black)
- F75 Engine cooling fan fuse
- F76 Blower relay fuse

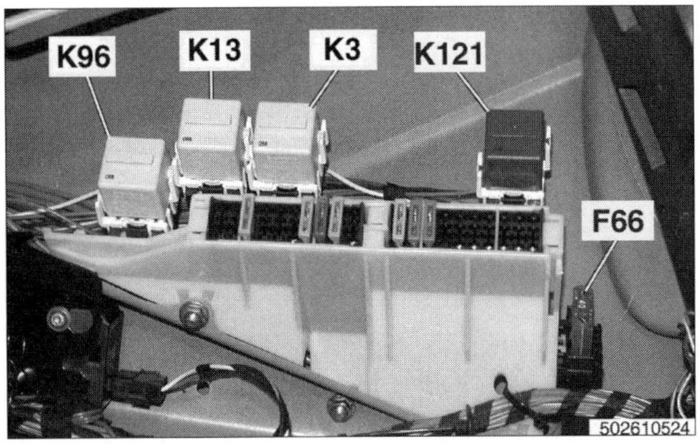

Fig. 9 Relay panel 3

Right side trunk or cargo compartment, above battery

- K3 Unloader relay (terminal R)
- X57 Unloader relay (terminal R) connector (9–pin, black)
- K13 Rear window defogger relay
- X292 Rear window defogger relay connector (9–pin, black)
- K62 Parked car (independent heating) blower motor relay (not shown)
- X1024 Parked car (independent heating) blower motor relay connector (9–pin, black)
- K70 Trunk lid motor relay (not shown)
- K90 Rear window motor relay (not shown)
- K93 Unloader relay (not shown)
- X1110 Unloader relay connector (9–pin, black)
- K96 Fuel pump relay 1
- X10156 Fuel pump relay 1 connector (9–pin, black)
- K121 Central locking fuel tank flap relay
- X1589 Central locking fuel tank flap relay connector (9–pin, black)
- F66 Rear window defogger fuse

Fig. 10 Relay panel 4

◄ Under left side of dash

- K2 Horn relay
- X56 Horn relay connector (9–pin, black)

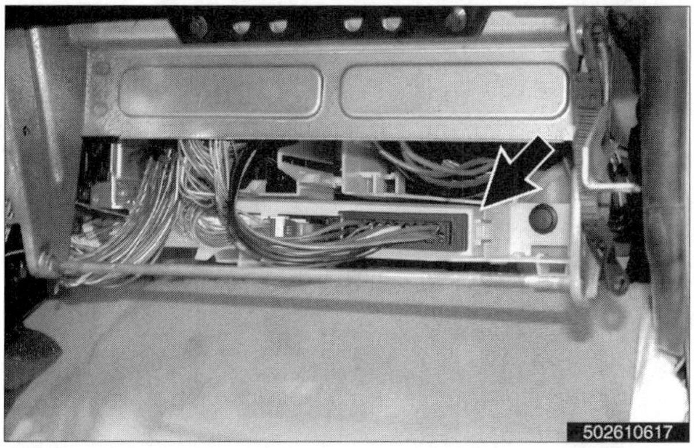

Fig. 11 General module (GM III) (A1)

◄ Behind glove compartment

- X254 General module connector (20–pin, black)

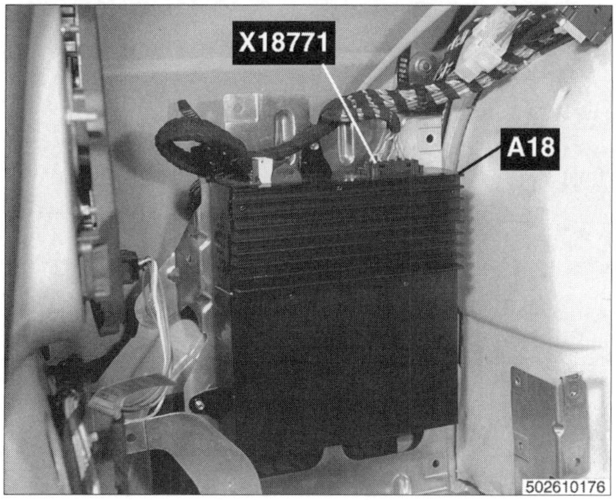

Fig. 12 Amplifier (A18)

◄ Trunk, left side

- X18771 Amplifier connector (15–pin, black)

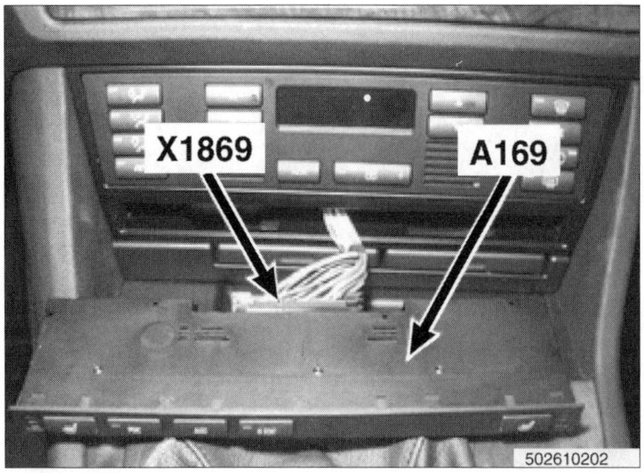

Fig. 13 Switching center (A169)

∢ Center console below radio

- X1869 Switching center connector (23–pin black)

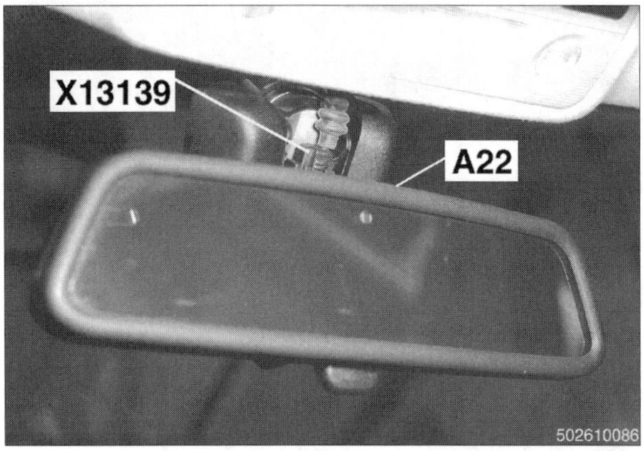

Fig. 14 Electrochromic rear view mirror (A22)

∢ In rear view mirror bracket

- X13139 Electrochromic rear view mirror connector (10–pin, natural)

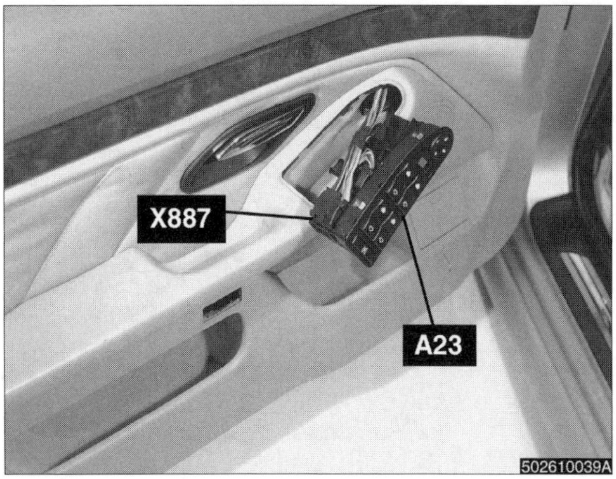

Fig. 15 Driver's door module (A23)

∢ Driver's door

- X887 Driver's door module connector (5–pin, black)

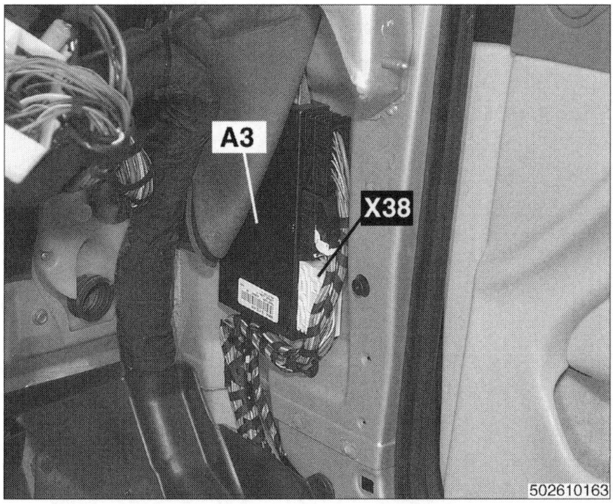

Fig. 16 Light control module (A3)

Right footwell

- X38 Light control module connector (15–pin, white)

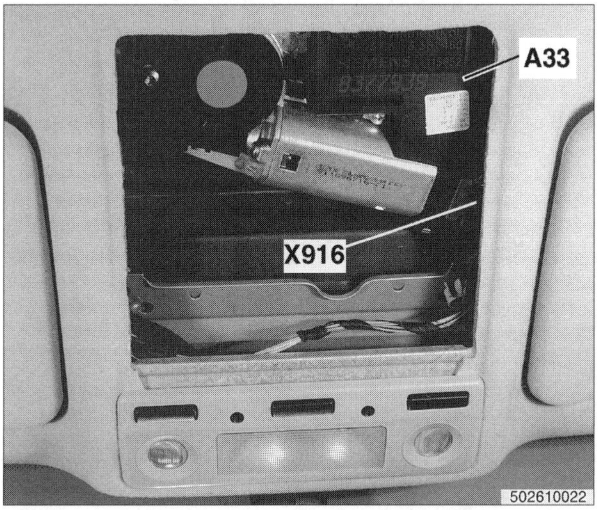

Fig. 17 Sunroof module (A33)

Behind front roof trim panel

- X916 Sunroof module connector (13–pin, black)

Fig. 18 A/C compressor (Y2)

Engine compartment, lower front right

- X163 A/C compressor connector (2–pin, black)

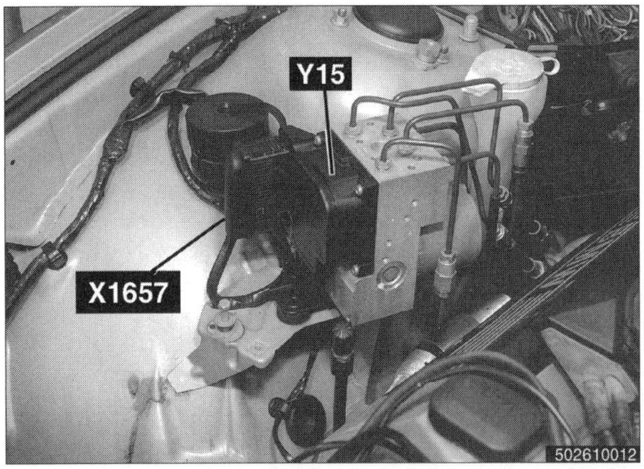

Fig. 19 DSC III version 5.3 hydraulic unit (Y15) (9/1998 — 9/1999 models)

◄ Front of strut tower, right side

- X1657 ABS/DSC hydraulic unit connector (black)

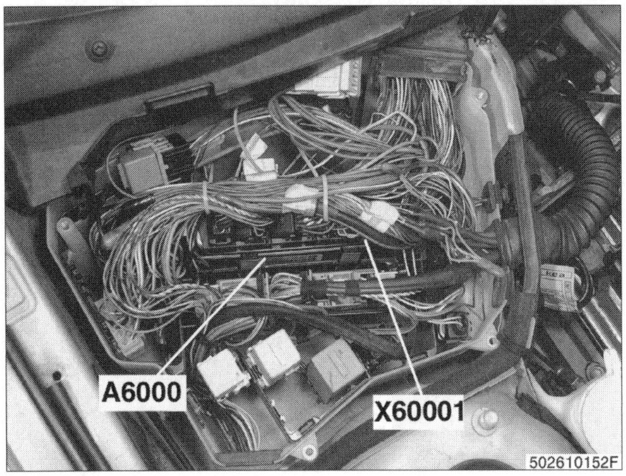

Fig. 20 Engine control module (DME) (A6000)

◄ E-box, right rear of engine compartment

- X60001 Engine control module connector (9–pin, black)

Fig. 21 Integrated instrument cluster control module (IKE) (A63)

◄ Behind instrument cluster

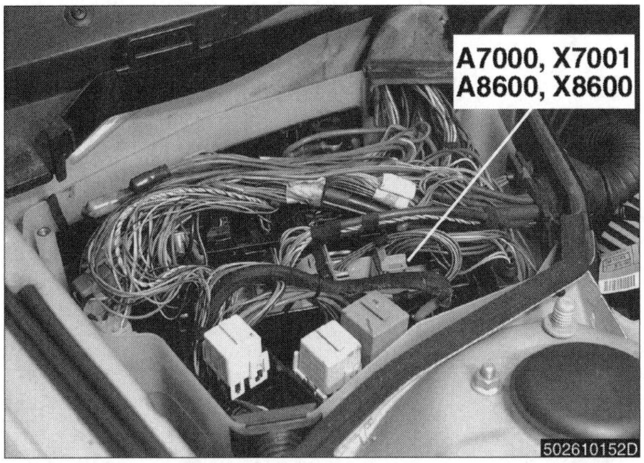

Fig. 22 Automatic transmission control module (AGS) (A7000, A8600)

E-box, right rear of engine compartment

- X70001, X8600 Automatic transmission control module (AGS) connector (9–pin, blue)

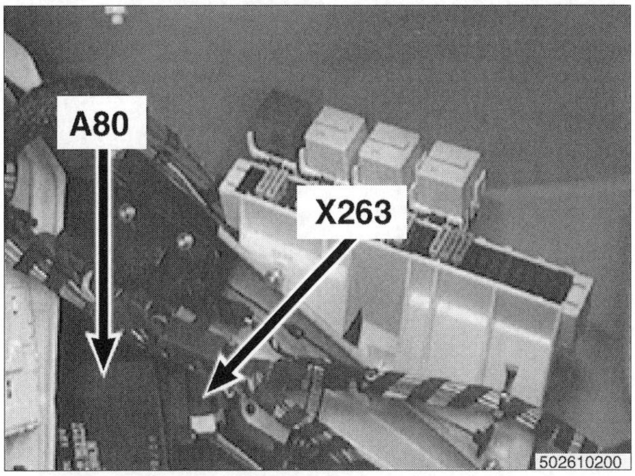

Fig. 23 Electronic shock absorber control module (A80)

Right side of trunk

- X263 Electronic shock absorber control module (EDC) connector (10–pin white)

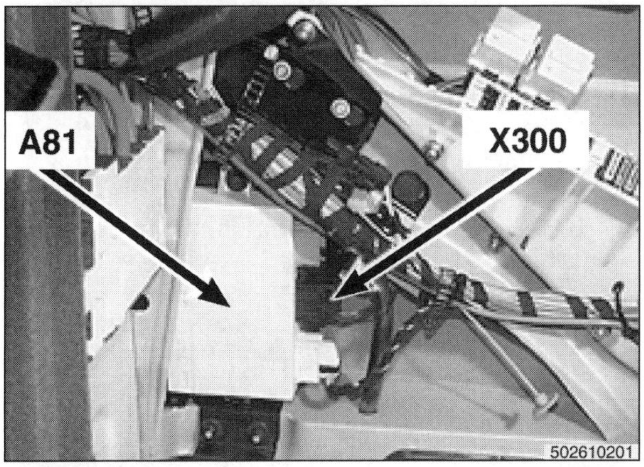

Fig. 24 Park distance control module (A81)

Right side of trunk

- X300 Park distance control module connector (12–pin black)

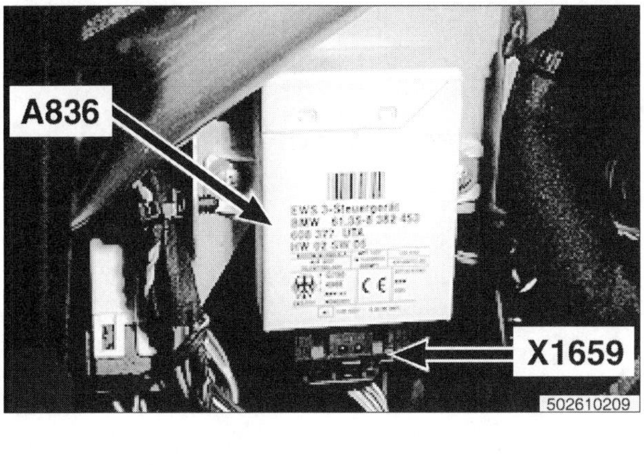

Fig. 25 EWS (electronic immobilizer) control unit (A836)

Under left side dash (sedan models from 3/1997)

- X1659 EWS (electronic immobilizer) control unit connector (13–pin black)

Fig. 26 Coolant valves (Y4)

Inner wheel well, front left

- X85 Coolant valve connector (3–pin, black)

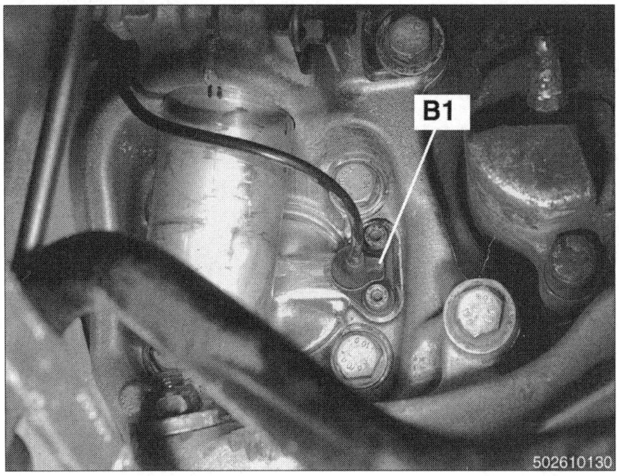

Fig. 27 ABS wheel speed sensor, right front (B1)

Right front wheel, inside wheel hub

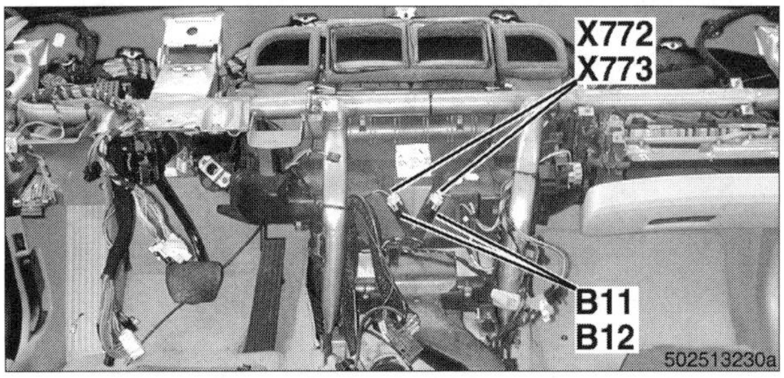

Fig. 28 Heat exchanger temperature sensors (B11, B12)

Behind center console

- X772, X773 Heat exchanger temperature sensor connectors (2–pin white)

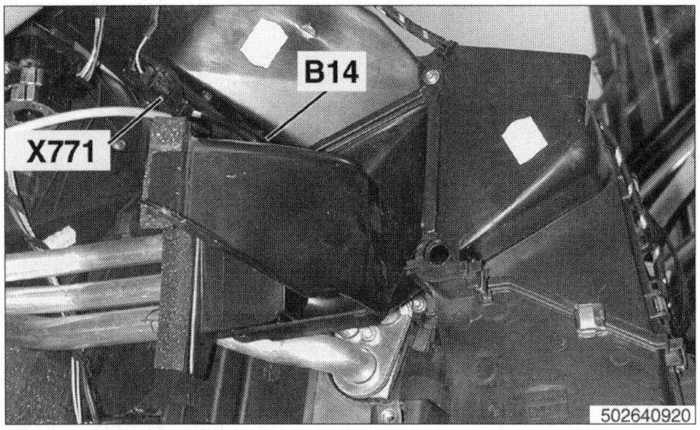

Fig. 29 A/C evaporator temperature sensor (B14) (IHKA to 3/2000)

Left side of heater housing, behind floor outlet

- X771 Temperature sensor connector (2–pin black)

Fig. 30 Brake pad wear sensor, left front (B16)

Brake caliper, front left

- X118 Left front brake pad wear sensor connector (2–pin, black)

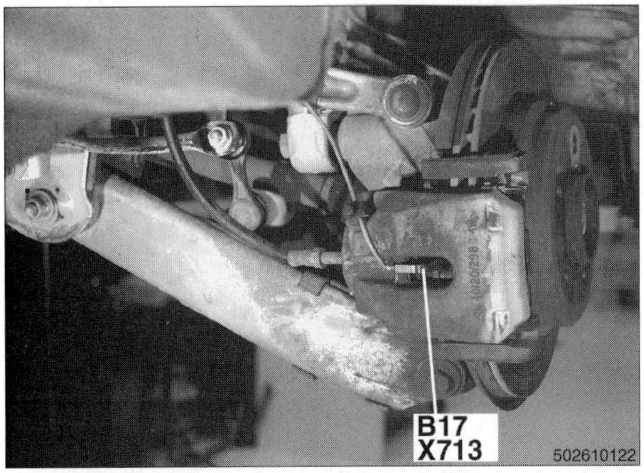

Fig. 31 Brake pad wear sensor, right rear (B17)

Brake caliper, right rear

- X713 Right rear brake pad wear sensor connector (2–pin, black)

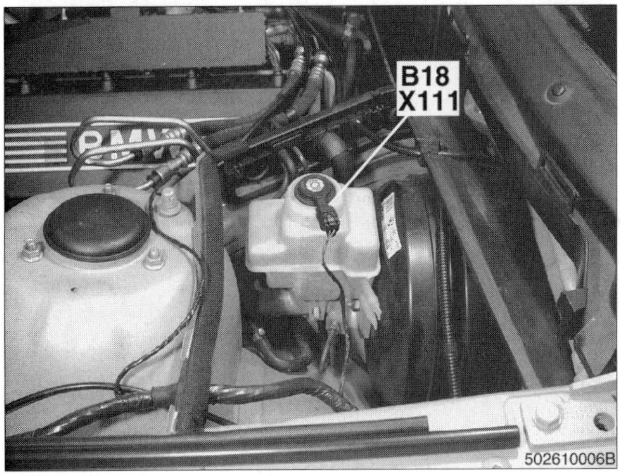

Fig. 32 Brake fluid level switch (B18)

Engine compartment, left rear

- X111 Brake fluid level switch connector (2–pin, black)

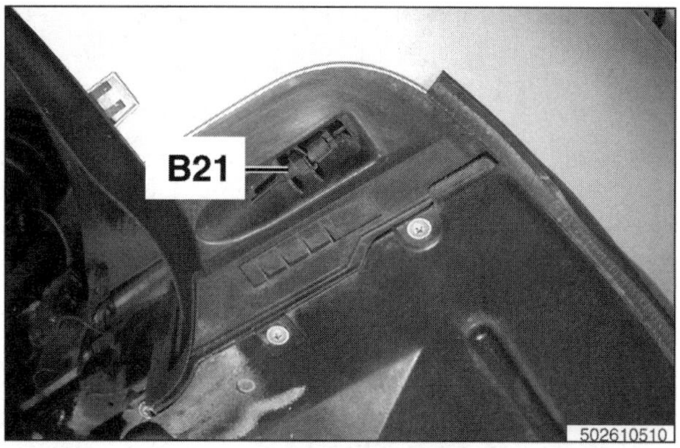

Fig. 33 Outside air temperature sensor (B21)

Under front of vehicle at bumper cover, right

- X770 Temperature sensor connector (2–pin, black)

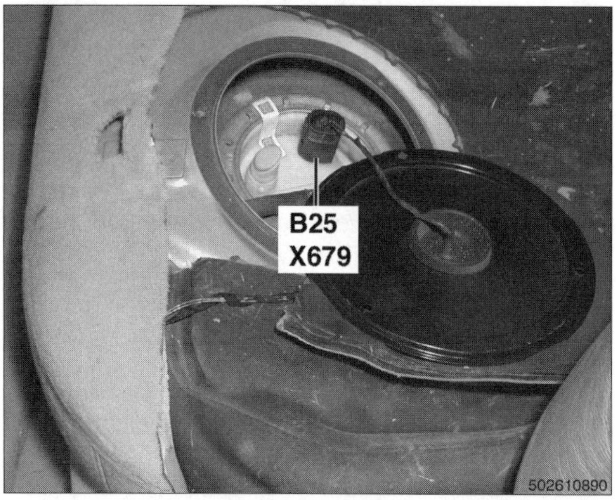

Fig. 34 Fuel level sensor II (B25)

Beneath rear seat, left side

- X679 Fuel level sensor II connector (2–pin, black)

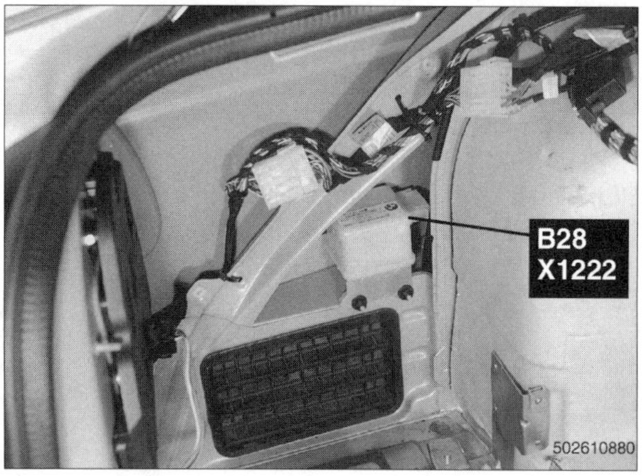

Fig. 35 Tilt sensor (B28)

Left side of trunk, behind radio amplifier

- X1222 Tilt sensor connector (6–pin white)

Fig. 36 ABS wheel speed sensor, right rear (B3)

< Right rear wheel, inside wheel hub

Fig. 37 Pneumatic speaker, left (B404)

< Behind front bumper support

- X3143 Pneumatic speaker connector (2–pin, black)

Fig. 38 Automatic air recirculation sensor (AUC) (B414)

< Engine cooling fan housing, lower right

- X3211 Automatic air recirculation sensor connector (4–pin, black)

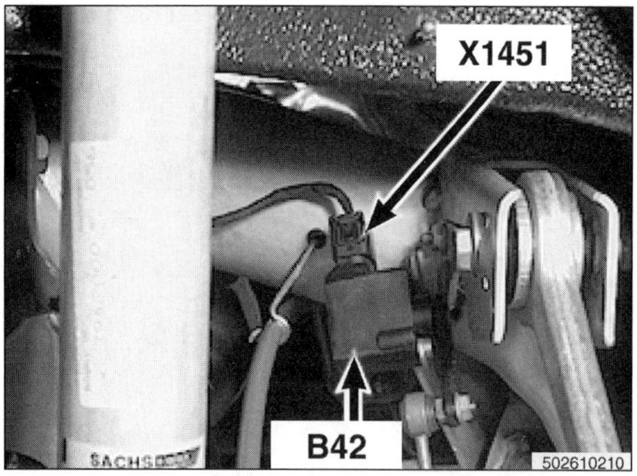

Fig. 39 Level sensor, right rear (B42)

Right rear wheel well

- X1451 Right rear level sensor connector (6–pin black)

Fig. 40 Crankshaft position/RPM sensor (V-8) (B6203)

Transmission bell housing, lower

Fig. 41 Mass air flow sensor (V-8) (B6207)

Air intake tube, near air filter housing

- X6207 Mass air flow sensor connector (4–pin, black)
- X6219 Camshaft position (Hall) sensor connector (3–pin, black)

Fig. 42 Camshaft position sensor I (intake camshaft, 6–cylinder) (B6214)

Cylinder head, front left (6–cylinder for intake camshaft, with single or double VANOS)

Fig. 43 Camshaft position sensor I (intake camshaft, M62 V-8) (B6219)

Front of cylinder head, right (V-8, without VANOS)

Fig. 44 Intake air temperature (IAT) sensor (V–8) (B6215)

Air filter housing, front

- X6215 IAT sensor connector (2–pin, black)

Fig. 45 Data link component connector (20–pin, black) (X6002)

Engine compartment, right front (to 6/2000)

- D100 Data link connector

Fig. 46 Camshaft position sensor II (exhaust camshaft, 6–cylinder) (B6224)

Right front of engine, top (6–cylinder)

- X6224 Camshaft sensor II connector (3–pin, black)

Fig. 47 Oil pressure switch (6–cylinder) (B6231)

Engine compartment, left, on side of oil filter housing

- X6231 Oil pressure switch connector (2–pin, black)

Fig. 48 Knock sensors (6–cylinder) (B6240)

Below intake manifold

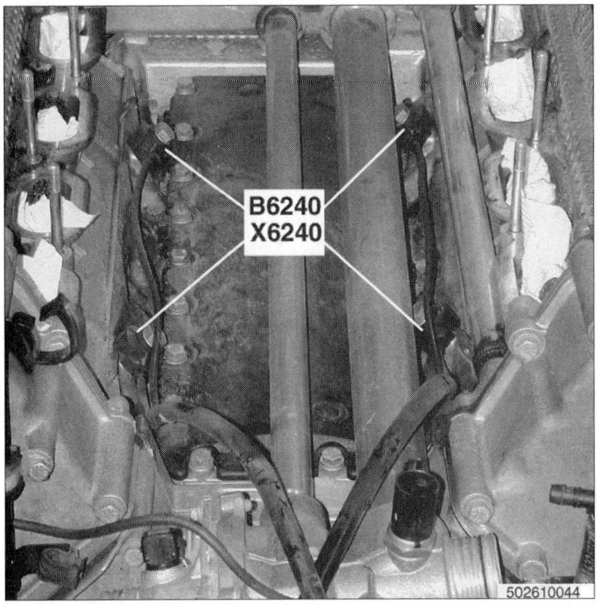

Fig. 49 Knock sensors (V-8) (B6240)

Center of engine, below intake manifold

- X6240 Knock sensor connector, at top of cylinder heads on wiring duct (4–pin, black)

Fig. 50 Oil level sensor (6254)

Oil pan, bottom

- X6254 Oil level sensor connector (3–pin, black)

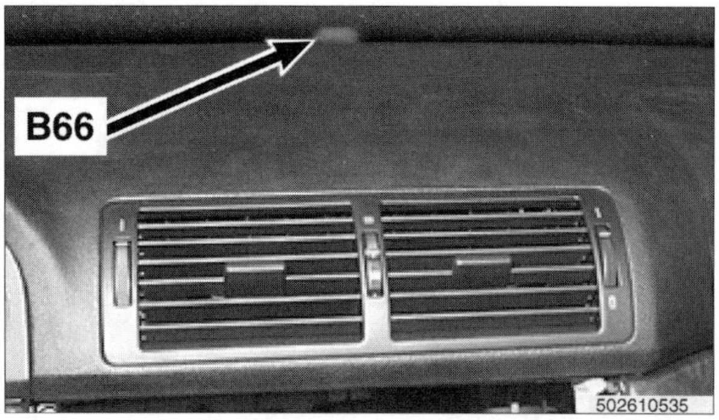

Fig. 51 Solar sensor (B66)

Above center dash vent at base of windshield

- X10669 Solar sensor connector (4–pin natural)

Fig. 52 Transverse (lateral) acceleration sensor (B74)

Under left front seat carpet

- X1655 Transverse acceleration sensor connector (3–pin, natural)

Fig. 53 RPM rate (rotational rate or yaw) sensor (B75)

Under front seat carpet, right

- X1653 RPM rate sensor connector (5–pin, black)

Fig. 54 DSC precharge pump (M118)

Engine compartment, left (1998 V-8)

- B76 DSC pressure sensor
- X1654 Pressure sensor connector (3–pin, black)

Fig. 55 A/C high pressure switch (B8)

Engine compartment, front right

- X126 A/C high pressure switch connector (4–pin, black)

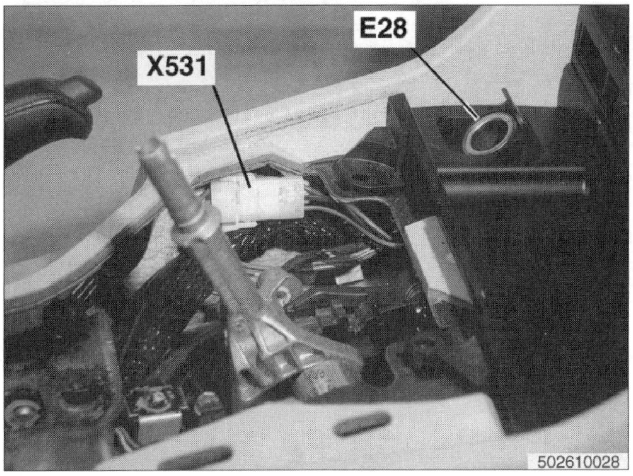

Fig. 56 Cigarette lighter (front) (E28)

Center console, near shift lever

- X531 Front cigarette lighter connector (3–pin, white)

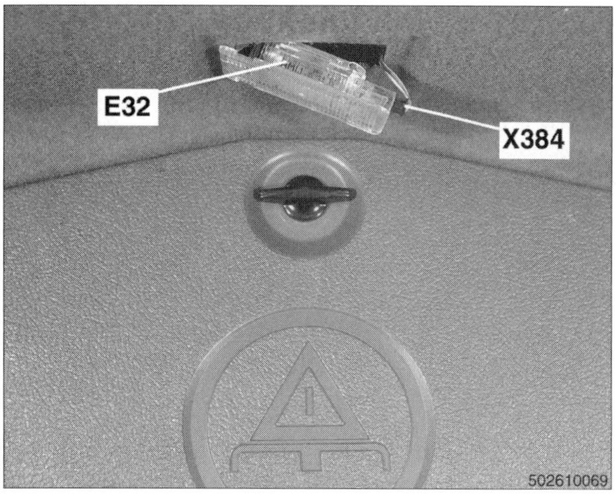

Fig. 57 Trunk light (E32)

Trunk lid, inside

- X384 Trunk light connector (3–pin, yellow)

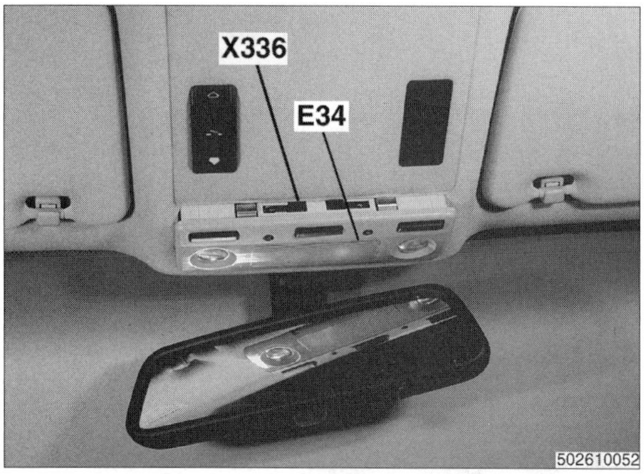

Fig. 58 Interior/reading lamp, front (E34)

In headliner, front

- X336 Interior/reading light connector (6–pin, black)

Fig. 59 Tail light assembly, left rear (E46)

Luggage compartment, inside left rear

- X319 Rear tail light connector with trailer adapter (8–pin, black)

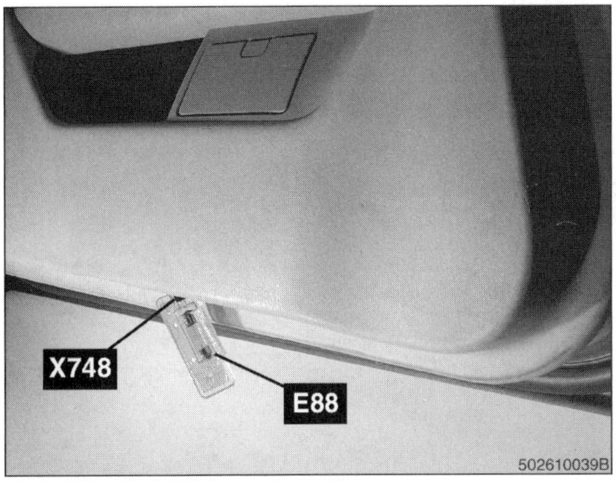

Fig. 60 Door access light, driver's door (E88)

Driver's door, bottom

- X748 Driver's door access light connector (3–pin, black)

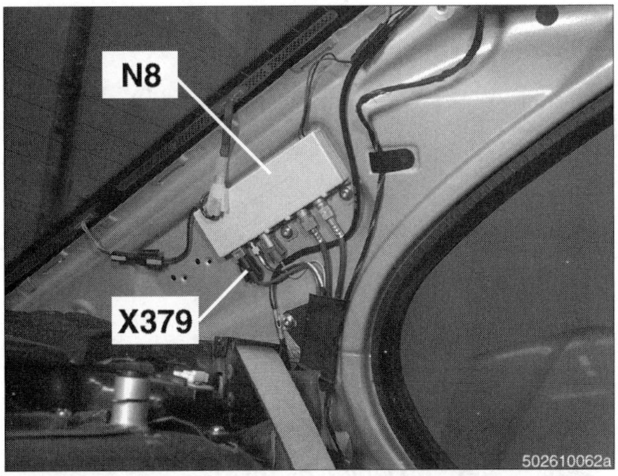

Fig. 61 Antenna amplifier with remote central locking (FZV) (N8)

Left C pillar, behind trim

- X379 Antenna amplifier connector (1–pin, black)

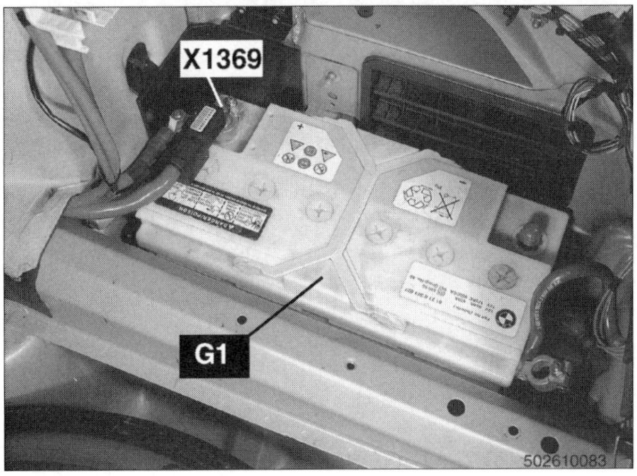

Fig. 62 Battery (G1)

Trunk, right side

- X1369 Cable shoe, battery

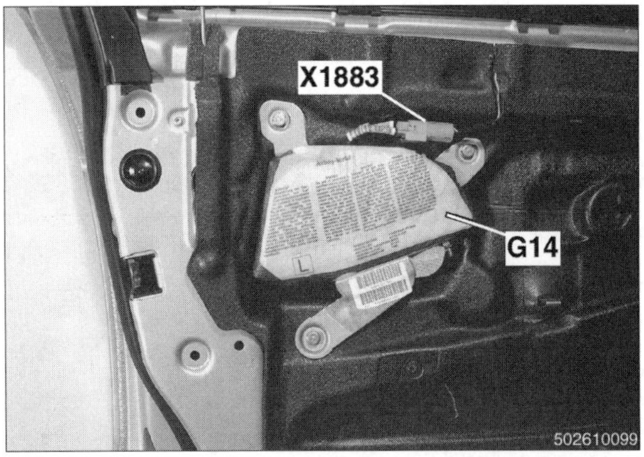

Fig. 63 Airbag, left front door (G14)

Left front door

- X1883 Left front side airbag connector (2–pin, orange)

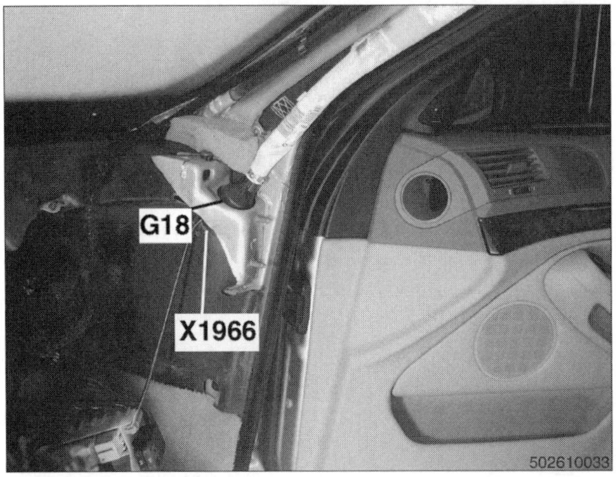

Fig. 64 Airbag, passenger side curtain (G18)

A-pillar, lower right

- X1966 Passenger side curtain airbag connector (3–pin, yellow)

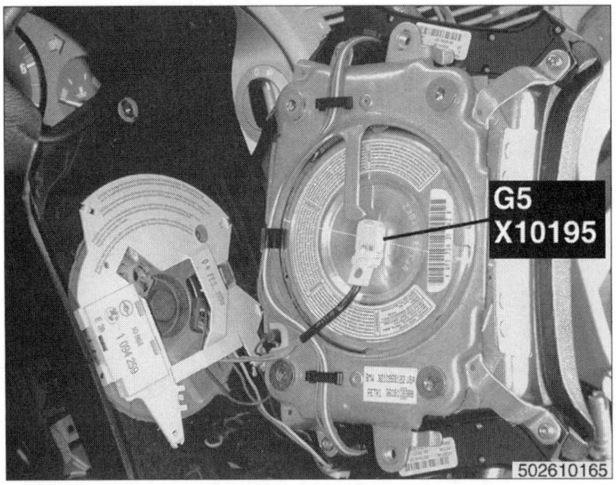

Fig. 65 Airbag, steering wheel (G5)

Steering wheel

- X10195 Driver's airbag connector (2–pin, yellow)

Fig. 66 Alternator (generator) (G6524)

◄ Engine, lower left

- X6524 Alternator connector (3–pin, black)

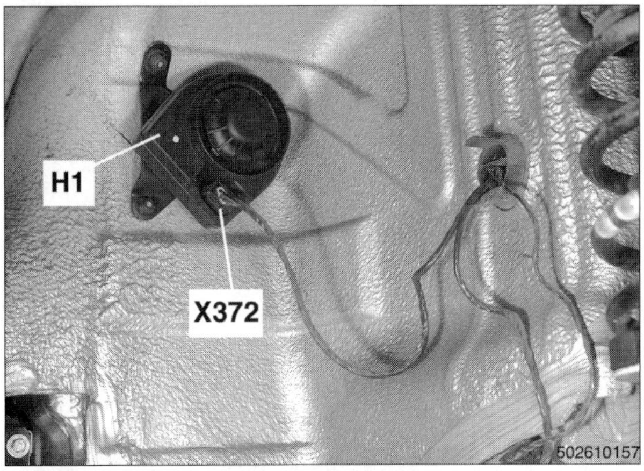

Fig. 67 Alarm (anti-theft) horn (DWA) (H1)

◄ Right rear wheel well behind inner panel

- X372 Anti-theft horn connector (2–pin, black)

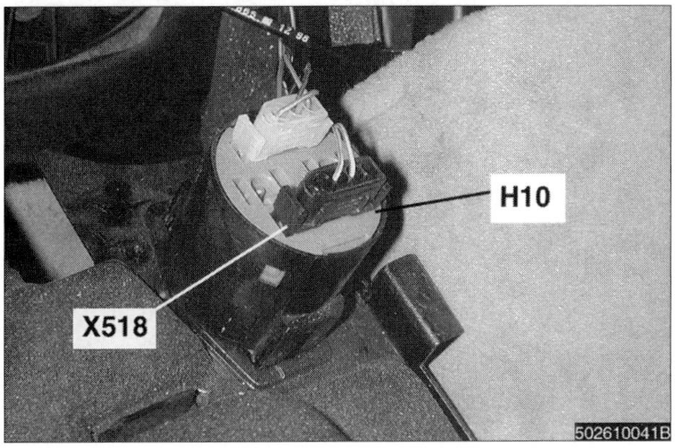

Fig. 68 Chime module (H10)

◄ Dash panel above driver's footwell

- X518 Chime module connector (4–pin, black)

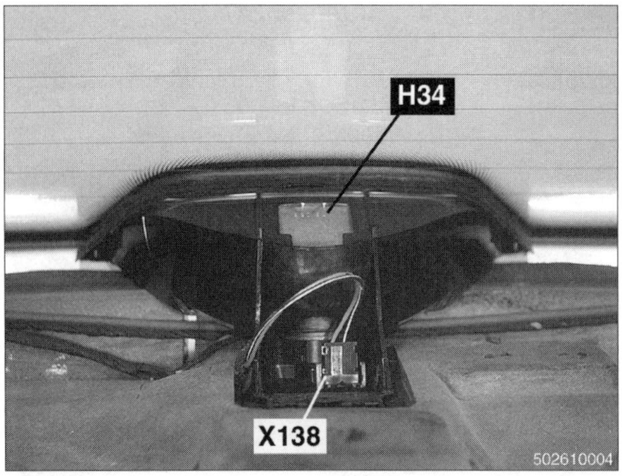

Fig. 69 Center brake light, sedan (H34)

Rear window shelf

- X138 High level stop light connector (2–pin, black)

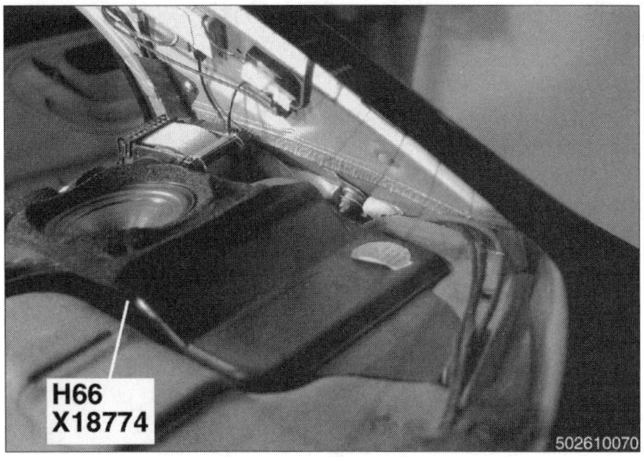

Fig. 70 Rear speaker, subwoofer (H66)

Rear window shelf

- X18774 Subwoofer speaker connector (8–pin, black)

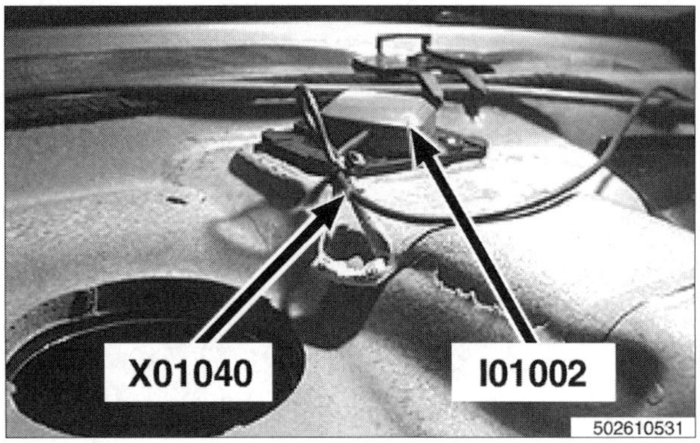

Fig. 71 GPS antenna (I01002)

Left side rear window shelf (sedan models)

- X01040 GPS antenna connector

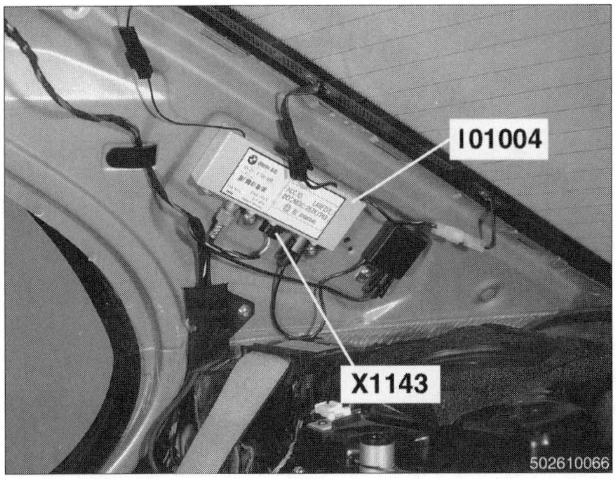

Fig. 72 Amplifier FM, lockout circuit (I01004)

Right C-pillar, lower

- X1143 FM amplifier connector (3–pin, black)

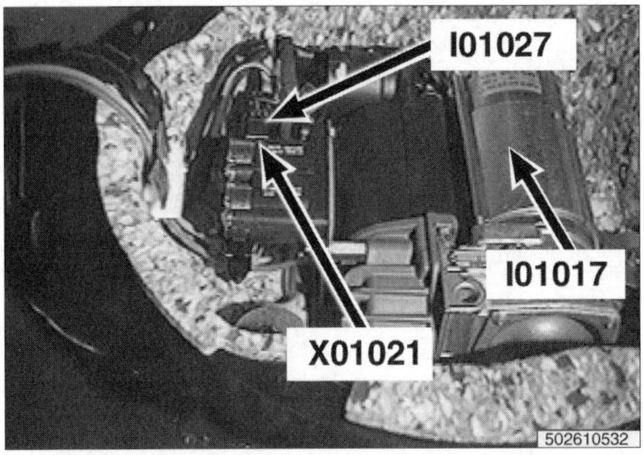

Fig. 73 Air suspension compressor pump assembly (I01017)

Spare tire well (under tire)

- X01021 Connector, relay, compressor pump control
- I01027 Relay, compressor pump control

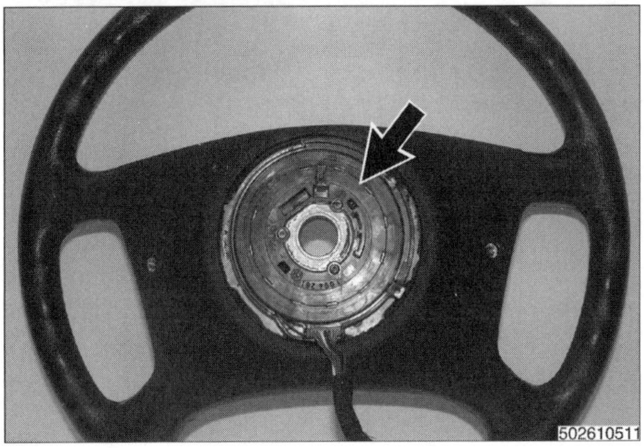

Fig. 74 Driver's airbag contact spring (I01030)

Between steering wheel and column switches

- X01031 Coil spring connector (2–pin, bordeaux)

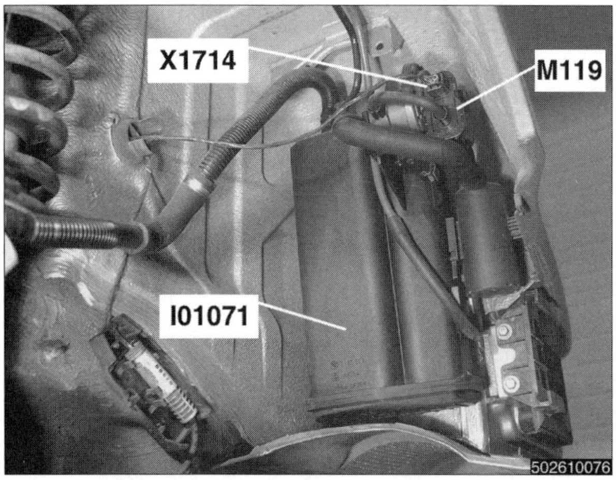

Fig. 75 Fuel tank leak diagnostic module (LDP or DMTL) (M52 TU, M54, M62 TU) (I01071)

Back of wheel well, left rear, behind liner

- X1714 Leak diagnosis connector (3 – pin, black)
- M119 Leak diagnostic pump

Fig. 76 Interference suppression capacitor, ignition coils 1 – 4 (V-8) (I01100)

Wire loom, top of right cylinder head

Fig. 77 Interference suppression capacitor, ignition coils 5 – 8 (V-8) (I01101)

Wire loom, top of left cylinder head

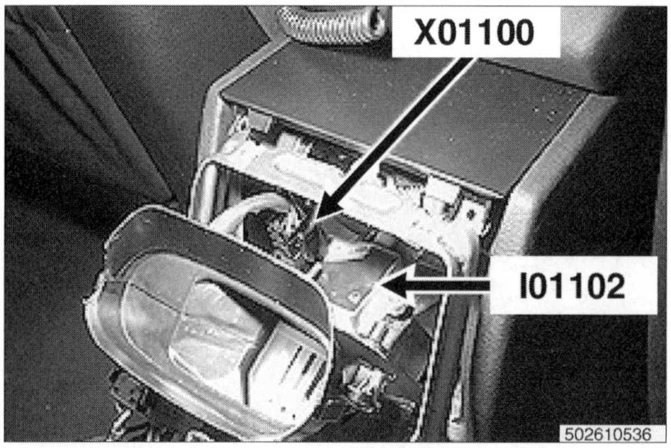

Fig. 78 A/C blower motor output stage, rear compartment (I01102)

◄ Rear of center console

- X01100 A/C blower motor output stage connector, rear compartment (5–pin black)

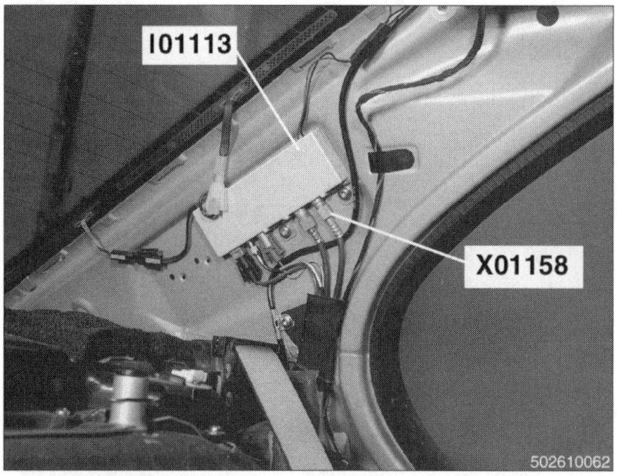

Fig. 79 Antenna, diversity (I01113)

◄ Left C-pillar

- X01158 Diversity antenna connector (1–pin)

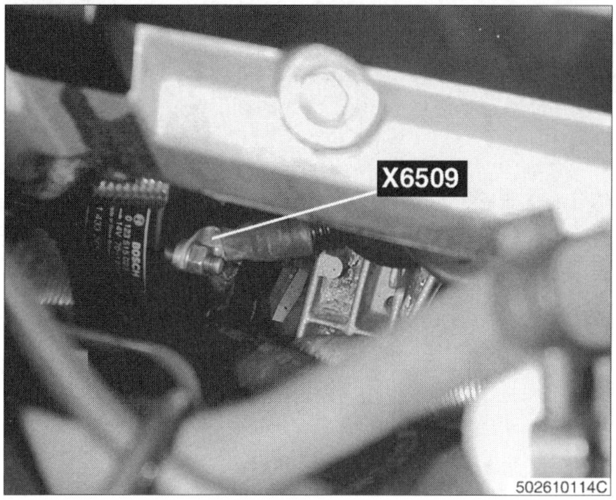

Fig. 80 Cable shoe, alternator (generator) (X6509)

◄ Engine compartment, lower left, on back of alternator (generator)

Fig. 81 Terminal 87 splice (X6820) (V-8 models)

◄ Wire loom, top of right cylinder head

Fig. 82 Terminal 87 splices (X6821, X6822))

◄ E-box, right rear of engine compartment

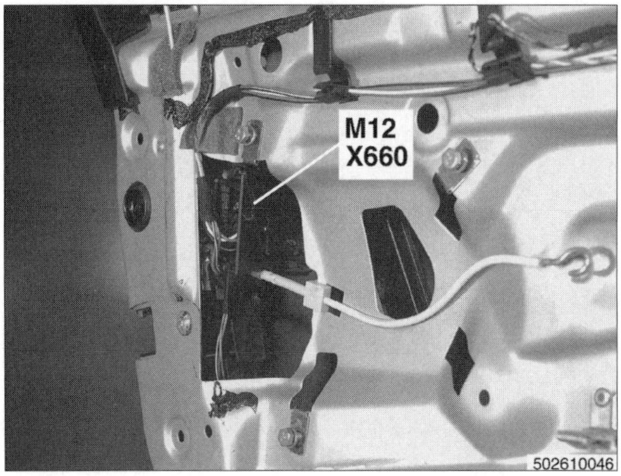

Fig. 83 Door lock motor, driver's door (M12)

◄ Driver's door

- X660 Driver's door lock motor connector (6–pin, black)

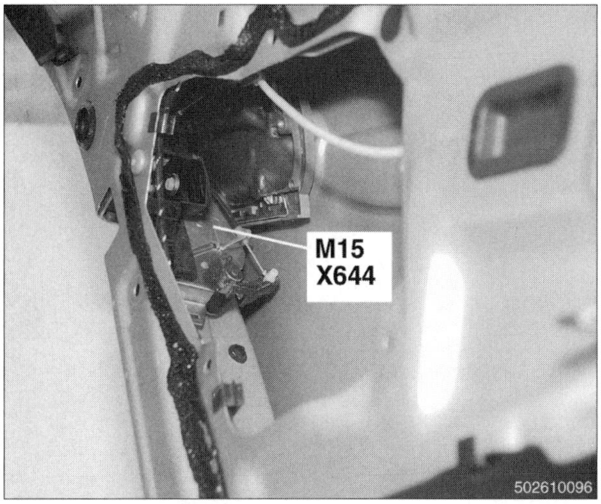

Fig. 84 Door lock motor, left rear (M15)

< Rear door, left

- X644 Left rear door lock motor connector (6–pin, black)

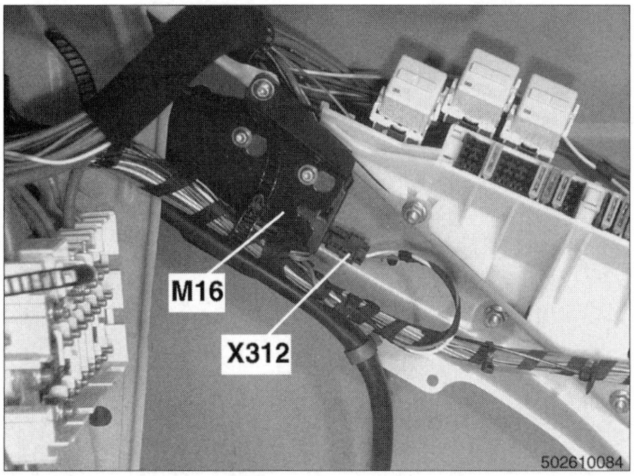

Fig. 85 Fuel tank access flap lock motor (M16)

< Luggage compartment, right

- X312 Fuel tank flap lock motor connector (2–pin, black)

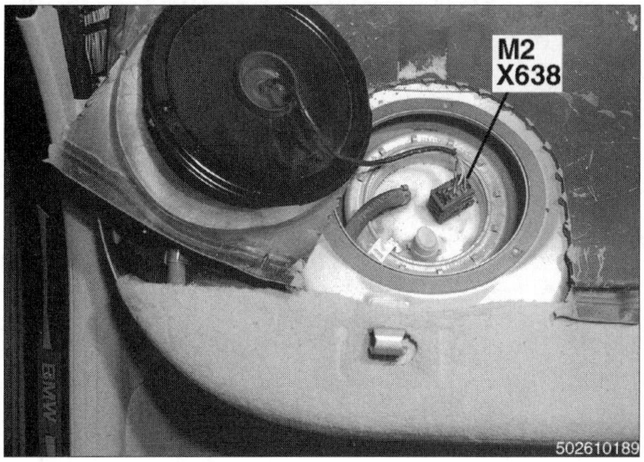

Fig. 86 Fuel pump (EKP I) (M2)

< Under rear seat, right

- X638 Electric fuel pump connector (6–pin, black)

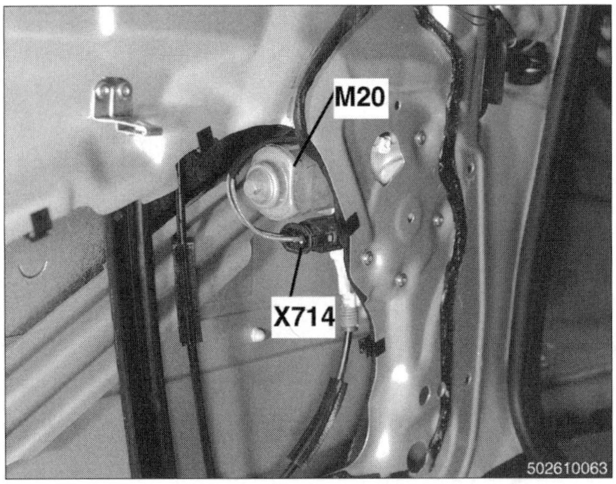

Fig. 87 Window motor, rear left (M20)

Rear door, left

- X714 Left rear window motor connector (2–pin, grey)

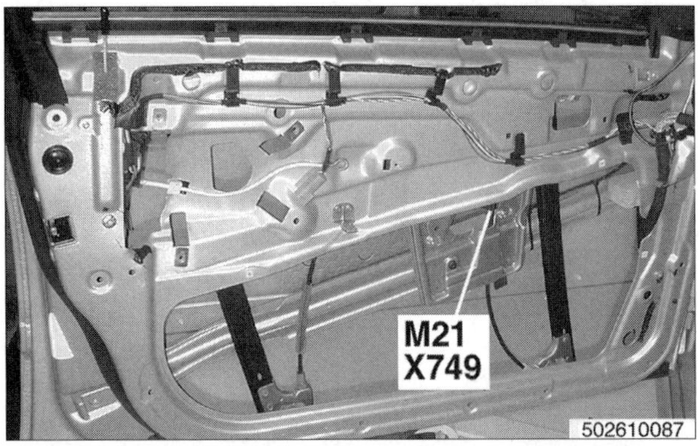

Fig. 88 Window motor, driver's door (M21)

Front door, left

- X749 Driver's window motor connector (2–pin, grey)

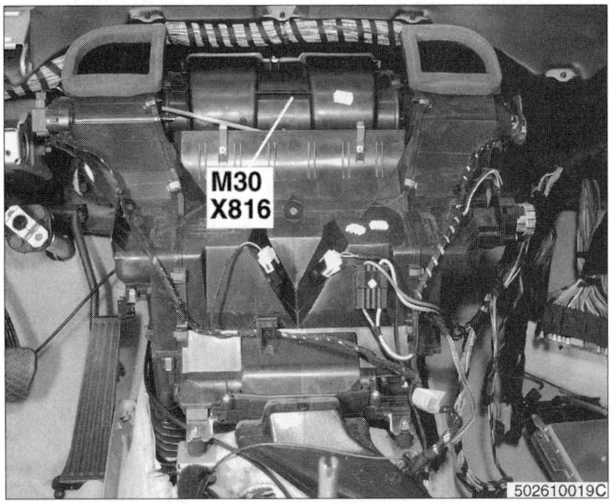

Fig. 89 A/C blower motor (M30)

Under dashboard, center

- X816 Blower motor connector (2–pin, black)

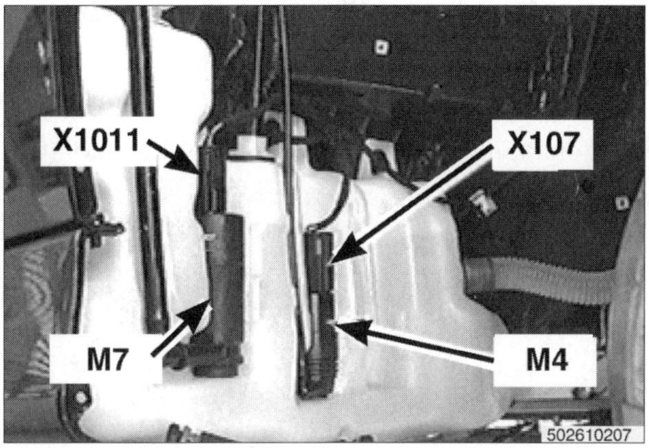

Fig. 90 Windshield washer pump (M4)

◀ Back of right front wheel well behind inner fender panel, on reservoir

- X107 Windshield washer pump connector (2–pin blue)
- M7 Headlight washer pump
- X1001 Headlight washer pump connector (2–pin, gray)

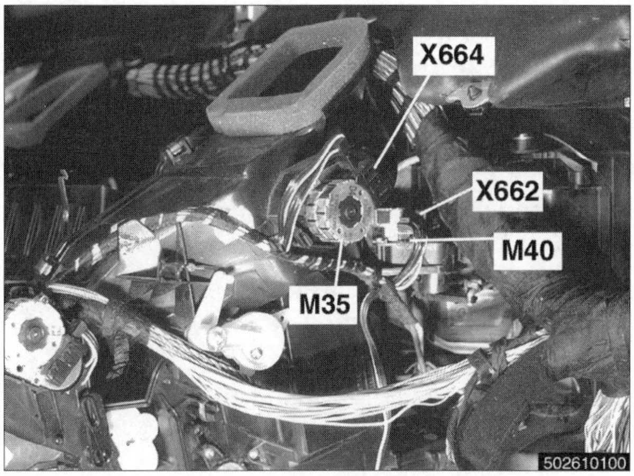

Fig. 91 Recirculation stepper motor (M40)

◀ Heater housing, right, behind dash

- X664 Defroster stepper motor connector (3–pin, black)
- X662 Recirculation stepper motor connector (3–pin, black)
- M35 Defroster stepper motor

Fig. 92 3/2 way valve (fuel changeover circuit) (Y31)

◀ Under left front of vehicle

- X1713 3/2-way valve (fuel changeover circuit) connector (2–pin, black)

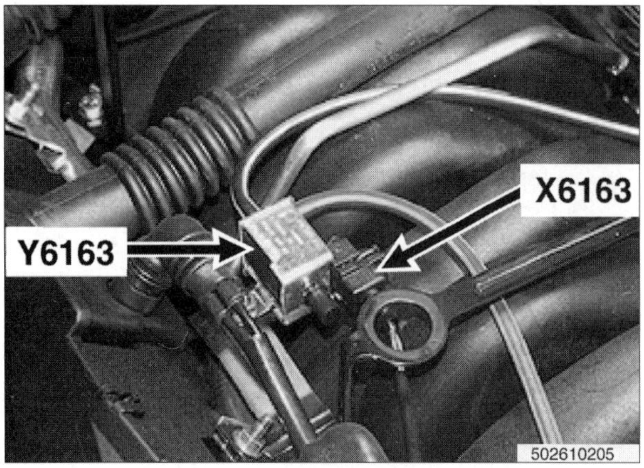

Fig. 93 Secondary air injection pump valve (Y6163)

Top center of engine

- X6163 Secondary air injection pump valve connector (2–pin black)

Fig. 94 Steering column angle adjustment motor (M83)

Steering column

- M82 Steering column length adjustment motor
- X18096 Steering column angle adjustment motor connector (3–pin, black)
- X18097 Steering column length adjustment motor connector (3–pin, black)

Fig. 95 Engine cooling fan, electric (M9)

Front of radiator

- X18193 Engine cooling fan connector (4–pin, black)

Fig. 96 Auxiliary throttle position motor (ADS) (M93)

X10094 Auxiliary throttle position motor connector (2–pin, black)

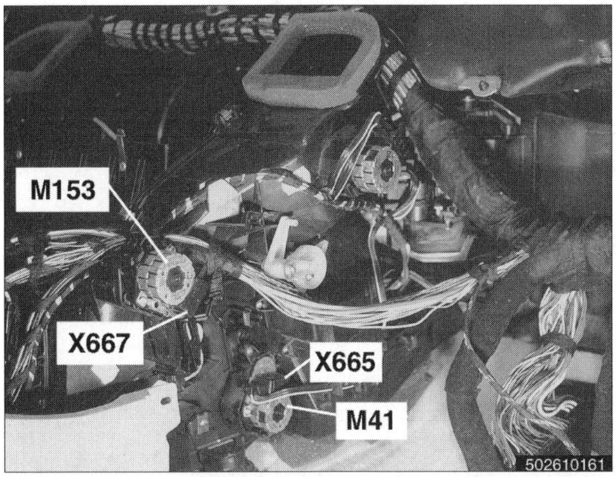

Fig. 97 Footwell ventilation stepper motor (M153)

Heater housing, right

- M41 Footwell/rear compartment ventilation stepper motor
- X665 Footwell/rear compartment stepper motor connector (3–pin, black)
- X667 Footwell ventilation stepper motor connector (3–pin, black)

Fig. 98 Trunk lid servo motor (M407)

Trunk lid

Fig. 99 E-box fan (M6506)

Under E-box, engine compartment right rear

Fig. 100 Starter (6–cylinder) (M6510)

Under intake manifold, right side

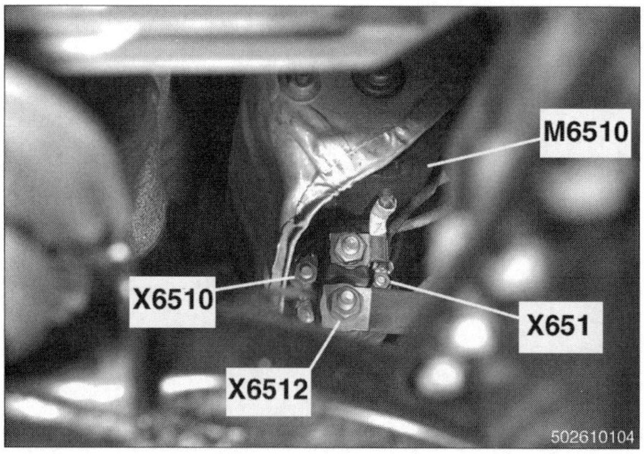

Fig. 101 Starter (V-8) (M6510)

Under engine, right side

- X651 Starter solenoid connector (Black/green wire, 4.0)
- X6510 Starter solenoid connector (Black wire, 4.0)
- X6512 Starter solenoid connector (B+, red wire, 35.0)

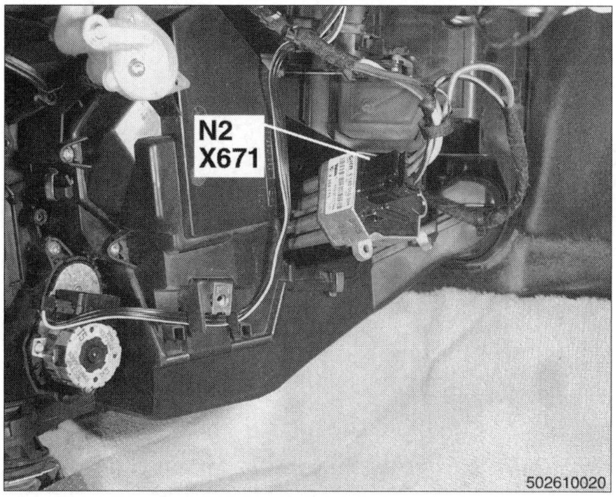

Fig. 102 Heater blower final stage (resistor) (N2)

◄ Heater housing, lower right

- X671 Final stage connector (5–pin, black)

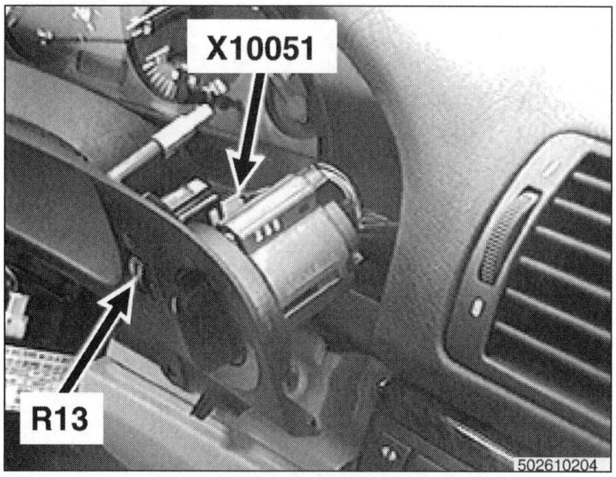

Fig. 103 Headlight widening potentiometer (R13)

◄ Left side of dash

- X10051 Headlight widening potentiometer connector (3–pin black)

Fig. 104 ABS/DSC steering angle sensor (R33)

◄ Steering column

- X1658 Steering angle sensor connector (6–pin, black)

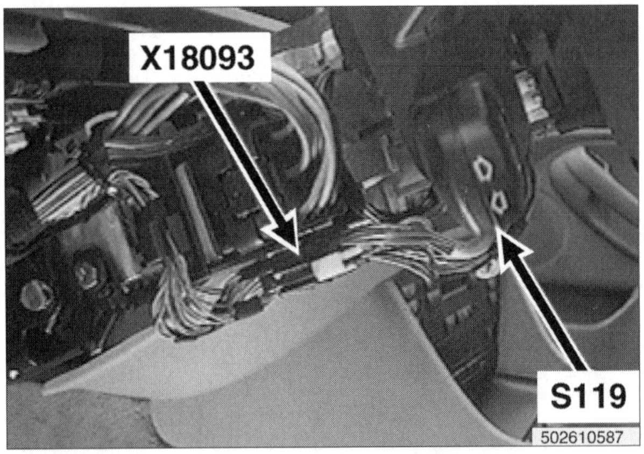

Fig. 105 Steering column position switch (S119)

◄ Left side of steering column

- X18093 Steering column position switch connector (6–pin, black)

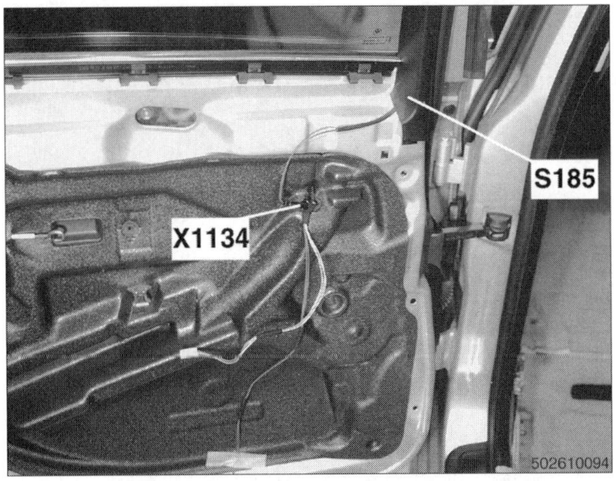

Fig. 106 Pressure sensitive finger guard, left rear window (anti-trap strip) (S185)

◄ Left rear door, upper front

- X1134 Left rear window pressure sensitive finger guard connector (3–pin, black)

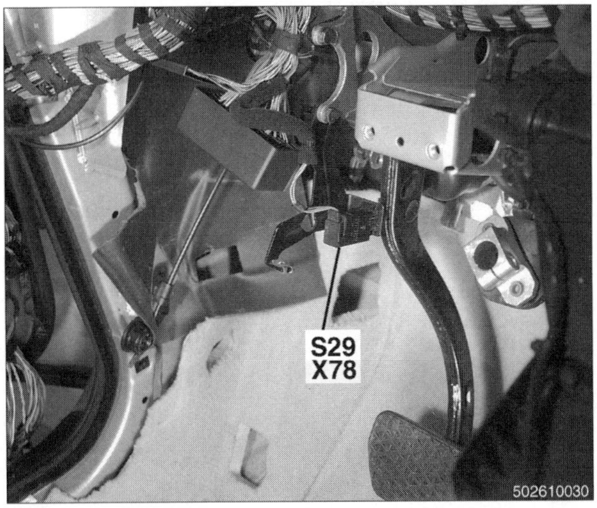

Fig. 107 Brake light switch (S29)

◄ Brake pedal, upper

- X78 Brake light switch connector (4–pin, black)

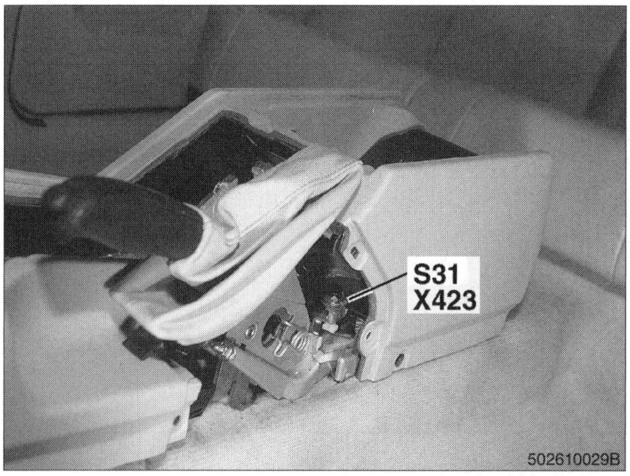

Fig. 108 Parking brake switch (S31)

Below center console, rear

- X423 Parking brake switch connector (2–pin, black)

Fig. 109 Engine cooling fan switch (dual) (S36)

Engine compartment, front right

- X87 Fan switch connector (3–pin, black)

Fig. 110 Glove compartment light switch (S37)

Glove compartment, top left

- X540 Glove compartment light switch (2–pin, black)

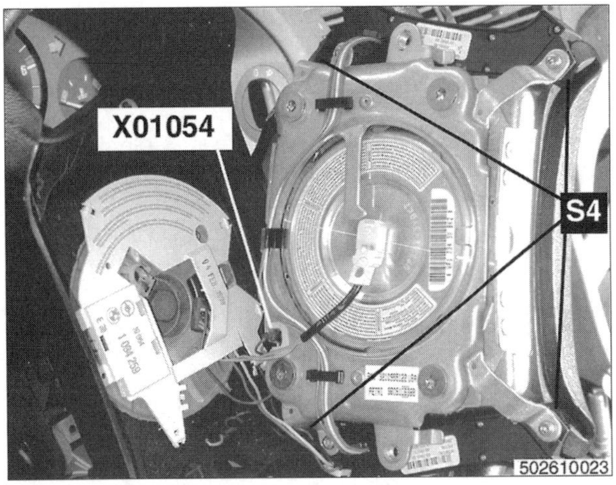

Fig. 111 Horn button (S4)

Steering wheel, behind impact cushion

- X01054 Horn button cable shoe (1–pin)

Fig. 112 Engine coolant level switch (S63)

Radiator shroud, lower right

- X112 Engine coolant level sensor connector (2–pin, black)

Fig. 113 Airbag sensor (crash sensor), left front (S71)

Under driver's seat, under carpet

- X1885 Left front airbag sensor connector (3–pin, black)

Fig. 114 Airbag sensor (crash sensor), right front (S72)

Under passenger seat, under carpet

- X1886 Right front airbag sensor connector (3–pin, black)

Fig. 115 Oil pressure switch (S95)

Engine compartment, left front on oil filter housing

- X145 Oil pressure switch connector (2–pin, black)

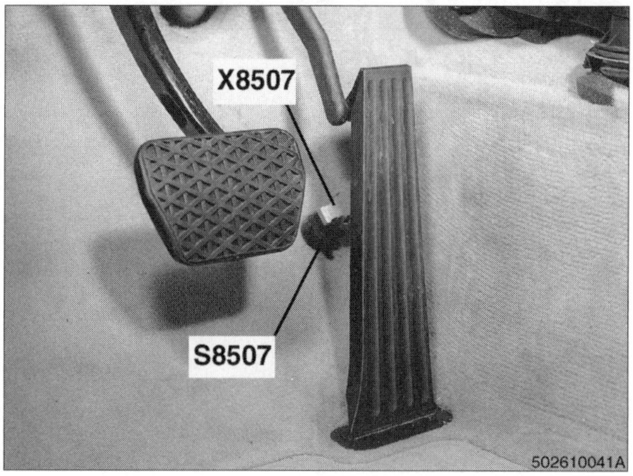

Fig. 116 Kick-down switch (S8507)

Driver's side floor, under accelerator pedal

- X8507 Kick-down switch connector (1–pin, black)

Fig. 117 Automatic transmission range switch (S8532)

◄ Transmission, lower left

- X8532 Automatic transmission range switch connector (10–pin, black)

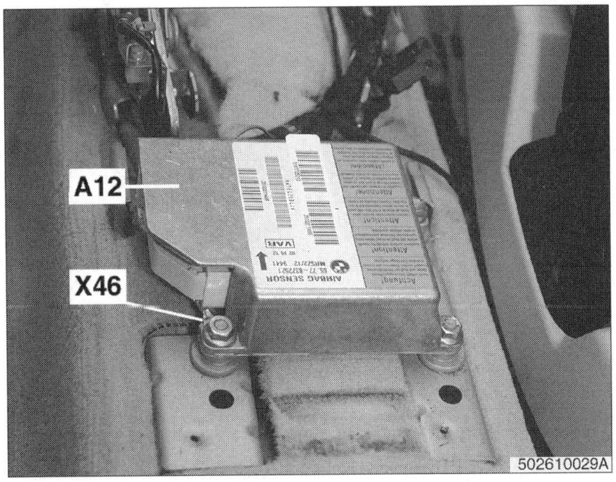

Fig. 118 Airbag control module (A12)

◄ Below center console, rear

- X46 Ground connector for airbag control module

Fig. 119 Ground cable shoe (X151)

◄ Under driver's seat carpet

- X173 ground cable shoe

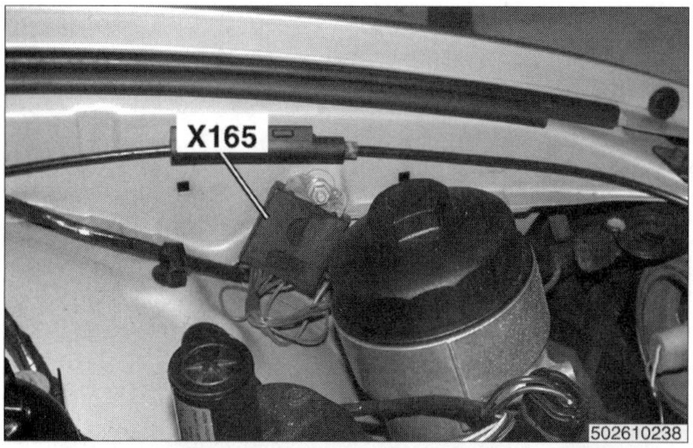

Fig. 120 Ground cable shoe (X165)

< Left front inner fender panel

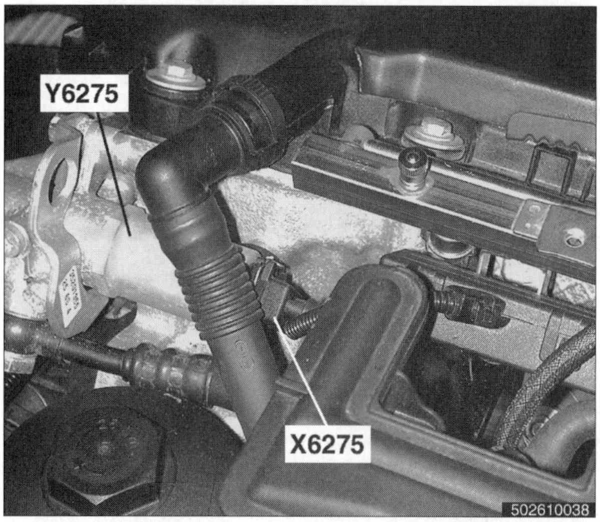

Fig. 121 Intake camshaft VANOS solenoid (6–cylinder) (Y6275)

< Cylinder head

- X6275 VANOS solenoid connector (2–pin, black)

Fig. 122 Characteristic map thermostat (Y6279)

< Front of engine, below air intake boot

- X6279 Characteristic map thermostat connector

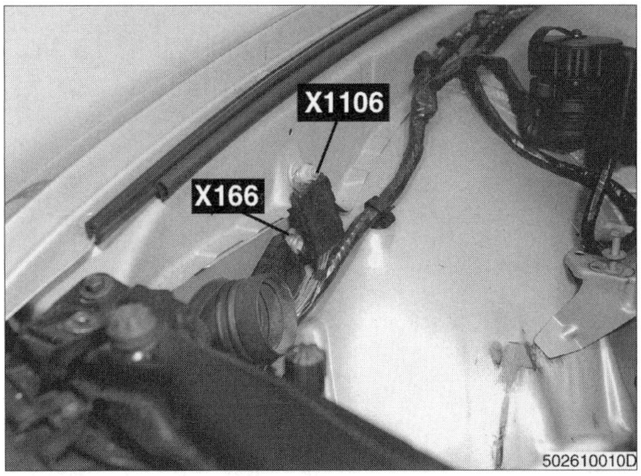

Fig. 123 Ground cable shoe (X166)

◄ Engine compartment, front right

- Ground cable shoe (X1106)

Fig. 124 Ground cable shoe (X6454)

◄ Engine compartment, right rear on outside of E-box

Fig. 125 Ground cable shoe (X490)

◄ Right side footwell under carpet

- X492 Ground cable shoe
- X218 Splice ground
- X10012 Ground cable shoe

Fig. 126 Transmission valve (Y8521)

Transmission, lower right

- X8521 Transmission control unit connector (9–pin, black)

Fig. 127 Ground cable shoe (X498)

Right side of trunk behind battery cover trim panel

- X13075 Ground cable shoe

Fig. 128 Ground cable shoe (X961)

Right side footwell under carpet, beneath cover

Fig. 129 Blower motor final stage connector (4–pin, black) (X18722)

⊲ Behind center console

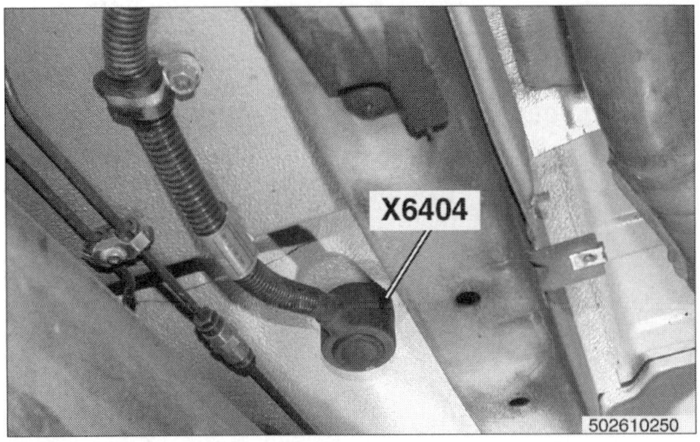

Fig. 130 Cable shoe, B+ junction (X6404)

⊲ Right side of transmission next to frame rail

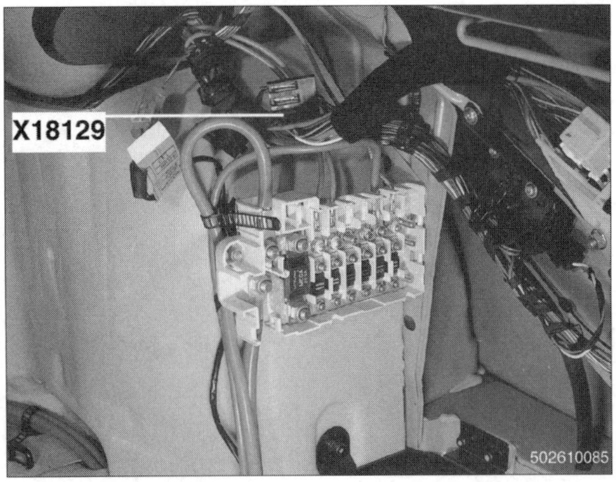

Fig. 131 Terminal 30 splice (X18129)

⊲ Trunk, upper right

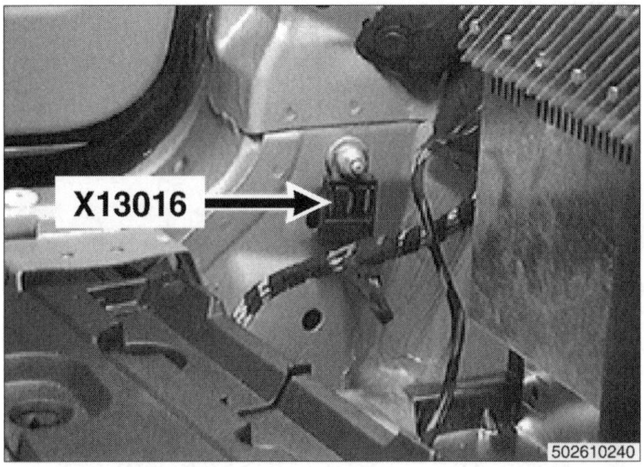

Fig. 132 Ground cable shoe (X13016)

◄ Left side of trunk behind trim panel

Fig. 133 Cable shoe, fuse panel 4 voltage supply (X13020)

◄ Fuse panel 4, under carpet beneath passenger seat

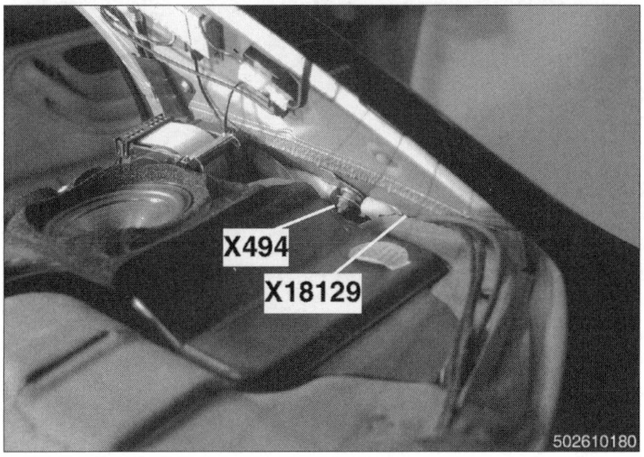

Fig. 134 Cable shoe ground (X494)

◄ Under rear window shelf, right

- X18129 Splice terminal 30

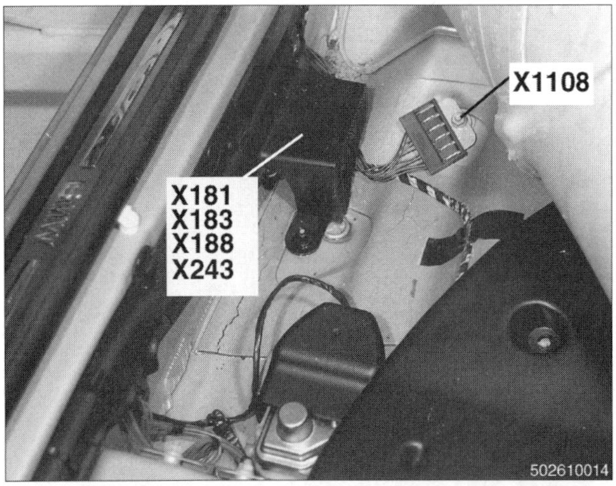

Fig. 135 Cable shoe ground (X1108)

Under driver's seat carpet

- X181 Brake light splice
- X183 Data link TXD splice
- X188 Speed signal splice
- X243 Engine speed signal splice (TD)

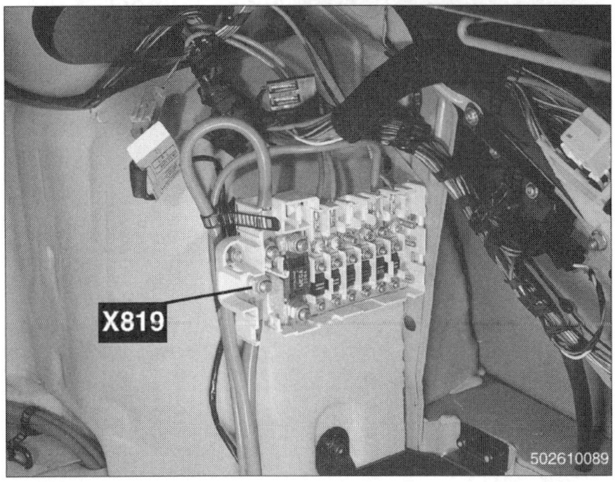

Fig. 136 Cable shoe, B+ supply, fuse panel 5 (X819)

Luggage compartment, right

Fig. 137 Terminal R splice (X1264)

Behind dash, left on steering column

- X1169 Splice back up signal (AGS)

Sport Wagon component locations

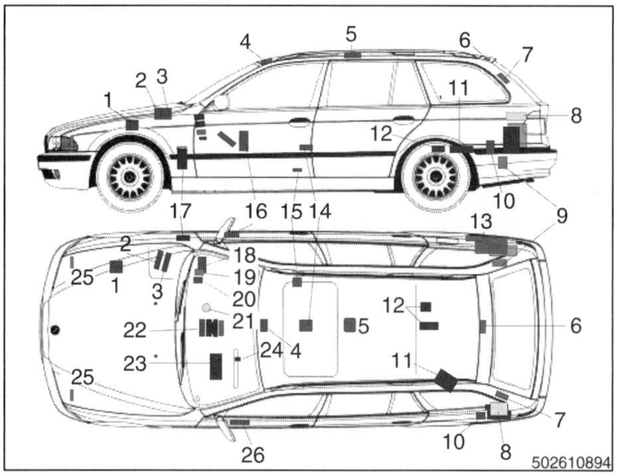

Fig. 138 Sport Wagon control modules

Module locations apply to 1999 models. Keep in mind that electrical component locations may vary by year and model.

1. Traction control module (DSC III version 5.7)
2. Engine control module, DME (ECM)
3. Transmission control module (AGS)
4. Sunroof control module (SM)
5. Interior motion sensor (UIS)
6. FM1 antenna amplifier
7. FZV / FM2 antenna amplifier
8. GPS control module
9. Air suspension (EHC) control module
10. Tilt sensor
11. Radio electronics (with GPS)
12. Telephone transceiver or PSE box
13. Battery and trunk fuses
14. Multiple restraint system (MRS) control module
15. Seat control module (SBE)
16. Door module
17. Light control module (LCM III)
18. General module (GM III)
19. Electronic immobilizer control module (EWS)
20. LWR
21. GPS antenna
22. IHKA control module, multi-information display (MID) or BMBT, SZM, Radio and tape player (non-GPS)
23. Integrated instrument cluster control module (IKE)
24. Multifunction steering wheel (MFL)
25. Xenon headlight
26. Left door module switchblock

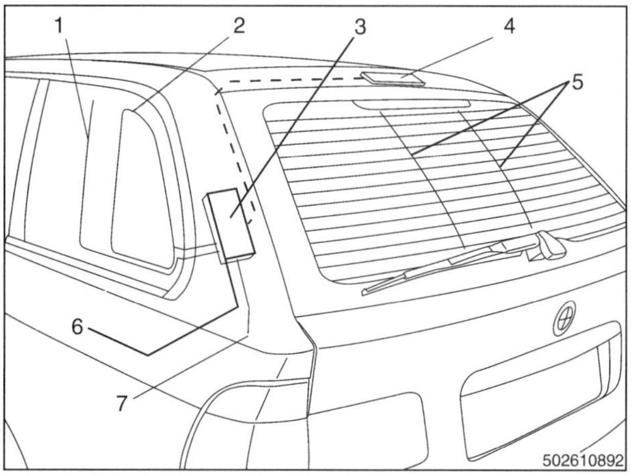

Fig. 139 Sport Wagon antennas

Sport Wagon antenna configuration is unique.

1. Remote (FZV) entry antenna
2. AM / FM2 antenna
3. FZV / FM2 antenna amplifier
4. FM1 amplifier
5. FM1 antenna
6. FZV connection to general module (GM)
7. Connection to radio

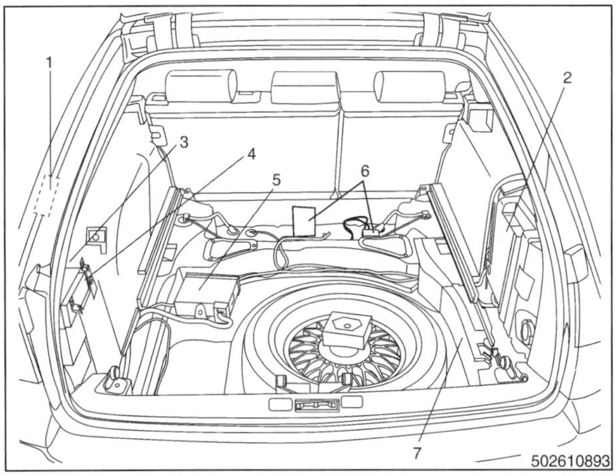

Fig. 140 Sport Wagon cargo compartment electrical components

◀ Under cargo compartment floor, or in side compartments

1. FZV / FM2 antenna amplifier
2. Audio subwoofer
3. Audio amplifier
4. GPS control module
5. Radio (with GPS)
6. Telephone transceiver or PSE box
7. Air suspension control module (EHC)

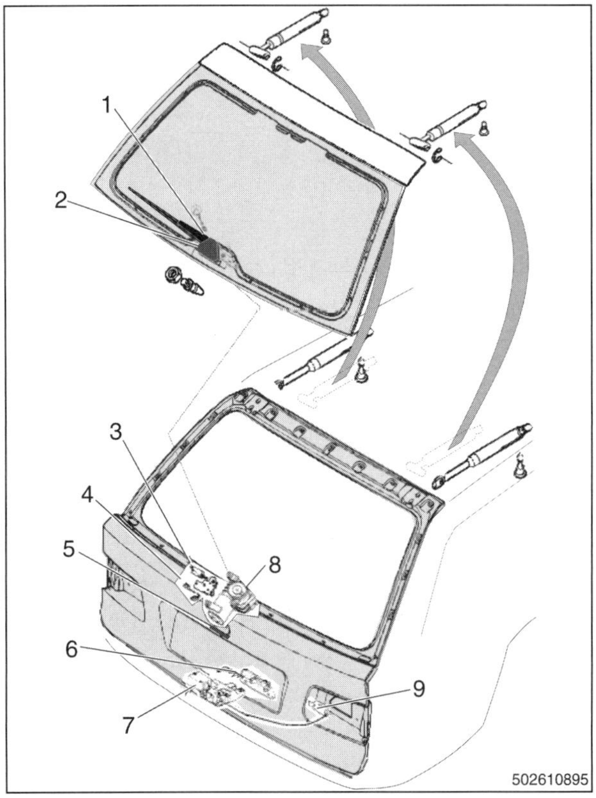

Fig. 141 Sport Wagon tailgate

◀ Electric components in tailgate

1. Wiper arm and drive linkage
2. Tailgate window unlock switch pad (signal to GM III)
3. Tailgate window latch actuator (GM III controlled)
4. Tailgate “window open” signal to rear wiper module
5. Tailgate unlock switch pad (signal to GM III)
6. Tailgate soft close (SCA) motor (GM III controlled)
7. Tailgate latch actuator (GM III controlled)
8. Tailgate window wiper module / motor
9. Tailgate emergency release (accessed from tool kit, inside car)

611 Wipers and Washers

GENERAL

This repair group covers repair information for windshield, headlight (optional) and rear window (Sport Wagon) wiper and washer systems.

Replacement of the wiper/washer stalk switch assembly is covered in **612 Switches.** Electrical wiring diagrams and relays for the wiper/washer system are covered in **ELE Electrical Wiring Diagrams**.

Special tools

Although most wiper system repairs can be carried out with normal shop tools, a few special tools may be necessary as well.

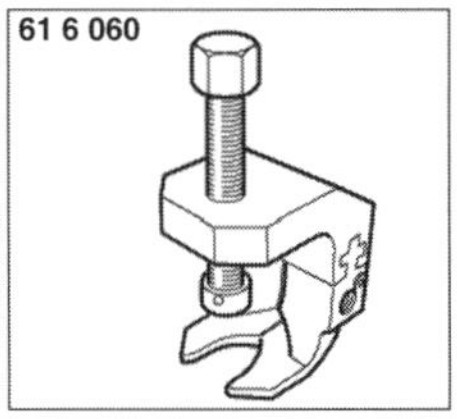

◄ Puller (Tool No. 61 6 060)

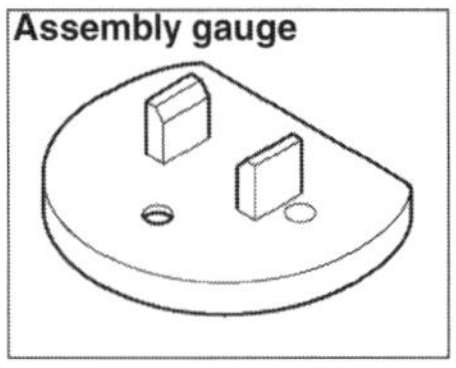

◄ Assembly gauge (Tool No. 61 1 320)

◄ Washer nozzle adjusting tool (Tool No. 00 9 100)

WIPER AND WASHER SYSTEM

The wiper and washer functions in E39 vehicles are controlled by the general module (GM III). Driver input to the system is via the multi-function stalk switch to the right of steering column.

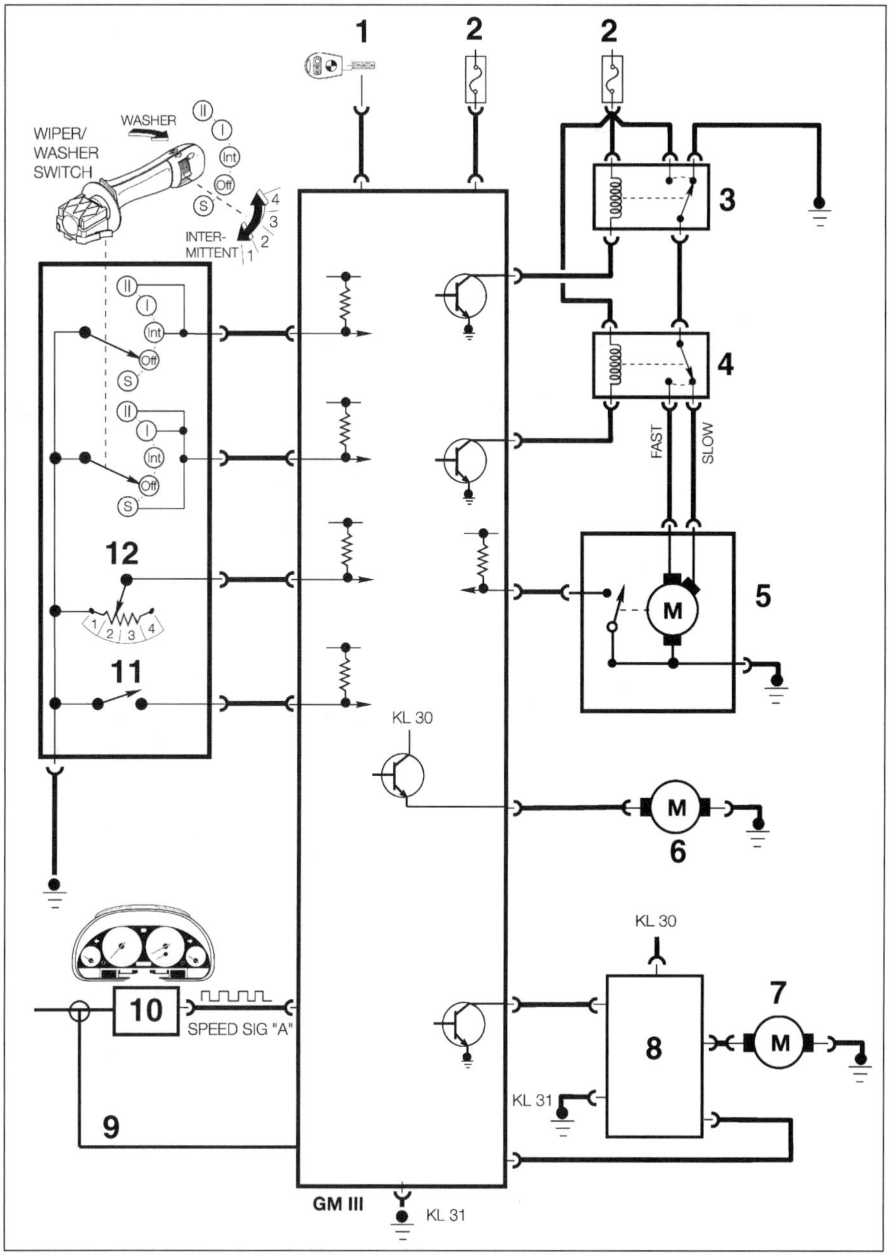

Windshield wiper/washer system

1. KL R (power with ignition in accessory position)
2. KL 30 (power at all times)
3. Stage I relay
4. Stage II relay
5. Wiper motor (front)
6. Windshield washer pump
7. Headlight washer pump
8. Headlight washer relay module
9. K-Bus (headlight on, vehicle speed signals)
10. IKE (instrument cluster electronics)
11. Speed signal (A)
12. Windshield washer switch
13. General module III

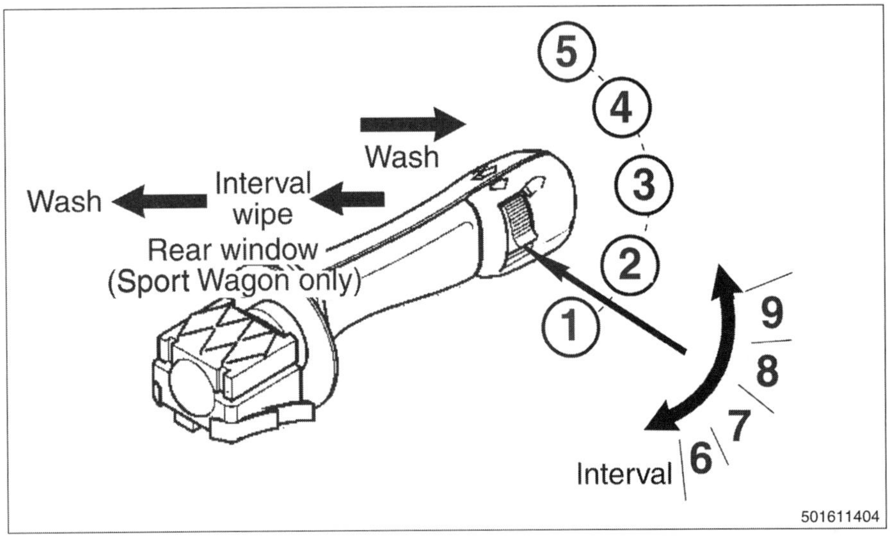

Windshield wiper switch

1. **Single wipe (hold stalk switch down)**
2. **Off**
3. **Interval control (thumb wheel on stalk switch)**
4. **Slow (automatically switches to interval when car is stopped)**
5. **Fast (automatically switches to slow speed when car is stopped)**

Wiper switch interval control

The interval control sets the wiping interval. Interval time will vary from 26 seconds with car at rest to 2 seconds at high speeds depending on the interval setting selected.

Wiping intervals (1 through 4) are dependent on road speed. As road speed increases, the wiping interval is shortened. See the table below.

Thumb wheel position	Vehicle speed (mph)					
	4	5 - 22	23 - 45	46 - 60	61 - 87	87
	Interval time (seconds)					
1	26	19	17	15	15	13
2	17	12	11	10	9	7
3	10	6	6	5	4	3
4	5	3	3	2	2	2

Wiping speed in stage I and stage II are also dependent on road speed. Stage I switches to intermittent when the vehicle is stopped. Stage II switches to stage I when the vehicle is stopped.

To protect the wiper motor from excessive loads, the return contact (parking contact) is used as an input signal for wiper operation. If the contact signal is not present for 16 seconds, indicating a blocked wiper arm, the wiper motor will switch off.

Windshield wiper relay

502611405

◄ Located on right side of engine compartment (**arrow**) under interior ventilation filter housing.

Windshield washer pump

502611407

◄ Pump is mounted on washer tank (**arrow**) located behind right front wheel inner fender cover.

Models equipped with optional headlight washers use a second pump that is mounted to right of windshield washer pump.

Windshield washer nozzle jets

– Washer jets are located on the engine hood. With the ignition ON, washer jets are automatically heated. The nozzle heaters, being of positive temperature coefficient (PTC) design, increase resistance as they heat up and automatically cut back on current consumption.

Headlight washer system (optional)

502611990

◄ Washer nozzles are on top of the front bumper. The headlight washer pump uses fluid from the front washer tank. If headlights are on, they will be cleaned every fifth time the windshield washers are activated.

Rear window wiper assembly (Sport Wagon)

Wiper assembly is mounted to the tailgate and linked to the rear wiper shaft via a mechanical coupling. See **Rear window wiper/washer system (Sport Wagon)**.

Rain sensor (optional)

The optional rain sensor system uses an infrared sensor, located at top of the windshield in front of rear view mirror, to detect the presence of water drops on the windshield. The signal from the sensor is communicated to GM III (General Control Module III), which activates interval wipe cycle if the wiper switch interval control is activated. The rain sensor is 'active' whenever the ignition is on.

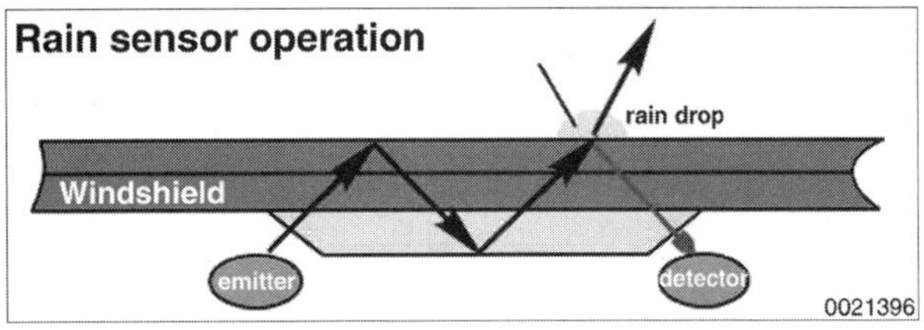

The rain sensor functions by aiming a beam of infrared light through the windshield at a set angle. The beam is reflected back and forth within the windshield until it is detected by the rain sensor. Rain drops (or other impurities) on the outside of the windshield cause some of the infrared to be dissipated outside the windshield. As a result the detector "sees" less infrared intensity. This is interpreted as a need for the wiper to be turned on.

Rain sensor operation

The rain sensor continuously monitors the windshield for rain accumulation and signals the GM III to activate the wipers based on the interval control position and how fast rain accumulates on thc windshield.

The interval control signal (1 - 4) via K-bus informs the rain sensor of the selected level of sensitivity:

- Position 1 (least sensitive) delays wiper activation signal.
- Position 4 (most sensitive) sends wiper activation signal to GM III module sooner.

Depending on the intensity of rain the wipers can operate continuously as if set in a normal wiper stalk switch position (stage I or stage II) regardless of interval control setting. For this reason, vehicle speed signal on K-bus is not utilized on rain sensor equipped wiper systems.

If ignition switch is turned off with wiper switch in intermittent position, the rain sensor will only become active after ignition is switched back on and one of the following occurs:

- Stalk switch is moved from intermittent position and then back.
- Knurled wheel setting is adjusted.
- Wash function is activated.

The rain sensor control module adapts to the sensor optics as follows:

- Windshield aging: As the vehicle ages, windshield pitting in the rain sensor monitoring area may cause a loss of light in the optics system. The control module adapts for loss of light based on the intensity of the detected infrared light with a cleared windshield.
- Dirty windows: Rain sensor adaptation reacts less sensitively to a dirty windshield (dirt, road salt, wax residue) after a completed wipe cycle. A dirty windshield has a film on it that diminishes the ability of infrared to refract into water droplets that are present. This causes a delay in the rain sensor detection capabilities and lengthens time intervals on an intermittent wipe.

> ***CAUTION—***
> *On rain sensor equipped models, make sure the wiper blades are in perfect condition. Only use window cleaner to clean the windshield.*

NOTE—
A dirty windshield can cause the rain sensor control module to set a fault due to approaching limits of its adaptation abilities.

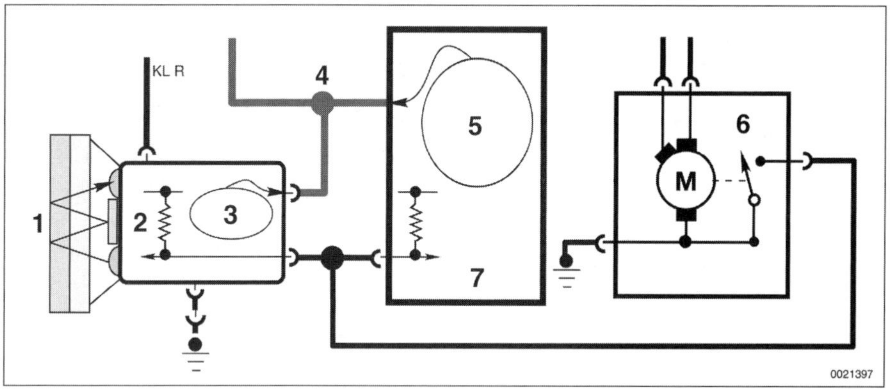

Rain sensor system

1. **Windshield**
2. **Rain sensor module**
3. **Activate wipers**
4. **K-Bus**
5. **Interval position selection**
6. **Wiper motor**
7. **General module III**

Rear wiper functions:

The rear wiper/washer is controlled by the wiper/washer steering column stalk switch via the ZKE III system. The functions of the system are:

- Intermittent rear window wiping.
- Programmed rear window wiping interval.
- Operation of the rear window washer.

Additionally, the system automatically controls the following safety and convenience features.

- Wiper interrupt with rear window open.
- Wiping interrupt with a blocked wiper arm.

Continuous wiping is activated any time the rear wiper is on and the transmission is in reverse. A signal is provided by the back-up light switch via the light control module.

Programmed wiping intervals are activated as follows:

- Switch the rear wiper on and off.
- Wait the desired interval time.
- Switch the rear wiper back on.

NOTE—
After washing, the rear wiper will remain in interval (normal) wiping mode until switched OFF.

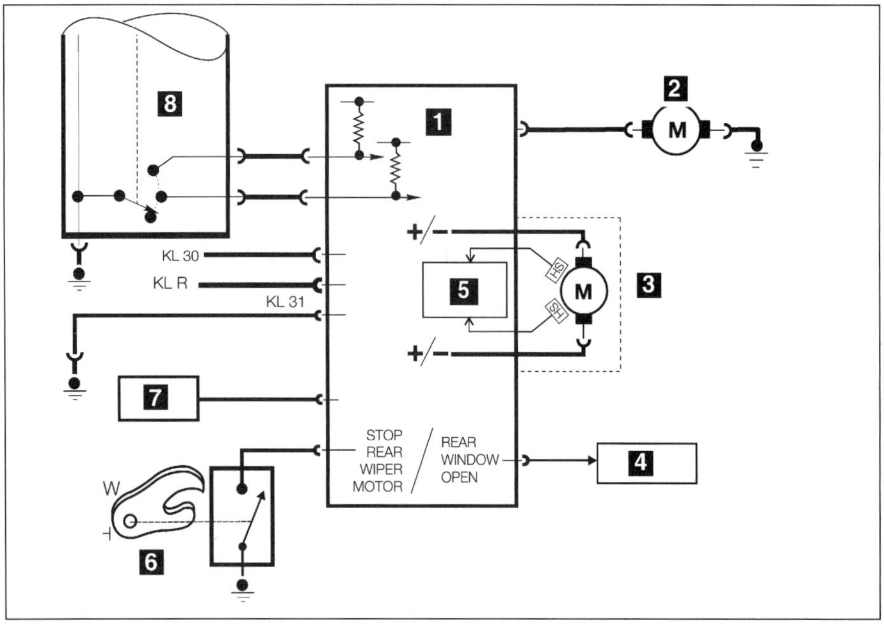

Rear window wiper/washer system (Sport Wagon)

1. **Rear window wiper/washer module**
2. **Rear window washer pump (located in right front wheel well)**
3. **Rear window wiper motor**
4. **GM III module (to turn interior lights /rear window open)**
5. **Motor operation monitoring (Hall effect)**
6. **Rear window latch switch**
7. **Reverse signal from light control module**
8. **Wiper/washer switch**

WIPER BLADES

Wiper blade cleaning problems

– Common cleaning problems with wipers include streaking or sheeting, water drops after wiping, and blade chatter.

Streaking is usually caused when wiper blades are coated with road film or car wash wax. Clean the blades using soapy water. If cleaning does not cure the problem, the blades should be replaced. BMW recommends replacing the wiper blades twice a year, before and after the cold season.

Water drops that remain behind after wiping are usually caused by oil, road film, or diesel exhaust residue on the glass. Use an alcohol or ammonia solution or a non-abrasive cleaner (such as Bon-Ami®) to clean windshield.

Chatter may be caused by dirty or worn blades, or by wiper arms that are out of alignment. Clean the blades and windshield as described above. Adjust the wiper arm so that there is even pressure along the blade, and so that the blade at rest is perpendicular to the windshield. If problems persist, blades and wiper arms should be replaced.

NOTE—
BMW has available a special tool/gauge (BMW special tool 00 9 210) to align the angle of the wiper arm to the windshield glass.

– The wiper blades can be renewed in one of two ways:
  - Complete blade replacement
  - Rubber insert replacement

– Insert replacement is the most economical method, although over time wiper blade frame itself will become worn. One rule of thumb would be to replace just the inserts every second time.

Wiper blade inserts, replacing

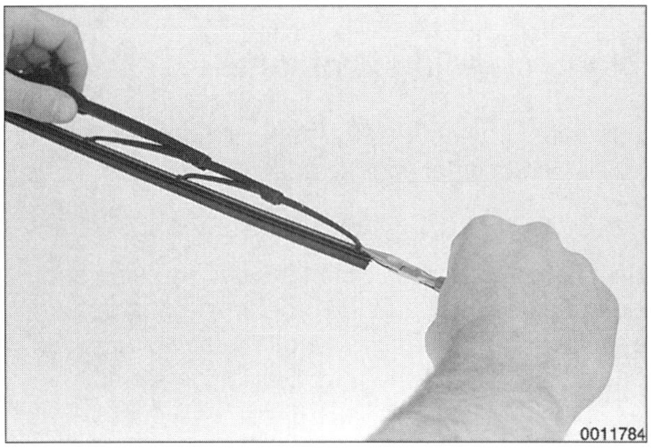
0011784

To replace wiper inserts:

- Remove wiper blade. See **Wiper blade, replacing**.
- Unhook wiper blade insert from wiper arm guides. If necessary, spread guide slightly using needle nose pliers.
- Pull old insert from wiper arm guides, noting installation position.
- Remove metal support strips from old insert and install into slots in new insert, noting installation direction of cutouts in support strips.
- Slide new insert through wiper blade guides. Lock insert in place at end guides.

NOTE—
Some wiper blade versions may have two retaining tabs.

Wiper blade, replacing

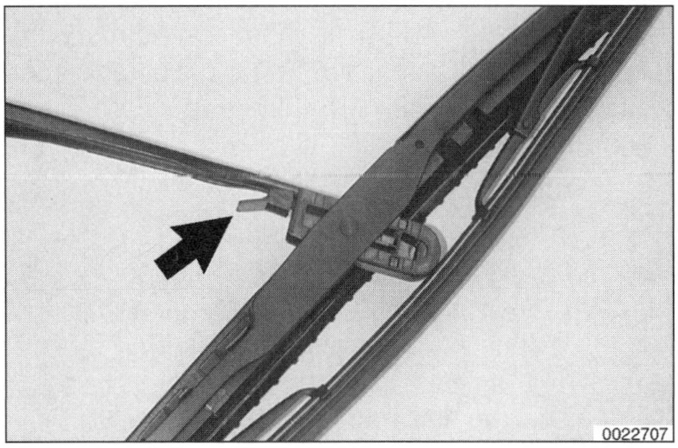
0022707

To replace wiper blades:

- Pivot wiper arm off windshield.
- Position wiper blade approximately perpendicular to wiper arm.
- Remove wiper blade from wiper arm by depressing retaining tab (**arrow**) and sliding blade out of arm.

Wiper arm, removing and installing

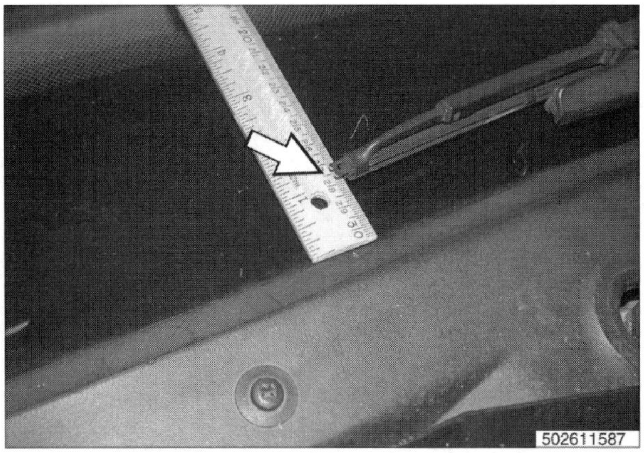
502611587

Mark the position of the wiper blades by measuring the distance between wiper blade and windshield gasket (**arrow**). Note the distance.

NOTE—
Wiper arm removal and installation on the Sport Wagon rear window is similar.

CAUTION—
- *Make sure wipers are parked (stalk switch in OFF position) and the ignition is also OFF.*
- *Use fender cover to protect windshield.*

To remove wiper arm:

- Open hood. Gently pry off caps covering wiper arm retaining nuts.
- Remove left wiper arm retaining nut (**A**).
- Remove spacer (**B**).
- Remove wiper arm from shaft.

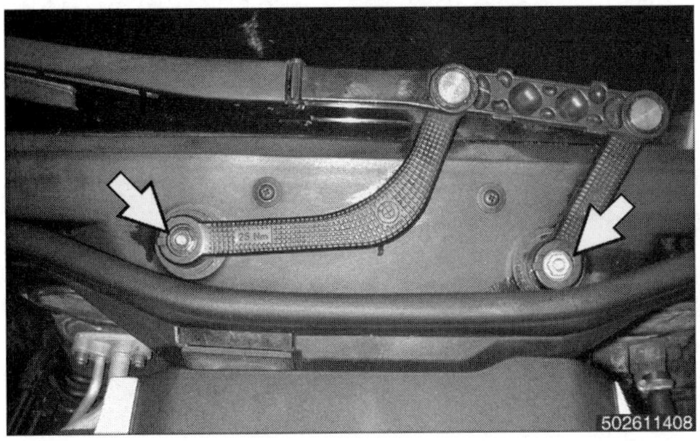

Remove right wiper arm retaining nuts (**arrows**). Disconnect arms from shafts.

NOTE —
Use BMW special tool 61 6 060 or equivalent puller to remove arm.

– If wiper arm sleeve at shaft is loose, it must be replaced.

– Install arms using measurement from step 1, torque nuts and recheck measurement.

Tightening torque

Left front wiper arm to wiper shaft	40 Nm (30 ft-lb)
Right front wiper arm to wiper shaft	25 Nm (18 ft-lb)
Rear wiper arm to wiper shaft	9.5 Nm (7 ft-lb)

WIPER ASSEMBLY

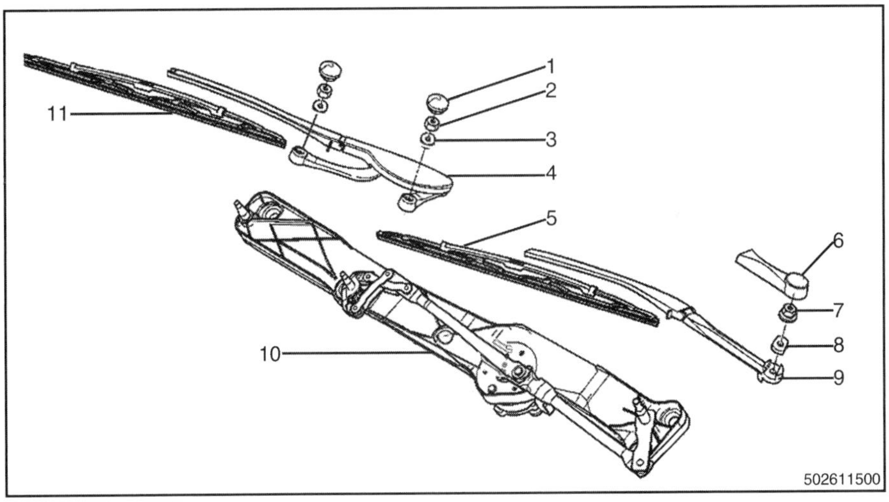

Wiper assembly diagram

1. **Wiper arm fastener cover**
2. **Wiper arm fastener**
3. **Wave washer**
4. **Right wiper arm**
5. **Wiper blade**
6. **Left side wiper arm fastener cover**
7. **Wiper arm fastener**
8. **Wiper arm locating spacer**
9. **Left wiper arm**
10. **Motor and rod assembly**
11. **Wiper blade**

Windshield wiper assembly, removing and installing

The windshield wiper assembly (linkage and motor) is removed as a single unit. Once the assembly is removed, wiper motor and other linkage parts can be repaired or replaced.

> *CAUTION—*
> - *Make sure wipers are parked (stalk switch in OFF position) and the ignition is also OFF.*
> - *Use fender cover to protect windshield.*
> - *To avoid damaging the wiper arms and pivots, do not manually slide or force the wiper arms across the windshield.*

– Remove wiper arms. See **Wiper arm, removing and installing**.

– Remove left and right microfilter housings. See **020 Maintenance**.

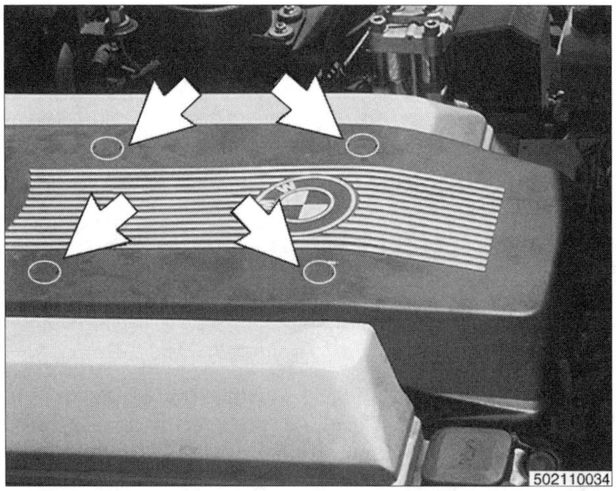

◄ V–8 models. Remove top engine cover by pushing down on tabs (**arrows**).

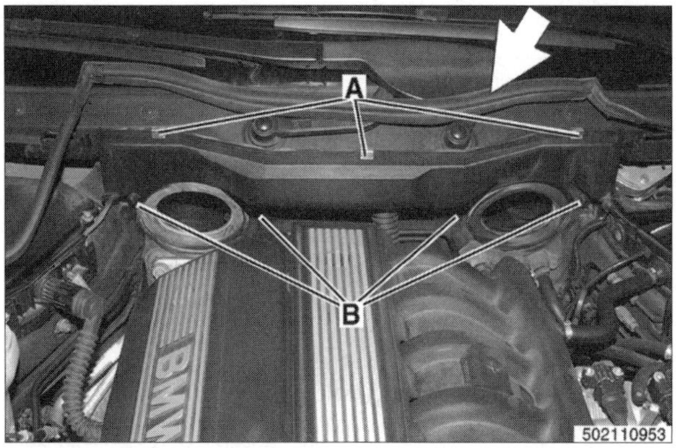

◄ Remove rear engine bulkhead cover:

- Remove mounting clips (**A**).
- Remove thumb screws (**B**).
- Remove engine harness lock tab by pulling straight up on tab.
- Turn locking knobs (**arrows**) and remove panel.

◄ Remove left wiper arm mounting spacer (**arrow**) with BMW special tool 61 6 060.

– Remove wiper assembly sealing washers.

Remove plastic expansion rivets (**arrows**) and remove cowl tray.

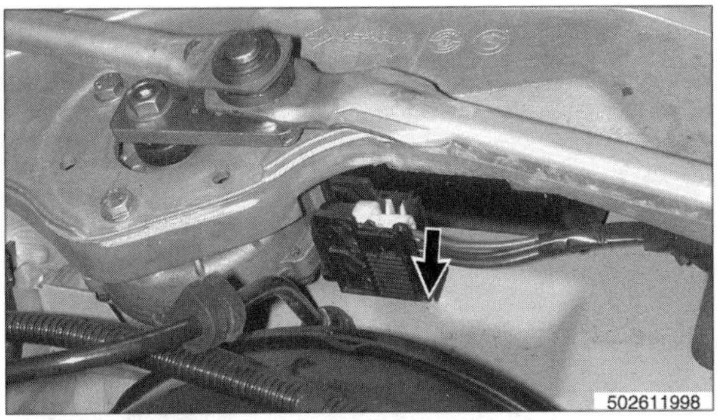

Push down (**arrow**) on wiper motor wiring harness plug lock and disconnect plug.

Remove wiper drive assembly mounting fasteners (**A**) and lift out wiper assembly.

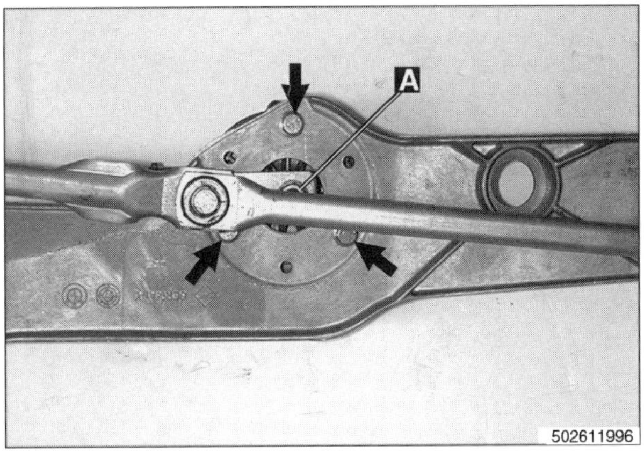

Remove wiper motor from wiper assembly:

- Remove nut (**A**) and pry off drive arm.
- Remove wiper motor mounting fasteners (**arrows**) and remove motor.

– Installation is reverse of removal, noting the following:
  - Fit center mounting rubber dampers over wiper assembly.
  - Install all fasteners finger-tight, then torque to specification below when satisfied with alignment.
  - Run wiper motor to parked position and switch off.
  - Install wiper arms but not blades.
  - Close hood and fit wiper blades.
  - Recheck wiper blade position as described earlier in **Wiper arm, removing and installing**.
  - Check all electrical harness fittings and sealing grommets for correct reinstallation.
  - Replace any wire ties cut off during removal.

Tightening torques

Wiper assembly	12 Nm (9 ft-lb)
Wiper motor to wiper assembly	12 Nm (9 ft-lb)
Left wiper arm to wiper shaft	40 Nm (25 ft-lb)
Right wiper arm to wiper shafts	25 Nm (18 ft-lb)

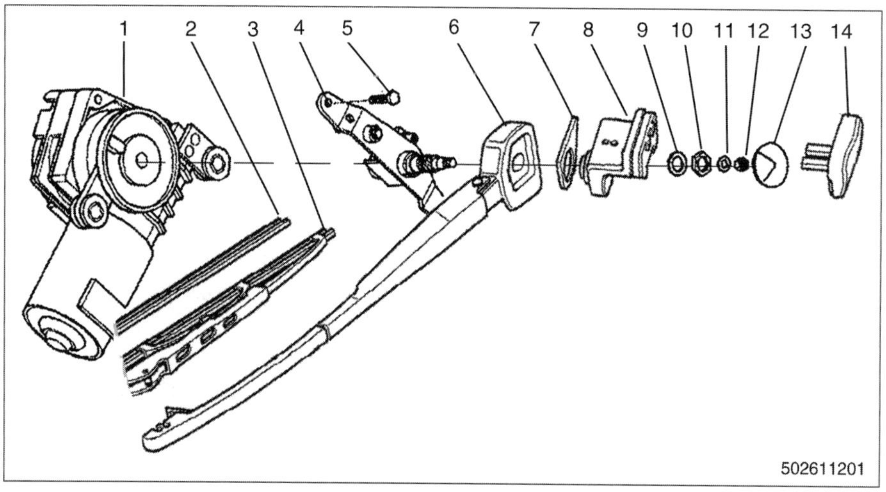

Rear wiper assembly

1. **Wiper motor**
2. **Wiper insert**
3. **Wiper blade assembly**
4. **Wiper shaft pivot**
5. **Bolt**
6. **Wiper arm**
7. **Gasket**
8. **Key button**
9. **Washer**
10. **Nut**
11. **Wave washer**
12. **Nut**
13. **Button cover**
14. **Wiper axle cover**

Rear window wiper motor, removing and installing (Sport Wagon)

- Remove rear wiper arm. See **Wiper arm, removing and installing**.
- Remove rear deck interior trim panel.
- Disconnect wiper motor electrical harness.
- Remove wiper motor mounting fasteners (3).
- Installation is reverse of removal, noting the following:
  - Install wiper motor assembly and thread mounting bolts finger tight.
  - Place BMW special tool 61 1 320 on rear window wiper drive and close rear window.
  - With rear wiper vertical, allow rear wiper shaft mechanical coupling to snap into special tool bore.
  - Tighten down wiper motor assembly. Remove special tool.

Tightening torque

Wiper motor to rear deck (Torx)	10 Nm (8 ft-lb)

Rear window wiper shaft, removing and installing (Sport Wagon)

- Remove rear wiper arm.
- Remove wiper shaft assembly mounting nut. Pull shaft and bearing out of housing.
- Installation is reverse of removal. Adjust wiper arm position.

Tightening torques

Rear window button to rear window	7 Nm (62 in-lb)
Wiper arm to wiper shaft	13.5 Nm (10 ft-lb)
Wiper shaft housing to rear window	10 Nm (8 ft-lb)

Washer Systems

The windshield washer system includes heated spray nozzles in the engine hood, the washer fluid pump, and washer fluid reservoir in the right front wheel well.

The headlight washer system (optional) consists of front washer fluid tank (shared with windshield washer system), a separate washer pump, and spray nozzles in the front bumper.

The rear window washer system (Sport Wagon only) consists of a washer tank and pump (shared with windshield washer system), and a spray nozzle at the top of the rear window frame.

Windshield spray nozzle, removing and installing

– Working under open engine hood, remove split rivets and remove sound damping mat.

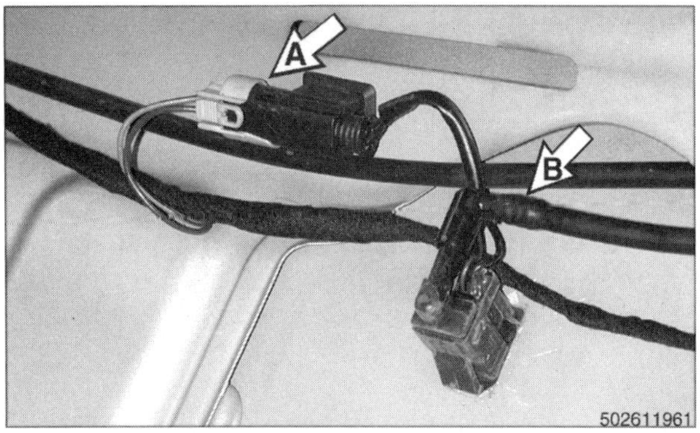

◀ Disconnect harness connector (**A**) for nozzle heater. Carefully disconnect hose (**B**) from nozzle.

◀ Gently squeeze retaining clip (**arrow**) on nozzle and remove from hood.

– Installation is reverse of removal.

– Check and adjust nozzles before driving.

NOTE—
The windshield spray nozzles can be aimed by using a sewing needle or a similar diameter stiff piece of wire.

Headlight washer spray nozzle, removing and installing

- Prior to removal, cover spray nozzle with shop rag to avoid washer spray.
- Gently pry spray nozzle out of bumper and disconnect hose.
- Transfer trim to new nozzle (if replacing) before installing.
- Connect washer fluid hose to nozzle before installing nozzle in bumper.

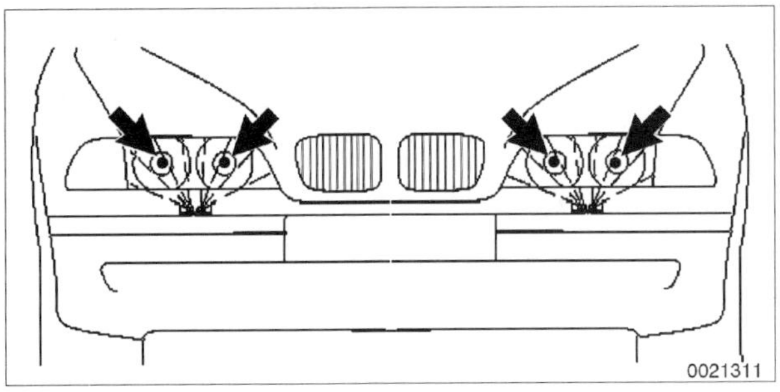

- Using BMW special tool 00 9 100 or equivalent, adjust headlight washers so that spray jets strike approximately in center of each beam (**arrows**).

NOTE—
To turn on headlight washer jets, turn on ignition, lights and windshield washer system. To repeat spray procedure, turn off ignition, then back on again. Otherwise the headlight washers are disabled for 3 minutes.

Washer fluid reservoir, removing and installing

- Remove right front wheel and inner fender trim. See **410 Fenders, Engine Hood**.

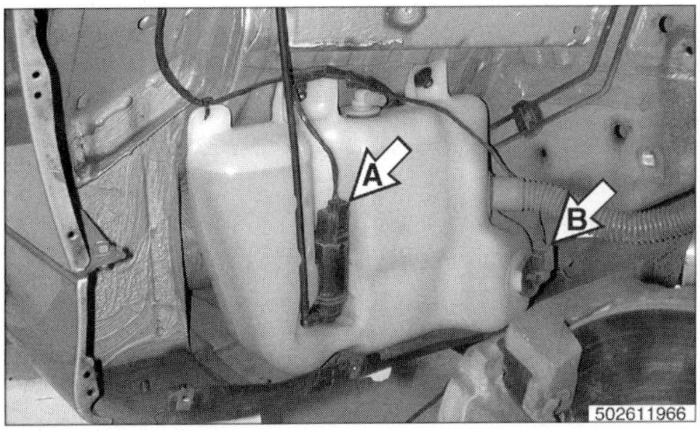

- Detach washer pump (**A**) and fluid level sensor (**B**) harness connectors.

- Remove filler tube (**arrow**) from reservoir.

NOTE—
Have drain pan ready to catch dripping washer fluid.

- Cut off wire tie to release washer pump electrical harness from reservoir.
- Remove reservoir retaining fastener and remove reservoir.
- Installation is reverse of removal.

Windshield washer pump, removing and installing

- Remove right front wheel and inner fender trim. See **410 Fenders, Engine Hood.**

- To remove windshield washer pump (**arrow**) and headlight washer pump if equipped:

  NOTE—
  - *Have drain pan ready to catch dripping washer fluid.*

- Disconnect washer pump electrical harness and fluid hose.
- Twist washer pump to remove from reservoir.
- Installation is reverse of removal, noting the following:
  - Coat fluid pump sealing ring with anti-friction agent.
  - On installation, check that fluid hoses are not kinked.
  - Make sure reservoir heat shield is correctly engaged.
  - Replace wire tie. Refill reservoir.

Washer fluid level sensor, removing and installing

- Remove right front wheel and inner fender trim. See **410 Fenders, Engine Hood.**

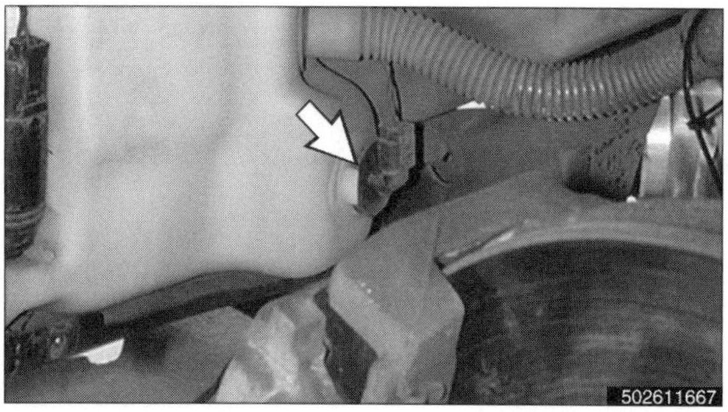

- Twist washer fluid level sensor (**arrow**) clockwise to remove from base of reservoir.

  NOTE—
  Have drain pan ready to catch dripping washer fluid.

- Installation is reverse of removal, noting the following:
  - Coat washer fluid level sensor sealing ring with anti-friction agent.
  - On installation, check that fluid hoses are not kinked.
  - Make sure reservoir heat shield is correctly engaged.
- Replace wire tie. Refill reservoir.

612 Switches

GENERAL

This section covers replacement of electrical switches at the steering wheel, steering column, dashboard, pedal cluster, center console and other locations.

See also the following sections:

- **250 Gearshift Linkage**
- **515 Central Locking and Anti-Theft**
- **520 Seats**
- **540 Sunroof**
- **610 Electrical Component Locations**
- **630 Lights**
- **ELE Electrical Wiring Diagrams**

> ***CAUTION—***
> - *When working on electrical switches or lights, always disconnect the negative (–) cable from the battery and insulate the cable end to prevent accidental reconnection. Prior to disconnecting the battery, read the battery disconnection cautions given in* **001 General Warning and Cautions**.
> - *To prevent marring the trim when working on interior components, work with plastic prying tools or wrap the tips of screwdrivers and pliers with tape before prying out switches or electrical accessories.*

STEERING WHEEL SWITCHES

E39 vehicles are equipped with either the multi-function (MFL) steering wheel or sport steering wheel. Incorporated into each steering wheel are an SRS airbag, horn contacts, selected cellular phone and radio controls and cruise control buttons.

To replace the steering wheel switches, remove the airbag first. See **721 Airbag System (SRS).**

> ***WARNING—***
> - *To prevent marring the trim when working on interior components, work with plastic prying tools or wrap the tips of screwdrivers and pliers with tape before prying out switches or electrical accessories.*
> - *Special test equipment is required to retrieve SRS fault codes, diagnose system faults, and reset/turn off the SRS indicator light. The SRS indicator light will remain on until any problem has been corrected and the fault memory has been cleared.*

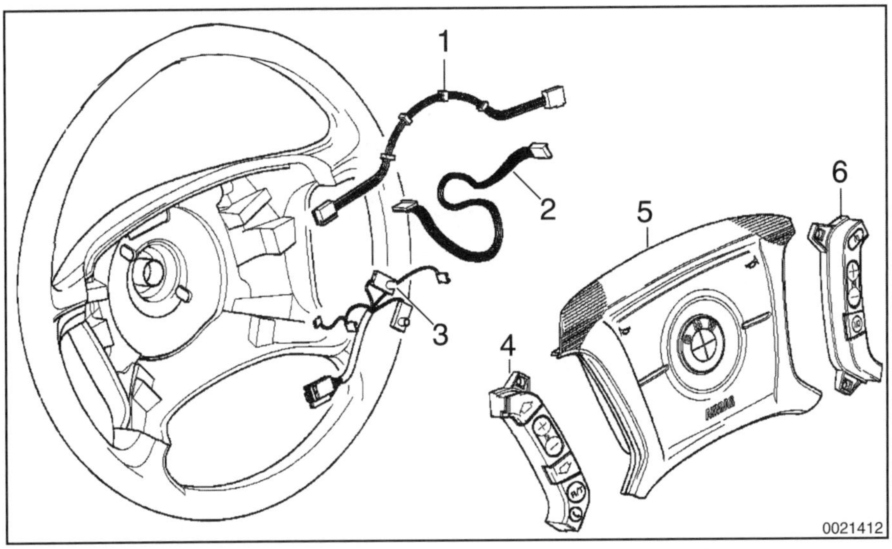

Multi-function steering wheel switches

1. Cruise control radio/telephone electrical harness
2. Horn button electrical harness
3. Airbag electrical harness
4. Radio/telephone control switches
5. Airbag unit
6. Cruise control switch set

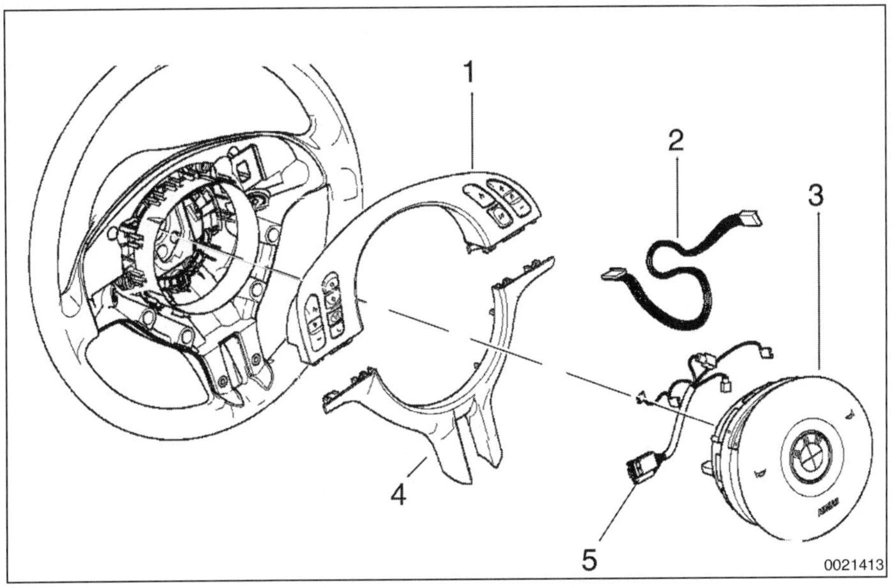

Sport steering wheel switches

1. Switch carrier
2. Steering wheel switch harness
3. Airbag
4. Lower cover
5. Horn button and airbag harness

Steering wheel switches, removing and installing

- MFL steering wheel and sport steering wheel are similar. See **320 Steering and Wheel Alignment** for more information.

- Remove airbag. See **721 Airbag System (SRS).**

> *WARNING —*
> *The BMW airbag system (Supplemental Restraint System or SRS) is complex. Special precautions must be observed when servicing. Serious injury may result if SRS system service is attempted by persons unfamiliar with the BMW SRS and its approved service procedures. BMW specifies that all inspection and service should be preformed by an authorized BMW dealer.*

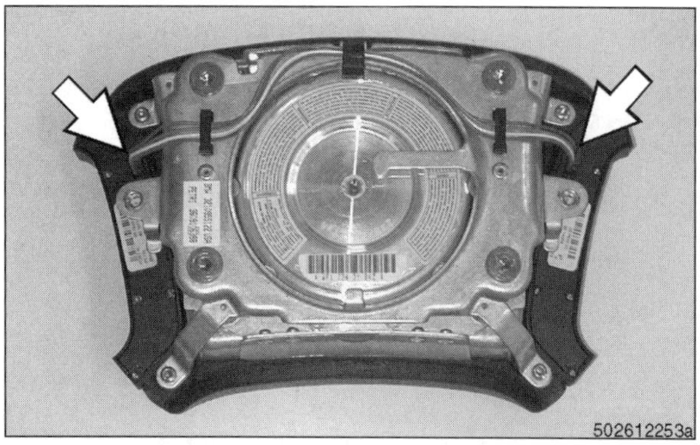

502612253a

- Disconnect switch electrical harness connectors (**arrows**).

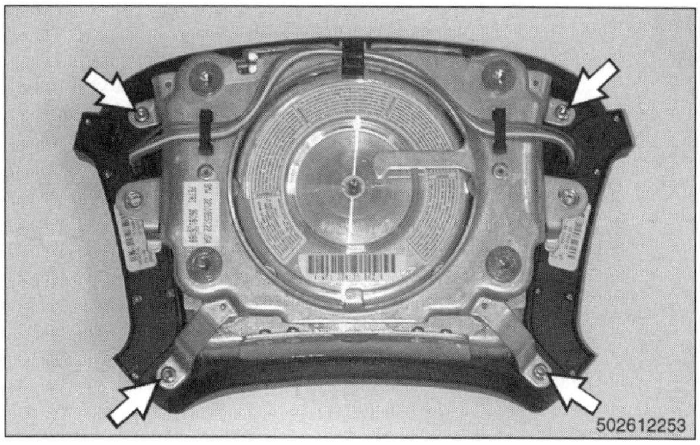

502612253

- Remove fasteners (**arrows**) from back side of airbag pad to release switch pack.

NOTE —
BMW does not provide the horn contact switch as a separate part.

- Installation is reverse of removal.

STEERING COLUMN SWITCHES

To remove any of the steering column switches, it is necessary to first remove the upper and lower column trim pieces. See **320 Steering and Wheel Alignment** for more information.

> *CAUTION—*
> *To prevent marring interior trim, work with plastic prying tools or wrap the tips of screwdrivers and pliers with tape before prying out switches or electrical accessories.*

Ignition lock cylinder, removing and installing

- To remove the ignition lock cylinder, first remove steering column trim. See **320 Steering and Wheel Alignment**.

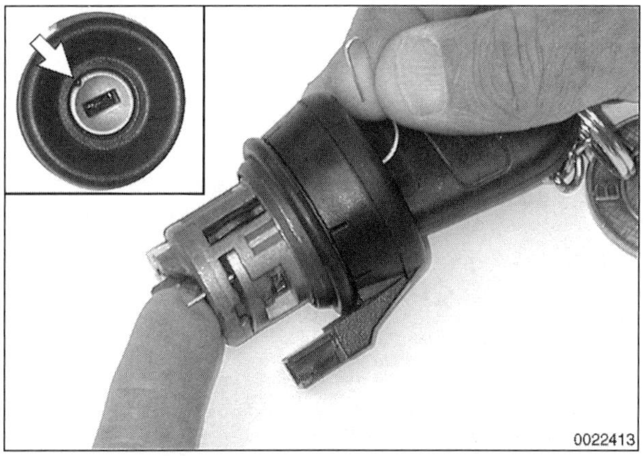

To remove the EWS (Electronic Immobilization) ring antenna prior to removing ignition lock cylinder, use BMW special tool 61 3 300 to gently pry off the ring antenna. Alternatively, remove ignition switch key cylinder first.

– With ignition key in ON position (60° from LOCKED):
  - Insert a thin piece of stiff wire into opening (**arrow**) in lock cylinder and pull lock cylinder out.
  - Disconnect ring antenna harness connector.
  - Gently work ring antenna off key cylinder.
  - Installation is reverse of removal.

Ignition switch, removing and installing

– Disconnect negative (–) cable from battery and cover terminal with insulating material.

> ***WARNING —***
> *Prior to disconnecting the battery, read the battery disconnection cautions given* **001 General Warnings and Cautions**.

Remove steering column trim panels. See **320 Steering and Wheel Alignment**.

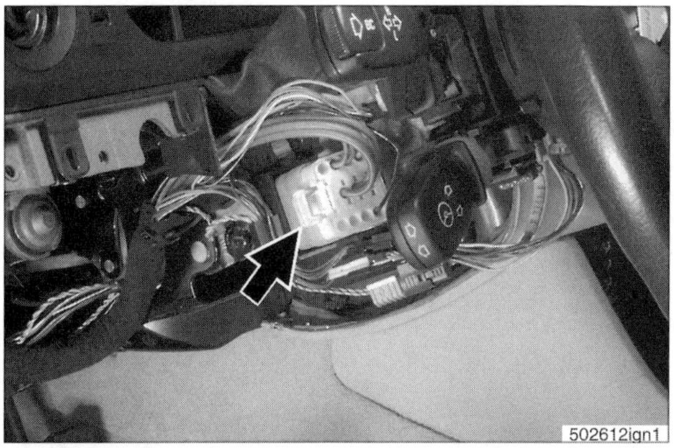

Pry out electrical connector lock (**arrow**) and disconnect connector.

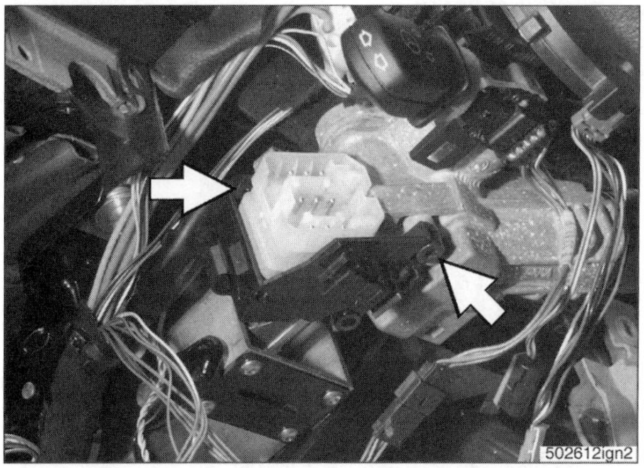

If applicable, remove fasteners (**arrows**) from wiring harness support and remove support.

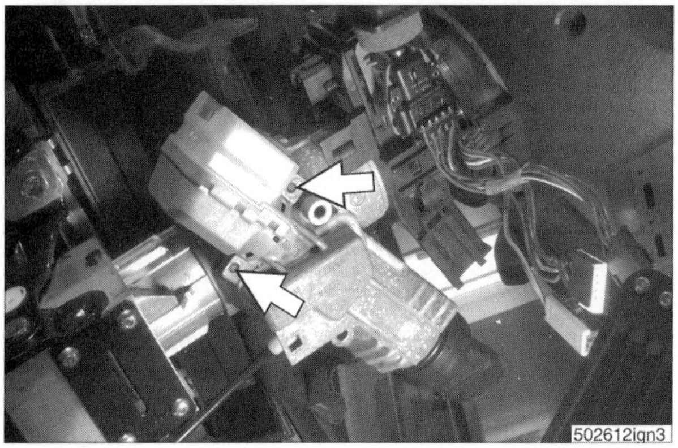

Remove protective paint covering ignition switch fasteners (**arrows**) and remove fasteners.

– Installation is reverse of removal noting the following:
  - Correctly align switch drive to ignition lock drive.
  - Secure ignition fasteners with paint after installation.

Wiper switch assembly, removing and installing

- Disconnect negative (–) cable from battery and cover terminal with insulating material.

> ***WARNING —***
> *Prior to disconnecting the battery, read the battery disconnection cautions given* ***001 General Warnings and Cautions****.*

- Remove steering column trim panels. See **320 Steering and Wheel Alignment**.

> ***CAUTION—***
> *To prevent marring interior trim, work with plastic prying tools or wrap the tips of screwdrivers and pliers with tape before prying out switches or electrical accessories.*

NOTE —
In the accompanying photos, the steering wheel is shown removed for clarity.

- Disconnect wiper/washer switch electrical harness connector.

◄ Squeeze locking tabs to release switch (**arrows**) and slide switch out of support.

- Installation is reverse of removal.

Turn signal/headlight dimmer switch, removing and installing

- Disconnect negative (–) cable from battery and cover terminal with insulating material.

> ***CAUTION—***
> *Prior to disconnecting the battery, read the battery disconnection cautions given* ***001 General Warnings and Cautions****.*

NOTE —
In the accompanying photos, the steering wheel is shown removed for clarity.

- Remove steering column trim panels. See **320 Steering and Wheel Alignment**.

- Disconnect switch electrical harness connector.

502612488

◀ Squeeze locking tabs to release switch (**arrows**) and slide switch out of support.

– Installation is reverse of removal, noting the following:
  - Place turn signal indicator in center position before installing.
  - Ensure that self cancelling cams on turn signal switch are not damaged during installation.

Steering column positioning switch, removing and installing

– Disconnect negative (–) cable from battery and cover terminal with insulating material.

> ***CAUTION—***
> *Prior to disconnecting the battery, read the battery disconnection cautions given* ***001 General Warnings and Cautions****.*

NOTE—
In the accompanying photos, the steering wheel is shown removed for clarity.

– Remove steering column trim panels. See **320 Steering and Wheel Alignment**.

– Disconnect switch electrical harness connector.

502612489

◀ Squeeze locking tabs to release switch (**arrow**) and slide switch out of support.

– Installation is reverse of removal.

Pedal Cluster Switches

To access either the brake pedal or the clutch pedal switch, remove left footwell trim (above pedals). See **513 Interior Trim.**

Brake light switch, replacing

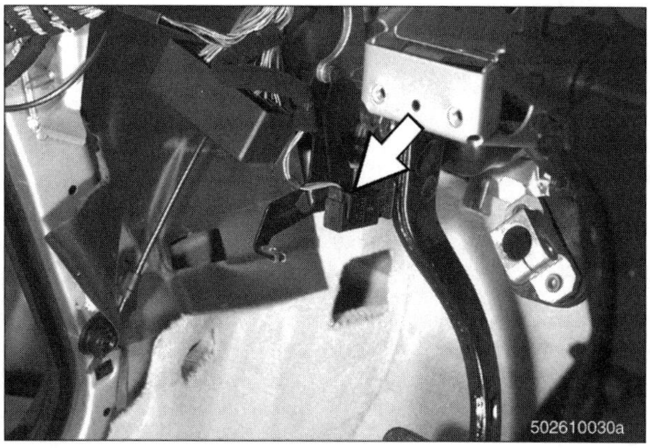

◀ Working at pedal cluster:

- Disconnect electrical harness connector (**arrow**) from brake light switch.
- Slide switch out of support.

NOTE—
The brake light switch is held in place via a serrated mounting. Remove switch mounting from pedal cluster bracket.

– Push brake pedal down, install new switch, then allow brake pedal to spring back slowly, automatically adjusting switch position.

Clutch pedal control switch, replacing

– Working at pedal cluster:

- Push clutch pedal to floor and lock in position using a pedal stop.
- Disconnect electrical harness connector from switch.
- Squeeze together retaining clips at front of switch to release from bracket.
- Slide switch out of holder.

– Install new switch, then allow clutch pedal to spring back slowly, automatically adjusting switch position.

Other Interior Switches

Headlight switch, removing and installing

– Disconnect negative (–) cable from battery and cover terminal with insulating material.

> ***CAUTION—***
> *Prior to disconnecting the battery, read the battery disconnection cautions given* **001 General Warnings and Cautions**.

NOTE—
In the accompanying photos, the steering wheel is shown removed for clarity.

502612390

< Pry gently on dashboard trim to remove.

502513710

< Remove upper instrument cluster trim fasteners (**arrows**).

502612387

< Remove lower instrument cluster trim fasteners (**arrows**).

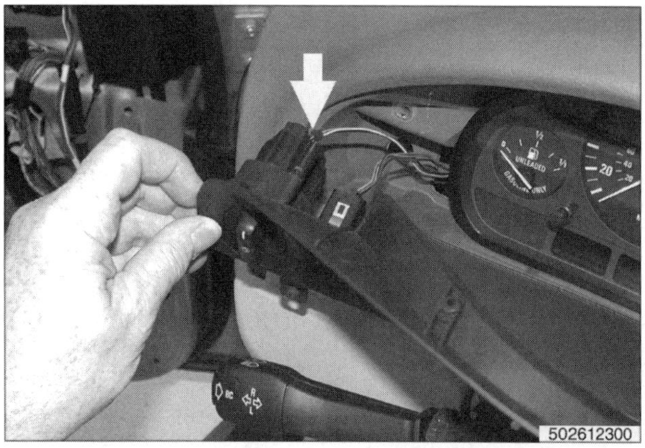

Pull panel out and disconnect electrical harness connector form head light switch (**arrow**).

Remove head light switch knob by pulling straight off.

Remove head light switch mounting nut (**arrow**).

Remove switch from back side of instrument cluster trim panel.

– Installation is reverse of removal.

Hazard warning and central locking switches, replacing

The central locking switch and hazard warning switch are behind shifter mechanism in center console.

– Remove center console wooden trim panel. See **513 Interior Trim**.

> ***CAUTION—***
> *To prevent marring interior trim, work with plastic prying tools or wrap the tips of screwdrivers and pliers with tape before prying out switches or electrical accessories.*

– Pull switches up from beneath console wooden trim panel to remove.

– Installation is reverse of removal.

Driver's door module, replacing

The front and rear window switches are ganged with the child safety switch in the driver's door module on the left front door arm rest.

◄ To remove driver's door module:

– Gently pry complete assembly out of arm rest starting at arrow (**A**) and working around to arrow (**D**).

> ***CAUTION—***
> *To prevent marring interior trim, work with plastic prying tools or wrap the tips of screwdrivers and pliers with tape before prying out switches or electrical accessories.*

– Disconnect electrical harnesses and remove module.

– Installation is reverse of removal.

Passenger door power window switch, replacing

– Gently pry door switch unit from door arm rest.

> ***CAUTION—***
> *To prevent marring interior trim, work with plastic prying tools or wrap the tips of screwdrivers and pliers with tape before prying out switches or electrical accessories.*

– Disconnect harness connector from switch unit.

– Installation is reverse of removal.

ASC/DSC / seat heater switches, replacing

ASC or DSC switch is located front of center console. Seat heater switches are also located here, if equipped.

◀ Gently pry out switch panel using plastic pry tool.

> ***CAUTION—***
> *To prevent marring interior trim, work with plastic prying tools or wrap the tips of screwdrivers and pliers with tape before prying out switches or electrical accessories.*

- Disconnect plug connectors and remove switch panel.

– Installation is reverse of removal.

620 Instruments

General

This repair group covers removal and installation of the instrument cluster and Global Positioning System (GPS) onboard monitor. Instrument cluster self-test procedures are also included.

Instrument cluster configurations

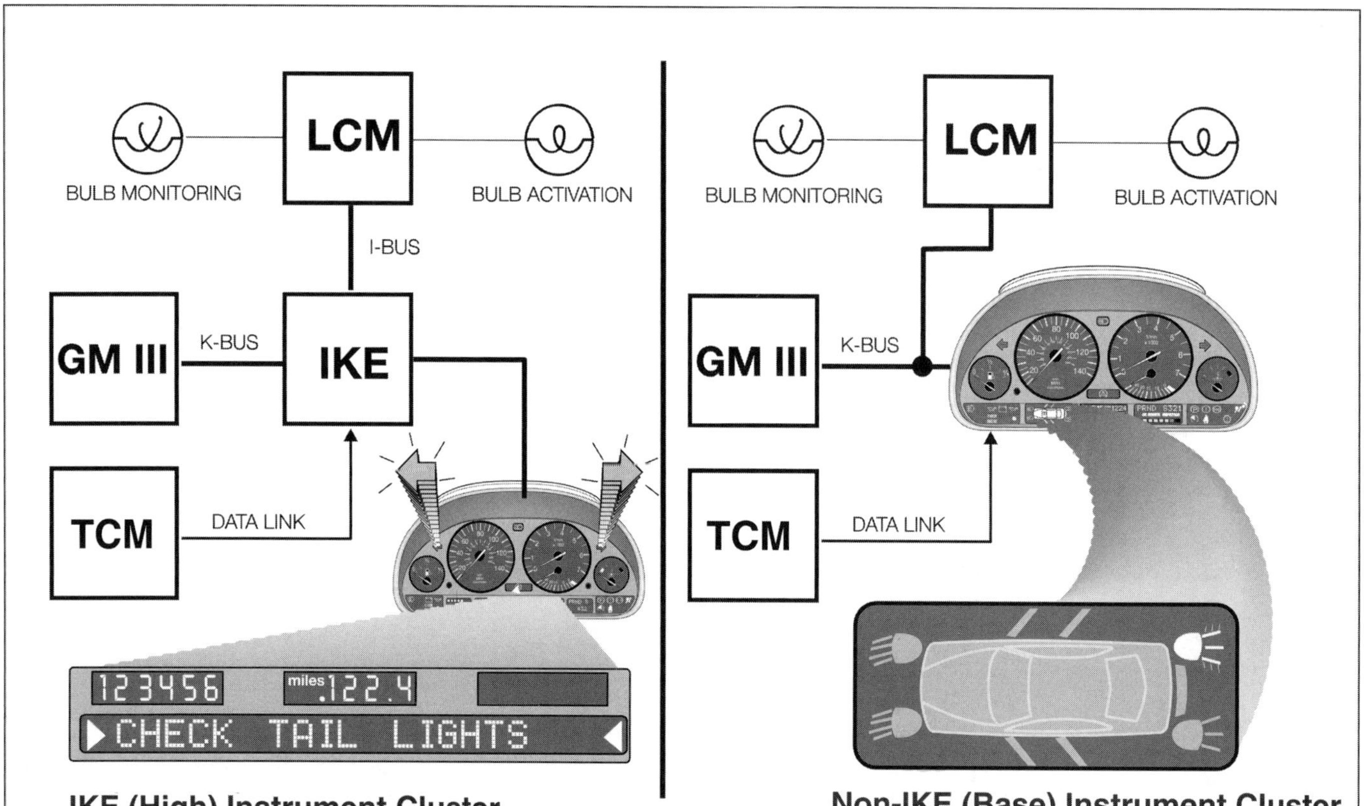

IKE (High) Instrument Cluster

Non-IKE (Base) Instrument Cluster

502620324

INSTRUMENT CLUSTER

Two types of instrument cluster configuration are used in the 5 series. The IKE (High) cluster configuration contains the on-board computer display and additional electronics.

The dashboard mounted instrument cluster is the control and information center of the E39 cars. It is connected to most of the systems and sensors in the car through the use of "Bus" networks:

K-Bus connects the Central Body Electronics (ZKE III) to heating /A/C (IHKA), rain sensor system, exterior and interior lights, Multiple Restraint System (MRS III), and Driveway Protection (EWS III).

CAN-Bus connects the engine management (DME), transmission control (AGS) and traction/stability control (ASC/DSC).

D-Bus connects the 20-pin Diagnostic Link Connector (DLC) and/or 16-pin OBD II diagnostic connector.

The instrument cluster stores and communicates Diagnostic Trouble Codes (DTCs) via the D-bus diagnostic link.

If the vehicle is equipped with On-Board Computer, pushing the button at the end of the directional stalk switch brings up on the cluster information of interest to the driver:

- Time
- Outside temperature
- Average fuel consumption
- Cruising range
- Average vehicle speed

These functions are more fully explained in the Owner's Manual.

The cluster also stores important vehicle memory functions such as total mileage and service interval data. Instrument cluster replacement must be followed by special procedures, using BMW service tester (DIS, GT1 or MoDiC), to synchronize vehicle memory and mileage with the new cluster unit.

NOTE —
- *Specific vehicle information is stored redundantly in the instrument cluster and the light control module. This information includes:*
- *Vehicle identification number (VIN)*
- *Total vehicle mileage*
- *Service interval data*

Instrument cluster layout

1. High beam warning light
2. Tachometer
3. Right directional
4. Temperature gauge
5. Warning lights
6. Right reset button
7. Automatic transmission selector position
8. Trip odometer
9. ASC/DSC Indicator light
10. Check control display
11. Service interval indicator
12. Trip odometer reset button
13. Warning lights
14. Fuel gauge
15. Left directional
16. Speedometer

Instrument cluster inputs and outputs

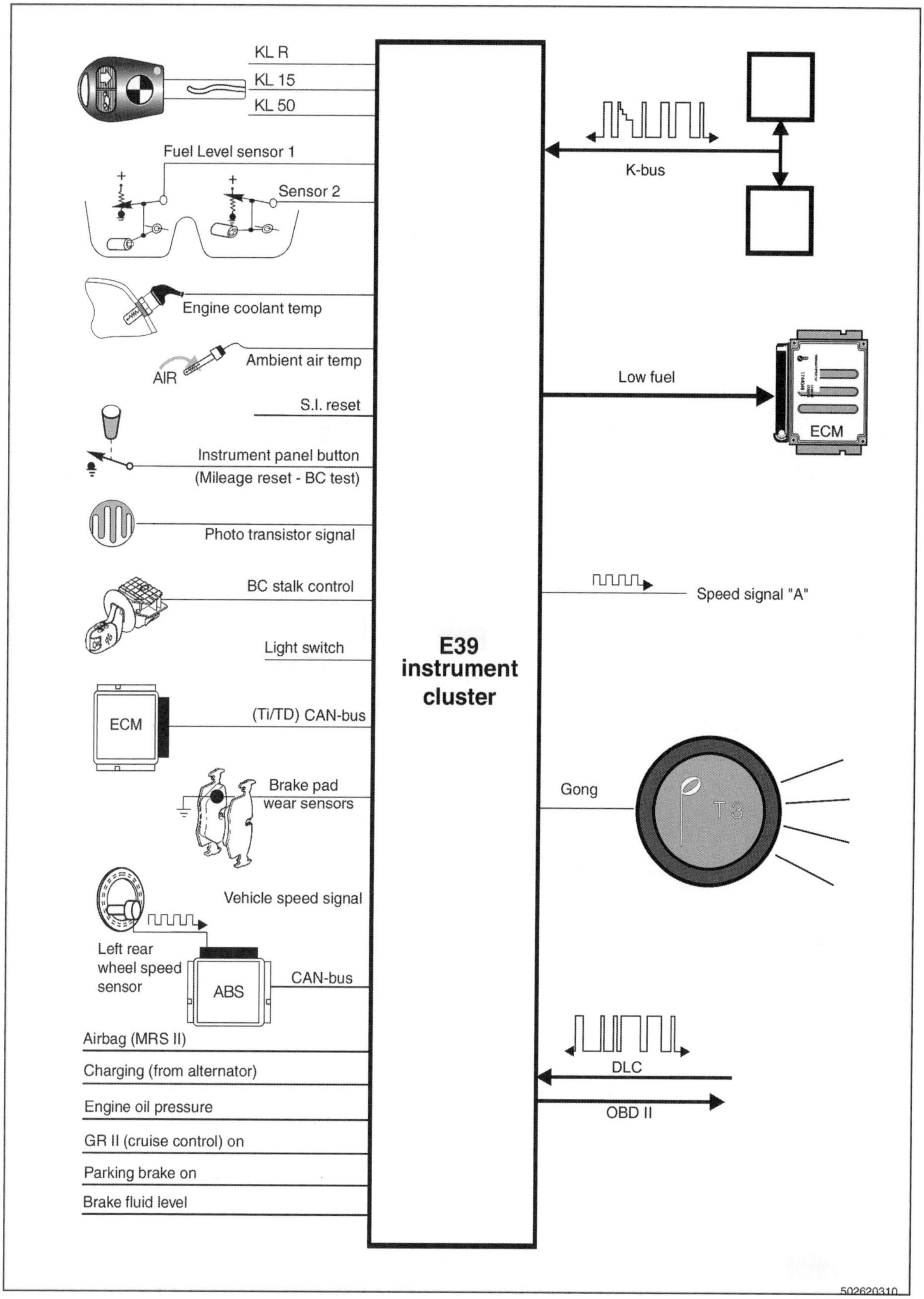
KL R
KL 15
KL 50
Fuel Level sensor 1
Sensor 2
Engine coolant temp
Ambient air temp
AIR
S.I. reset
Instrument panel button
(Mileage reset - BC test)
Photo transistor signal
BC stalk control
Light switch
ECM
(Ti/TD) CAN-bus
Brake pad
wear sensors
Vehicle speed signal
Left rear
wheel speed
sensor
ABS
CAN-bus
Airbag (MRS II)
Charging (from alternator)
Engine oil pressure
GR II (cruise control) on
Parking brake on
Brake fluid level
E39
instrument
cluster
K-bus
Low fuel
ECM
Speed signal "A"
Gong
T3
DLC
OBD II
502620310

Instrument cluster test functions

In addition to fault memory via the diagnostic link, the instrument cluster contains a series of self tests that can be used to check various functions and values. The test functions are displayed in the mileage LCD block. The table below lists the instrument cluster test menus and submenus.

Menu	Sub menu	Sample output	Meaning
Test 1: Vehicle specific data	1.0	12345	VIN
	1.1	4812	Body number
	6_1.2	834762	Part number of cluster
	1.3	010203	Coding/Diagnosis/Bus index
	1.4	3495	Manufacturing data (calendar week/year)
	1.5	04_600	Hardware/software number of cluster
	3_1.6	415_06	Injection status, number of cylinders, engine factor
Test 2: Cluster system test - Activates test for gauge drivers, indicators and LEDs to confirm function			
Test 3: SI data	3.0	1500	Liters
	3.1	0	Periodic inspection days (not applicable for US)
Test 4: Fuel consumption data (current)	4.0	0267	26.7 liters/1000 km
	4.1	0073	7.3 liters per hour
Test 5: Fuel consumed/distance traveled	5.0	0195	19.5 liters /100 km
	5.1	226	Momentary distance to go (22 km)
Test 6: Fuel level sensor input in liters	6.0	237415	Fuel level averaged • LH sensor input = 23.7 liters • RH sensor input = 41.5 liters
	6.1	0652	Total tank level averaged = 65.2 liters
	1_6.2	0667	Indicated value and tank phase • 1 = both sensors OK • 2 = One sensor fault • 3 = Implausible input
Test 7: Temperature and speed	7.0	032	Coolant temperature input 32° C (90° F)
	7.1	245	Outside temperature input 24.5° C (76° F)
	7.2	5283	Engine speed 5,283 RPM
	7.3	058	Vehicle speed 58 km/h (36 mph)
Test 8: Input values in HEX code	8.0 — 8.3	XXX	Hex code, instrument cluster inputs
Test 9: Battery voltage	9.0	125	12.5 Volts
Test 10: Country coding	10.0	02	US 02
Test 11: Cluster code	11.0	000003	Cluster code

Menu	Sub menu	Sample output	Meaning
Test 12: Not used	Not used		
Test 13: Gong test	13.0	Gong	Activate gong by pressing button (gong response is delayed).
Test 14: Fault memory (not for diagnosis)			
Tests 15 - 18: Not used	Not used		
Test 19: Lock/unlock (see Note below)	19.0	L-ON L-OFF	Lock / unlock specific test functions. See **Instrument cluster self test, unlocking**.
Test 20: Average fuel consumption correction factor (see Note below)	20.0	XXX9	Press button when correct 1s position is attained.
	20.1	XX5X	Press button when correct 10s position is attained.
	20.2	12XX	Press button when correct 100s position is attained.
Test 21: Software reset	21.0	reset	Reset software

Instrument cluster, self testing

Perform the following steps to access the instrument cluster self test functions:

1. Remove and insert ignition key (ignition OFF).
2. Press and hold RIGHT cluster button. "CHECK CONTROL OK" is displayed.
3. Without releasing button, turn ignition switch to first detent (RADIO position). "TEST-NR. 01" is displayed.
4. Press LEFT cluster button for test sub-menus.
5. Press RIGHT cluster button to scroll to next test.

NOTE —
- *Test 1 and 2 are always unlocked.*
- *Tests 3 - 21 are only accessible after unlocking using TEST-NR. 19 lock / unlock function. See* **Instrument cluster self test, unlocking**.

Instrument cluster self test, unlocking

To unlock a specific test:

1. Remove and insert ignition key (ignition OFF).
2. Press and hold RIGHT cluster button. "CHECK CONTROL OK" is displayed.
3. Without releasing button, turn ignition switch to first detent (RADIO position). "TEST-NR. 01" is displayed.
4. Use RIGHT cluster button to scroll to TEST-NR. 19 (lock / unlock).
5. Press LEFT cluster button once to access TEST-NR. 19 submenu. "LOCK : ON" is displayed.
6. Use LEFT cluster button to scroll to test you wish to unlock.

7. Press RIGHT cluster button once to unlock desired test. Display returns to TEST-NR. 01.
8. Scroll to unlocked test using RIGHT cluster button.
9. Press LEFT cluster button to perform desired test or access that tests submenu.
10. Repeat unlock sequence for each test required.
11. Switch ignition OFF to cancel self test mode.

NOTE—
Display shows no visual confirmation of test unlock.

Instrument cluster, software reset

To reset instrument cluster software:

1. Remove and insert ignition key (ignition OFF).
2. Press and hold RIGHT cluster button. "CHECK CONTROL OK" is displayed.
3. Without releasing button, turn ignition switch to first detent (RADIO position). "TEST-NR. 01" is displayed.
4. Use RIGHT cluster button to scroll to TEST-NR. 19 (lock / unlock).
5. Press LEFT cluster button once to access TEST-NR. 19 submenu. "LOCK : ON" is displayed.
6. Use LEFT cluster button to scroll to TEST-NR 21. "LOCK : 21" is displayed.
7. Press RIGHT cluster button to unlock TEST-NR. 21. Display returns to TEST-NR. 01.
8. Use RIGHT cluster button to scroll to TEST-NR. 21.
9. Press LEFT cluster button to access TEST-NR. 21 submenu. "RESET ?" is displayed.
10. Press LEFT cluster button again to perform reset.
11. Switch ignition OFF to cancel self test mode.

NOTE—
Display shows no visual confirmation of test unlock.

Instrument cluster, removing and installing

502513710

< Remove upper instrument cluster trim panel fasteners (**arrows**).

NOTE—
The steering wheel is shown removed for clarity.

⊲ Gently pry of dashboard trim on left and right side of steering column.

⊲ Remove lower instrument cluster trim panel fasteners (**arrows**).

– Remove cluster trim panel and disconnect light switch harness connectors.

⊲ Remove instrument cluster fasteners (**arrows**).

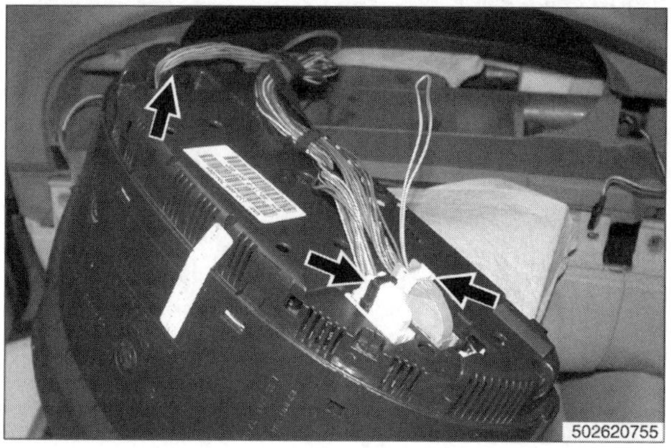

⊲ Unlock and disconnect harness connectors (**arrows**) from back of cluster.

– Installation is reverse of removal, noting the following:

- Instrument cluster harness connector locking levers must be in up position before installing connector.
- Recode new or replacement cluster using BMW scan tools DISplus, MoDiC or equivalent.

GLOBAL POSITIONING SYSTEM (GPS)

The navigation system operates in conjunction with the Global Positioning System (GPS). Utilization of GPS improves accuracy and provides redundancy for the navigation system, which also incorporates a dead reckoning system.

The BMW navigation system is based on the CARiN™ (Car Information and Navigation System) system developed by Phillips Electronics. The driver can enter a destination through the On-Board Monitor and the navigation system will select a mapped route from the current location to the destination. The route maps are stored digitally on a navigational database CD that is installed in a dedicated CD drive in the navigation computer.

GPS component and signal diagram

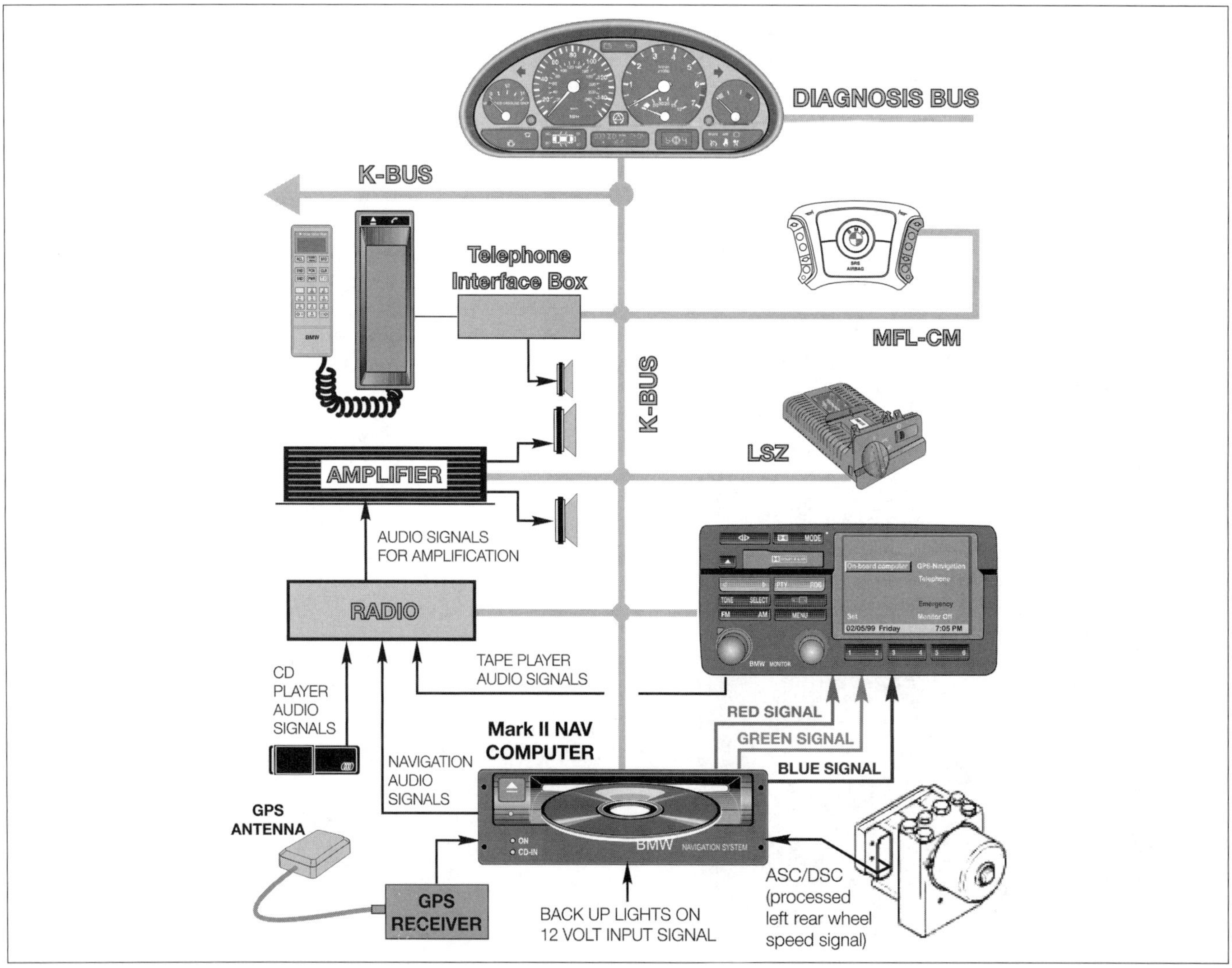

GPS tire size calibration

Tire calibration is required so that the navigation computer can calculate the tire rotation ratio. Calibration should be performed whenever original equipment tires are replaced with tires or wheels of a different size.

To calibrate tires:

- Press tire calibration button on vehicle position screen. The following message is displayed noting the overwrite of existing values once the procedure is completed.
- Press “continue” to access tire adjustment screen.
- Press tire size and rotate knob to see if the tire size is listed.
- Select correct tire size and press button once again. Note that tire circumference size automatically changes to set tire size.
- If tire size is not listed the tire circumference value must be entered manually by rotating tire size button to “???” position.
- Press and enter actual tire circumference in millimeters.
- This value is available from the tire manufacture or it can be measured as shown below.

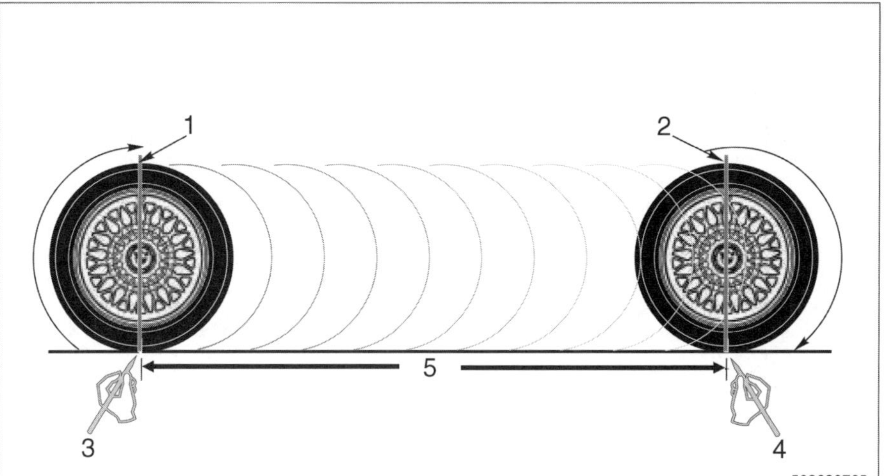

502620765

Tire circumference measurement

1. **Place a straight edge up against tire directly in the vertical center line of tire.**
2. **Mark bottom of tire and surface in line with the straight edge.**
3. **Roll vehicle forward until tire rotates one complete revolution.**
4. **Place a straight edge up against tire directly in the vertical center line of tire. Align previous tire mark with straight edge.**
5. **Mark surface and measure distance between surface marks.**

GPS on-board monitor

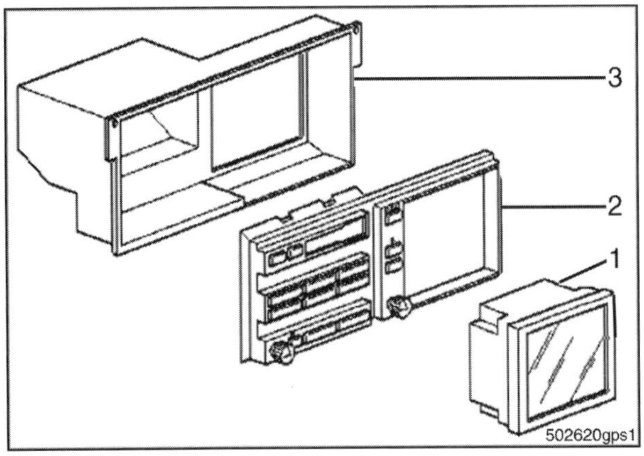

The On-Board monitor assembly is mounted in the center console and consists of 3 parts:

1. 5 1/4 inch color LCD display screen.
2. On-Board Monitor control module/panel.
3. Monitor housing with cassette tape player.

GPS monitor assembly, removing and installing

CAUTION—
The navigation computer must not be disconnected from the power supply while the LED on the computer remains lit (the LED goes out after approx. 1 minute).

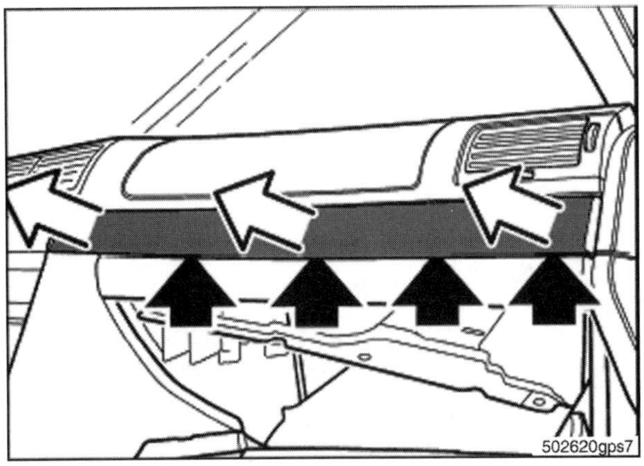

Remove wood trim panel (**arrows**) from right side of On-Board Monitor.

Remove wood trim panel (**arrow**) from left side of On-Board Monitor.

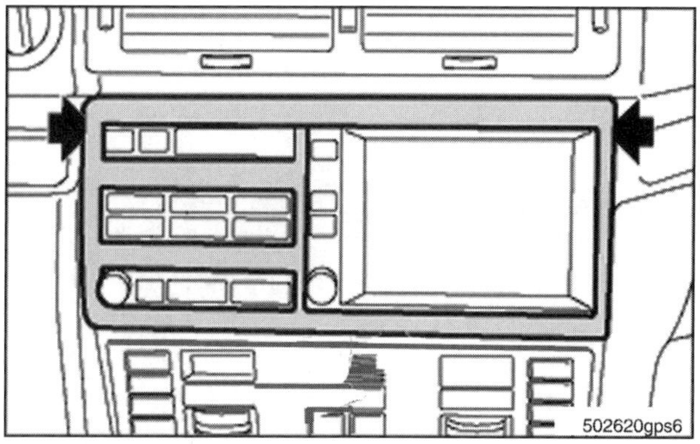

◄ Remove left and right side fasteners (**arrows**).

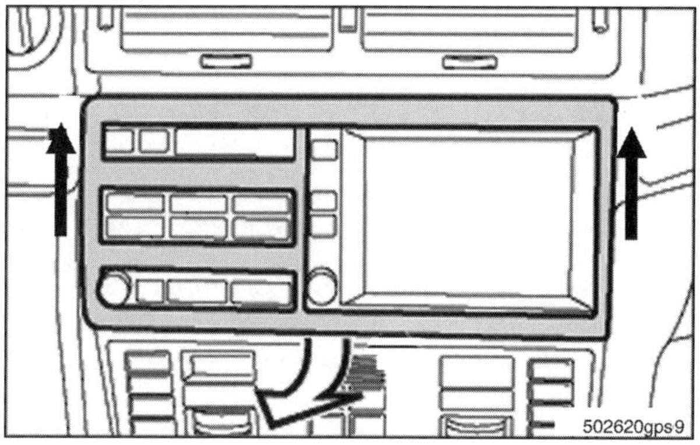

◄ Raise left and right side mounting levels (**arrows**) and pull down and out to remove panel.

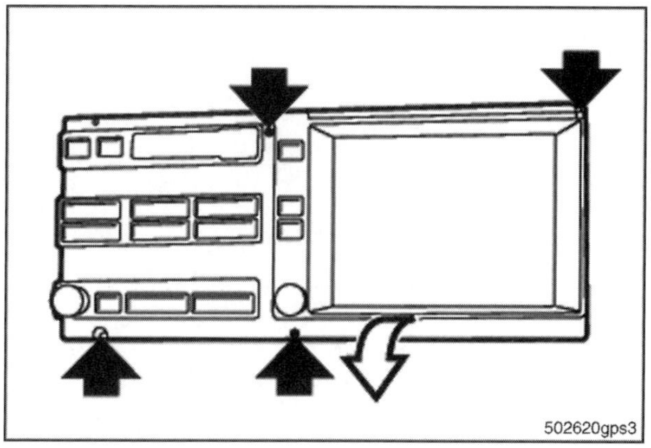

◄ Remove face plate fasteners (**arrows**) and pull down on face plate to remove.

◄ Remove display fasteners (**arrows**) and slide display out of housing.

– Installation is reverse of removal. Take care not to damage display ribbon cable while installing face plate.

GPS antenna receiver module, removing and installing

- Remove trunk floor panel.
- Loosen and remove receiver mounting fasteners.
- Disconnect electrical harness and antenna lead and remove receiver.
- Installation is reverse of removal.

630 Lights

GENERAL

This repair group covers interior and exterior lighting, including repairs to the light switch assembly.

NOTE—
Light switch assembly removal and installation is covered in **612 Switches**.

Bulb applications

Bulb applications for E39 cars are listed in the table below.

E39 bulb applications

Location	Type & rating
Headlights	
• Low beam (Halogen)	H7 55W
• Low beam (Xenon)	D2–S (Osram)
• High beam	HB3 60W
Foglights	
• Front	H7 55W
• Front (M-Technik)	HB4 51W
Turn signal and tail lights	
• Back-up	21W
• Brake	21W
• Tail light	5W
• Licence plate	5W
• Side turn signal	W5
• Third brake light	LED
• Turn signal (front and rear)	55W
Interior lights	
• Footwell	5W
• Glove compartment	5W
• Trunk compartment	10W halogen
• Interior light	10W
• Reading light	5W

LIGHT CONTROL MODULE (LCM)

The Light Control Module (LCM) is mounted behind right front kick panel. Both versions (base or high cluster configuration) of instrument clusters use the LCM for processing Check Control data and controlling the exterior lighting functions. See **620 Instruments**. The LCM communicates with other modules over the Bus systems. Functions of the LCM include:

- Monitoring of all Check Control inputs
- Output of Check Control messages or signals
- Control of vehicle external lighting
- Monitoring of external lighting
- Instrument panel illumination dimming signal
- Control of instrument cluster indicator lights (high beam, turn signal and fog light indicators).

A replacement LCM must be coded using the BMW Service Tester (select Central Coding Key or ZCS).

Lamp control monitoring

All exterior lighting is controlled by the LCM. It contains transistor power output stages for activating the lights. This eliminates the need for fuses and relays previously used for this purpose.

The LCM receives the input request for light illumination from the various switches and data inputs from other control modules. The LCM then switches the power output stages ON for lamp activation.

Other control modules that communicate with the LCM include:

- IKE (Instrument Cluster Electronics) over the I/K bus for turn signal, high beam and fog lamp indicator illumination.
- MRS (Multiple Restraint/Airbag Electronics) for crash alarm indication.
- AGS (Adaptive Automatic Transmission Control) control module for back up lamp activation.

All exterior lighting is monitored (both on and off) by the LCM. When the monitored value exceeds an acceptable level (high or low) the LCM generates and sends the signal to the IKE or base instrument cluster for Check Control display.

For safety purposes, the LCM is designed with emergency functions. An LCM failure will still allow various lamps to function. These lamps include:

- Side marker lights
- Taillights
- Low beam head lamps
- Brake lights
- Turn signal lights

NOTE—
Headlight switch replacement is covered **612 Switches**.

HEADLIGHTS

E39 cars are equipped with Halogen headlights as standard equipment. Halogen bulb replacement is performed from the back (engine) side of the headlight assembly. The front face of each headlight assembly is a removable plastic cover.

Xenon headlights

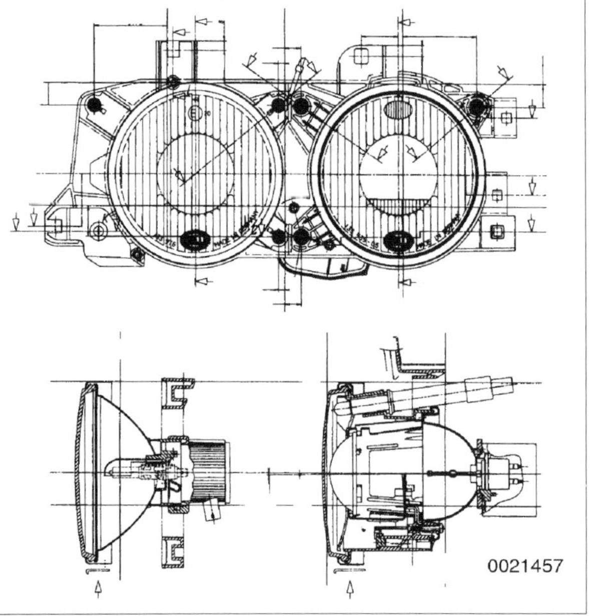

Cars equipped with the optional Xenon headlights also feature automatic headlight adjustment control (LWR) for varying passenger and cargo loads.

The illustrations on following pages identify headlight components.

Headlight aim, adjusting

Adjust headlight aim with correct tire pressures, fuel tank full, and weight of one person (approximately 75 Kg/165 lb) in driver seat.

CAUTION—
Headlights must be aimed using a headlight aiming tool. DO NOT aim headlights by eye.

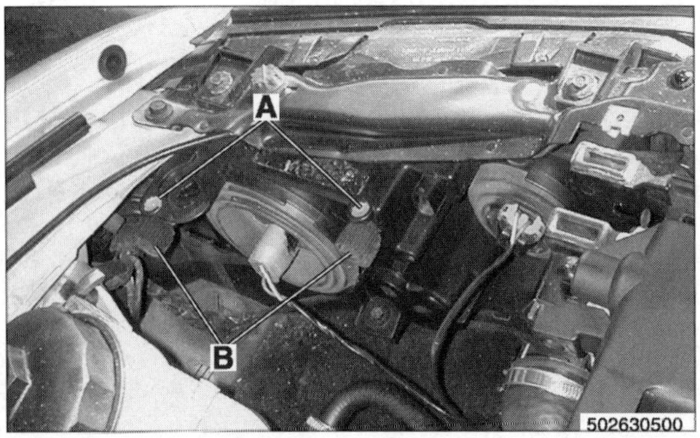

Use 6 mm Allen wrench to turn screws (**A**) or use hand to adjust headlight by turning adjusting knobs (**B**).

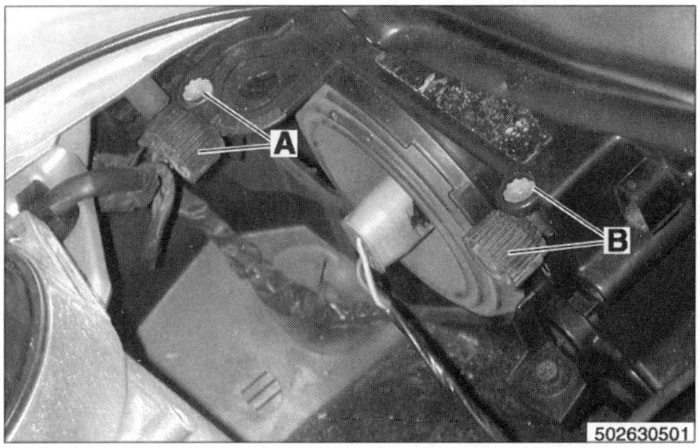

Turn adjuster (**A**) for lateral movement and adjuster (**B**) for vertical movement.

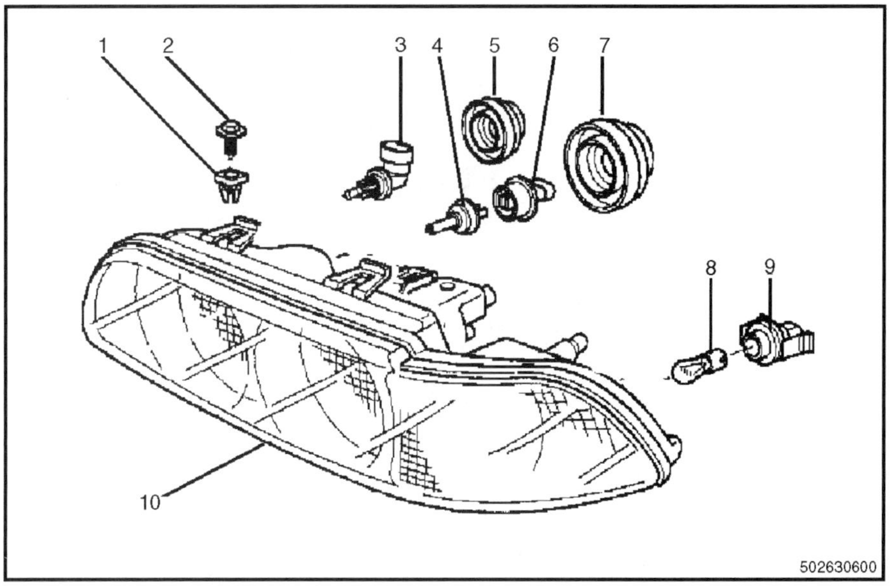

Halogen headlight assembly

1. **Expanding nut**
2. **Screw**
3. **Low beam bulb**
4. **High beam bulb**
5. **Low beam bulb cover**
6. **Bulb adapter**
7. **High beam bulb cover**
8. **Parking light bulb**
9. **Parking light bulb socket**
10. **Head light housing assembly**

Xenon headlight assembly

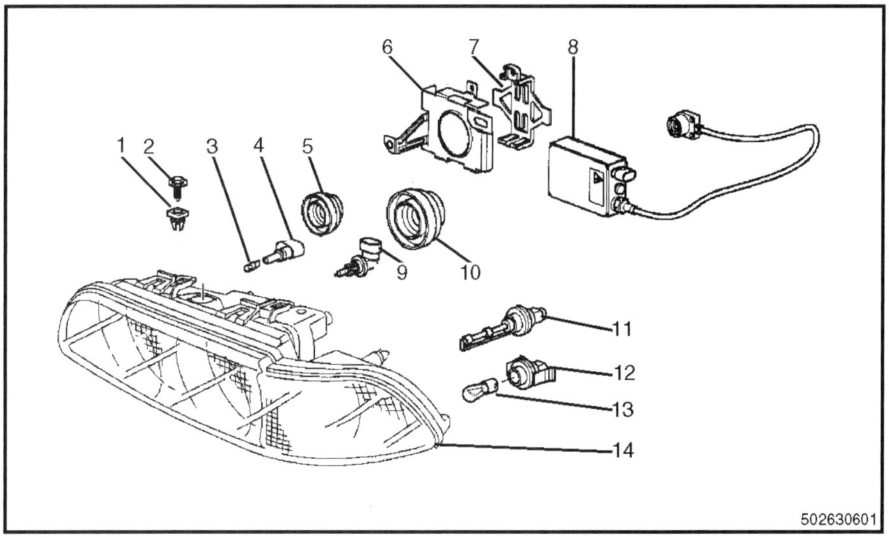

1. **Expanding nut**
2. **Screw**
3. **Parking light bulb**
4. **Parking light bulb socket**
5. **High beam bulb cover**
6. **Support bracket**
7. **Support frame**
8. **Xenon light control unit (manuf. up to 9/2000)**
9. **High beam bulb**
10. **High beam bulb cover**
11. **Xenon low beam bulb**
12. **Bulb socket**
13. **Corner marker bulb**
14. **Headlight housing assembly**

Halogen headlight bulb, replacing

< Remove headlight bulb from headlight assembly.

– Working in back of headlight assembly:
  - Rotate headlight bulb socket (**arrows**) counterclockwise.
  - Pull bulb socket and bulb out of headlight assembly.
  - Disconnect harness connector from socket.
  - Gently wiggle bulb and pull straight out of socket.
  - Replace bulb by pushing firmly into socket.
  - Installation is reverse of removal.

NOTE—
It may be necessary to remove air filter housing in order to remove the headlight bulbs. See **020 Maintenance.**

> ***CAUTION—***
> *Do not touch halogen bulbs with your bare hands. If necessary wipe bulb using a clean cloth dampened with rubbing alcohol.*

Xenon headlight bulb, replacing

– Working in back of headlight assembly:
  - Remove low beam (Xenon) cover.
  - Rotate headlight bulb counterclockwise.
  - Pull bulb out of headlight assembly.
  - Installation is reverse of removal.

> ***CAUTION—***
> *Do not touch bulbs with your bare hands. If necessary wipe bulb using a clean cloth dampened with rubbing alcohol.*

Headlight assembly, removing and installing

> ***CAUTION—***
> *Following headlight assembly work, headlight beam aim must be adjusted using special equipment.*

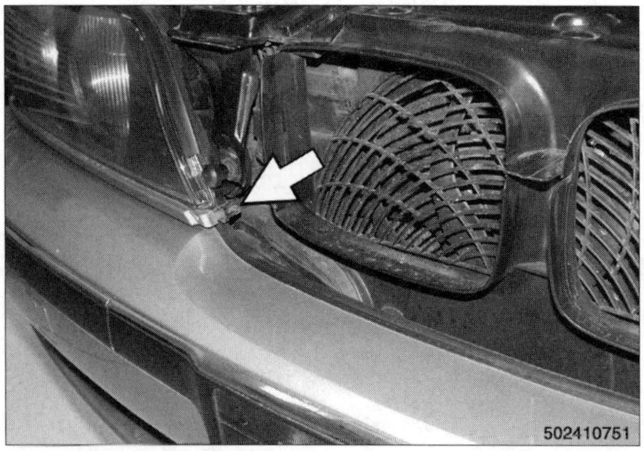

< Unclip inner trim (**arrow**) by pressing down to release locks. Swing trim panel out to remove.

– Disconnect harness connectors from headlight assembly.

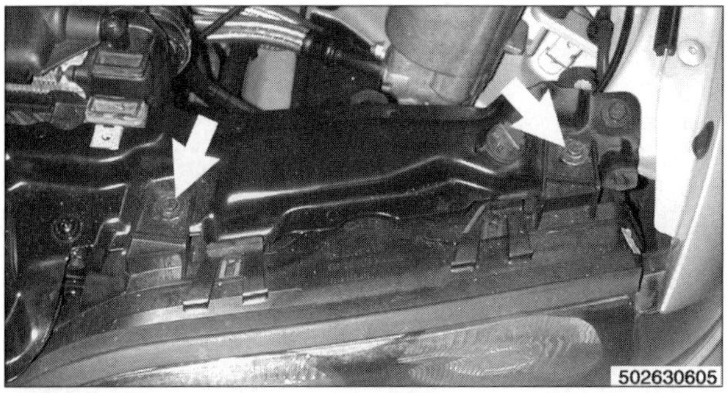

< Remove upper headlight mounting screws (**arrows**).

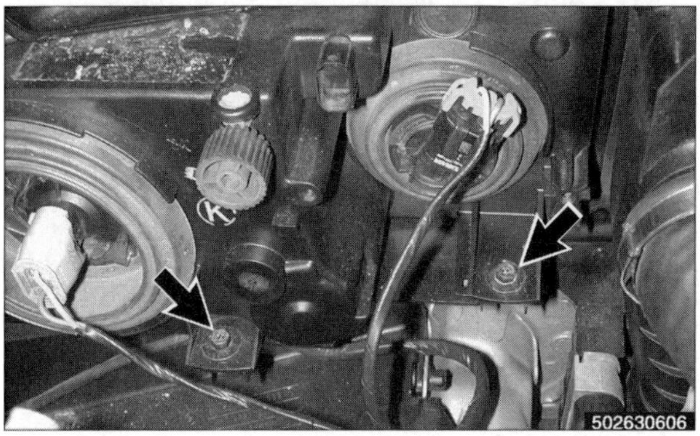

< Remove lower headlight mounting screws (**arrows**). Lift headlight assembly forward and out of car.

– During reassembly:
  - Install top mounting screws hand tight.
  - Pull headlight assembly toward front of car.
  - Close engine hood and check to make sure that gap between hood and headlight assembly is correct (see the table below).
  - Open hood and tighten down mounting screws.
  - Make sure rubber seal is in place on lower trim panel.
  - Remainder of assembly is reverse of removal.

– Adjust headlight aim as described earlier.

Automatic headlight adjustment (LWR)

Vehicles equipped with the optional Xenon low-beam headlight bulbs also feature automatic headlight adjustment (LWR). This system automatically adjusts the vertical positioning of the headlights. The system compensates for vehicle load angle changes.

LWR monitors vehicle load via two Hall effect sensors mounted to the front and rear suspension members. When an adjustment to the angle of the headlight beams is necessary, LWR simultaneously activates two stepper motors (one in each headlight assembly) to change the vertical aim of the headlights.

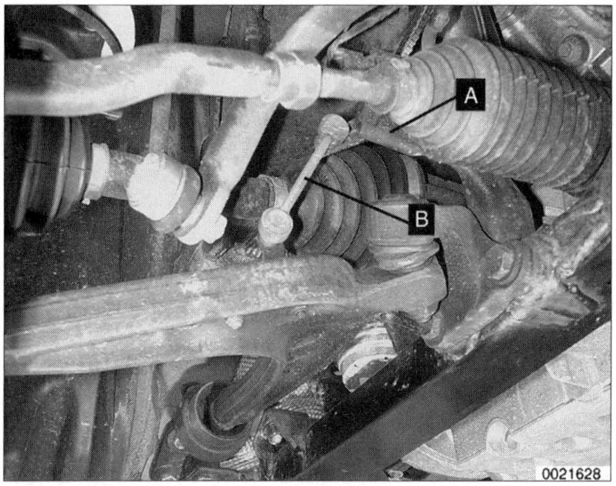

< At each axle of vehicle, the LWR sensor (**A**) is mounted to a fixed point on suspension subframe. Rod (**B**) is connected to the moving suspension member. The sensor output voltage changes as suspension moves up and down.

LWR diagnosis is accessed through the Light Control Module.

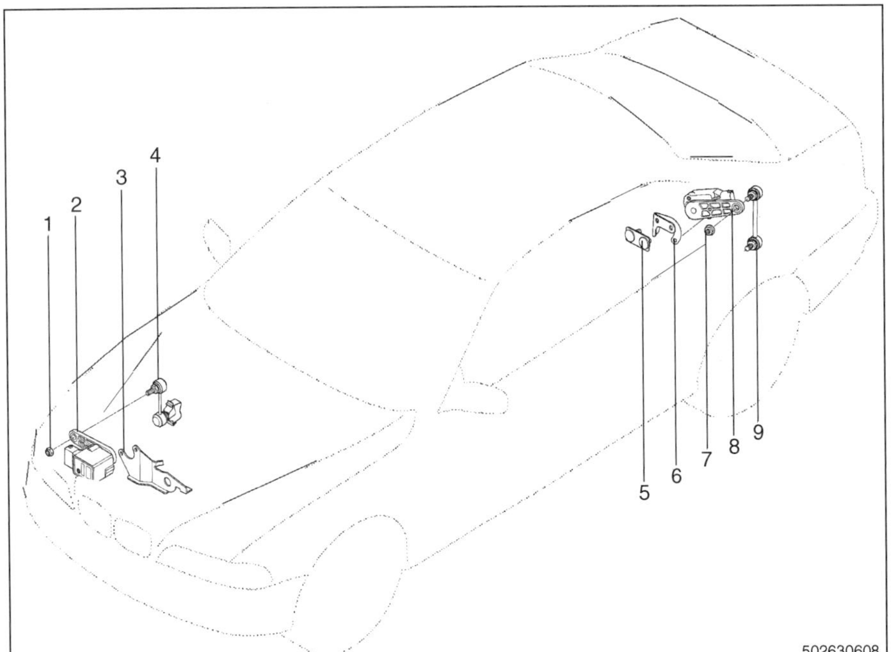

502630608

Headlight vertical aim system components

1. **Locking nut**
2. **Front level sensor**
3. **Front level sensor bracket**
4. **Front level sensor control arm**
5. **Locking plate**
6. **Rear level sensor bracket**
7. **Locking nut**
8. **Rear level sensor**
9. **Rear level sensor rod**

Exterior Lights

Foglight aim, adjusting

502630444

◄ Using a Phillips screwdriver turn plastic adjuster (**arrow**) on inner edge of foglight.

Foglight bulb, removing and installing

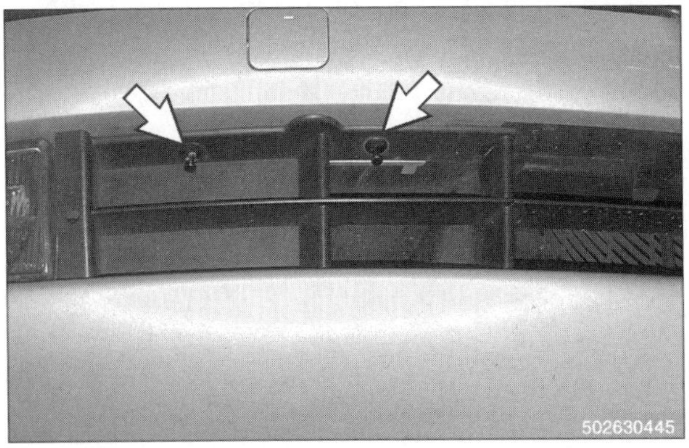
502630445

◄ Pry out plastic expansion rivets (**arrows**) and remove grill panel.

Remove two fasteners (**arrows**) and remove fog light.

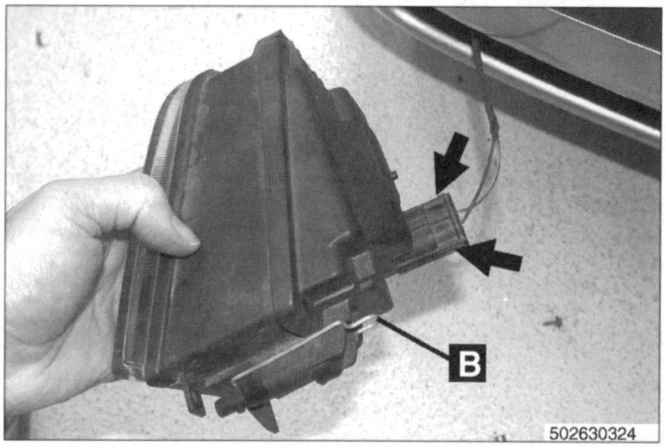

Disconnect electrical plug locks by squeezing locks (**arrows**). Release housing latch (**B**) and open housing.

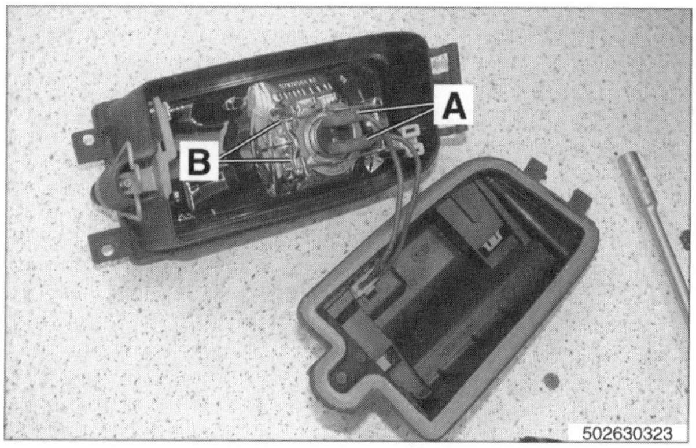

Disconnect connectors (**A**) and release spring lock (**B**) to remove bulb.

Side turn signal assembly, removing and installing

Remove turn signal by sliding lens assembly forward and carefully pulling assembly out of fender at rear.

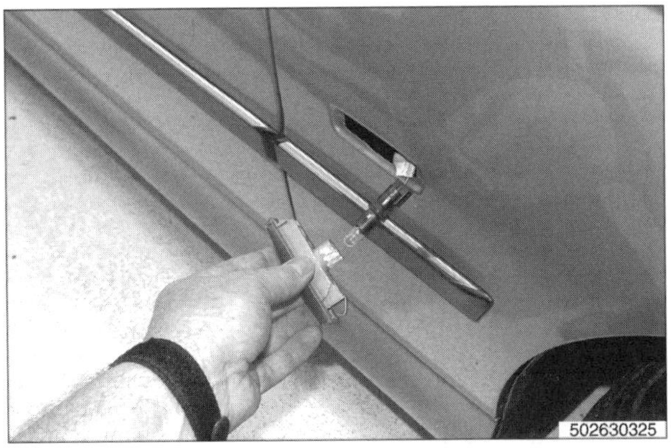

While holding lens, turn bulb socket to release.

Taillight assembly, removing and installing

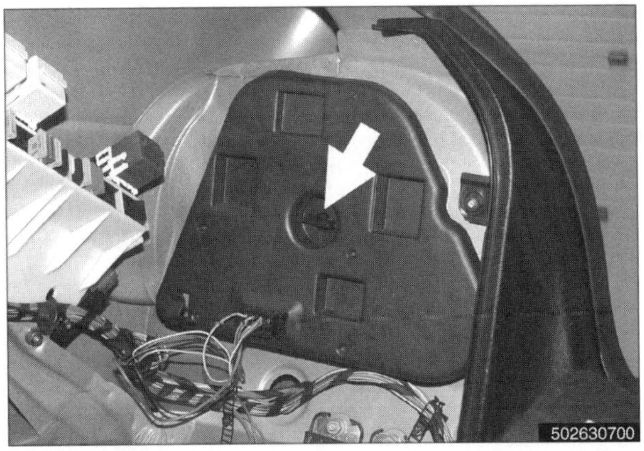

NOTE—
The procedure given here applies to 2001 and earlier models. 2002 models use a redesigned taillight.

– To access taillight bulbs carriers, open trunk lid or tailgate and open trim panel.

Release bulb carrier locking fastener (**arrow**) and remove carrier.

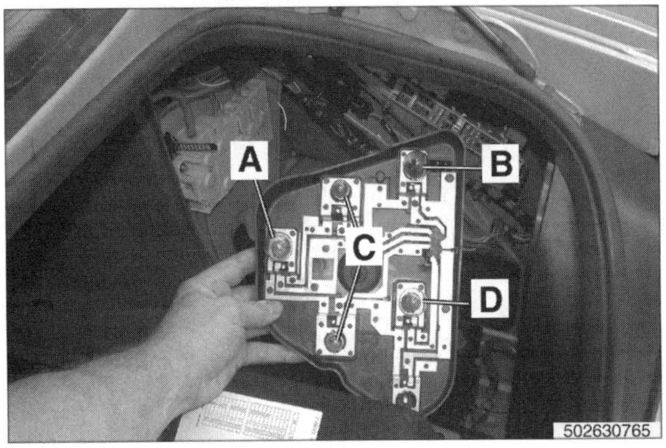

Bulb carriers contain:

- Turn signal bulb (**A**)
- Brake light bulb (**B**)
- Taillight bulb (**C**)
- Back-up light bulb (**D**)

Licence plate light, removing and installing

< Using a plastic tool, pry gently on side of license plate light with slot to remove plate light assembly.

< Replace bulb.

NOTE—
Inspect bulb contact springs for damage or corrosion. Replace socket assembly if necessary.

Center brake light, removing and installing (sedan)

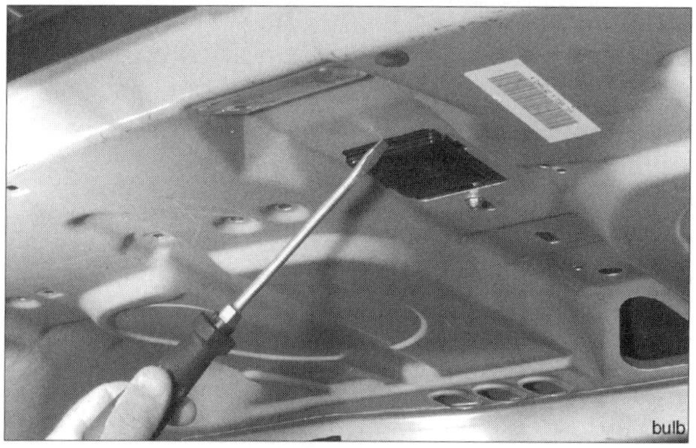

< Working inside luggage compartment, pry off bulb cover (**arrow**) directly below light housing.

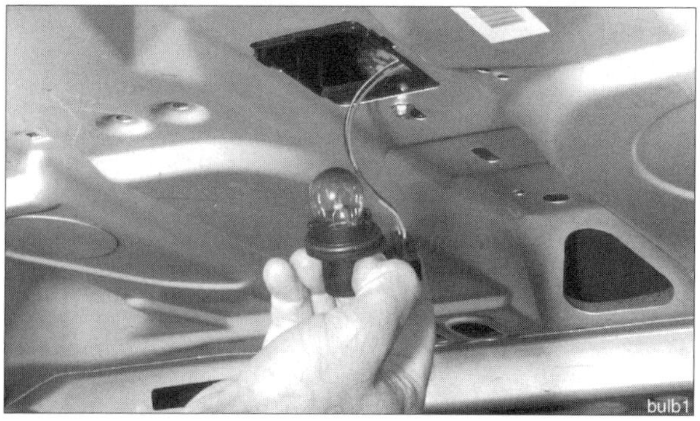

< Twist bulb holder 1/4 turn clockwise and pull holder down. Remove old bulb and install new bulb.

– Installation is reverse of removal.

Interior Lights

The general module (GM III) controls the interior lighting automatically using input from several monitors. The lighting can also be manually controlled.

Each door lock actuator contains a hall effect sensor for the purpose of monitoring door open/closed status. The hall effect sensor is located directly behind the rotary latch plate encased in the lock actuator. The sensor is activated by the rotary latch plate position.

- **Door closed**: Rotary latch plate in latched position. Current flow through hall sensor < 5 mA.
- **Door open**: Rotary latch plate in open position. Current flow through hall sensor > 12 mA.

A change in current flow informs the GM III when a door is opened or closed.

The overhead front seat interior/map light unit contains a single main interior light. The light is controlled by the GM III automatically or by momentarily pressing the interior light switch located on the light assembly. The switch provides a momentary ground signal that the GM III recognizes as a request to either turn the light on or turn the light off.

If the switch is held for more than 3 seconds, the GM III interprets the continuous ground signal as a request to turn the interior light circuit off (workshop mode). Workshop mode is stored in memory: Even if the GM III is removed from the power supply and reconnected, the lights do not come back on unless the switch is pressed again.

There are two reading/map lights located in the front interior light assembly. Each is mechanically controlled by depressing the corresponding switch. The power supply for the map lights is supplied by the GM III.

There is a courtesy light in each front footwell. These lights are only operated when the GM III provides power to the interior lighting circuit.

Interior light automatic controls

The GM III provides 12 volts to the interior lighting circuit when the status of one of the following input signals changes:

- Door contact hall sensor active (door open)
- "Unlock" request received from driver door key lock Hall sensor (ignition switch OFF)

- "Unlock" request from FZV keyless entry system received via K— Bus (ignition switch OFF)
- Vehicle exterior lights on for minimum of 2 minutes when ignition switch is OFF
- Active crash signal from MRS III control module
- Lock button of FZV key pressed with vehicle already locked (interior search function)
- Immediately after ignition switch is turned to "radio" position with driver door closed
- When vehicle is locked (single or double) with door contacts closed.
- When vehicle door contacts are closed. Lights remain on for 20 seconds, then go to soft off.
- After interior search function is activated, lights automatically turn off (soft off) after 8 seconds.
- After 16 minutes with door contact active (open door) and key off, lights are switched off (consumer cutoff function).

The component activation function of DIS plus also has the ability to switch the lights.

Interior light applications	
Footwell light bulb	Softlite 5W
Glove compartment light bulb	Softlite 5W
Passenger compartment bulb, front or rear	Softlite 5W
Reading bulb, front or rear	6W
Tailgate courtesy light bulb	Softlite 10W
Visor vanity light bulb	Softlite 10W

Interior lights, removing and installing

◀ Working beneath front door, pry door marker light assembly out of door trim panel.

– Installation is reverse of removal.

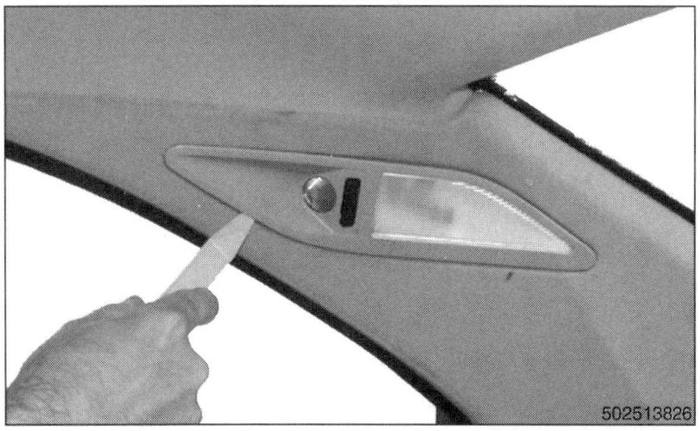

◄ Working at rear roof pillar (C pillar) gently pry out interior light to remove.

– Installation is reverse of removal.

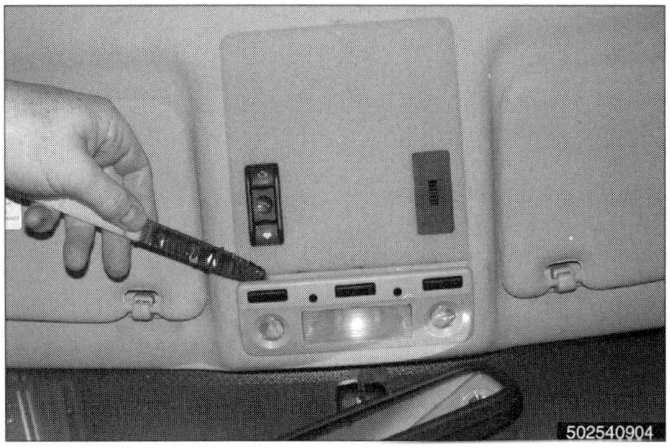

◄ Gently pry interior light assembly out of head liner.

– Installation is reverse of removal.

Trunk light bulb, replacing

◄ Working at left side of light trunk assembly, gently pry light assembly out of trim cover to remove.

– Installation is reverse of removal.

640 Heating and Air Conditioning

GENERAL

Many of the procedures given in this group require that the A/C refrigerant charge be evacuated. See **A/C system warnings and cautions**.

For information on the engine cooling system, see **170 Radiator and Cooling System**.

NOTE—
A/C system recharging procedures are beyond the scope of this manual.

A/C system warnings and cautions

WARNING—
- *Always wear hand and eye protection (gloves and goggles) when working around the A/C system. If refrigerant does come in contact with your skin or eyes:*
- *Do not rub skin or eyes.*
- *Immediately flush skin or eyes with cool water for 15 minutes.*
- *Rush to a doctor or hospital.*
- *Do not attempt to treat yourself.*
- *Work in a well ventilated area. Switch on exhaust/ventilation systems when working on the refrigerant system.*
- *Do not expose any component of the A/C system to high temperatures (above 80°C / 176°F) or open flames. Excessive heat causes a pressure increase which could burst the system.*
- *Keep refrigerant away from open flames. Poisonous gas is produced if it burns. Do not smoke near refrigerant gases for the same reason.*
- *The A/C system is filled with refrigerant gas which is under pressure. Pressurized refrigerant in the presence of oxygen may form a combustible mixture. Never introduce compressed air into any refrigerant container (full or empty).*
- *Electric welding near refrigerant hoses causes R-134a to decompose. Discharge system before welding.*

CAUTION—
- *Any person who services a motor vehicle air conditioner must, by law, be properly trained and certified, and use approved refrigerant recycling equipment. Technicians must complete an EPA-approved recycling course to be certified.*
- *State and local governments may have additional requirements regarding air conditioning servicing. Always comply with state and local laws.*
- *It is recommended that all A/C service be left to an authorized BMW dealer or other qualified A/C service facility.*
- *Do not top off a partially charged refrigerant system. Discharge system, evacuate and then recharge system.*
- *The mixture of refrigerant oil (PAG oil) and refrigerant R-134a attacks some metals and alloys (for example, copper) and breaks down certain hose materials. Use only hoses and lines that are identified with a green mark (stripe) or the lettering “R-134a”.*
- *Immediately plug open connections on A/C components and lines to prevent dirt and moisture contamination.*
- *Do not steam clean A/C condensers or evaporators. Use only cold water or compressed air.*

Heating and climate control outlets

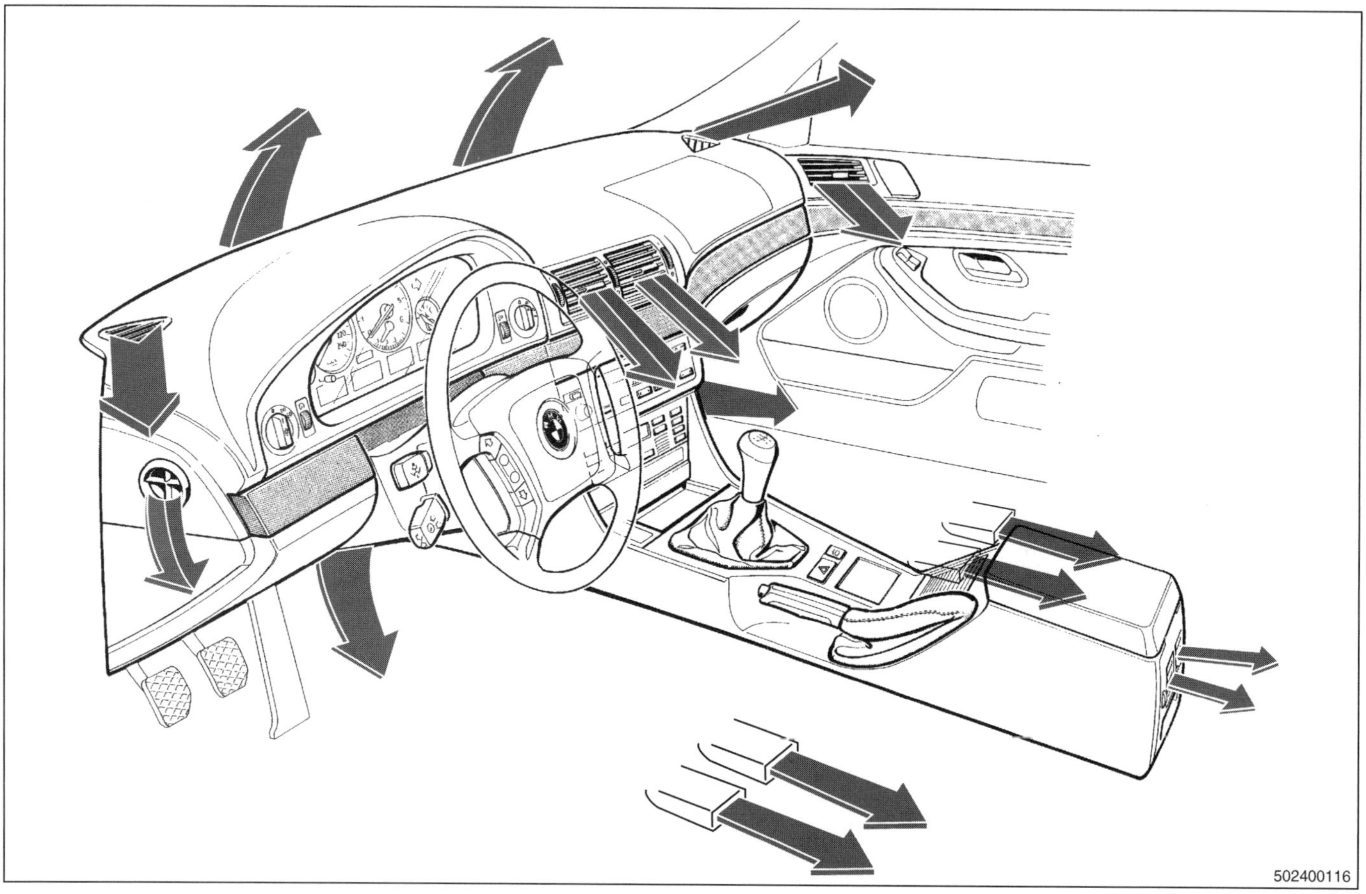

Heating and climate control systems

Depending on year and model, two versions of the basic climate control system were offered. See **E39 heating and climate control applications** table.

E39 heating and climate control applications

System	Distinguishing features	Comments
IHKA	Dual heater valve Push button control panel with separate controls for driver and passenger	Optional on 525i and 530i models until 3/2000
IHKR	Single heater valve Rotary knob control panel	Installed in 1999 — 2000 525i and 530i models

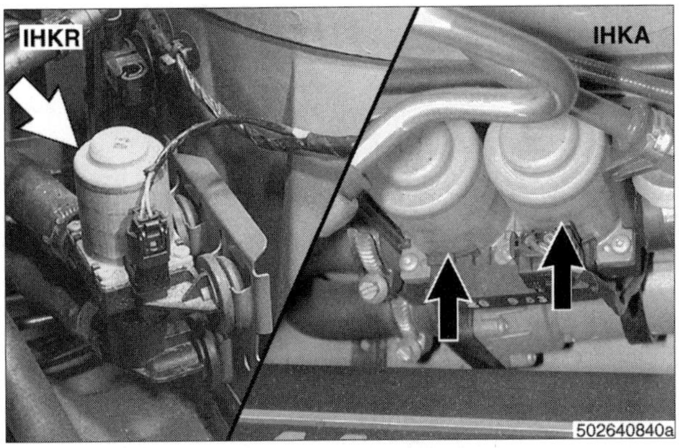

The IHKR system uses a single heater valve. The IHKA system uses two heater valves. Heater valves are located in the engine compartment, near left strut tower (**arrows**).

Integrated automatic heating and air conditioning system (IHKA)

The major components of the IHKA system:

- Automatic heating and air conditioning control panel and module.
- Dual heater core with separate engine coolant inlets and one common outlet.
- Two heater core temperature sensors and one evaporator temperature sensor.
- Evaporator with expansion valve.
- 1997 models are equipped with five stepper motors: Four controlled by the stepper motor bus (M-Bus) link, one conventionally controlled. 1998 and later models use six stepper motors: Five controlled by the M-Bus link, one conventionally controlled. Each stepper motor has a unique ID which is electronically recognized by diagnostic software.
- Auxiliary coolant pump.
- Blower motor and relay with final stage output control (final stage located in air flow on passenger side of IHKA housing).
- Interior ventilation micro-filters.

IHKA control module inputs and outputs

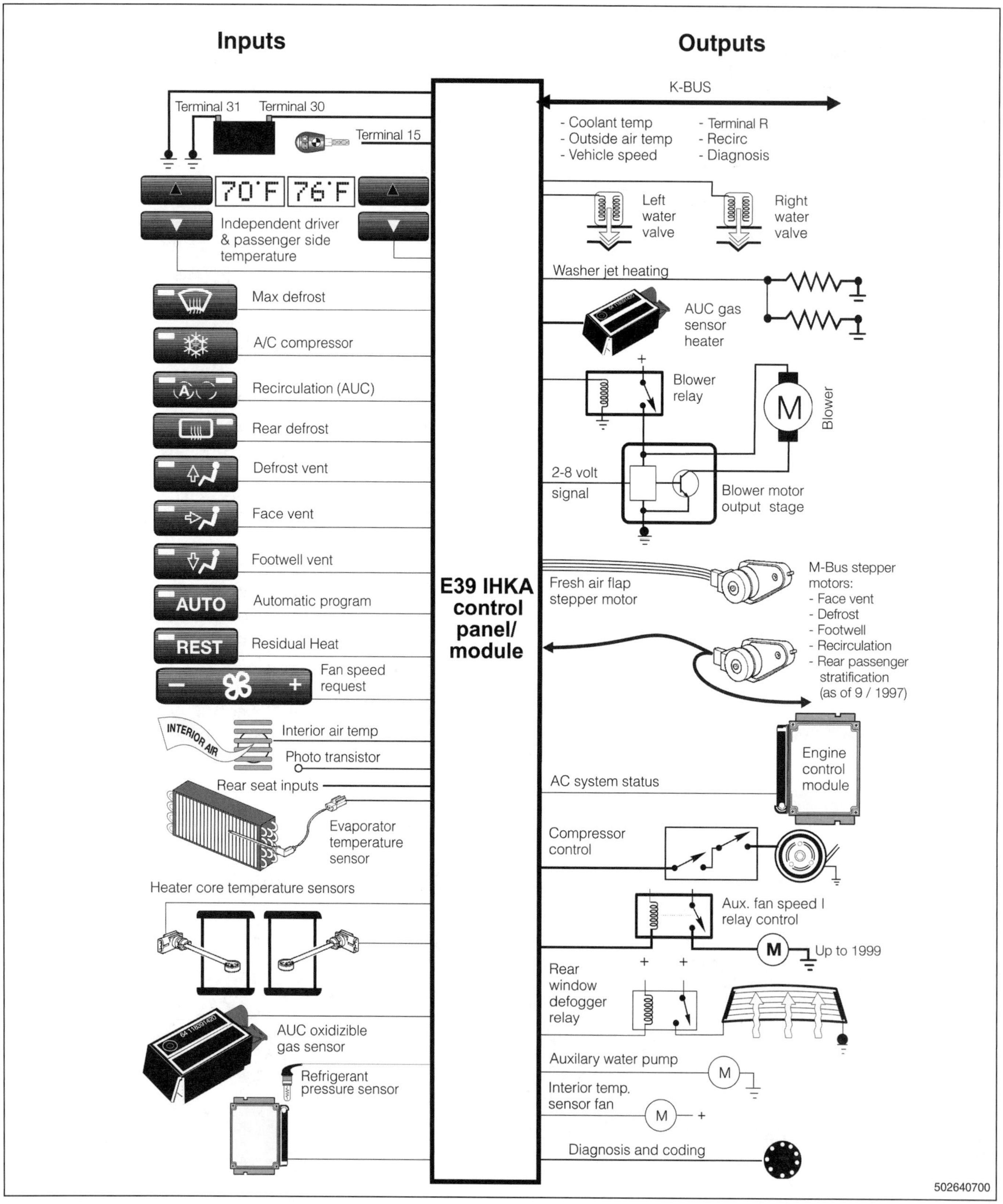
Inputs
Outputs
Terminal 31
Terminal 30
Terminal 15
70°F
76°F
Independent driver & passenger side temperature
Max defrost
A/C compressor
Recirculation (AUC)
Rear defrost
Defrost vent
Face vent
Footwell vent
AUTO
Automatic program
REST
Residual Heat
Fan speed request
INTERIOR AIR
Interior air temp
Photo transistor
Rear seat inputs
Evaporator temperature sensor
Heater core temperature sensors
AUC oxidizible gas sensor
Refrigerant pressure sensor
E39 IHKA control panel/ module
K-BUS
- Coolant temp
- Outside air temp
- Vehicle speed
- Terminal R
- Recirc
- Diagnosis
Left water valve
Right water valve
Washer jet heating
AUC gas sensor heater
Blower relay
M
Blower
2-8 volt signal
Blower motor output stage
Fresh air flap stepper motor
M-Bus stepper motors:
- Face vent
- Defrost
- Footwell
- Recirculation
- Rear passenger stratification (as of 9 / 1997)
Engine control module
AC system status
Compressor control
Aux. fan speed I relay control
Up to 1999
Rear window defogger relay
Auxilary water pump
Interior temp. sensor fan
Diagnosis and coding
502640700

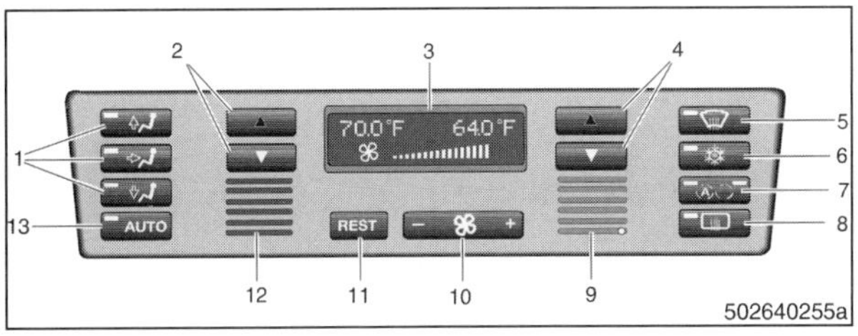

IHKA control panel functions

Heating and air conditioning functions are programmed via the center console mounted control panel.

1. Air vent control (windshield, face level, foot level).
2. Driver temperature selection (up or down).
3. LCD display panel (displays automatic blower speed mode, AUTO mode and actual blower speed, indicated numerically and by number of bars displayed.
4. Passenger temperature selection (up or down).
5. Windshield defroster. Maximum windshield defrost overrides other distribution settings (also switches on rear defroster).
6. A/C control
7. Recirculation / automatic recirculation. Toggles system between fresh / recirculated air flap activation and automatic recirculation control (AUC). AUC system incorporates a sensor in the engine compartment that reacts to high levels exterior air pollution. When levels exceed set value stored in IHKA control module, system switches automatically to recirculation.
8. Rear window defroster. When button is pressed rear window defrost is switched on for 10 minutes with outside temperature above -10° C / 14° F, 17 minutes with outside temperature below -8° C / 17° F. After initial timed duration, each subsequent pressing of button will switch rear defroster on for 5 minutes.
9. Interior air temperature sensor intake, passenger (small blower fan continuously draws interior air over temperature sensor).
10. Air volume control toggle switch (air volume adjusted through 16 steps, setting is displayed as wedge on display panel).
11. Residual heat (REST). With engine OFF, vehicle interior can be heated using REST feature. Pressing REST button activates auxiliary coolant pump and blower motor. System supplies heat up to 15 minutes after engine shutoff, or until engine coolant temperature drops below 30° C / 86° F.
12. Interior air temperature sensor intake, driver (small blower fan continuously draws interior air over temperature sensor).
13. Automatic operation. AUTO button overrides manual settings and provides pre-programmed cooling / heating.

NOTE—
If the control module is replaced it must be coded using BMW electronic service tools (DISplus, MoDiC, GT1 or equivalent).

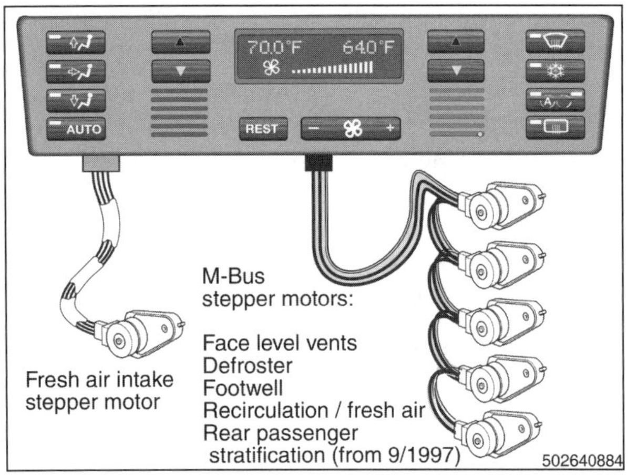

IHKA air distribution stepper motors on M-Bus

The IHKA system is equipped with stepper motors that control air distribution flaps. The motors are controlled by the IHKA control module via the M-Bus.

Each stepper motor is connected through a ribbon cable that contains three wires (power, ground and signal). A command for motor movement is sent over the signal wire and addressed to a specific motor. All of the motor processors receive the signal, but only the addressed motor will respond and move to the desired position. Because of the unique address stored in the processor, all stepper motors have a unique part number and cannot be interchanged.

Integrated heating and air conditioning system with regulation (IHKR)

Starting with 9/1999 production, 6–cylinder models (525i and 530i) were equipped with a semiautomatic regulated heating and climate control system (IHKR).

NOTE—
IHKA was available in 525i and 530i models as an option. Starting with models produced from 3/2000, IHKA was standard on all E39 models.

The E39 IHKR is a single zone system that automatically regulates cabin temperature as dialled in by occupant(s). Blower speed control and air distribution settings are set manually.

The major components of the IHKR system:

- IHKR control panel and module
- Integrated heater and A/C components housing
- Heater core temperature sensor
- Evaporator temperature sensor
- Interior temperature sensor located in driver's footwell
- Double cage blower motor and final stage
- Heater valve (duty cycle controlled)
- Auxiliary coolant pump
- Fresh air / recirculating air stepper motor
- Auxiliary engine cooling fan (DME controlled)
- Refrigerant pressure sensor
- Blower motor and relay with final stage output control
- Interior ventilation micro-filters

IHKR control module input and outputs

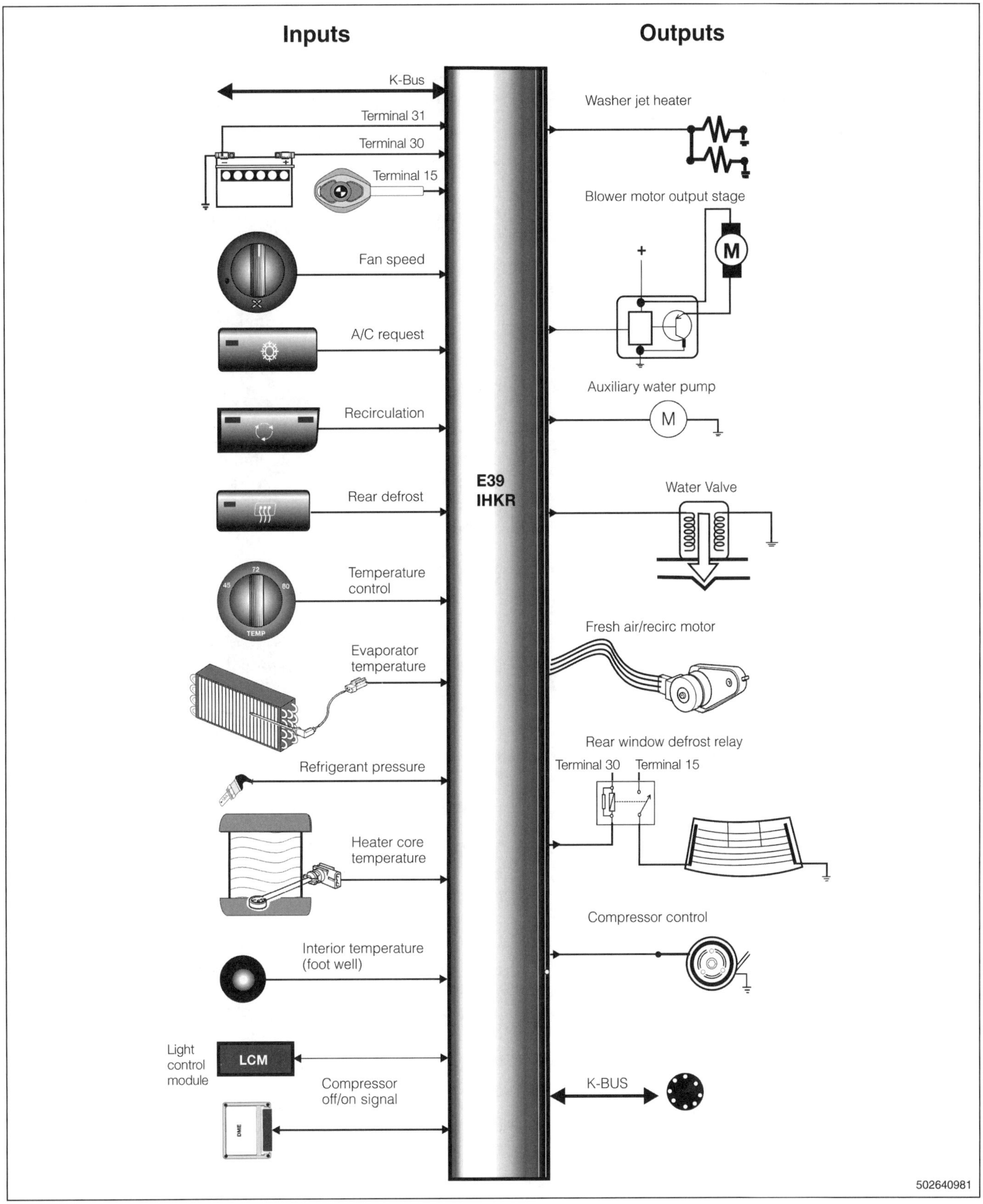
Inputs
Outputs
K-Bus
Terminal 31
Terminal 30
Terminal 15
Fan speed
A/C request
Recirculation
Rear defrost
Temperature control
Evaporator temperature
Refrigerant pressure
Heater core temperature
Interior temperature (foot well)
Light control module
LCM
Compressor off/on signal
E39 IHKR
Washer jet heater
Blower motor output stage
Auxiliary water pump
Water Valve
Fresh air/recirc motor
Rear window defrost relay
Terminal 30
Terminal 15
Compressor control
K-BUS
502640981

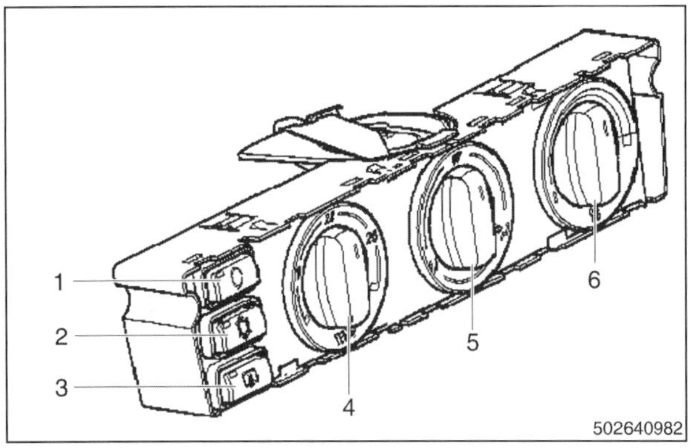

IHKR control panel

Heating and air conditioning functions are programmed via the center console mounted control panel.

1. Recirculation control
2. A/C control
3. Rear window defrost
4. Temperature control potentiometer
5. Air distribution control
6. Blower fan control potentiometer

Other special features

Heating and A/C system features listed here may not be available on all models.

Cold start interlock

The cold start interlock is active in the AUTO program with a driver's side heater core temperature below 20° C (68° F). In this program, the defrost flaps are 100% open, the footwell and face vents are closed. The blower fan will run at a set speed.

Service station feature

This feature prevents hot engine coolant from entering the heater cores after the engine is switched off. It is designed to prevent a blast of hot air on restart.

When engine coolant temperature is above 15° C (59° F), the heater valves are closed for 3 minutes when the engine is switched off.

Parked car ventilation

The system is operational at outside temperatures above 60° F (16° C), or manually and is only available in V-8 (540i) models.

When the vehicle is unattended, this system can be programmed to ventilate the interior and lower its temperature by using the IHKA blower. Two different activation times may be preselected, using the Multi-Information Display (MID) or on-board computer. Once activated, ventilation continues for 30 minutes. Ventilation can also be turned on and off manually.

Because of its high current consumption, do not use the system twice in succession without allowing the battery to be recharged by driving.

Windshield washer spray jet heating

The windshield washer spray jets are heated if outside temperature is below 3° C (37° F). Jet heating is switched off when outside temperature is above 6° C (43° F) or if battery voltage is below 11.4 volts.

Multi–function (MFL) steering wheel recirculation button

The recirculation button on the MFL steering wheel communicates with the IHKA module.

HEATING AND A/C CONTROLS

The IHKA control module is integrated with the control panel in the center console below the radio. There is a built-in interior temperature sensor and fan.

The IHKR control panel is also in the center console. Bowden cables attach it to the air distribution flaps in the IHKR housing.

Models with GPS navigation are equipped with a center console-mounted Multi-Information Display (MID). This combines sound system control functions, GPS monitoring and heating/A/C control functions.

Heating and A/C control panel, removing

– Models with IHKA:
  - Remove radio. See **650 Radio**.
  - Push out IHKA control panel through radio opening.
  - Disconnect electrical harness connectors.

NOTE—
Recode new IHKA control panel using the BMW service tool DISplus, MoDiC, GT1 or equivalent.

– Models with IHKR:
  - Remove switch panel below IHKR panel.
  - Push out IHKR control panel by reaching through switch panel opening.
  - Disconnect electrical harness connectors.
  - Disconnect Bowden cables from back of panel.

CAUTION—
Note color coding of Bowden cables. When reinstalling, re-attach cables to correct control levers.

Heater core temperature sensor(s)

– Remove radio. See **650 Radio**.

– If necessary, remove Multi-Information Display (MID).

< Disconnect heater core temperature sensor harness connector(s) (**arrows**).

NOTE—
Dashboard is shown disassembled for clarity.

– Pull out temperature sensor(s).

Evaporator temperature sensor

The IHKA system evaporator temperature sensor is under the left side of the dashboard on models produced until 3/2000. After that date it is under the right side of the dashboard.

The IHKR system evaporator temperature sensor is under the right side of the dashboard.

IHKA system

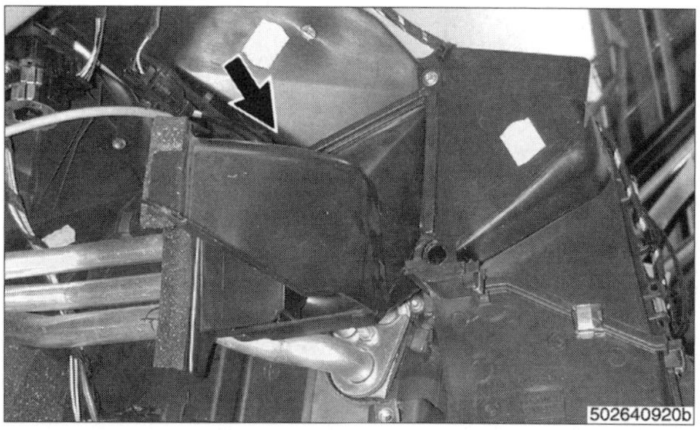

– Models to 3/2000: Remove left side trim above pedal cluster.

< Remove evaporator temperature sensor (**arrow**) behind left footwell outlet.

– Models after 3/2000: Remove section of carpet against right front of center console.

– Remove right footwell air duct.

– Remove right side center console trim cover.

– Pull out evaporator temperature sensor, which is just below and ahead of rear compartment air control stepper motor. Remove stepper motor, if necessary.

IHKR system

– Remove glove compartment. See **513 Interior Trim**.

– Remove right footwell air duct.

– Remove evaporator cover.

– Disconnect electrical harness connector from evaporator sensor and pull out sensor.

Stepper Motors

The IHKA air distribution system includes air distribution motors (stepper motors). Stepper motors are connected to the IHKA control module via M-Bus. Each is identified by a letter-number code unique to its location. See illustrations that follow.

> ***CAUTION—***
> *Stepper motors are not interchangeable. Replacement units must bear the same letter-number code.*

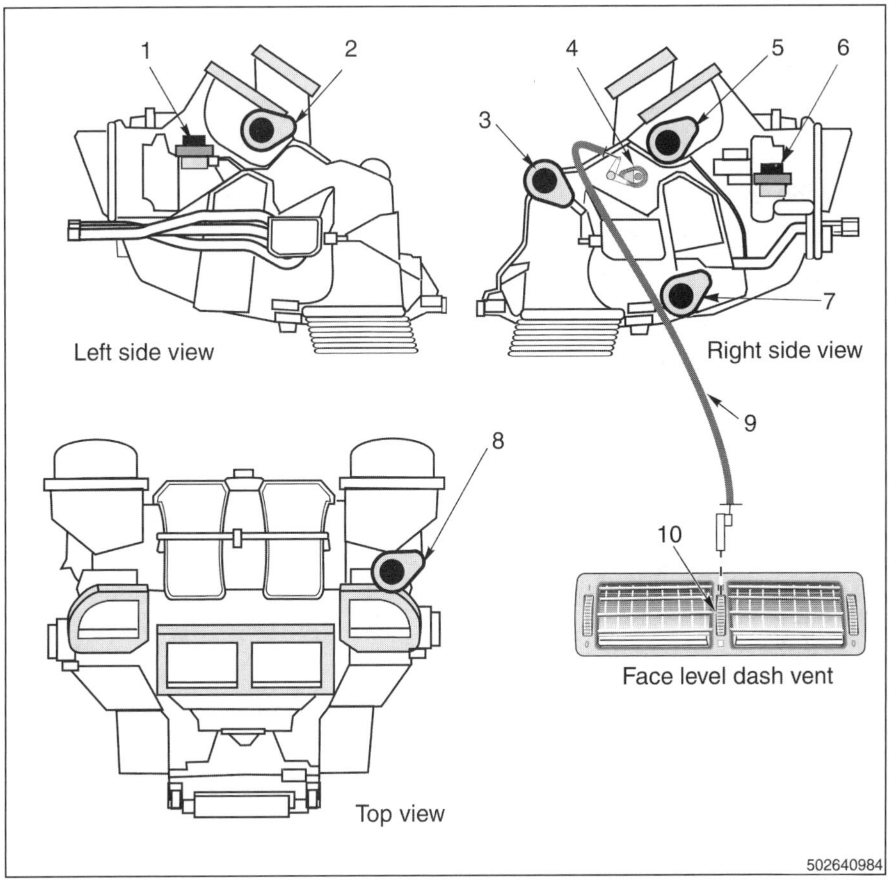

Air distribution controls

1. **Fresh air control stepper motor**
2. **Face level vents control stepper motor (B1)**
3. **Footwell air control stepper motor (F3)**
4. **Stratified air control linkage**
5. **Defroster control stepper motor (D4)**
6. **Recirculated air stepper motor (to 3/2000) (U2)**
7. **Rear air control stepper motor (from 3/2000) (T5)**
8. **Rear stratified air control stepper motor (from 9/1997)**
9. **Stratified air control Bowden cable**
10. **Stratified air outlet control thumb wheel**

Left side stepper motors

– Remove pedal cluster trim and left center console covering.

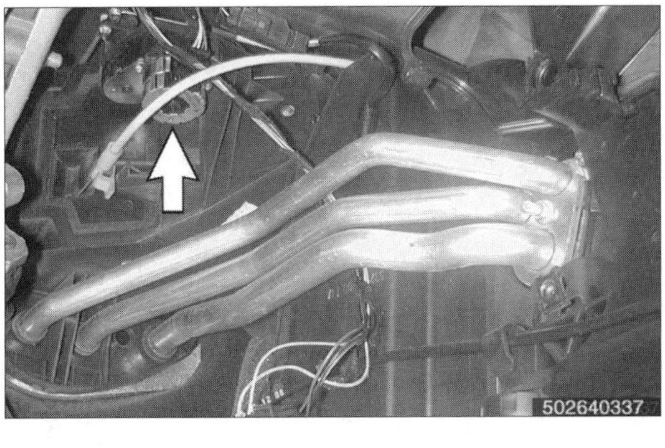

< Fresh air control stepper motor (**arrow**) is mounted vertically in IHKA housing, ahead and above coolant pipes to heater core.

Face level vent stepper motor (**B1**) is mounted above coolant pipes to heater core.

- Remove steering column covering to access motor.

Right side stepper motors

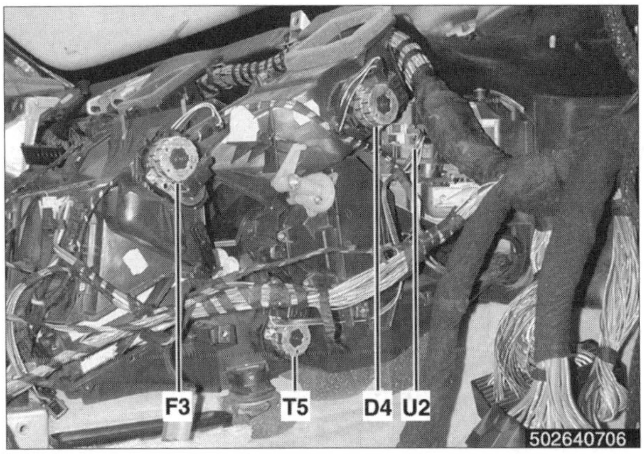

Remove right center console covering.

- Footwell air control stepper motor (**F3**): Remove glove compartment for access. See **513 Interior Trim**.
- Rear air control stepper motor (**T5**) is accessible.
- Defroster control (**D4**) or recirculated air (**U2**) stepper motors: Remove glove compartment and right footwell air duct for access. See **513 Interior Trim**.

– Disconnect electrical harness connector at stepper motor.

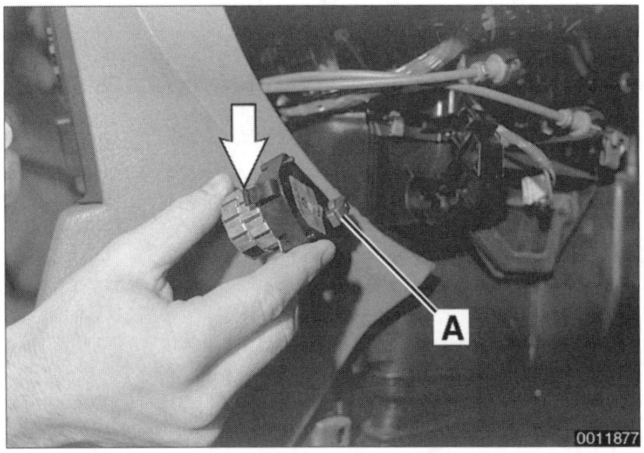

Squeeze plastic clip (**arrow**) to release motor.

- Tilt motor out of housing.
- During installation, be sure to align air distribution flap and motor drive (**A**).

Blower

Removal of the blower motor involves dashboard removal. Read the procedure through before beginning the job.

Blower motor, removing and installing

– Disconnect battery negative (–) cable.

> ***CAUTION—***
> *See battery disconnection warnings and cautions in* **001 General Warnings and Cautions**.

– Remove upper dash panel. See **513 Interior Trim**.

– Remove protective foam rubber mat from components under dash panel.

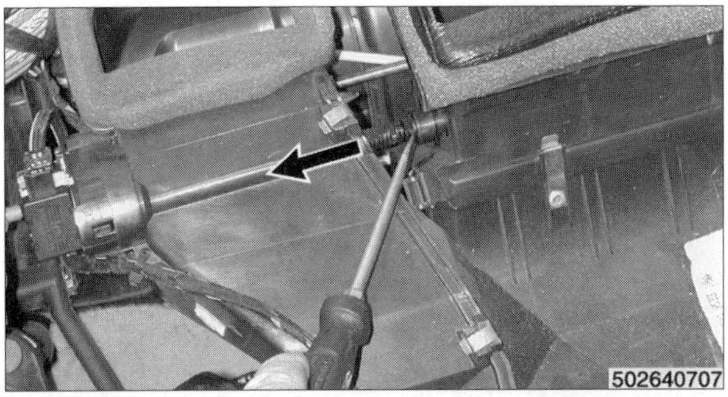

< Working at top of IHKA housing, slide connector to left (**arrow**) to disengage flap rail.

< Pry off ventilation duct cover retaining clips (**arrows**) and remove duct.

< Slide vent flap connecting rail (**A**) to one side and pull both rails out of vent flaps (**long arrow**).

< Pry off blower housing retaining clips (**arrows**). Lift off outer blower housing cover.

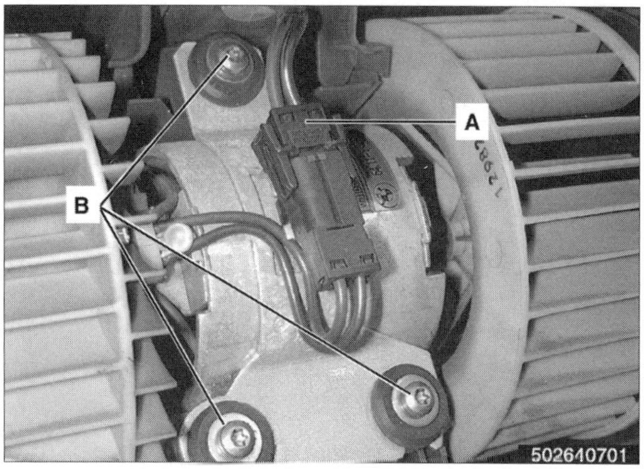

< Disconnect blower fan electrical connector (**A**).

- Remove blower fan mounting fasteners (**B**) and remove fan.

– Installation is reverse of removal. Note the following:

- Align slot in blower motor with mounting tab in blower motor housing.

< When installing flap rails be sure both ends are visible through hole (**arrow**) in center of connector.

– Insert clips at bottom of cover first.

– Remainder of installation is reverse of removal.

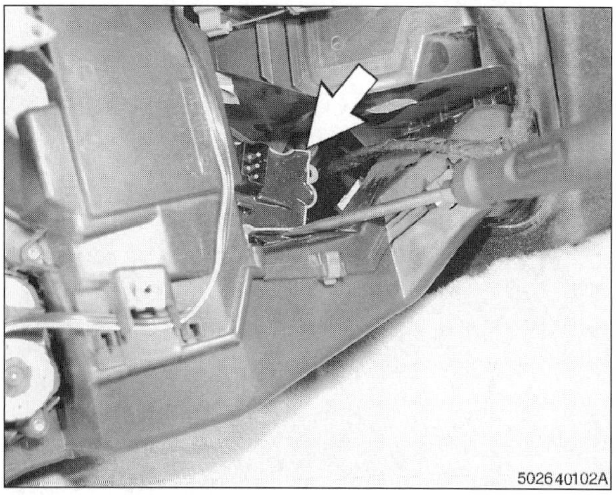

Blower motor final stage (resistor pack), replacing

– Working in passenger side of cabin, remove right side carpeted panel retaining screws. Remove panel.

– Remove right side lower dashboard trim (below glove compartment).

– Disconnect electrical connector from blower motor final stage.

< Release mounting clip and remove final stage unit (**arrow**).

Interior ventilation filter housing, removing

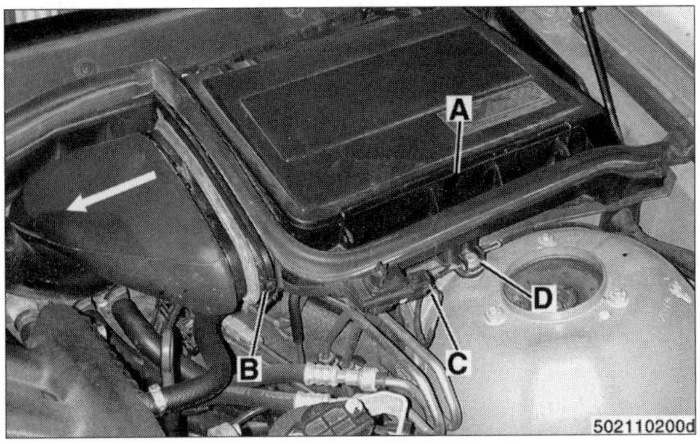

< Remove left interior ventilation filter housing:

- Release ventilation filter cover latch (**A**) and remove cover.
- Release plastic locking tab (**B**) or release locking tabs on top of duct (later models).
- Rotate duct counterclockwise to unlock from bulkhead and remove (**arrow**).
- Disconnect electrical harness from hood switch (**C**).
- Release spring lock (**D**).
- Slide filter housing away from inner fender to remove.

– Removal of right side ventilation filter housing is similar.

HEATER COMPONENTS

The heater valve is located in the left side of the engine compartment, attached to the left strut tower. The solenoid operated valve controls coolant flow through the heater core.

The IHKA or IHKR housing, located underneath the center of the dashboard, houses the heater core, the A/C evaporator, the heating and A/C blower and associated sensors and air distribution stepper motors.

Heater valve, replacing

– Drain engine coolant. See**170 Radiator and Cooling System.**

> ***WARNING —***
> *Allow the engine to cool thoroughly before opening or draining the cooling system.*

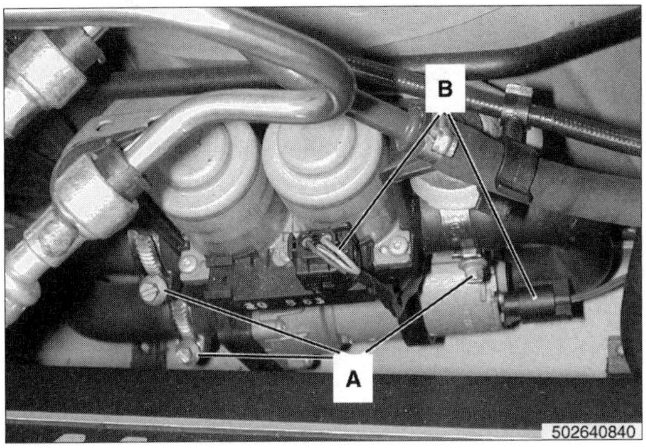

< Working in engine compartment at left strut tower, loosen hose clamps (**A**) and detach electrical harness connectors (**B**) at heater valve.

NOTE —
Illustration shows V-8 (540i) model with IHKA. Models with IHKR are similar.

– Carefully pull heater valve out of rubber mounting and pull up and out of engine compartment.

– Installation is reverse of removal.
  - Inspect hoses and rubber mounts. Replace as necessary. Use new hose clamps.
  - Fill and bleed cooling system as described in **170 Radiator and Cooling System**.

Tightening torque	
Coolant hose clamp 32 - 48 mm ($1\frac{1}{4}$ - 2 in.)	2.5 Nm (22 in-lb)

Heater core, replacing (IHKA)

– Disconnect negative (–) battery cable. See **020 Maintenance**.

> ***CAUTION—***
> *Prior to disconnecting the battery, read the battery disconnection cautions given in* **001 General Cautions and Warnings**.

– Drain engine coolant. See **170 Radiator and Cooling System**.

> ***WARNING—***
> *Allow the engine to cool thoroughly before opening or draining the cooling system.*

NOTE—
In the following illustrations a V-8 (540i) model with IHKA is shown. Other models are similar.

◄ Working in engine compartment, remove left and right interior ventilation ducts by releasing locking clips. Twist ducts inward (**arrows**) to remove.

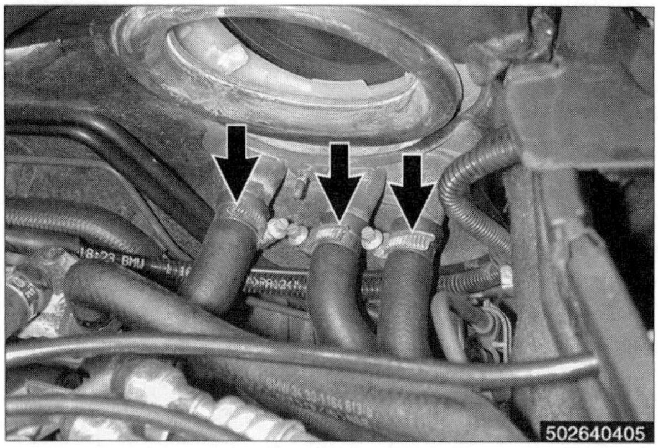

◄ Working at left rear of engine compartment, disconnect heater hoses (**arrows**) at heater core ducts.
  - Gently blow compressed air into heater core ducts to clear out residual coolant.
  - Plug hose and duct ends to prevent contamination.

– Working inside passengers compartment:
  - Remove center console. See **513 Interior Trim**.
  - Remove trim panel above pedal cluster.
  - Remove lower steering column casing with footwell trim. See **320 Steering and Wheel Alignment**.
  - Remove glove compartment. See **513 Interior Trim**.
  - Remove left and right footwell air ducts.

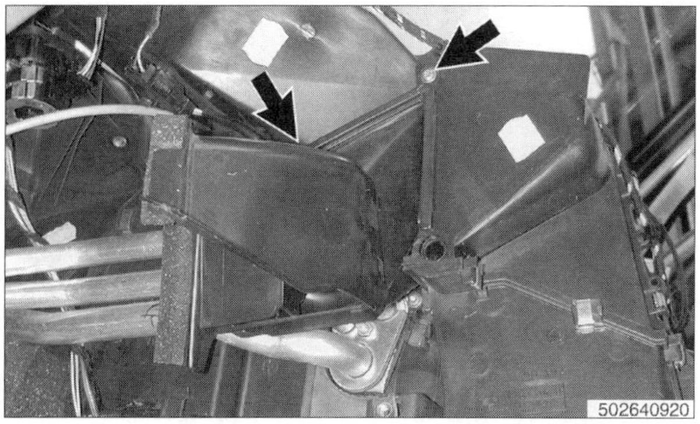

502640920

Remove left footwell outlet vent fasteners (**arrows**) and remove vent.

502640921

Working under left side of dashboard, remove coolant pipe mounting nut (**arrow**) at heater core. Remove pipe assembly.

502640925

Working under left side of dashboard, release footwell air distribution stepper motor mounting clip (**arrow**). Remove motor and set aside. Note motor ID number.

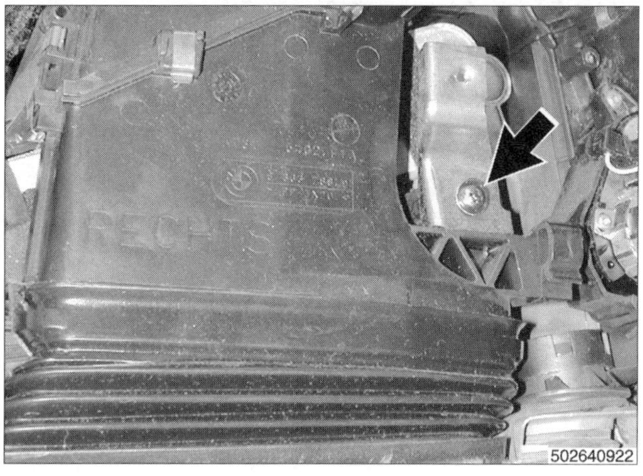

502640922

Working under right side of dashboard, remove heater core support bracket screw (**arrow**). Remove bracket.

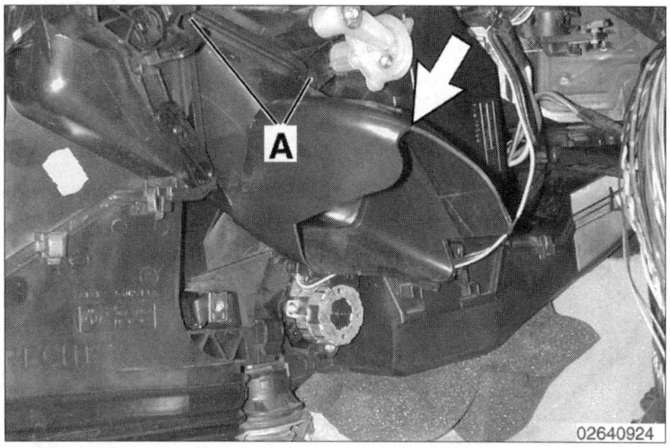

Remove right footwell outlet vent mounting fasteners (**A**) and remove vent (**arrow**).

NOTE—
Right footwell vent removal procedure may differ among models.

Pry off locking clips (**arrows**) from rear compartment heat duct and remove duct.

– If applicable: Pull out evaporator temperature sensor from right side of IHKA housing and set aside.

Remove fasteners (**arrows**) from right side of heater core cover and remove cover.

– Remove heater core from right side of housing.

> ***CAUTION—***
> *Be careful not to bend cooling fins on heater core.*

– Installation is reverse of removal.

- Use new sealing O-rings when mounting coolant pipes to heater core.
- Use new hose clamps to reattach heater hoses.
- Fill and bleed cooling system. See **170 Radiator and Cooling System**.

Tightening torque

Coolant hose clamp 32 - 48 mm ($1^1/_4$ - 2 in.)	2.5 Nm (22 in-lb)

IHKA housing, removing and installing

> *CAUTION—*
> - *IHKA housing removal requires that the dashboard first be removed. Before starting work, disconnect the battery negative (–) cable in the trunk.*
> - *IHKA housing removal requires evacuating the A/C system. Be sure to read* **A/C system warnings and cautions**.

– Disconnect negative (–) battery cable. See **020 Maintenance.**

> *CAUTION—*
> *Prior to disconnecting the battery, read the battery disconnection cautions given in* **001 General Cautions and Warnings** *and airbag warnings in* **721 Airbag System (SRS)**.

– Following manufacturer's instructions, connect an approved refrigerant recovery / recycling / recharging unit to A/C system and discharge system.

> *WARNING —*
> *Do not discharge/charge the A/C system without proper equipment and training. Damage to the vehicle and personal injury may result.*

– Drain engine coolant. See **170 Radiator and Cooling System.**

NOTE —
In the following illustrations, a V-8 (540i) model with IHKA is shown. Other models are similar.

< Working in engine compartment, remove left and right interior ventilation ducts by releasing locking clips. Twist ducts inward (**arrows**) to remove.

< Working in right rear of engine compartment, remove A/C line fasteners (**arrows**) at expansion valve double pipe.

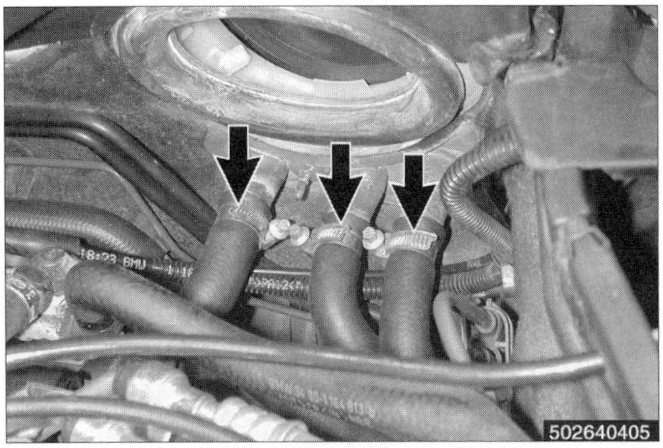

Working at left rear of engine compartment, loosen heater hose clamps (**arrows**).

- Remove coolant hoses and gently blow compressed air into heater core ducts to clear out residual coolant.
- Plug hose and duct ends to prevent contamination.

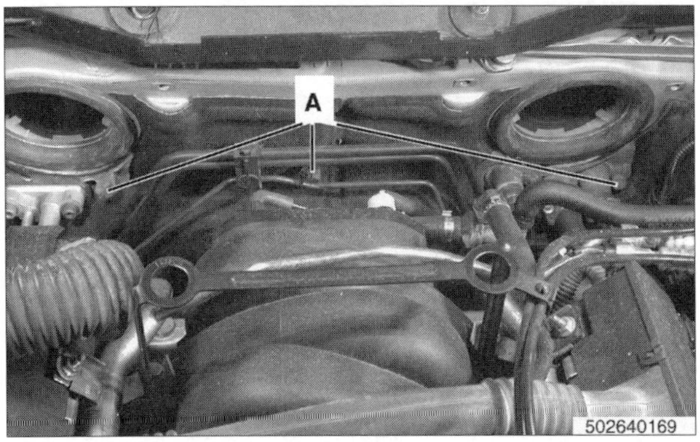

Remove IHKA housing fasteners (**A**).

– Working inside passengers compartment, remove center console, lower and upper dashboard sections. See **513 Interior Trim**.

– Unbolt steering column from transverse dashboard reinforcement bar. See **320 Steering and wheel alignment**.

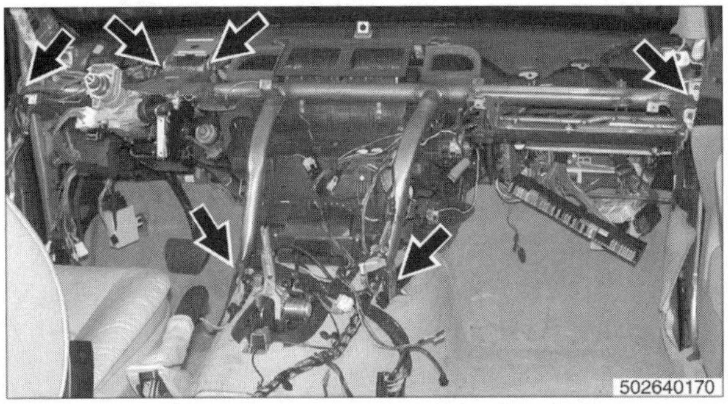

Remove transverse dashboard reinforcement bar fasteners (**arrows**).

– Cut wire ties and remove transverse dashboard reinforcement bar.

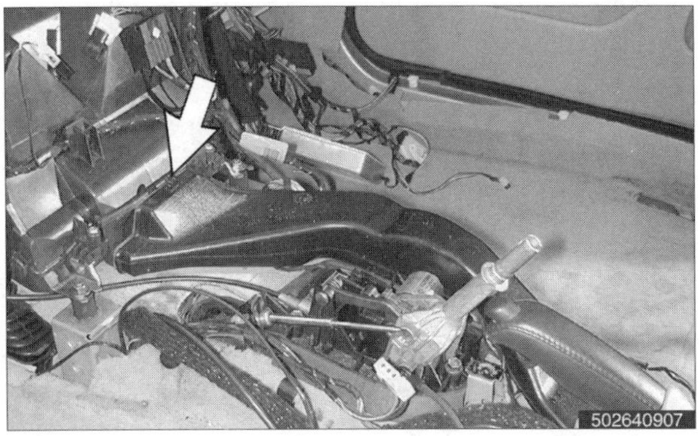

Remove plastic expanding rivet (**arrow**) and remove passenger compartment rear air duct.

< Remove heater housing mounting fasteners (**arrows**).

– Lift out housing carefully while checking for lines, hoses or harnesses that might get snagged.

– Installation is reverse of removal.
  - Make sure electrical harnesses are routed as before.
  - Align guides and clips correctly.
  - Recharge system following equipment manufacturer's instructions.
  - Fill and bleed cooling system as described in **170 Radiator and Cooling System**.

CAUTION—
Always replace sealing O-rings when reconnecting refrigerant lines.

A/C system fluid specifications	
R-134a refrigerant capacity	
• Models built up to 12/1997	1225 ±25 grams (2.70 ±0.05 lb)
• Models built after 12/1997	750 ±10 grams (1.65 ±0.03 lb)
Refrigerant oil	PAG oil

Tightening torque	
Coolant hose clamp 32 - 48 mm ($1^1/_4$ - 2 in.)	2.5 Nm (22 in-lb)

Air Conditioning Components

This section covers removal and installation of air conditioning refrigerant components. A/C testing and diagnosis, refrigerant discharge, evacuation and recharge are not covered here.

The A/C condenser, compressor, receiver / dryer, pressure sensor, refrigerant lines and expansion valve are either installed in the engine compartment or accessible from the engine compartment.

Be sure to read **A/C system warnings and cautions**.

NOTE—
The air conditioning system is filled with R-134a refrigerant.

A/C compressor, replacing

– Following manufacturer's instructions, connect an approved refrigerant recovery / recycling / recharging unit to A/C system and discharge system.

> ***WARNING —***
> *Do not attempt to discharge or charge the A/C system without proper equipment and training. Damage to the vehicle and personal injury may result.*

– Remove splash shield from under engine.

– Mark A/C drive belt with direction of rotation. Then remove belt. See **020 Maintenance**.

0022961

– V-8 (540i) models: Remove intake air filter housing.

– Disconnect electrical harness connector from A/C compressor.

◄ Remove A/C pressure hose and suction hose flange bolts (**arrows**) from compressor. Plug hoses immediately.

0021811

◄ Support compressor while removing compressor mounting bolts (**arrows**). Remove compressor.

NOTE —
Depending on model, compressor may be mounted with 3 or 4 bolts.

– Installation is reverse of removal.

- Always replace O-rings when reconnecting refrigerant lines.
- If installing a new compressor, or if compressor has been off the vehicle for more than 24 hours, receiver/drier unit should be replaced. See **A/C receiver / drier, replacing**.
- Install and tension A/C drive belt, noting previously made direction mark. See **020 Maintenance**.
- Recharge A/C system following equipment manufacturer's instructions.

Tightening torque

A/C lines to compressor (replace sealing O-rings)	20 Nm (15 ft-lb)

- When starting a new compressor for the first time, carry out the following break-in procedure:
  - Switch on A/C system.
  - Set all instrument cluster air vents to OPEN.
  - Start engine and allow to idle.
  - Set blower output to minimum 75% of maximum.
  - Run A/C for at least 2 minutes at idle speed.

> ***CAUTION—***
> *The new compressor may be damaged if run at higher than idle speed at start-up.*

- Top off refrigerant.

A/C system fluid specifications

R-134a refrigerant capacity	
• Models built up to 12/1997	1225 ±25 grams (2.70 ±0.05 lb)
• Models built after 12/1997	750 ±10 grams (1.65 ±0.03 lb)
Refrigerant oil	PAG oil

A/C condenser, replacing

The A/C condenser is located in front of the radiator.

- Following manufacturer's instructions, connect an approved refrigerant recovery / recycling / recharging unit to A/C system and discharge system.

> ***WARNING—***
> *Do not discharge/charge A/C system without proper equipment and training. Damage to the vehicle and personal injury may result.*

- Remove engine cooling fan. Drain coolant and remove radiator. See **170 Radiator and Cooling System**.

> ***WARNING—***
> *Allow the engine to cool thoroughly before opening or draining the cooling system.*

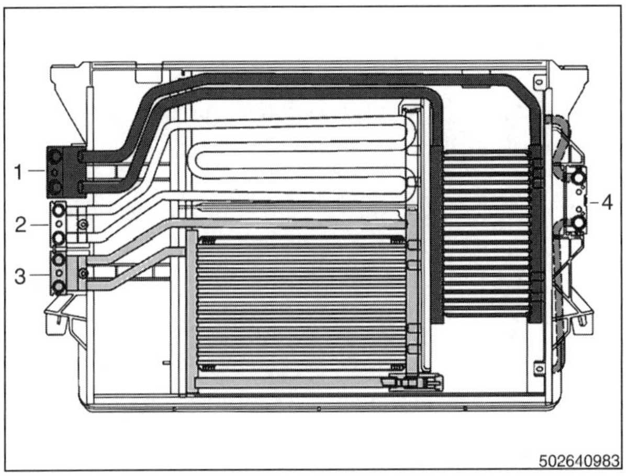

◀ Detach lines from coils on cooling cassette:

1. Engine oil cooler
2. Steering fluid cooler
3. Transmission oil cooler
4. A/C condenser

> ***CAUTION—***
> *Use shop rags to catch dripping fluid(s). Plug open lines and cooling coil ports immediately to prevent contamination.*

– Tilt cassette slightly backward to remove.

– Unclip A/C condenser and remove.

– Installation is reverse of removal.
  - Replace rubber profile seal gaskets.
  - Align rubber insulators between cassette and radiator.
  - Replace sealing O-rings at line connections.
  - If installing a new condenser, or if condenser has been off the vehicle for more than 24 hours, receiver/drier unit should be replaced. See **A/C receiver / drier, replacing**.
  - Fill and bleed cooling system. See **170 Radiator and Cooling System**.
  - Recharge A/C system following equipment manufacturer's instructions.

A/C system fluid specifications

R-134a refrigerant capacity	
• Models built up to 12/1997	1225 ±25 grams (2.70 ±0.05 lb)
• Models built after 12/1997	750 ±10 grams (1.65 ±0.03 lb)
Refrigerant oil	PAG oil

A/C receiver / drier, replacing

The receiver / drier is mounted in the front right corner of the engine compartment behind and below the headlight assembly.

> ***CAUTION—***
> *The receiver/drier must be replaced when:*
> - *There is dirt in the A/C system*
> - *The compressor has seized or has been replaced*
> - *The condenser or evaporator are replaced*
> - *The A/C system is leaking and there is no more refrigerant*
> - *The A/C system was open for 24 hours or more*

– Following manufacturer's instructions, connect an approved refrigerant recovery / recycling / recharging unit to A/C system and discharge system.

– Remove right headlight assembly. See **630 Lights**.

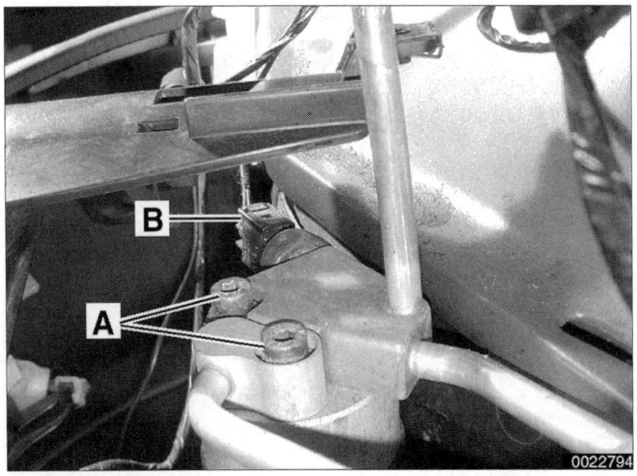

◄ Remove refrigerant pressure line mounting bolts (**A**) from receiver / drier.
  - Plug lines and ports immediately.
  - Disconnect high pressure switch harness connector (**B**).

– Remove receiver / dryer mounting bolts. Pull unit upward to remove.

– Installation is reverse of removal.
  - Replace sealing O-rings at line connections.
  - Recharge A/C system following equipment manufacturer's instructions.

A/C system fluid specifications

R-134a refrigerant capacity	
• Models built up to 12/1997	1225 ±25 grams (2.70 ±0.05 lb)
• Models built after 12/1997	750 ±10 grams (1.65 ±0.03 lb)
Refrigerant oil	PAG oil

A/C expansion valve, removing and installing

– Following manufacturer's instructions, connect an approved refrigerant recovery / recycling / recharging unit to A/C system and discharge system.

> ***WARNING —***
> *Do not discharge/charge the A/C system without proper equipment and training. Damage to the vehicle and personal injury may result.*

NOTE —
In the following illustrations, a V-8 (540i) model with IHKA is shown. Other models are similar.

◄ Working in engine compartment, remove right interior ventilation duct by releasing locking clips. Twist duct inward (**arrow**) to remove.

◄ Working in right rear of engine compartment, remove A/C line fasteners (**arrows**) at expansion valve double pipe.

– Working in right side of passenger cabin, remove glove compartment. See **513 Interior Trim**.

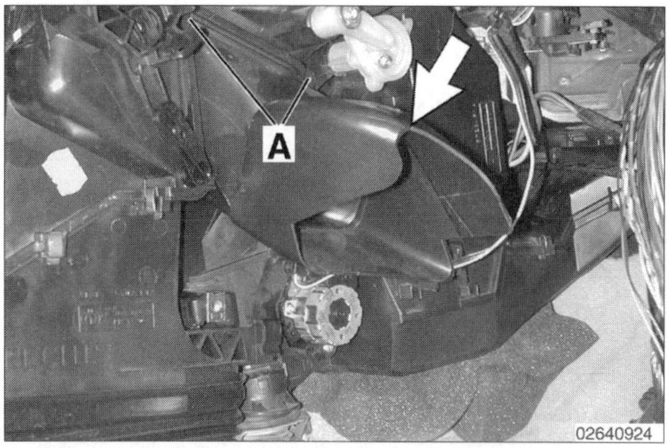

Remove right side footwell outlet vent mounting fasteners (**A**) and remove vent (**arrow**).

NOTE—
Right footwell vent removal procedure may differ among models.

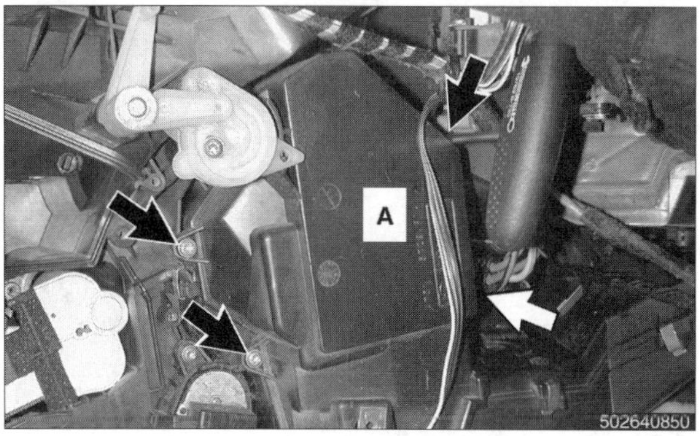

Remove evaporator / expansion valve cover screws (**arrows**) and remove cover (**A**).

Remove expansion valve mounting bolt (**arrow**). Push refrigerant lines slightly apart and remove expansion valve.

– Installation is reverse of removal.
  - Always replace O-rings when reconnecting refrigerant lines.
  - If installing a new expansion valve, or if expansion valve has been off the vehicle for more than 24 hours, replace receiver/drier unit. See **A/C receiver / drier, replacing**.
  - Recharge A/C system following equipment manufacturer's instructions.

A/C system fluid specifications

R-134a refrigerant capacity	
• Models built up to 12/1997	1225 ±25 grams (2.70 ±0.05 lb)
• Models built after 12/1997	750 ±10 grams (1.65 ±0.03 lb)
Refrigerant oil	PAG oil

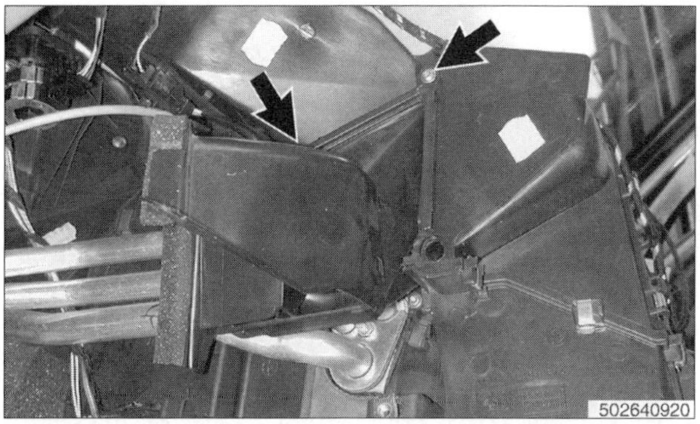

A/C evaporator, removing and installing (IHKA)

– Remove IHKA housing as described earlier. See **IHKA housing, removing and installing**.

◄ Working at IHKA housing on shop bench, remove left footwell outlet vent fasteners (**arrows**) and remove vent.

– Repeat with right air outlet.

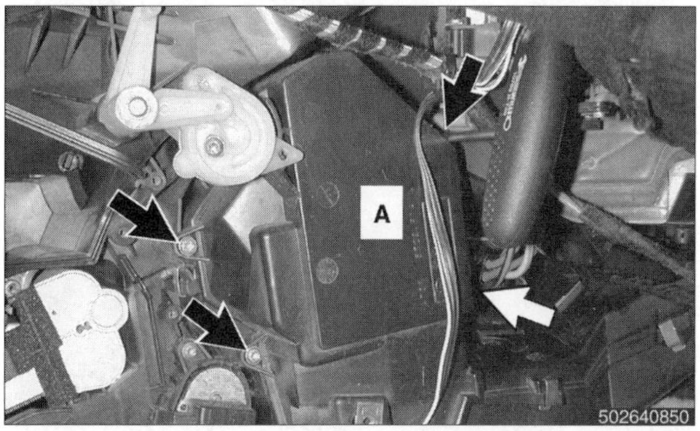

◄ Remove evaporator / expansion valve cover screws (**arrows**) and remove cover (**A**).

– Unfasten clips along bottom cover of IHKA housing. Remove cover.

– Remove footwell vent outlet.

– Remove heater core cover.

– Remove screw and separate upper and lower sections of IHKA housing.

◄ Remove expansion valve mounting bolt (**arrow**). Push refrigerant lines slightly apart and remove expansion valve.

– Pull out evaporator, taking care not to bend cooling fins.

– Installation is reverse of removal.
  - Always replace O-rings when reconnecting refrigerant lines.
  - If installing a new evaporator, or if evaporator has been off the vehicle for more than 24 hours, replace receiver/drier unit. See **A/C receiver / drier, replacing**.
  - Fill and bleed cooling system. See **170 Radiator and Cooling System**.
  - Recharge A/C system following equipment manufacturer's instructions.

A/C system fluid specifications	
R-134a refrigerant capacity	
• Models built up to 12/1997	1225 ±25 grams (2.70 ±0.05 lb)
• Models built after 12/1997	750 ±10 grams (1.65 ±0.03 lb)
Refrigerant oil	PAG oil

650 Radio

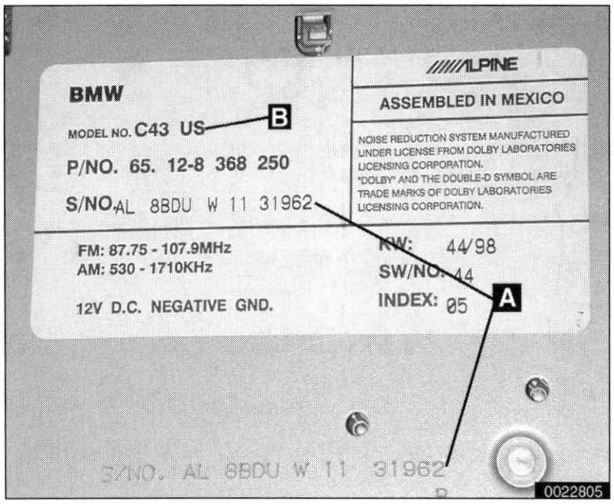

General

This section covers the BMW factory-installed sound system, including radio, amplifier and speaker removal. Radio antenna information is also included.

Radio installations can vary by year and model.

A tag on the bottom of the radio contains the serial number (**A**) and model number (**B**).

Sound system

The standard E39 radio features a cassette player. The optional radio has a CD player. Both radios are prewired for the optional CD changer that mounts in the trunk. Another option, the On-Board Monitor, integrates GPS navigation with radio and IHKA controls. Basic radio controls are also incorporated in the steering wheel.

Sound system components are interconnected via K-bus. Theft proofing of the radio by code is no longer required as the radio will not function without the K-bus connection and a valid signal from the instrument cluster.

Other features of the sound system include:

- Autostoring of stations
- Speed dependent volume
- Telephone muting

Diversity antenna, described later in this group, is optional on some models and standard on the Sport Wagon models.

Radio troubleshooting

Although electronic radio and sound system troubleshooting is beyond the scope of this manual, there are number of self-tests that are possible with the standard BMW radio installed in E39 cars.

Radio test functions are activated by pressing the M button within 8 seconds of switching the radio on. Hold it pressed in for 8 seconds to start the tests.

The test functions include:

- Radio serial number
- Software version display
- Speed dependent volume control adjustment
- Station signal strength, including FM frequency set, quality of signal received, AM frequency set and signal strength

The test also checks antenna functions:

- Antenna signal strength (F number) indicates the quality of the signal received by the antenna. The scale ranges from 0 to 15, with the optimum value being 15. If the value falls below 10, radio stations can not be listened to in stereo.
- The seek sensitivity allows for the choice between two levels of sensitivity.

Radio and Audio Accessories

Radio, removing and installing

> ***CAUTION—***
> - *Before beginning work on the radio or sound system, verify that the radio is an original equipment BMW radio and that the wiring harness has not been modified.*
> - *Servicing of aftermarket sound equipment should be referred to an authorized agent of the equipment's manufacturer.*

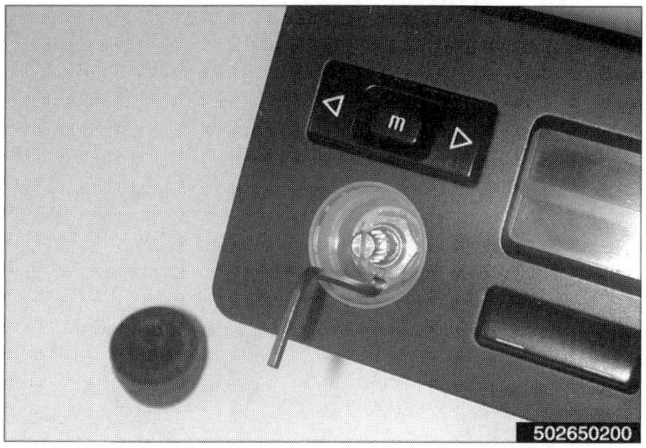

⮜ Carefully remove volume control knob. Insert a 2 mm allen wrench as shown and turn approximately 90° to release locking tabs.

– Pull radio out of instrument cluster and disconnect electrical harness connector.

– Installation is reverse of removal.

Tape player, removing and installing

– Remove radio. See **Radio, removing and installing**.

⮜ Use a 2.5 mm allen wrench to loosen left and right tape player locking tabs (**arrows**).

– Pull tape player out of instrument cluster and disconnect electrical harness connector.

– Installation is reverse of removal.

Amplifier, removing and installing

– The sound system amplifier is located behind trim panel on left side of luggage compartment.

– To access amplifier, remove CD changer if equipped. See **CD Changer, removing and installing**.

< Disconnect wiring harness connector.

– Remove mounting fasteners at base of amplifier and remove amplifier.

– Installation is reverse of removal.

CD Changer, removing and installing

– The optional CD changer is located in the left side of the trunk behind the trim panel. An access door allows loading of up to 6 CDs.

< To remove CD changer:
- Disconnect wiring harness connector.
- Remove mounting fasteners.
- Carefully lift CD changer out of mounting bracket.

– Installation is reverse of removal.

SPEAKERS

Speaker locations also vary depending on the type of sound system installed. Some of the common speaker installations are covered in this section.

Sedan and Sport Wagon speakers

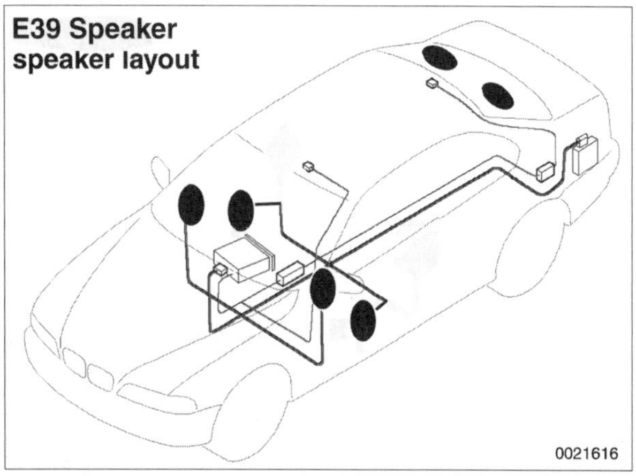

< The standard installation is six speakers, two in each front door and two in the rear of the vehicle. Rear speakers in sedan models are in the parcel shelf. Rear speakers in Sport Wagon models are mounted on the left and right wheel housings behind trim covers.

Door speakers, removing and installing

> ***WARNING —***
> *All E39 cars are equipped with front door airbags. Rear door airbags are optional. Before performing any work involving airbags, disconnect the negative (–) battery cable. See* **721 Airbag System (SRS)**.

> ***CAUTION—***
> *Prior to disconnecting the battery, read the battery disconnection cautions given in* **001 General Cautions and Warnings**.

– Remove interior door panel. See **513 Interior Trim**.

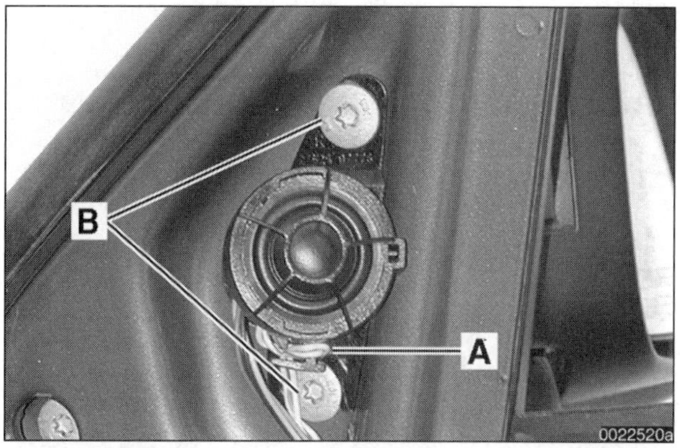

Door post speaker

– Pry back window/speaker trim to access speaker.

◄ Disconnect electrical harness connector (**A**) and remove speaker mounting screws (**B**).

– Installation is reverse of removal.

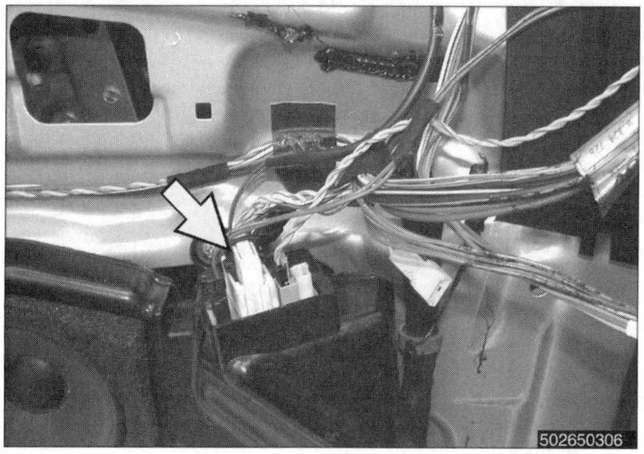

Lower front door speaker

◄ Disconnect speaker wiring harnesses (**arrow**).

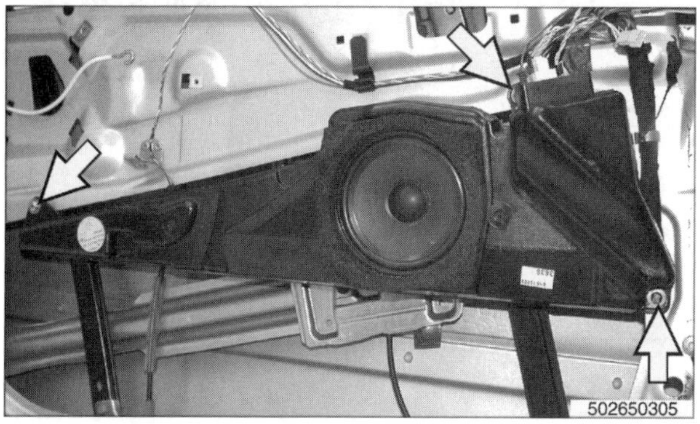

◄ Remove speaker mounting fasteners (**arrow**).

– Installation is reverse of removal.

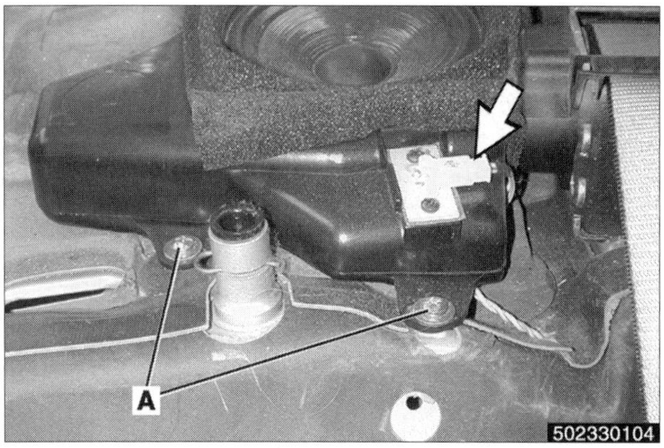

Rear speakers, removing and installing

– Remove rear parcel shelf. See **513 Interior Trim.**

< Disconnect speaker wiring harness (**arrow**) and remove fasteners (**A**).

– Installation is reverse of removal.

Antenna

Standard and Diversity antenna

The antenna used for radio, telephone and FZV remote entry system is integrated with the rear window defogger in sedan models and Sport Wagon models.

Some models are equipped with the Diversity antenna. In this system there are two (or more) antennas. Both main and auxiliary antenna(s) receive radio signals and both signals are amplified in separate amplifiers. Signals are then transmitted to the diversity switching module, which locks onto the strongest signal and sends it to the radio receiver.

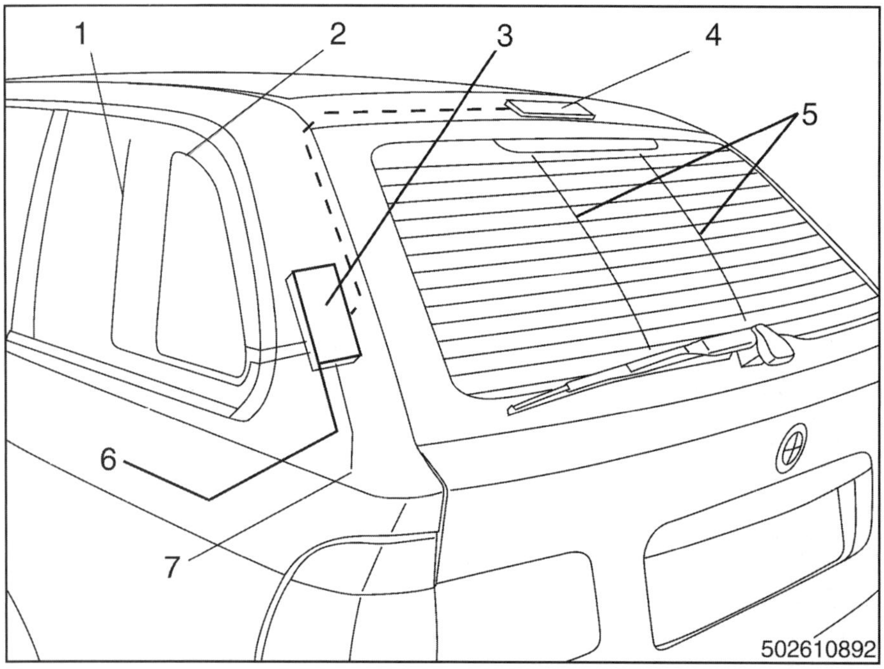

Diversity antenna system

1. **FZV antenna in left rear side window**
2. **AM/FM2 antenna in left rear side window**
3. **FZV/FM 2 antenna amplifier**
4. **FM 1 Antenna amplifier**
5. **FM 1 antenna**
6. **To General Module III (FZV)**
7. **To Radio**

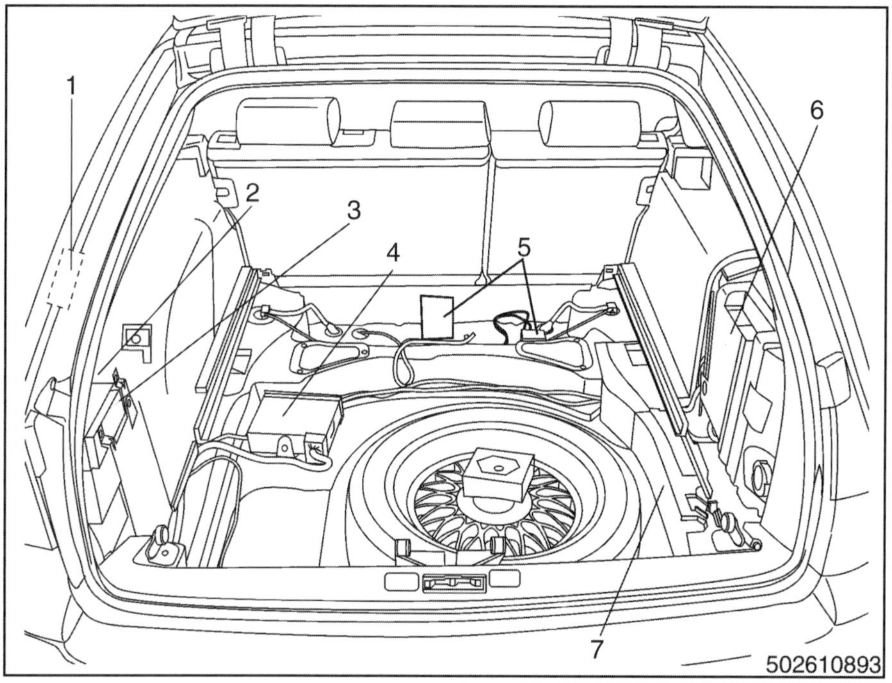

Sport Wagon rear module locations

1. **FZV/FM2 Antenna amplifier**
2. **Audio amplifier**
3. **Navigation Computer**
4. **Radio (with navigation)**
5. **Telephone transceiver or PSE box (6000)**
6. **Audio system sub woofer**
7. **EHC control module**

Antenna amplifier, accessing

Sedan

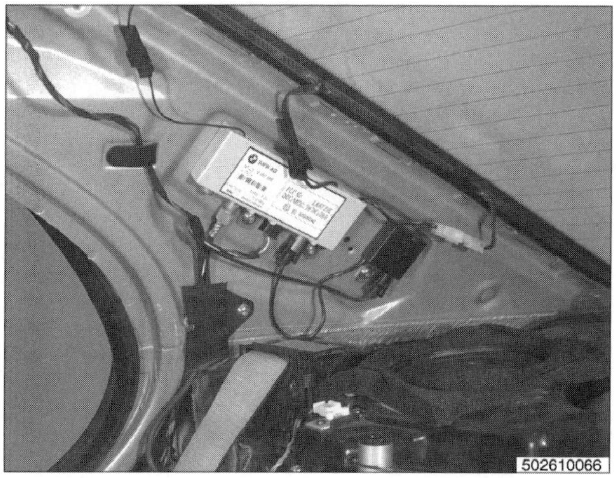

◄ Antenna amplifier:

– Remove left roof pillar (C-pillar) trim panel as described in **513 Interior Trim** to access amplifier.

Sport Wagon

– FZV / FM2 amplifier in left rear D-pillar.

– FM 1 amplifier in tailgate frame above rear window.

ELE Electrical Wiring Diagrams

NOTE—
- *Common BMW abbreviations are explained in* **600 Electrical System—General**.
- *Electronic driveaway protection is also referred to as electronic immobilization or EWS.*
- *Every attempt has been made in this repair manual to standardize component names. However, in some cases, the same component may appear with different names. Regardless of the component name, the alphanumeric component designation (BMW code) is consistent throughout.*

GENERAL

The wiring schematics given in this section represent detailed electrical circuit information for BMW E39 5 Series models. Each diagram shows the wiring, connectors, terminals, and electrical or electronic components of the circuit. It also identifies the wires by color or terminal coding.

Wiring diagrams are necessary to troubleshoot and repair electrical or electronic circuits. Remember that electrical and electronic circuits often have more than one source of power and/or ground. In many cases the ground may also be a switched ground. Take time to study the schematics of the entire system to understand the circuit logic prior to circuit troubleshooting.

When working on electrical or electronic circuits, general precautions should be observed. The following is a listing of common sense safety precautions that you must observe at all times:

CAUTION—

- *On cars equipped with airbags and pyrotechnic seatbelt retractors, special precautions apply to any electrical testing or repair. These components are explosive devices and must be handled with extreme care. Before starting any work, refer to the warnings and cautions in* **720 Seat Belts** *and* **721 Airbag Systems (SRS)**.
- *Prior to disconnecting the battery, read the battery disconnection cautions in* **001 General Cautions and Warning**.
- *Connect and disconnect ignition system wires, multiple connectors and ignition test equipment leads only while ignition is switched off. Keep clothing, hands, and feet dry if possible.*
- *Always switch a test meter to the appropriate function and range before making test connections.*
- *Always switch the ignition off and disconnect the negative (–) battery cable before removing any electrical components.*

Special tools

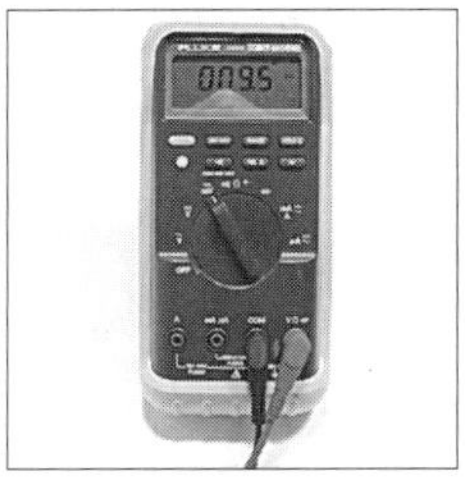

Automotive digital multimeter
(Fluke 87)

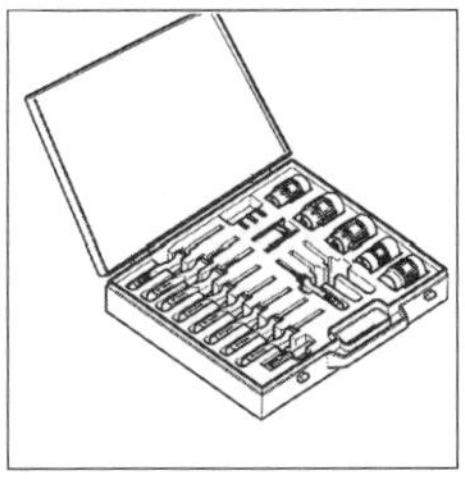

Wiring harness end repair tools
(BMW tool no. BMW 61 1 150)

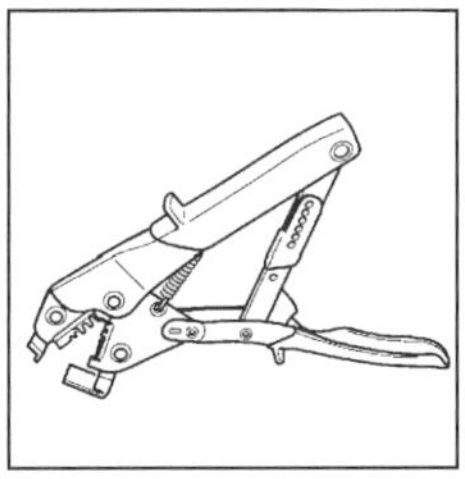

Wire end crimp tool
(BMW tool no. BMW 61 9 041)

Circuit and terminal descriptions

BMW designates electrical circuits, including junctions and grounds, with unique designations, most of which follow the German DIN standard. See **Table a**. For example, if a relay terminal is labeled '30', it tells you that positive (+) voltage is supplied to that terminal at all times directly from the battery.

Electrical components are identified in the schematics using a letter followed by a number. For example, A6000 is the DME control module. The letter A identifies the component as an electronic control module. **Table b** lists the component alpha-codes.

Electrical Wiring Diagrams

Table a. Electrical terminal designations (according to DIN 72 552 standard)

Number	Circuit Description
1	Low voltage switched terminal of coil
4	High voltage center terminal of coil
+X	Originates at ignition switch. Supplies power when ignition switch is in PARK, RUN or START position.
15	Originates at ignition switch. Supplies power when ignition switch is in RUN or START position.
30	Battery positive (+) voltage. Supplies power whenever battery is connected. (Not dependent on ignition switch position, unfused)
31	Ground, battery negative (-) terminal
50	Supplies power from battery to starter solenoid when ignition switch is in START position only.
+54	Originates at ignition switch. Supplies power when ignition switch is in the RUN position only.
85	Ground side (-) or relay coil
86	Power-in side (+) of relay coil
87	Power out when the relay coil is energized (usually terminal 87 connects to terminal 30 power when relay is energized)
D	Alternator warning light and field energizing circuit

Table b. BMW electrical component designation

Letter	Function	Example
A	Electronic control modules, electronic assemblies	A6000 (DME Engine control module)
B	Sensors, transducers	B48 (Right rear acceleration sensor)
E	Lights, electric heaters	E46 (Left trunk-lid light)
F	Fuses	F3 (Fuse 3 in fuse panel)
G	Power supply	G6524 (Alternator), G1 (Battery)
H	Warning lamps, signal indicators	H10 (Chime module)
K	Relays	K6300 (DME relay)
M	Electric motors, actuators	M6510 (Starter)
S	Switches, coding plugs	S204 (Trunk lid release switch)
T	Ignition coils	T6151 (Cylinder 1 ignition coil)
U	Radio/interference suppression	U4 (Tandem telephone)
X	Connectors; splice connectors; grounds	X166 (Left front EDC valve)
Y	Electromechanical components	Y6100 (Fuel injectors, solenoids)
Z	Interference suppression coils	Z400 (Noise suppression coil)

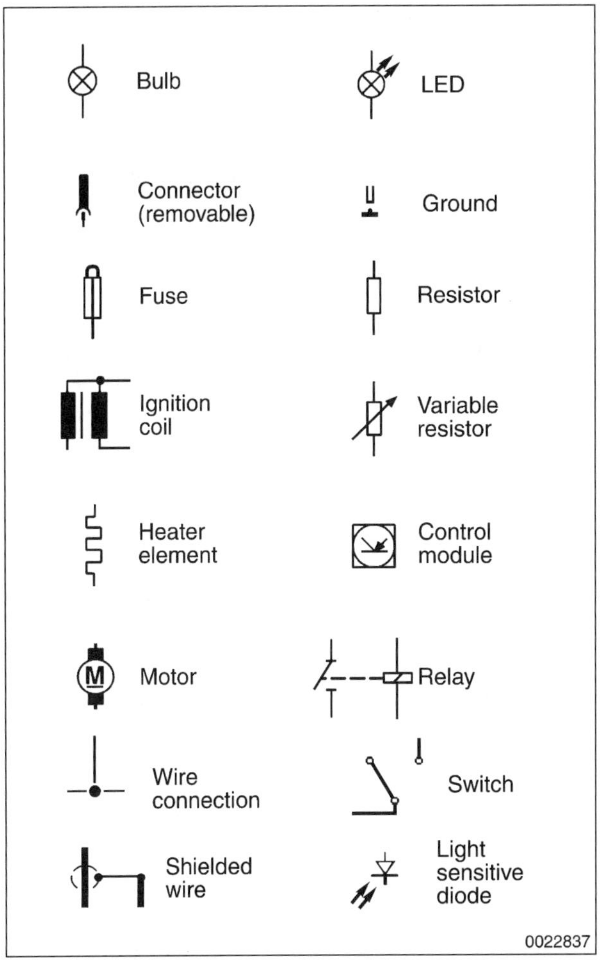

Electrical schematic symbols

The schematics utilize simplified electrical symbols.

Wire insulation colors in this section are given with German color abbreviations. Wire sizes follow the DIN (European) convention.

NOTE —
For example, an 0.5 wire is ½ mm^2 in cross-section area. This corresponds to approx. SAE 16 gauge wire.

Sample wiring schematic

A sample wiring diagram is shown below. It identifies many of the elements found in the diagrams within this section. Note that a dashed line indicates that only a partial view is given and more information on that component or circuit can be found elsewhere in the schematics.

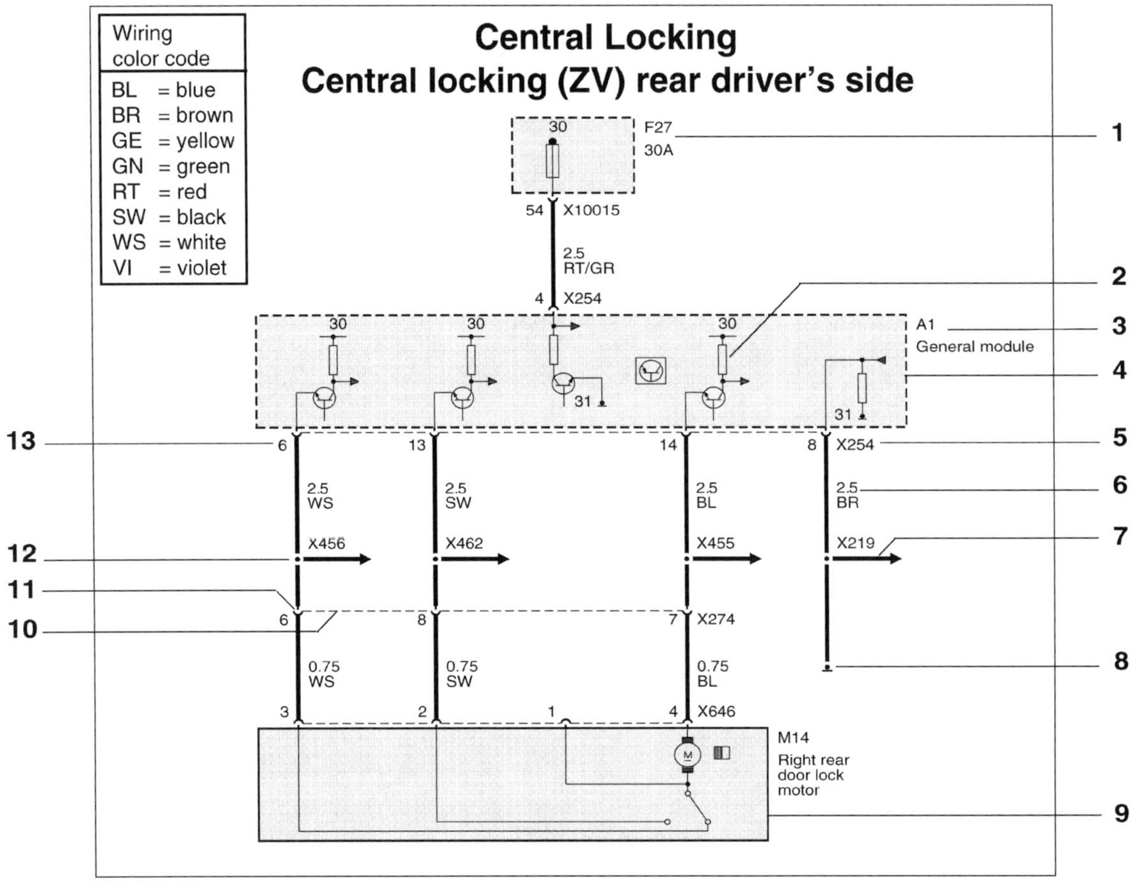

1 - Fuse location. F27 is a fuse in position 27, and is rated 30 amp.

2 - Indicates internal component circuitry in the electronic control module (A1, General Module).

3 - Alpha-numeric designation and name of component. A1 is the General Module, central body electronics.

4 - Dashed border: Indicates that only a portion of component is shown. Complete component is not shown.

5 - Connector alpha-numeric designation. Indicates the connector designation of X254.

6 - Wire size (mm^2) and color.

7 - Arrow indicates that wiring continues to additional diagram. Use main wiring index to locate diagram for splice X219.

8 - Ground.

9 - Solid border: Complete component illustrated.

10 - Dashed line represents a multipin connector.

11 - Connector is removable.

12 - Indicates a splice in wiring harness.

13 - Indicates the pin number on the connector. For example, pin 6 in connector X254.

502ele001i

Electrical Wiring Diagram–Main Index

Electrical Wiring Diagram–Main Index

Electrical Wiring Diagram–Main Index

ELECTRICAL WIRING DIAGRAM–MAIN INDEX

Electrical Wiring Diagram–Main Index

Electrical Wiring Diagram–Main Index

ELECTRICAL WIRING DIAGRAM–MAIN INDEX

Electrical Wiring Diagram–Main Index

ABS/Traction Control
ABS/DSC control module (A65)
(1 of 4)

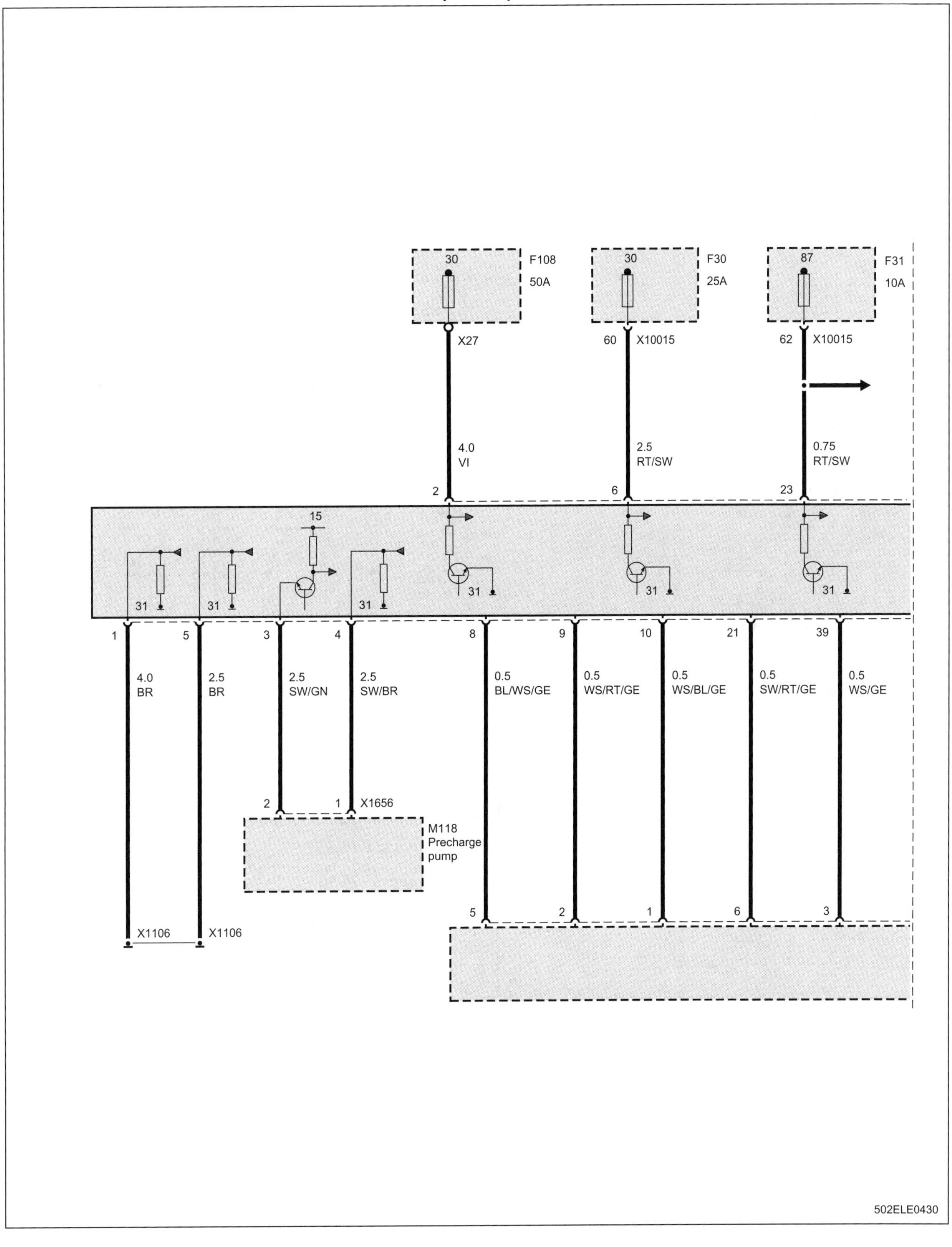

ABS/Traction Control
ABS/DSC control module (A65)
(2 of 4)

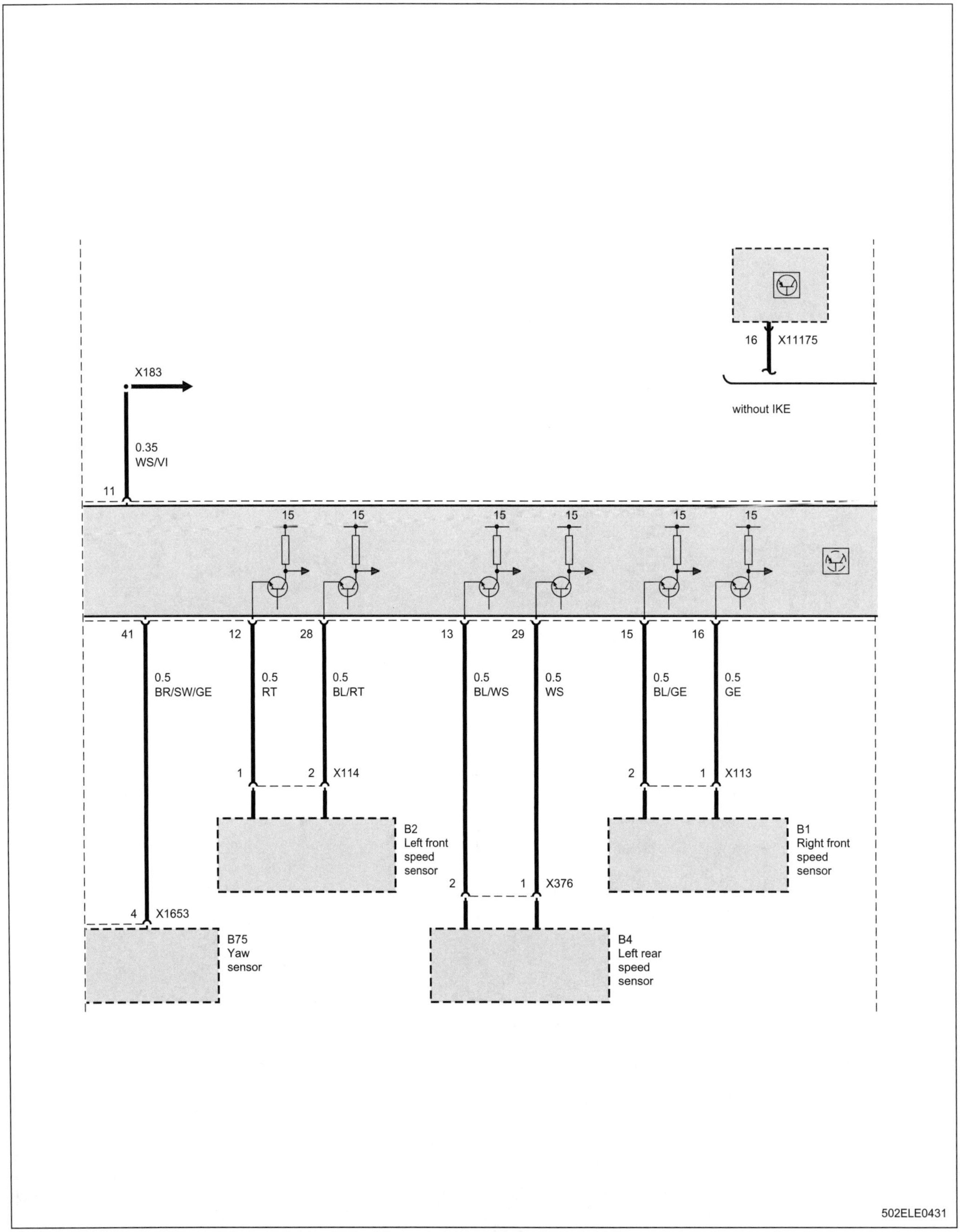

ABS/Traction Control
ABS/DSC control module (A65)
(3 of 4)

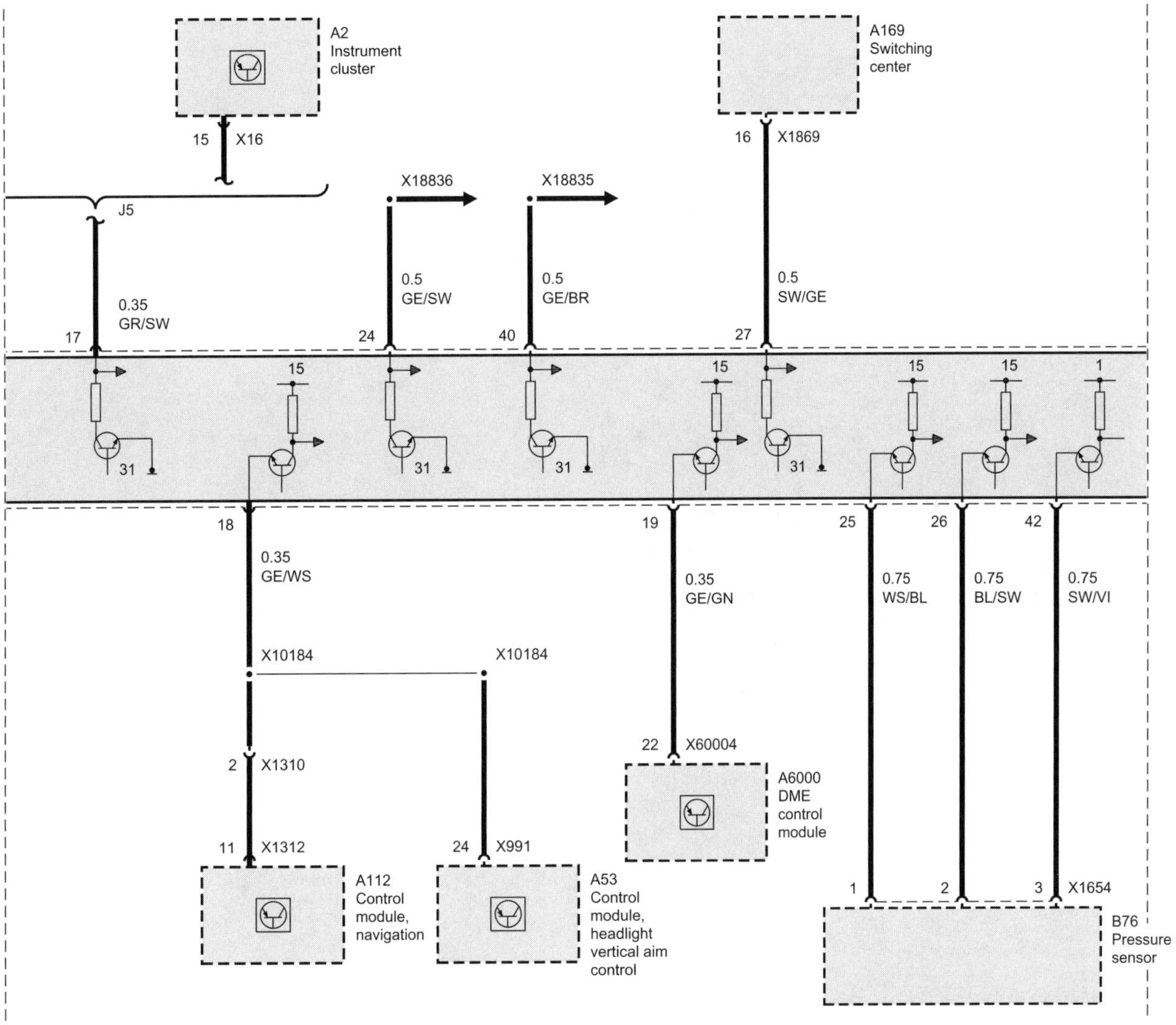

502ELE0432

ABS/Traction Control
ABS/DSC control module (A65)
(4 of 4)

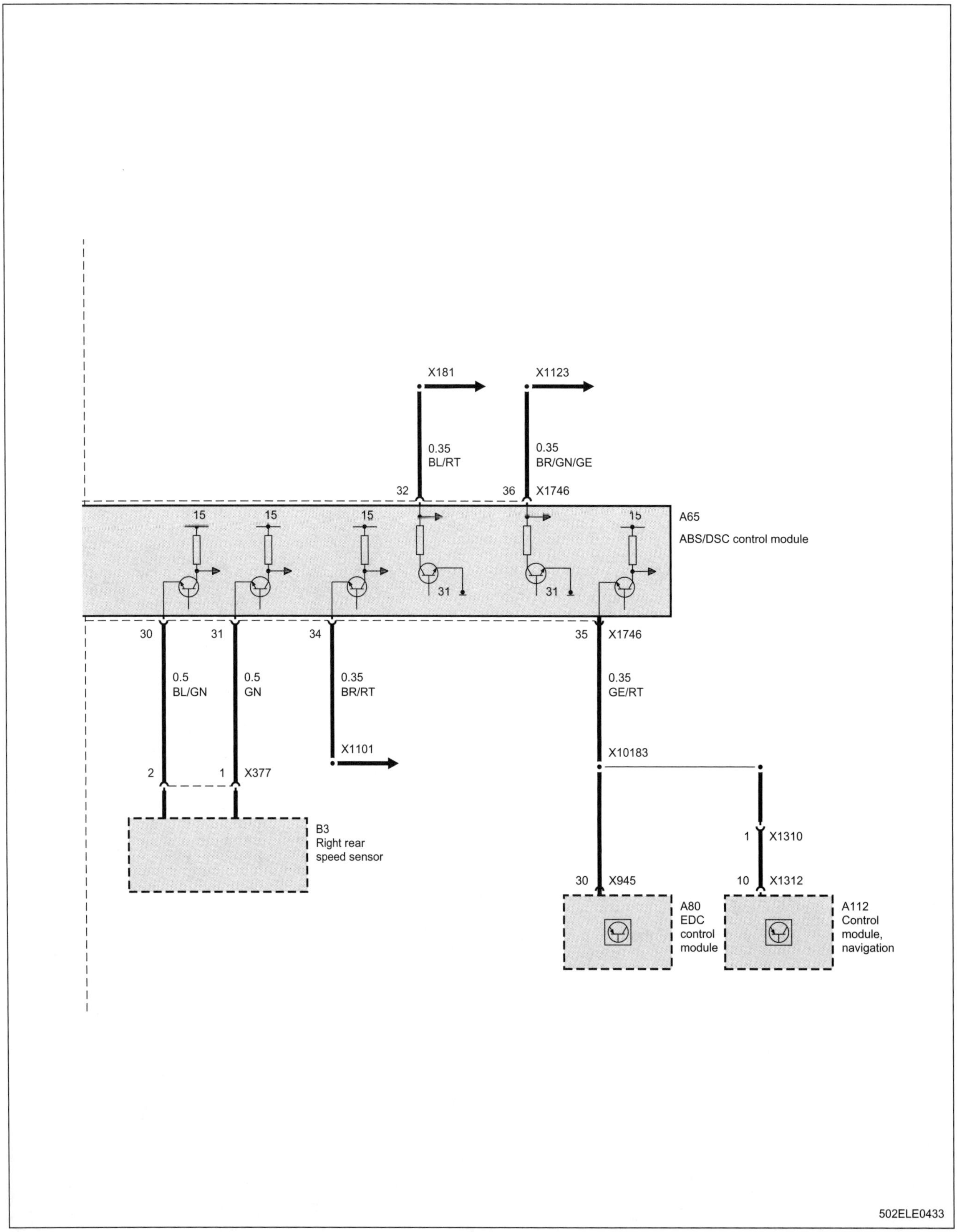

ABS/Traction Control
Wheel speed

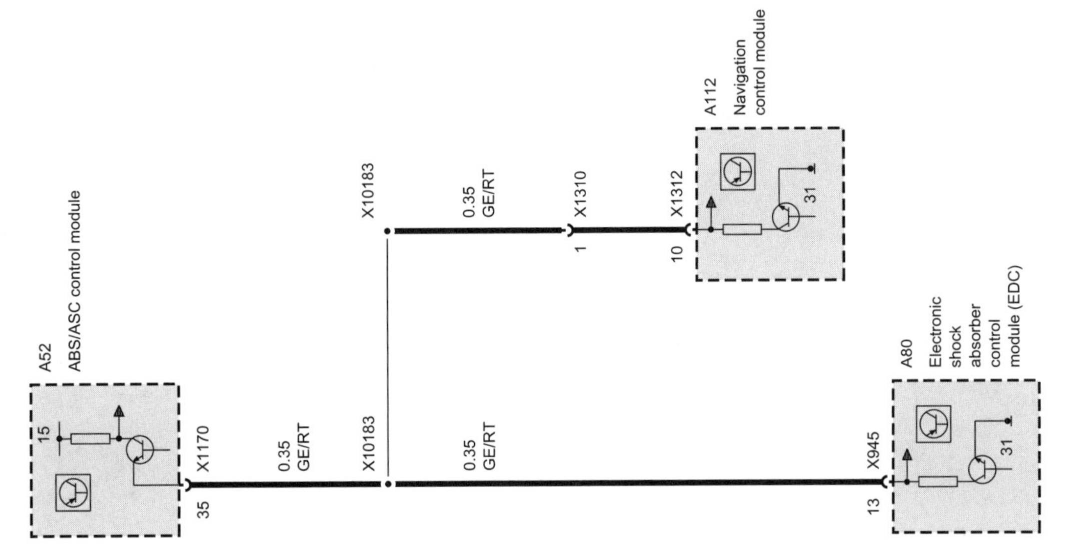

502ELE0266a

ABS/Traction Control
Wheel speed

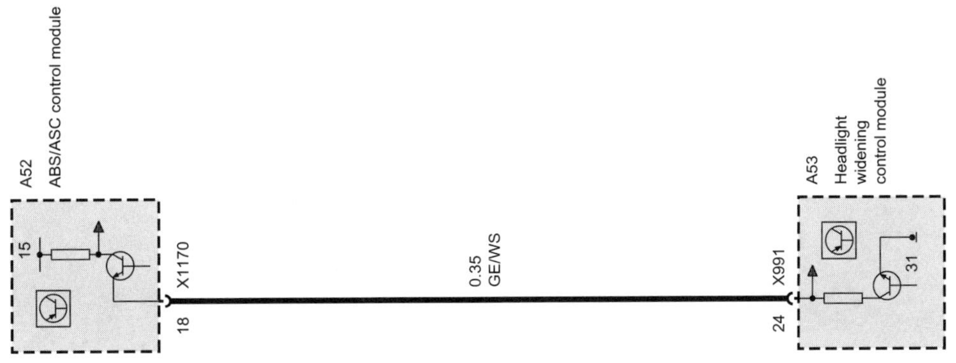

502ELE0266b

ABS/Traction Control
ABS/ASC indicator lamp

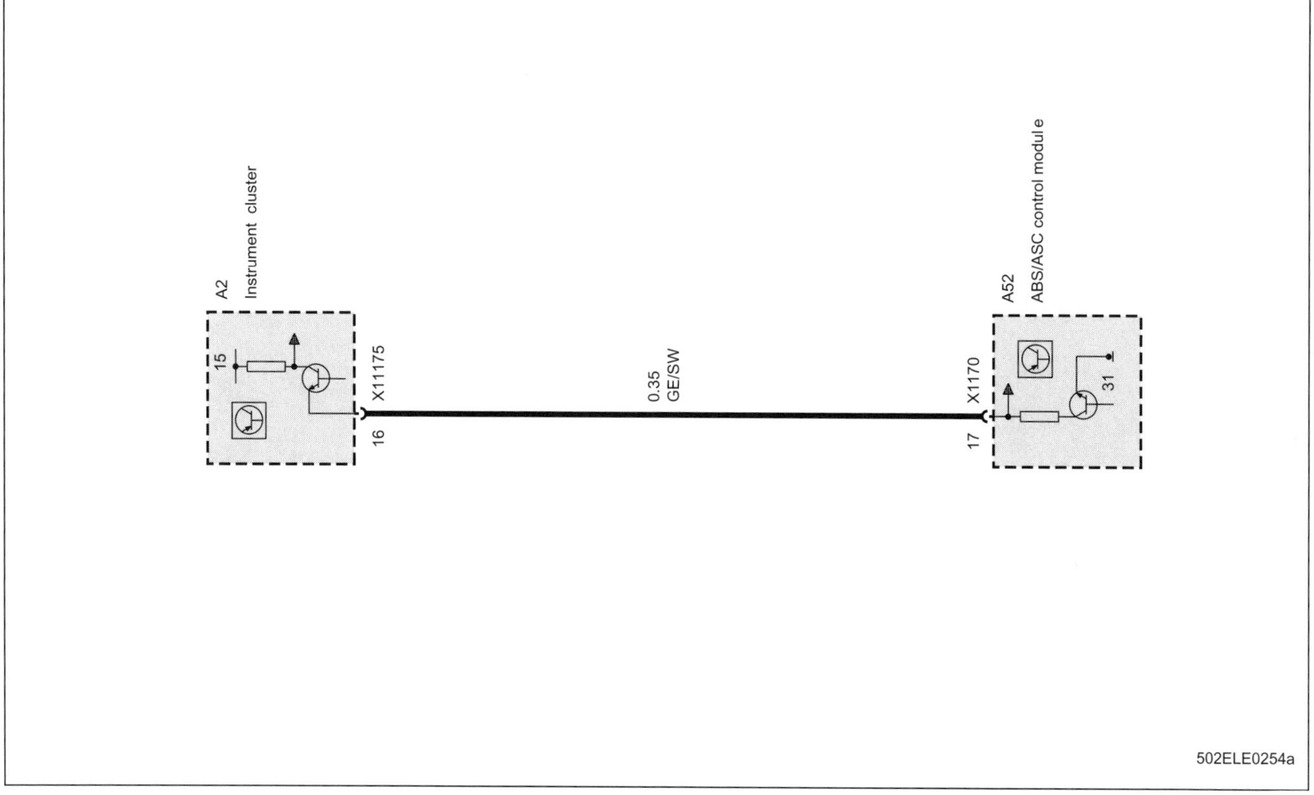

ABS/Traction Control
ASC button

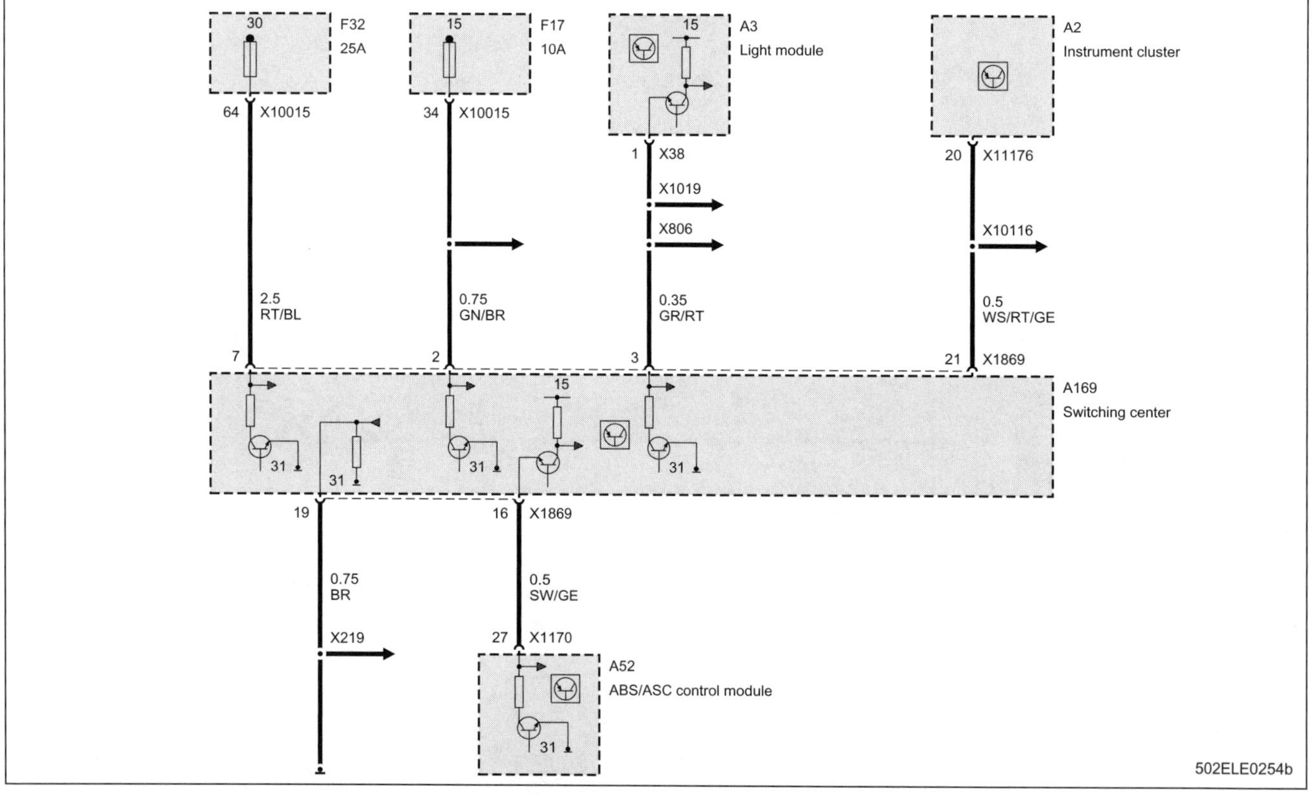

ABS/Traction Control
ABS/ASC Power
(1 of 1)

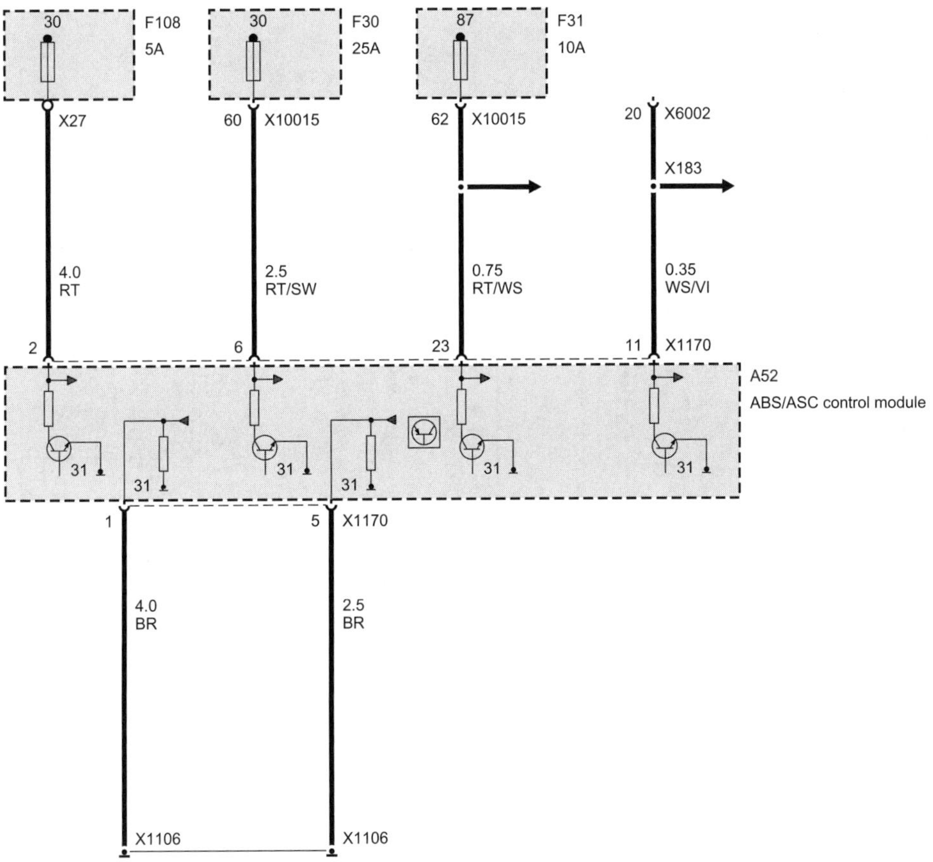

ABS/Traction Control
EDC acceleration sensors, light signal
(1 of 1)

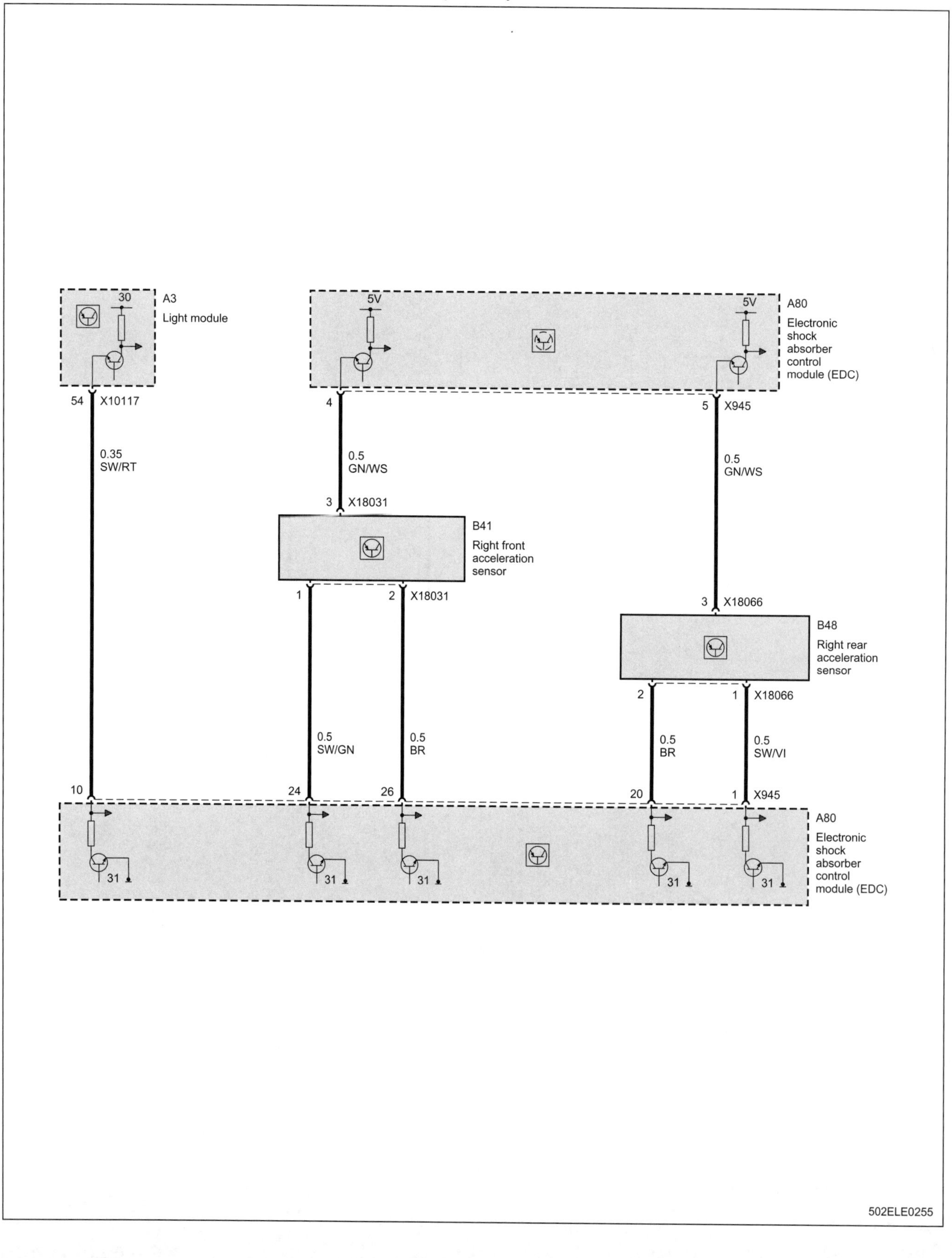

ABS/Traction Control ASC/DME interfaces (1 of 1)

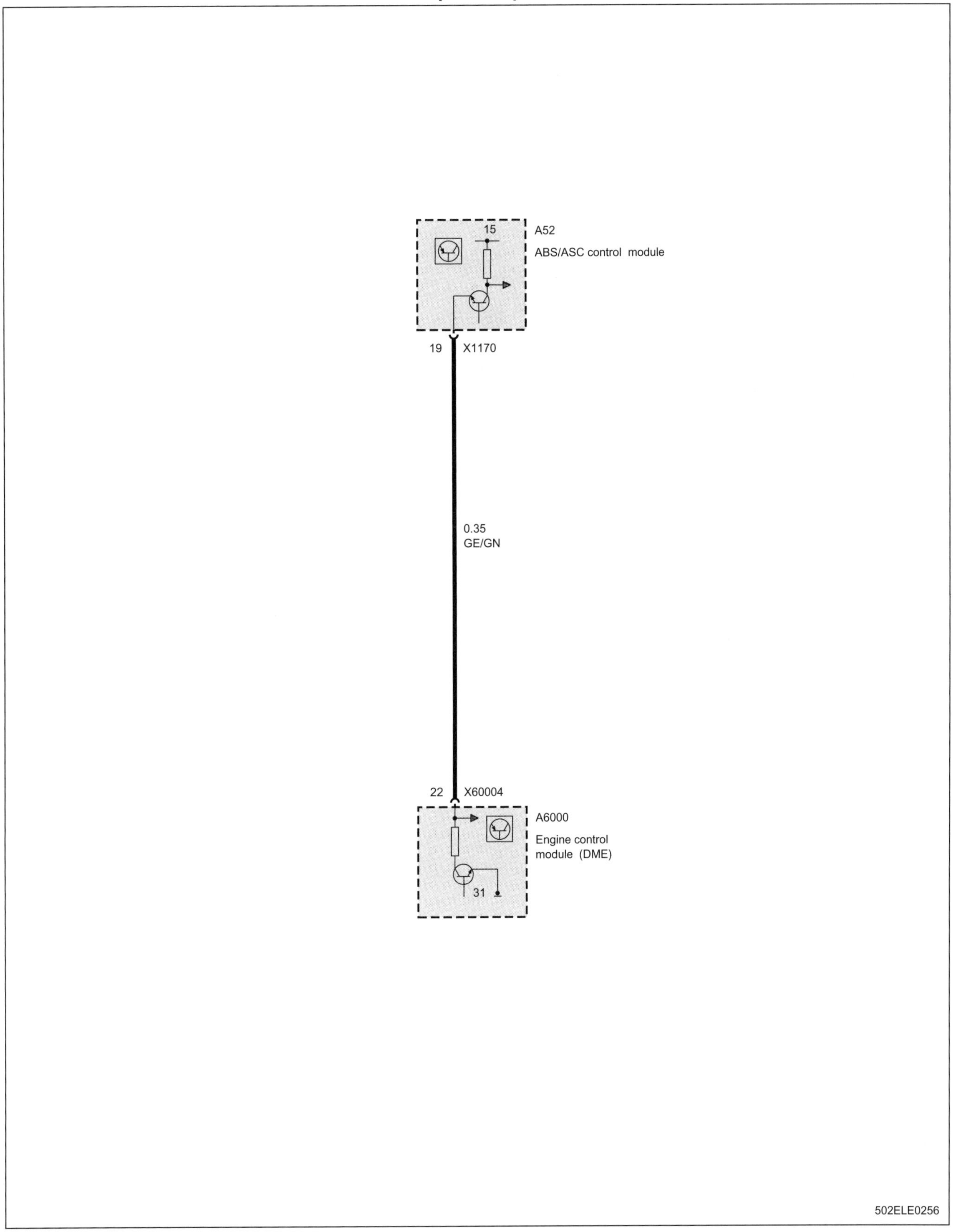

ABS/Traction Control
Rear right wheel speed (ABS/ASC)

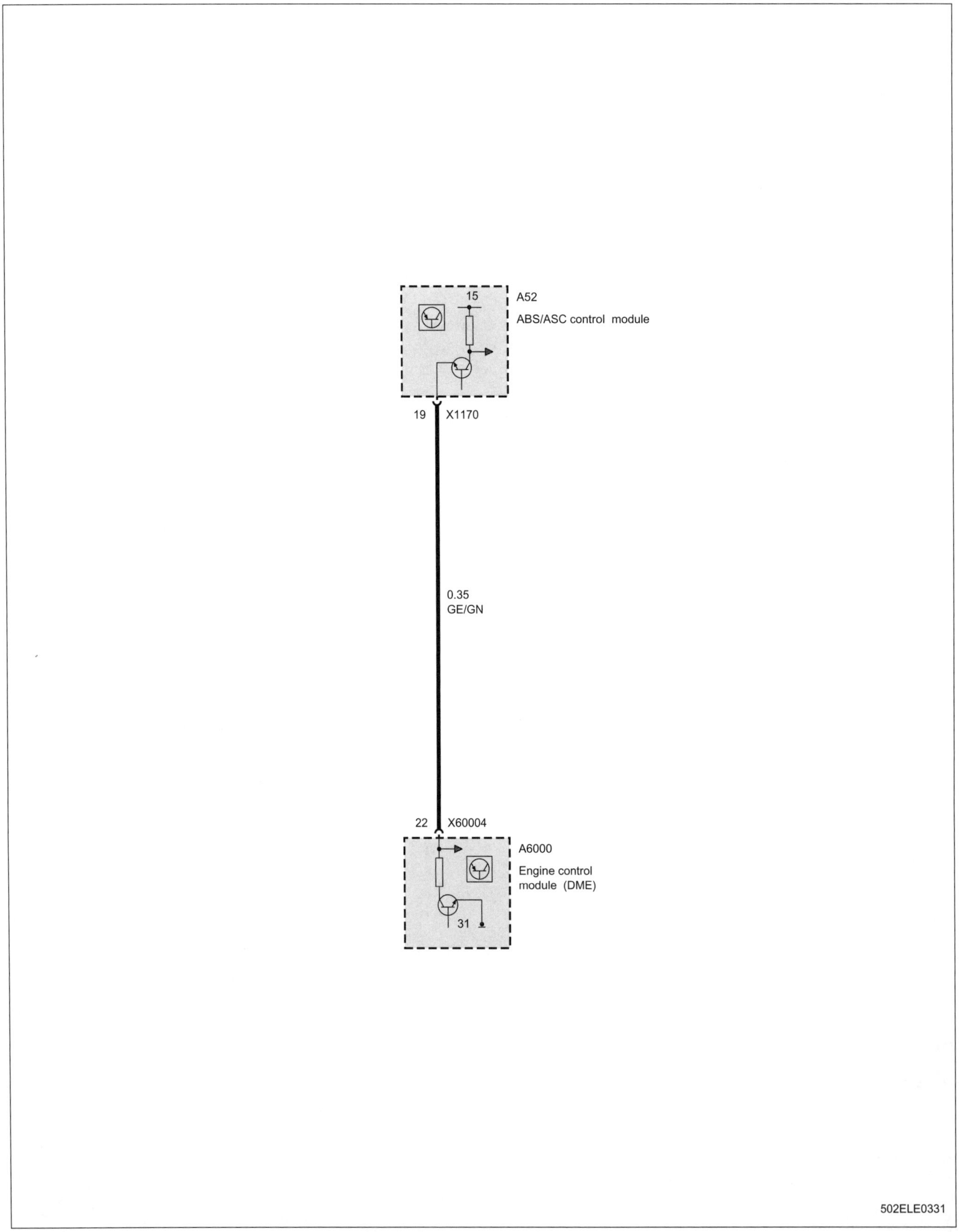

ABS/Traction Control
ABS/ASC rear wheel speed sensors
(1 of 1)

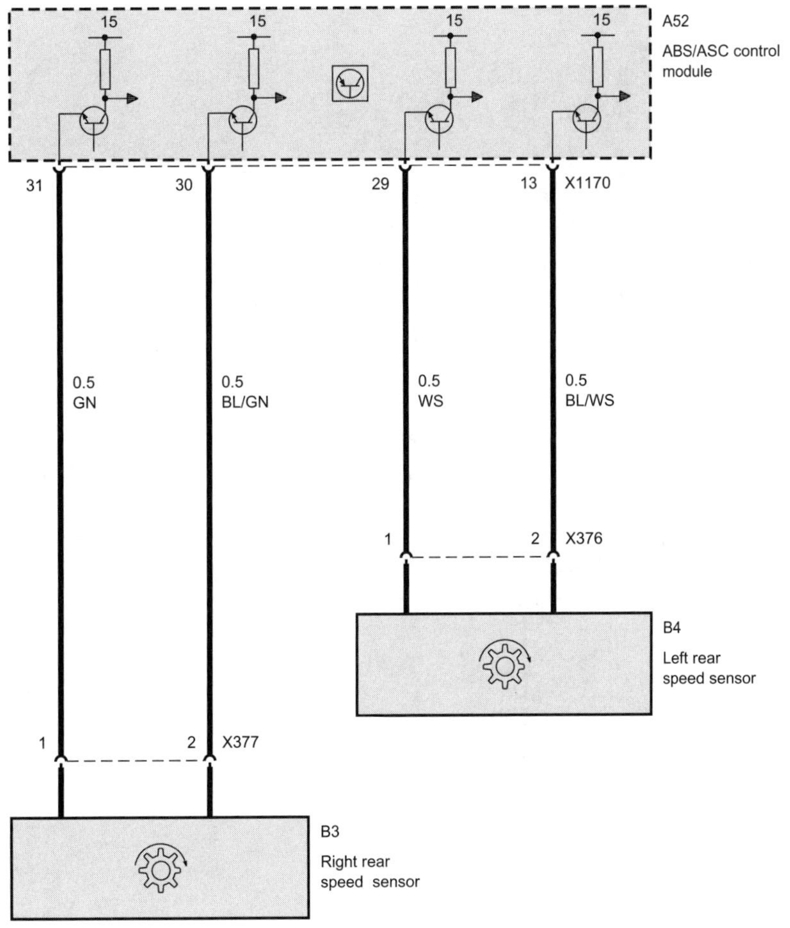

ABS/Traction Control
Steering-angle sensor
(1 of 1)

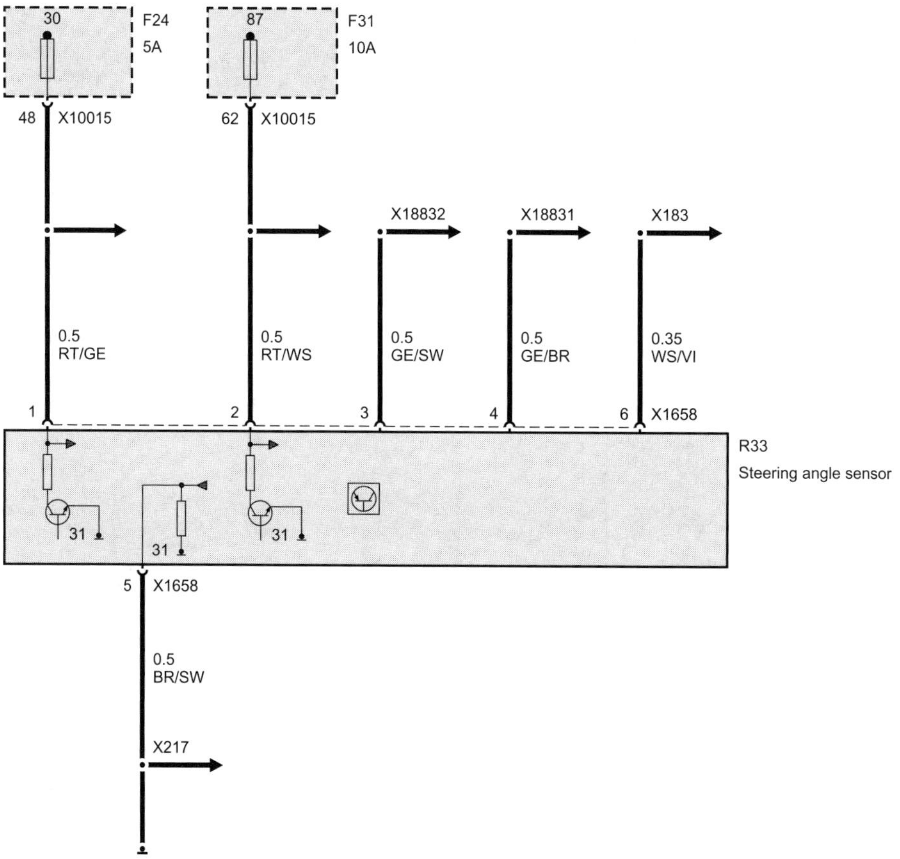

502ELE0279

ABS/Traction Control
ABS/ASC front wheel speed sensors
(1 of 1)

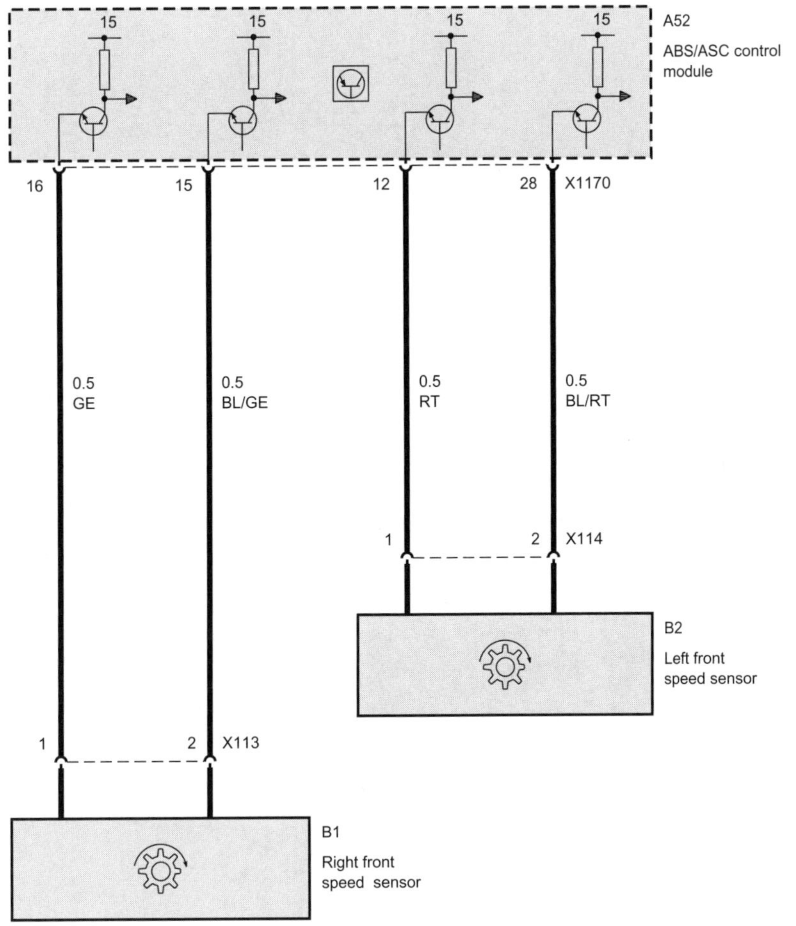

ABS/Traction Control
ABS/ASC wheel speed, left rear
(1 of 1)

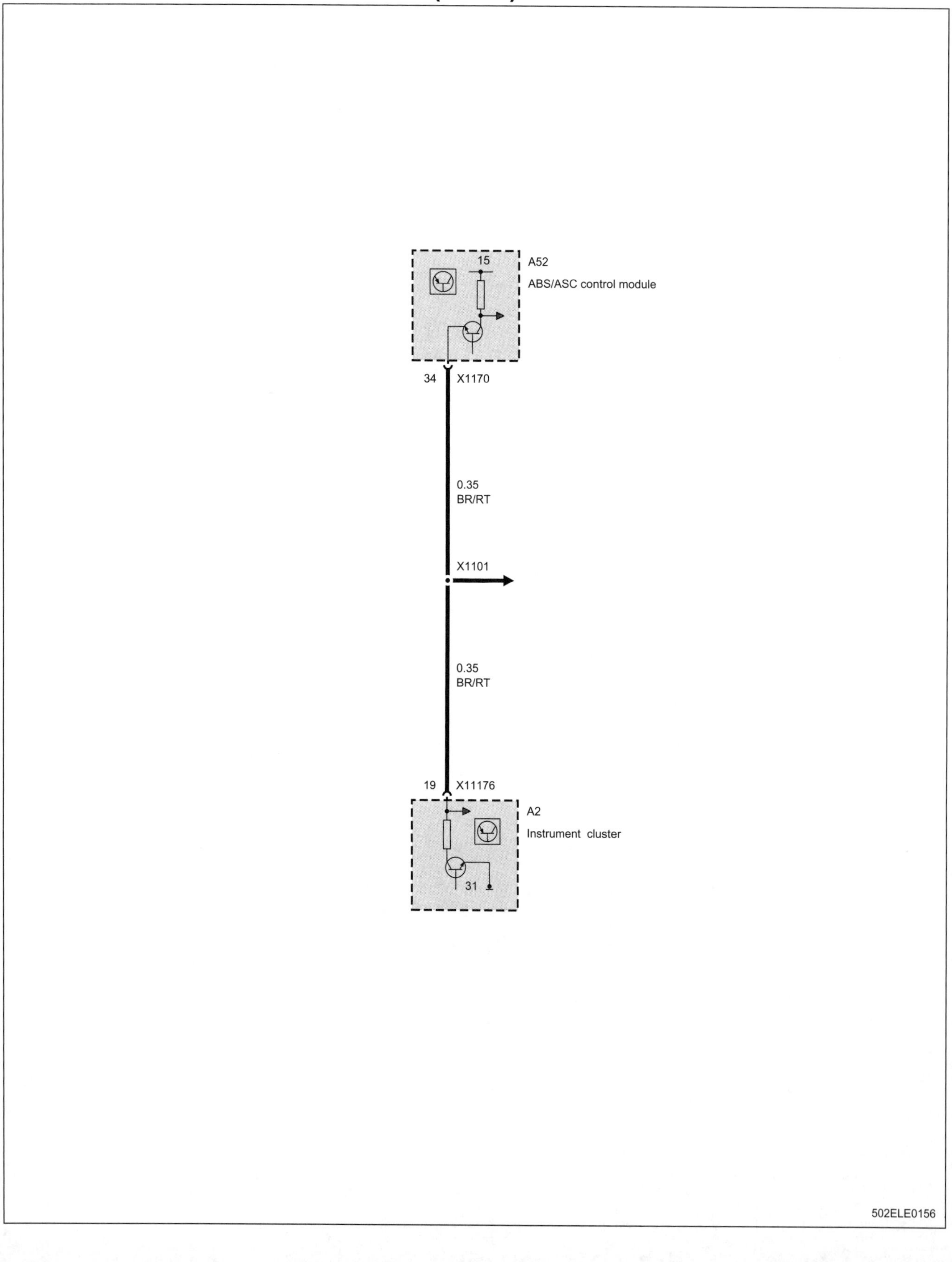

ABS/Traction Control
ABS/ASC wheel speed, right front
(1 of 1)

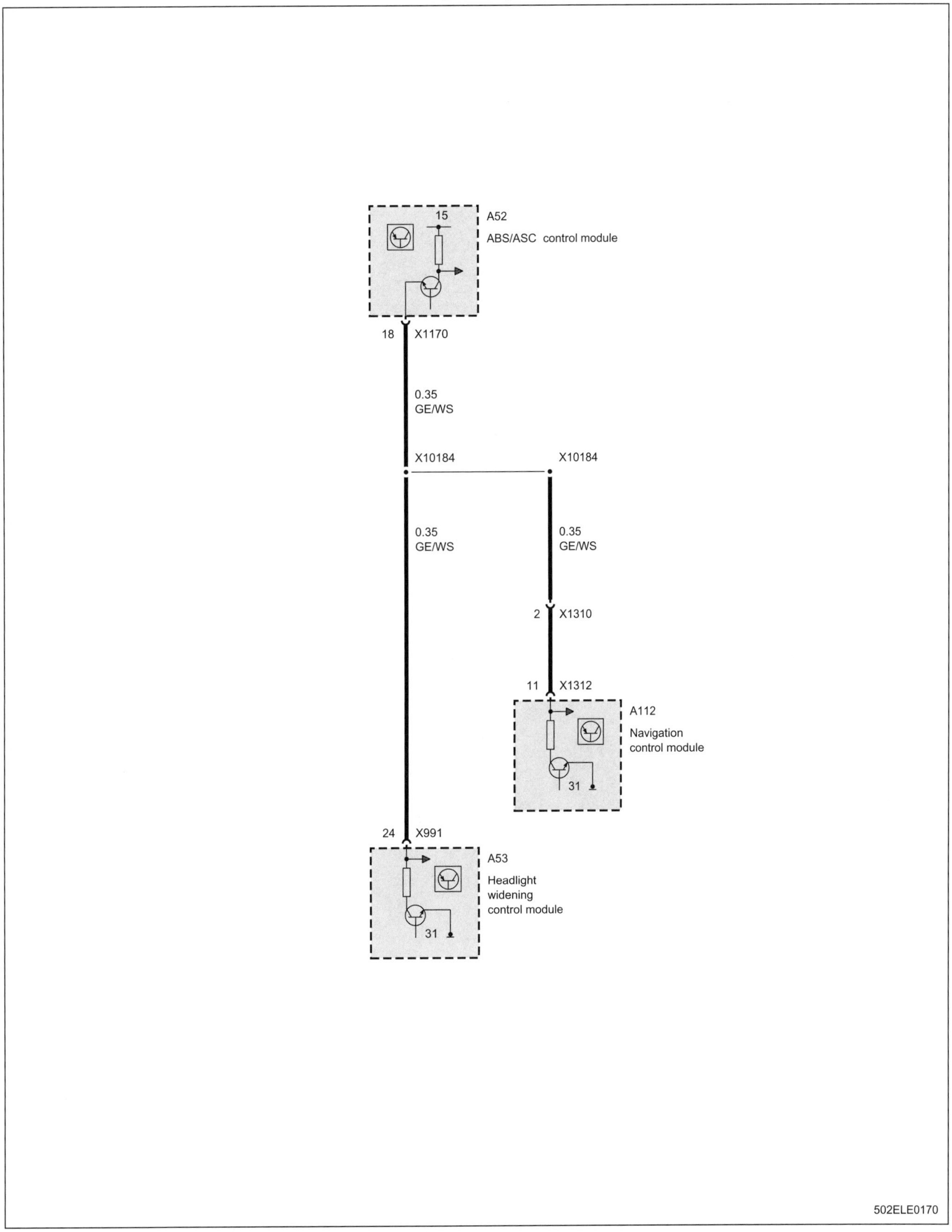

ABS/Traction Control
ABS/DSC indicator lamp
(1 of 1)

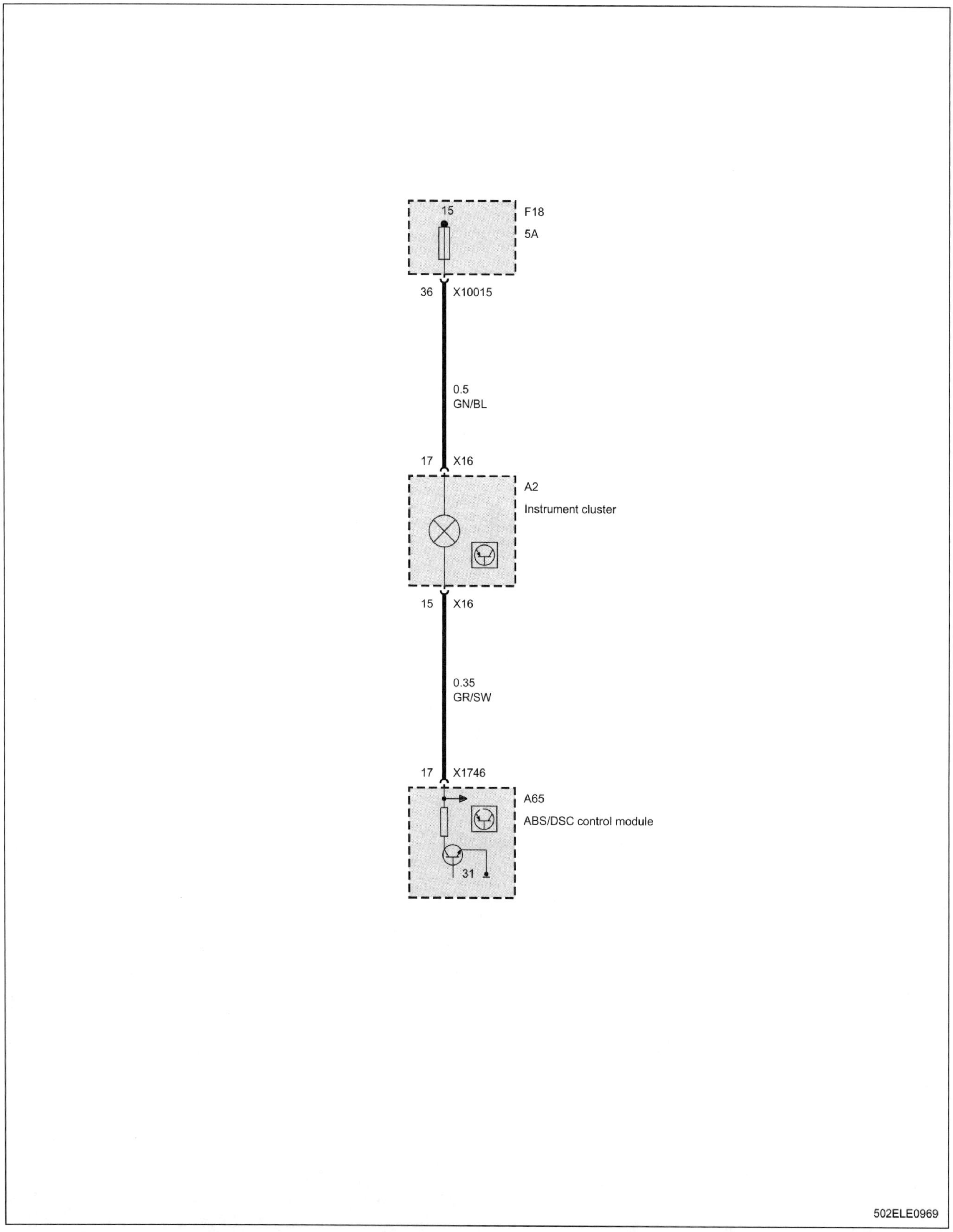

ABS/Traction Control
ABS/DSC power
(1 of 1)

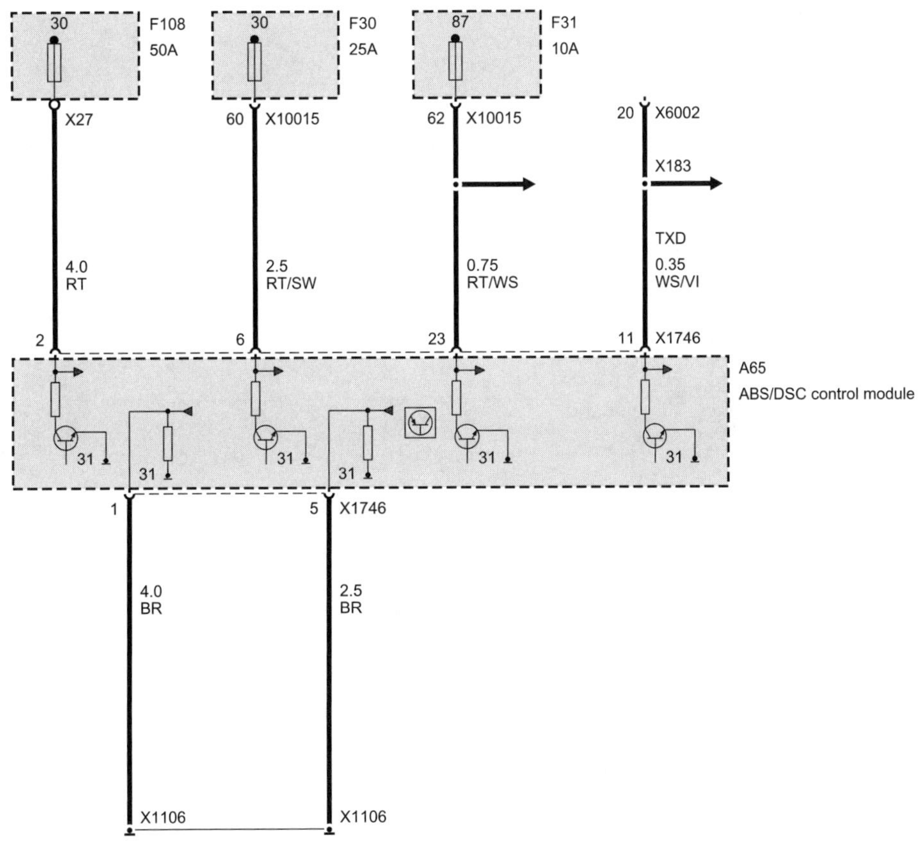

502ELE0970

ABS/Traction Control
CAN interface (DSC)
(1 of 2)

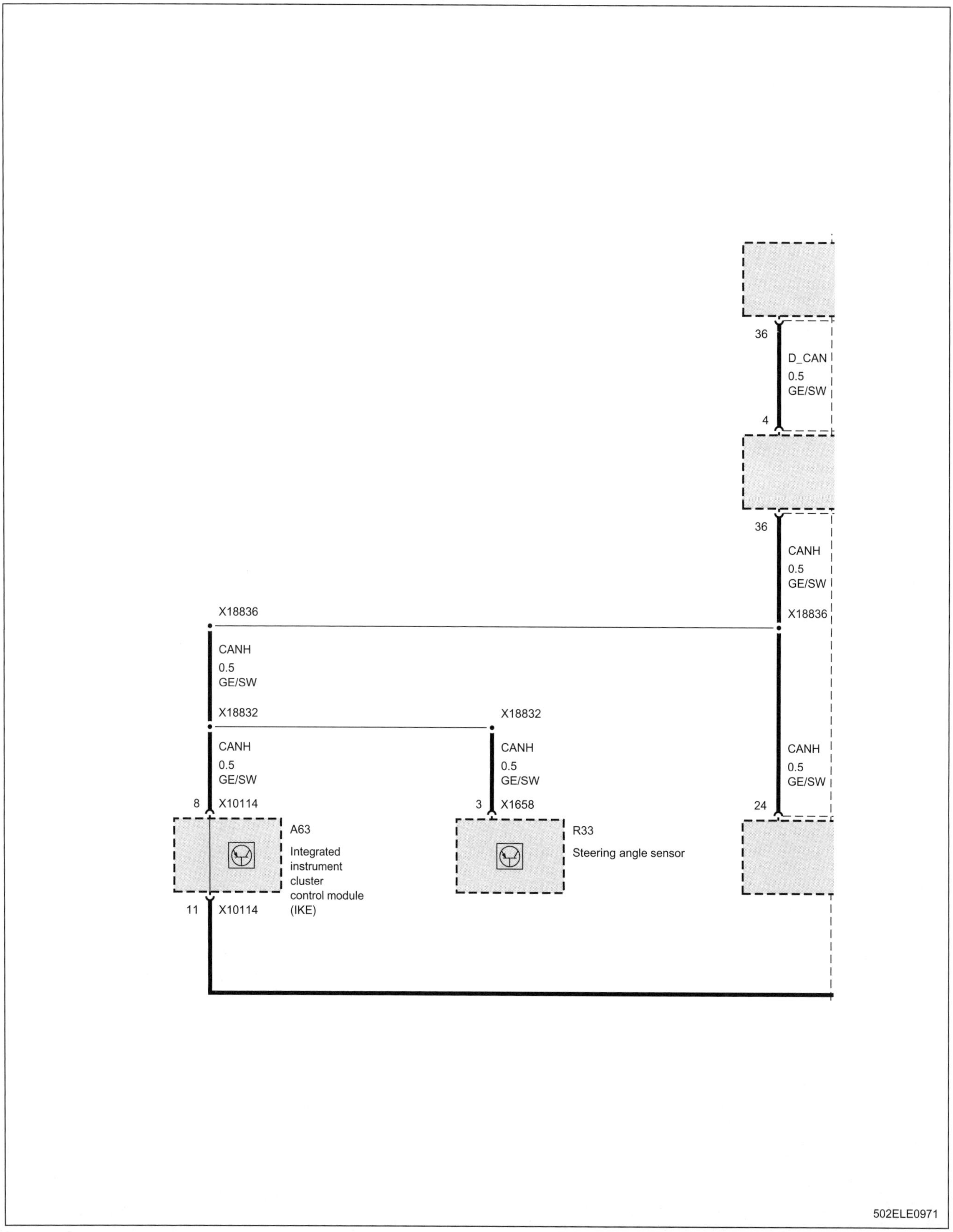
36
D_CAN
0.5
GE/SW
4
36
CANH
0.5
GE/SW
X18836
X18836
CANH
0.5
GE/SW
X18832
X18832
CANH
0.5
GE/SW
8
X10114
CANH
0.5
GE/SW
3
X1658
CANH
0.5
GE/SW
24
A63
Integrated instrument cluster control module (IKE)
R33
Steering angle sensor
11
X10114
502ELE0971

ABS/Traction Control
CAN interface (DSC)
(2 of 2)

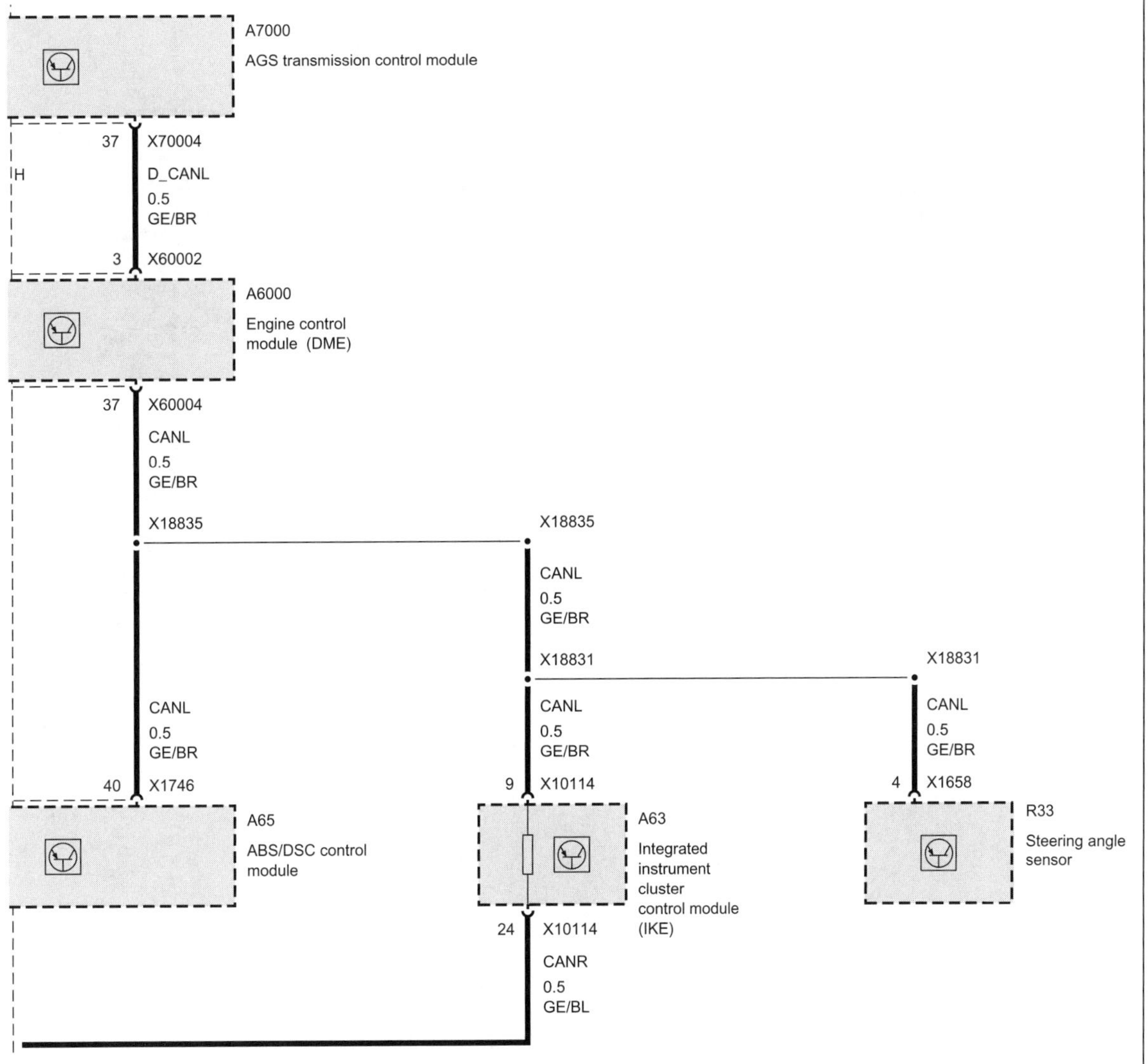
A7000
AGS transmission control module
37
X70004
H
D_CANL
0.5
GE/BR
3
X60002
A6000
Engine control module (DME)
37
X60004
CANL
0.5
GE/BR
X18835
X18835
CANL
0.5
GE/BR
X18831
X18831
CANL
0.5
GE/BR
CANL
0.5
GE/BR
CANL
0.5
GE/BR
40
X1746
9
X10114
4
X1658
A65
ABS/DSC control module
A63
Integrated instrument cluster control module (IKE)
R33
Steering angle sensor
24
X10114
CANR
0.5
GE/BL
502ELE0972

ABS/Traction Control
DSC button
(1 of 1)

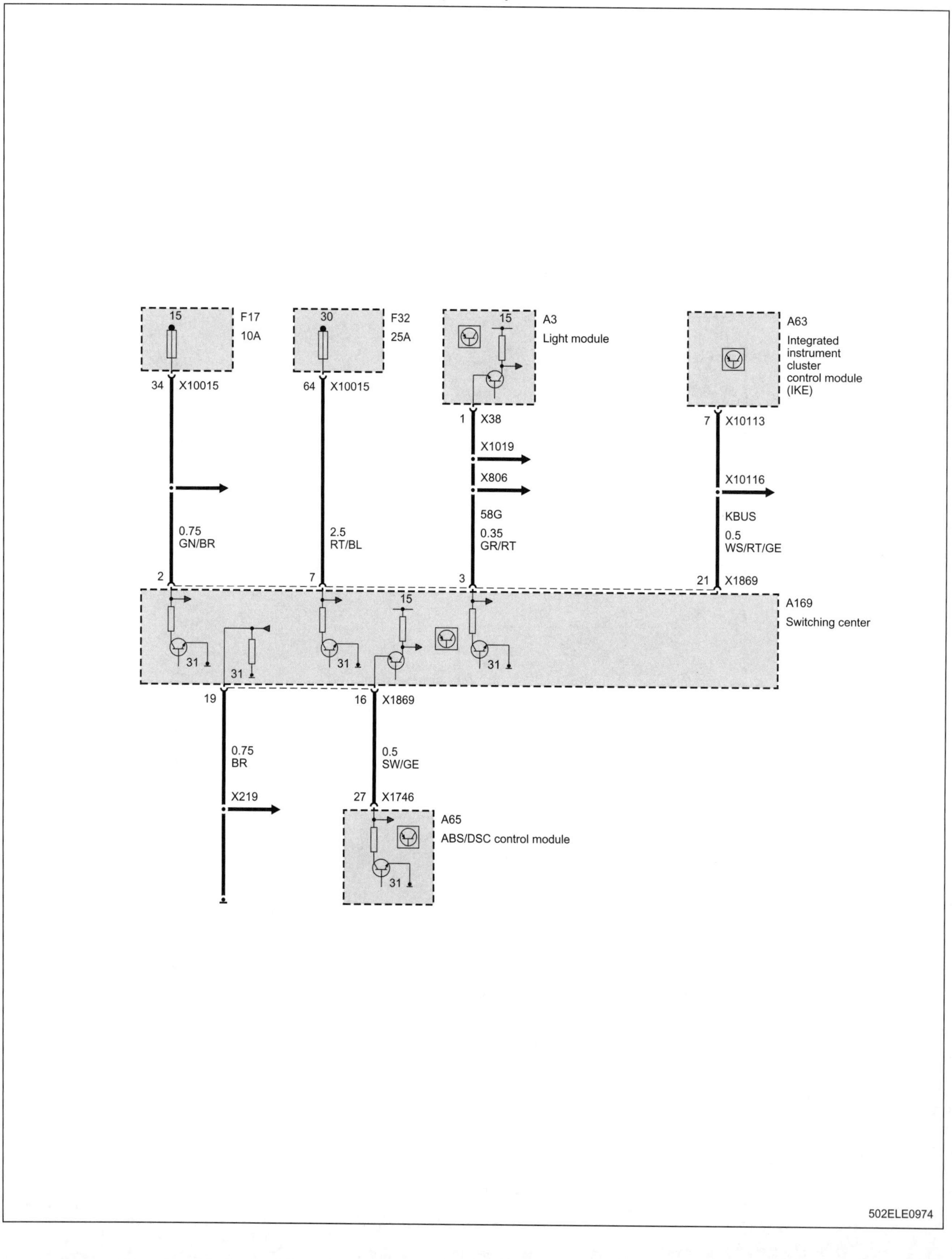

502ELE0974

ABS/Traction Control
Front wheel speed sensor (DSC)
(1 of 1)

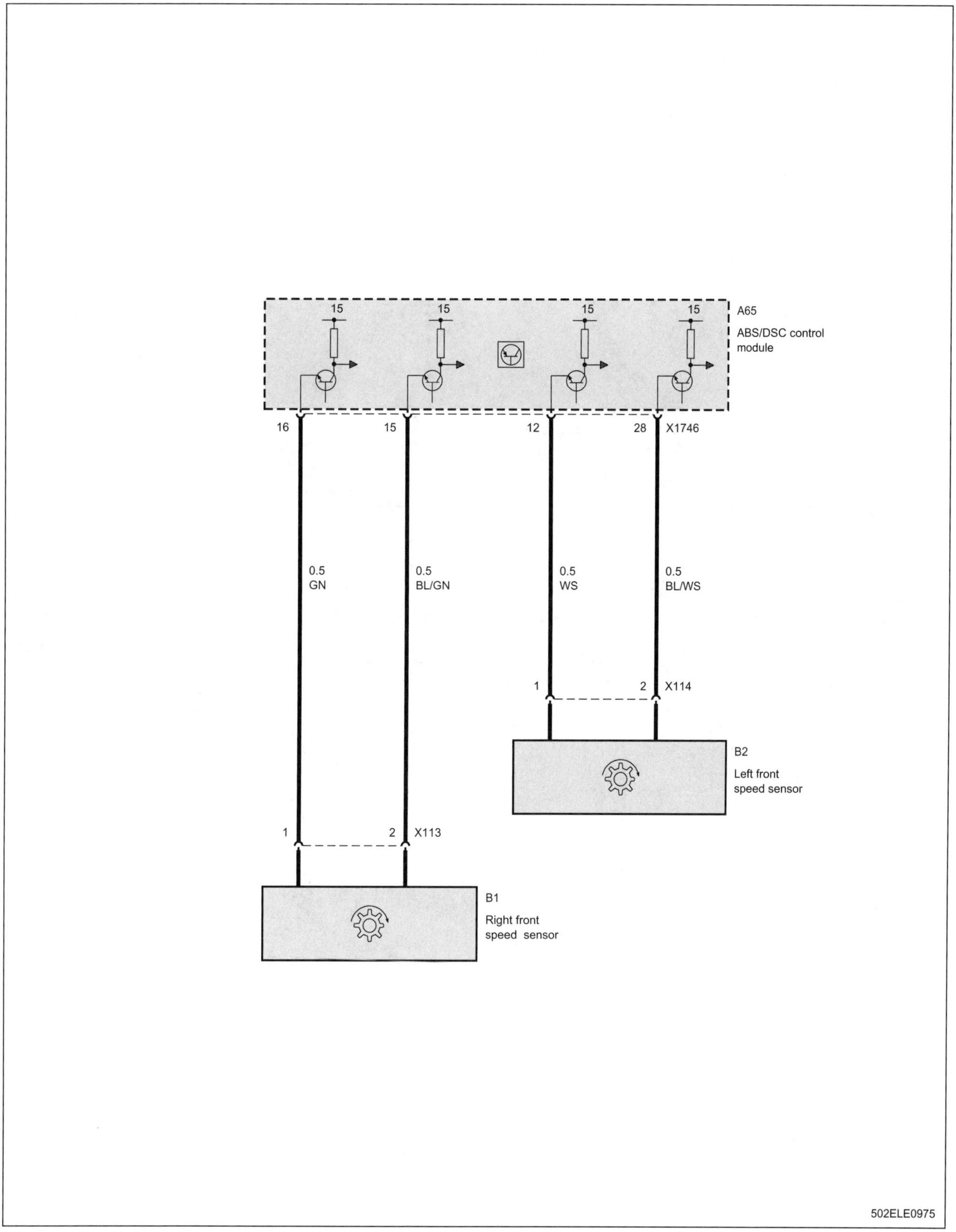

ABS/Traction Control
Hydraulic unit - solenoid valves (DSC)
(1 of 2)

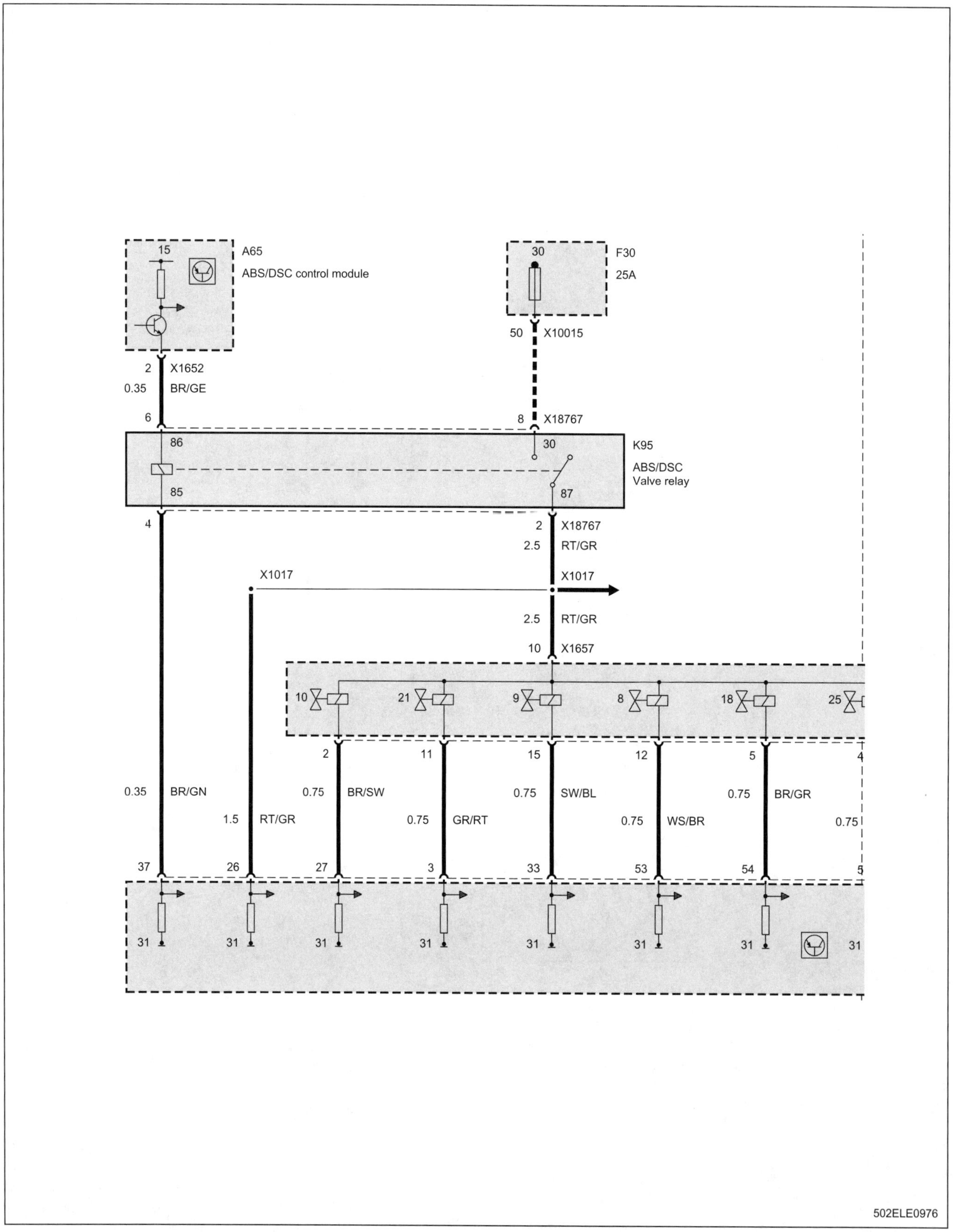

ABS/Traction Control
Hydraulic unit - solenoid valves (DSC)
(2 of 2)

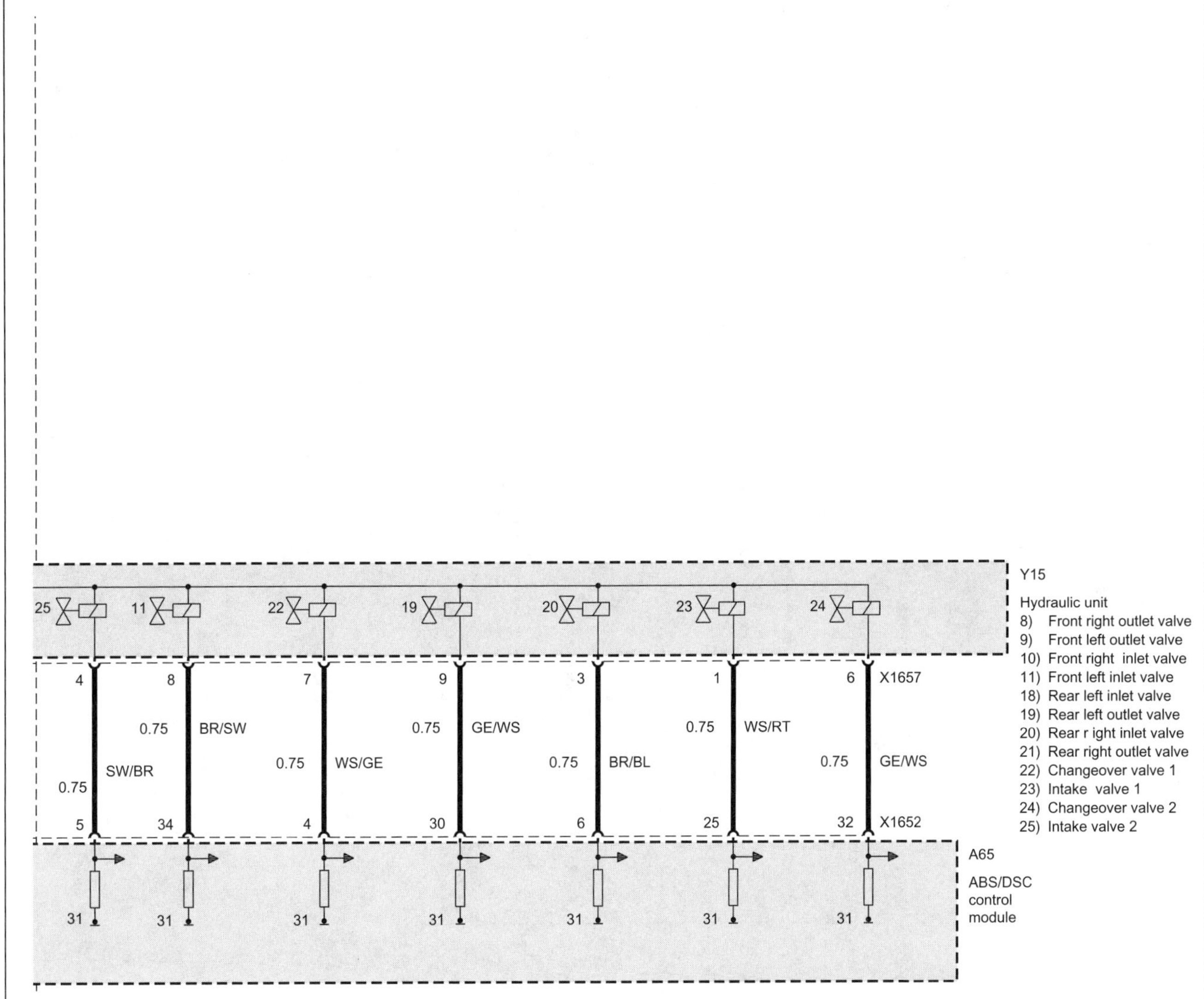

502ELE0977

ABS/Traction Control
Precharge pump (DSC)
(1 of 1)

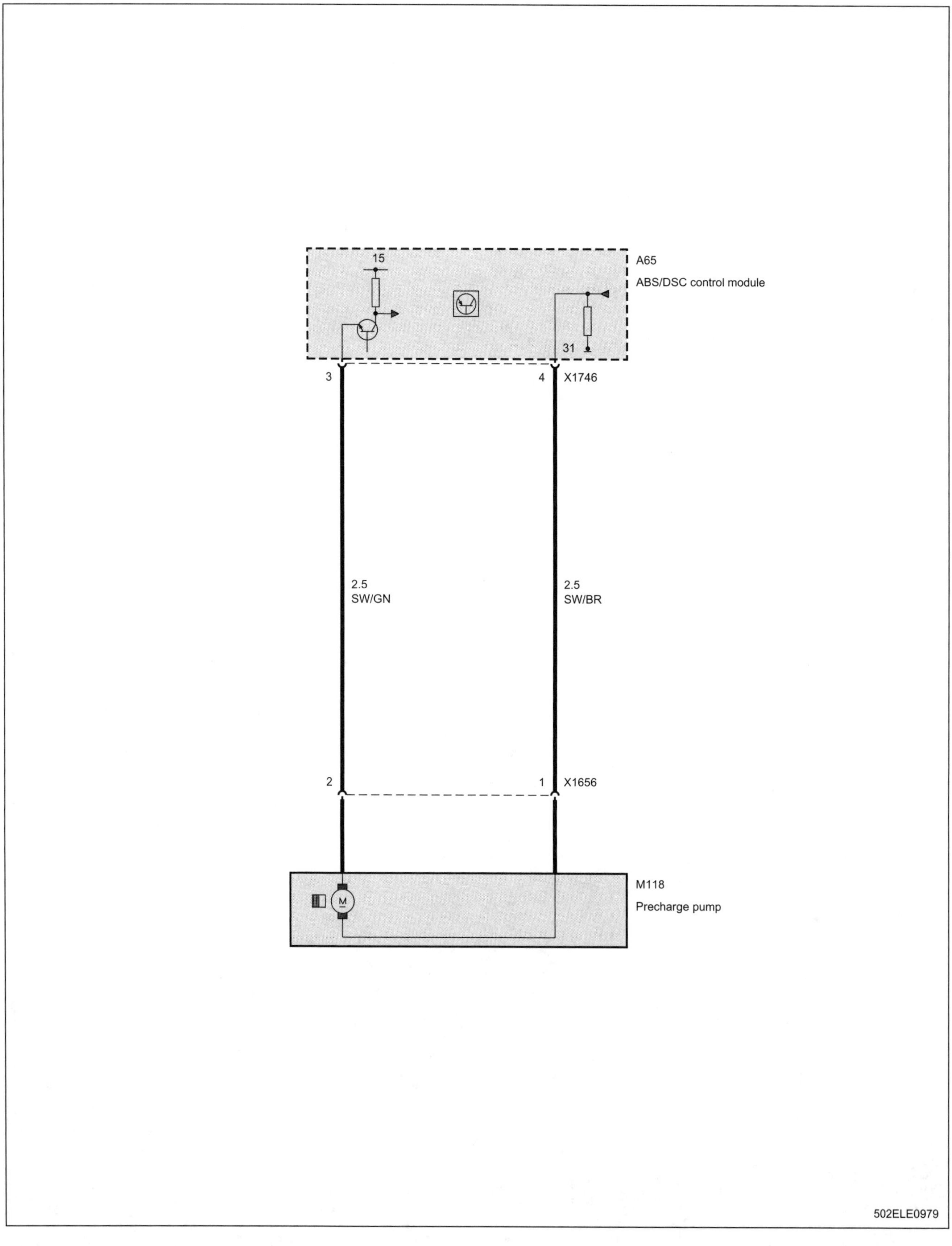

ABS/Traction Control
Pressure sensor (DSC)
(1 of 1)

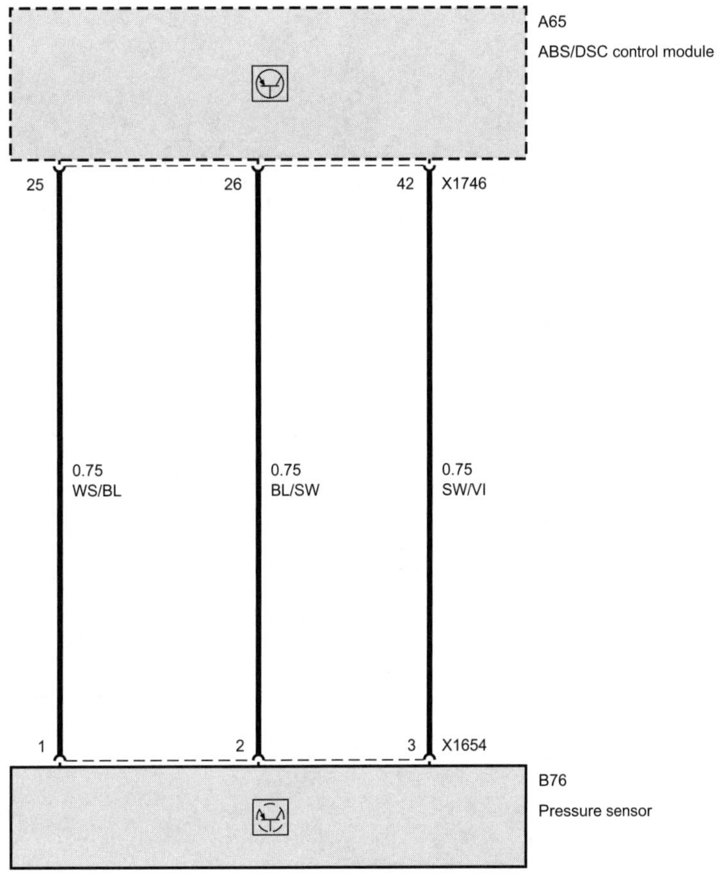
A65
ABS/DSC control module
25
26
42
X1746
0.75
WS/BL
0.75
BL/SW
0.75
SW/VI
1
2
3
X1654
B76
Pressure sensor
502ELE0980

ABS/Traction Control
Rear wheel speed sensor (DSC)
(1 of 1)

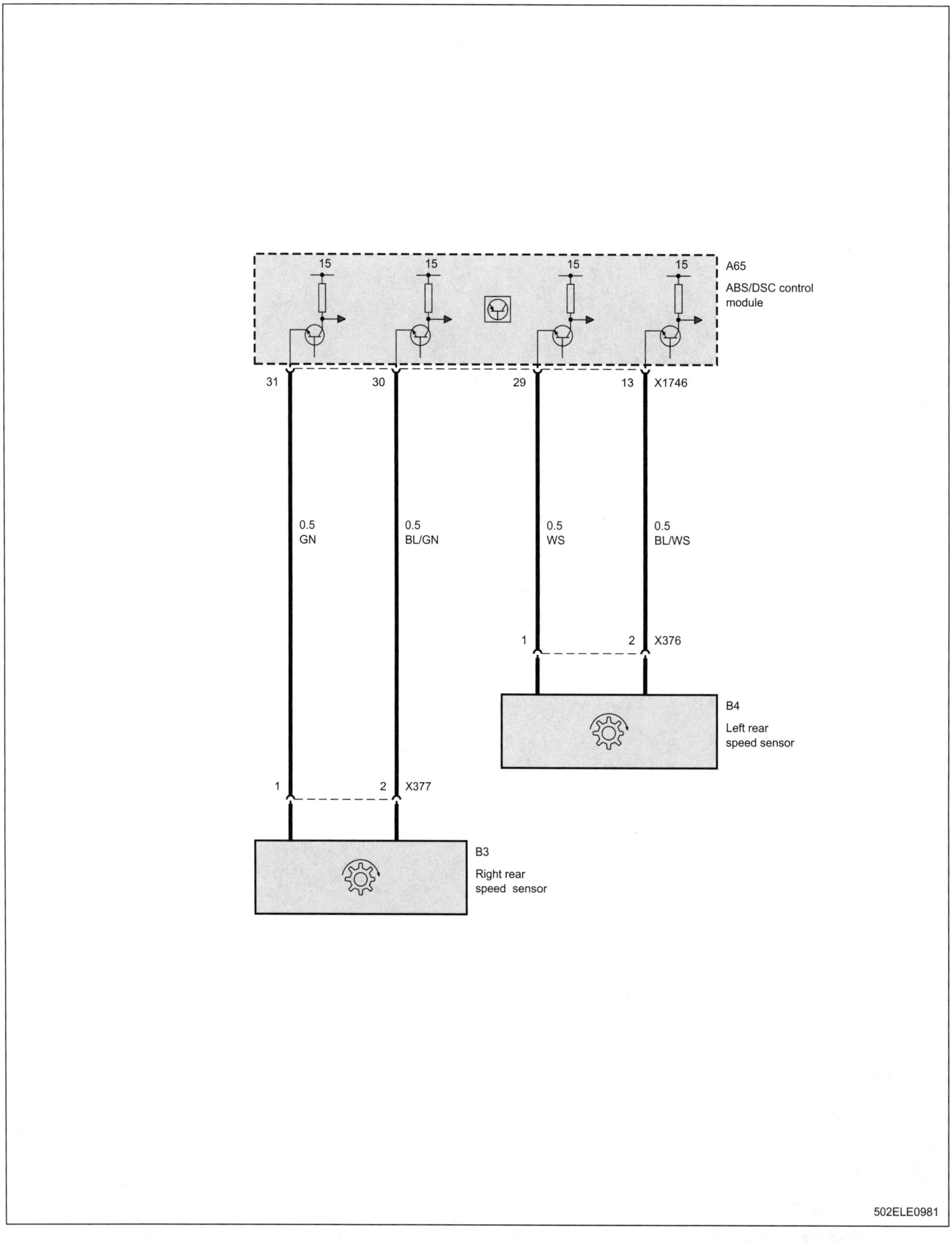

ABS/Traction Control
Steering-angle sensor (DSC)
(1 of 1)

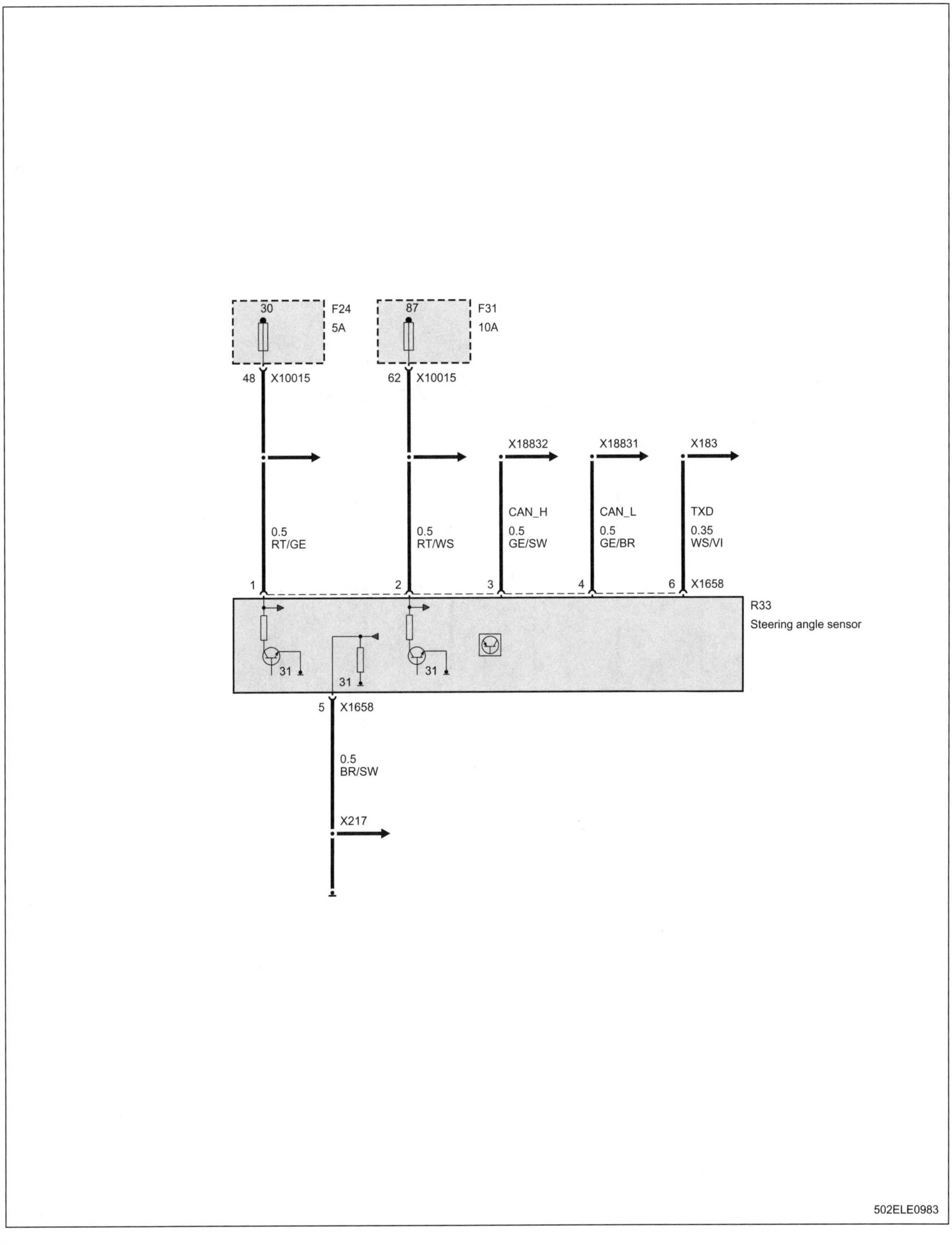

ABS/Traction Control
Yaw sensor (DSC)
(1 of 1)

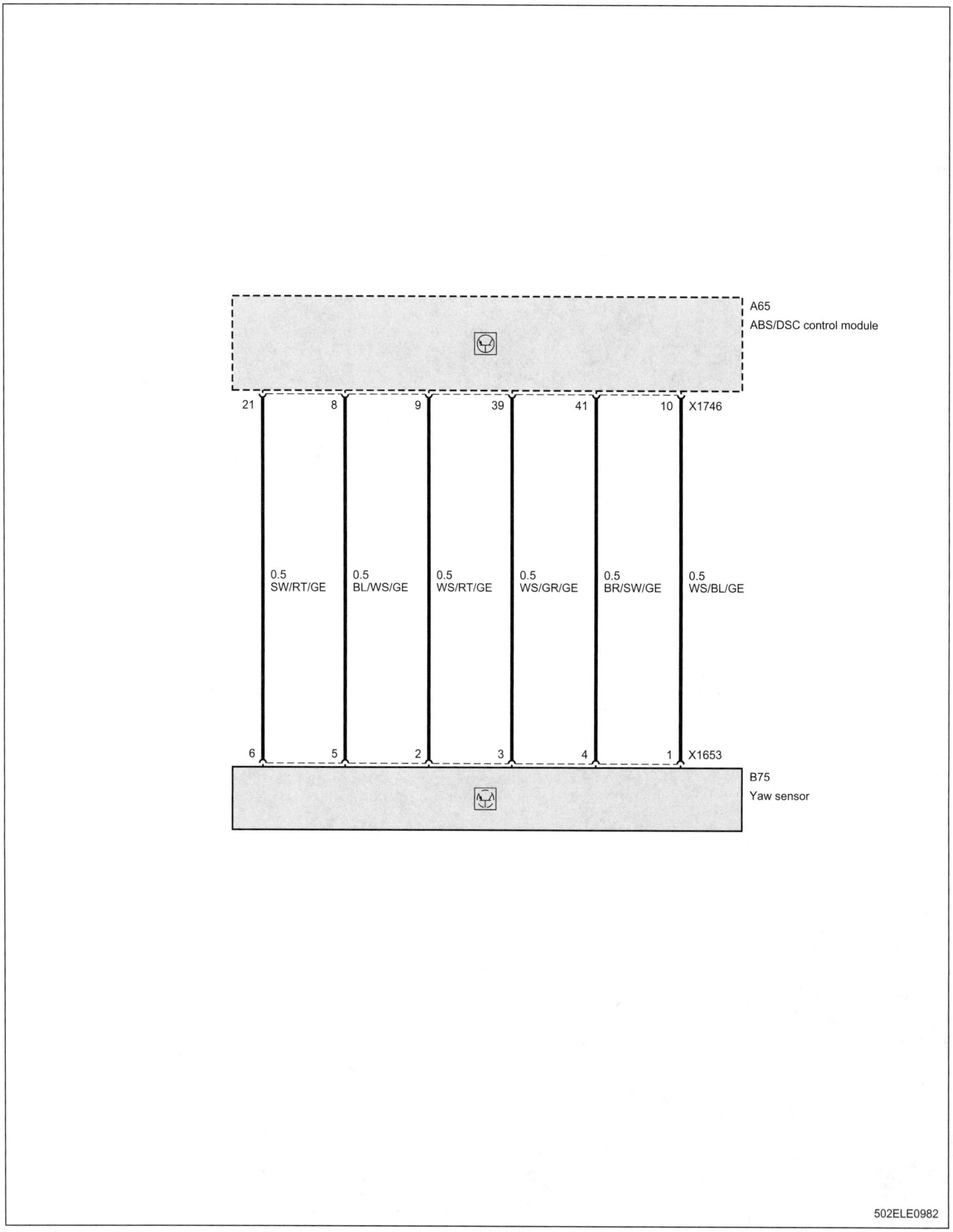
A65
ABS/DSC control module
21
8
9
39
41
10
X1746
0.5
SW/RT/GE
0.5
BL/WS/GE
0.5
WS/RT/GE
0.5
WS/GR/GE
0.5
BR/SW/GE
0.5
WS/BL/GE
6
5
2
3
4
1
X1653
B75
Yaw sensor
502ELE0982

Air Conditioning and Heating Functions (overview)
(1 of 4)

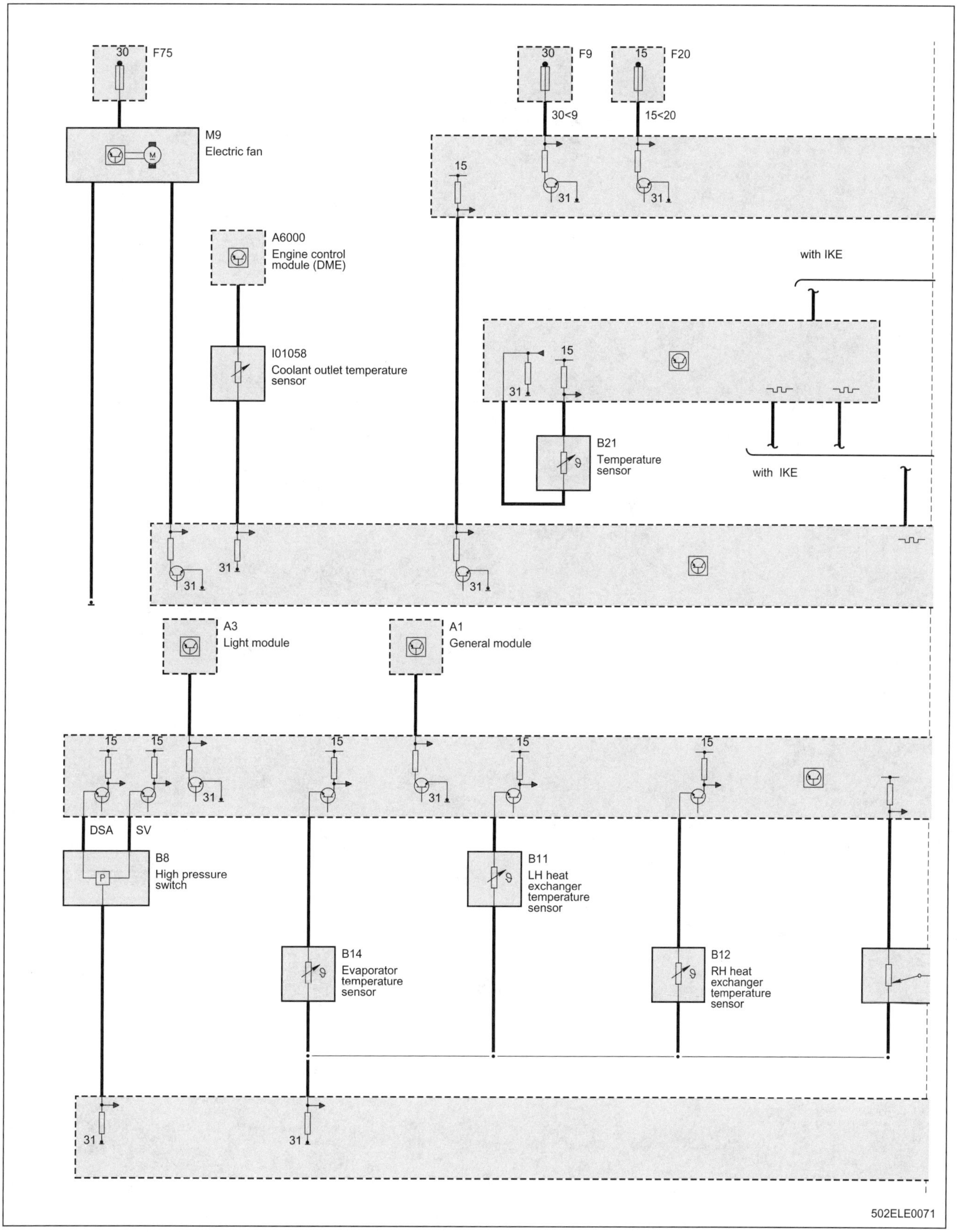

Air Conditioning and Heating Functions (overview)
(2 of 4)

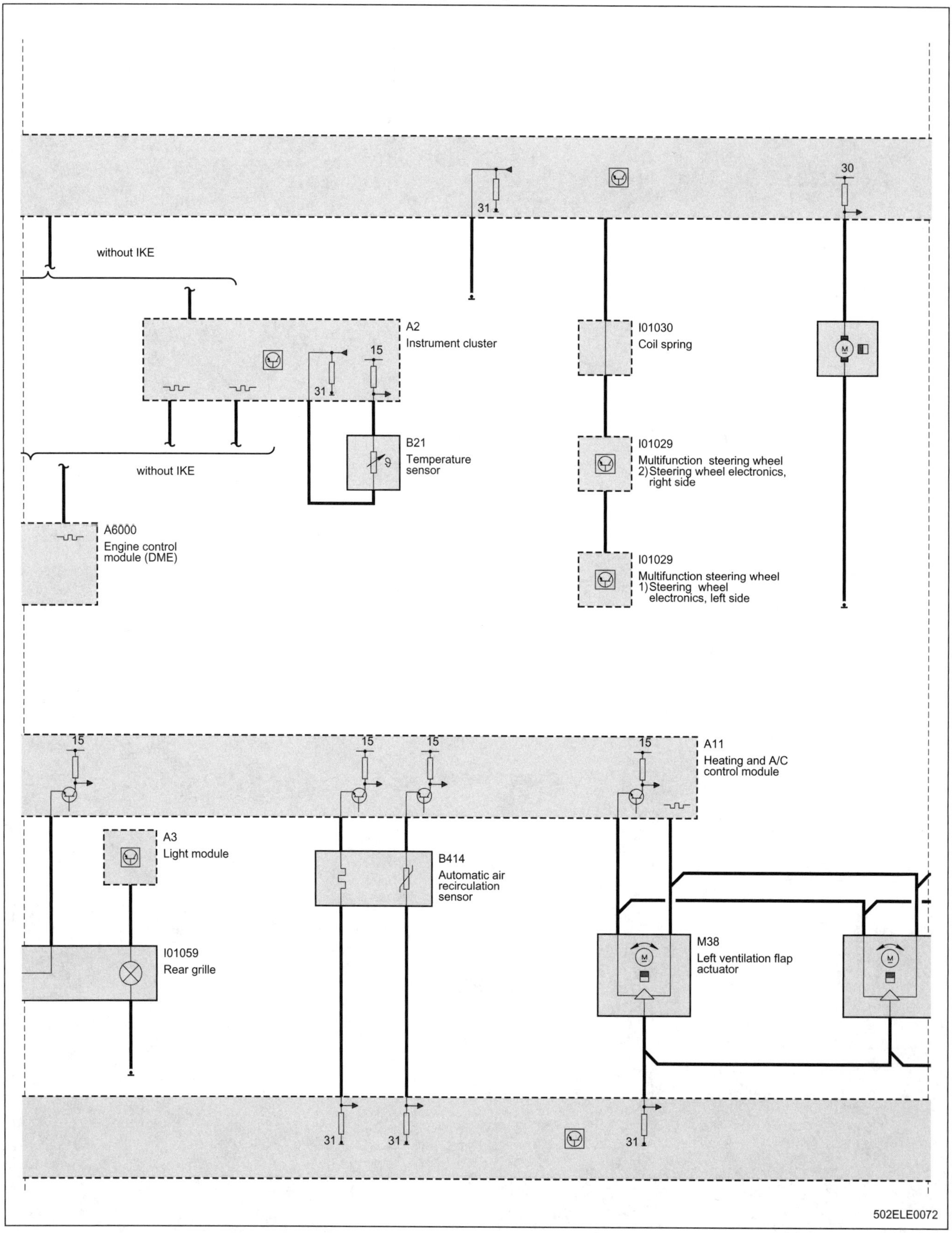

Air Conditioning and Heating Functions (overview)
(3 of 4)

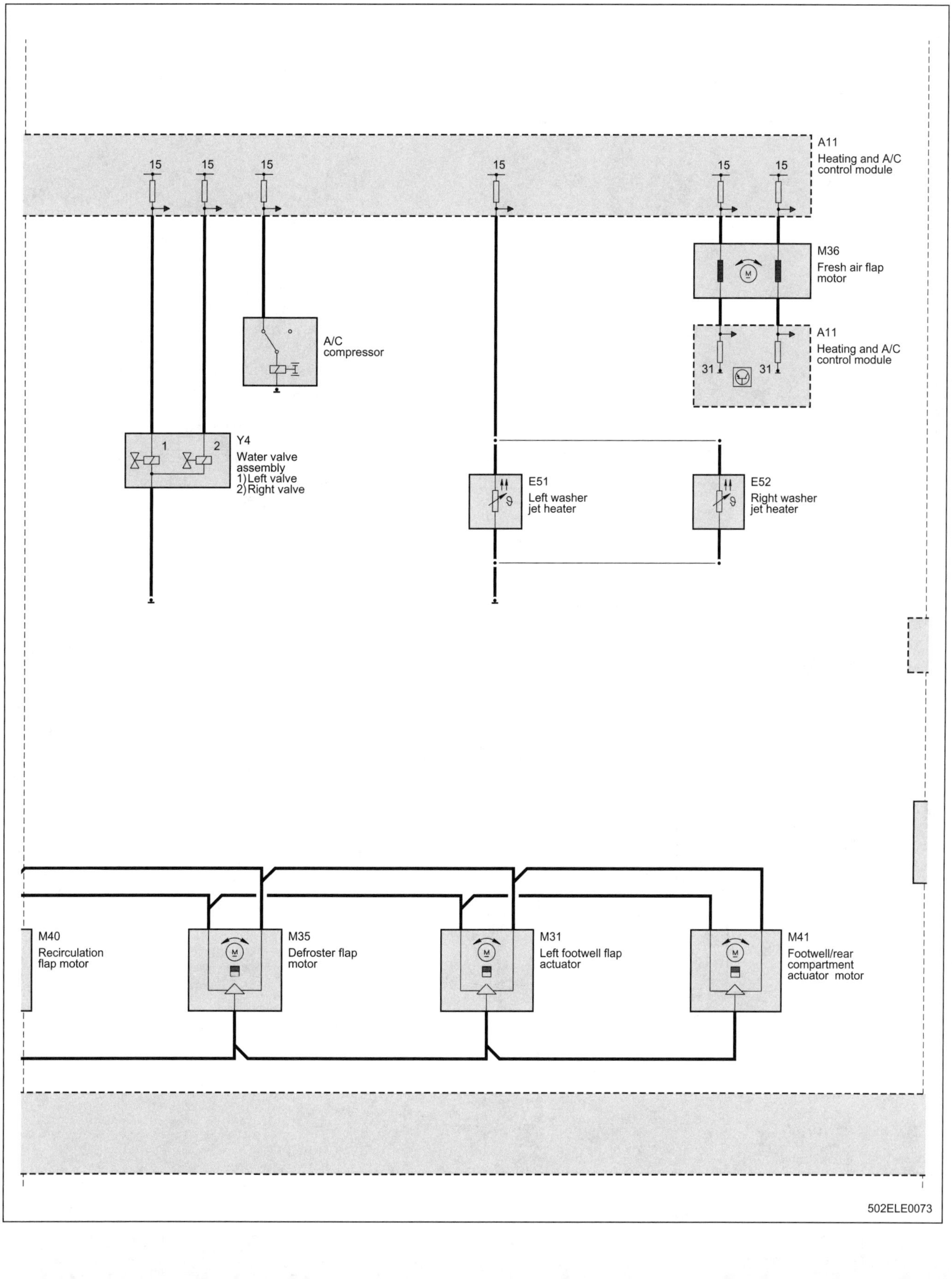

Air Conditioning and Heating Functions (overview)
(4 of 4)

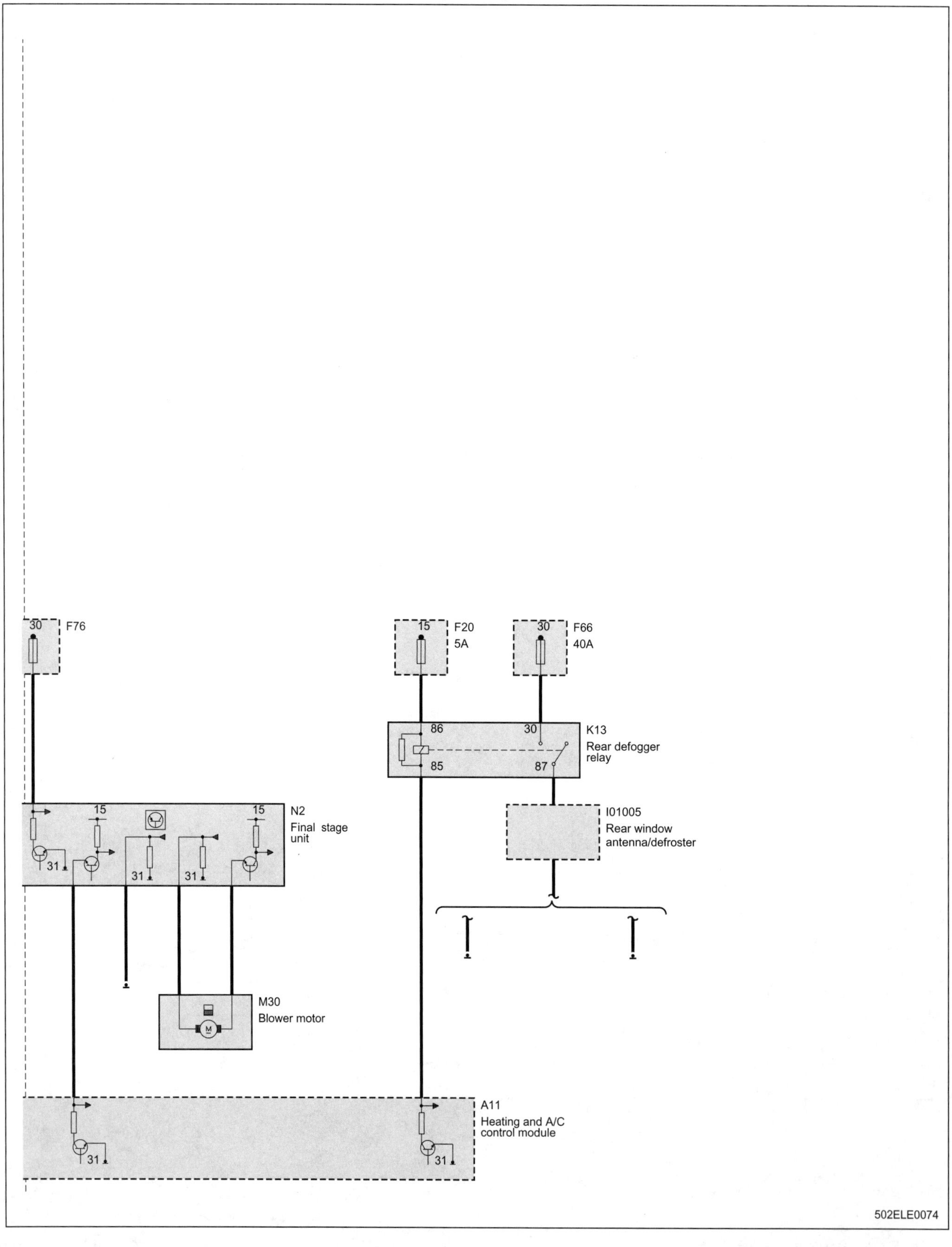

Air Conditioning and Heating
Heating and A/C control module (A11)
(1 of 4)

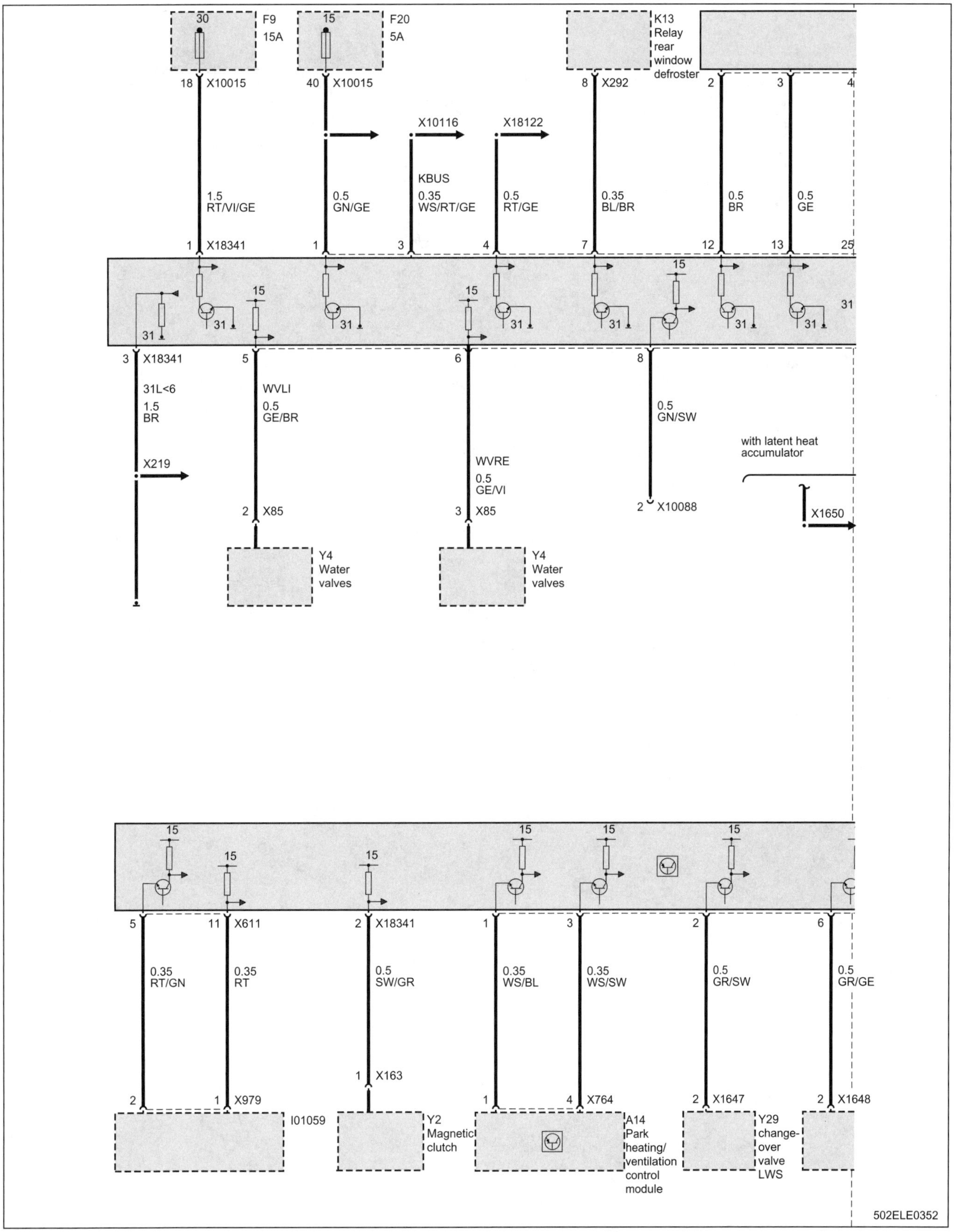

Air Conditioning and Heating
Heating and A/C control module (A11)
(2 of 4)

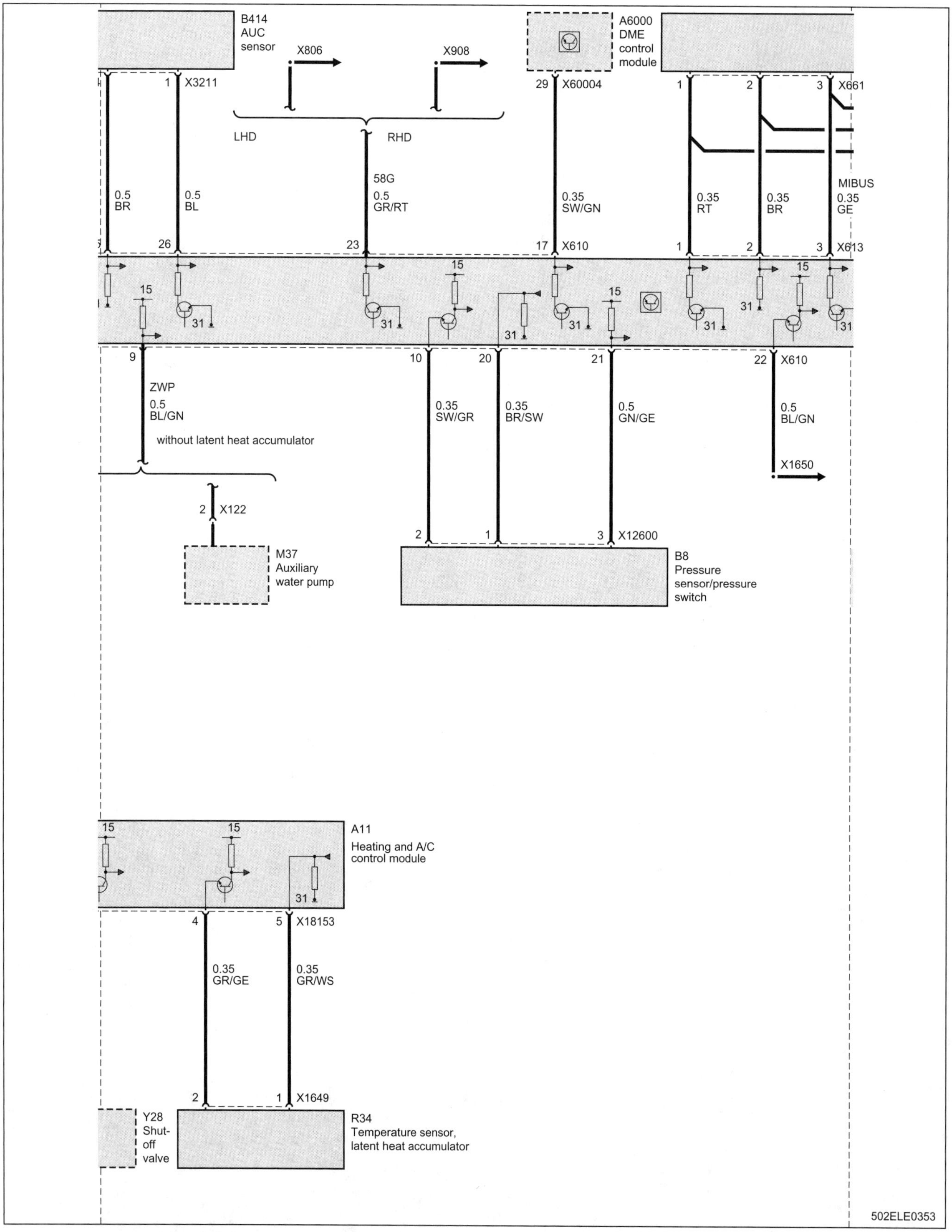

Air Conditioning and Heating
Heating and A/C control module (A11)
(3 of 4)

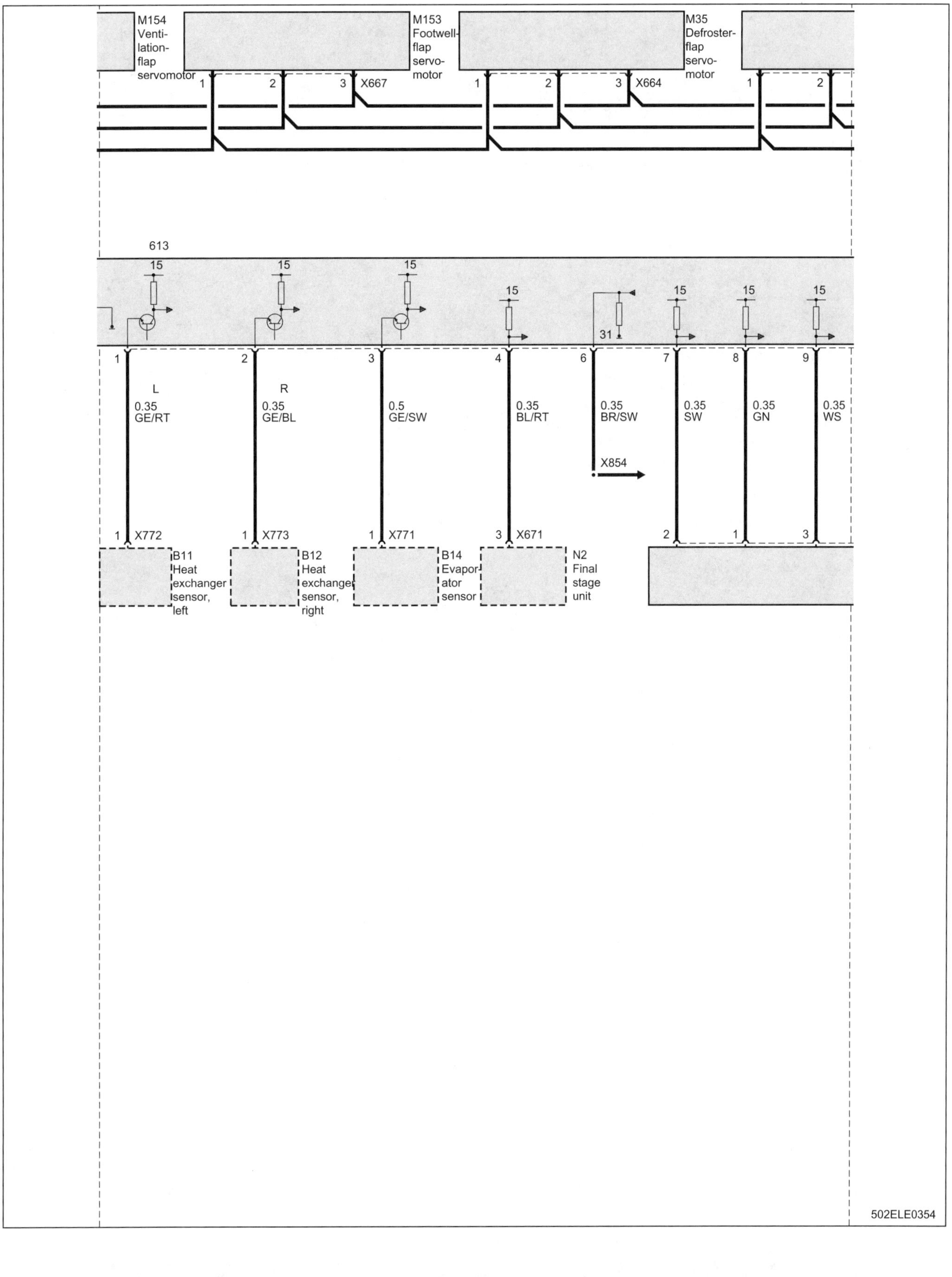

Air Conditioning and Heating
Heating and A/C control module (A11)
(4 of 4)

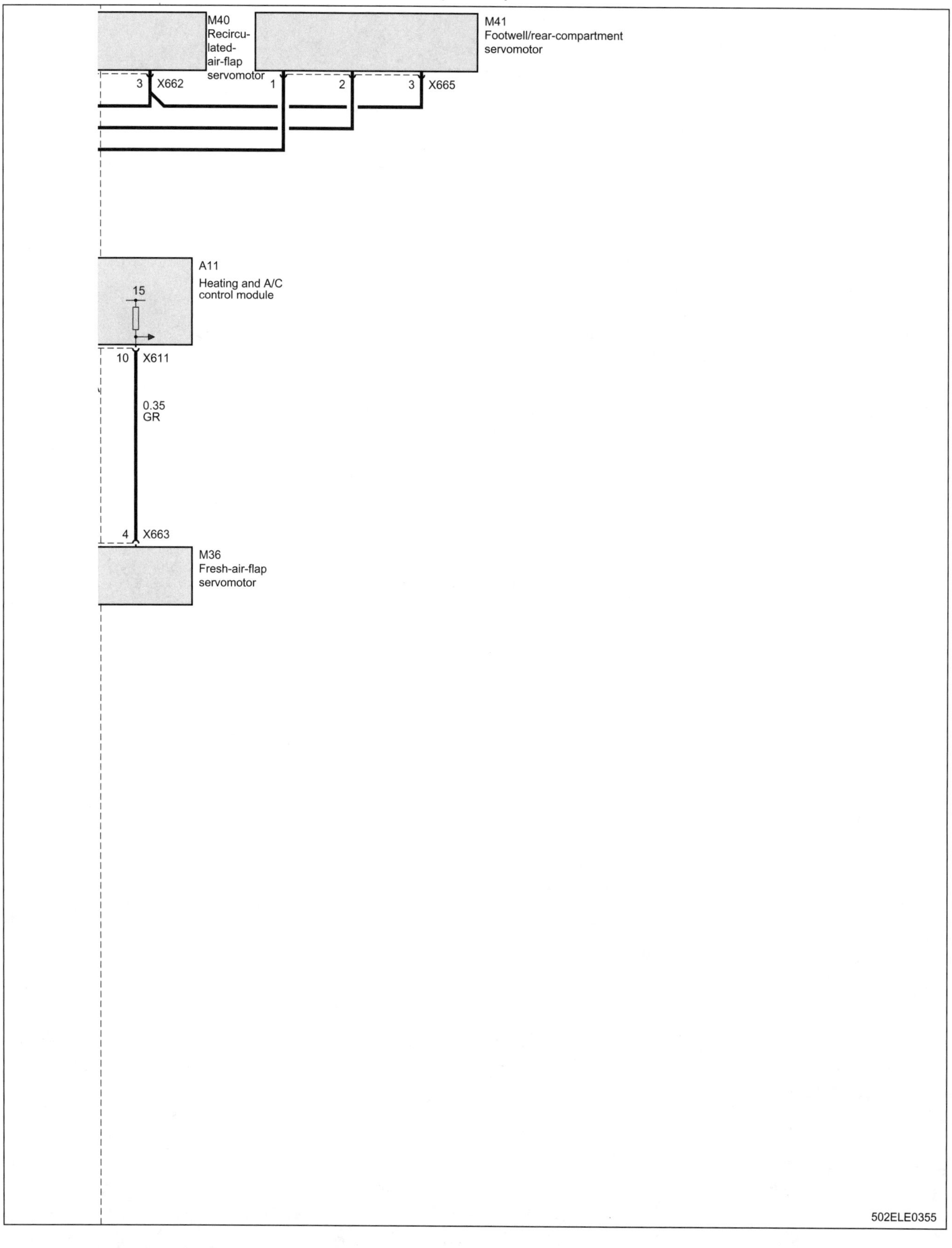

Air Conditioning and Heating
Heating and A/C control module (A11), power
(1 of 1)

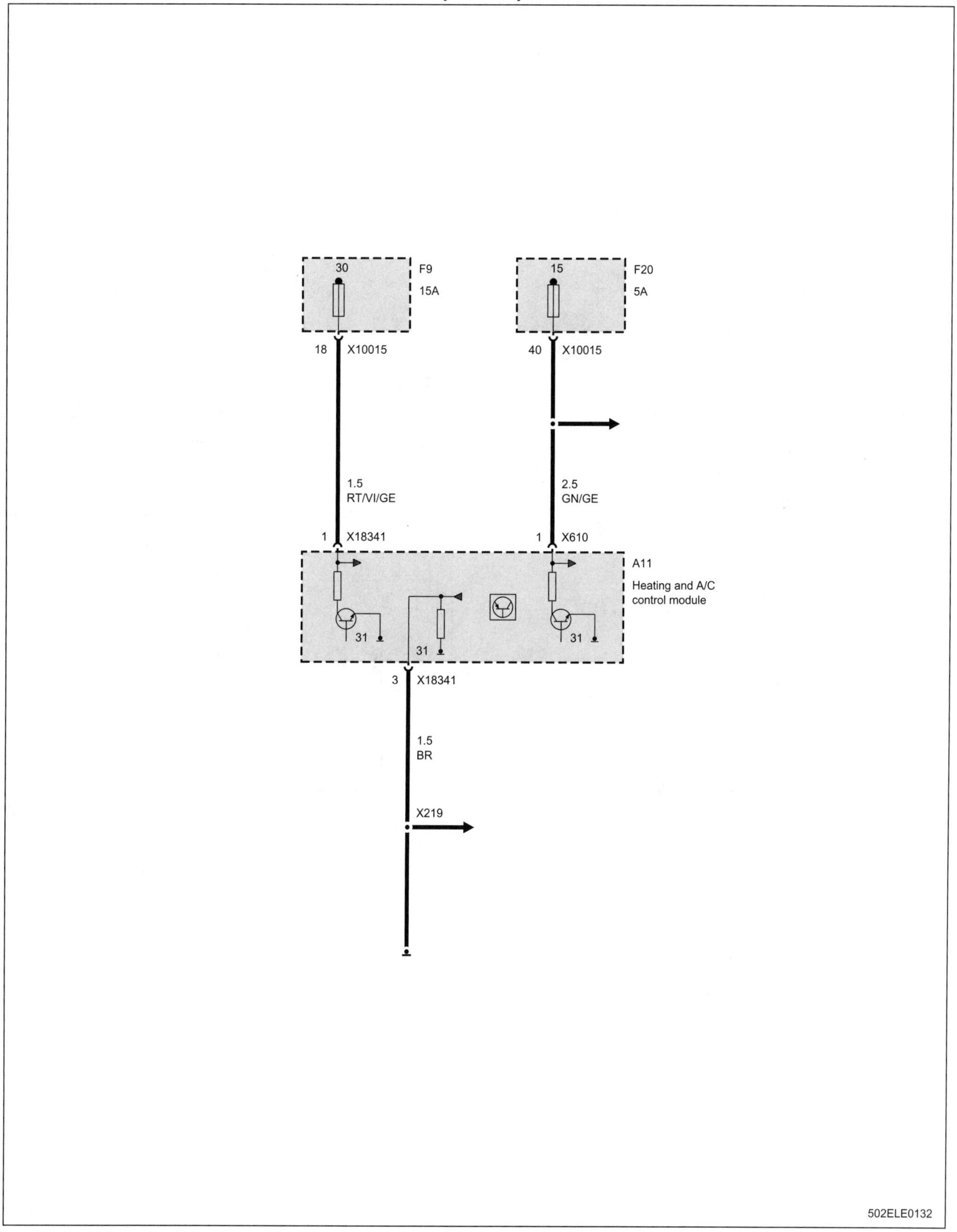

Air Conditioning and Heating
Air supply and defrost
(1 of 2)

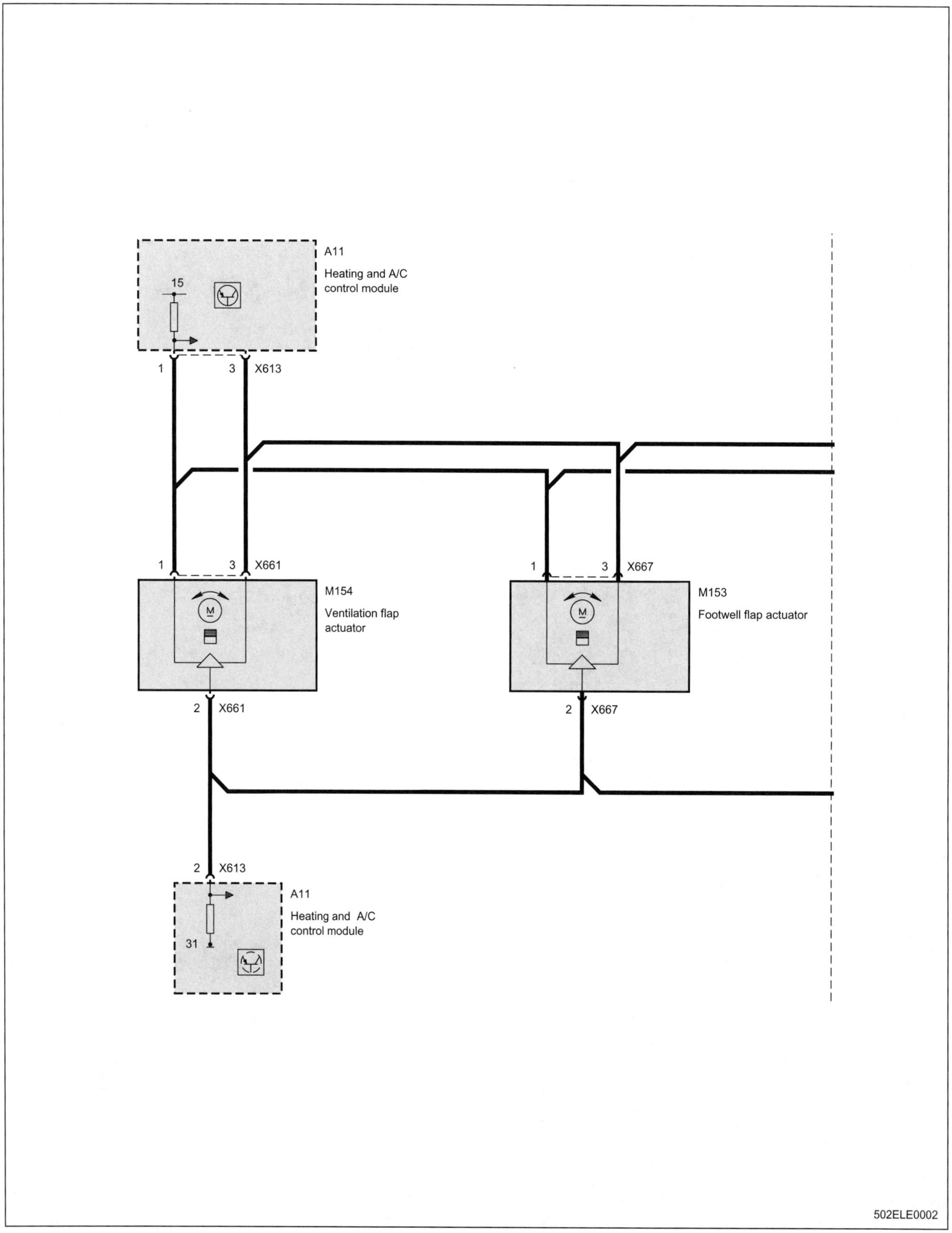

Air Conditioning and Heating
Air supply and defrost
(2 of 2)

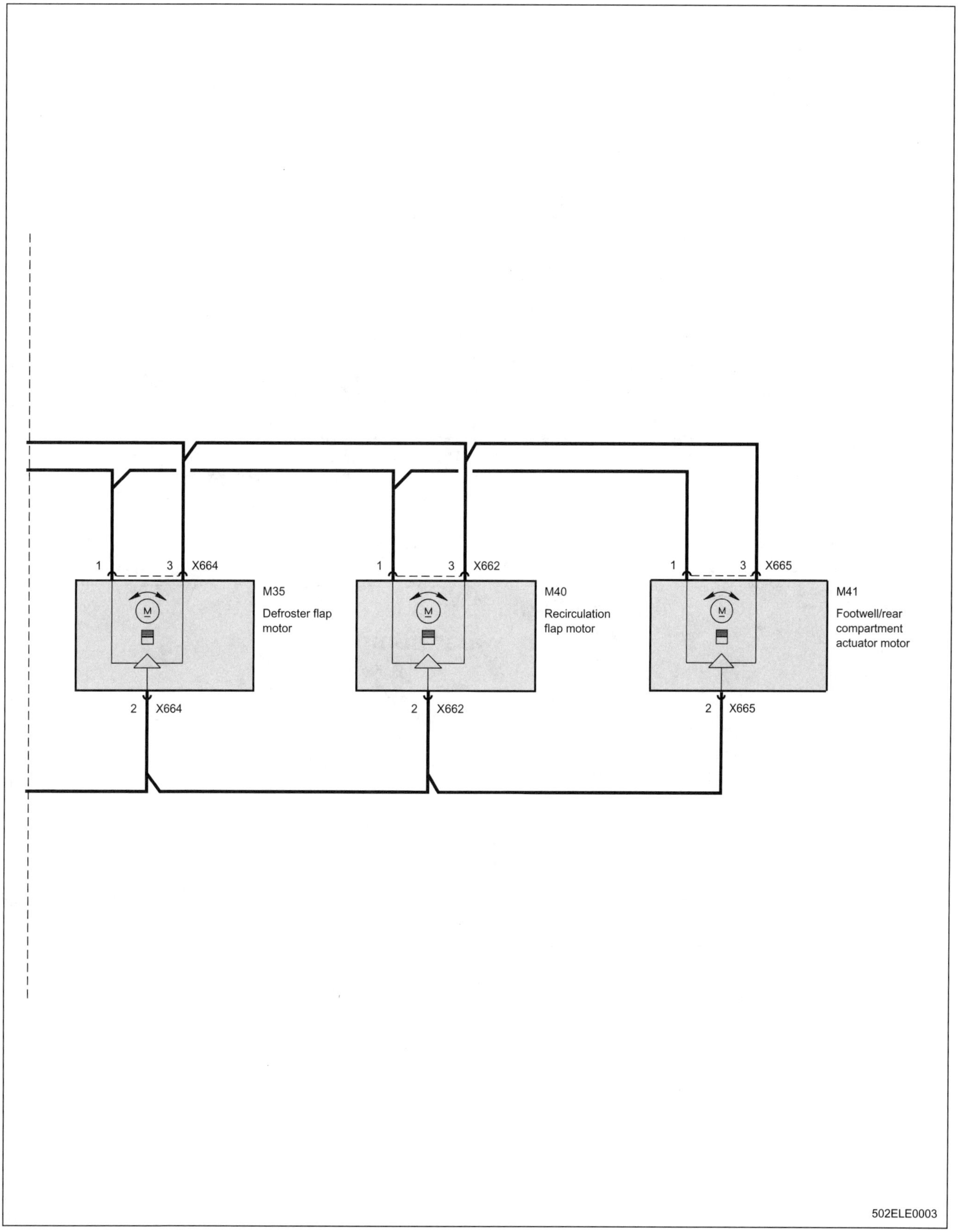

Air Conditioning and Heating
Automatic recirculated air control (AUC)

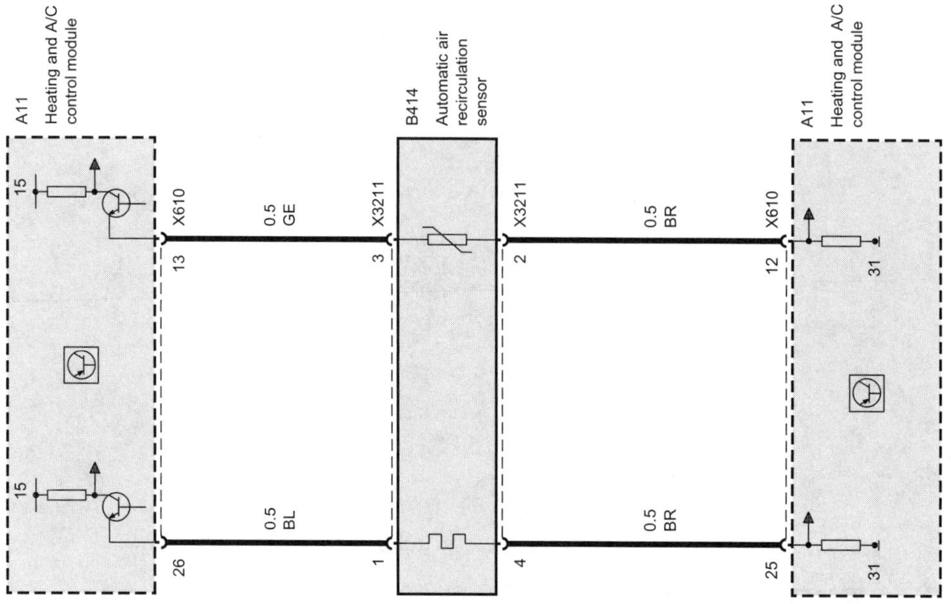

502ELE0012a

Air Conditioning and Heating
Auxiliary water pump

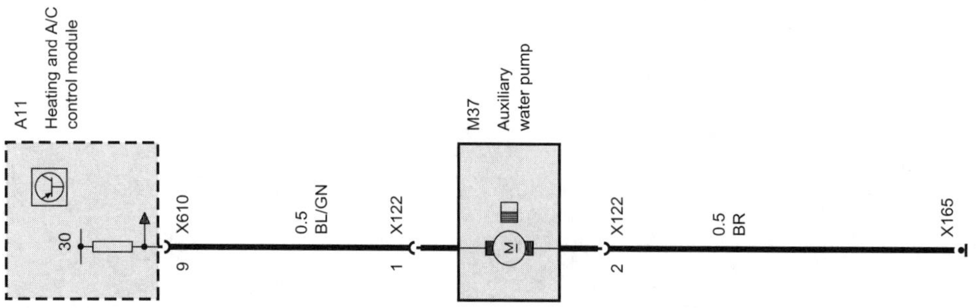

502ELE0012b

Air Conditioning and Heating
Blower motor control (final stage)

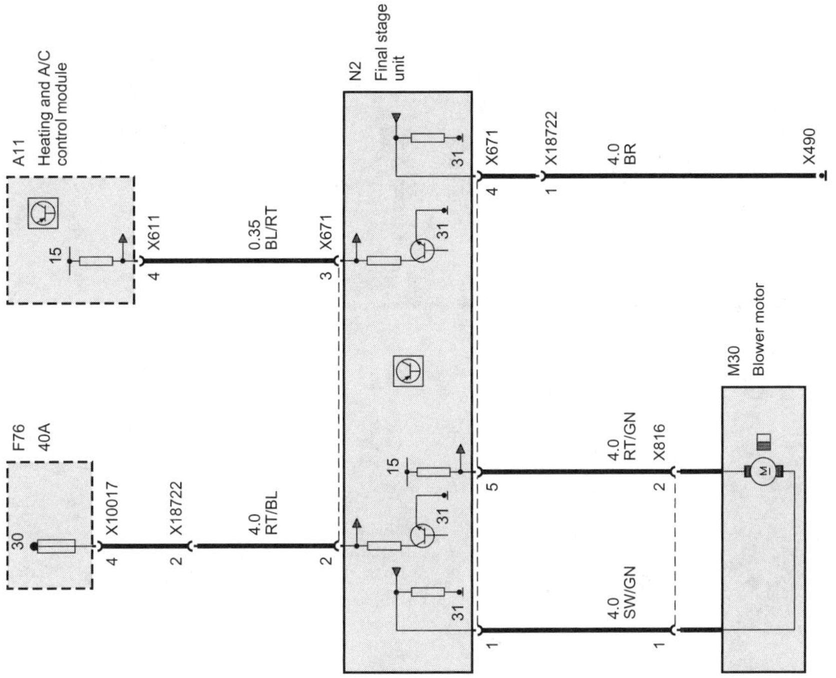

502ELE0016a

Air Conditioning and Heating
Rear blower motor control

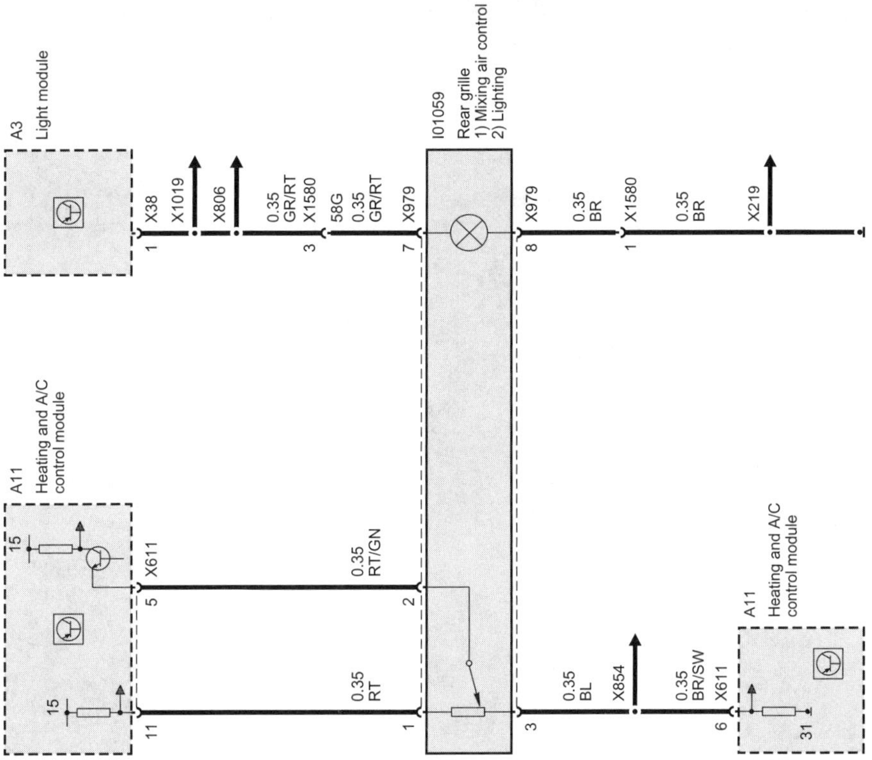

502ELE0016b

Headlights/Foglights
Fog lights

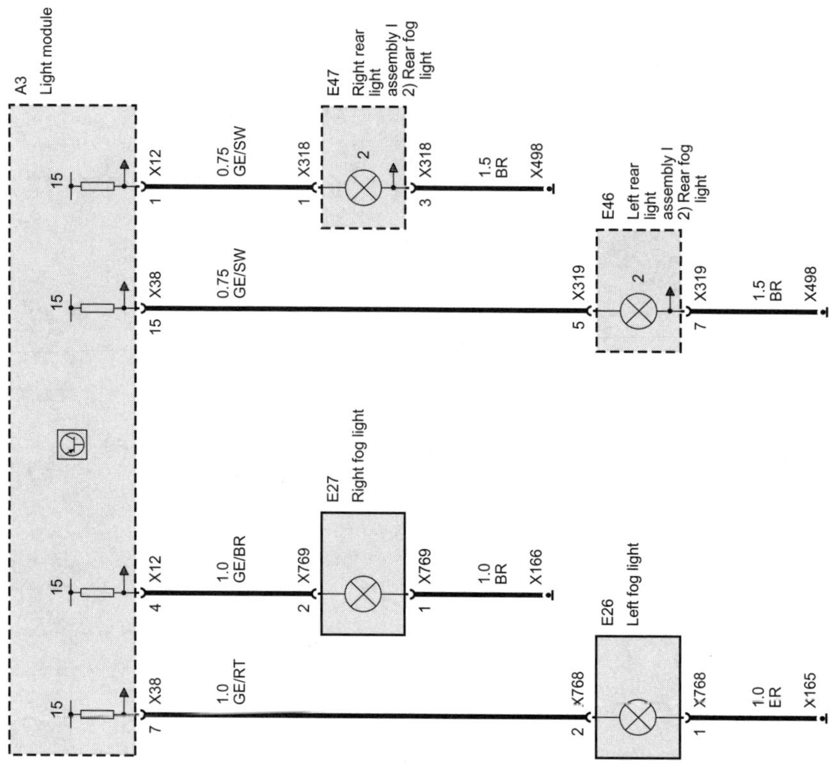

502ELE0052a

Air Conditioning and Heating
Fresh air actuator motor

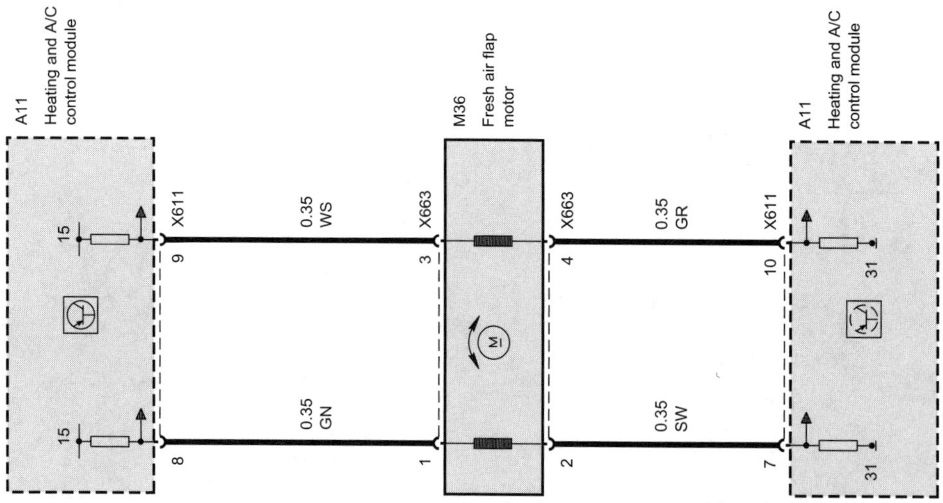

502ELE0052b

Air Conditioning and Heating
Heat exchanger sensor
(1 of 1)

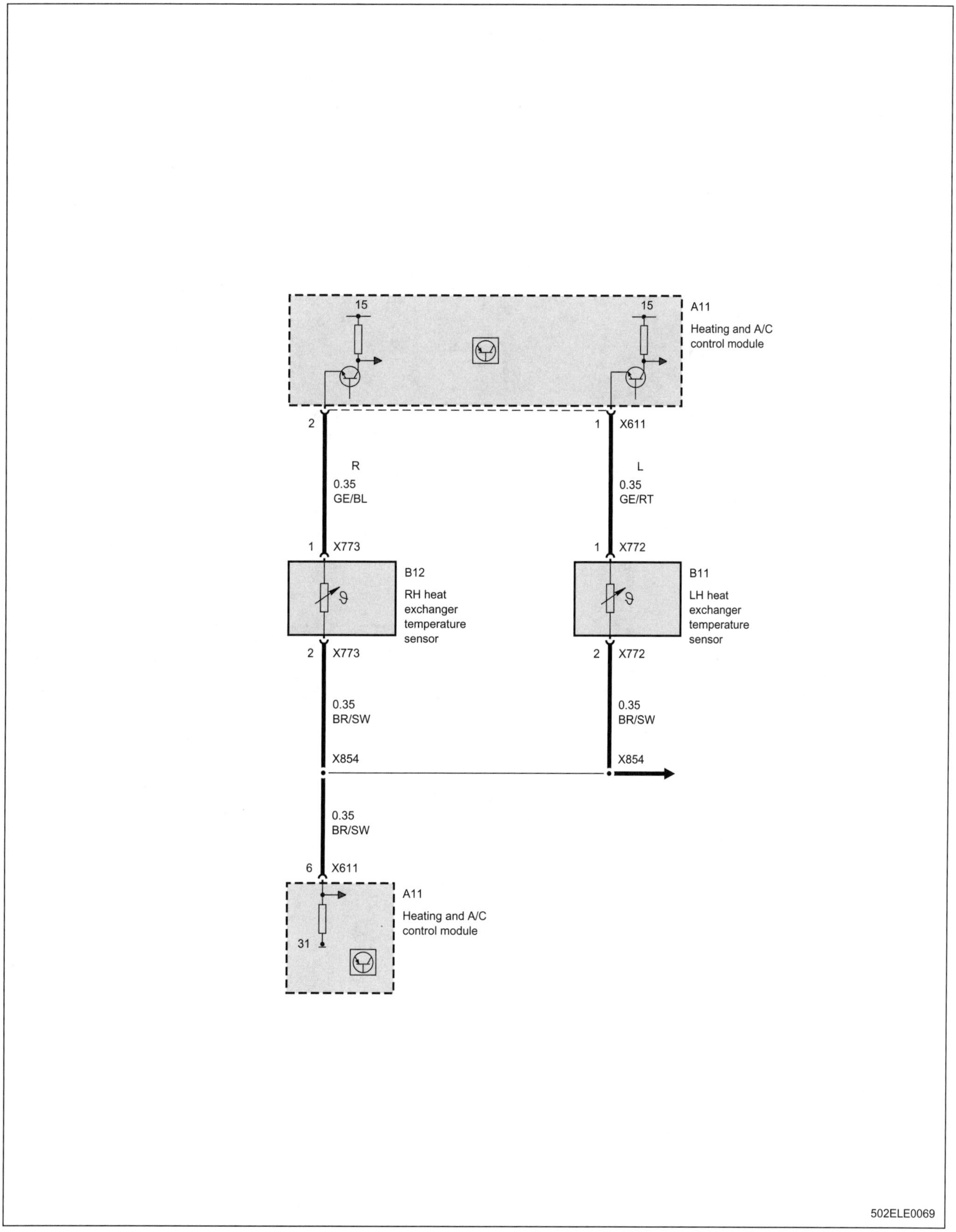

Air Conditioning and Heating
Rear blower
(1 of 3)

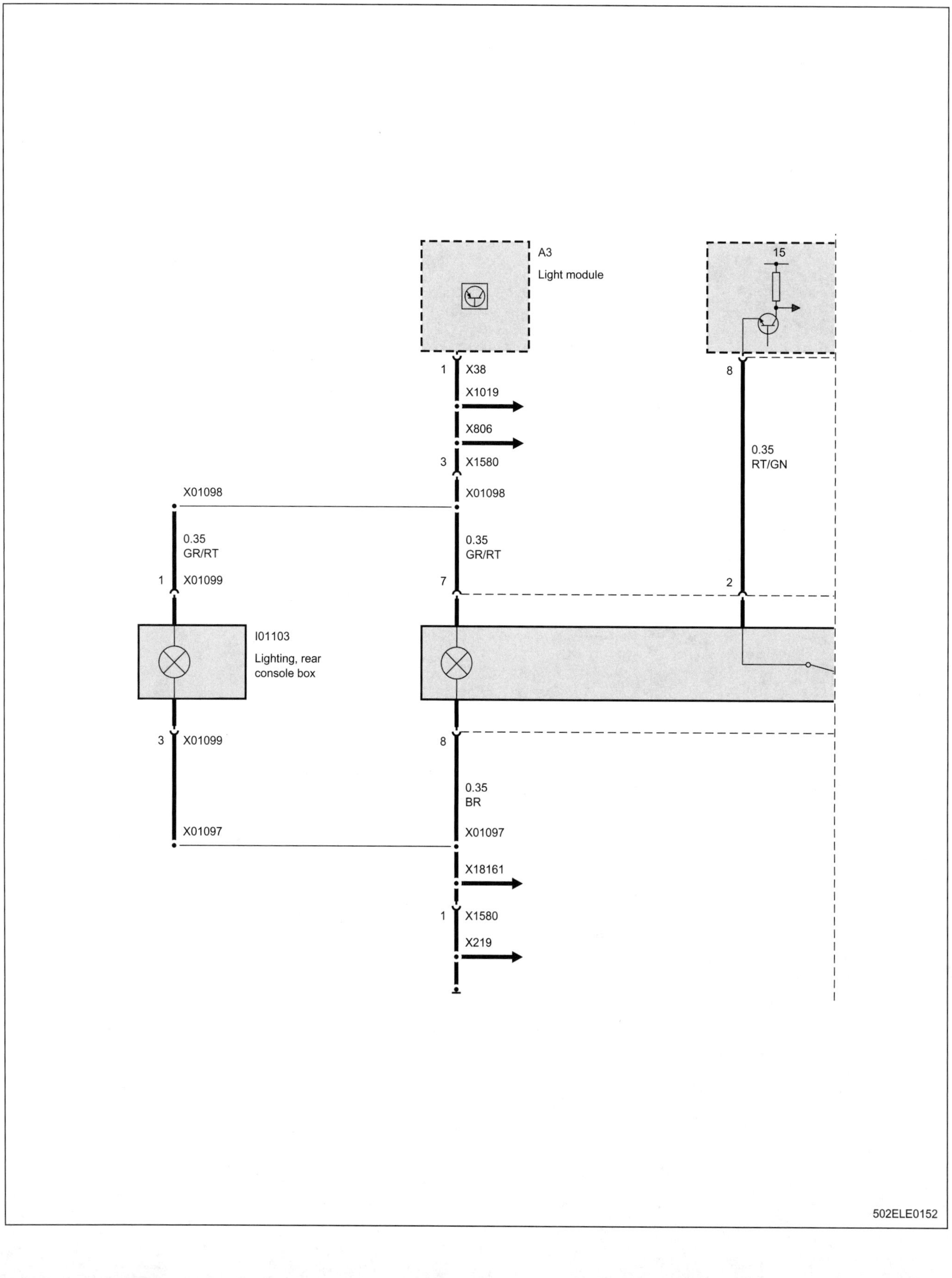
A3
Light module
15
1
X38
X1019
X806
3
X1580
X01098
8
0.35
RT/GN
X01098
0.35
GR/RT
1
X01099
X01098
0.35
GR/RT
7
2
I01103
Lighting, rear
console box
3
X01099
8
0.35
BR
X01097
X01097
X18161
1
X1580
X219
502ELE0152

Air Conditioning and Heating
Rear blower
(2 of 3)

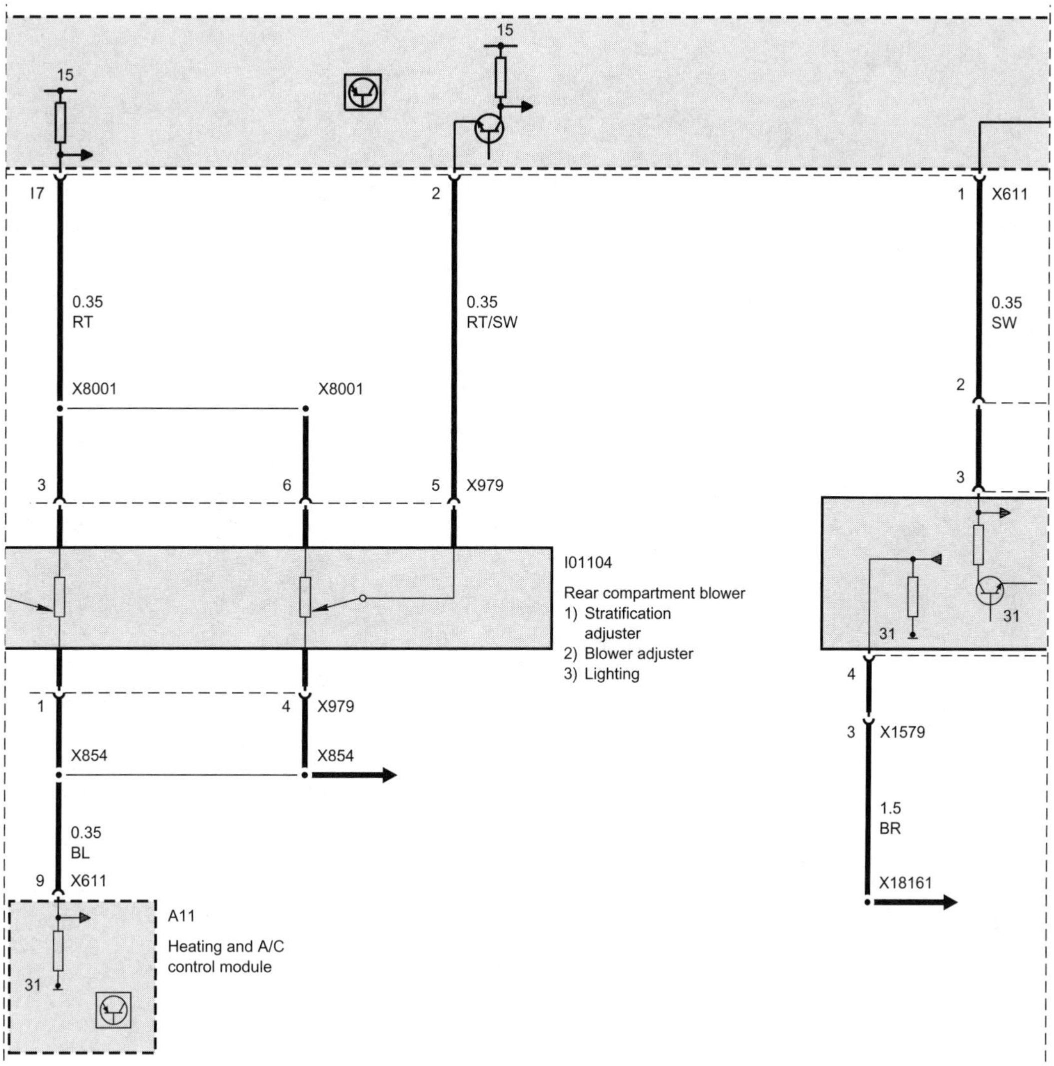

502ELE0153

Air Conditioning and Heating
Rear blower
(3 of 3)

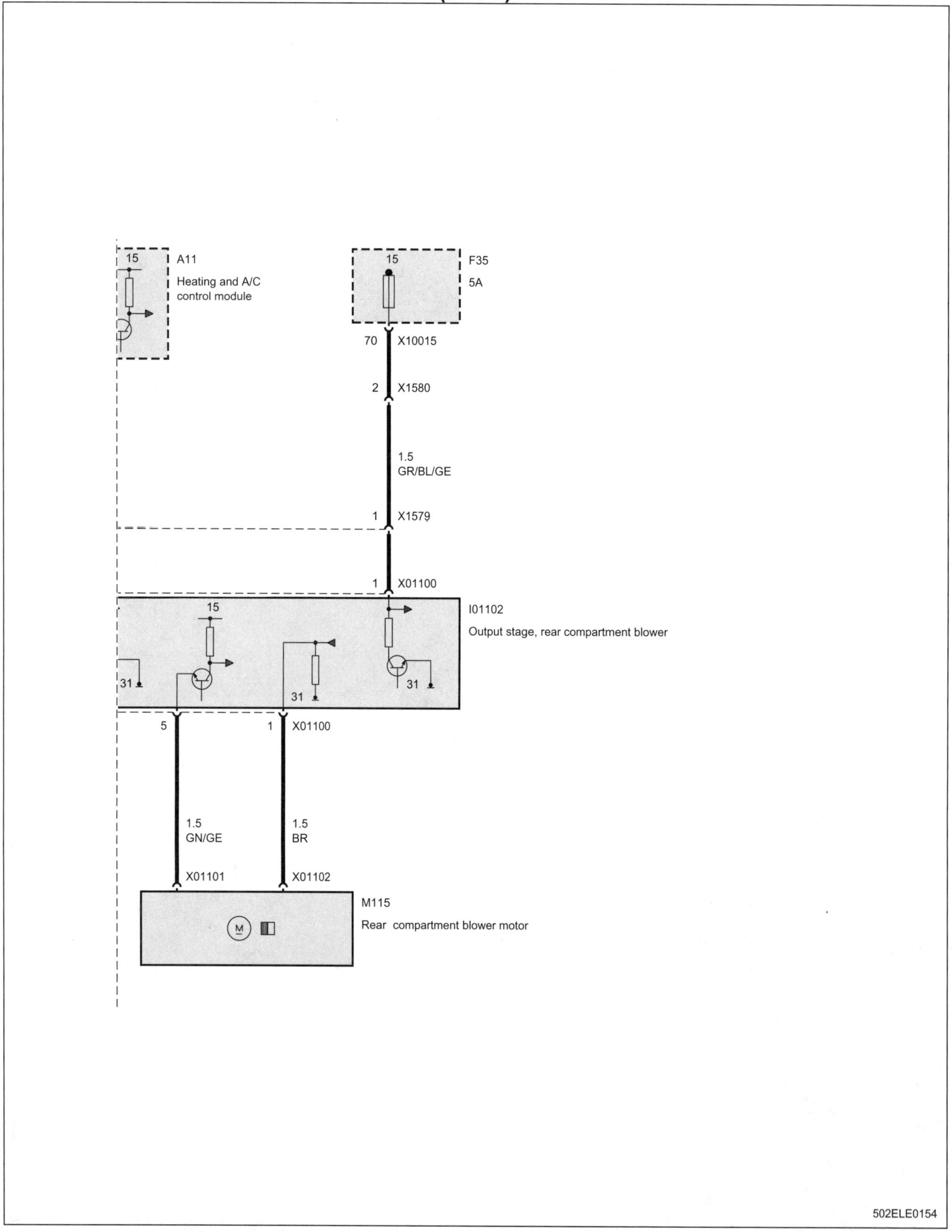
15
A11
Heating and A/C control module
15
F35
5A
70
X10015
2
X1580
1.5
GR/BL/GE
1
X1579
1
X01100
15
I01102
Output stage, rear compartment blower
31
31
31
5
1
X01100
1.5
GN/GE
1.5
BR
X01101
X01102
M115
Rear compartment blower motor
M
502ELE0154

Air Conditioning and Heating
Solenoid valve, evaporator sensor
(1 of 1)

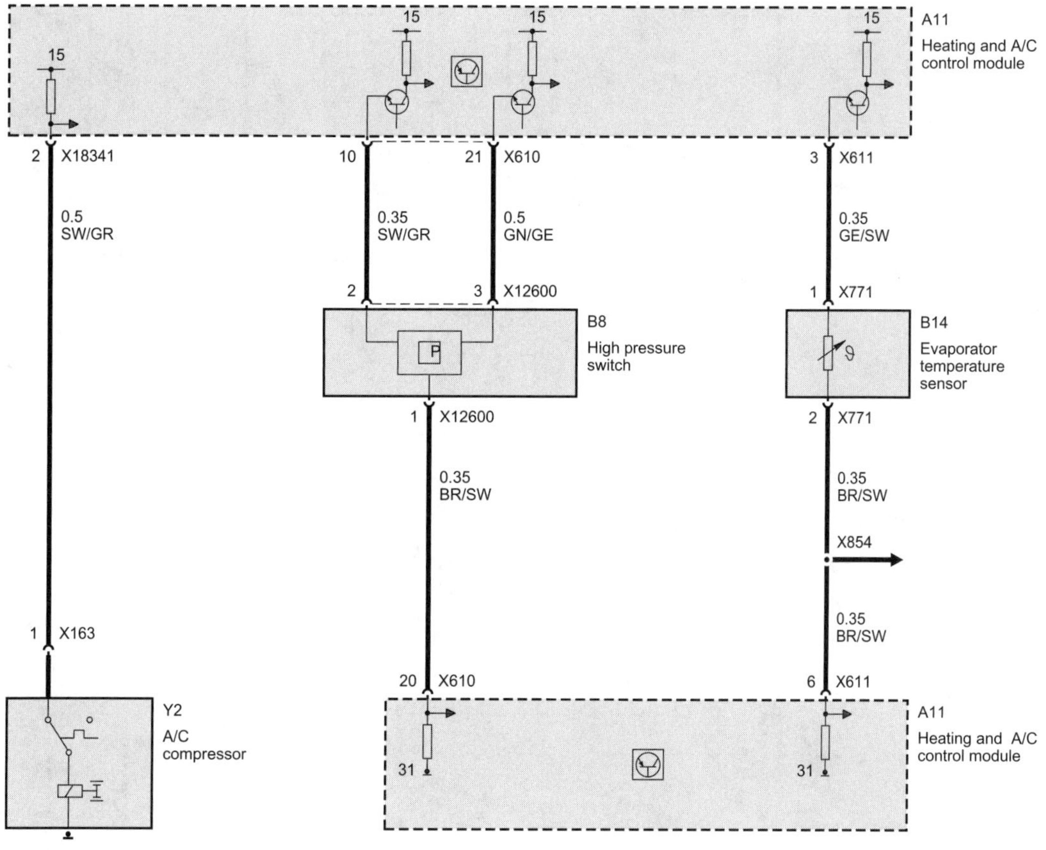

502ELE0216

Supplemental Restraint System (SRS)
Restraint functions (overview)
(1 of 3)

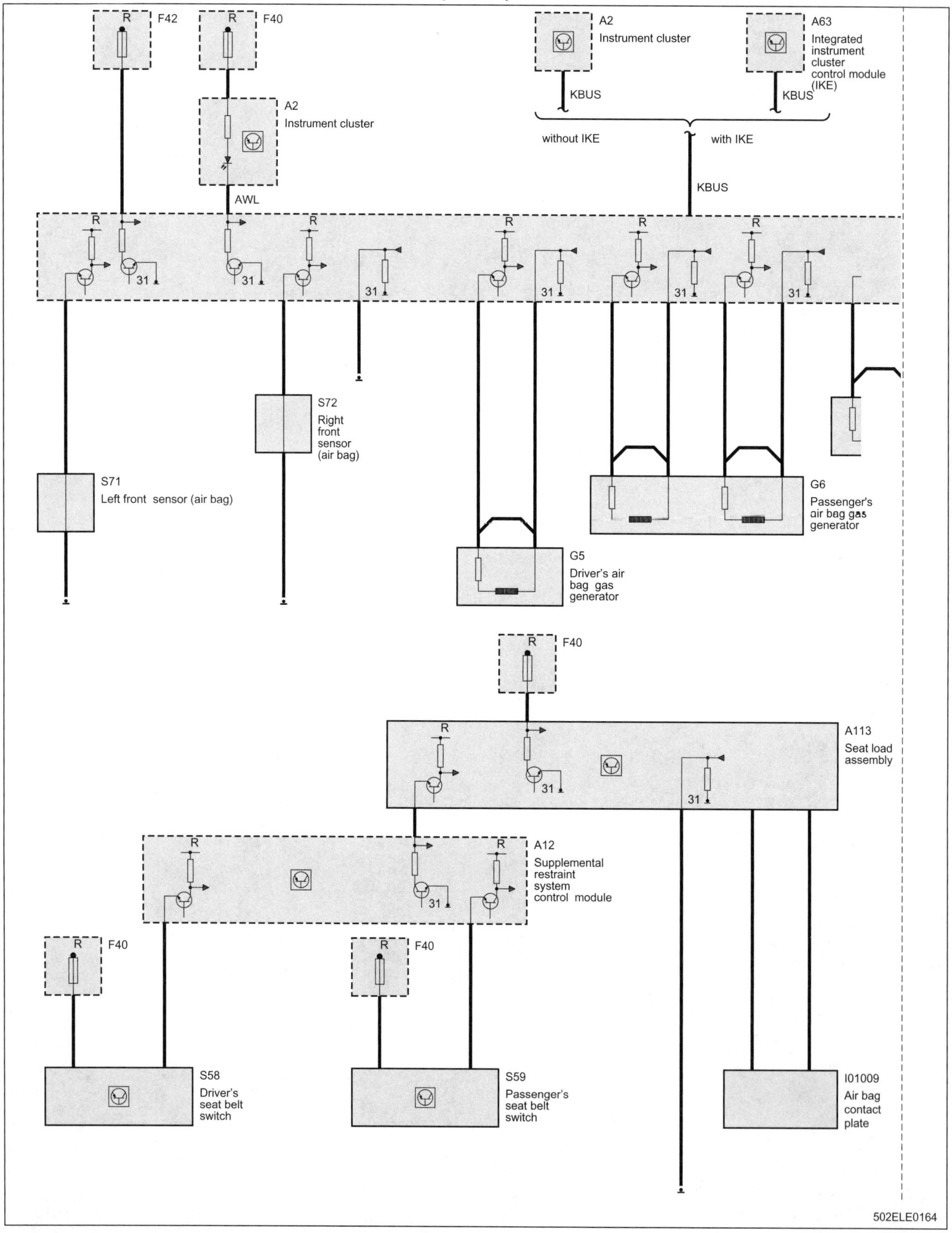

Supplemental Restraint System (SRS)
Restraint functions (overview)
(2 of 3)

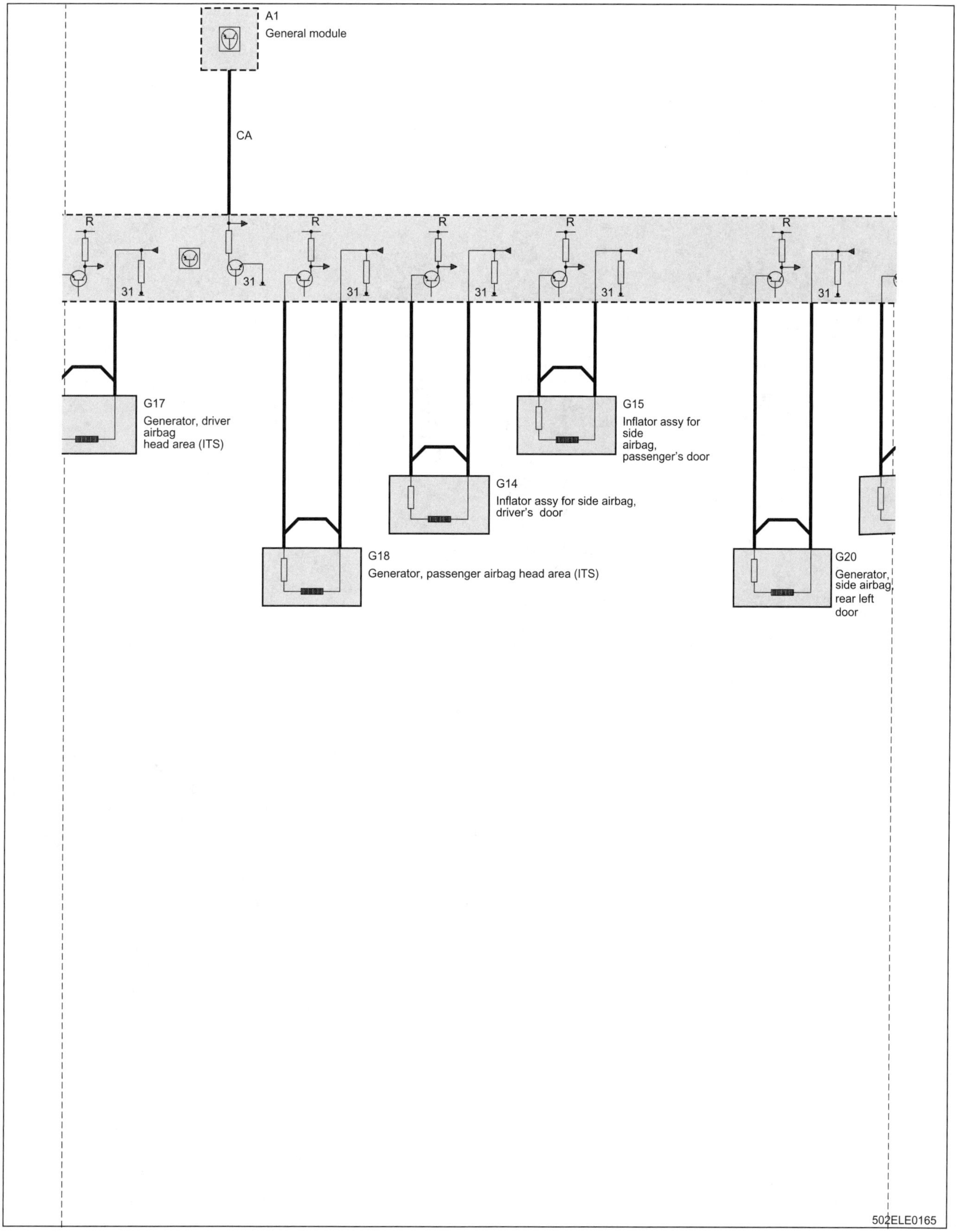

Supplemental Restraint System (SRS)
Restraint functions (overview)
(3 of 3)

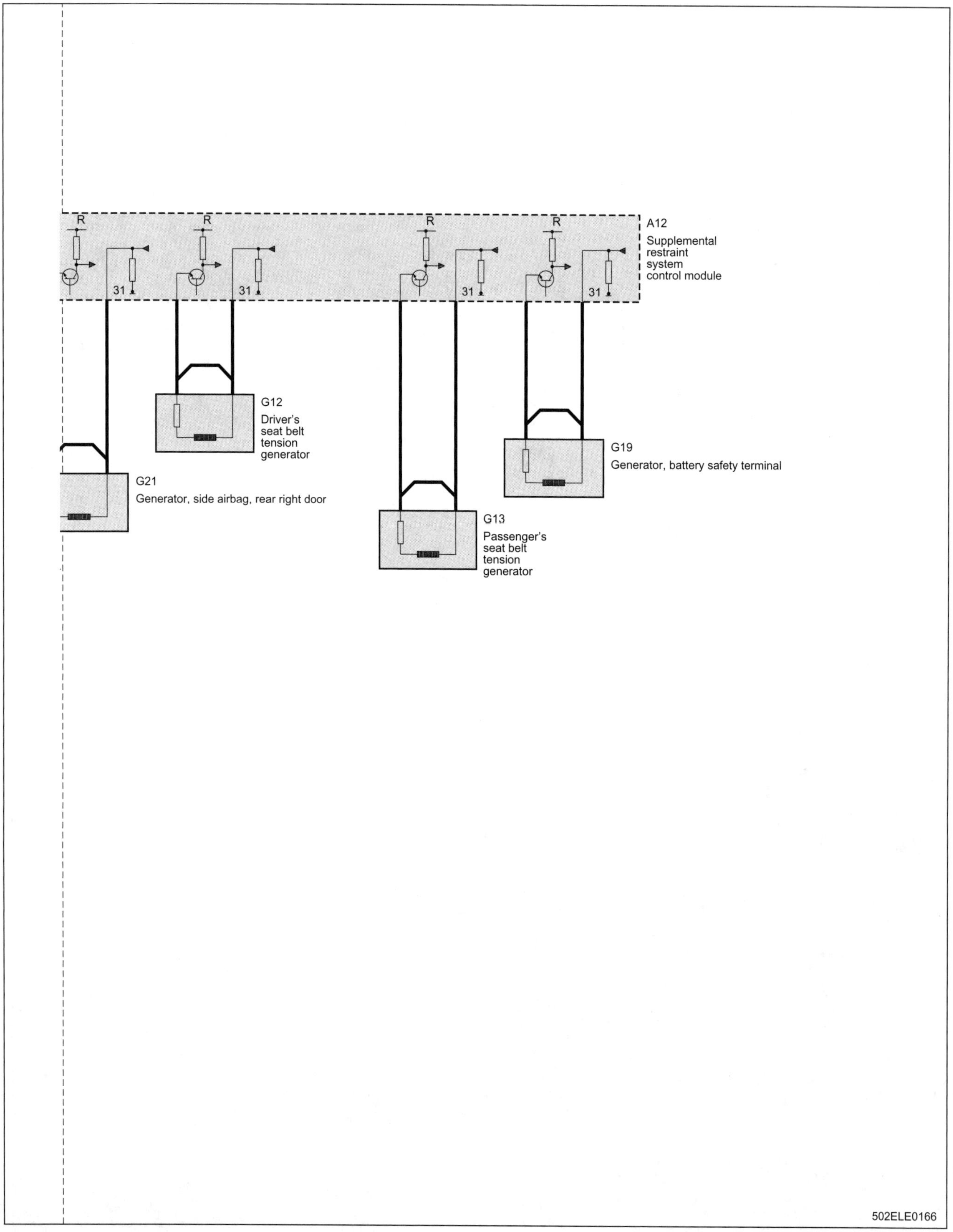

Supplemental Restraint System (SRS)
Battery safety terminal (BST)
(1 of 1)

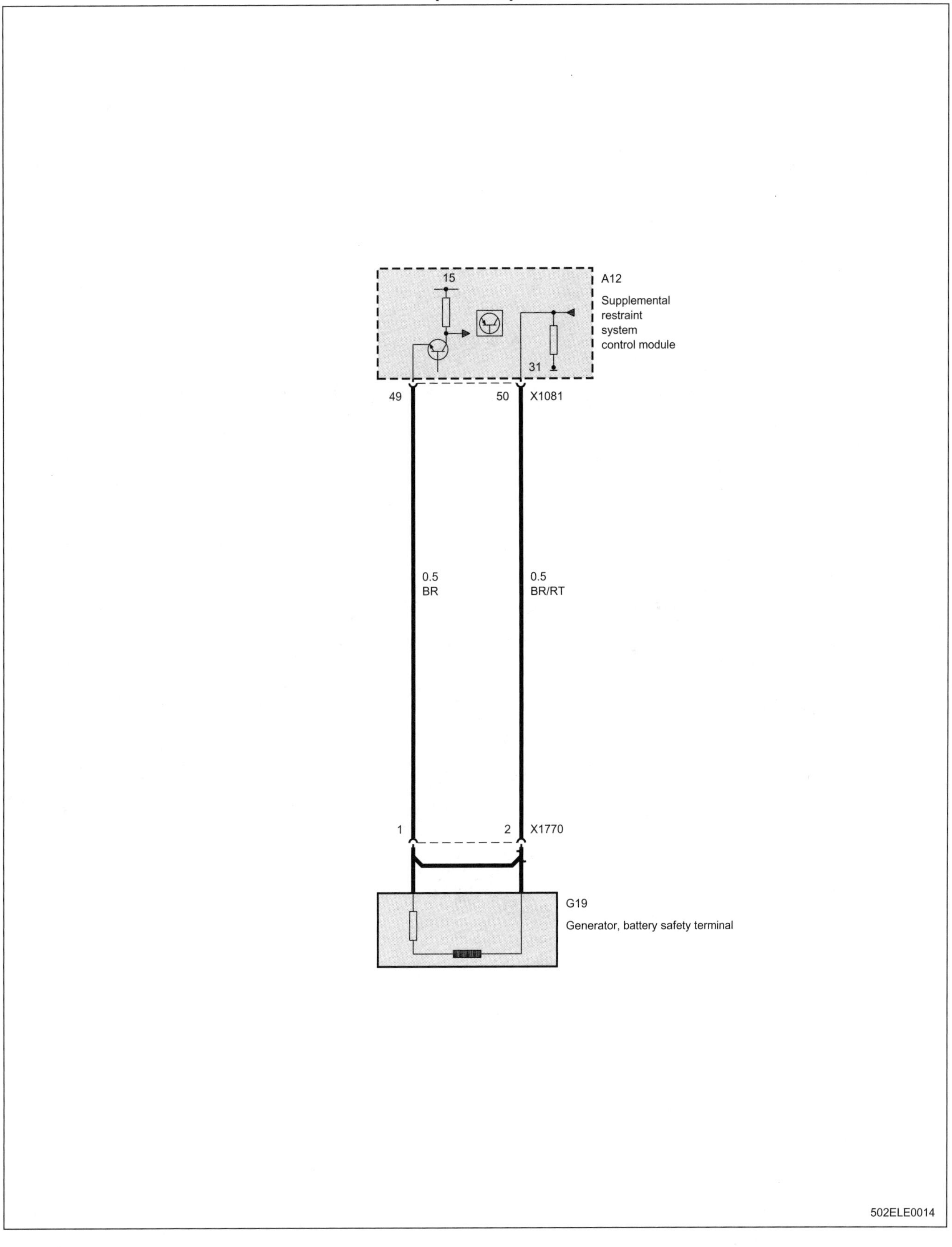

Supplemental Restraint System (SRS)
Seat belt tensioner

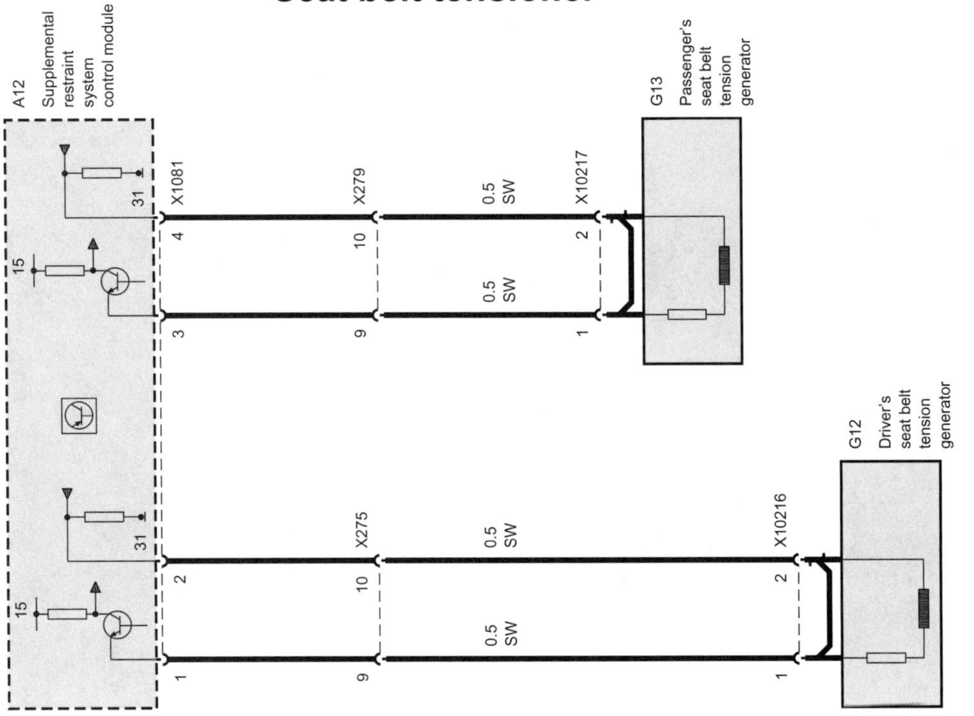

502ELE0015a

Supplemental Restraint System (SRS)
Belt-lock contact (driver's side)

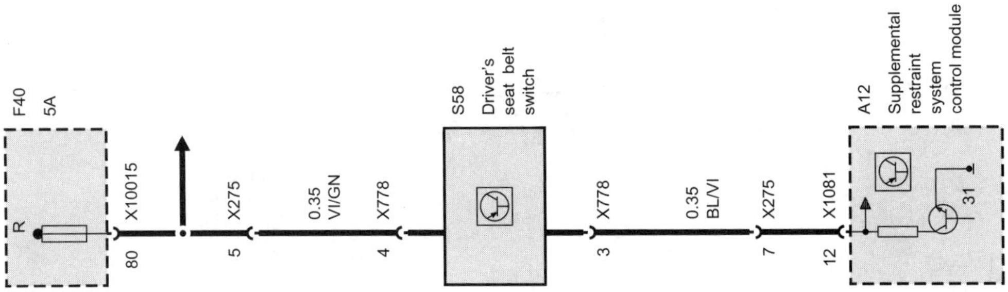

502ELE0015b

Supplemental Restraint System (SRS)
Front sensor side air bag
(1 of 1)

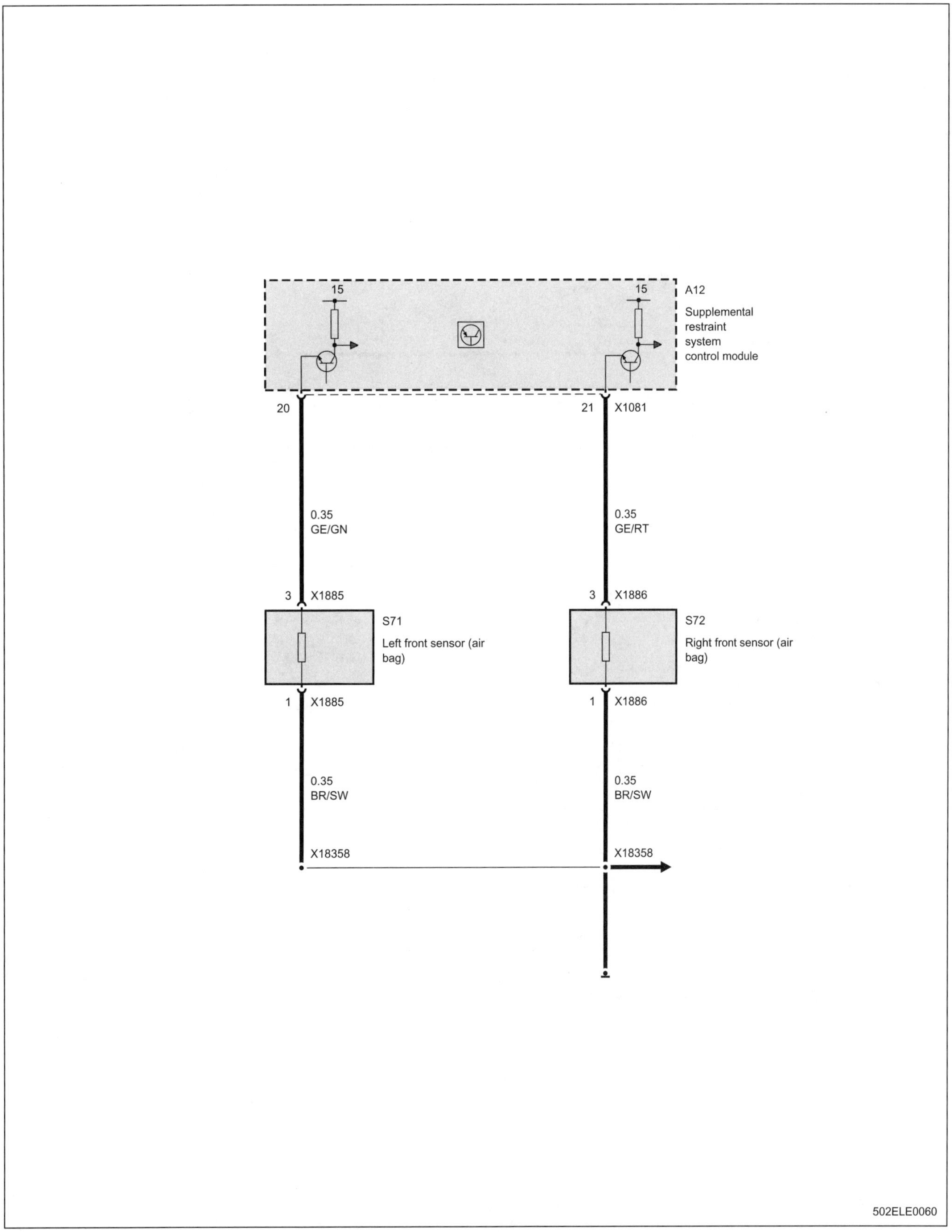

Supplemental Restraint System (SRS)
Gas generators
(1 of 1)

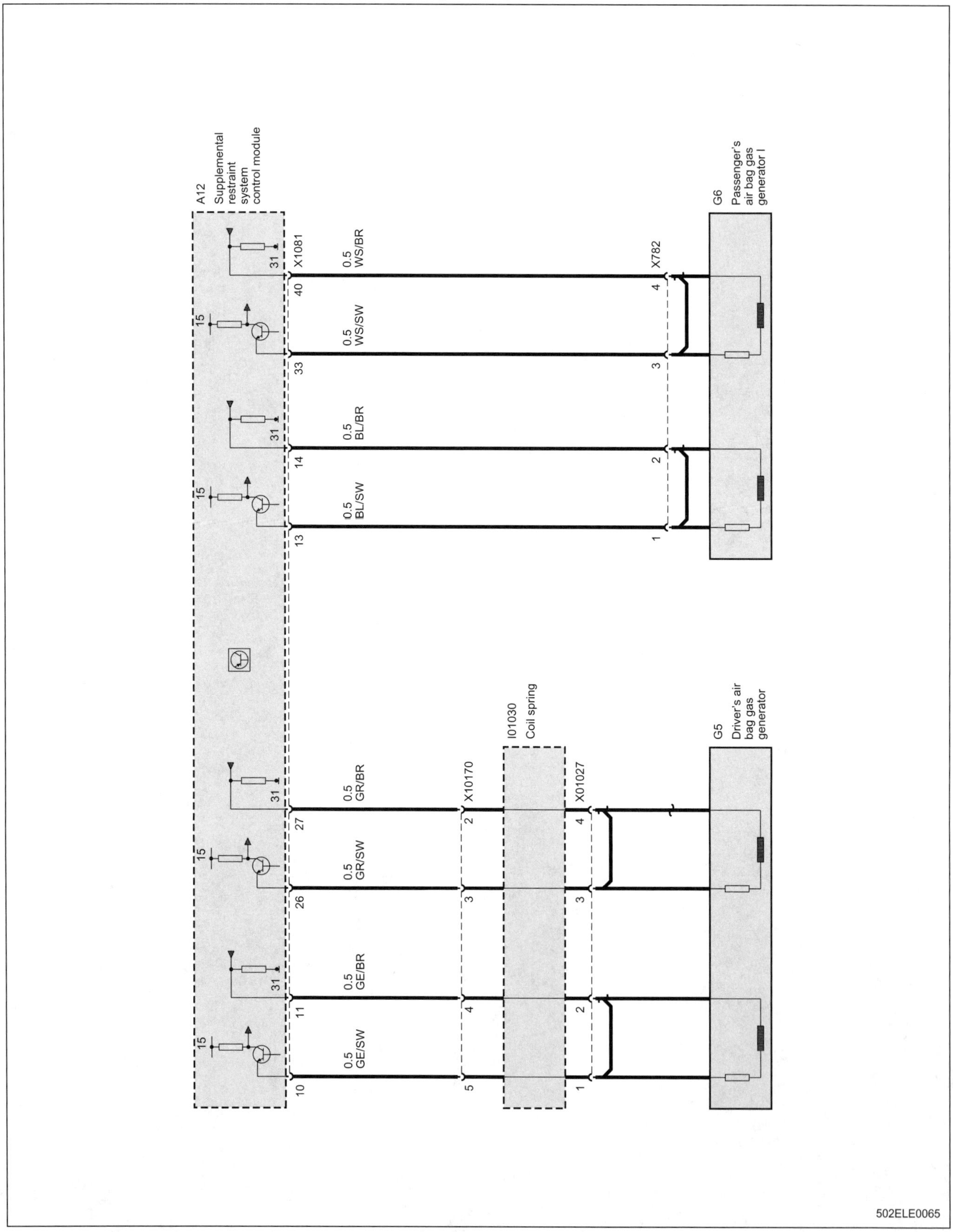

Supplemental Restraint System (SRS) Passenger's seatbelt switch (1 of 1)

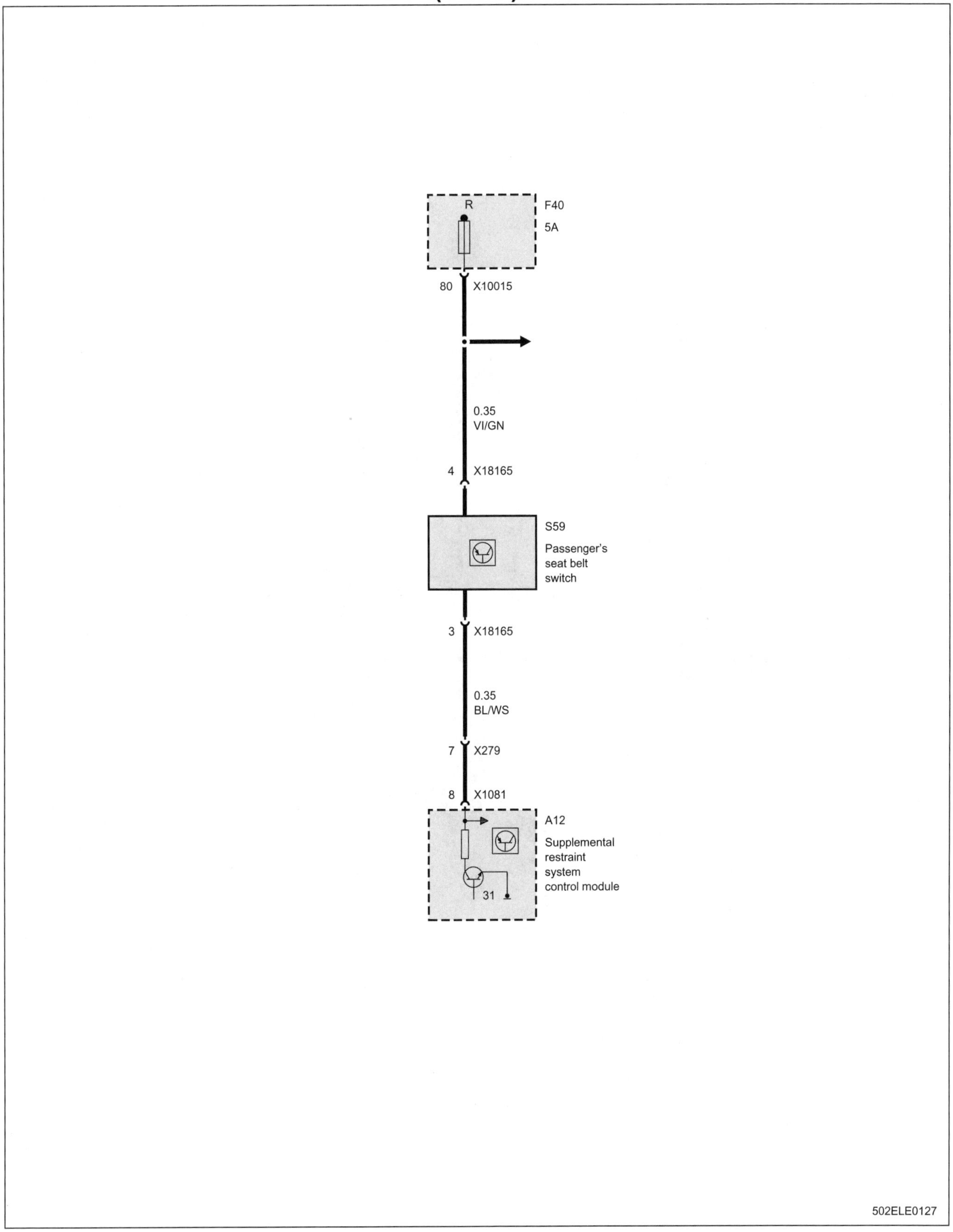

Supplemental Restraint System (SRS)
Power, signal inputs
(1 of 1)

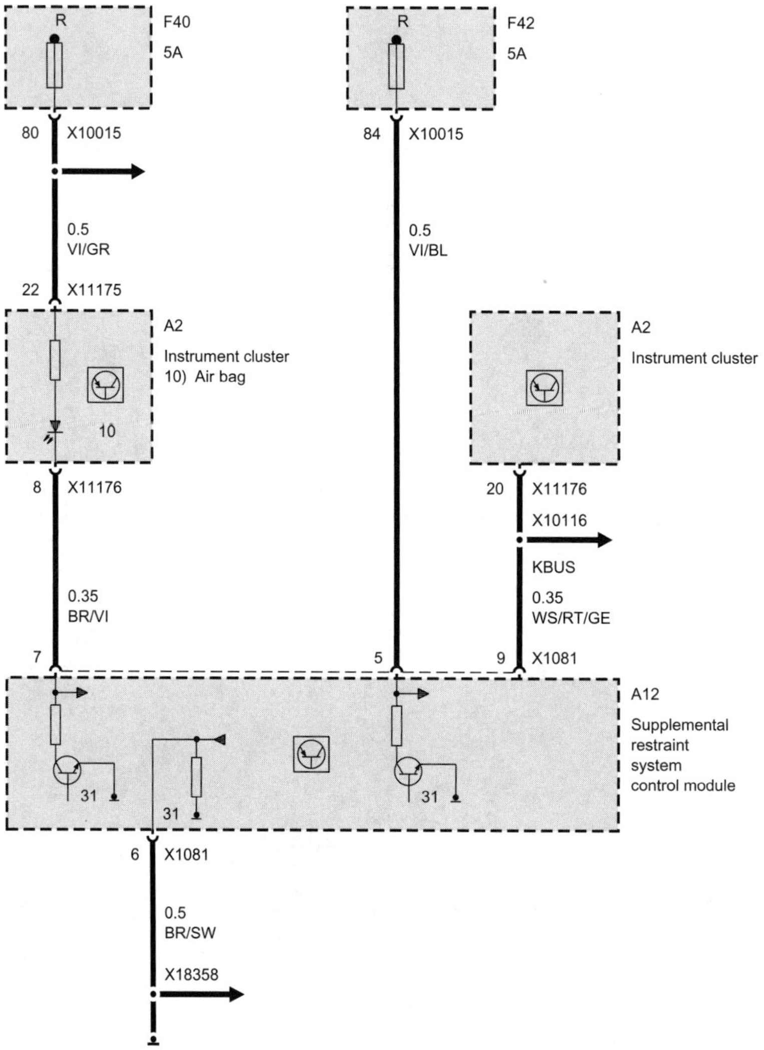

Supplemental Restraint System (SRS)
Seat occupancy recognition
(1 of 1)

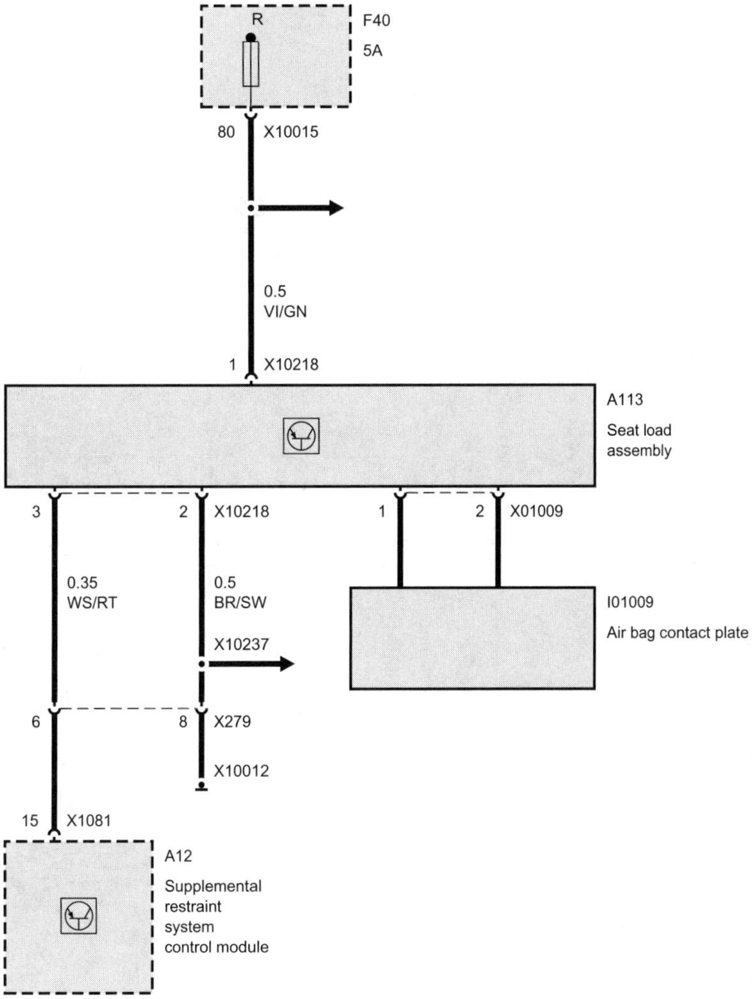

502ELE0205

Supplemental Restraint System (SRS)
Side air bag, front

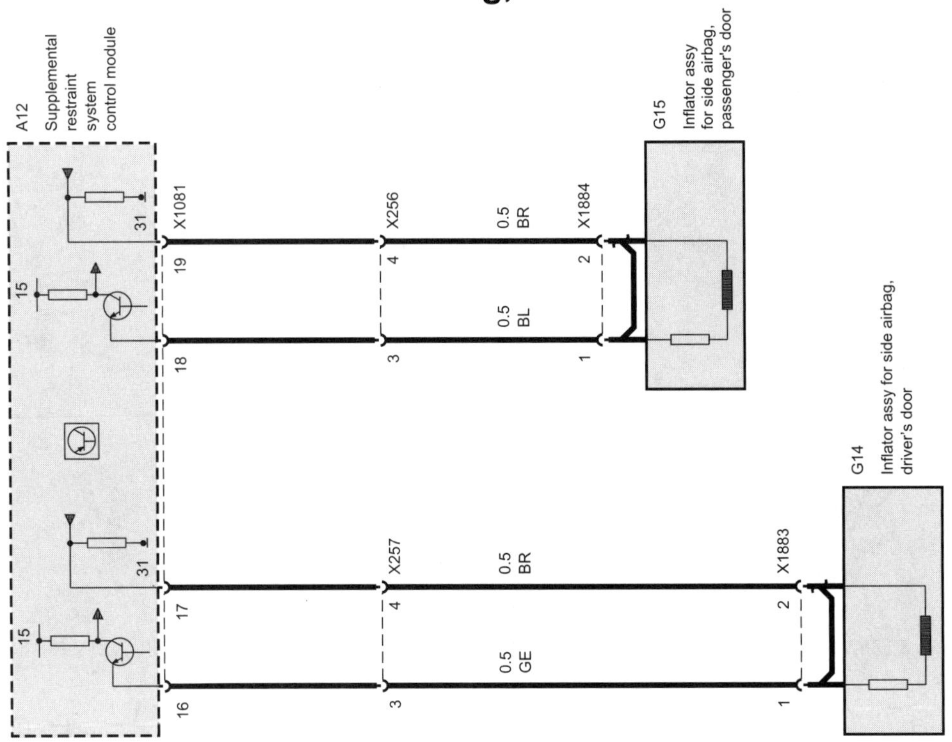

502ELE0211a

Supplemental Restraint System (SRS)
Side airbag, front head area (ITS)

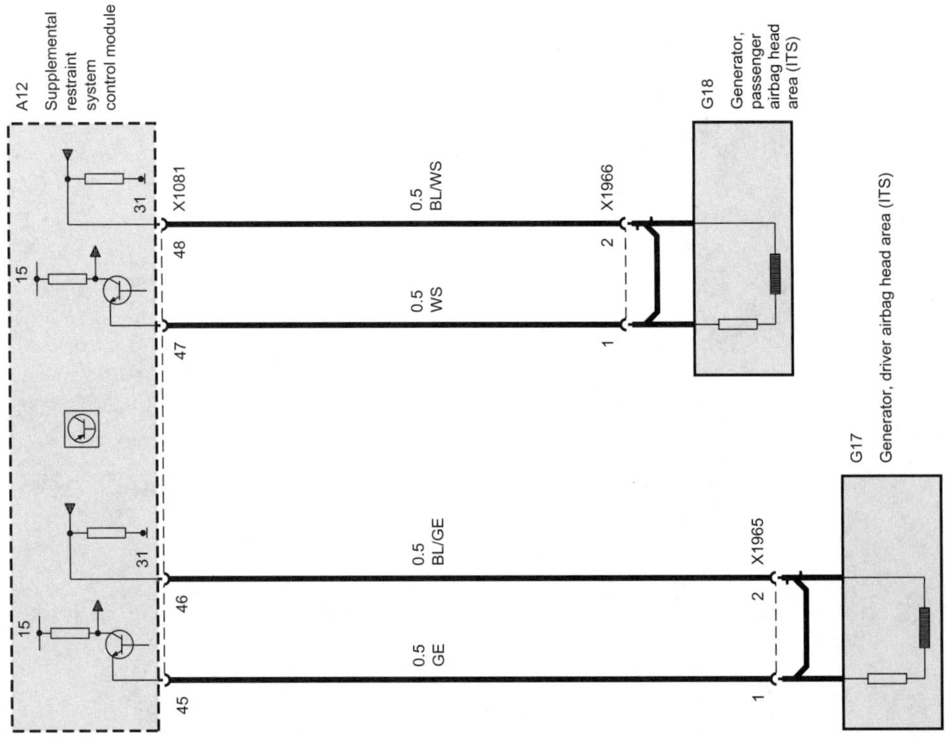

502ELE0211b

Supplemental Restraint System (SRS)
Side airbag, rear

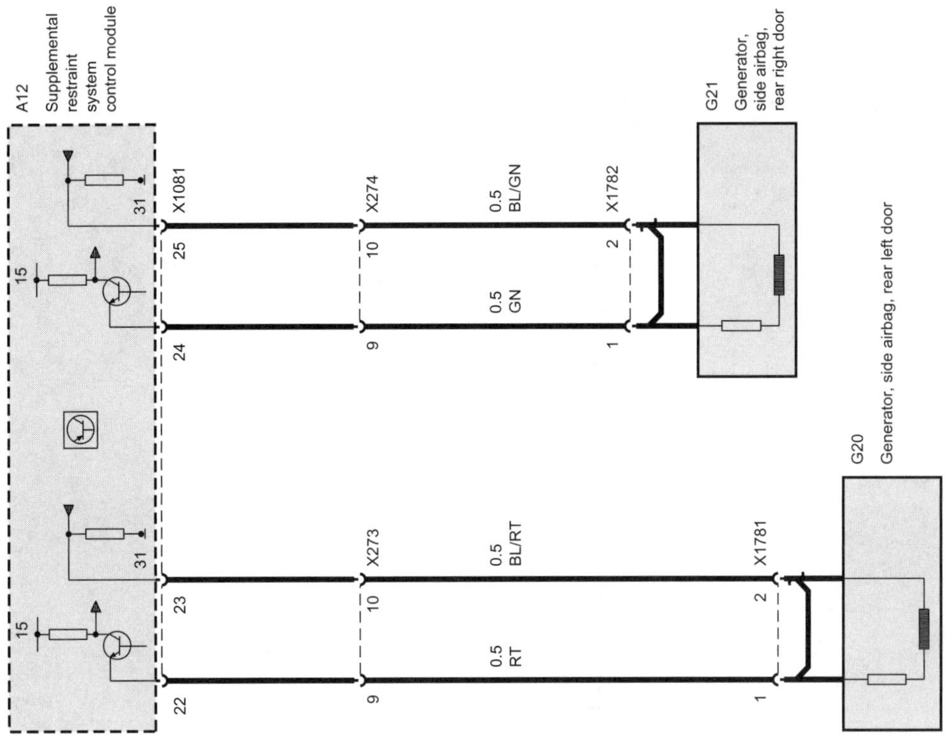

502ELE0212a

Supplemental Restraint System (SRS)
Side airbag, rear head area (ITS)

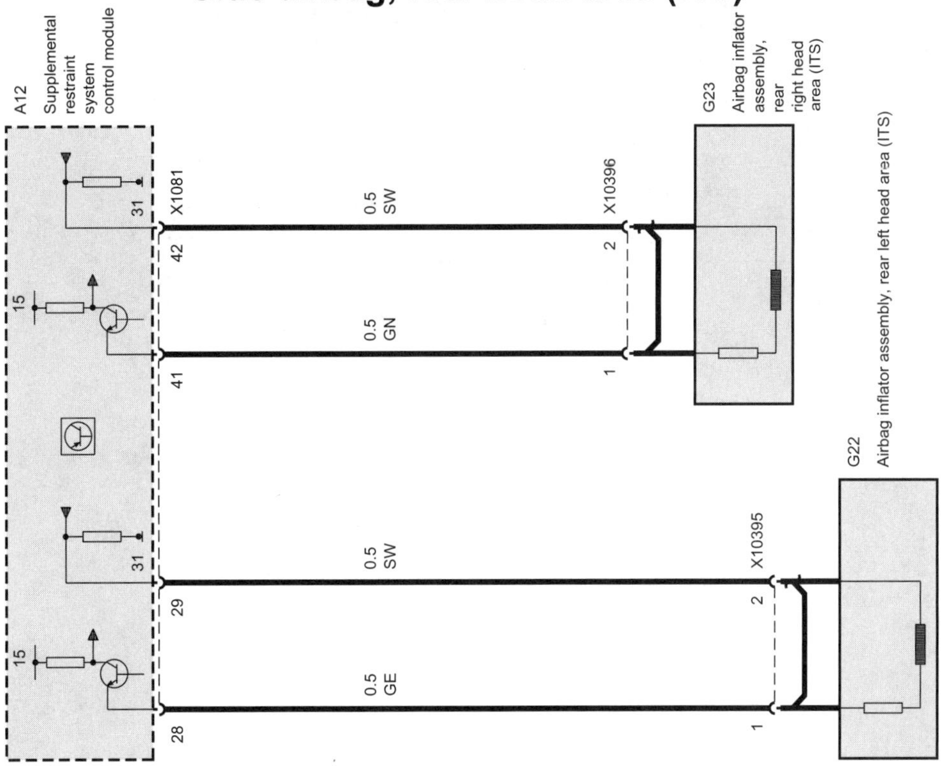

502ELE0212b

Supplemental Restraint System (SRS)
Supplemental restraint system control module
(1 of 1)

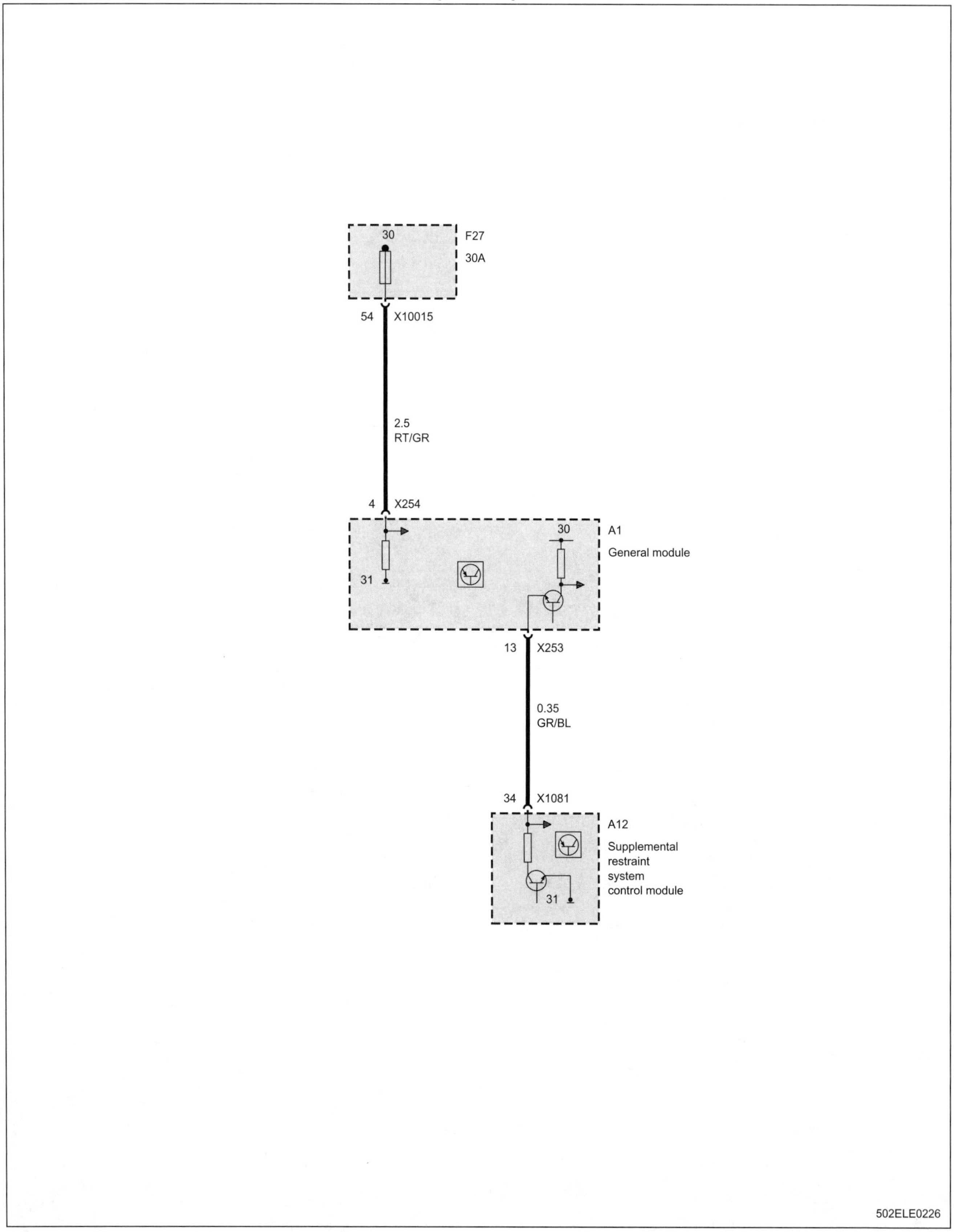

Anti-Theft
Antitheft alarm system (overview)
(1 of 4)

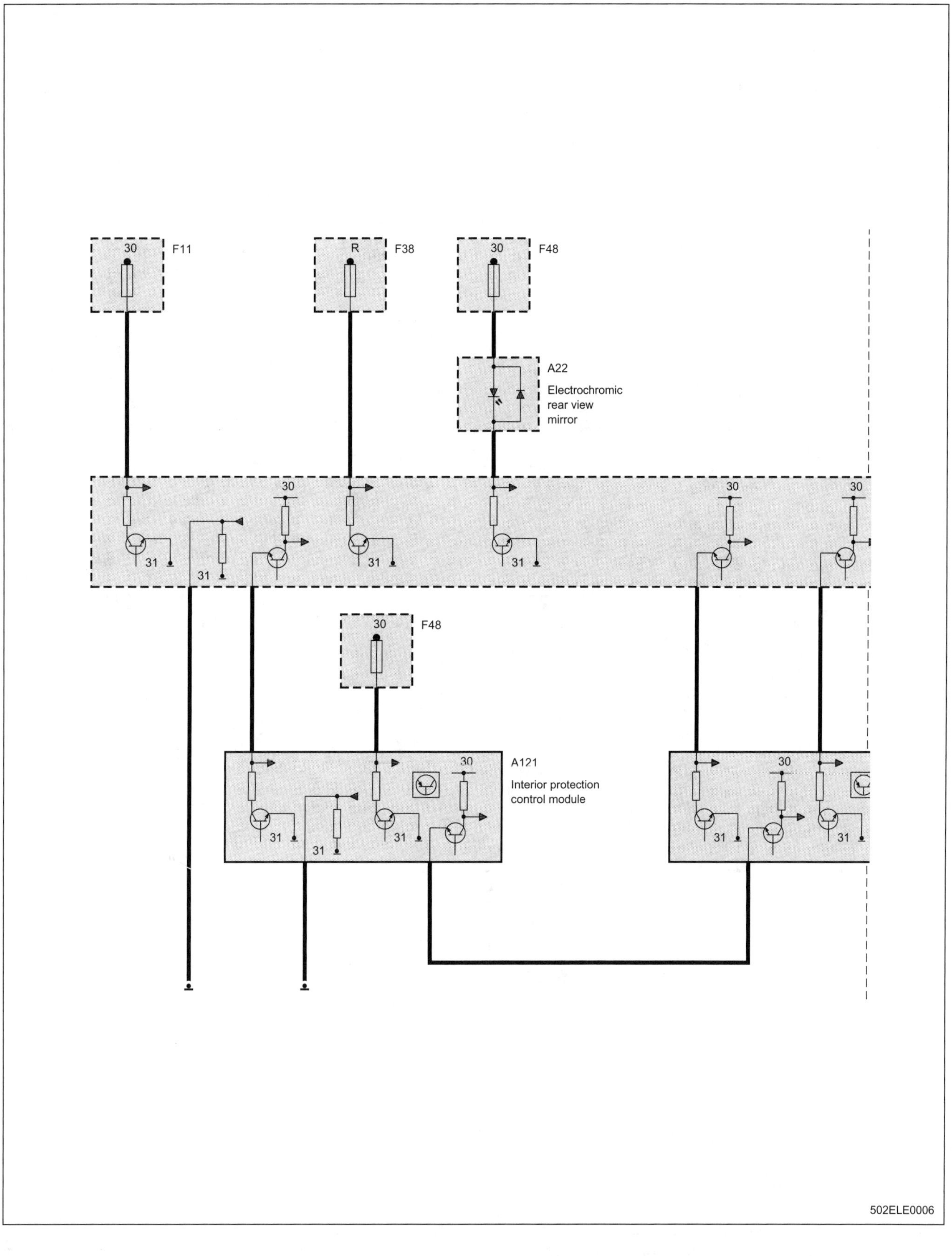

Anti-Theft
Alarm system (overview)
(2 of 4)

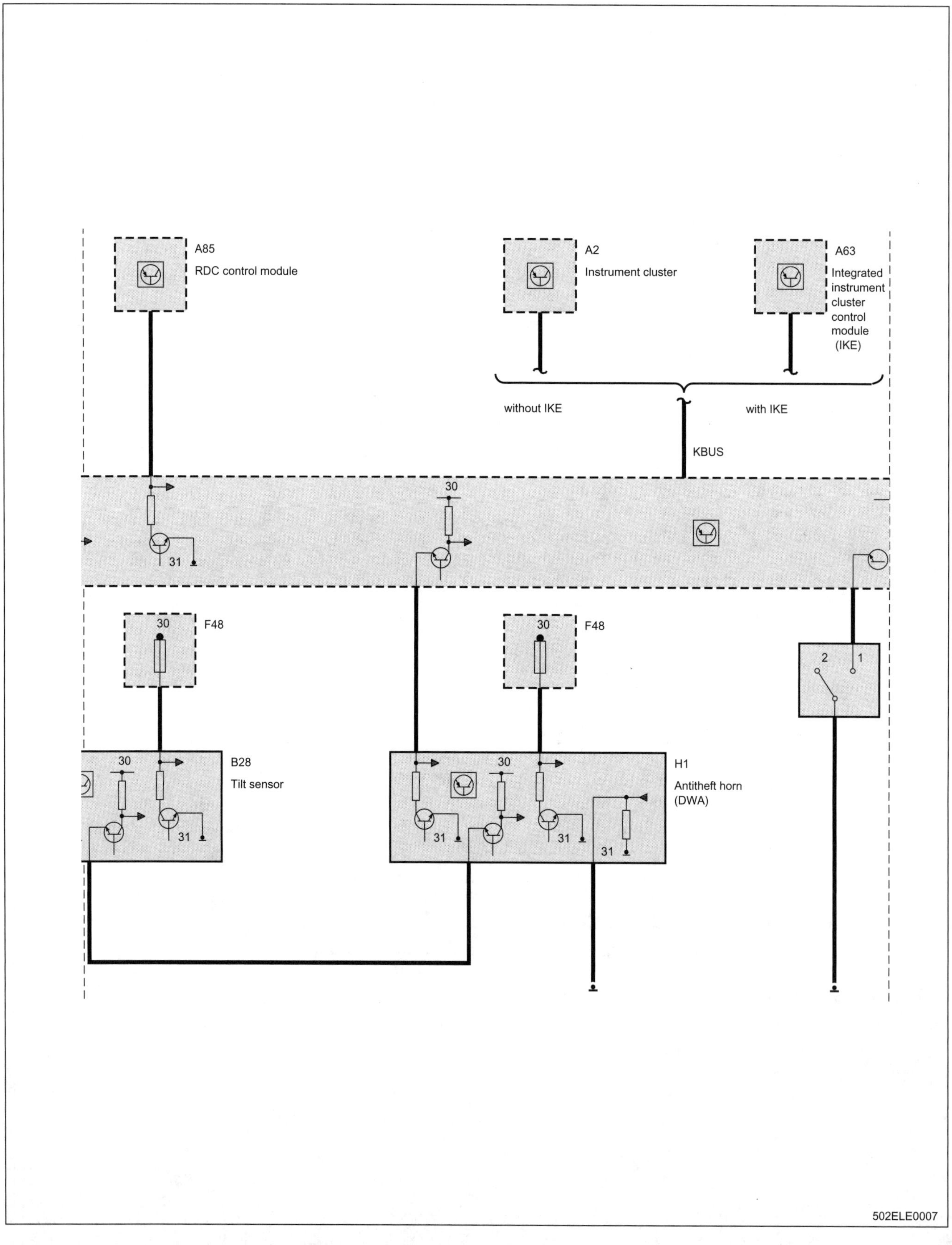
A85
RDC control module
A2
Instrument cluster
A63
Integrated instrument cluster control module (IKE)
without IKE
with IKE
KBUS
30
31
F48
30
2
1
B28
Tilt sensor
H1
Antitheft horn (DWA)
502ELE0007

Anti-Theft
Alarm system (overview)
(3 of 4)

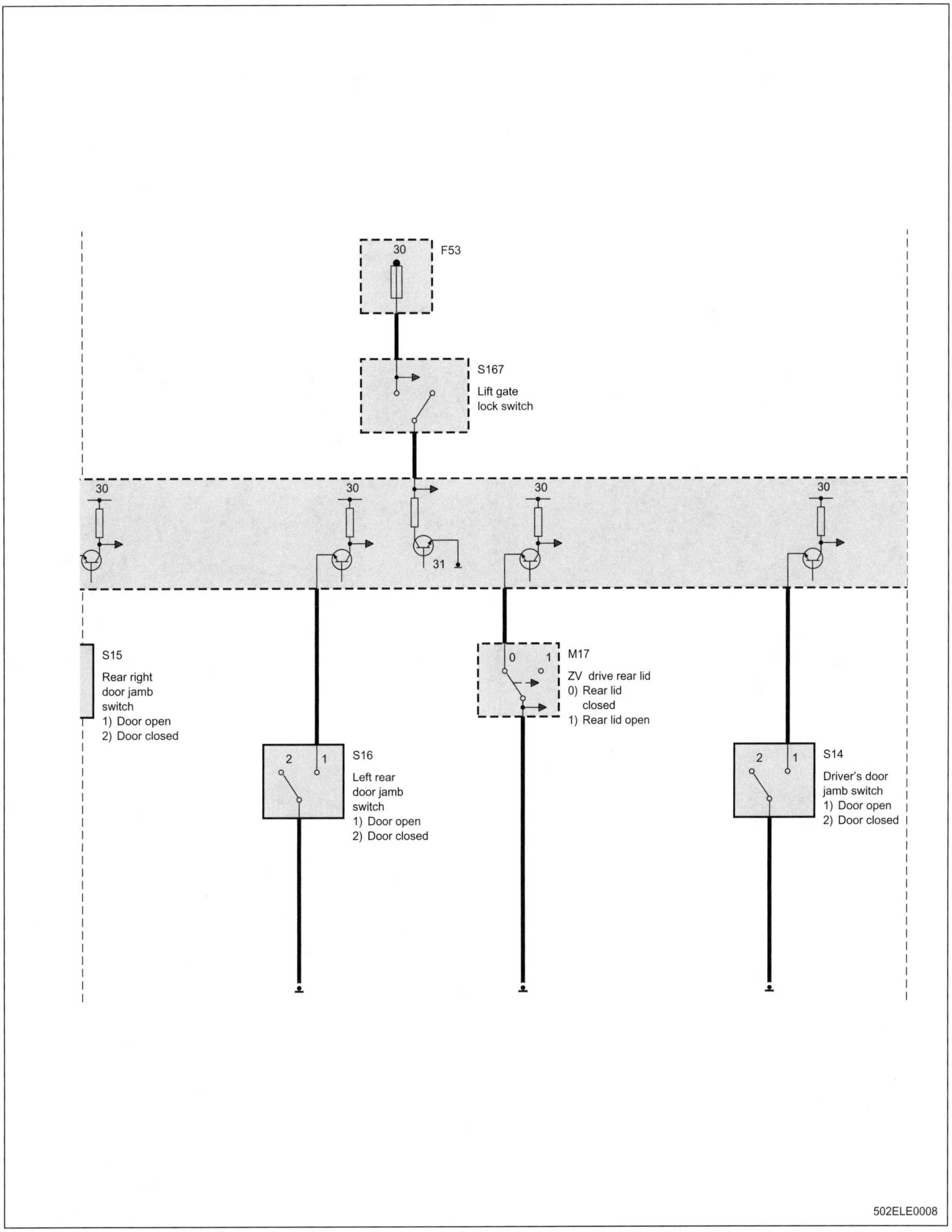
30
F53
S167
Lift gate
lock switch
30
30
30
30
31
S15
Rear right
door jamb
switch
1) Door open
2) Door closed
0
1
M17
ZV drive rear lid
0) Rear lid
closed
1) Rear lid open
2
1
S16
Left rear
door jamb
switch
1) Door open
2) Door closed
2
1
S14
Driver's door
jamb switch
1) Door open
2) Door closed
502ELE0008

Anti-Theft
Alarm system (overview)
(4 of 4)

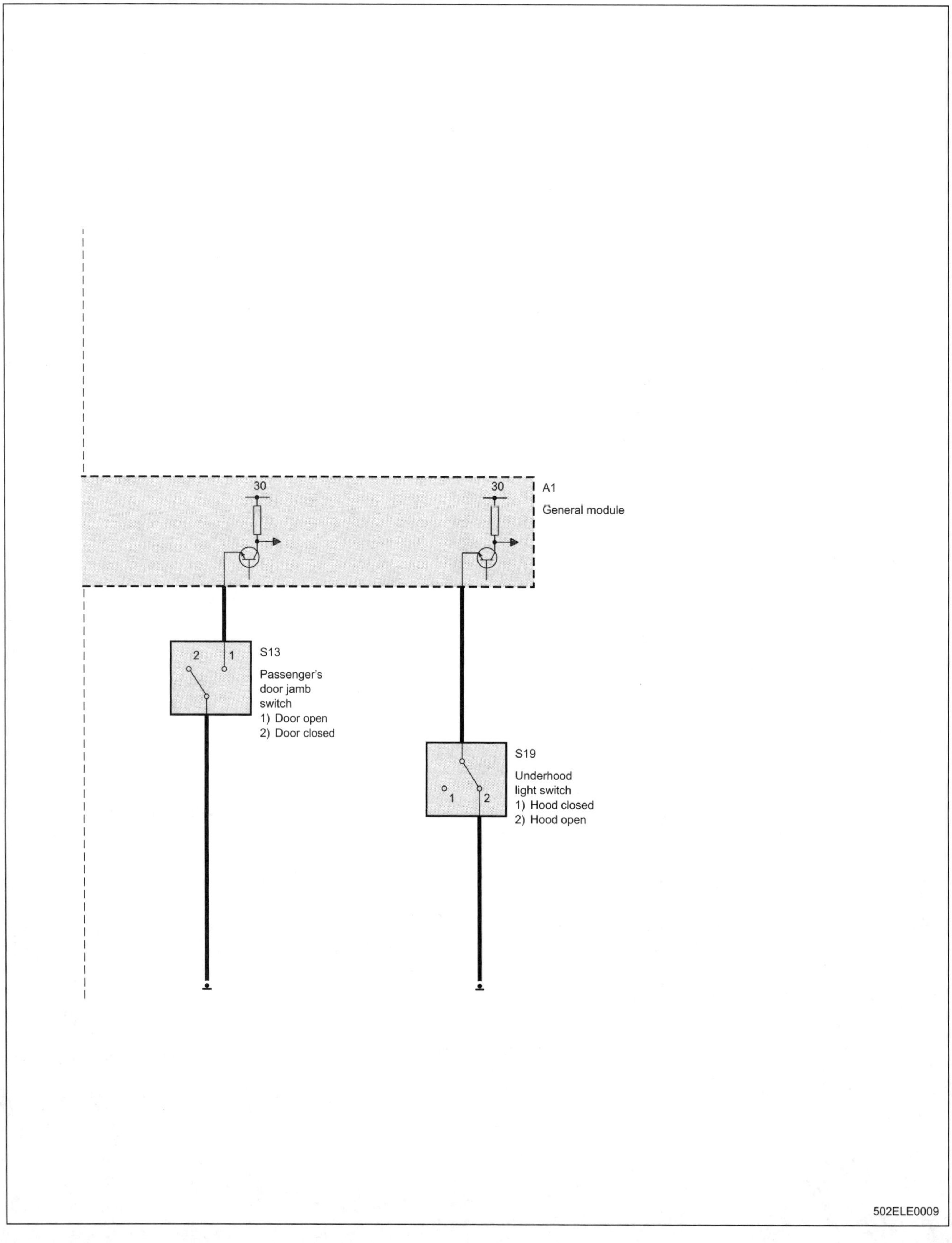
30
30
A1
General module
2
1
S13
Passenger's door jamb switch
1) Door open
2) Door closed
S19
Underhood light switch
1) Hood closed
2) Hood open
1
2
502ELE0009

Anti-Theft
Drive-away protection (overview)
(1 of 1)

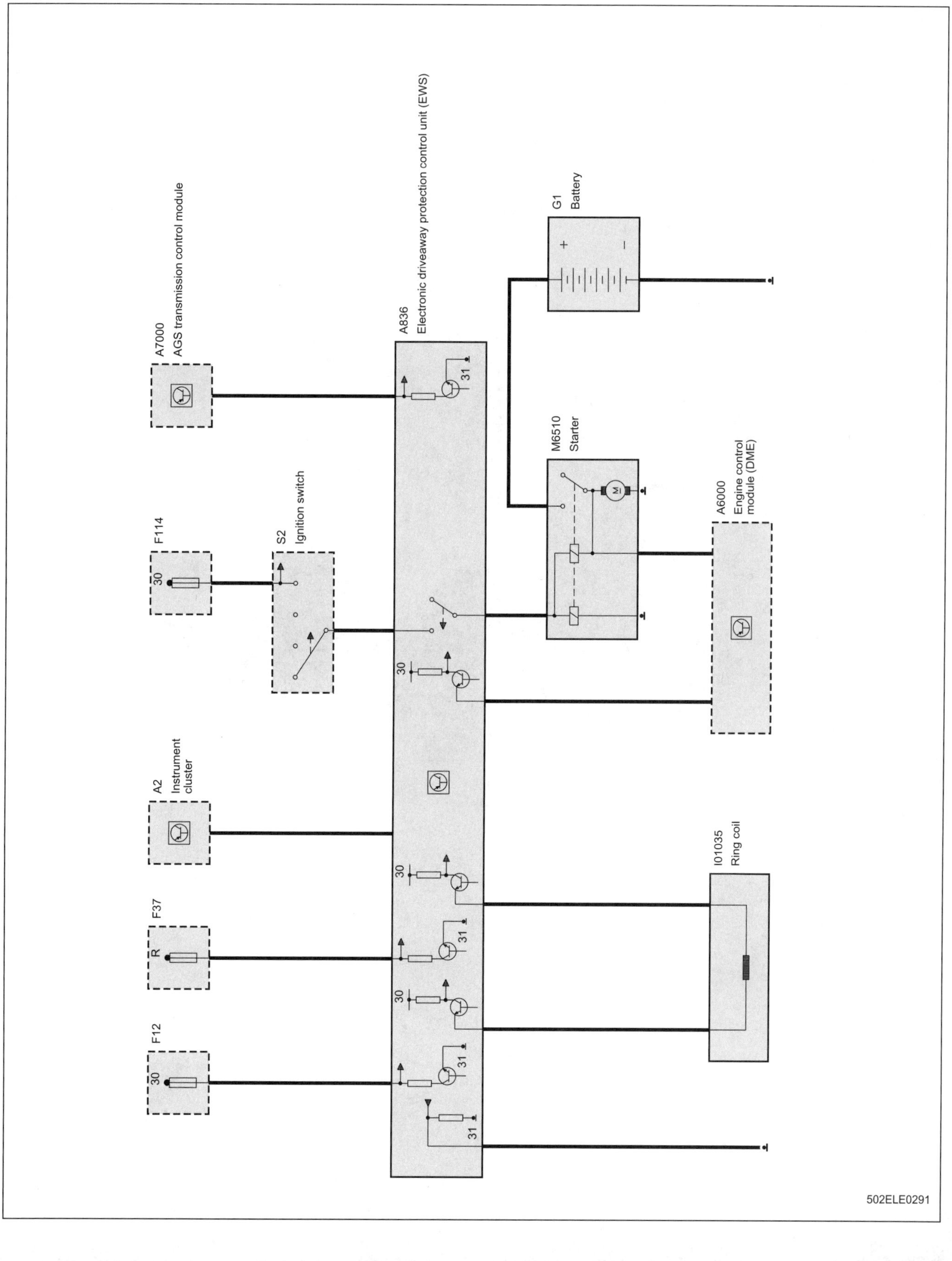

Anti-Theft
Alarm horn
(1 of 1)

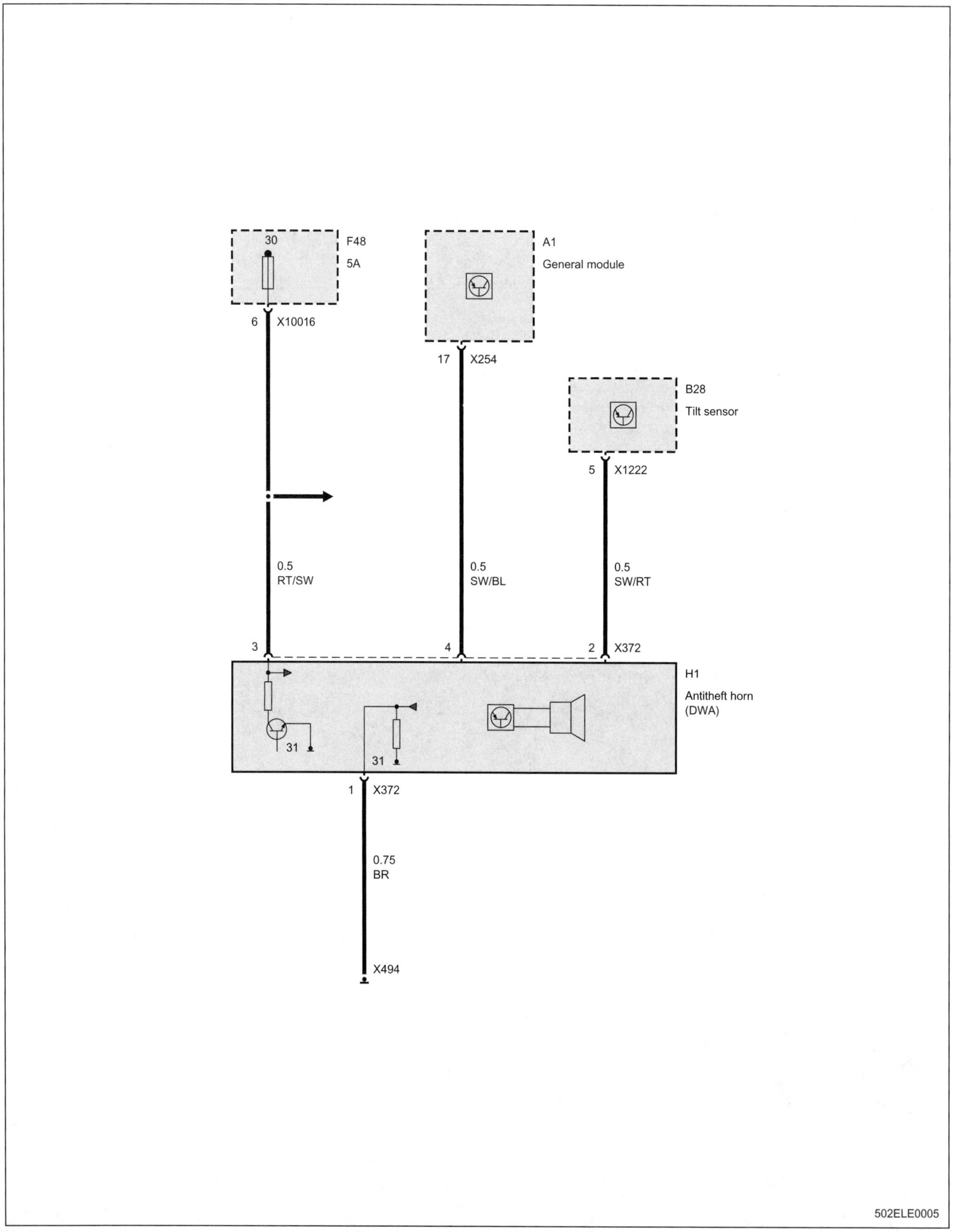
30
F48
5A
A1
General module
6
X10016
17
X254
B28
Tilt sensor
5
X1222
0.5
RT/SW
0.5
SW/BL
0.5
SW/RT
3
4
2
X372
H1
Antitheft horn
(DWA)
31
31
1
X372
0.75
BR
X494
502ELE0005

Anti-Theft
Tilt sensor
(1 of 1)

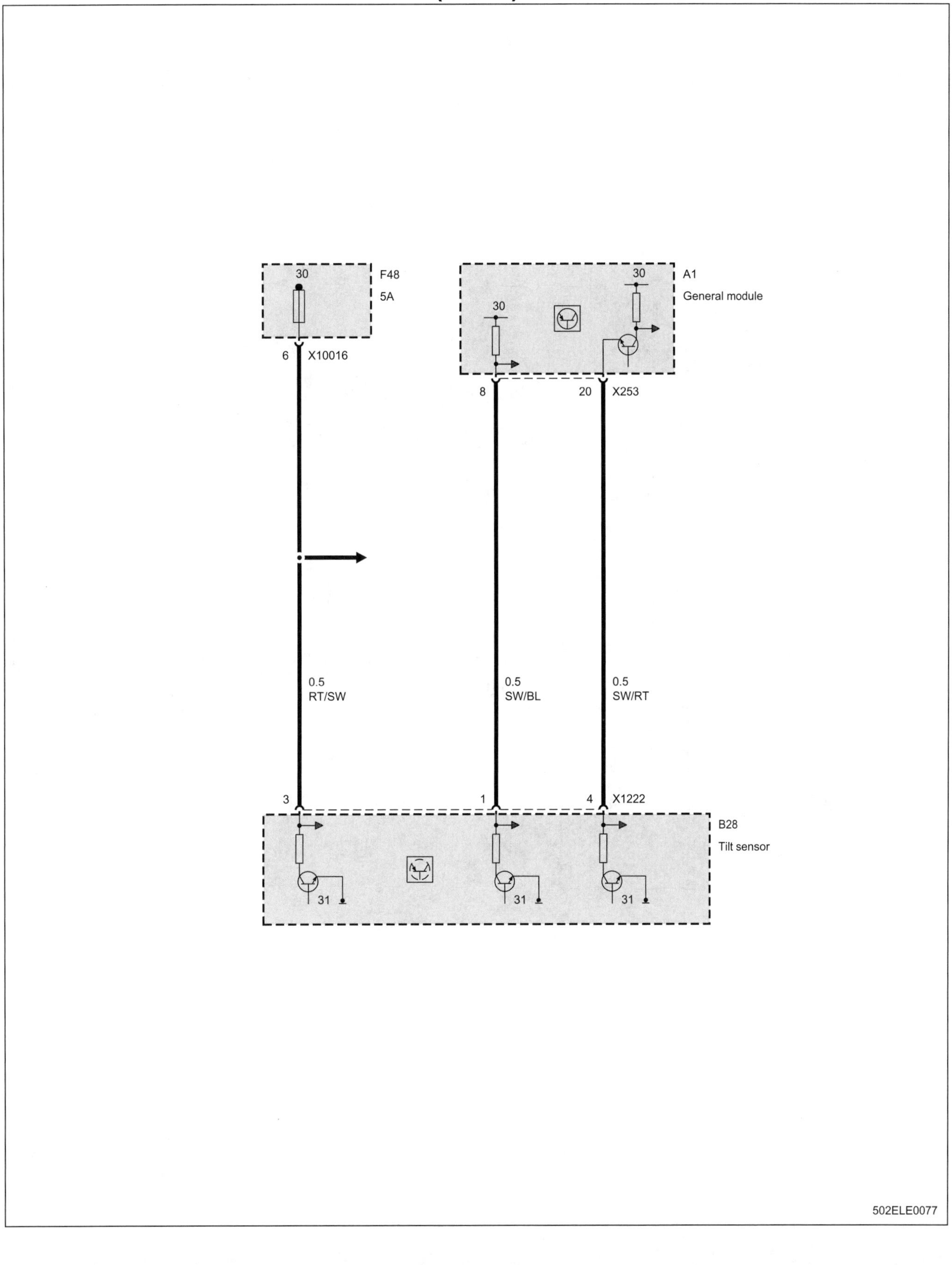
30
F48
5A
6
X10016
30
A1
General module
30
8
20
X253
0.5
RT/SW
0.5
SW/BL
0.5
SW/RT
3
1
4
X1222
B28
Tilt sensor
31
31
31

502ELE0077

Anti-Theft
Interior protection
(1 of 1)

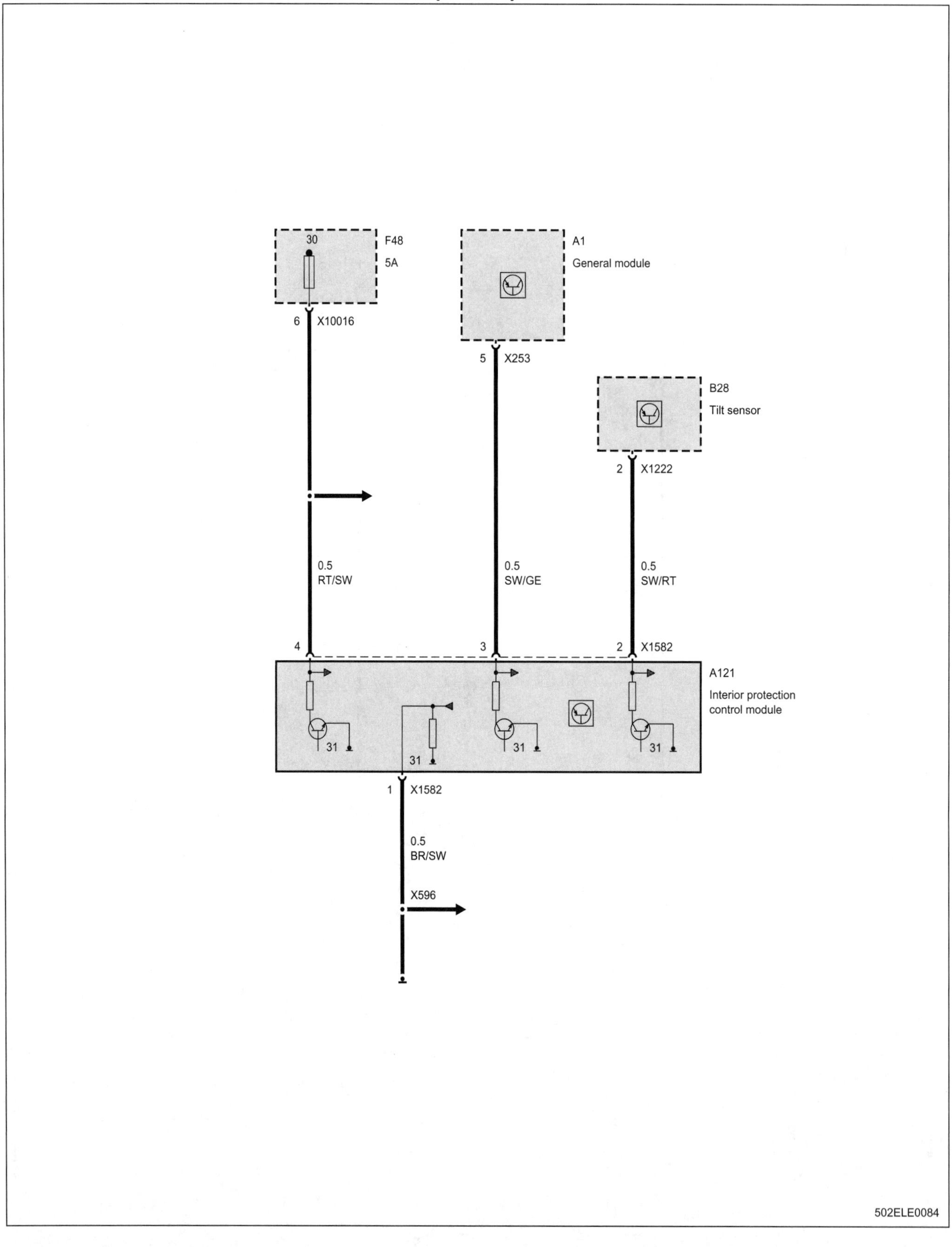
30
F48
5A
6 X10016
A1
General module
5 X253
B28
Tilt sensor
2 X1222
0.5
RT/SW
0.5
SW/GE
0.5
SW/RT
4
3
2 X1582
A121
Interior protection
control module
31
31
31
31
1 X1582
0.5
BR/SW
X596
502ELE0084

Anti-Theft
EWS Interface signals
(1 of 1)

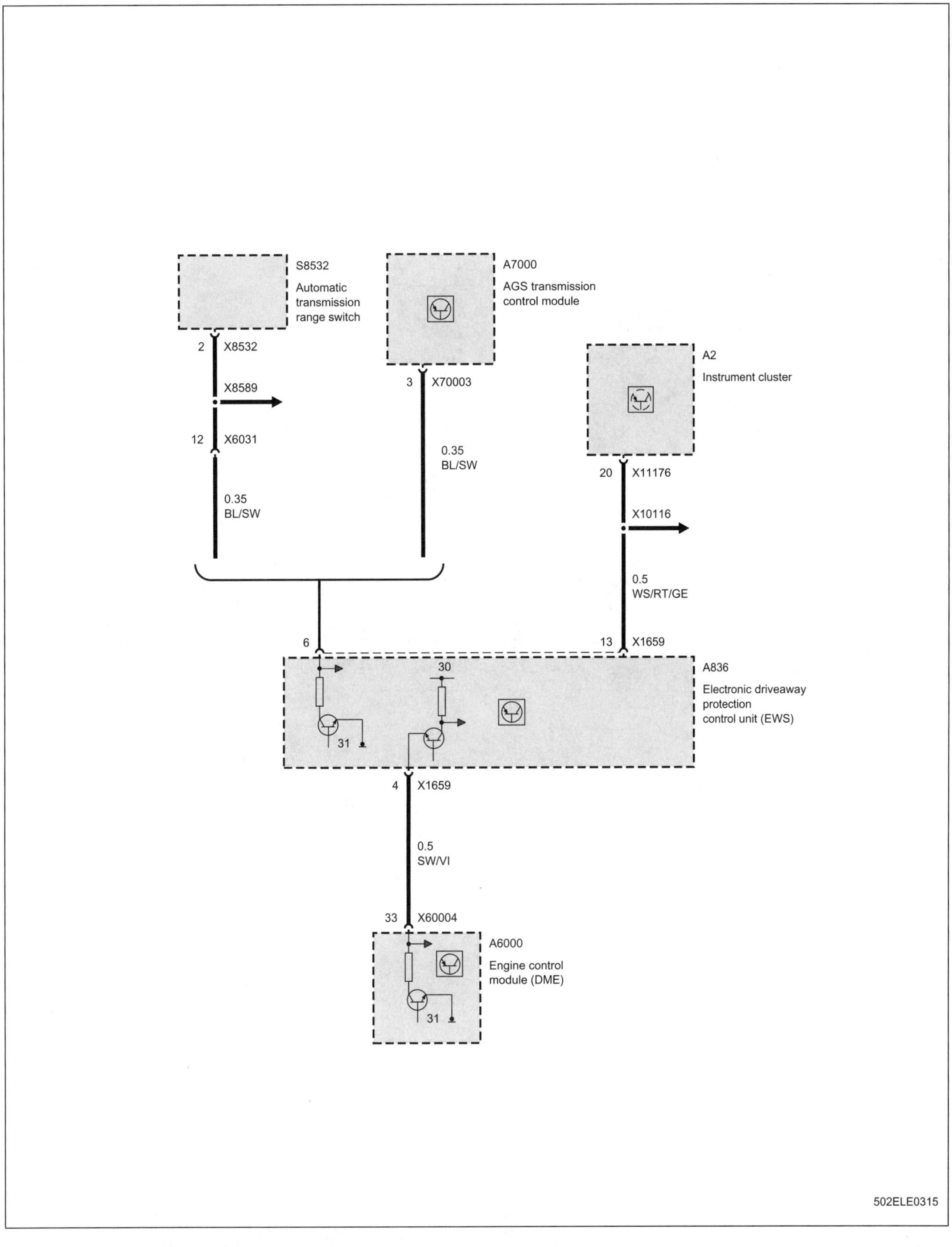
S8532
Automatic transmission range switch
A7000
AGS transmission control module
A2
Instrument cluster
2 X8532
X8589
12 X6031
0.35 BL/SW
3 X70003
0.35 BL/SW
20 X11176
X10116
0.5 WS/RT/GE
6
13 X1659
30
31
A836
Electronic driveaway protection control unit (EWS)
4 X1659
0.5 SW/VI
33 X60004
A6000
Engine control module (DME)
31
502ELE0315

Anti-Theft
EWS Control Unit, Power
(1 of 1)

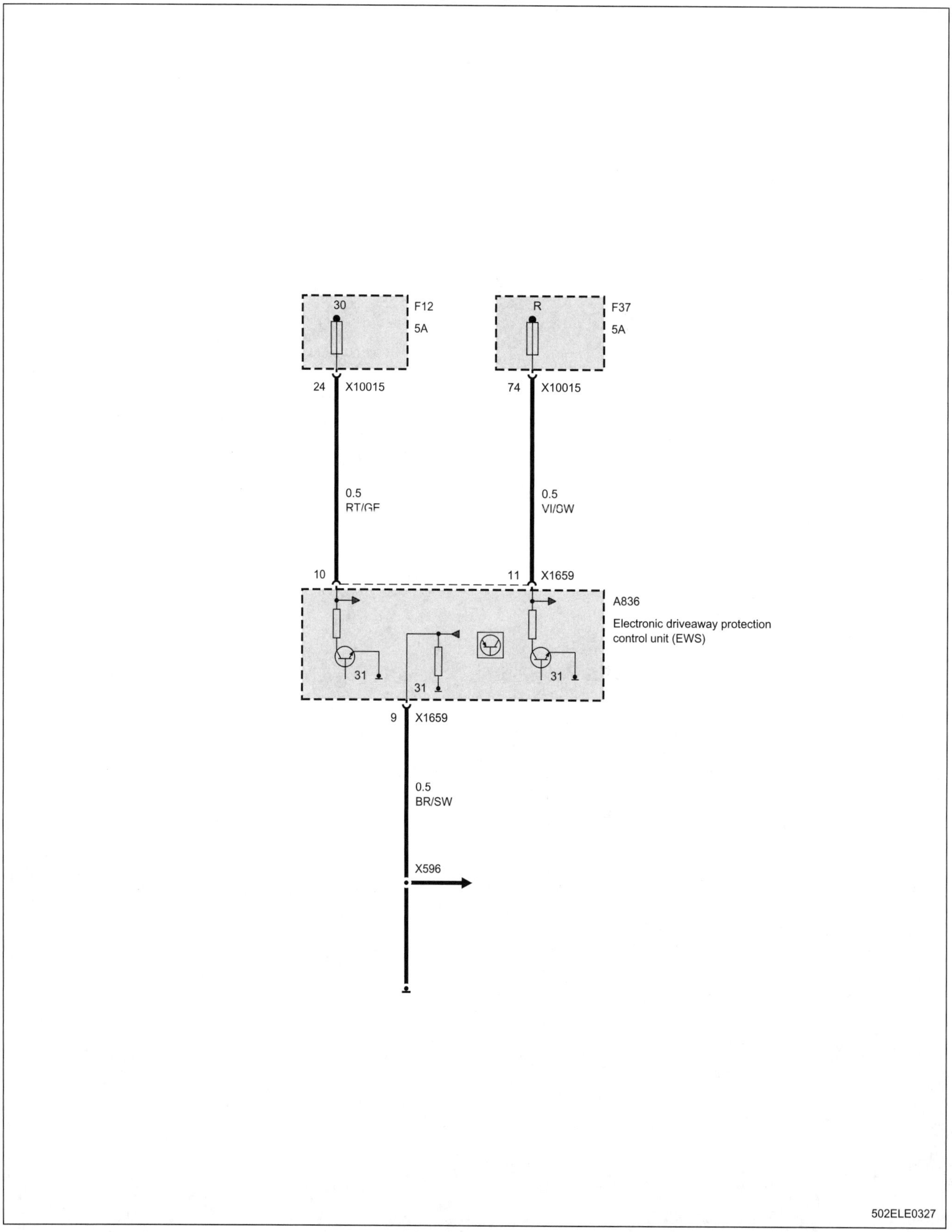
30
F12
5A
R
F37
5A
24
X10015
74
X10015
0.5
RT/GE
0.5
VI/SW
10
11
X1659
A836
Electronic driveaway protection
control unit (EWS)
31
31
31
9
X1659
0.5
BR/SW
X596
502ELE0327

Anti-Theft
Electronic drive-away protection control unit (EWS) (A836)
(1 of 2)

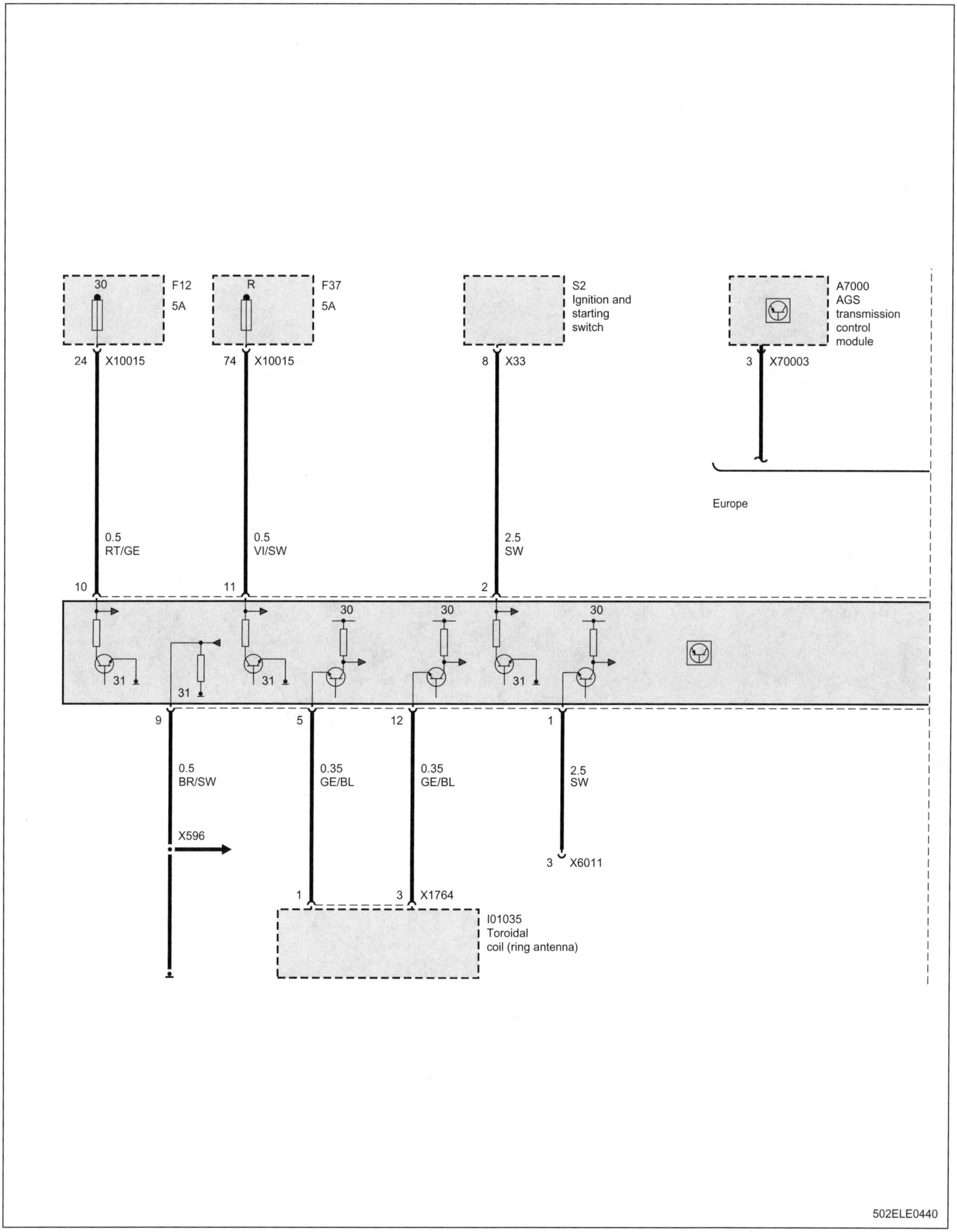

Anti-Theft
Electronic drive-away protection control unit (EWS) (A836)
(2 of 2)

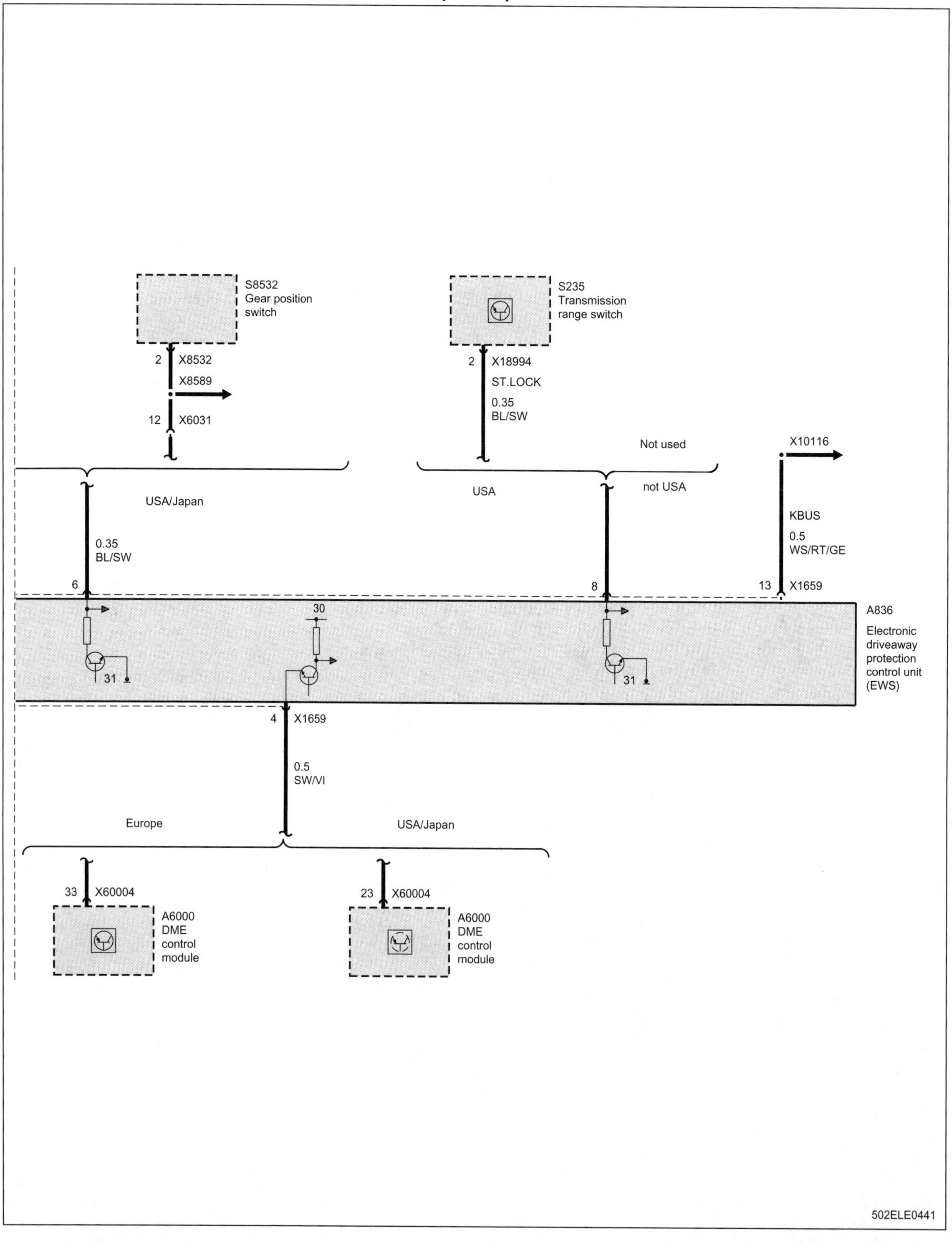

502ELE0441

Anti-Theft
EWS Ring coil 1
(1 of 1)

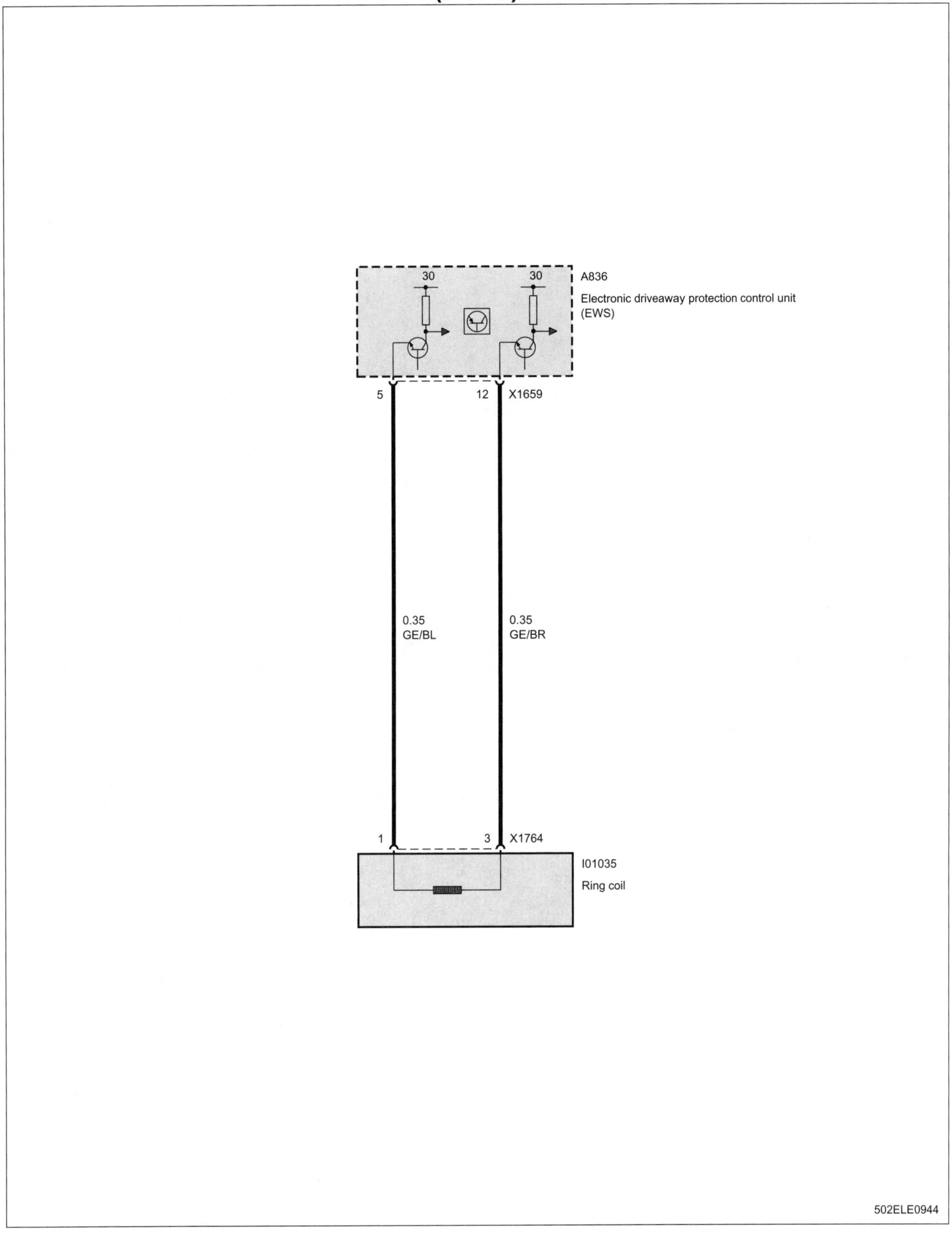
30
30
A836
Electronic driveaway protection control unit
(EWS)
5
12
X1659
0.35
GE/BL
0.35
GE/BR
1
3
X1764
I01035
Ring coil

502ELE0944

Central Locking

Central locking system (ZV) (overview)

(1 of 3)

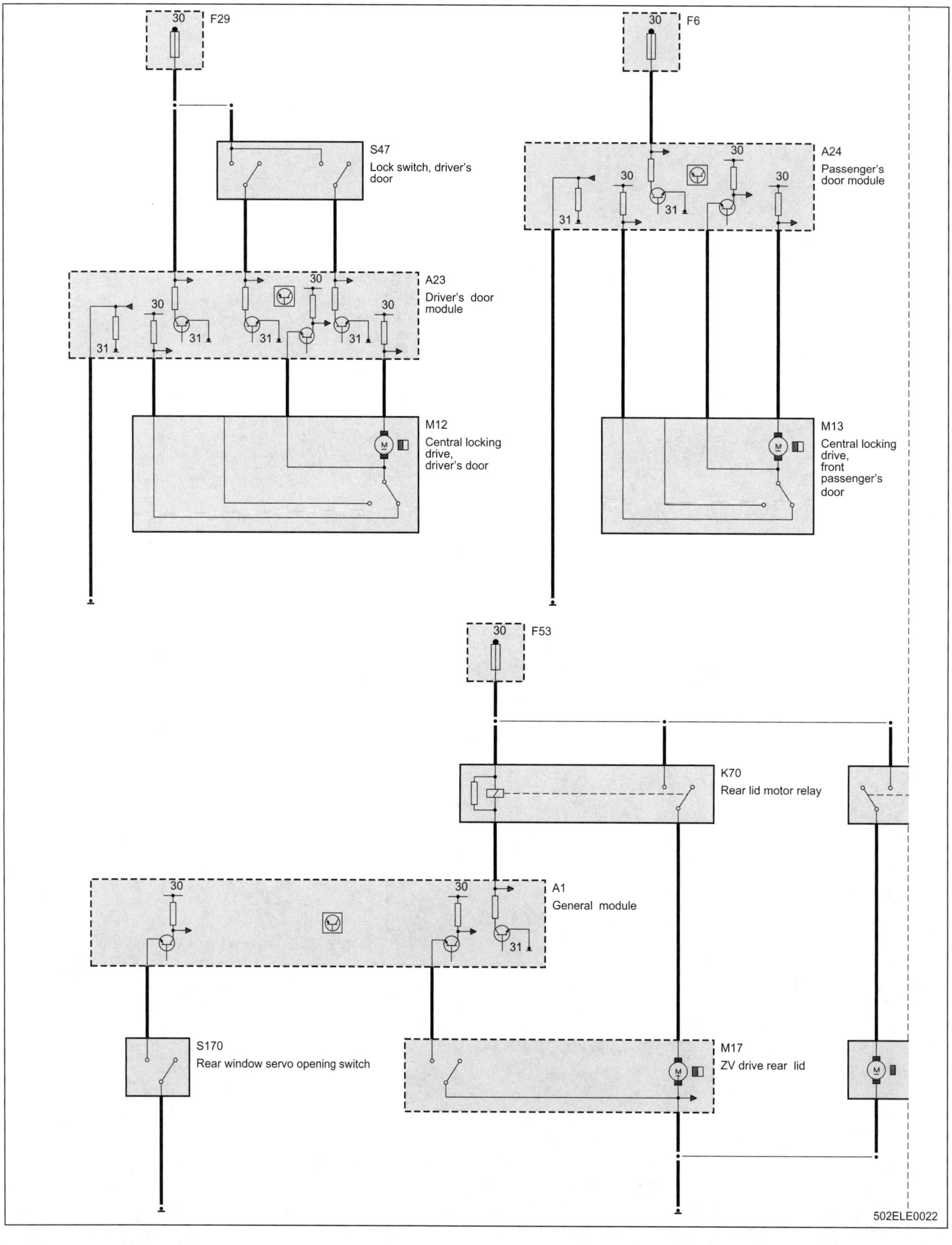

Central Locking
Central locking system (ZV) (overview)
(2 of 3)

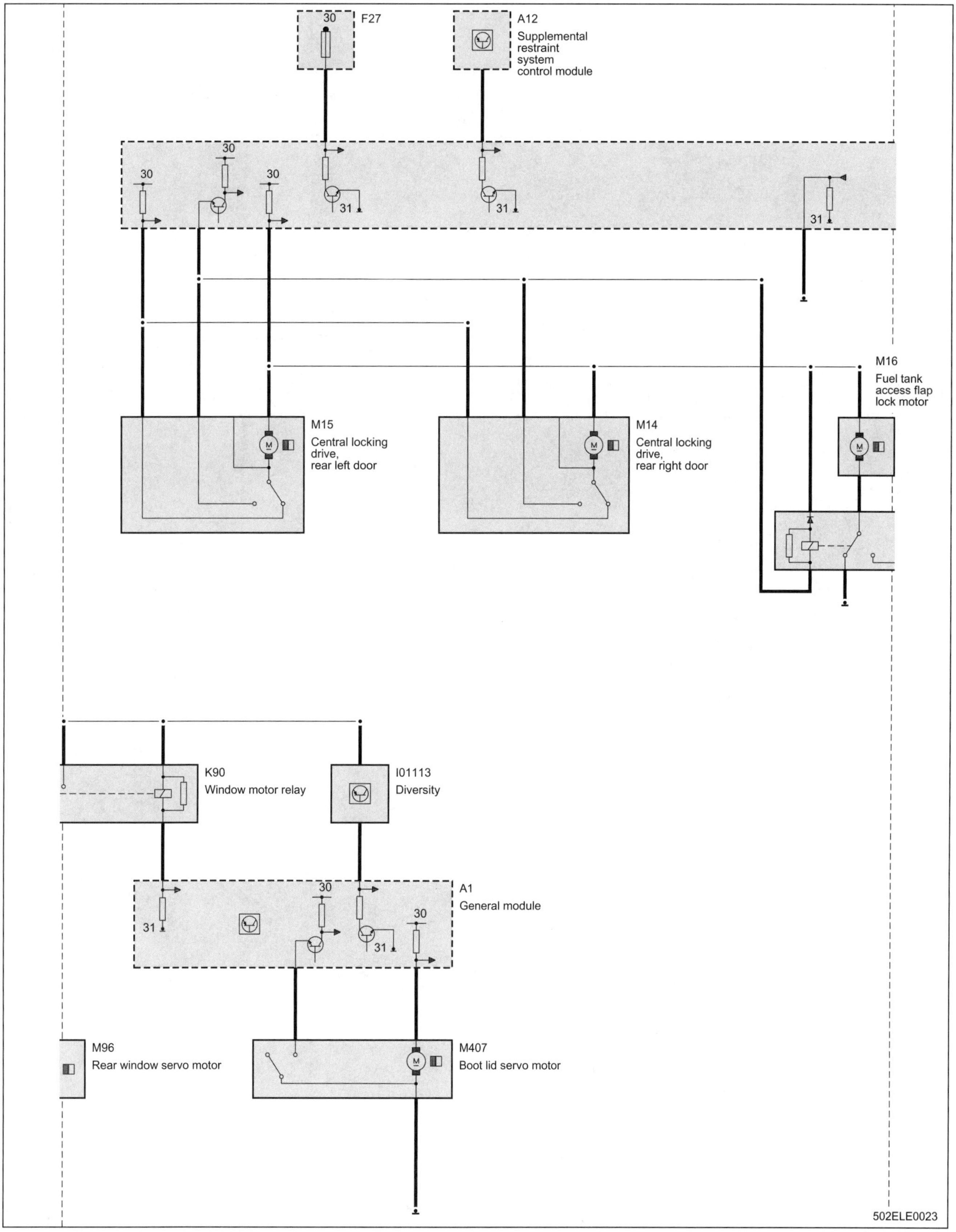

Central Locking
Central locking system (ZV) (overview)
(3 of 3)

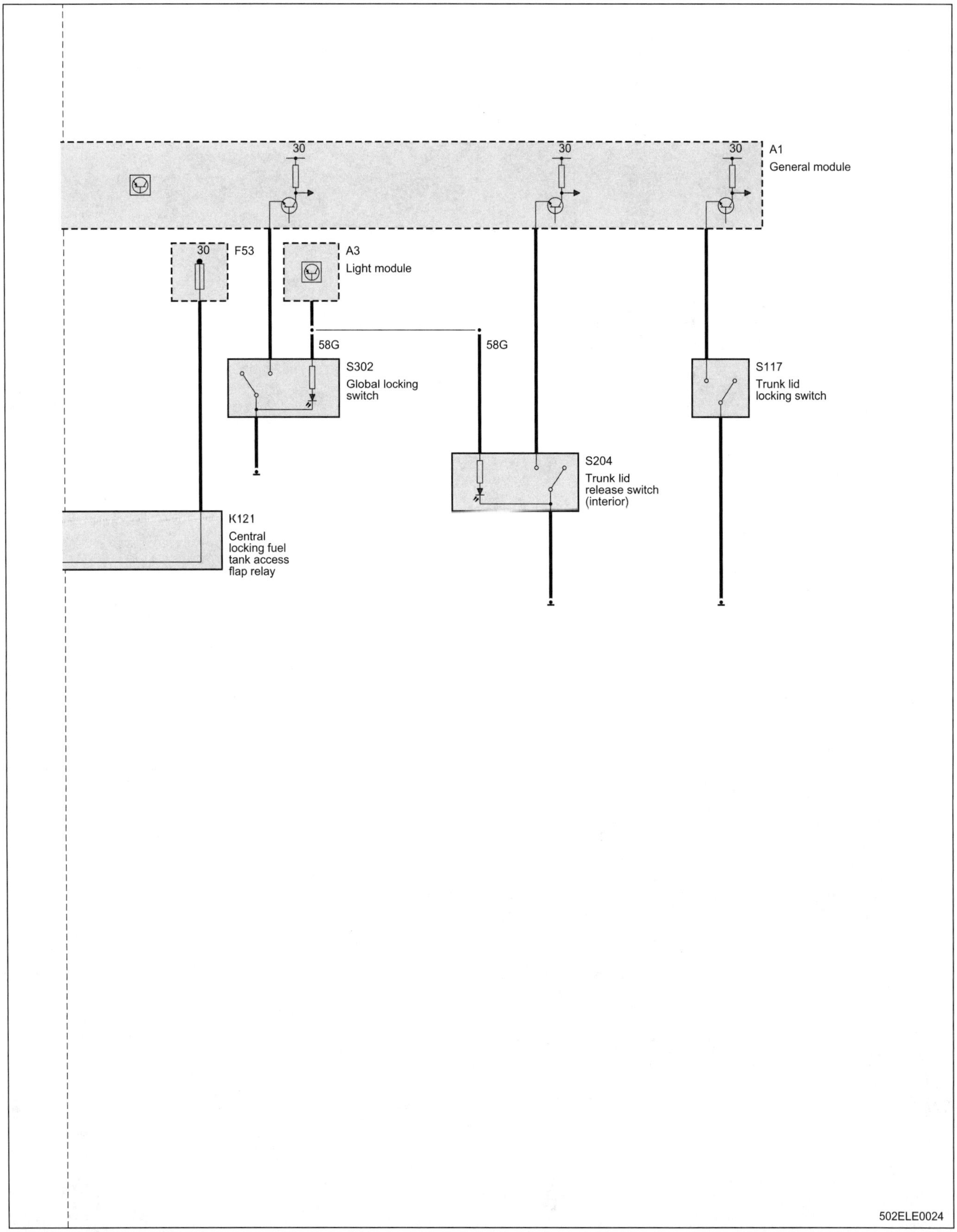

Central Locking
Trunk lid release
(1 of 1)

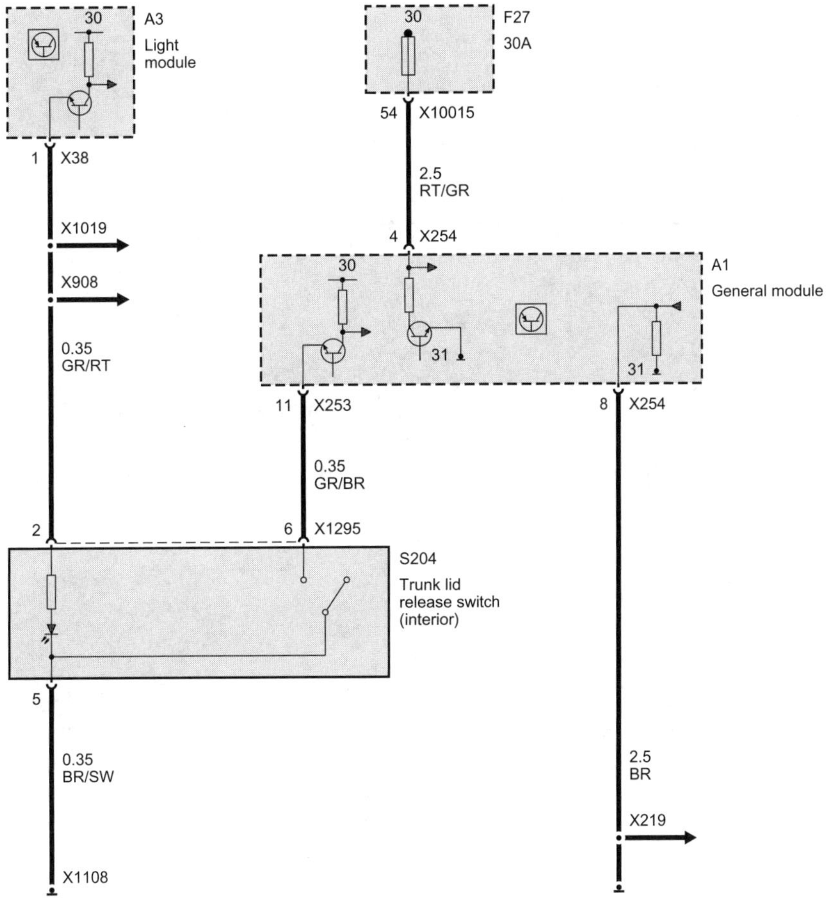

502ELE0017

Central Locking

Central locking (ZV) fuel tank access flap
(1 of 1)

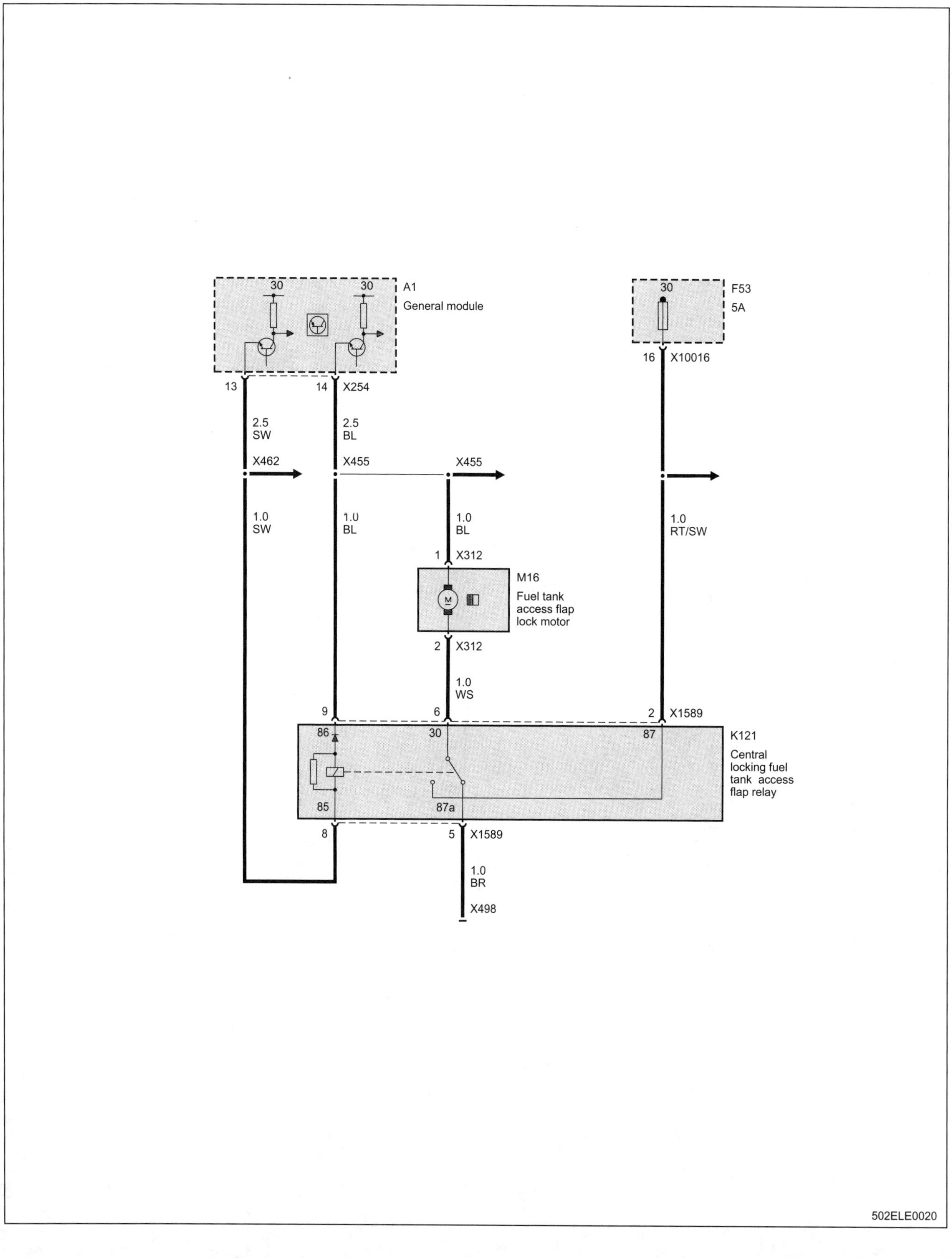

Central Locking
Central locking (ZV) rear driver's side

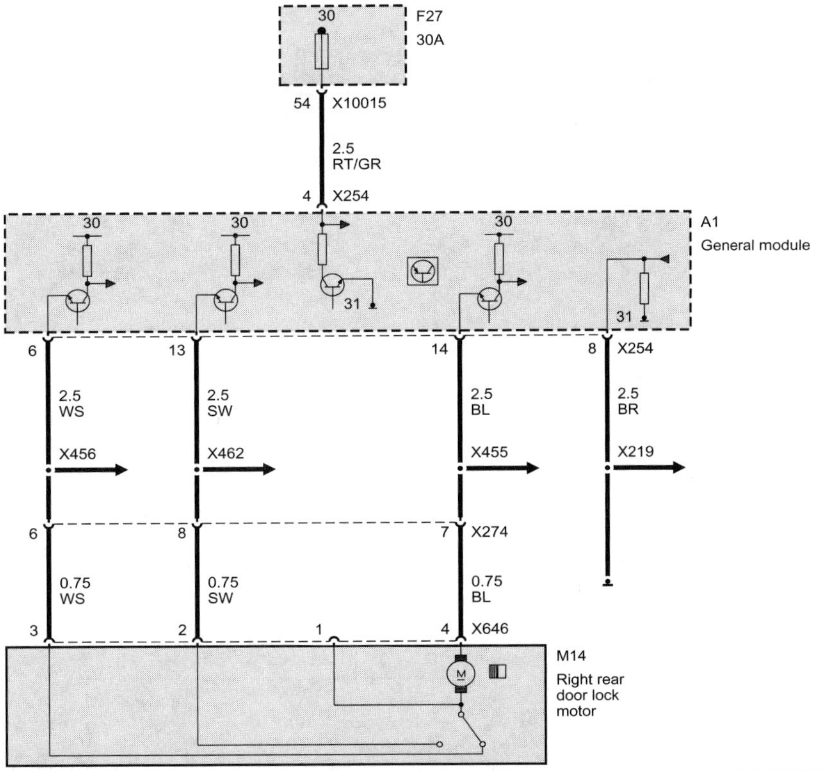

Central Locking
Central locking (ZV) rear passenger's side

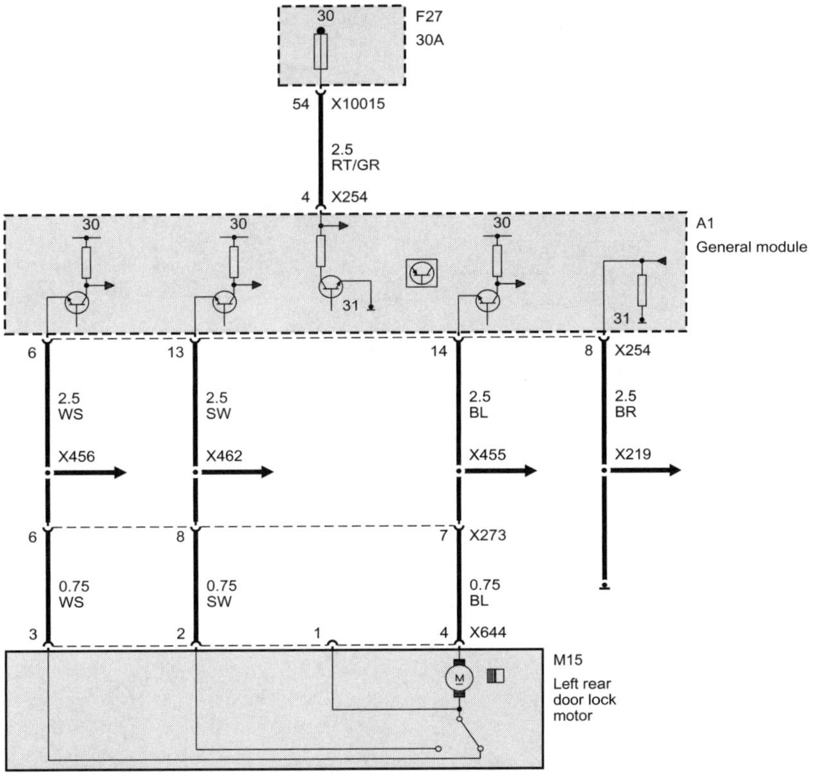

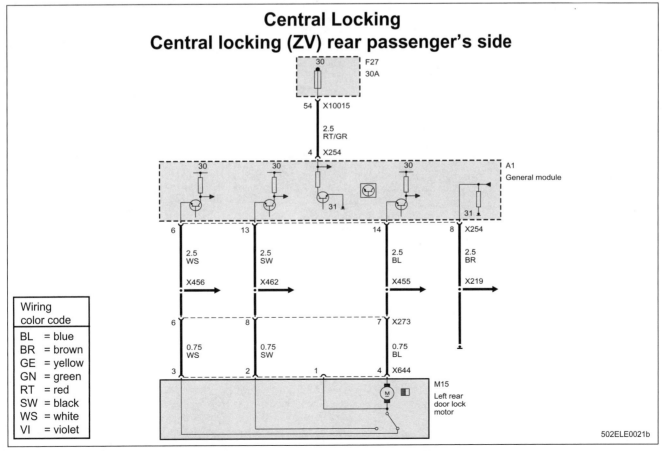

Wiring color code	
BL	= blue
BR	= brown
GE	= yellow
GN	= green
RT	= red
SW	= black
WS	= white
VI	= violet

Central Locking
Central-locking button
(1 of 1)

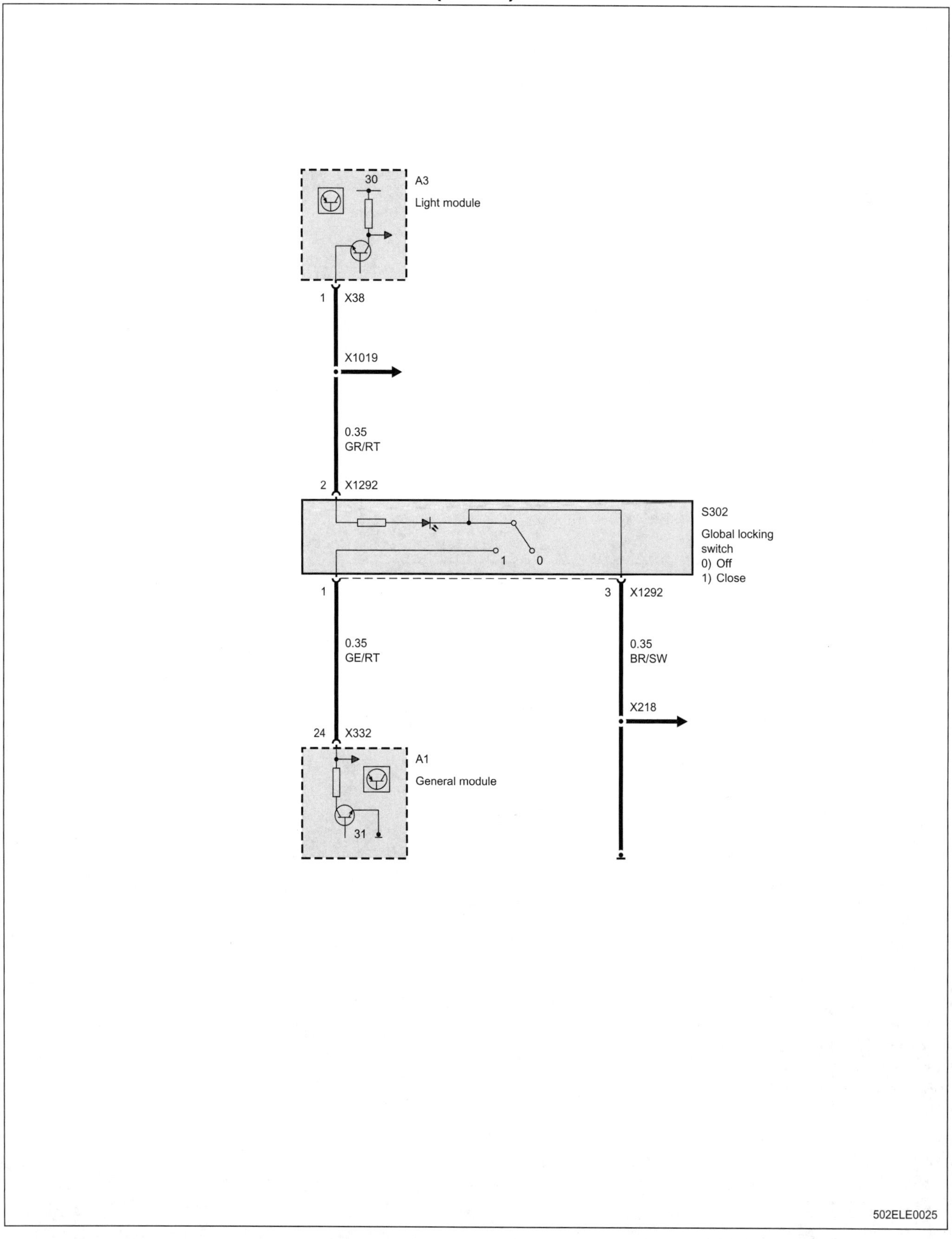
30
A3
Light module
1
X38
X1019
0.35
GR/RT
2
X1292
S302
Global locking
switch
0) Off
1) Close
1
0
1
3
X1292
0.35
GE/RT
0.35
BR/SW
X218
24
X332
A1
General module
31
502ELE0025

Central Locking
Driver's door
(1 of 1)

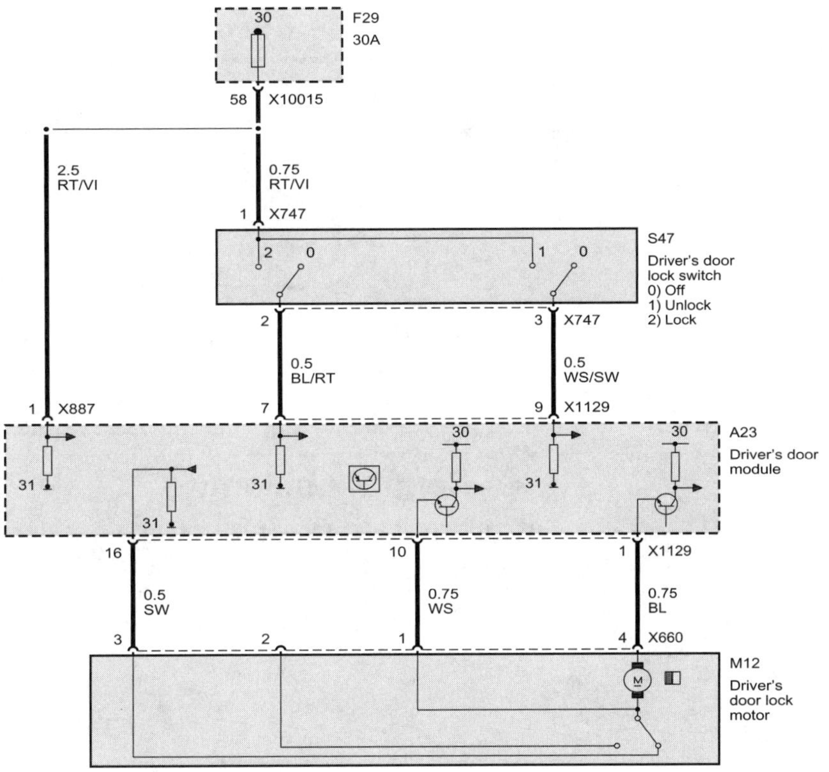
30
F29
30A
58
X10015
2.5
RT/VI
0.75
RT/VI
1
X747
2
0
1
0
S47
Driver's door
lock switch
0) Off
1) Unlock
2) Lock
2
3
X747
0.5
BL/RT
0.5
WS/SW
1
X887
7
9
X1129
30
30
A23
Driver's door
module
31
31
31
31
16
10
1
X1129
0.5
SW
0.75
WS
0.75
BL
3
2
1
4
X660
M
M12
Driver's
door lock
motor

502ELE0040

Central Locking
Passenger's door central locking (ZV)

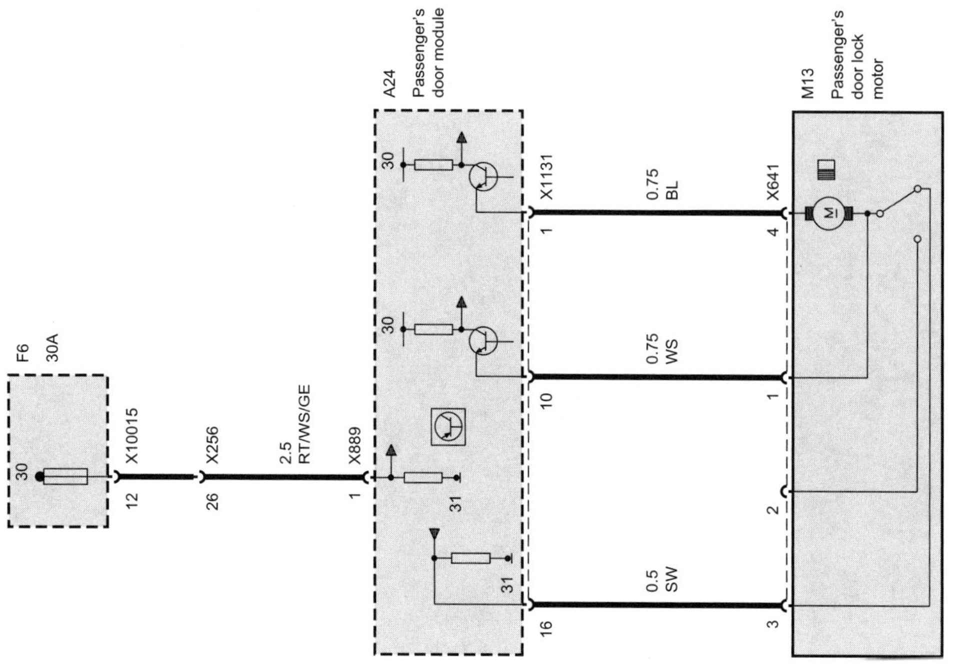

502ELE0120a

Central Locking
Passenger's door contact

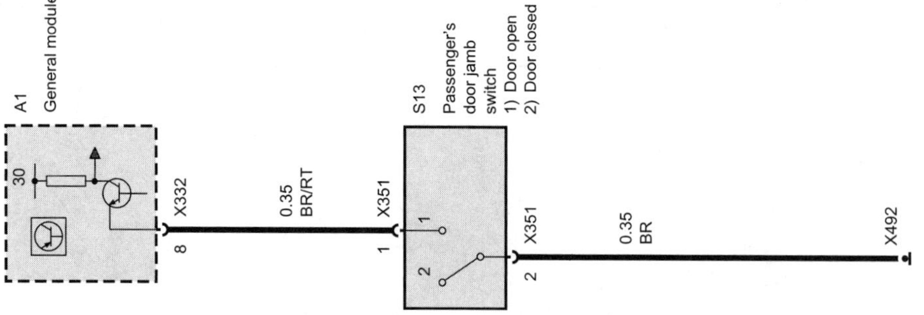

502ELE0120b

Central Locking
ZV drive, automatic rear lid
(1 of 1)

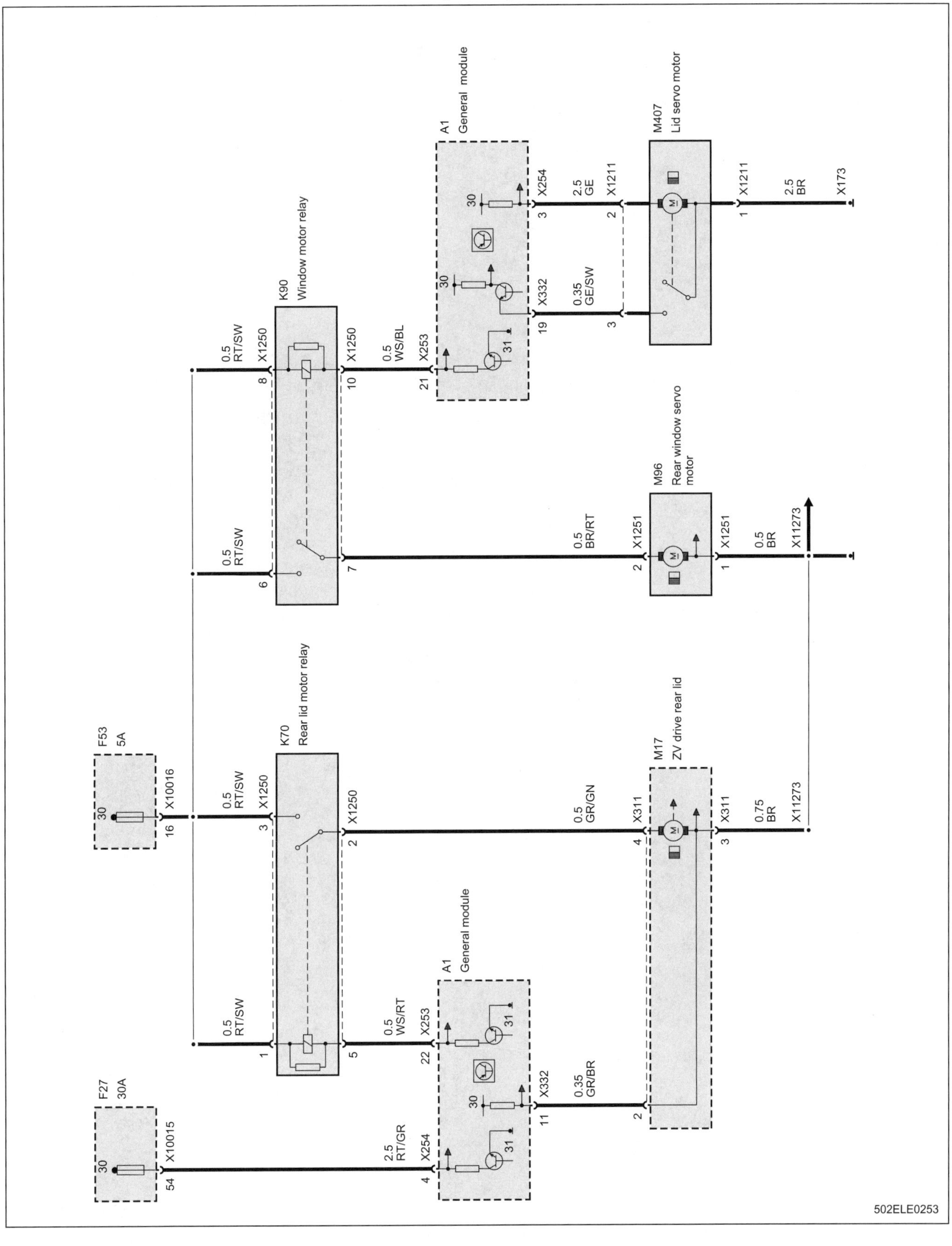

Charging System
Generator (alternator) (G2023)
(1 of 1)

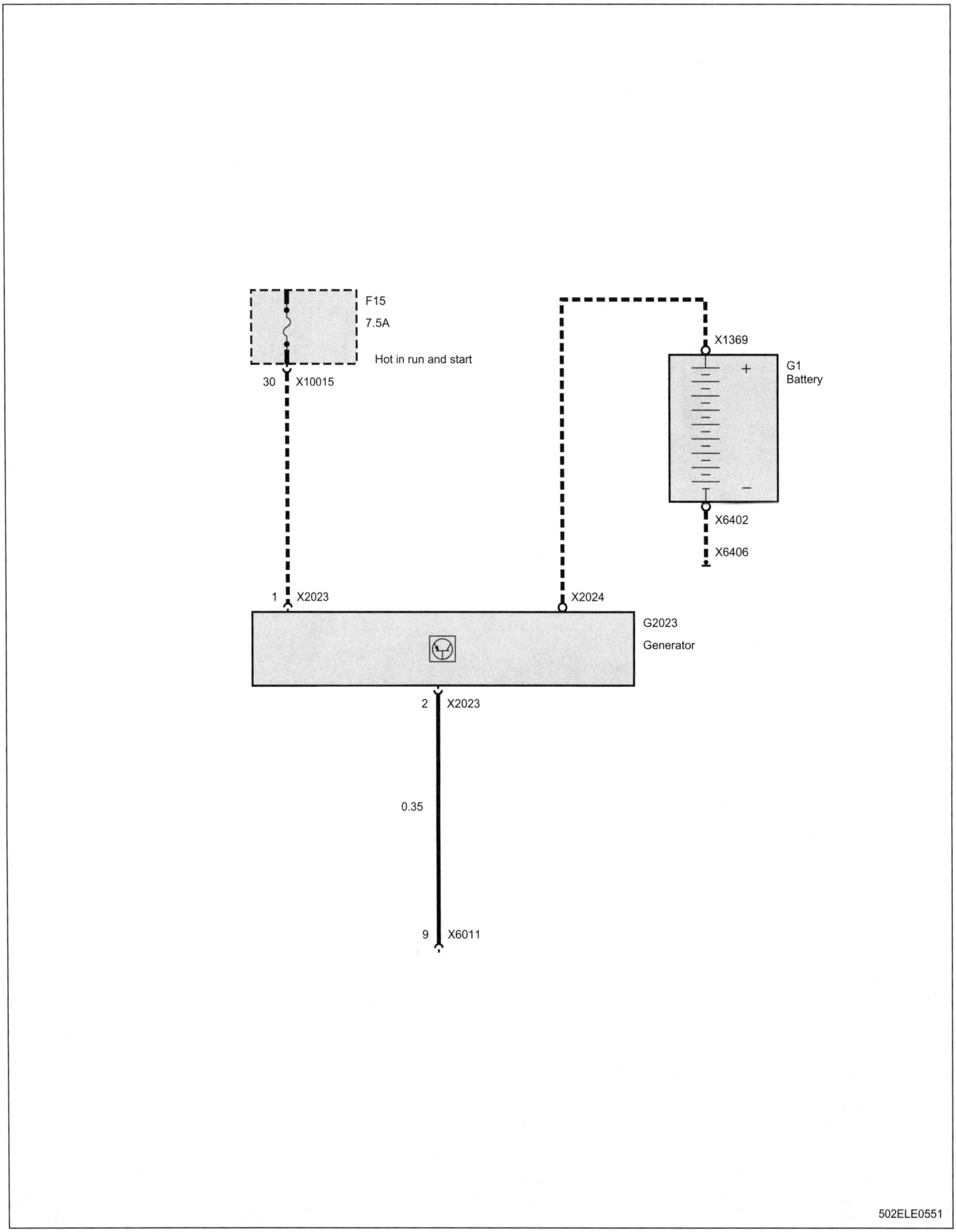

Charging System
Generator (alternator) (G6524)
(1 of 1)

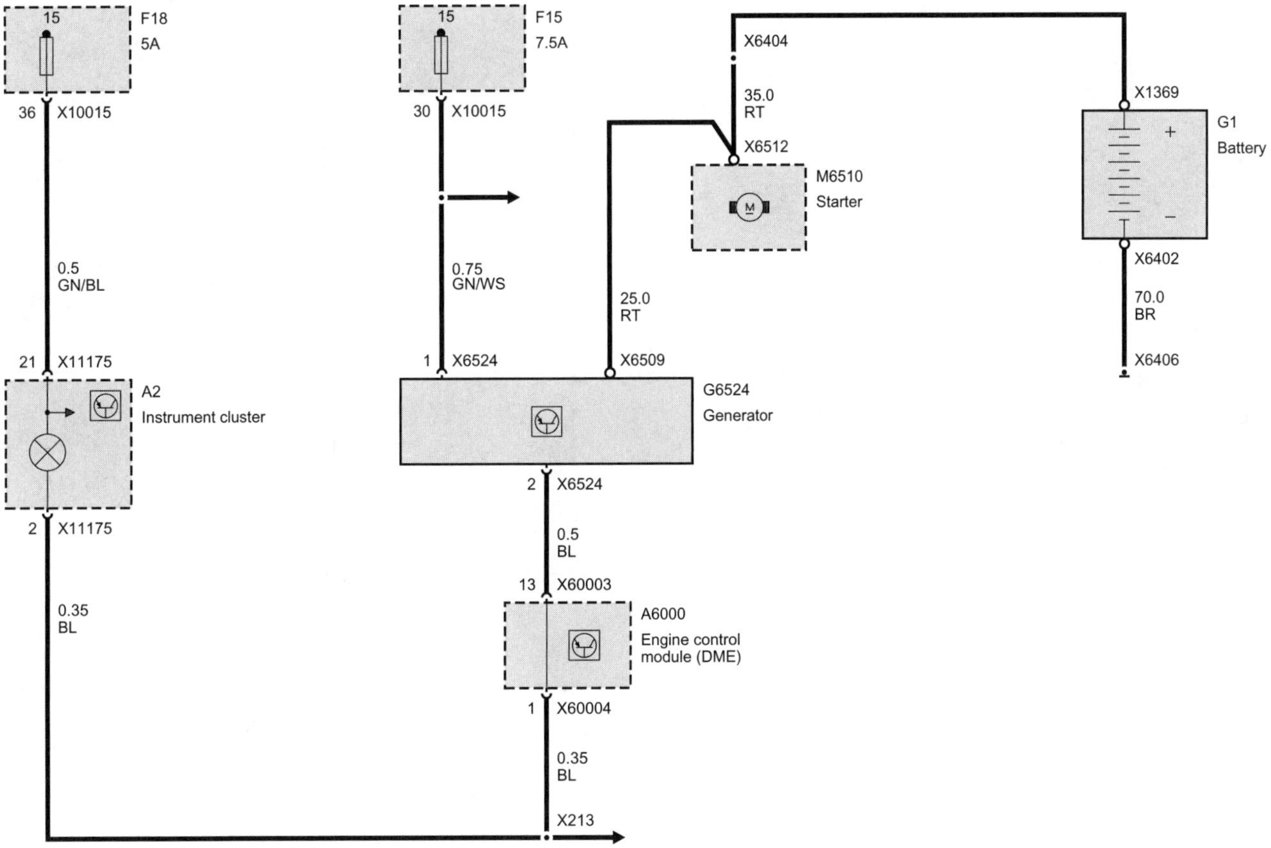

502ELE0308

Data Link Connector
X6002 Diagnostic connector
(1 of 2)

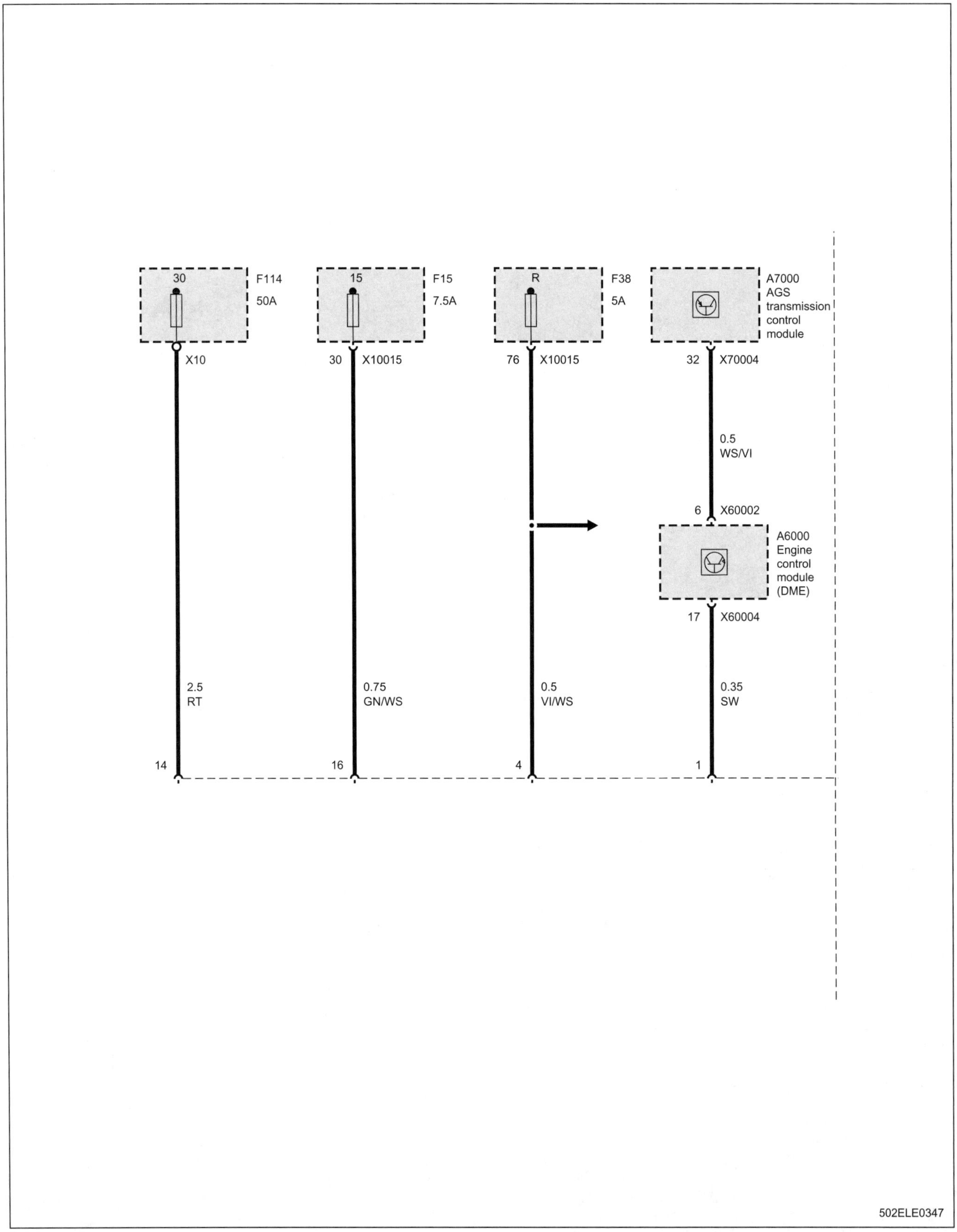

Data Link Connector
X6002 Diagnostic connector
(2 of 2)

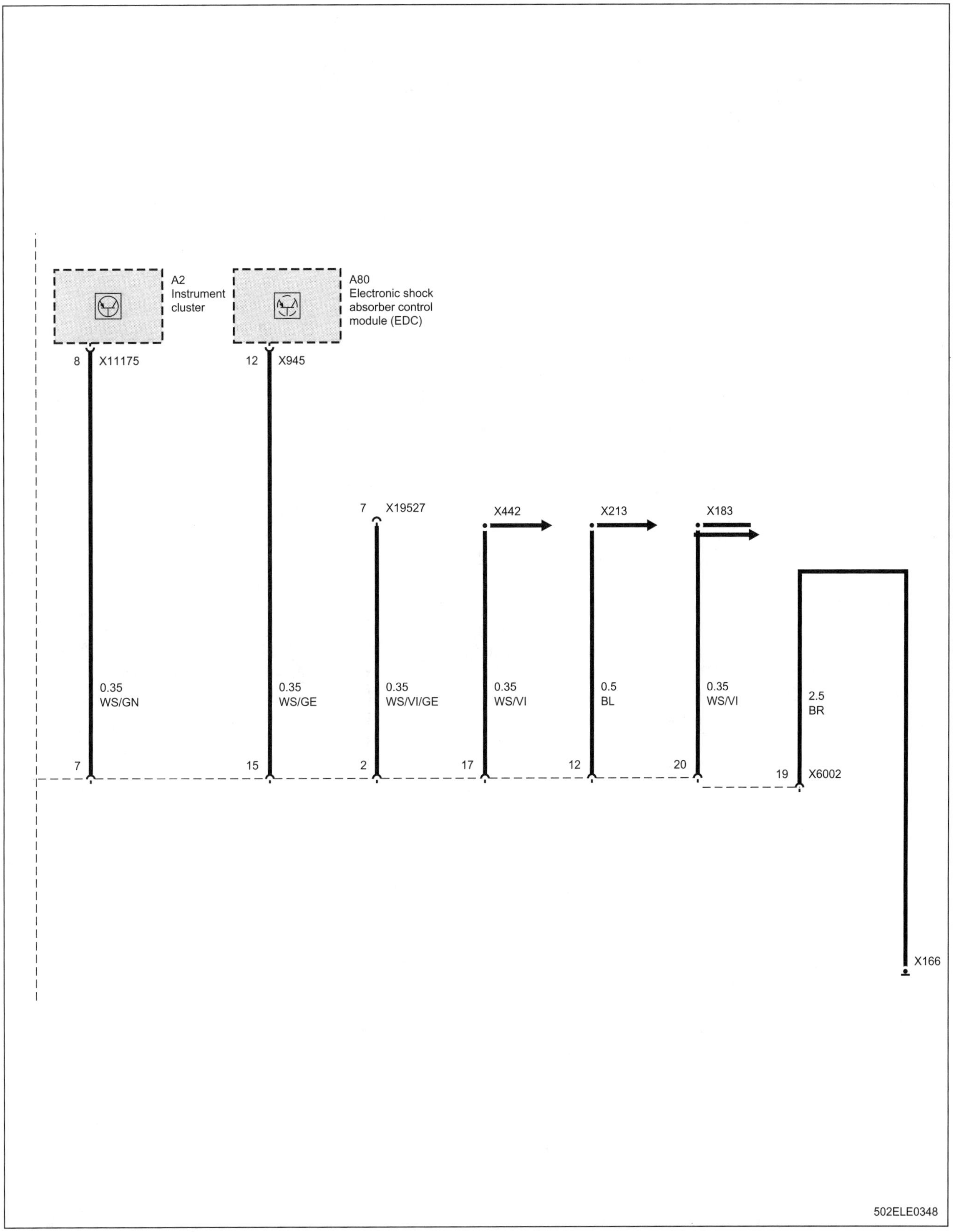

Defogger
Rear defogger relay
(1 of 1)

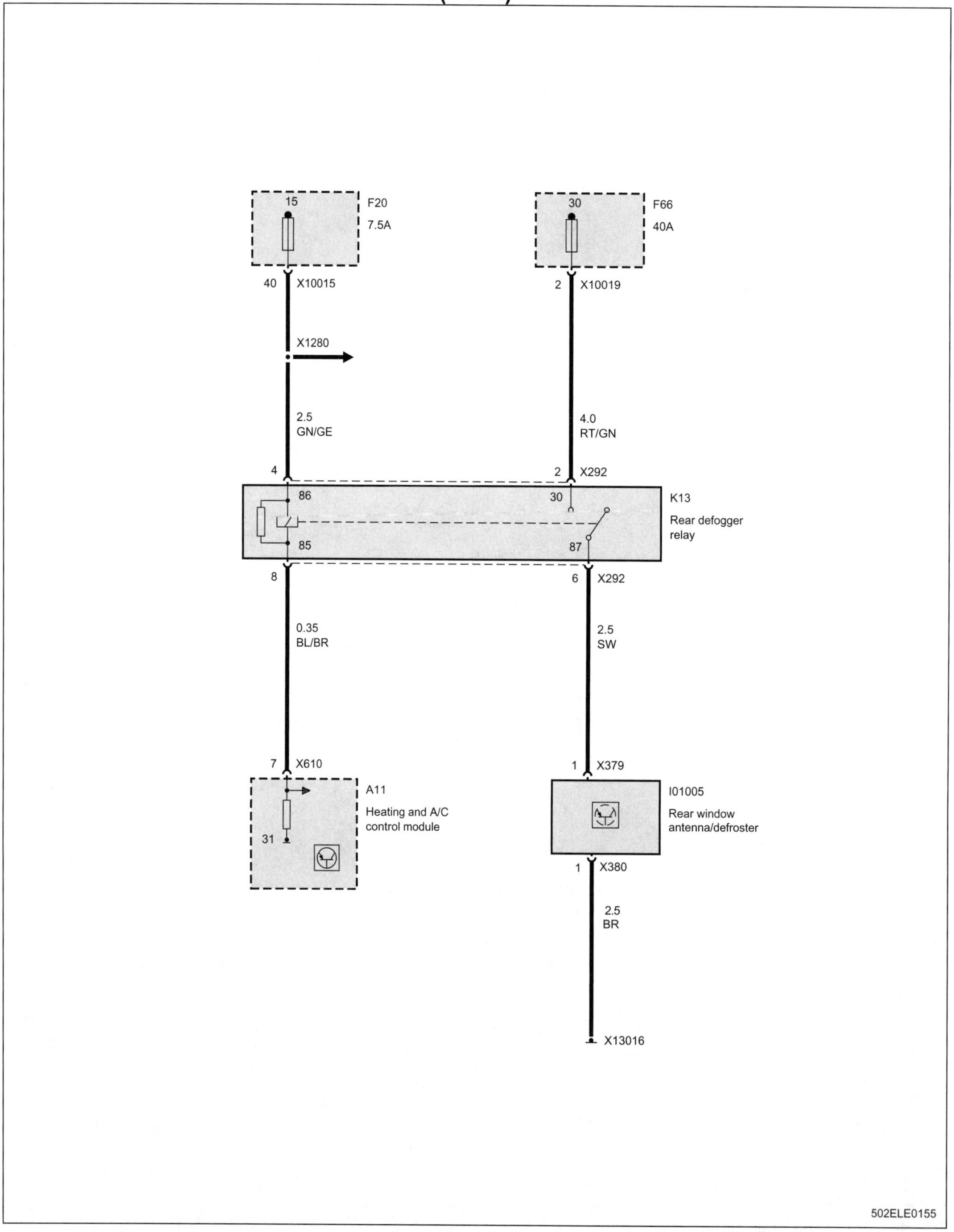
15
F20
7.5A
30
F66
40A
40
X10015
2
X10019
X1280
2.5
GN/GE
4.0
RT/GN
4
2
X292
86
30
K13
Rear defogger relay
85
87
8
6
X292
0.35
BL/BR
2.5
SW
7
X610
1
X379
A11
Heating and A/C control module
31
I01005
Rear window antenna/defroster
1
X380
2.5
BR
X13016
502ELE0155

Electronic Suspension
Automatic stability control (overview)
(1 of 3)

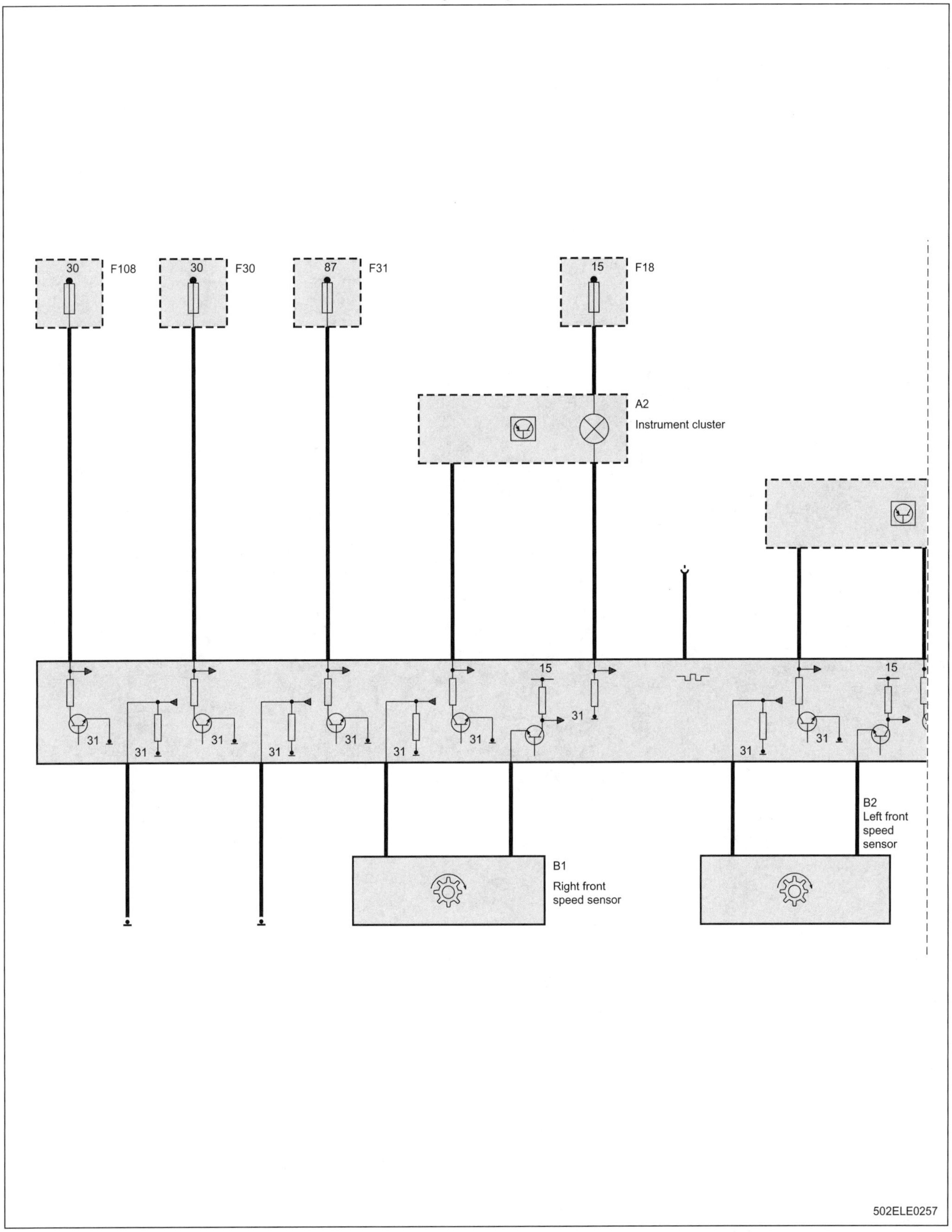

Electronic Suspension
Automatic stability control (overview)
(2 of 3)

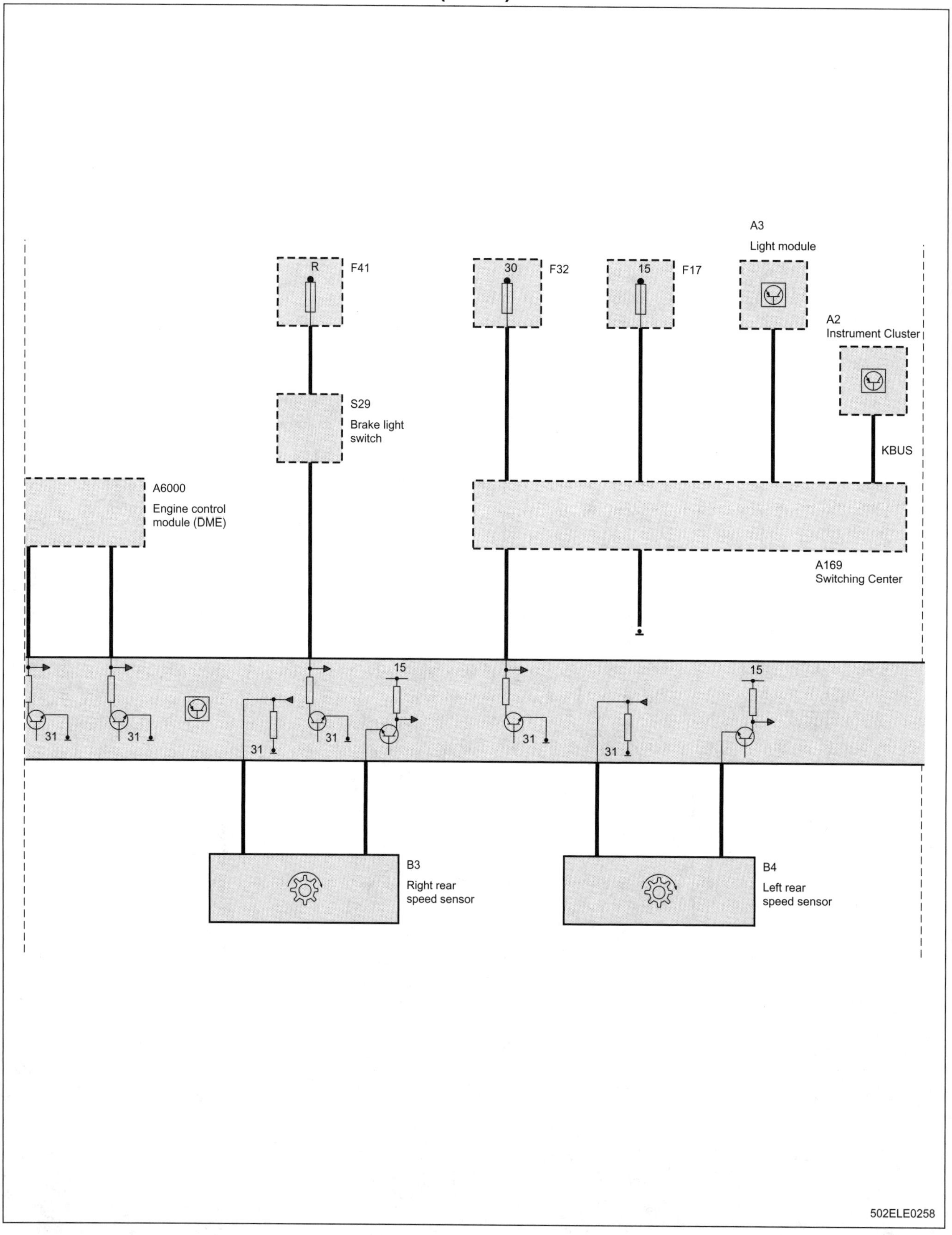

Electronic Suspension
Automatic stability control (overview)
(3 of 3)

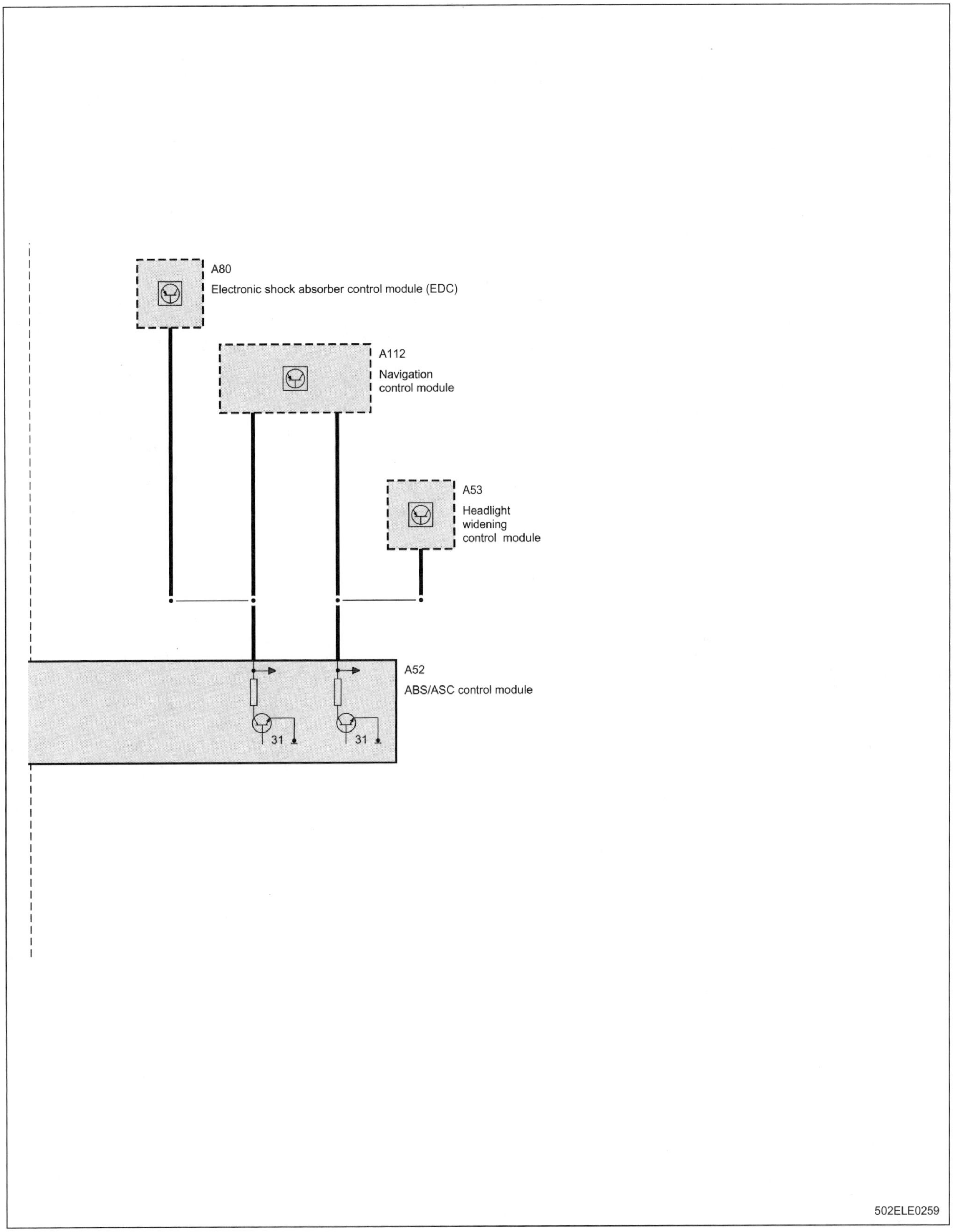

Electronic Suspension
Electronic damper control (EDC) (overview)
(1 of 3)

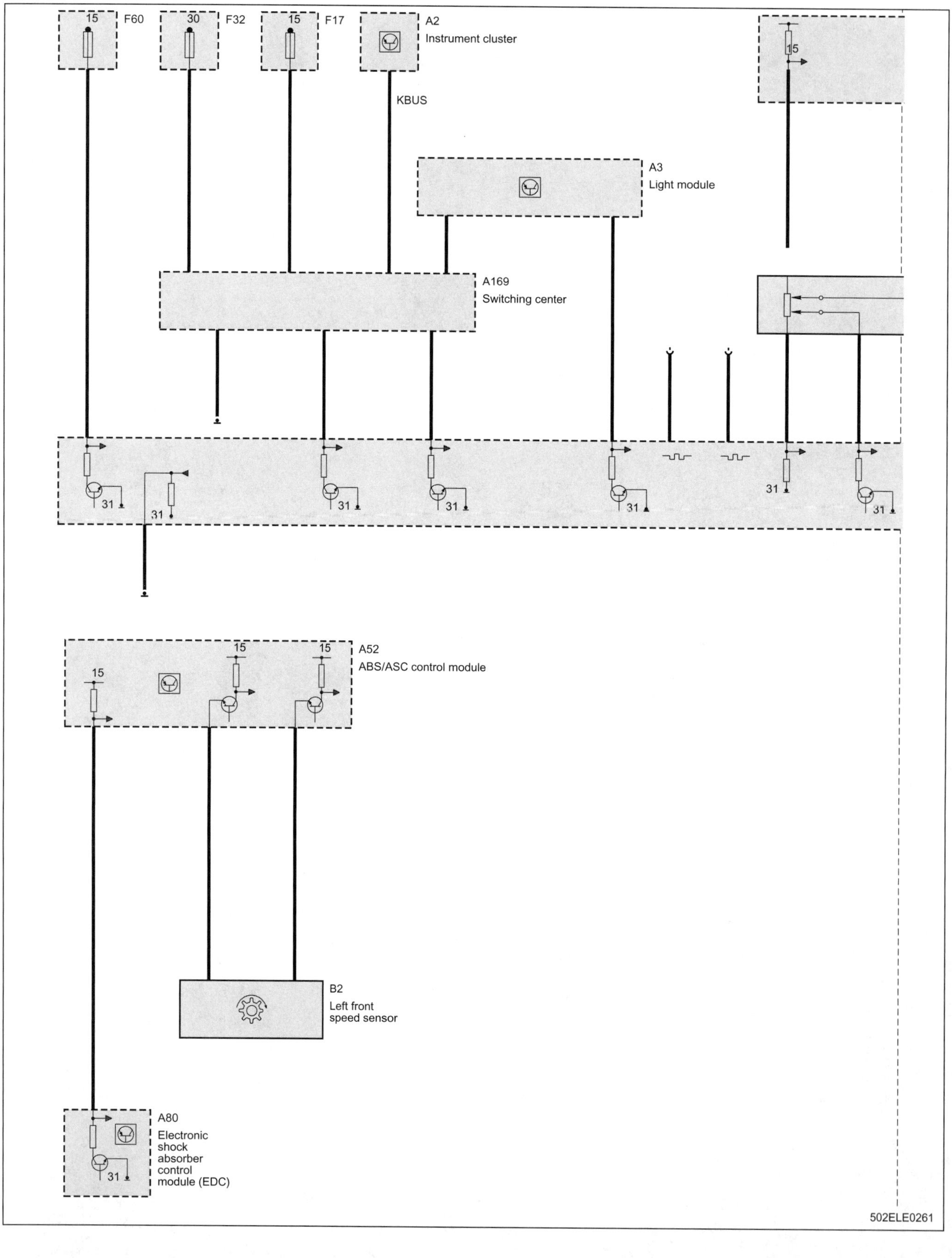

Electronic Suspension
Electronic damper control (EDC) (overview)
(2 of 3)

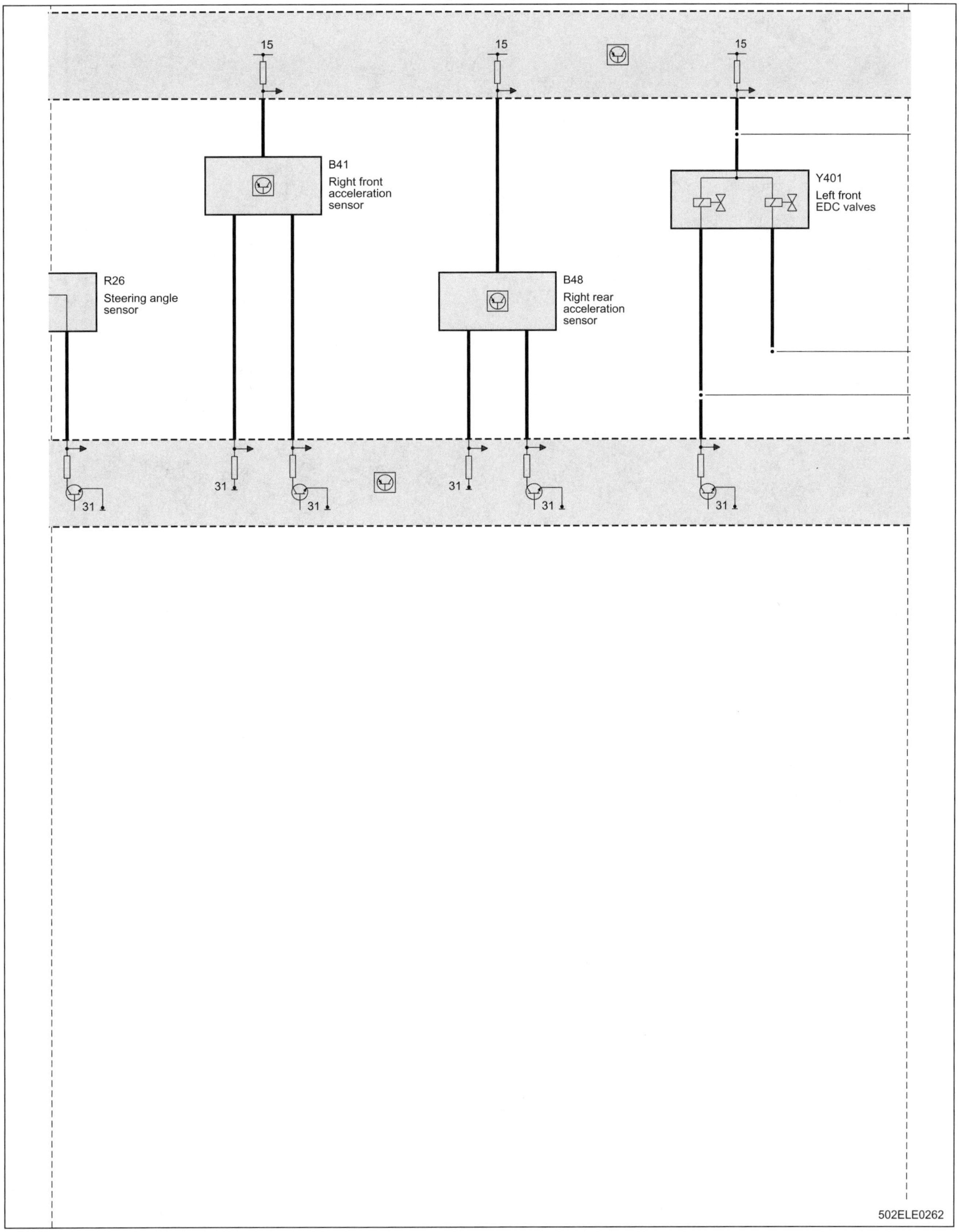

Electronic Suspension
Electronic damper control (EDC) (overview)
(3 of 3)

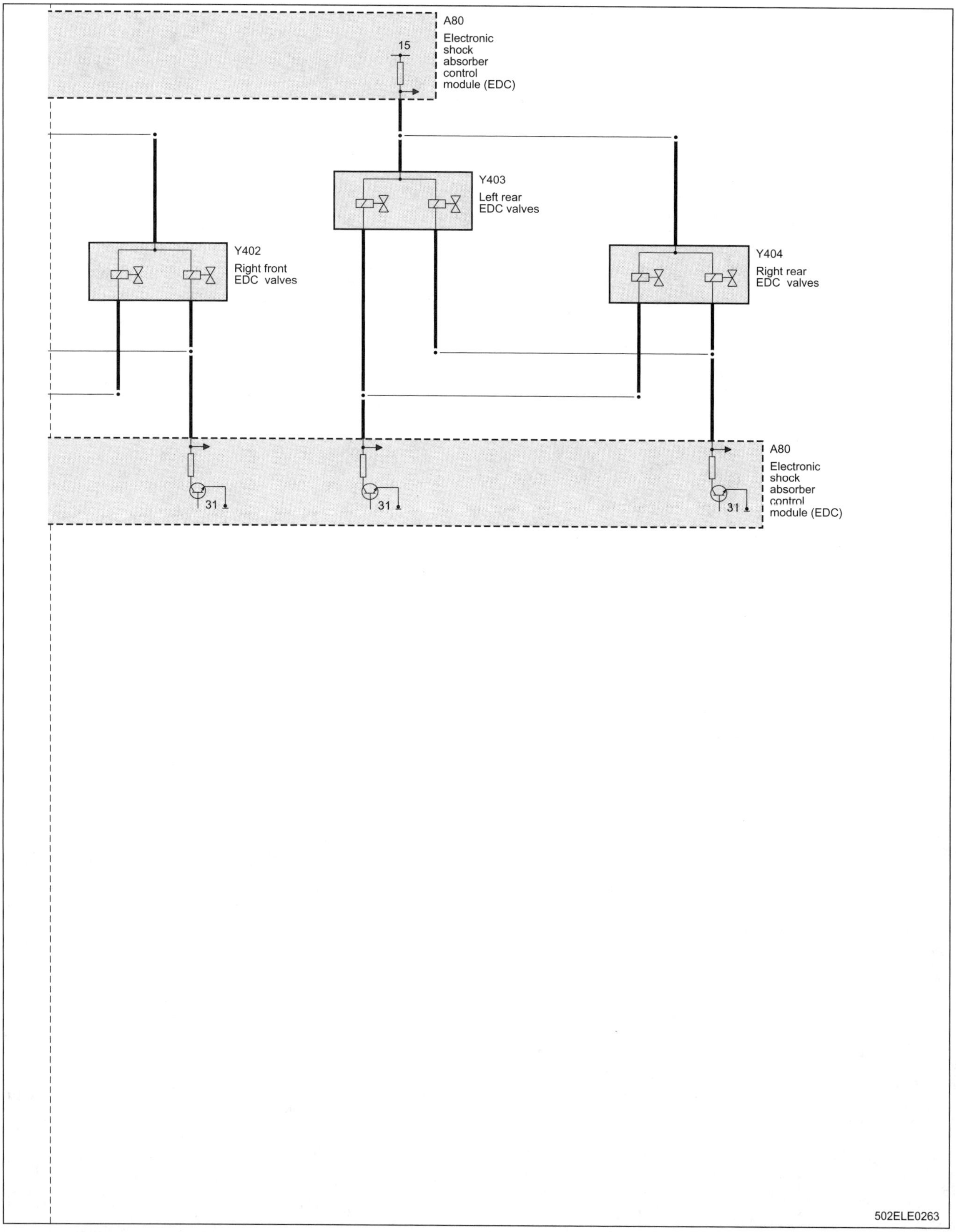

Electronic Suspension
Air suspension control unit, with LWR (A118)
(1 of 1)

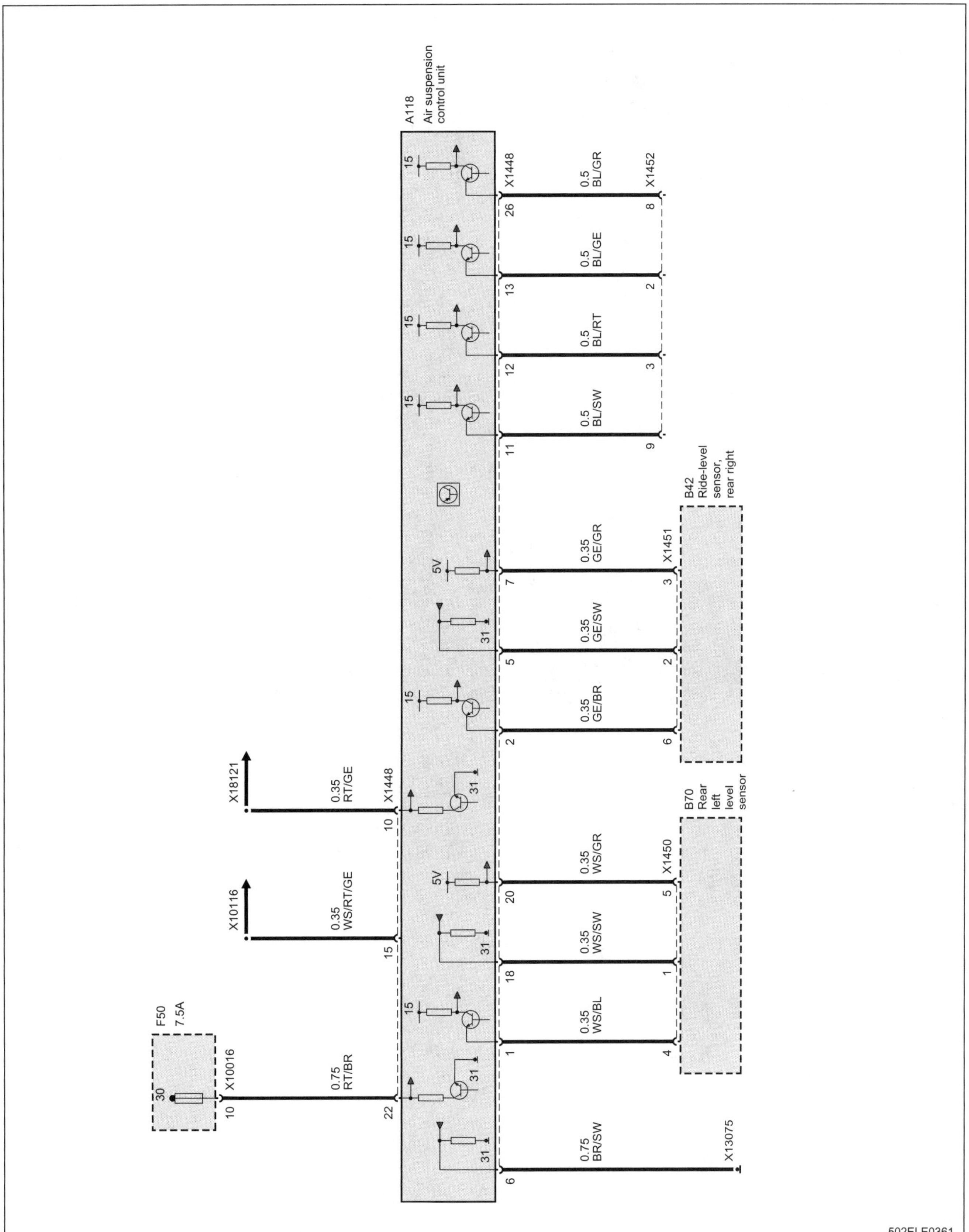

502ELE0361

Electronic Suspension
EDC Power
(1 of 1)

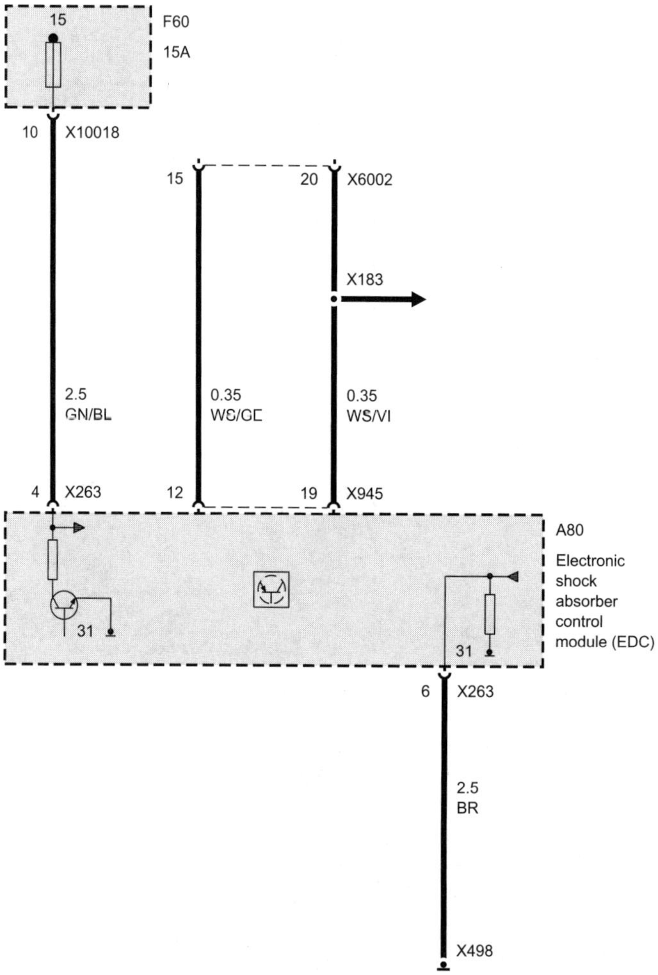

502ELE0270

Electronic Suspension
EDC switch
(1 of 1)

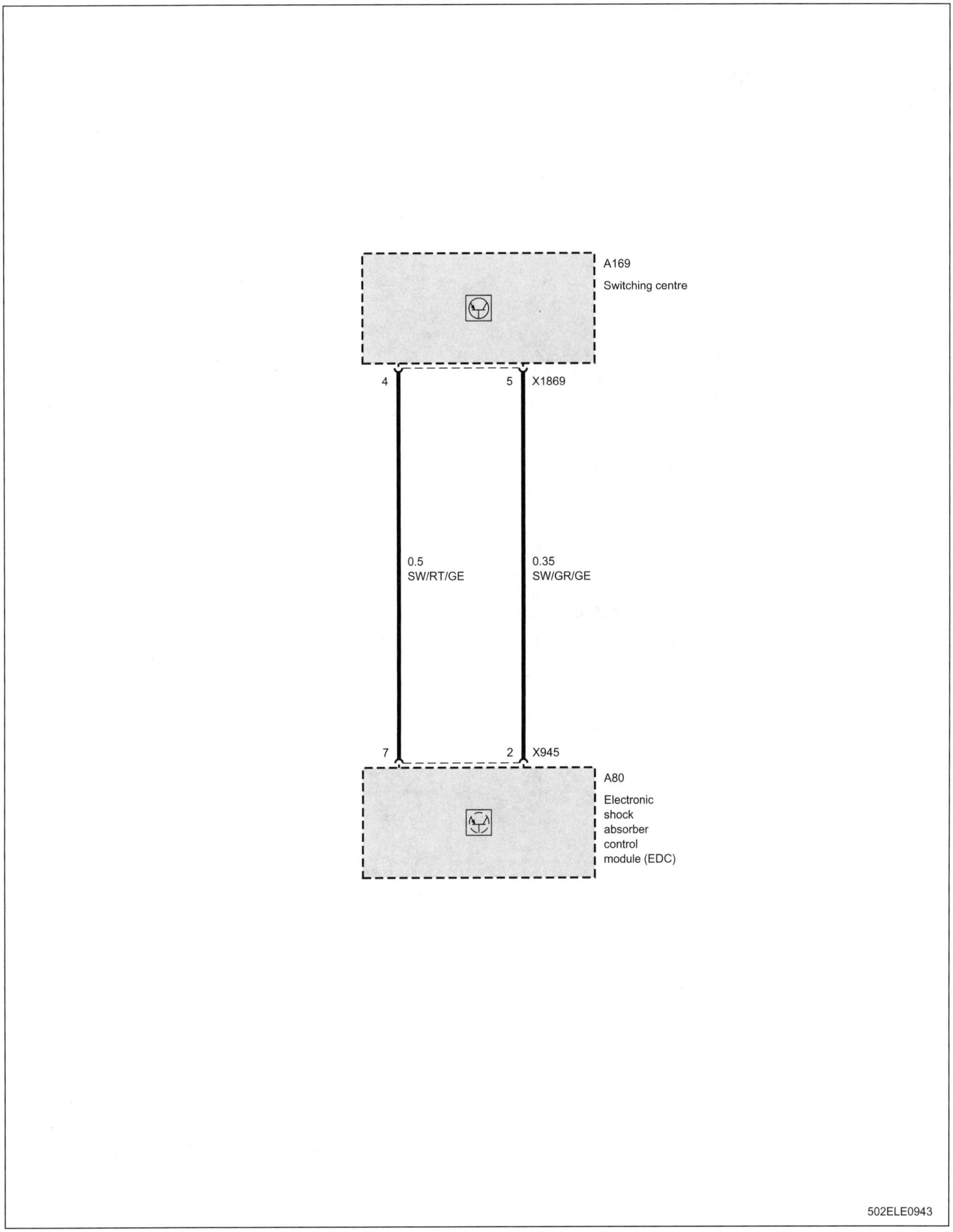

Electronic Suspension
Front EDC valves

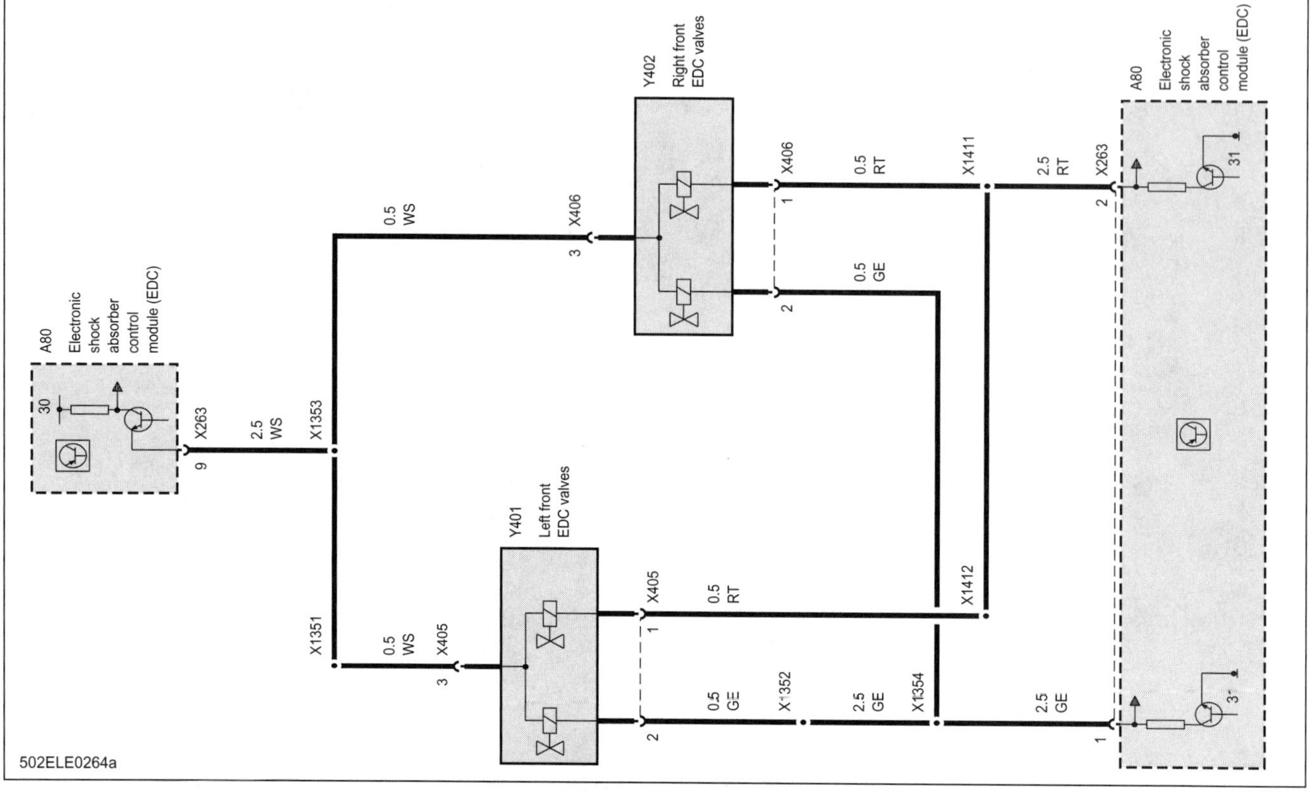

502ELE0264a

Electronic Suspension
Rear EDC valves

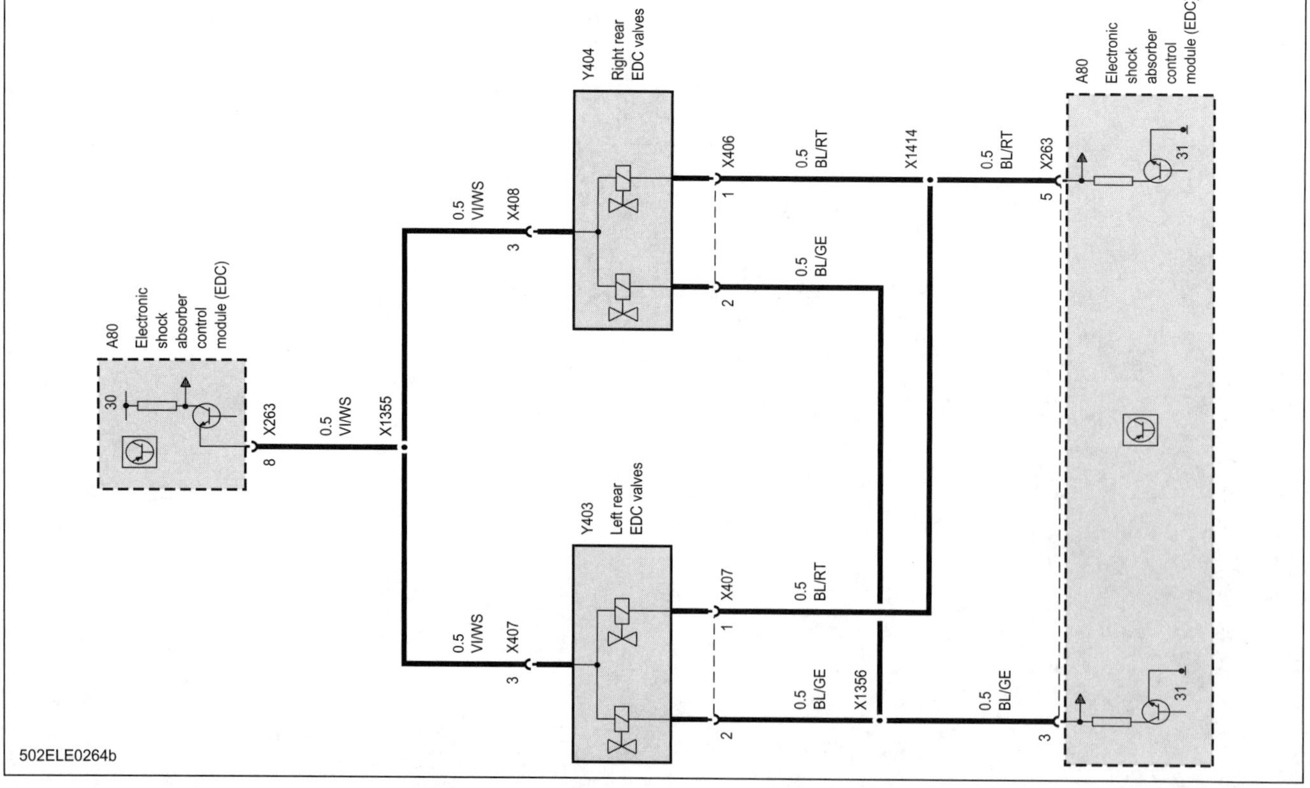

502ELE0264b

Electronic Suspension
Steering angle sensor (EDC)
(1 of 1)

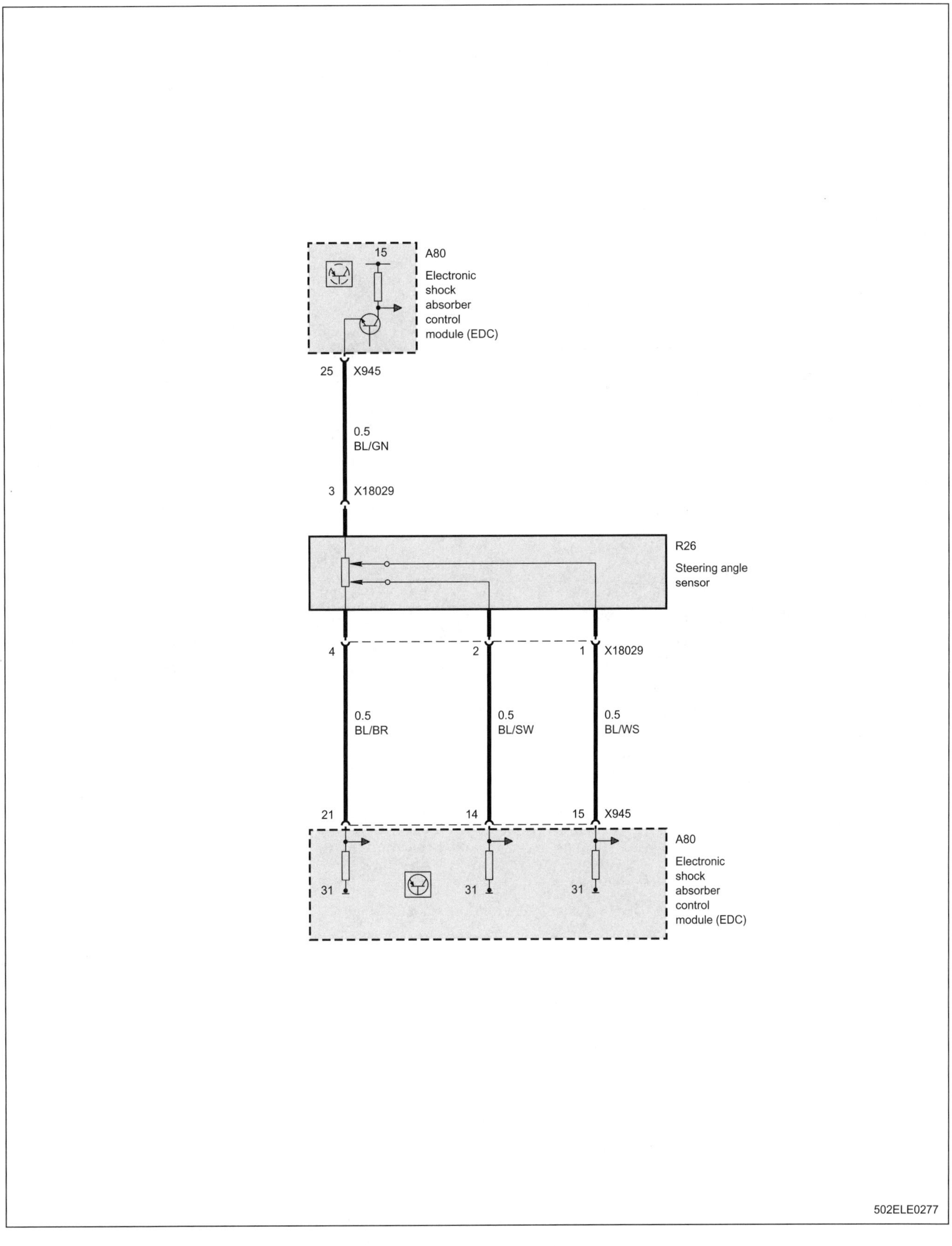

Engine Cooling
Coolant temperature/electric fan
(1 of 1)

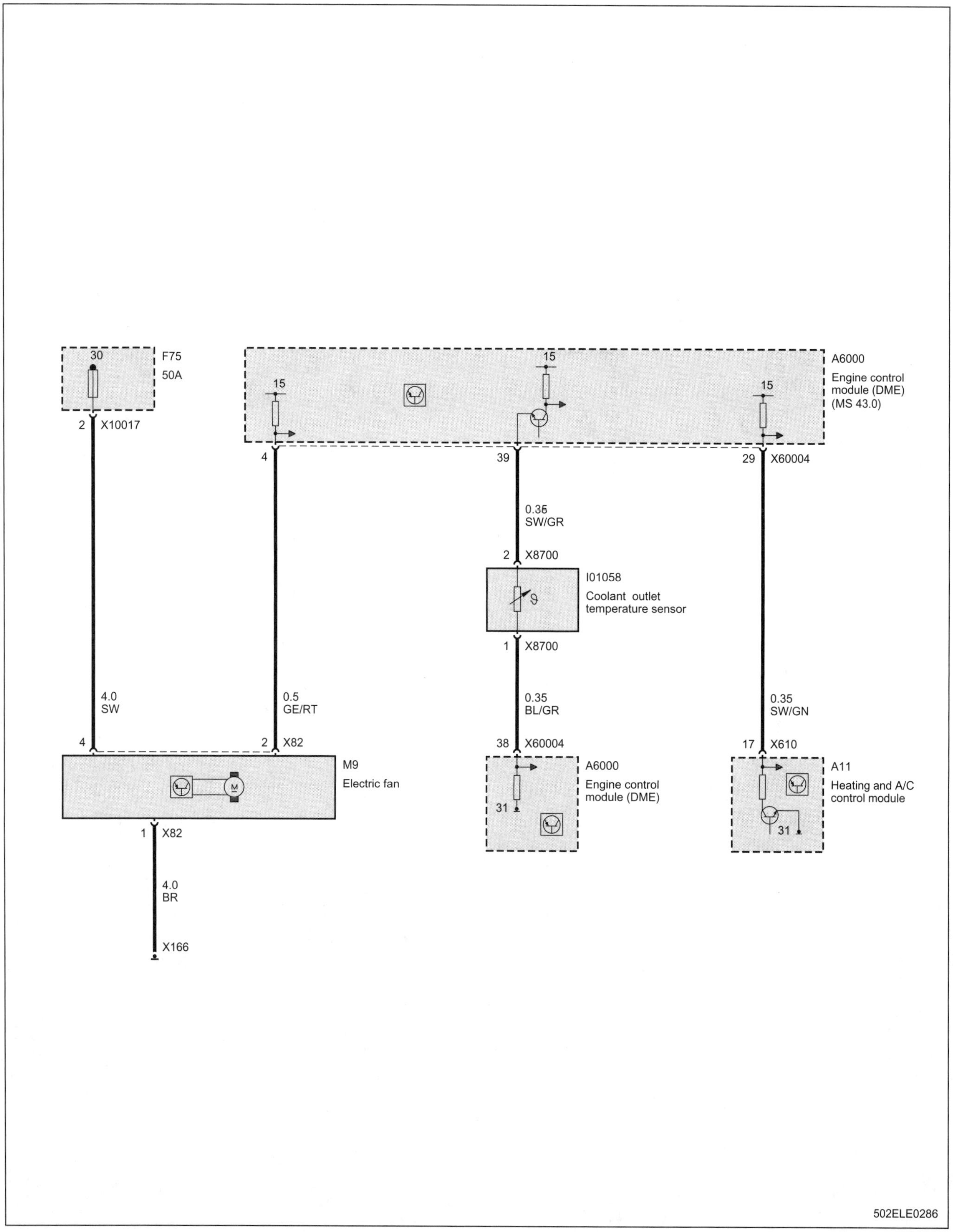

Engine Cooling
Thermostat (MS 42.0)
(1 of 1)

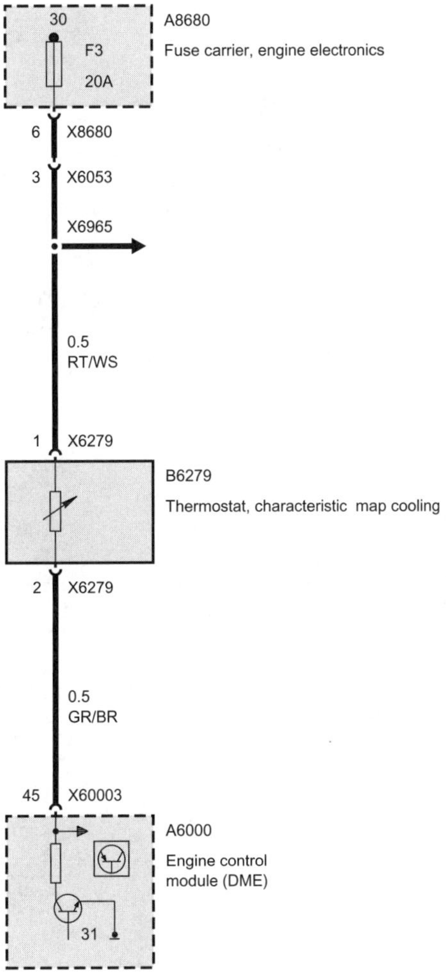

502ELE336

Engine Management (MS 42.0)
Auxiliary functions (overview)
(1 of 3)

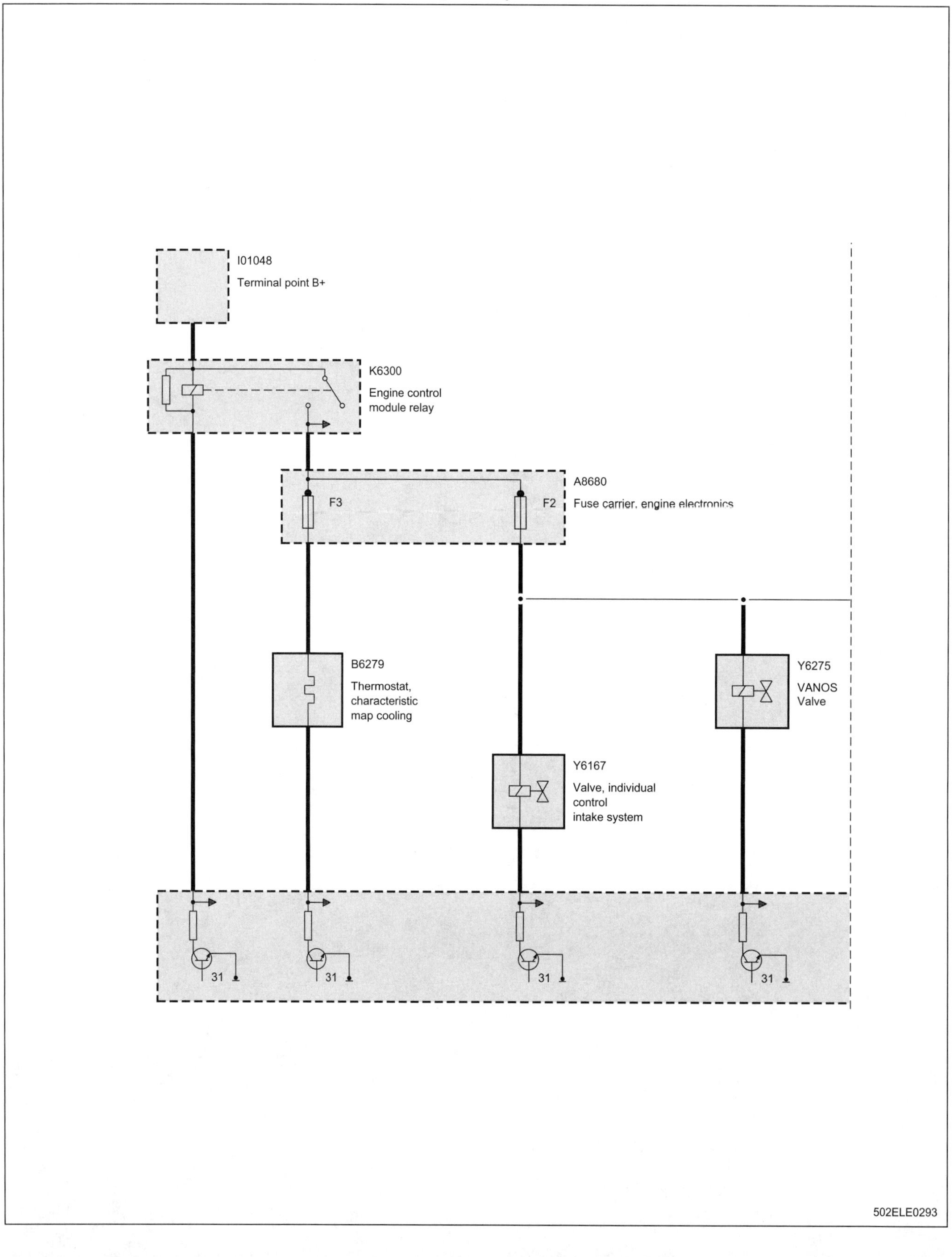

Engine Management (MS 42.0)
Auxiliary functions (overview)
(2 of 3)

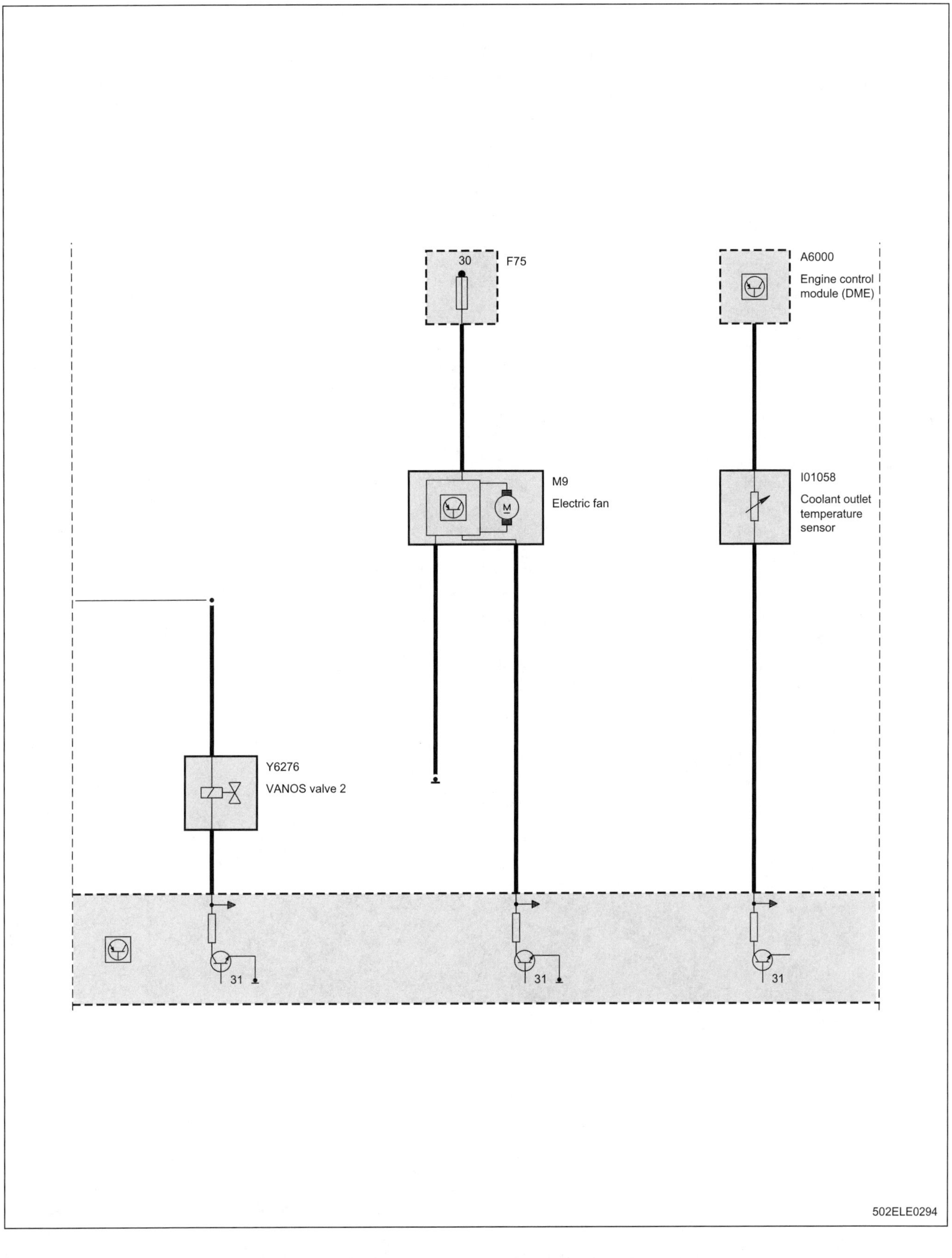

Engine Management (MS 42.0)
Auxiliary functions (overview)
(3 of 3)

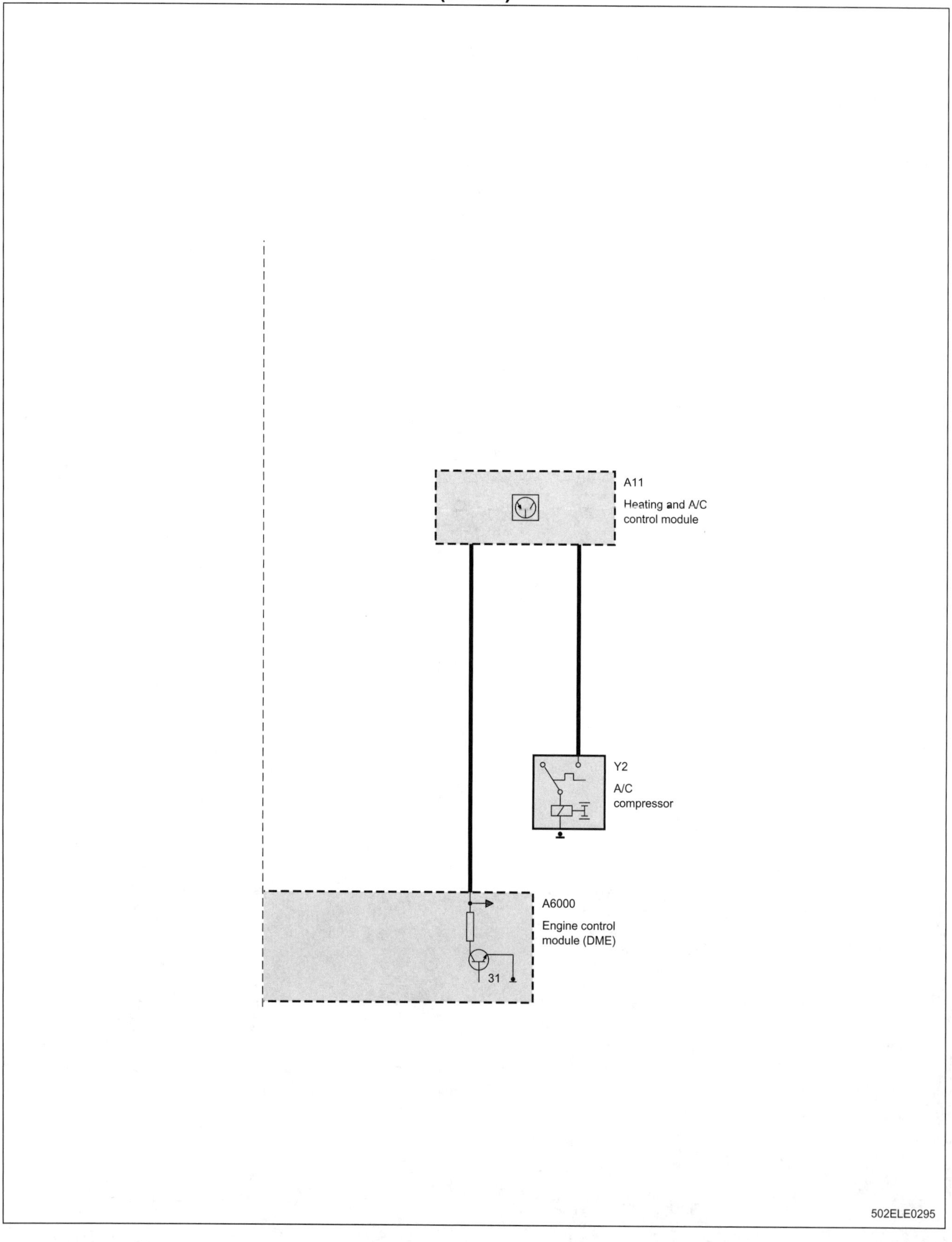

Engine Management (MS 42.0)
Exhaust emission control/monitoring (overview)
(1 of 4)

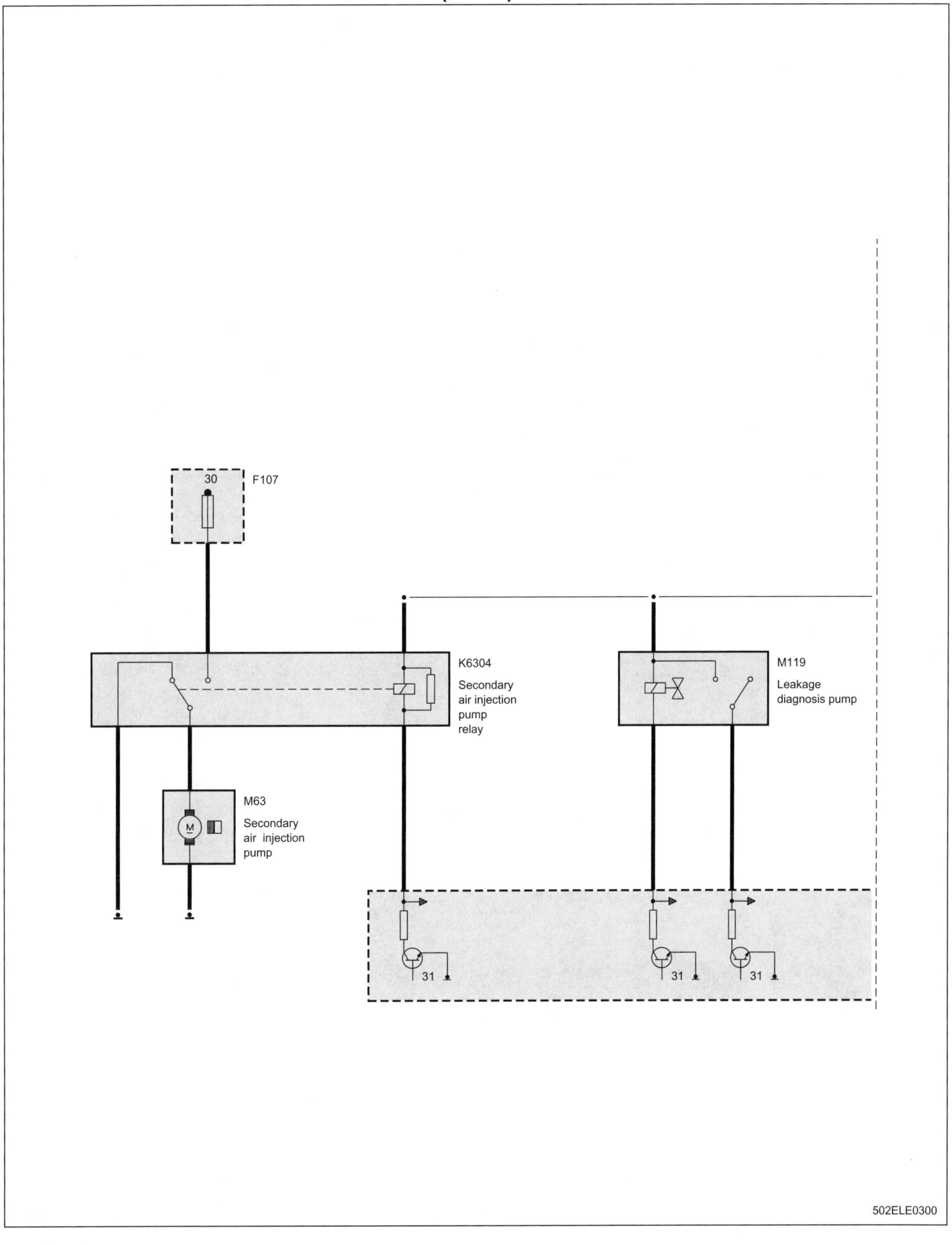

Engine Management (MS 42.0)
Exhaust emission control/monitoring (overview)
(2 of 4)

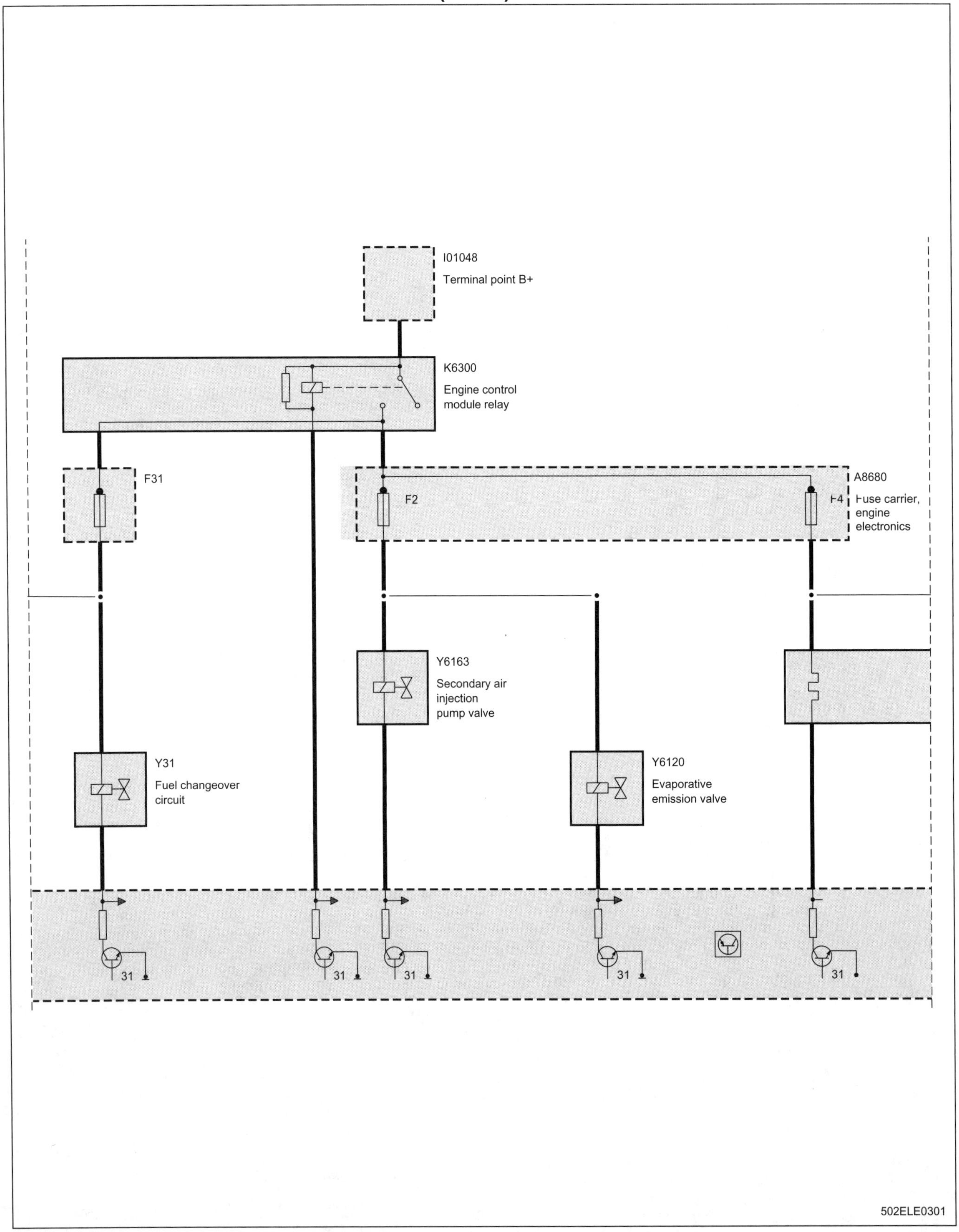

Engine Management (MS 42.0)
Exhaust emission control/monitoring (overview)
(3 of 4)

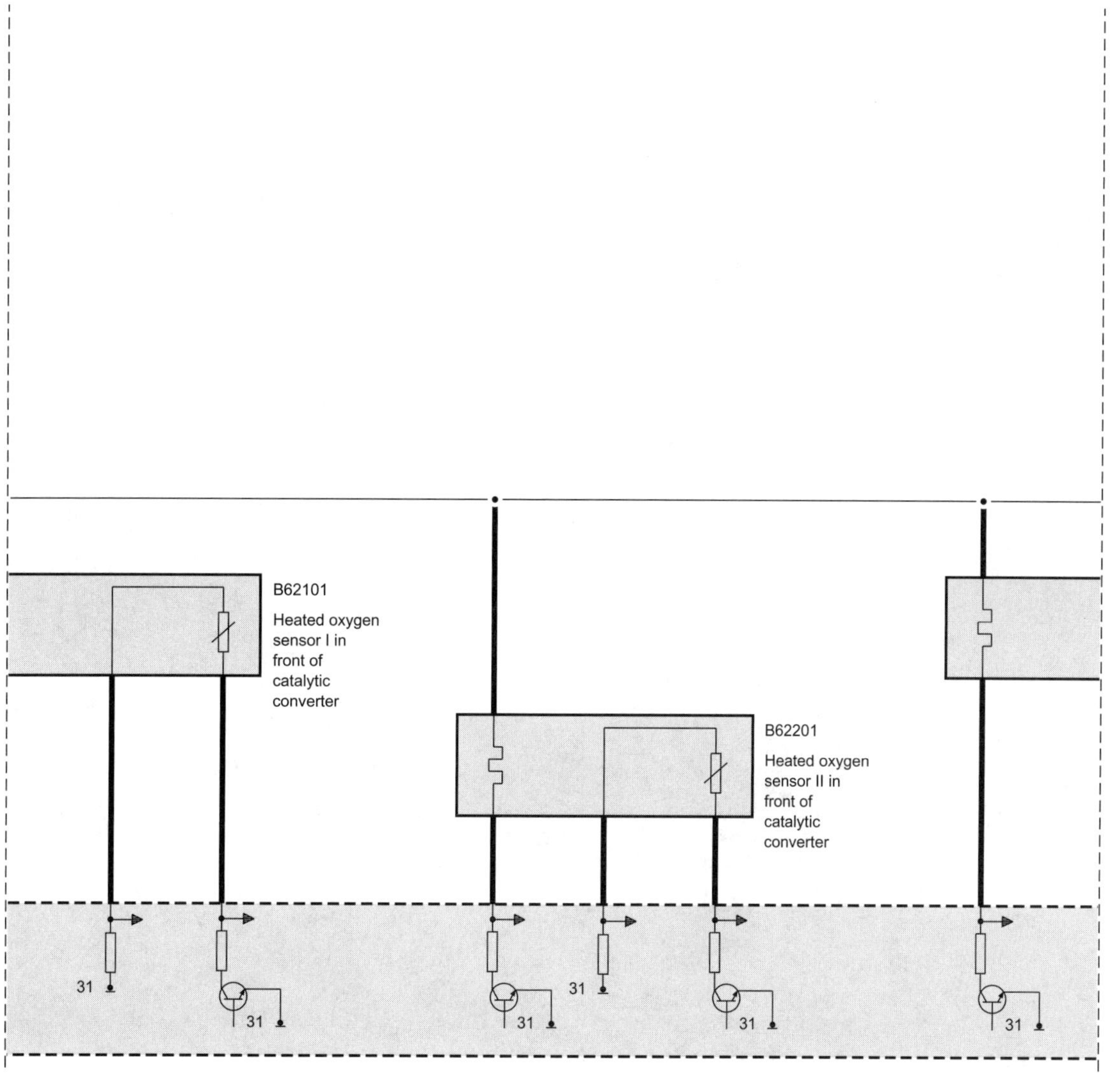

Engine Management (MS 42.0)
Exhaust emission control/monitoring (overview)
(4 of 4)

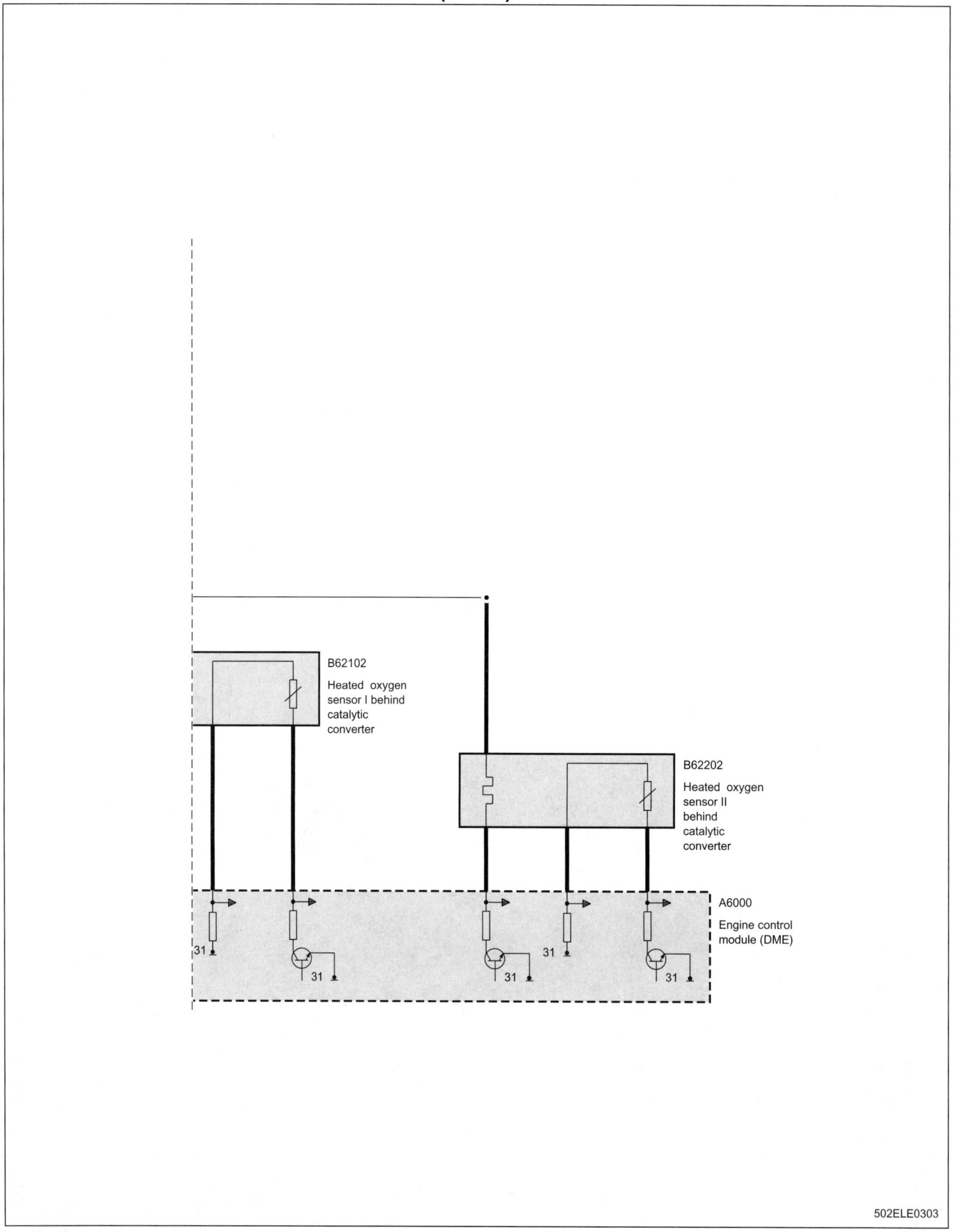

Engine Management (MS 42.0)
Input parameter, mixture/ignition (overview)
(1 of 4)

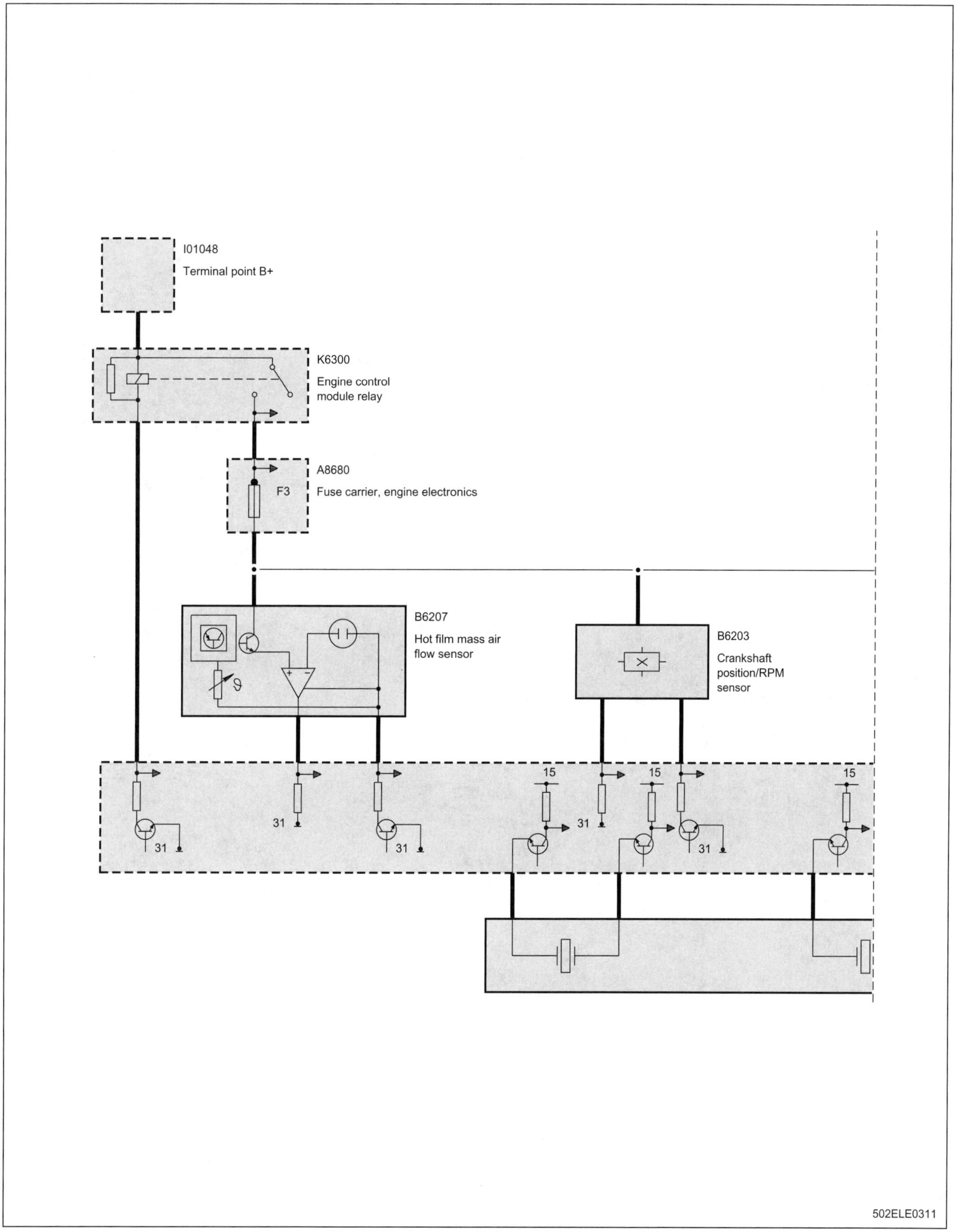

Engine Management (MS 42.0)
Input parameter, mixture/ignition (overview)
(2 of 4)

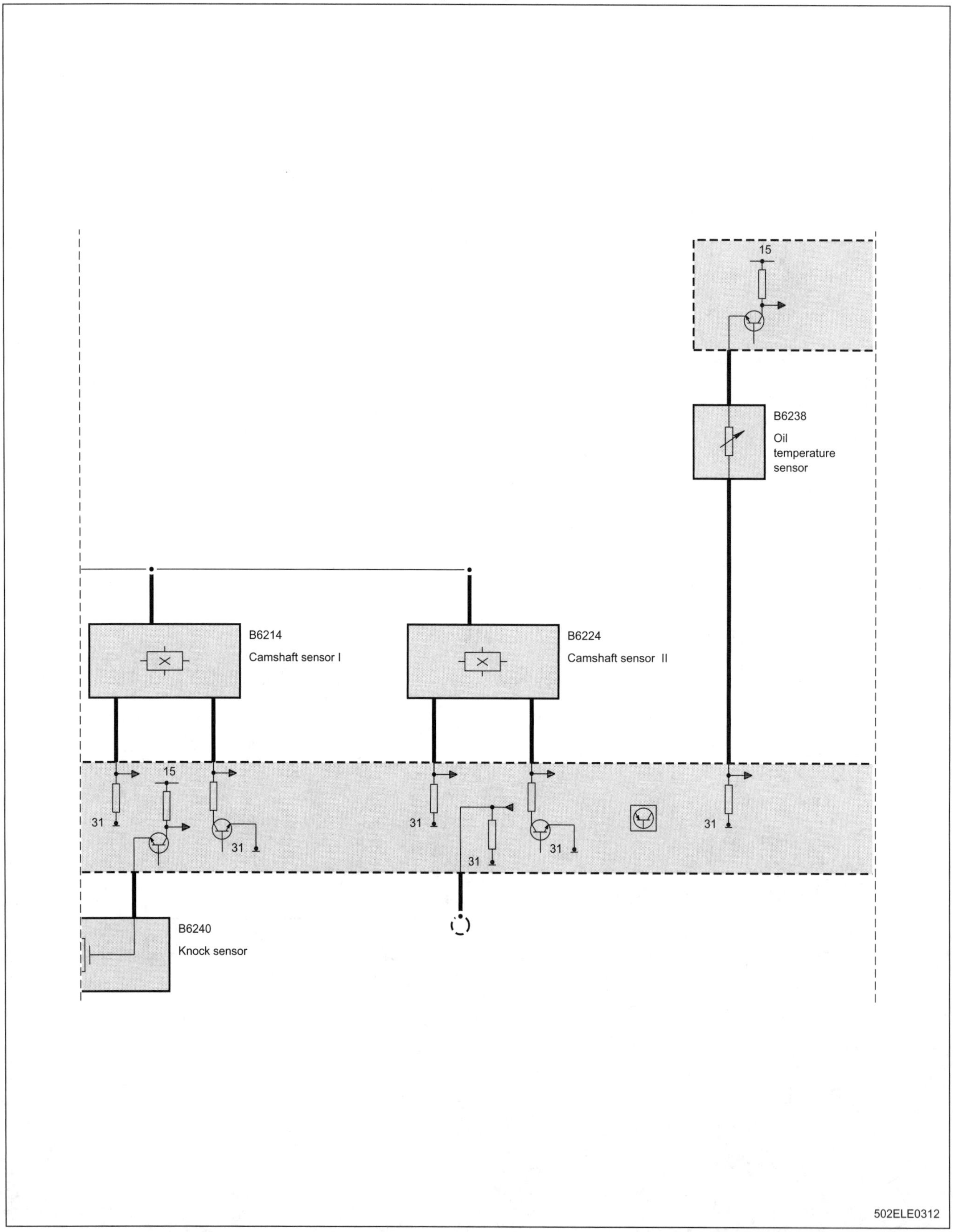

Engine Management (MS 42.0)
Input parameter, mixture/ignition (overview)
(3 of 4)

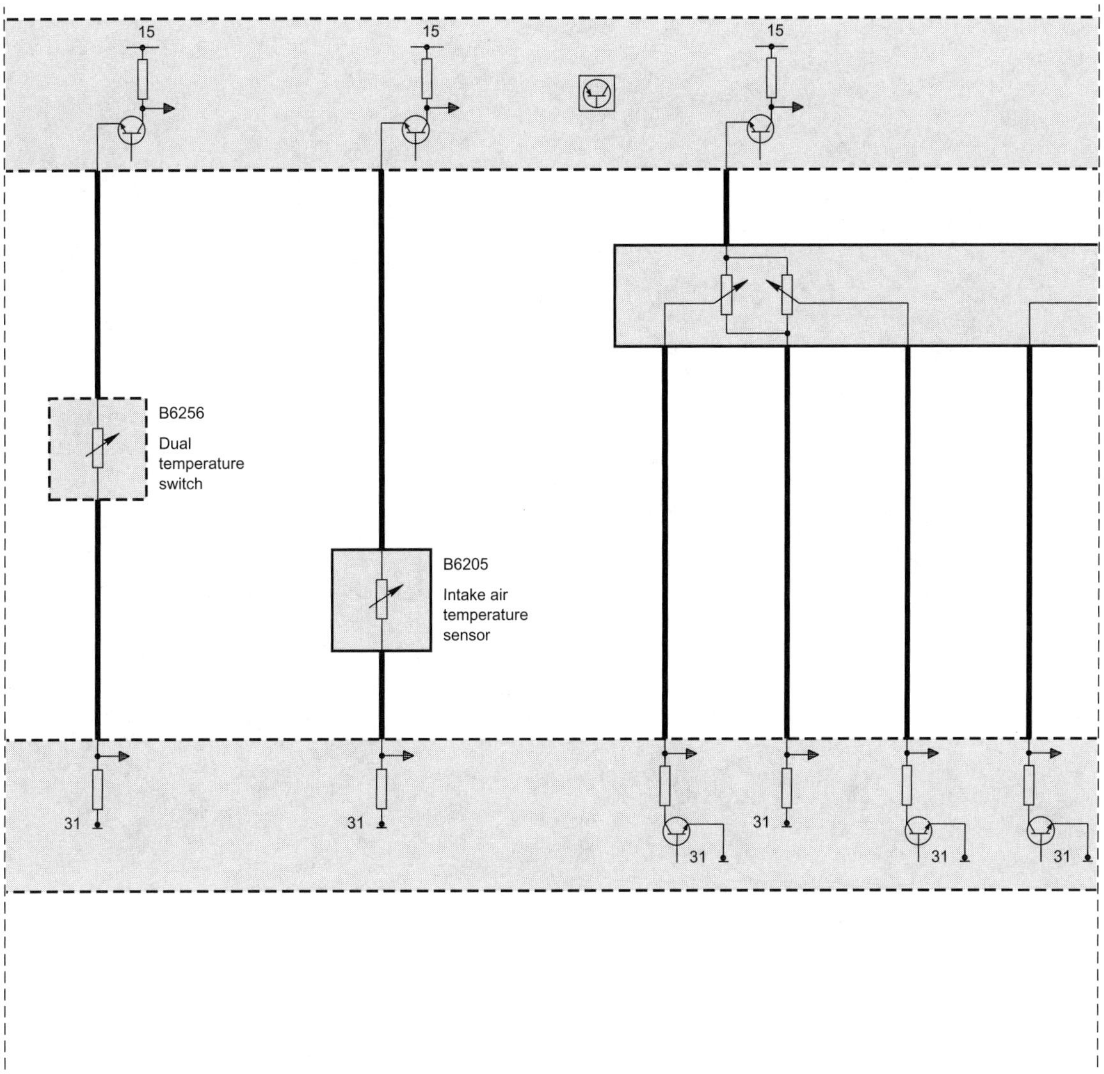

502ELE0313

Engine Management (MS 42.0)
Input parameter, mixture/ignition (overview)
(4 of 4)

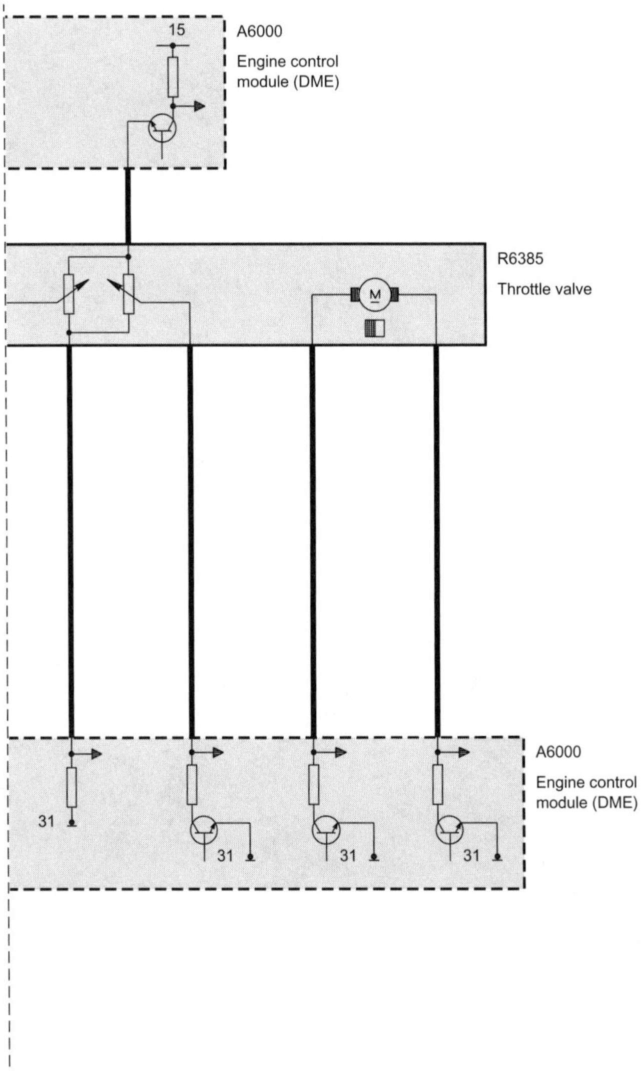

502ELE0314

Engine Management (MS 42.0)
Signals/auxiliary signals (overview)
(1 of 3)

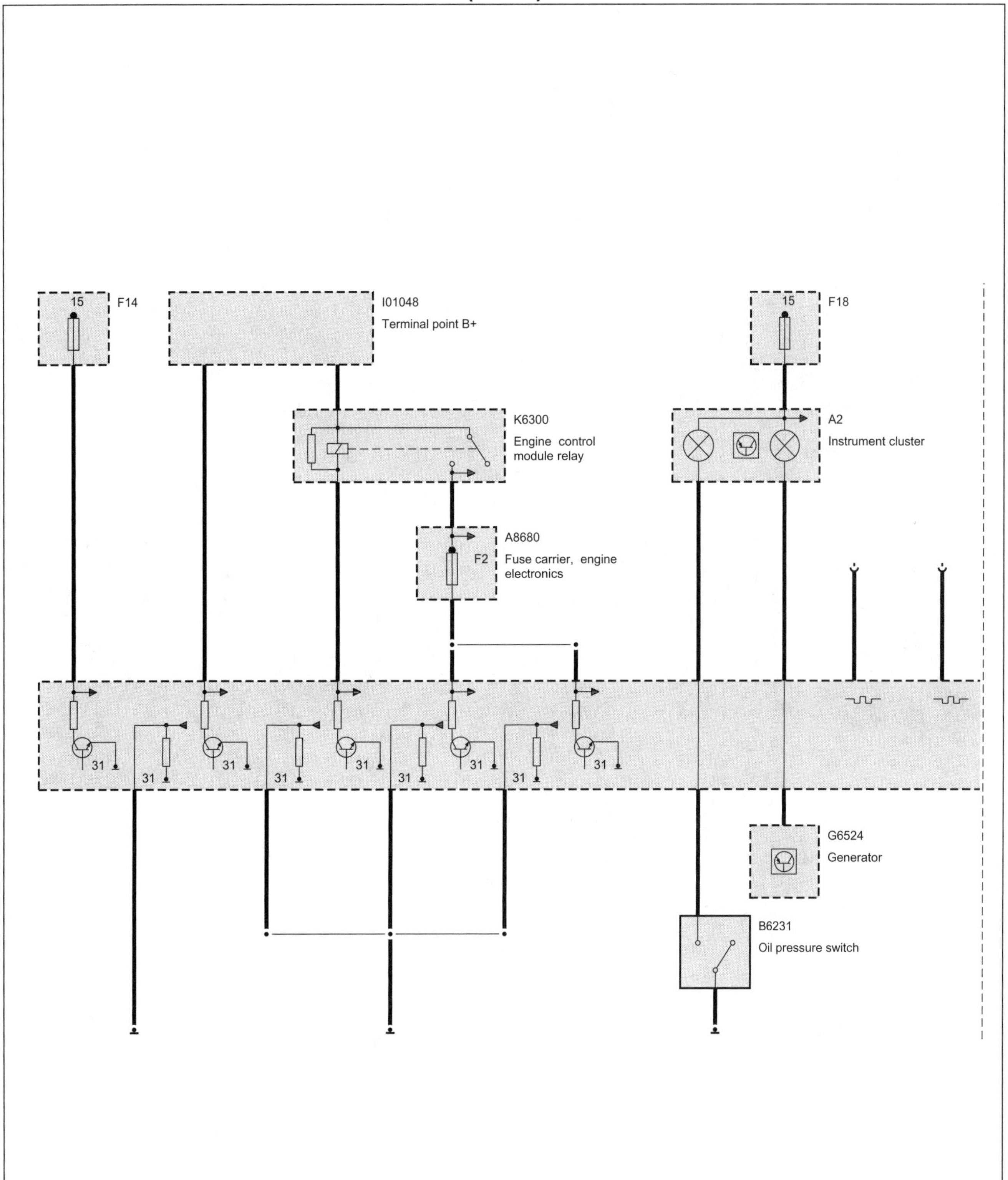

Engine Management (MS 42.0)
Signals/auxiliary signals (overview)
(2 of 3)

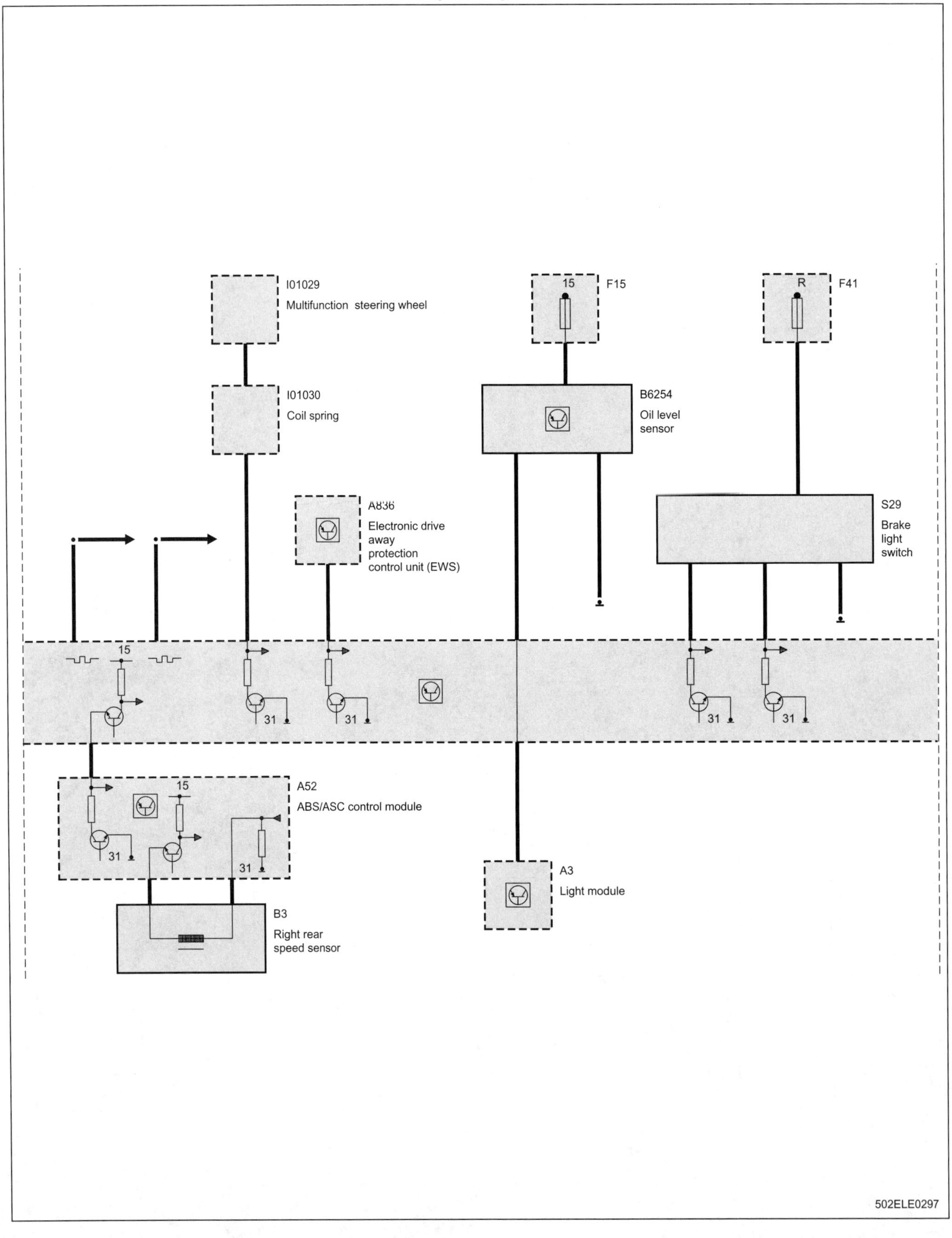

502ELE0297

Engine Management (MS 42.0)
Signals/auxiliary signals (overview)
(3 of 3)

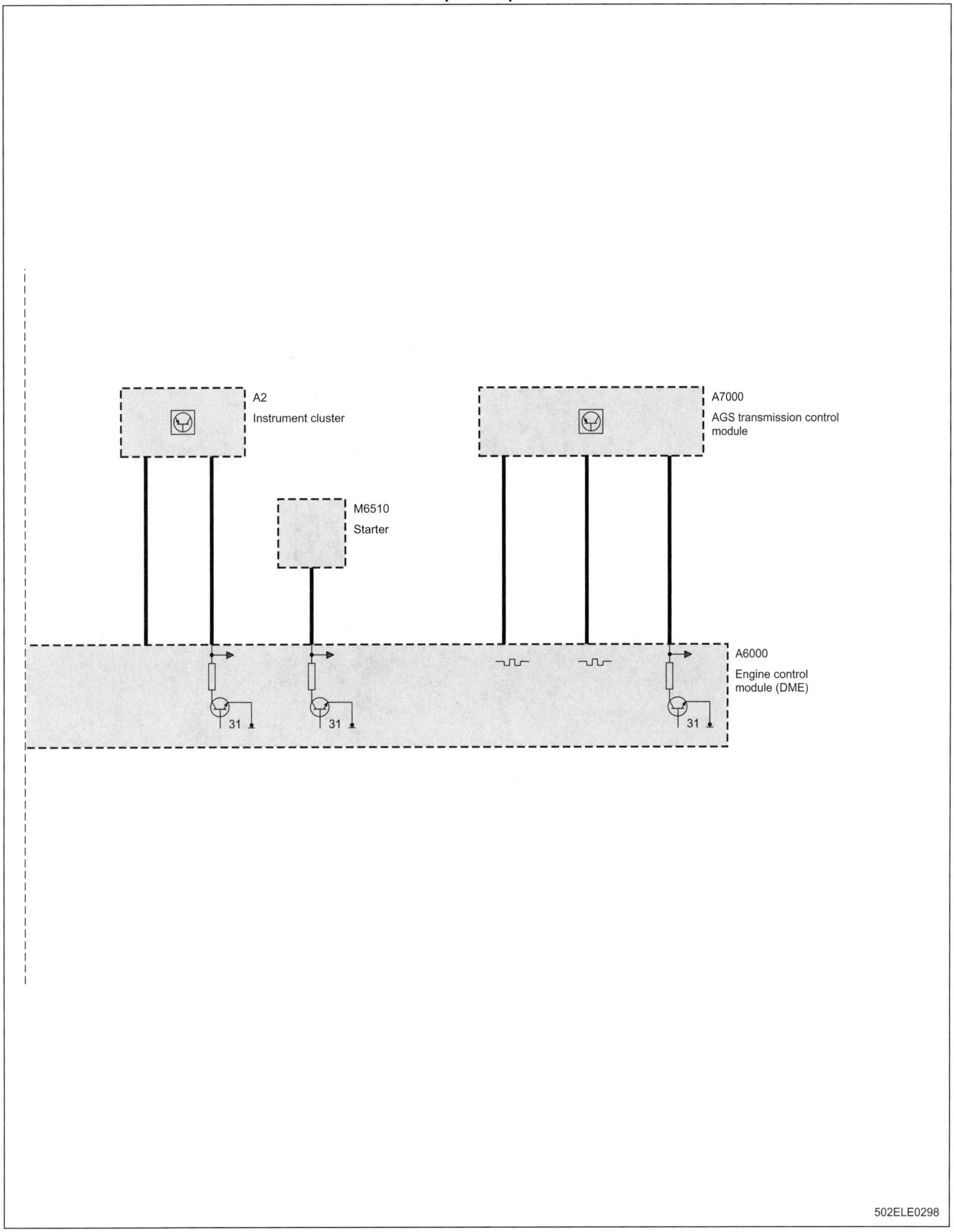

Engine Management (MS 42.0)
Engine control module (DME) Module 1 (A6000)
(1 of 1)

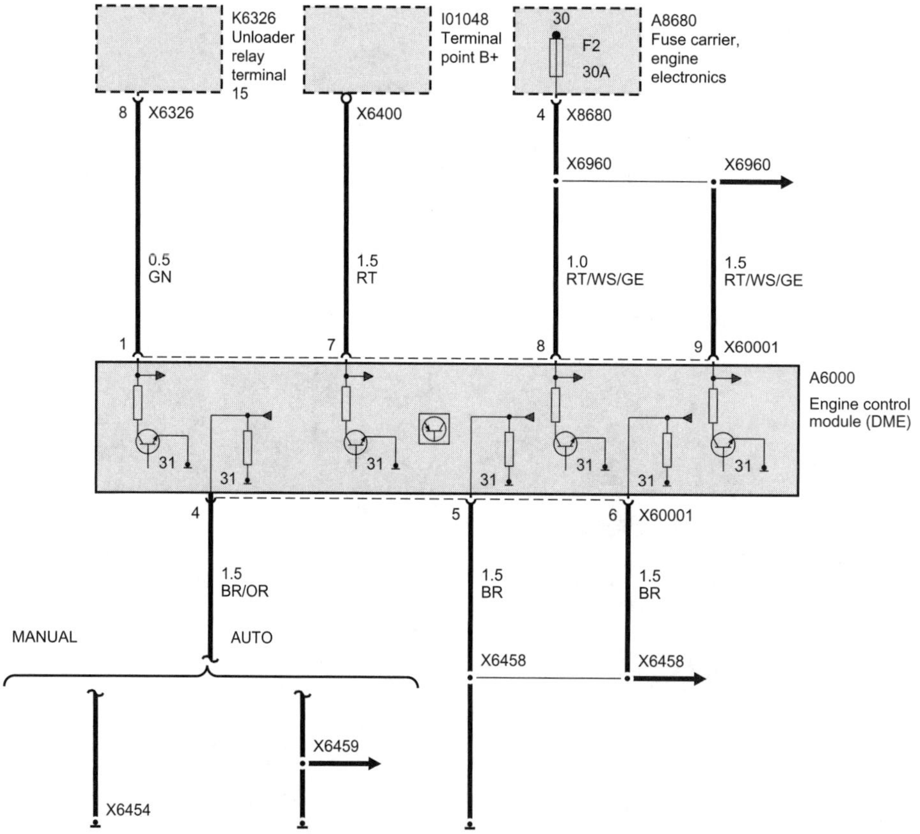

502ELE0415

Engine Management (MS 42.0)
Engine control module (DME) Module 2 (A6000)
(1 of 3)

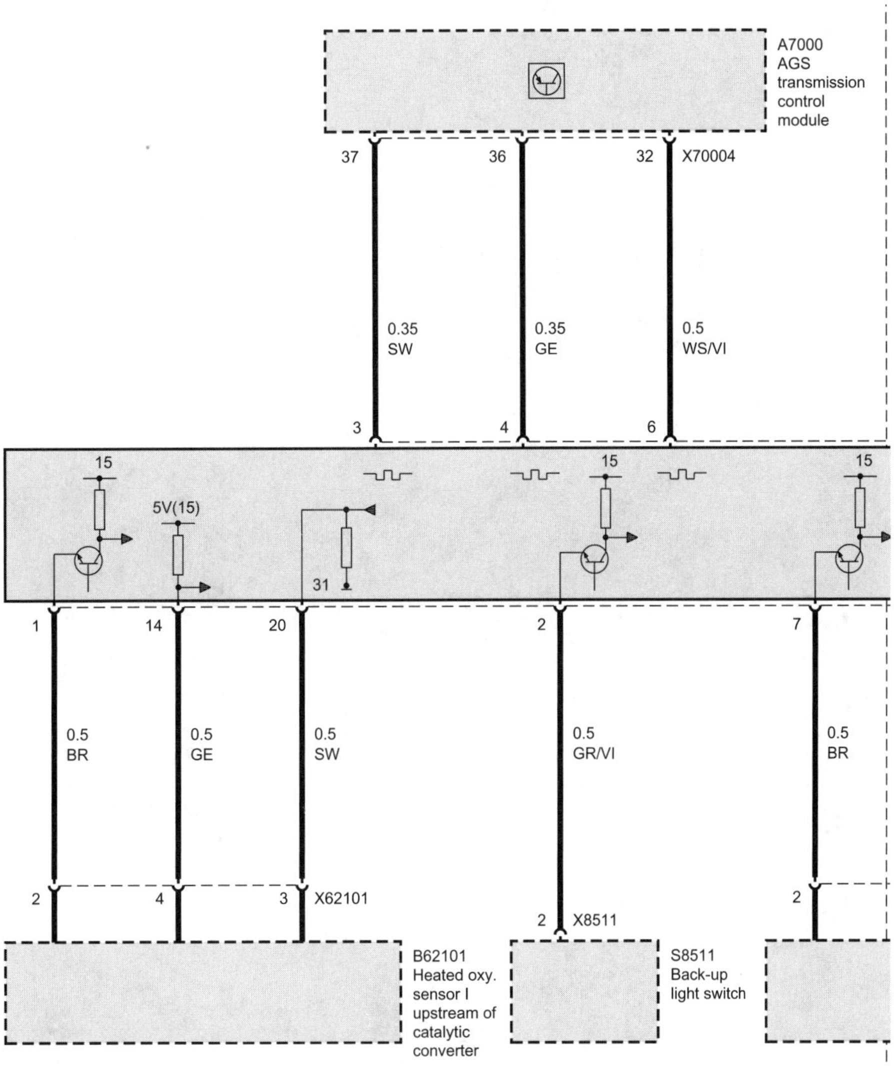

502ELE0416

Engine Management (MS 42.0)
Engine control module (DME) Module 2 (A6000)
(2 of 3)

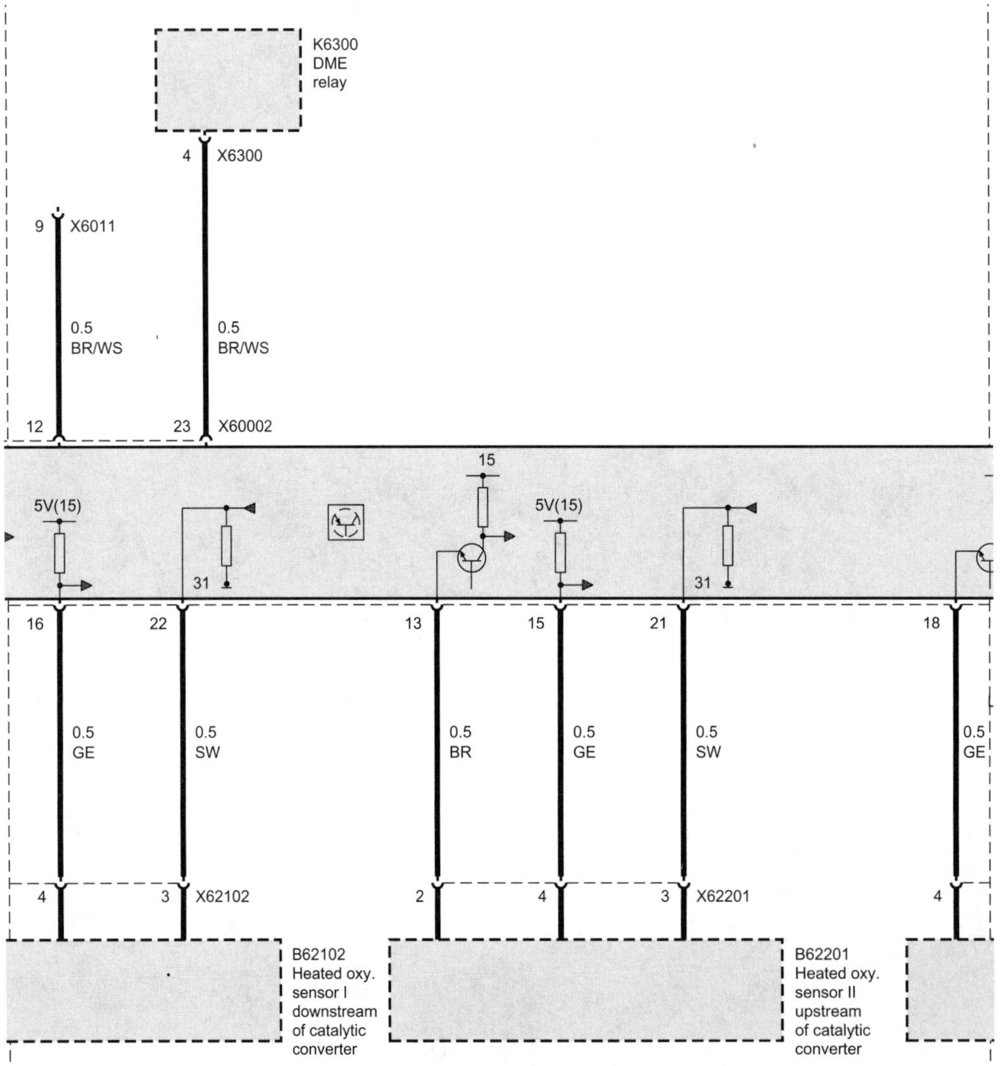

Engine Management (MS 42.0)
Engine control module (DME) Module 2 (A6000)
(3 of 3)

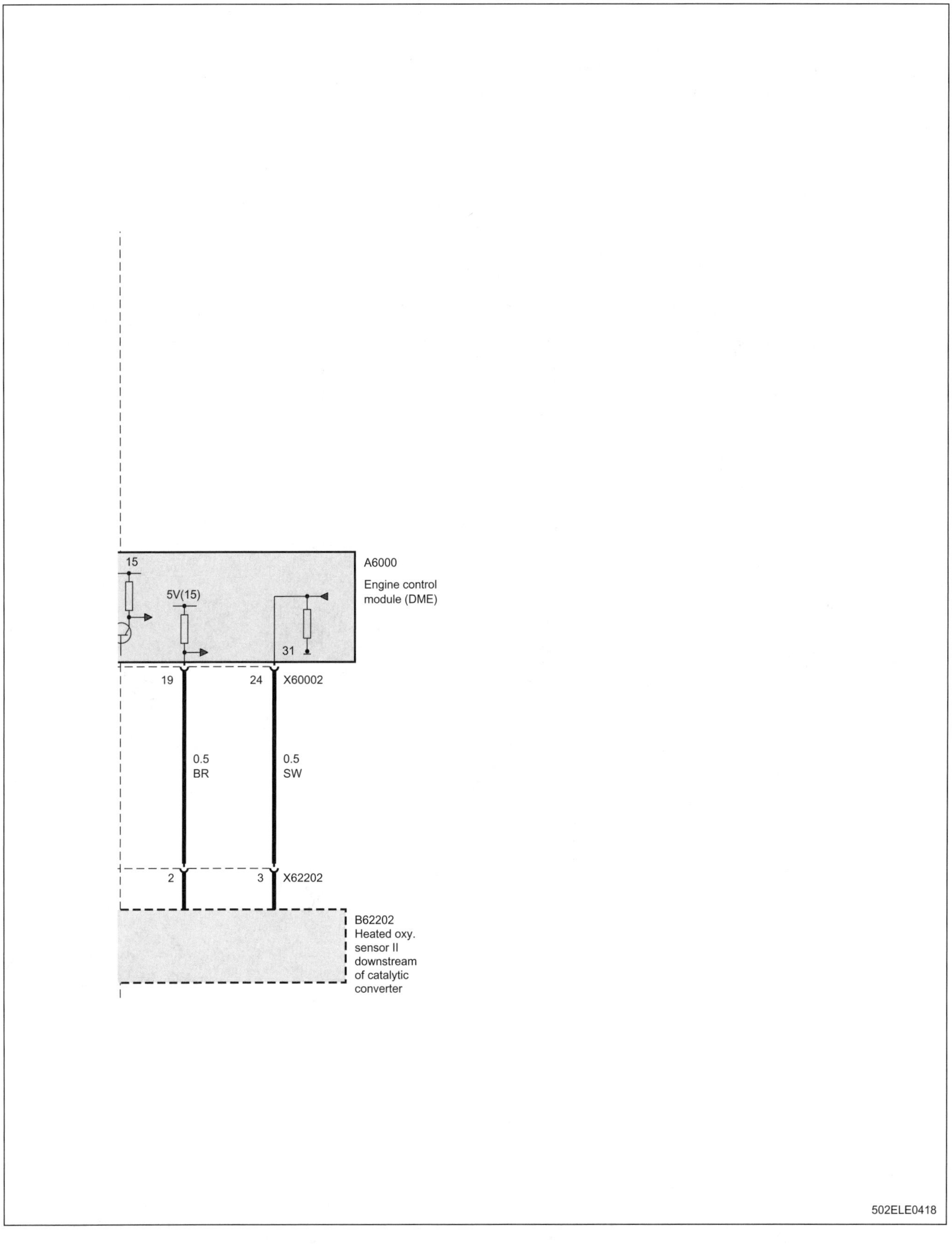

Engine Management (MS 42.0)
Engine control module (DME) Module 3 (A6000)
(1 of 3)

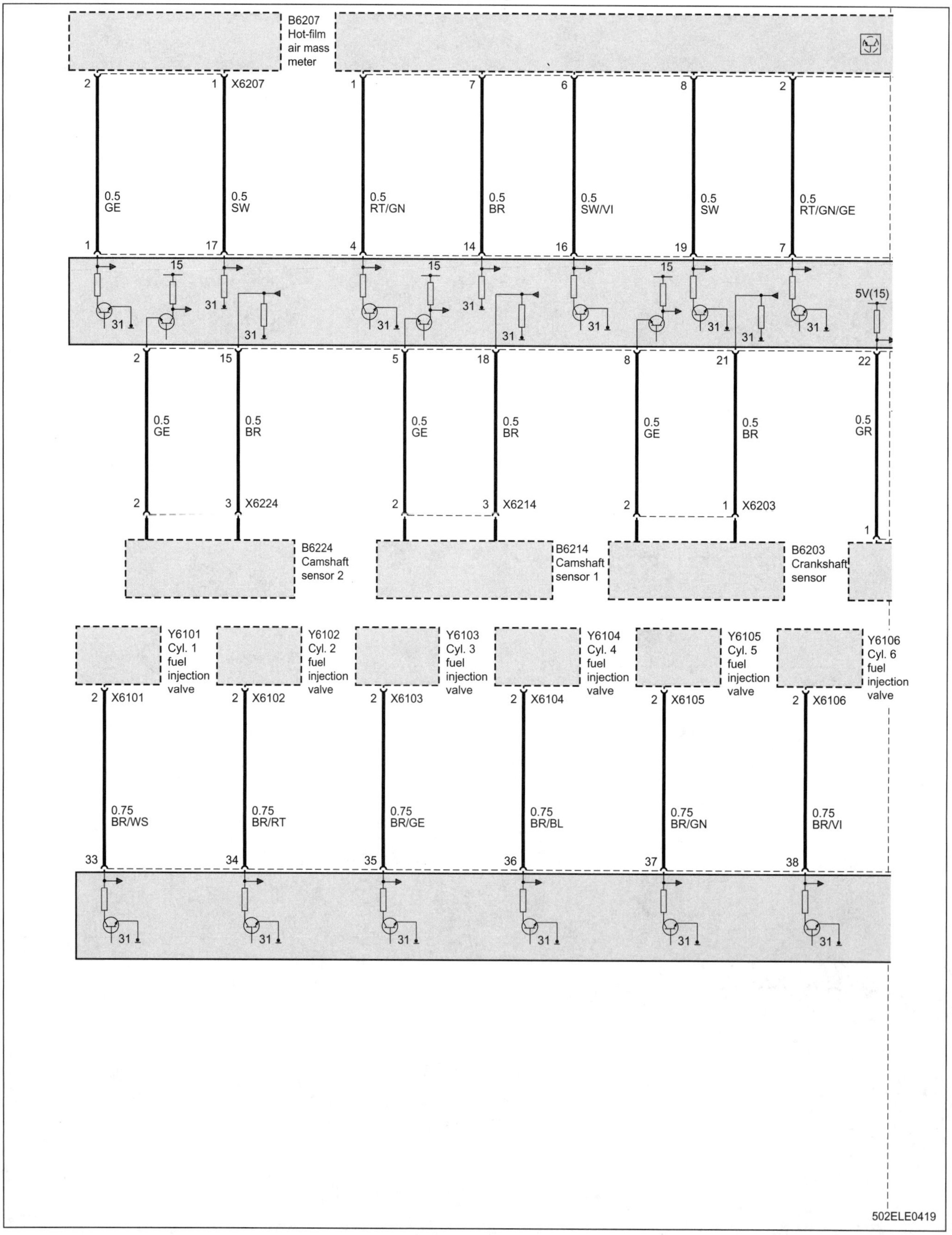

502ELE0419

Engine Management (MS 42.0)
Engine control module (DME) Module 3 (A6000)
(2 of 3)

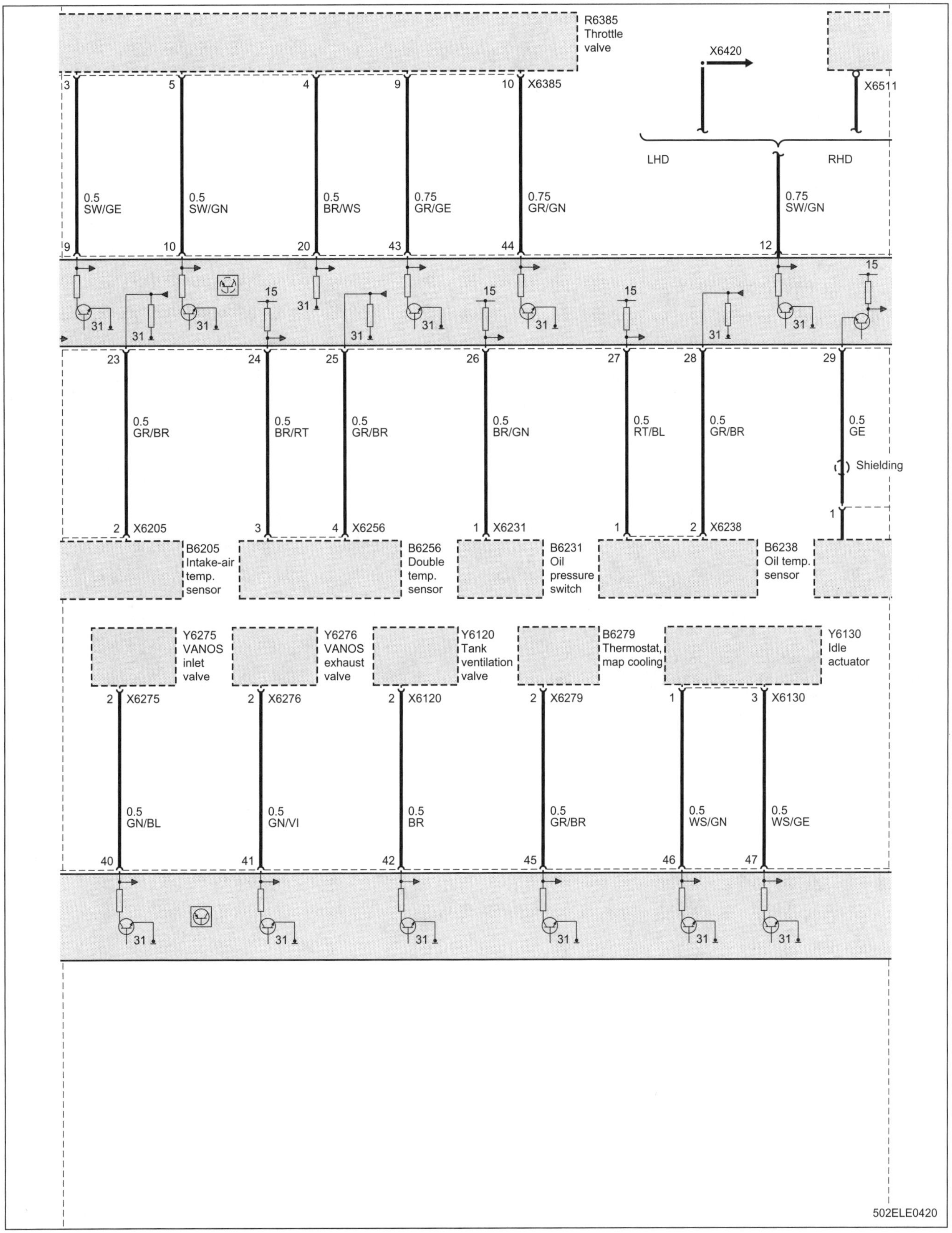

Engine Management (MS 42.0)
Engine control module (DME) Module 3 (A6000)
(3 of 3)

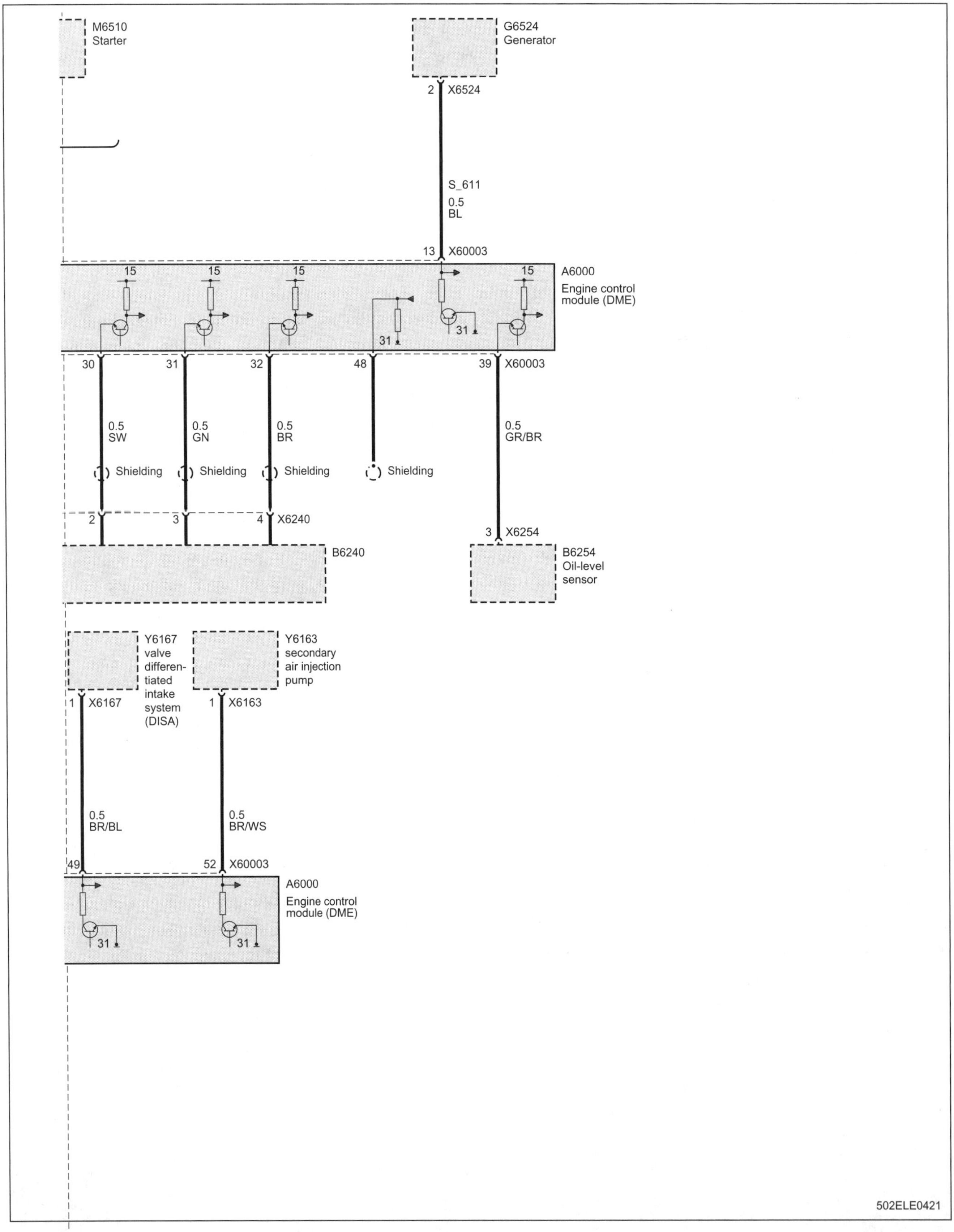

Engine Management (MS 42.0)
Engine control module (DME) Module 4 (A6000)
(1 of 4)

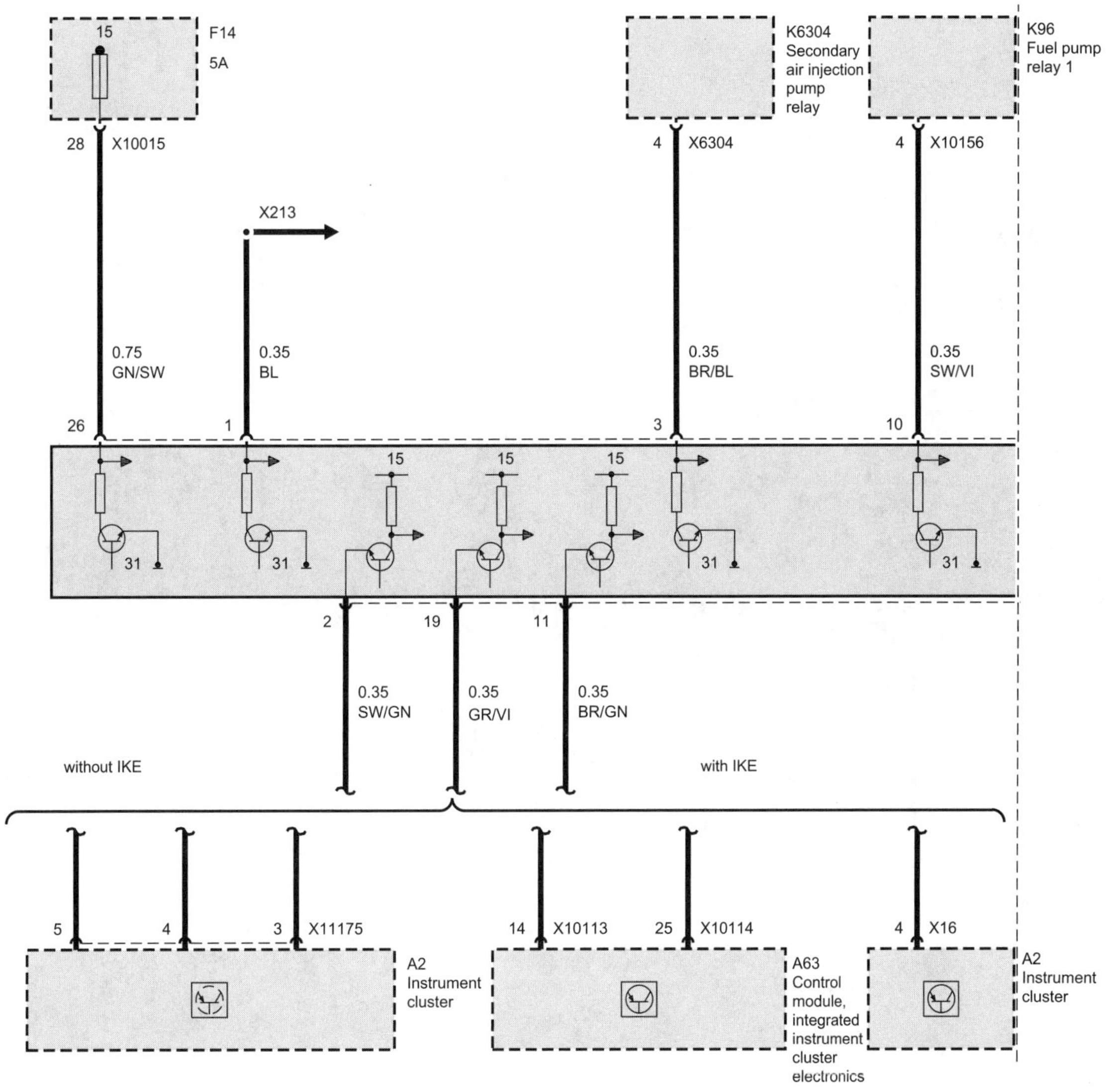

502ELE0422

Engine Management (MS 42.0)
Engine control module (DME) Module 4 (A6000)
(2 of 4)

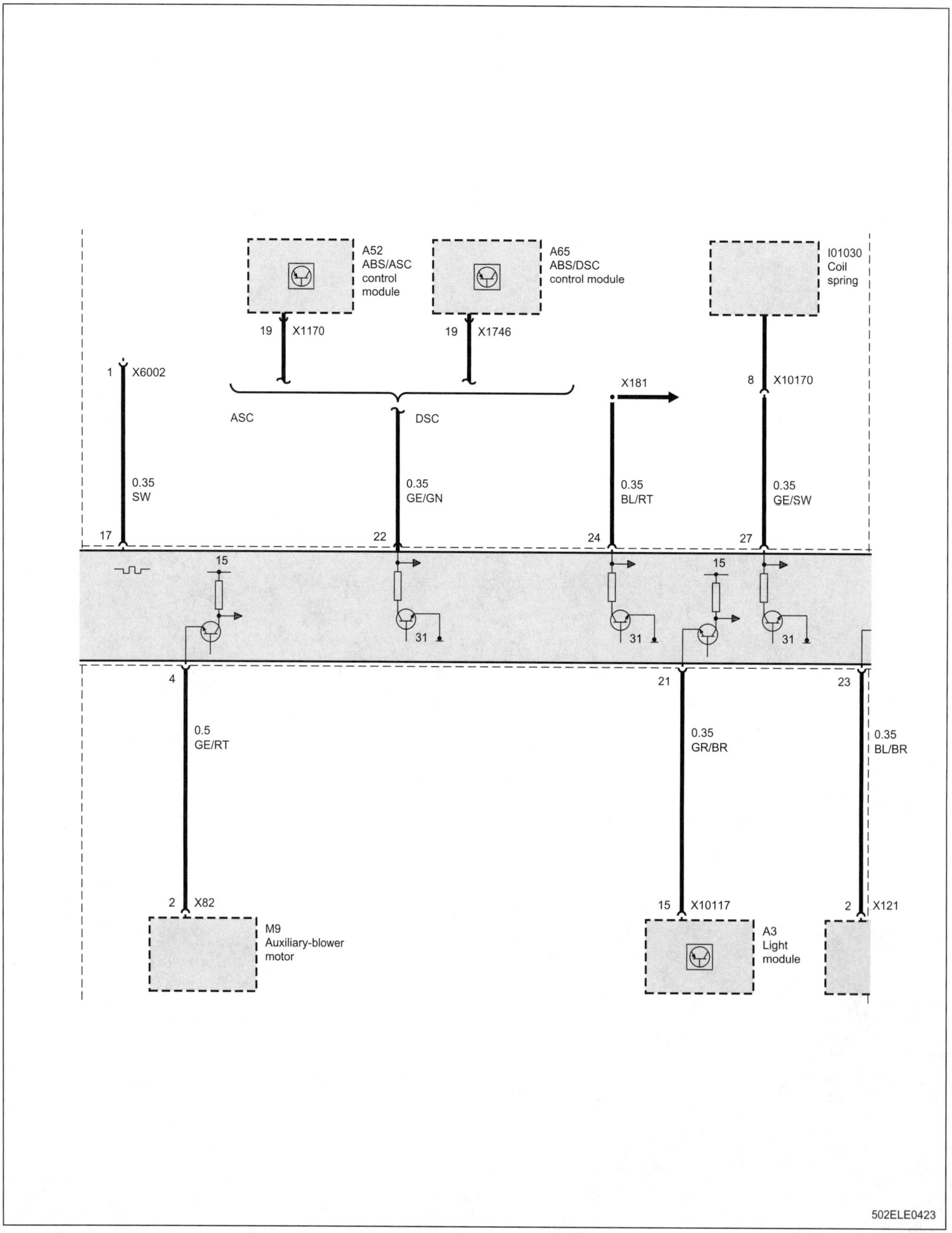

Engine Management (MS 42.0)
Engine control module (DME) Module 4 (A6000)
(3 of 4)

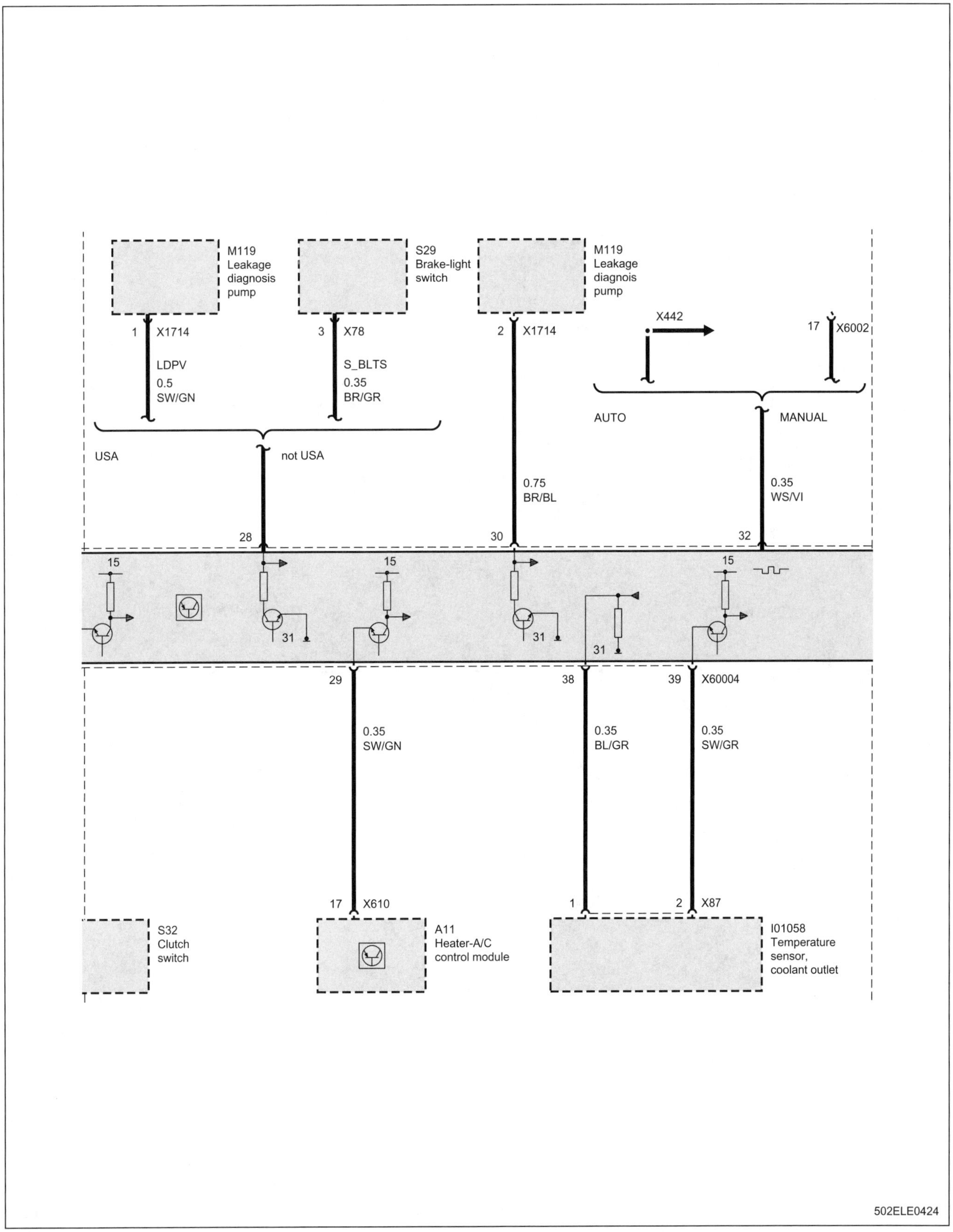

Engine Management (MS 42.0)
Engine control module (DME) Module 4 (A6000)
(4 of 4)

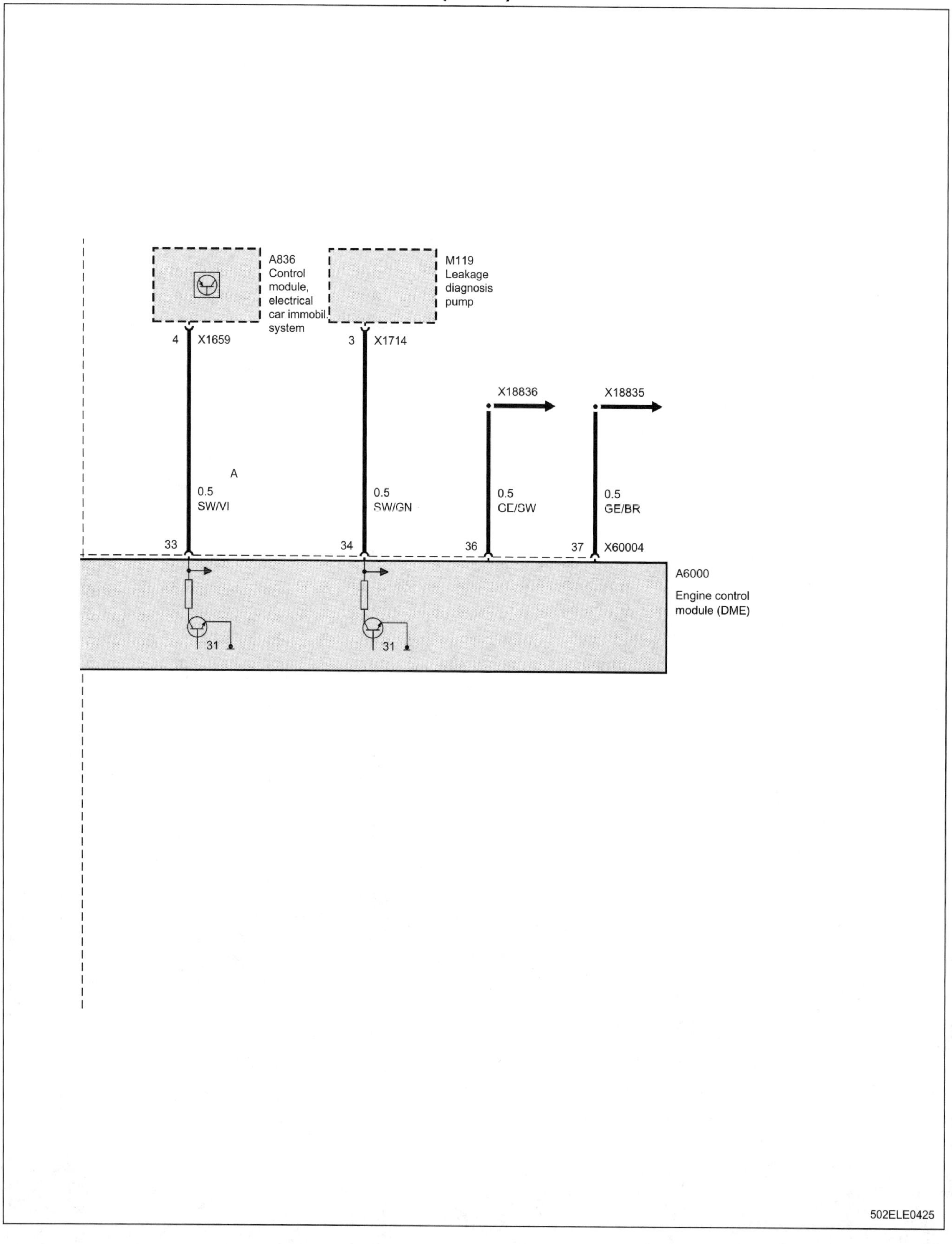

Engine Management (MS 42.0)
Engine control module (DME) Module 5 (A6000)
(1 of 1)

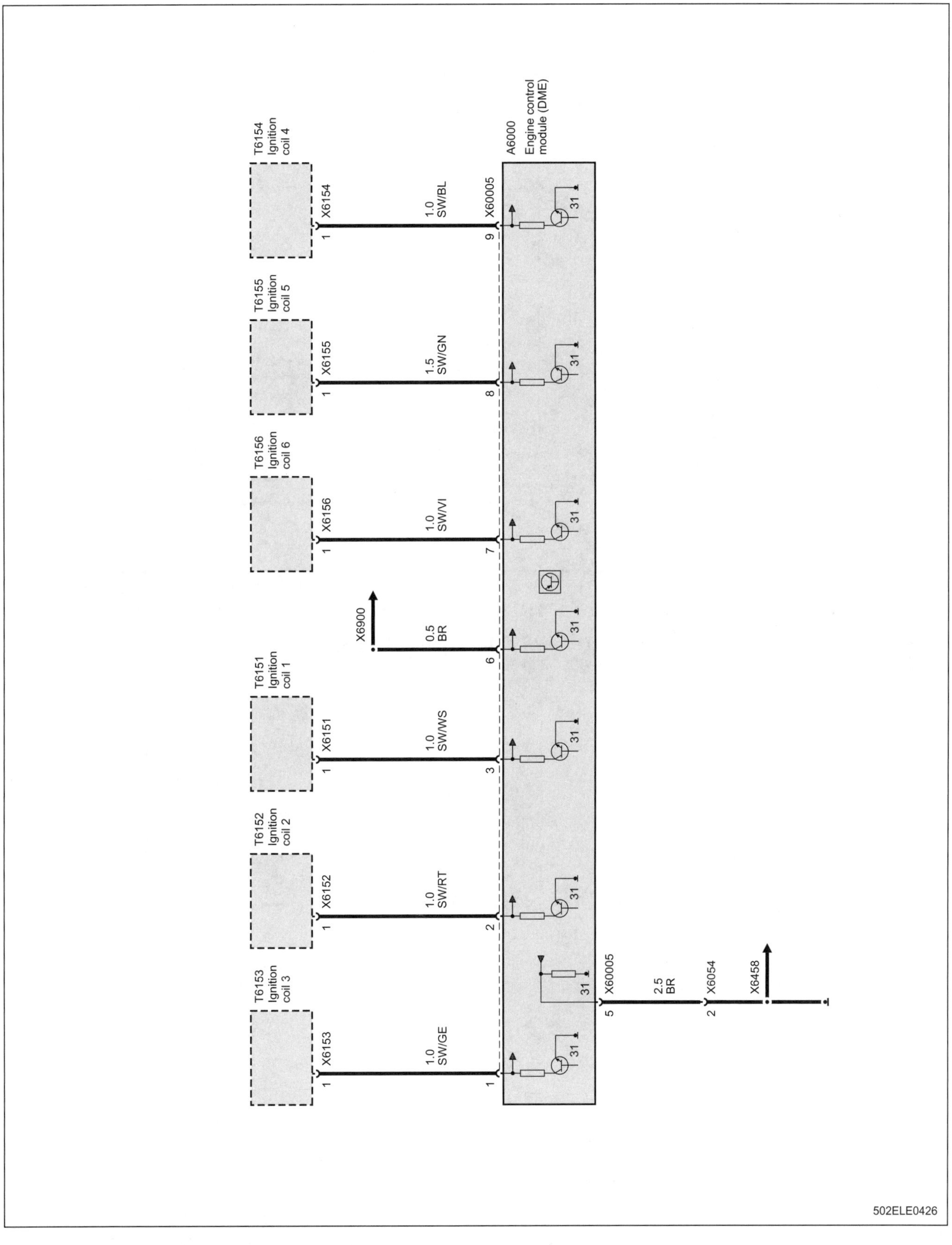

Engine Management (MS 42.0)
Fuel pump

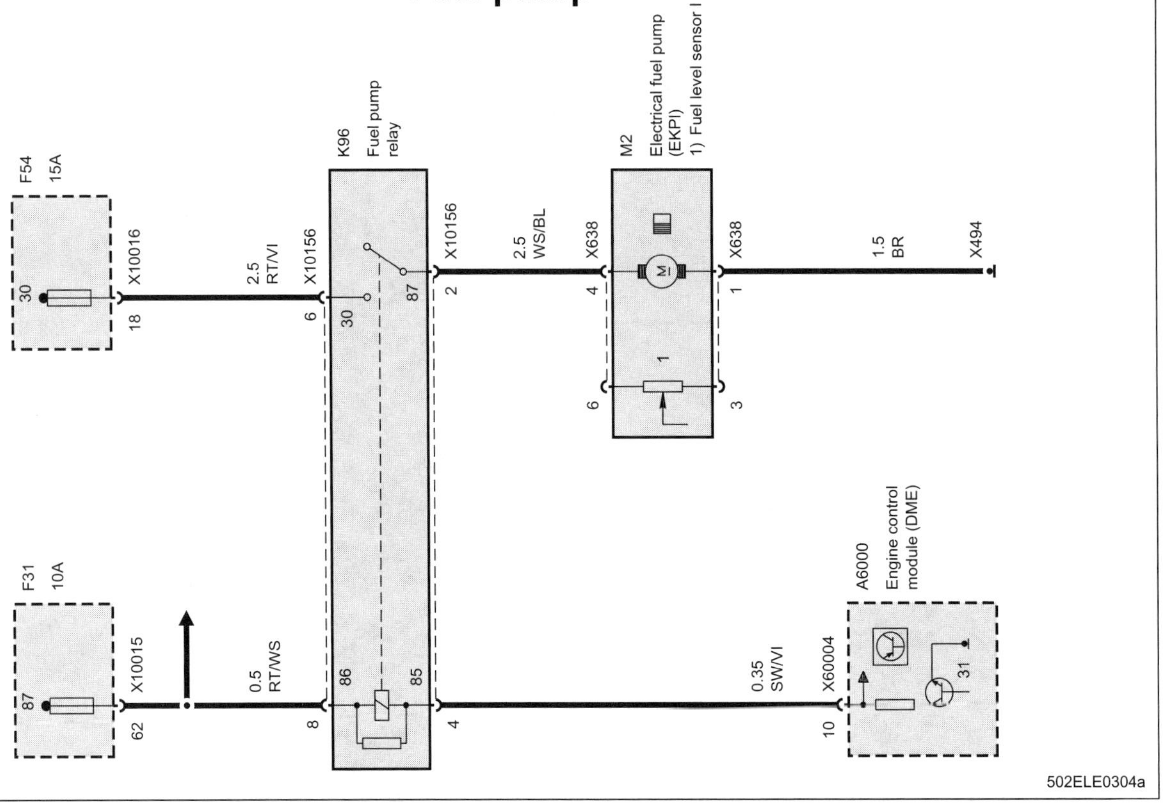

Engine Management (MS 42.0)
Fuel tank leak diagnosis pump

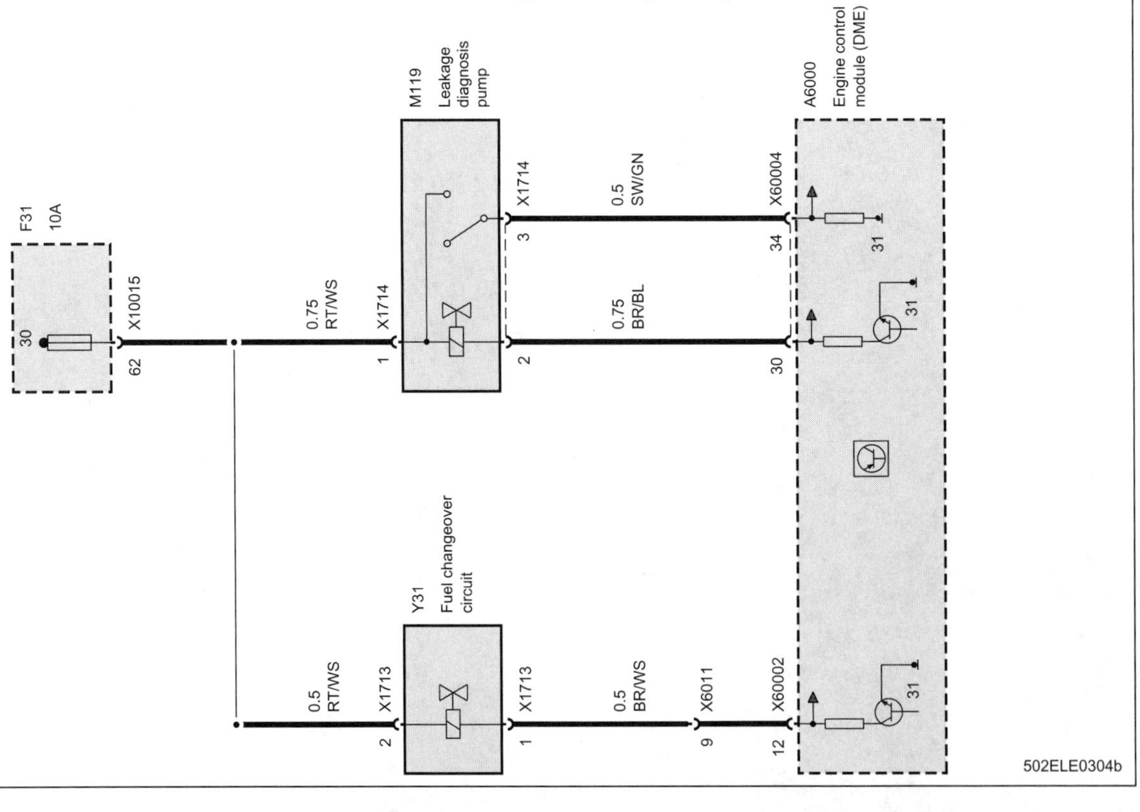

Engine Management (MS 42.0)
Hot-film mass air flow sensor
(1 of 1)

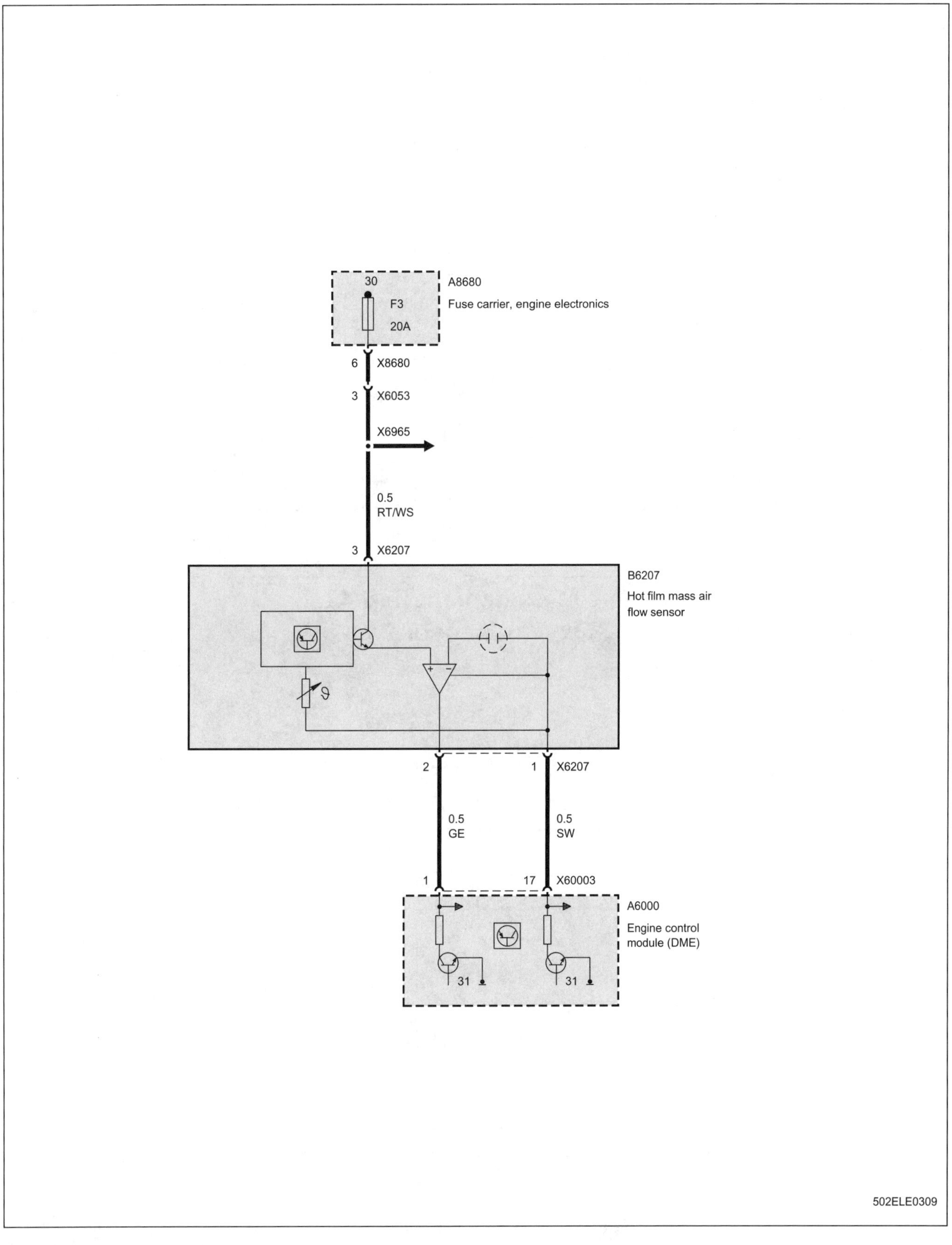

Engine Management (MS 42.0)
Oxygen sensor 1

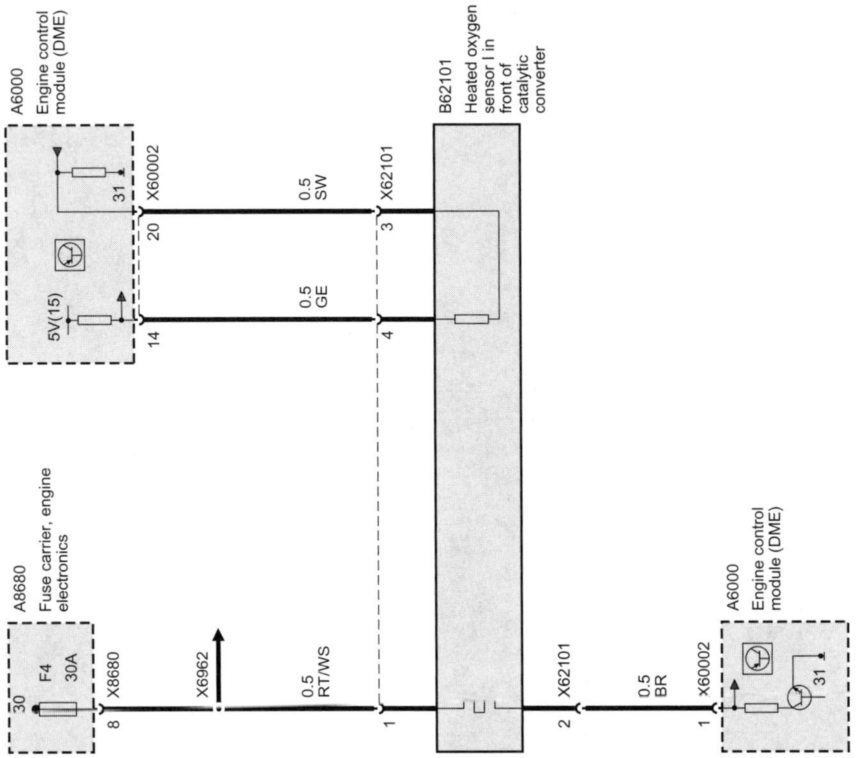

502ELE0325a

Engine Management (MS 42.0)
Oxygen sensor 2

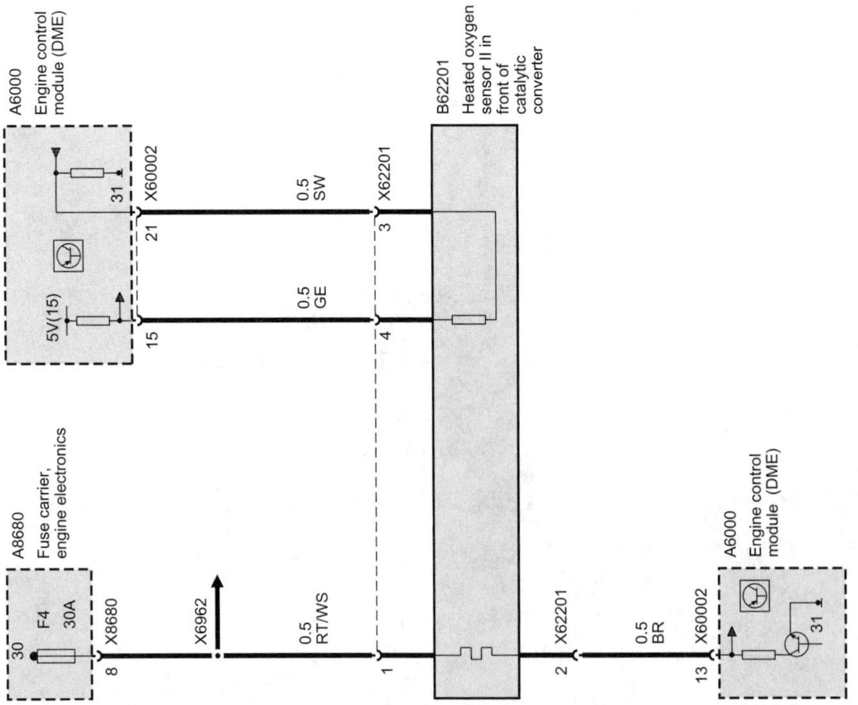

502ELE0325b

Engine Management (MS 42.0)
Oxygen sensor I behind catalytic converter

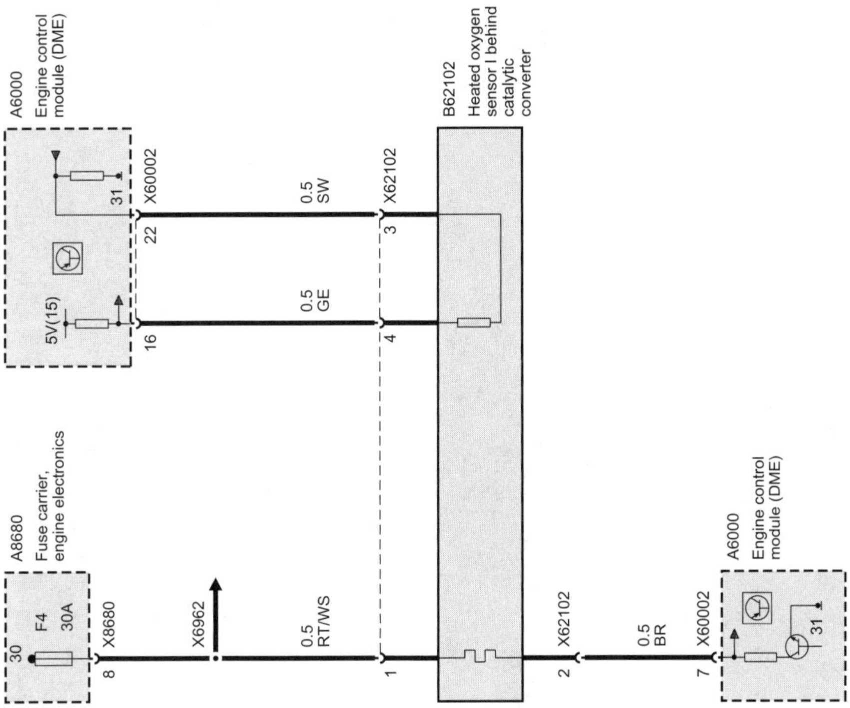

502ELE0326a

Engine Management (MS 42.0)
Oxygen sensor II behind catalytic converter

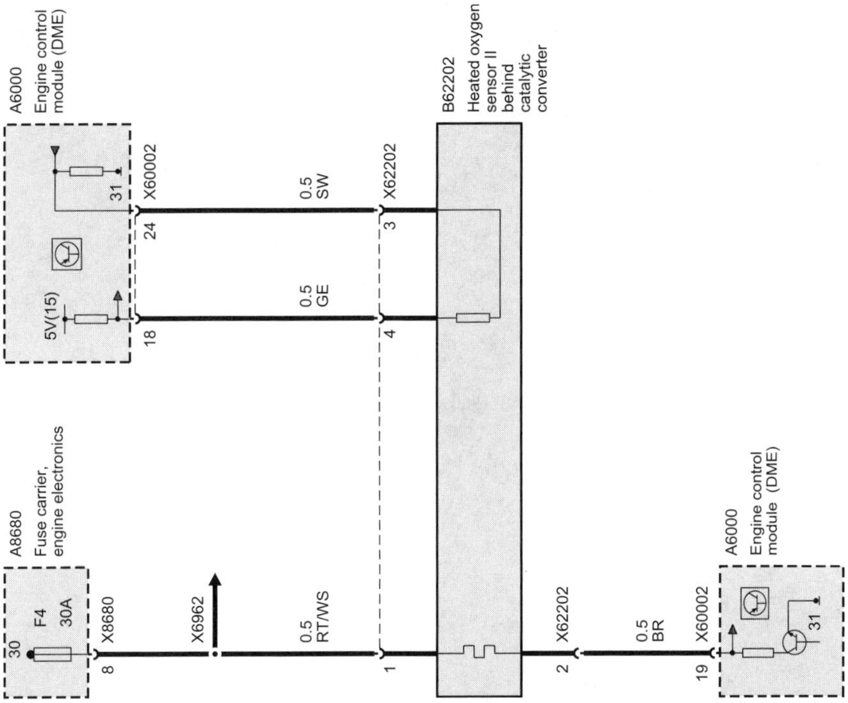

502ELE0326b

Engine Management (MS 42.0)
Idle speed control valve
(1 of 1)

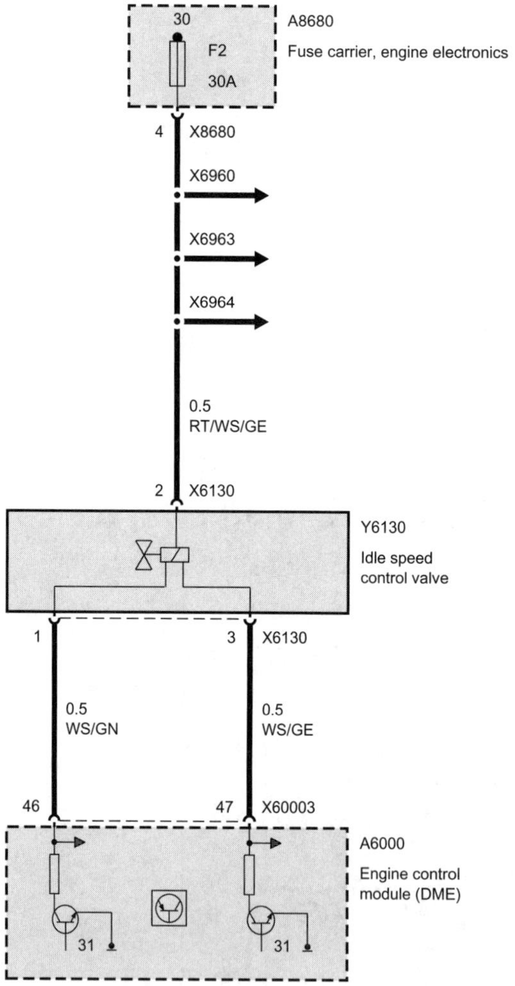

502ELE0310

Engine Management (MS 42.0)
Knock sensor
(1 of 1)

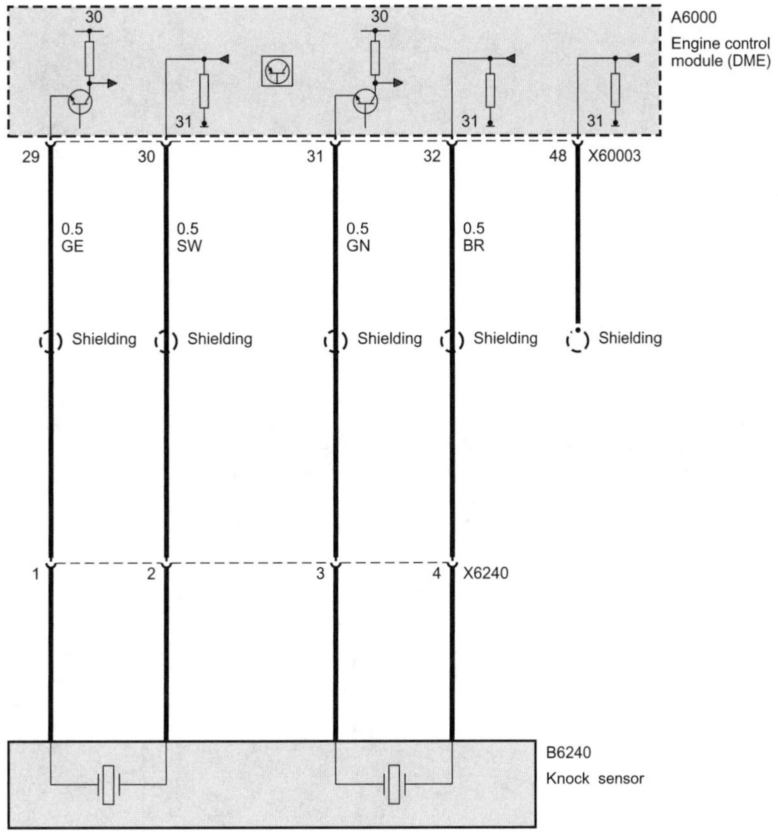
30
30
31
31
31
A6000
Engine control module (DME)
29
30
31
32
48
X60003
0.5 GE
0.5 SW
0.5 GN
0.5 BR
Shielding
Shielding
Shielding
Shielding
Shielding
1
2
3
4
X6240
B6240
Knock sensor
502ELE0317

Engine Management (MS 42.0)
Power, ignition coils
(1 of 1)

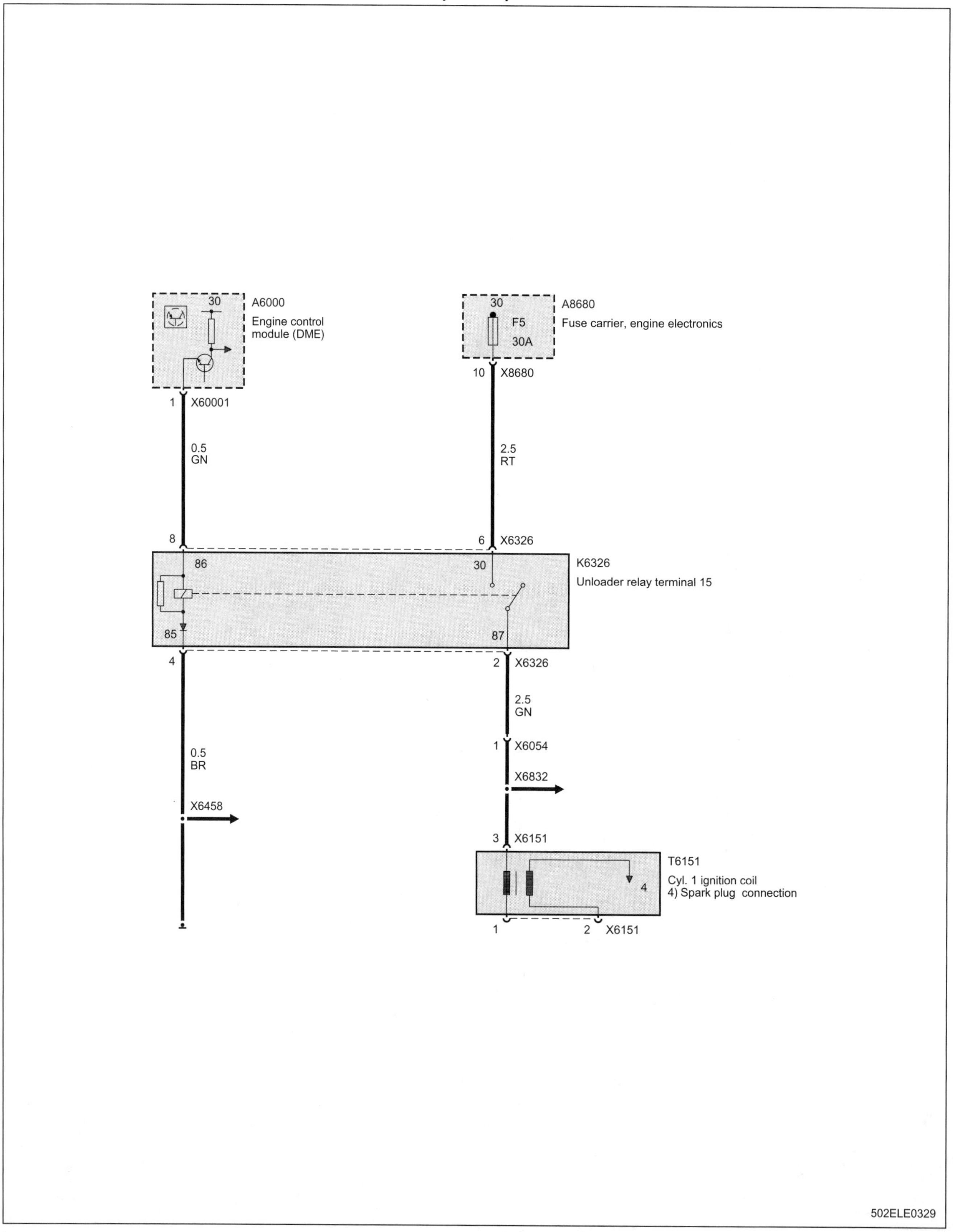

Engine Management (MS 42.0)
Changeover valve, intake (DISA)

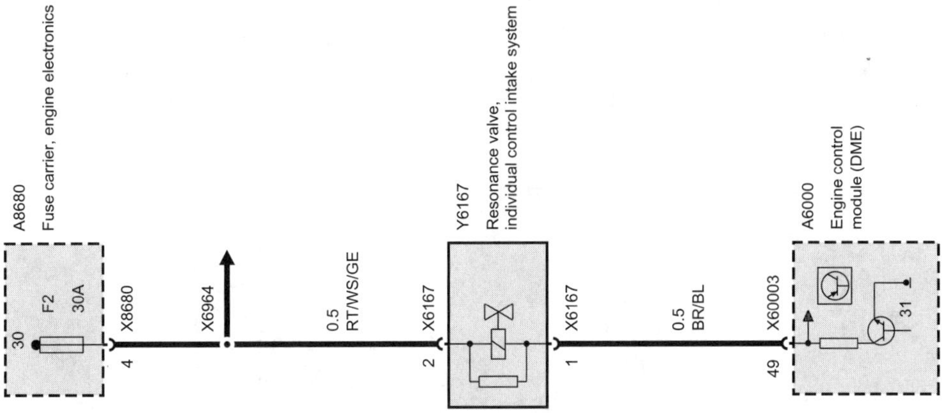

502ELE0285a

Engine Management (MS 42.0)
Crankshaft sensor

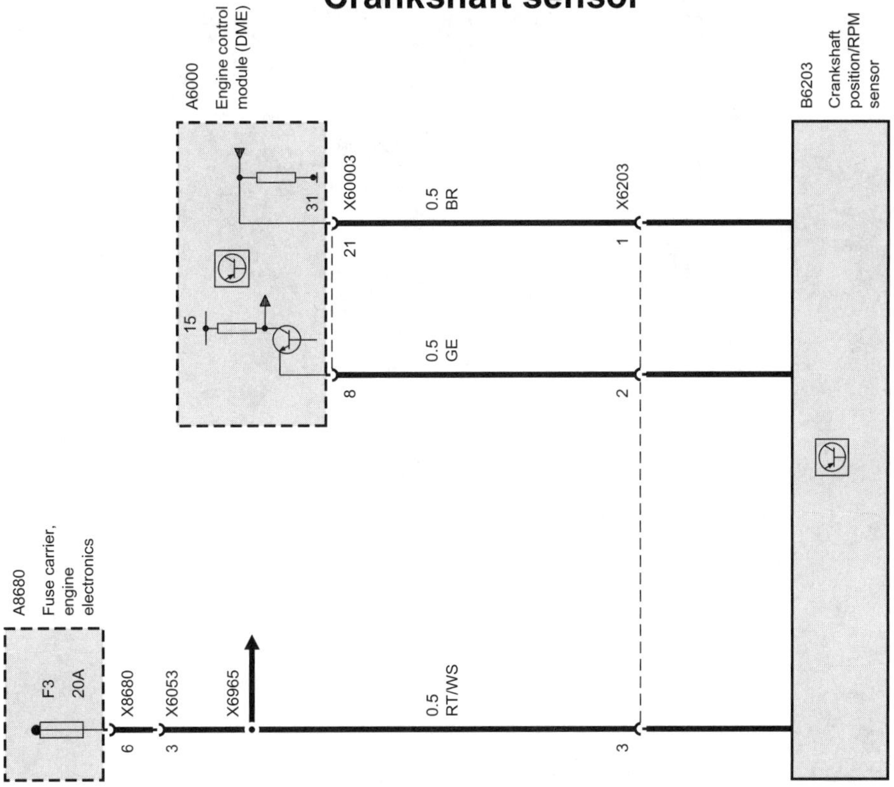

502ELE0285b

Engine Management (MS 42.0)
Secondary air system
(1 of 1)

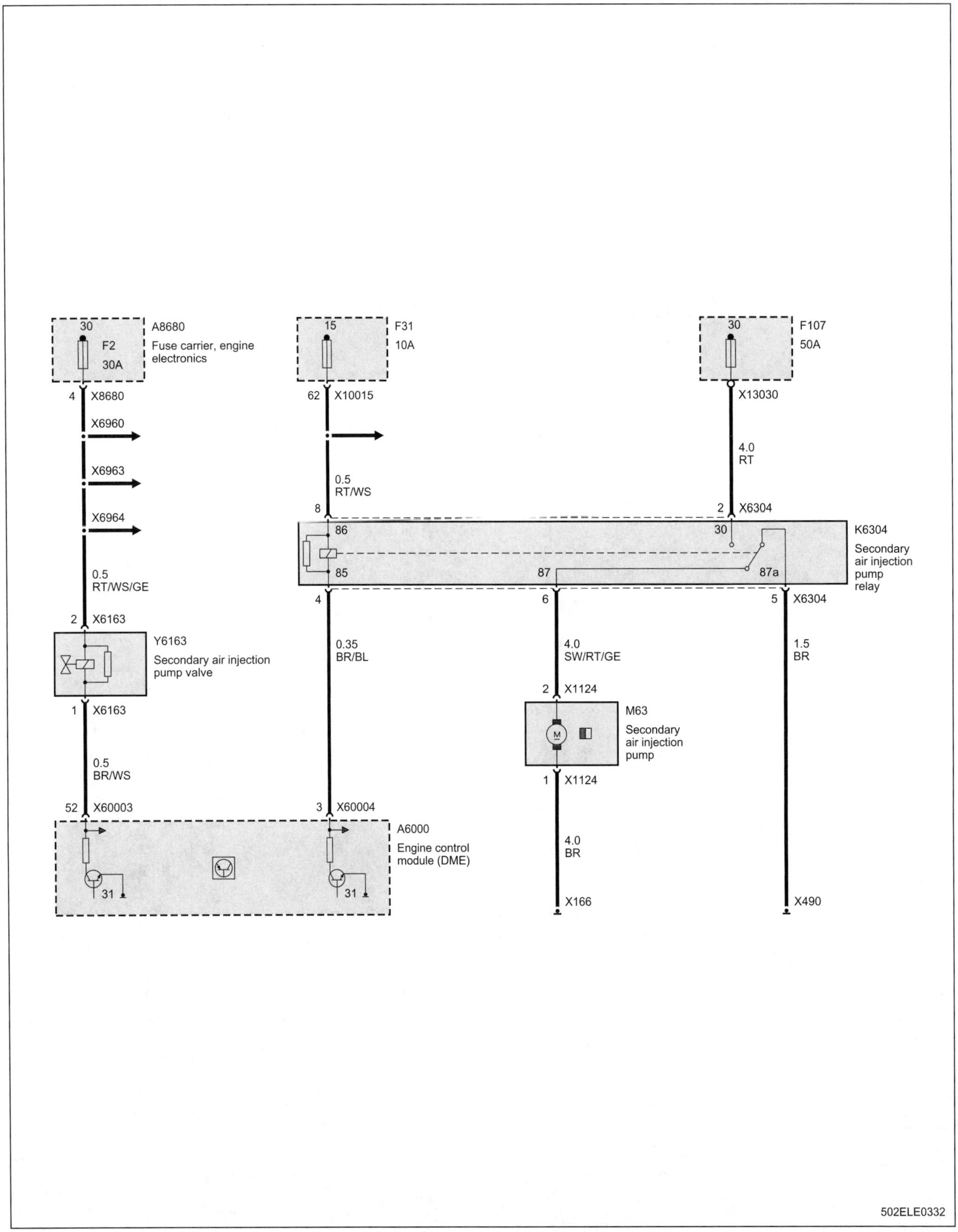

Engine Management (MS 42.0)
Throttle valve actuator
(1 of 1)

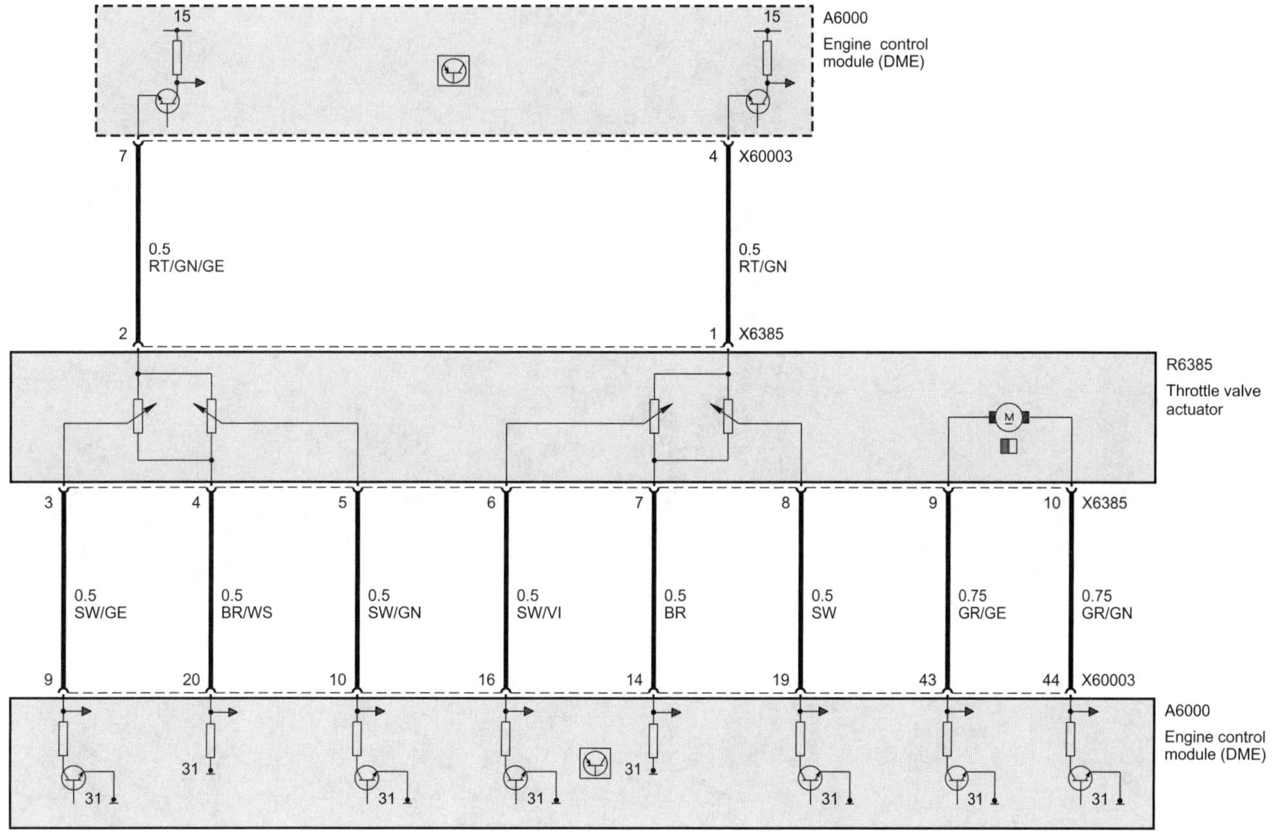

502ELE0337

Engine Management (MS 42.0)
Intake air temperature sensor
(1 of 1)

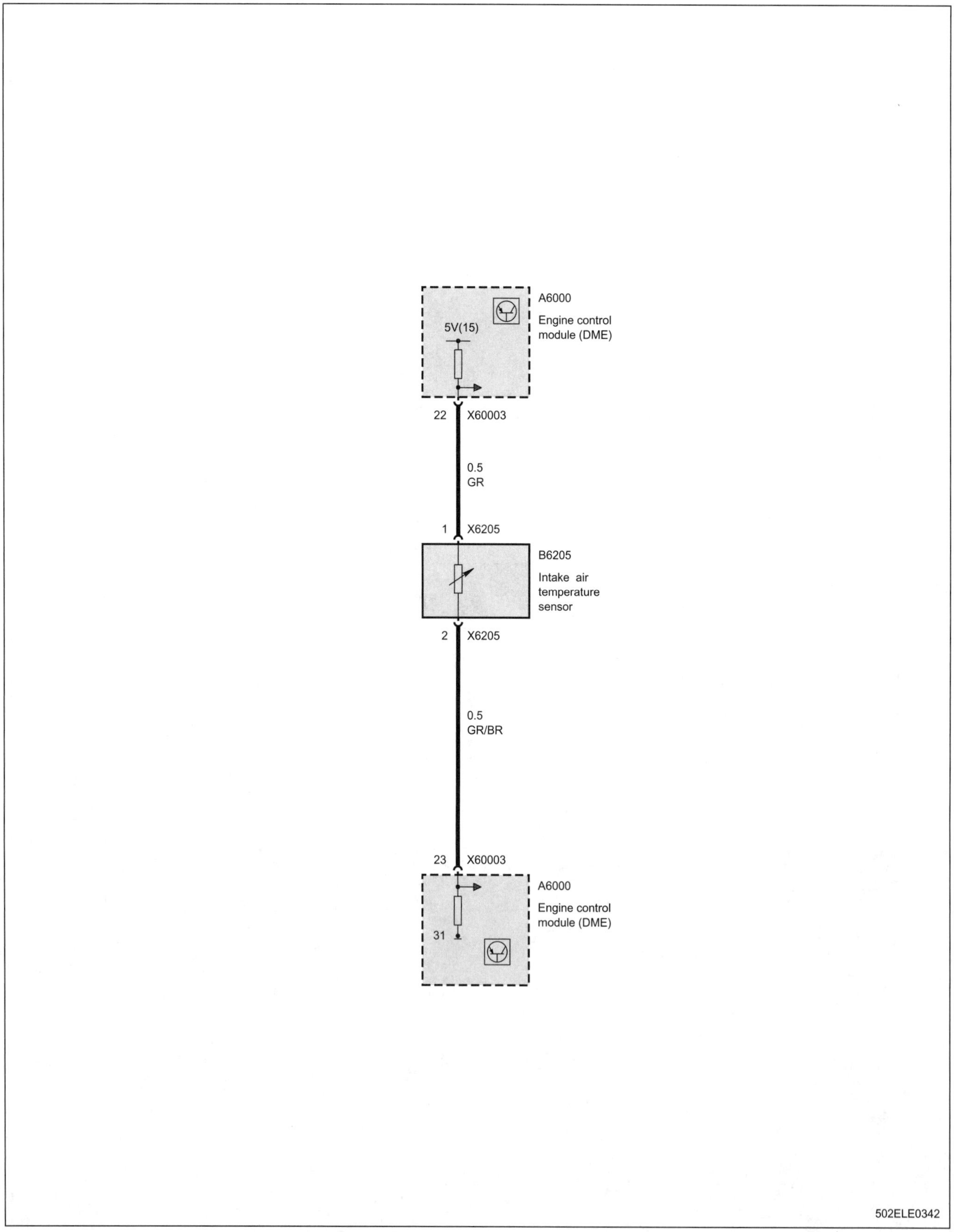

Engine Management (MS 42.0)
VANOS valves
(1 of 1)

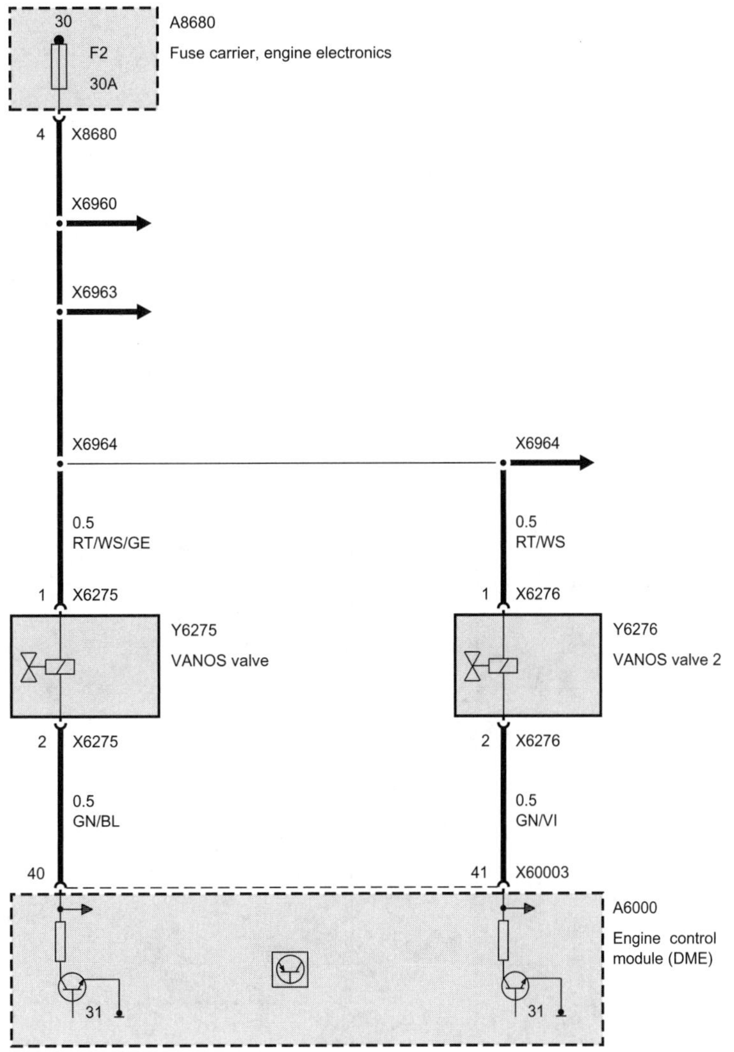
30
F2
30A
A8680
Fuse carrier, engine electronics
4
X8680
X6960
X6963
X6964
X6964
0.5
RT/WS/GE
0.5
RT/WS
1
X6275
1
X6276
Y6275
VANOS valve
Y6276
VANOS valve 2
2
X6275
2
X6276
0.5
GN/BL
0.5
GN/VI
40
41
X60003
A6000
Engine control
module (DME)
31
31
502ELE0343

Engine Management (MS 42.0)
Camshaft position (CMP) sensor
(1 of 1)

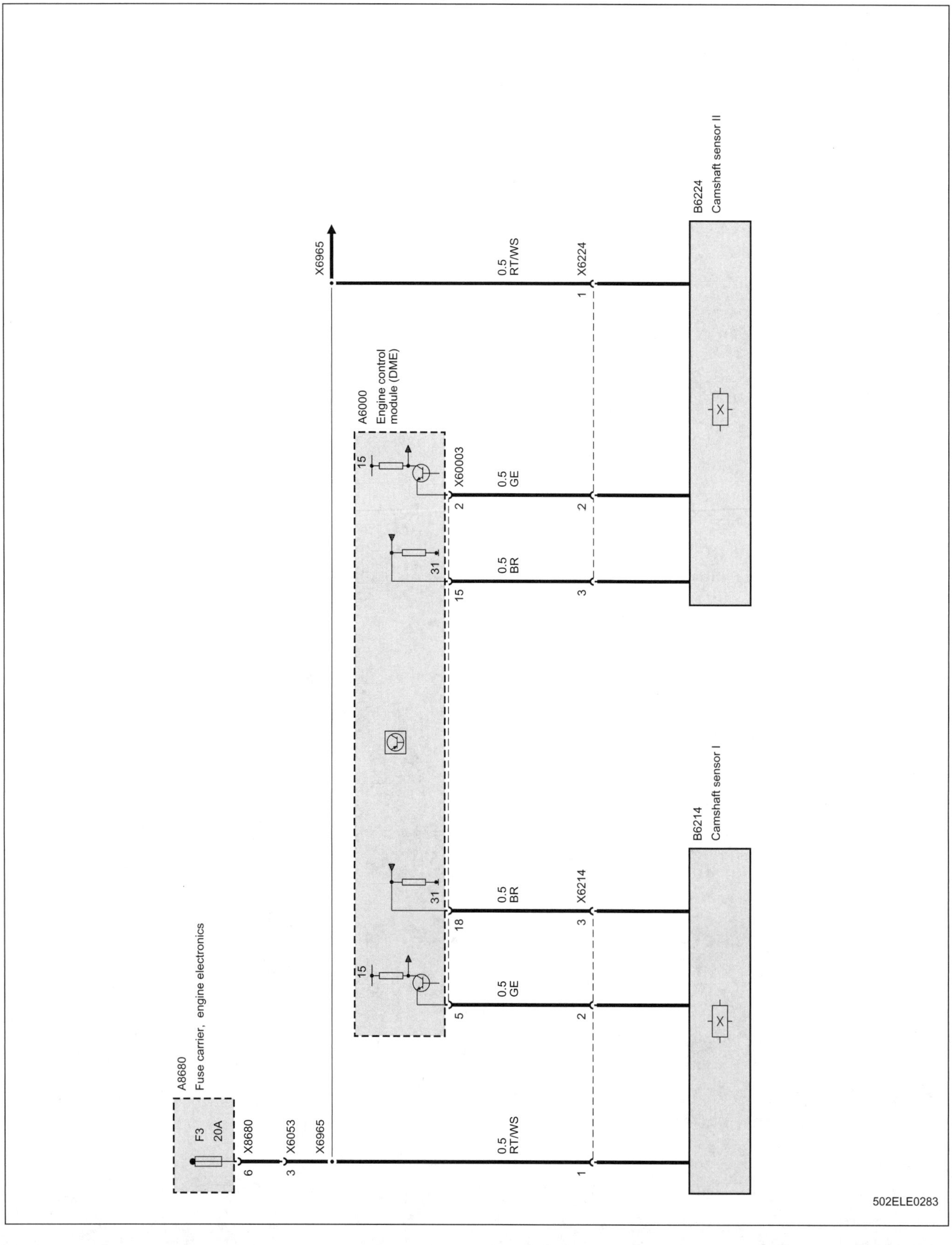

Engine Management (MS 42.0)
Power, DME control module
(1 of 1)

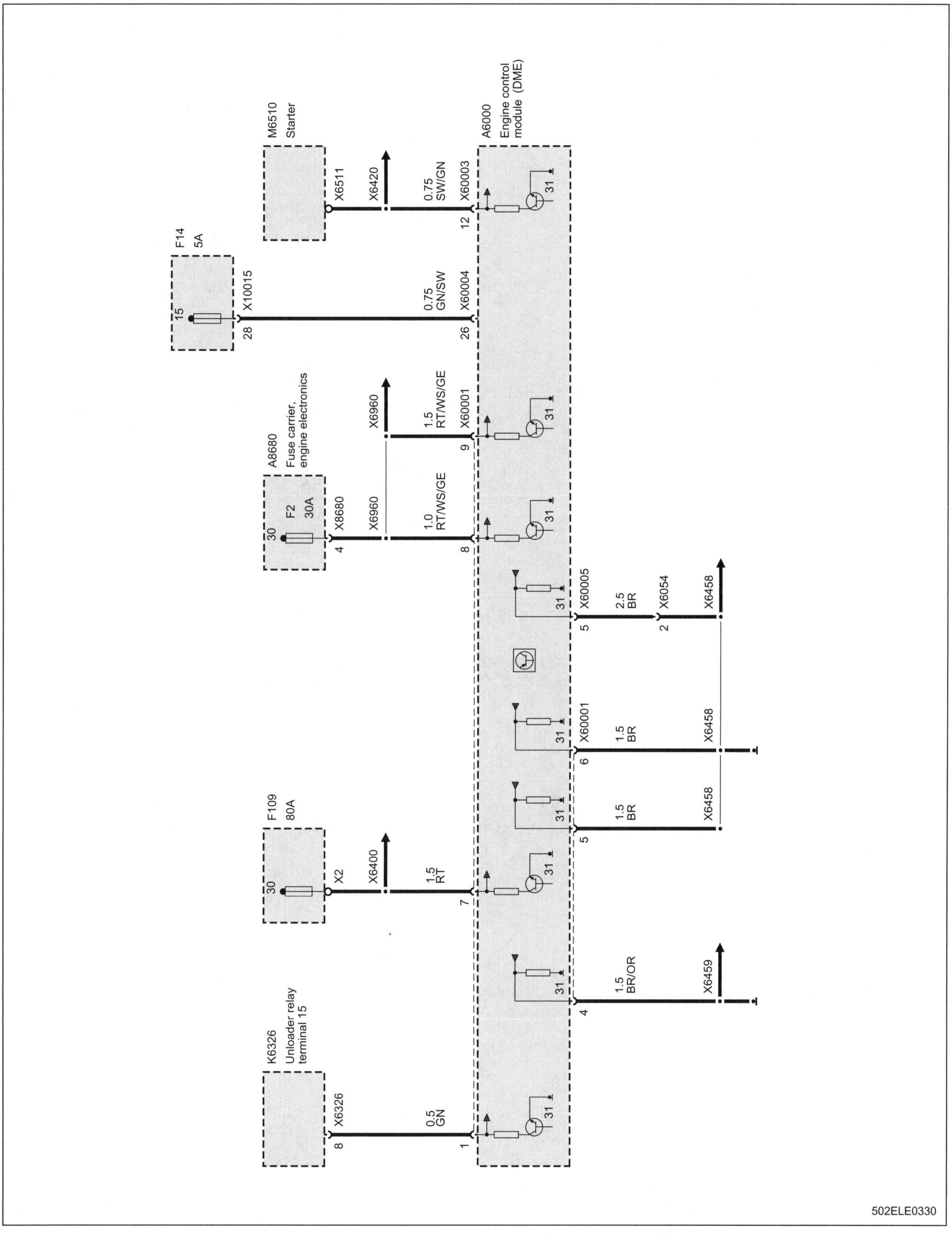

Engine Management (MS 42.0)
Cyl. 1 and 2 fuel injection valves

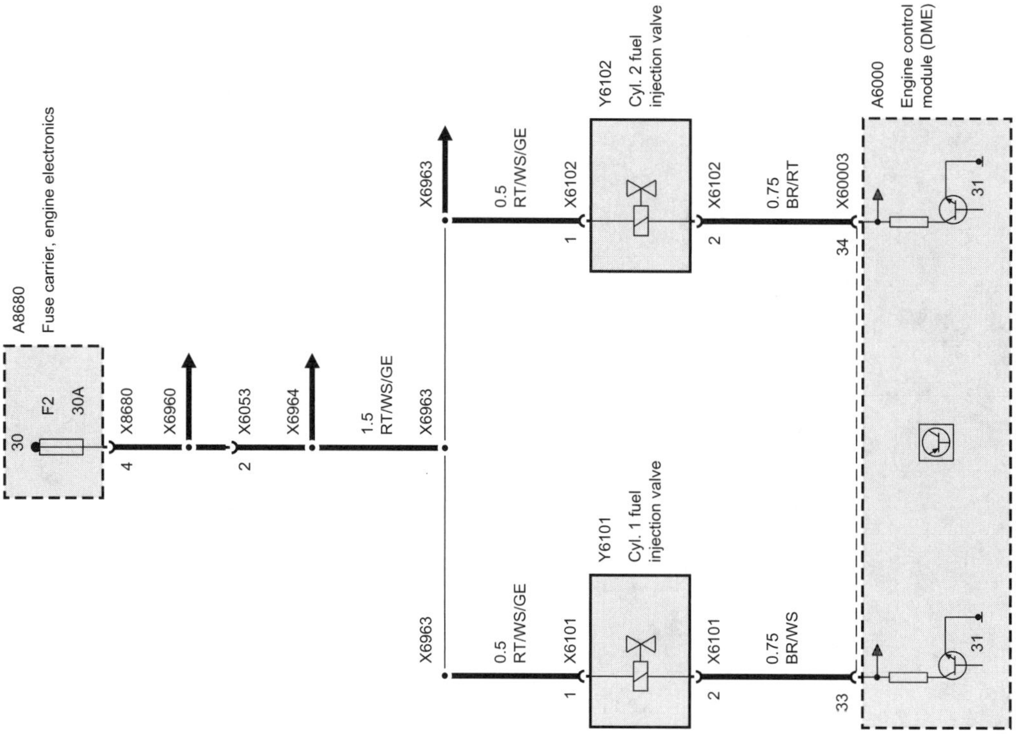

502ELE0287a

Engine Management (MS 42.0)
Cyl. 3 and 4 fuel injection valves

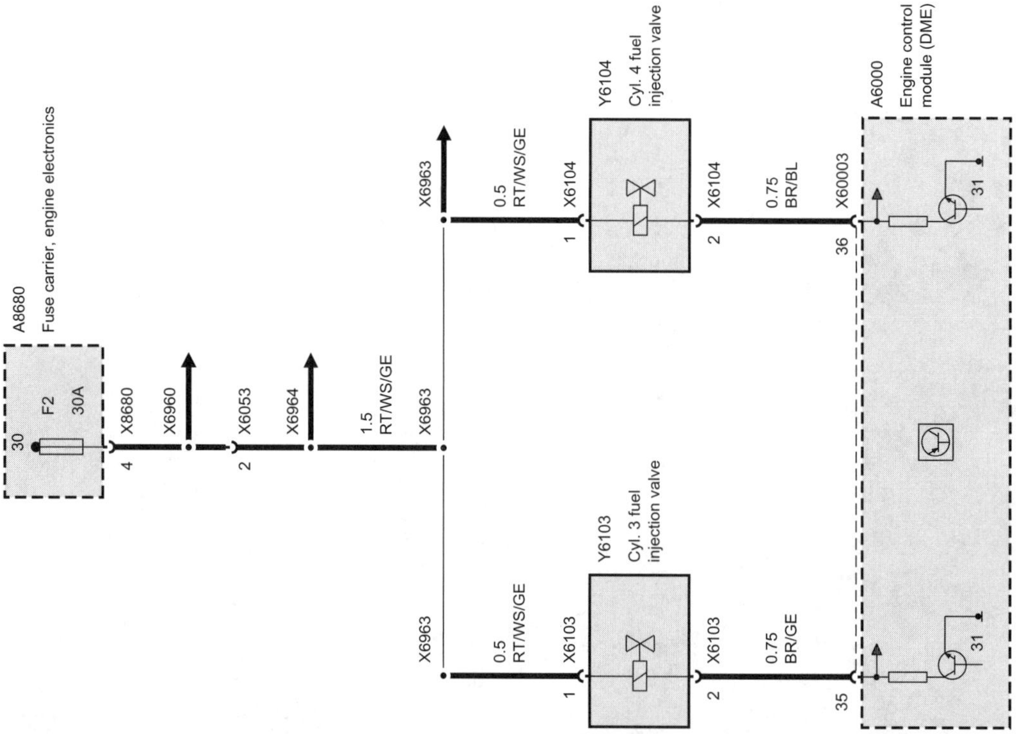

502ELE0287b

Engine Management (MS 42.0)
Cyl. 5 and 6 fuel injection valves

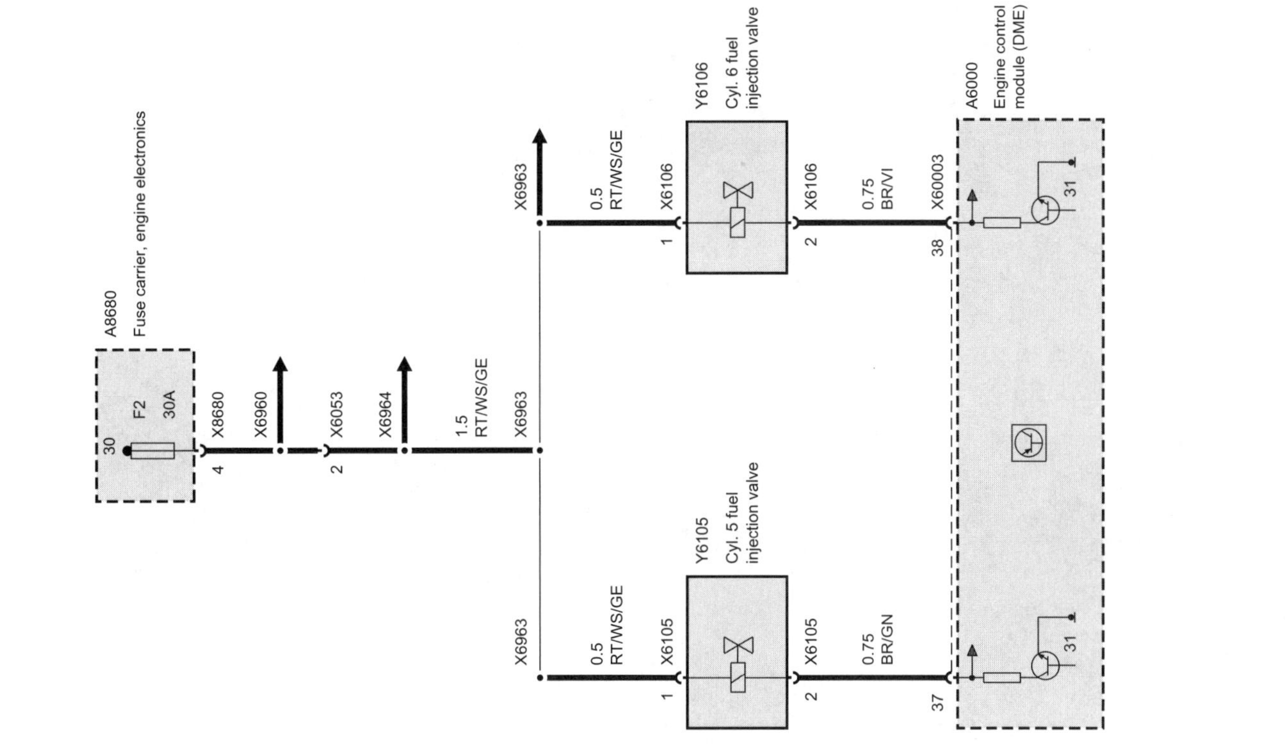

502ELE0288a

Engine Management (MS 42.0)
Cyl. 1 and 2 ignition coils

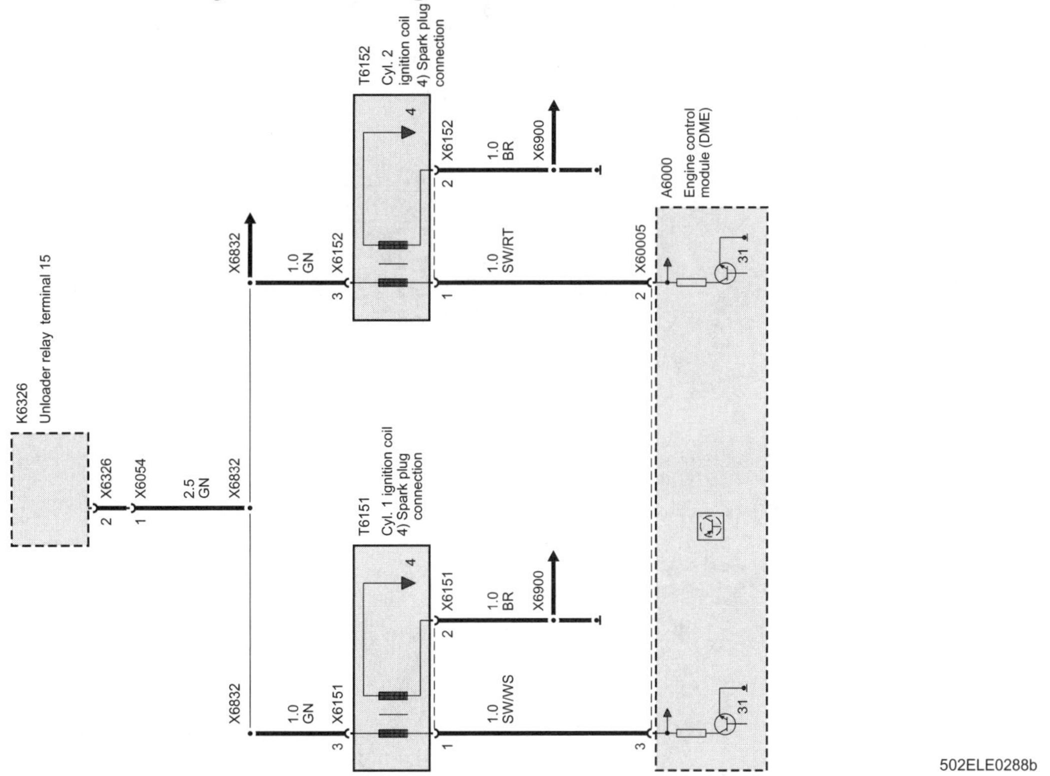

502ELE0288b

Engine Management (MS 42.0)
Cyl. 3 and 4 ignition coils

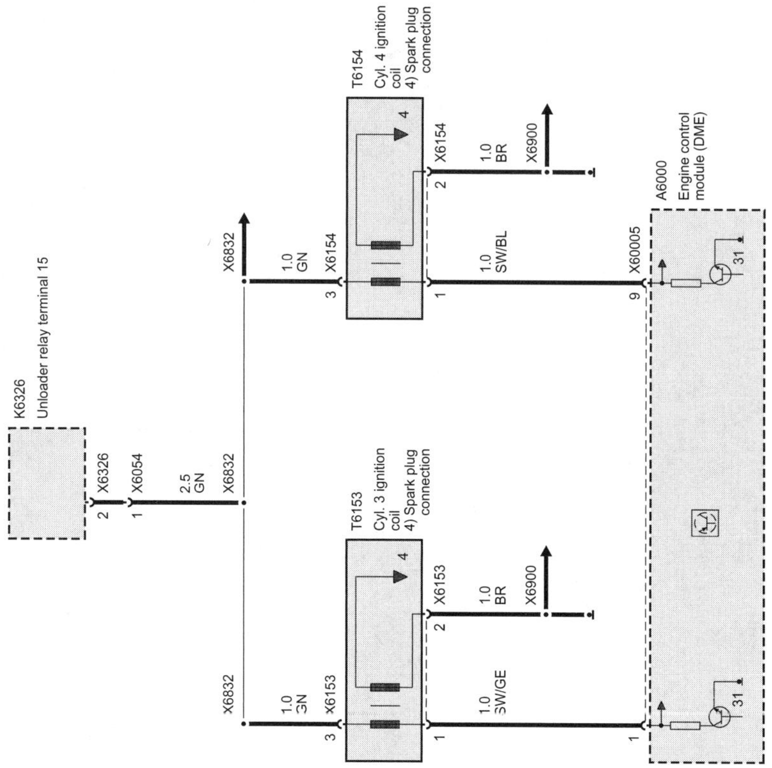

502ELE0289a

Engine Management (MS 42.0)
Cyl. 5 and 6 ignition coils

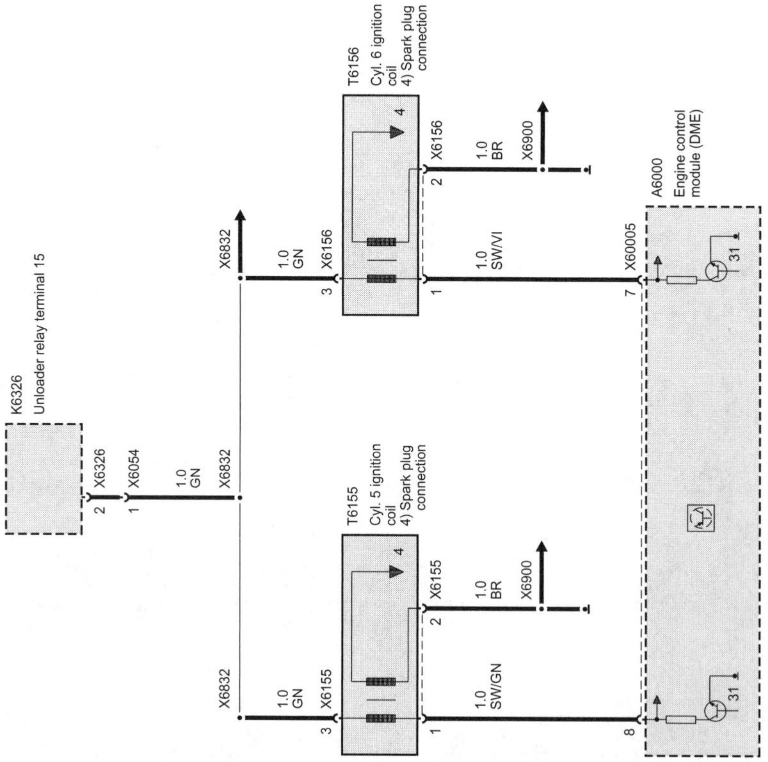

502ELE0289b

Engine Management (MS 42.0)
DME/climate control interfaces

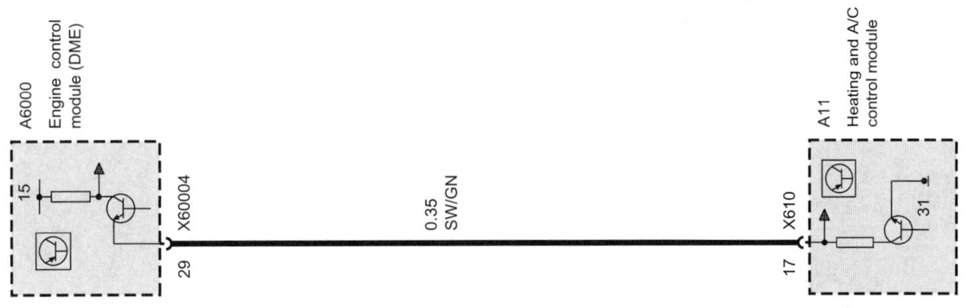

502ELE0290a

Engine Management (MS 42.0)
E-Box fan

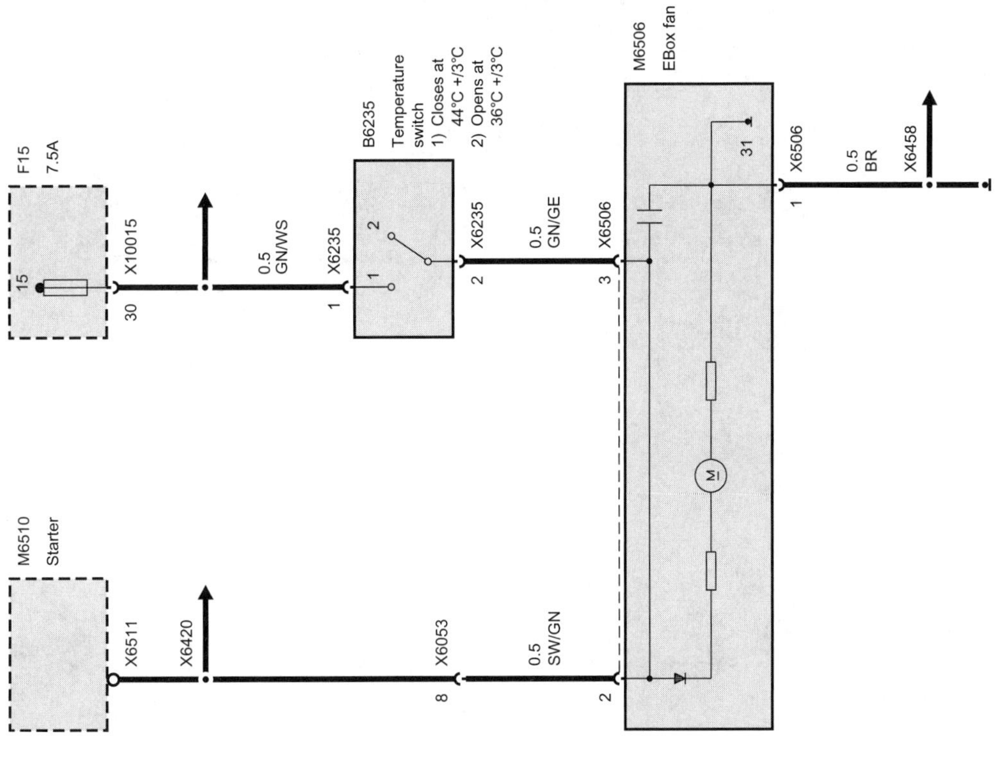

502ELE0290b

Engine Management (MS 42.0)
Engine control module relay

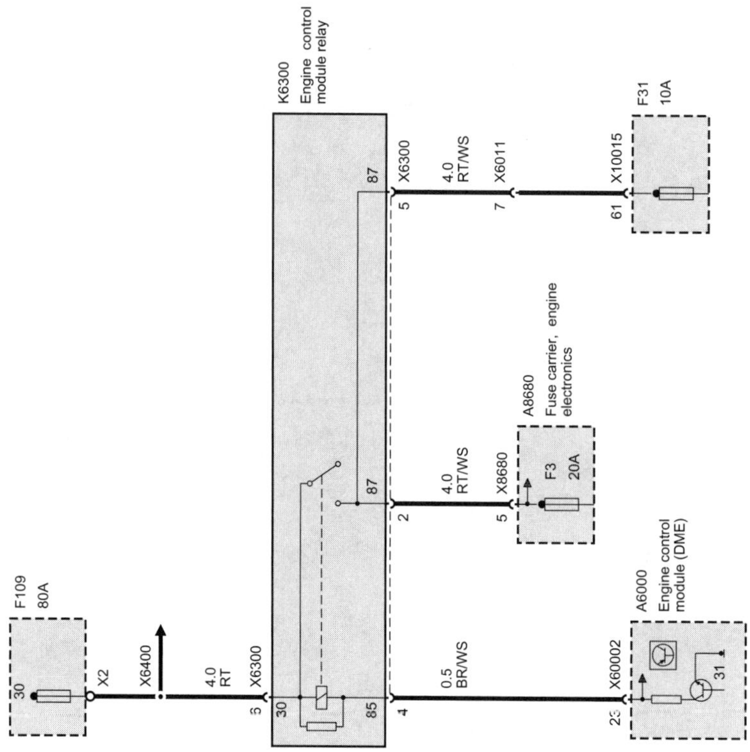

502ELE0292a

Engine Management (MS 42.0)
Engine coolant dual temperature sensor

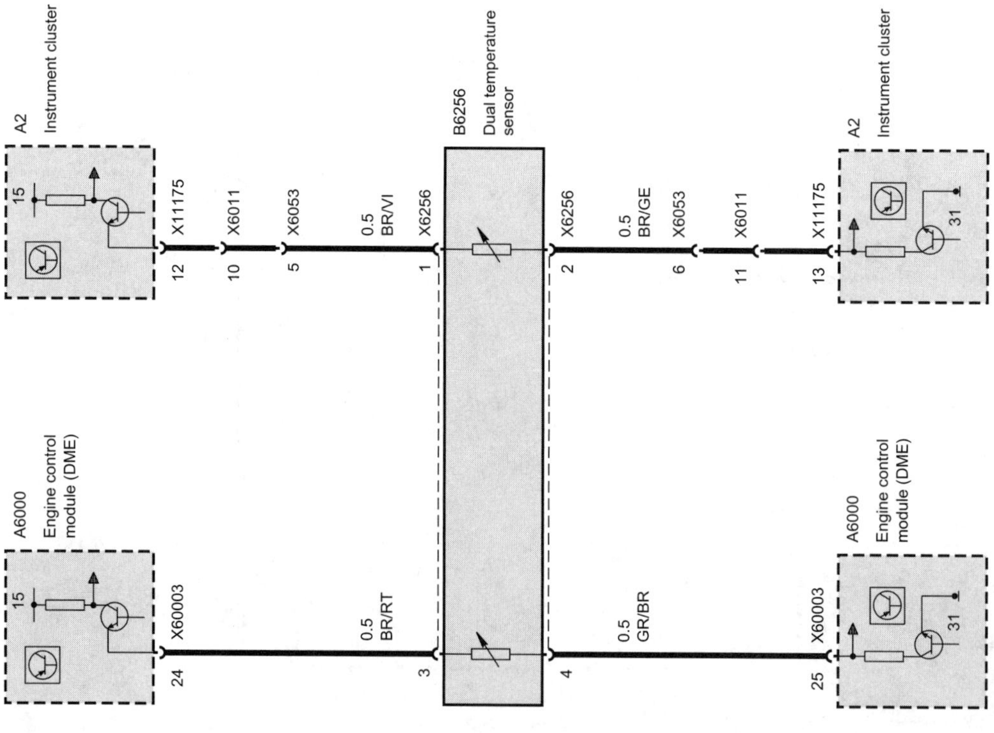

502ELE0292b

Engine Management (MS 42.0)
Engine oil temperature sensor

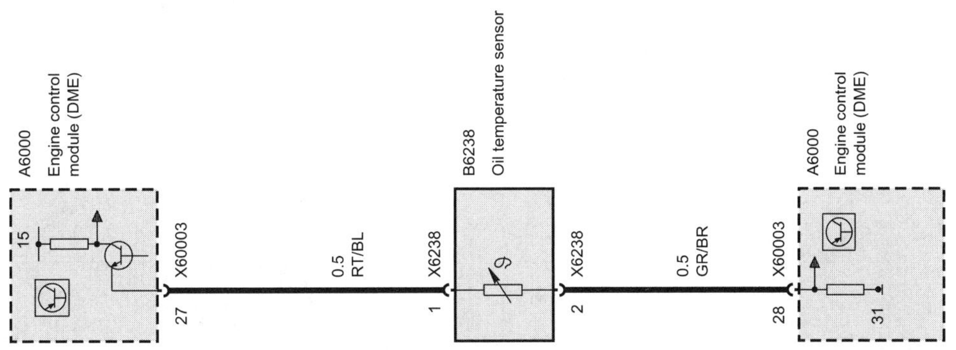

502ELE0299a

Engine Management (MS 42.0)
Evaporative emission valve

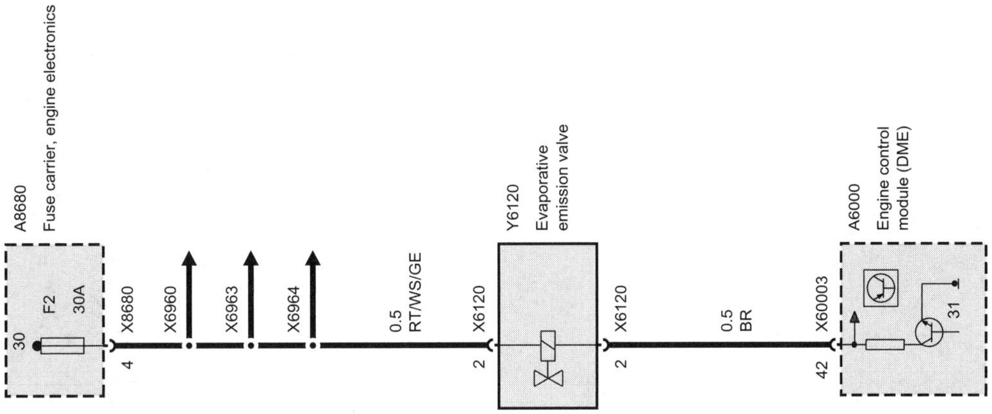

502ELE0299b

Engine Management (MS 41.1)
A6000 Engine control module (DME)
(1 of 3)

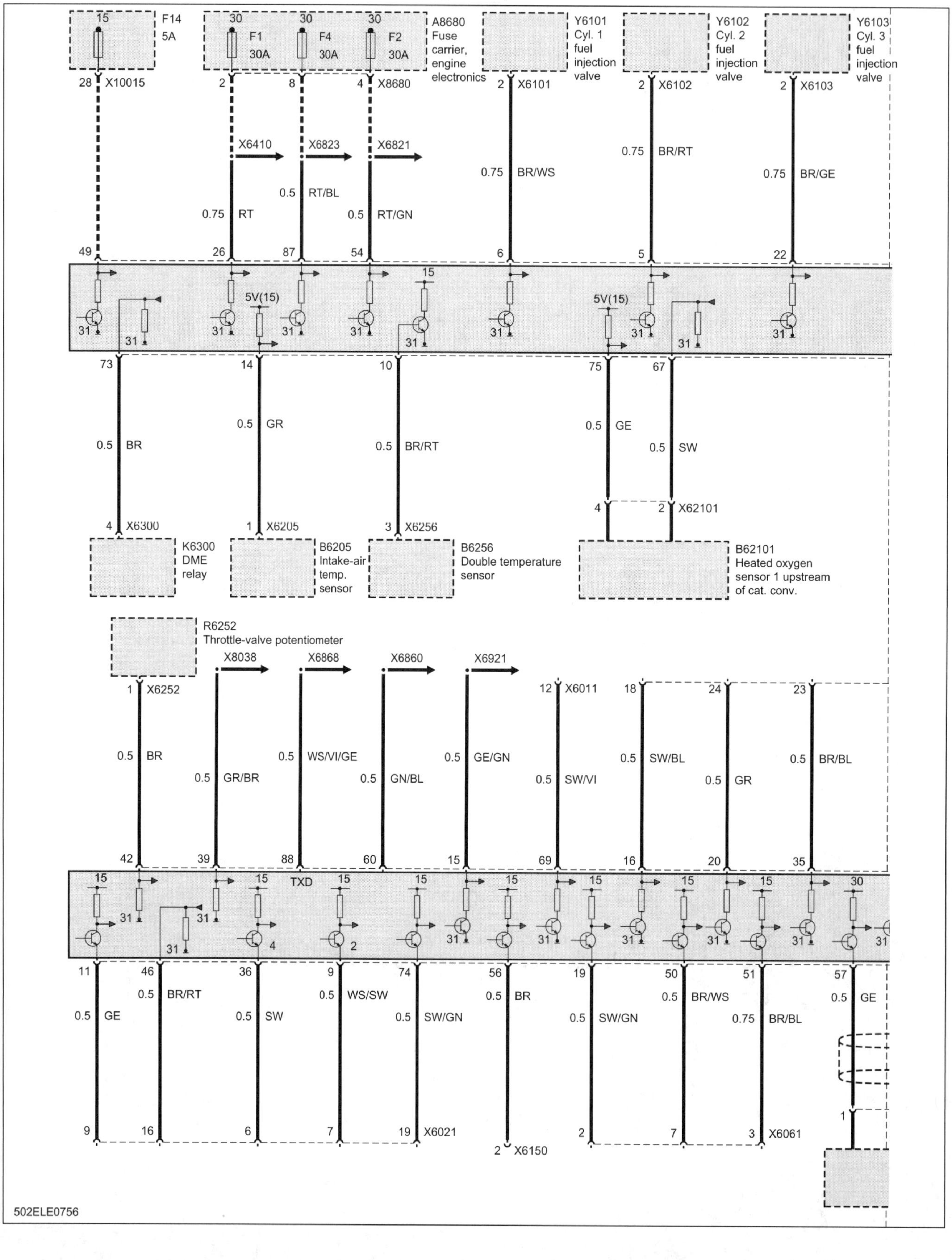

502ELE0756

Engine Management (MS 41.1)
A6000 Engine control module (DME)
(2 of 3)

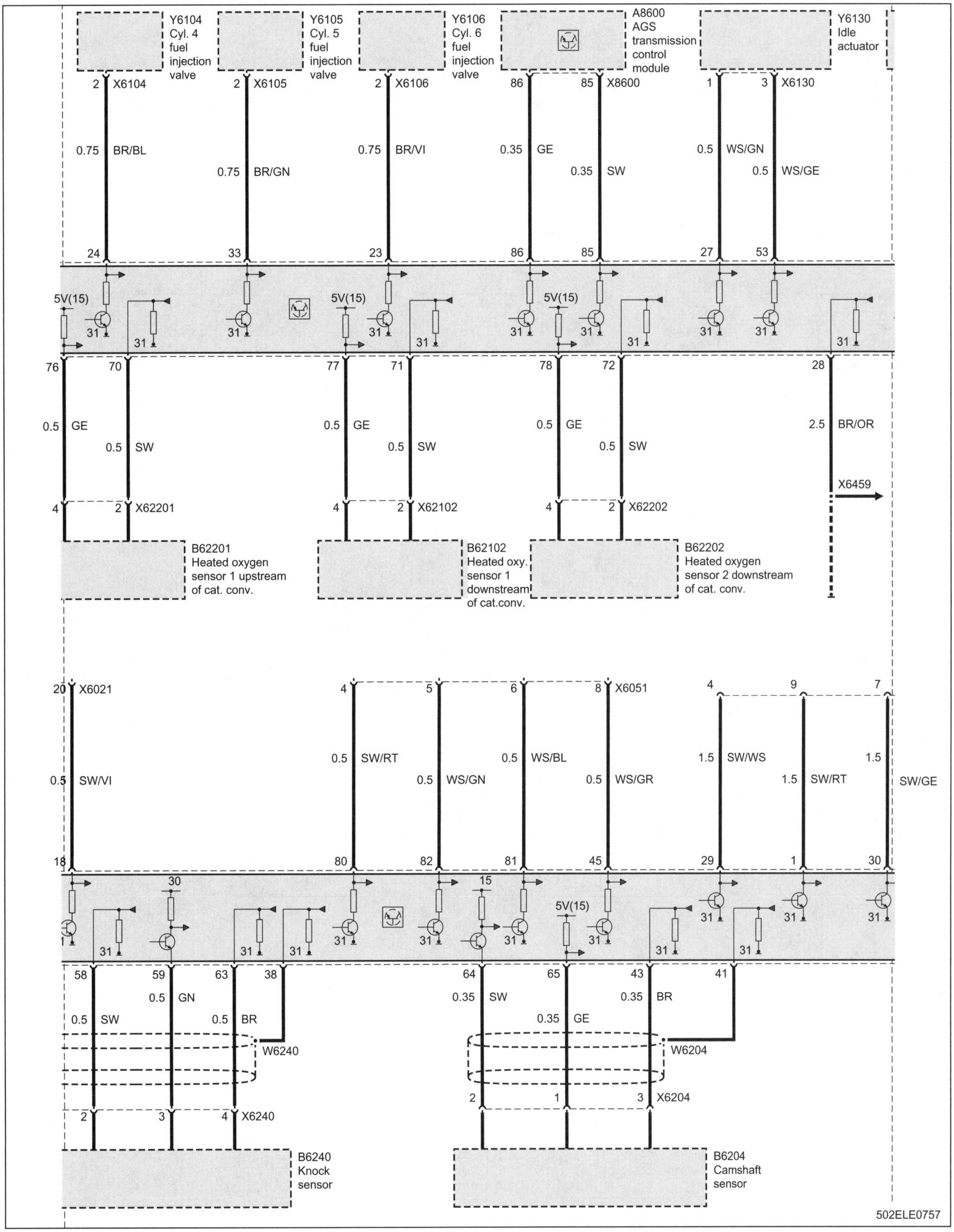

Engine Management (MS 41.1)
A6000 Engine control module (DME)
(3 of 3)

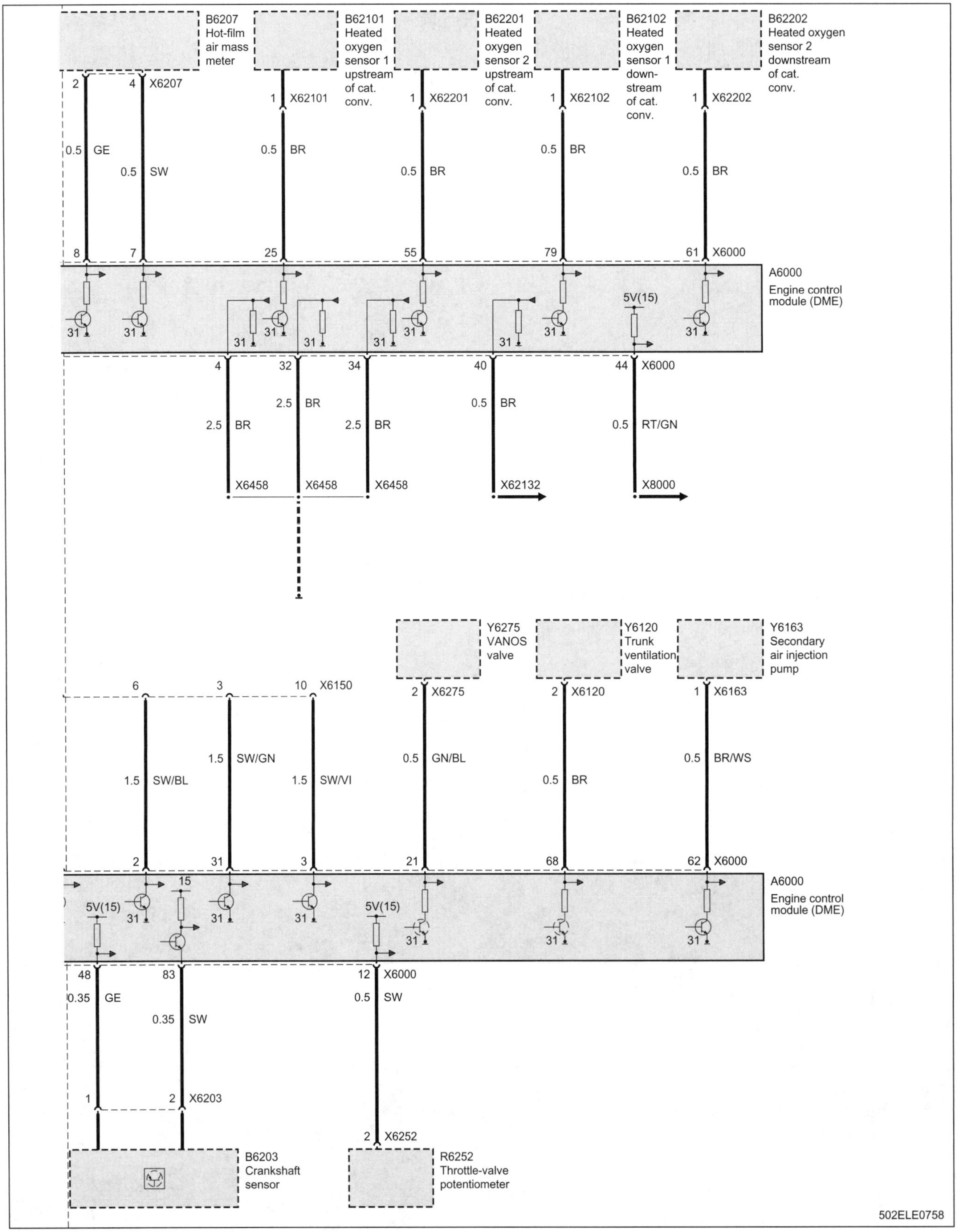

Engine Management (MS 41.1)
OBDII plug
(1 of 1)

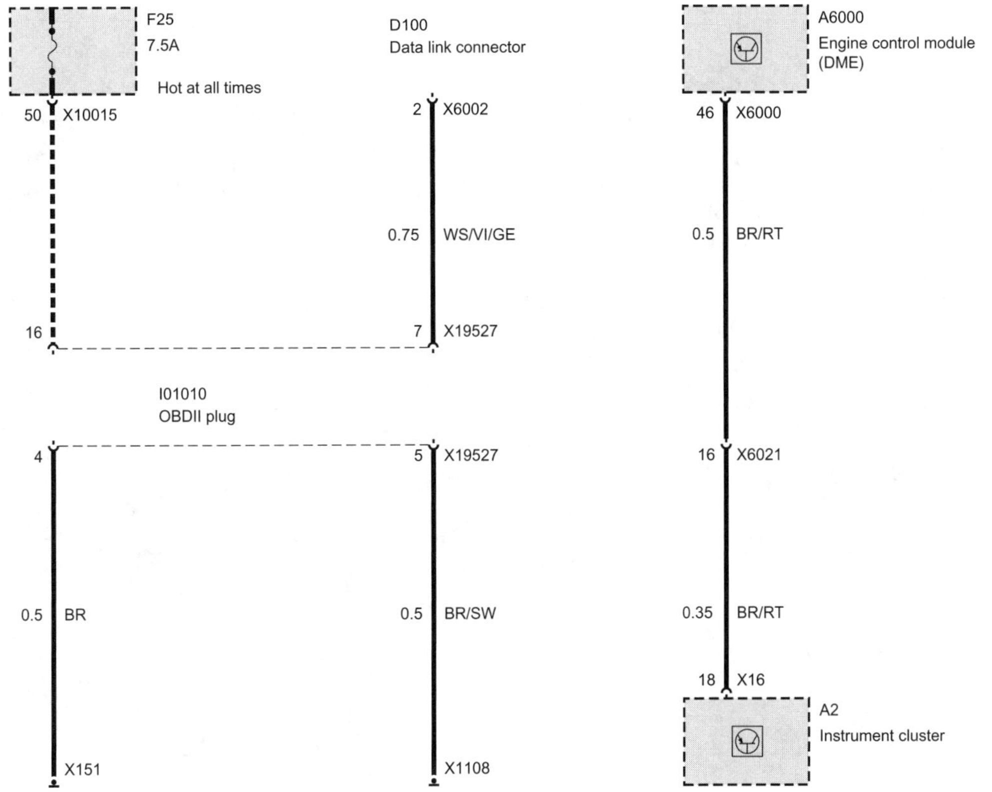
F25
7.5A
Hot at all times
50 X10015
16
D100
Data link connector
2 X6002
0.75 WS/VI/GE
7 X19527
A6000
Engine control module
(DME)
46 X6000
0.5 BR/RT
I01010
OBDII plug
4
0.5 BR
X151
5 X19527
0.5 BR/SW
X1108
16 X6021
0.35 BR/RT
18 X16
A2
Instrument cluster
502ELE0752

Engine Management (MS 41.1)
Power, DME control module
(1 of 1)

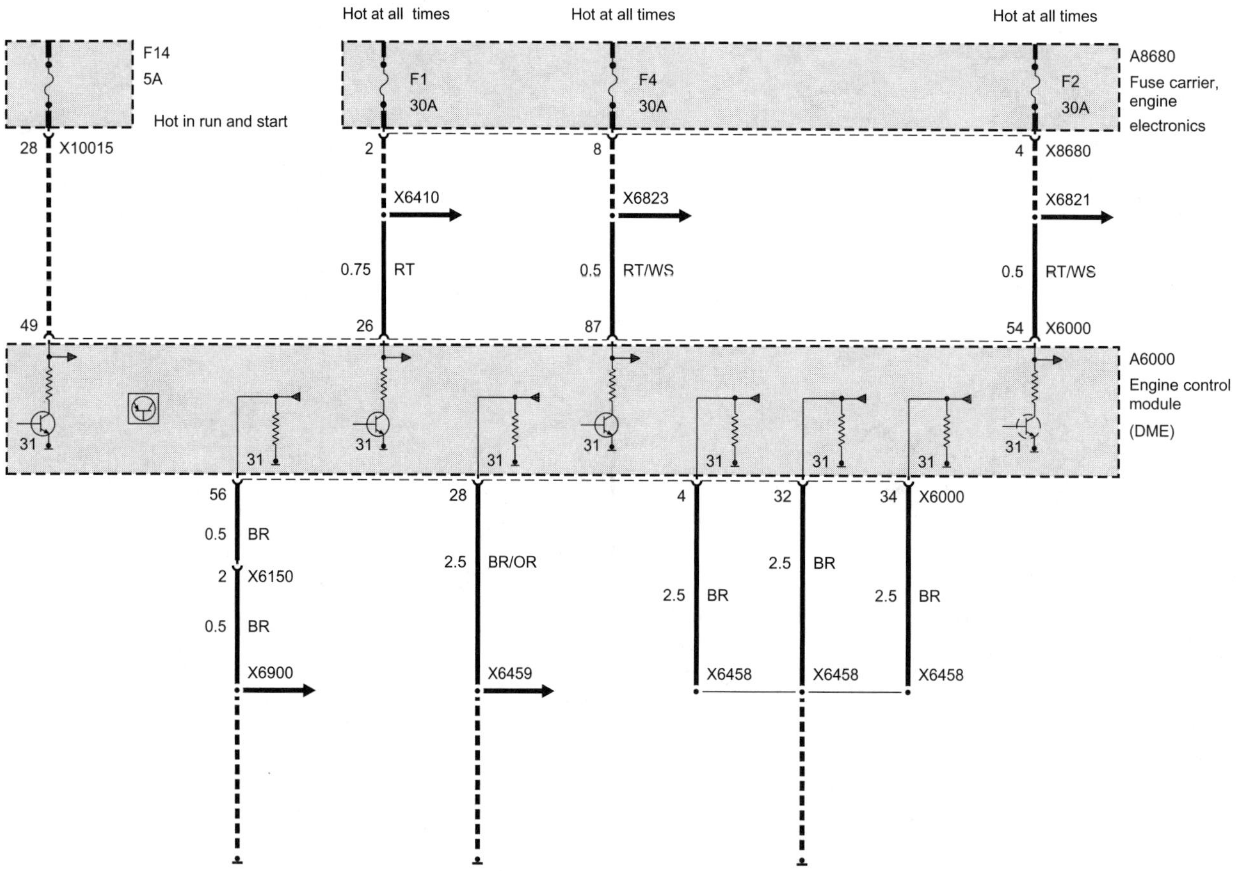

502ELE0721

Engine Management (MS 41.1)
Engine control (DME) relay
(1 of 1)

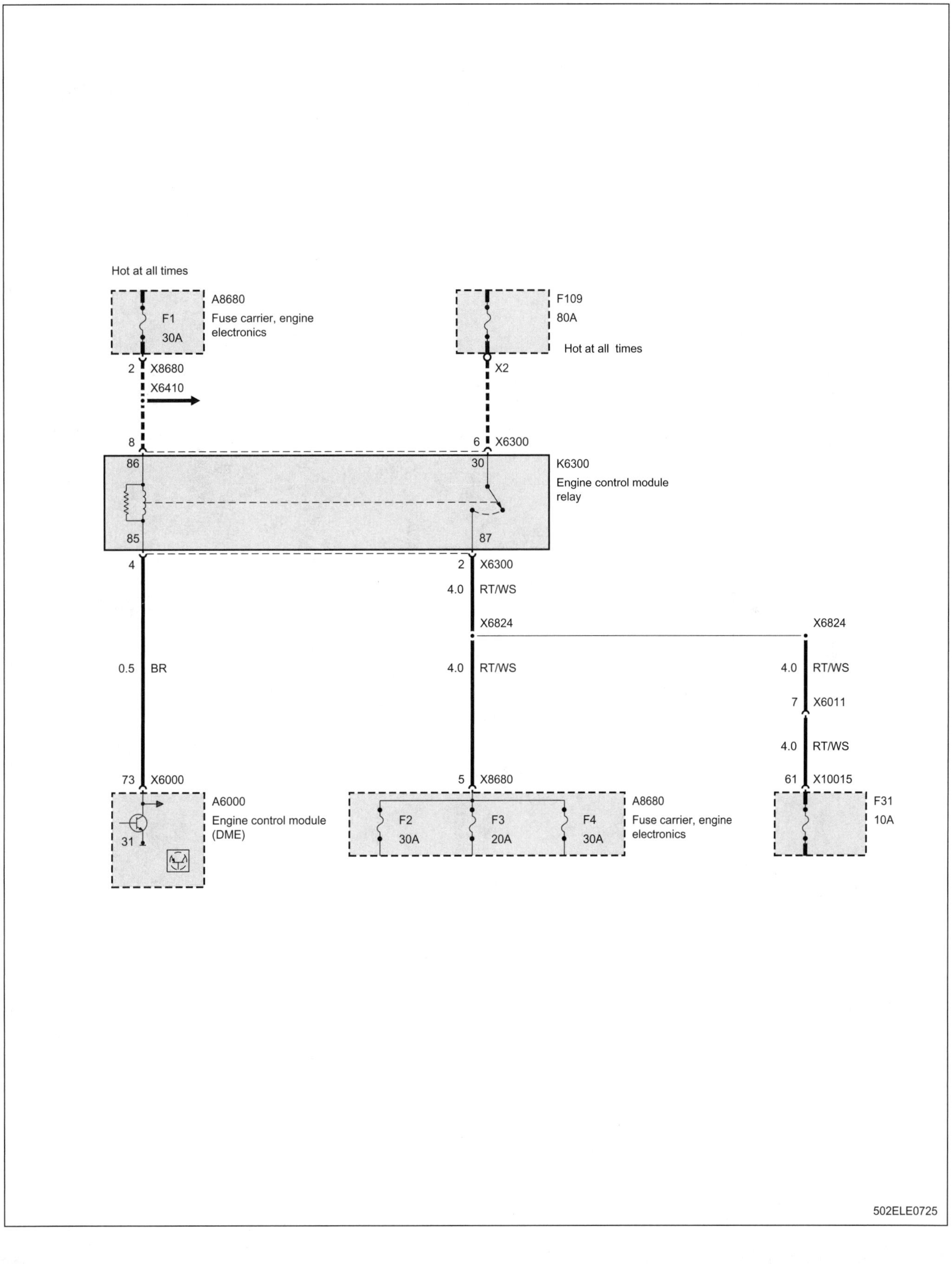

Engine Management (MS 41.1)
Mass air flow sensor
(1 of 1)

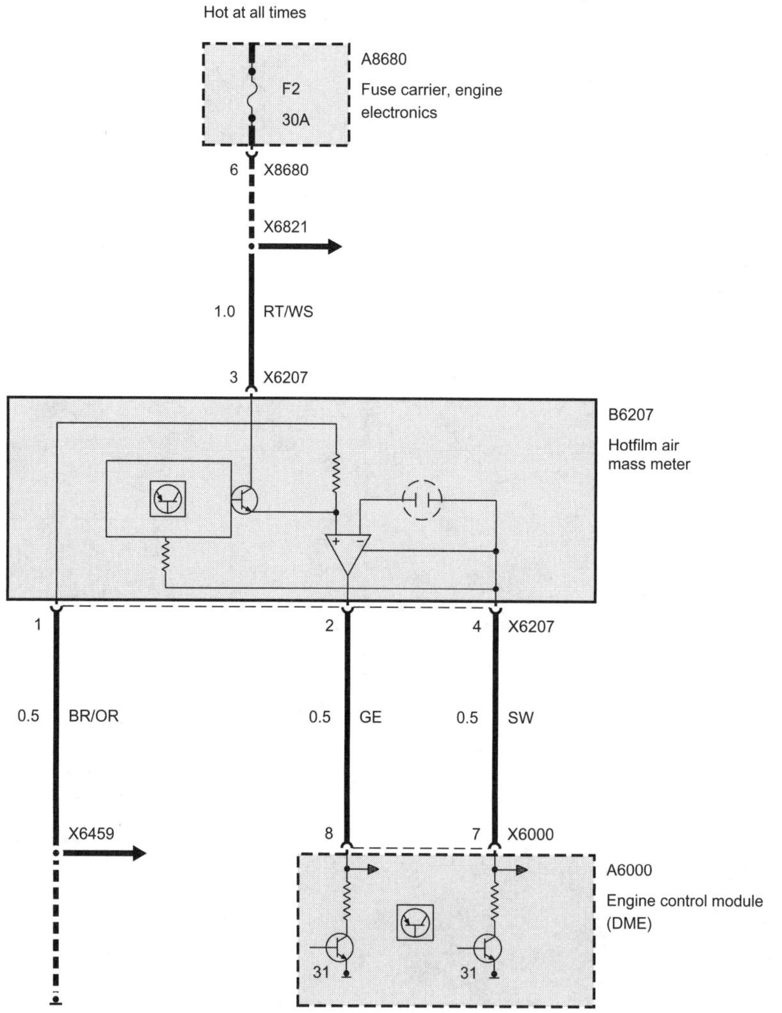

502ELE0722

Engine Management (MS 41.1)
Engine coolant dual temperature sensor (without IKE)
(1 of 1)

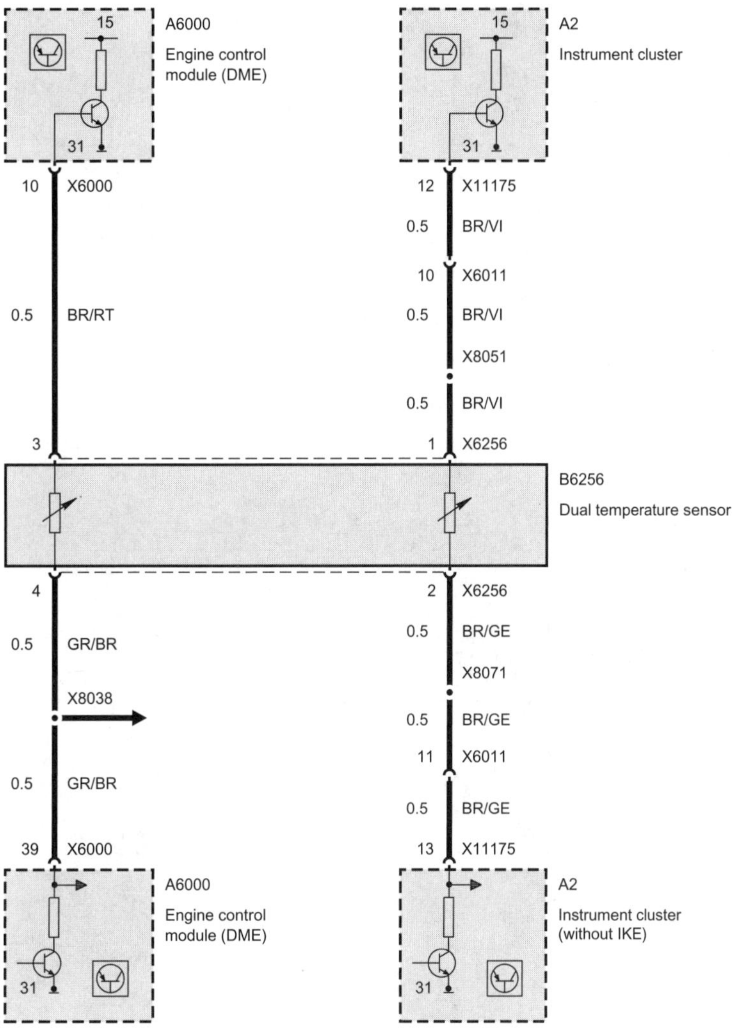

Engine Management (MS 41.1)
Engine coolant dual temperature sensor (with IKE)
(1 of 1)

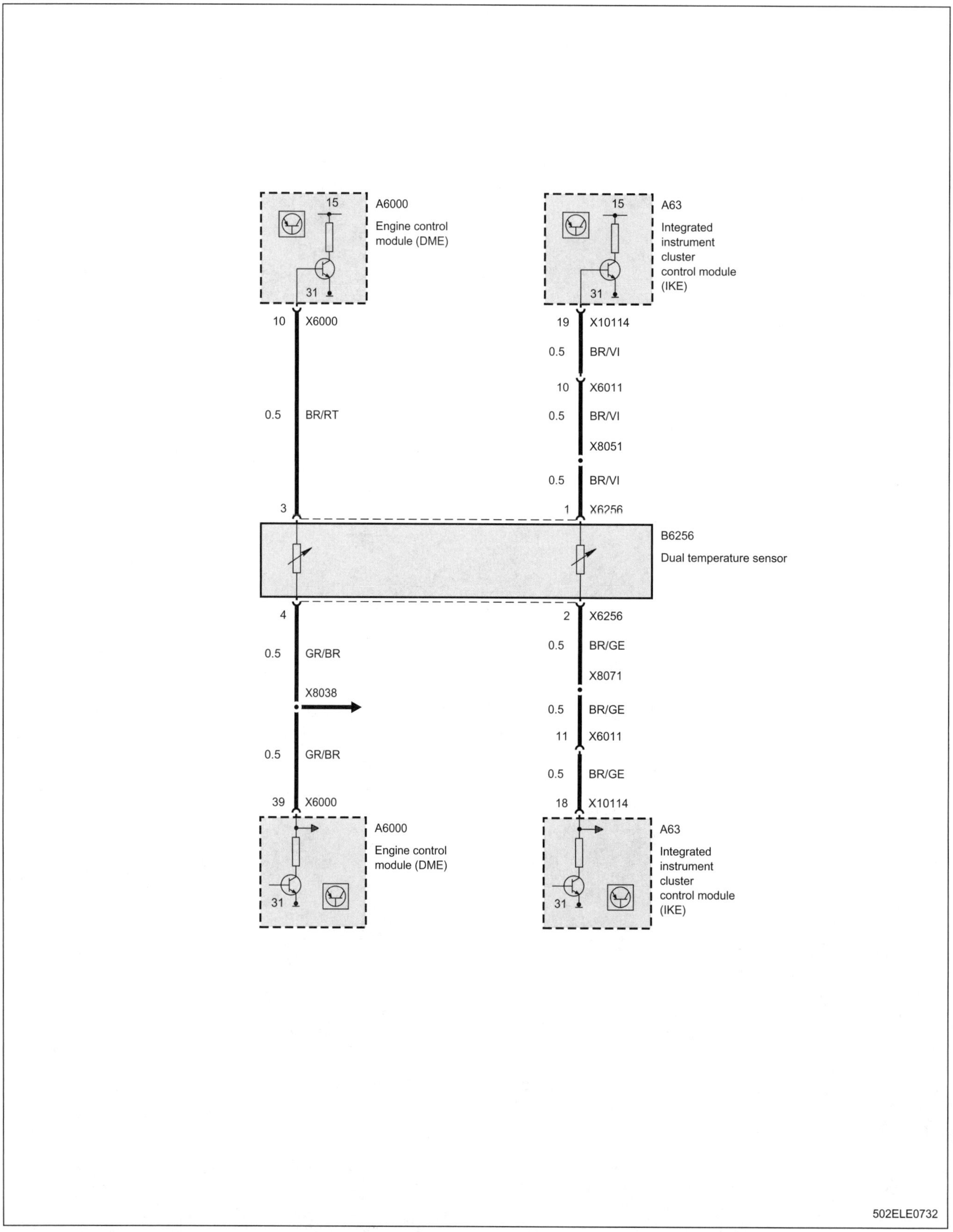

Engine Management (MS 41.1)
Intake air temperature sensor
(1 of 1)

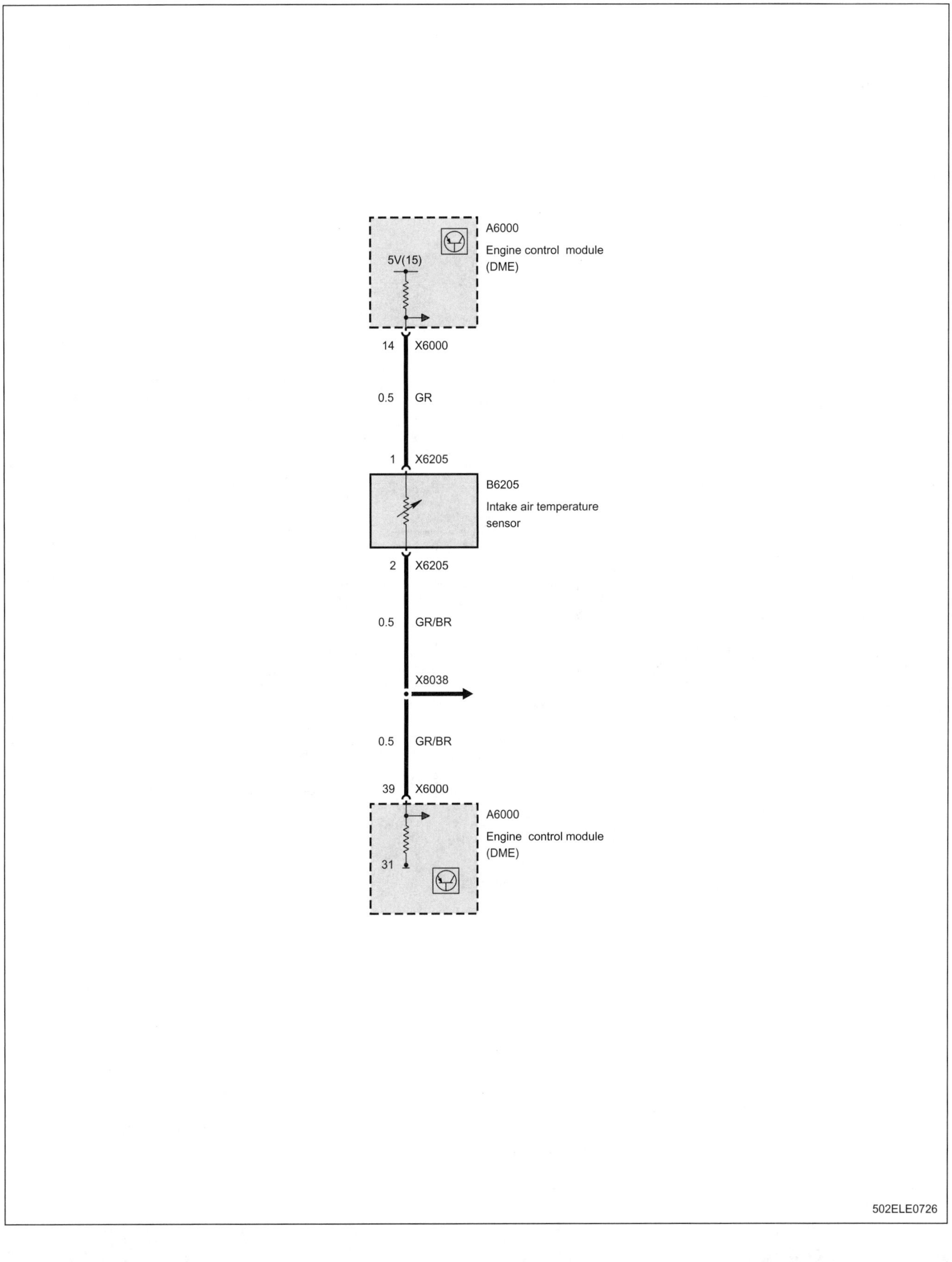

Engine Management (MS 41.1)
Idle speed control
(1 of 1)

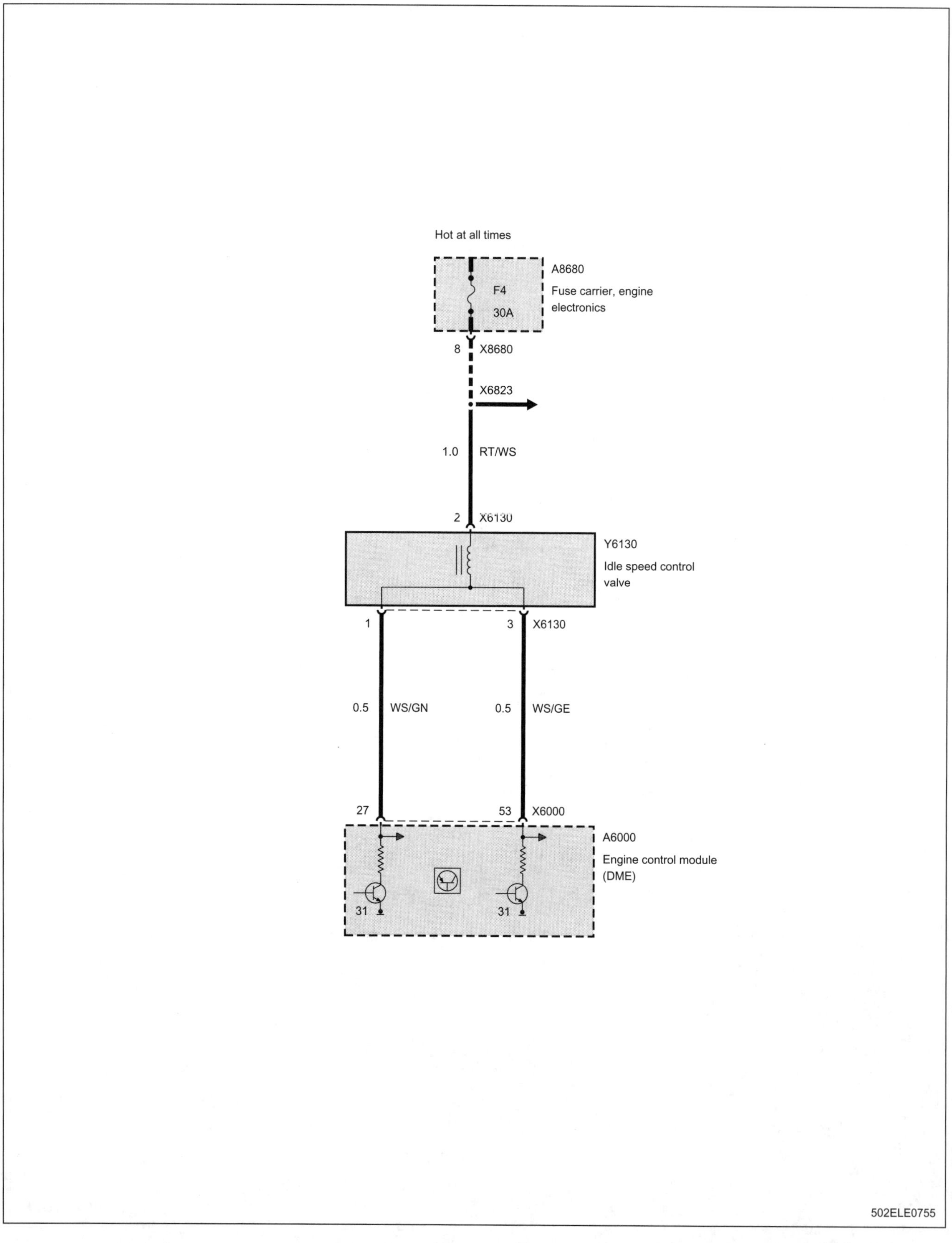

Engine Management (MS 41.1)
Cyl. 1 and 2 fuel injection valves
(1 of 1)

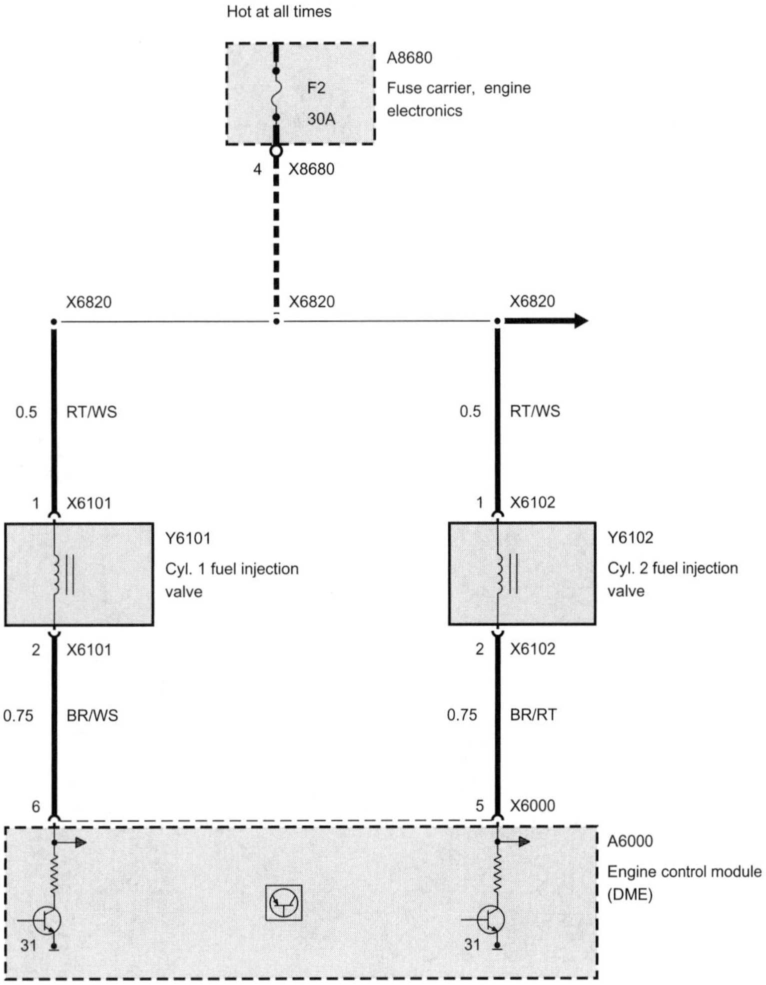

502ELE0728

Engine Management (MS 41.1)
Cyl. 3 and 4 fuel injection valves
(1 of 1)

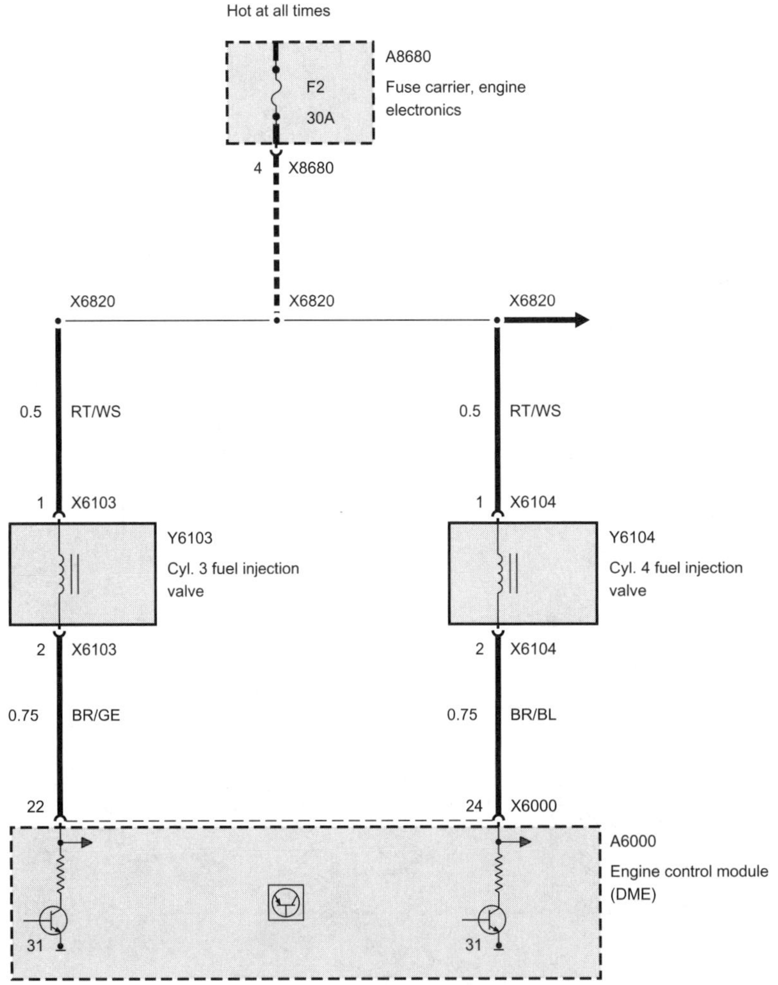

Engine Management (MS 41.1)
Cyl. 5 and 6 fuel injection valves
(1 of 1)

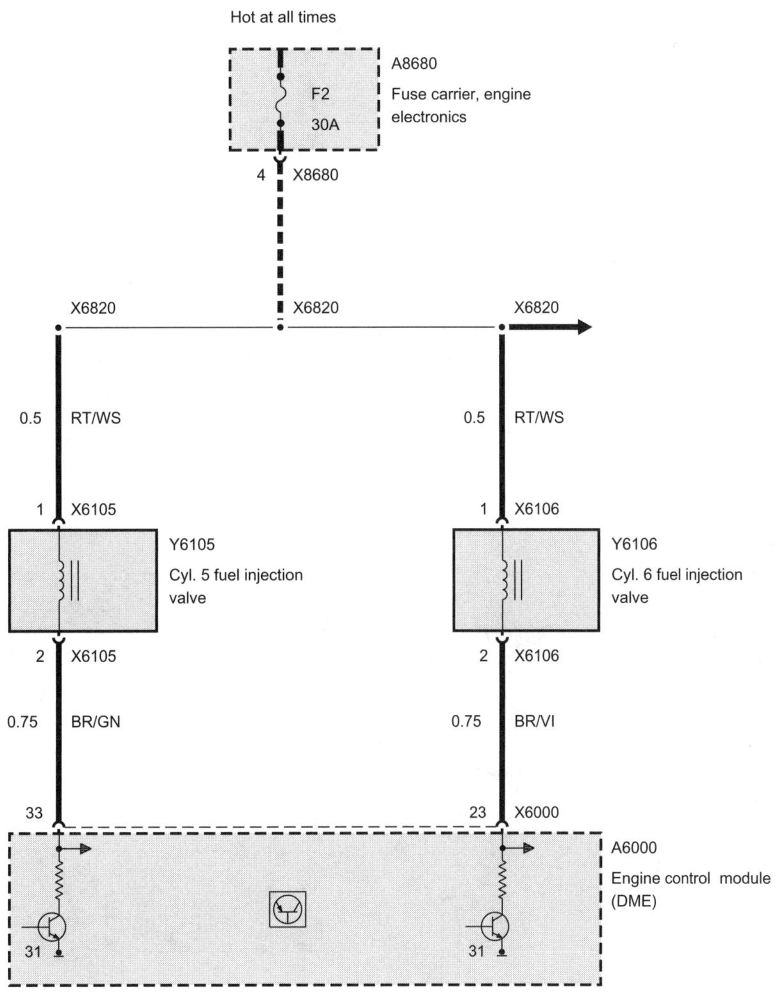

502ELE0727

Engine Management (MS 41.1)
Secondary air injection pump
(1 of 1)

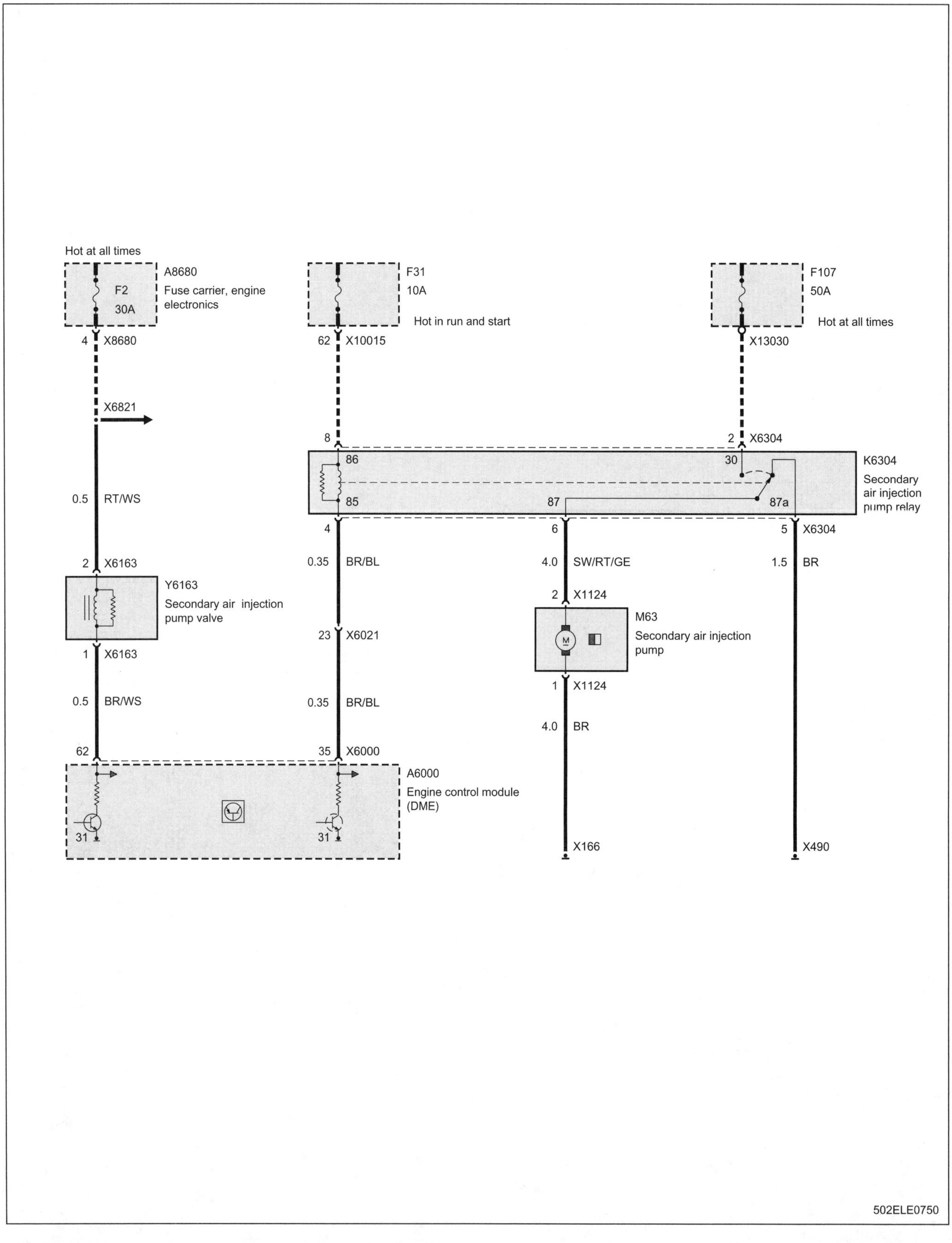

Engine Management (MS 41.1)
Knock sensor
(1 of 1)

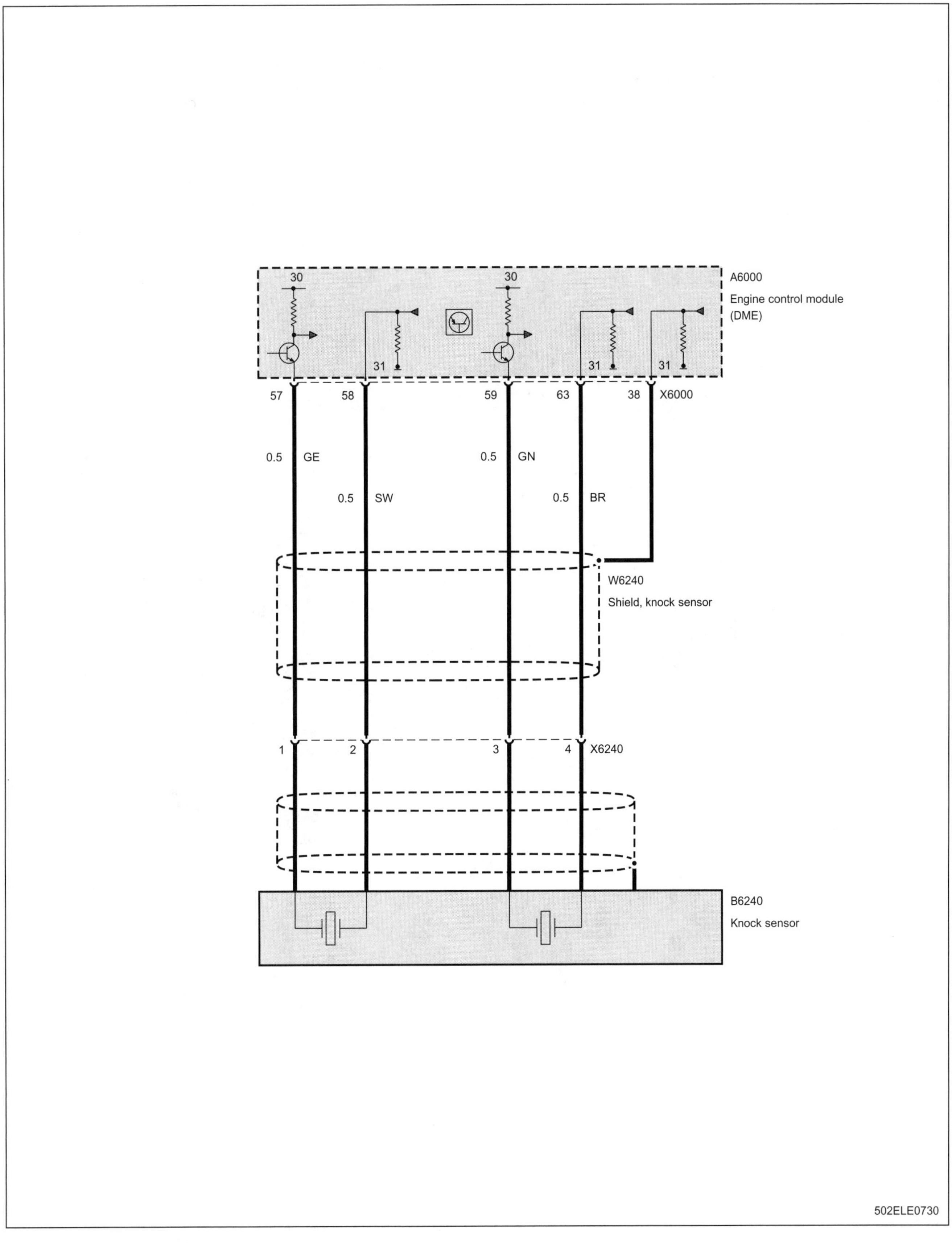

Engine Management (MS 41.1)
Cyl. 1 and 2 ignition coils
(1 of 1)

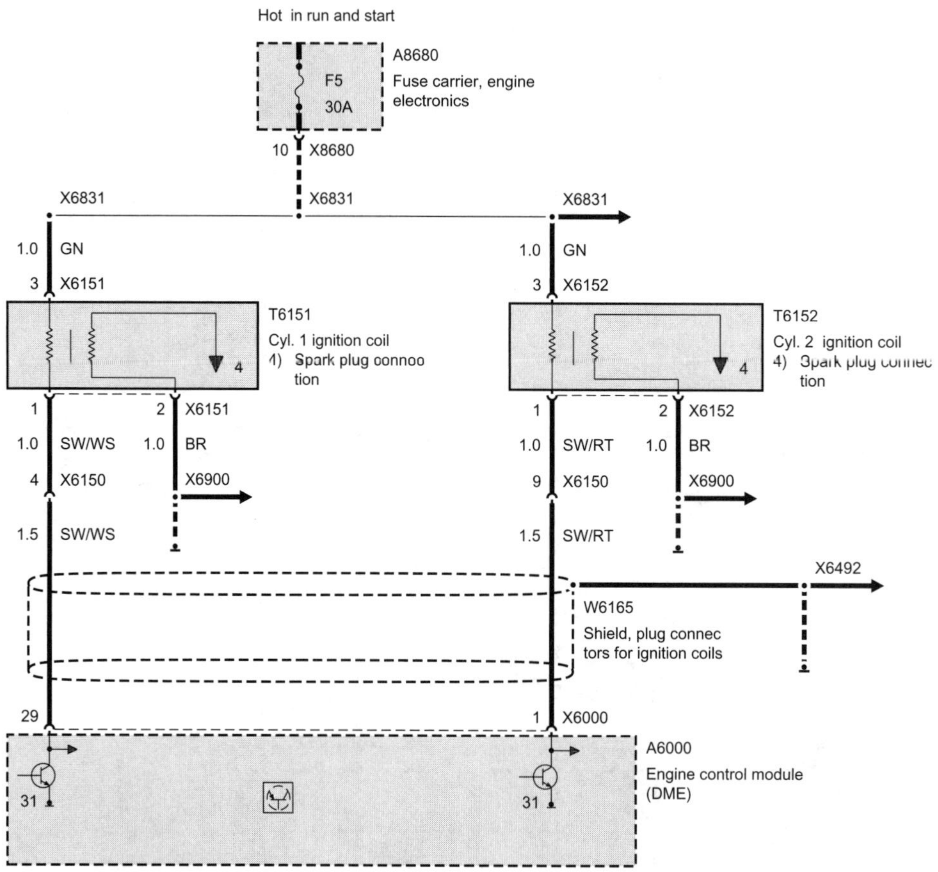

Engine Management (MS 41.1)
Cyl. 3 and 4 ignition coils
(1 of 1)

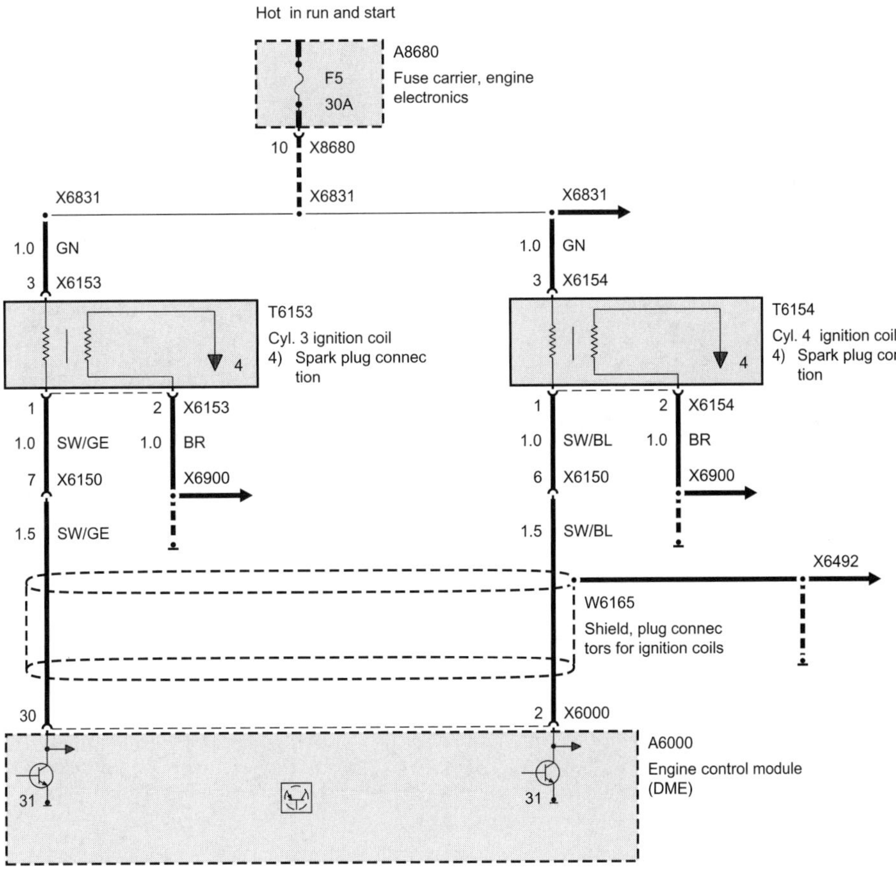

502ELE0751

Engine Management (MS 41.1)
Cyl. 5 and 6 ignition coils
(1 of 1)

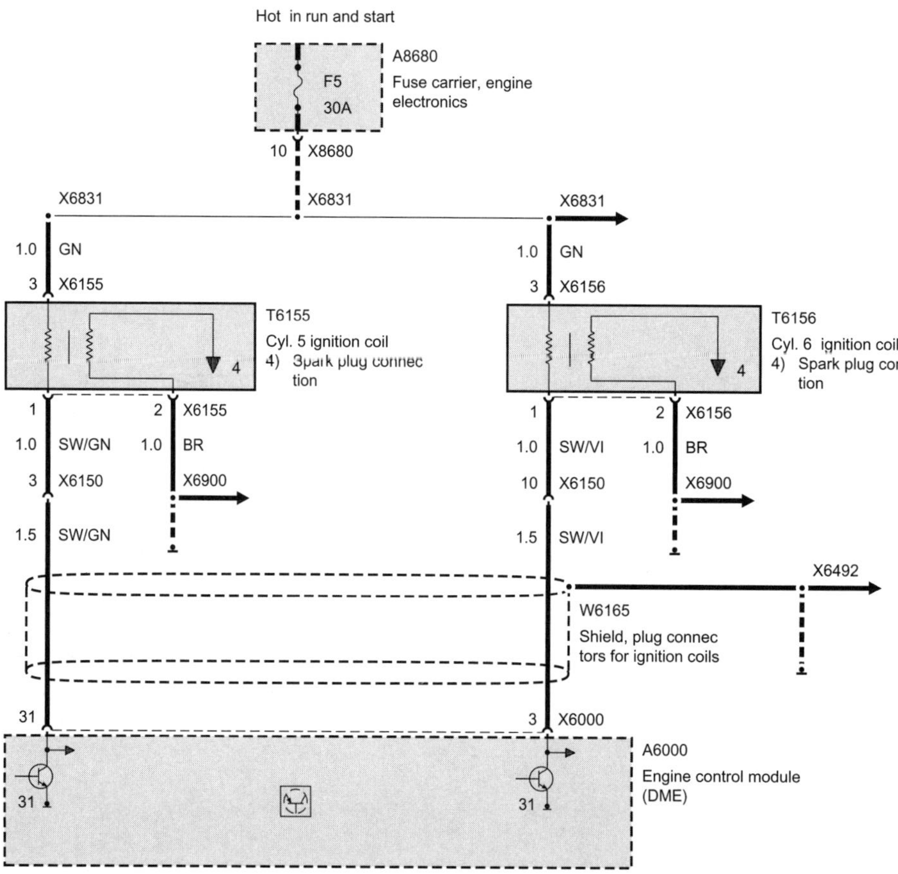

502ELE0753

Engine Management (MS 41.1)
Oxygen sensor 1 in front of catalytic converter
(1 of 1)

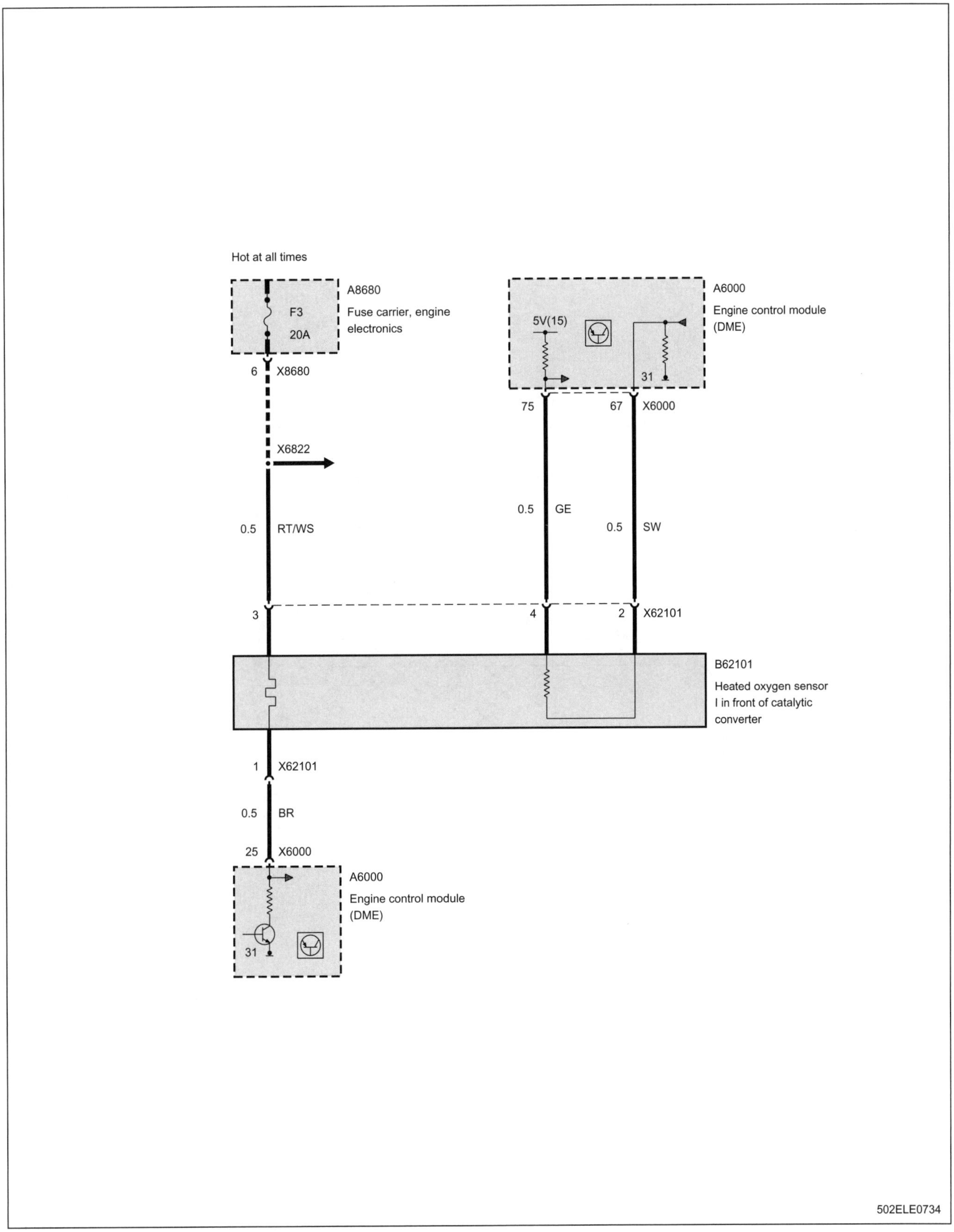

Engine Management (MS 41.1)
Oxygen sensor 1 behind catalytic converter
(1 of 1)

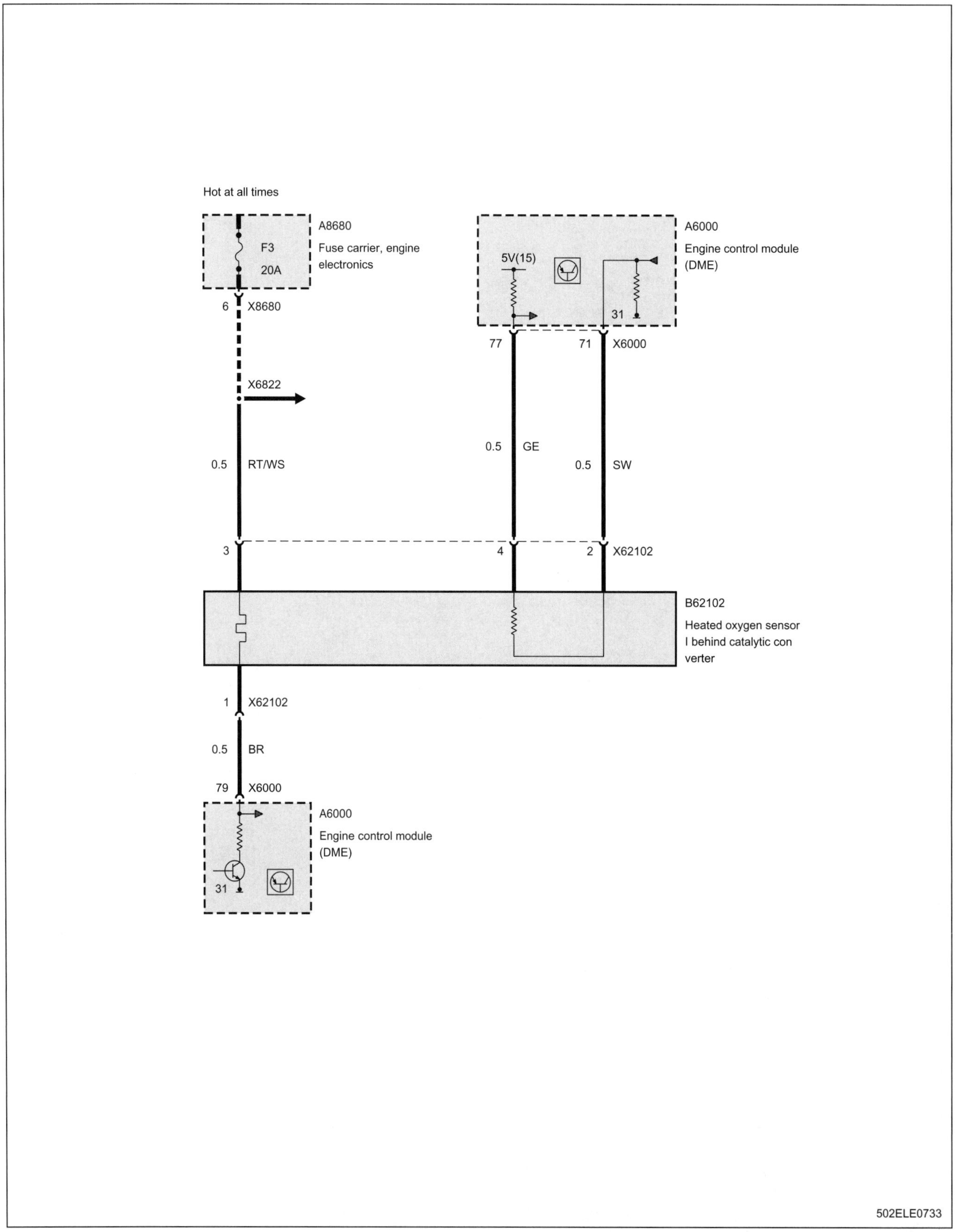

Engine Management (MS 41.1)
Oxygen sensor 2 in front of catalytic converter
(1 of 1)

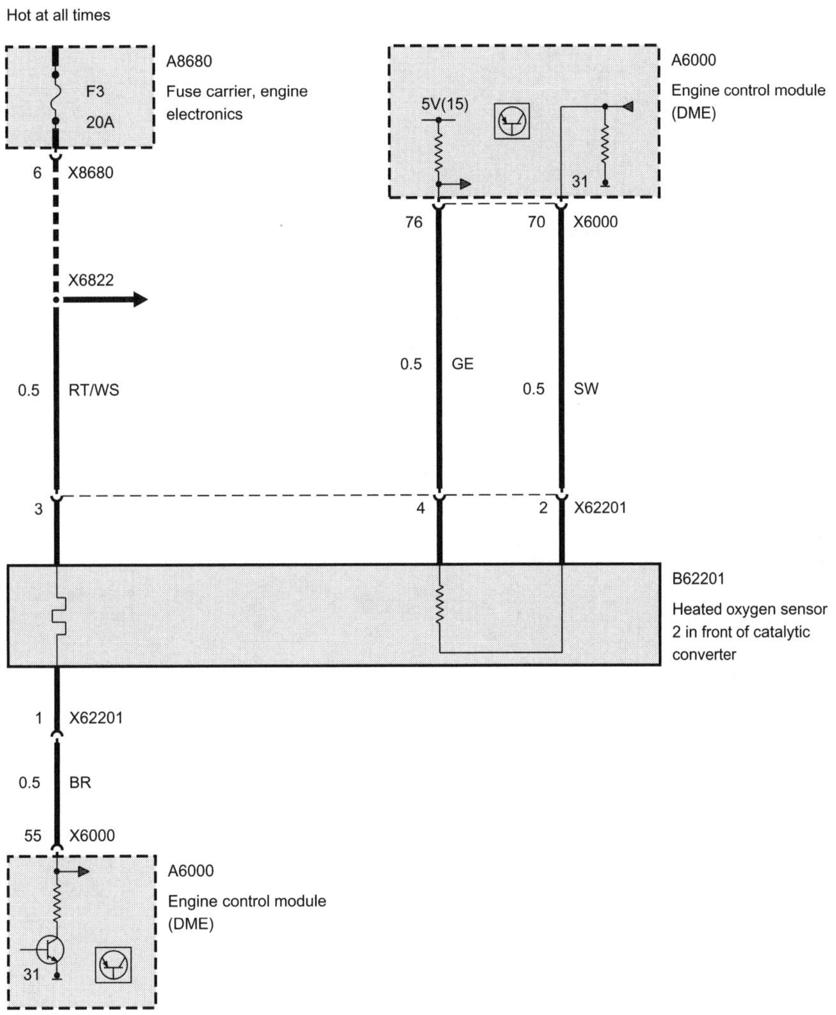

502ELE0731

Engine Management (MS 41.1)
Oxygen sensor 2 behind catalytic converter
(1 of 1)

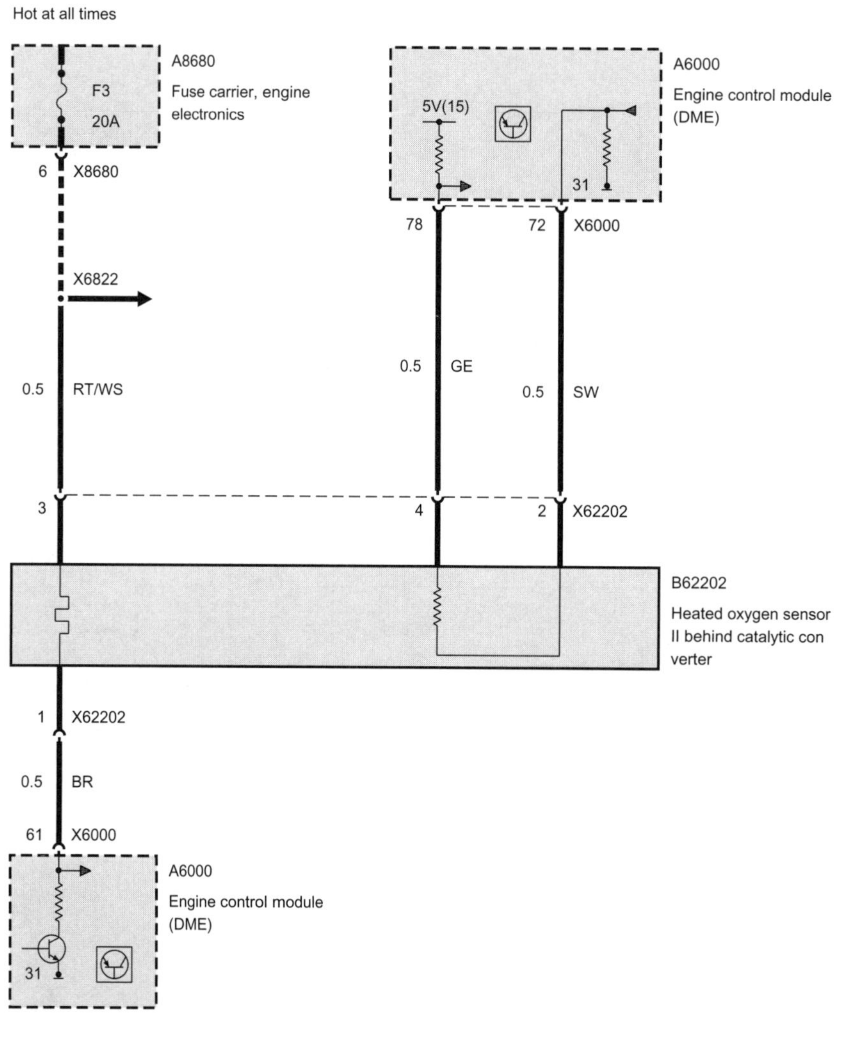

502ELE0737

Engine Management (MS 41.1)
Camshaft and crankshaft position sensors
(1 of 1)

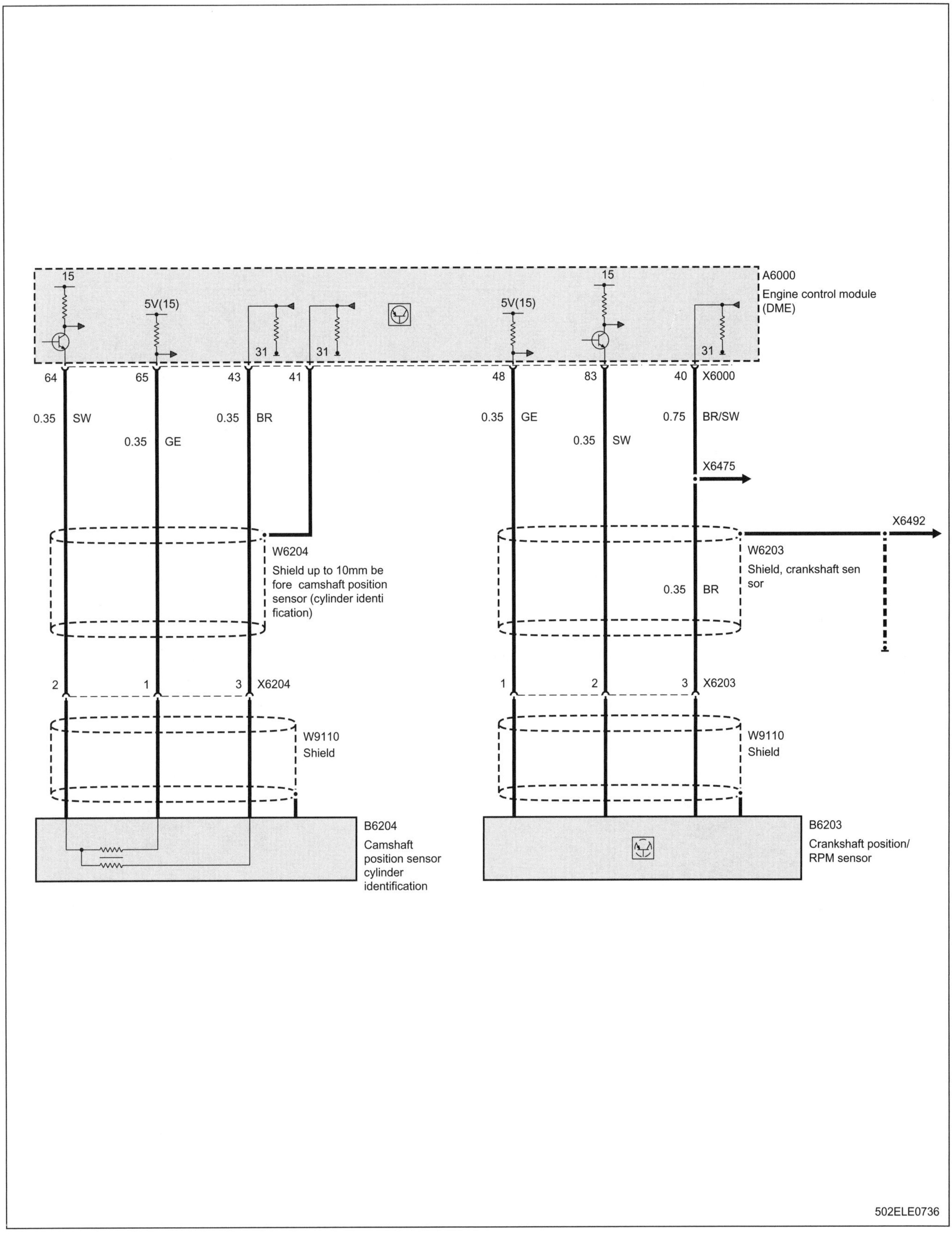

Engine Management (MS 41.1)
Fuel pump
(1 of 1)

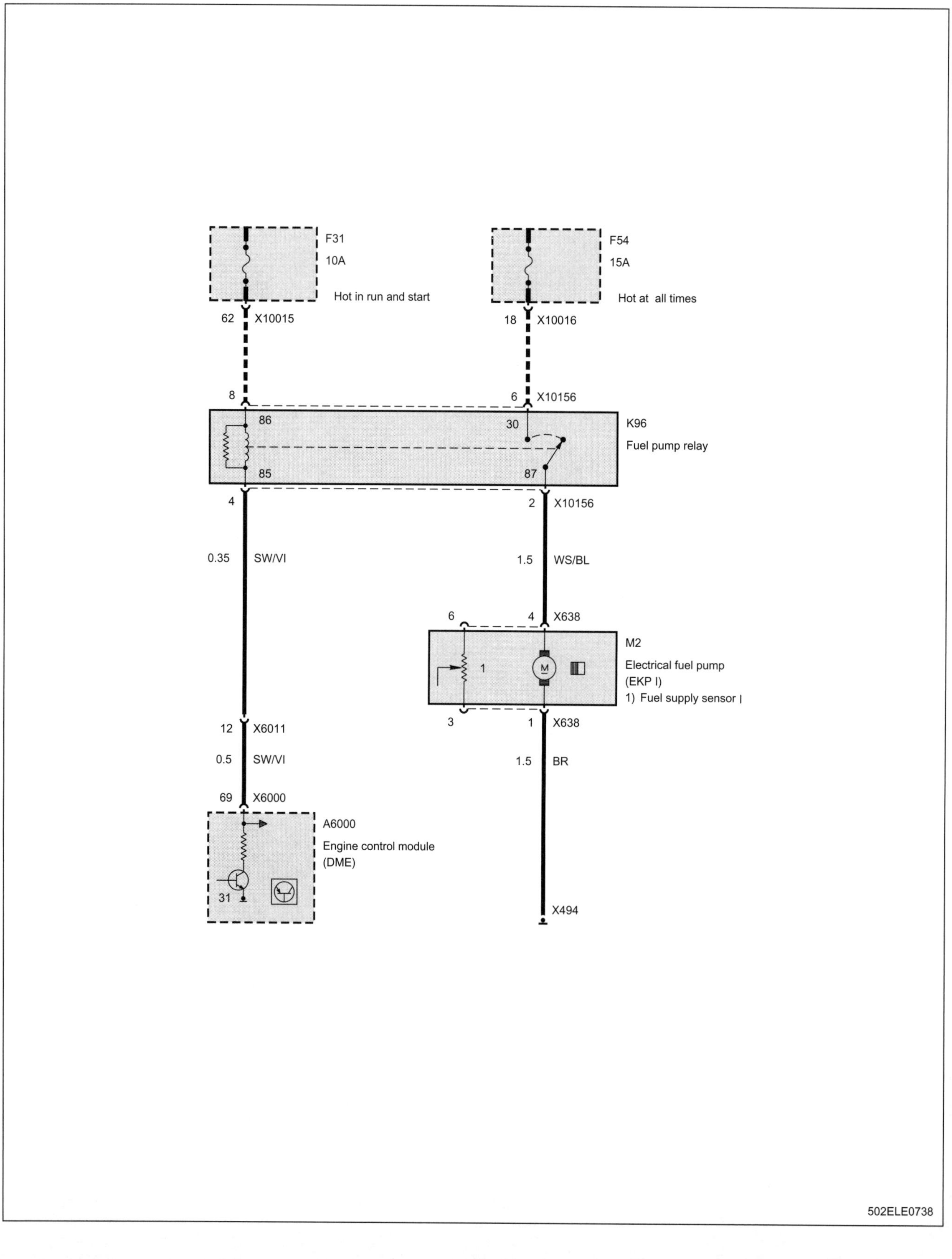
F31
10A
Hot in run and start
62
X10015
F54
15A
Hot at all times
18
X10016
8
6
X10156
86
30
K96
Fuel pump relay
85
87
4
2
X10156
0.35
SW/VI
1.5
WS/BL
6
4
X638
M2
Electrical fuel pump
(EKP I)
1) Fuel supply sensor I
1
M
3
1
X638
12
X6011
0.5
SW/VI
1.5
BR
69
X6000
A6000
Engine control module
(DME)
31
X494
502ELE0738

Engine Management (MS 41.1)
Throttle position sensor
(1 of 1)

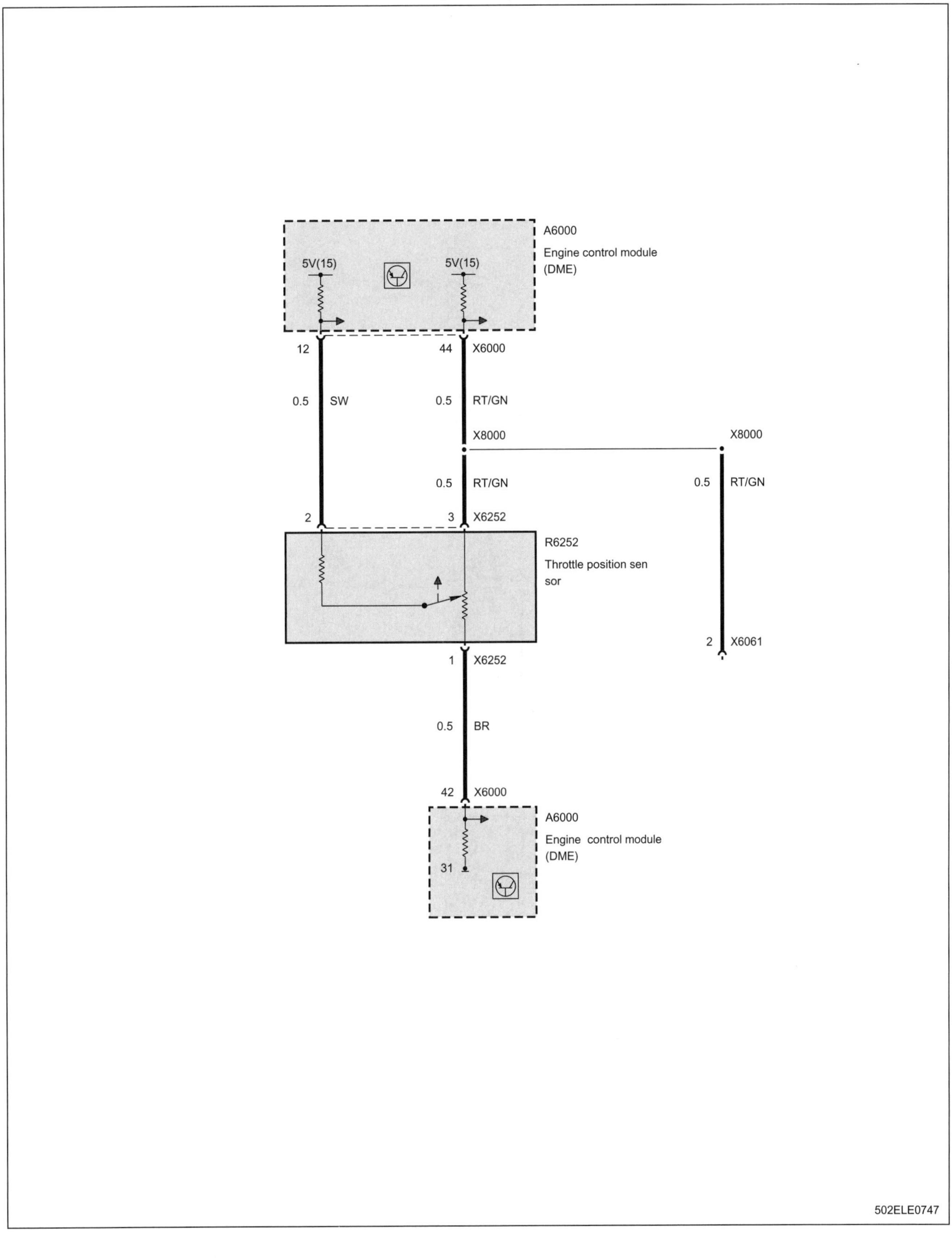

Engine Management (MS 41.1)
Evaporative emission valve
(1 of 1)

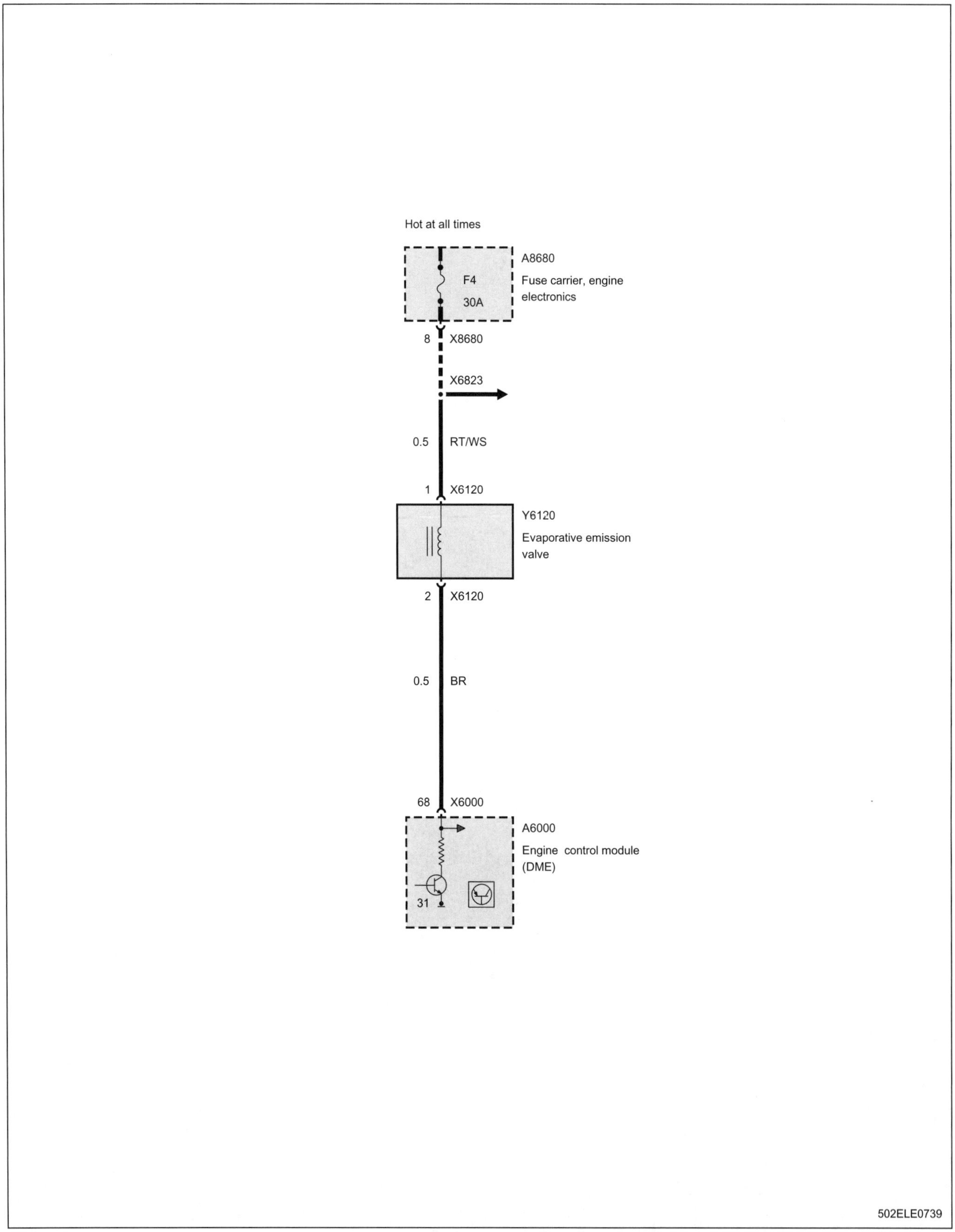

Engine Management (MS 41.1)
VANOS valve
(1 of 1)

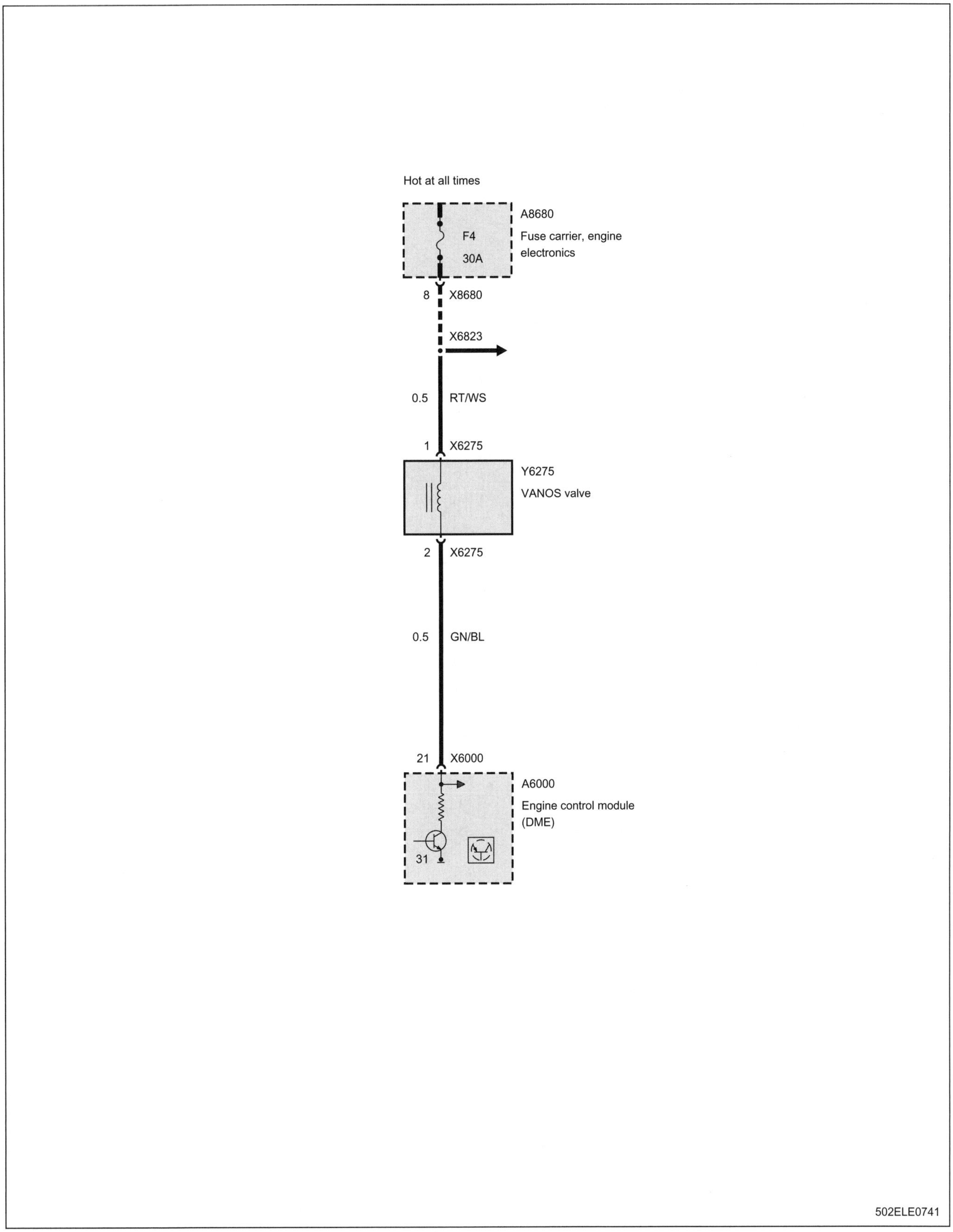
Hot at all times
A8680
Fuse carrier, engine electronics
F4
30A
8
X8680
X6823
0.5
RT/WS
1
X6275
Y6275
VANOS valve
2
X6275
0.5
GN/BL
21
X6000
A6000
Engine control module (DME)
31
502ELE0741

Engine Management (MS 41.1)
DME/climate control interfaces
(1 of 1)

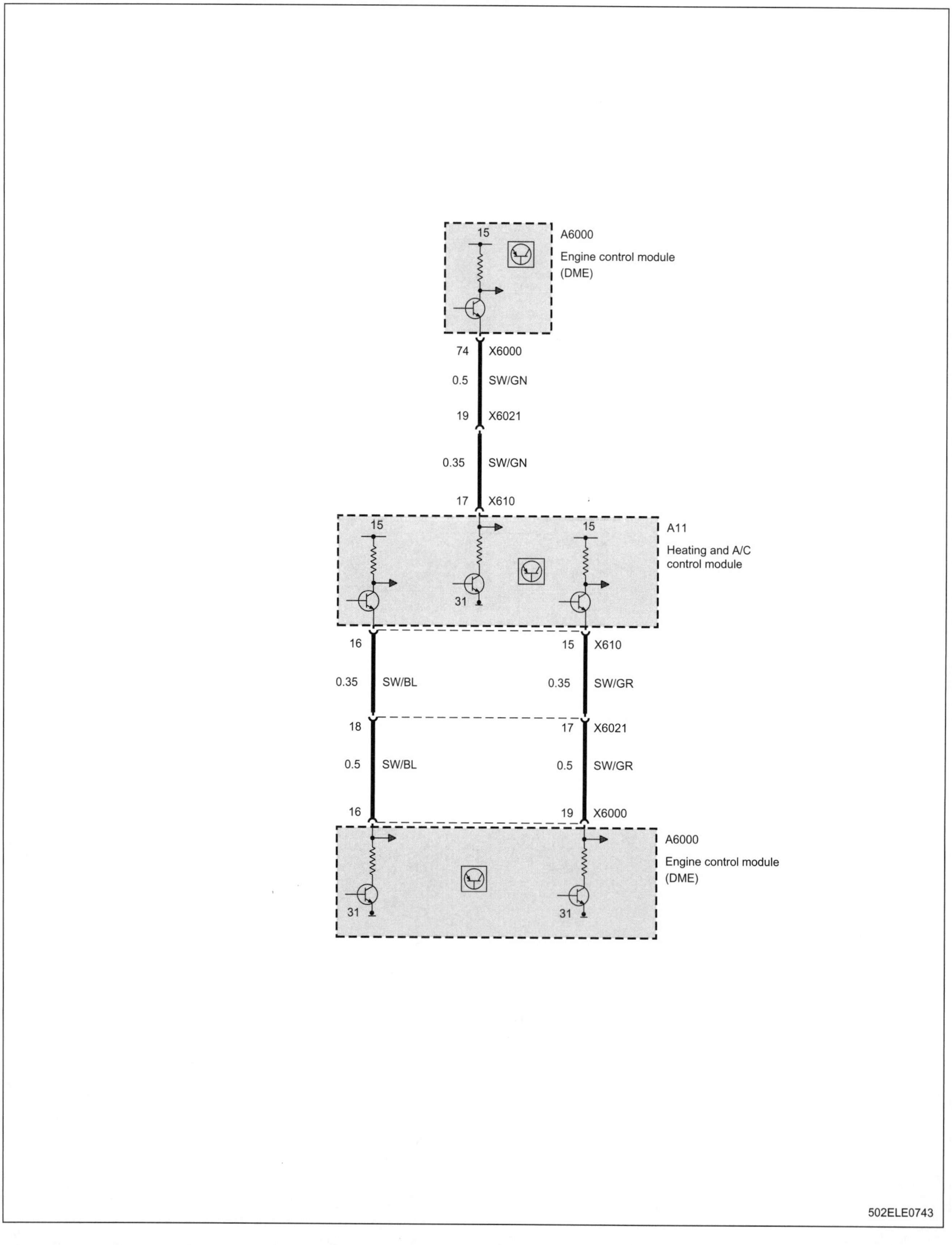

Engine Management (MS 41.1)
DME/AGS interfaces
(1 of 2)

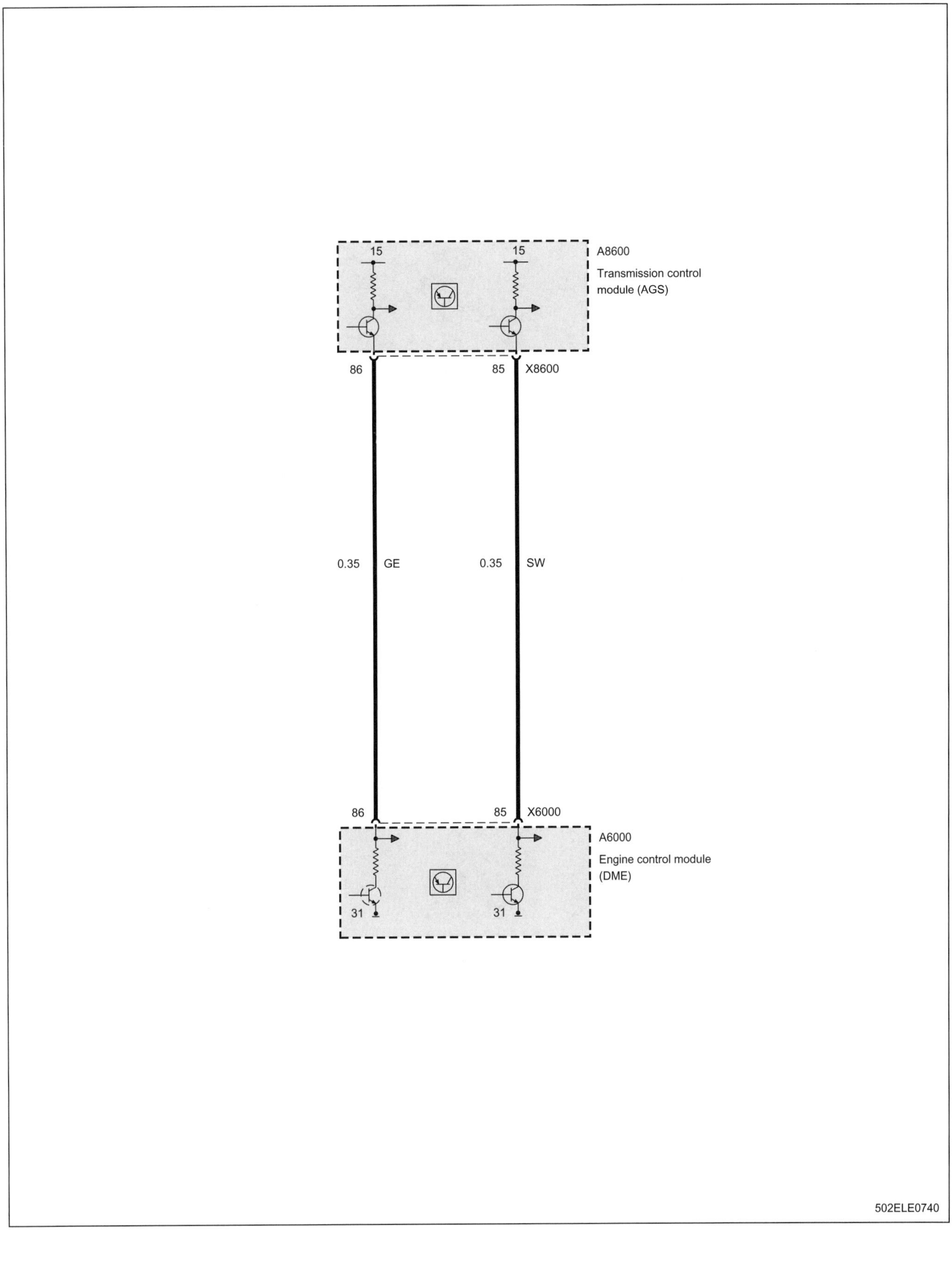

Engine Management (MS 41.1)
DME/AGS interfaces
(2 of 2)

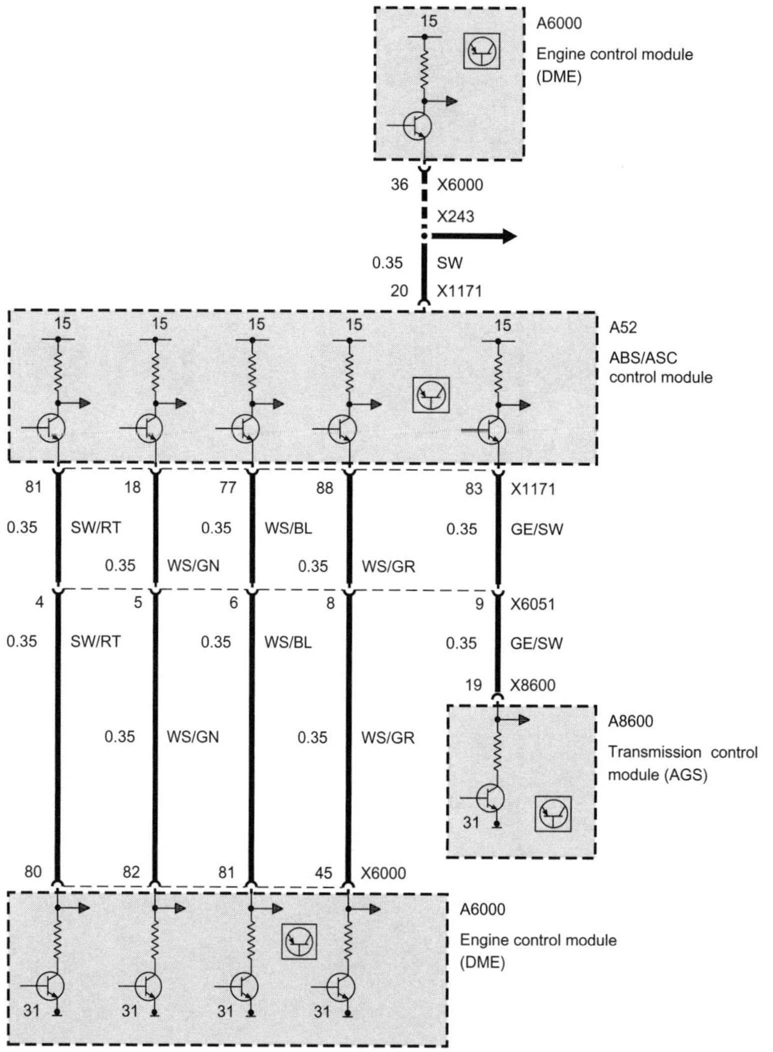

Engine Management (MS 41.1)
DME/instrument cluster interface
(1 of 1)

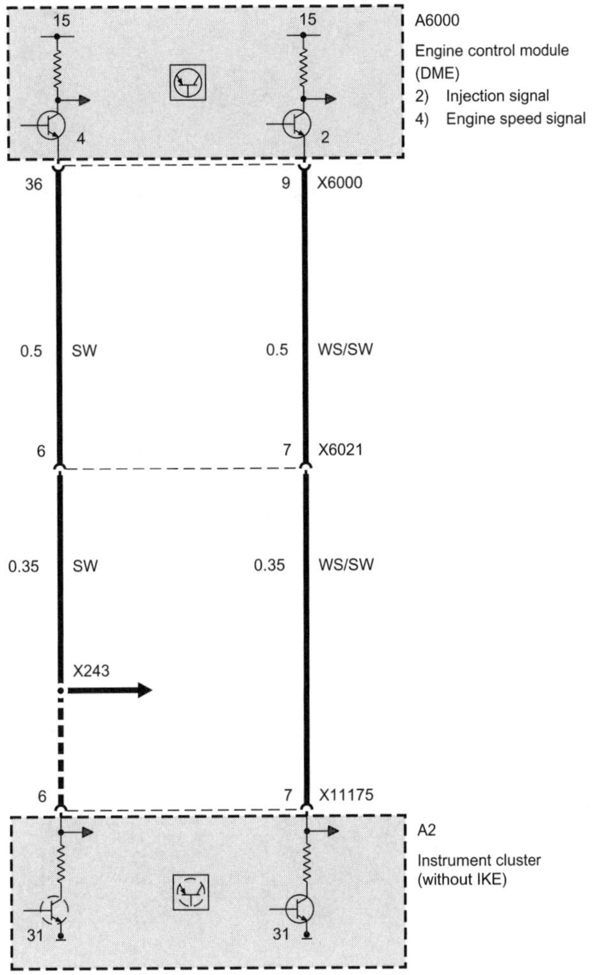

502ELE0749

Engine Management (MS 41.1)
DME/IKE interface
(1 of 1)

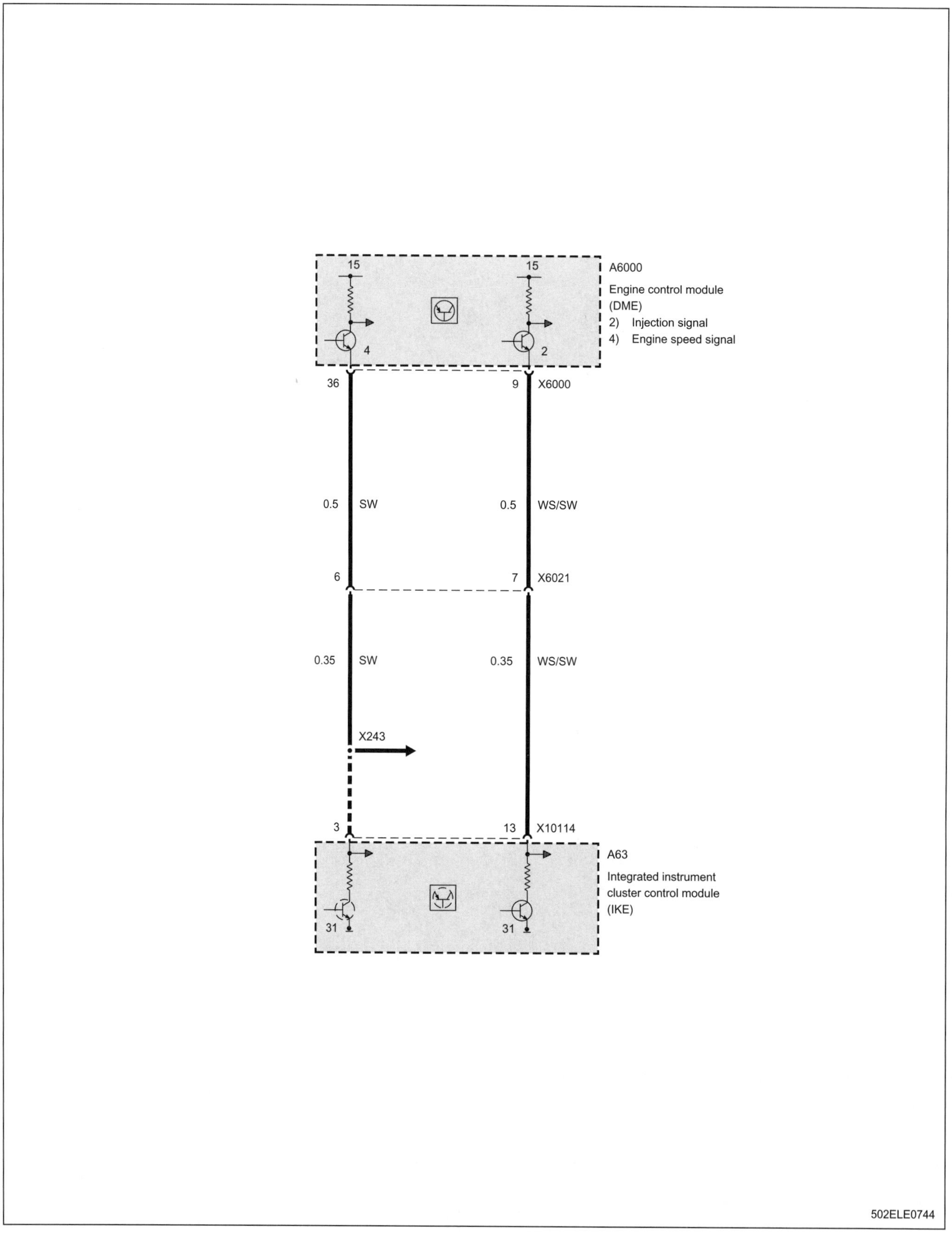
15
15
4
2
A6000
Engine control module
(DME)
2) Injection signal
4) Engine speed signal
36
9
X6000
0.5
SW
0.5
WS/SW
6
7
X6021
0.35
SW
0.35
WS/SW
X243
3
13
X10114
A63
Integrated instrument
cluster control module
(IKE)
31
31
502ELE0744

Engine Management (MS 41.1)
Data link connector pin assignments
(1 of 1)

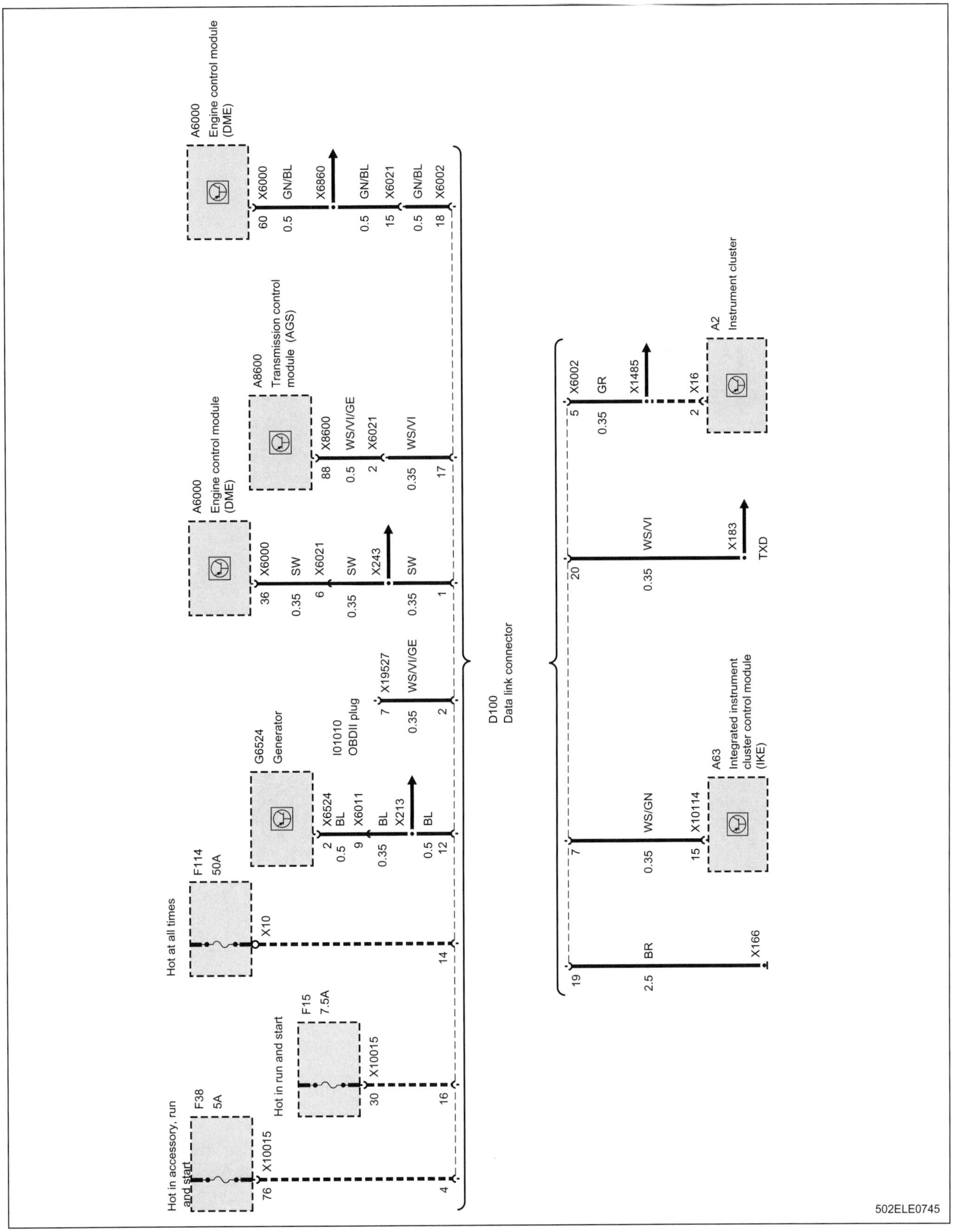

Engine Management (MS 41.1)
ASC/DME interfaces
(1 of 1)

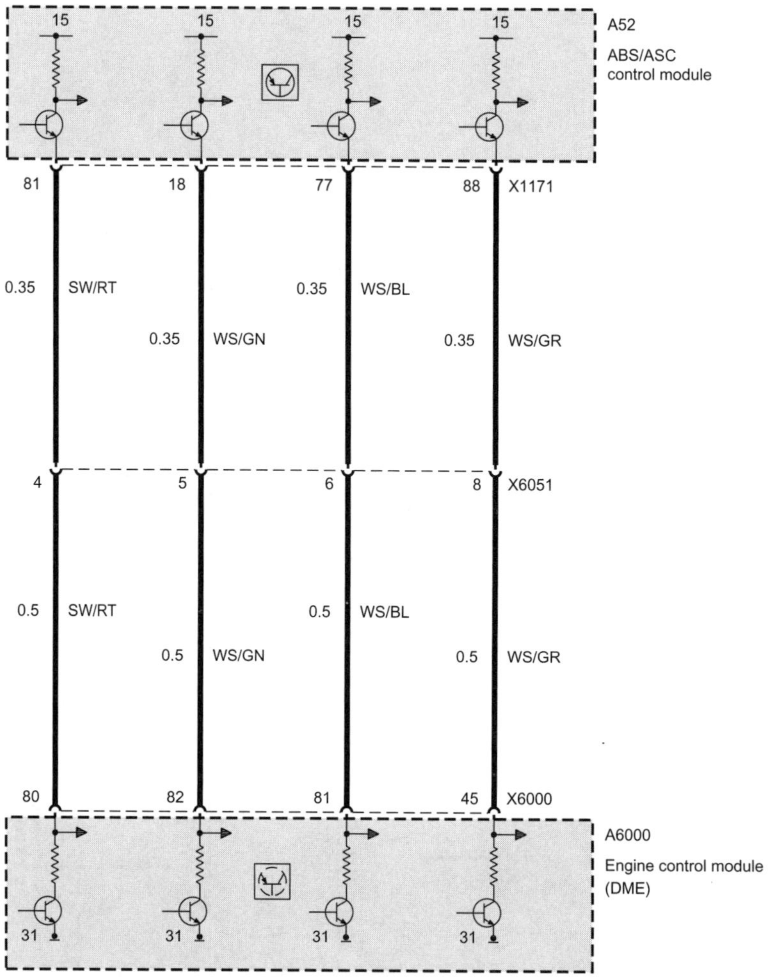

502ELE0746

Engine Management (MS 41.1)
Diagnosis, terminating resistor
(1 of 1)

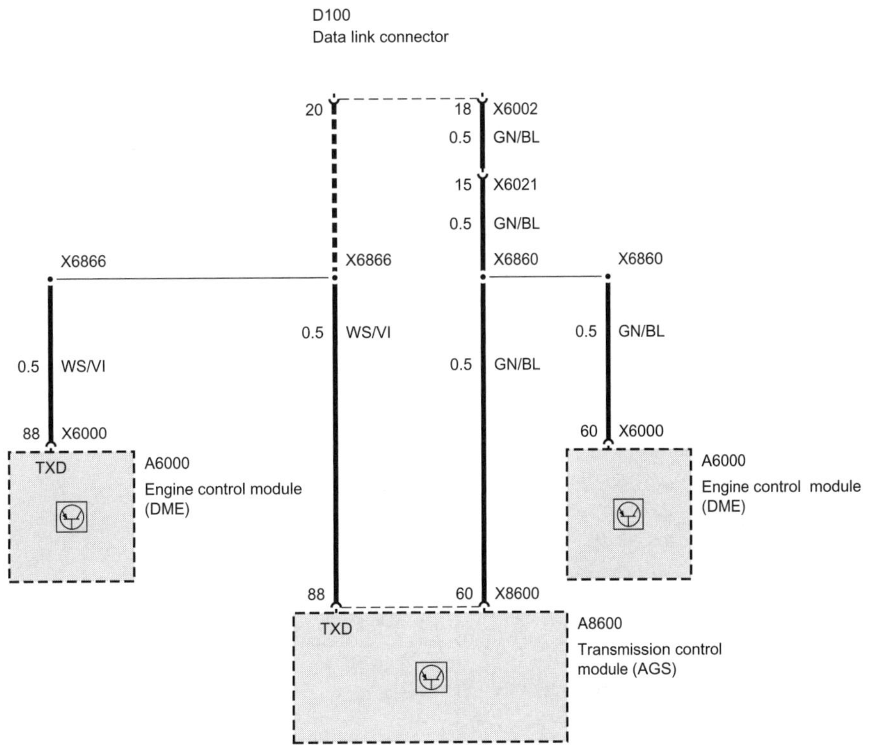

Engine Management (MS 41.1)
X6900 - Ground splice
(1 of 1)

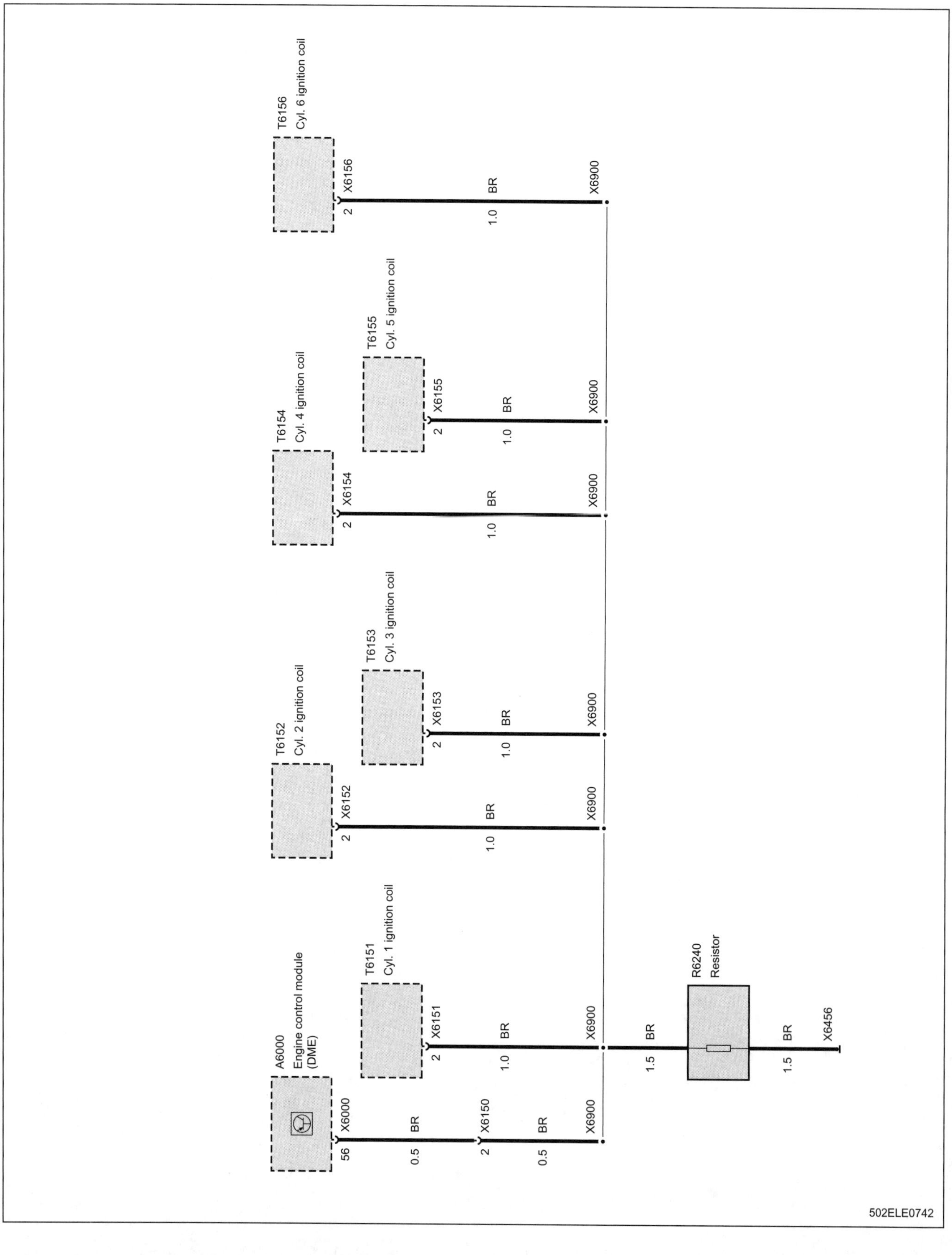

Engine Management (MS 43.0)
Cruise control (overview)
(1 of 2)

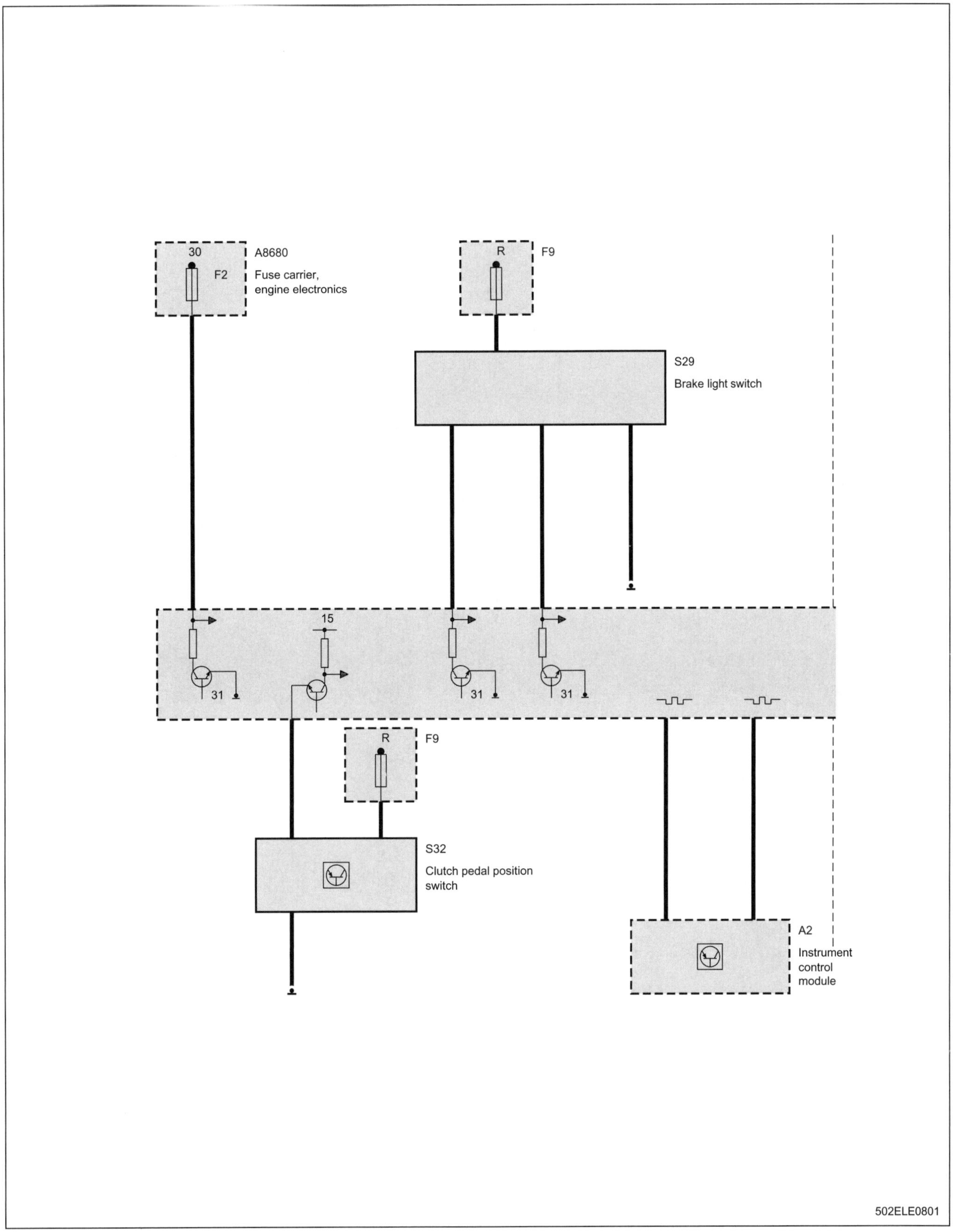

Engine Management (MS 43.0)
Cruise control (overview)
(2 of 2)

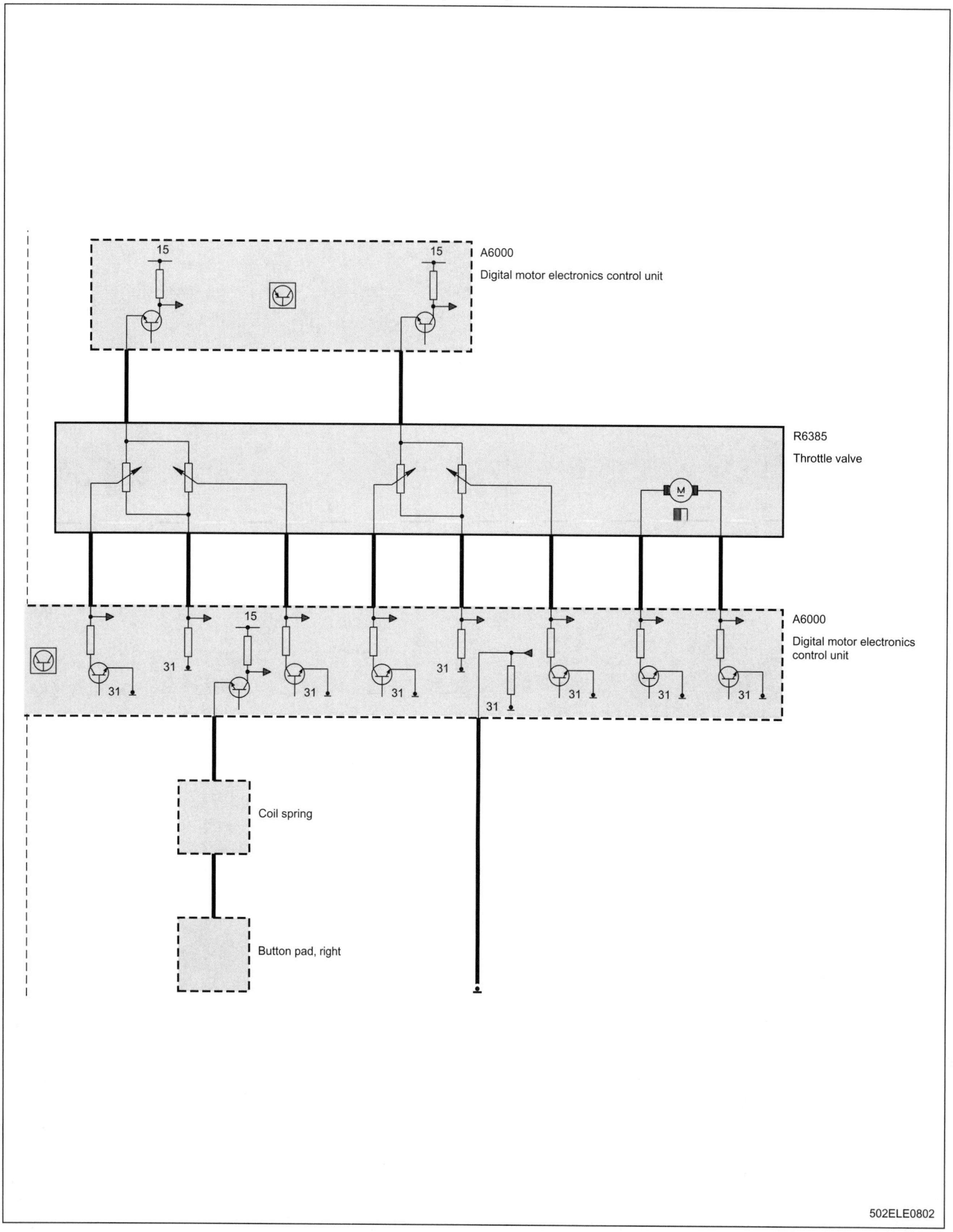

Engine Management (MS 43.0)
A6000 Engine control module (DME) Module 1
(1 of 1)

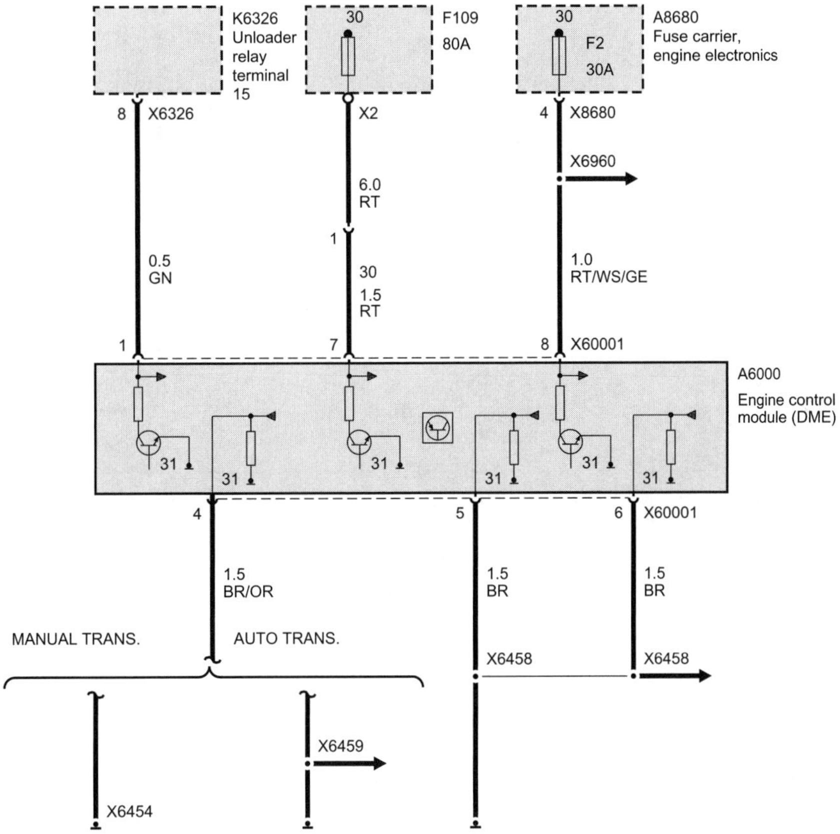

Engine Management (MS 43.0)
A6000 Engine control module (DME) Module 2
(1 of 3)

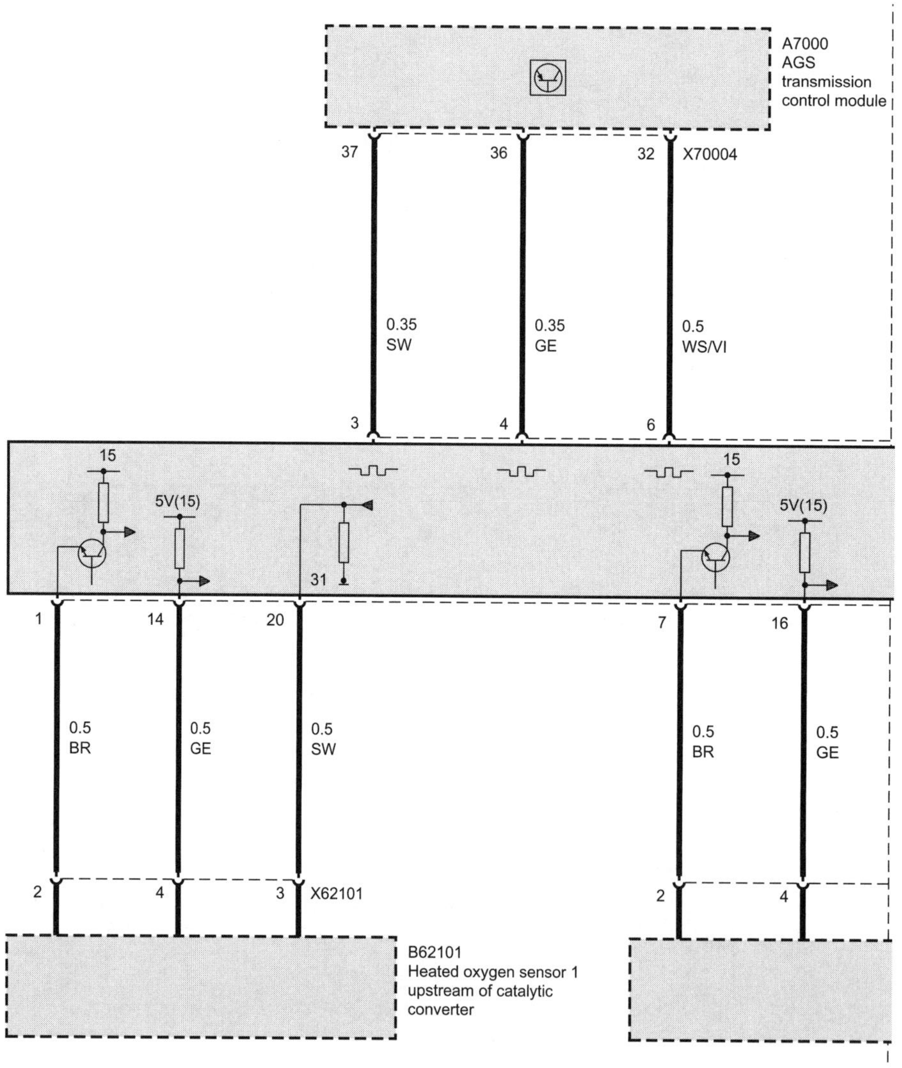

502ELE818

Engine Management (MS 43.0)
A6000 Engine control module (DME) Module 2
(2 of 3)

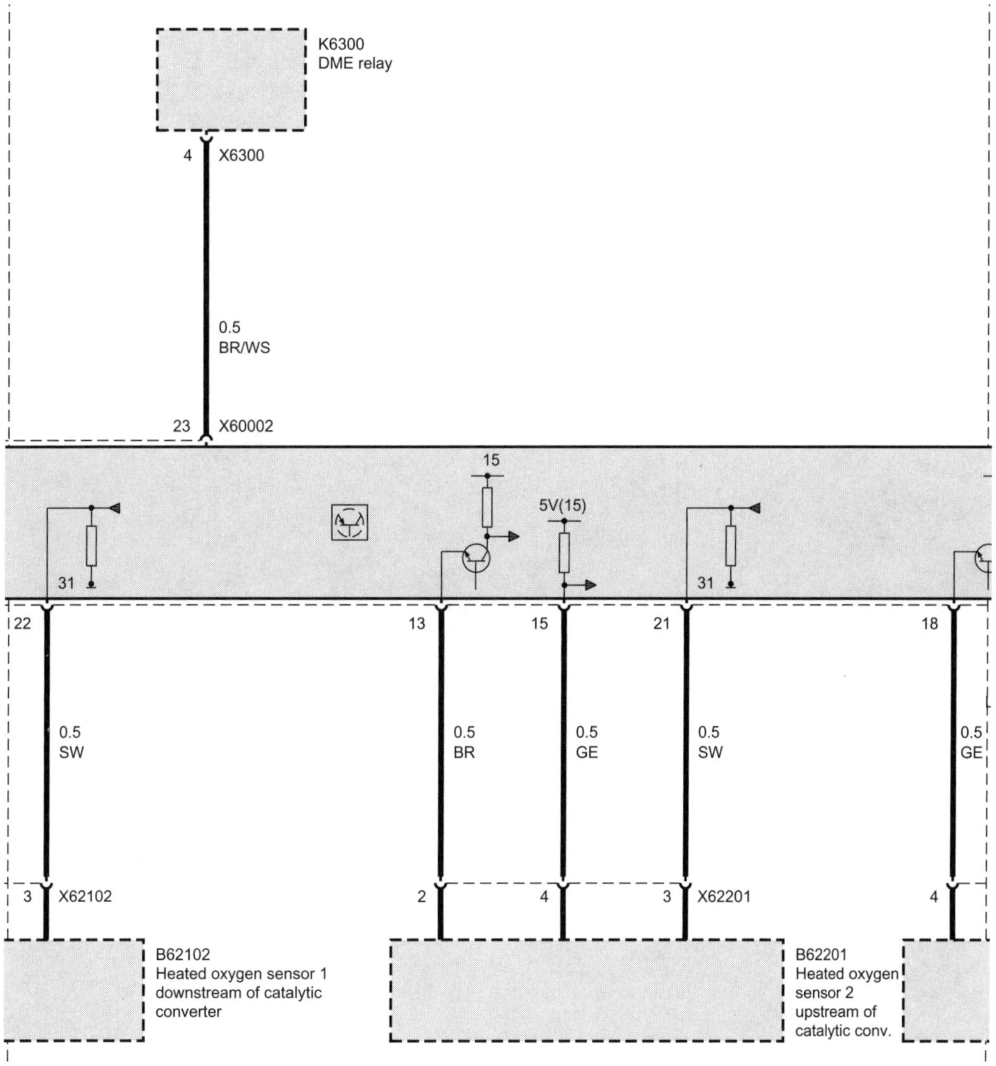

502ELE0819

Engine Management (MS 43.0)
A6000 Engine control module (DME) Module 2
(3 of 3)

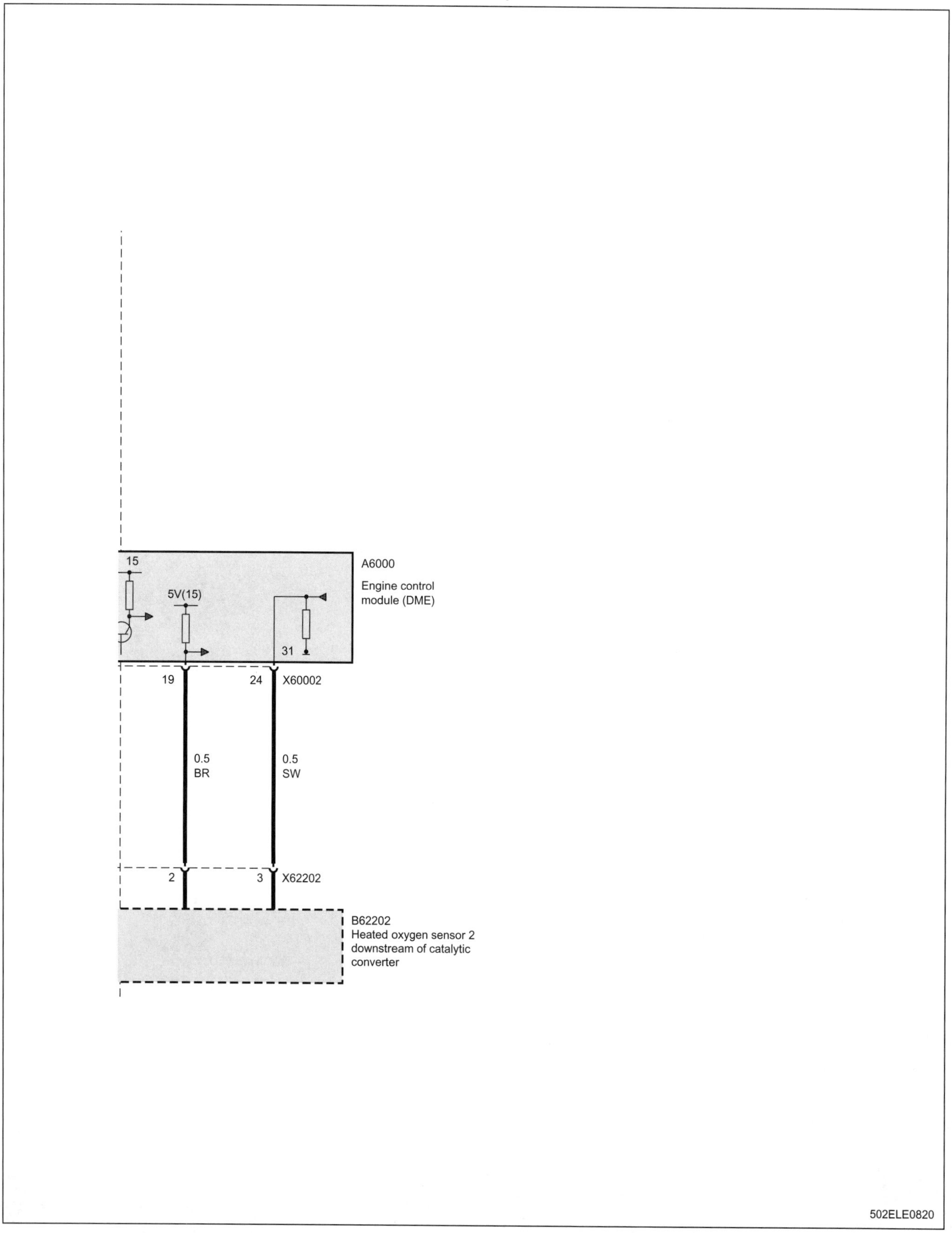

Engine Management (MS 43.0)
A6000 Engine control module (DME) Module 3
(1 of 3)

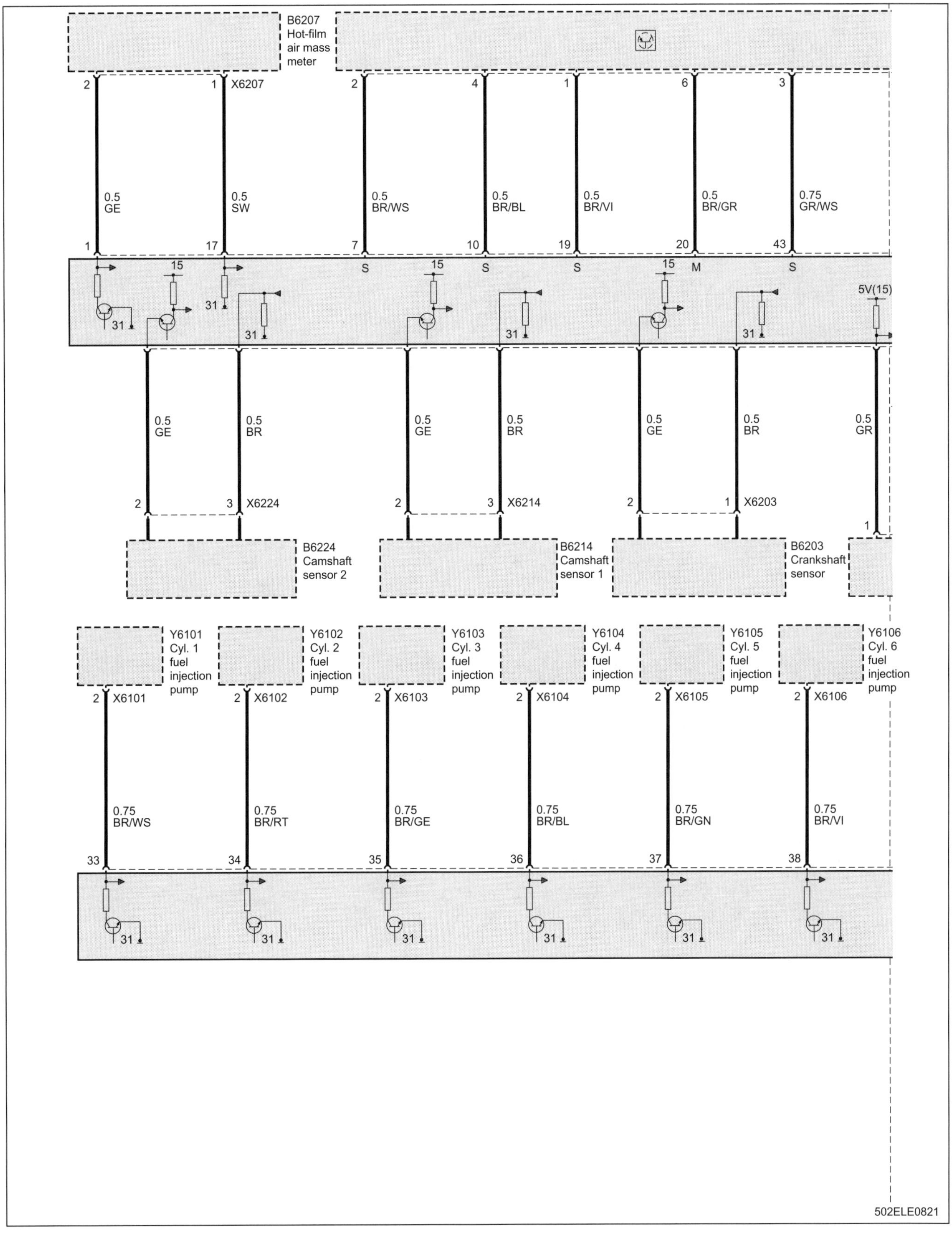

Engine Management (MS 43.0)
A6000 Engine control module (DME) Module 3
(2 of 3)

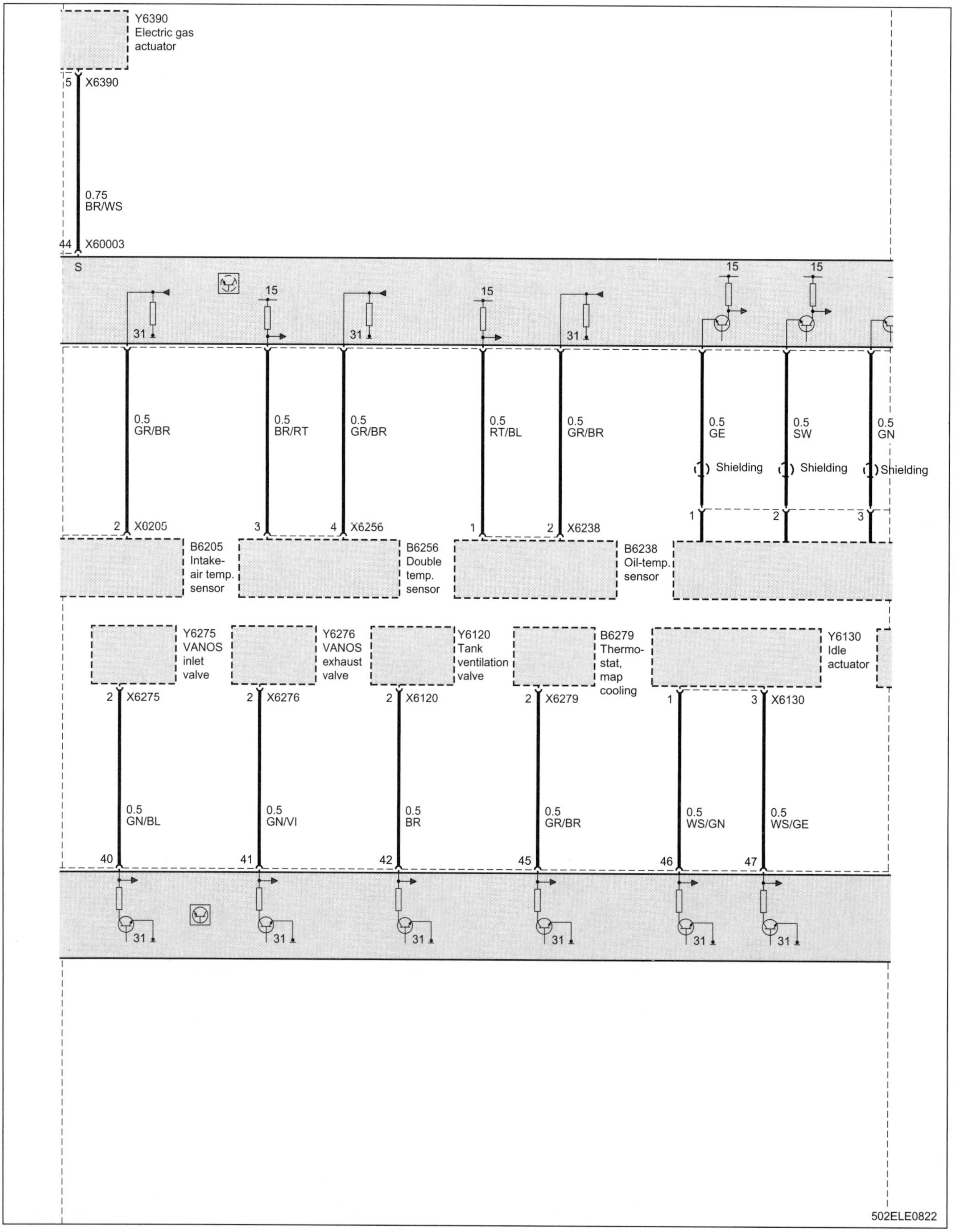

Engine Management (MS 43.0)
A6000 Engine control module (DME) Module 3
(3 of 3)

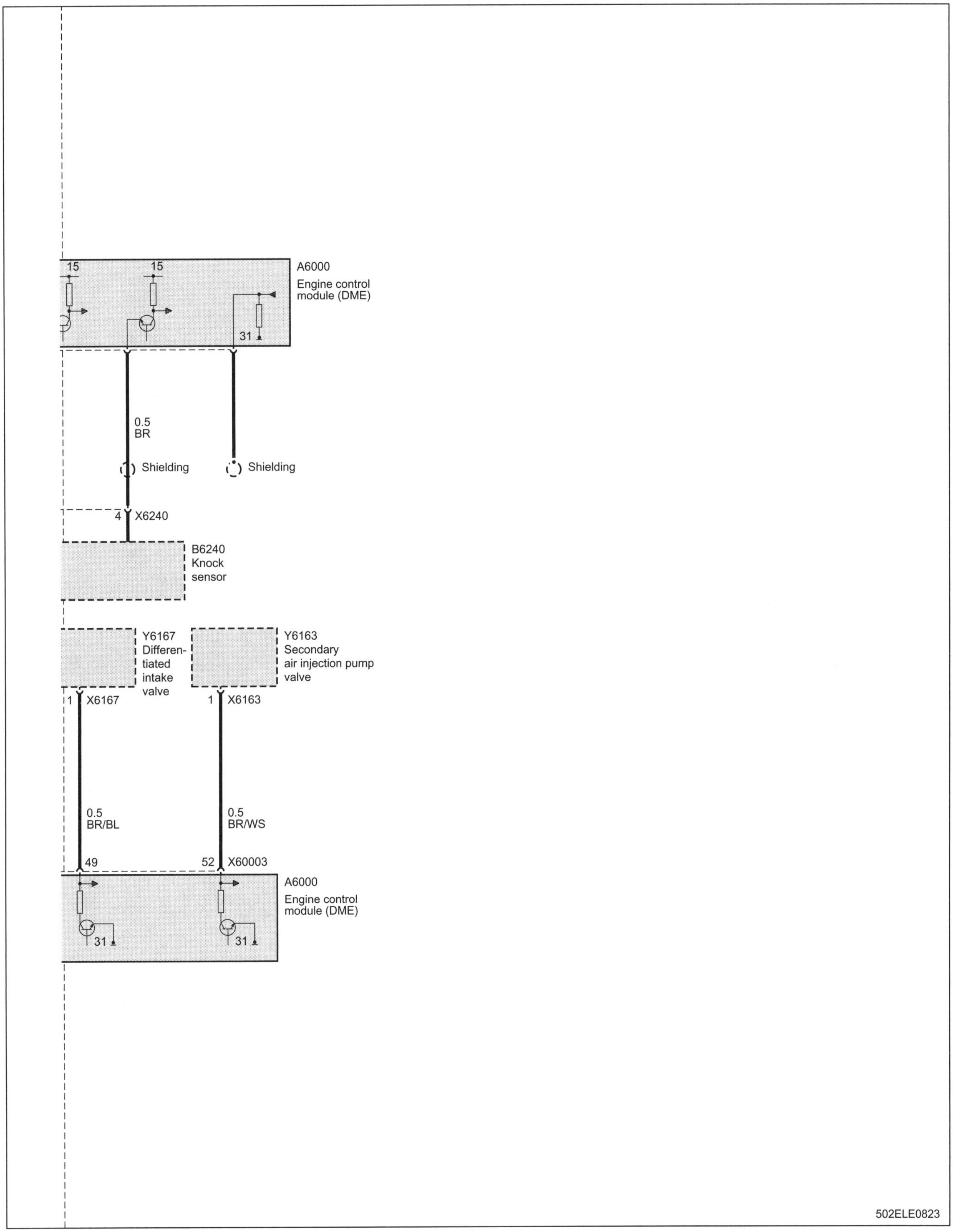

Engine Management (MS 43.0)
A6000 Engine control module (DME) Module 4
(1 of 4)

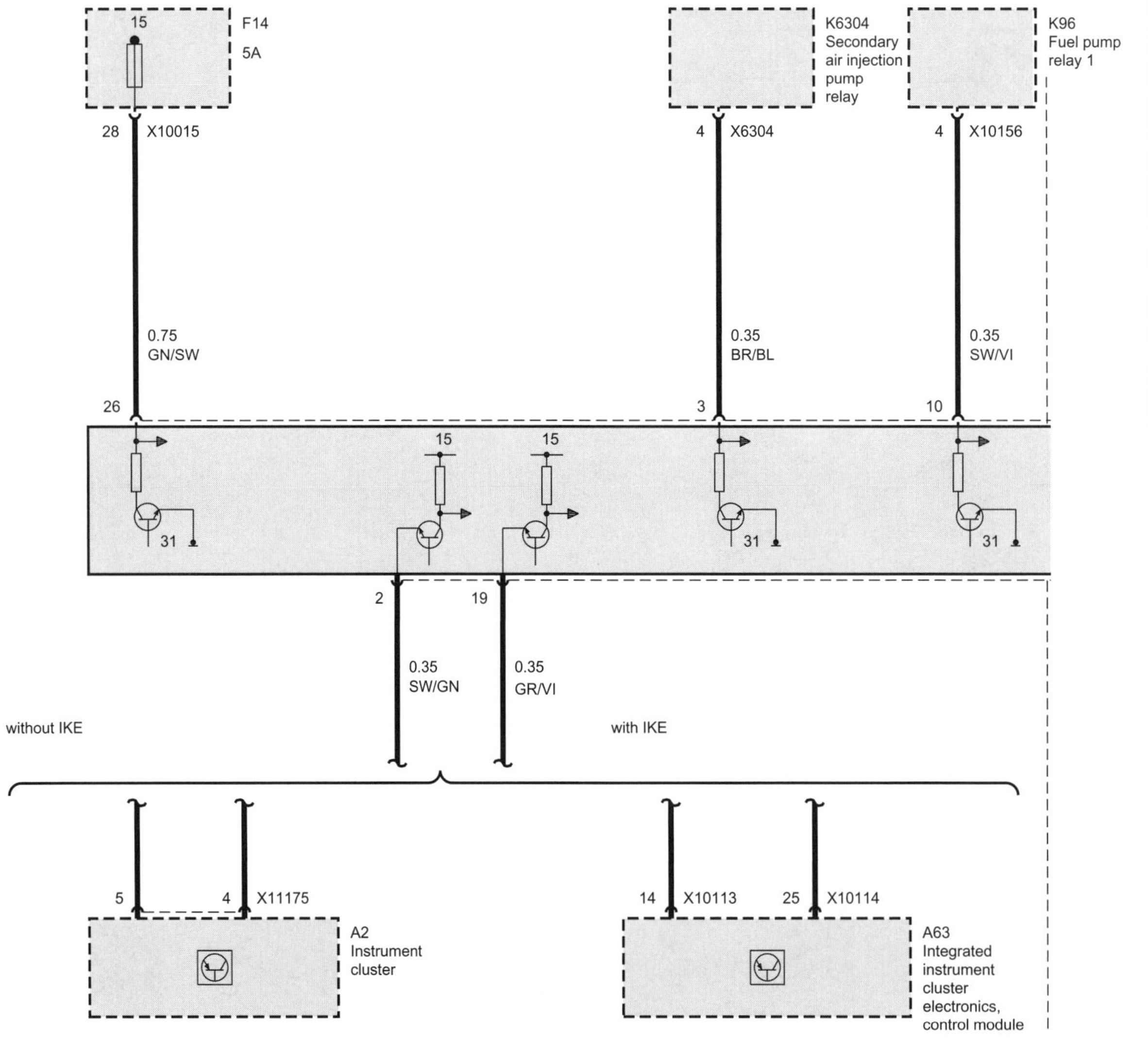

Engine Management (MS 43.0)
A6000 Engine control module (DME) Module 4
(2 of 4)

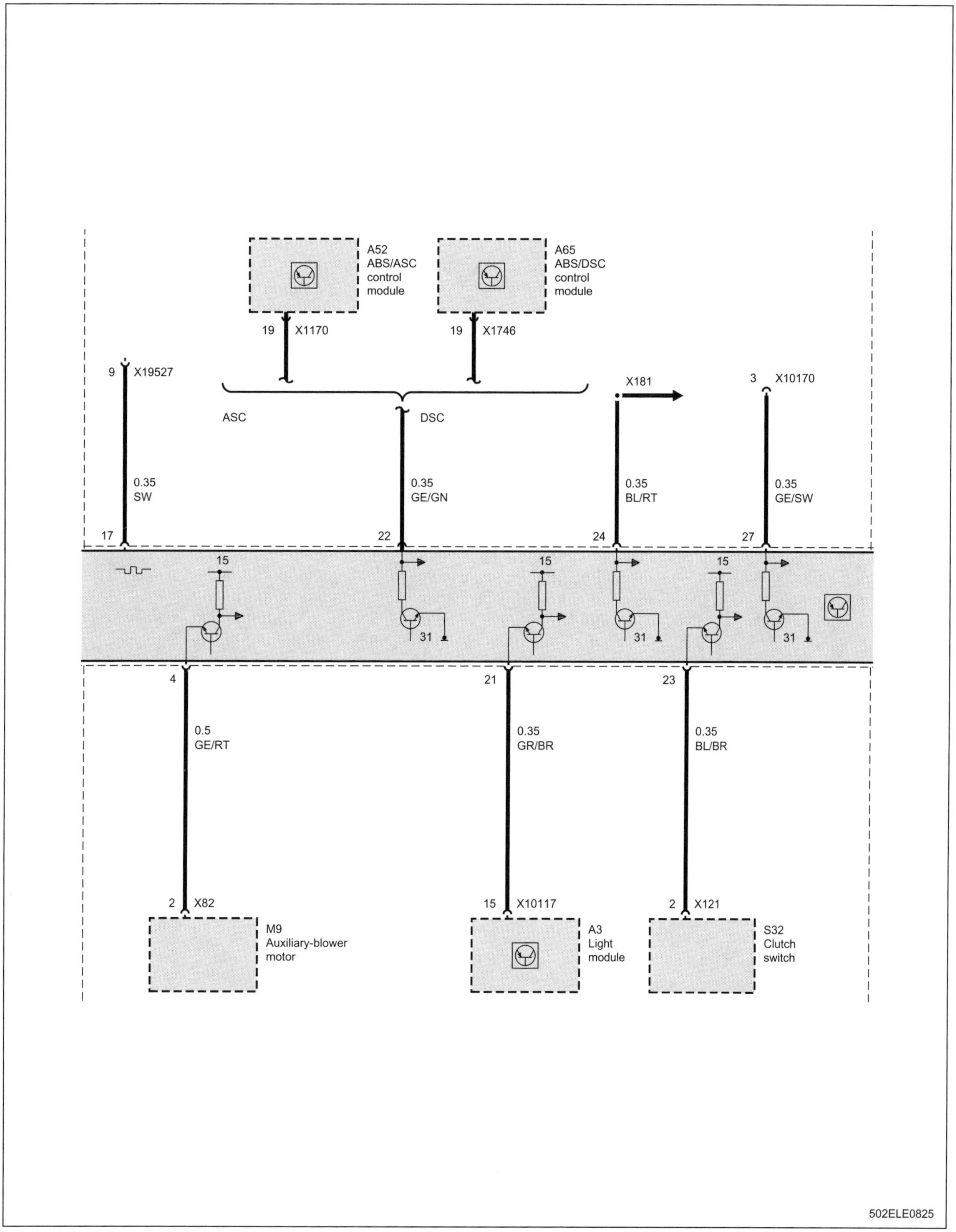

Engine Management (MS 43.0)
A6000 Engine control module (DME) Module 4
(3 of 4)

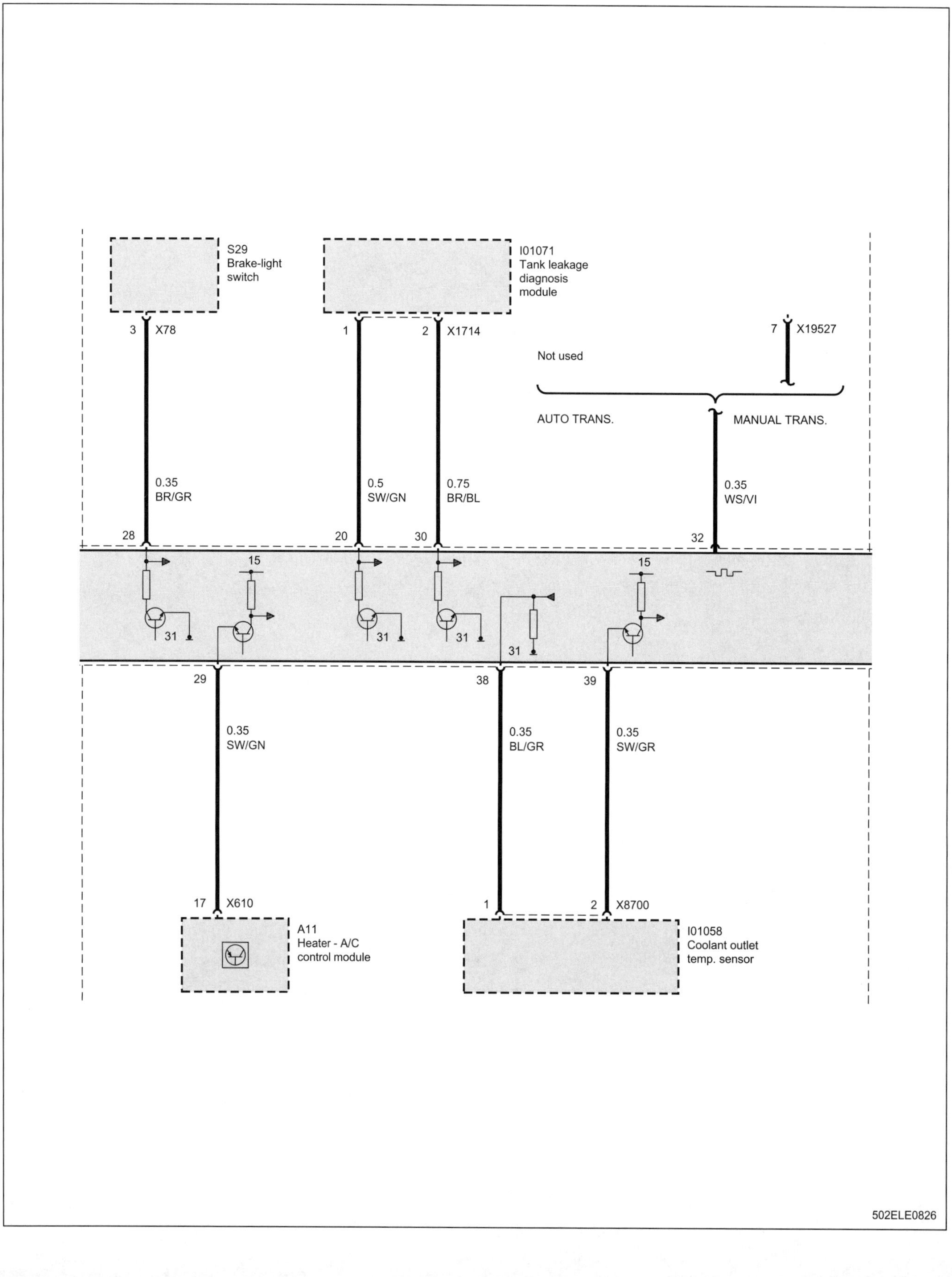

Engine Management (MS 43.0)
A6000 Engine control module (DME) Module 4
(4 of 4)

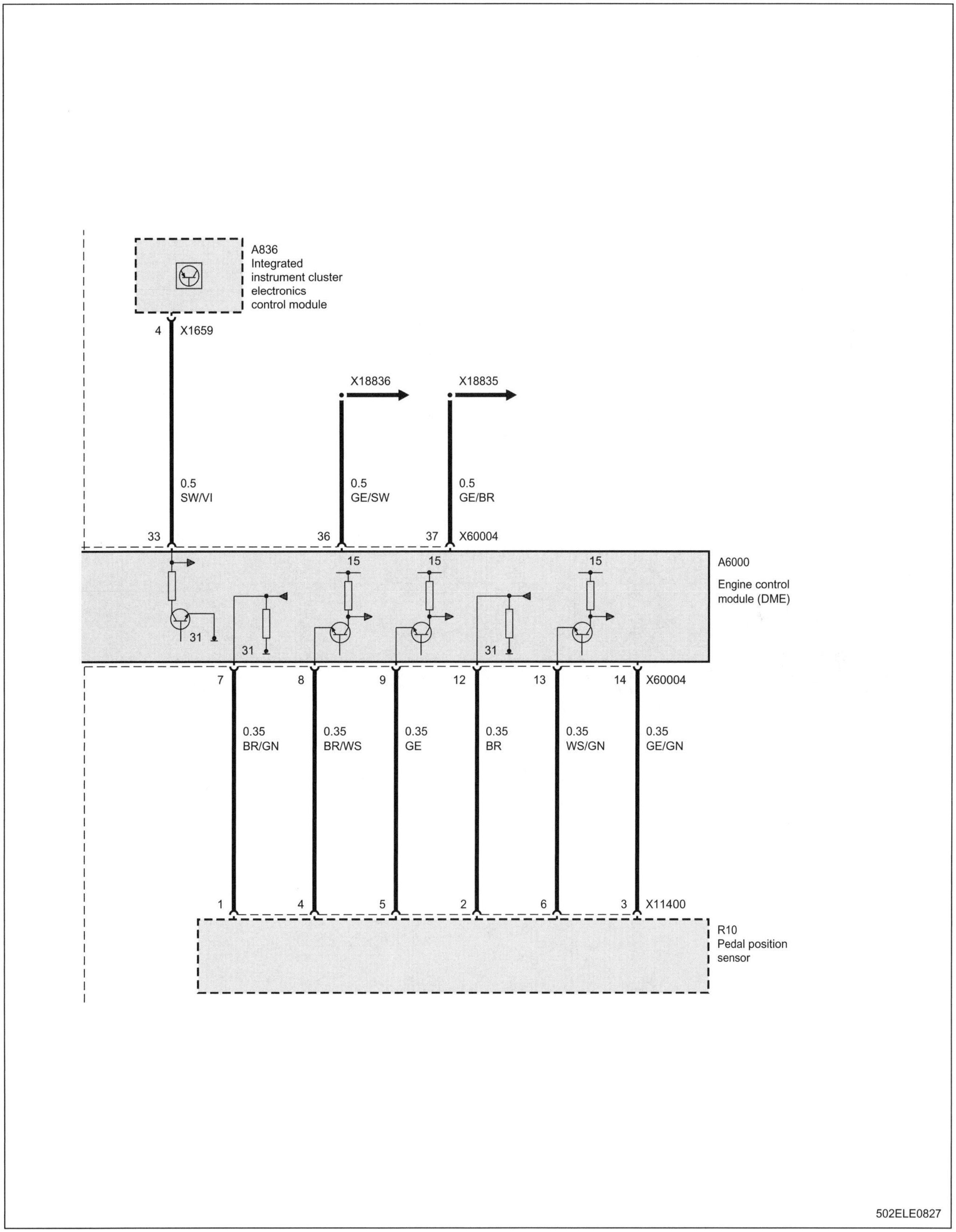

Engine Management (MS 43.0)
A6000 Engine control module (DME) Module 5
(1 of 1)

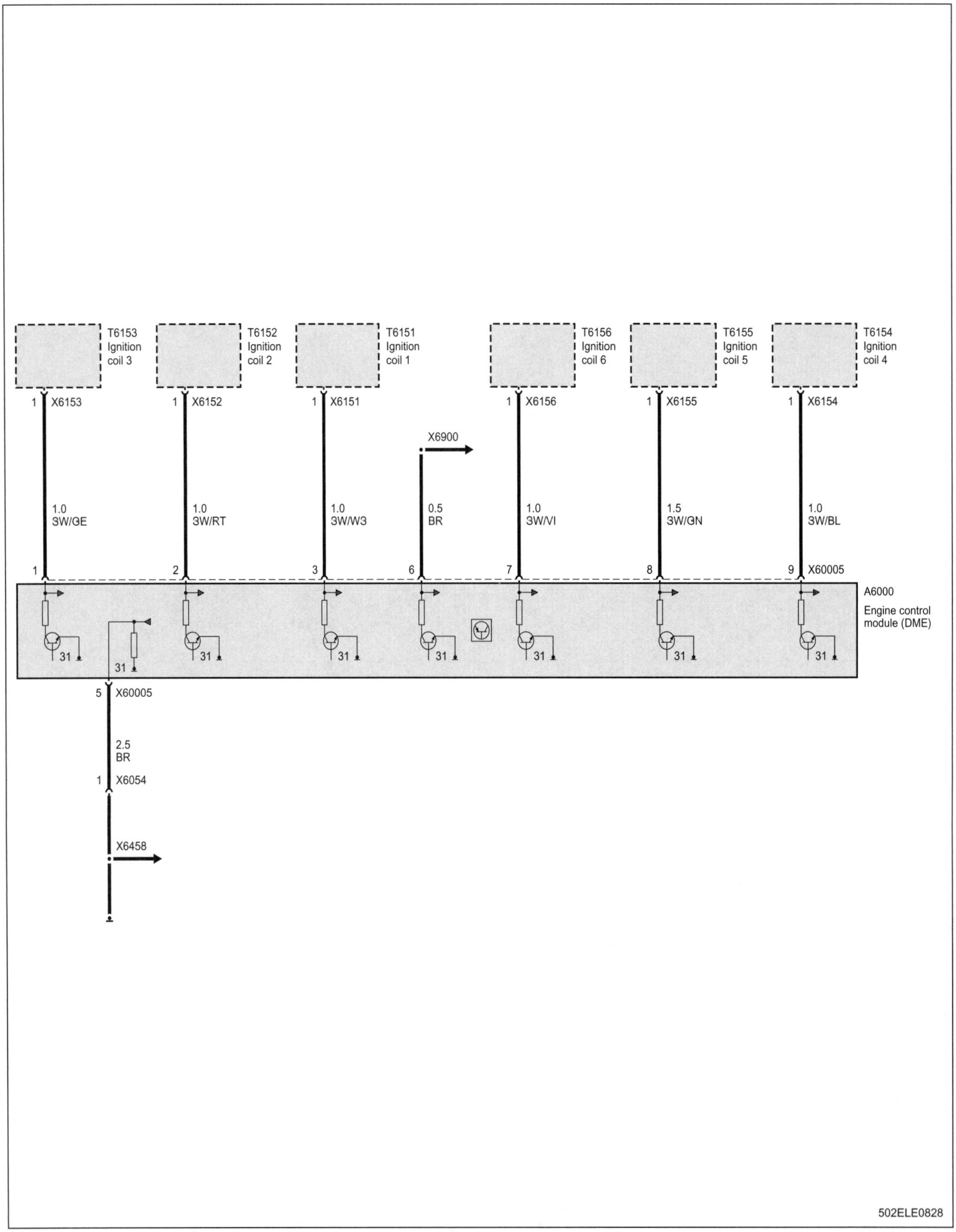

Engine Management (MS 43.0)
X19527 OBDII socket
(1 of 1)

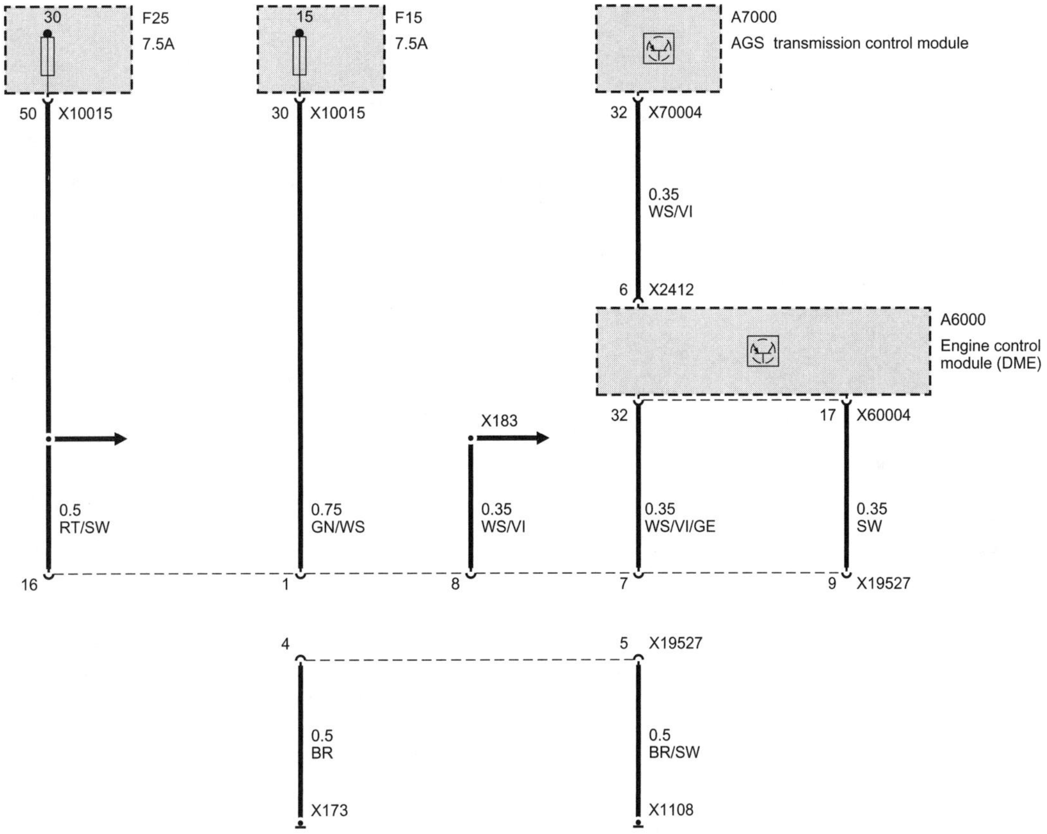

502ELE0767

Engine Management (MS 43.0)
Engine control module relay
(1 of 1)

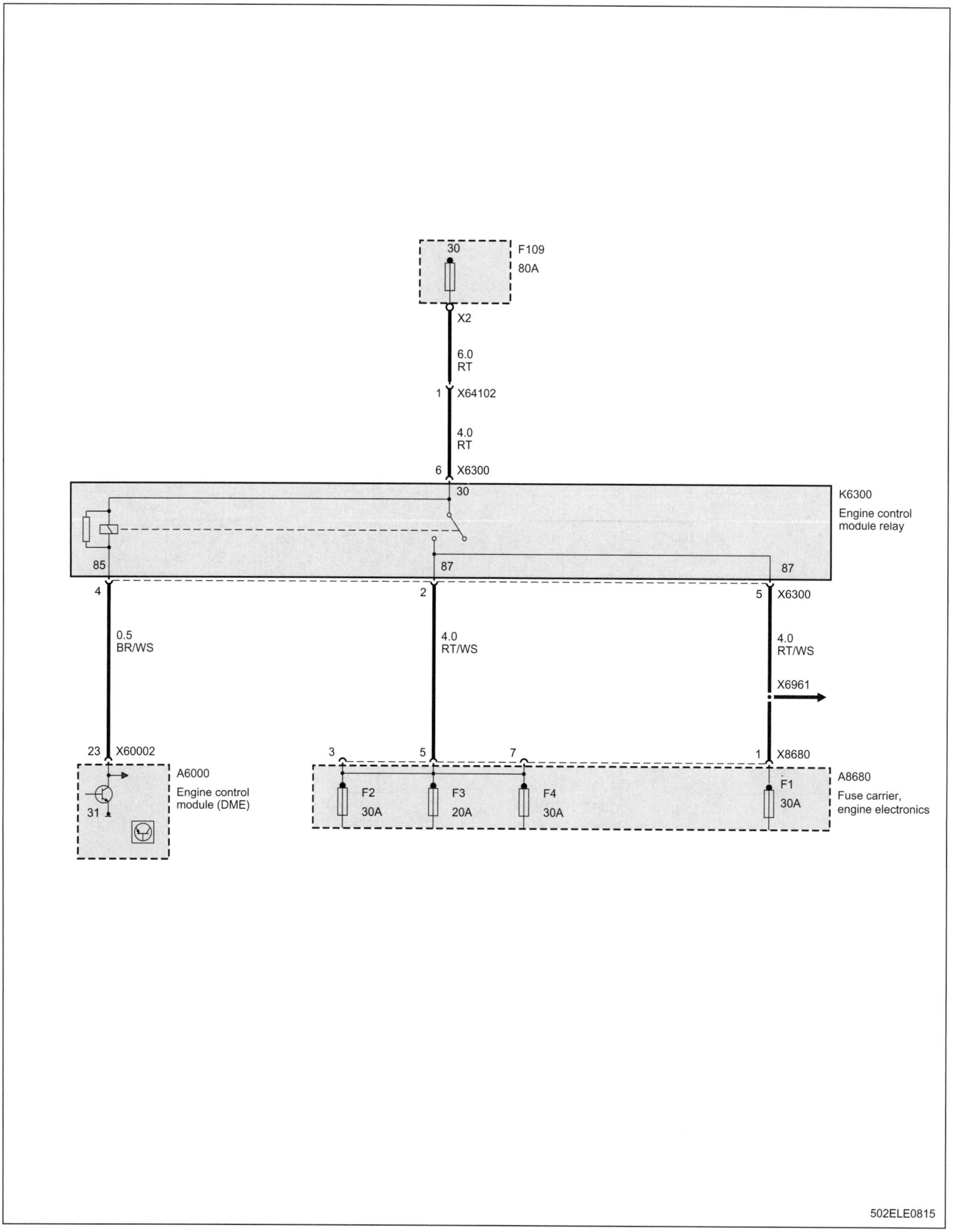

Engine Management (MS 43.0)
Fuel pump
(1 of 1)

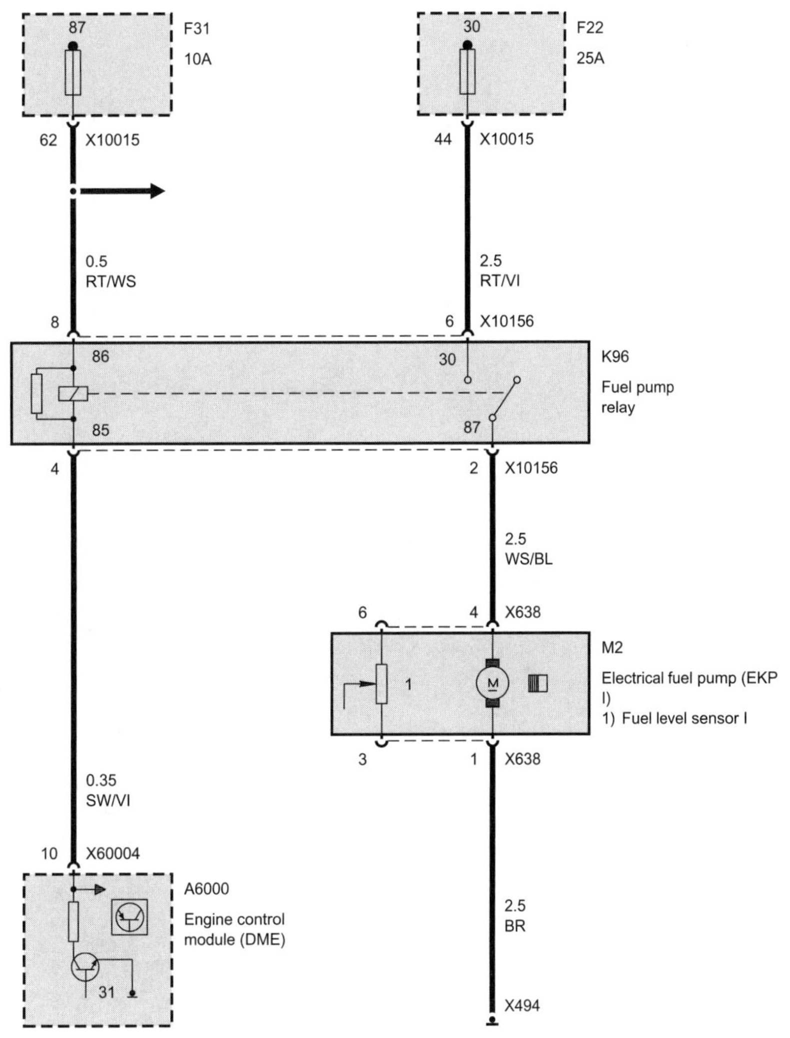

502ELE0786

Engine Management (MS 43.0)
Hot-film mass air flow sensor
(1 of 1)

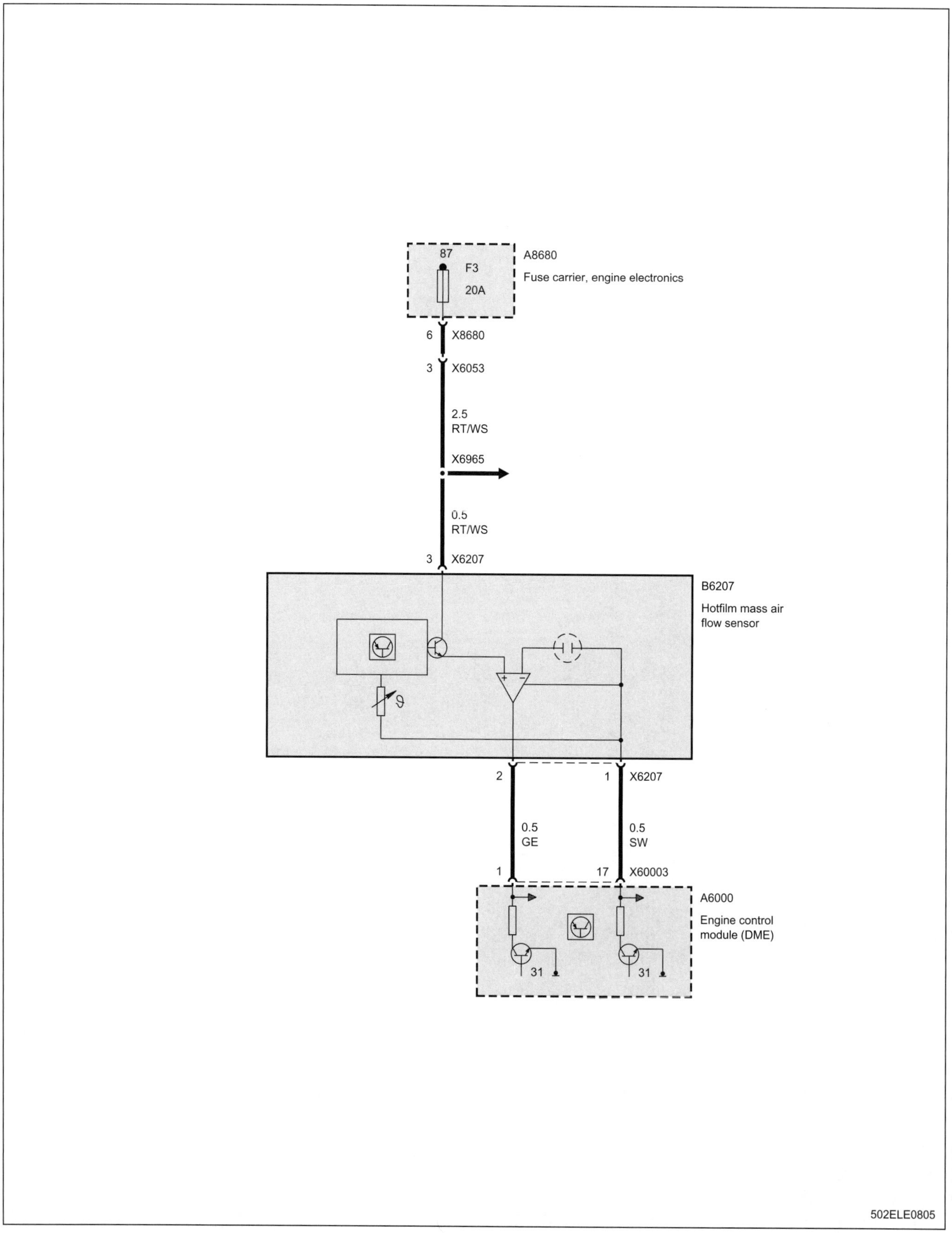

Engine Management (MS 43.0)
Idle speed control valve
(1 of 1)

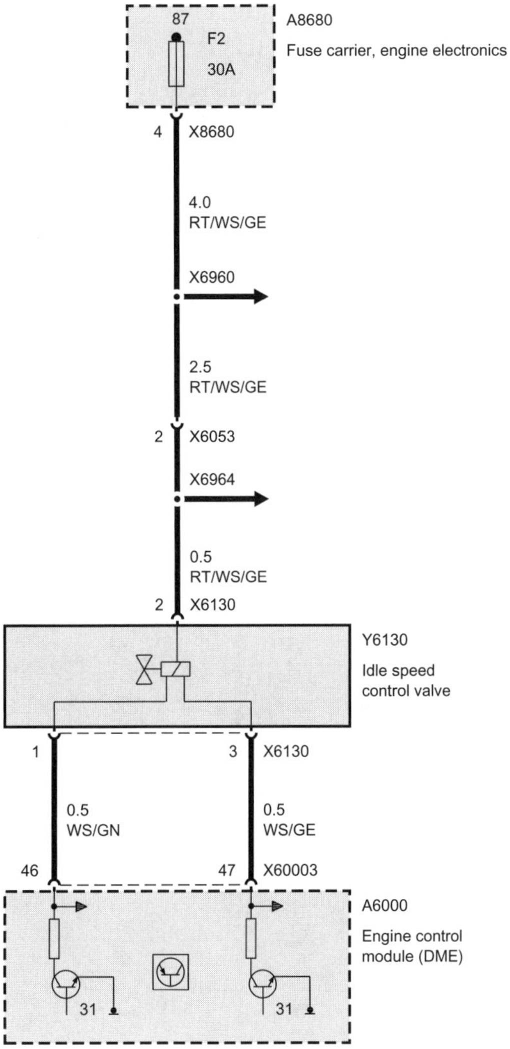

502ELE0795

Engine Management (MS 43.0)
Electric throttle actuator
(1 of 1)

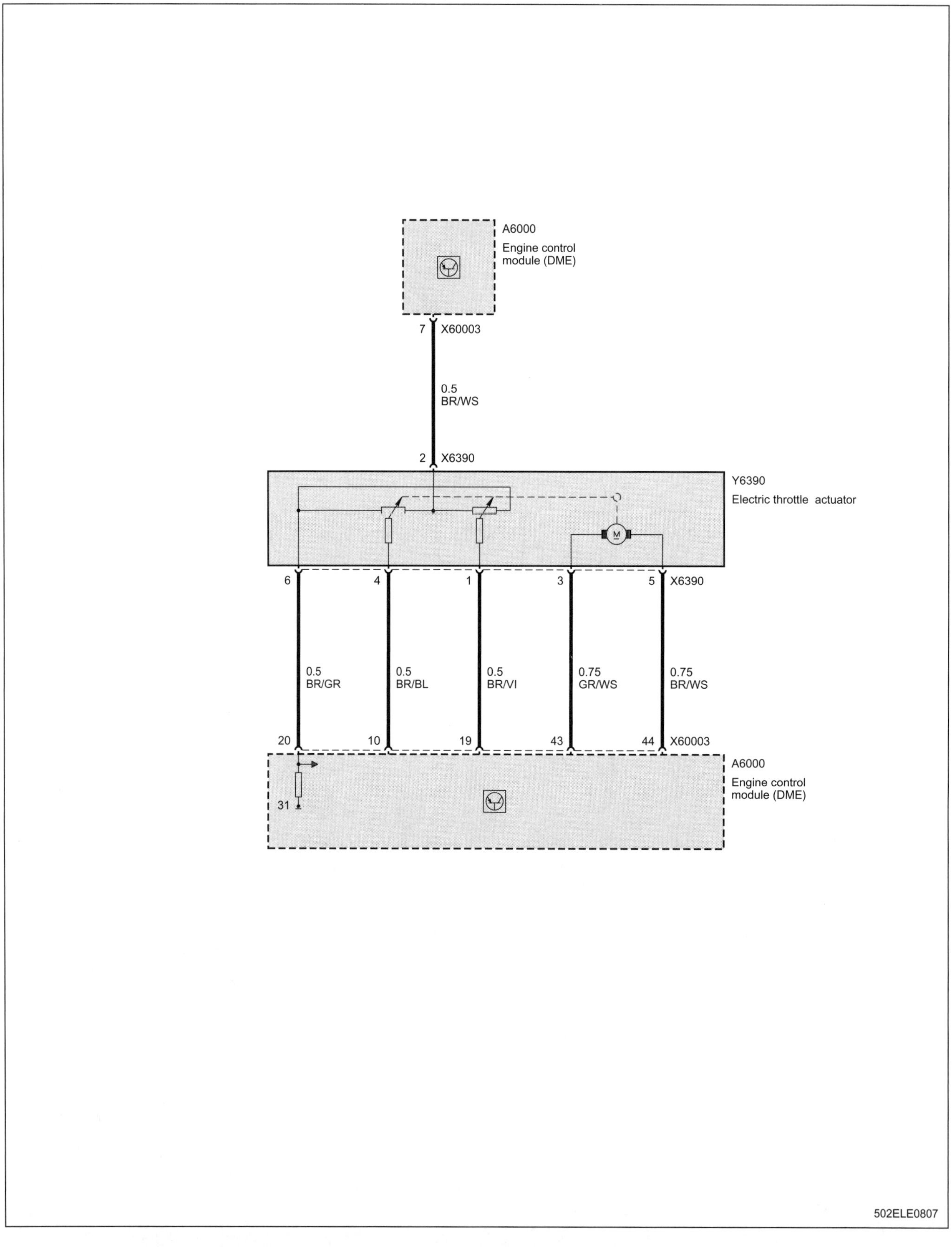

Engine Management (MS 43.0)
Pedal position sensor
(1 of 1)

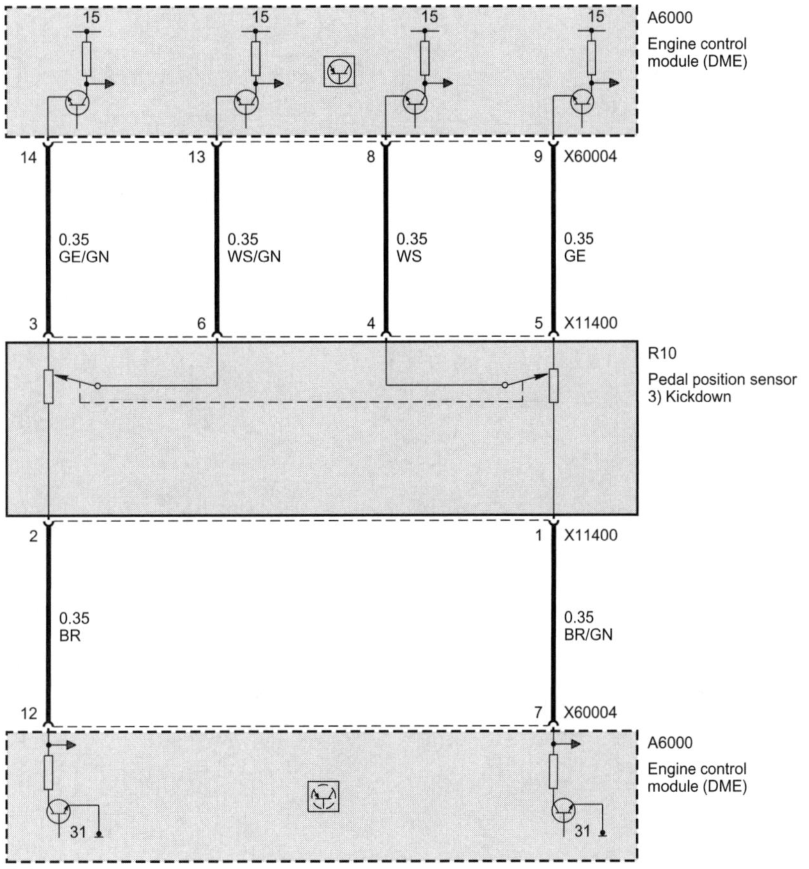

502ELE0769

Engine Management (MS 43.0)
Engine coolant dual temperature sensor
(1 of 1)

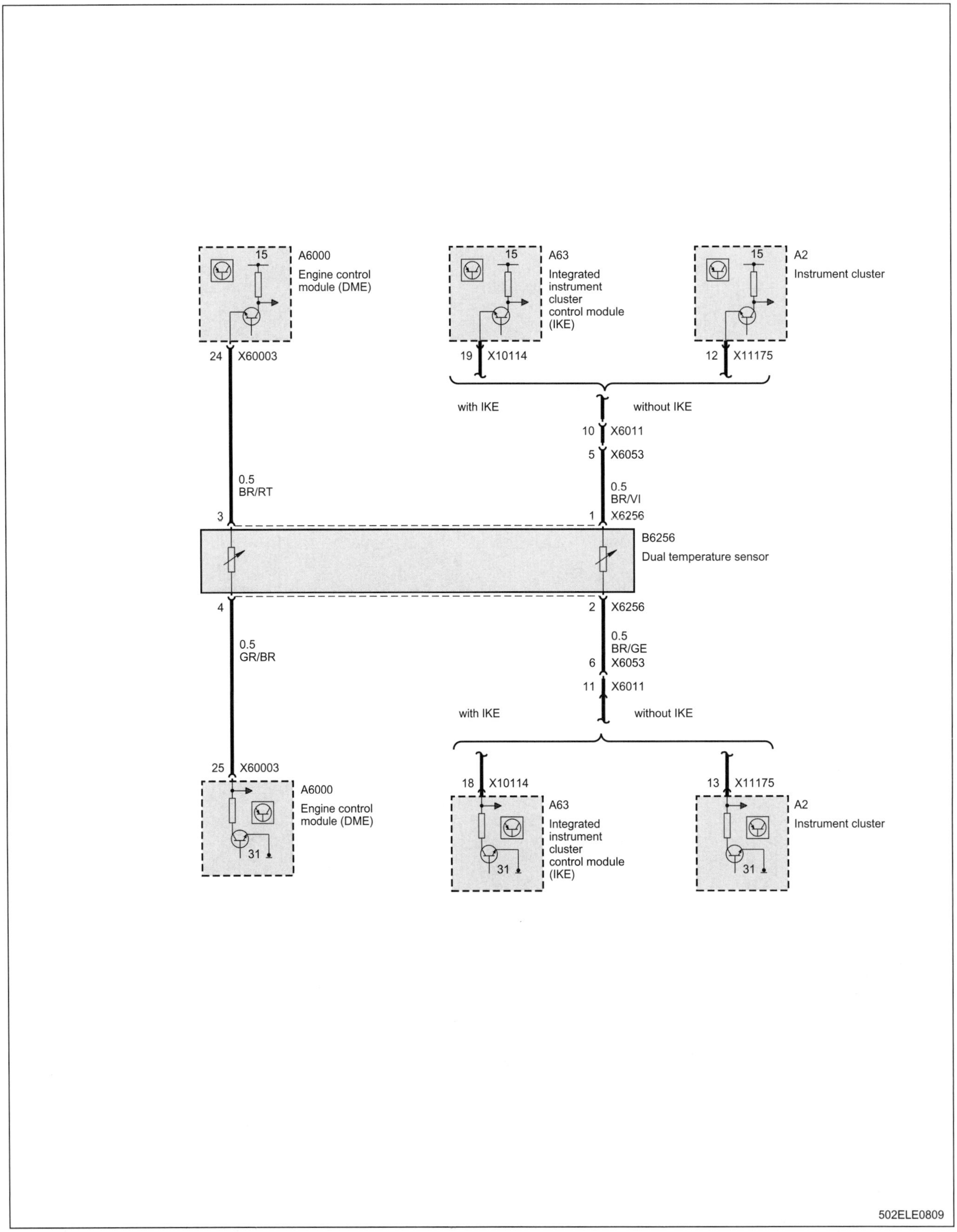

Engine Management (MS 43.0)
Intake air temperature sensor
(1 of 1)

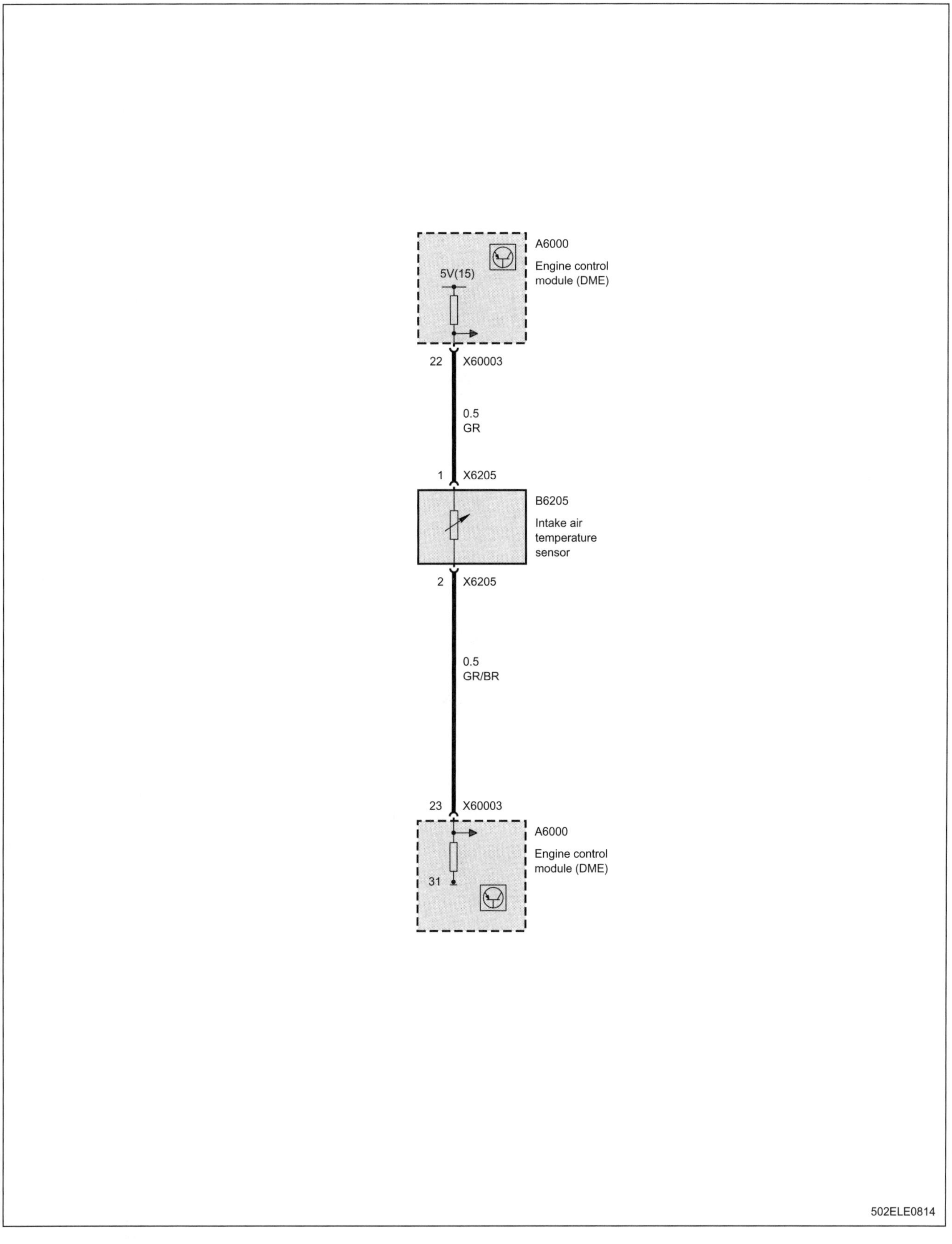

Engine Management (MS 43.0)
Changeover valve, intake pipe (DISA)
(1 of 1)

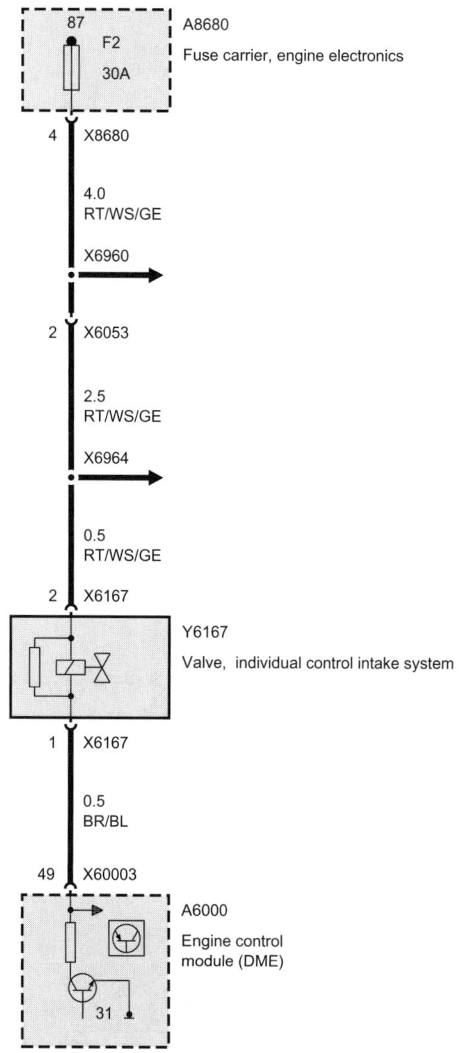

502ELE0813

Engine Management (MS 43.0)
Thermostat
(1 of 1)

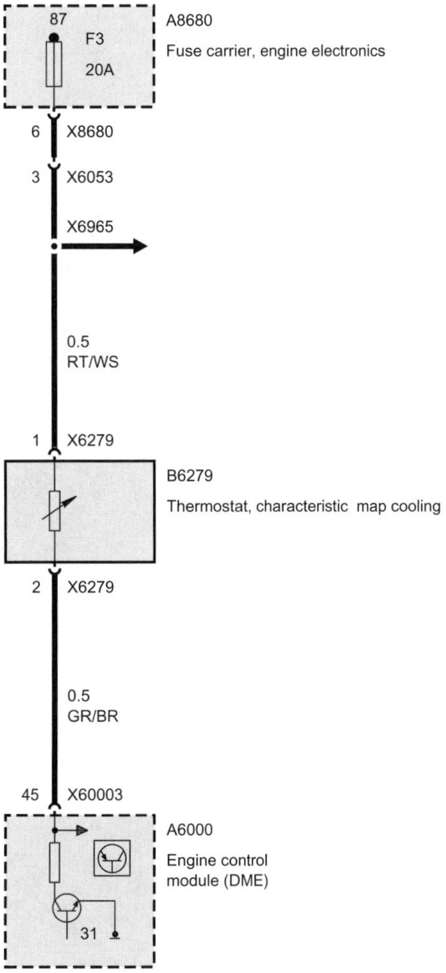

502ELE0759

Engine Management (MS 43.0)
Coolant temperature/electric fan
(1 of 1)

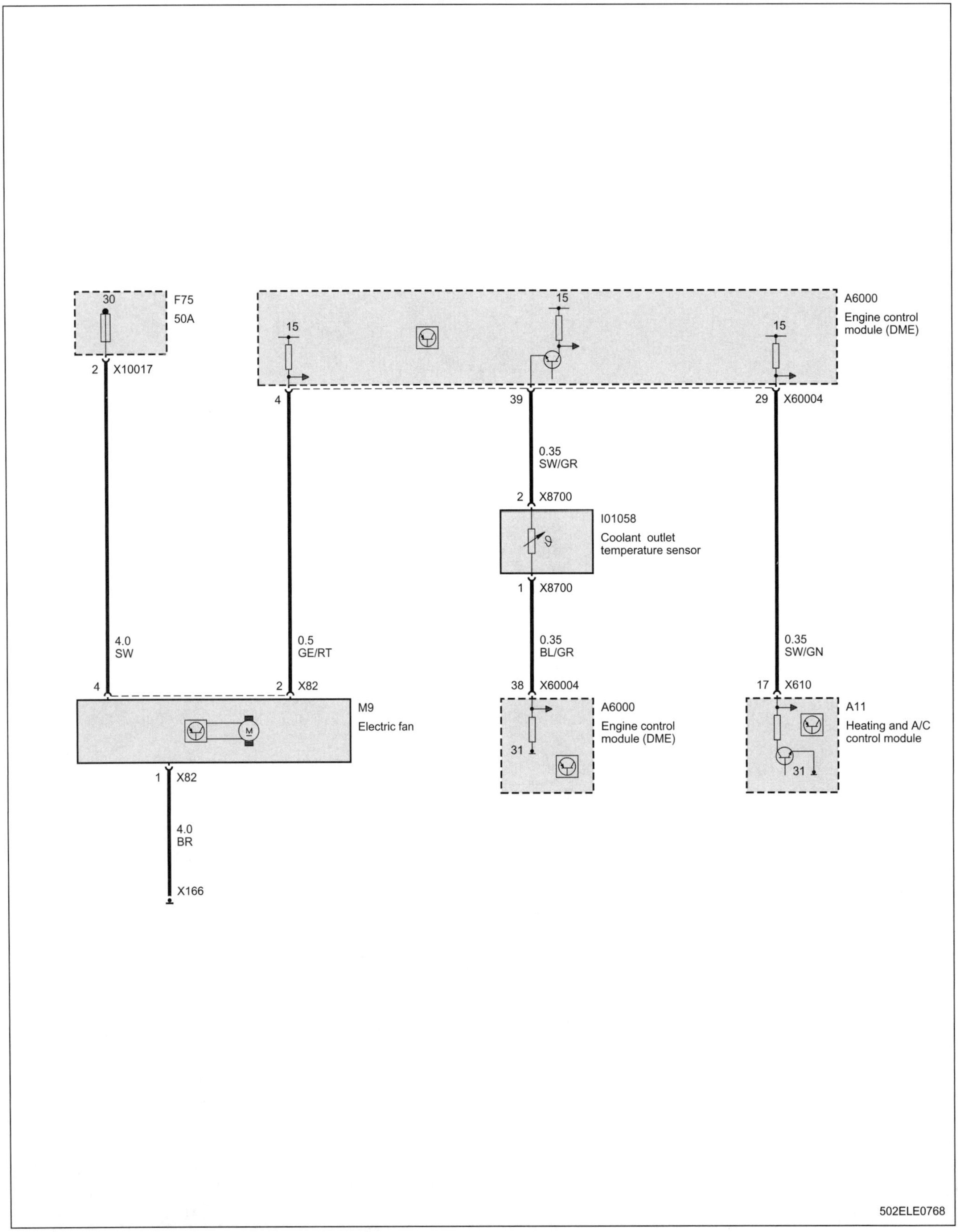

Engine Management (MS 43.0)
Oxygen sensor 1 in front of catalytic converter
(1 of 1)

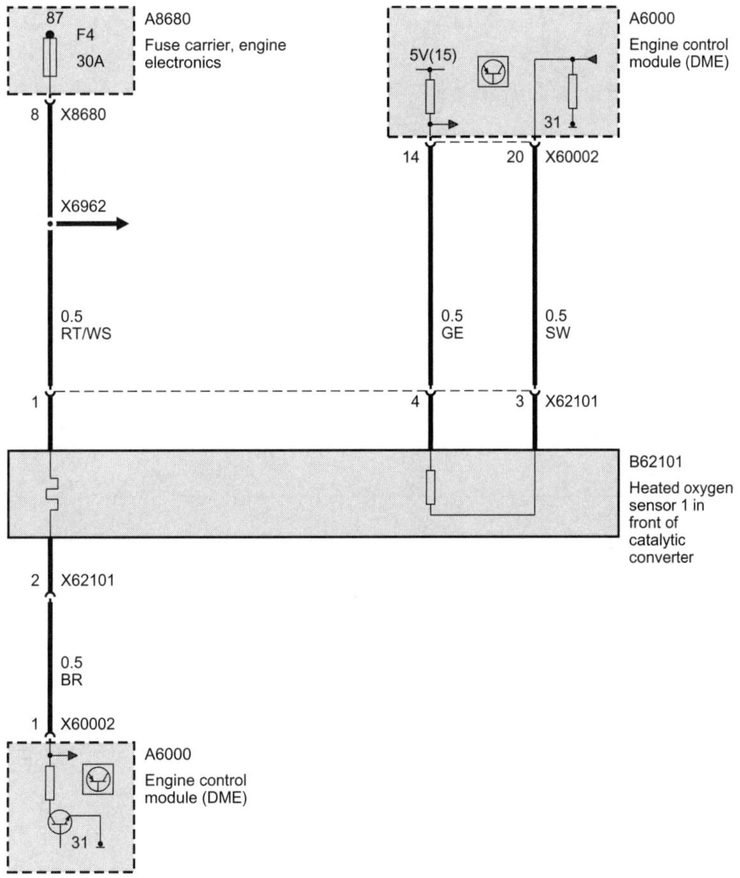

502ELE0816

Engine Management (MS 43.0)
Oxygen sensor 1 behind catalytic converter
(1 of 1)

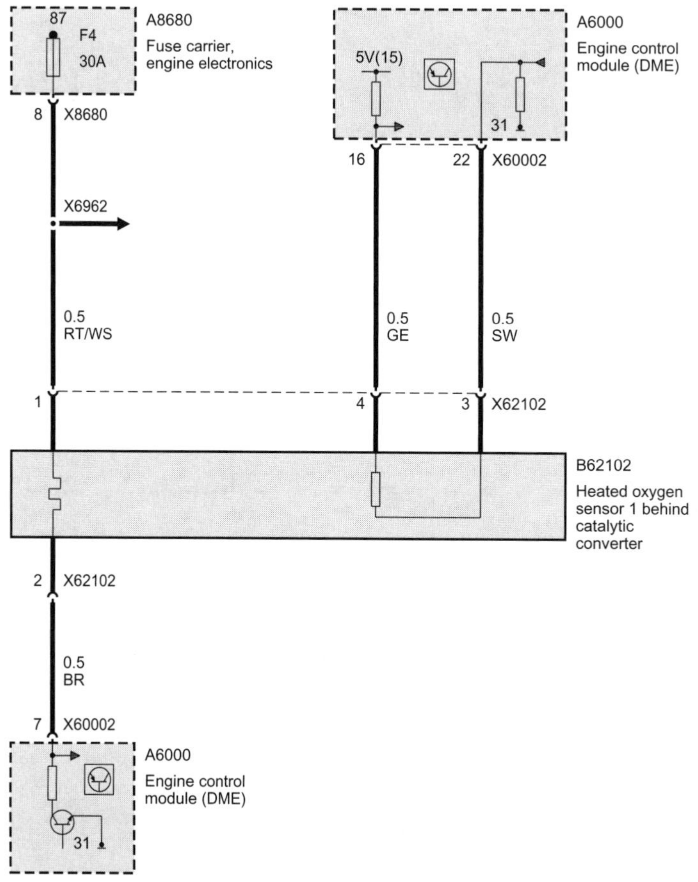

502ELE0766

Engine Management (MS 43.0)
Oxygen sensor 2 in front of catalytic converter
(1 of 1)

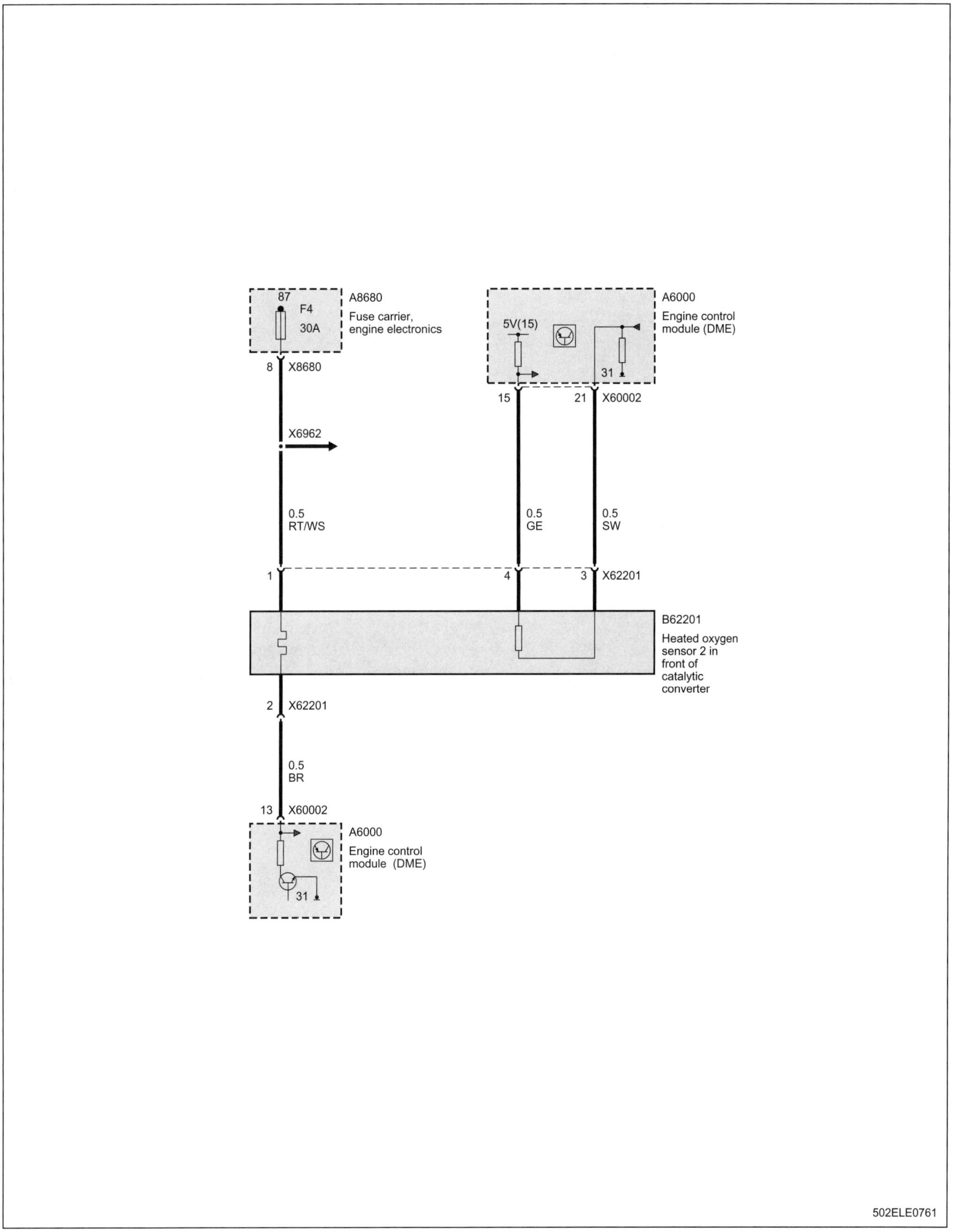

Engine Management (MS 43.0)
Oxygen sensor 2 behind catalytic converter
(1 of 1)

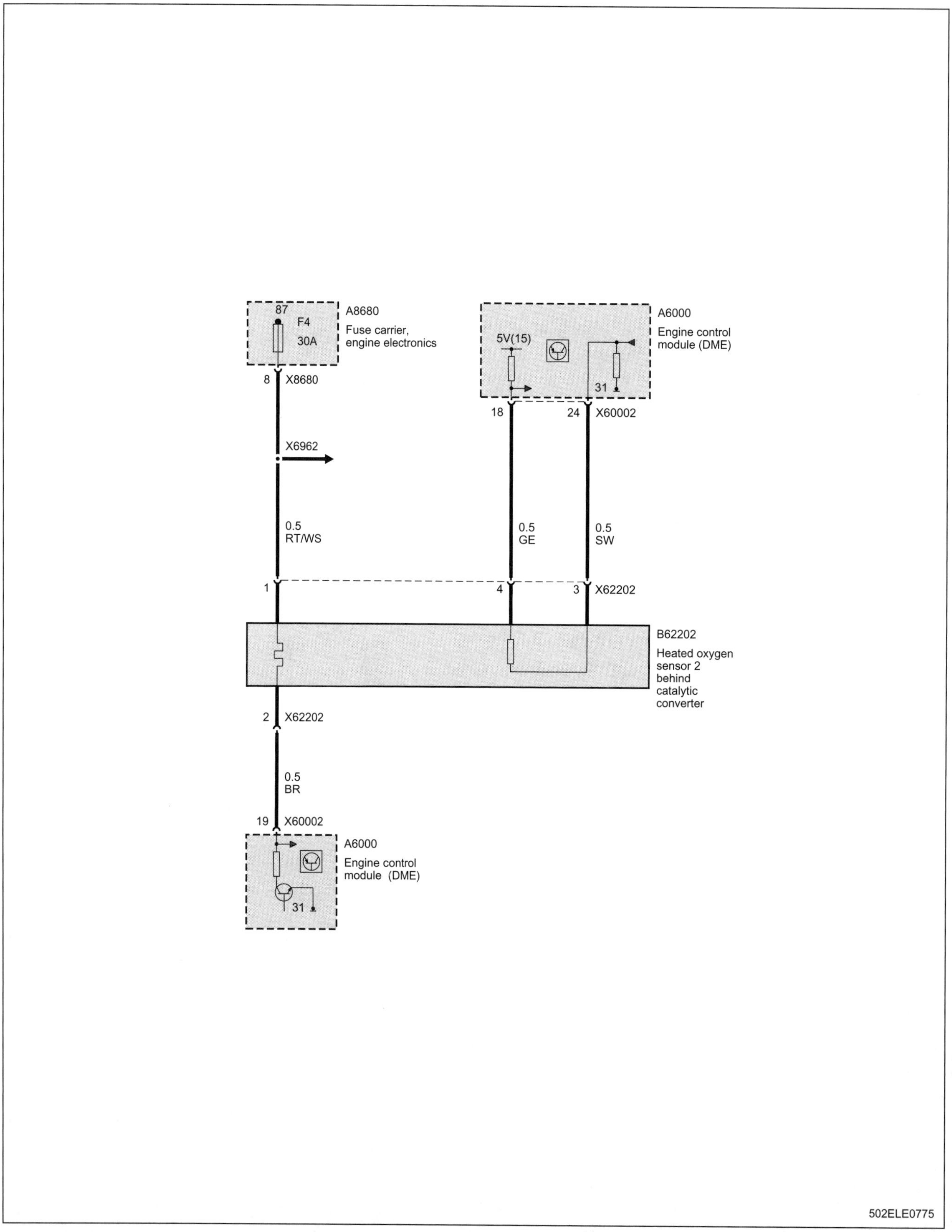

Engine Management (MS 43.0)
VANOS valves
(1 of 1)

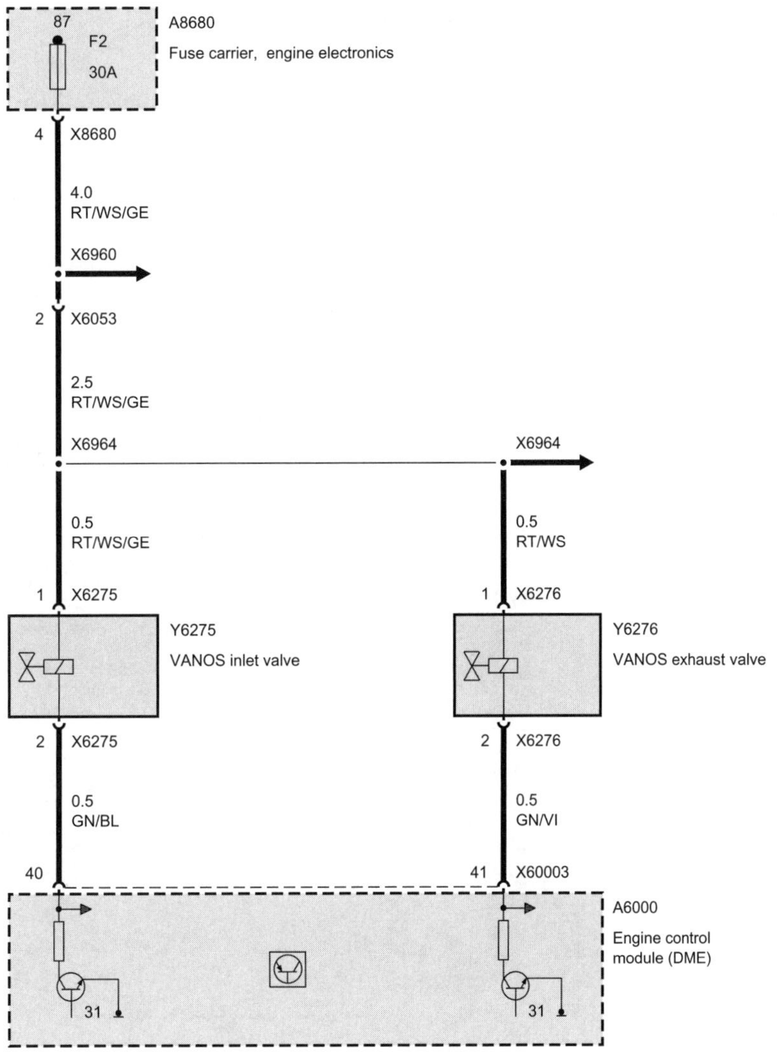
87
F2
30A
A8680
Fuse carrier, engine electronics
4
X8680
4.0
RT/WS/GE
X6960
2
X6053
2.5
RT/WS/GE
X6964
X6964
0.5
RT/WS/GE
0.5
RT/WS
1
X6275
1
X6276
Y6275
VANOS inlet valve
Y6276
VANOS exhaust valve
2
X6275
2
X6276
0.5
GN/BL
0.5
GN/VI
40
41
X60003
A6000
Engine control
module (DME)
31
31
502ELE0785

Engine Management (MS 43.0)
Camshaft position sensor
(1 of 1)

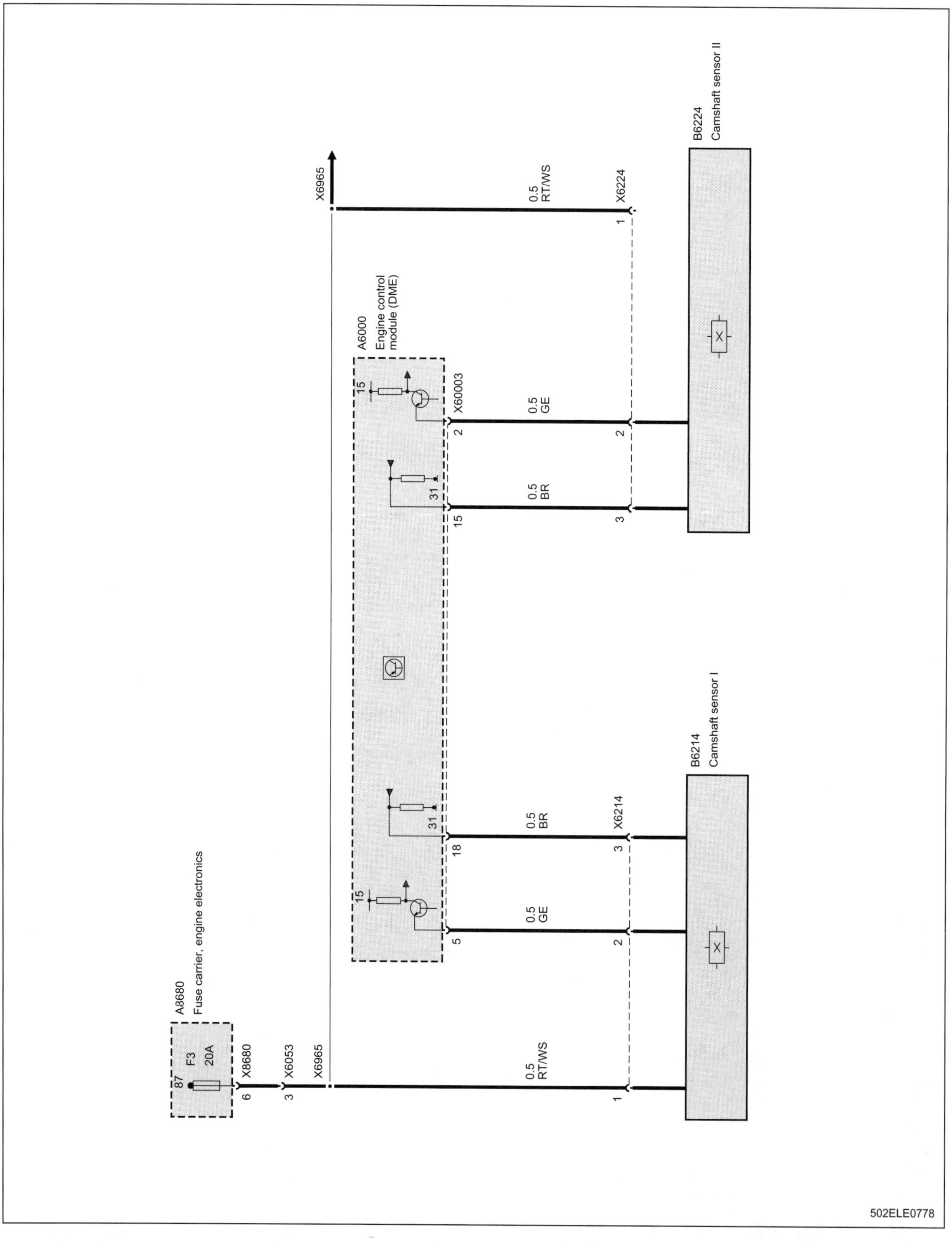

Engine Management (MS 43.0)
Crankshaft sensor
(1 of 1)

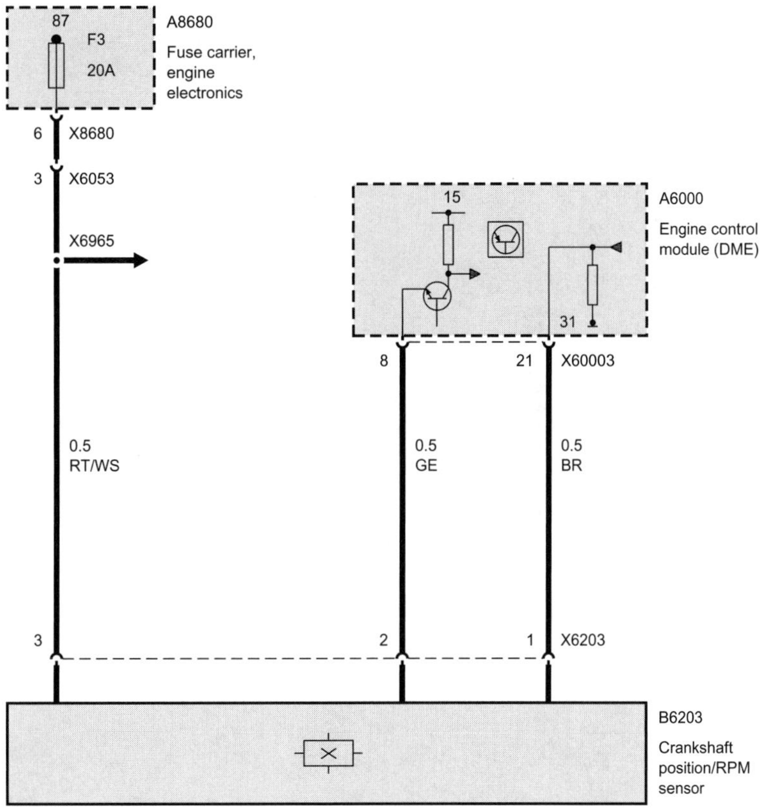

Engine Management (MS 43.0)
Knock sensor
(1 of 1)

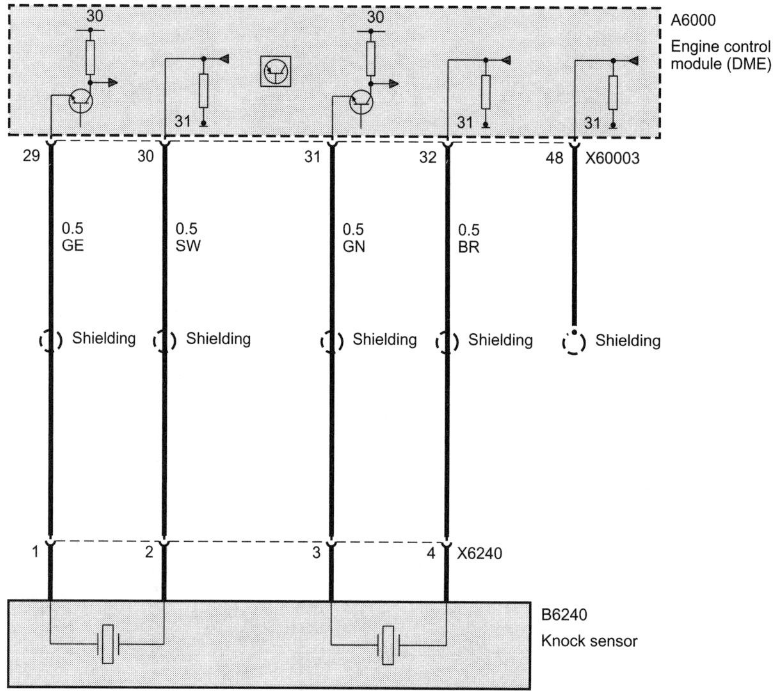
30
30
31
31
31
A6000
Engine control module (DME)
29
30
31
32
48
X60003
0.5
GE
0.5
SW
0.5
GN
0.5
BR
Shielding
Shielding
Shielding
Shielding
Shielding
1
2
3
4
X6240
B6240
Knock sensor
502ELE0776

Engine Management (MS 43.0)
Diagnostic module, fuel tank leakage
(1 of 1)

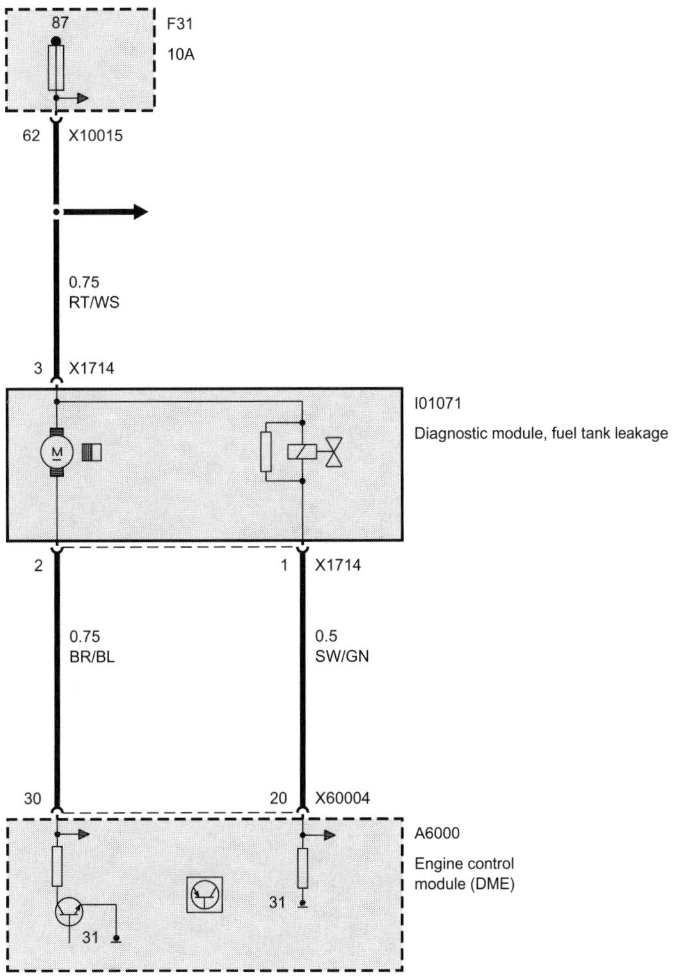

Engine Management (MS 43.0)
Evaporative emission valve
(1 of 1)

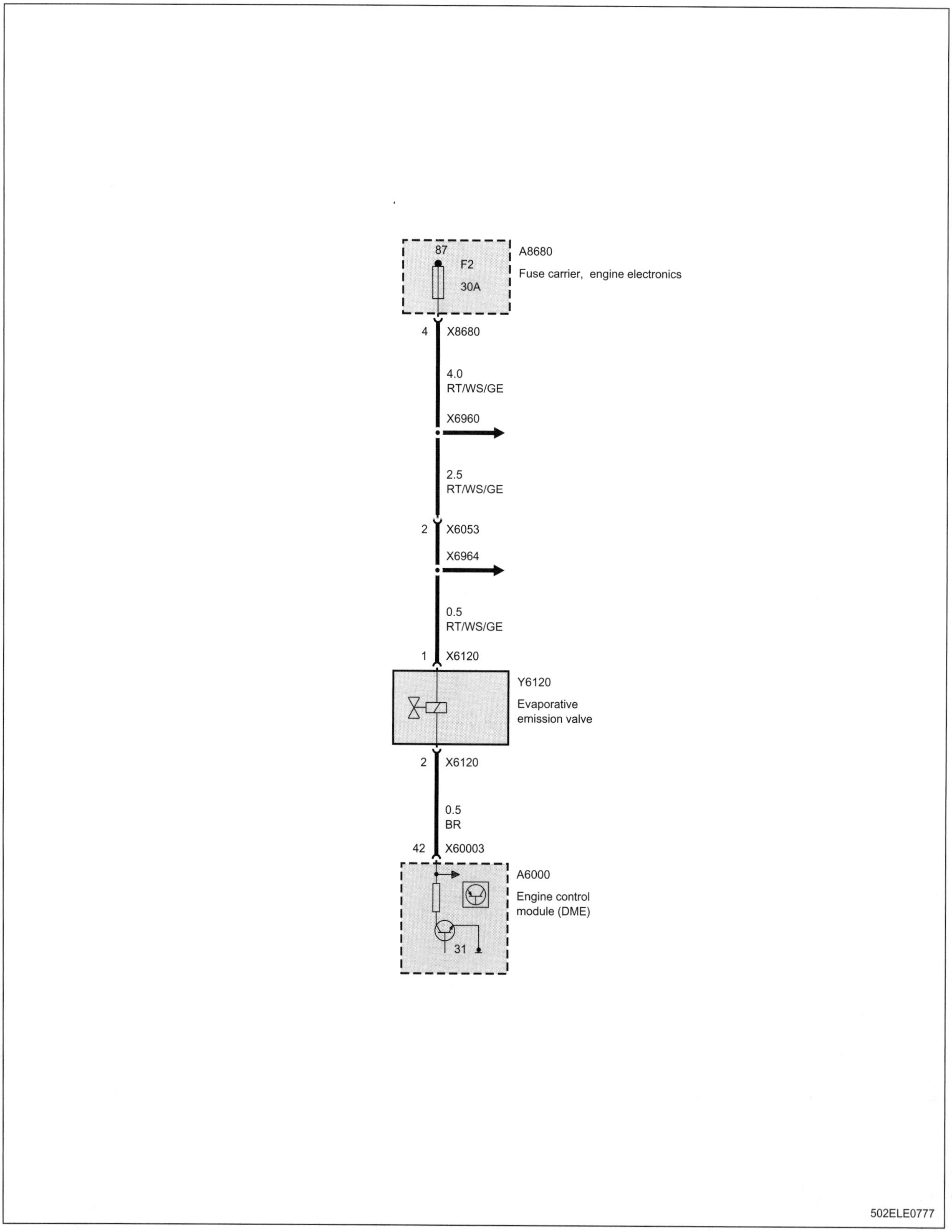

Engine Management (MS 43.0)
Secondary air system
(1 of 1)

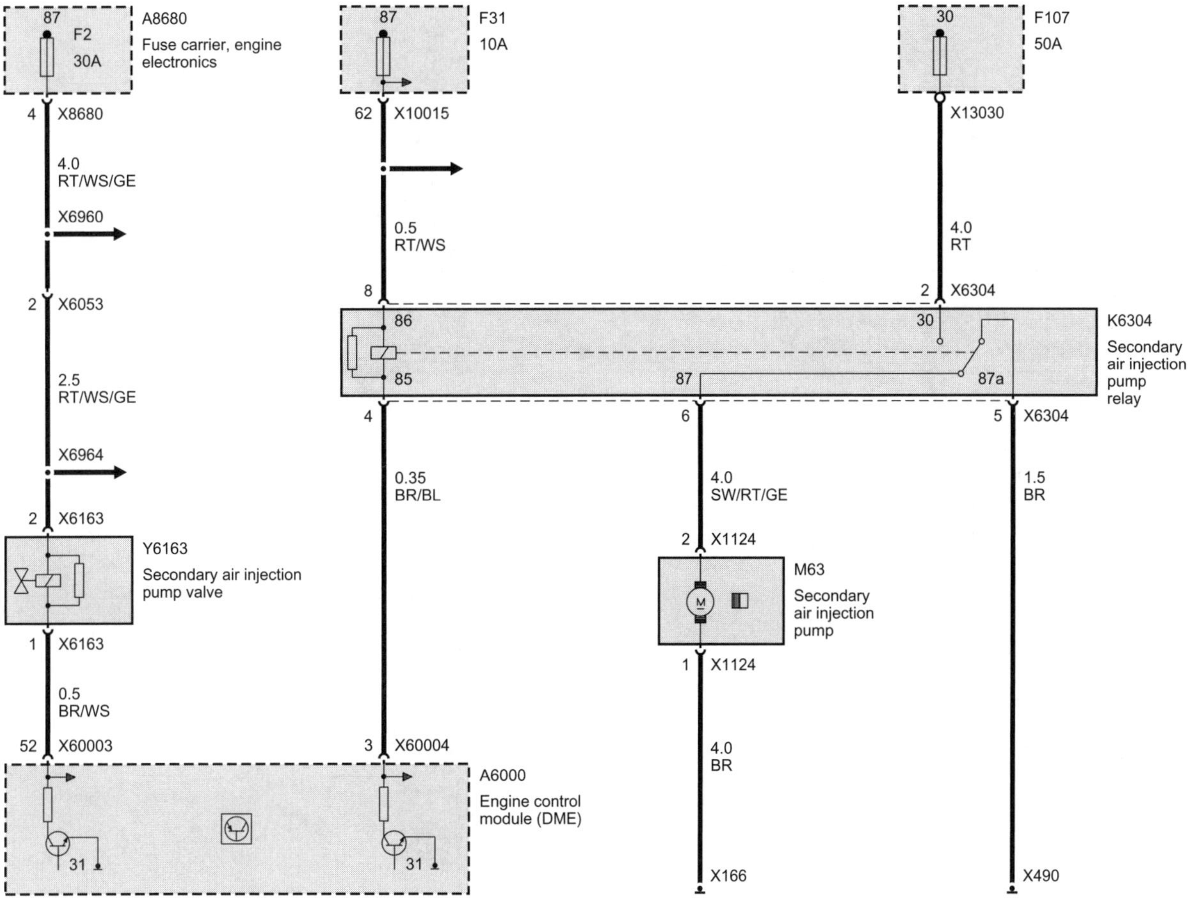

502ELE0784

Engine Management (MS 43.0)
Fuel injection valves
(1 of 3)

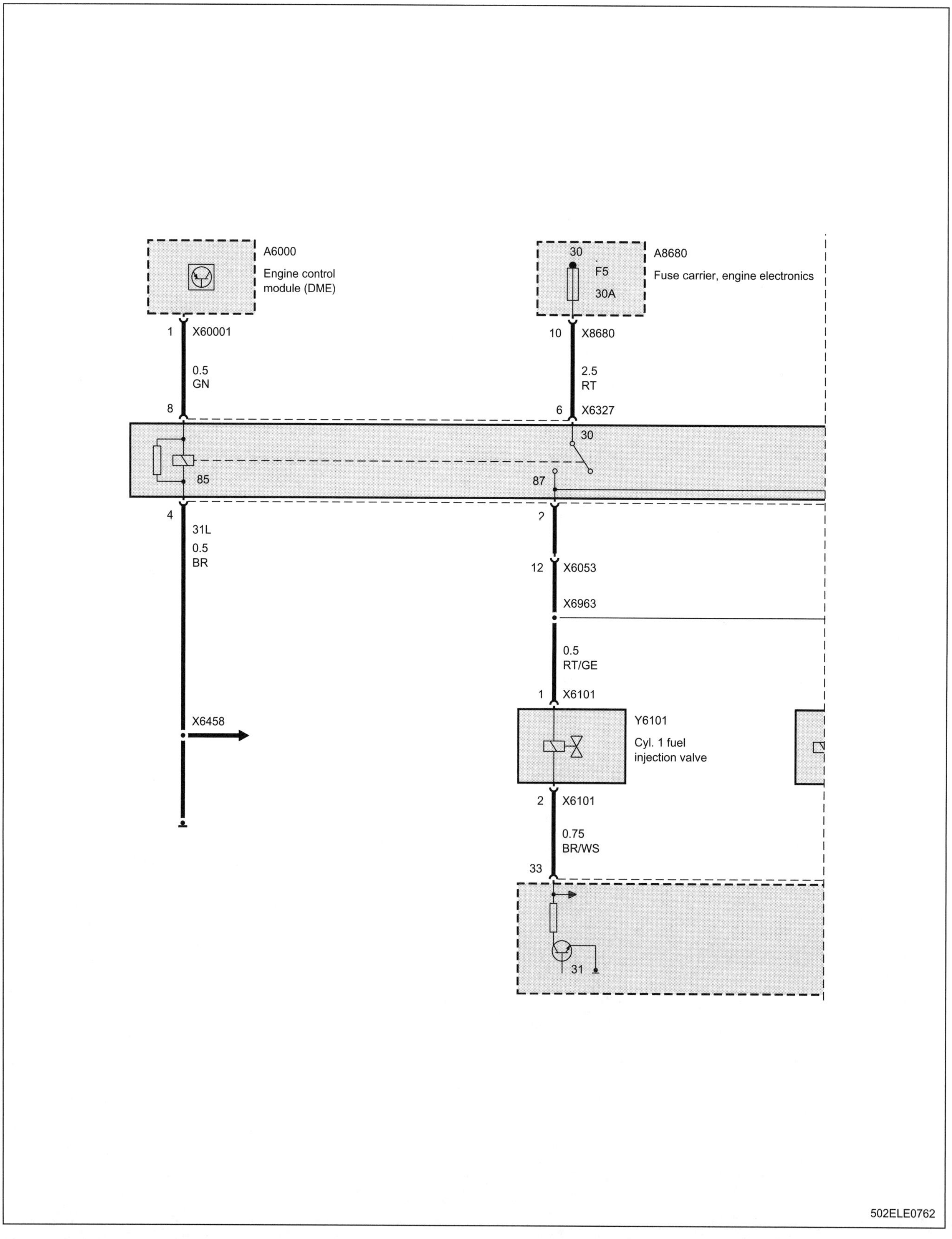

Engine Management (MS 43.0)
Fuel injection valves
(2 of 3)

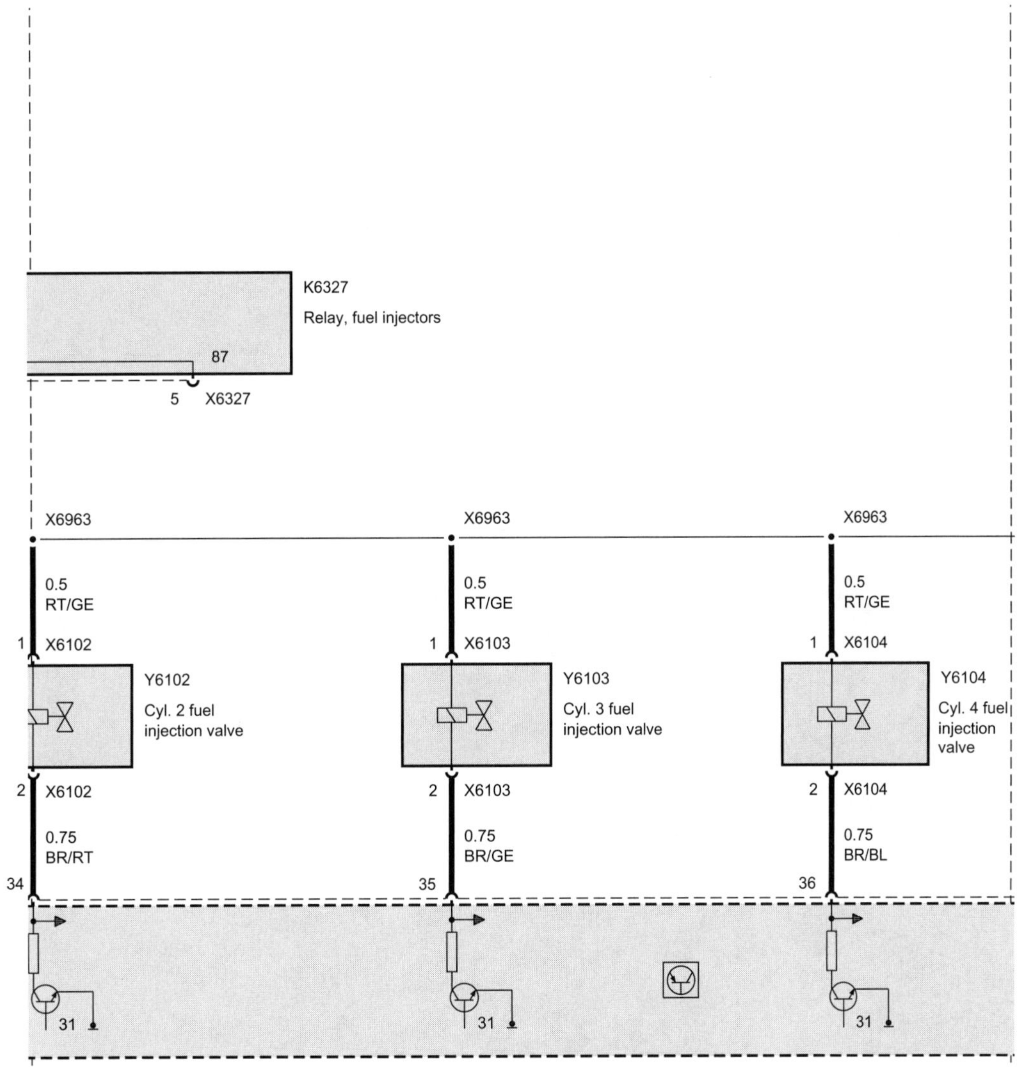

502ELE0763

Engine Management (MS 43.0)
Fuel injection valves
(3 of 3)

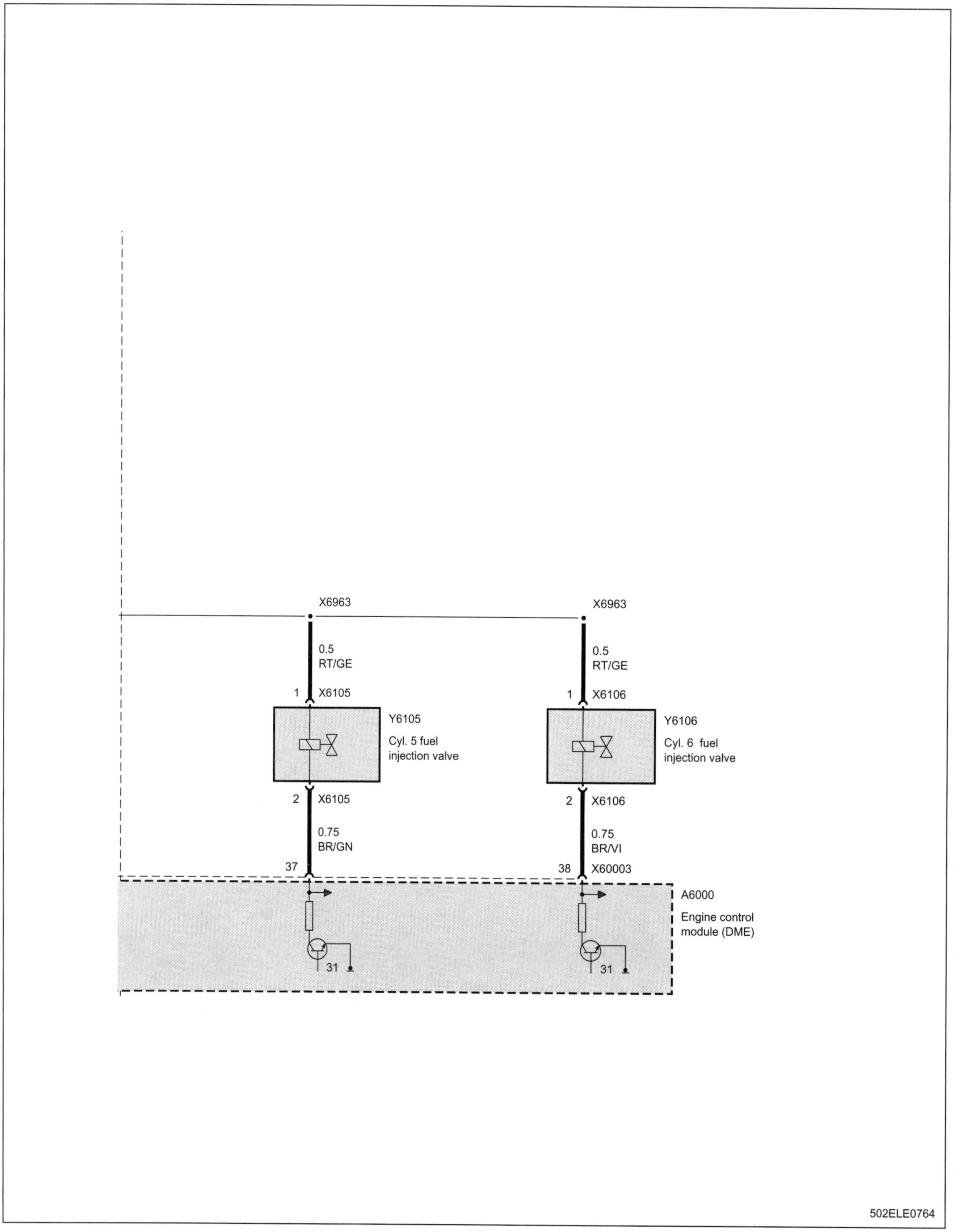

Engine Management (MS 43.0)
Ignition coils
(1 of 3)

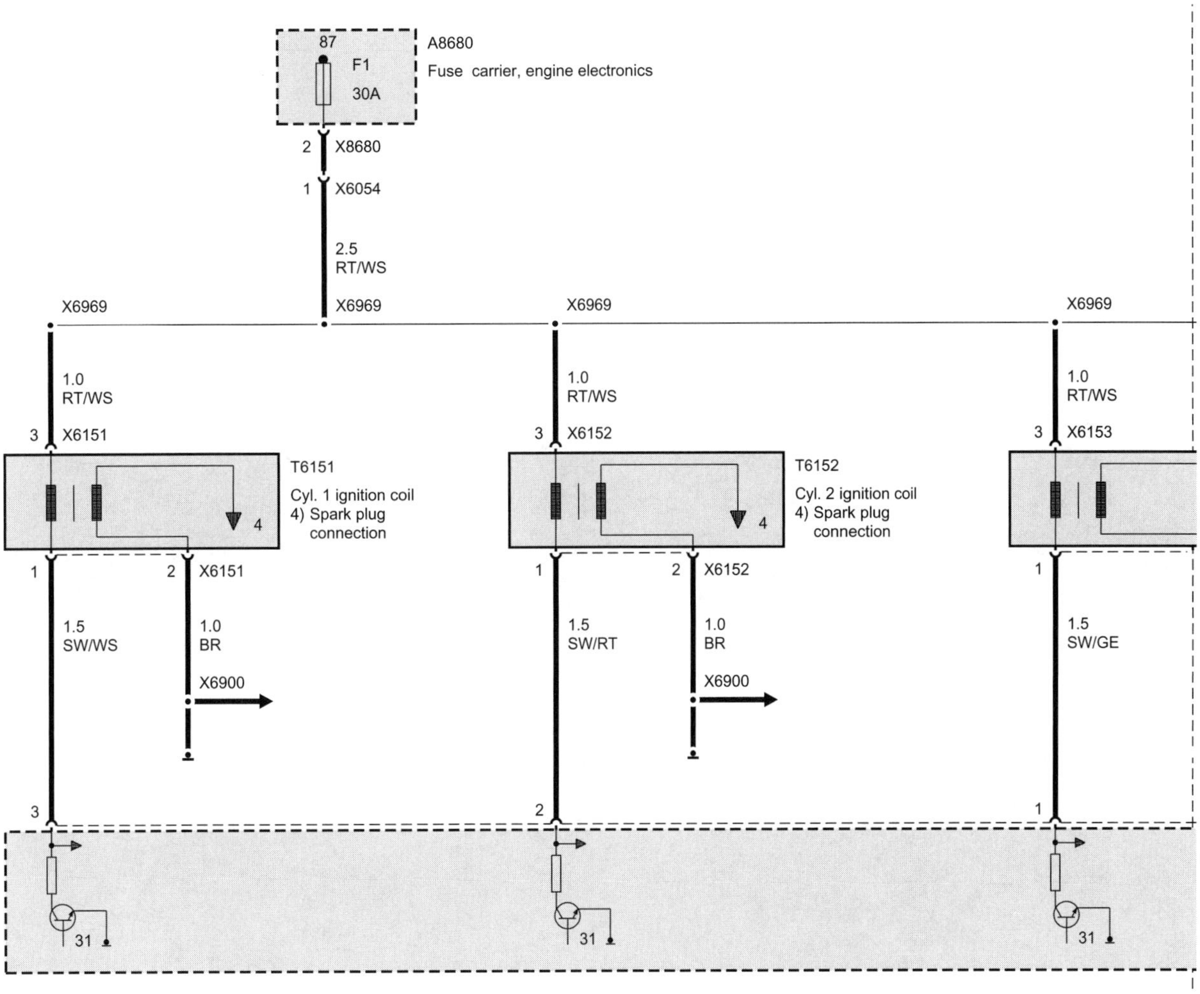
87
F1
30A
A8680
Fuse carrier, engine electronics
2 X8680
1 X6054
2.5
RT/WS
X6969
X6969
X6969
X6969
1.0
RT/WS
1.0
RT/WS
1.0
RT/WS
3 X6151
3 X6152
3 X6153
T6151
Cyl. 1 ignition coil
4) Spark plug connection
4
T6152
Cyl. 2 ignition coil
4) Spark plug connection
4
1
2 X6151
1
2 X6152
1
1.5
SW/WS
1.0
BR
X6900
1.5
SW/RT
1.0
BR
X6900
1.5
SW/GE
3
2
1
31
31
31
502ELE0788

Engine Management (MS 43.0)
Ignition coils
(2 of 3)

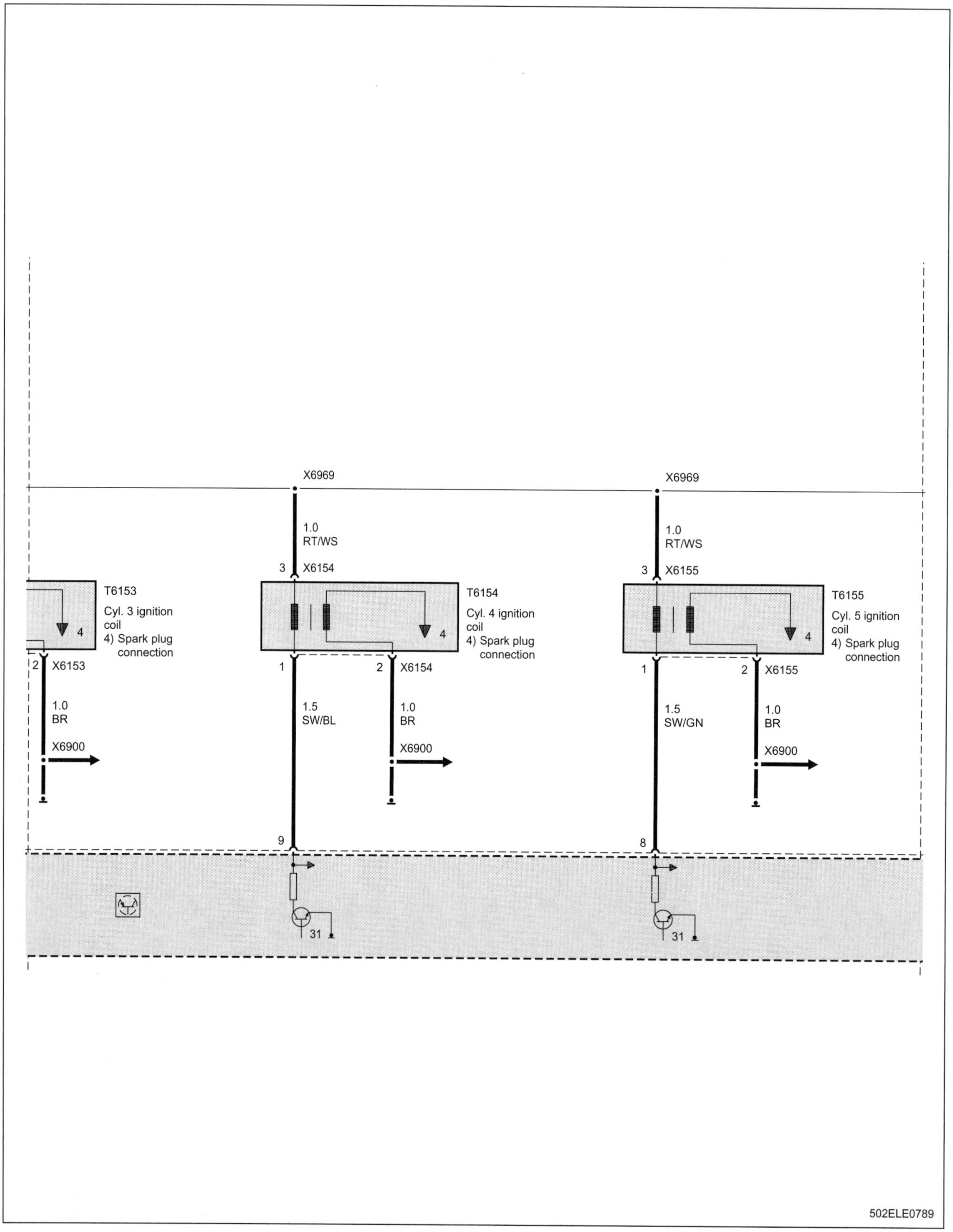
X6969
1.0
RT/WS
3
X6154
T6153
Cyl. 3 ignition coil
4) Spark plug connection
4
2
X6153
1.0
BR
X6900
T6154
Cyl. 4 ignition coil
4) Spark plug connection
1
2
X6154
1.5
SW/BL
1.0
BR
X6900
9
31
X6969
1.0
RT/WS
3
X6155
T6155
Cyl. 5 ignition coil
4) Spark plug connection
1
2
X6155
1.5
SW/GN
1.0
BR
X6900
8
31
502ELE0789

Engine Management (MS 43.0)
Ignition coils
(3 of 3)

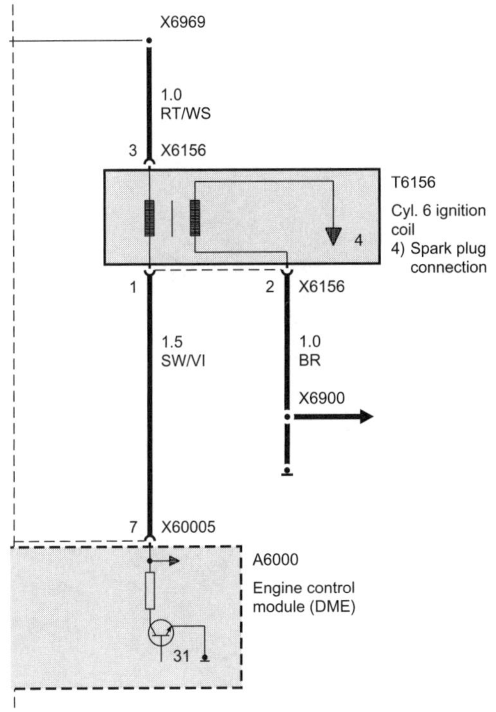
X6969
1.0
RT/WS
3
X6156
T6156
Cyl. 6 ignition coil
4) Spark plug connection
4
1
2
X6156
1.5
SW/VI
1.0
BR
X6900
7
X60005
A6000
Engine control module (DME)
31
502ELE0790

Engine Management (MS 43.0)
Engine oil temperature sensor
(1 of 1)

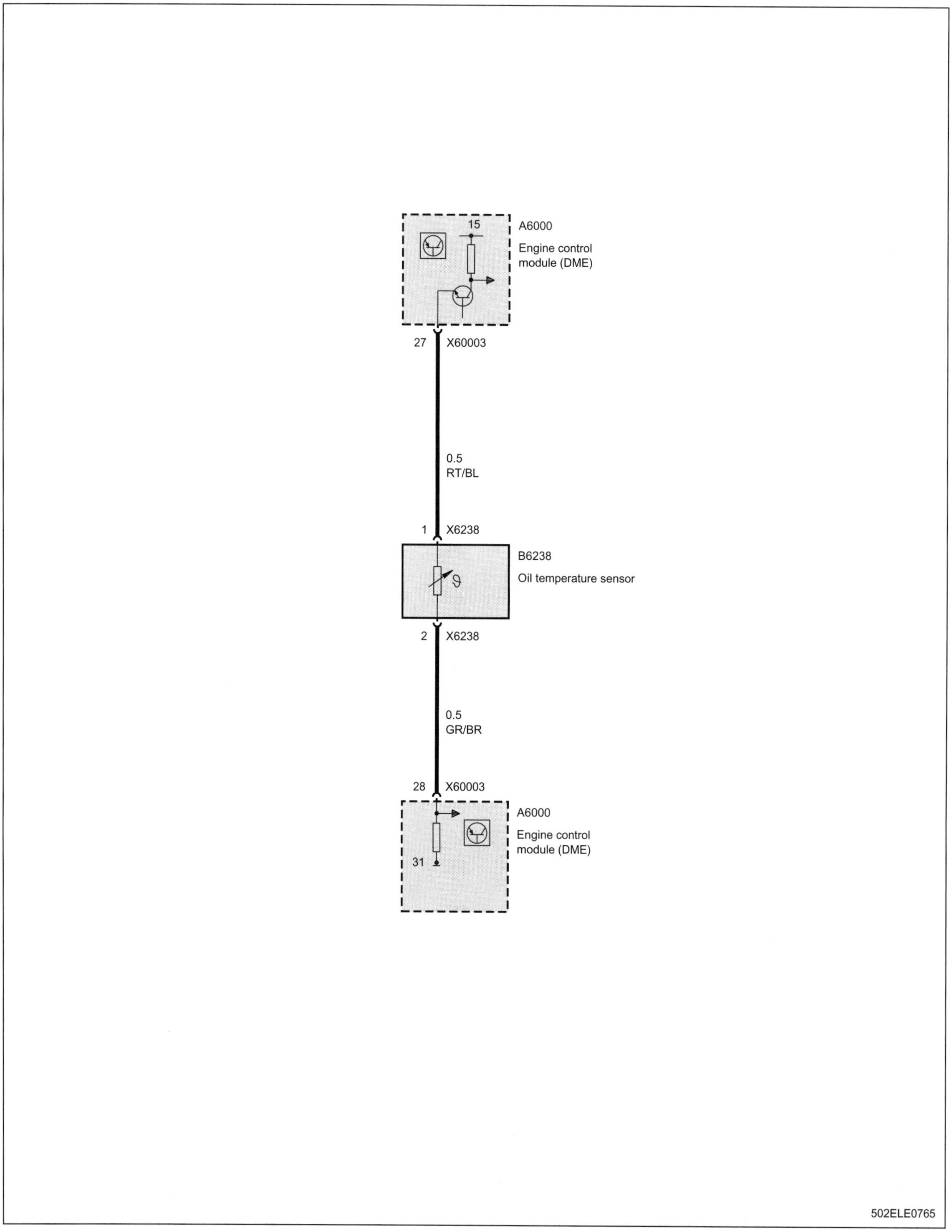

Engine Management (MS 43.0)
Starter
(1 of 1)

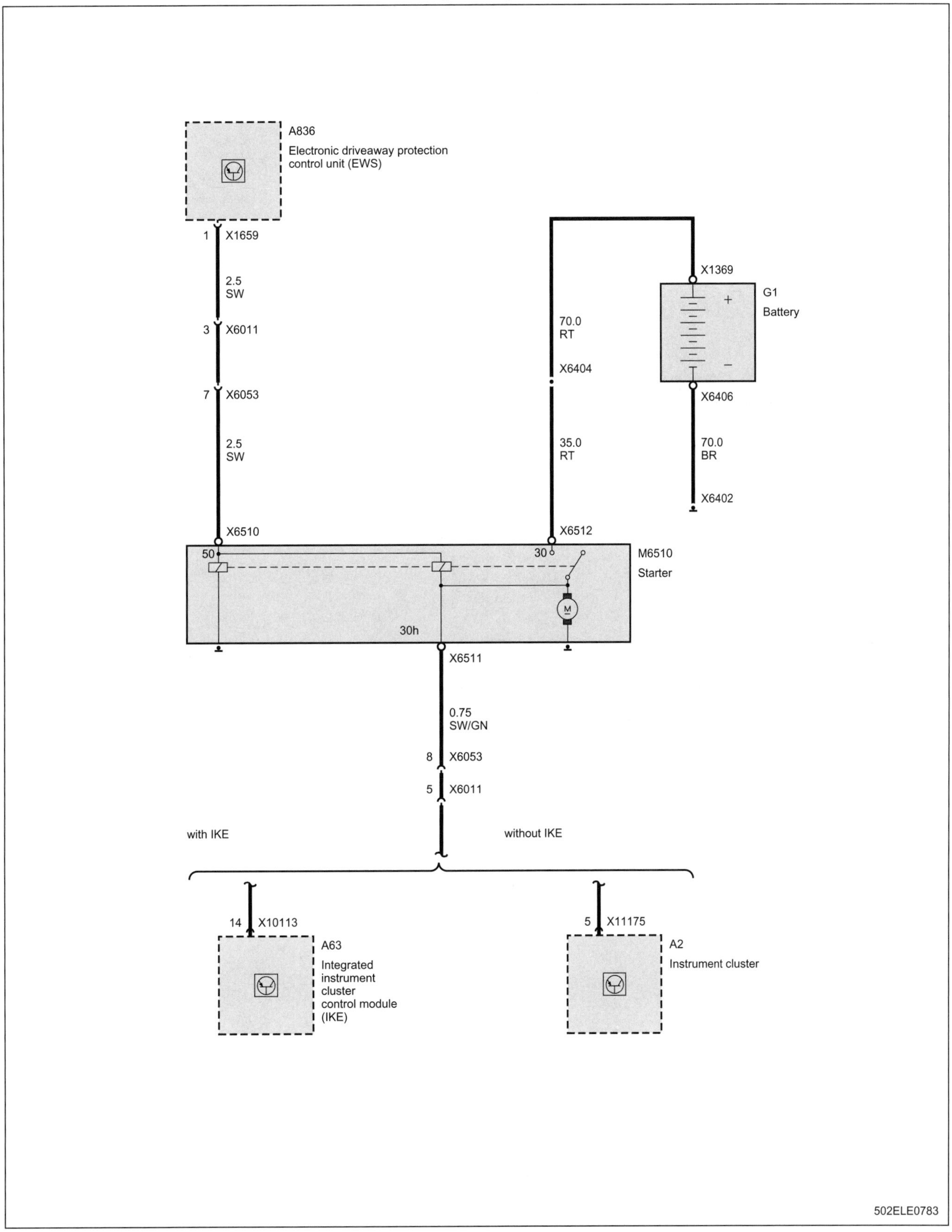
A836
Electronic driveaway protection control unit (EWS)
1 X1659
2.5 SW
3 X6011
7 X6053
2.5 SW
X6510
X1369
G1
Battery
+
–
70.0 RT
X6404
35.0 RT
X6406
70.0 BR
X6402
X6512
50
30
M6510
Starter
M
30h
X6511
0.75 SW/GN
8 X6053
5 X6011
with IKE
without IKE
14 X10113
A63
Integrated instrument cluster control module (IKE)
5 X11175
A2
Instrument cluster
502ELE0783

Engine Management (MS 43.0)
Power, ground splice X221
(1 of 1)

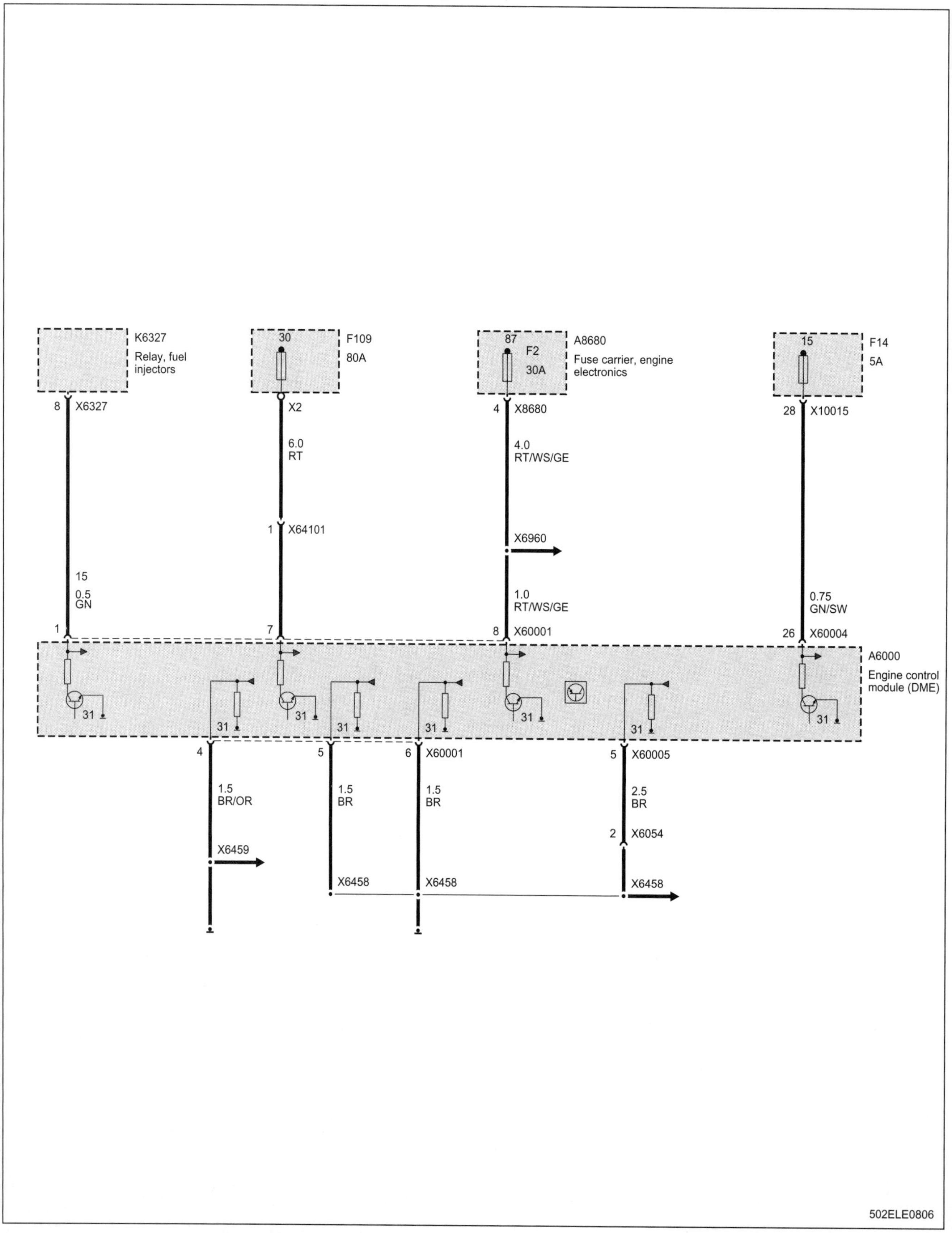

Engine Management (MS 43.0)
DME/climate control interfaces
(1 of 1)

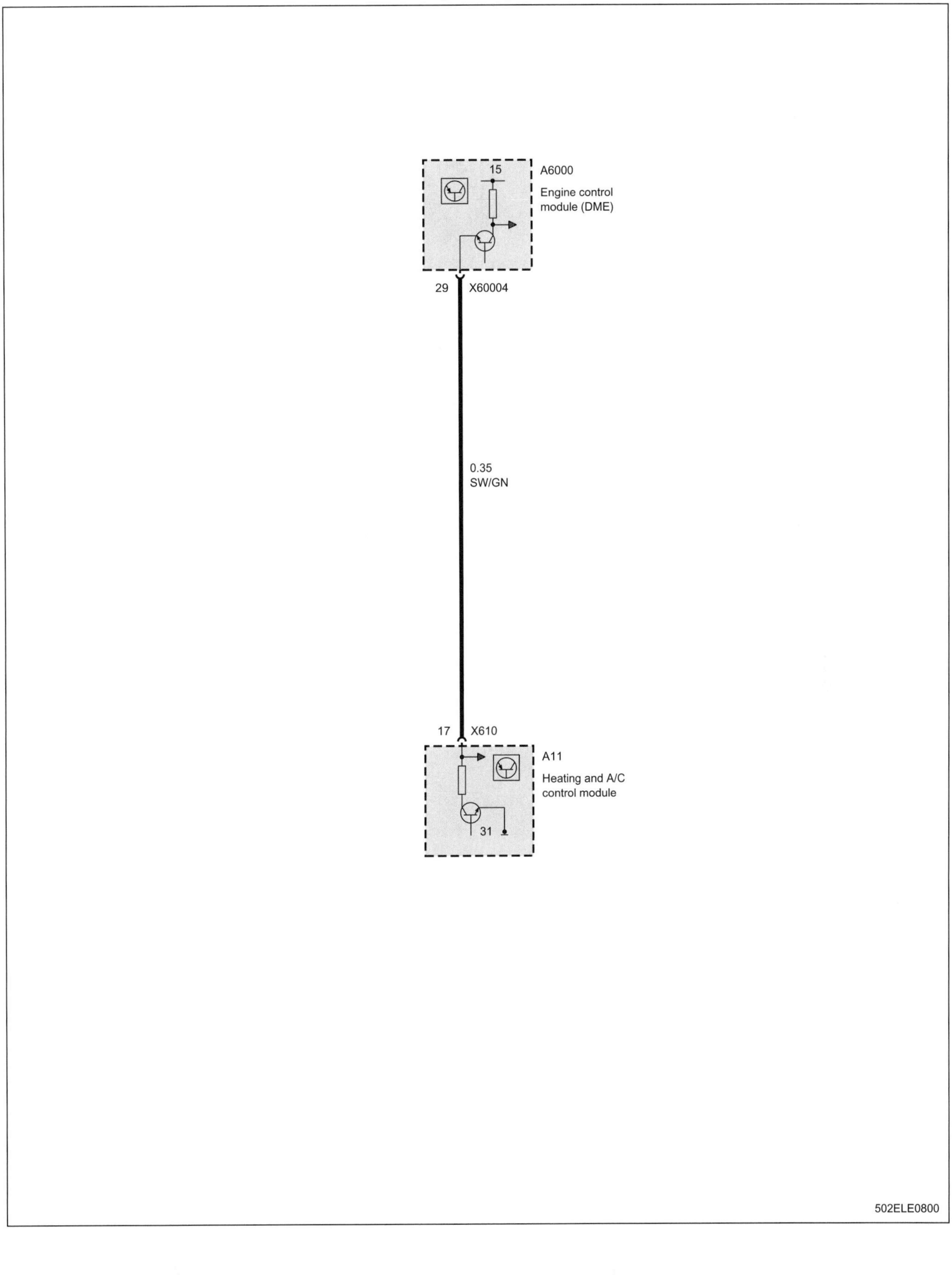

Engine Management (M 5.2)
A6000 Engine control module (DME)
(1 of 3)

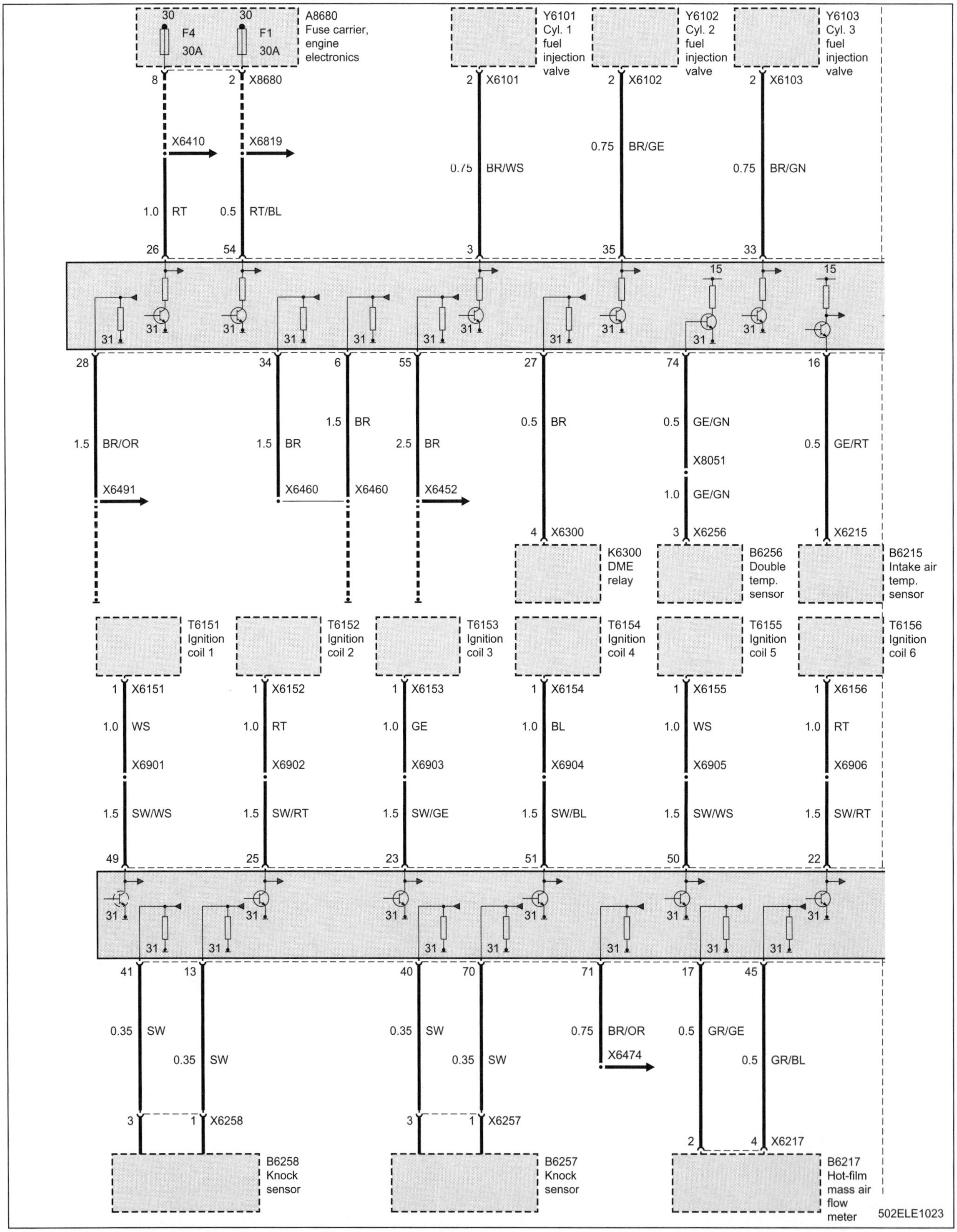

Engine Management (M 5.2)
A6000 Engine control module (DME)
(2 of 3)

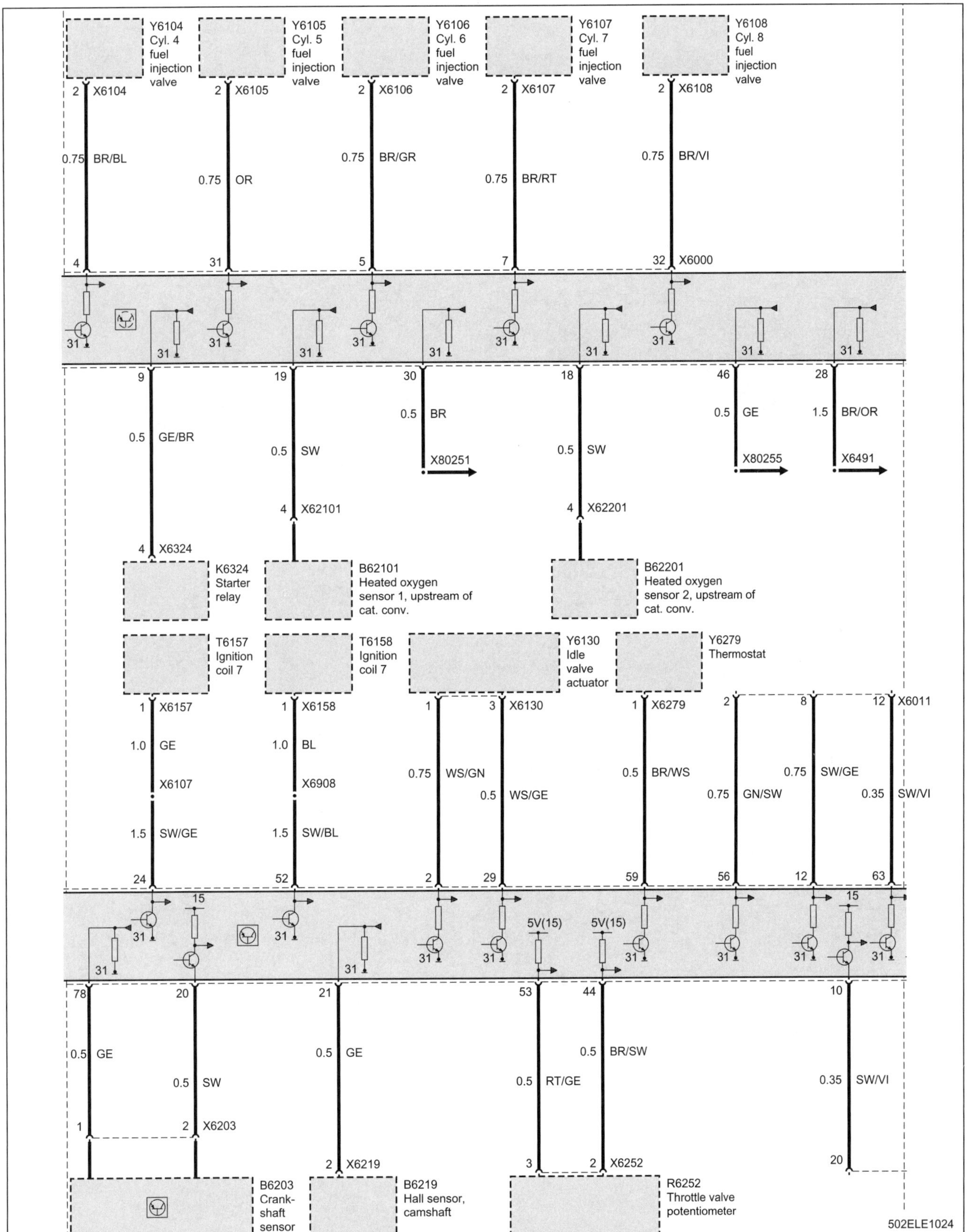

Engine Management (M 5.2)
A6000 Engine control module (DME)
(3 of 3)

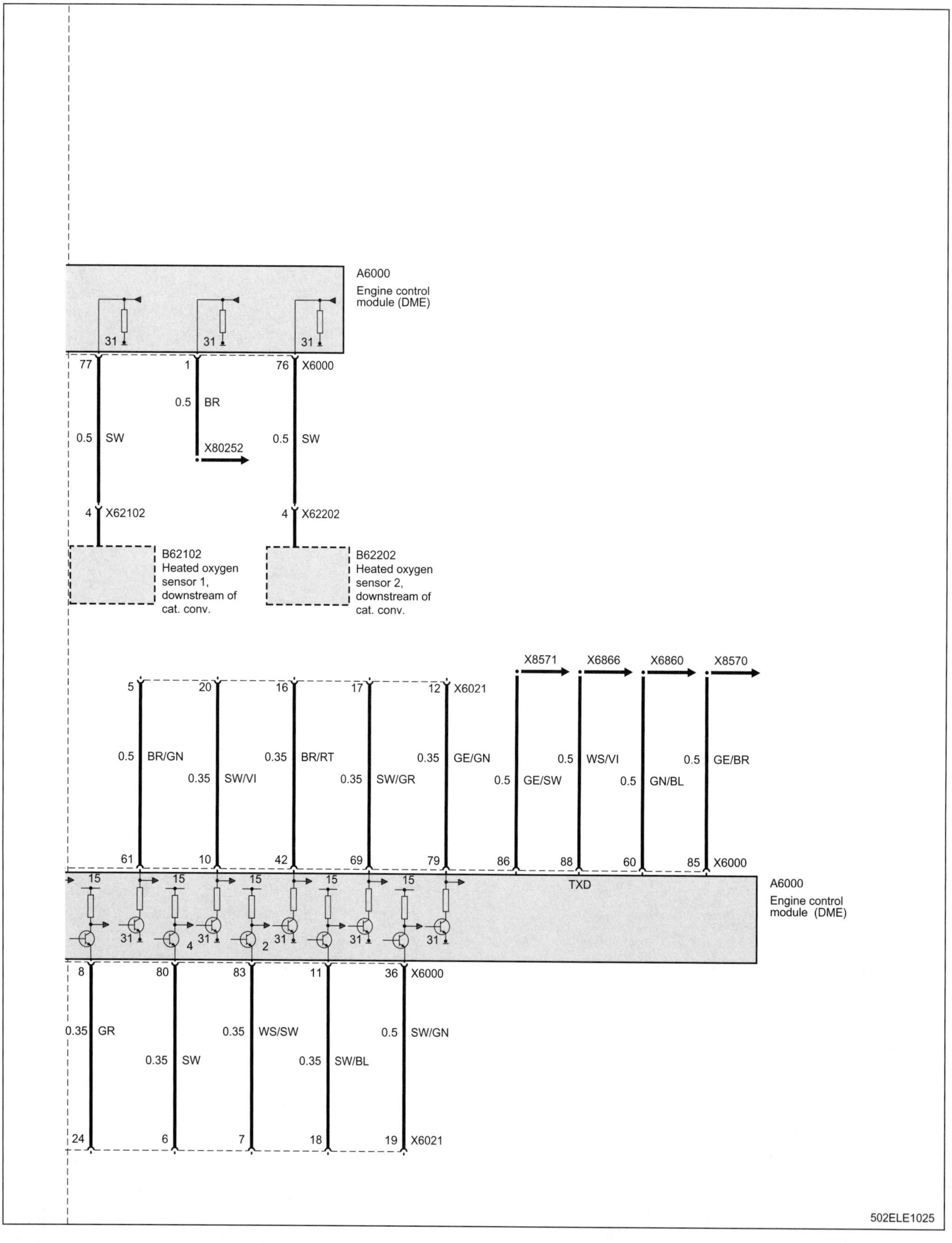

Engine Management (M 5.2)
OBDII plug
(1 of 1)

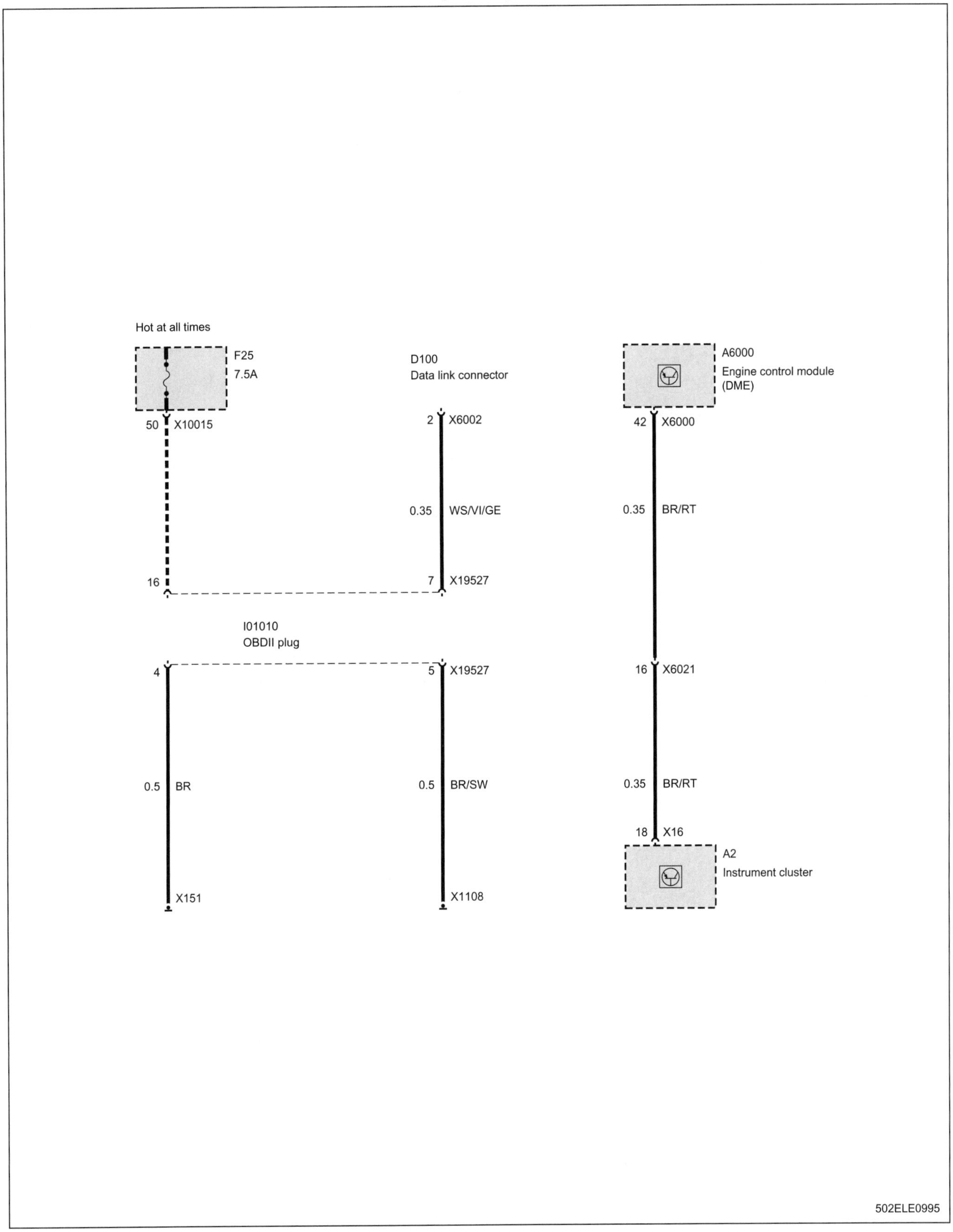
Hot at all times
F25
7.5A
50
X10015
16
D100
Data link connector
2
X6002
0.35
WS/VI/GE
7
X19527
A6000
Engine control module
(DME)
42
X6000
0.35
BR/RT
I01010
OBDII plug
4
5
X19527
16
X6021
0.5
BR
0.5
BR/SW
0.35
BR/RT
18
X16
A2
Instrument cluster
X151
X1108
502ELE0995

Engine Management (M 5.2)
Data link connector pin assignments
(1 of 3)

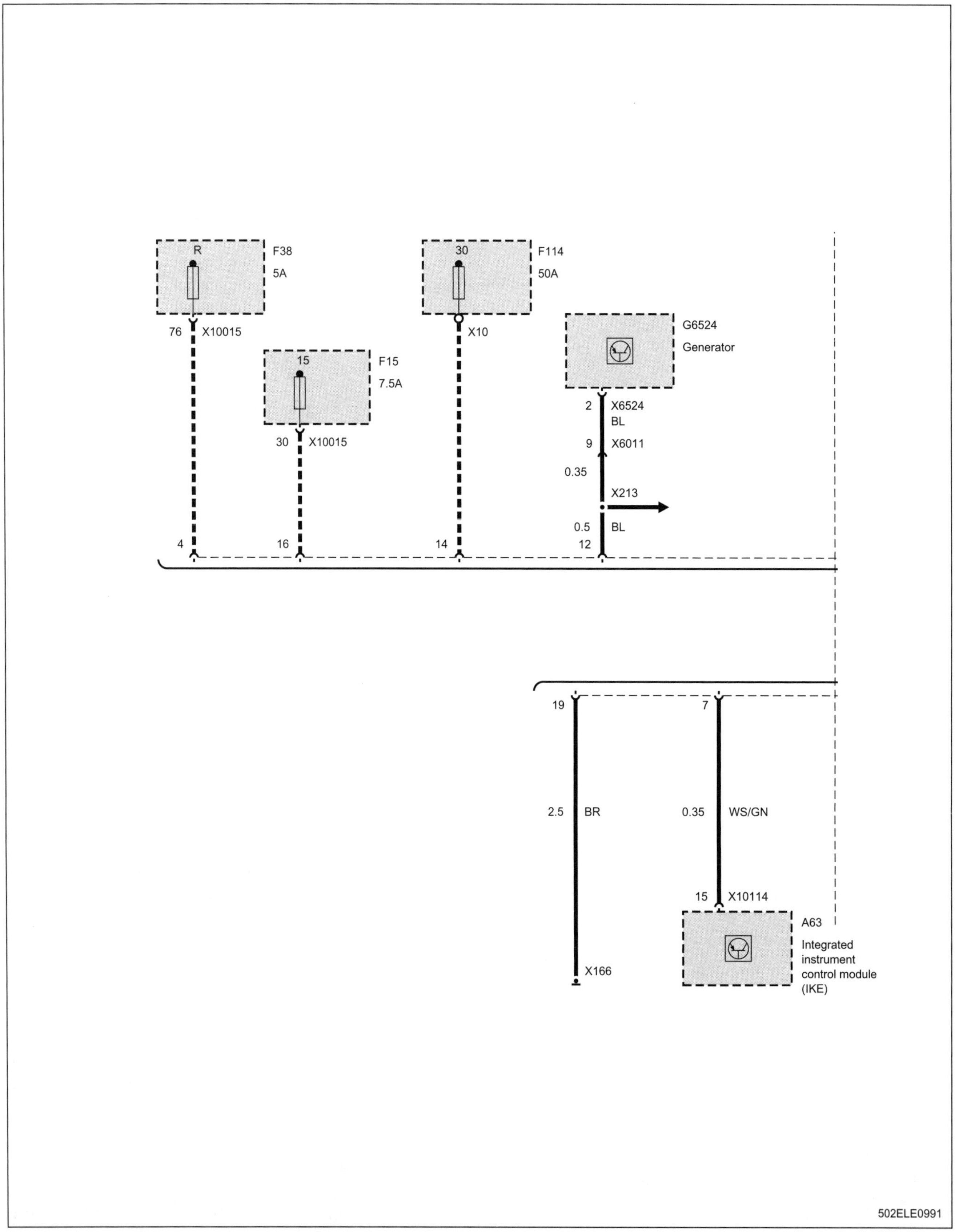

Engine Management (M 5.2)
Data link connector pin assignments
(2 of 3)

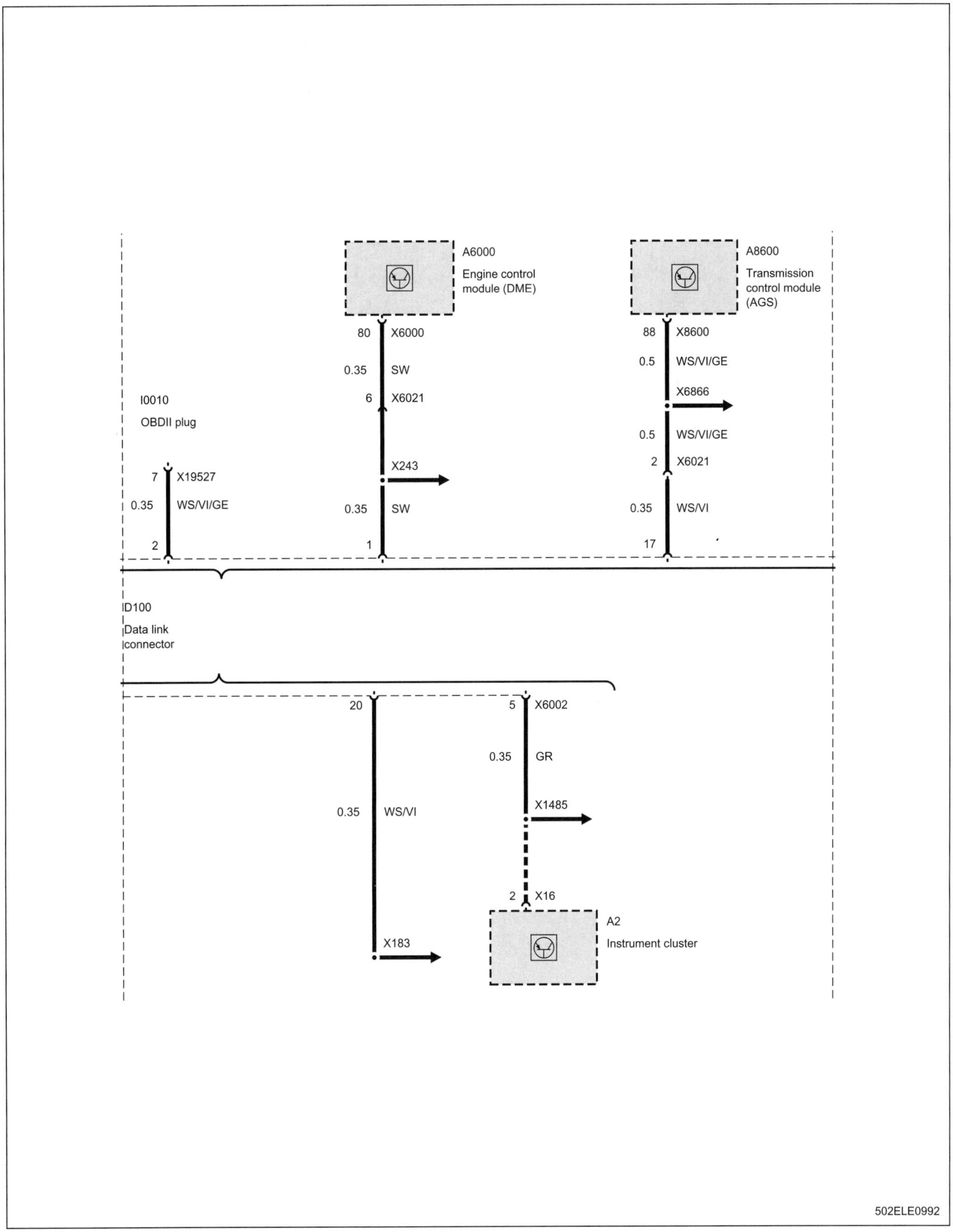

Engine Management (M 5.2)
Data link connector pin assignments
(3 of 3)

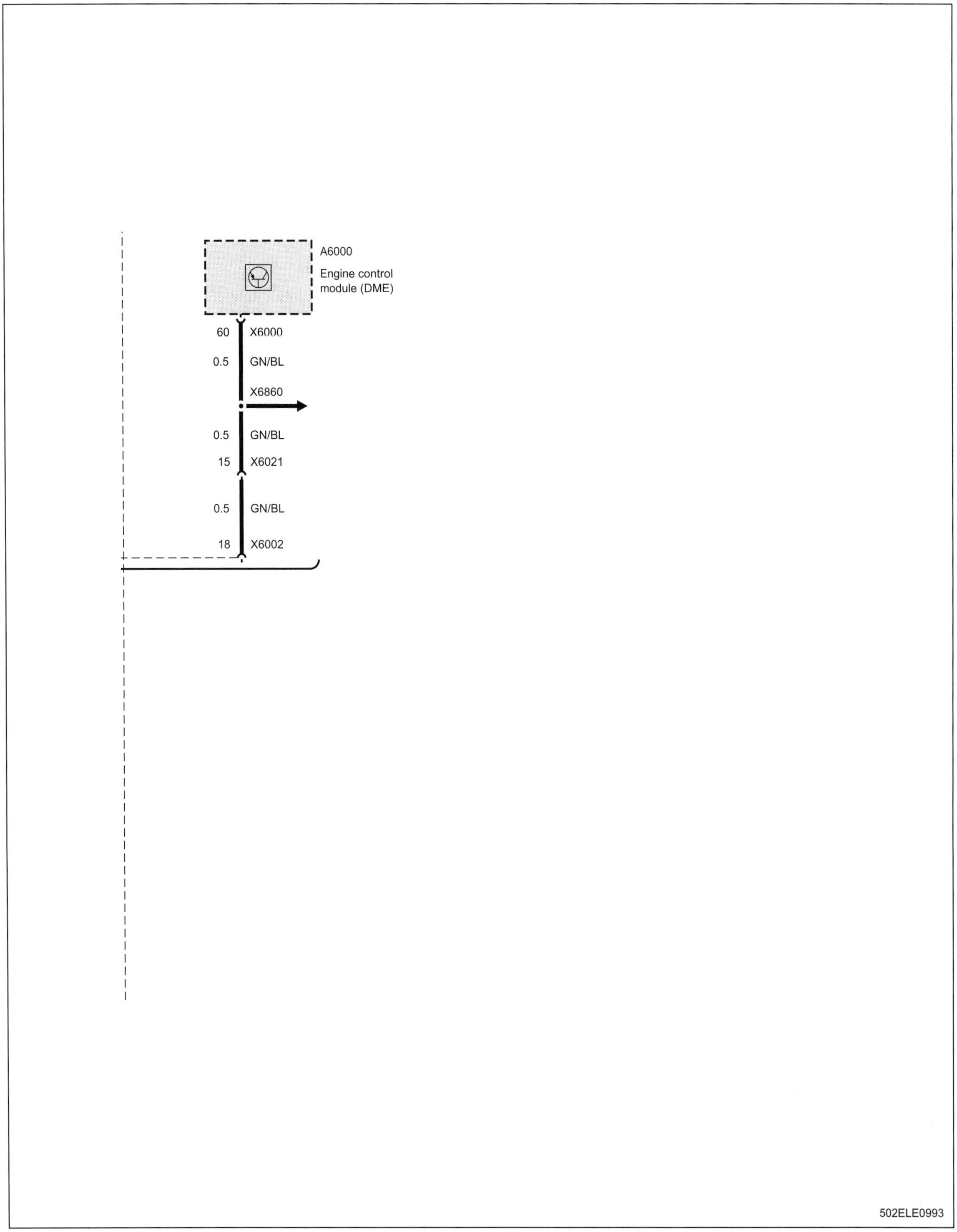

Engine Management (M 5.2)
Engine control module relay
(1 of 1)

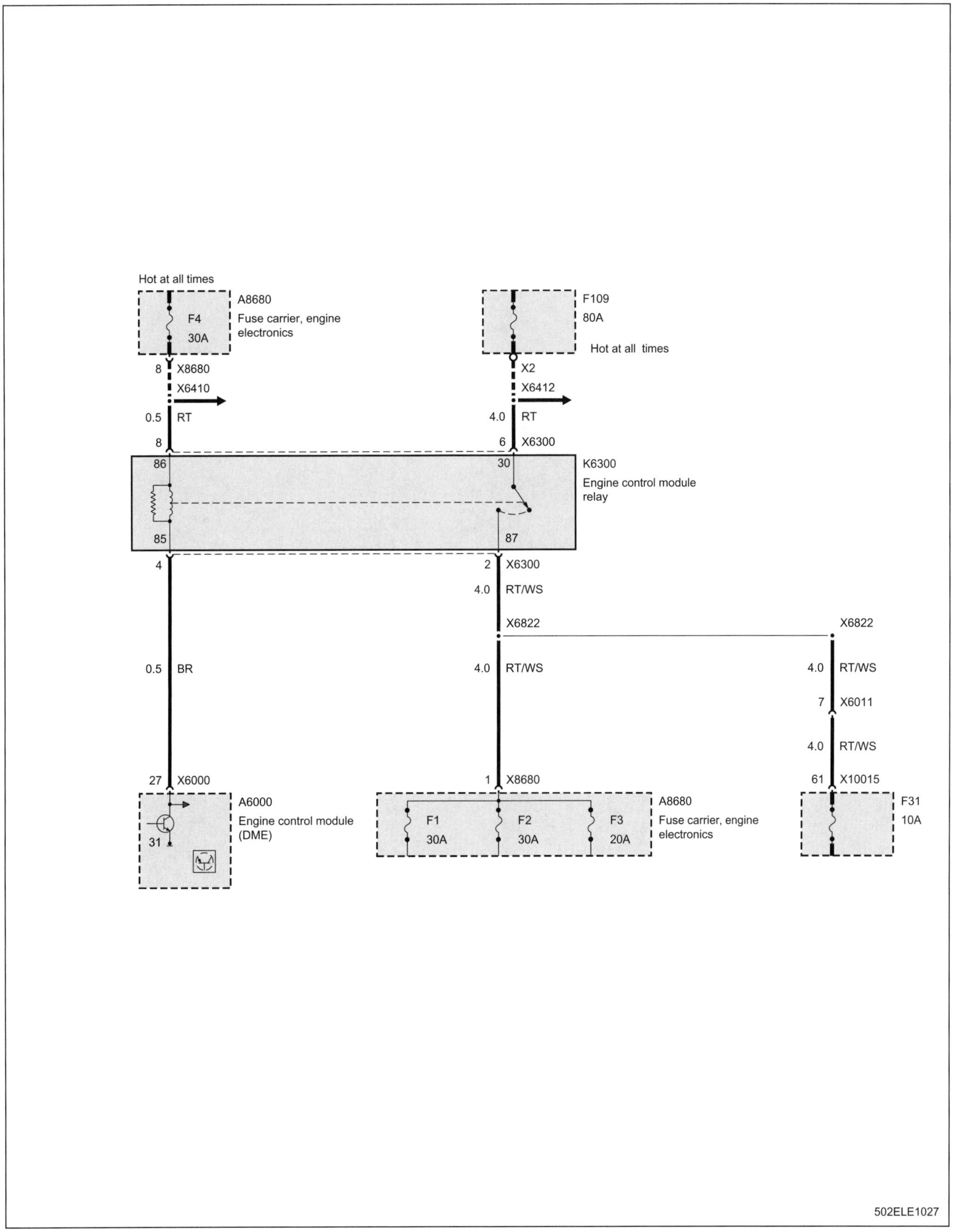

Engine Management (M 5.2)
Level sensor
(1 of 1)

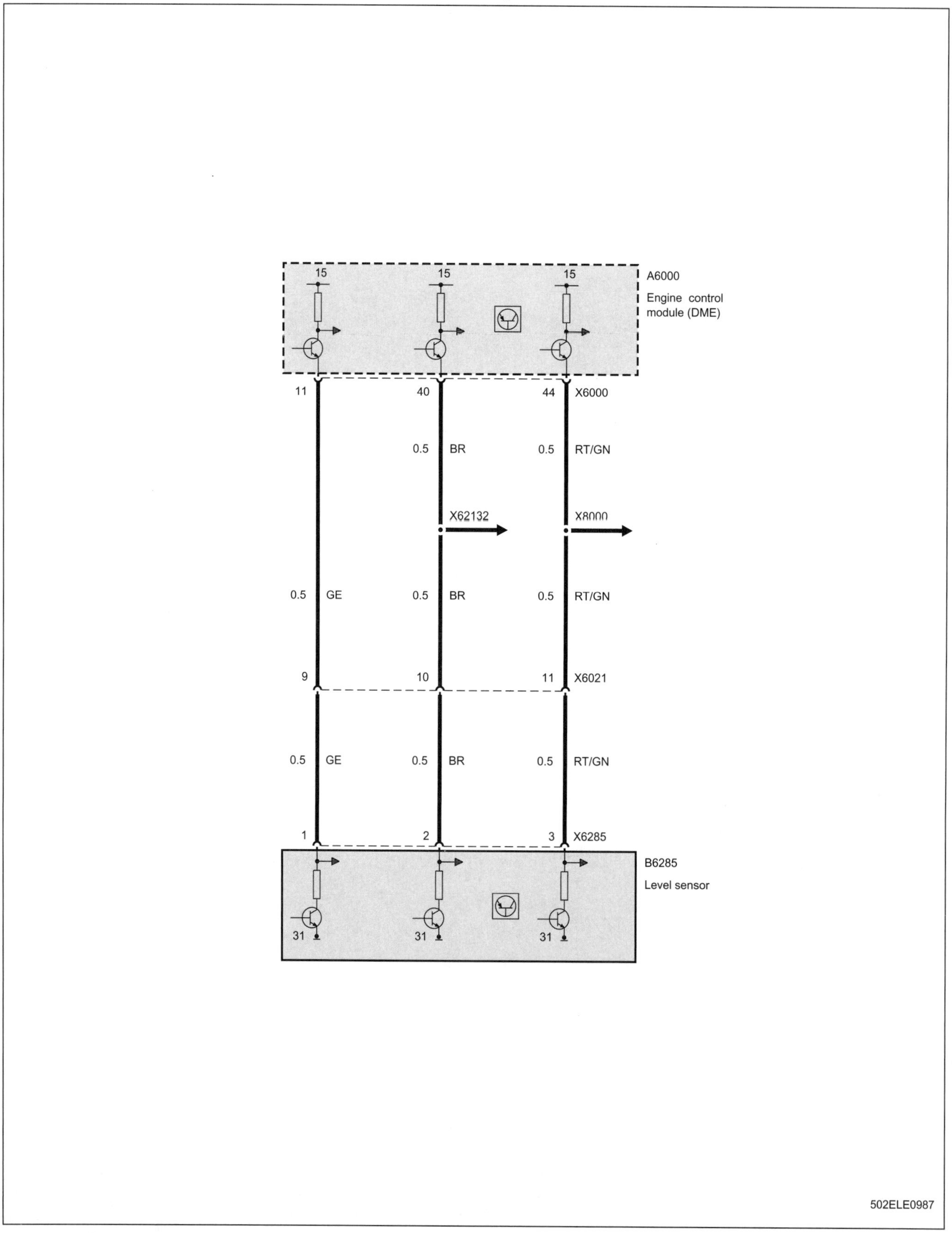

Engine Management (M 5.2)
Power, DME control module
(1 of 1)

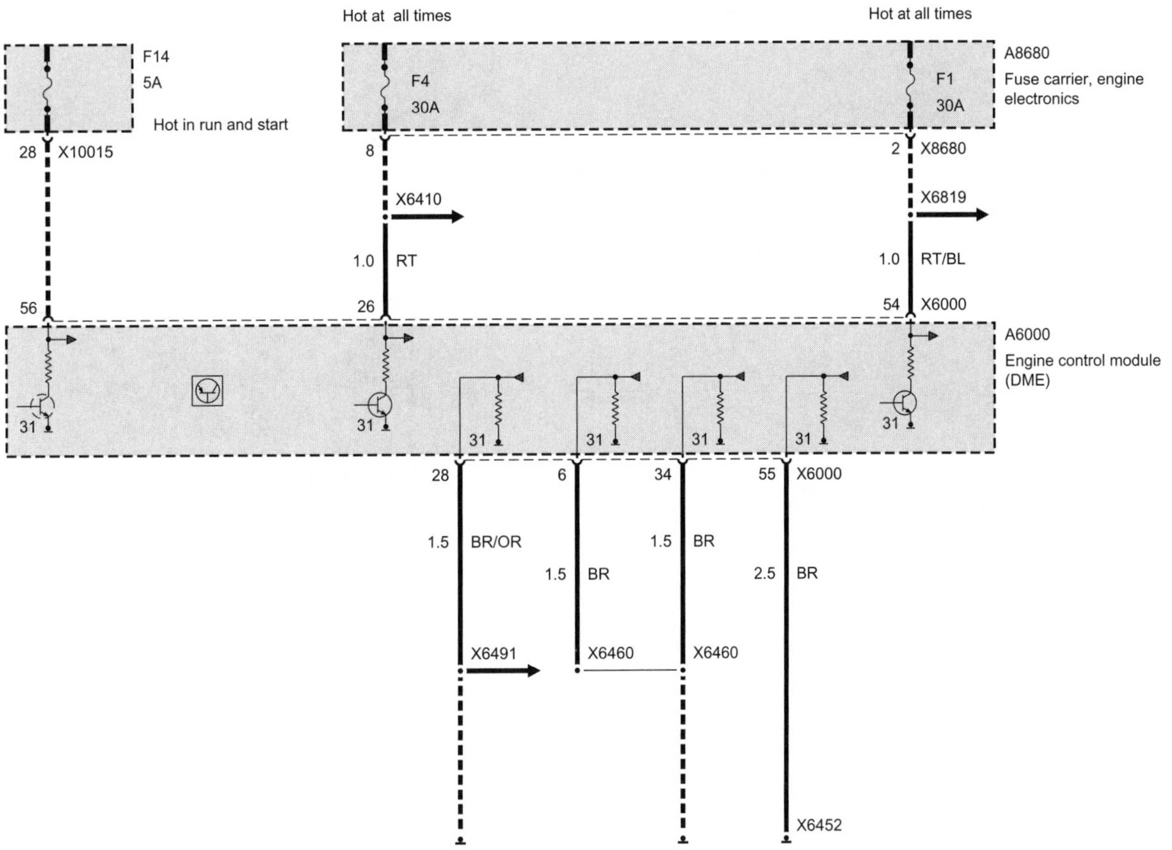

502ELE0996

Engine Management (M 5.2)
Fuel pump
(1 of 1)

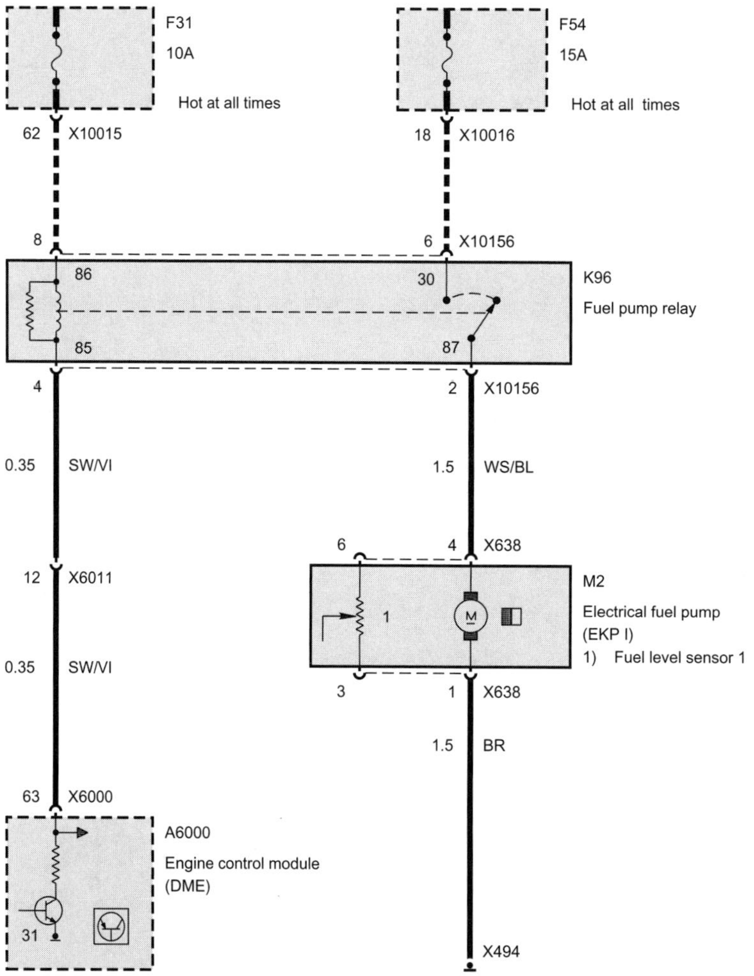

502ELE1022

Engine Management (M 5.2)
Idle speed control valve
(1 of 1)

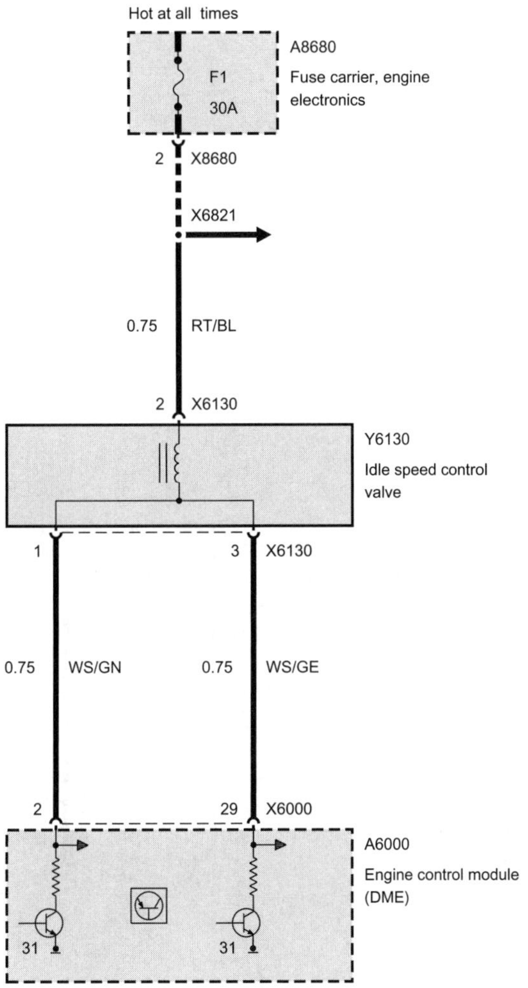

502ELE0998

Engine Management (M 5.2)
Hot-film mass air flow sensor
(1 of 1)

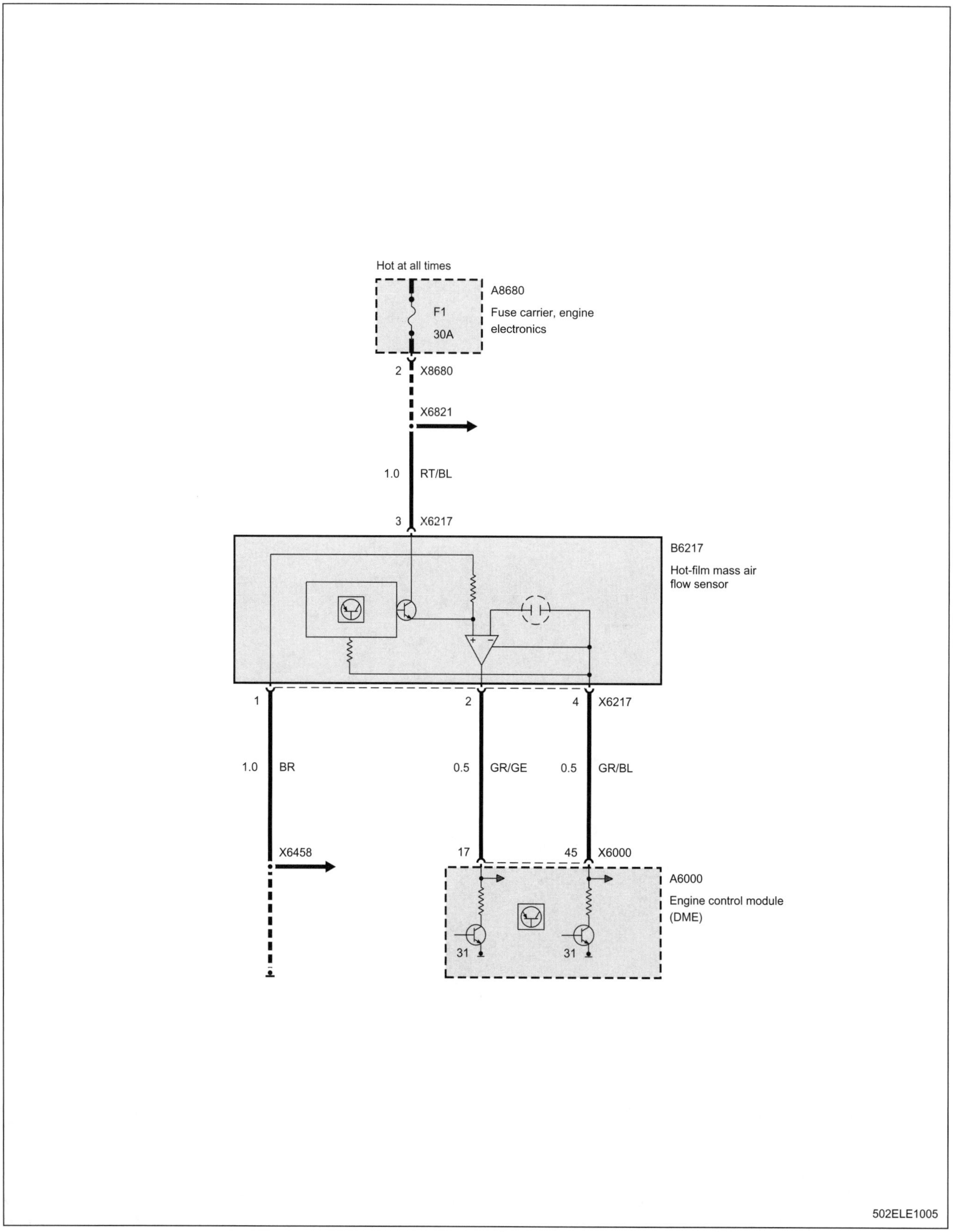

Engine Management (M 5.2)
Intake air temperature sensor
(1 of 1)

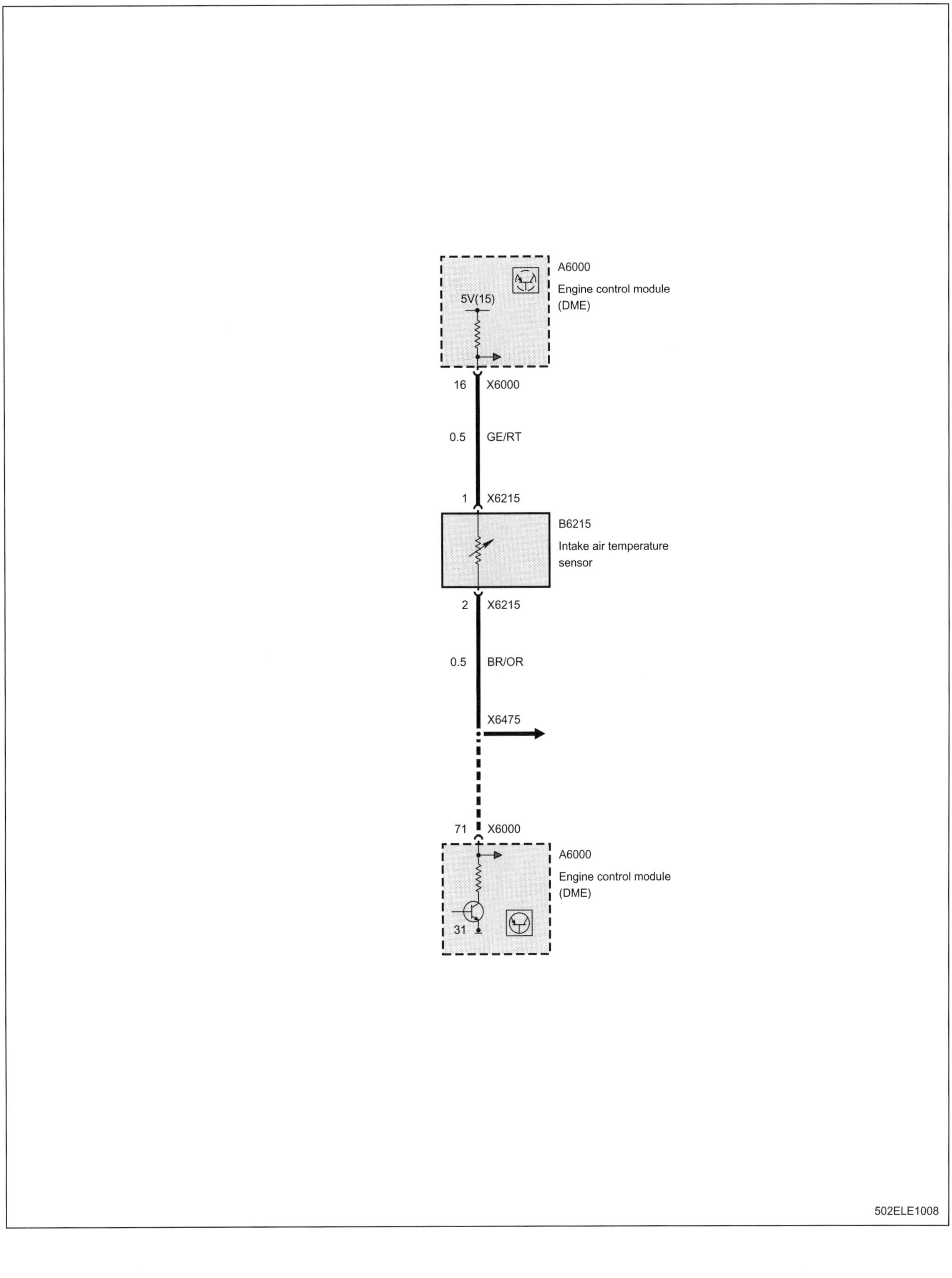

Engine Management (M 5.2)
Camshaft position sensor
(1 of 1)

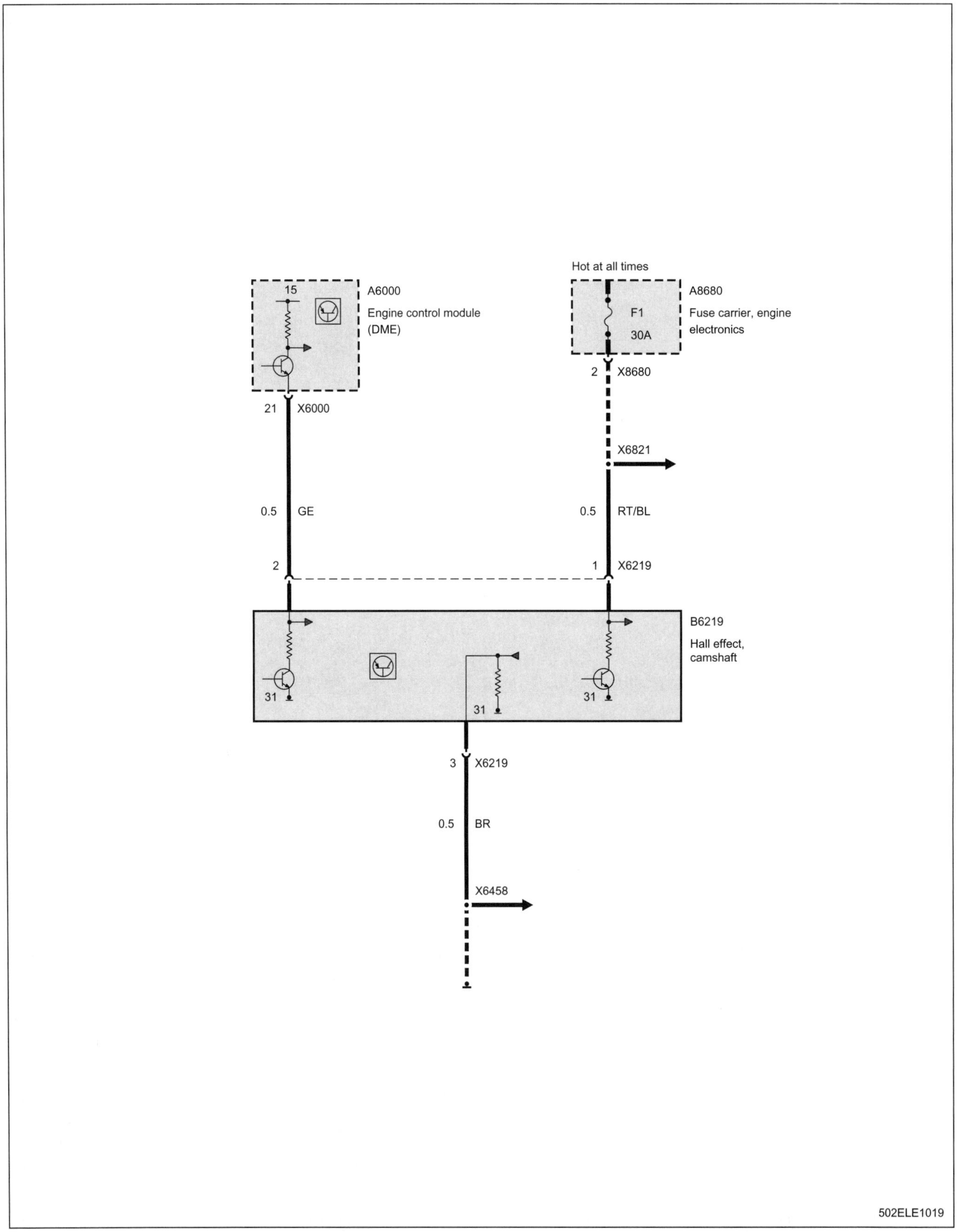

Engine Management (M 5.2)
Throttle position sensor
(1 of 1)

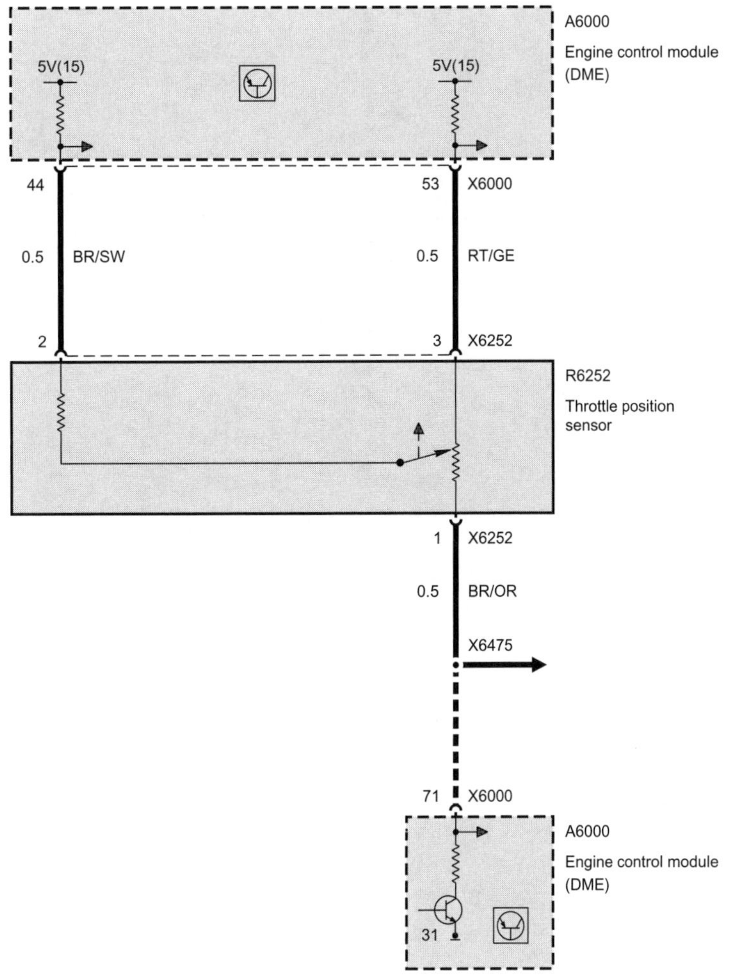

Engine Management (M 5.2)
Characteristic map, cooling (thermostat)
(1 of 1)

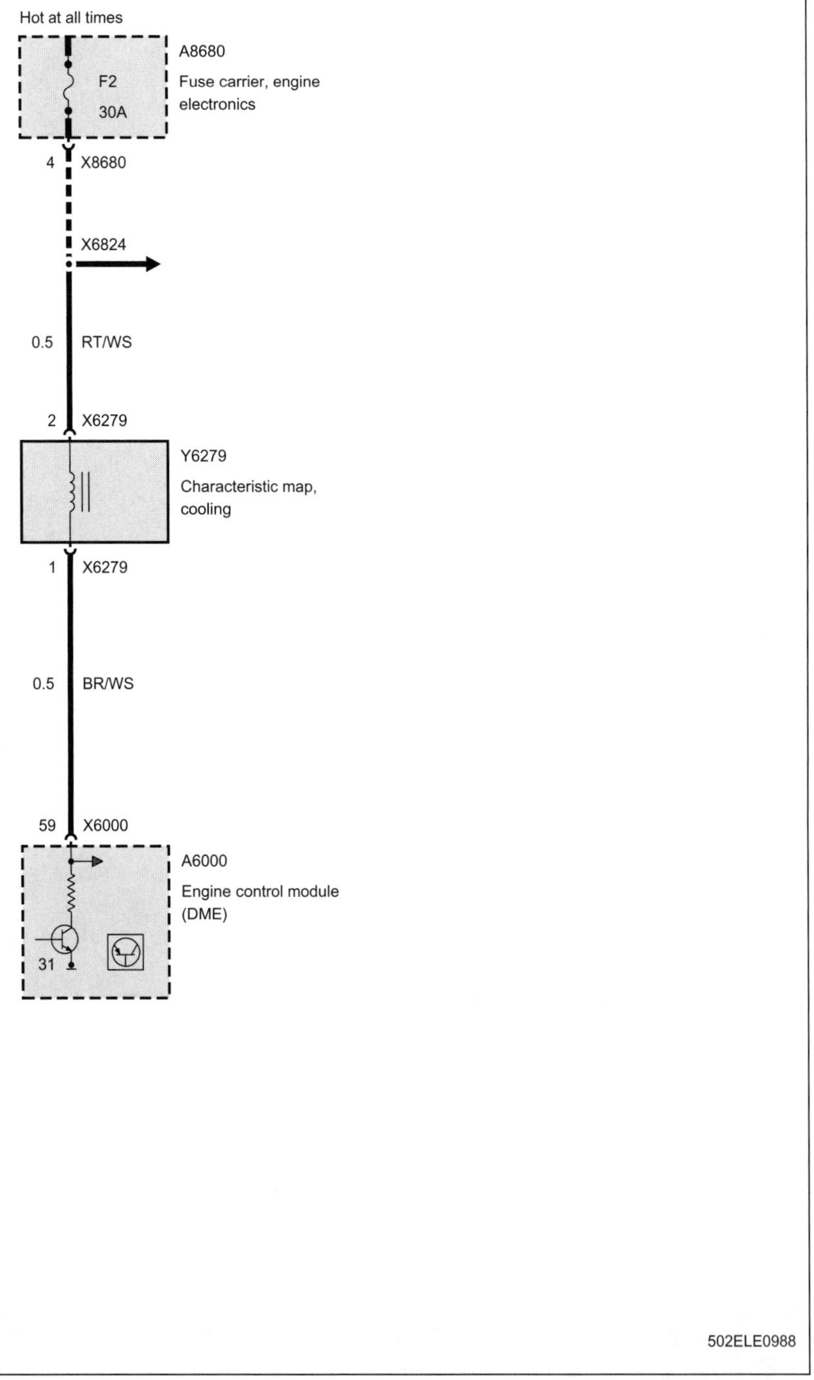

Engine Management (M 5.2)
Crankshaft position/RPM sensor 1
(1 of 1)

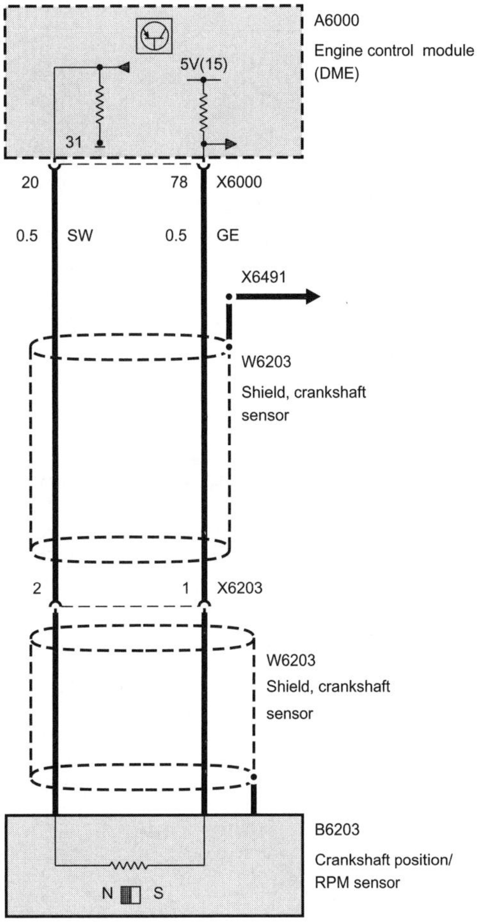

502ELE1012

Engine Management (M 5.2)
Dual temperature sensor
(1 of 1)

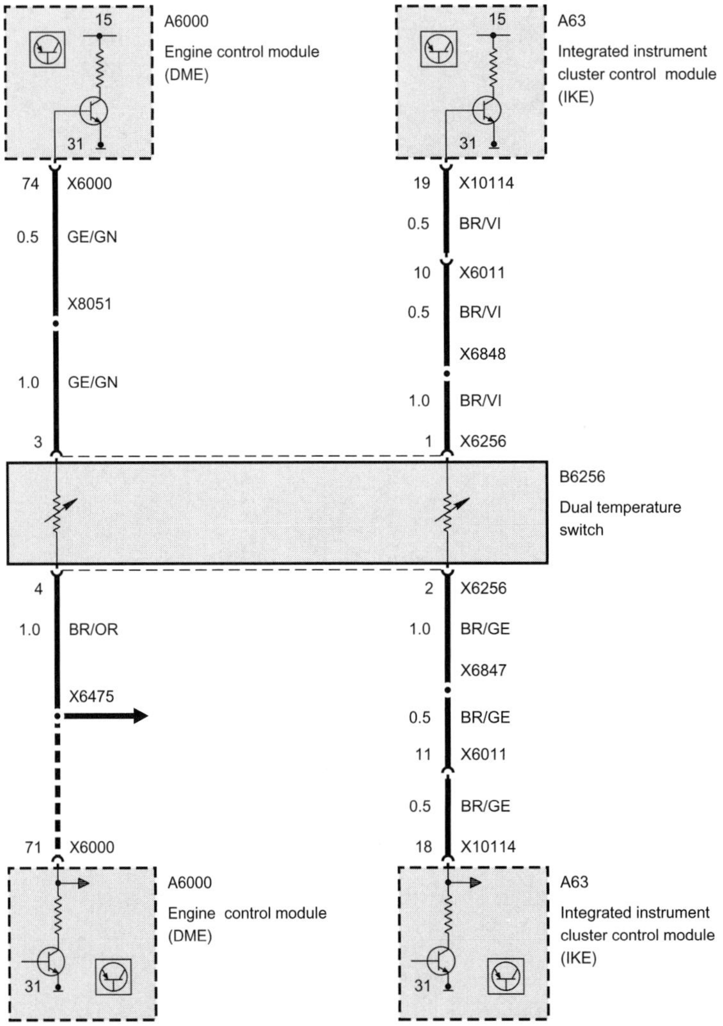

502ELE1010

Engine Management (M 5.2)
Engine coolant dual temperature sensor
(1 of 1)

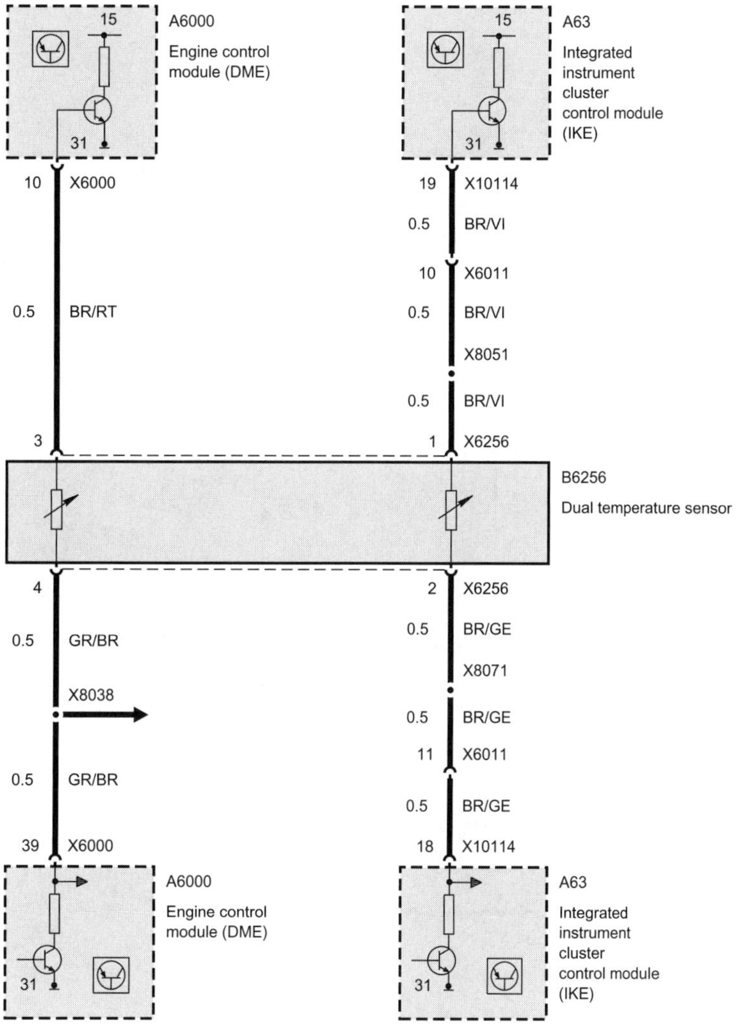

Engine Management (M 5.2)
Cyl. 1-2, 3-4 knock sensors
(1 of 1)

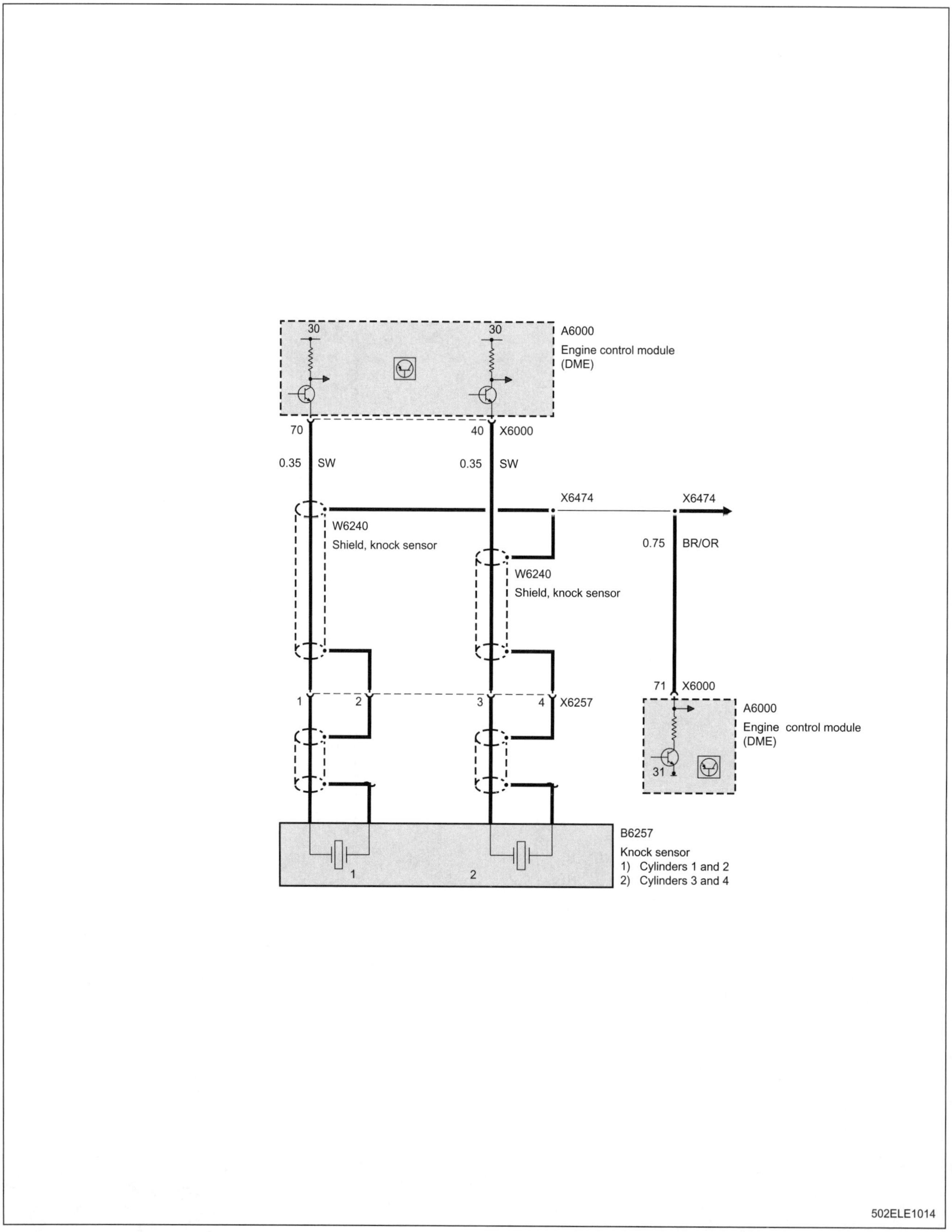

Engine Management (M 5.2)
Cyl. 5-6, 7-8 knock sensors
(1 of 1)

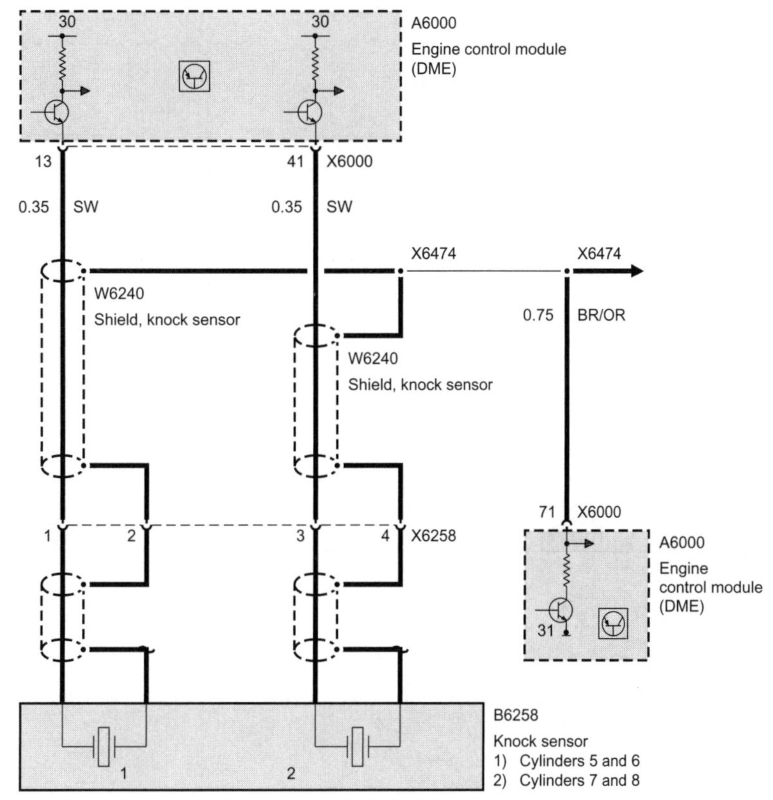

Engine Management (M 5.2)
Oxygen sensor 1 behind catalytic converter
(1 of 1)

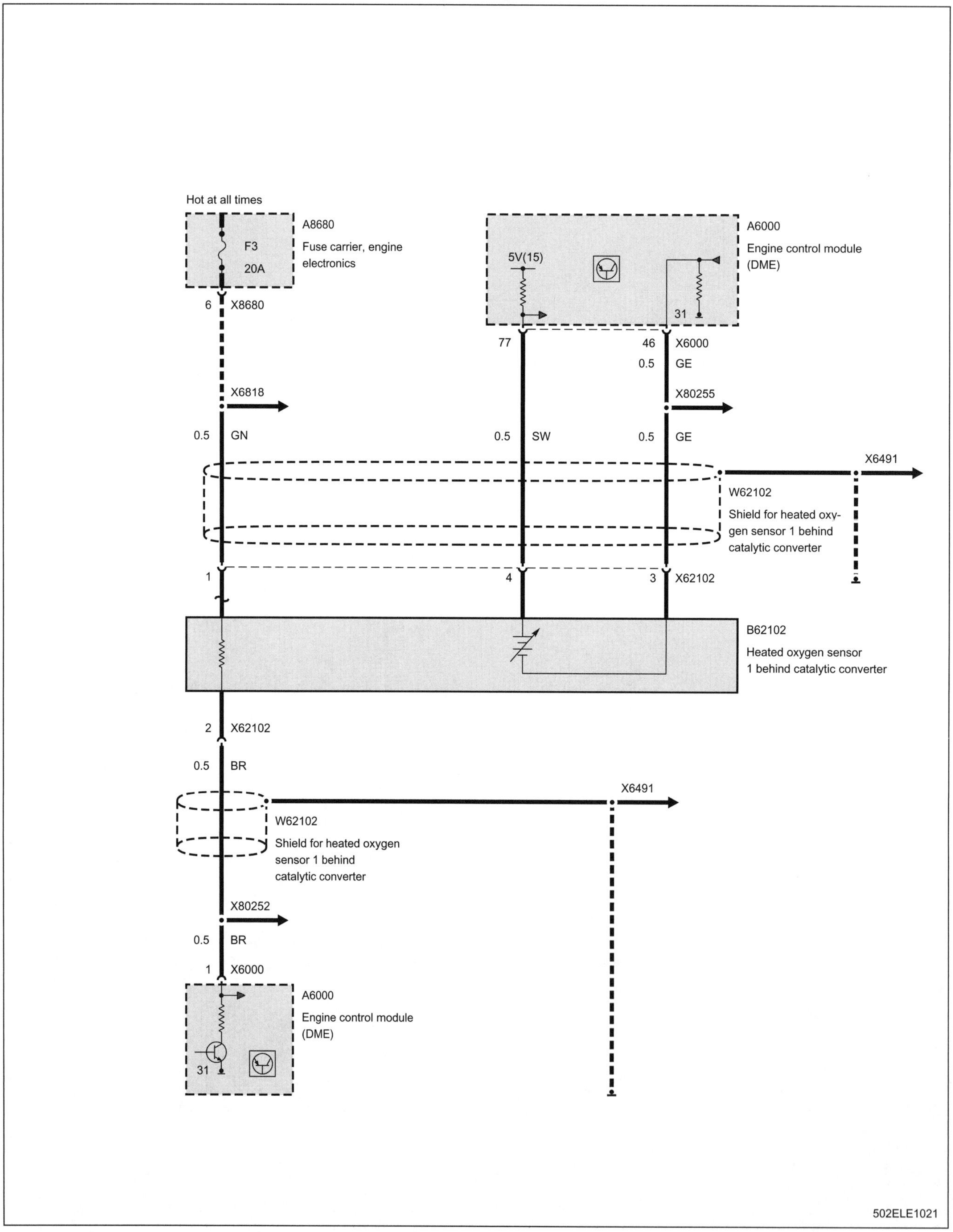

Engine Management (M 5.2)
Oxygen sensor 1 in front of catalytic converter
(1 of 1)

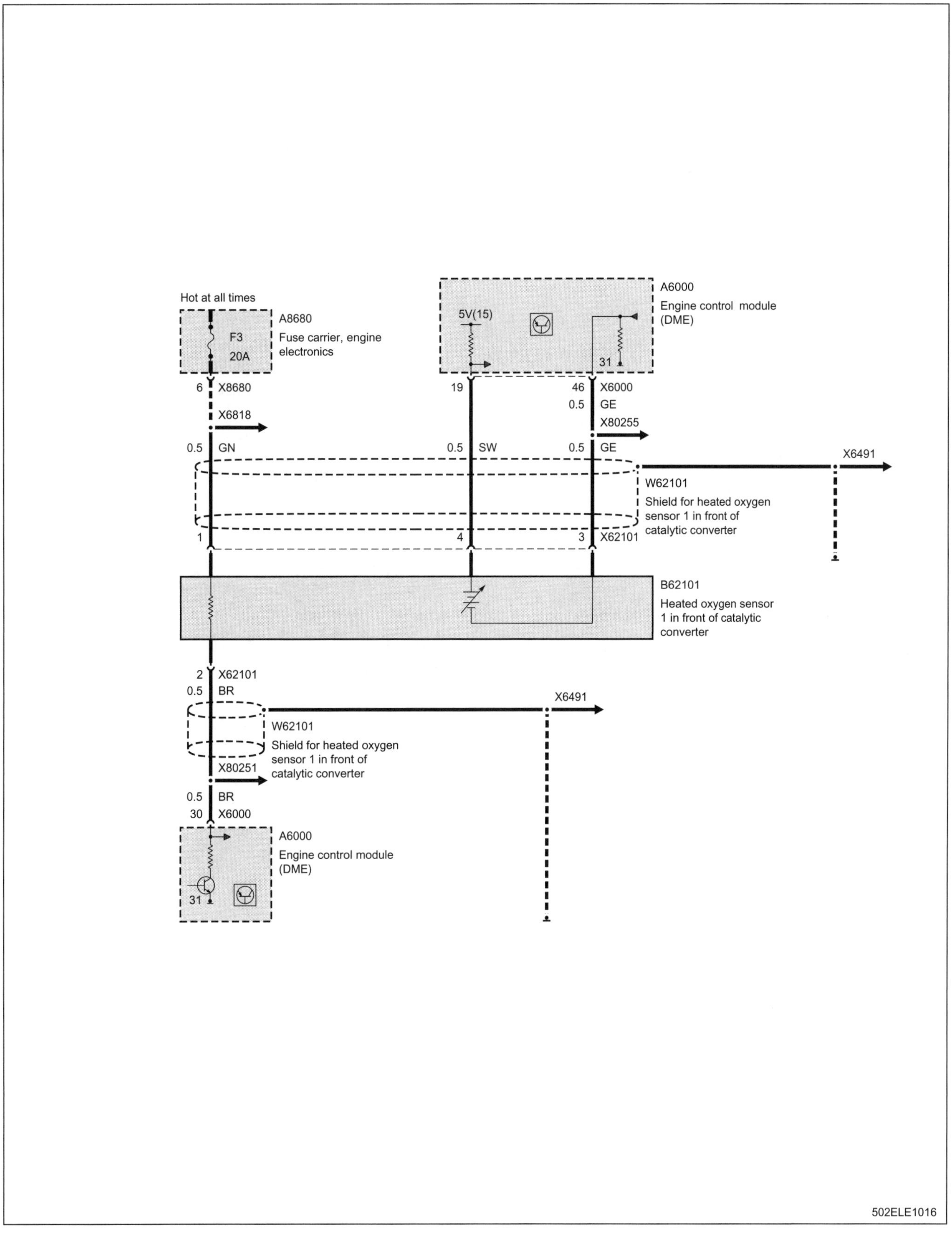

Engine Management (M 5.2)
Oxygen sensor 2 behind catalytic converter
(1 of 1)

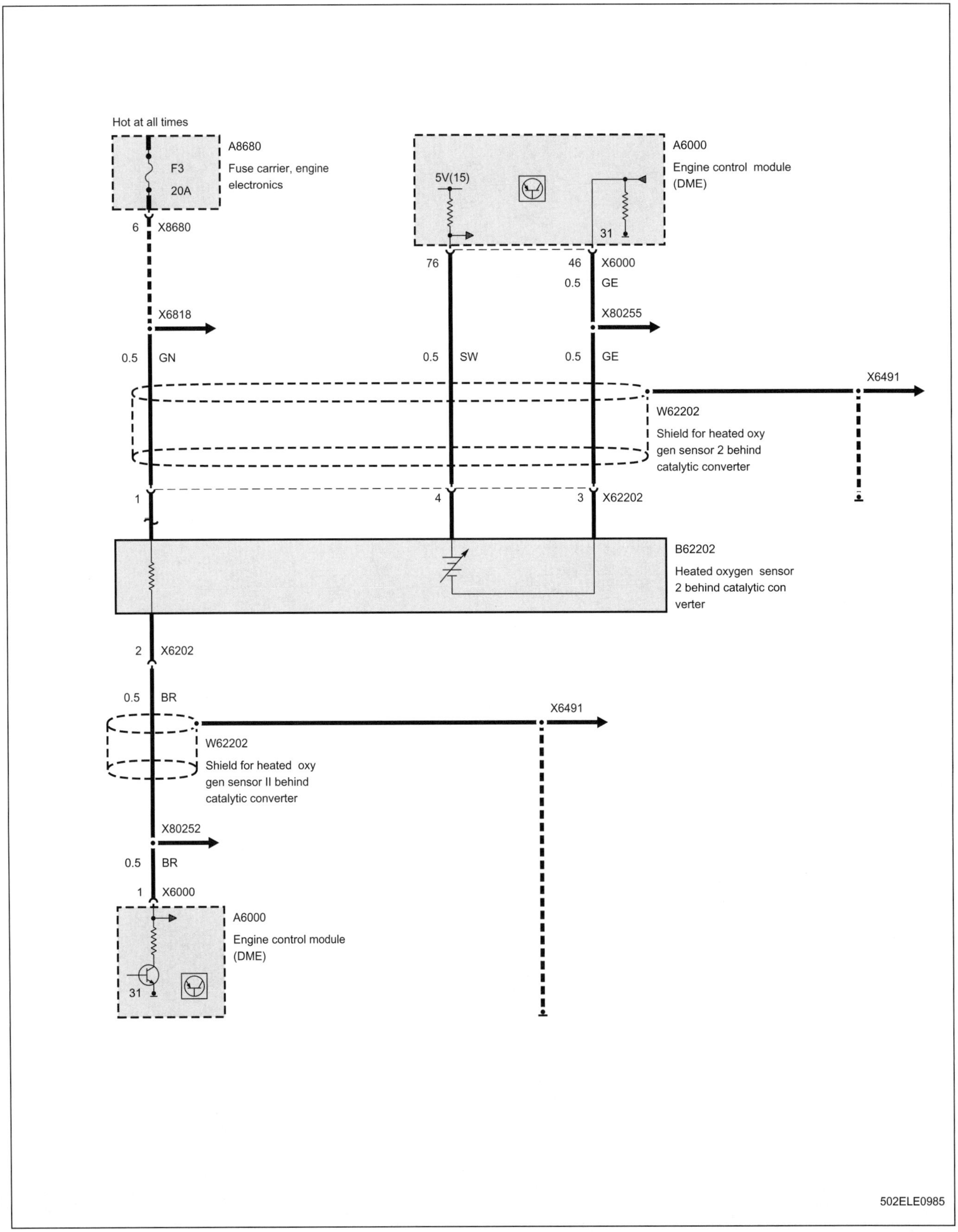

Engine Management (M 5.2)
Oxygen sensor 2 in front of catalytic converter
(1 of 1)

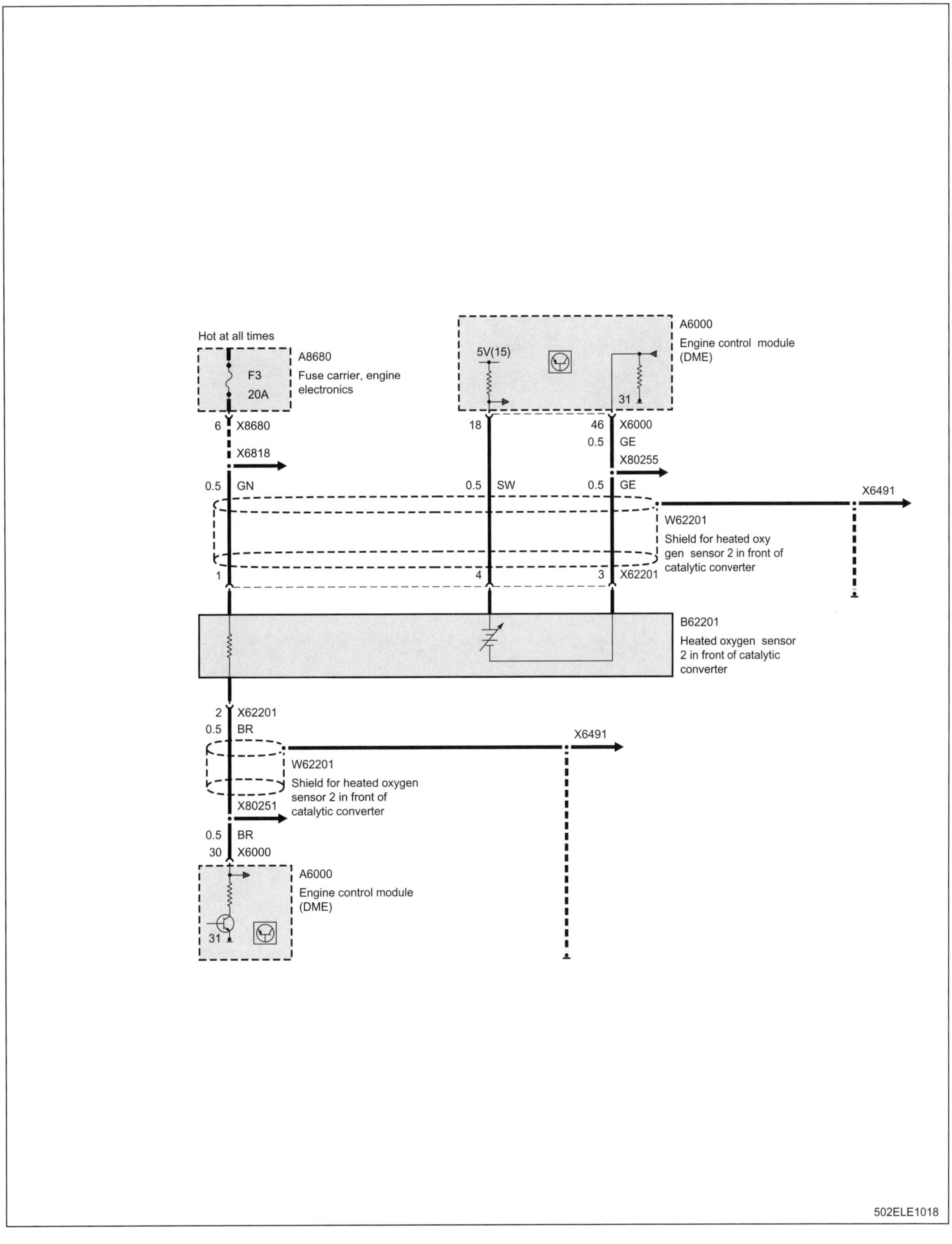

Engine Management (M 5.2)
ASC/DME interfaces
(1 of 1)

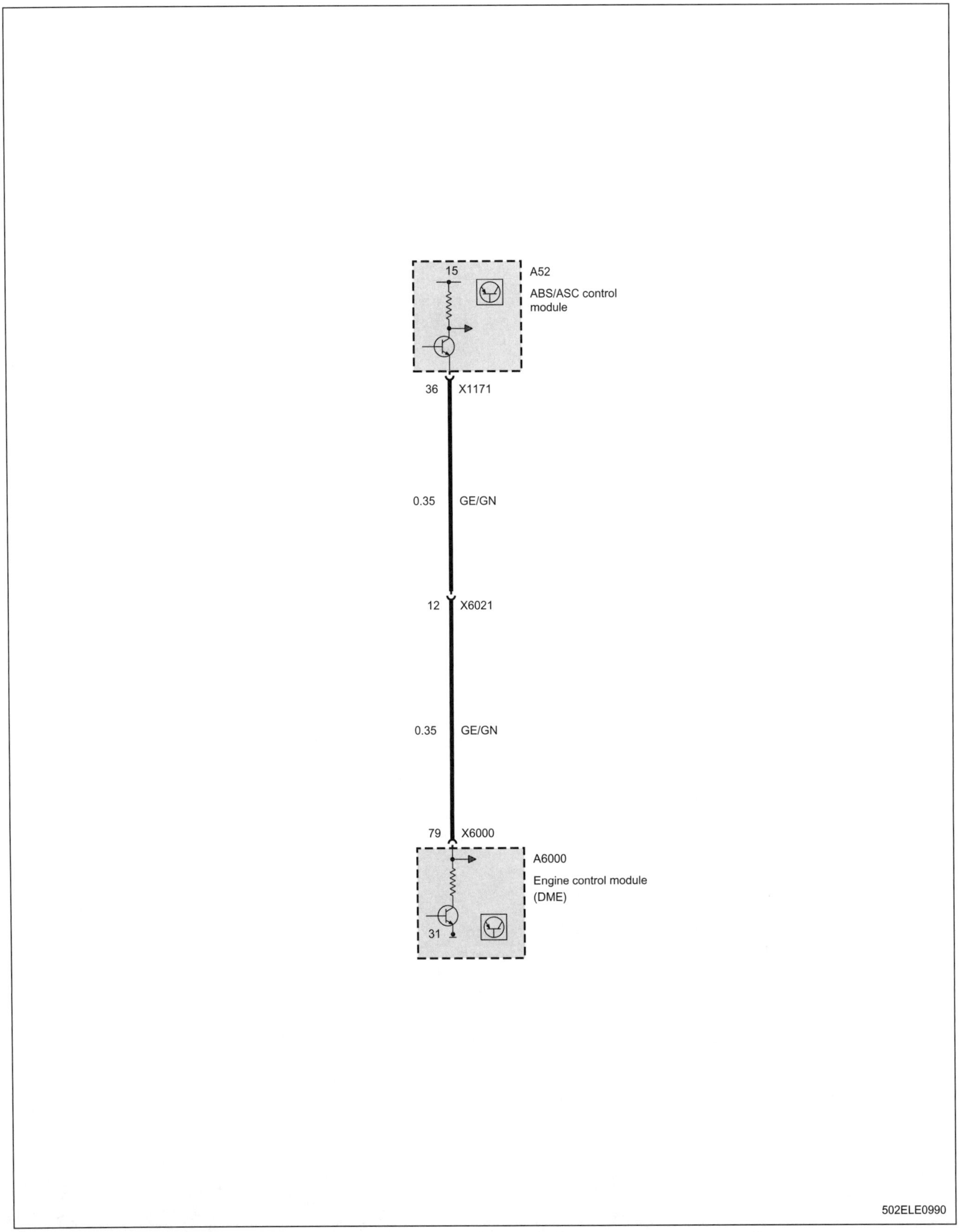

Engine Management (M 5.2)
Evaporative emission valve
(1 of 1)

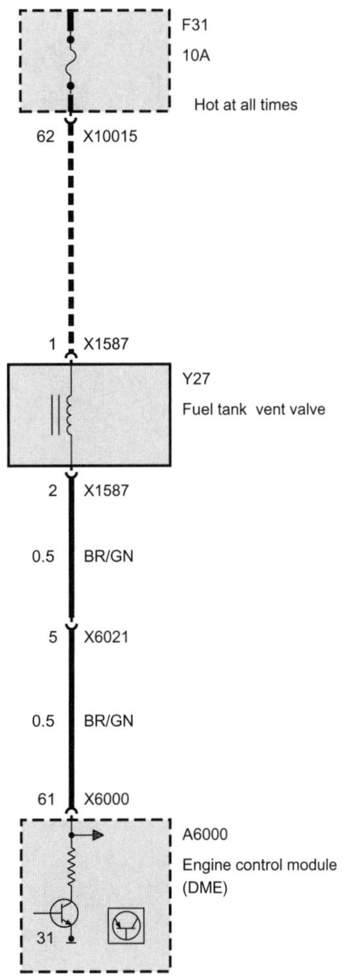

502ELE1026

Engine Management (M 5.2)
Cyl. 1 and 2 fuel injection valves
(1 of 1)

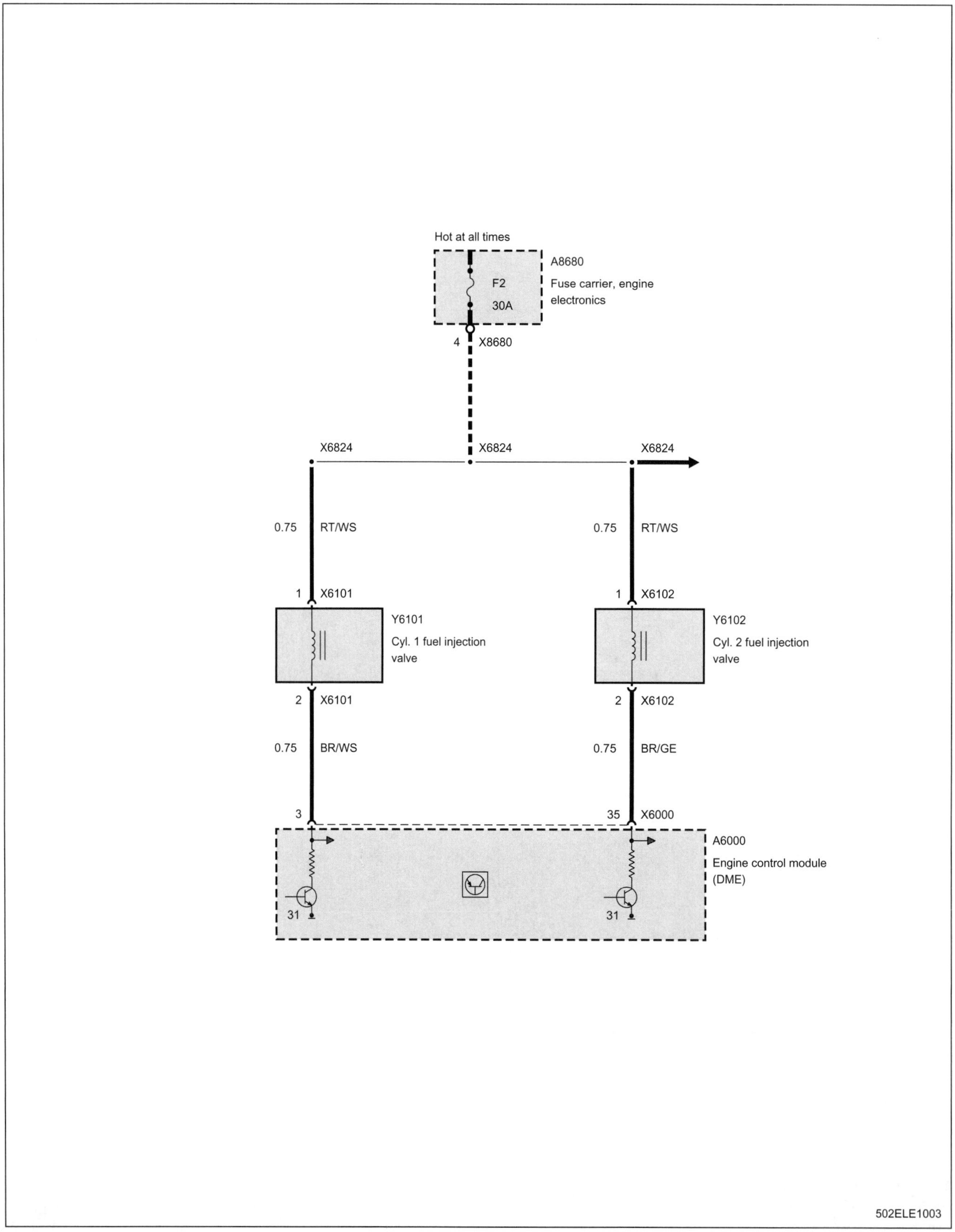

Engine Management (M 5.2)
Cyl. 3 and 4 fuel injection valves
(1 of 1)

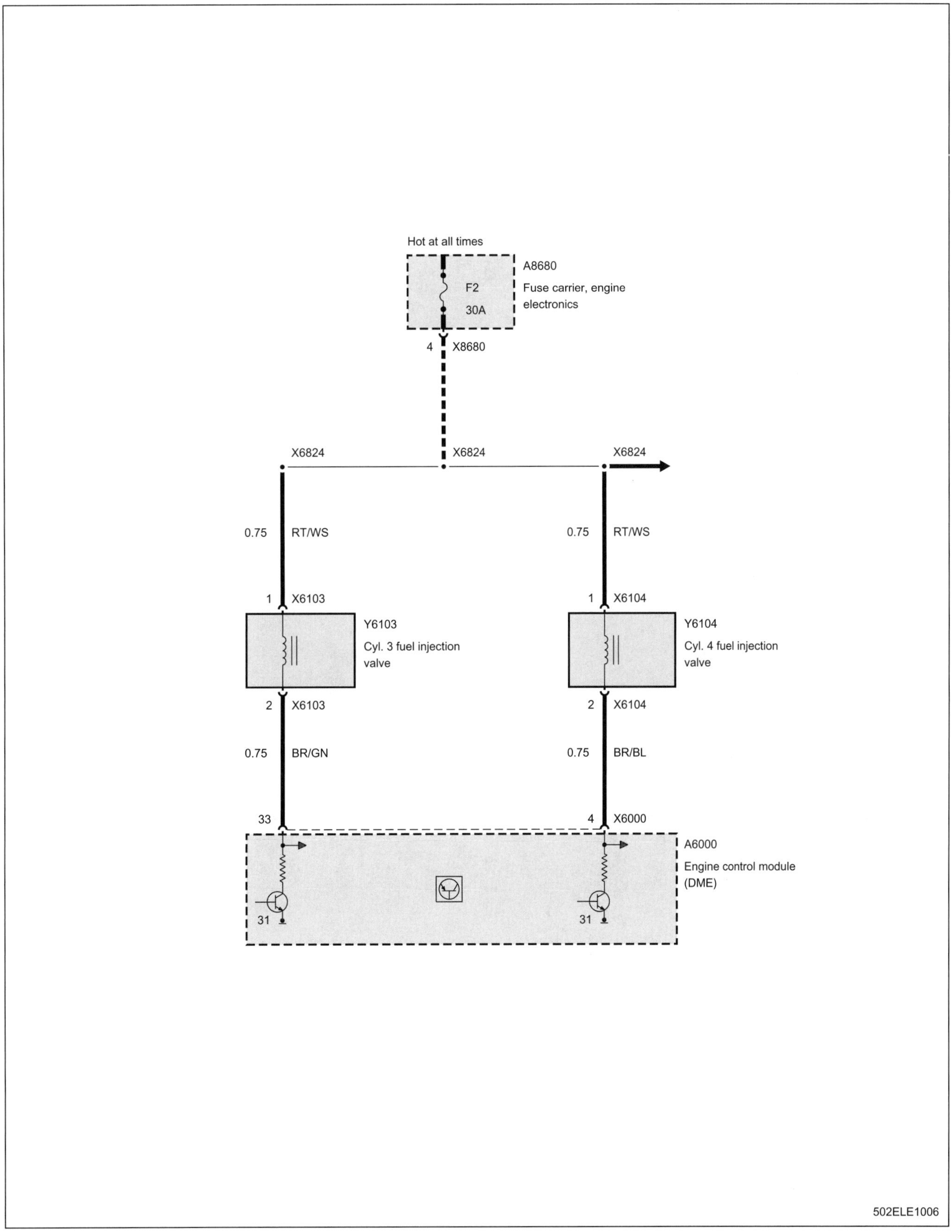

Engine Management (M 5.2)
Cyl. 5 and 6 fuel injection valves
(1 of 1)

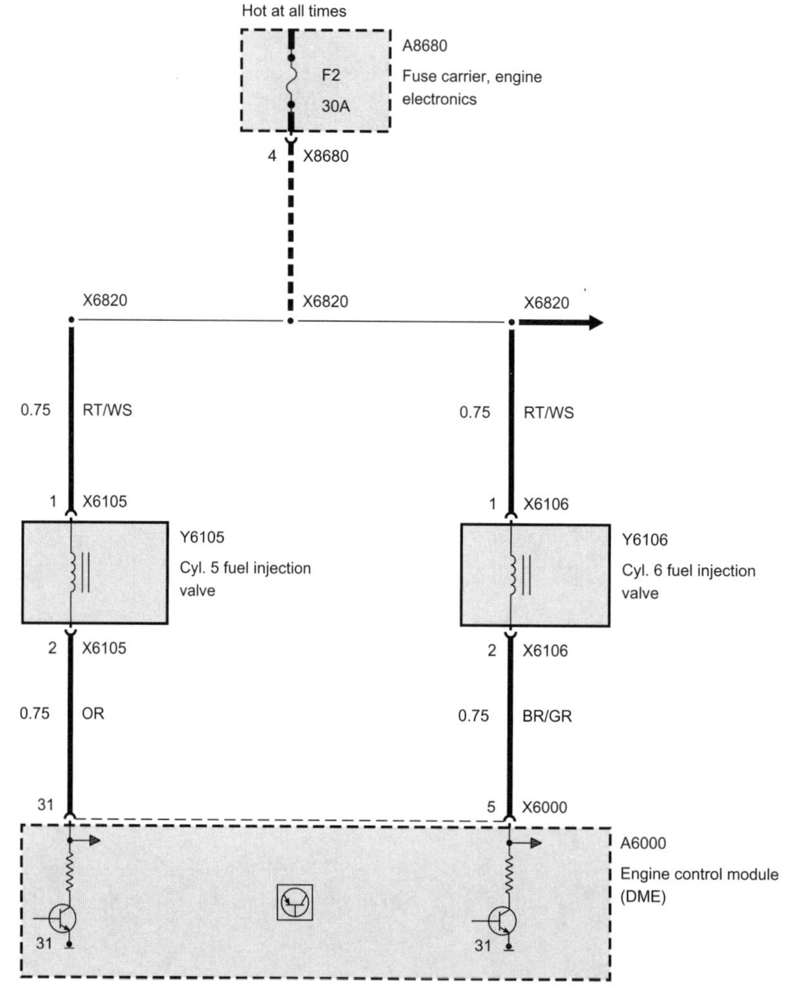

502ELE1009

Engine Management (M 5.2)
Cyl. 7 and 8 fuel injection valves
(1 of 1)

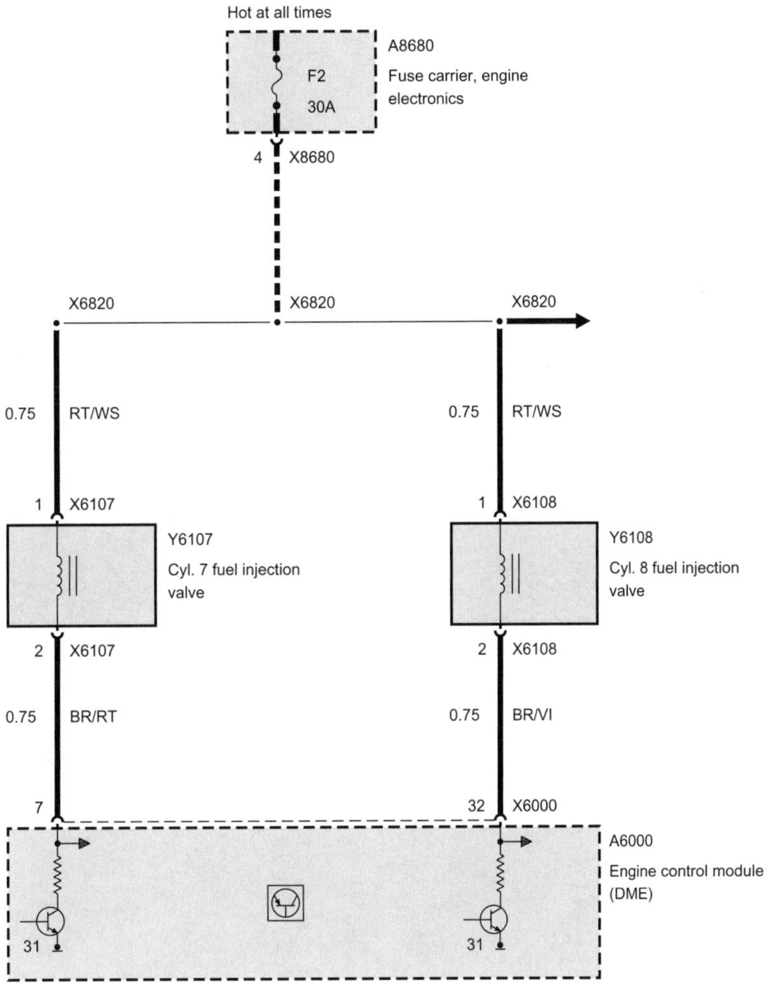

502ELE1011

Engine Management (M 5.2)
Ignition coils, power
(1 of 1)

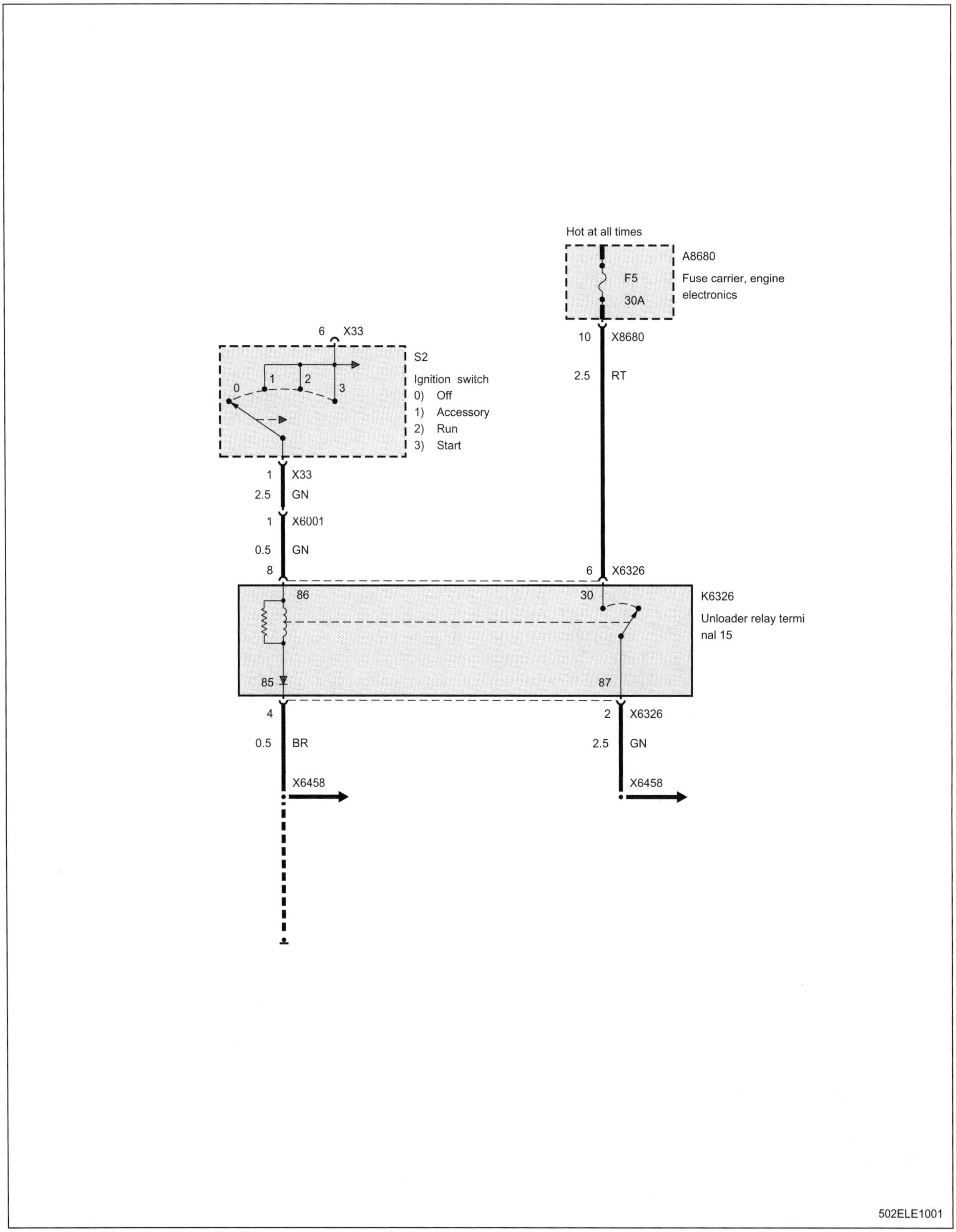

Engine Management (M 5.2)
Cyl. 1 and 2 ignition coils
(1 of 1)

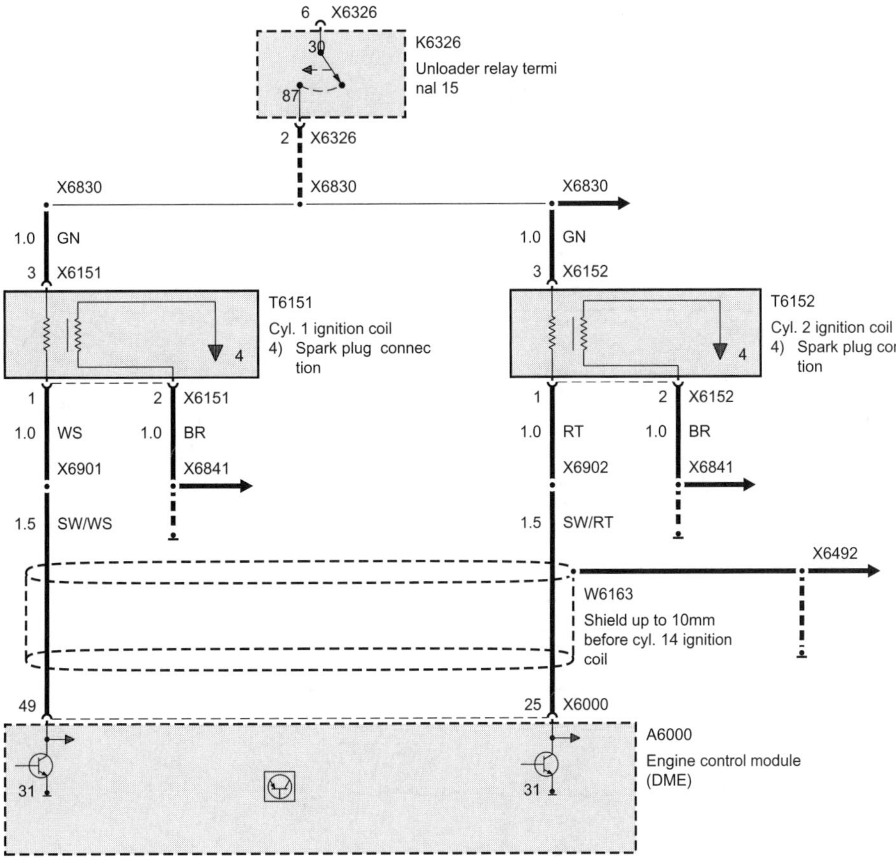

502ELE1000

Engine Management (M 5.2)
Cyl. 3 and 4 ignition coils
(1 of 1)

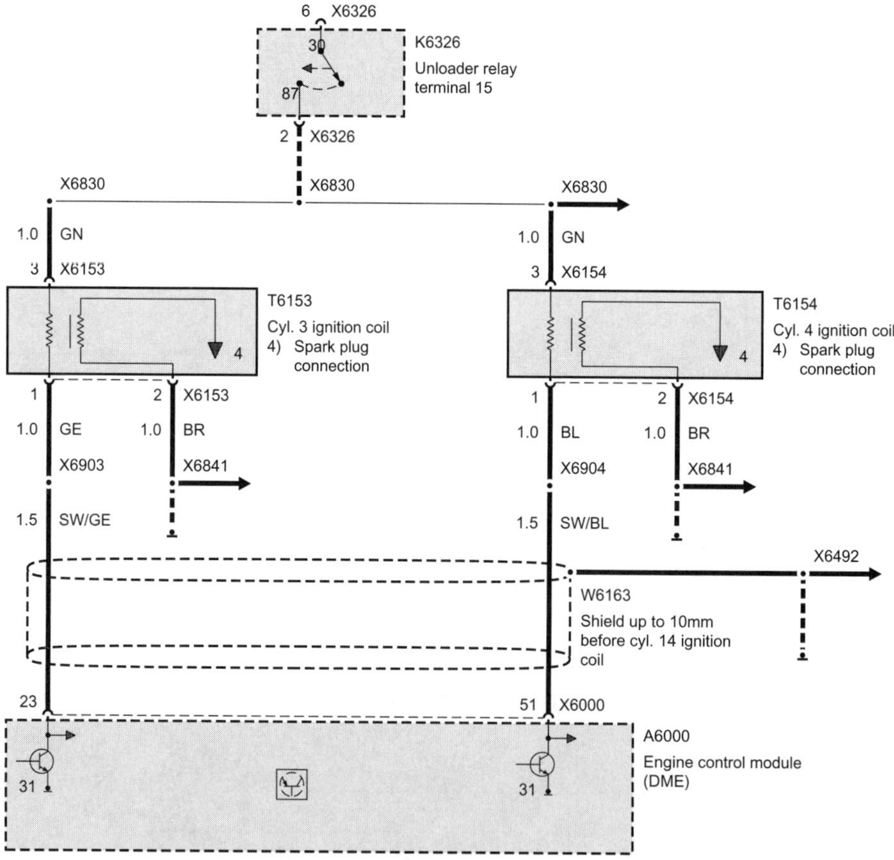

502ELE1004

Engine Management (M 5.2)
Cyl. 5 and 6 ignition coils
(1 of 1)

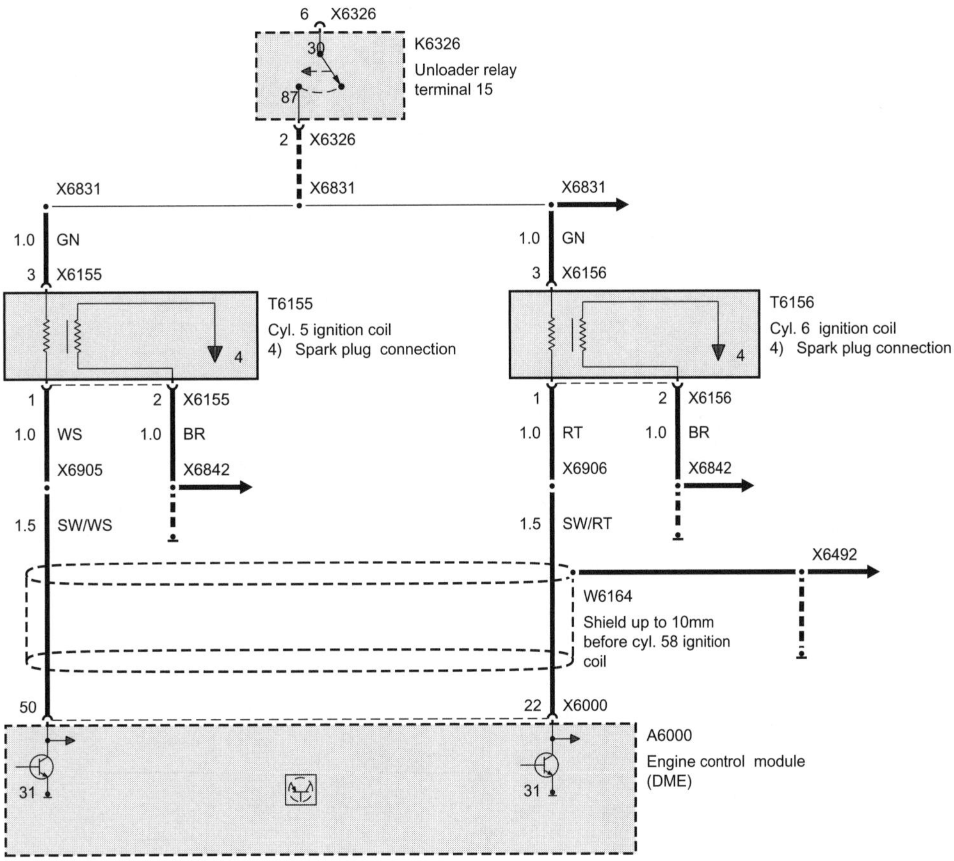

502ELE1007

Engine Management (M 5.2)
Cyl. 7 and 8 ignition coils
(1 of 1)

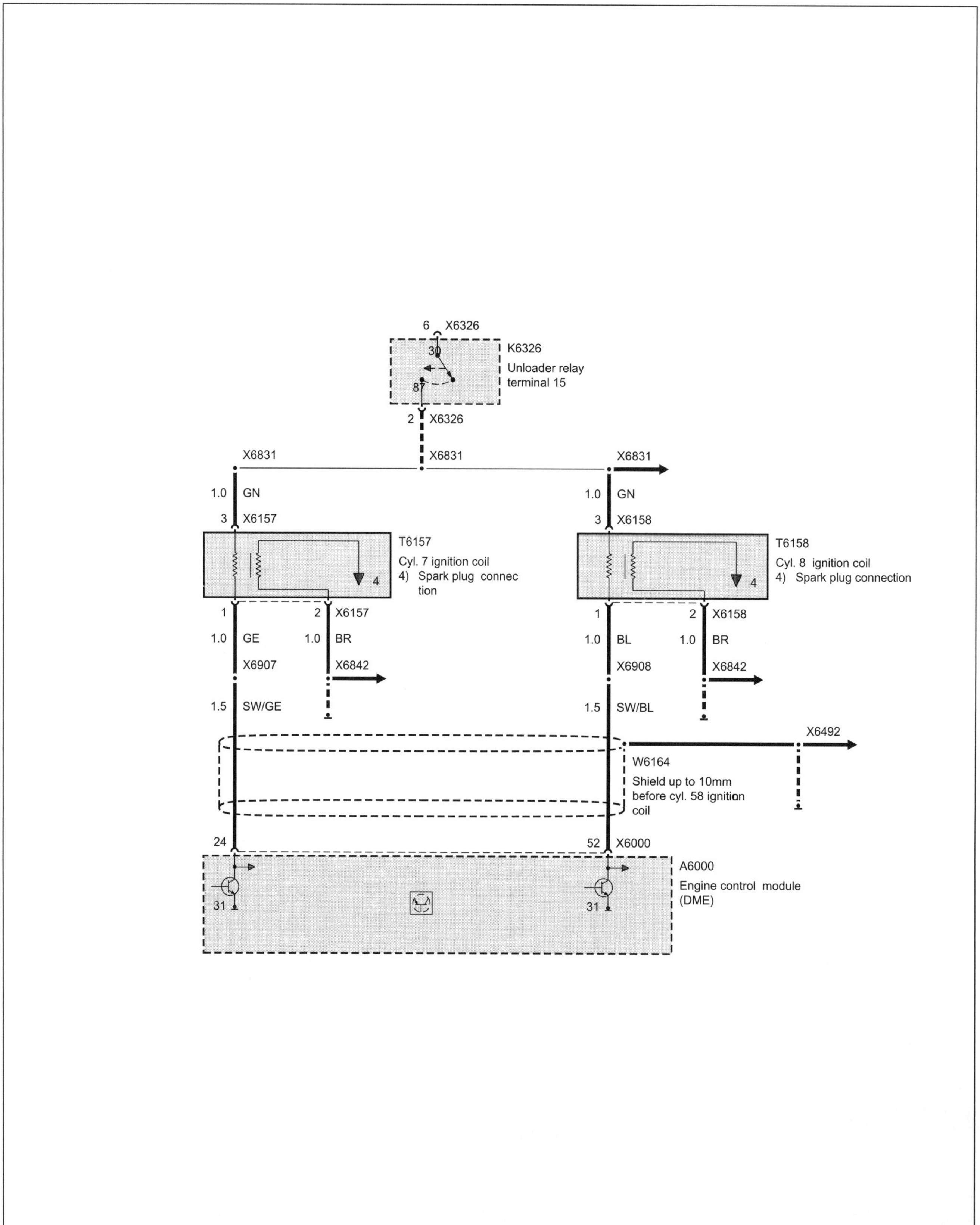

Engine Management (M 5.2)
Fuse supply, engine electronics
(1 of 1)

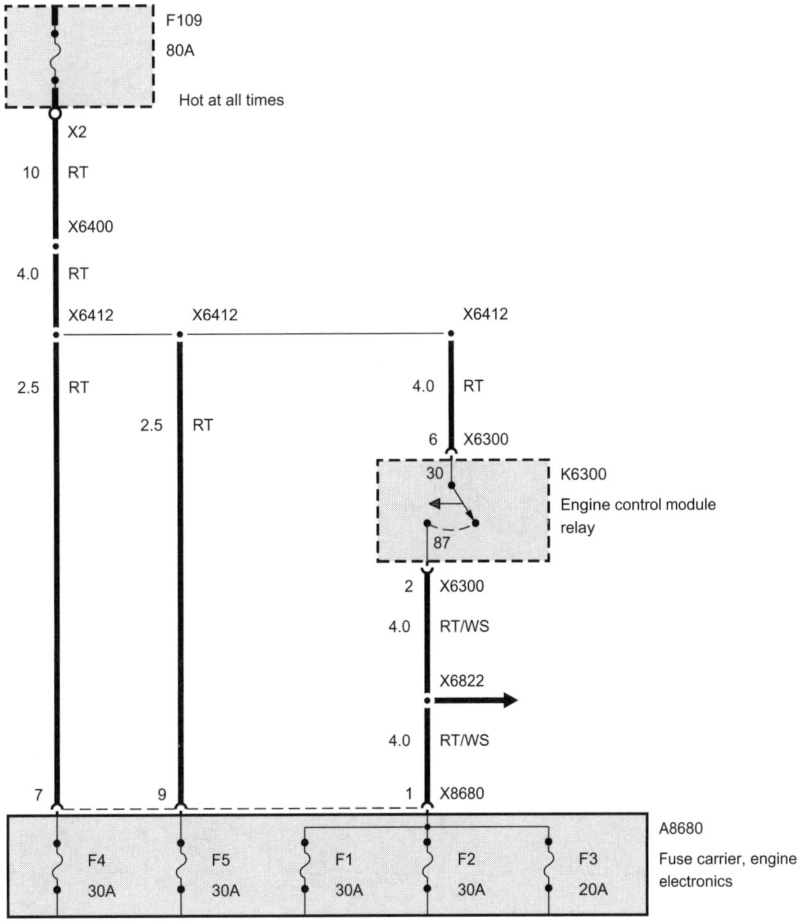

Engine Management (M 5.2)
Start detection
(1 of 1)

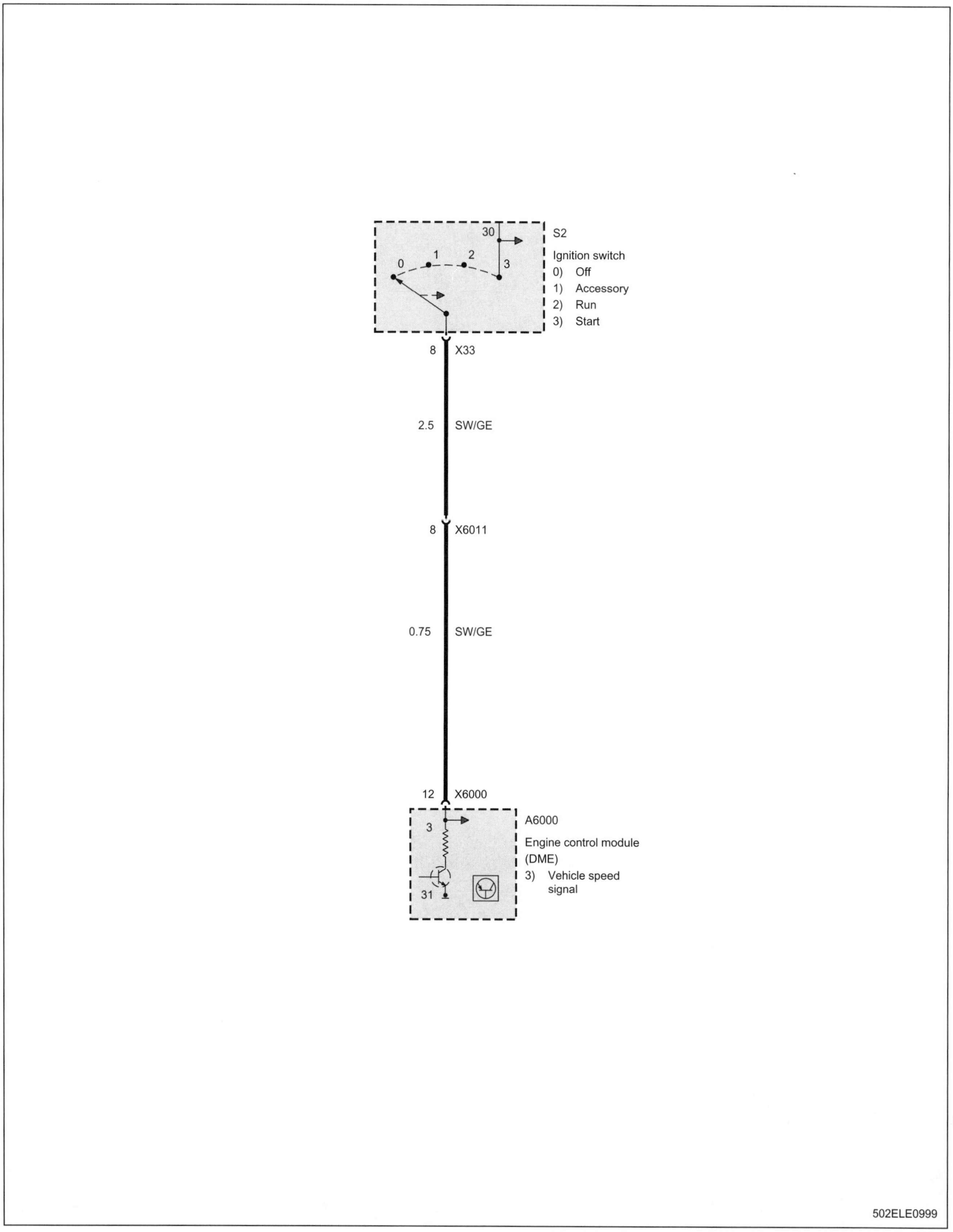
30
0
1
2
3
S2
Ignition switch
0) Off
1) Accessory
2) Run
3) Start
8 X33
2.5 SW/GE
8 X6011
0.75 SW/GE
12 X6000
3
31
A6000
Engine control module
(DME)
3) Vehicle speed
signal
502ELE0999

Engine Management (M 5.2)
Starter control (EWS II)
(1 of 1)

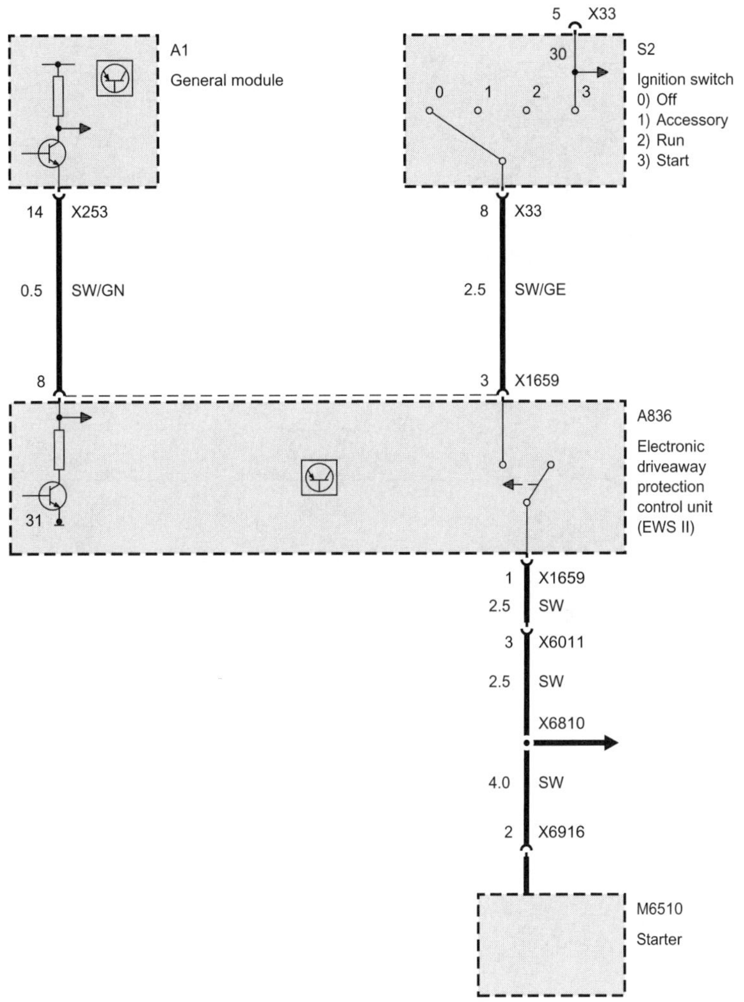

502ELE1020

Engine Management (M 5.2)
Starter control (starter relay)
(1 of 1)

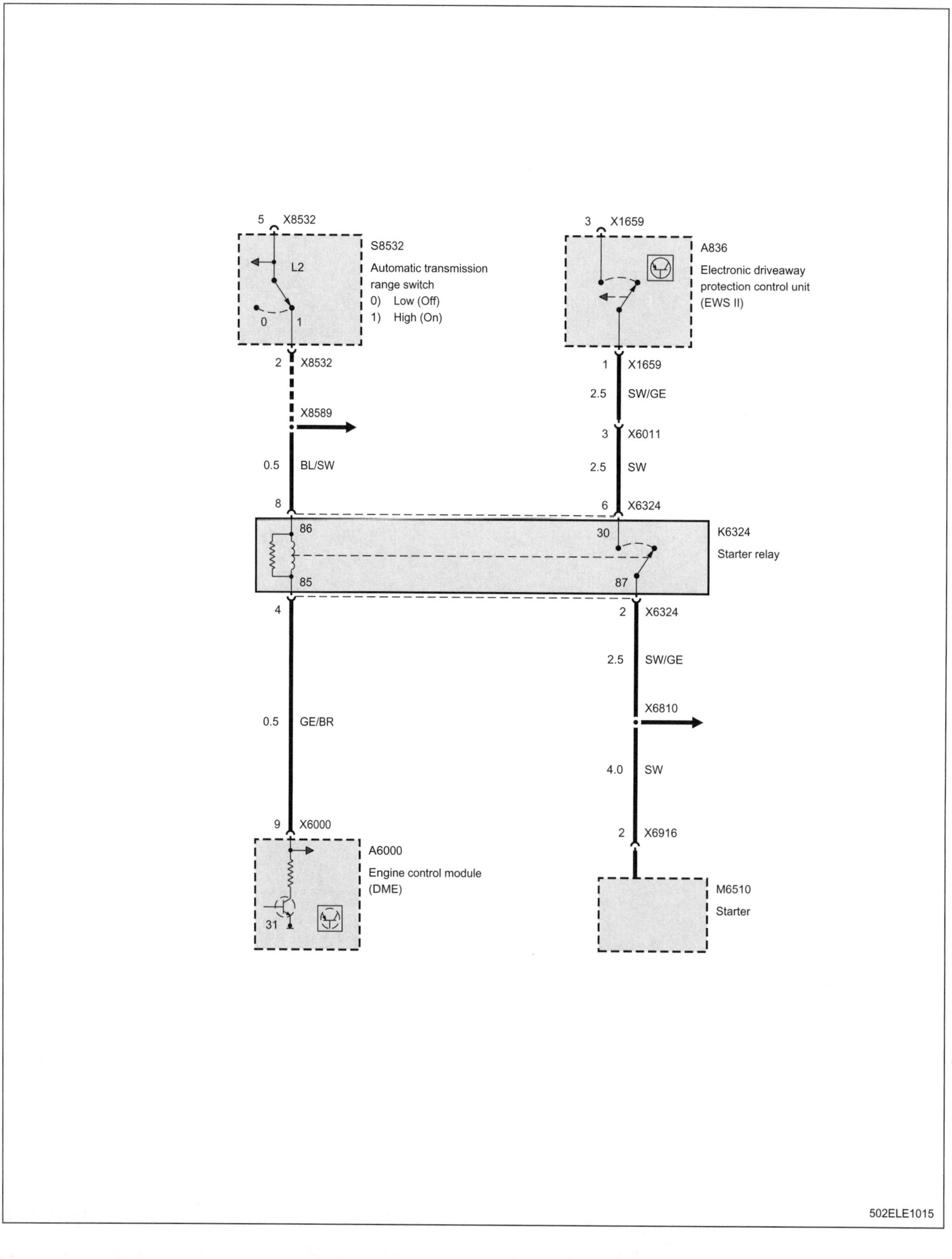

Engine Management (M 5.2)
CAN interface
(1 of 1)

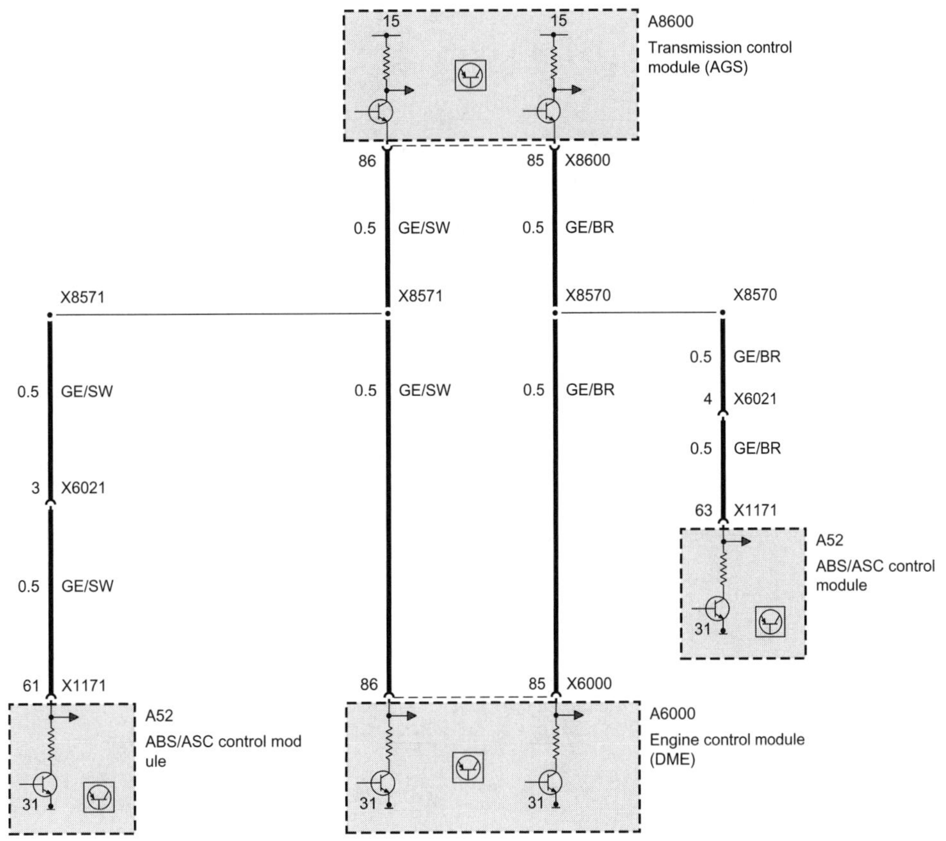

Engine Management (M 5.2)
DME/Climate control interfaces
(1 of 1)

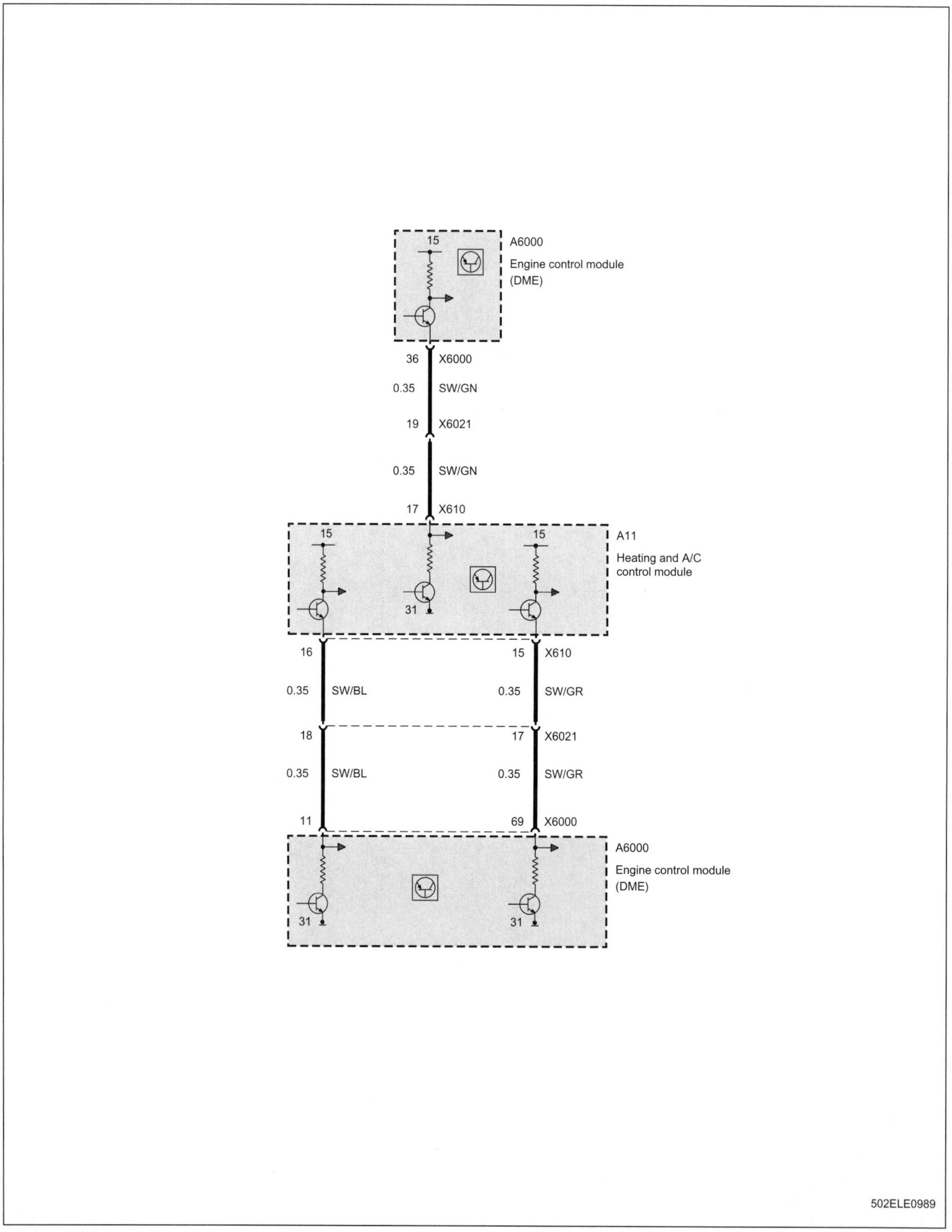

Engine Management (M 5.2)
DME/IKE interface
(1 of 1)

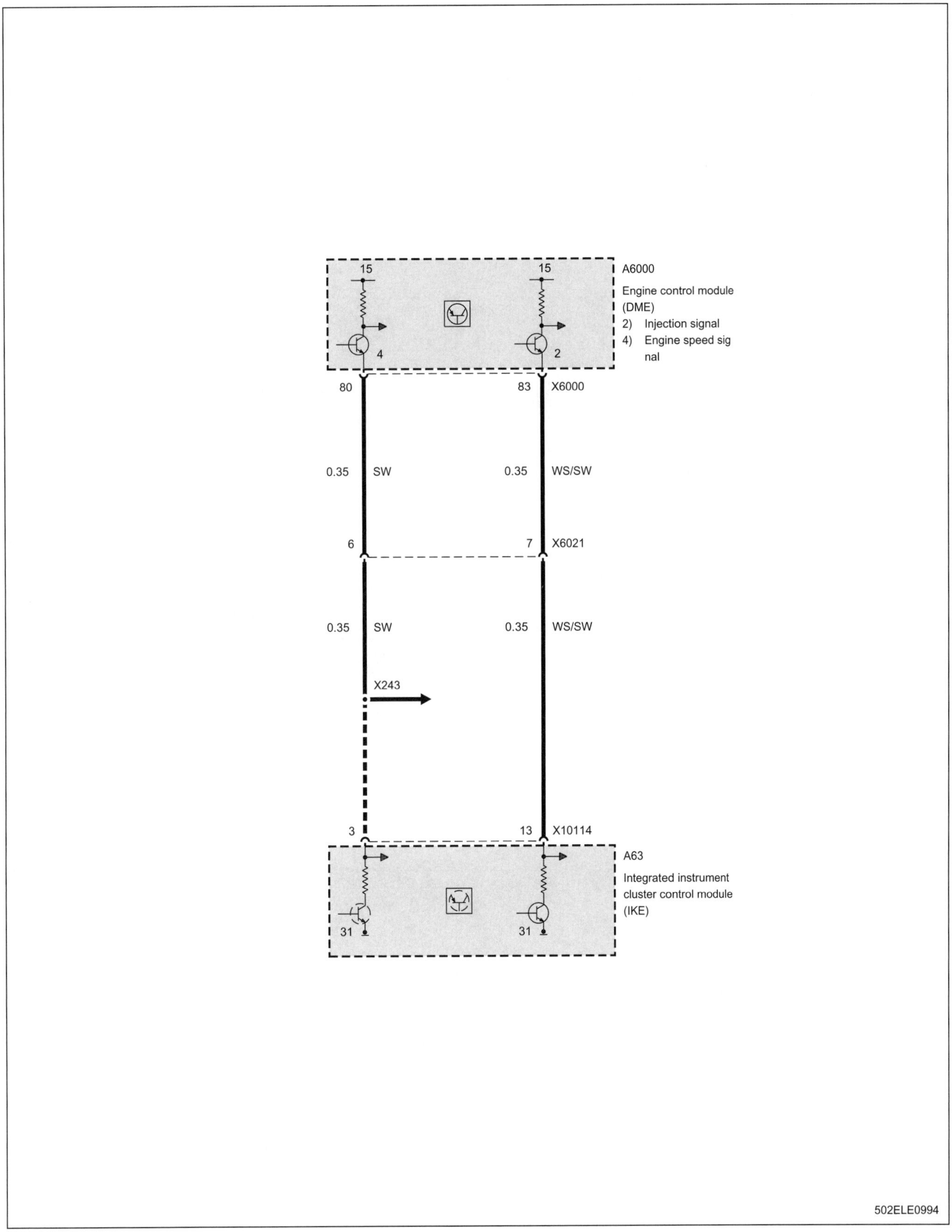

Engine Management (M 5.2.1)
A6000 Engine control module (DME)
(1 of 3)

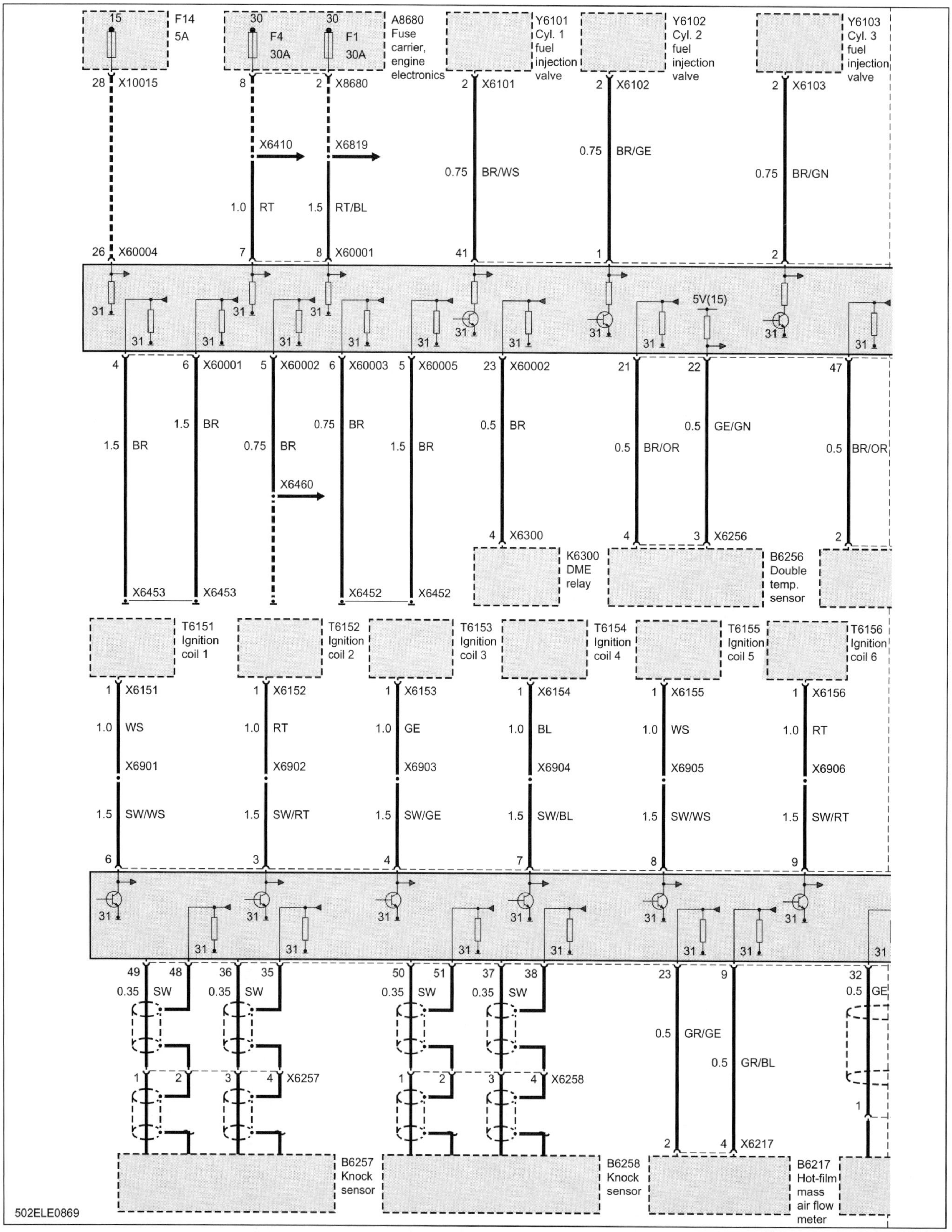

Engine Management (M 5.2.1)
A6000 Engine control module (DME)
(2 of 3)

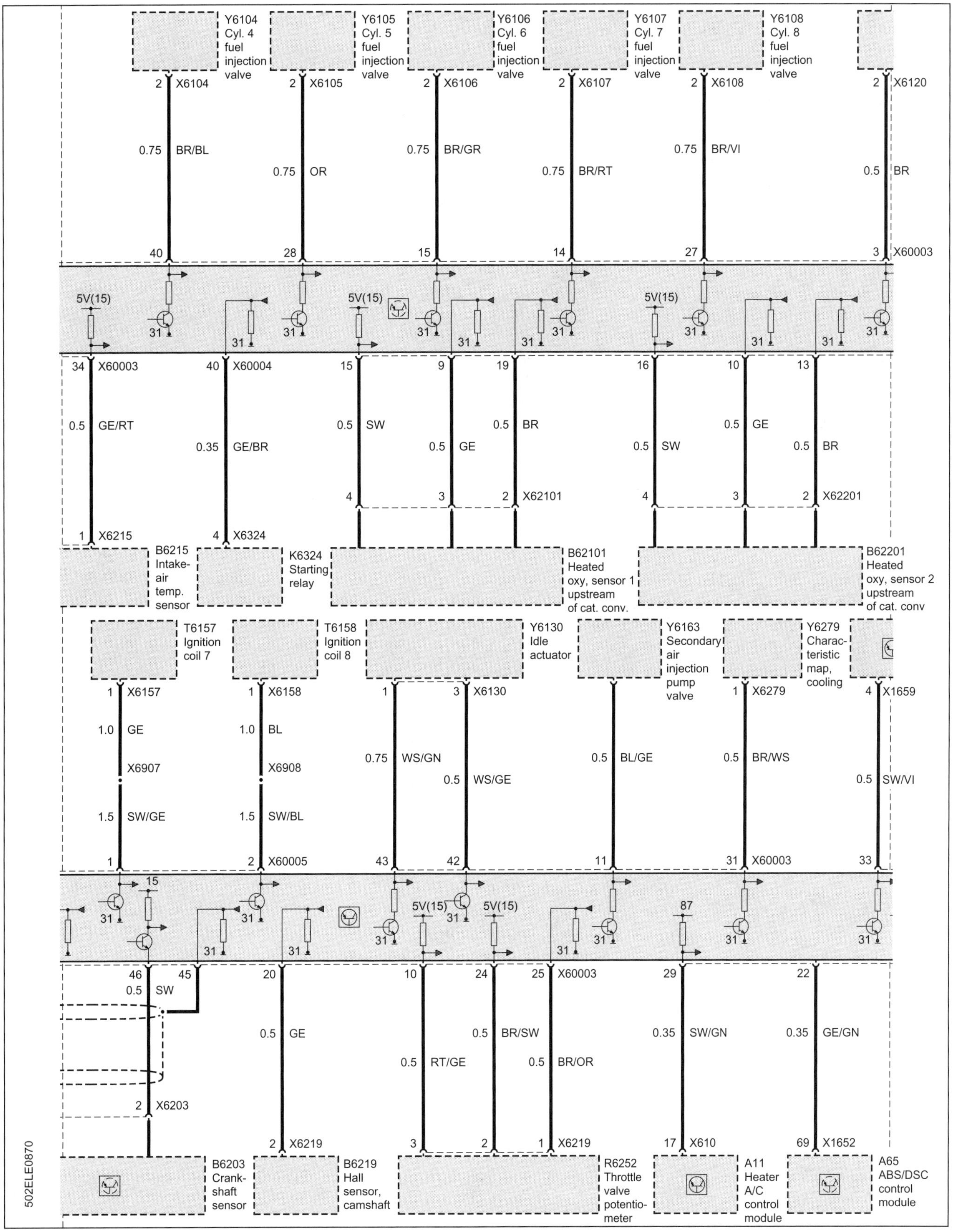

Engine Management (M 5.2.1)
A6000 Engine control module (DME)
(3 of 3)

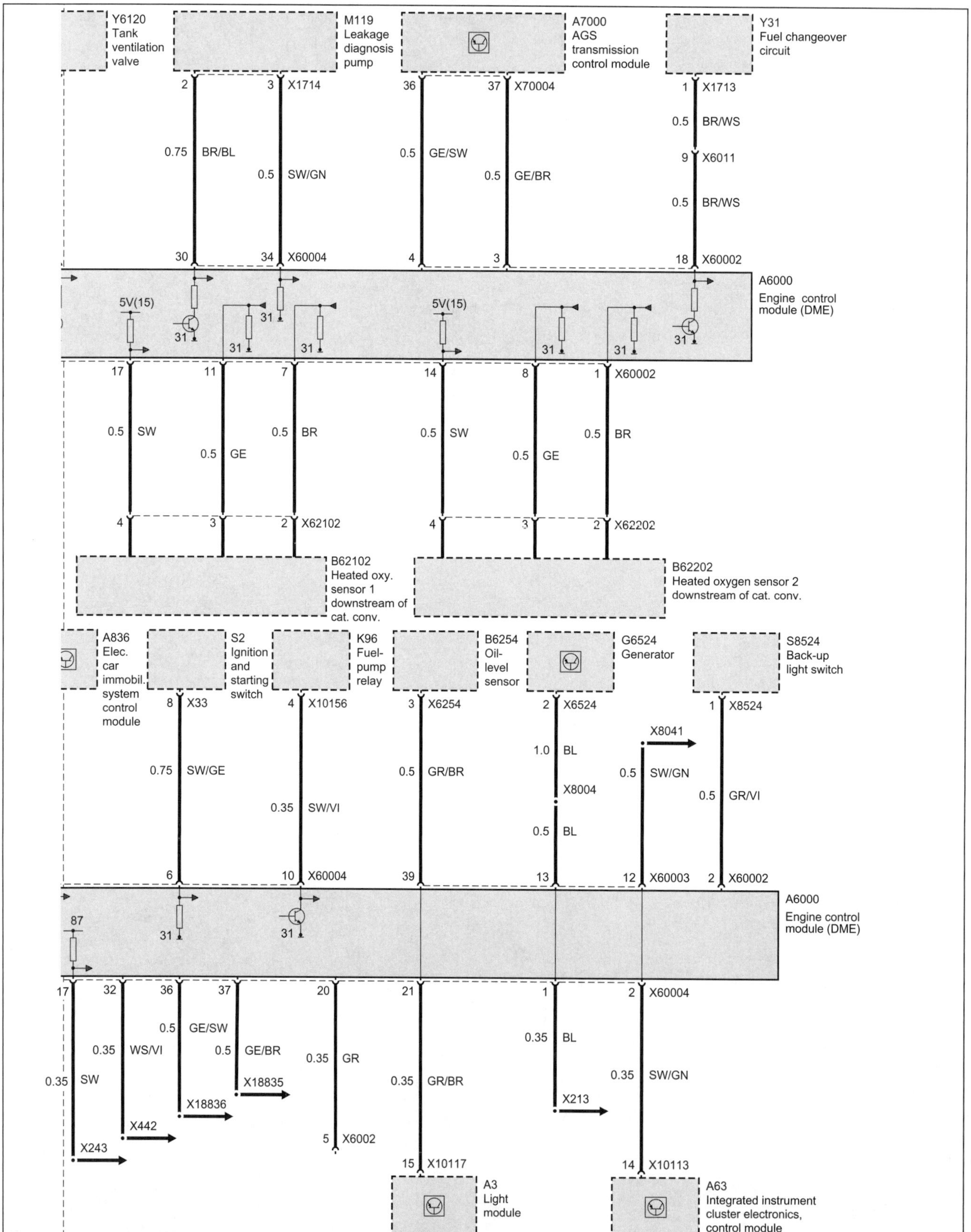

Engine Management (M 5.2.1)
OBDII plug
(1 of 1)

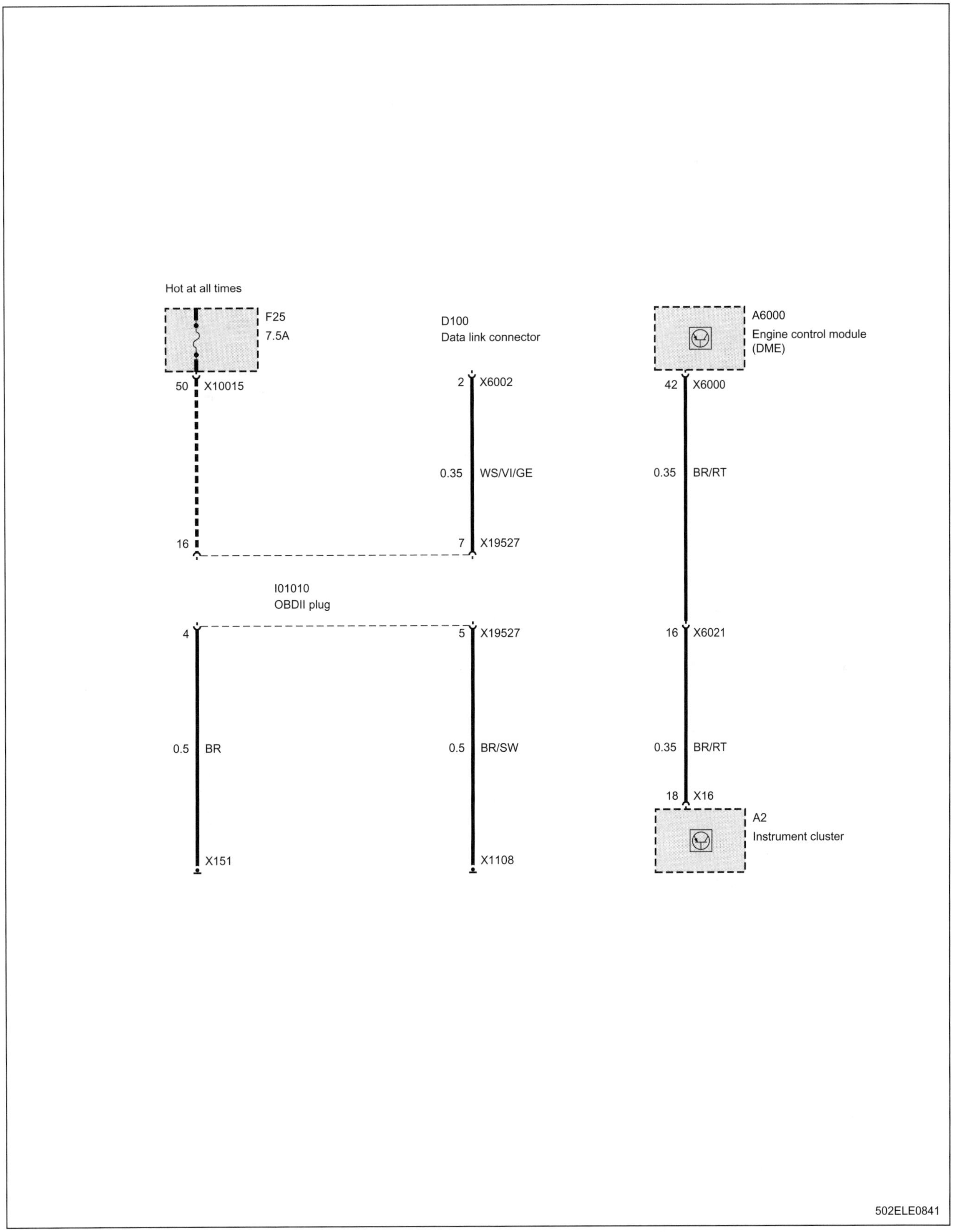

Engine Management (M 5.2.1)
Data link connector pin assignments
(1 of 1)

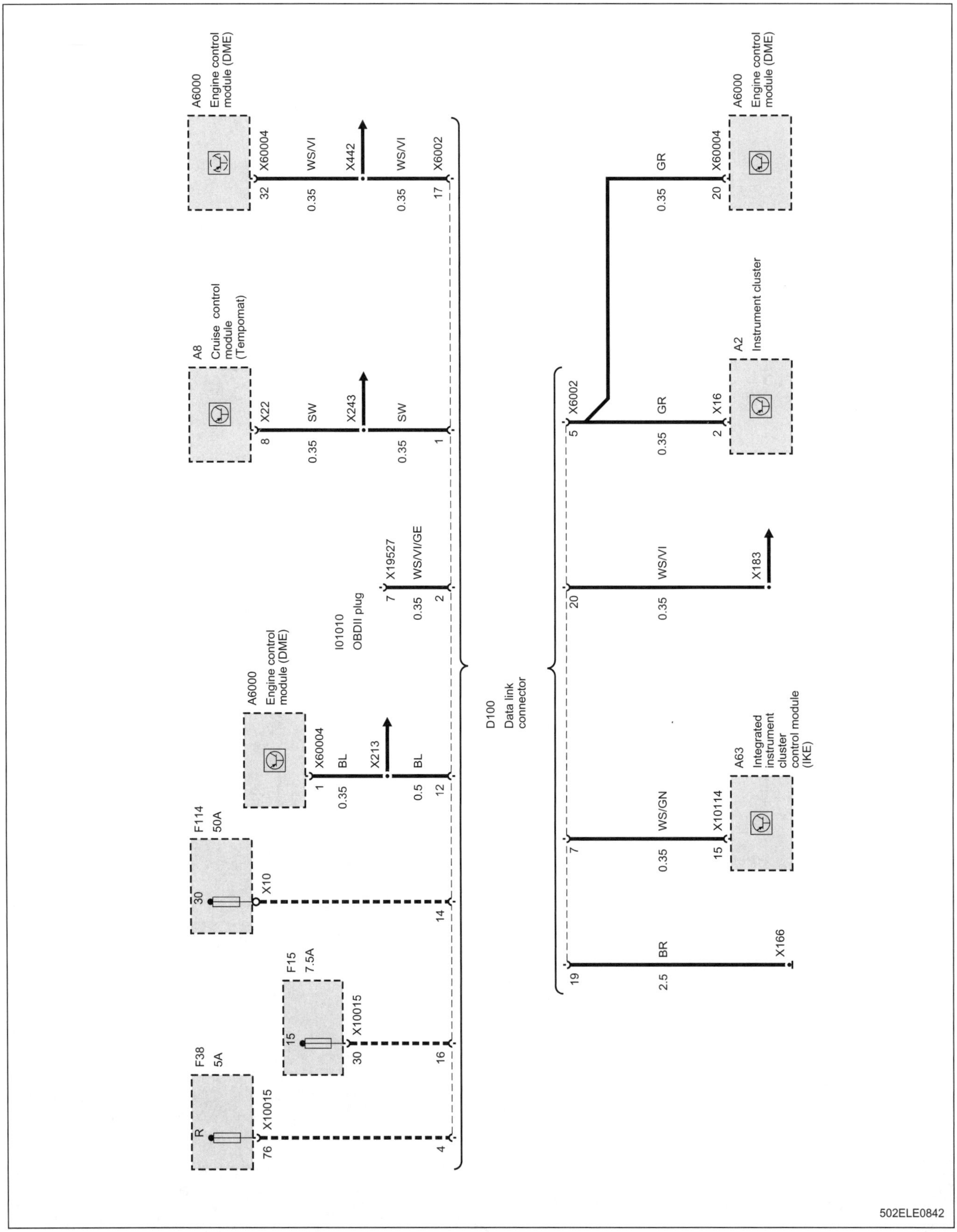

Engine Management (M 5.2.1)
Engine control module relay
(1 of 1)

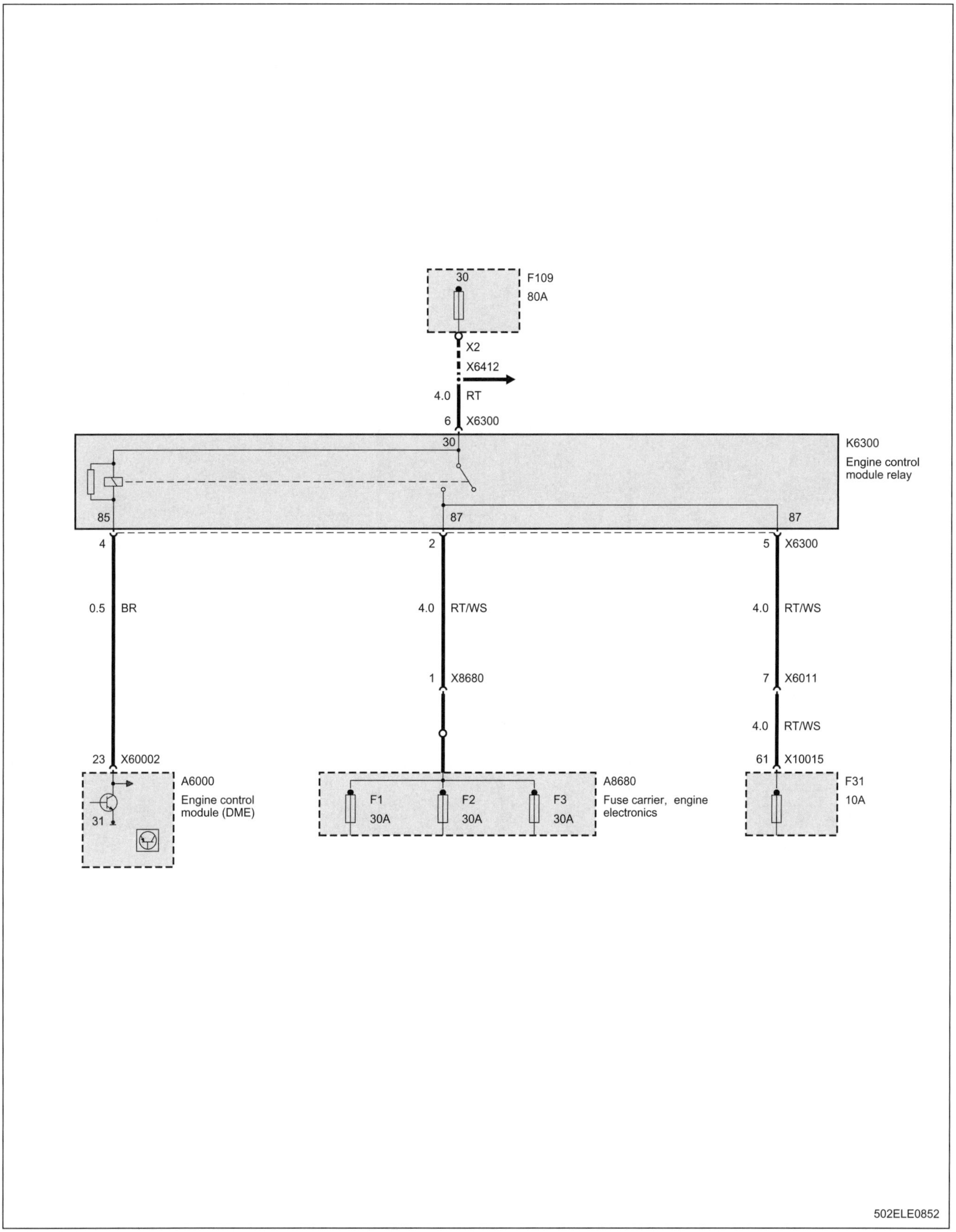

Engine Management (M 5.2.1)
Level sensor
(1 of 1)

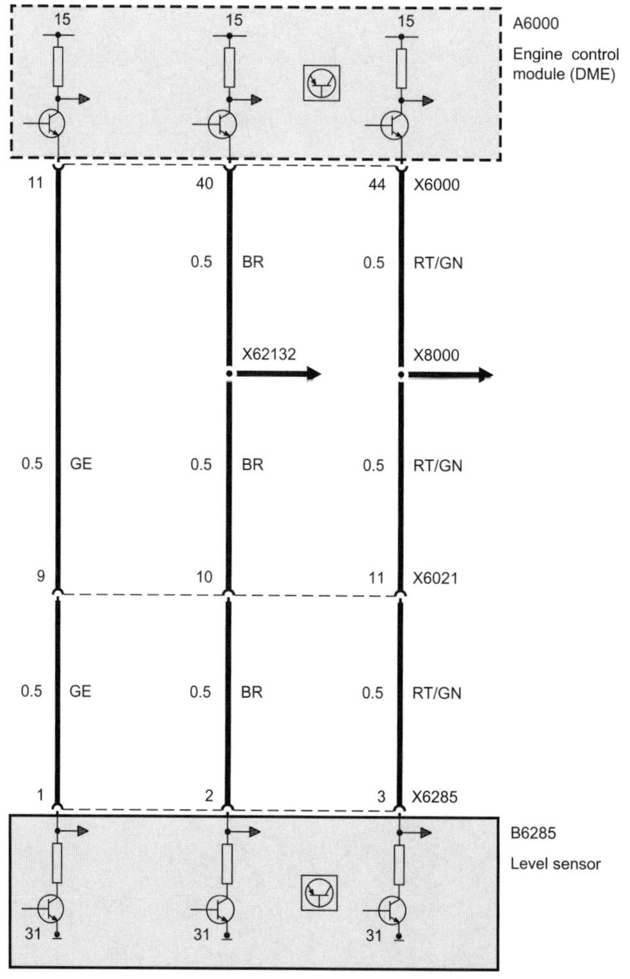

502ELE0832

Engine Management (M 5.2.1)
Power, DME control module
(1 of 1)

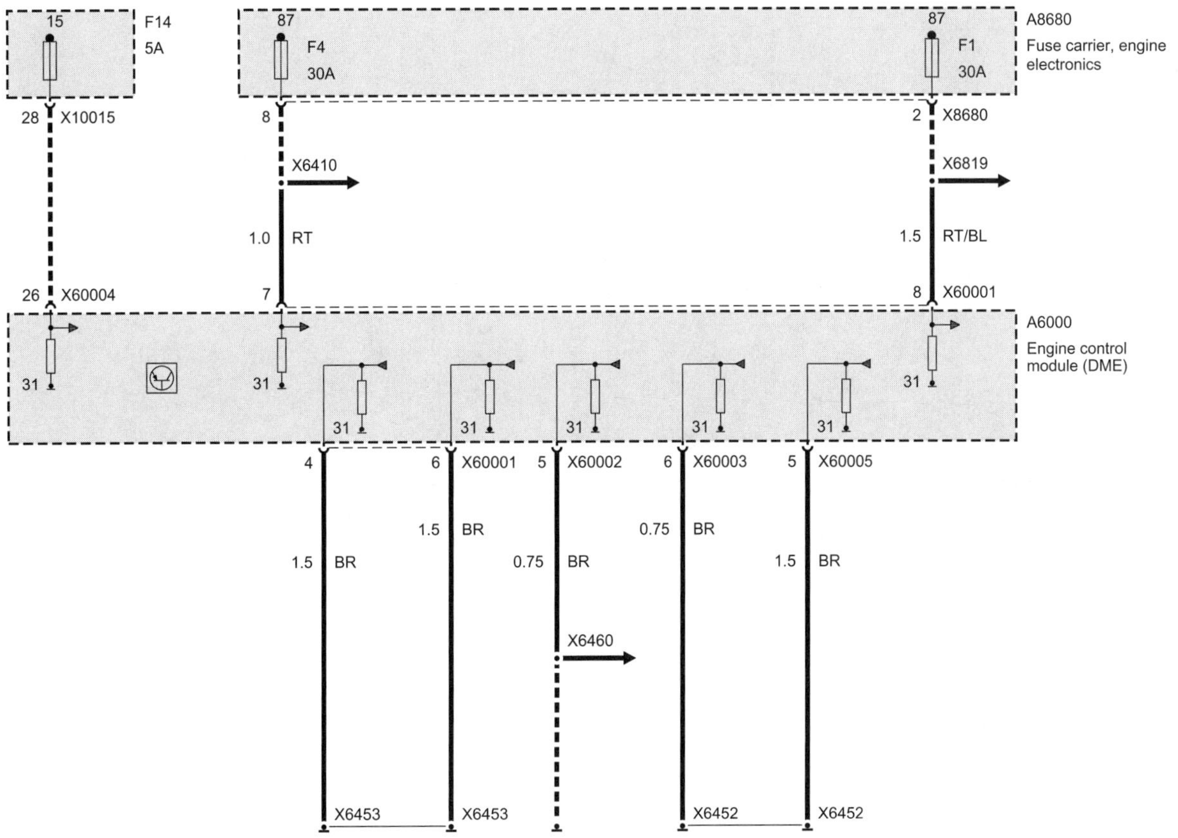

Engine Management (M 5.2.1)
Fuel pump
(1 of 1)

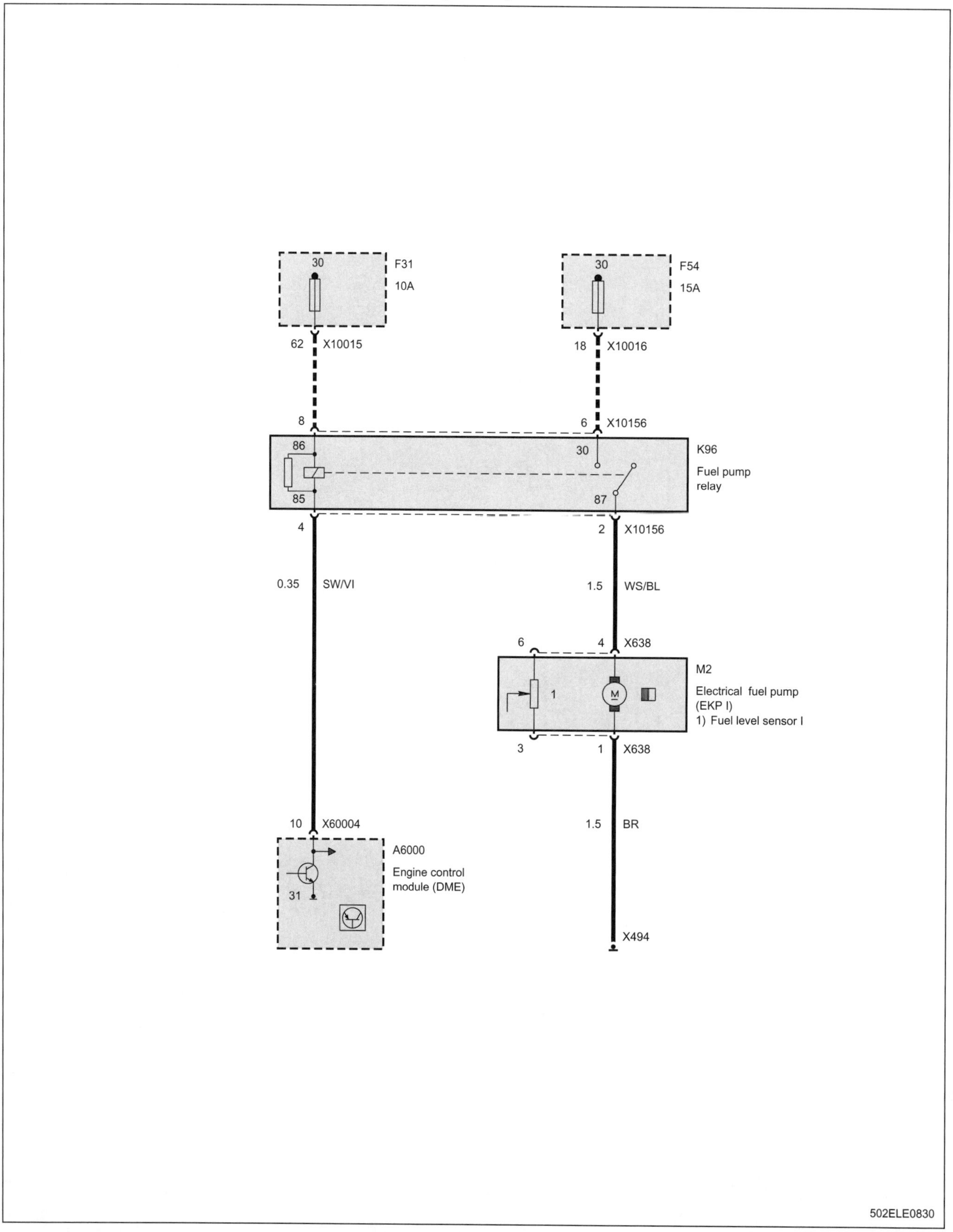
30
F31
10A
30
F54
15A
62
X10015
18
X10016
8
6
X10156
86
30
K96
Fuel pump
relay
85
87
4
2
X10156
0.35
SW/VI
1.5
WS/BL
6
4
X638
M2
Electrical fuel pump
(EKP I)
1) Fuel level sensor I
1
3
1
X638
10
X60004
1.5
BR
A6000
Engine control
module (DME)
31
X494
502ELE0830

Engine Management (M 5.2.1)
Idle speed control valve
(1 of 1)

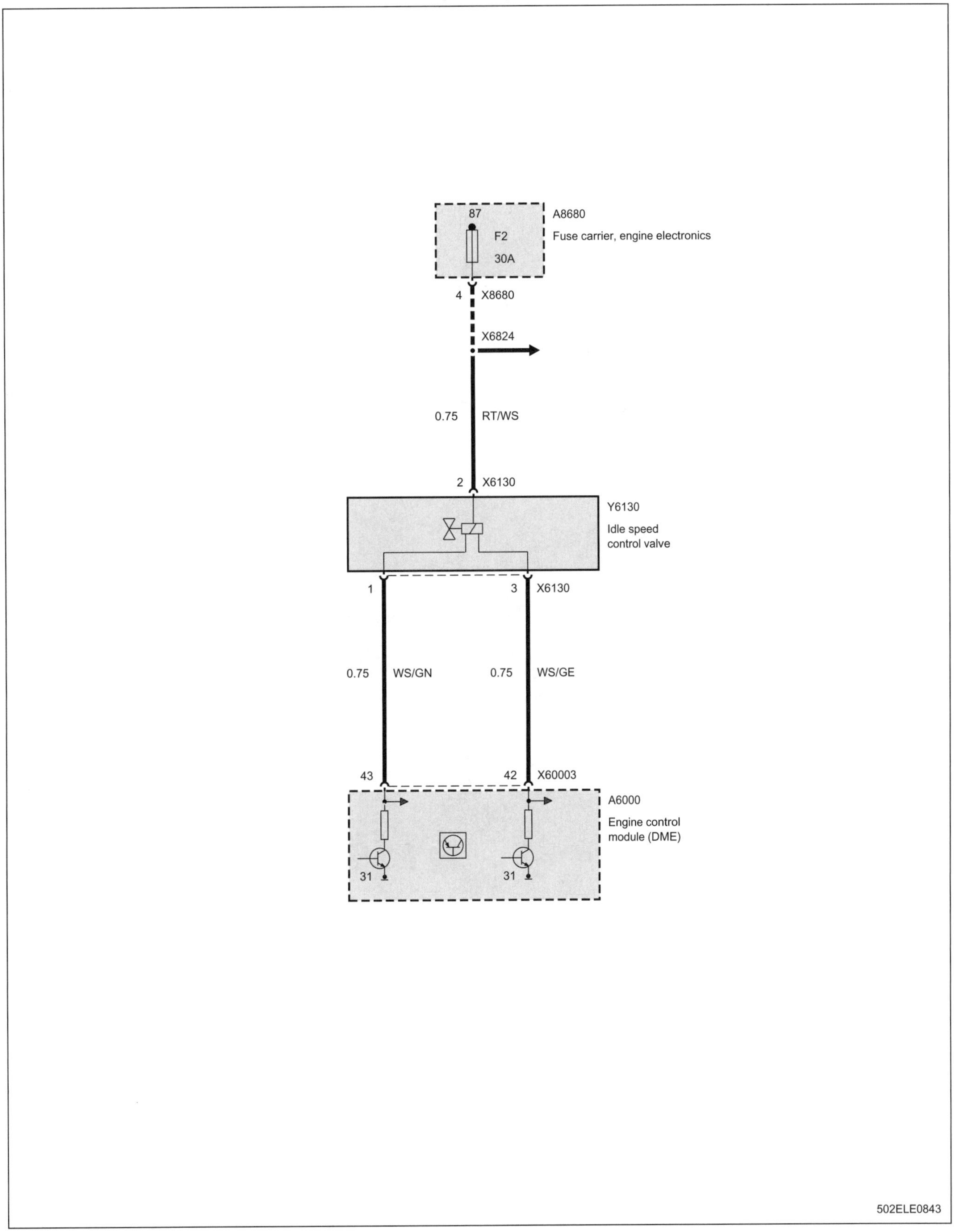

Engine Management (M 5.2.1)
Hot-film air mass meter
(1 of 1)

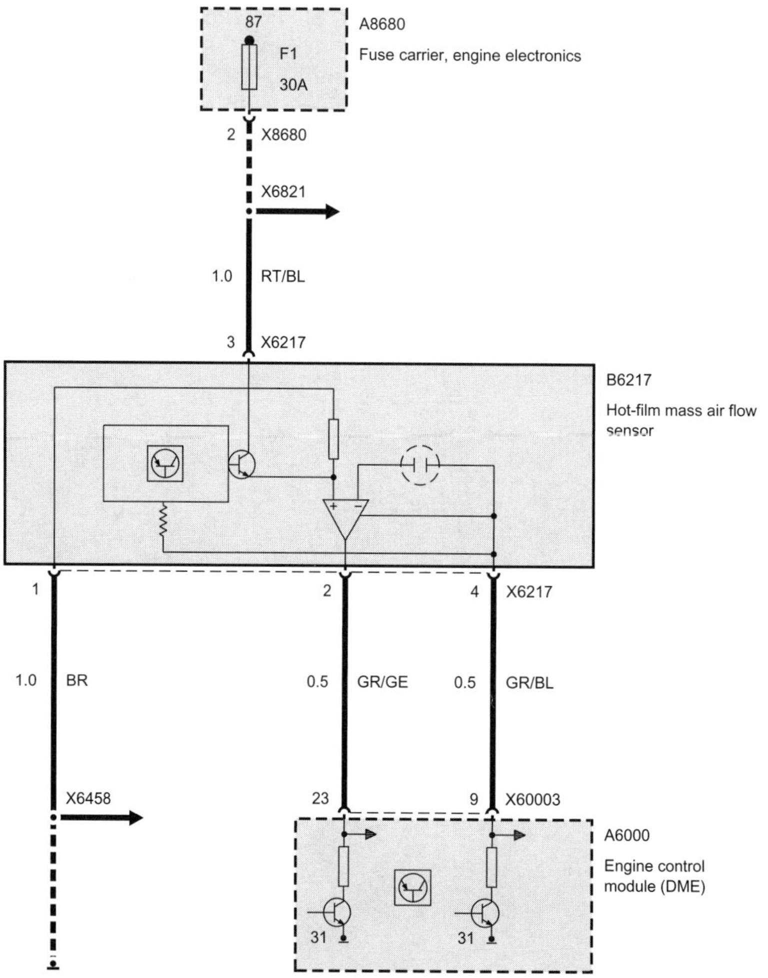

502ELE0850

Engine Management (M 5.2.1)
Intake air temperature sensor
(1 of 1)

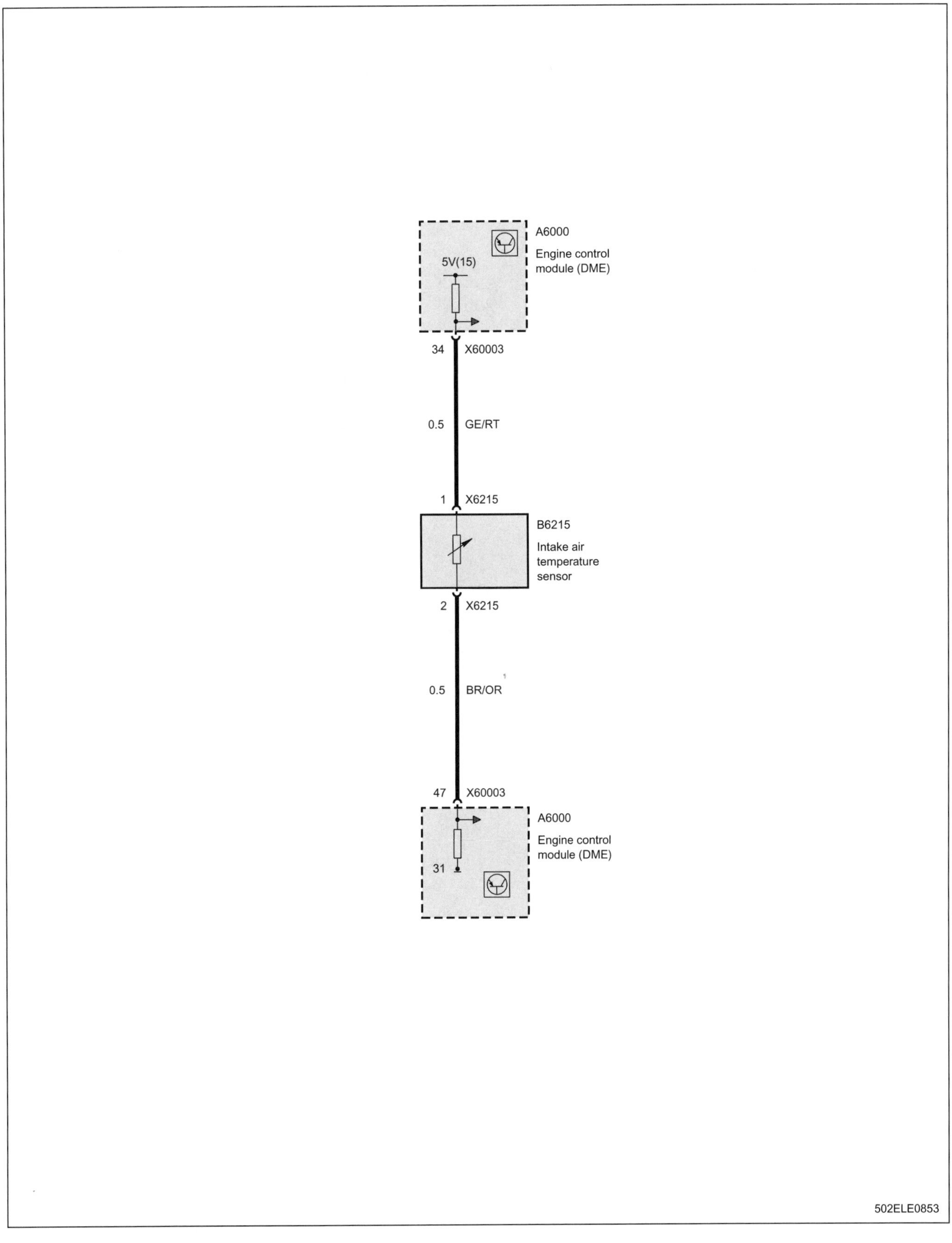

Engine Management (M 5.2.1)
Camshaft position sensor
(1 of 1)

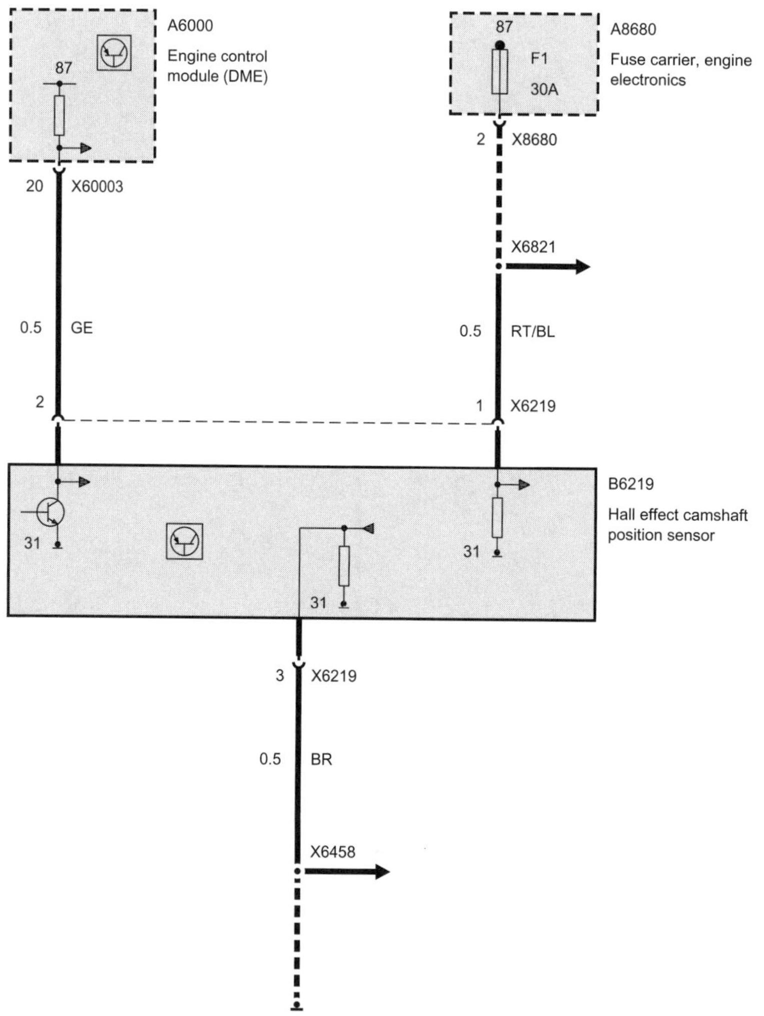

Engine Management (M 5.2.1)
Throttle position sensor
(1 of 1)

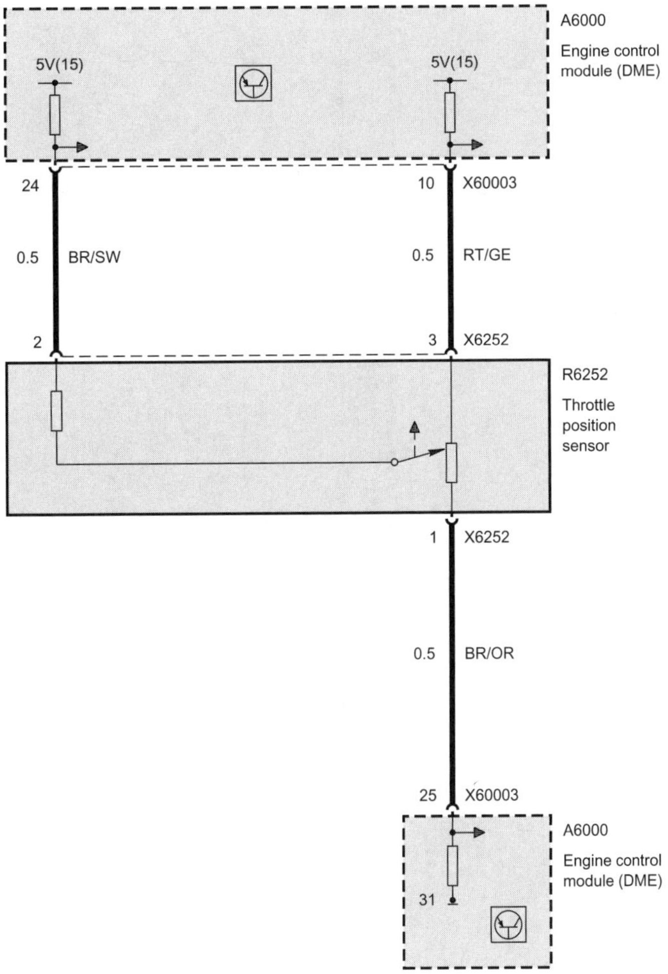

502ELE0839

Engine Management (M 5.2.1)
Characteristic map, cooling
(1 of 1)

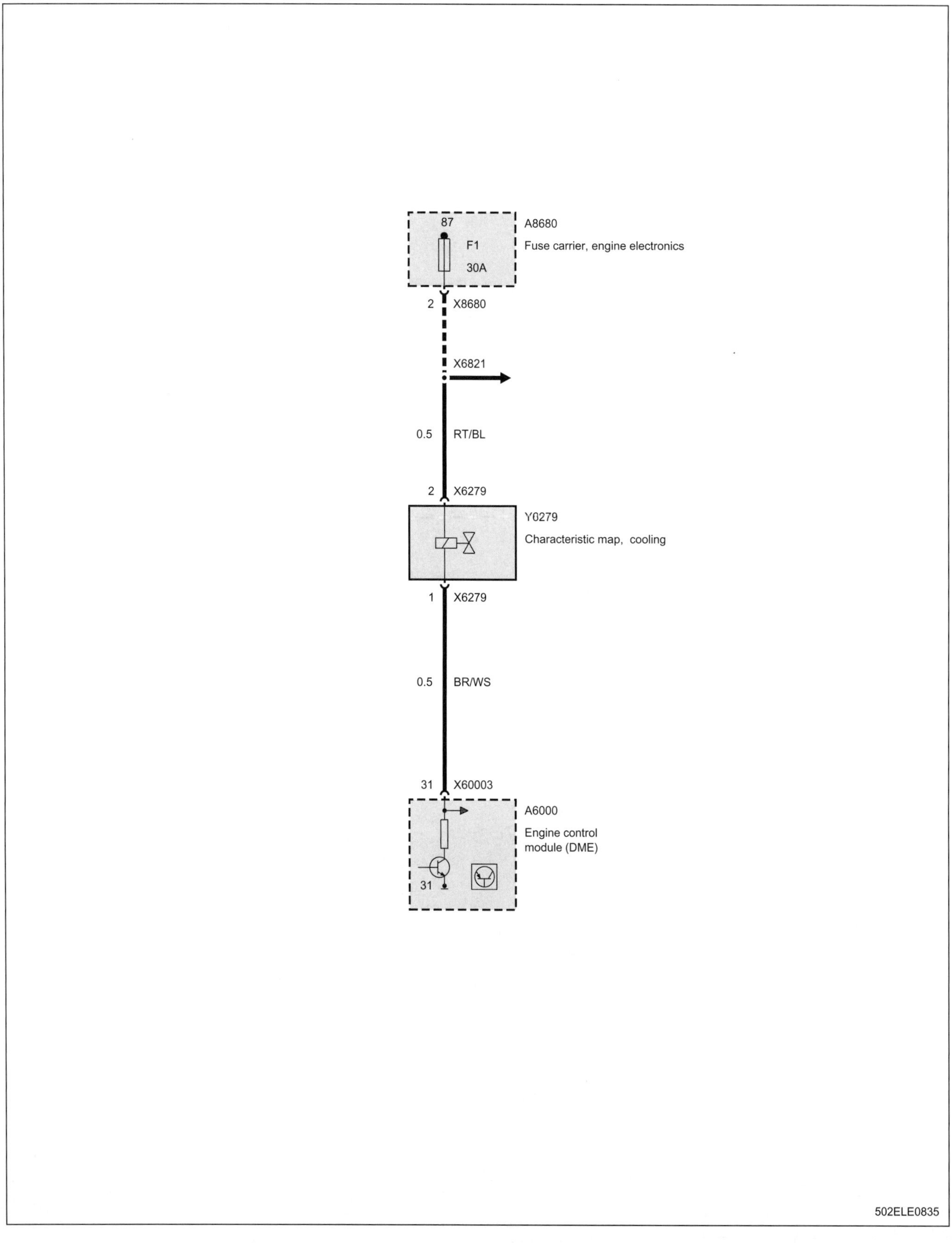

Engine Management (M 5.2.1)
Crankshaft position/RPM sensor 1
(1 of 1)

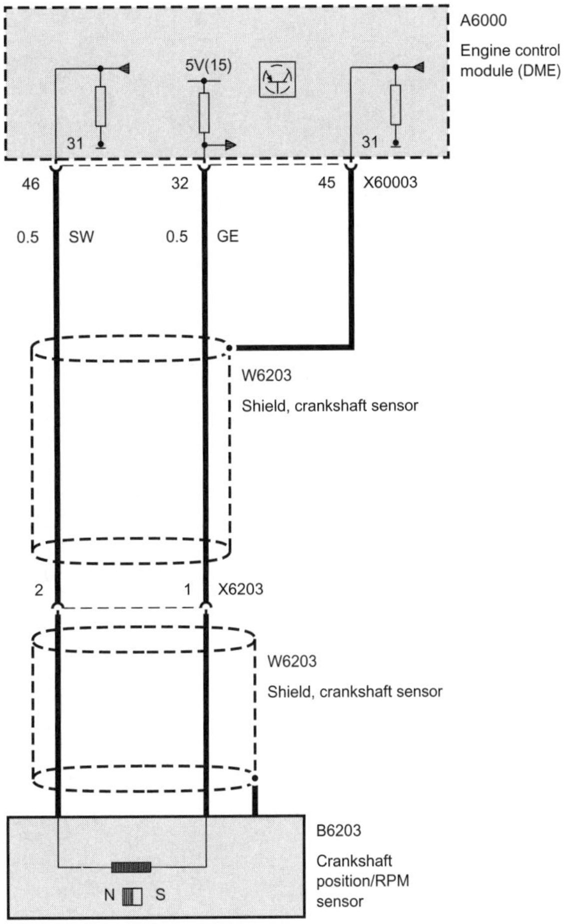

502ELE0859

Engine Management (M 5.2.1)
Dual temperature sensor
(1 of 1)

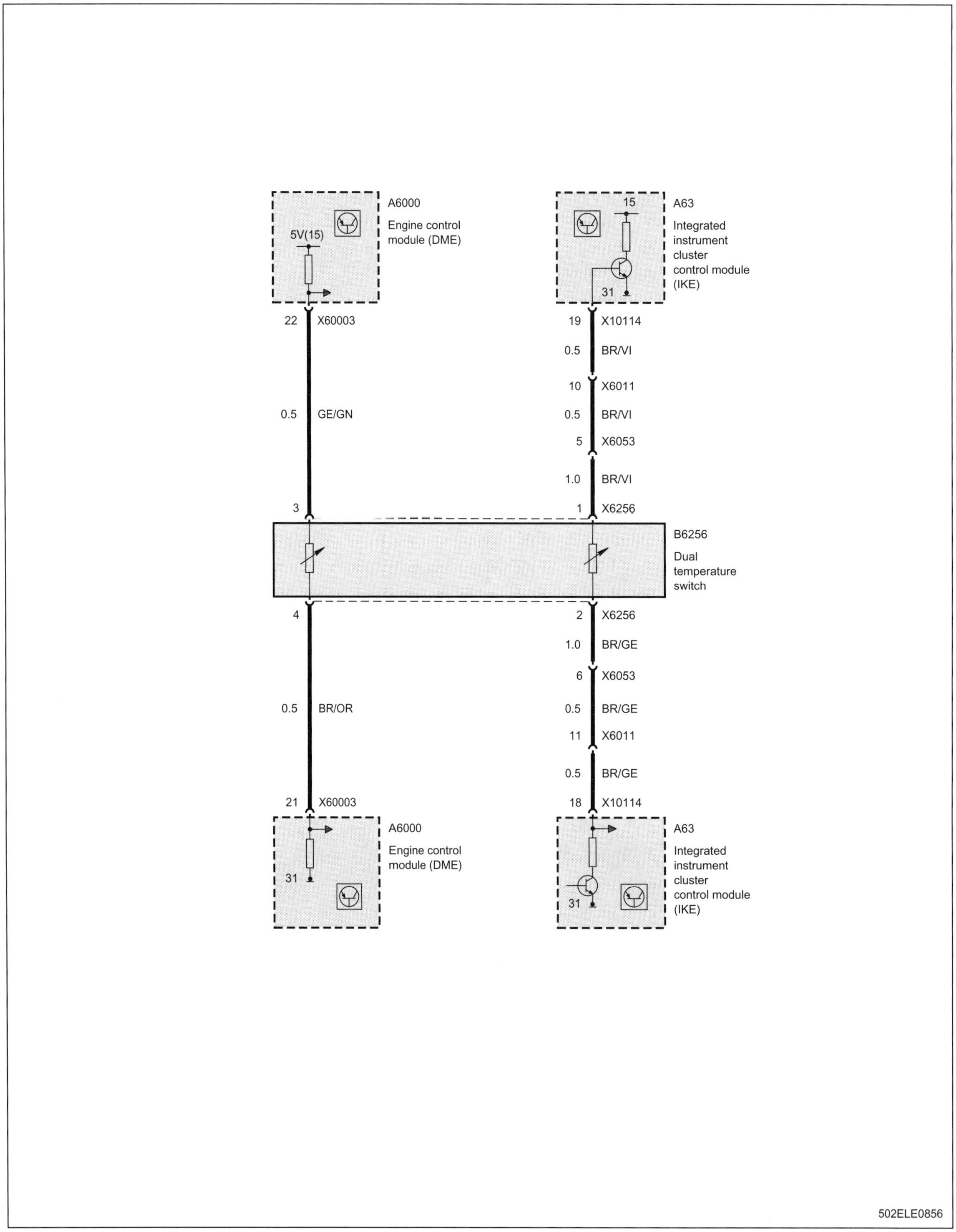

Engine Management (M 5.2.1)
Cyl. 1-2, 3-4 knock sensors
(1 of 1)

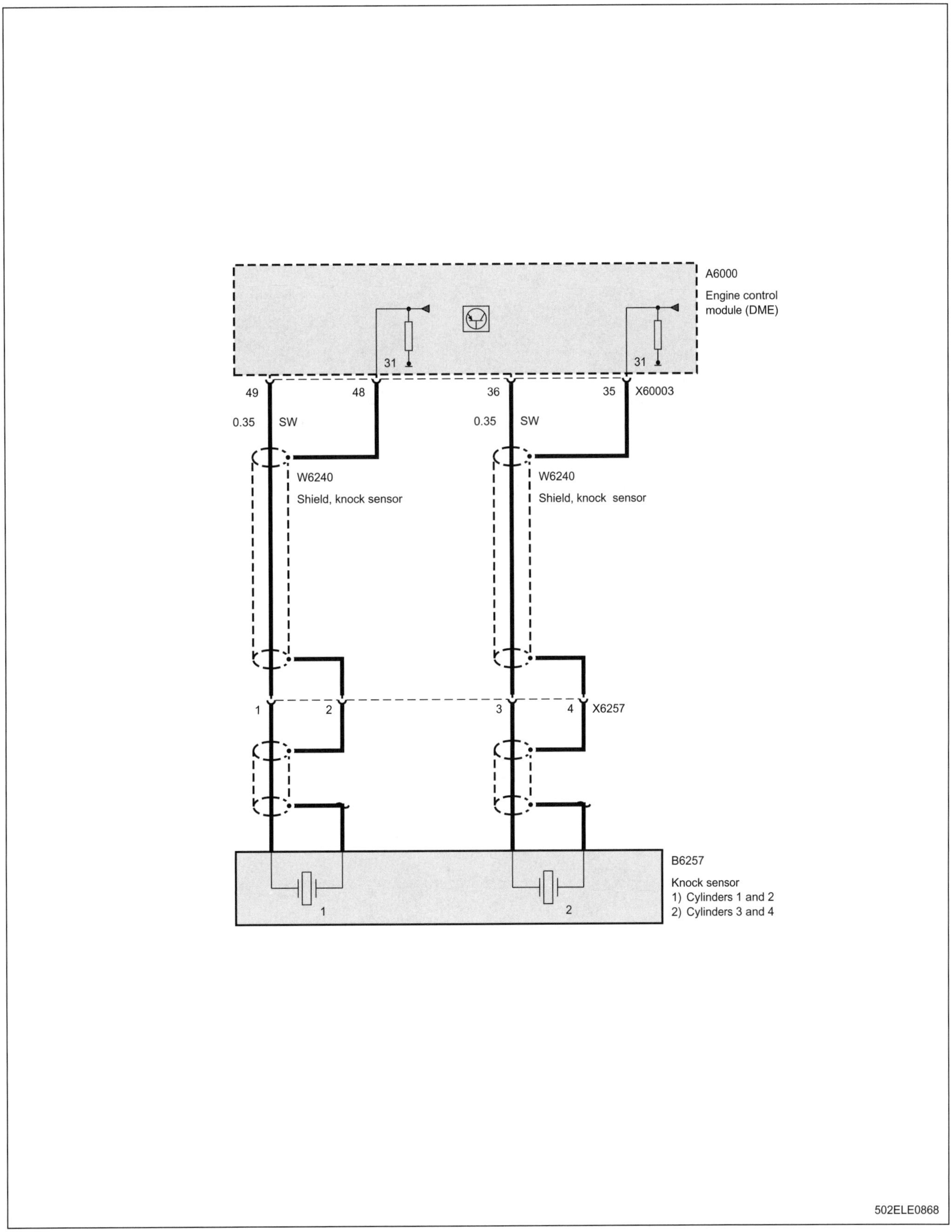

Engine Management (M 5.2.1)
Cyl. 5-6, 7-8 knock sensors
(1 of 1)

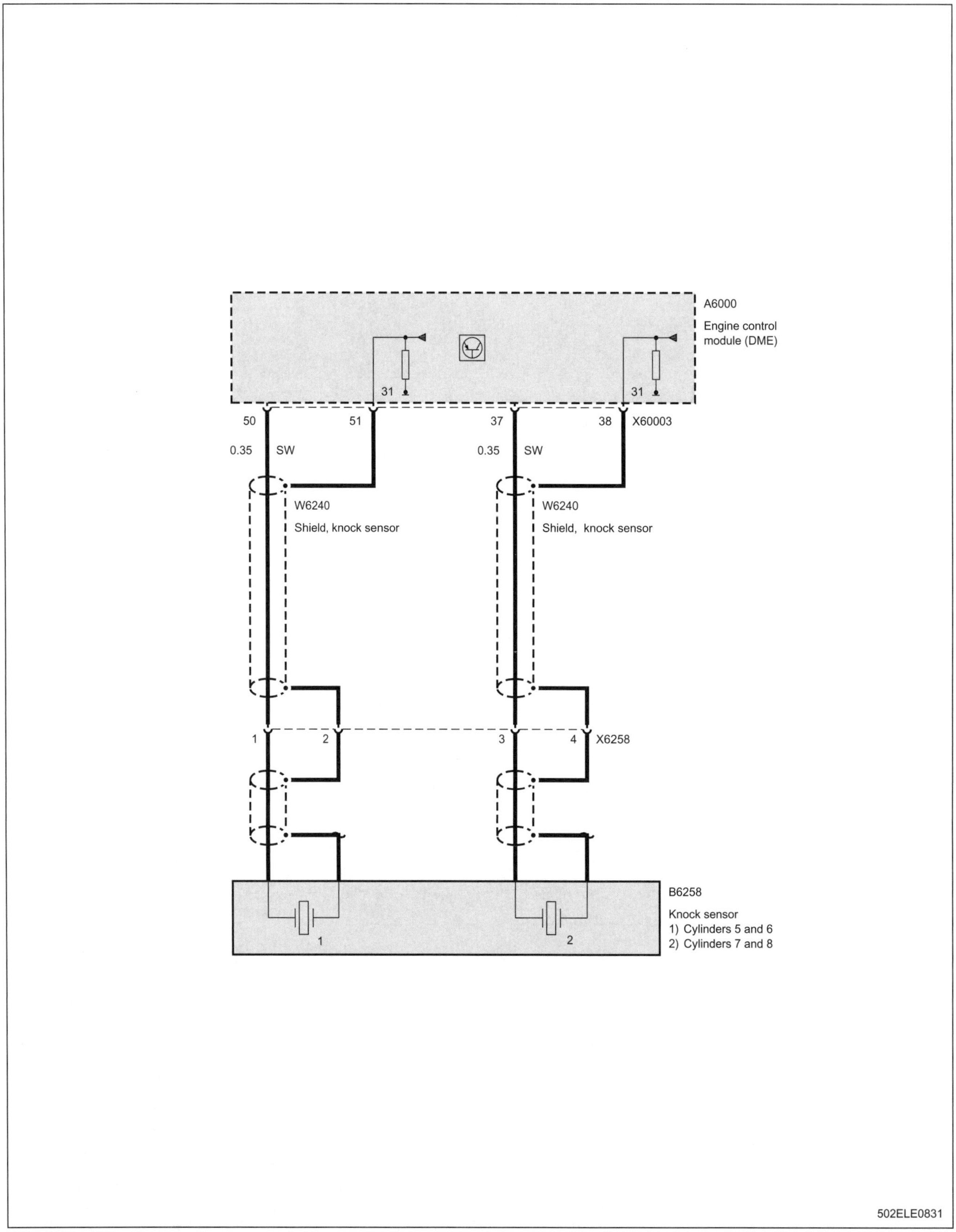

Engine Management (M 5.2.1)
Oxygen sensor 1 in front of catalytic converter
(1 of 1)

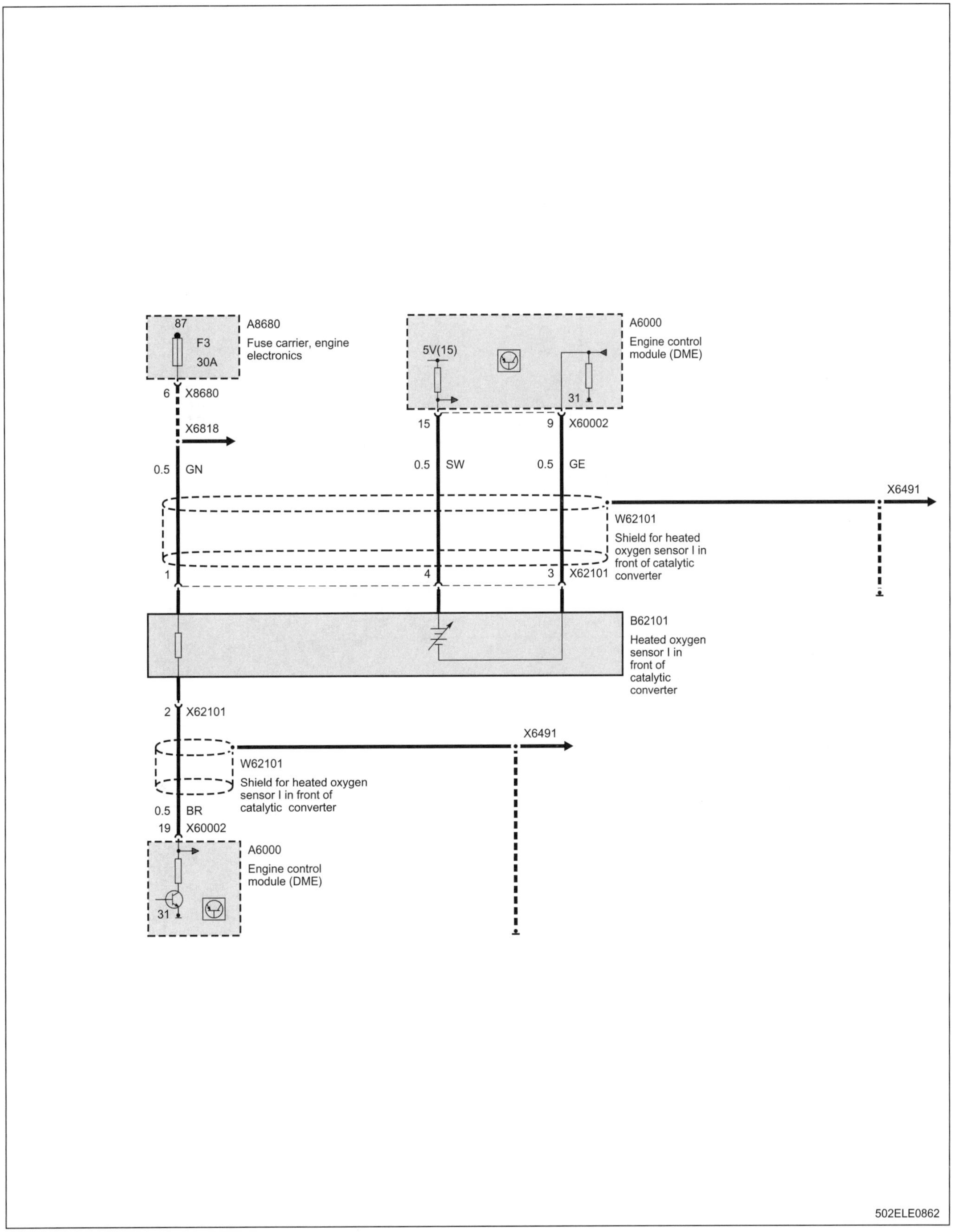

Engine Management (M 5.2.1)
Oxygen sensor 1 behind catalytic converter
(1 of 1)

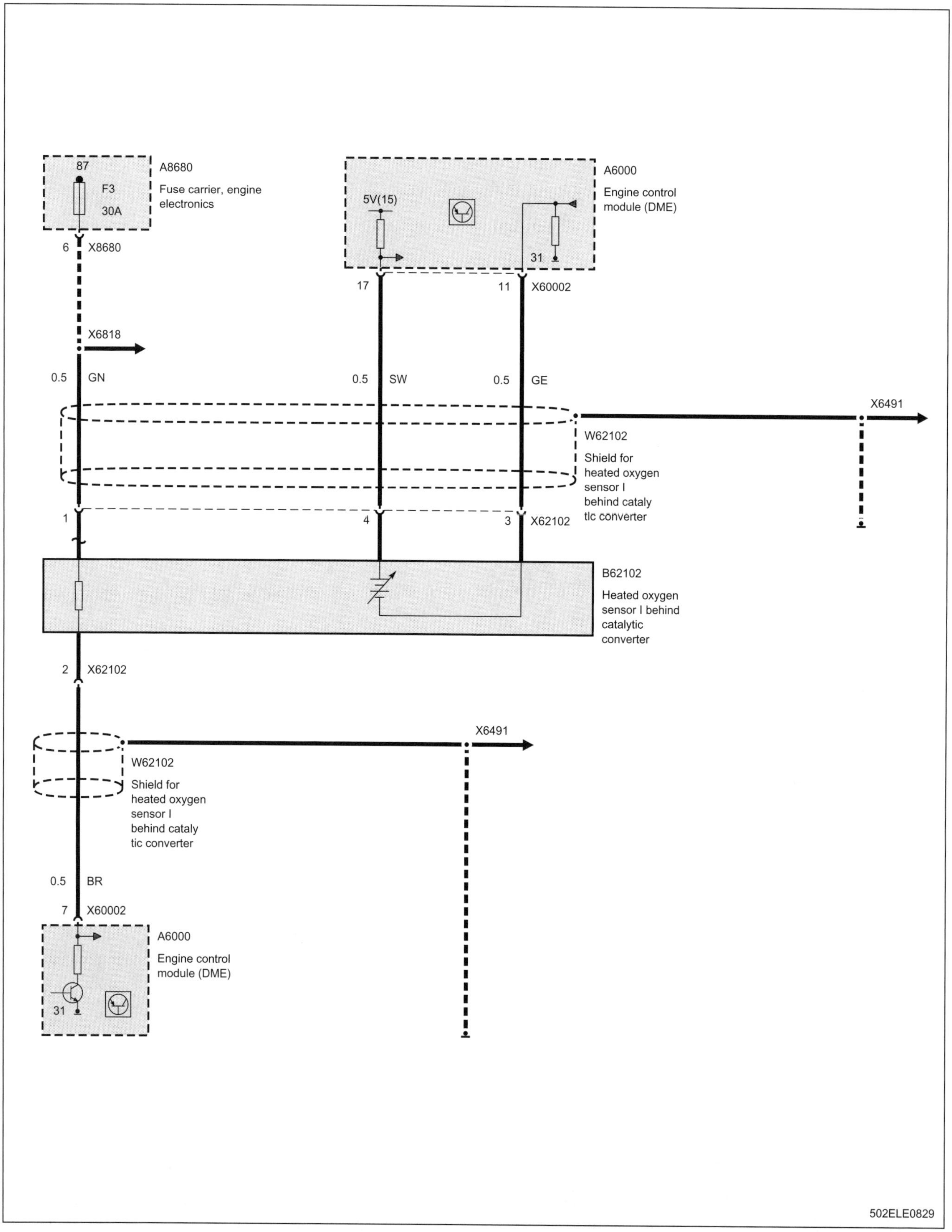

502ELE0829

Engine Management (M 5.2.1)
Oxygen sensor 2 in front of catalytic converter
(1 of 1)

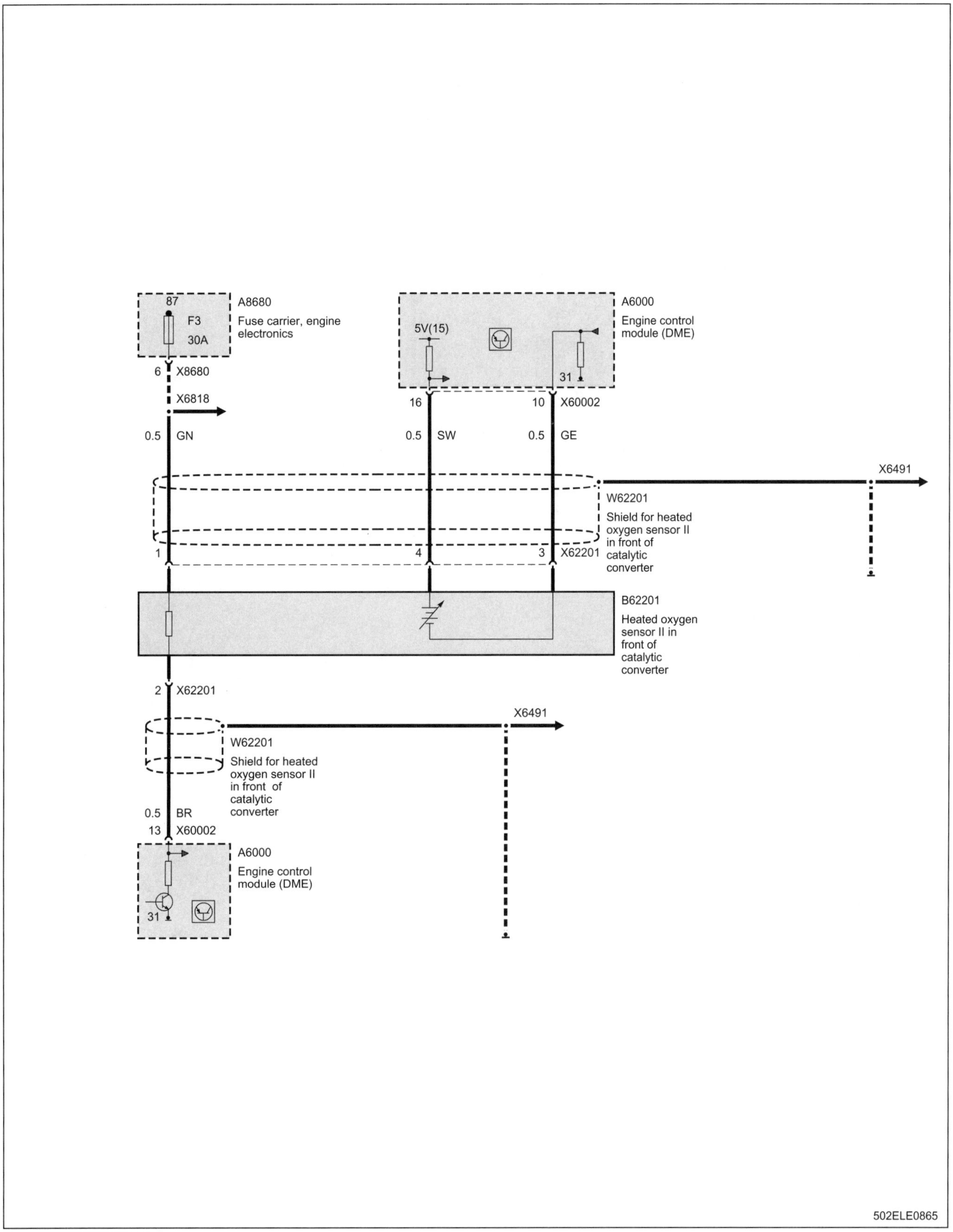

Engine Management (M 5.2.1)
Oxygen sensor 2 behind catalytic converter
(1 of 1)

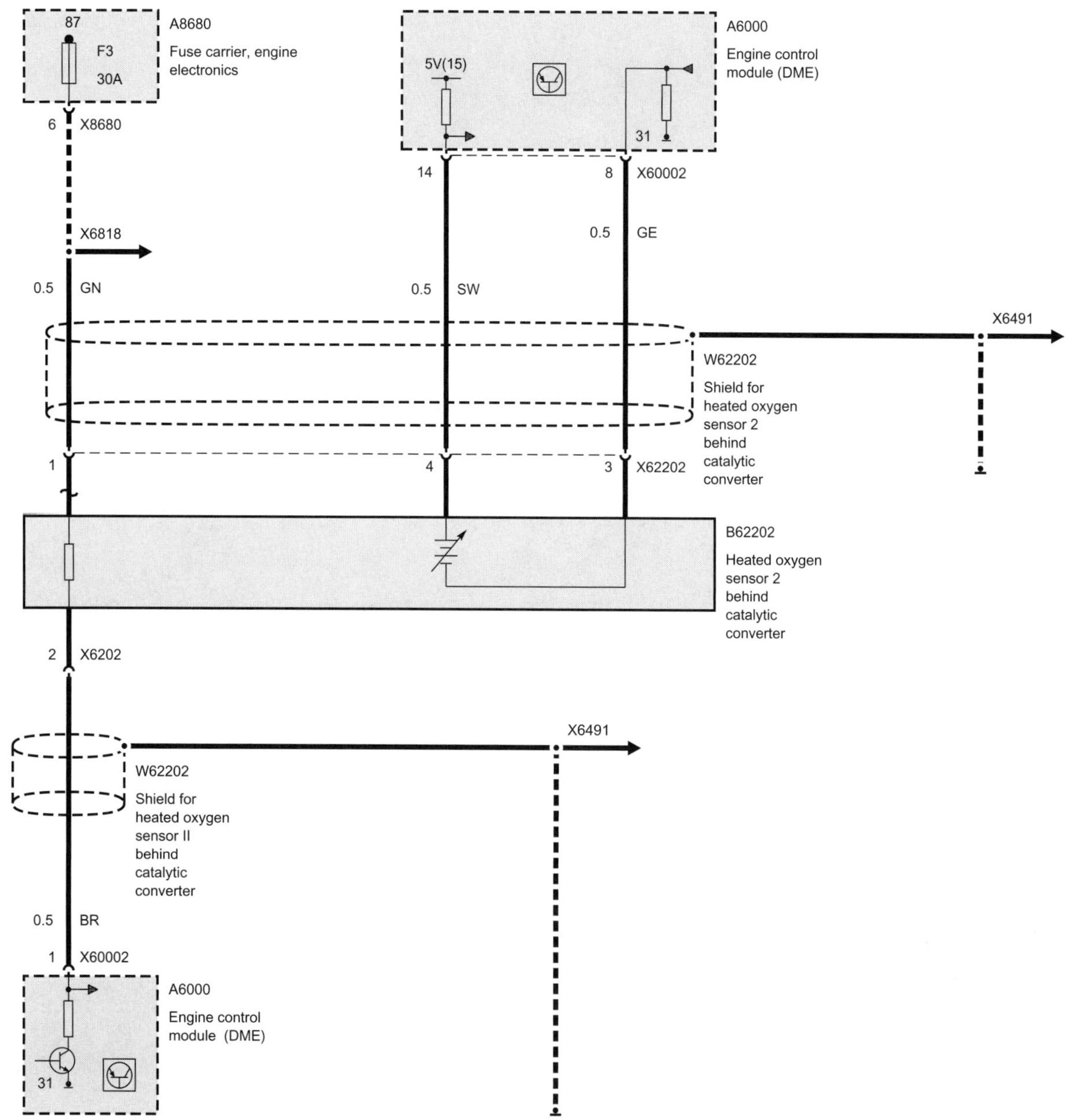

502ELE0833

Engine Management (M 5.2.1)
Evaporative emission valve
(1 of 1)

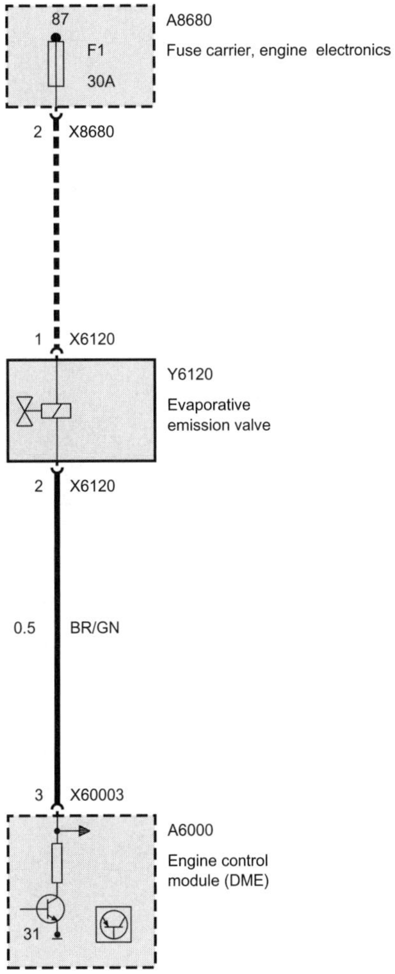

502ELE0836

Engine Management (M 5.2.1)
Running losses
(1 of 1)

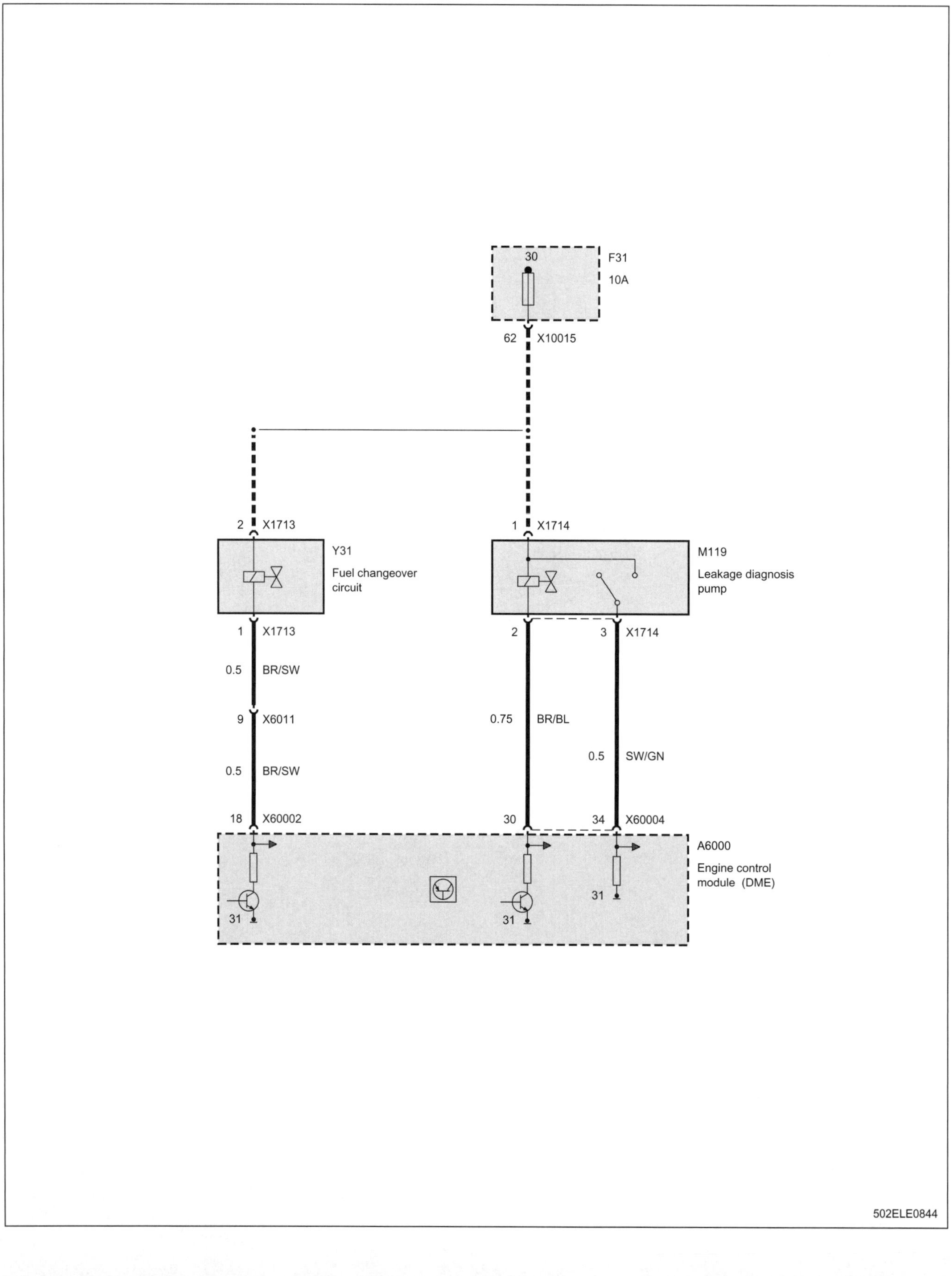
30
F31
10A
62
X10015
2
X1713
1
X1714
Y31
Fuel changeover circuit
M119
Leakage diagnosis pump
1
X1713
2
3
X1714
0.5
BR/SW
9
X6011
0.75
BR/BL
0.5
SW/GN
0.5
BR/SW
18
X60002
30
34
X60004
A6000
Engine control module (DME)
31
31
31
502ELE0844

Engine Management (M 5.2.1)
Cyl. 1 and 2 fuel injection valves
(1 of 1)

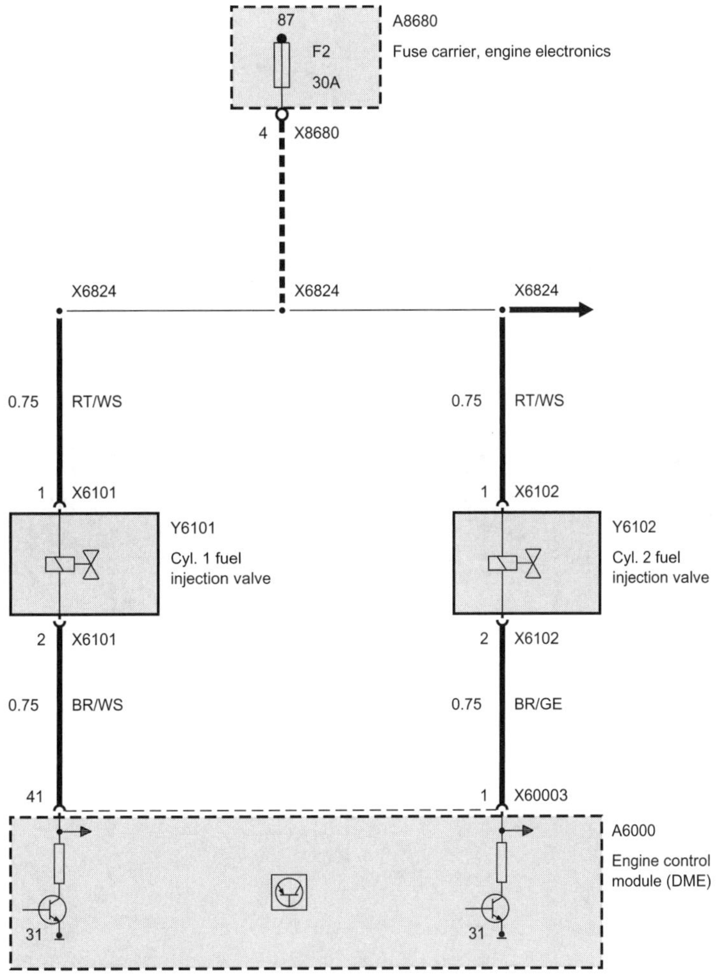

502ELE0855

Engine Management (M 5.2.1)
Cyl. 3 and 4 fuel injection valves
(1 of 1)

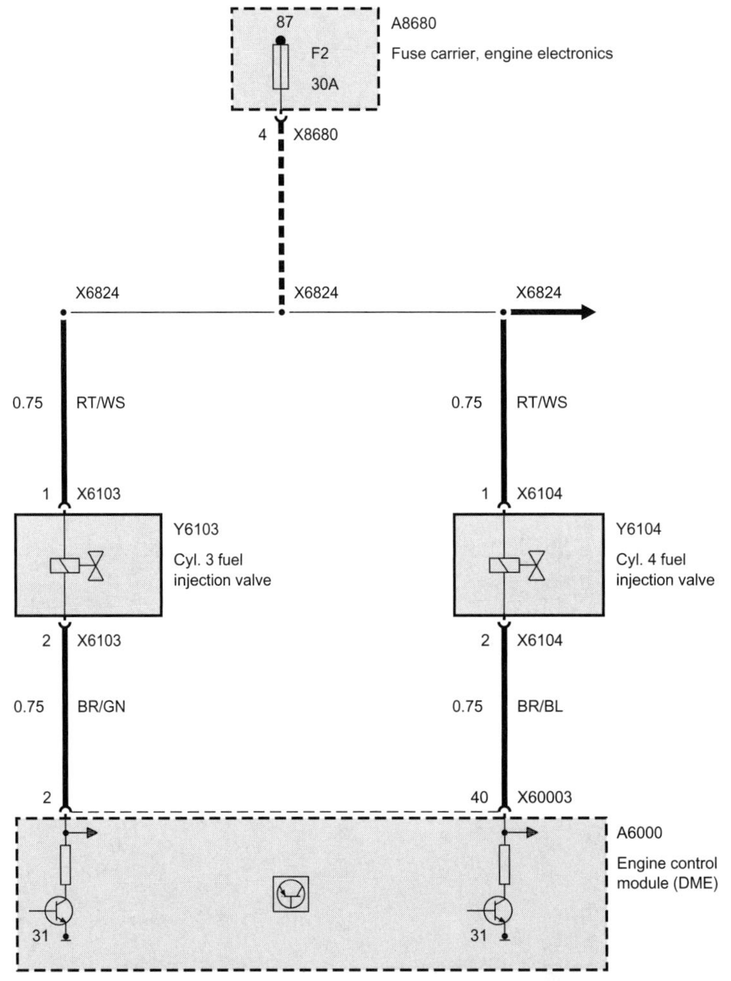

Engine Management (M 5.2.1)
Cyl. 5 and 6 fuel injection valves
(1 of 1)

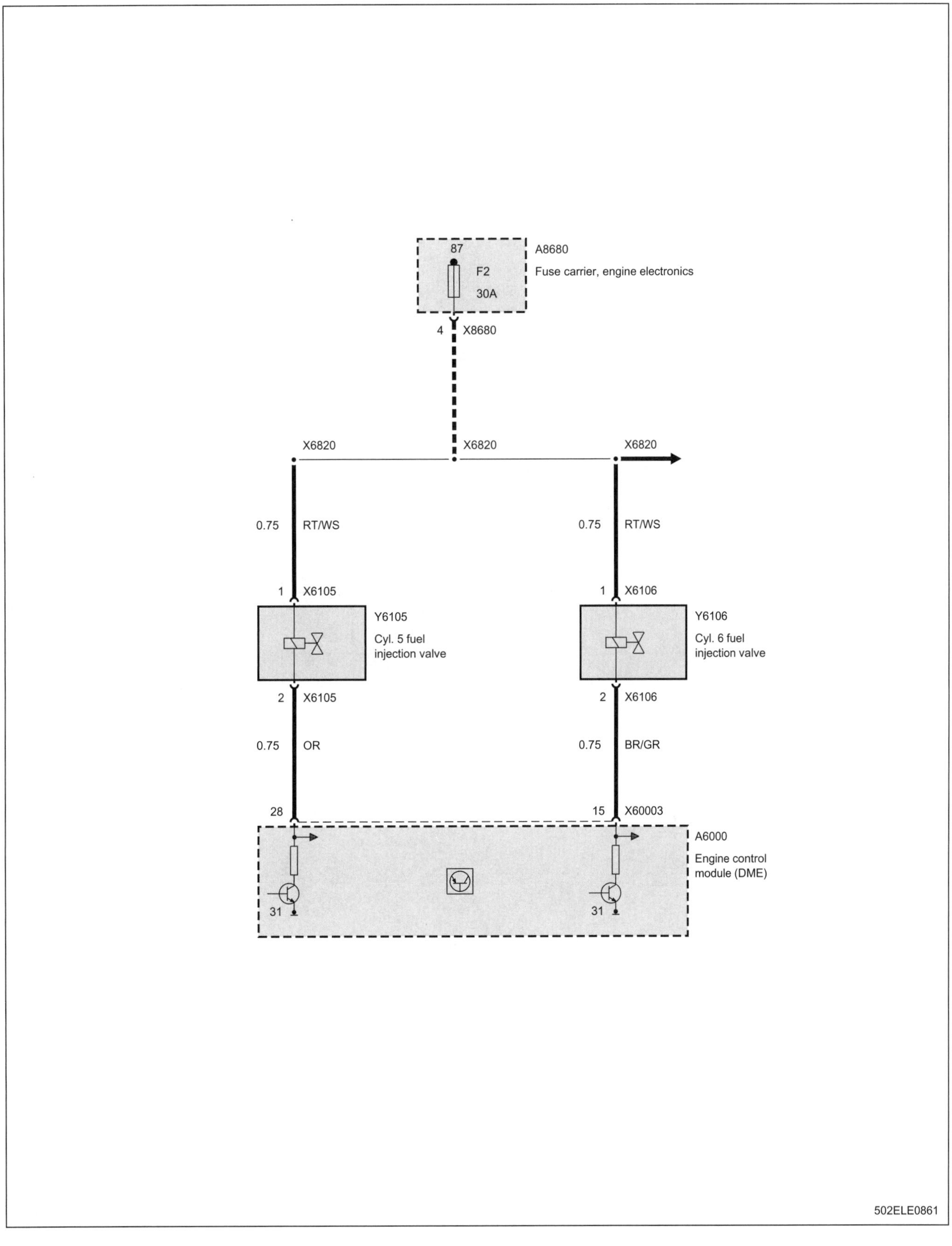

Engine Management (M 5.2.1)
Cyl. 7 and 8 fuel injection valves
(1 of 1)

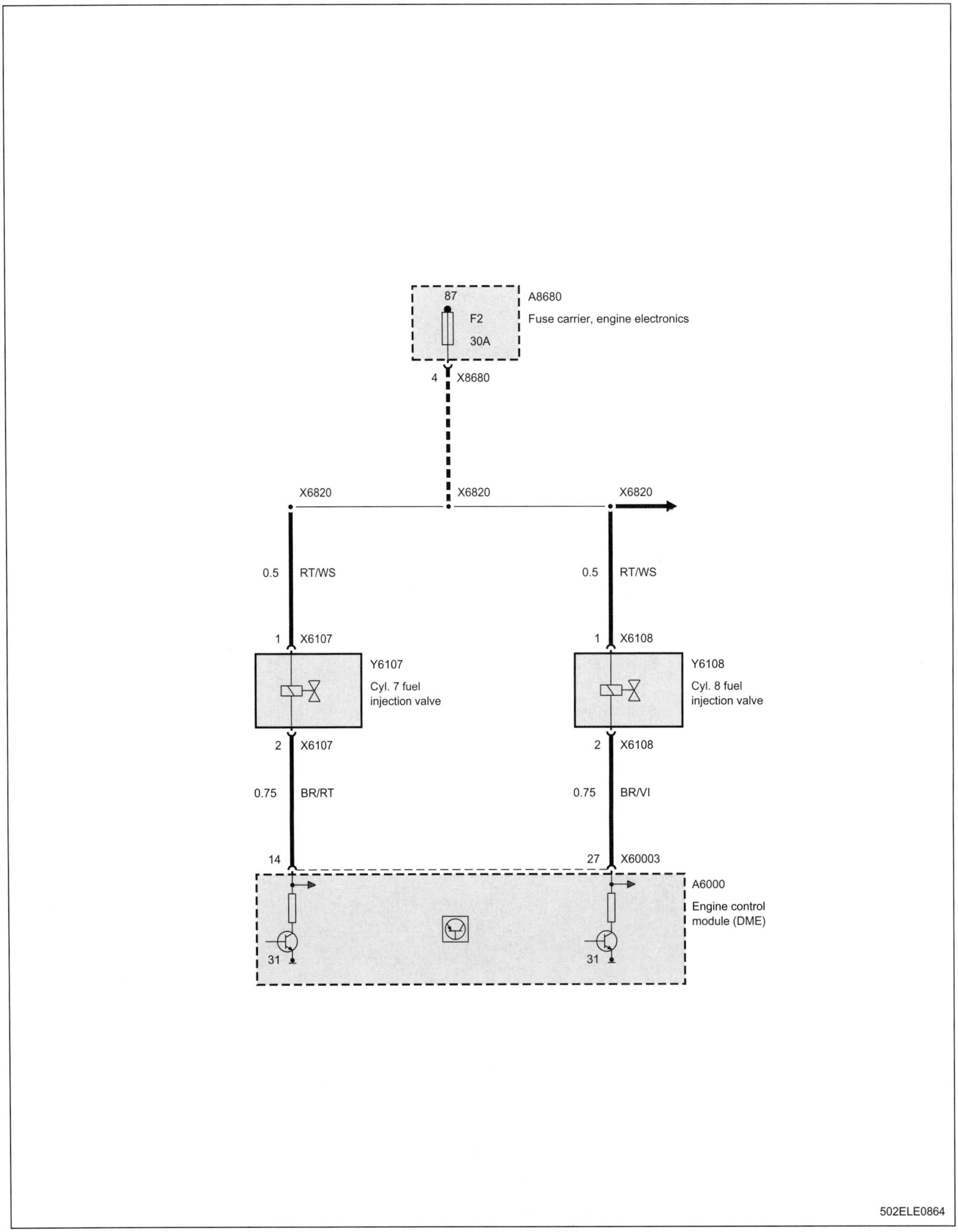

Engine Management (M 5.2.1)
Power, ignition coils
(1 of 1)

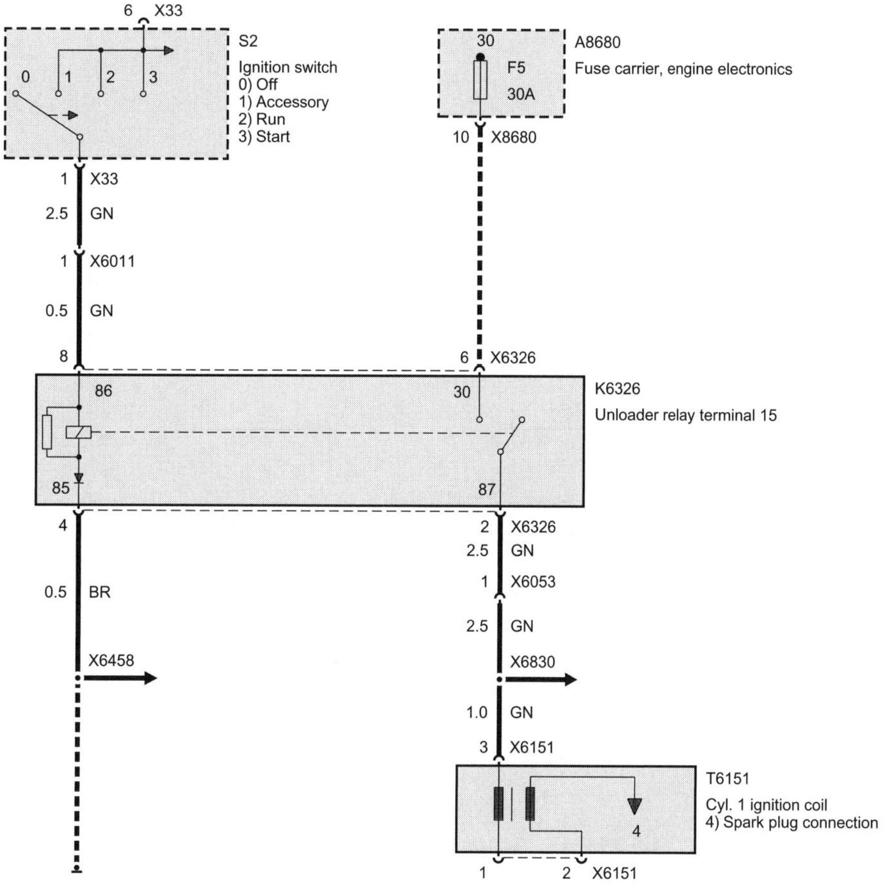

502ELE0846

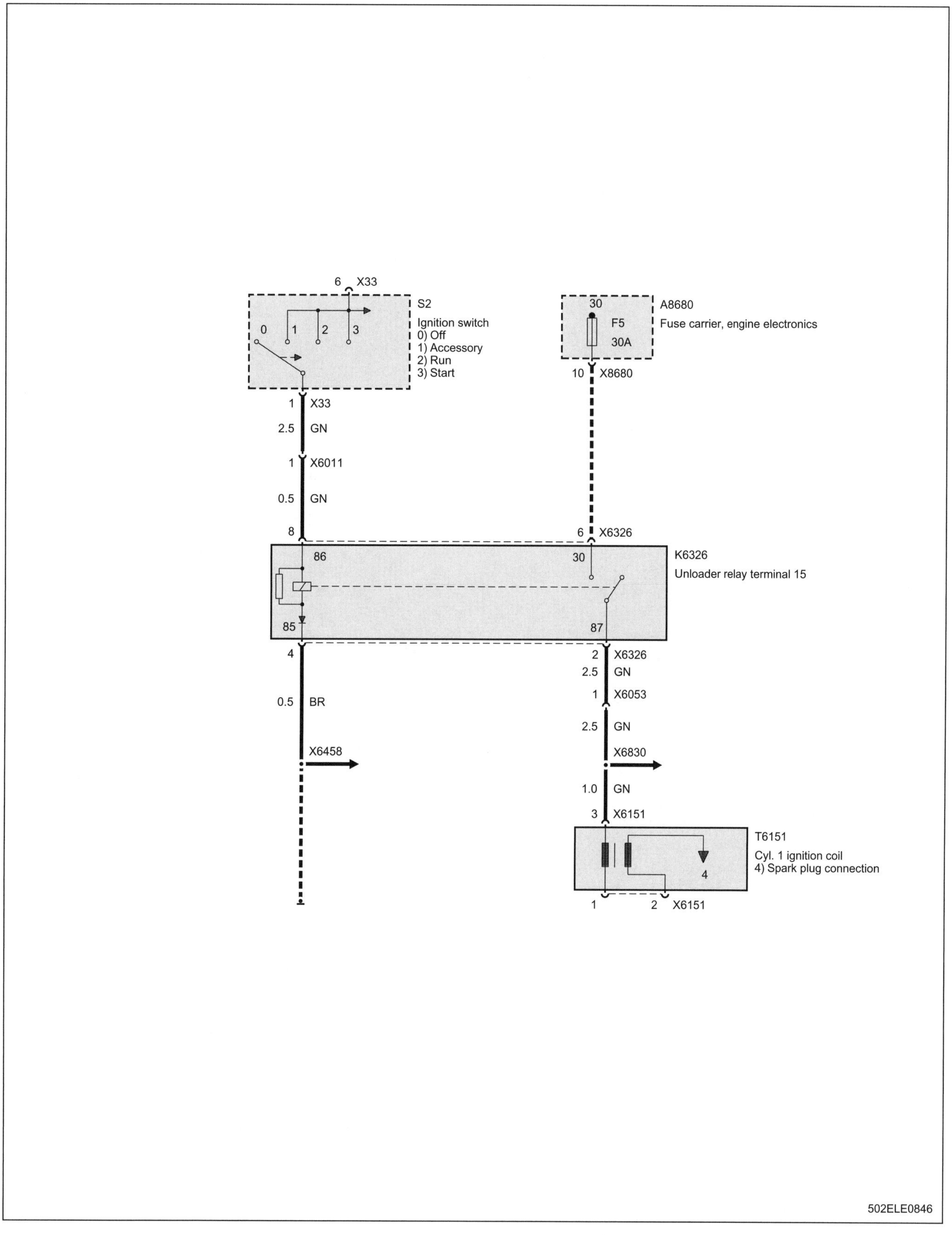

Engine Management (M 5.2.1)
Cyl. 1 and 2 ignition coils
(1 of 1)

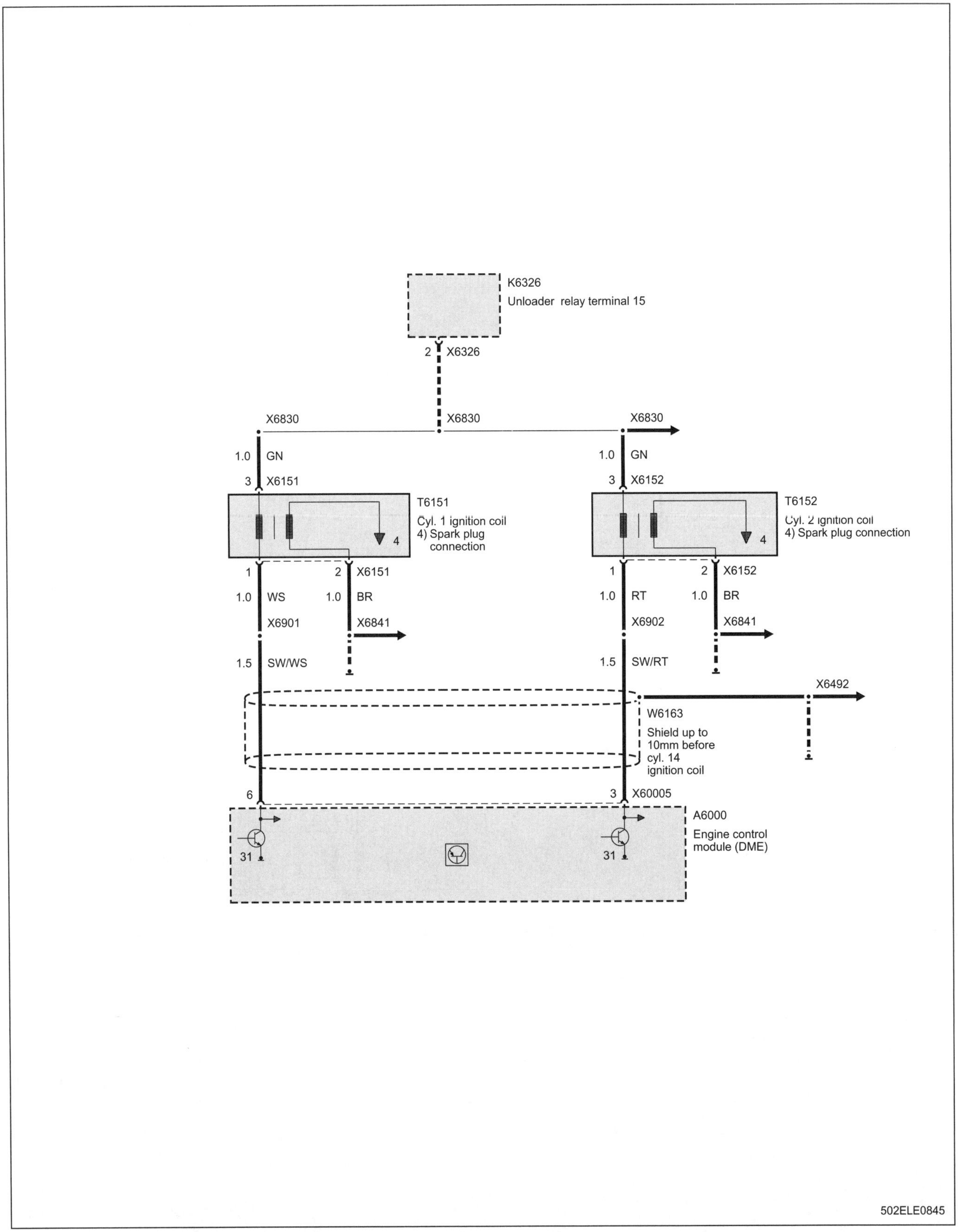

Engine Management (M 5.2.1)
Cyl. 3 and 4 ignition coils
(1 of 1)

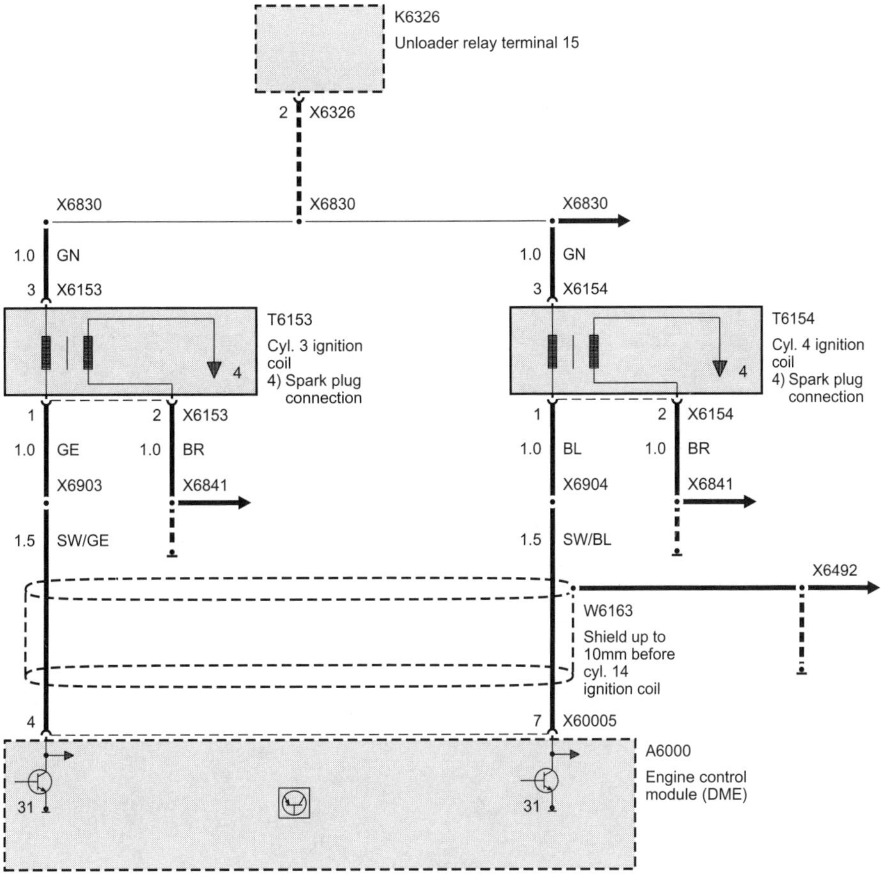

502ELE0847

Engine Management (M 5.2.1)
Cyl. 5 and 6 ignition coils
(1 of 1)

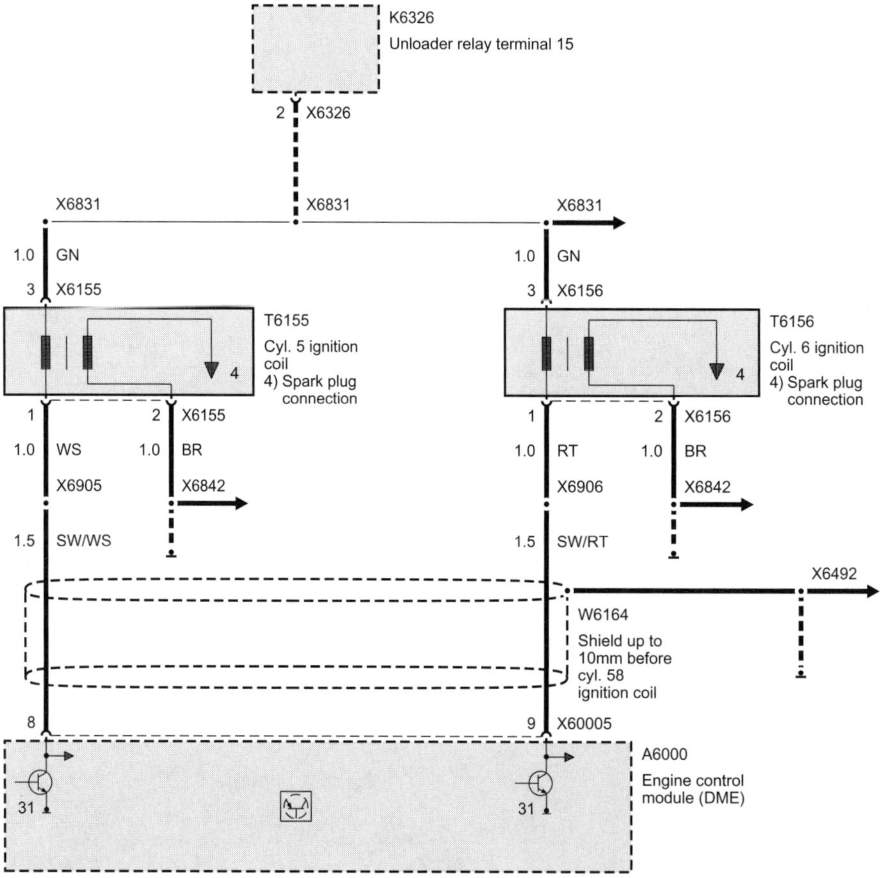

502ELE0851

Engine Management (M 5.2.1)
Fuse supply, engine electronics
(1 of 1)

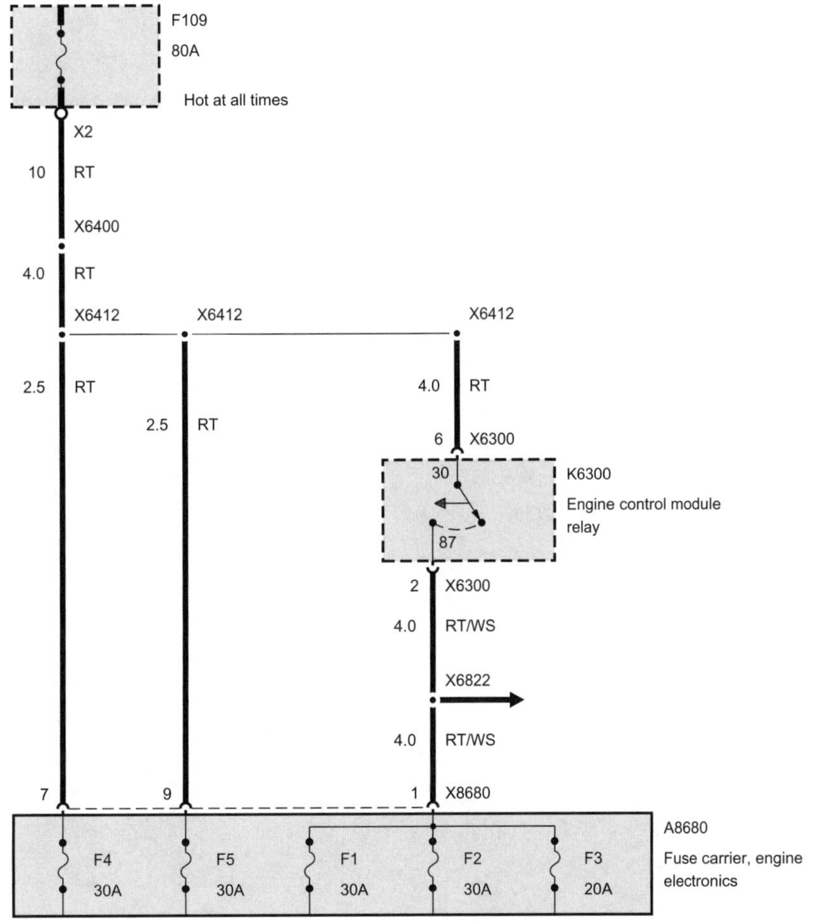

502ELE0857

Engine Management (M 5.2.1)
Cyl. 7 and 8 ignition coils
(1 of 1)

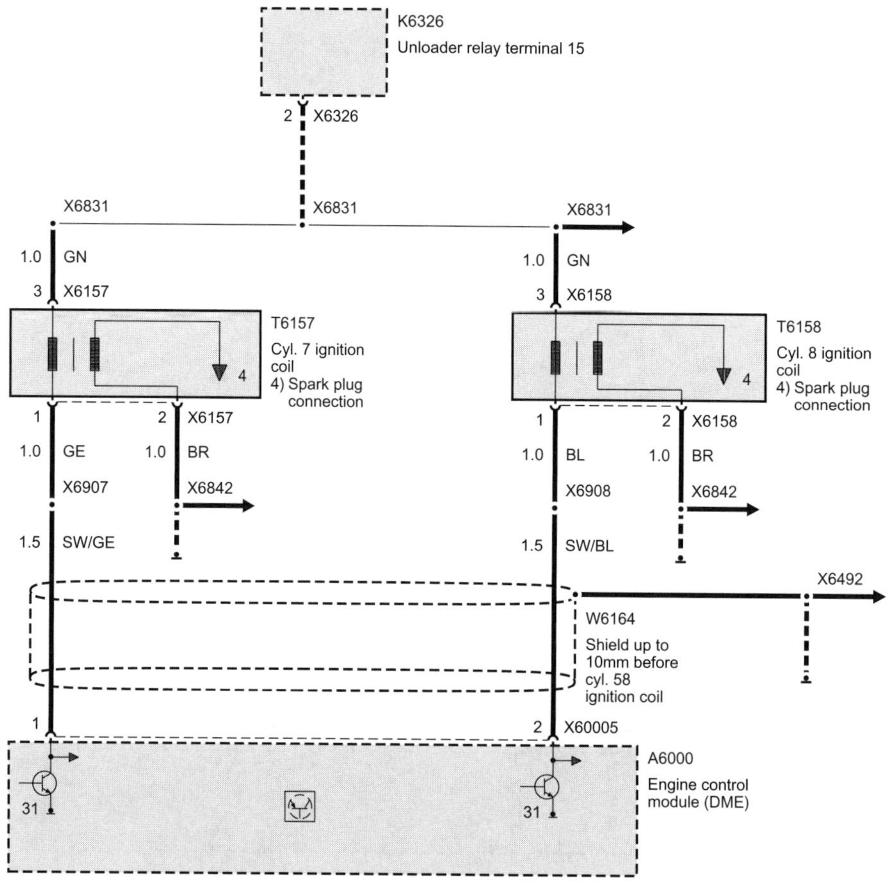

Engine Management (M 5.2.1)
Start detection
(1 of 1)

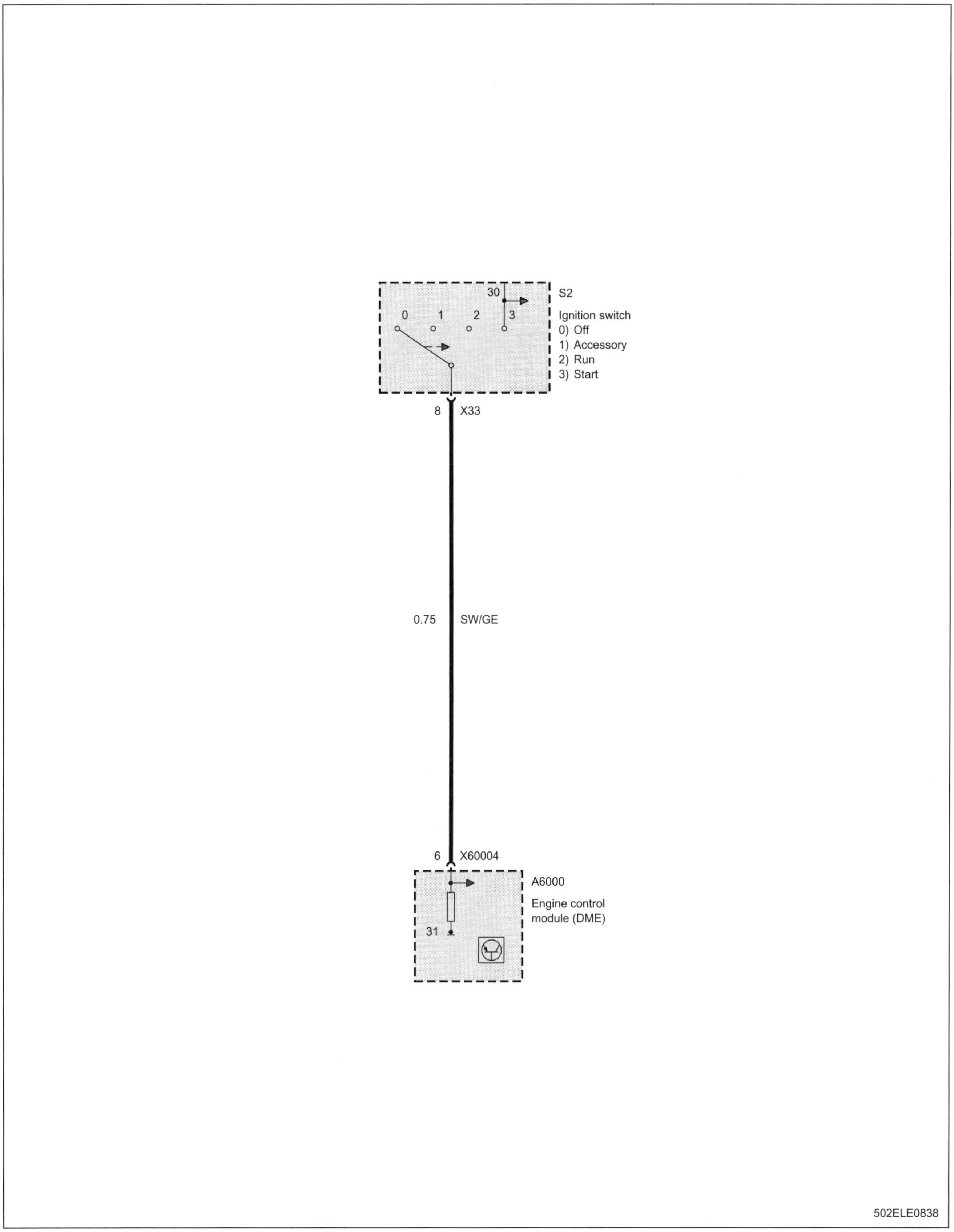
30
0
1
2
3
S2
Ignition switch
0) Off
1) Accessory
2) Run
3) Start
8
X33
0.75
SW/GE
6
X60004
A6000
Engine control
module (DME)
31
502ELE0838

Engine Management (M 5.2.1)
EWS starter control (AGS)
(1 of 1)

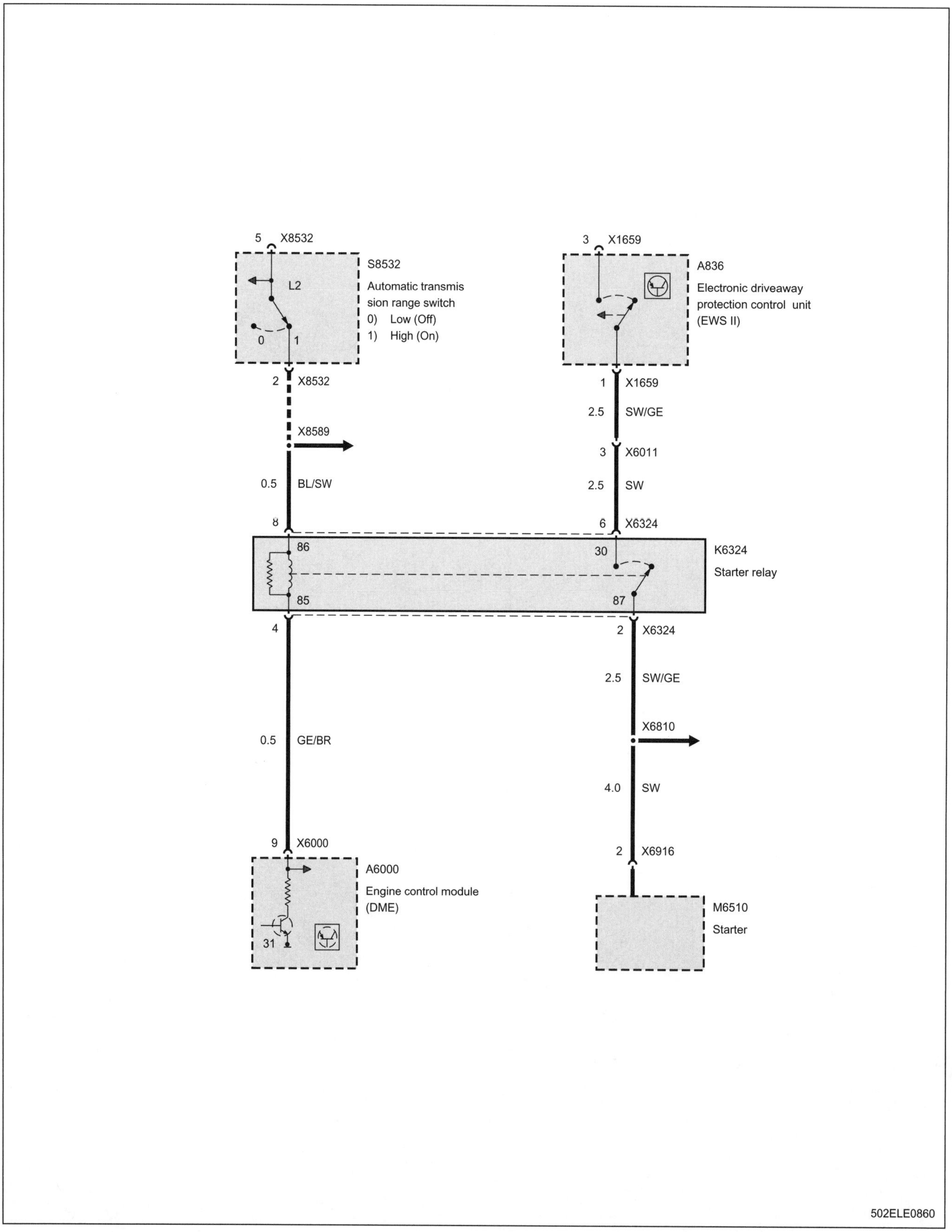

Engine Management (M 5.2.1)
EWS starter control (ex. AGS)
(1 of 1)

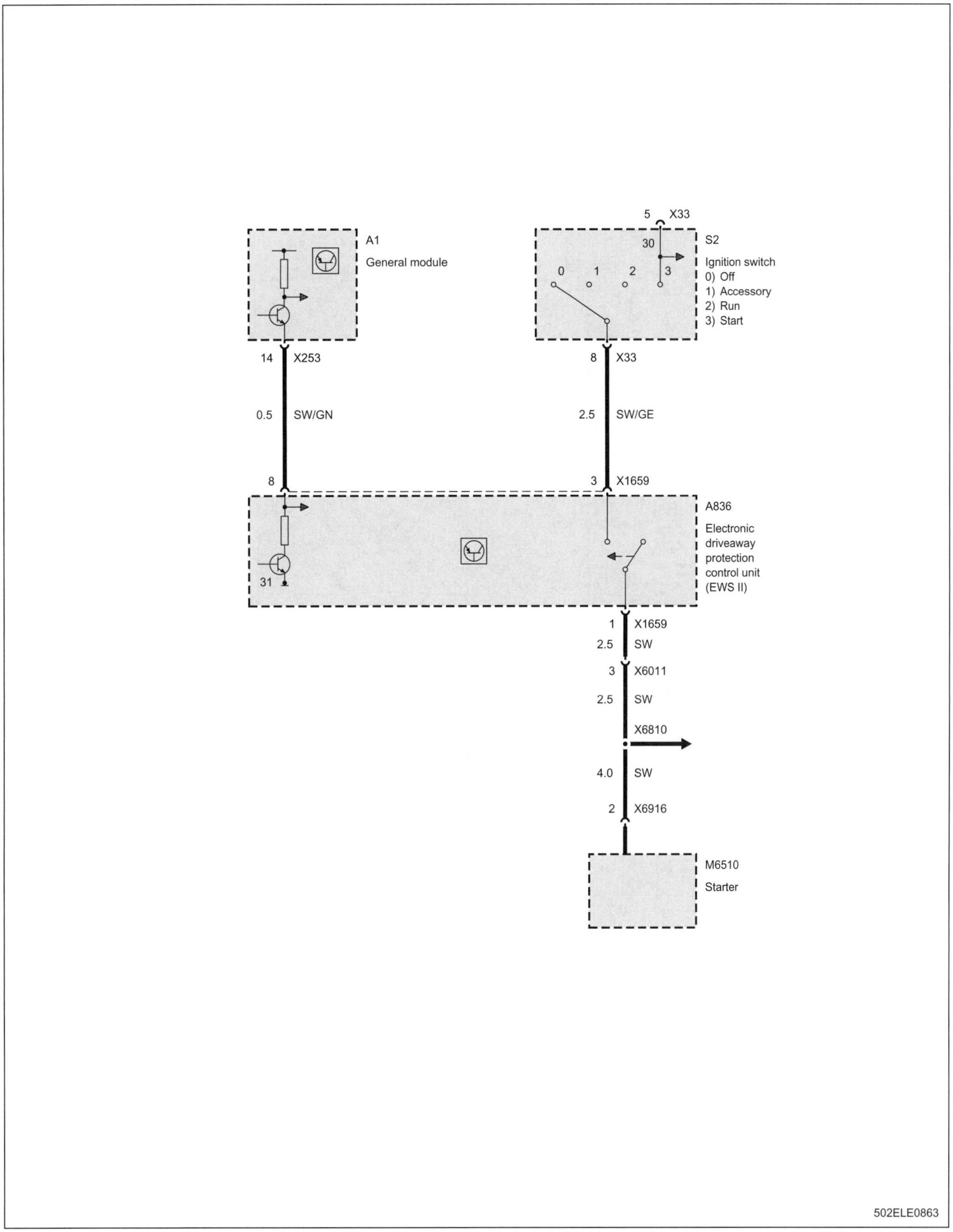

Engine Management (M 5.2.1)
CAN interface
(1 of 2)

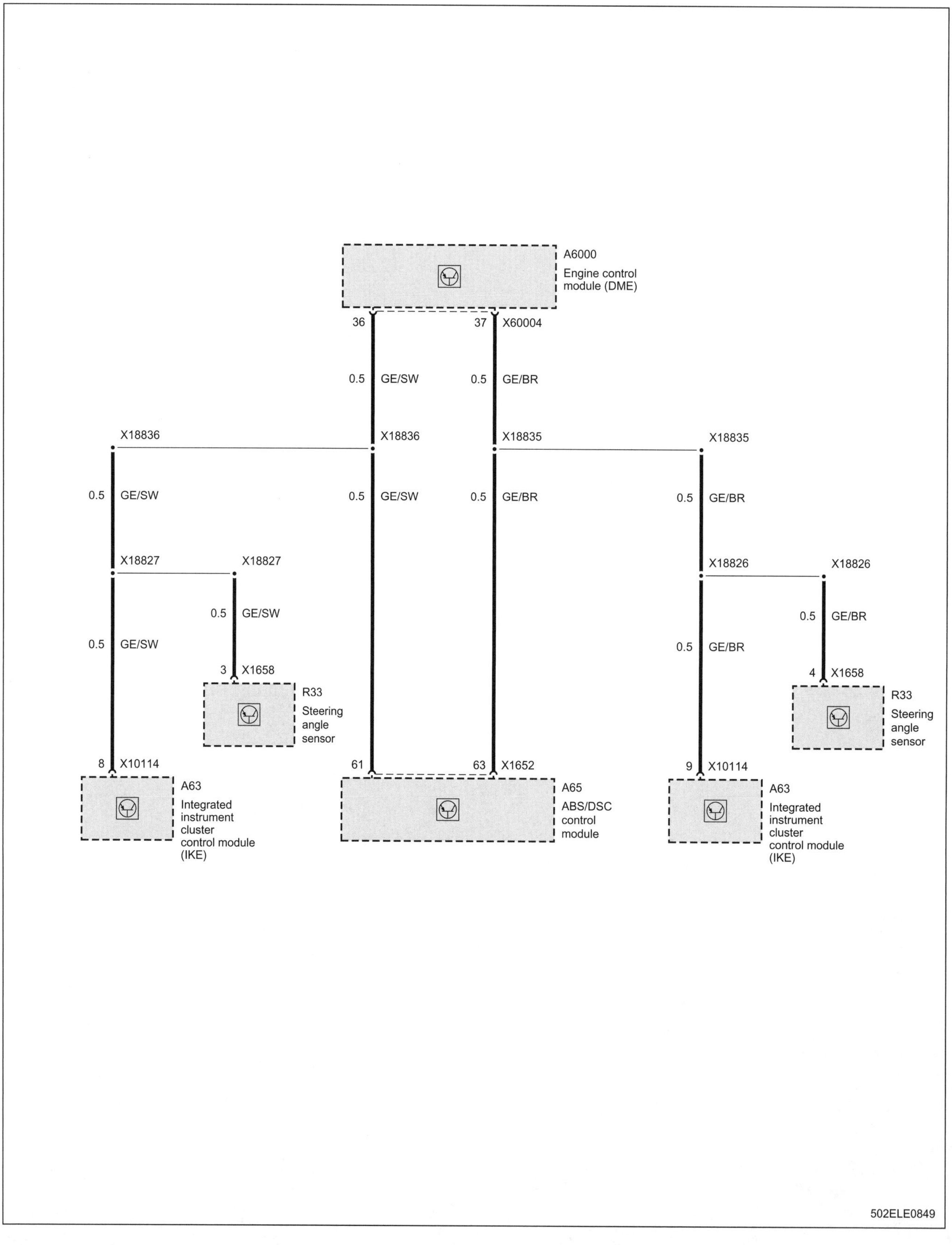
A6000
Engine control module (DME)
36
37
X60004
0.5
GE/SW
0.5
GE/BR
X18836
X18836
X18835
X18835
0.5
GE/SW
0.5
GE/SW
0.5
GE/BR
0.5
GE/BR
X18827
X18827
X18826
X18826
0.5
GE/SW
0.5
GE/SW
0.5
GE/BR
0.5
GE/BR
3
X1658
4
X1658
R33
Steering angle sensor
R33
Steering angle sensor
8
X10114
61
63
X1652
9
X10114
A63
Integrated instrument cluster control module (IKE)
A65
ABS/DSC control module
A63
Integrated instrument cluster control module (IKE)
502ELE0849

Engine Management (M 5.2.1)
CAN interface
(2 of 2)

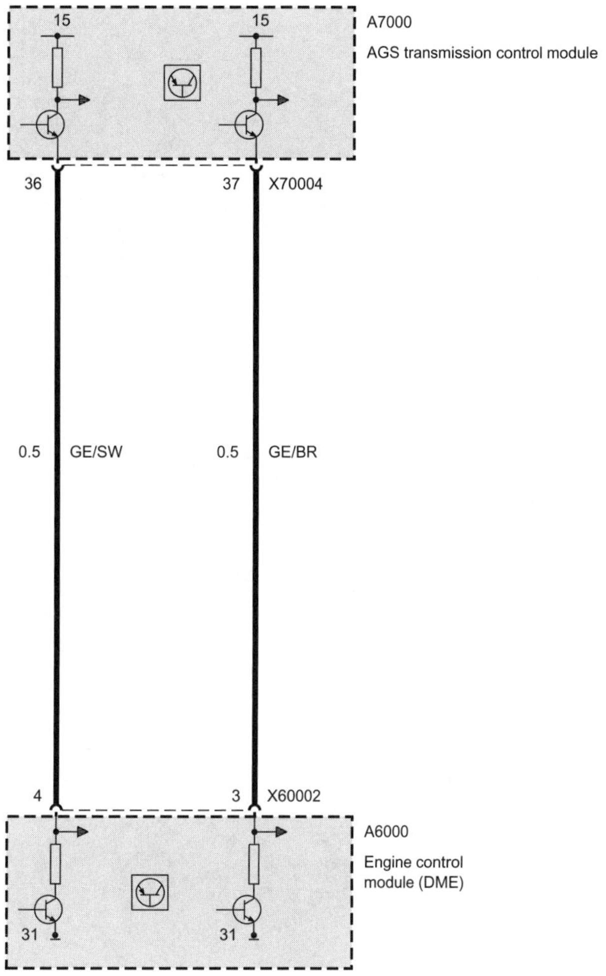

Engine Management (M 5.2.1)
DME/instrument cluster interface
(1 of 1)

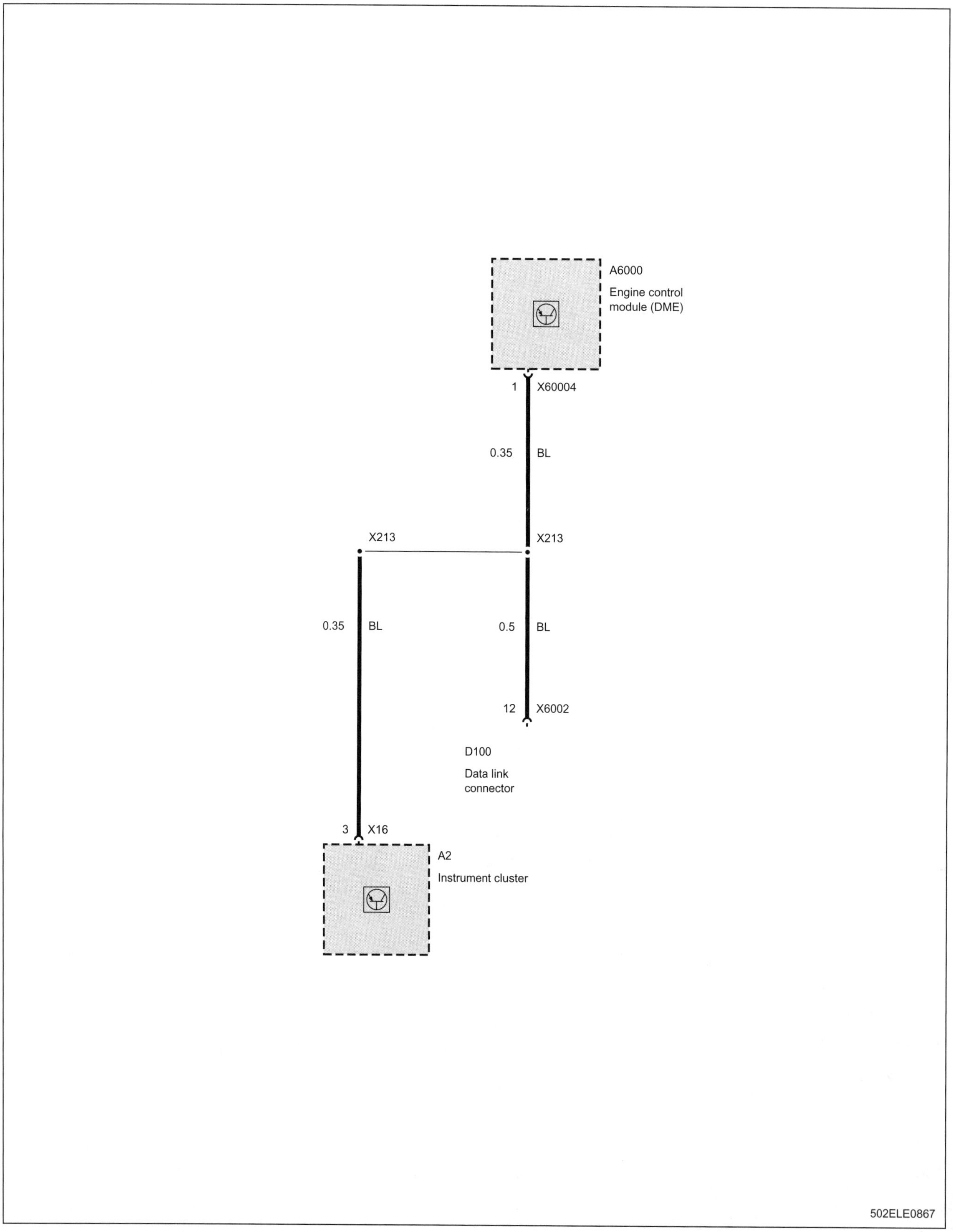

Engine Management (M 5.2.1)
DME/IKE interface
(1 of 1)

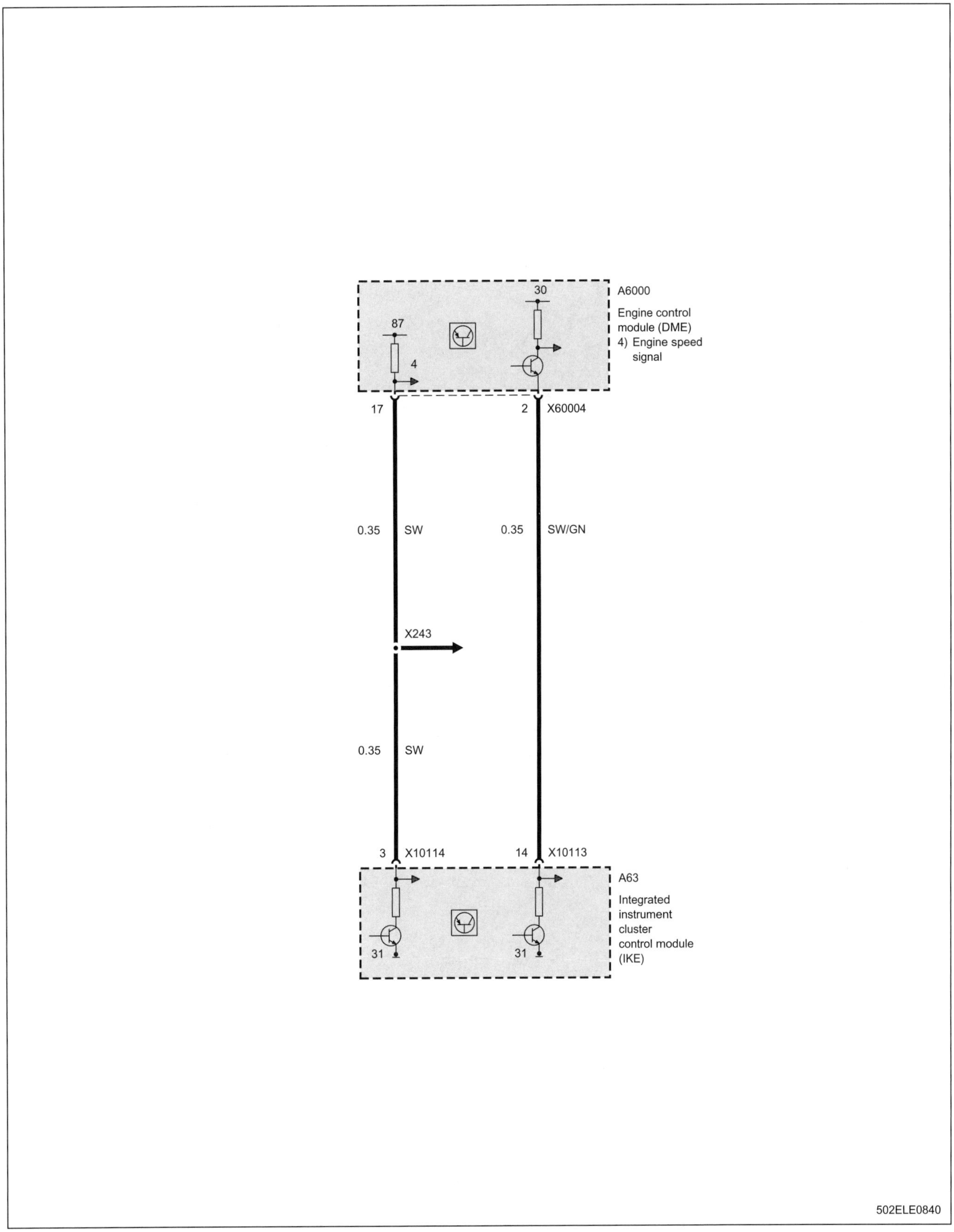

Engine Management (M 5.2.1)
DME/climate control interfaces
(1 of 1)

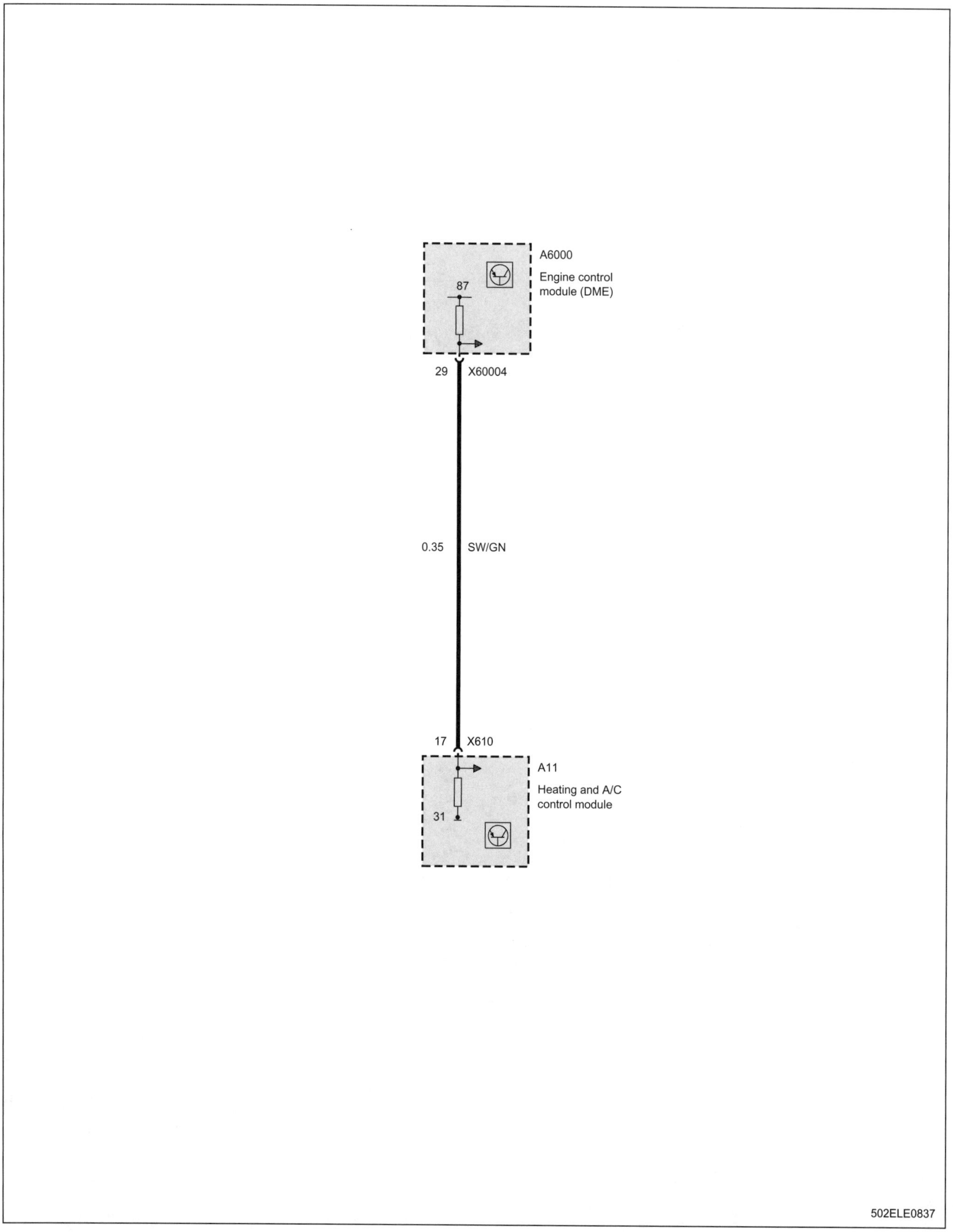

Engine Management (ME 7.2)
A6000 Engine control module (DME) Module 1
(1 of 1)

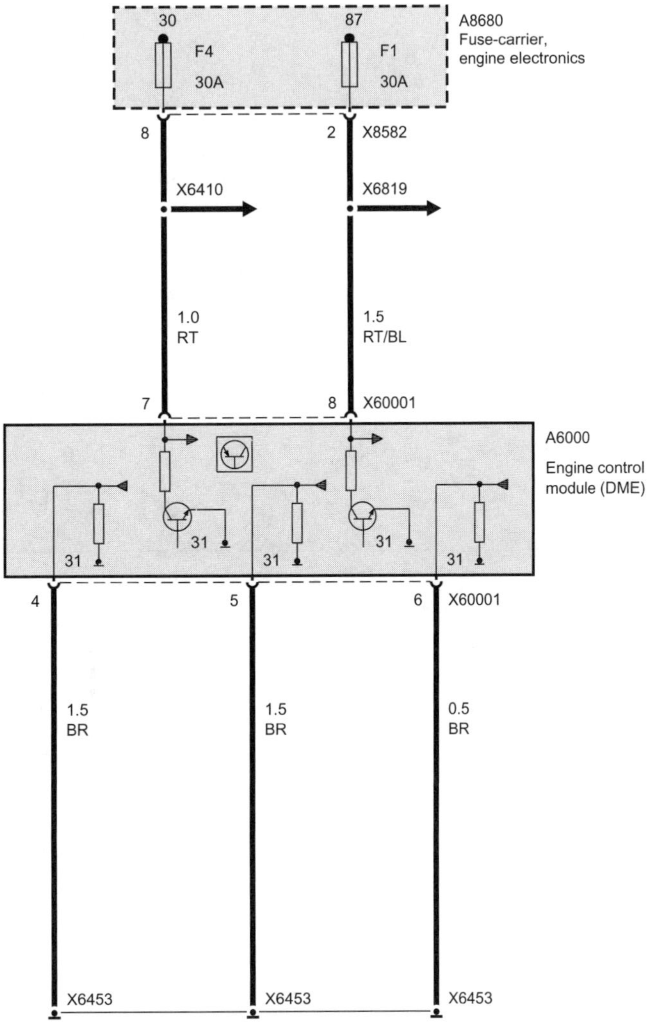

502ELE0929

Engine Management (ME 7.2)
A6000 Engine control module (DME) Module 2
(1 of 3)

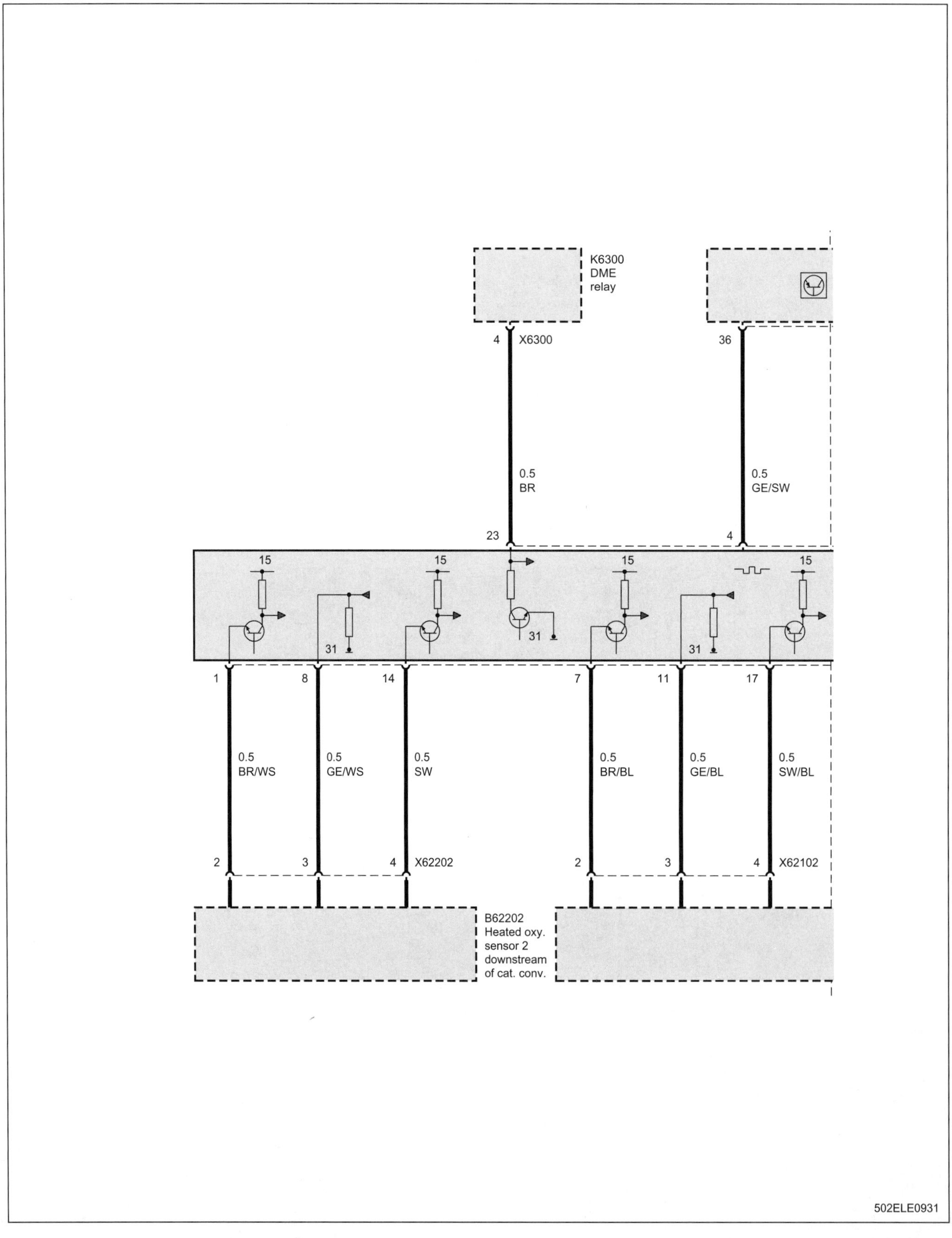

Engine Management (ME 7.2)
A6000 Engine control module (DME) Module 2
(2 of 3)

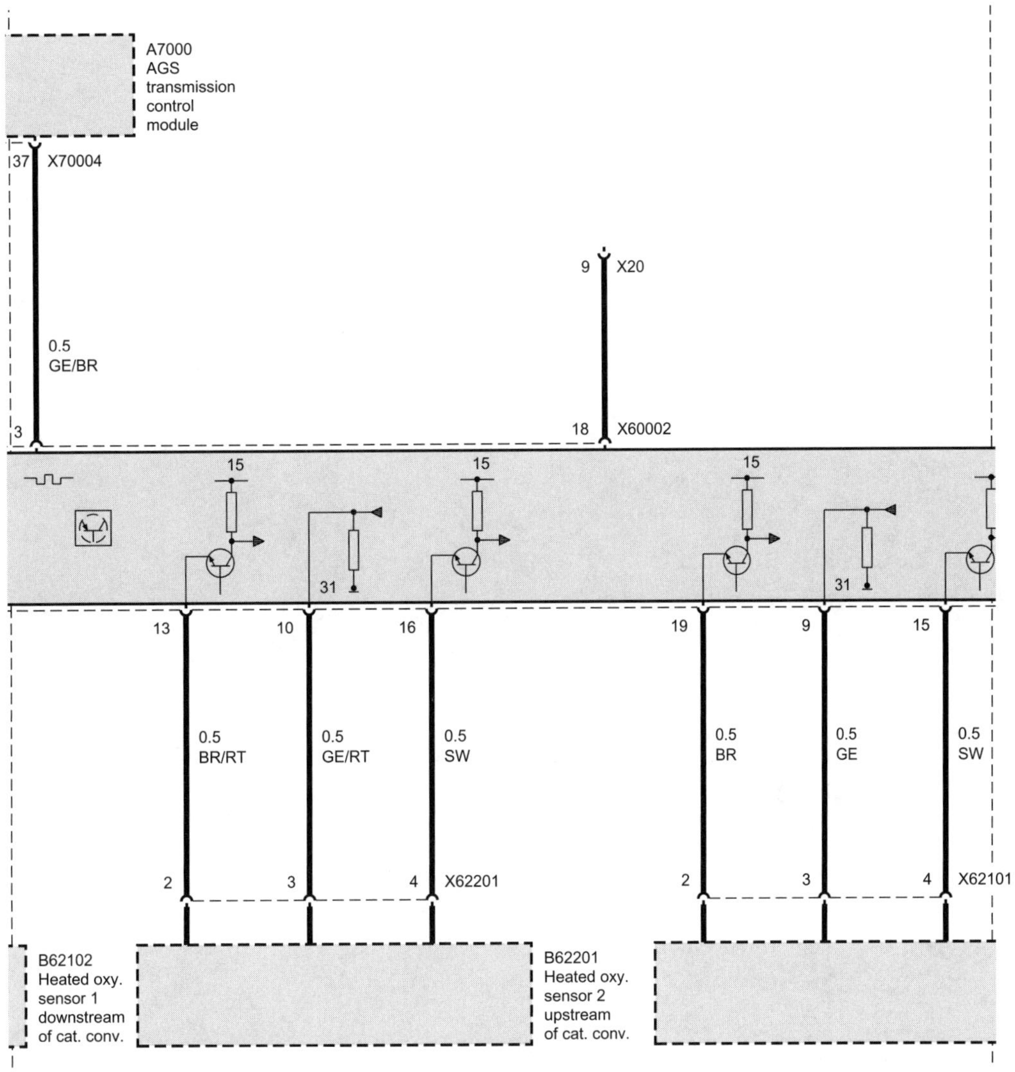

502ELE0932

Engine Management (ME 7.2)
A6000 Engine control module (DME) Module 2
(3 of 3)

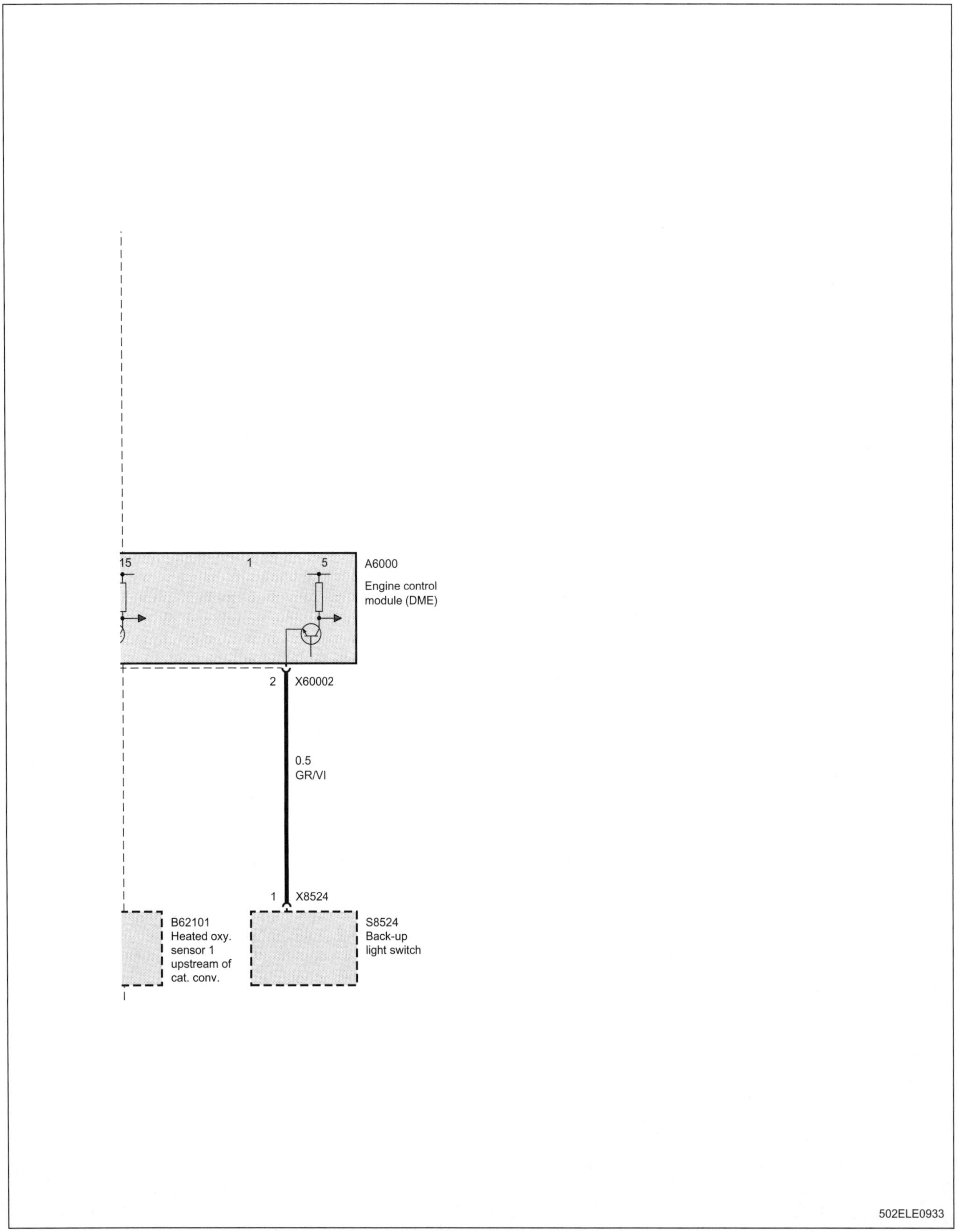

Engine Management (ME 7.2)
A6000 Engine control module (DME) Module 3
(1 of 3)

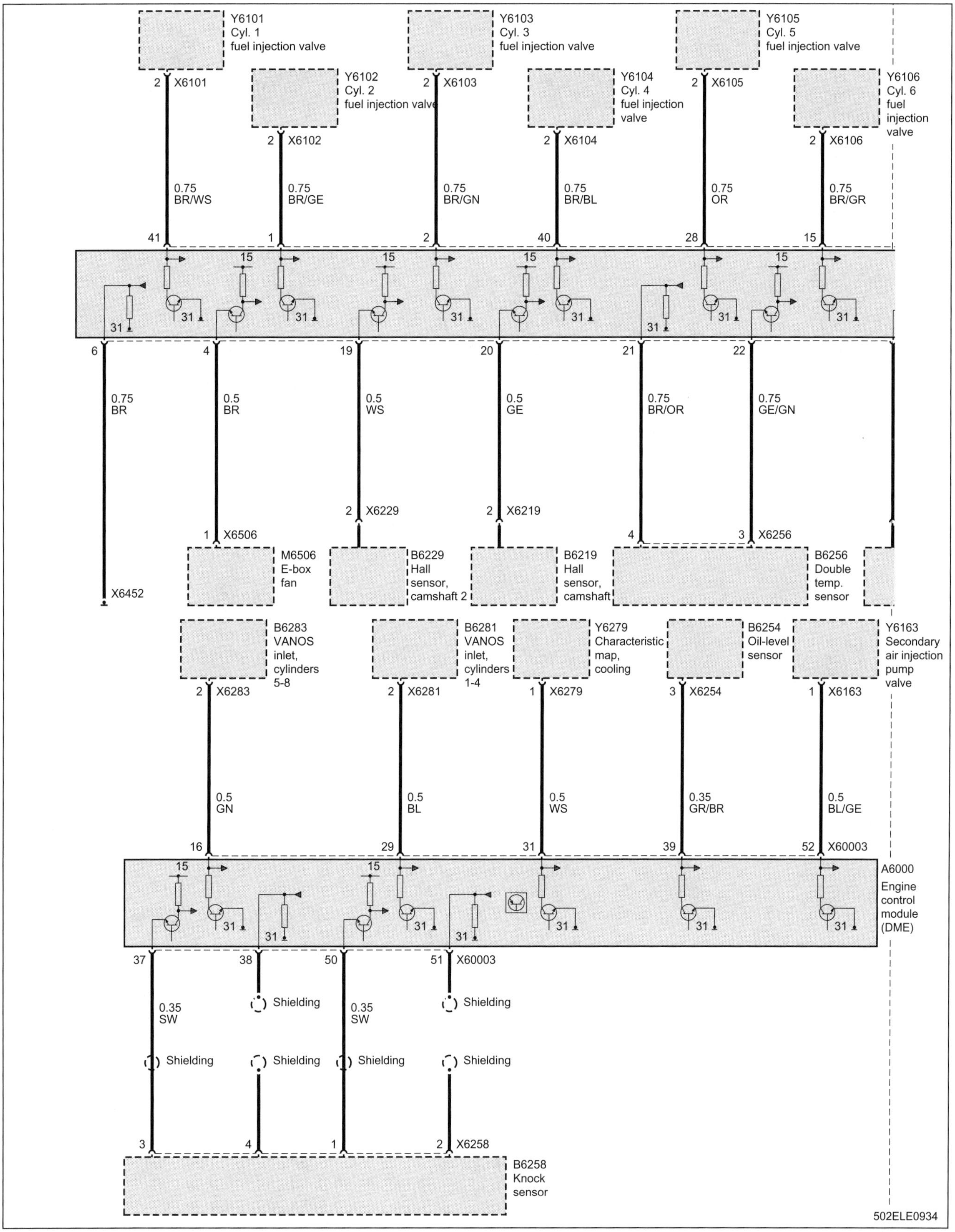

Engine Management (ME 7.2)
A6000 Engine control module (DME) Module 3
(2 of 3)

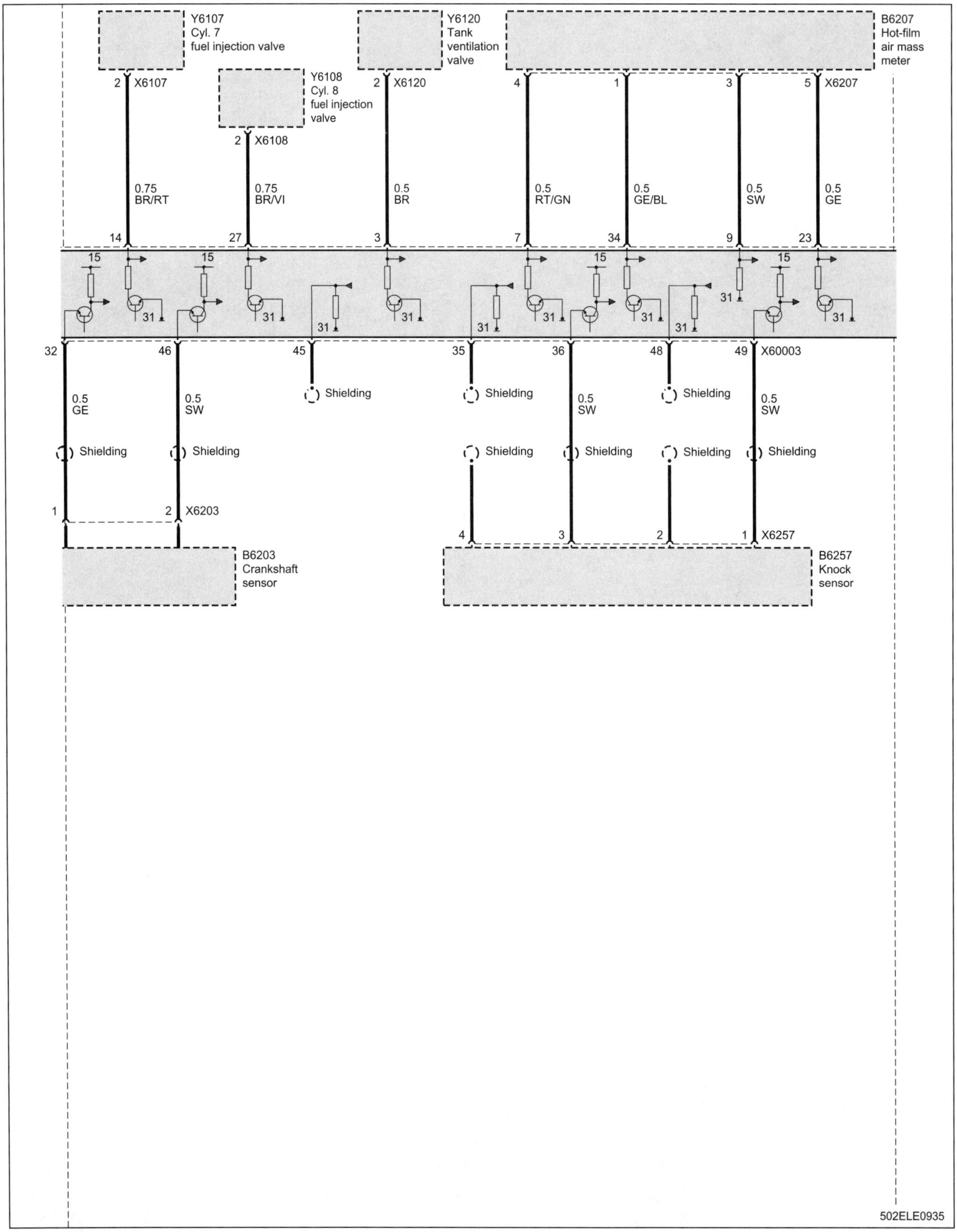

Engine Management (ME 7.2)
A6000 Engine control module (DME) Module 3
(3 of 3)

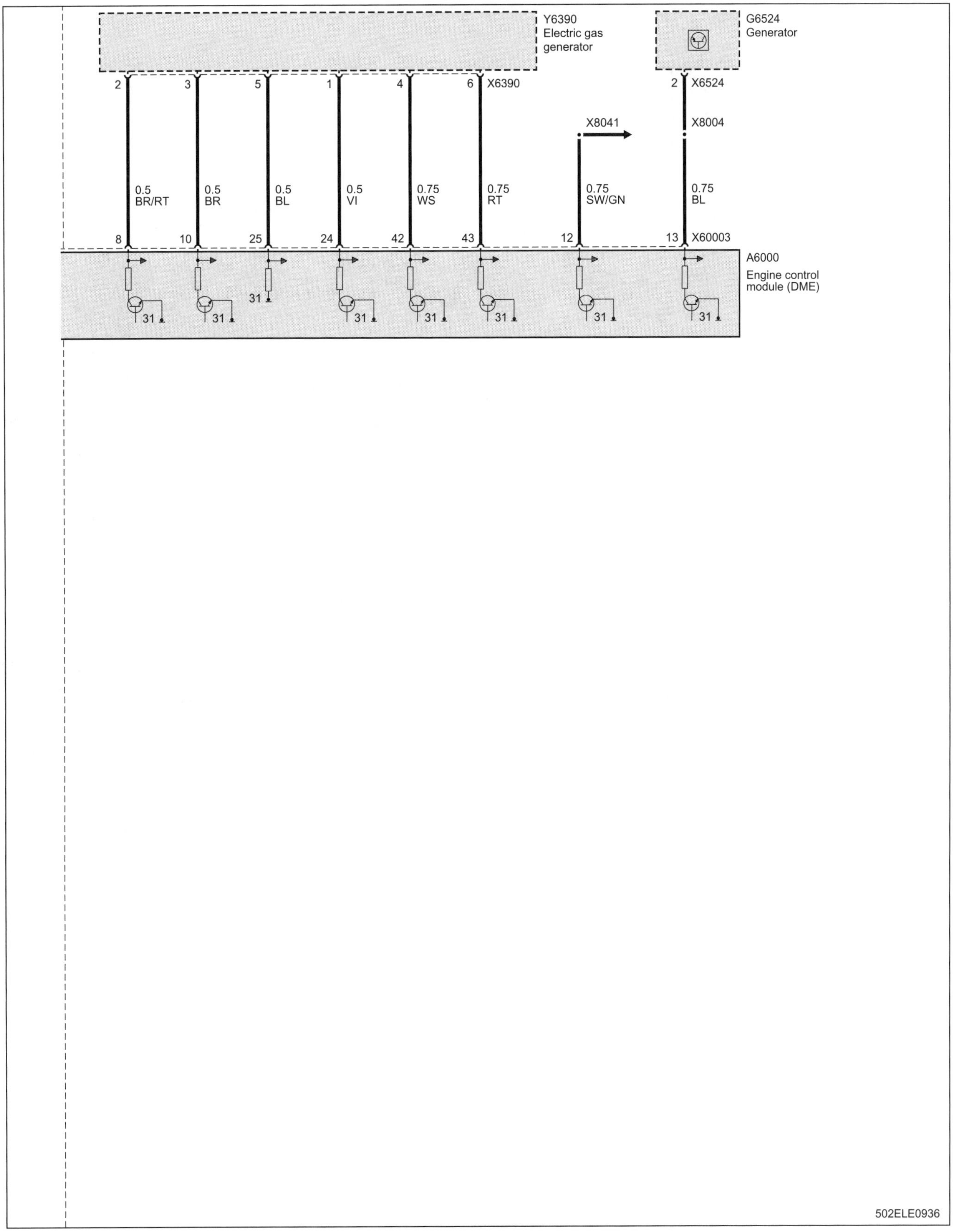

Engine Management (ME 7.2)
A6000 Engine control module (DME) Module 4
(1 of 4)

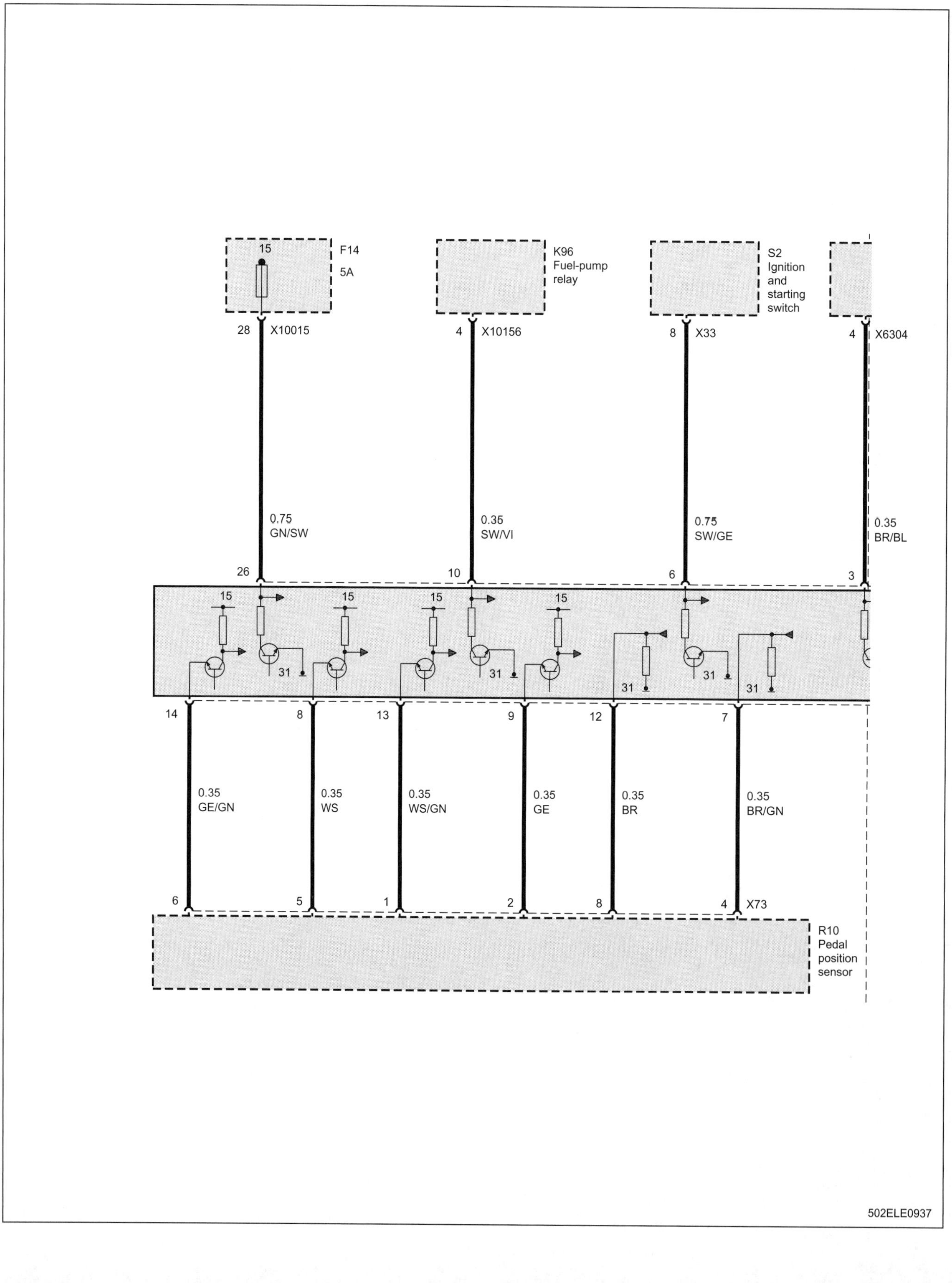

Engine Management (ME 7.2)
A6000 Engine control module (DME) Module 4
(2 of 4)

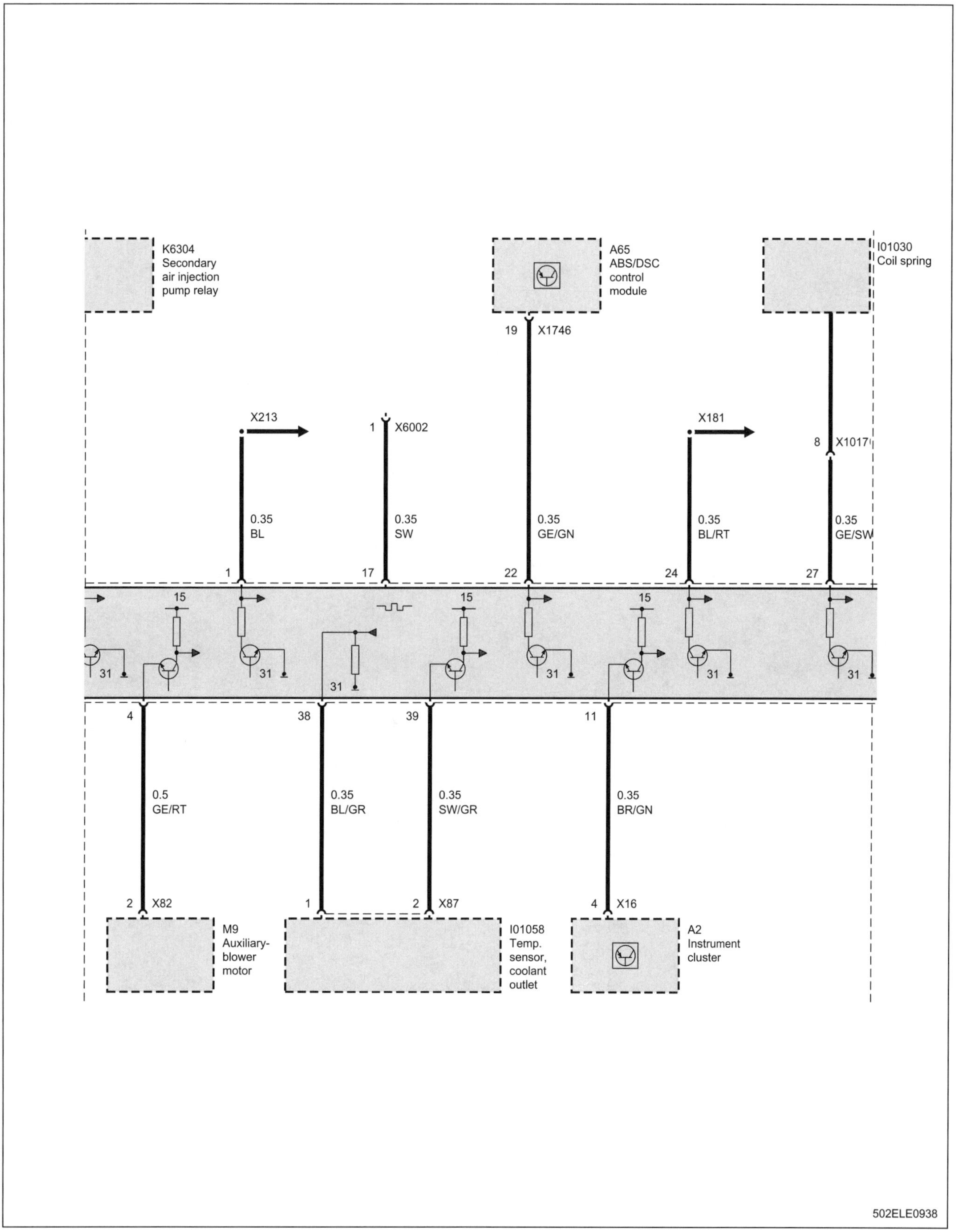

Engine Management (ME 7.2)
A6000 Engine control module (DME) Module 4
(3 of 4)

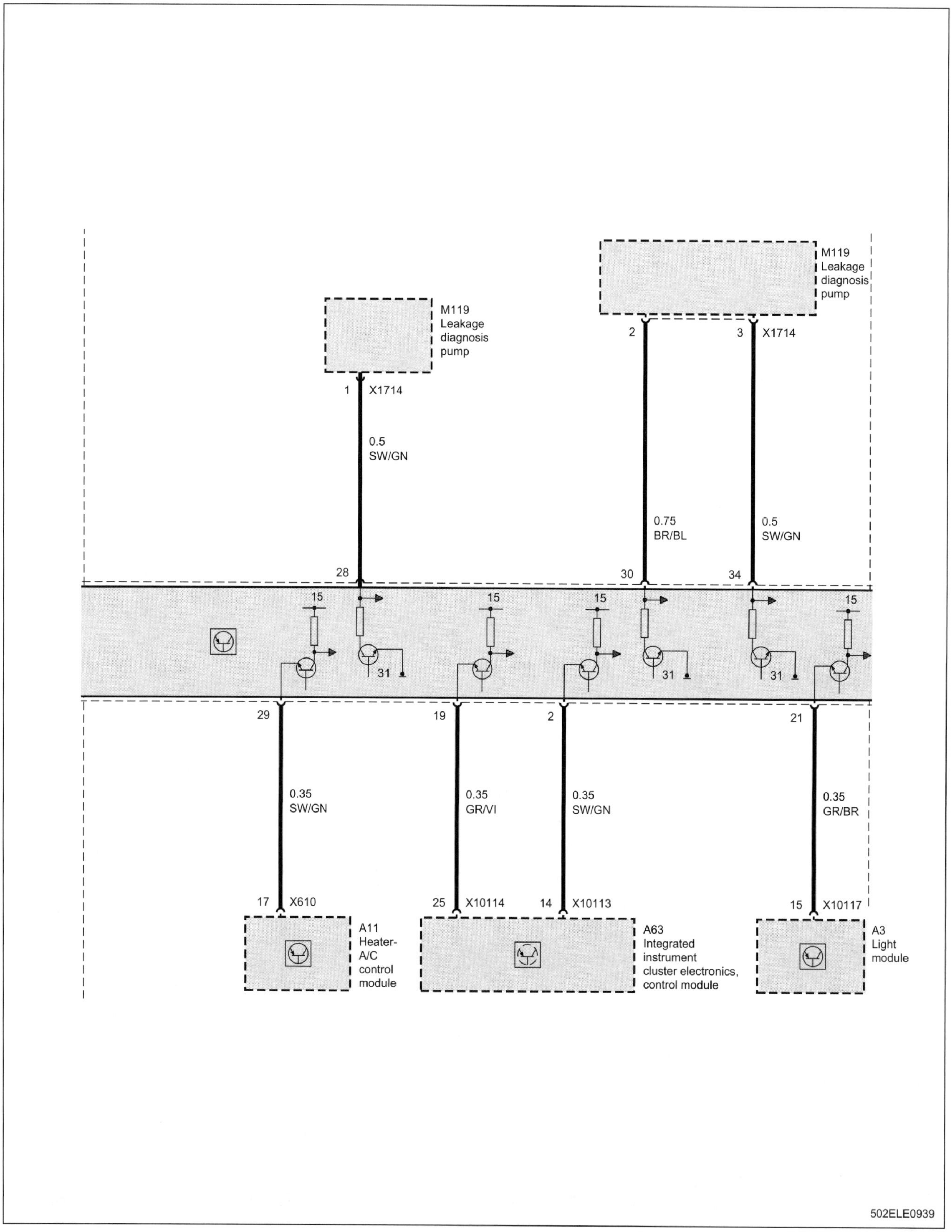

Engine Management (ME 7.2)
A6000 Engine control module (DME) Module 4
(4 of 4)

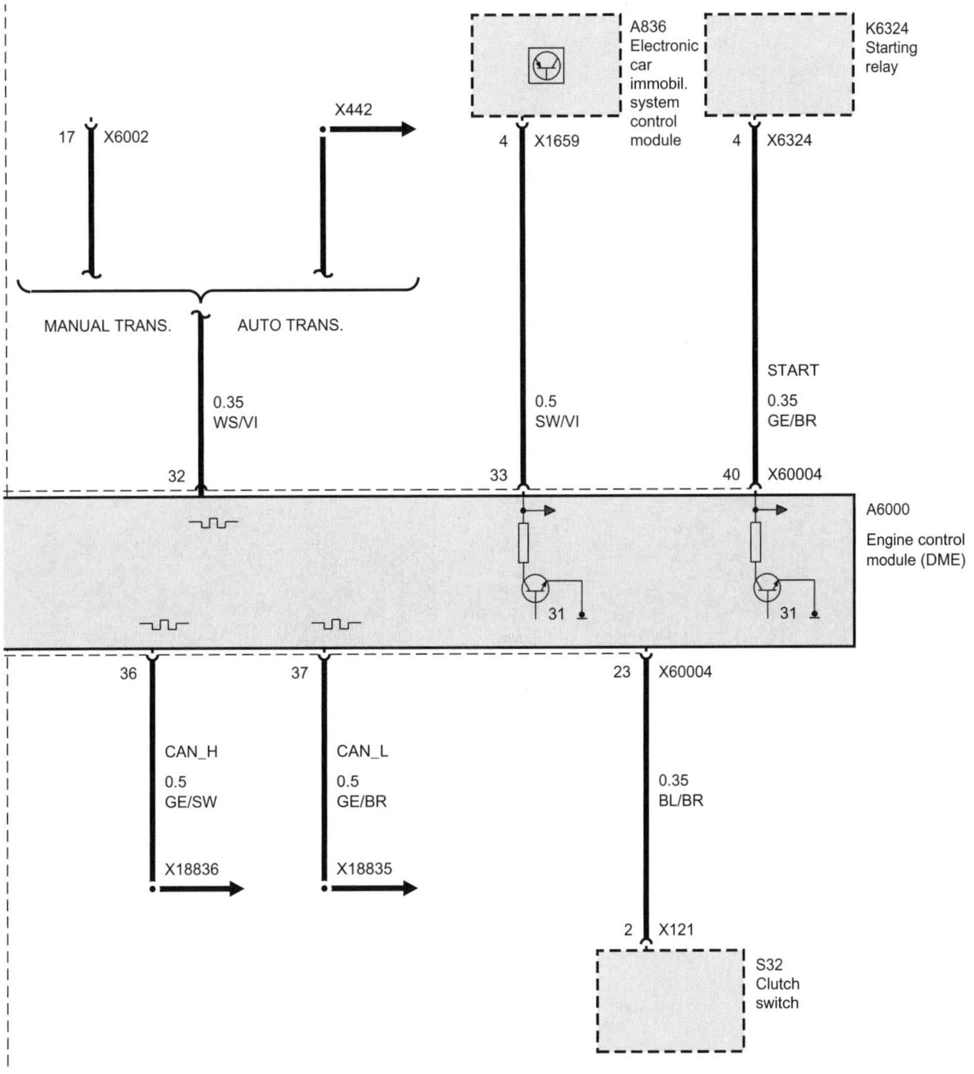

502ELE0940

Engine Management (ME 7.2)
A6000 Engine control module (DME) Module 5
(1 of 1)

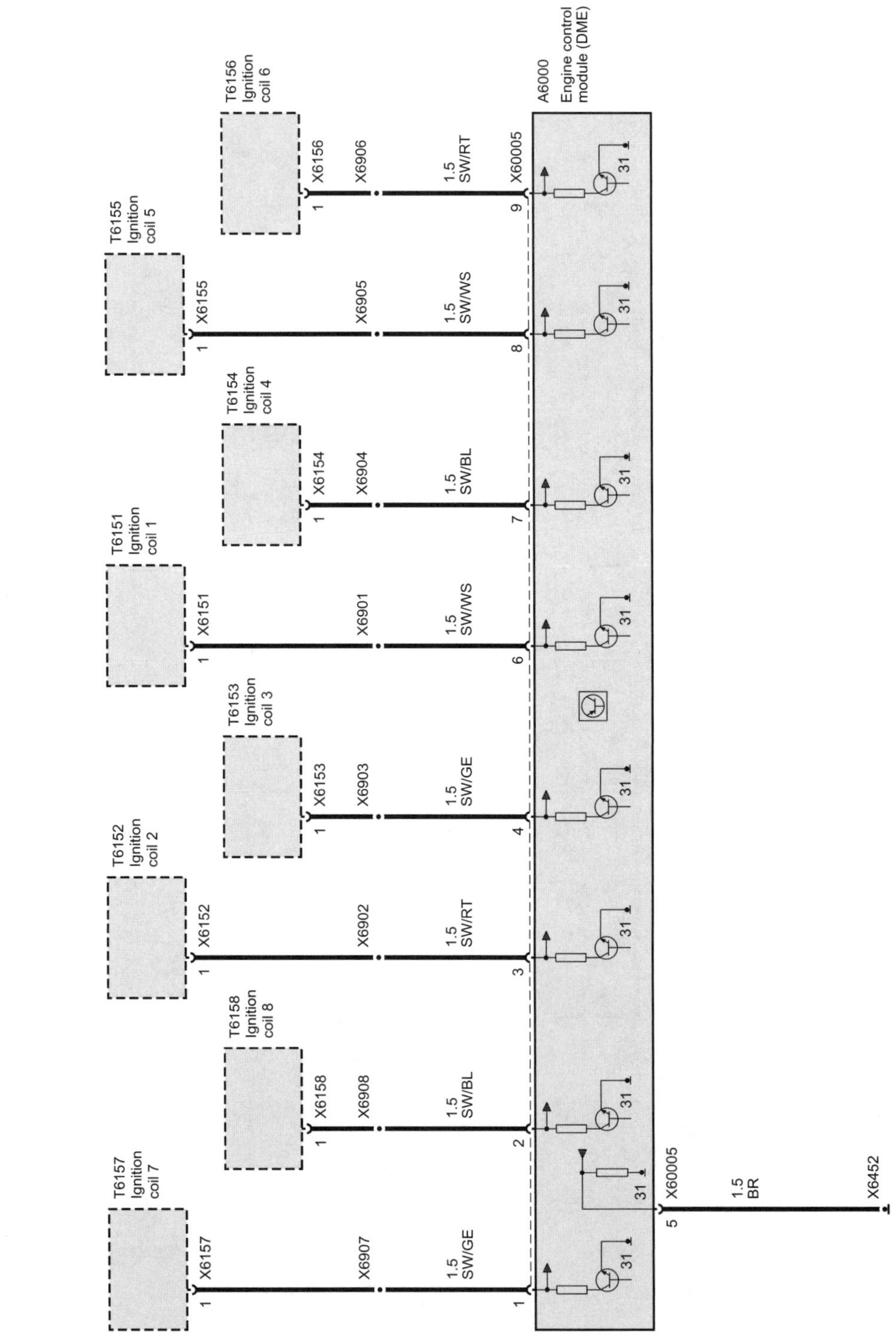

502ELE0930

Engine Management (ME 7.2)
X19527 OBDII socket
(1 of 1)

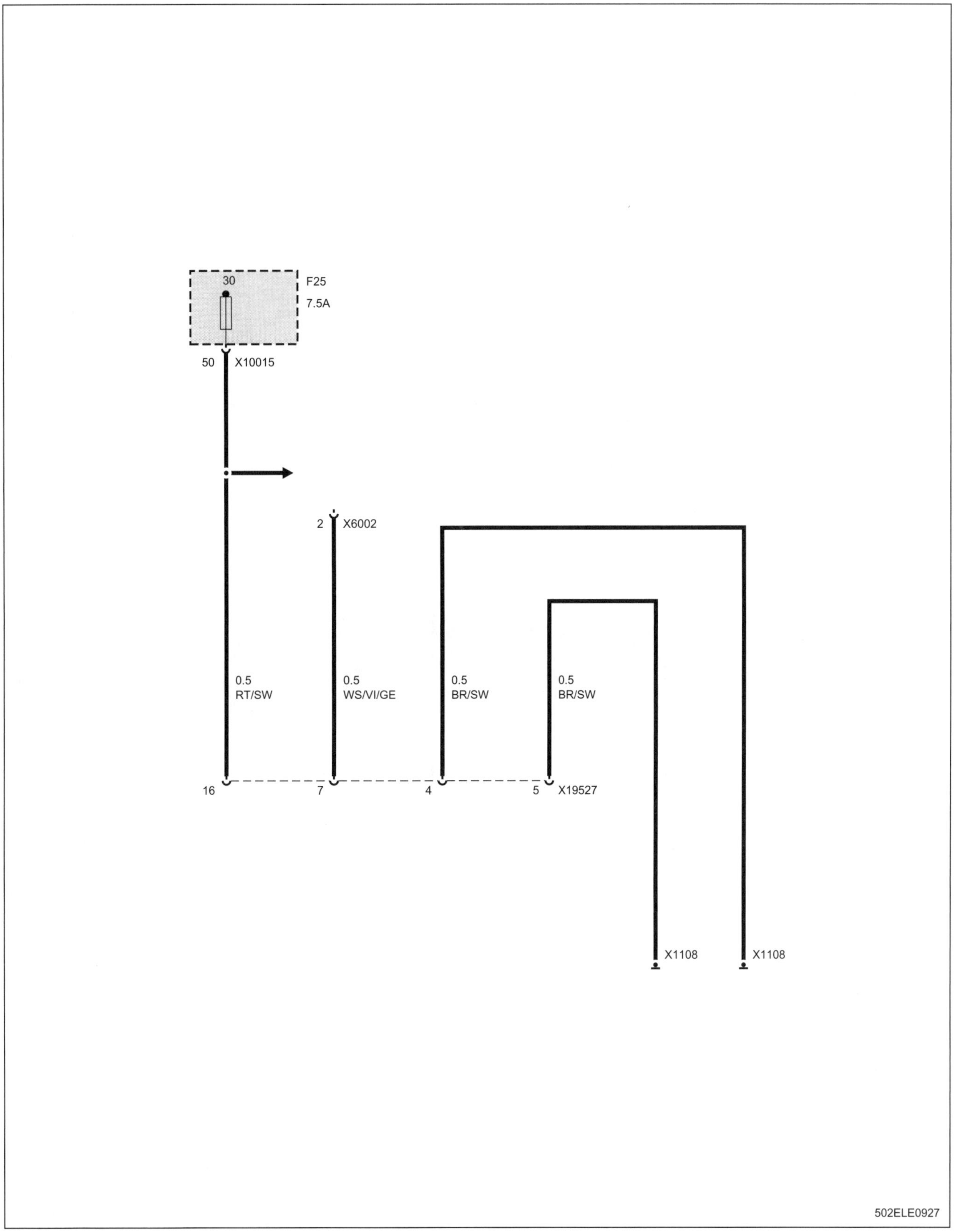

Engine Management (ME 7.2)
X6002 Diagnostic connector
(1 of 2)

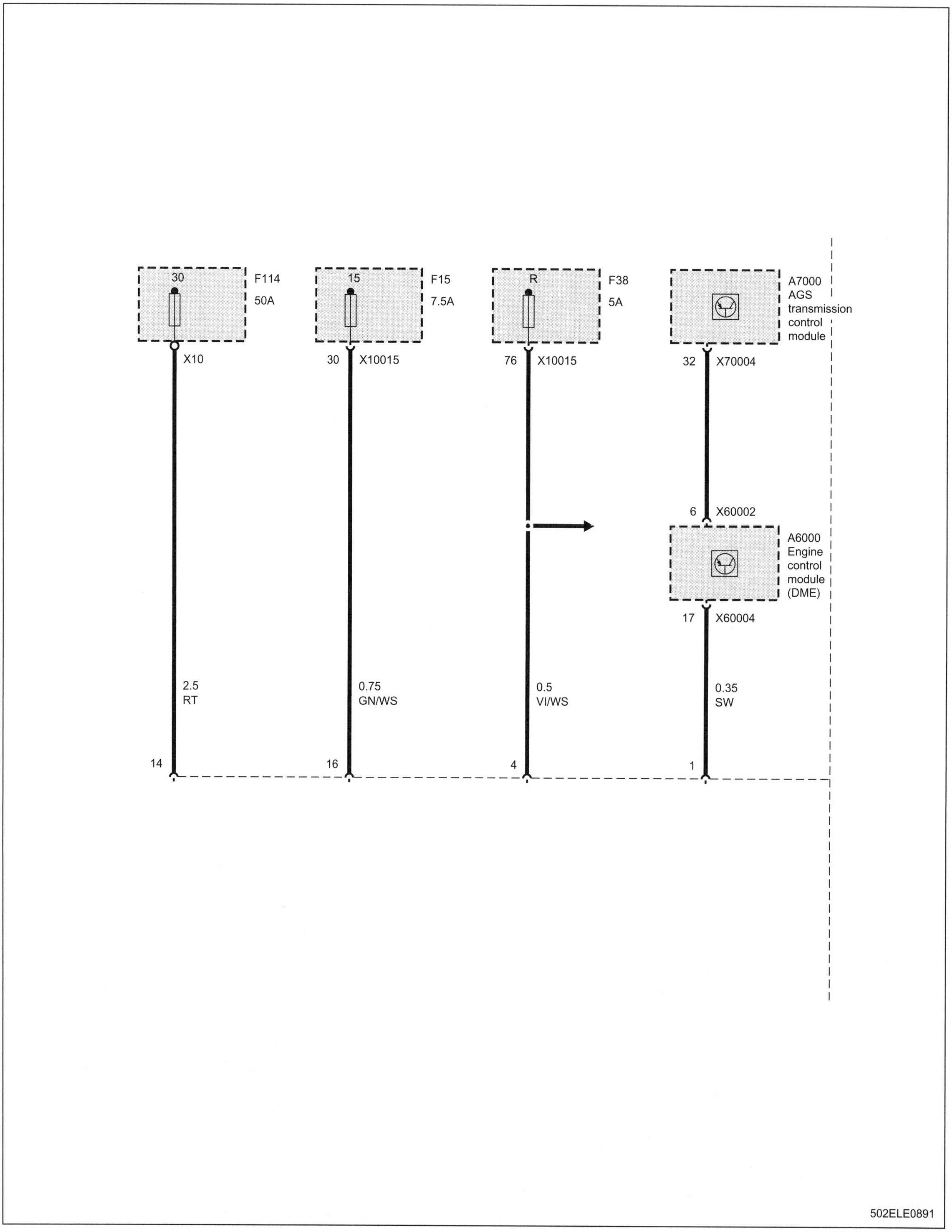

Engine Management (ME 7.2)
X6002 Diagnostic connector
(2 of 2)

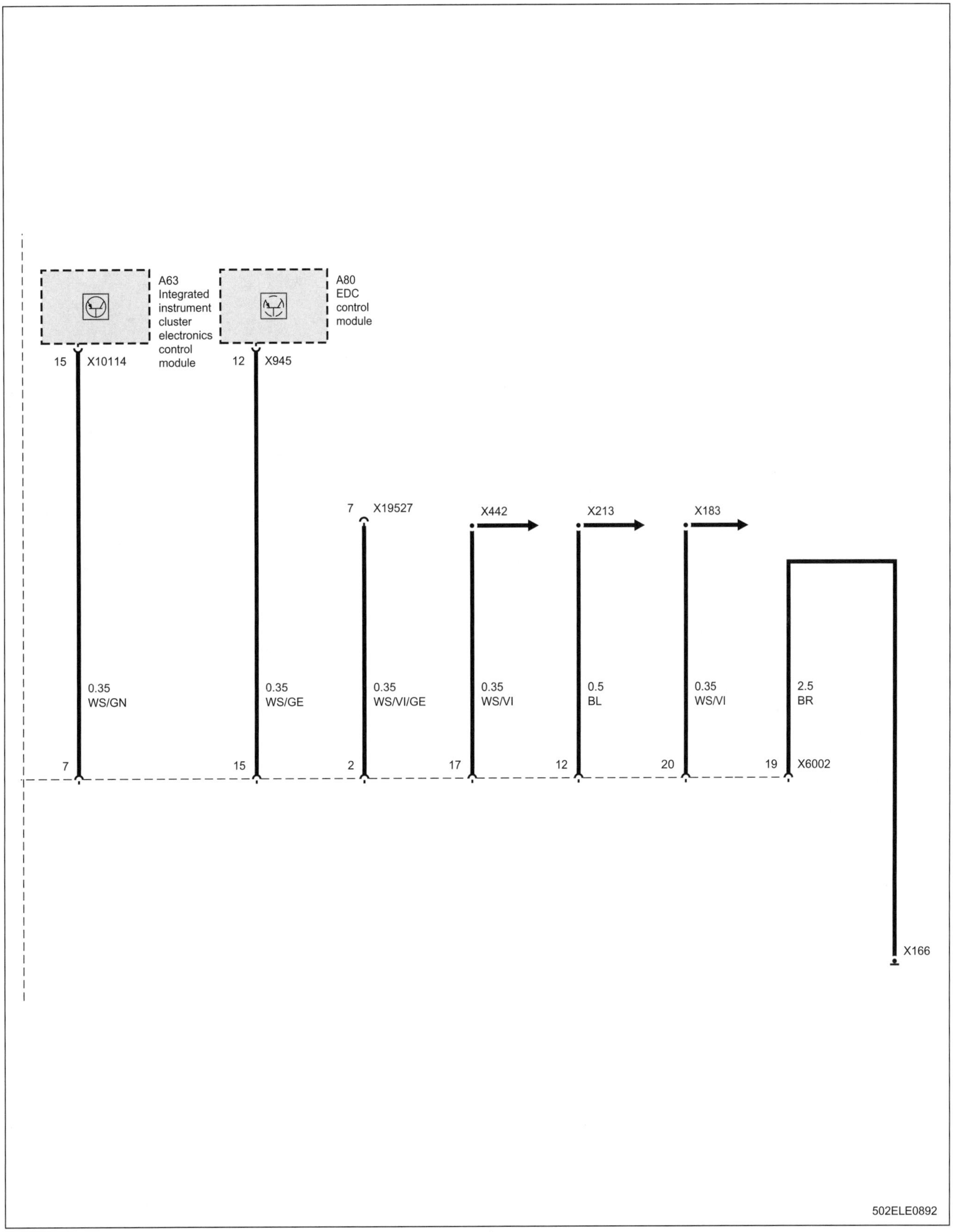

Engine Management (ME 7.2)
Engine control module relay
(1 of 1)

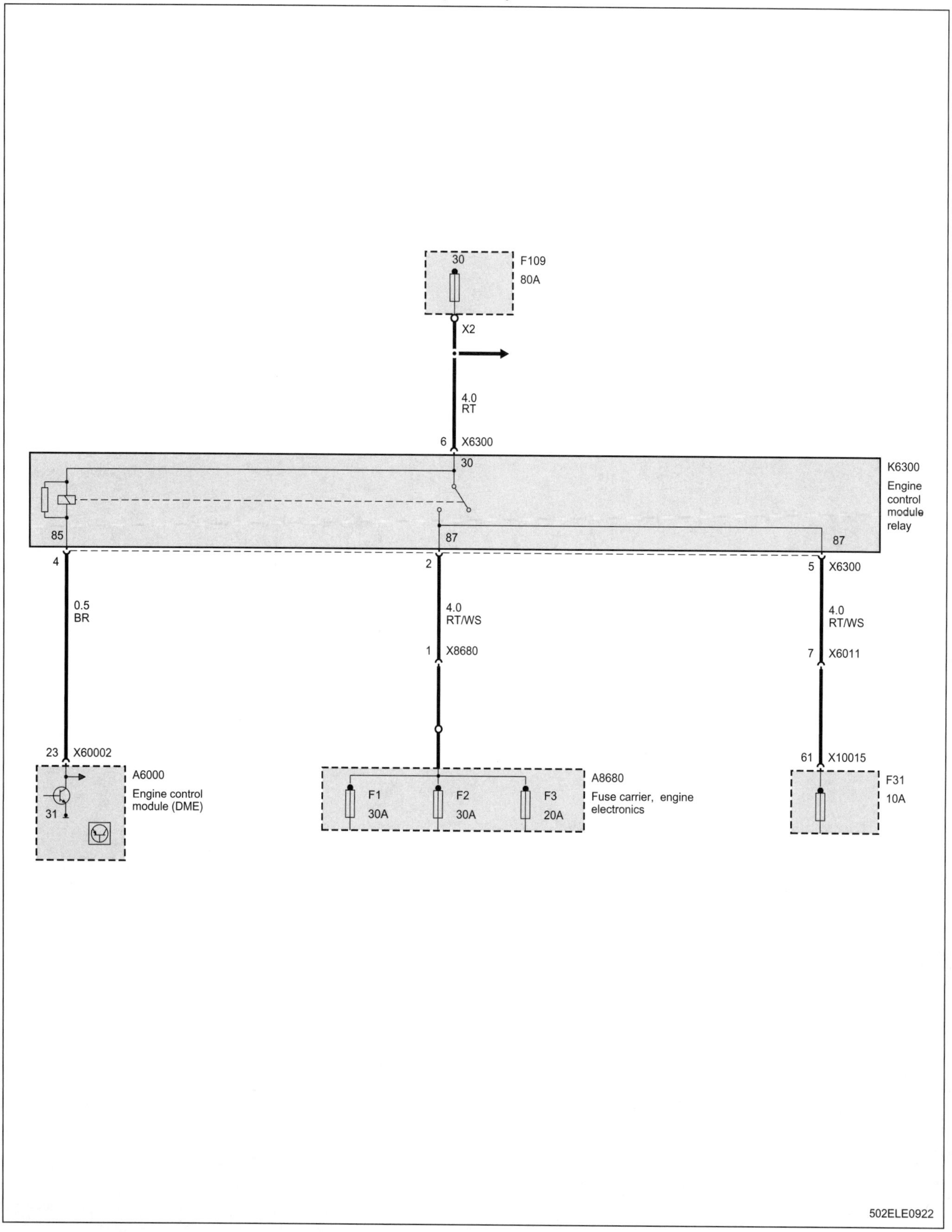

Engine Management (ME 7.2)
Power, DME control module
(1 of 1)

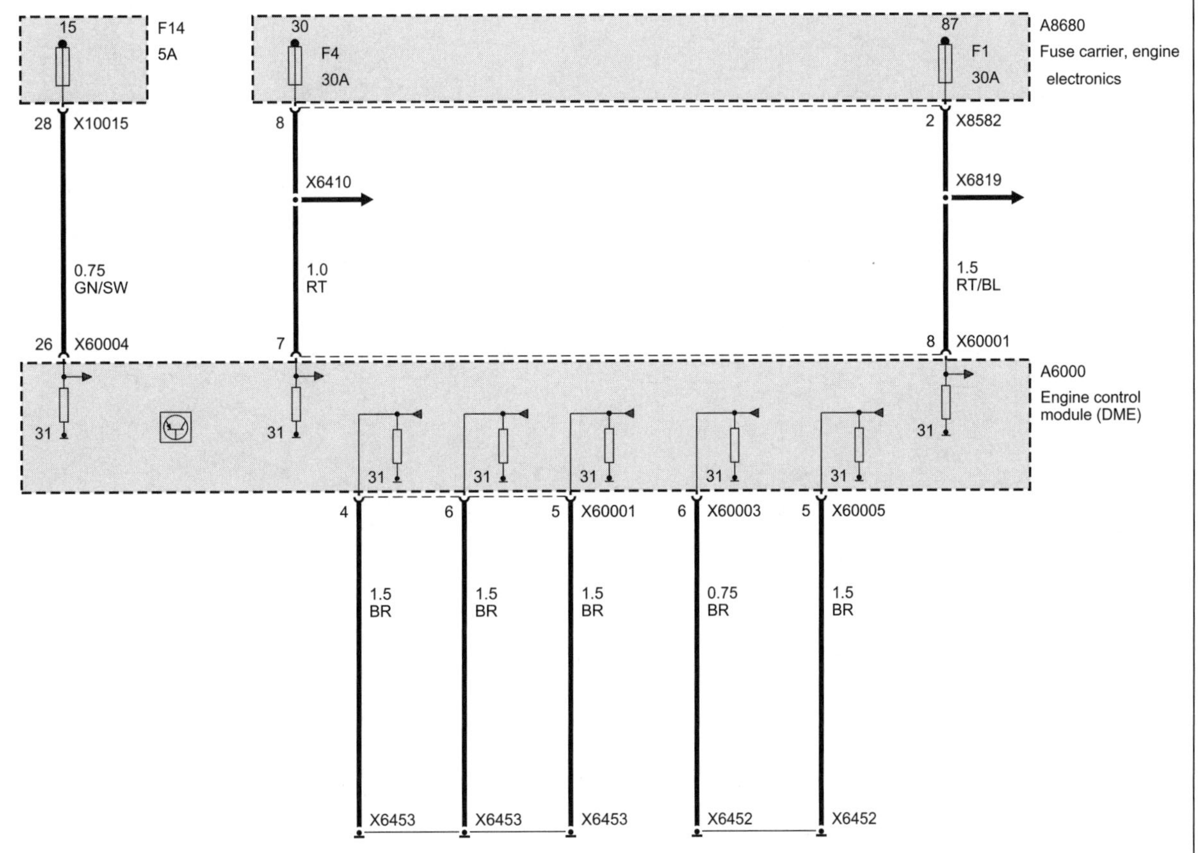

Engine Management (ME 7.2)
Fuel pump
(1 of 1)

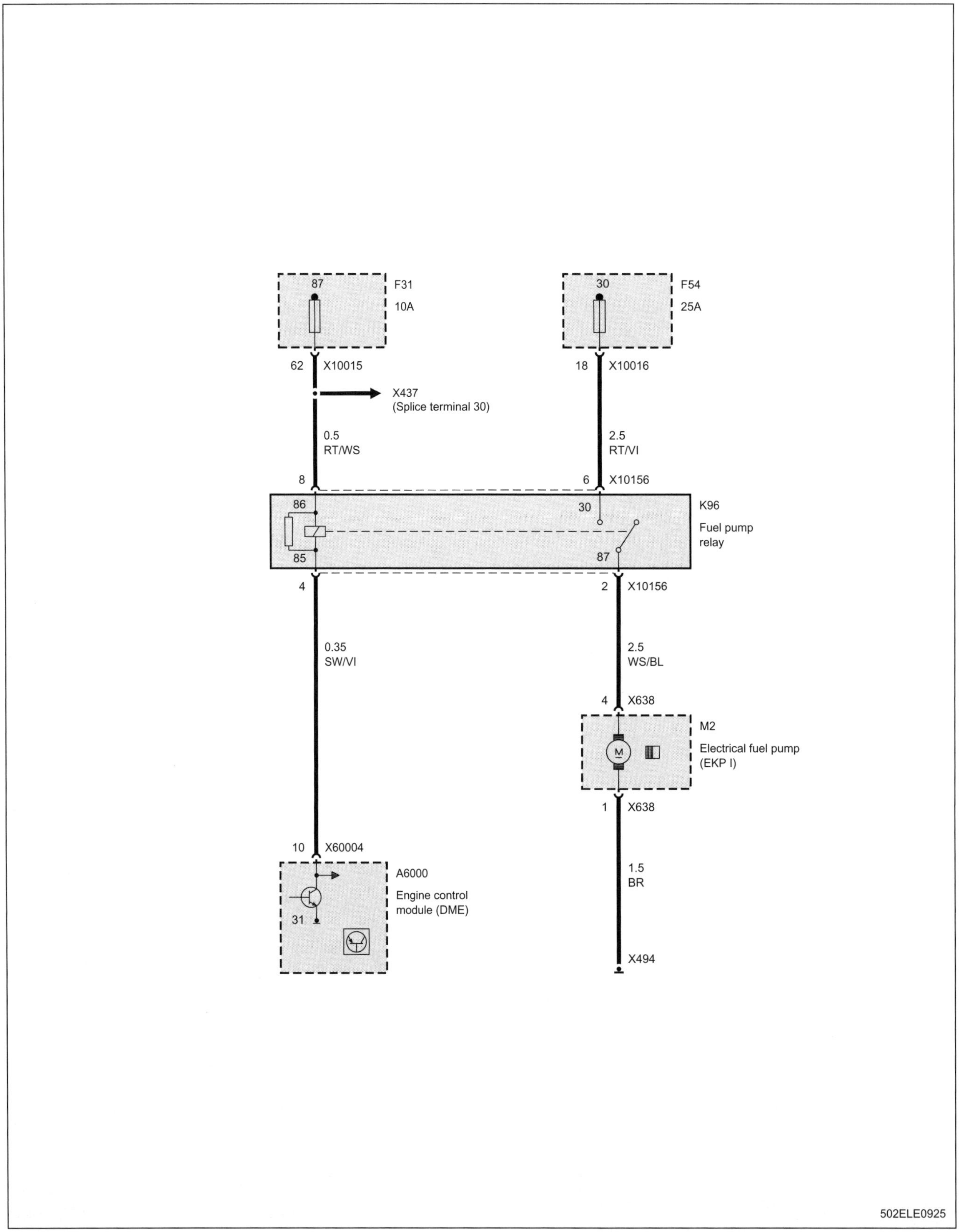
87
F31
10A
30
F54
25A
62
X10015
18
X10016
X437
(Splice terminal 30)
0.5
RT/WS
2.5
RT/VI
8
6
X10156
86
30
K96
Fuel pump
relay
85
87
4
2
X10156
0.35
SW/VI
2.5
WS/BL
4
X638
M2
Electrical fuel pump
(EKP I)
M
1
X638
10
X60004
A6000
Engine control
module (DME)
31
1.5
BR
X494
502ELE0925

Engine Management (ME 7.2)
Electric throttle actuator
(1 of 1)

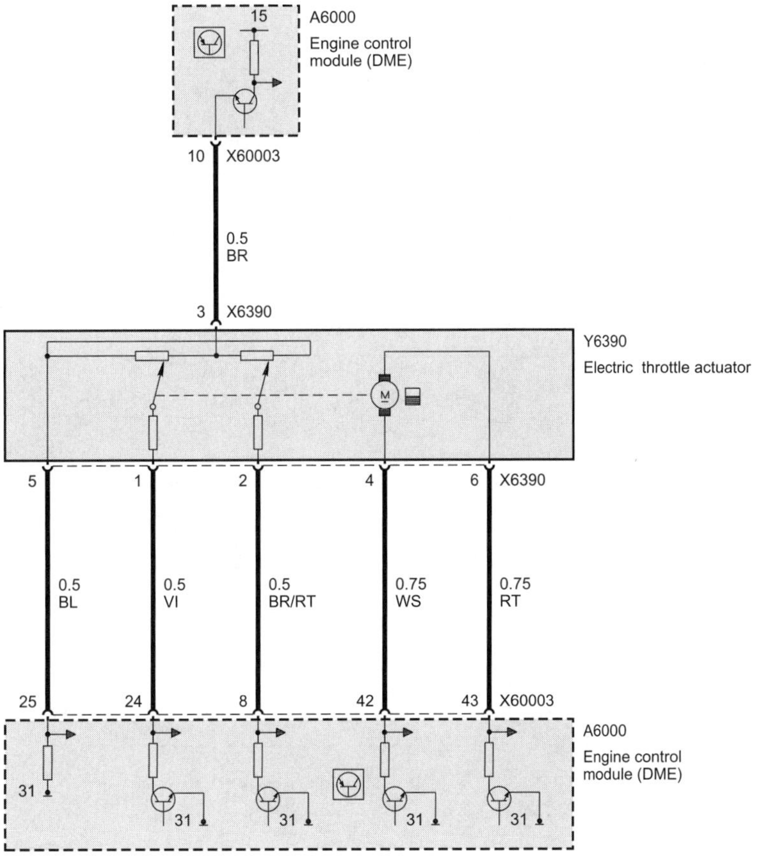

502ELE0902

Engine Management (ME 7.2)
Pedal position sensor
(1 of 1)

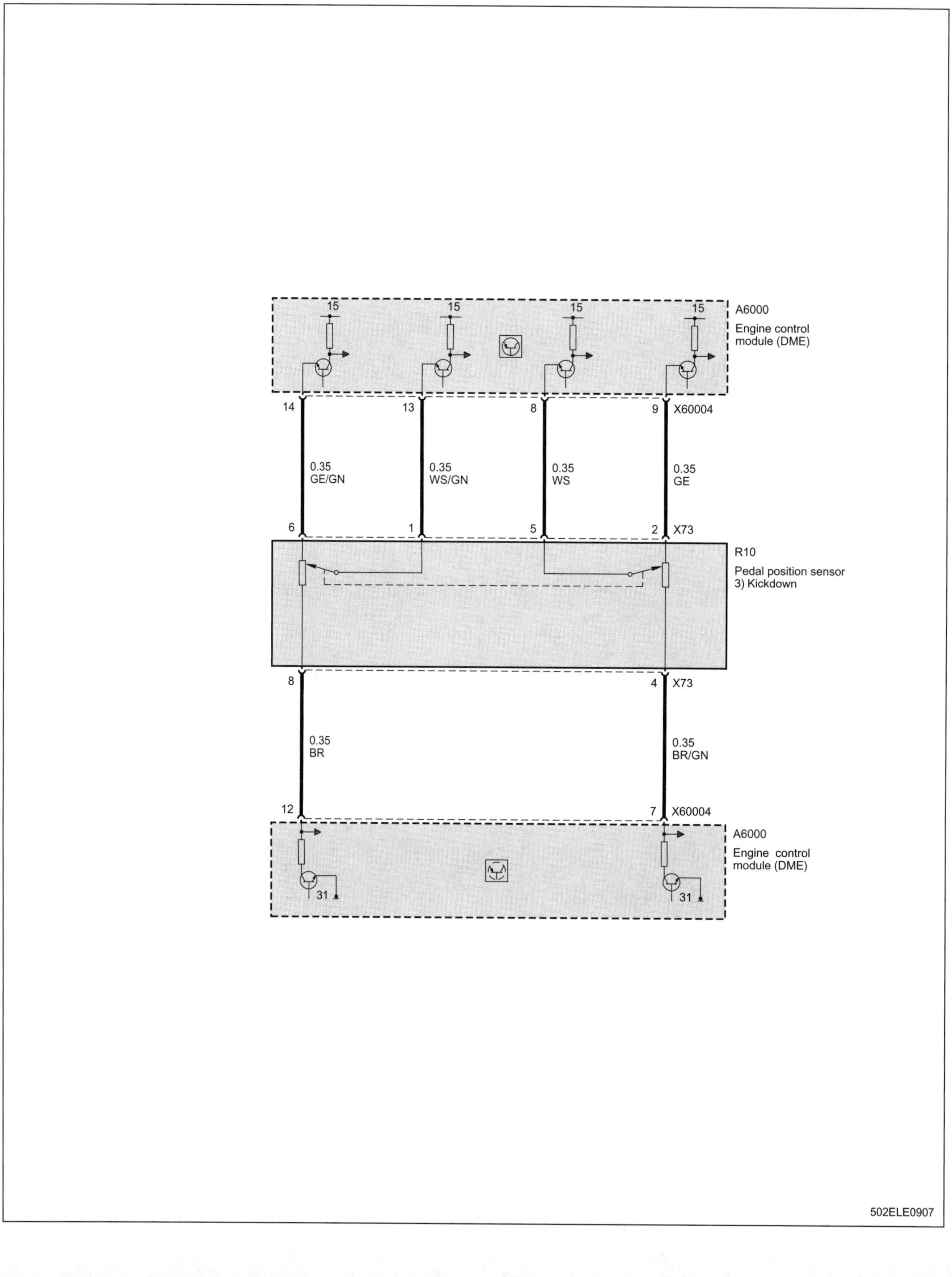

Engine Management (ME 7.2)
Engine coolant dual temperature sensor
(1 of 1)

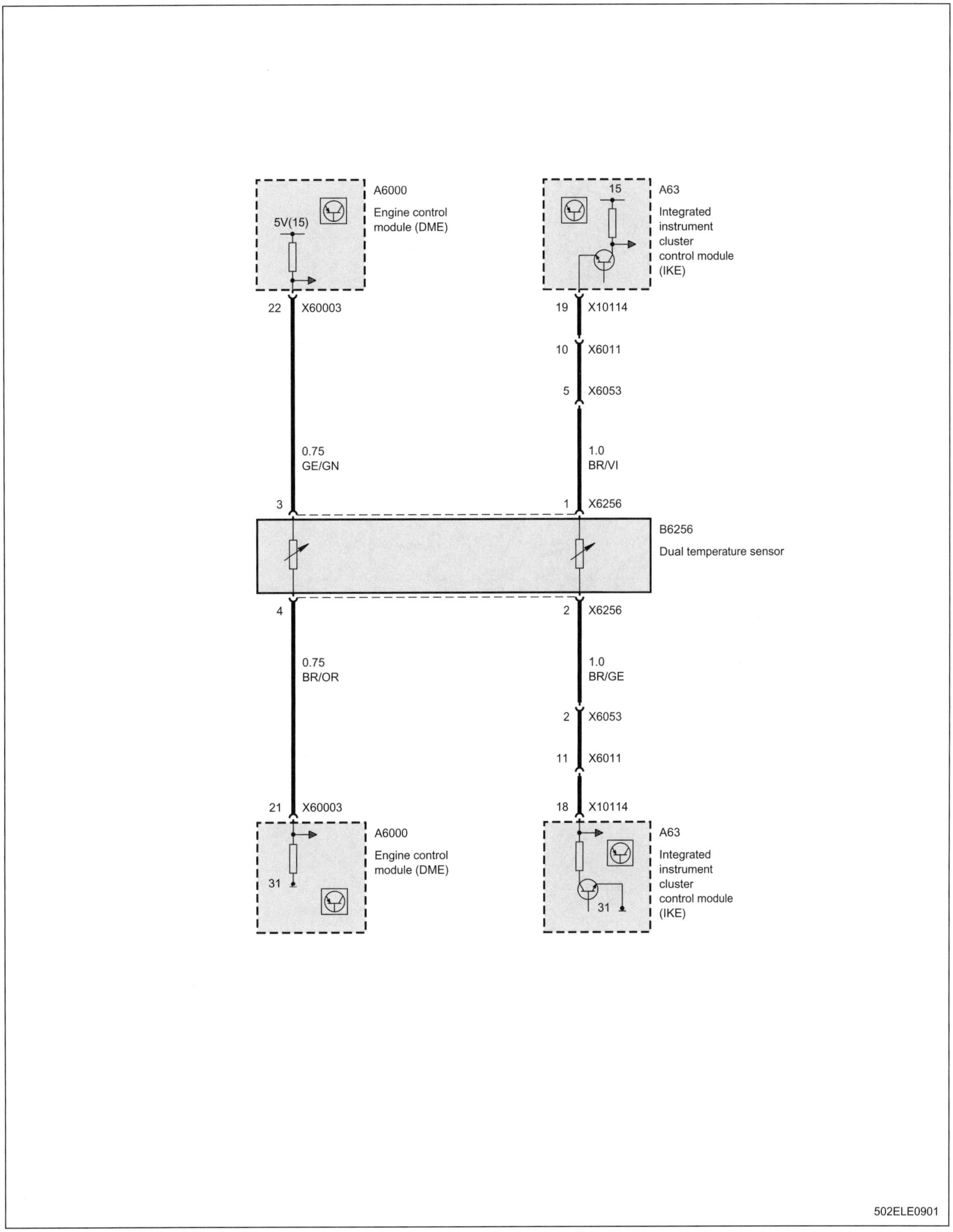

Engine Management (ME 7.2)
Hot-film mass air flow sensor
(1 of 1)

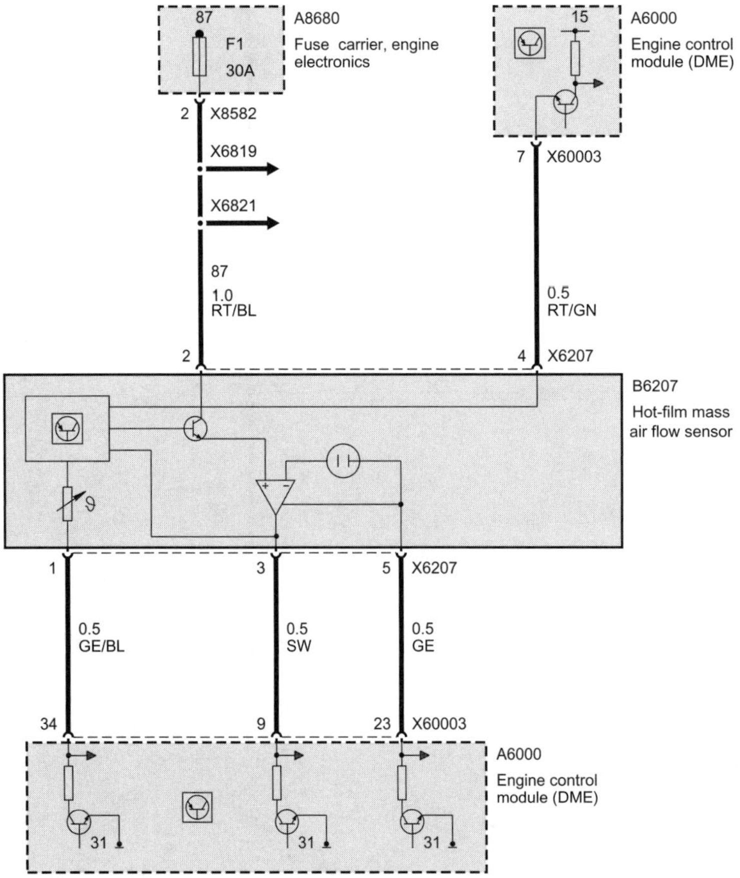

Engine Management (ME 7.2)
Camshaft sensor 1
(1 of 1)

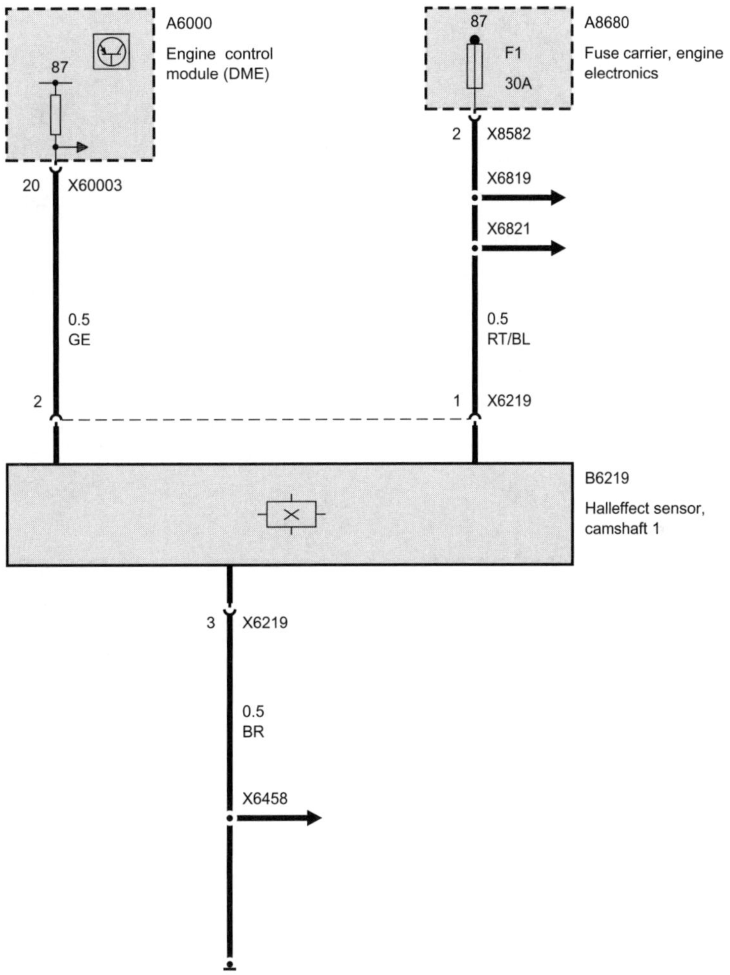
A6000
Engine control module (DME)
87
20
X60003
0.5
GE
2
A8680
Fuse carrier, engine electronics
87
F1
30A
2
X8582
X6819
X6821
0.5
RT/BL
1
X6219
B6219
Halleffect sensor, camshaft 1
3
X6219
0.5
BR
X6458
502ELE0895

Engine Management (ME 7.2)
Camshaft sensor 2
(1 of 1)

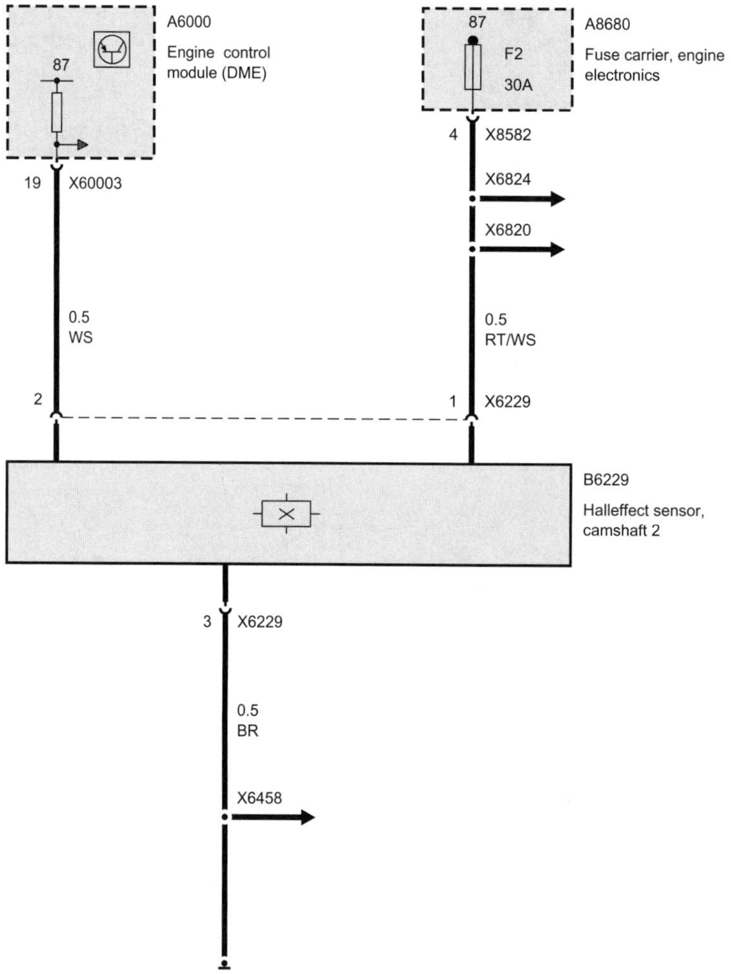
A6000
Engine control module (DME)
87
19
X60003
0.5
WS
2
A8680
Fuse carrier, engine electronics
87
F2
30A
4
X8582
X6824
X6820
0.5
RT/WS
1
X6229
B6229
Halleffect sensor, camshaft 2
3
X6229
0.5
BR
X6458
502ELE0894

Engine Management (ME 7.2)
Crankshaft sensor
(1 of 1)

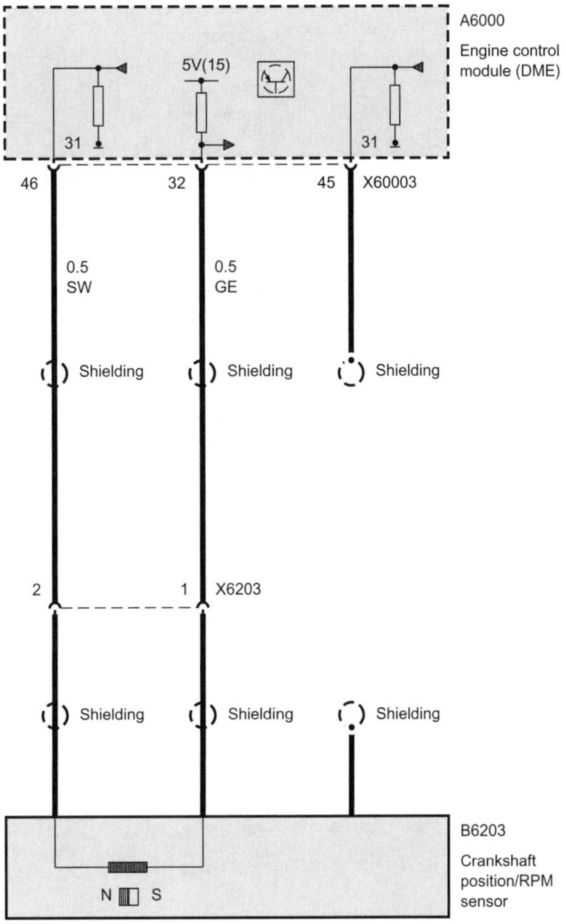

502ELE0896

Engine Management (ME 7.2)
Characteristic map, cooling (thermostat)
(1 of 1)

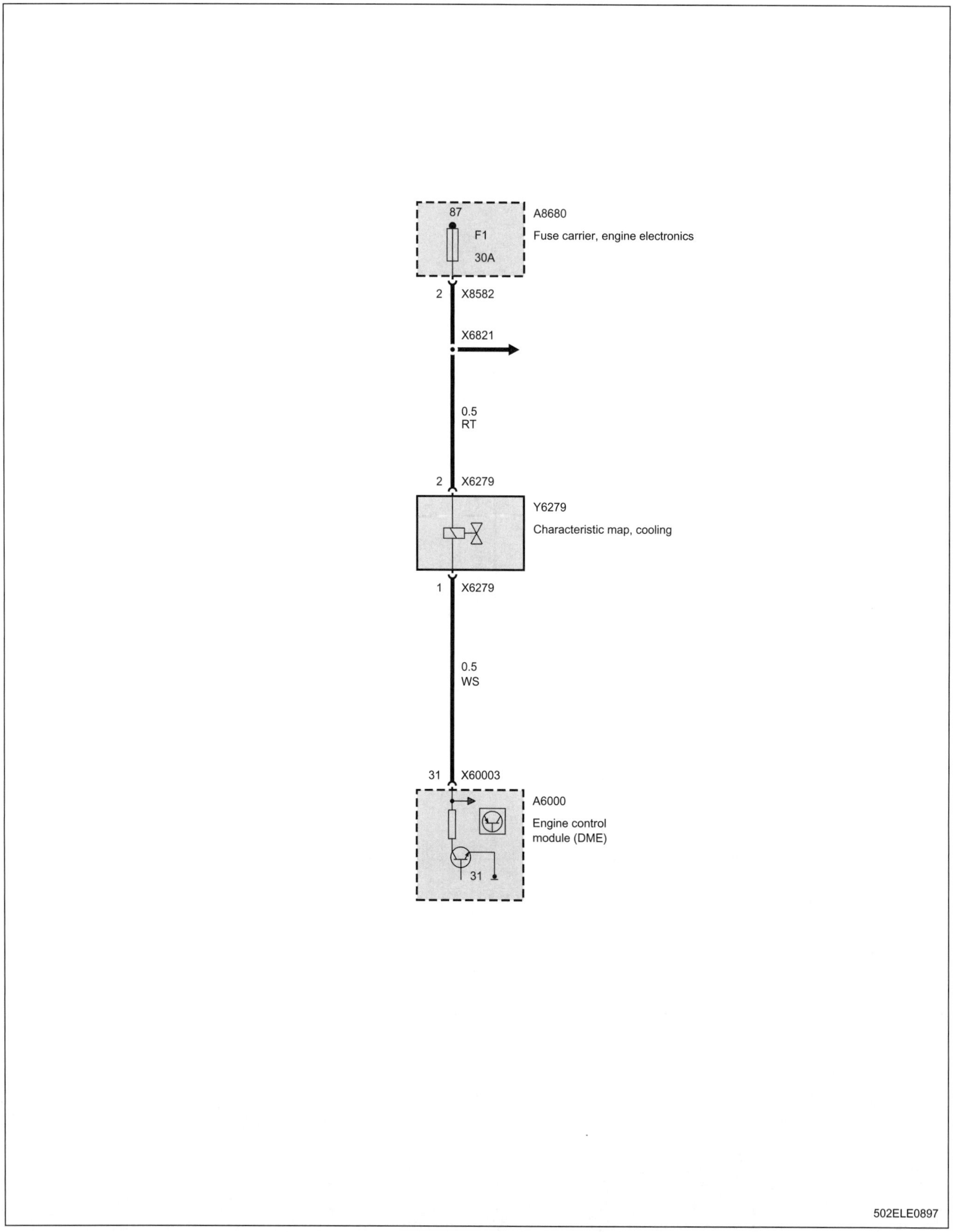

Engine Management (ME 7.2)
Coolant temperature/electric fan
(1 of 1)

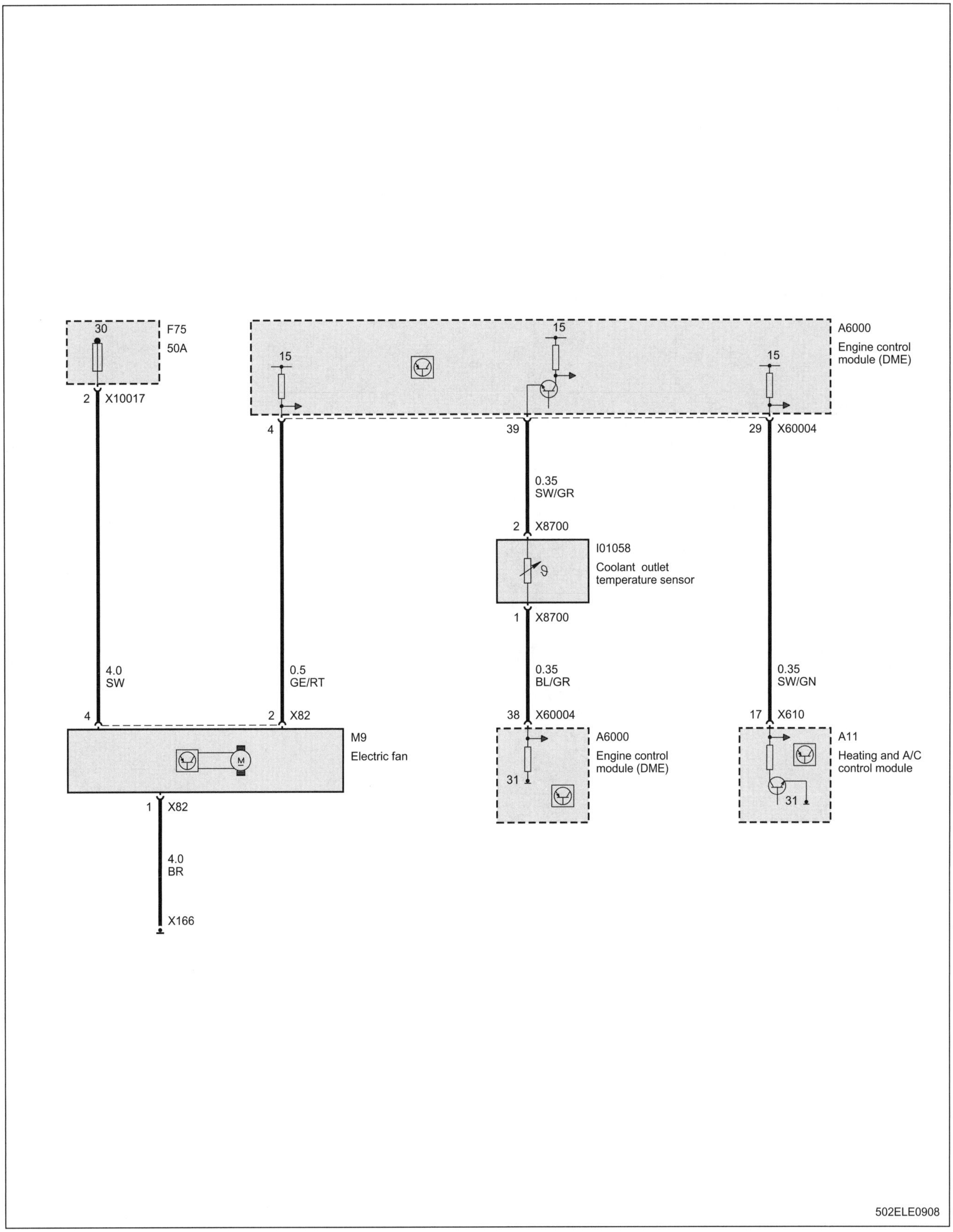

Engine Management (ME 7.2)
VANOS valve, cylinders 1-4
(1 of 1)

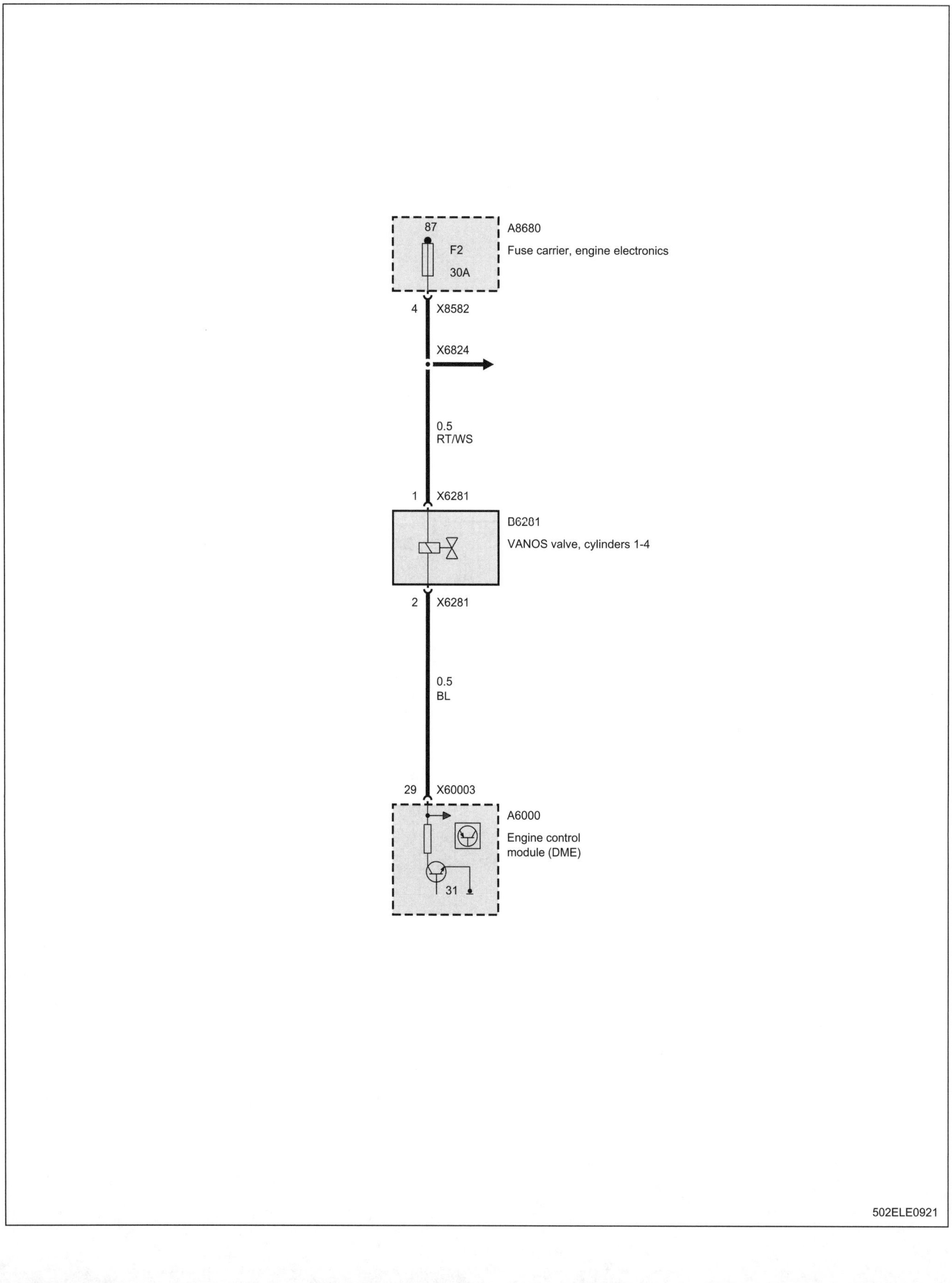

Engine Management (ME 7.2)
VANOS valve, cylinders 5-8
(1 of 1)

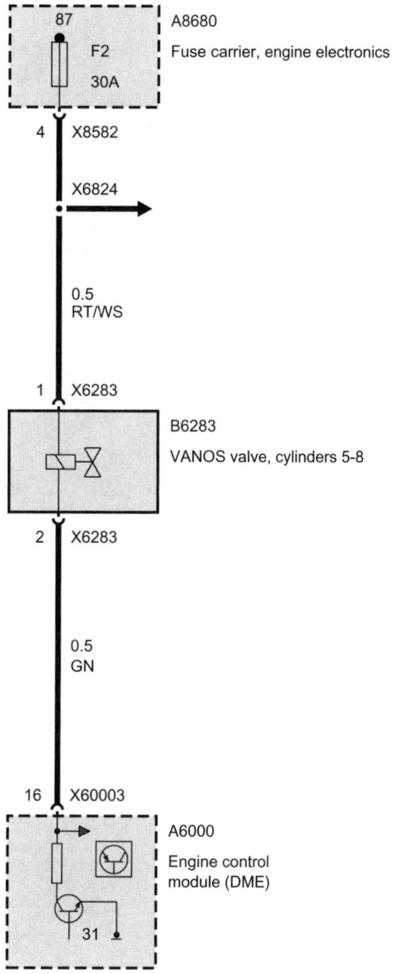

502ELE0920

Engine Management (ME 7.2)
Knock sensors 1 and 2
(1 of 1)

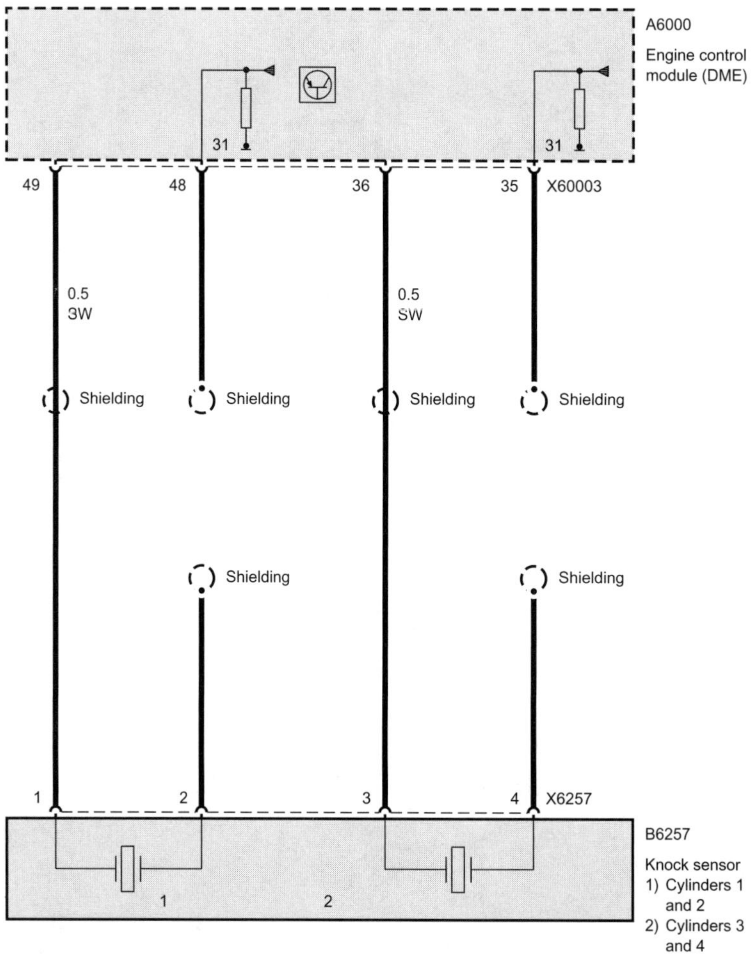

502ELE0899

Engine Management (ME 7.2)
Knock sensors 3 and 4
(1 of 1)

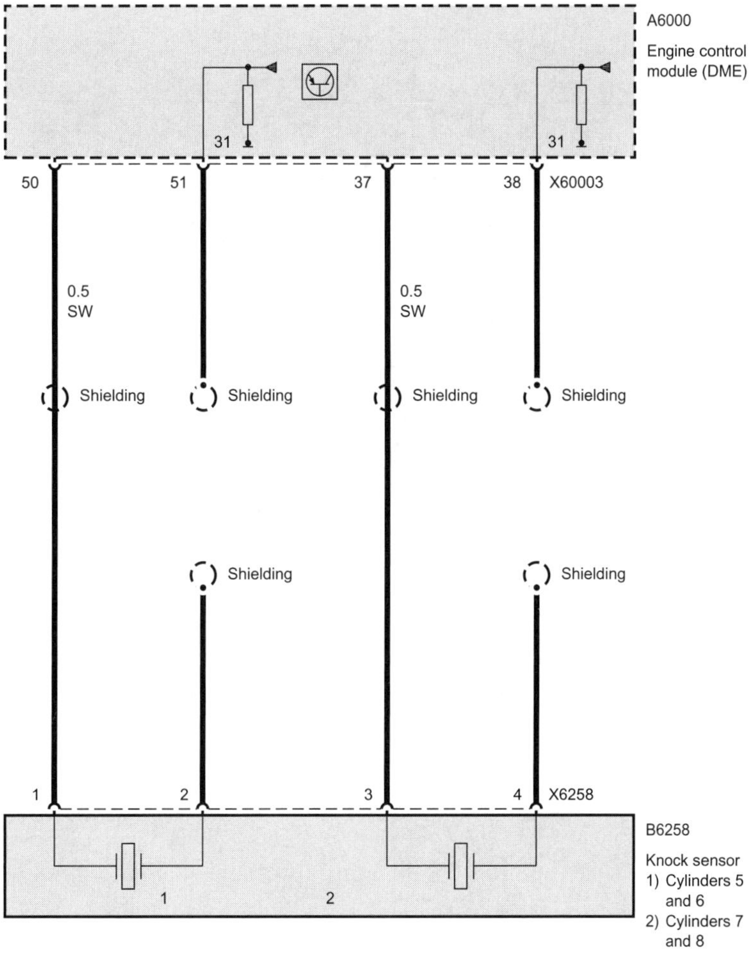

Engine Management (ME 7.2)
Evaporative emission valve
(1 of 1)

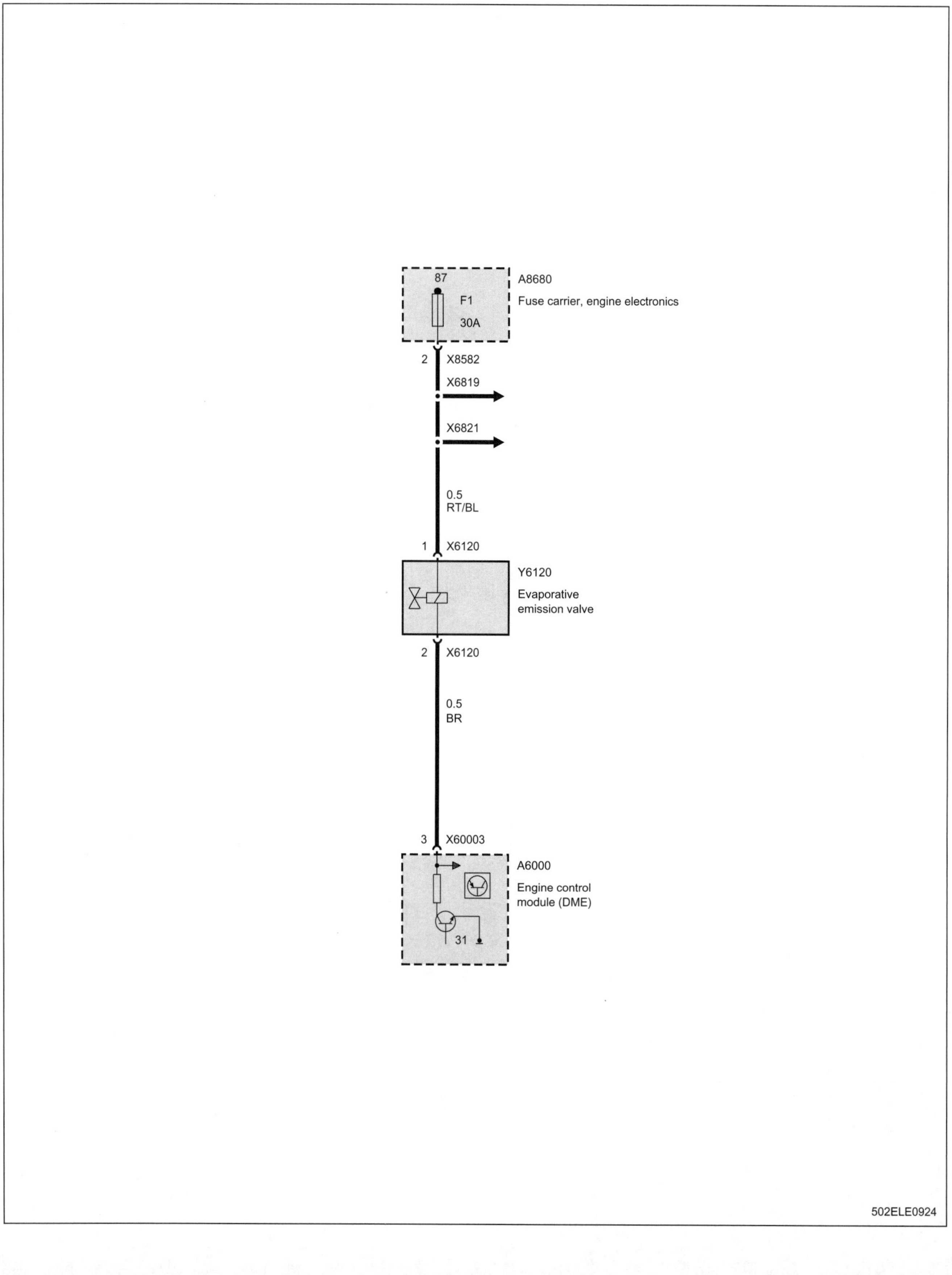

Engine Management (ME 7.2)
Fuel tank leak diagnosis pump
(1 of 1)

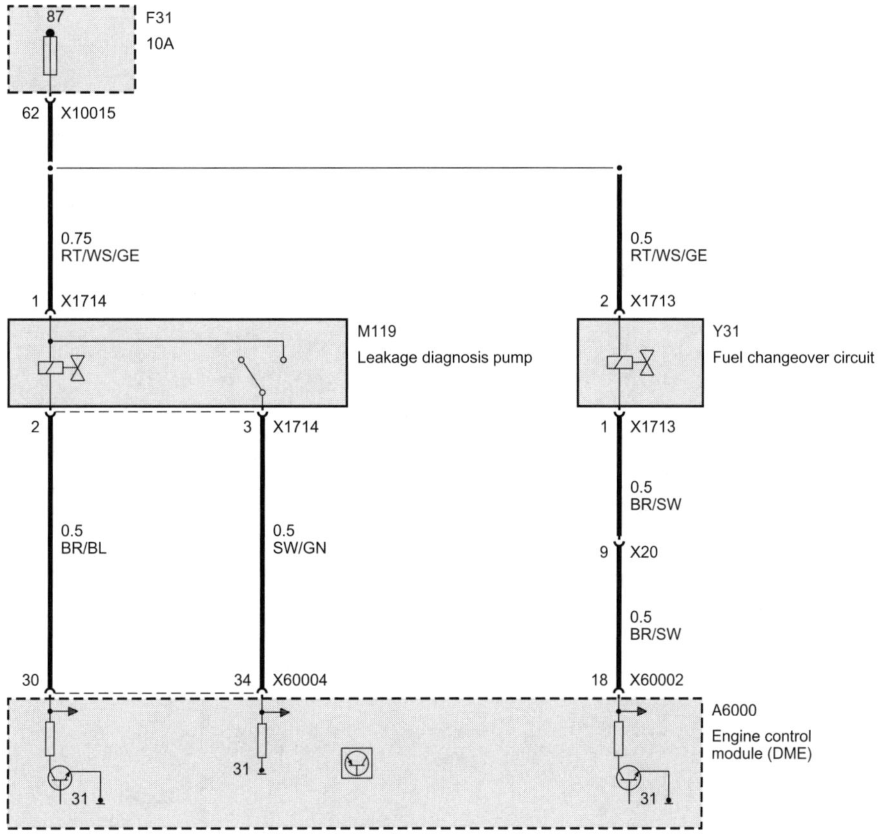

502ELE0923

Engine Management (ME 7.2)
Oxygen sensor 1 in front of catalytic converter
(1 of 1)

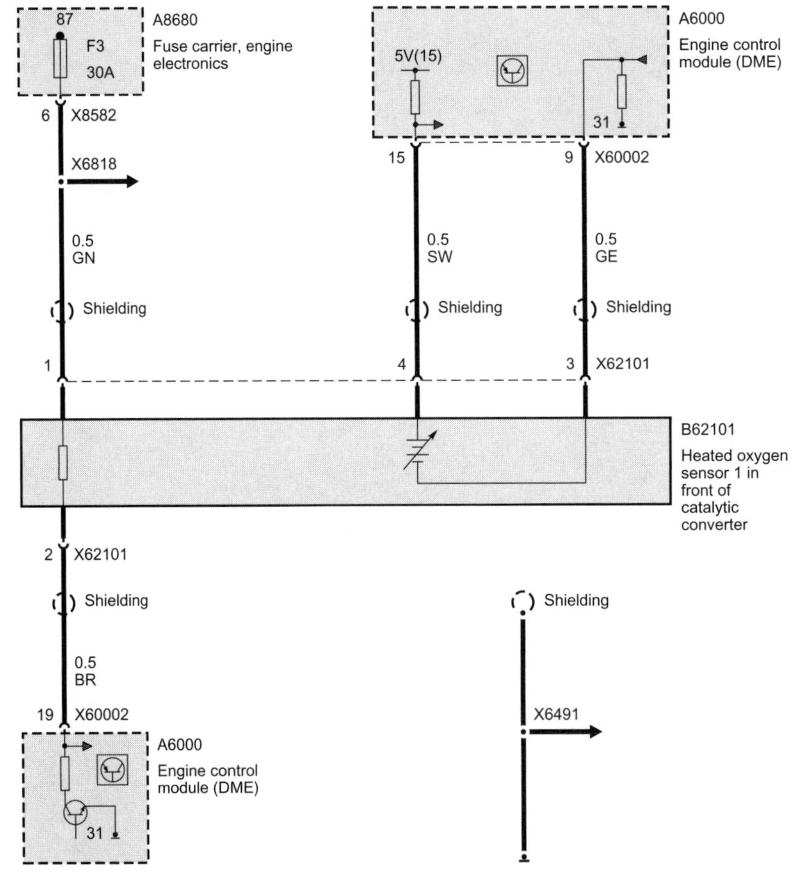

502ELE0906

Engine Management (ME 7.2)
Oxygen sensor 1 behind catalytic converter
(1 of 1)

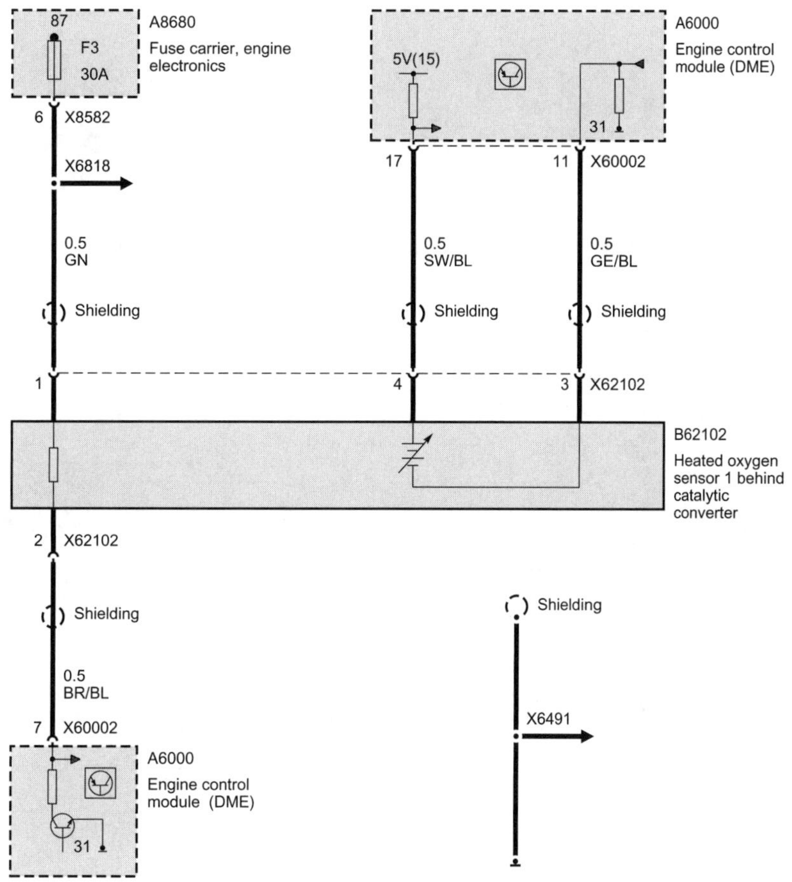

502ELE0904

Engine Management (ME 7.2)
Oxygen sensor 2 in front of catalytic converter
(1 of 1)

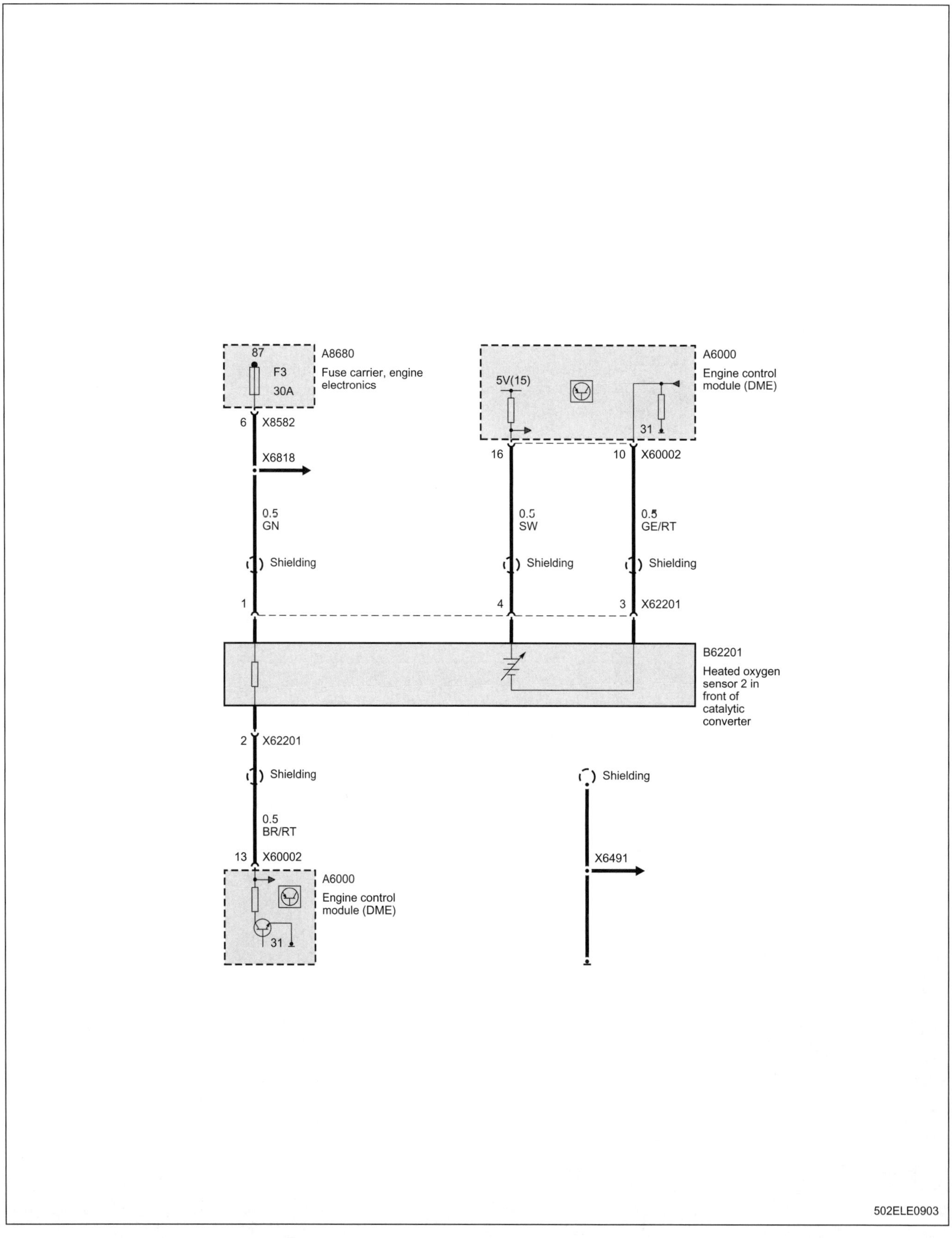

Engine Management (ME 7.2)
Oxygen sensor 2 behind catalytic converter
(1 of 1)

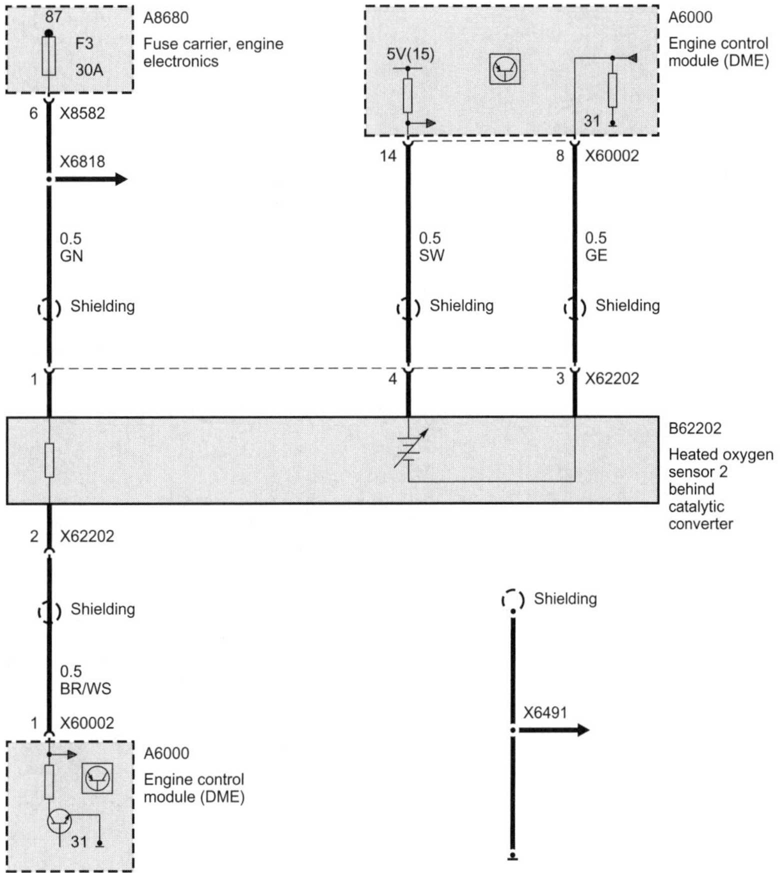

502ELE0905

Engine Management (ME 7.2)
Secondary air system
(1 of 1)

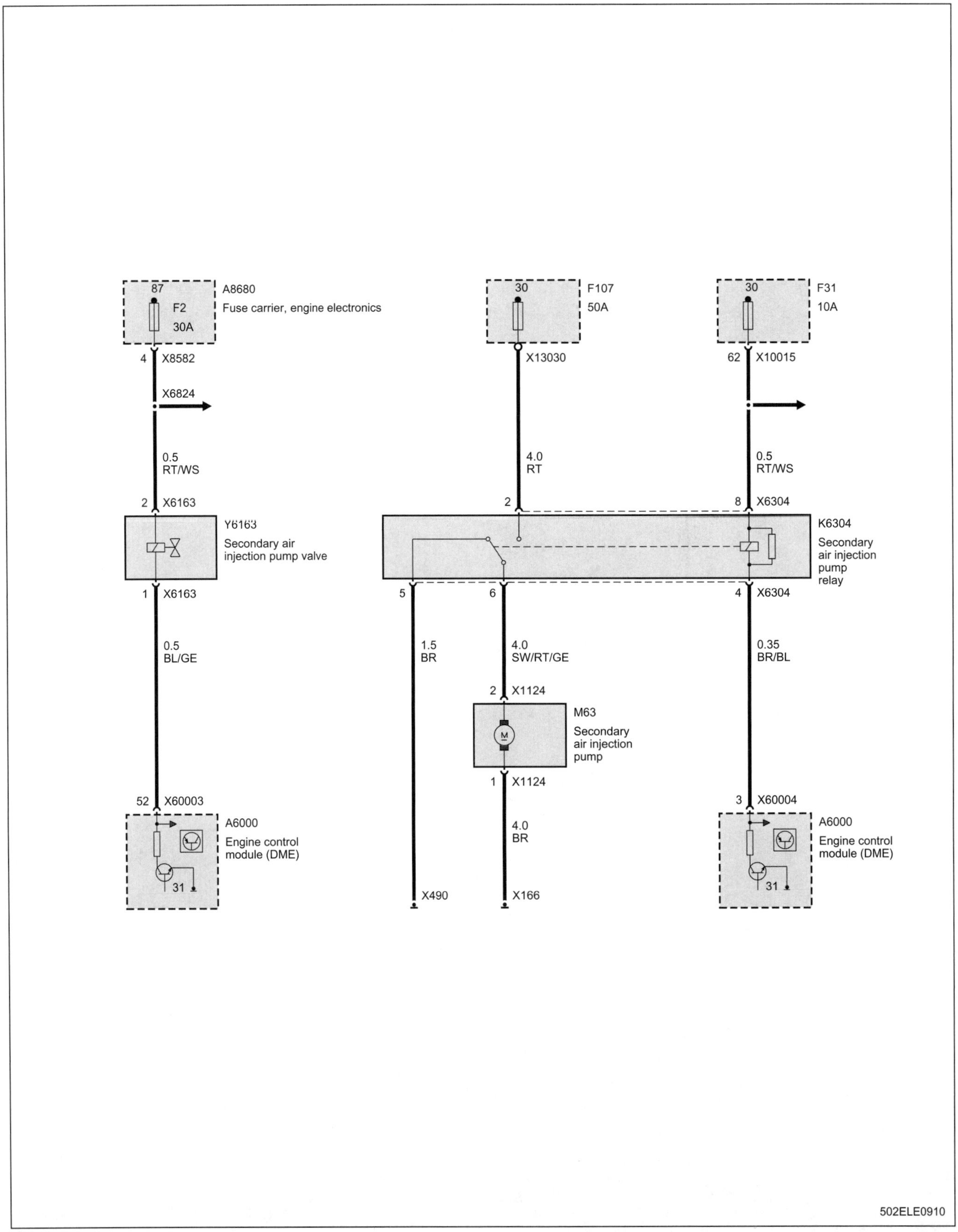

Engine Management (ME 7.2)
Cyl. 1 and 2 fuel injection valves
(1 of 1)

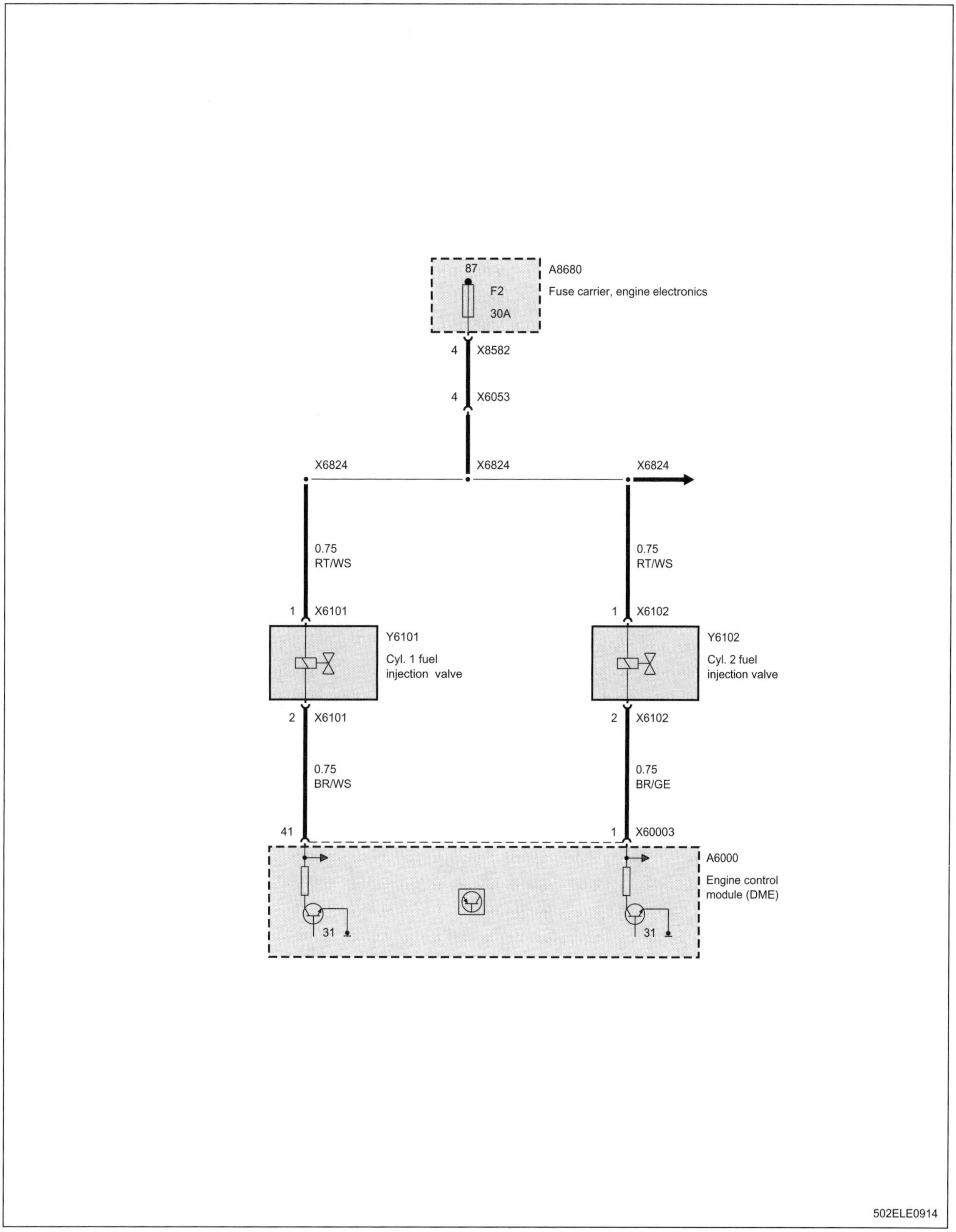

Engine Management (ME 7.2)
Cyl. 3 and 4 fuel injection valves
(1 of 1)

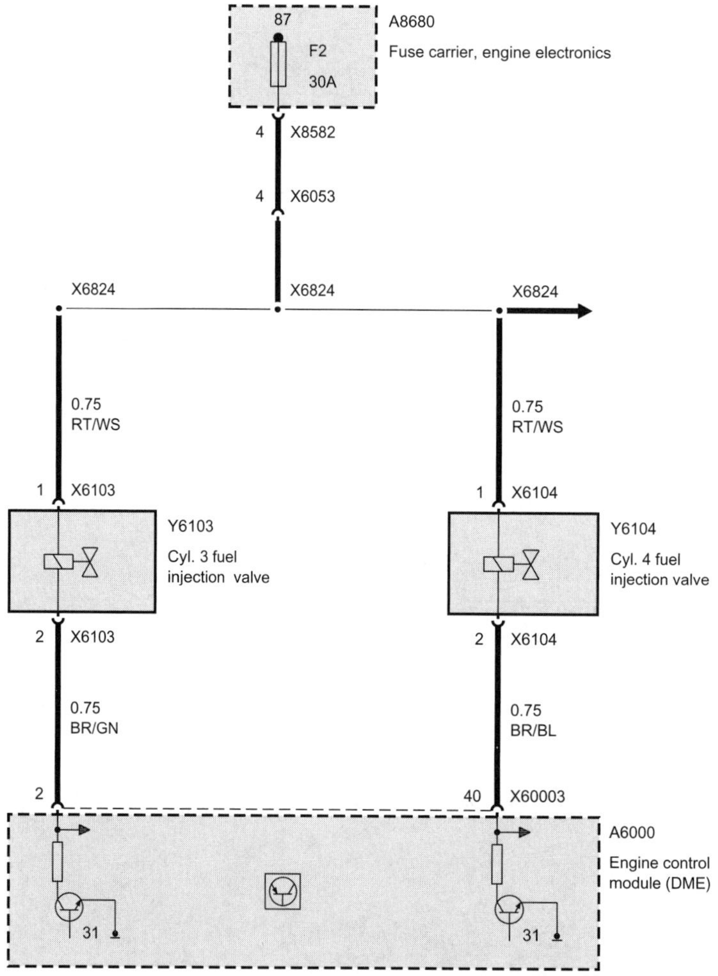

502ELE0911

Engine Management (ME 7.2)
Cyl. 5 and 6 fuel injection valves
(1 of 1)

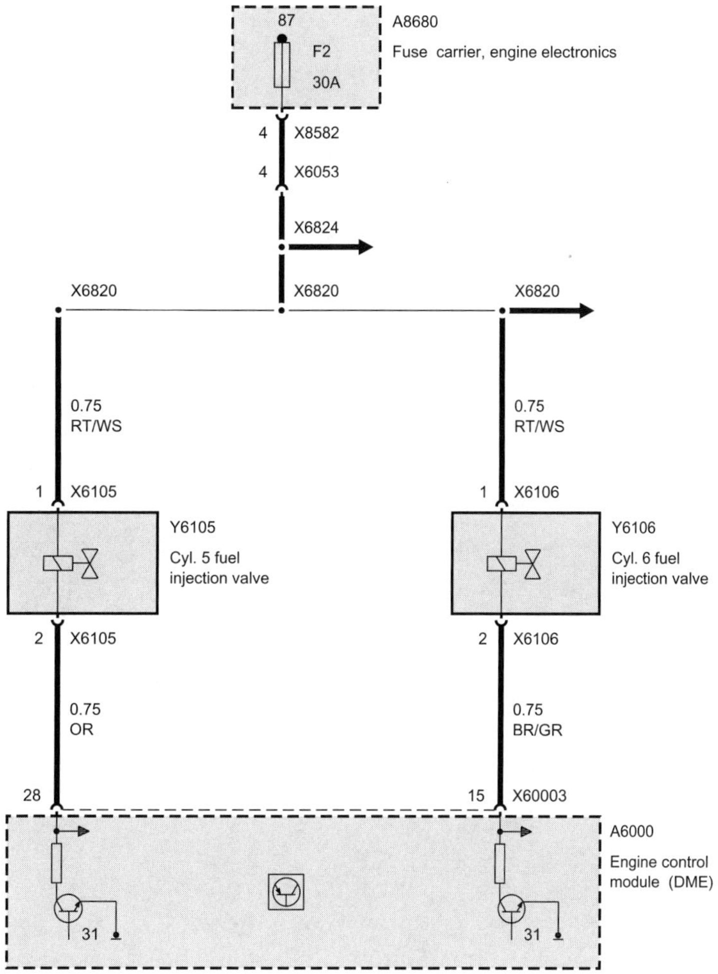

502ELE0912

Engine Management (ME 7.2)
Cyl. 7 and 8 fuel injection valves
(1 of 1)

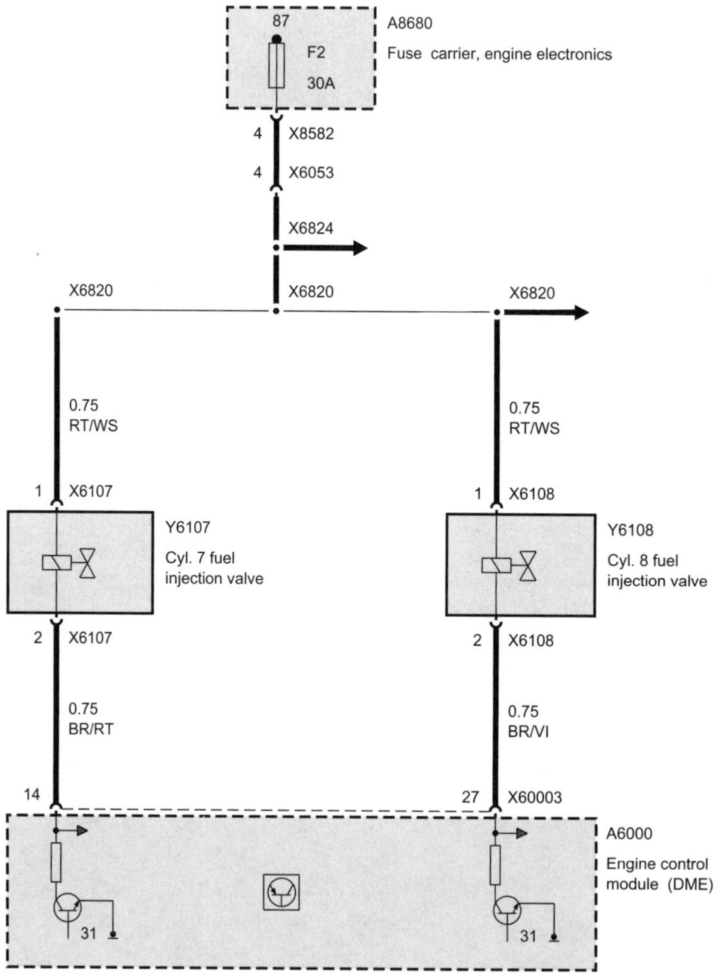

502ELE0913

Engine Management (ME 7.2)
Power, ignition coils
(1 of 1)

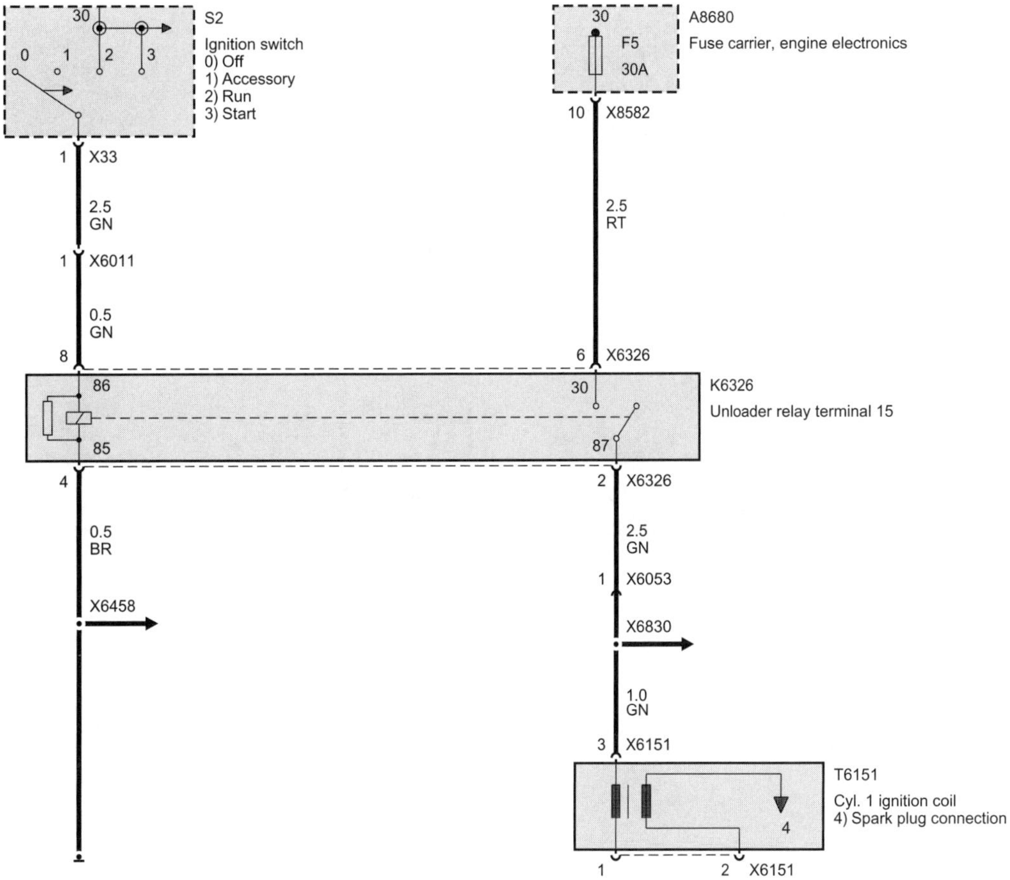

Engine Management (ME 7.2)
Cyl. 1 and 2 ignition coils
(1 of 1)

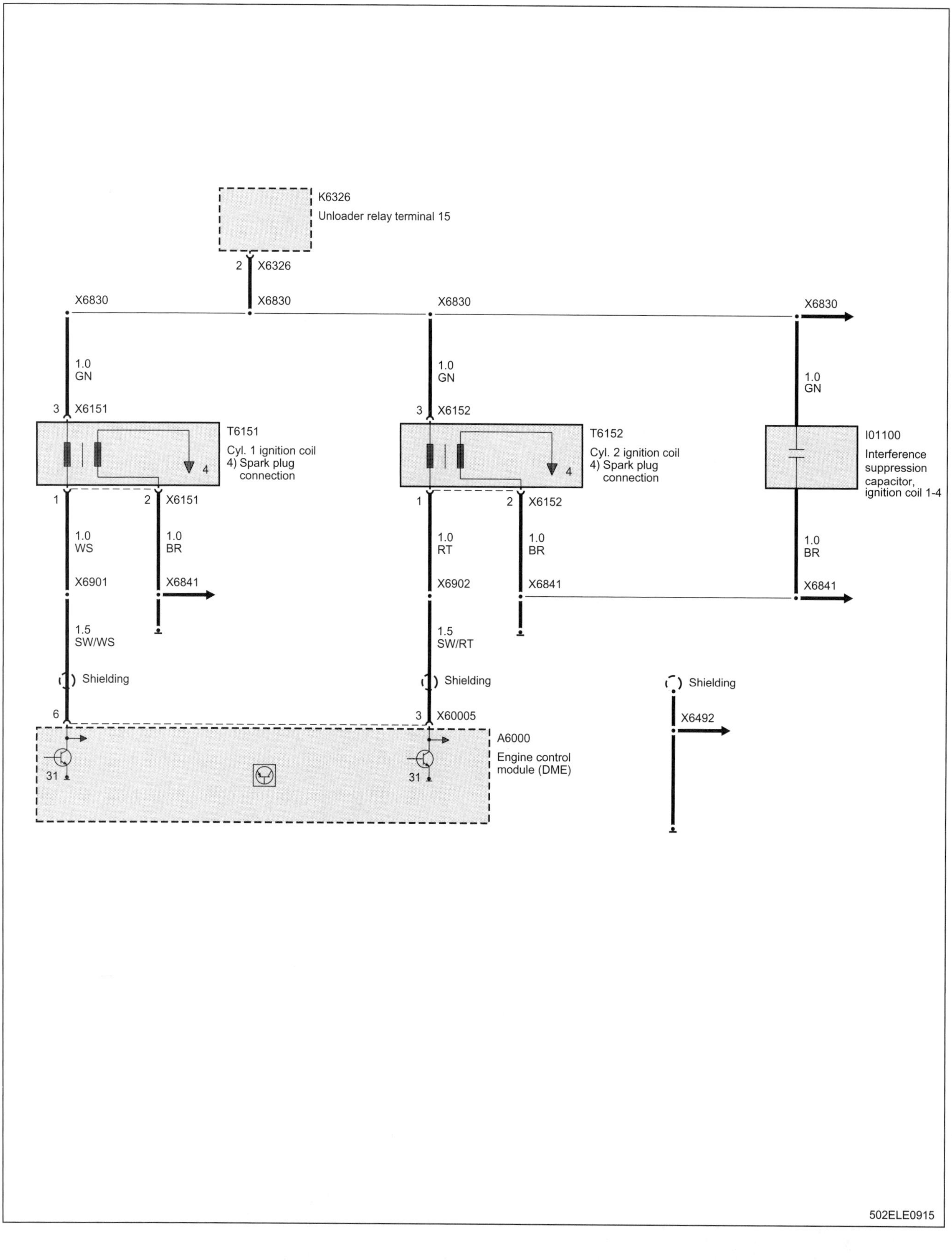

Engine Management (ME 7.2)
Cyl. 3 and 4 ignition coils
(1 of 1)

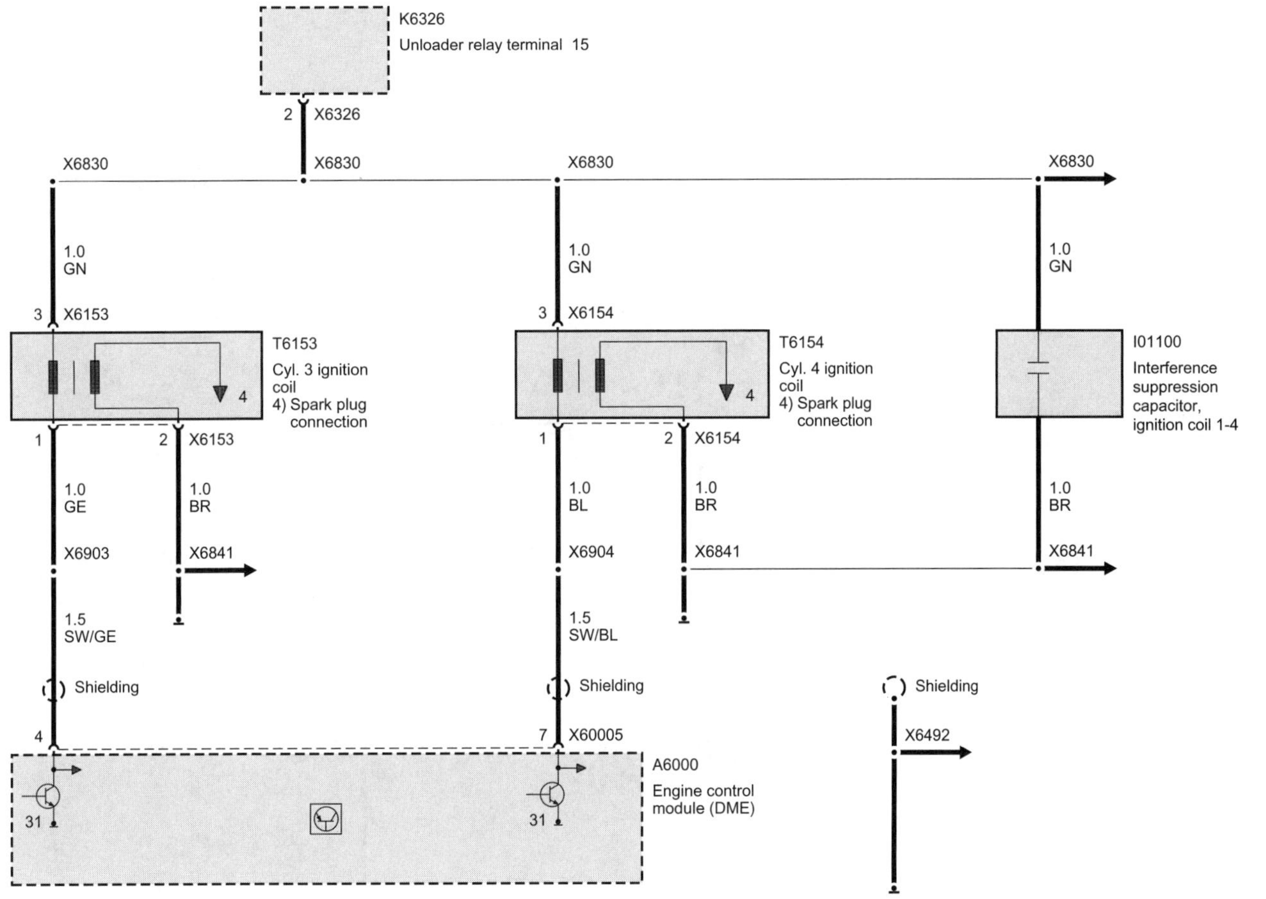

502ELE0916

Engine Management (ME 7.2)
Cyl. 5 and 6 ignition coils
(1 of 1)

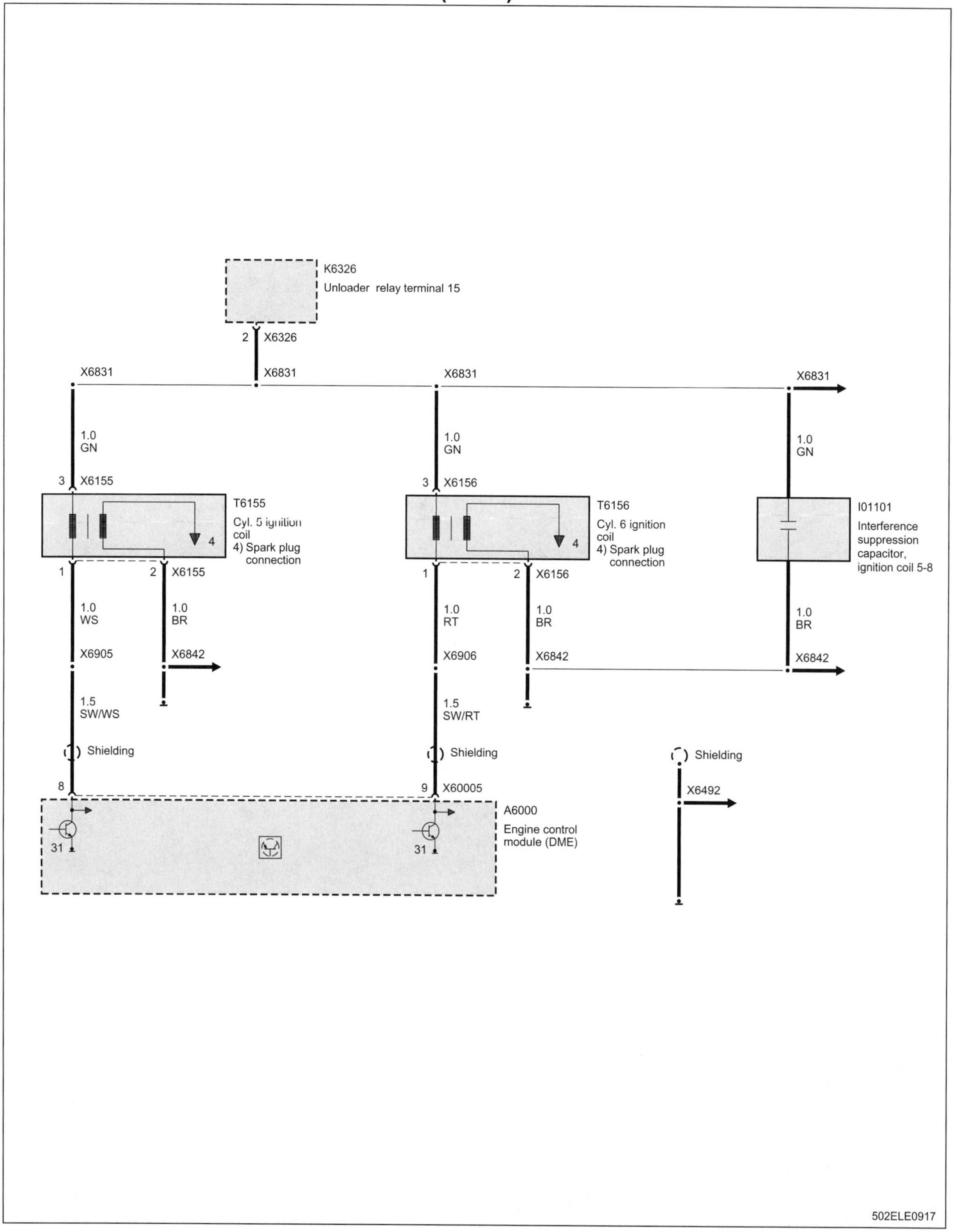

Engine Management (ME 7.2)
Cyl. 7 and 8 ignition coils
(1 of 1)

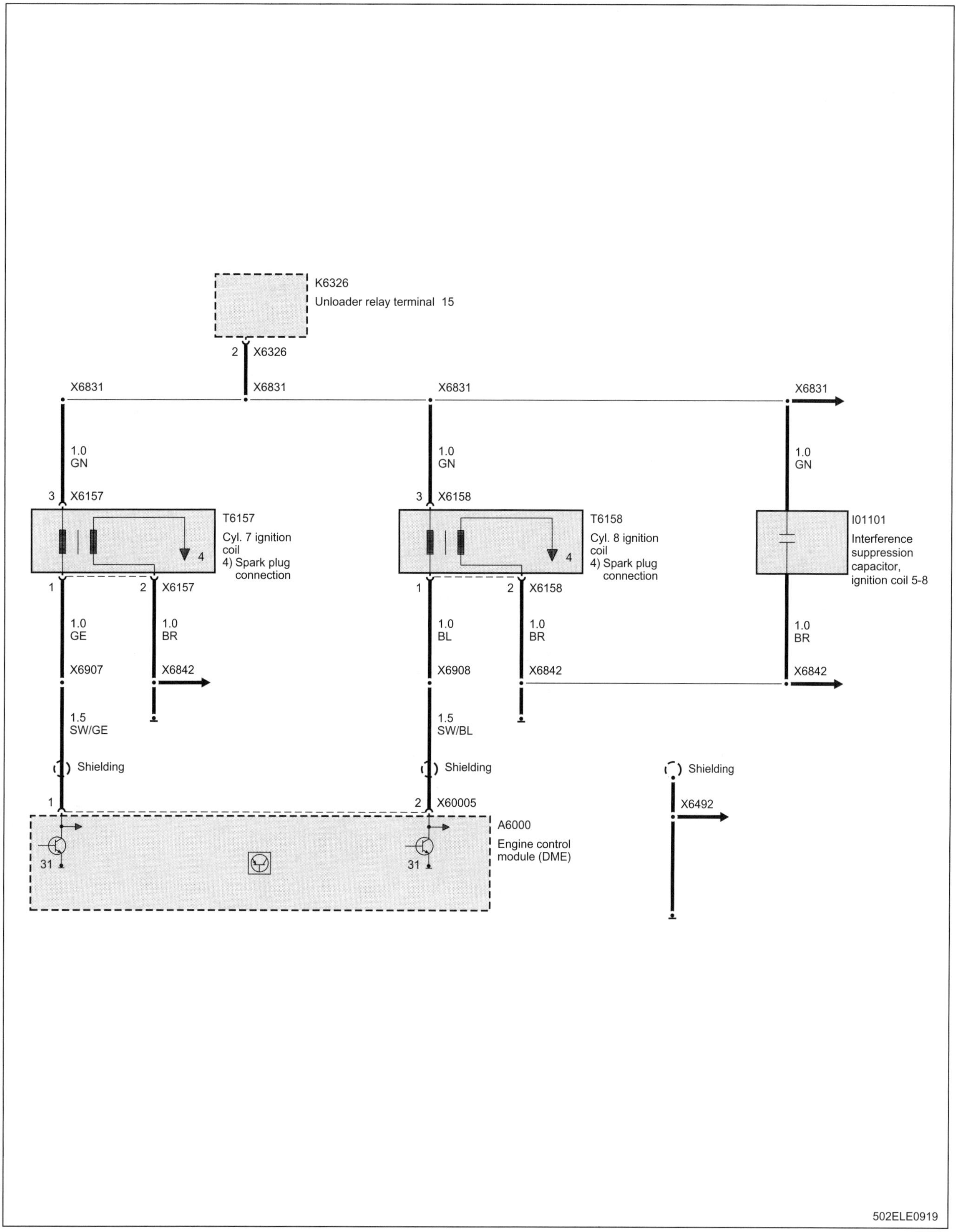

502ELE0919

Engine Management (ME 7.2)
Generator
(1 of 1)

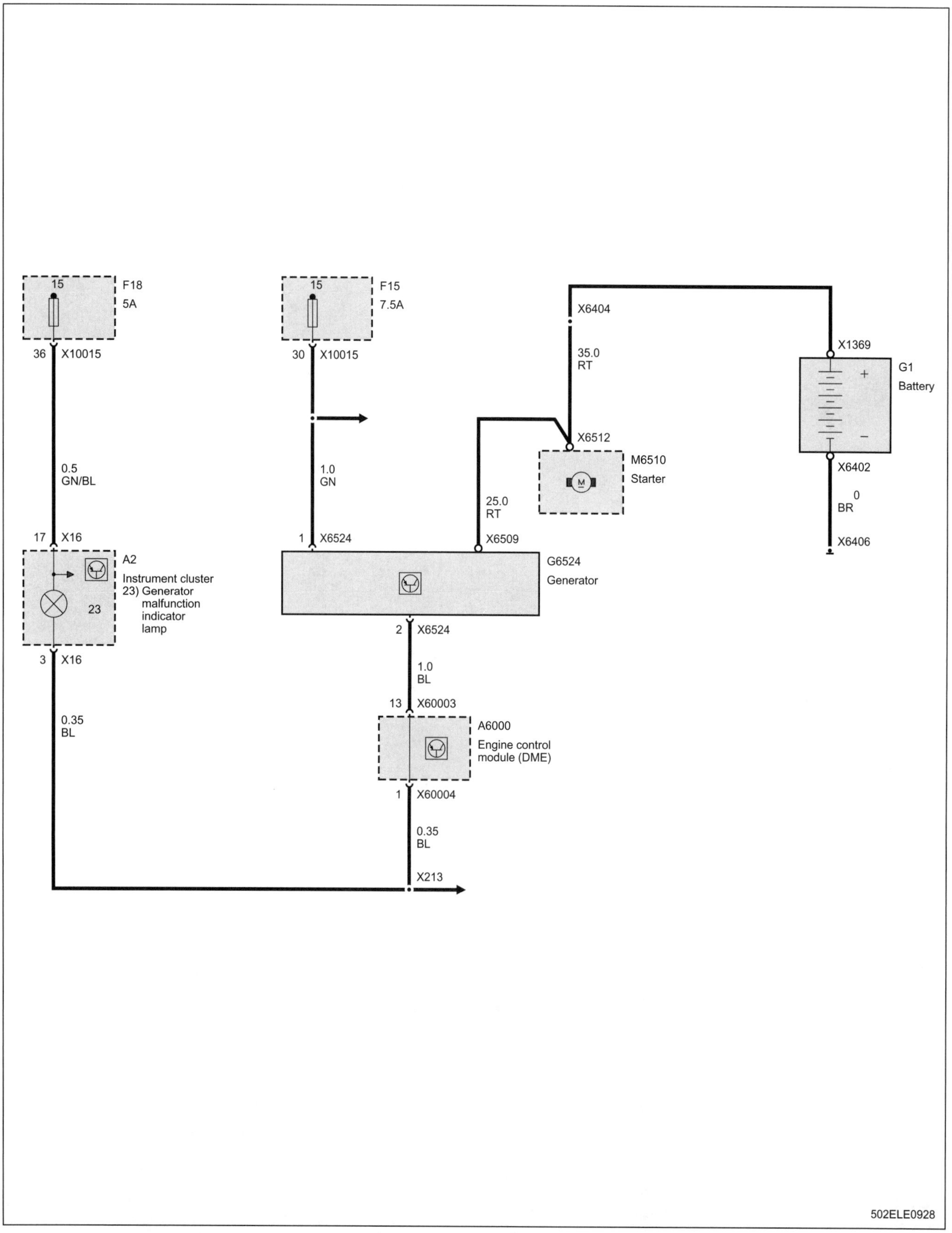
15
F18
5A
36 X10015
0.5
GN/BL
17 X16
A2
Instrument cluster
23) Generator
malfunction
indicator
lamp
23
3 X16
0.35
BL
15
F15
7.5A
30 X10015
1.0
GN
1 X6524
G6524
Generator
2 X6524
1.0
BL
13 X60003
A6000
Engine control
module (DME)
1 X60004
0.35
BL
X213
X6404
35.0
RT
X6512
M6510
Starter
25.0
RT
X6509
X1369
G1
Battery
X6402
0
BR
X6406
502ELE0928

Engine Management (ME 7.2)
Start detection
(1 of 1)

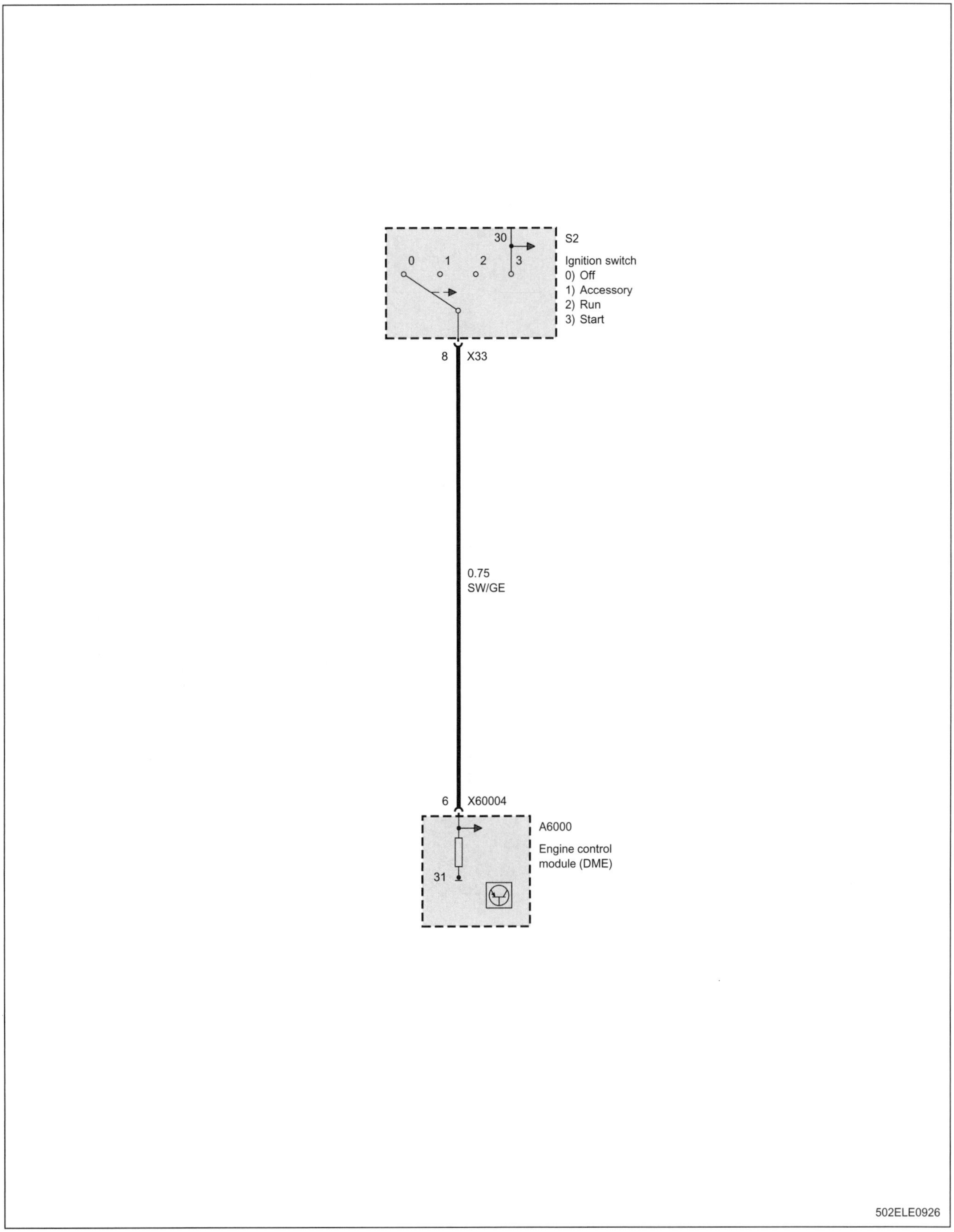

Engine Management (ME 7.2)
CAN interface
(1 of 2)

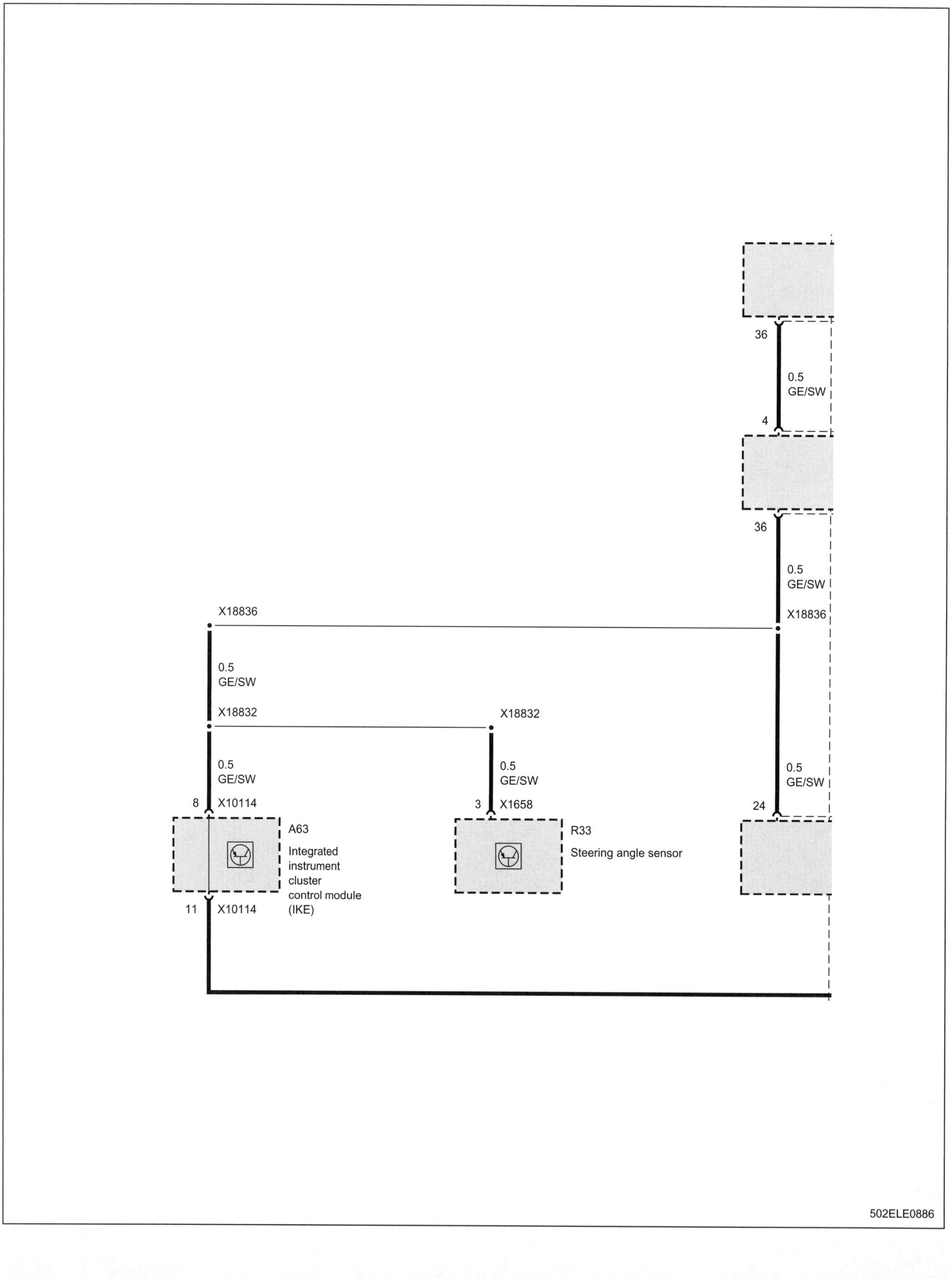
36
0.5
GE/SW
4
36
0.5
GE/SW
X18836
X18836
0.5
GE/SW
X18832
X18832
0.5
GE/SW
0.5
GE/SW
0.5
GE/SW
8
X10114
3
X1658
24
A63
Integrated
instrument
cluster
control module
(IKE)
R33
Steering angle sensor
11
X10114
502ELE0886

Engine Management (ME 7.2)
CAN interface
(2 of 2)

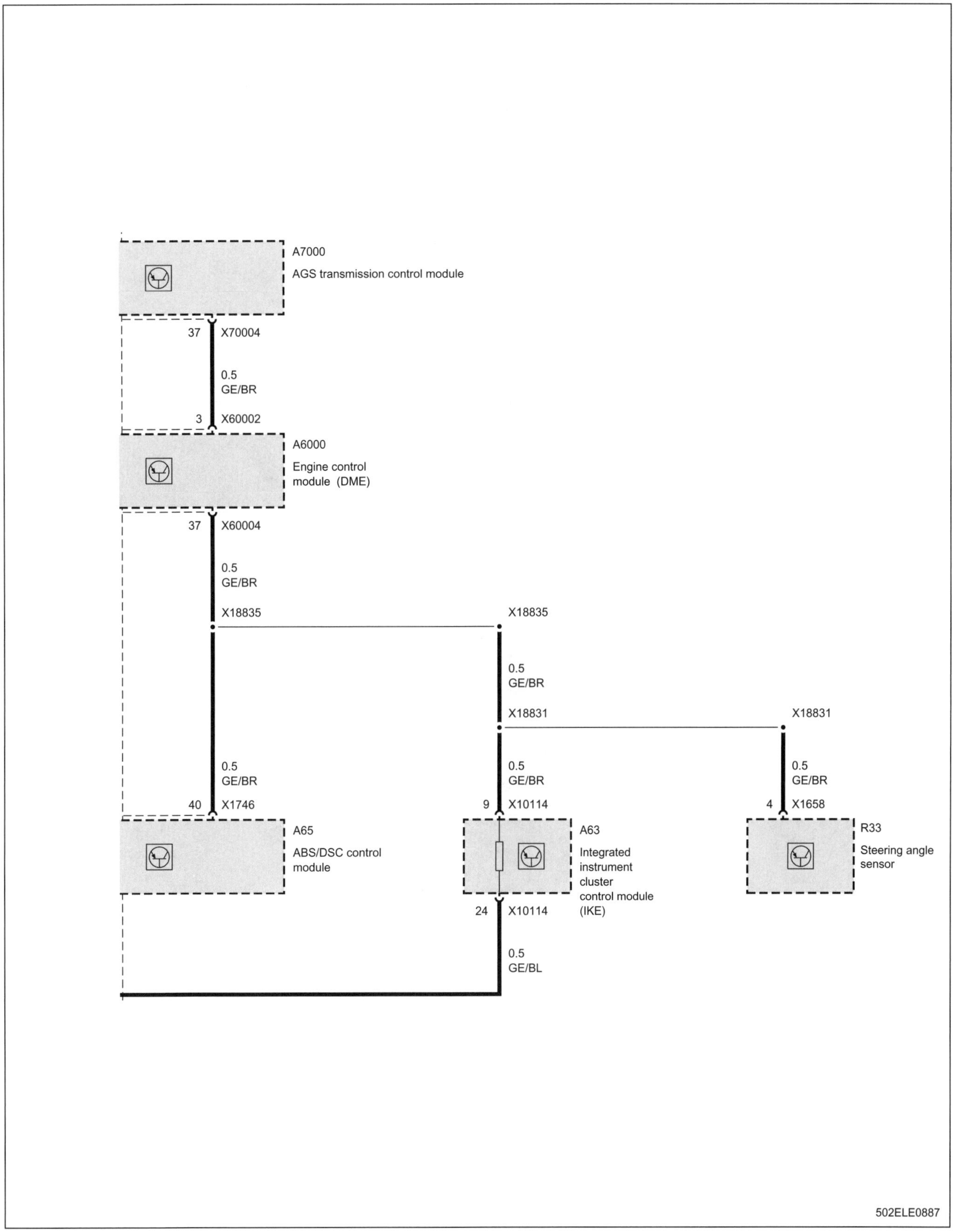
A7000
AGS transmission control module
37
X70004
0.5
GE/BR
3
X60002
A6000
Engine control
module (DME)
37
X60004
0.5
GE/BR
X18835
X18835
0.5
GE/BR
X18831
X18831
0.5
GE/BR
0.5
GE/BR
0.5
GE/BR
40
X1746
9
X10114
4
X1658
A65
ABS/DSC control
module
A63
Integrated
instrument
cluster
control module
(IKE)
R33
Steering angle
sensor
24
X10114
0.5
GE/BL
502ELE0887

Engine Management (ME 7.2)
DME/climate control interfaces
(1 of 1)

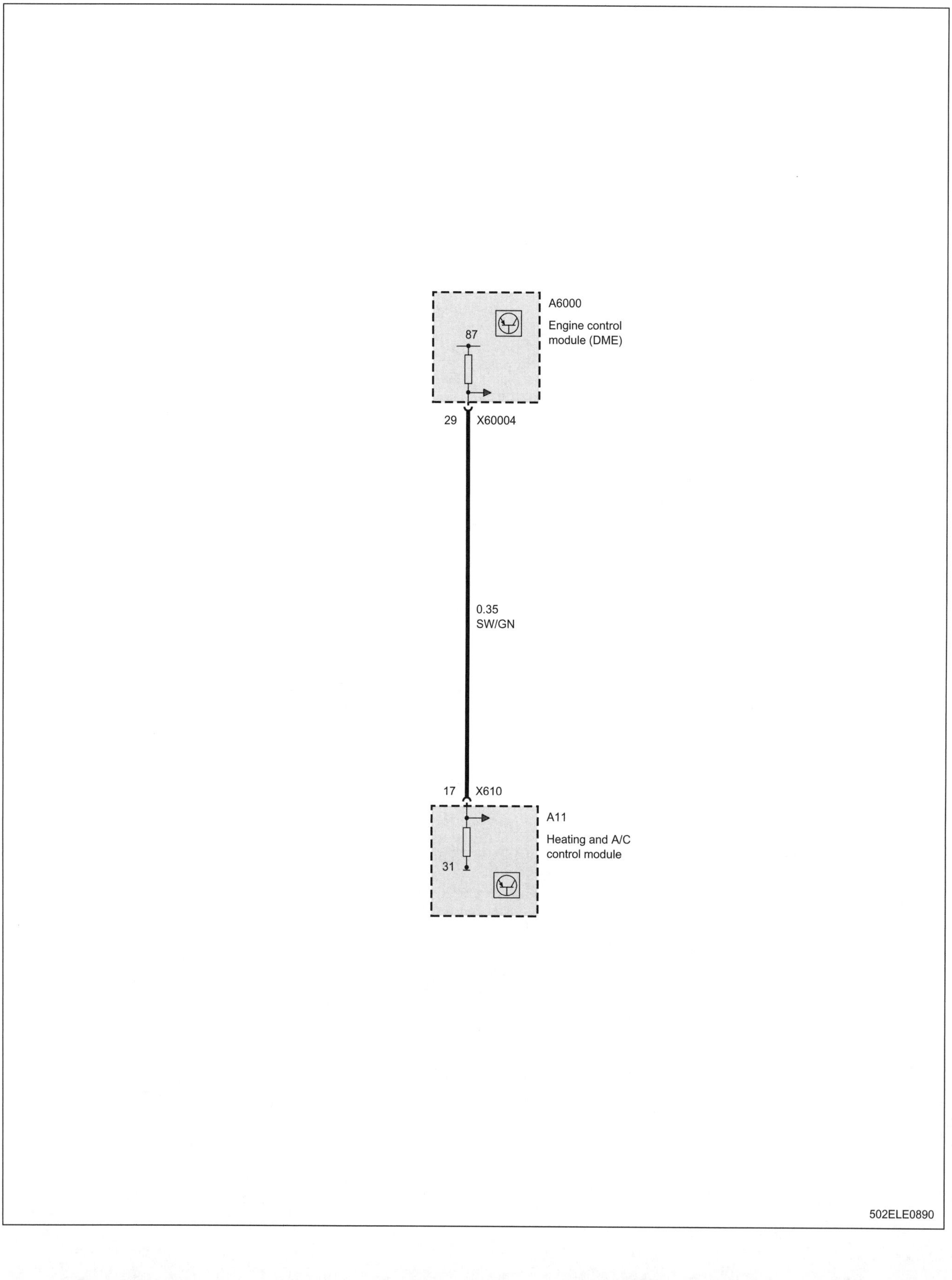

Engine Management (ME 7.2)
DME/IKE interface
(1 of 1)

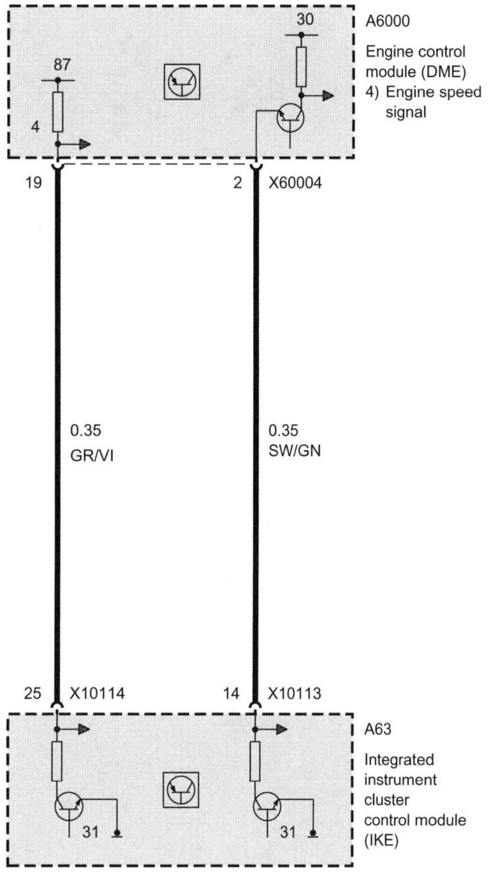

502ELE0889

Engine Management (ME 7.2)
Engine coolant level, oil level
(1 of 1)

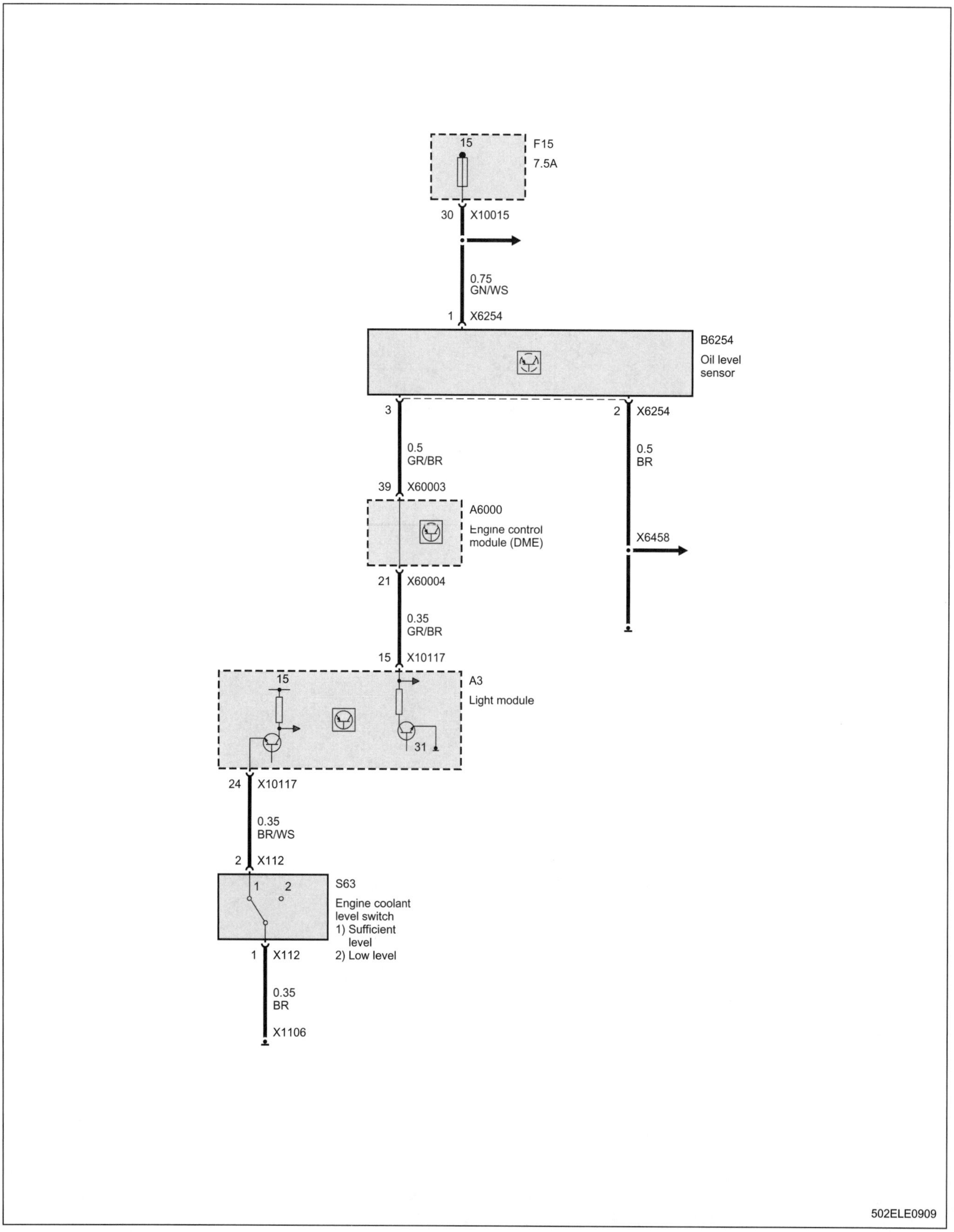

Exterior Lights
Lighting (overview)
(1 of 3)

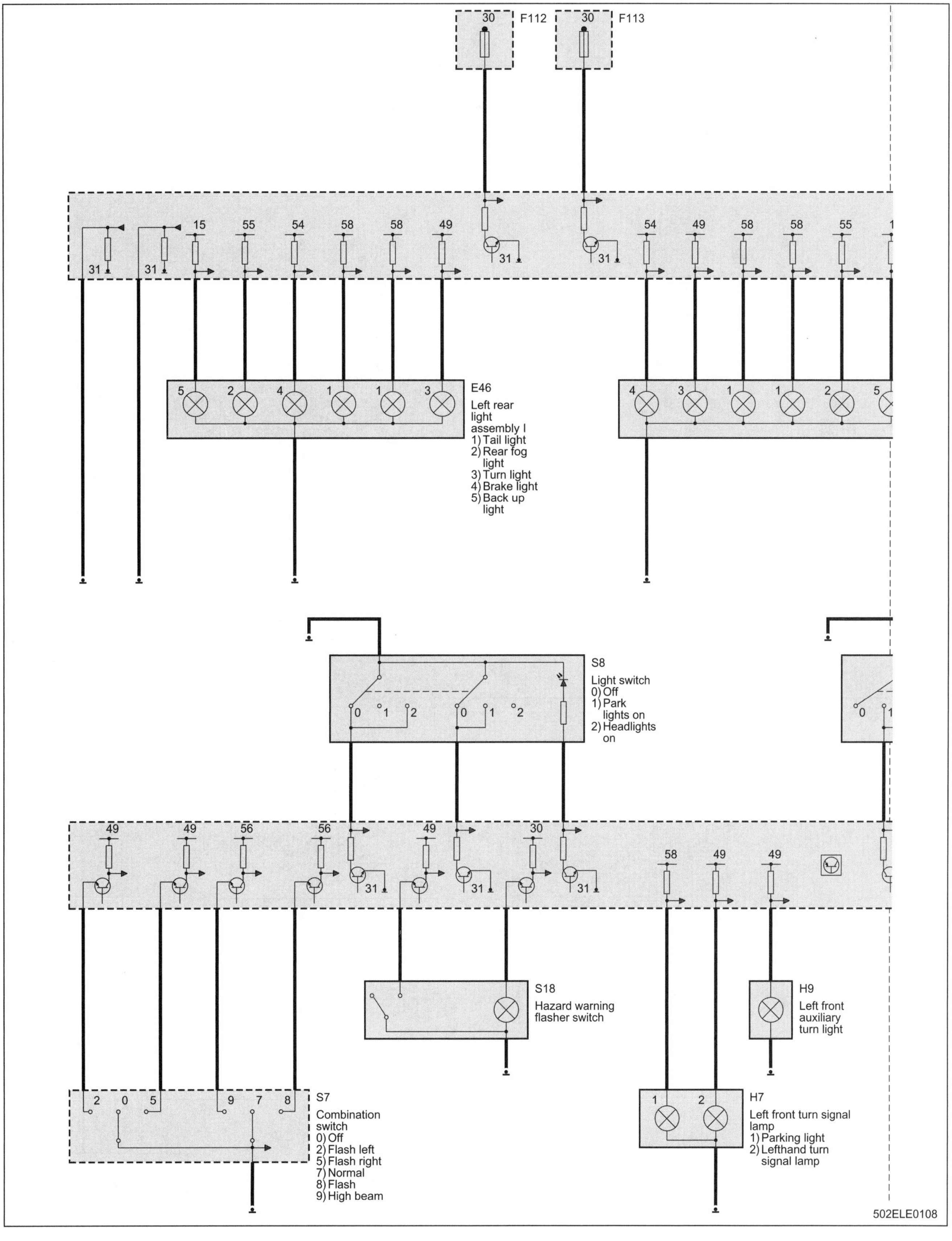
30
F112
30
F113
31
31
15
55
54
58
58
49
31
31
54
49
58
58
55
5
2
4
1
1
3
E46
Left rear light assembly I
1) Tail light
2) Rear fog light
3) Turn light
4) Brake light
5) Back up light
4
3
1
1
2
5
S8
Light switch
0) Off
1) Park lights on
2) Headlights on
0
1
2
0
1
2
49
49
56
56
49
30
31
31
31
58
49
49
S18
Hazard warning flasher switch
H9
Left front auxiliary turn light
2
0
5
9
7
8
S7
Combination switch
0) Off
2) Flash left
5) Flash right
7) Normal
8) Flash
9) High beam
1
2
H7
Left front turn signal lamp
1) Parking light
2) Lefthand turn signal lamp
502ELE0108

Exterior Lights
Lighting (overview)
(2 of 3)

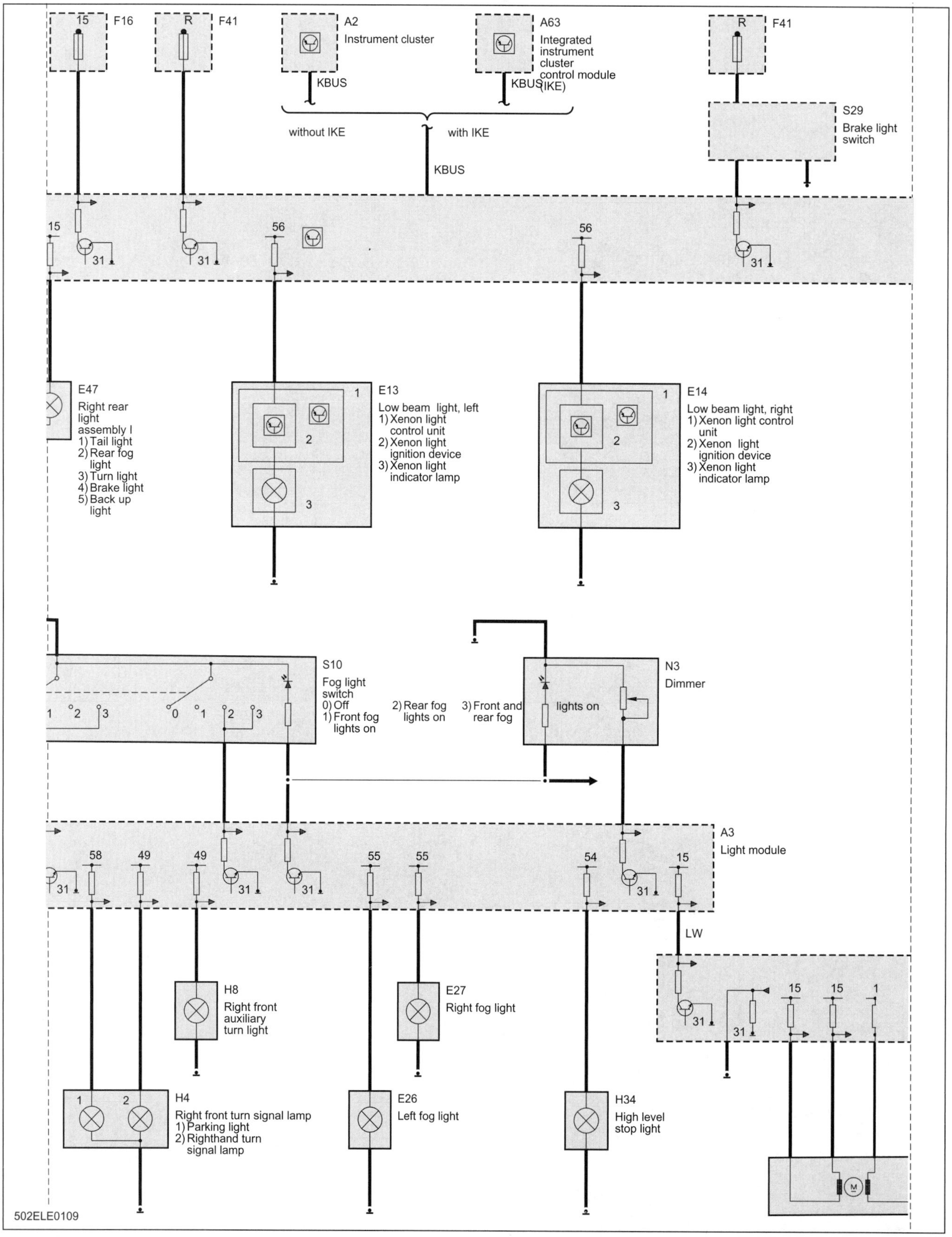
F16
F41
A2
Instrument cluster
KBUS
A63
Integrated instrument cluster control module (IKE)
KBUS
without IKE
with IKE
KBUS
S29
Brake light switch
E47
Right rear light assembly I
1) Tail light
2) Rear fog light
3) Turn light
4) Brake light
5) Back up light
E13
Low beam light, left
1) Xenon light control unit
2) Xenon light ignition device
3) Xenon light indicator lamp
E14
Low beam light, right
1) Xenon light control unit
2) Xenon light ignition device
3) Xenon light indicator lamp
S10
Fog light switch
0) Off
1) Front fog lights on
2) Rear fog lights on
3) Front and rear fog
lights on
N3
Dimmer
A3
Light module
LW
H8
Right front auxiliary turn light
E27
Right fog light
H4
Right front turn signal lamp
1) Parking light
2) Righthand turn signal lamp
E26
Left fog light
H34
High level stop light
502ELE0109

Exterior Lights
Lighting (overview)
(3 of 3)

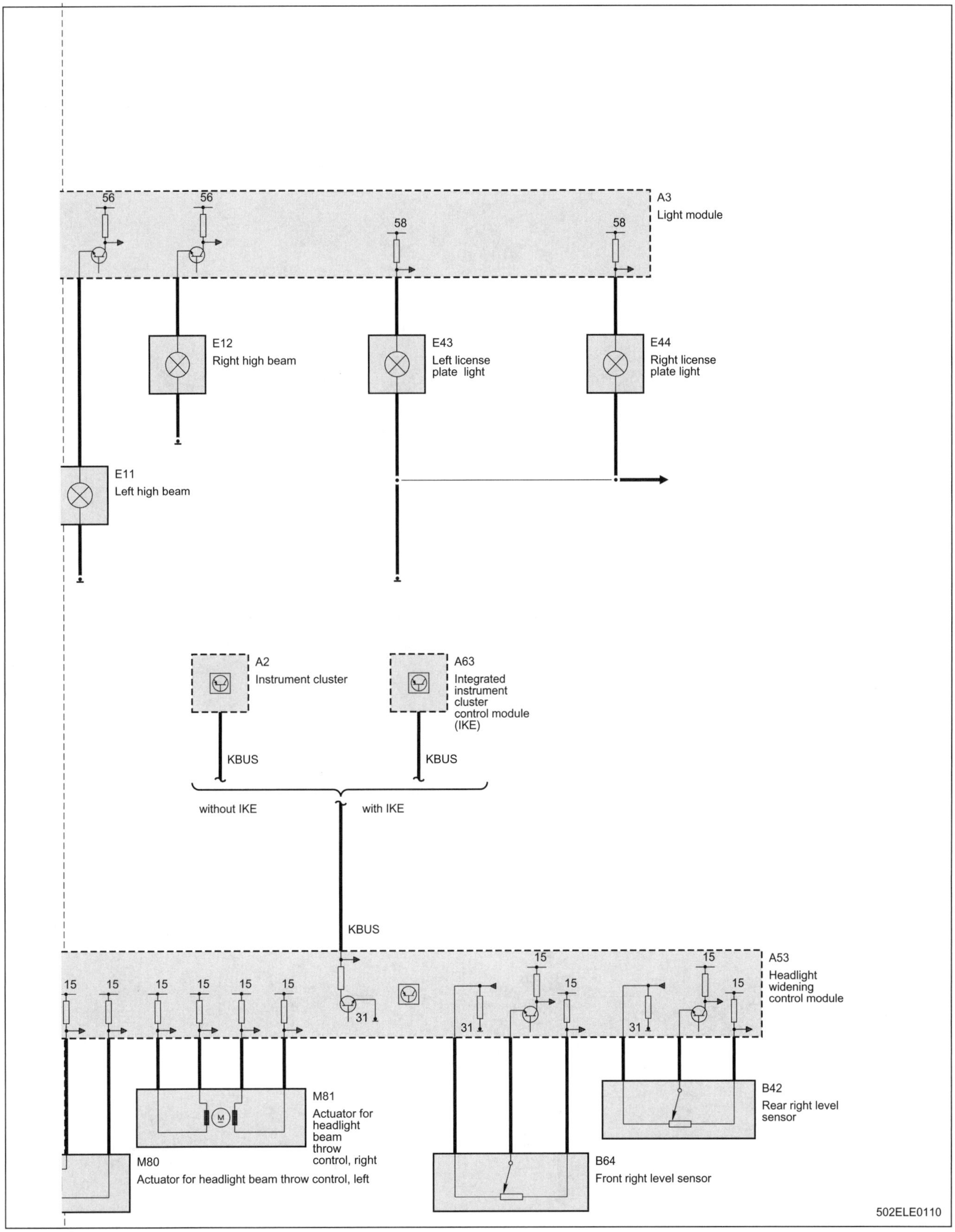
56
56
58
58
A3
Light module
E12
Right high beam
E43
Left license plate light
E44
Right license plate light
E11
Left high beam
A2
Instrument cluster
A63
Integrated instrument cluster control module (IKE)
KBUS
KBUS
without IKE
with IKE
KBUS
15
15
15
15
15
15
31
15
15
31
15
15
31
A53
Headlight widening control module
M81
Actuator for headlight beam throw control, right
M80
Actuator for headlight beam throw control, left
B42
Rear right level sensor
B64
Front right level sensor
502ELE0110

Exterior Lights
Back up light

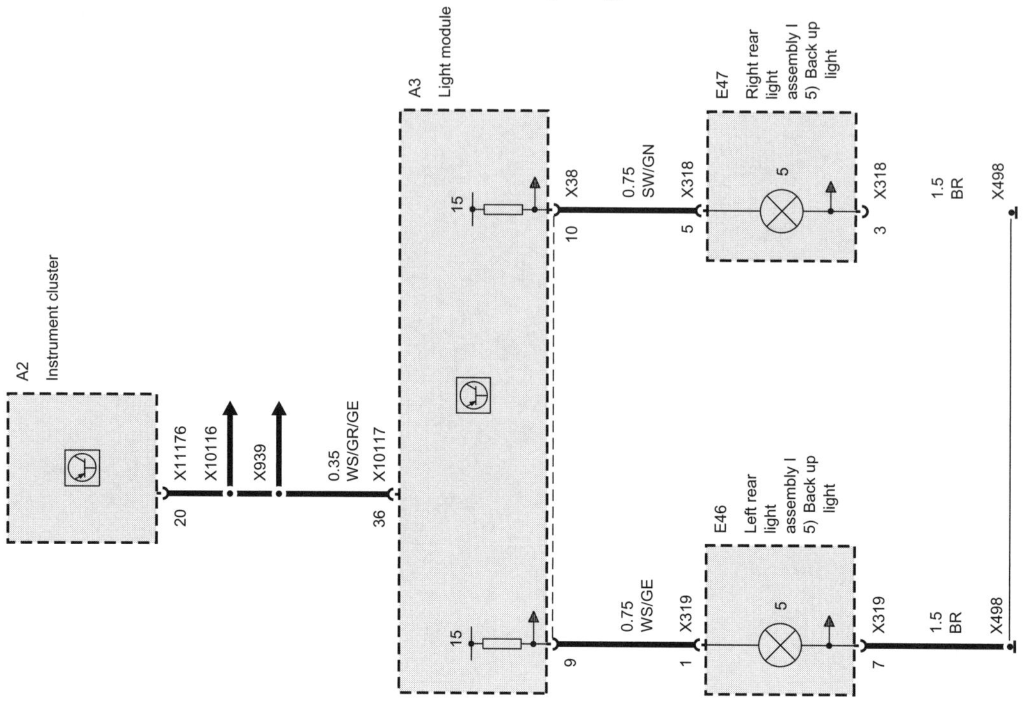

502ELE0013a

Exterior Lights
Back up light switch (manual transmission)

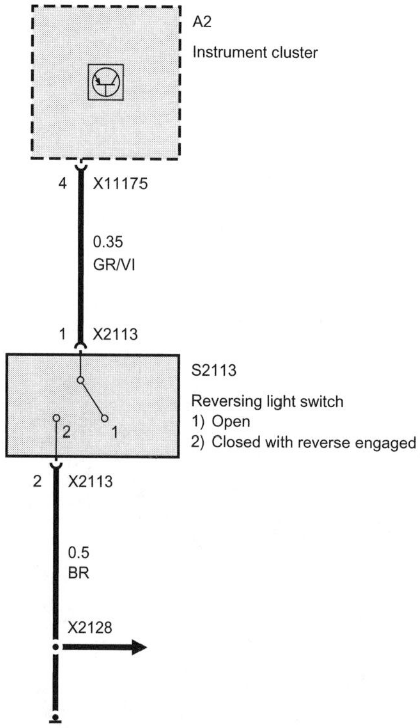

502ELE0013b

Exterior Lights
Brake light switch
(1 of 1)

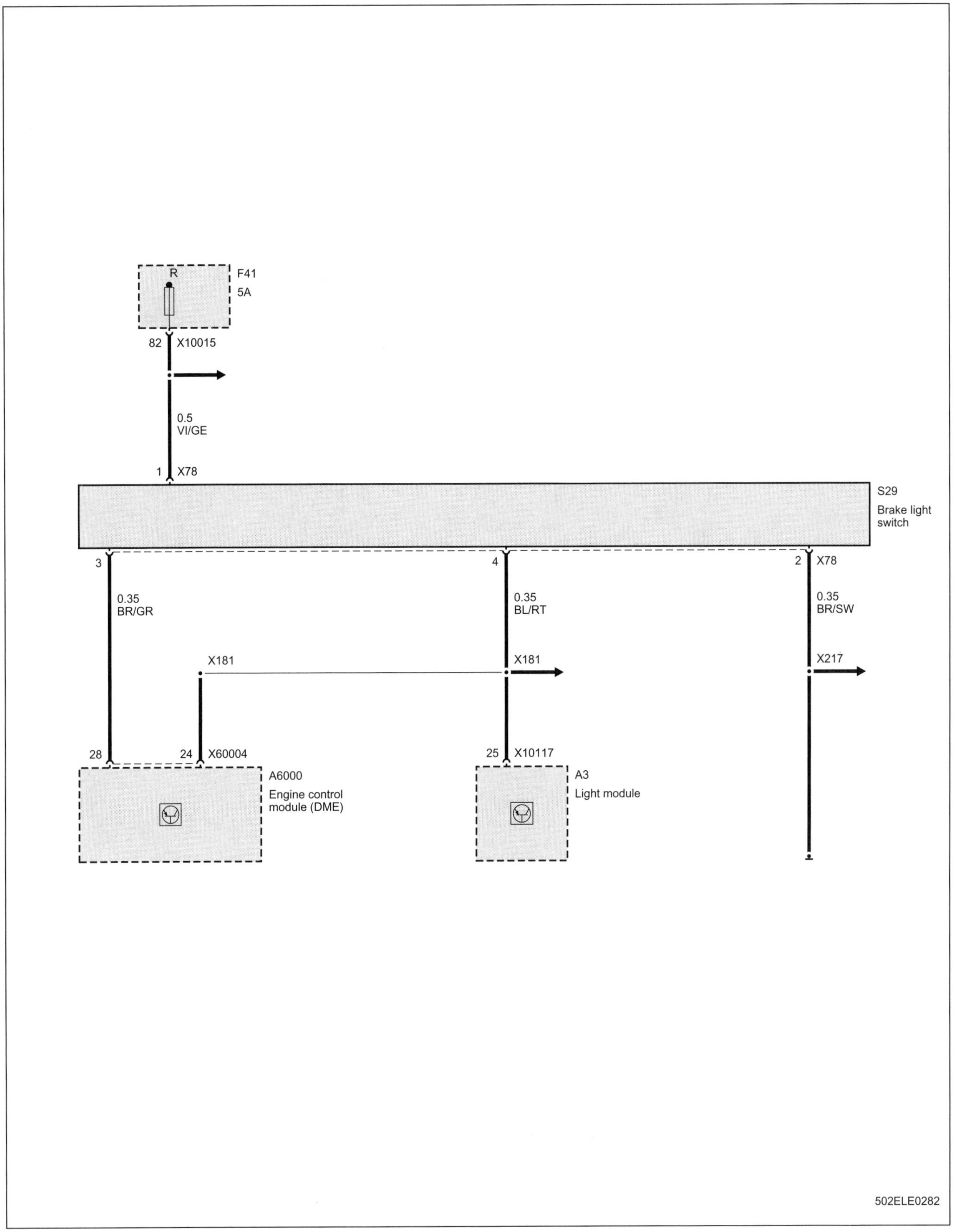
R
F41
5A
82
X10015
0.5
VI/GE
1
X78
S29
Brake light
switch
3
0.35
BR/GR
4
0.35
BL/RT
2
X78
0.35
BR/SW
X181
X181
X217
28
24
X60004
A6000
Engine control
module (DME)
25
X10117
A3
Light module
502ELE0282

Exterior Lights
Brake lights
(1 of 1)

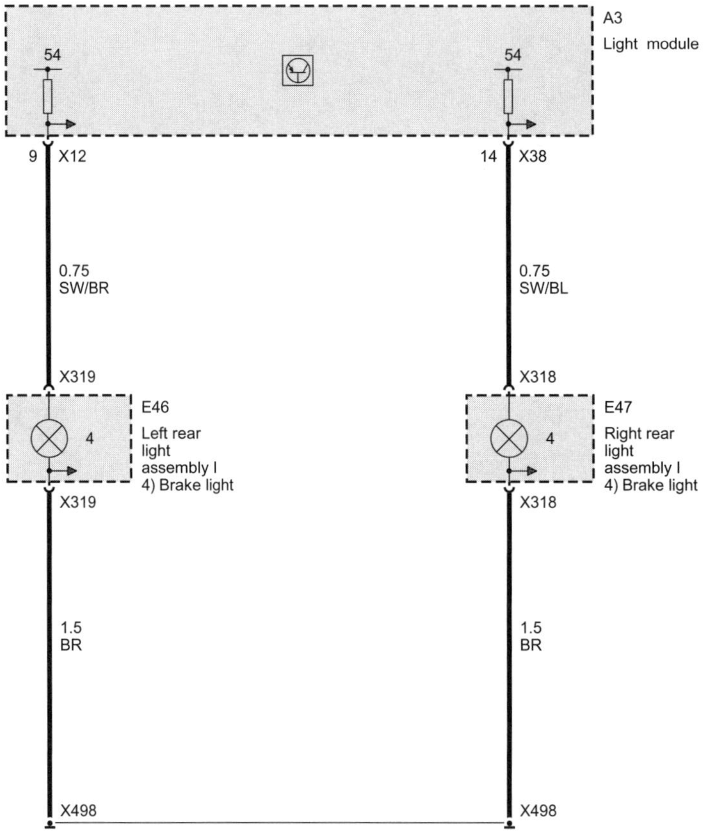
A3
Light module
54
54
9
X12
14
X38
0.75
SW/BR
0.75
SW/BL
X319
X318
E46
Left rear
light
assembly I
4) Brake light
4
E47
Right rear
light
assembly I
4) Brake light
4
X319
X318
1.5
BR
1.5
BR
X498
X498
502ELE0018

Exterior Lights
Emergency flasher (hazard) switch
(1 of 1)

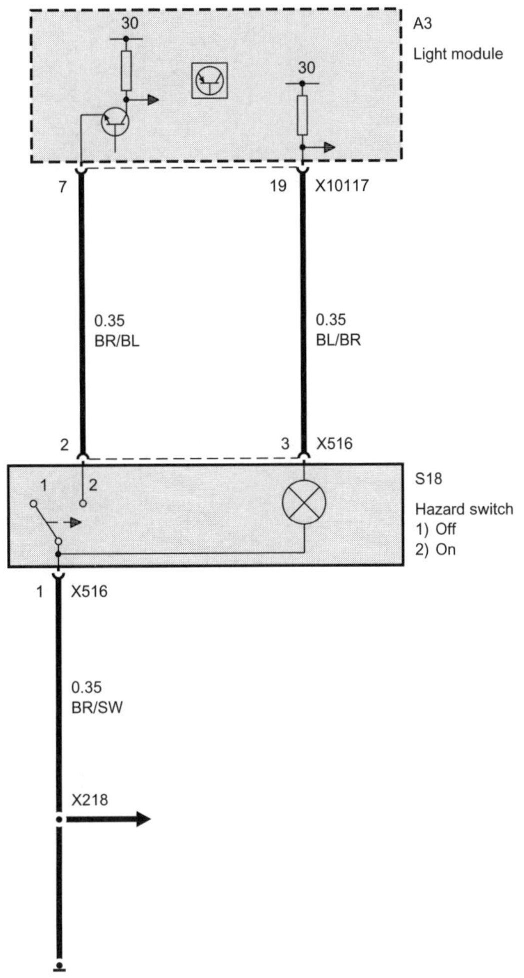

Exterior Lights
Engine compartment light
(1 of 1)

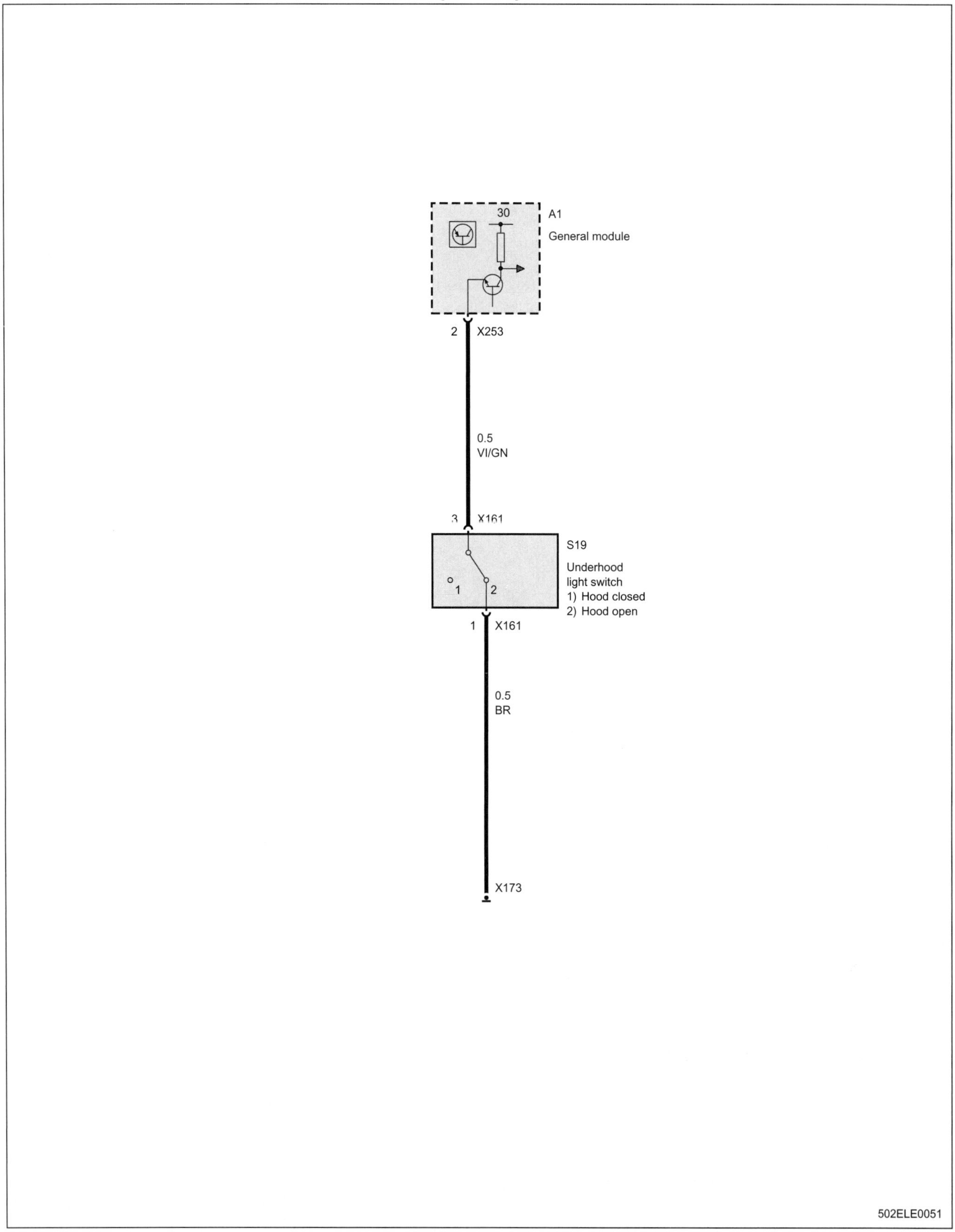
30
A1
General module
2
X253
0.5
VI/GN
3
X161
S19
Underhood
light switch
1) Hood closed
2) Hood open
1
2
1
X161
0.5
BR
X173
502ELE0051

Exterior Lights
High level brake light (H34)
(1 of 1)

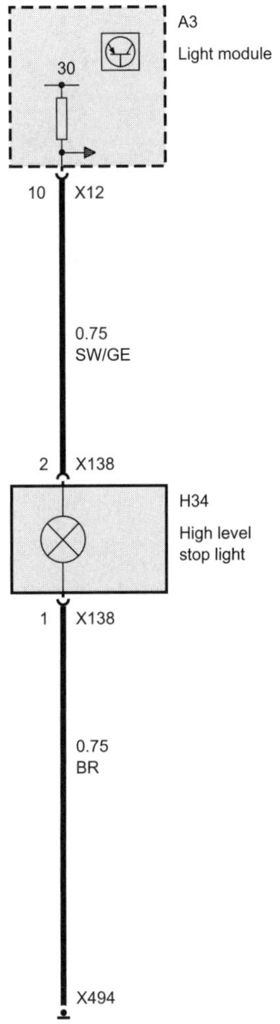

Exterior Lights
License plate lights
(1 of 1)

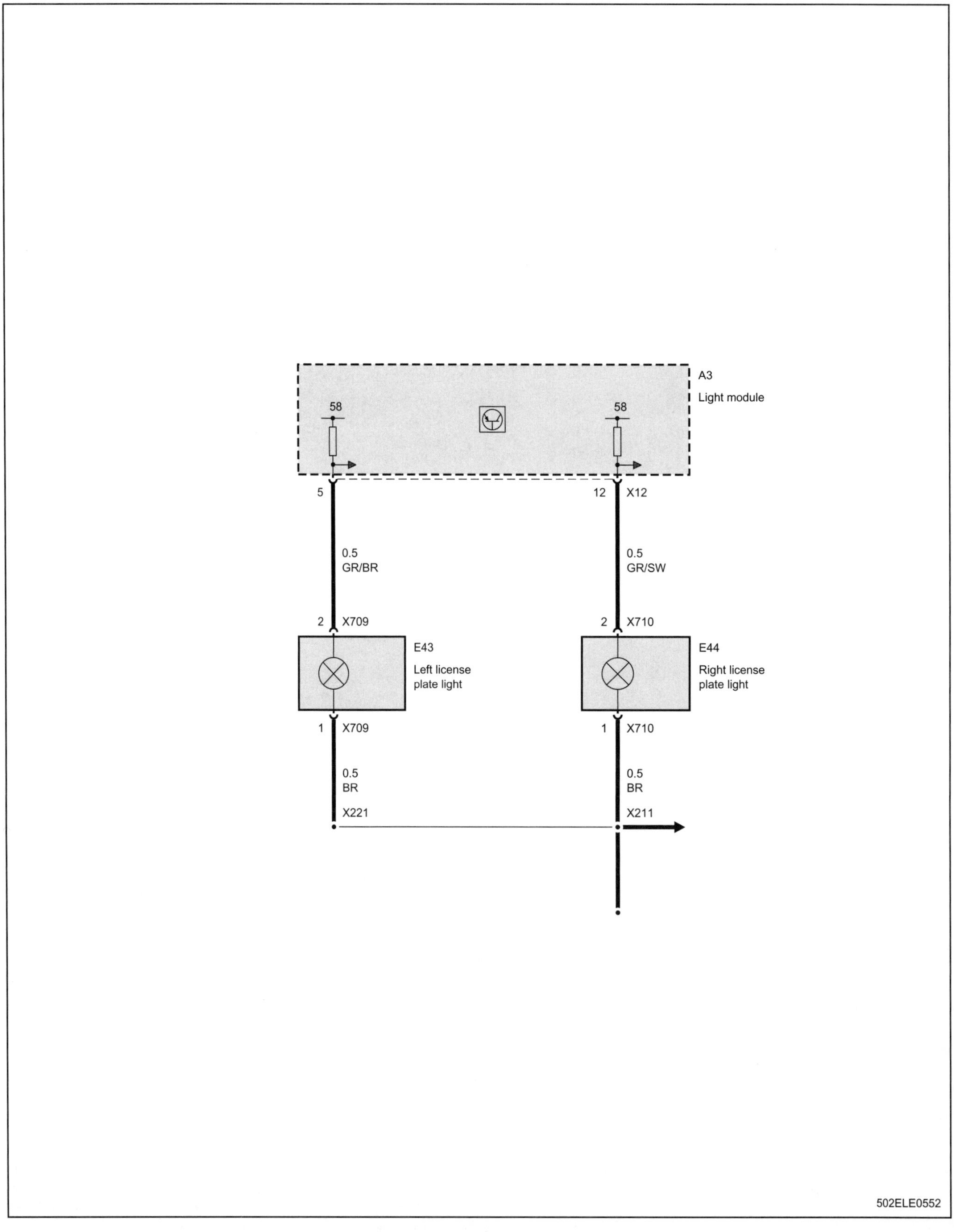
A3
Light module
58
58
5
12
X12
0.5
GR/BR
0.5
GR/SW
2
X709
2
X710
E43
Left license
plate light
E44
Right license
plate light
1
X709
1
X710
0.5
BR
0.5
BR
X221
X211
502ELE0552

Exterior Lights
Light switch
(1 of 1)

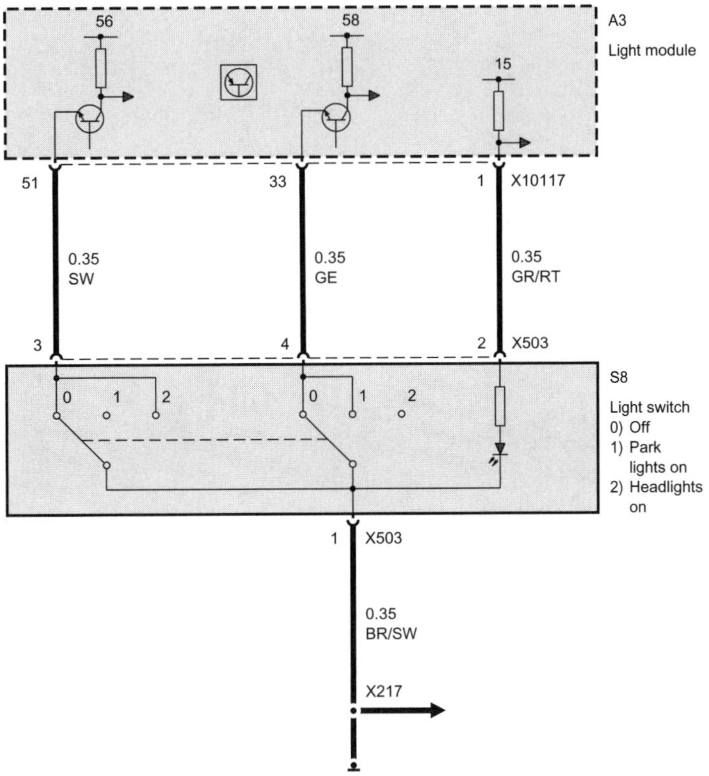
56
58
15
A3
Light module
51
33
1
X10117
0.35
SW
0.35
GE
0.35
GR/RT
3
4
2
X503
S8
Light switch
0) Off
1) Park lights on
2) Headlights on
0
1
2
0
1
2
1
X503
0.35
BR/SW
X217
502ELE107

Exterior Lights
Right tail light

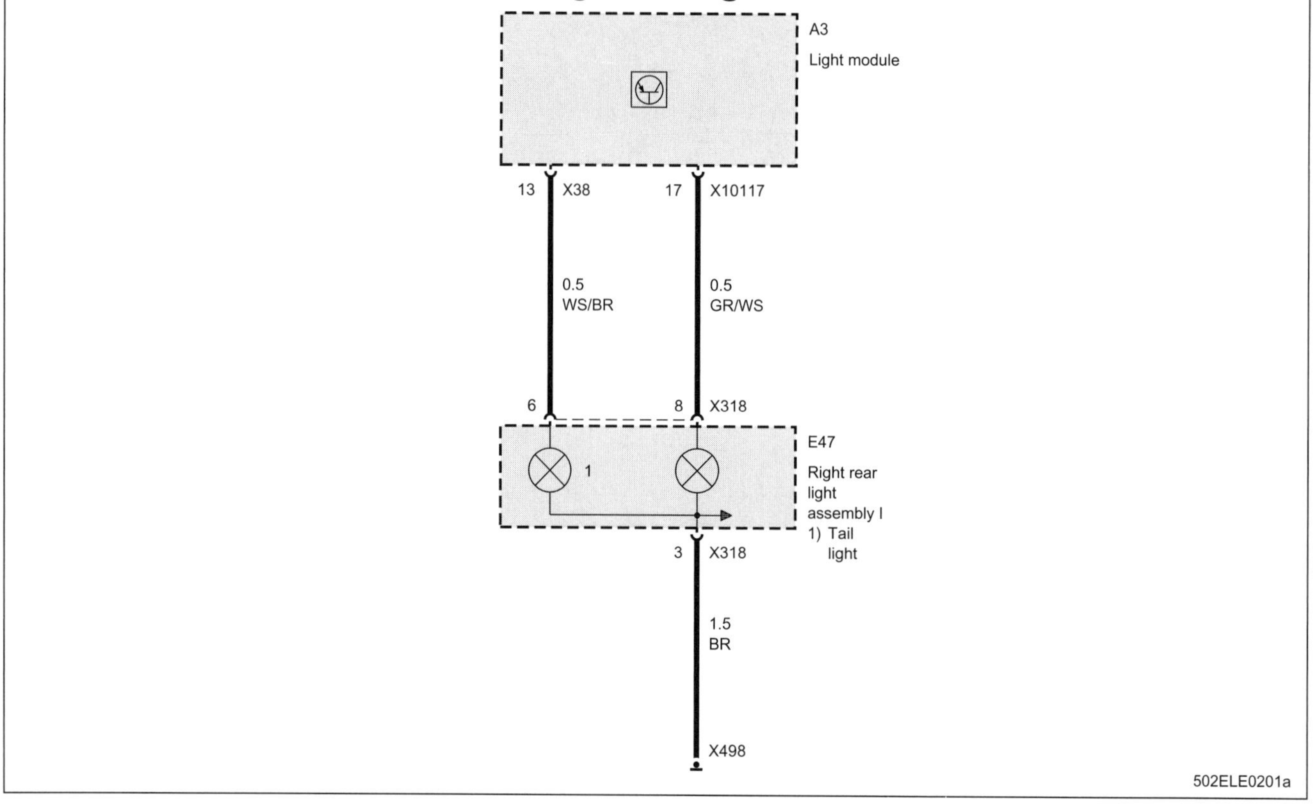

Exterior Lights
Right turn light

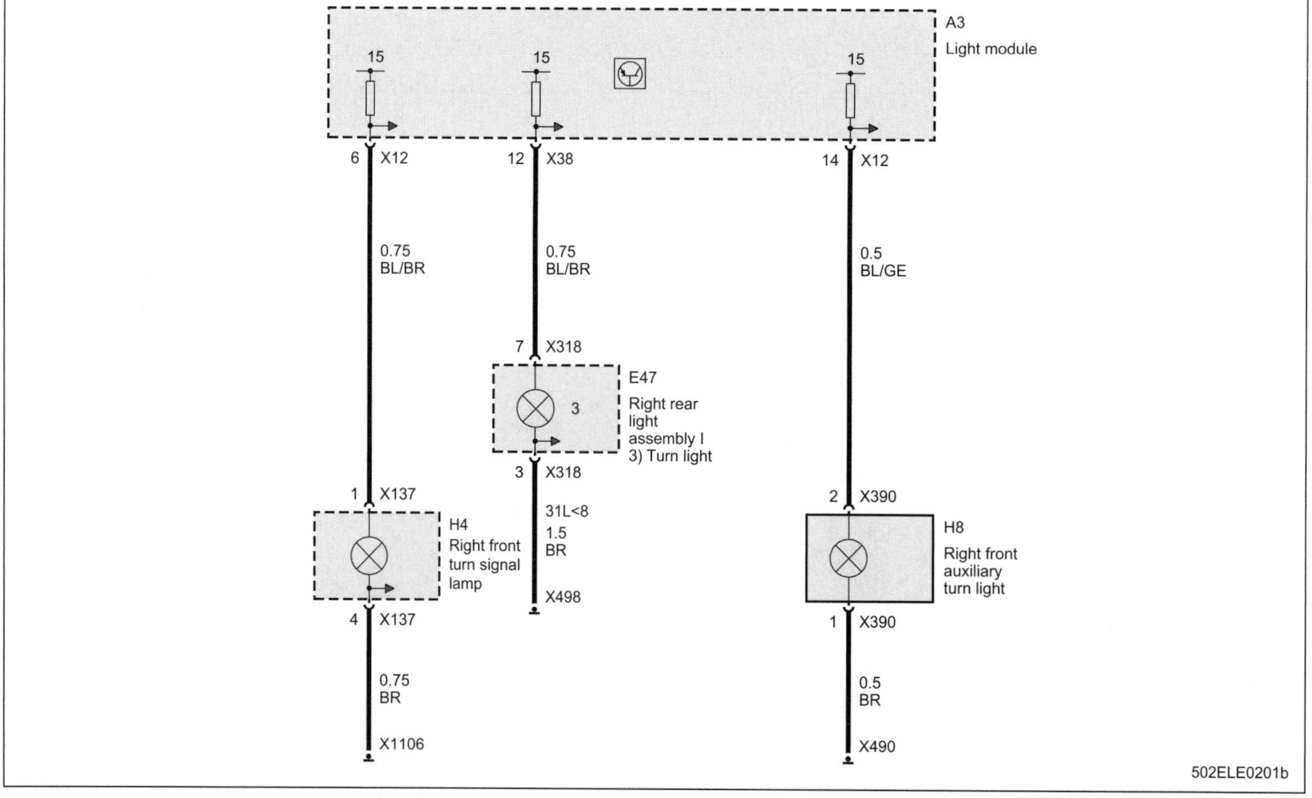

Exterior Lights
Tail light, left
(1 of 1)

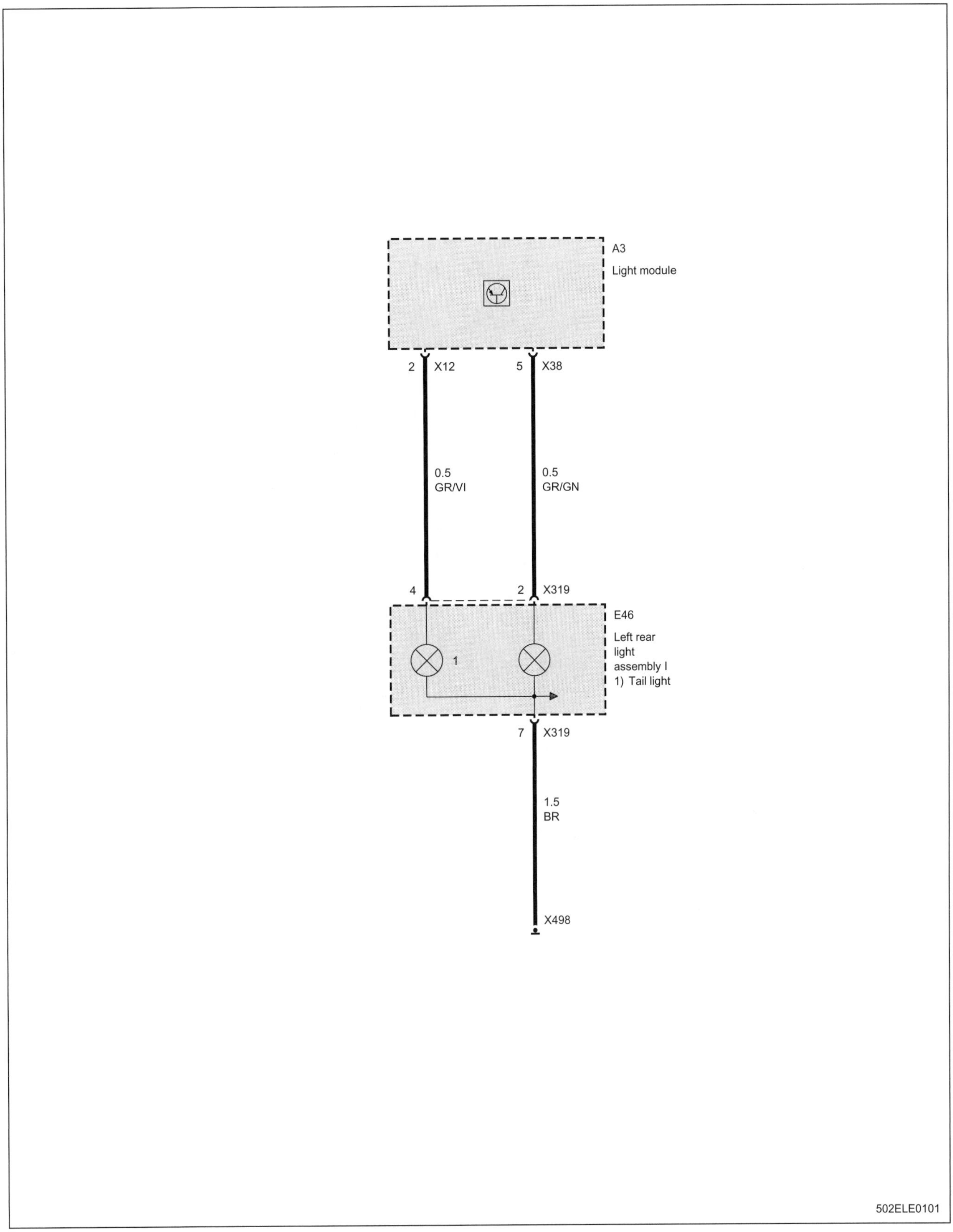

Exterior Lights
Tail lights
(1 of 1)

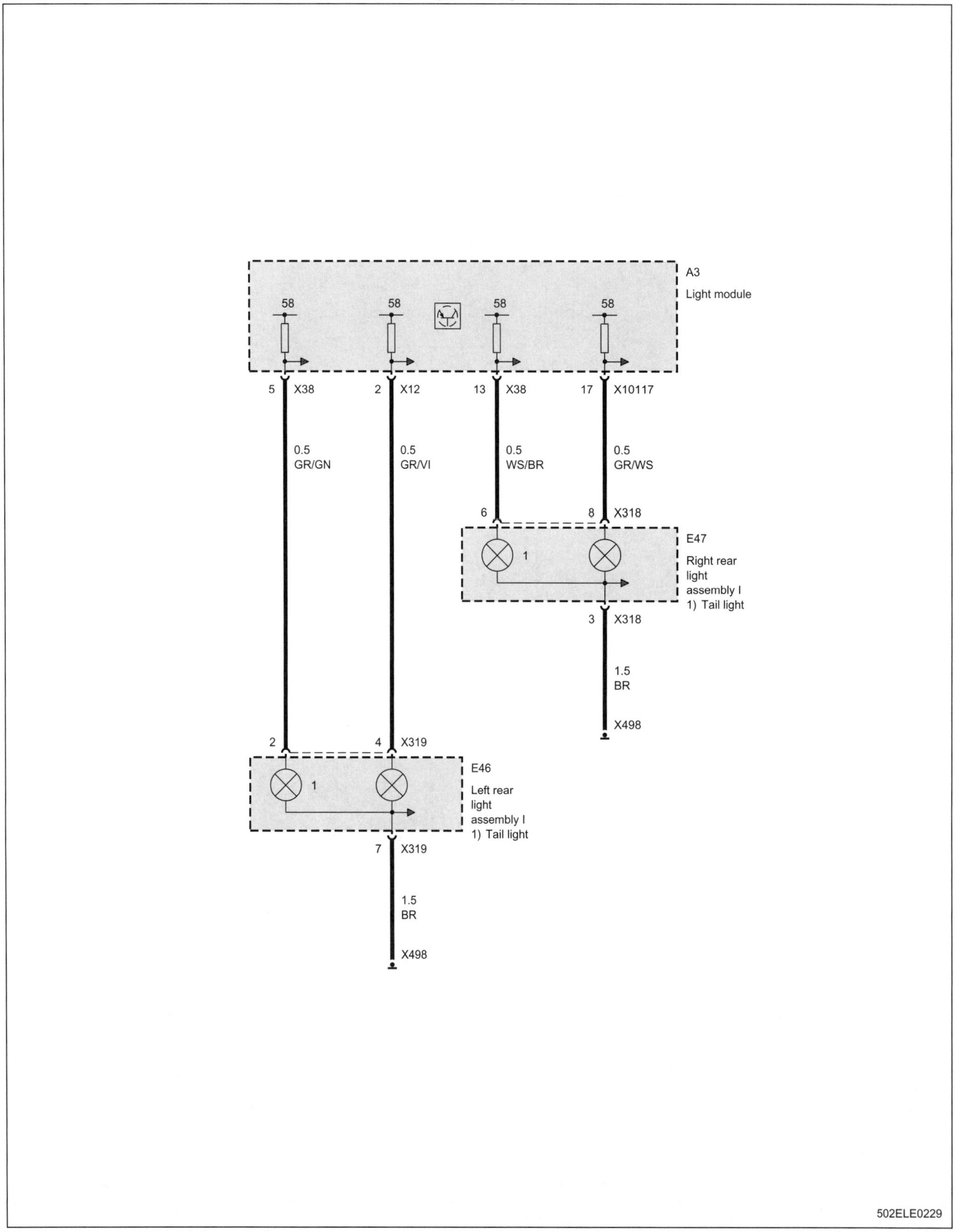
A3
Light module
58
58
58
58
5 X38
2 X12
13 X38
17 X10117
0.5
GR/GN
0.5
GR/VI
0.5
WS/BR
0.5
GR/WS
6
8 X318
E47
Right rear
light
assembly I
1) Tail light
1
3 X318
1.5
BR
X498
2
4 X319
E46
Left rear
light
assembly I
1) Tail light
1
7 X319
1.5
BR
X498
502ELE0229

Exterior Lights
Turn signal switch
(1 of 1)

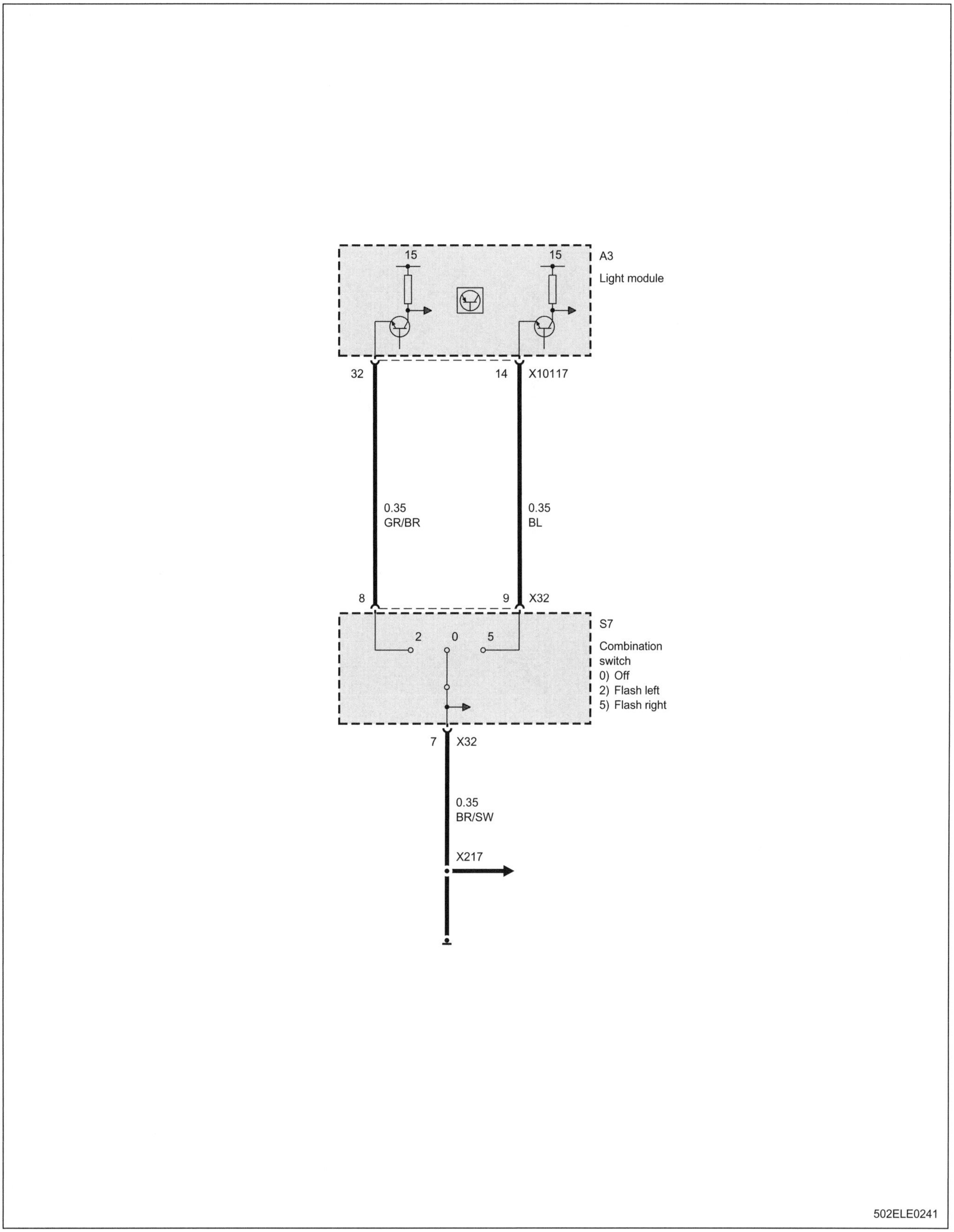

Exterior Lights
Turn signal light, left
(1 of 1)

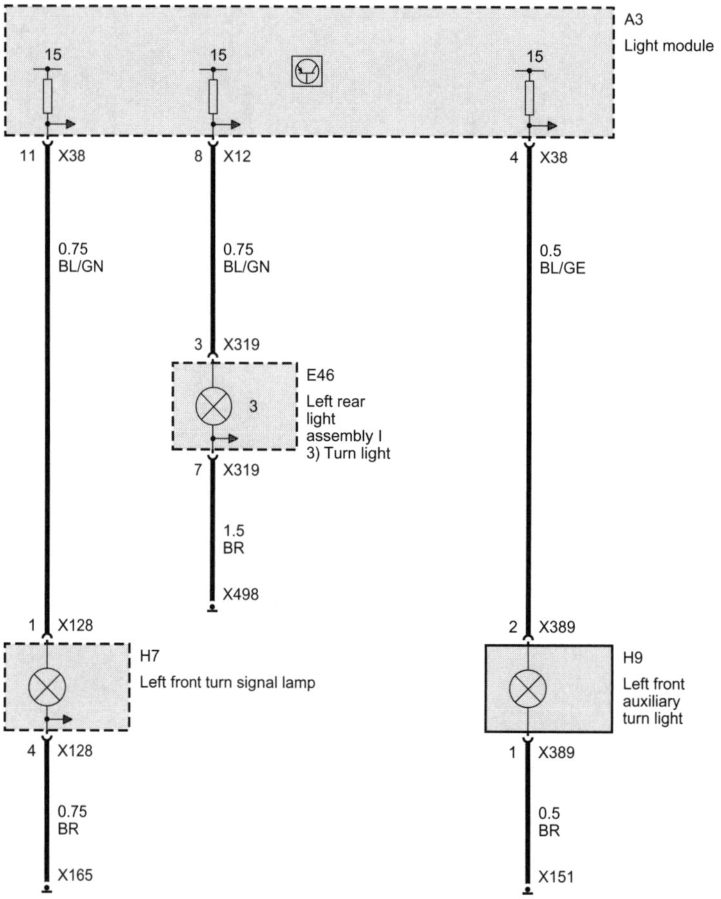
A3
Light module
15
15
15
11 X38
8 X12
4 X38
0.75
BL/GN
0.75
BL/GN
0.5
BL/GE
3 X319
E46
Left rear
light
assembly I
3) Turn light
3
7 X319
1.5
BR
X498
1 X128
H7
Left front turn signal lamp
4 X128
0.75
BR
X165
2 X389
H9
Left front
auxiliary
turn light
1 X389
0.5
BR
X151
502ELE0102

Headlights/Foglights
Headlight widening control module (A53)
(1 of 2)

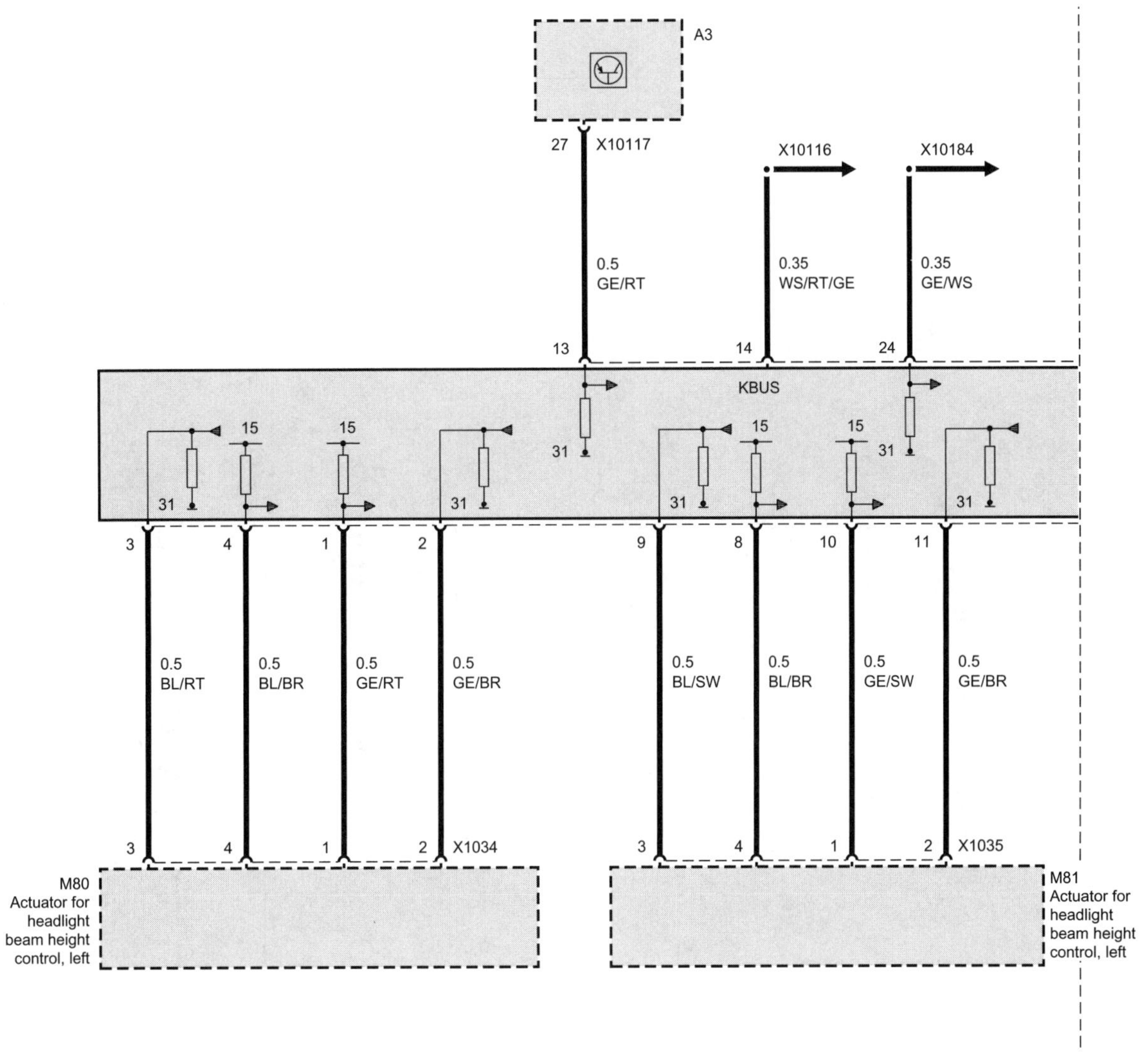

502ELE0413

Headlights/Foglights
Headlight widening control module (A53)
(2 of 2)

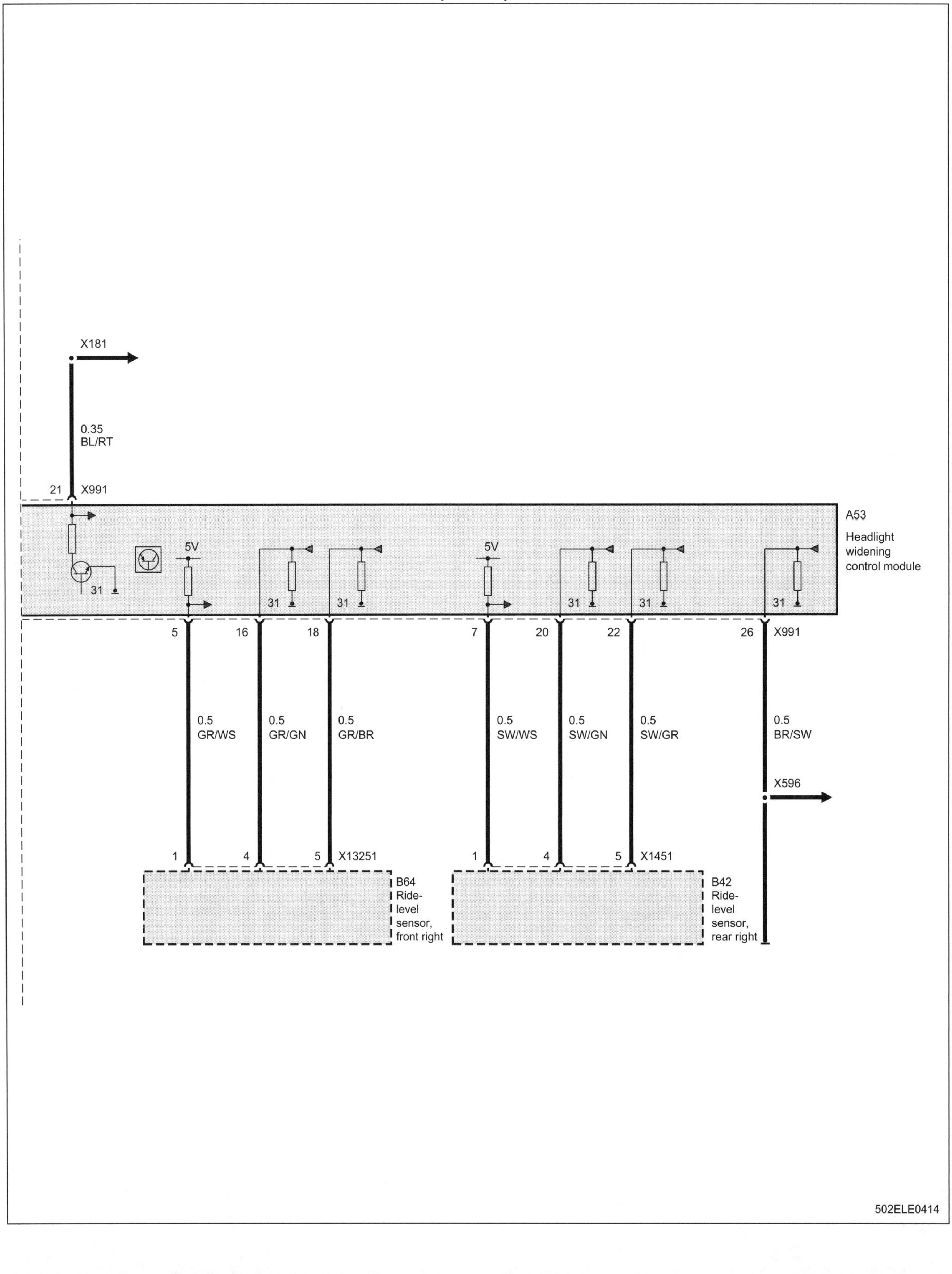

Headlights/Foglights
Auto. headlight widening (LWR) (actuator motors)
(1 of 1)

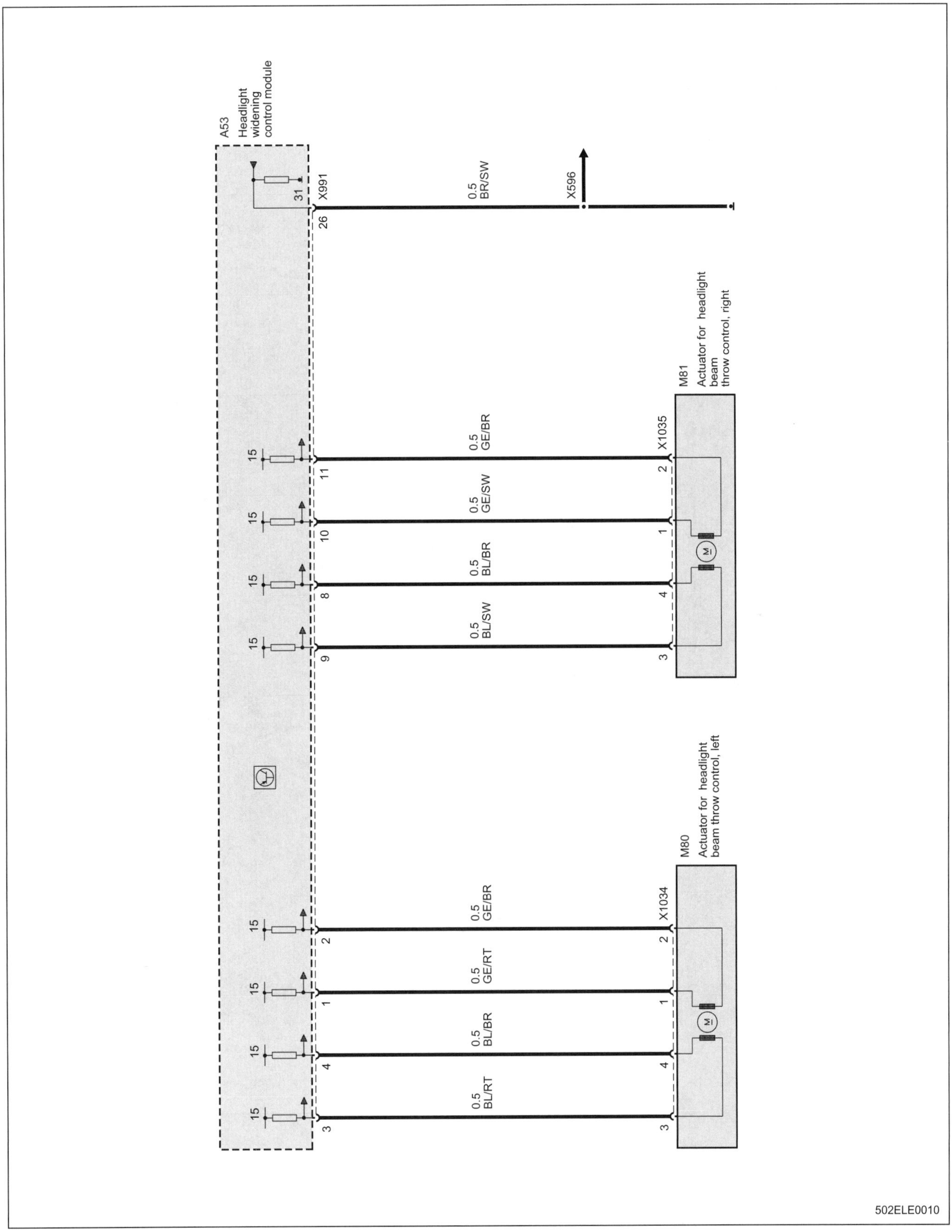

Headlights/Foglights
Auto. headlight widening (LWR) (load sensors)
(1 of 1)

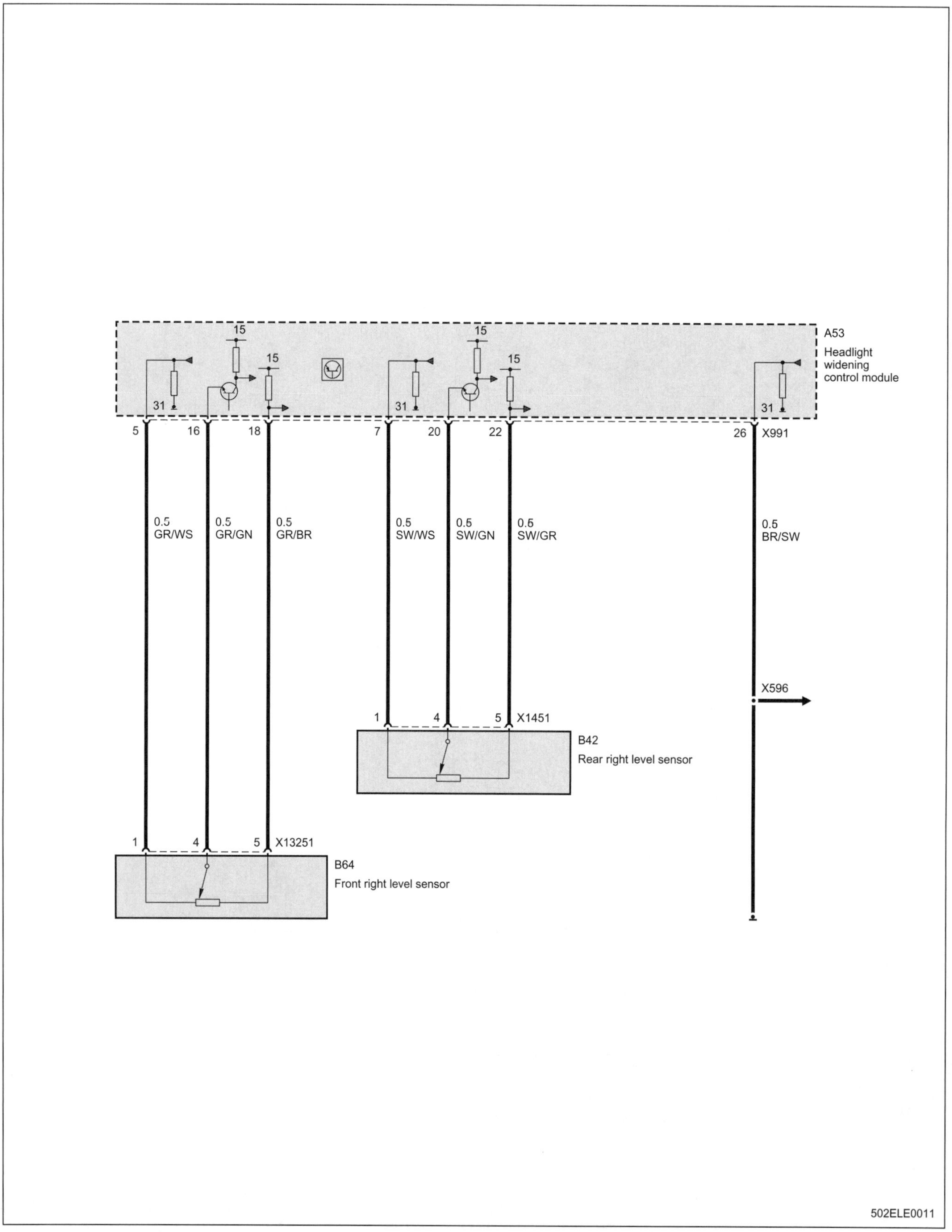

Headlights/Foglights
Fog light switch
(1 of 1)

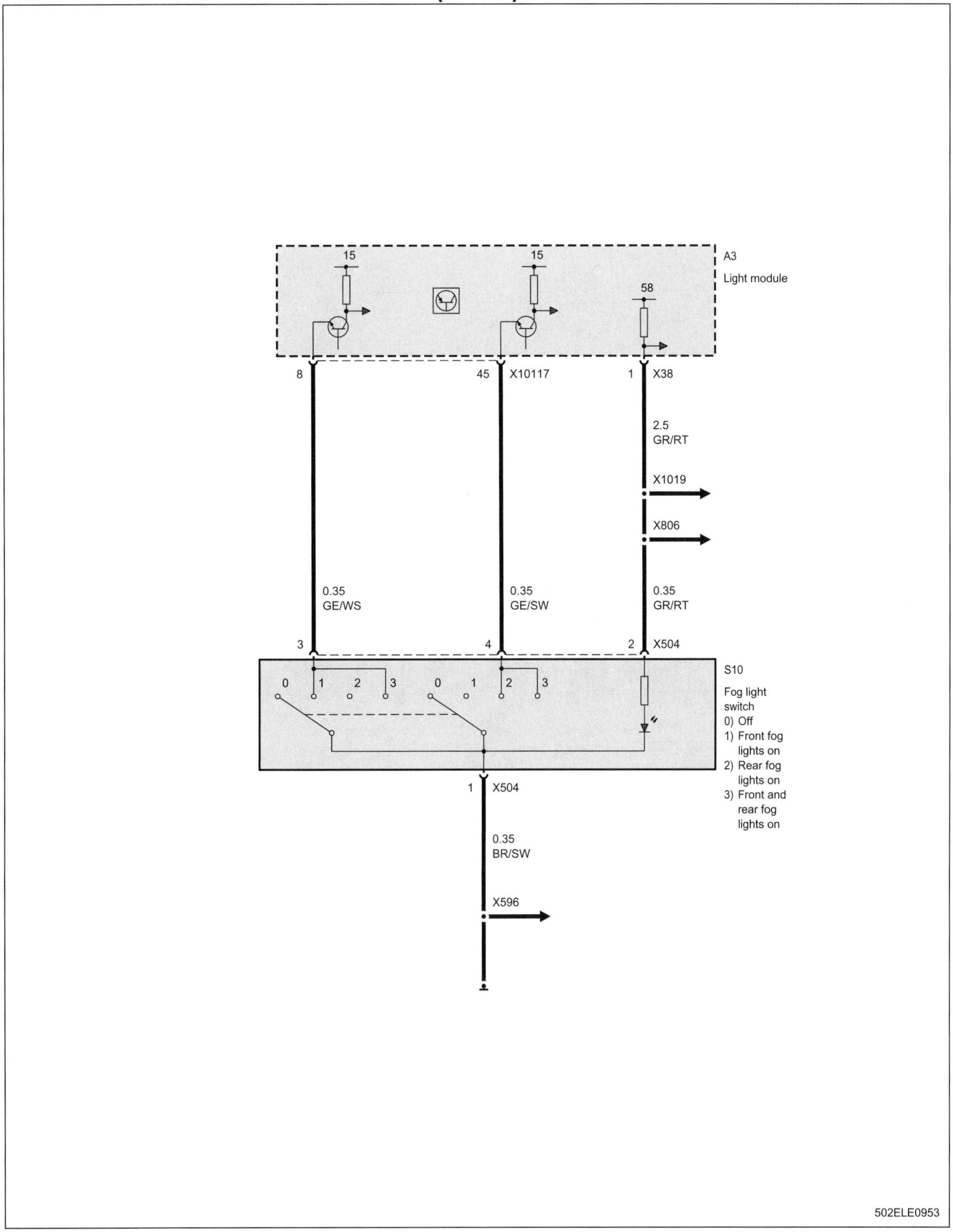
15
15
58
A3
Light module
8
45
X10117
1
X38
2.5
GR/RT
X1019
X806
0.35
GE/WS
0.35
GE/SW
0.35
GR/RT
3
4
2
X504
0
1
2
3
0
1
2
3
S10
Fog light switch
0) Off
1) Front fog lights on
2) Rear fog lights on
3) Front and rear fog lights on
1
X504
0.35
BR/SW
X596
502ELE0953

Headlights/Foglights
Fog lights
(1 of 1)

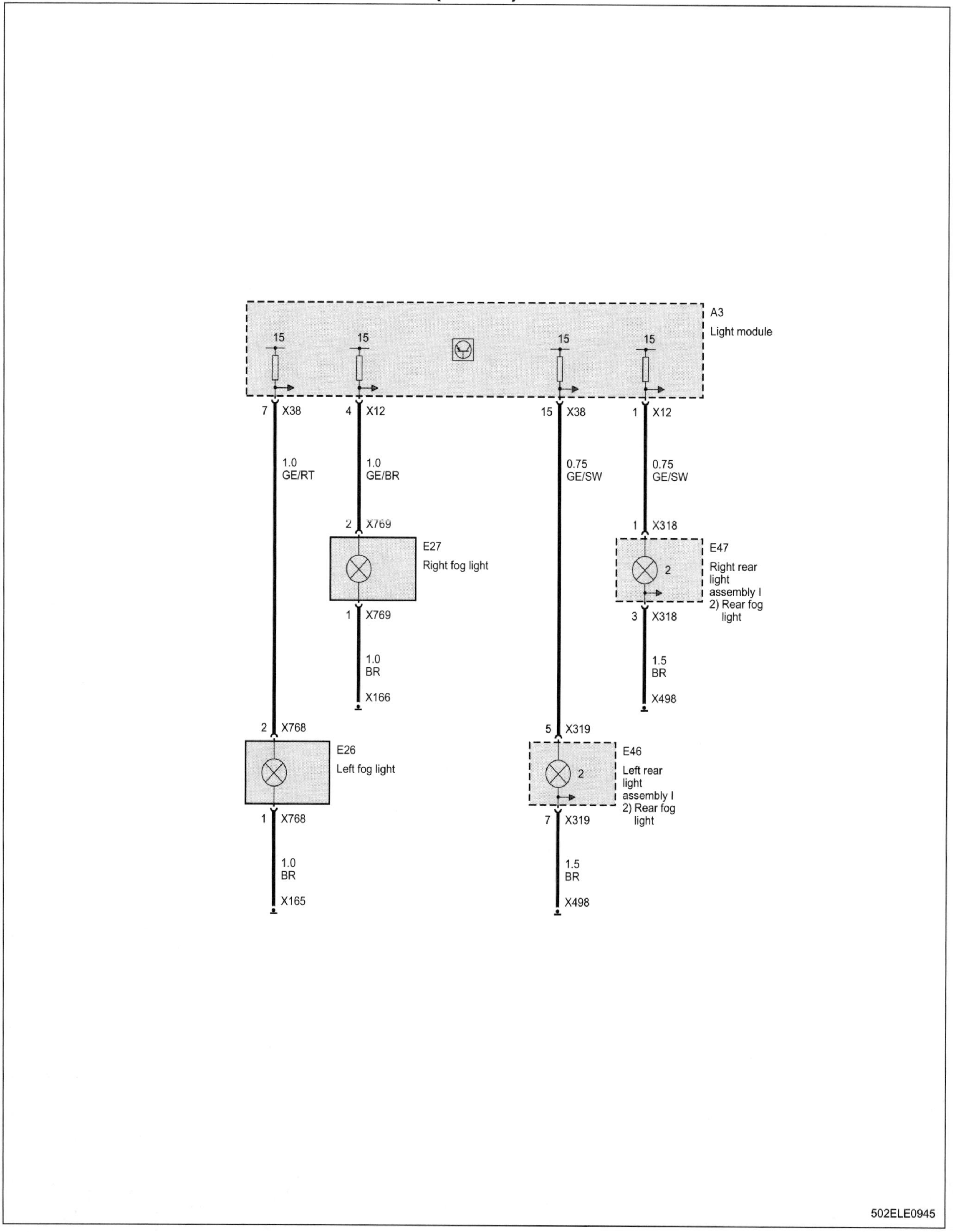
A3
Light module
15
15
15
15
7 X38
4 X12
15 X38
1 X12
1.0
GE/RT
1.0
GE/BR
0.75
GE/SW
0.75
GE/SW
2 X769
E27
Right fog light
1 X769
1.0
BR
X166
1 X318
E47
Right rear light assembly I
2) Rear fog light
3 X318
1.5
BR
X498
2 X768
E26
Left fog light
1 X768
1.0
BR
X165
5 X319
E46
Left rear light assembly I
2) Rear fog light
7 X319
1.5
BR
X498
502ELE0945

Headlights/Foglights
Headlights (xenon)
(1 of 2)

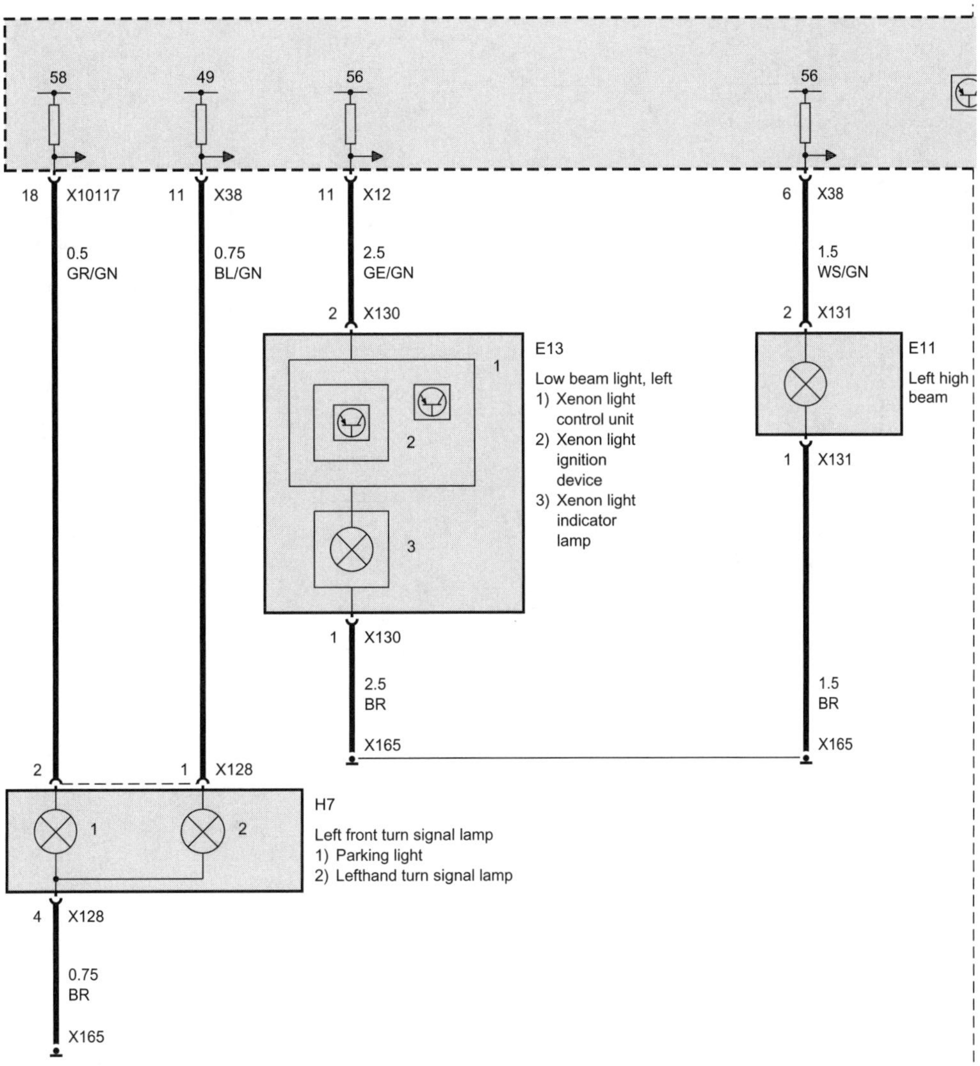

502ELE0055

Headlights/Foglights
Headlights (xenon)
(2 of 2)

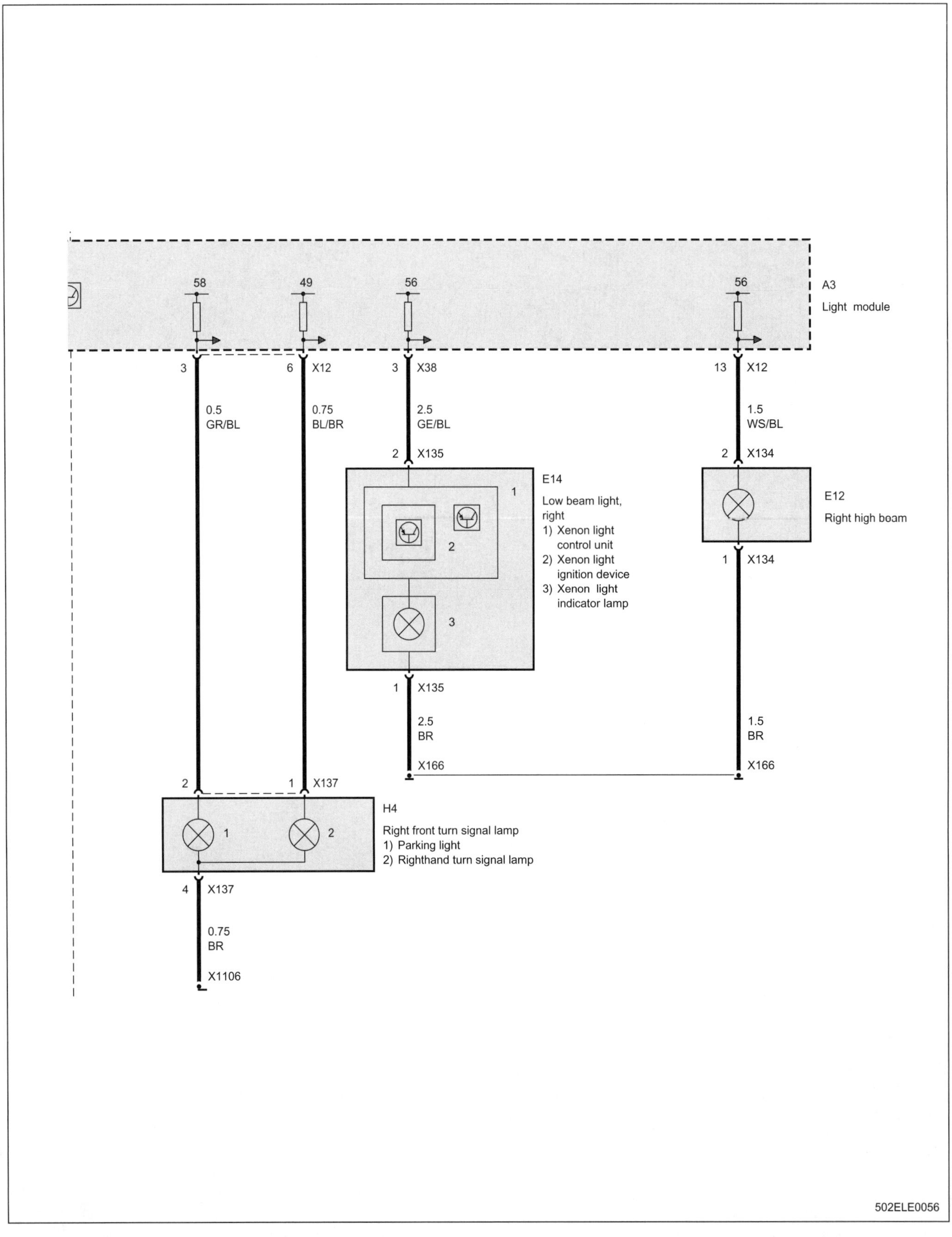
58
49
56
56
A3
Light module
3
6
X12
3
X38
13
X12
0.5
GR/BL
0.75
BL/BR
2.5
GE/BL
1.5
WS/BL
2
X135
2
X134
E14
Low beam light, right
1) Xenon light control unit
2) Xenon light ignition device
3) Xenon light indicator lamp
1
2
3
E12
Right high beam
1
X134
1
X135
2.5
BR
1.5
BR
X166
X166
2
1
X137
H4
Right front turn signal lamp
1) Parking light
2) Righthand turn signal lamp
4
X137
0.75
BR
X1106
502ELE0056

Headlights/Foglights
High beam, headlight flash switch
(1 of 1)

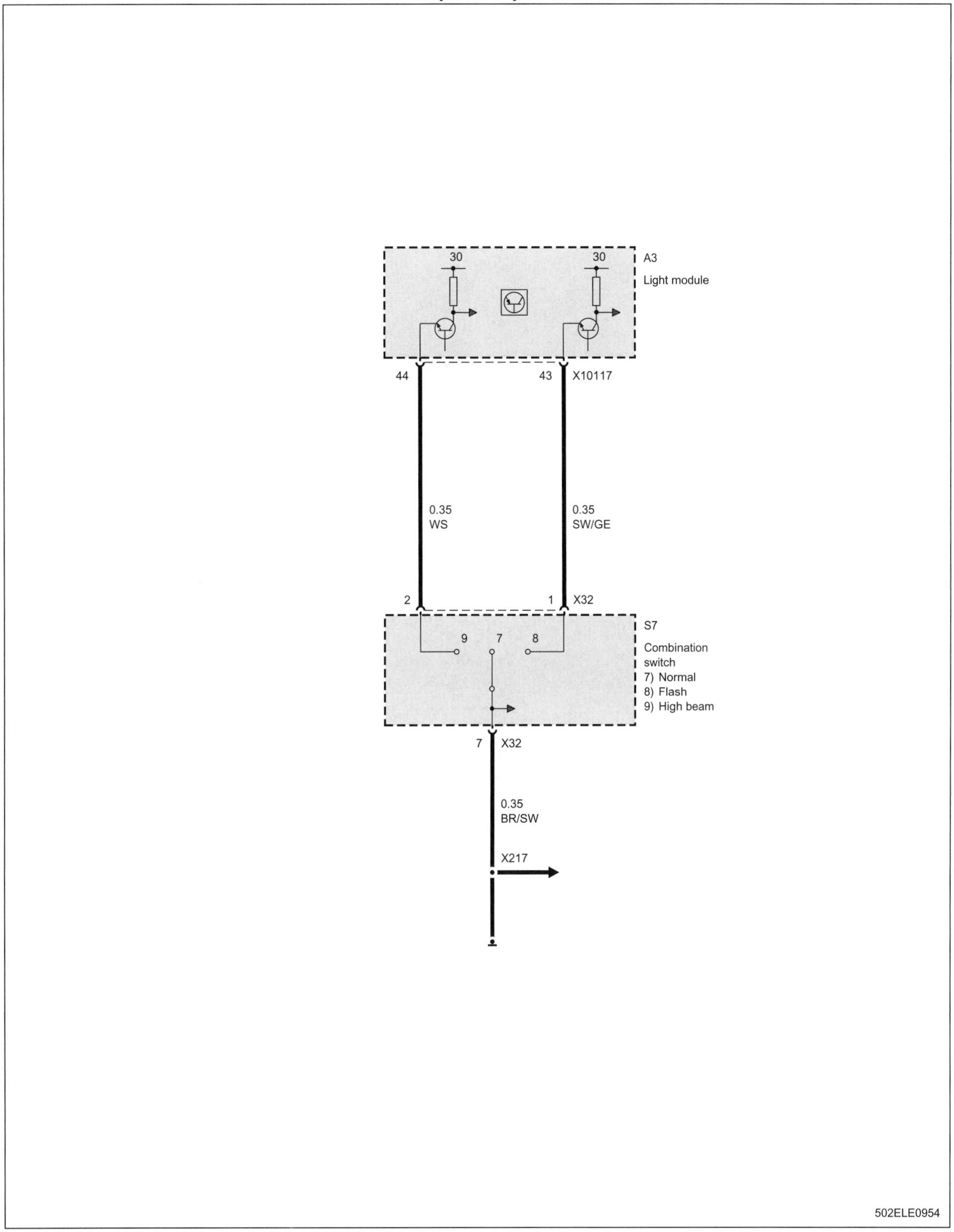

Horns

(1 of 1)

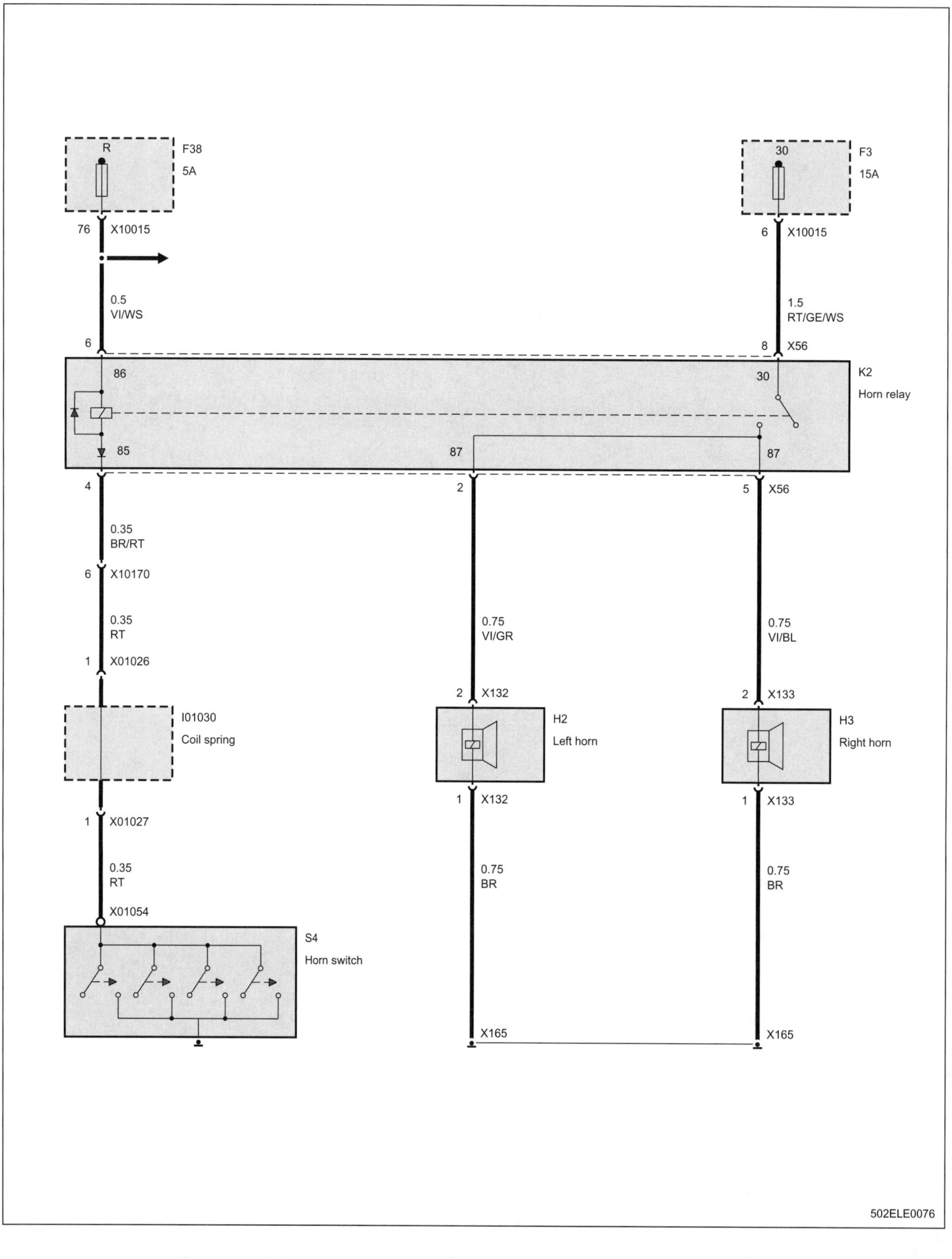
R
F38
5A
76
X10015
0.5
VI/WS
6
86
85
4
0.35
BR/RT
6
X10170
0.35
RT
1
X01026
I01030
Coil spring
1
X01027
0.35
RT
X01054
S4
Horn switch
30
F3
15A
6
X10015
1.5
RT/GE/WS
8
X56
30
K2
Horn relay
87
87
2
5
X56
0.75
VI/GR
2
X132
H2
Left horn
1
X132
0.75
BR
X165
0.75
VI/BL
2
X133
H3
Right horn
1
X133
0.75
BR
X165
502ELE0076

Instrument Panel
Display and information (overview)
(1 of 3)

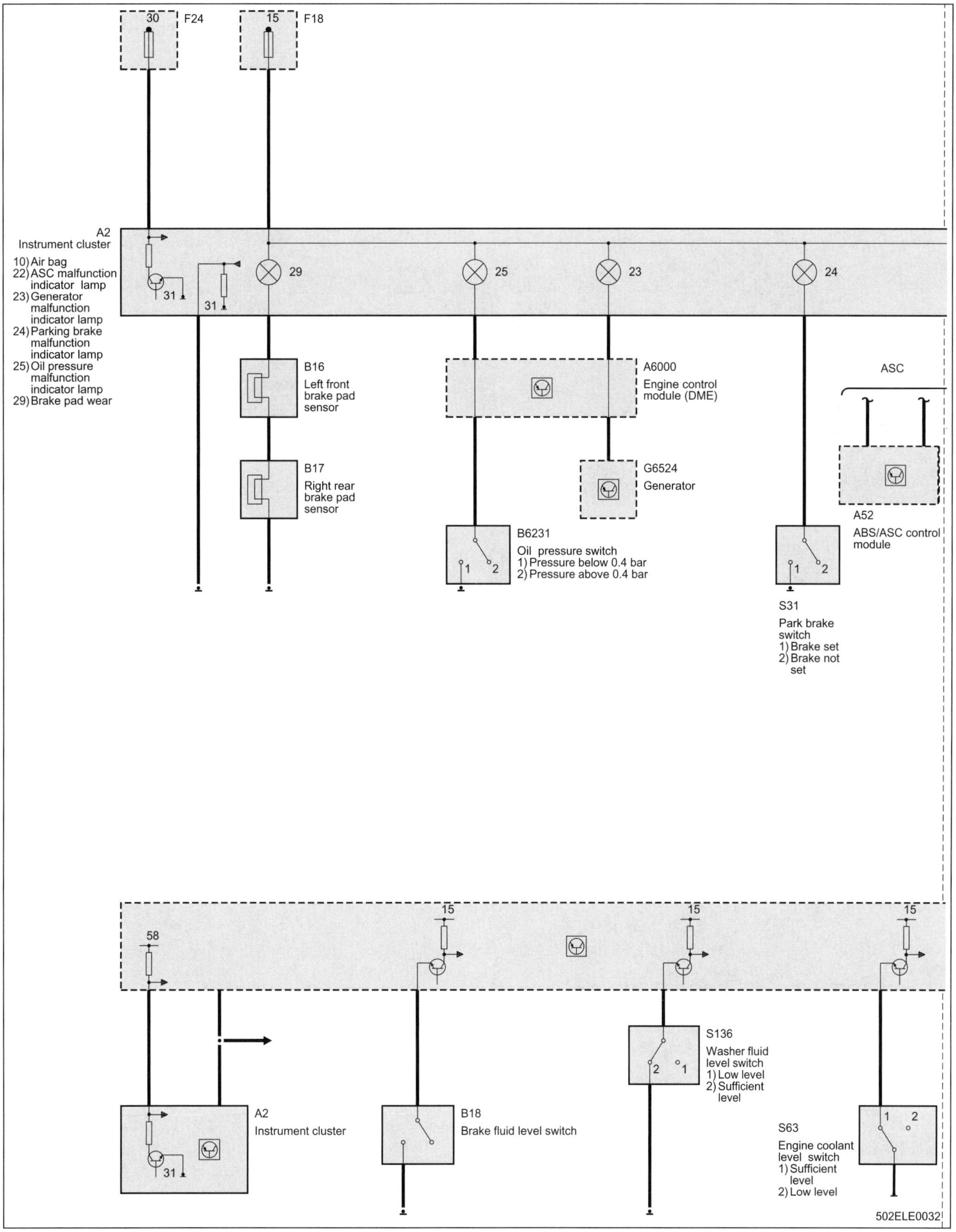
30
F24
15
F18
A2
Instrument cluster
10) Air bag
22) ASC malfunction indicator lamp
23) Generator malfunction indicator lamp
24) Parking brake malfunction indicator lamp
25) Oil pressure malfunction indicator lamp
29) Brake pad wear
31
31
29
25
23
24
B16
Left front brake pad sensor
A6000
Engine control module (DME)
ASC
B17
Right rear brake pad sensor
G6524
Generator
A52
ABS/ASC control module
B6231
Oil pressure switch
1) Pressure below 0.4 bar
2) Pressure above 0.4 bar
S31
Park brake switch
1) Brake set
2) Brake not set
58
15
15
15
S136
Washer fluid level switch
1) Low level
2) Sufficient level
A2
Instrument cluster
B18
Brake fluid level switch
S63
Engine coolant level switch
1) Sufficient level
2) Low level
31
502ELE0032

Instrument Panel
Display and information (overview)
(2 of 3)

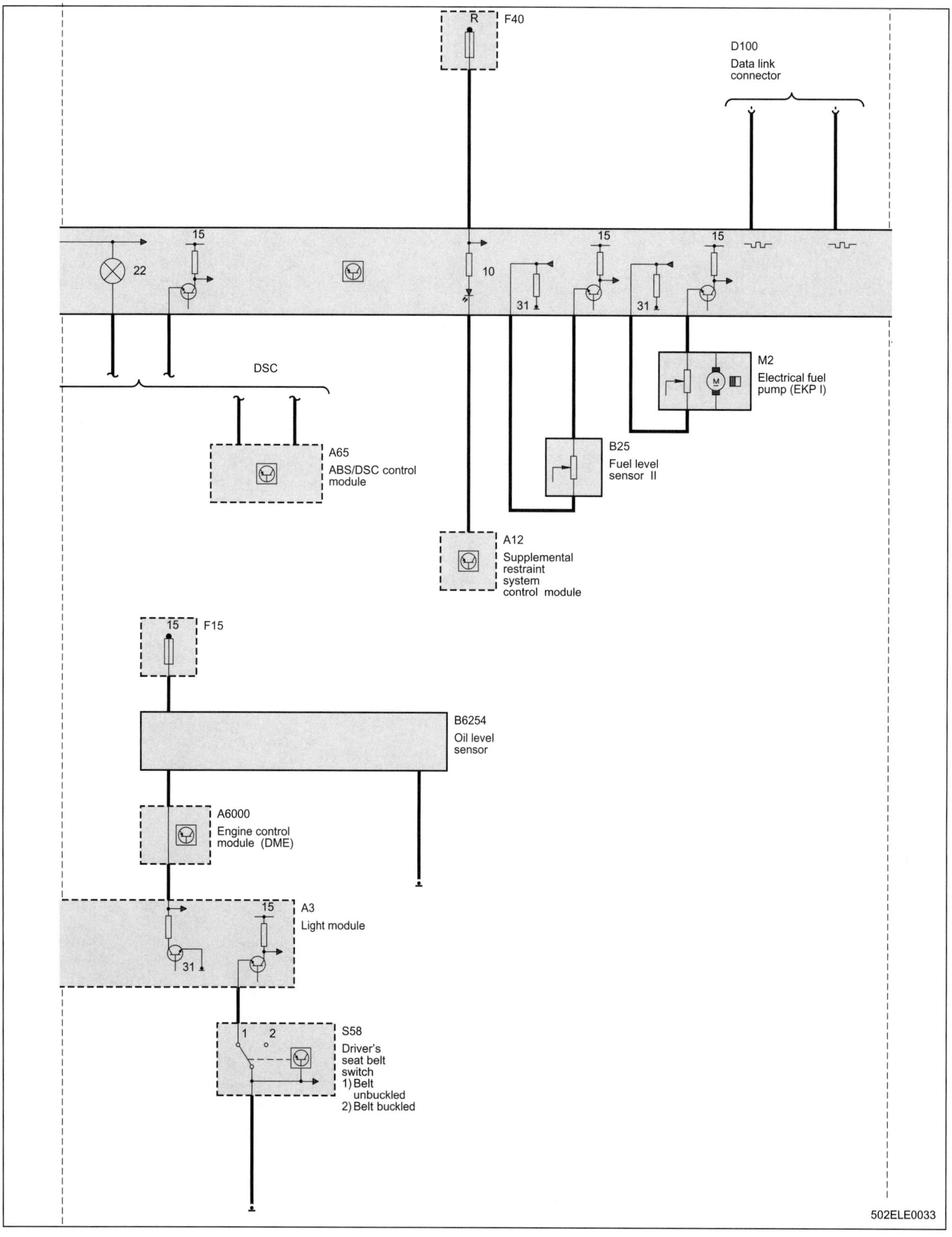

Instrument Panel
Display and information (overview)
(3 of 3)

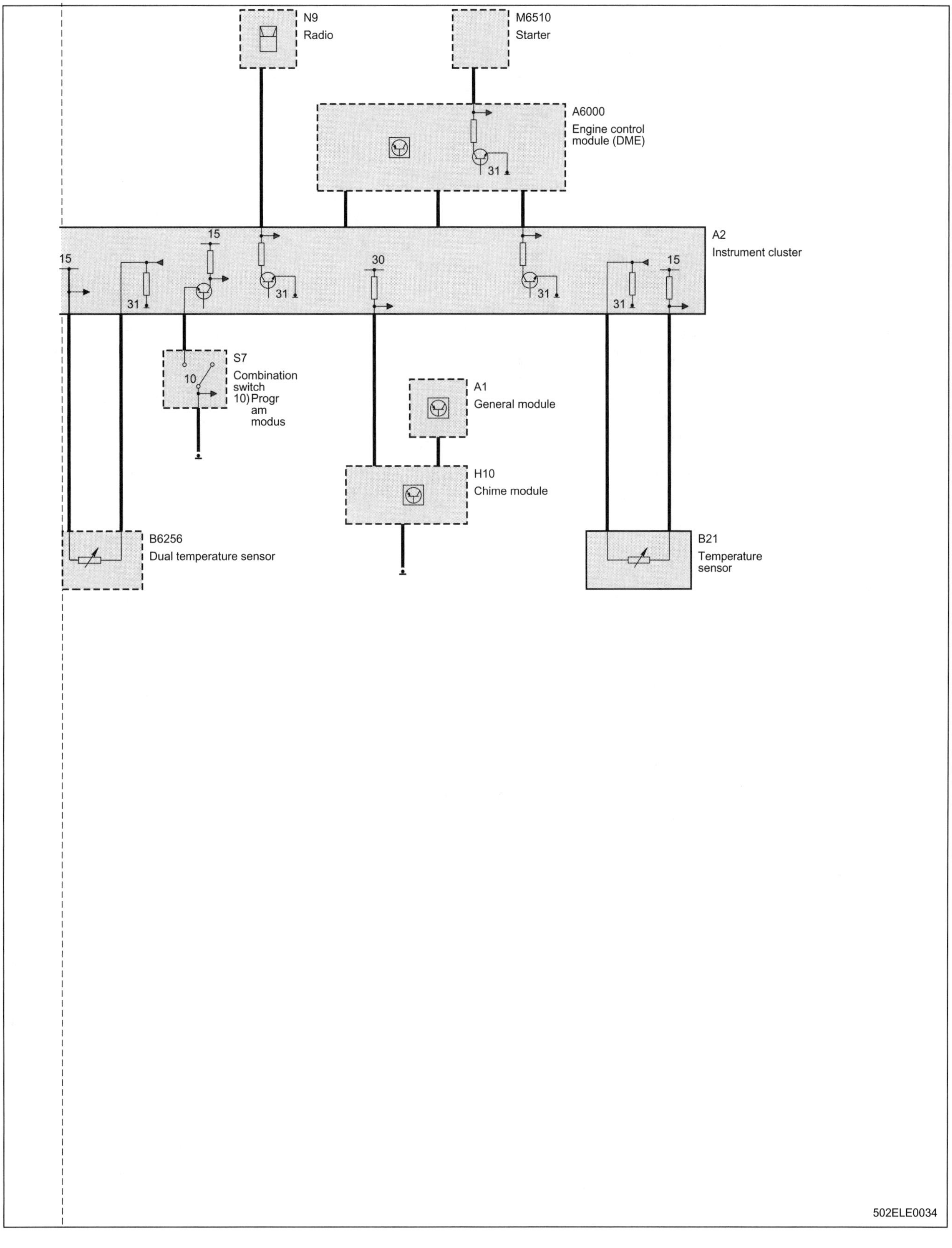

Instrument Panel
Integrated instrument cluster control module (IKE) (A63)
(1 of 3)

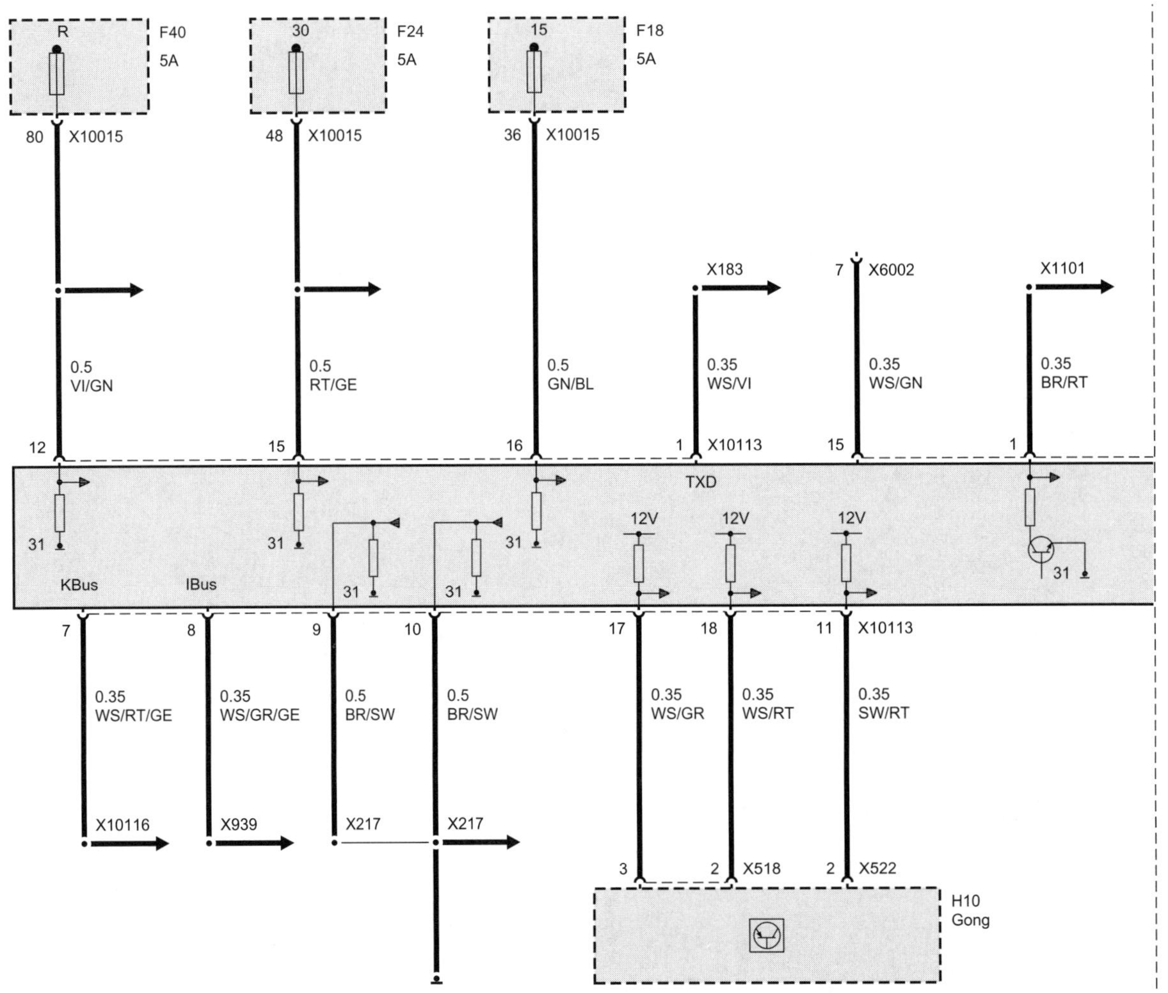

502ELE0427

Instrument Panel
Integrated instrument cluster control module (IKE) (A63)
(2 of 3)

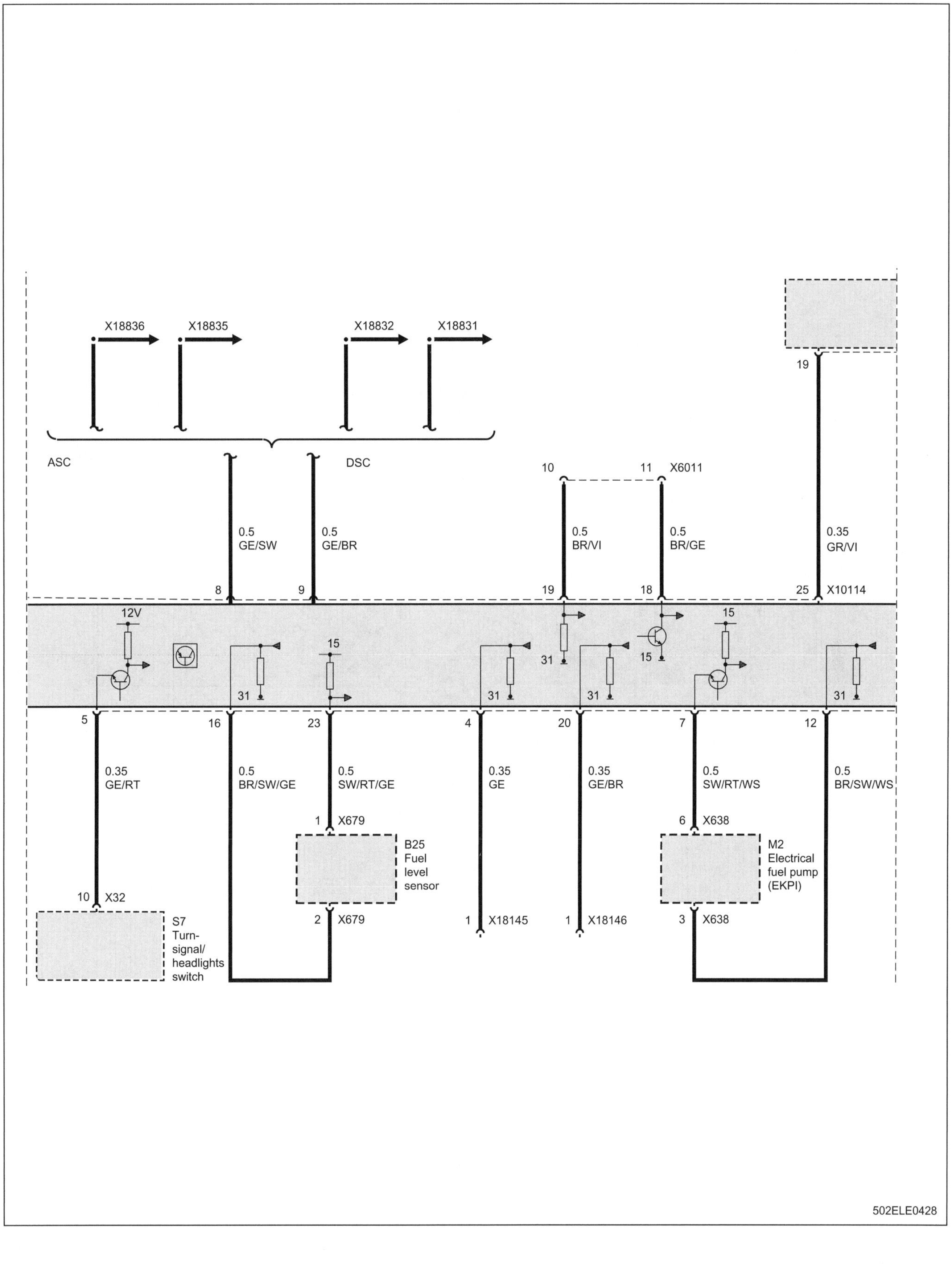

Instrument Panel
Integrated instrument cluster control module (IKE) (A63)
(3 of 3)

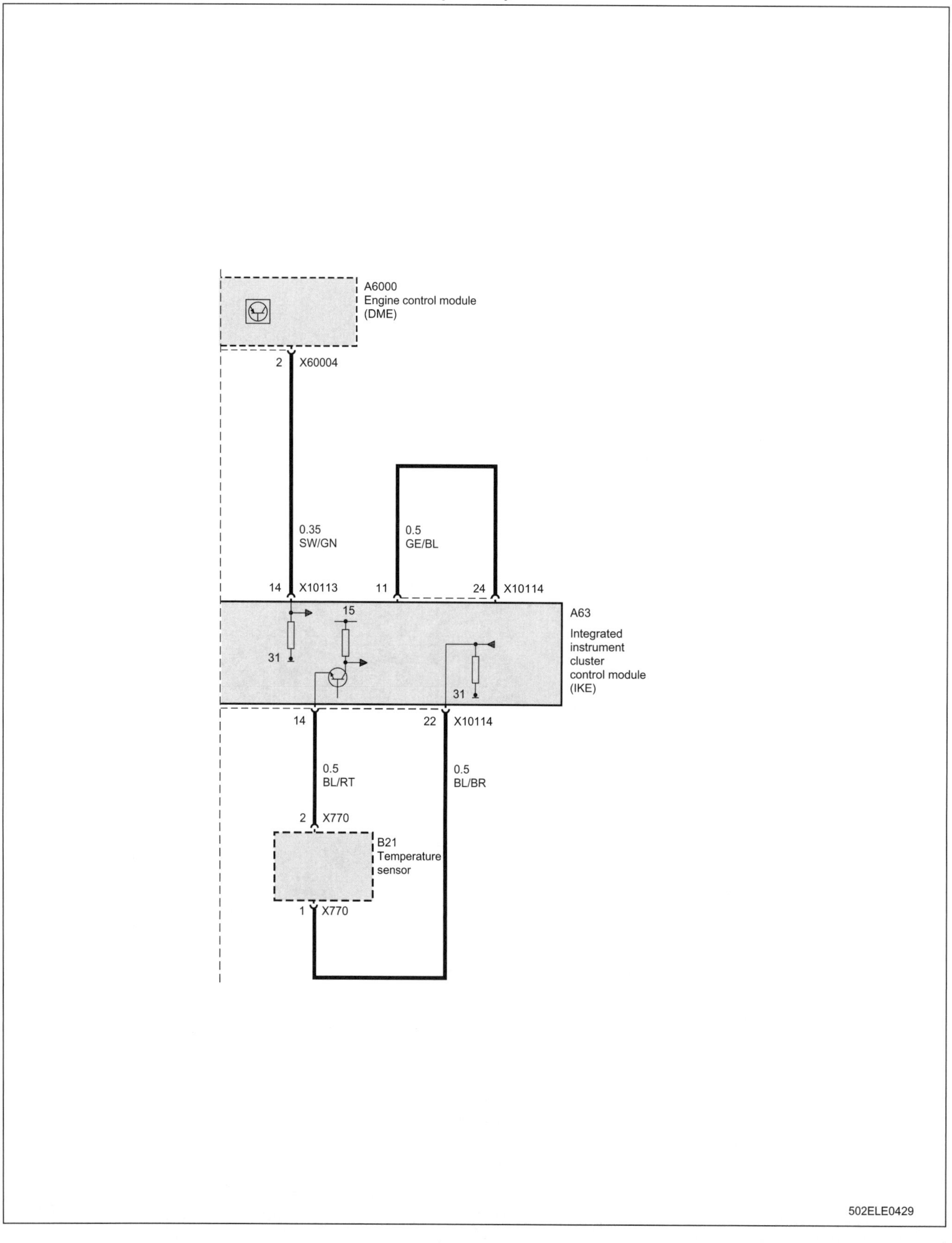

Instrument Panel
Instrument panel power supply
(1 of 1)

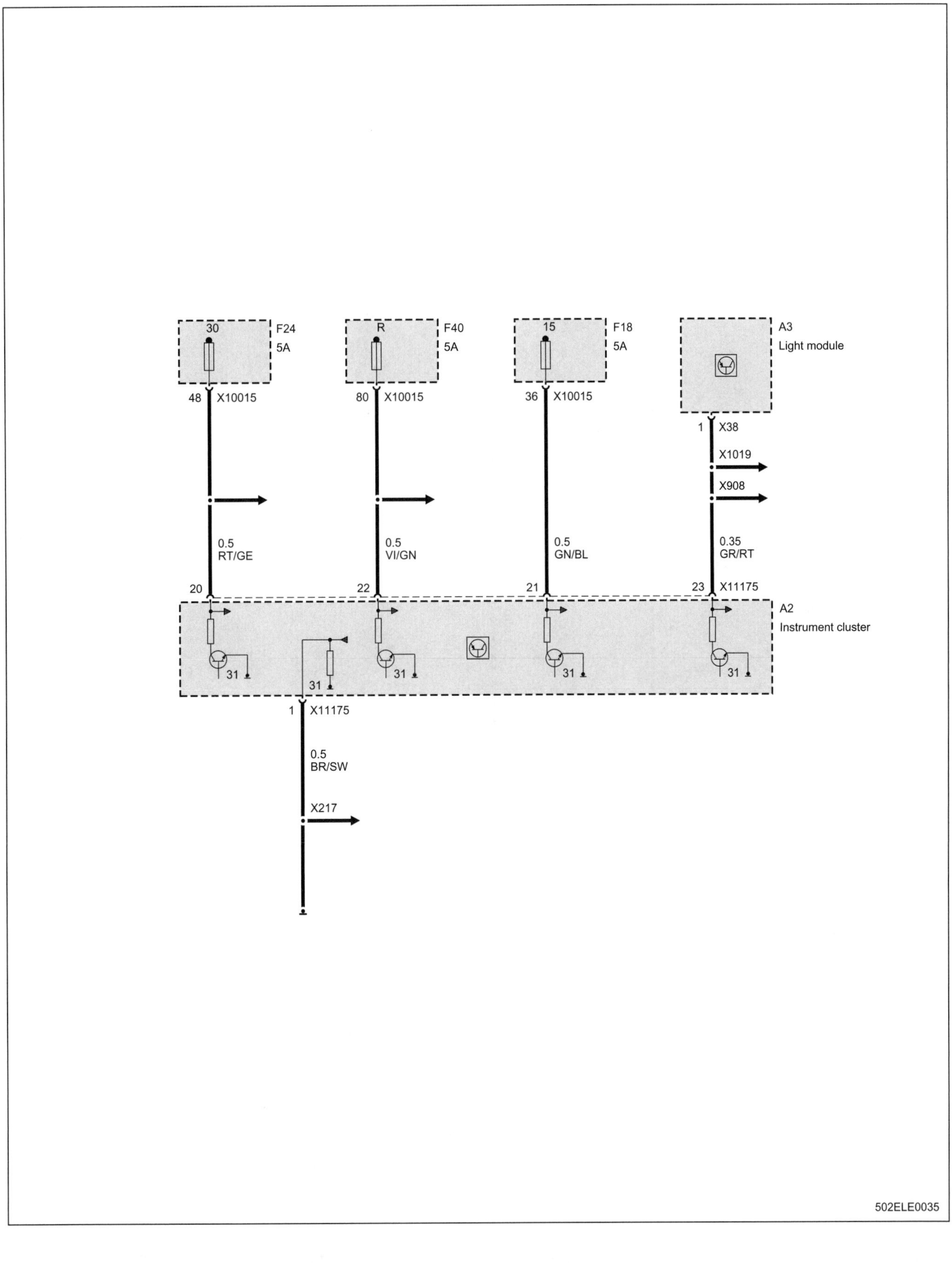

Instrument Panel
DME/instrument cluster interface
(1 of 1)

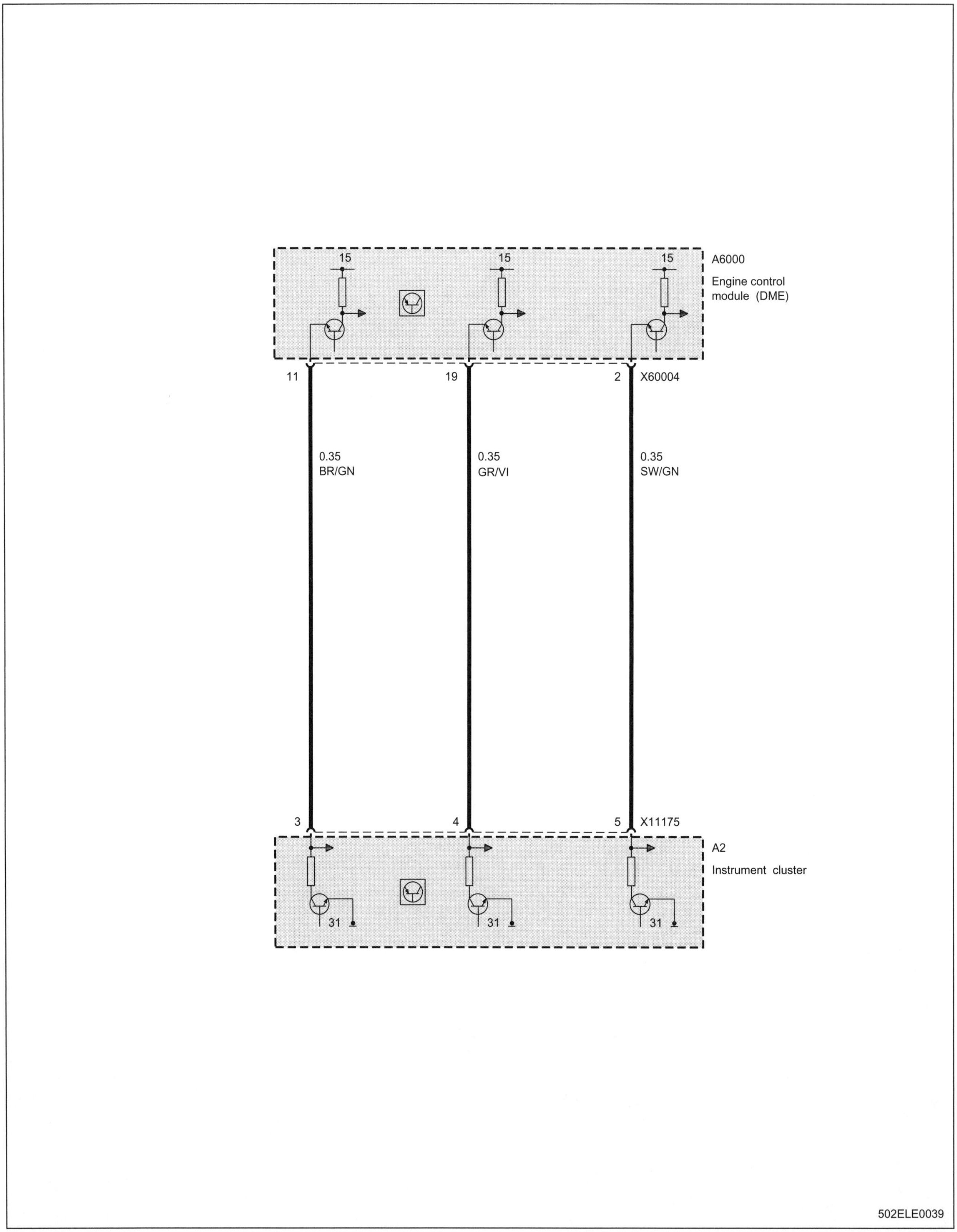

Instrument Panel
Fuel level sensors I and II
(1 of 1)

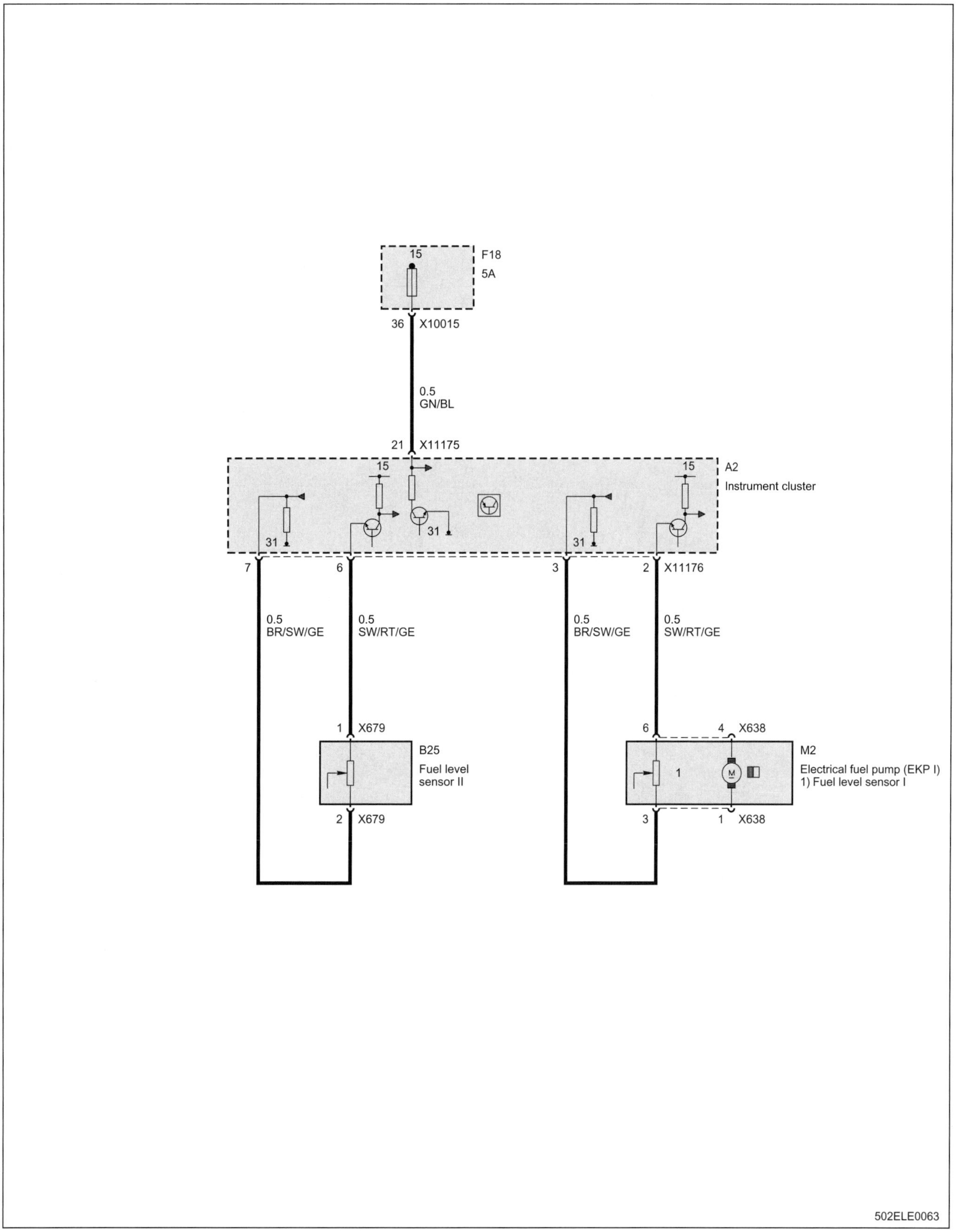

Instrument Panel
Garage door opener
(1 of 1)

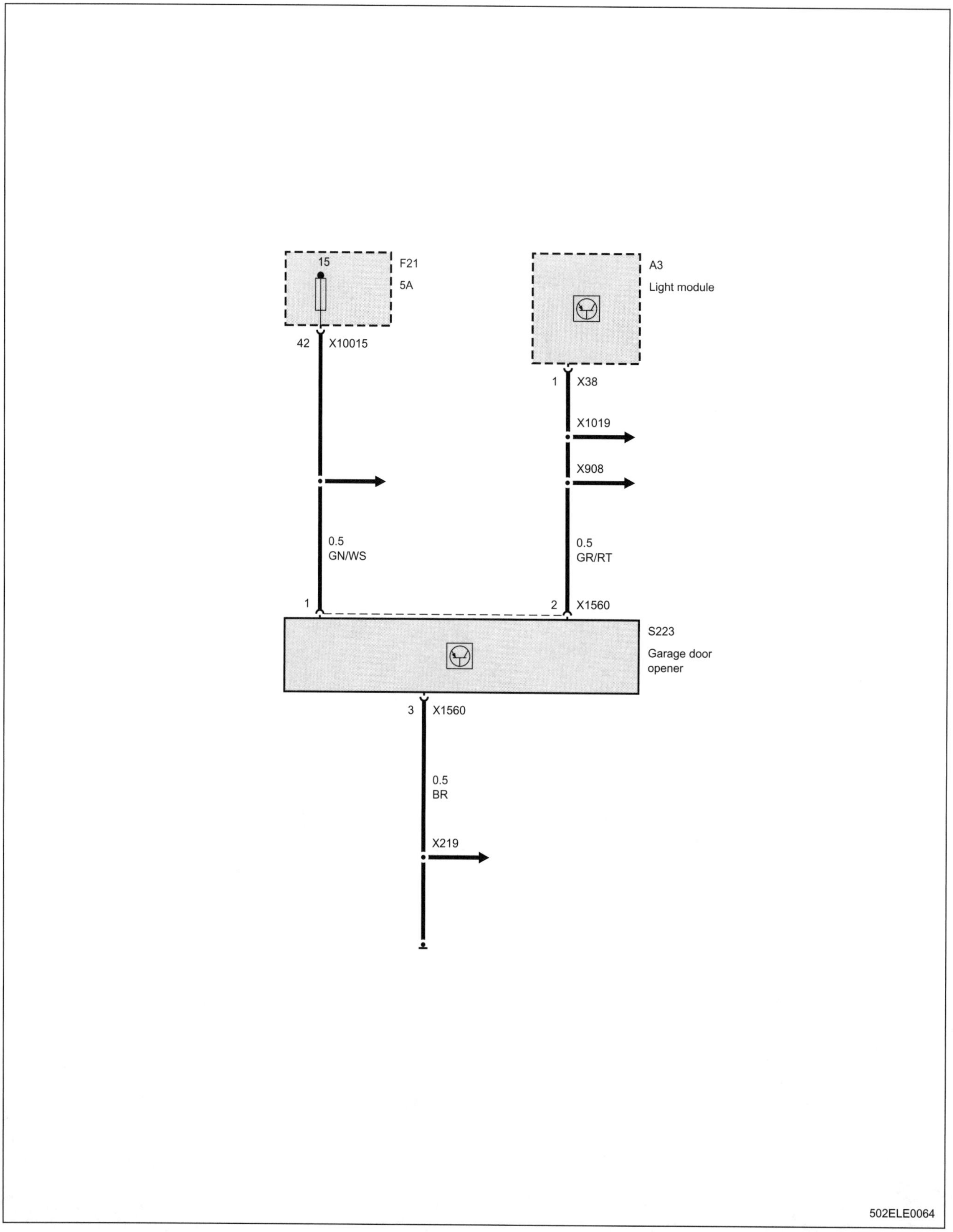
15
F21
5A
42
X10015
0.5
GN/WS
A3
Light module
1
X38
X1019
X908
0.5
GR/RT
1
2
X1560
S223
Garage door
opener
3
X1560
0.5
BR
X219
502ELE0064

Instrument Panel
Power
(1 of 1)

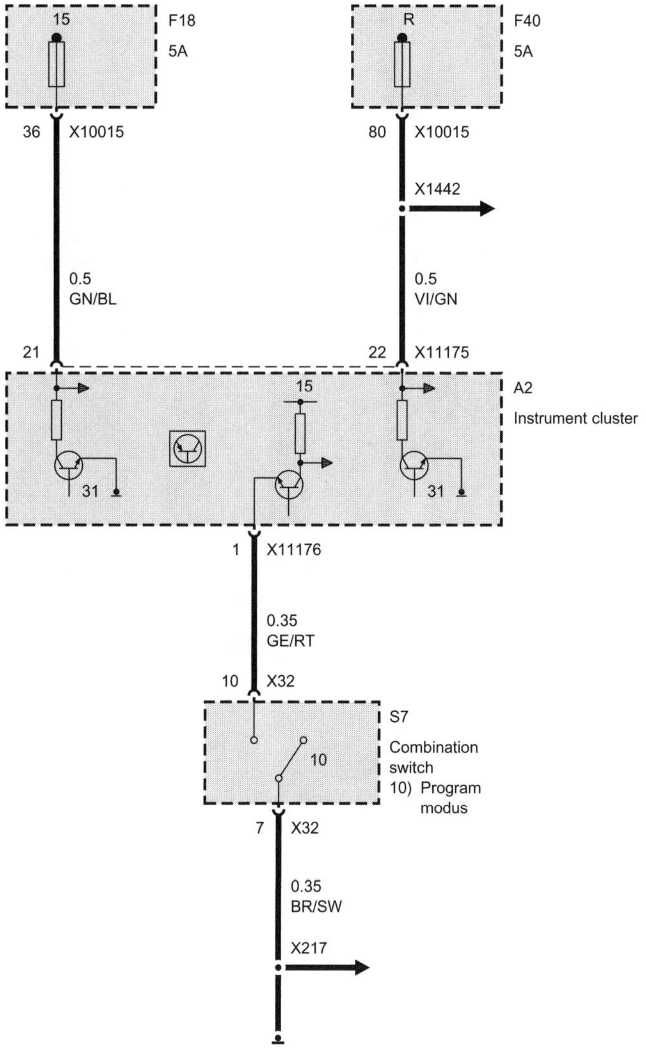
15
F18
5A
R
F40
5A
36
X10015
80
X10015
X1442
0.5
GN/BL
0.5
VI/GN
21
22
X11175
15
A2
Instrument cluster
31
31
1
X11176
0.35
GE/RT
10
X32
S7
Combination switch
10) Program modus
10
7
X32
0.35
BR/SW
X217
502ELE0133

Interior Lights/Illumination
Interior (overview)
(1 of 3)

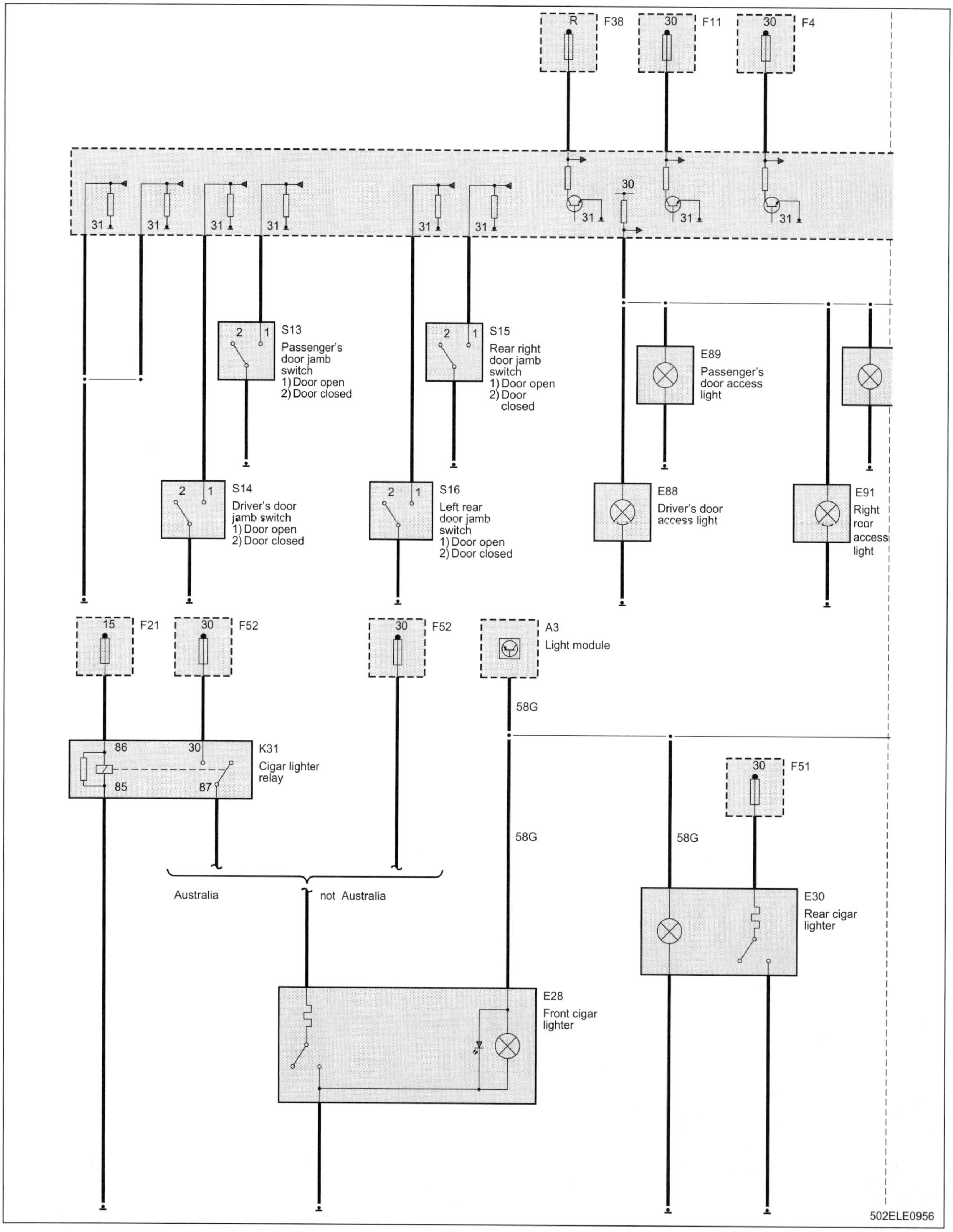
R
F38
30
F11
30
F4
30
31
31
31
31
31
31
31
31
31
31
2
1
S13
Passenger's door jamb switch
1) Door open
2) Door closed
2
1
S15
Rear right door jamb switch
1) Door open
2) Door closed
E89
Passenger's door access light
2
1
S14
Driver's door jamb switch
1) Door open
2) Door closed
2
1
S16
Left rear door jamb switch
1) Door open
2) Door closed
E88
Driver's door access light
E91
Right rear access light
15
F21
30
F52
30
F52
A3
Light module
58G
86
30
85
87
K31
Cigar lighter relay
30
F51
58G
58G
Australia
not Australia
E30
Rear cigar lighter
E28
Front cigar lighter
502ELE0956

Interior Lights/Illumination
Interior (overview)
(2 of 3)

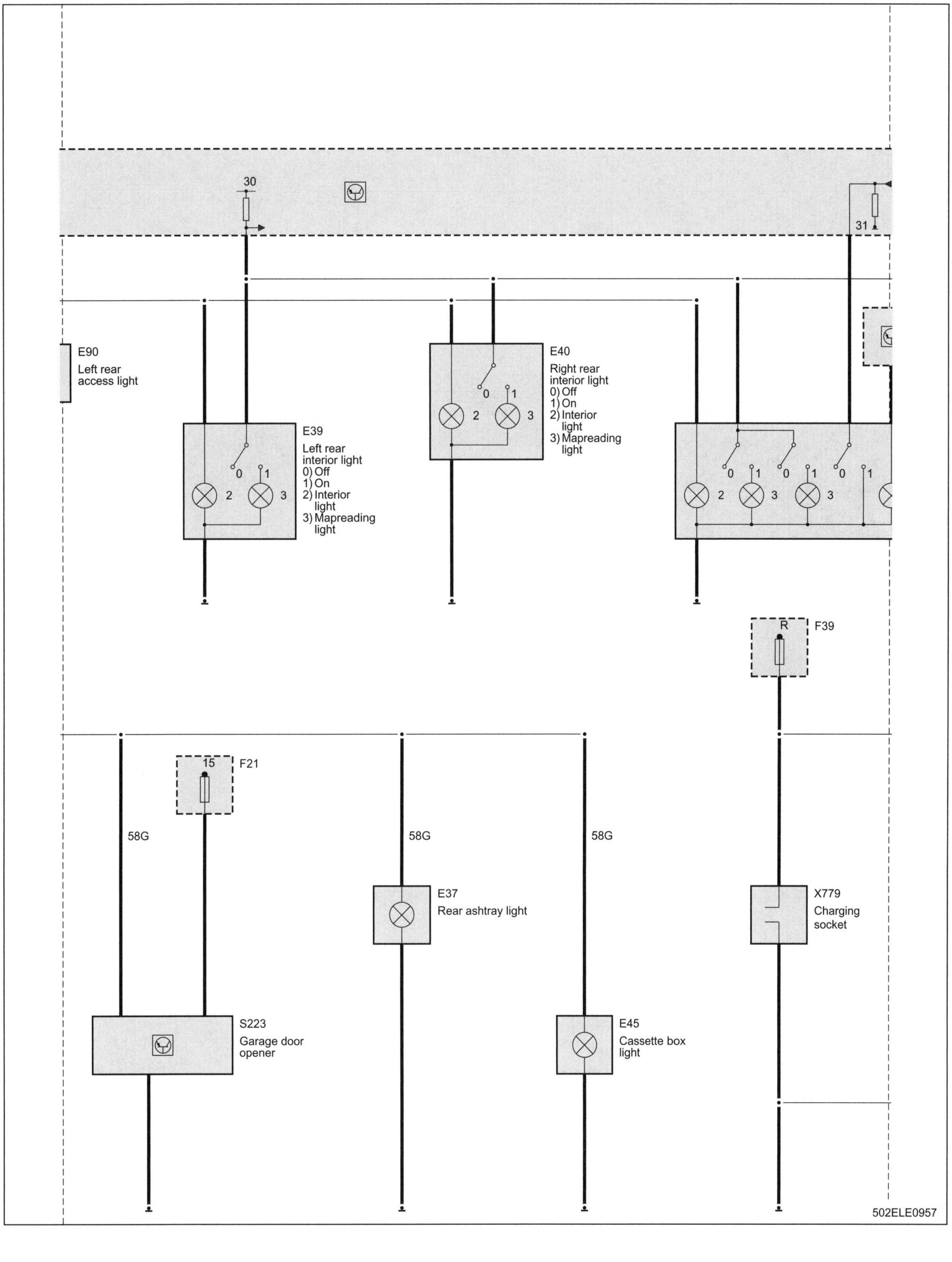

Interior Lights/Illumination
Interior (overview)
(3 of 3)

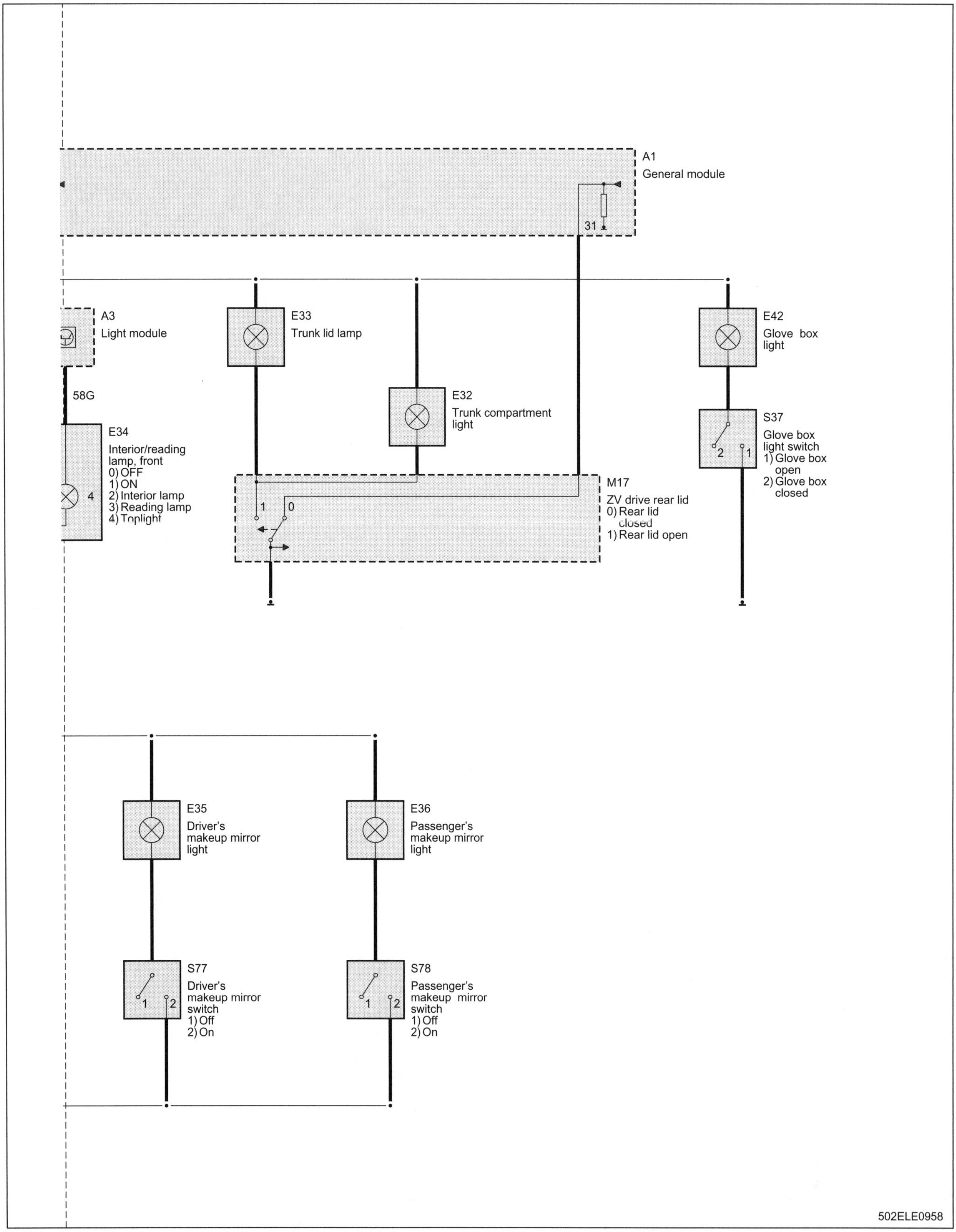

Interior Lights/Illumination
Lighting module (A3), power
(1 of 1)

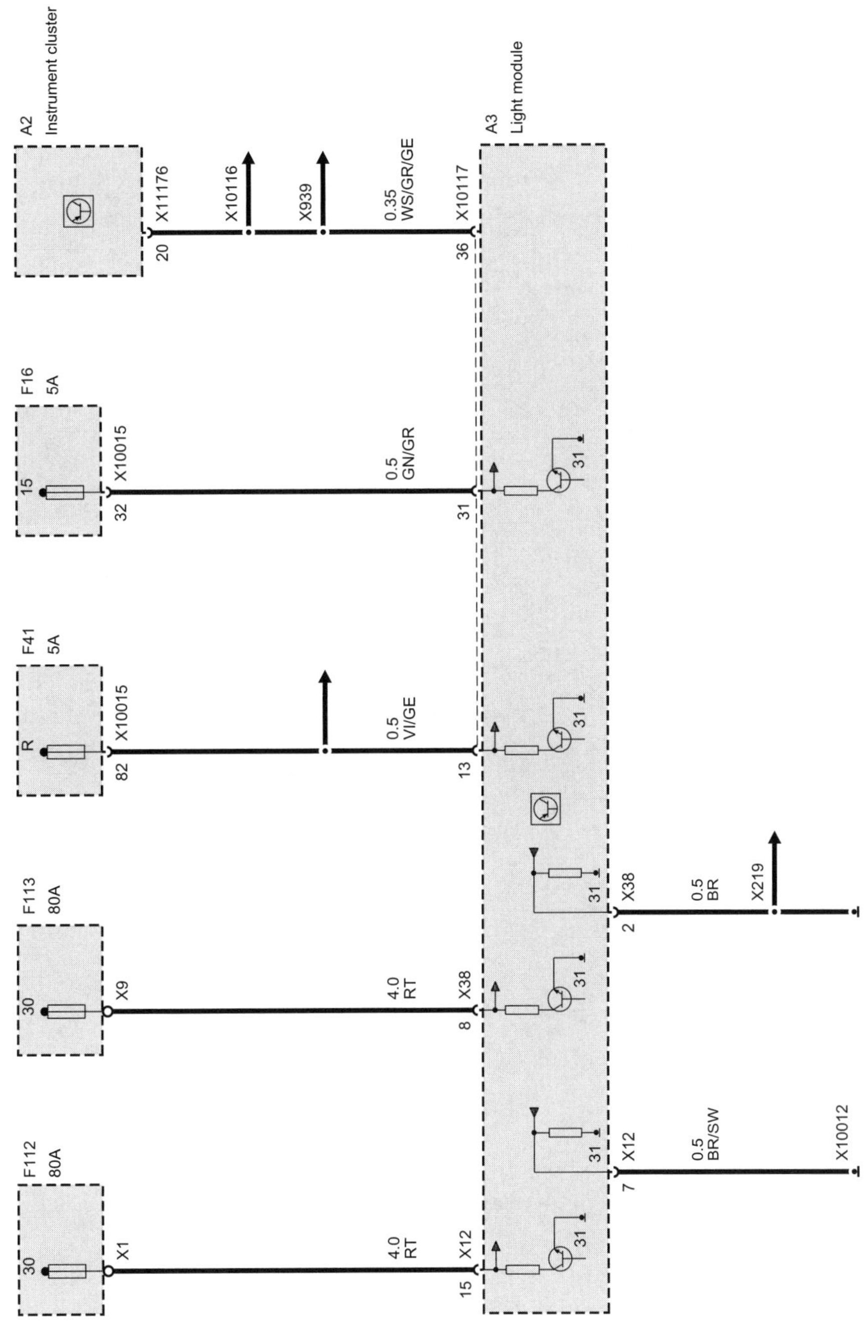

Interior Lights/Illumination
Charging socket, cassette box light
(1 of 1)

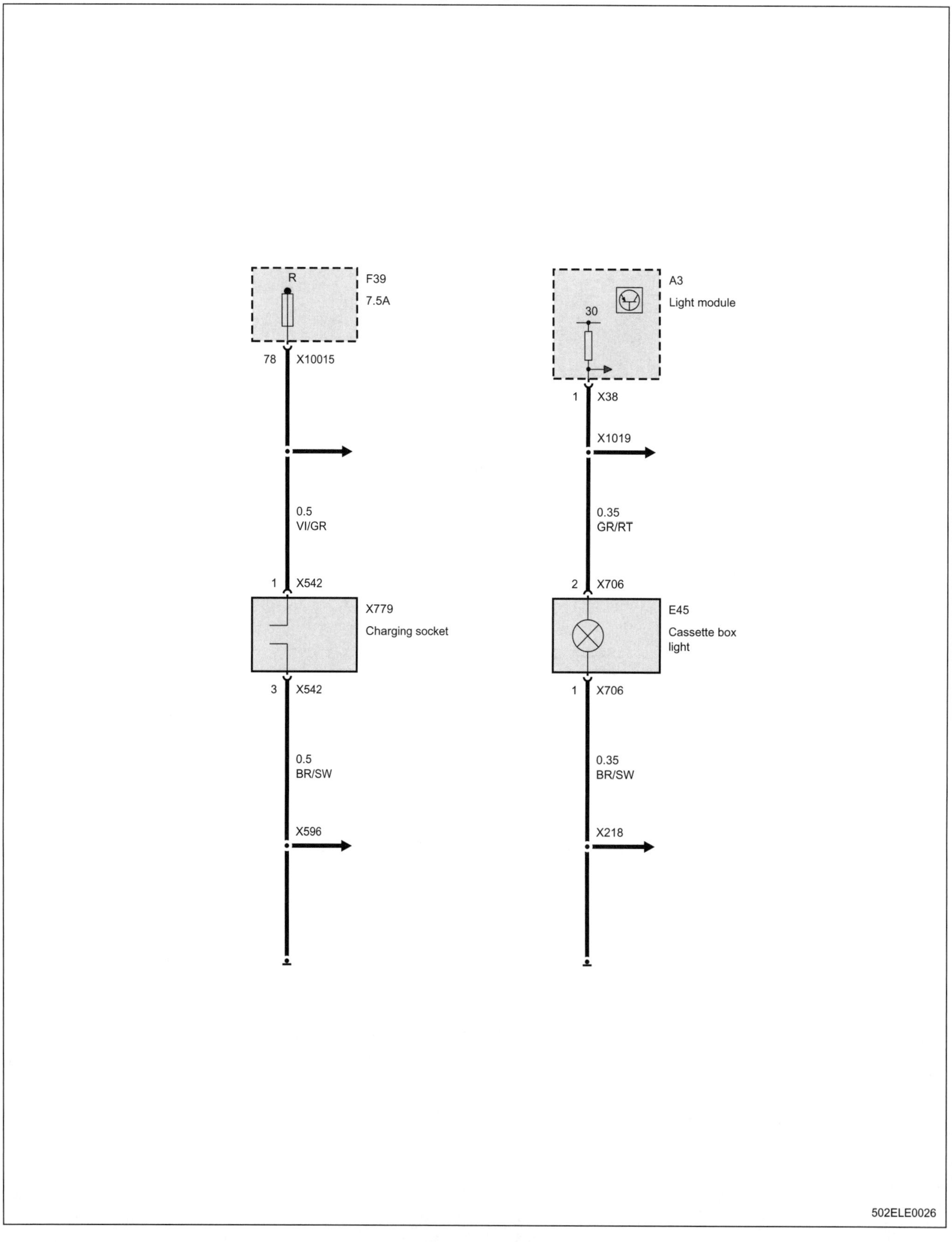

Interior Lights/Illumination
Dimmer
(1 of 1)

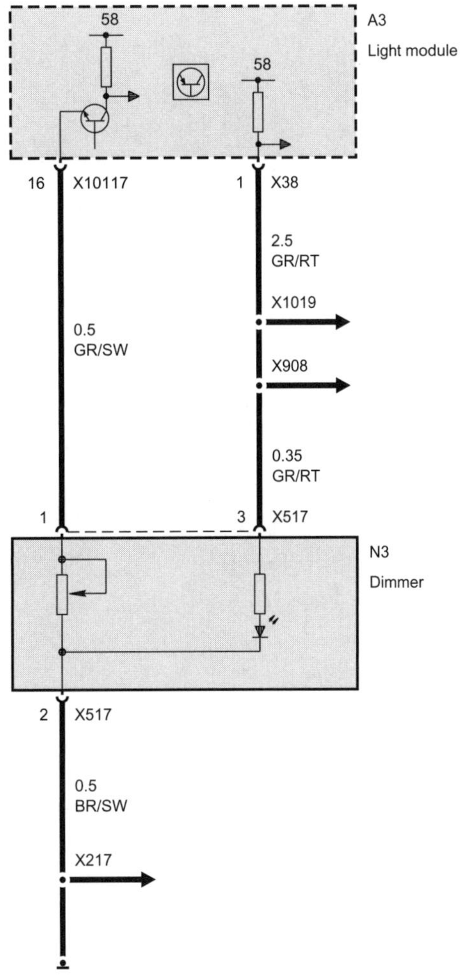

502ELE0031

Interior Lights/Illumination
Driver's door switch (door jamb)
(1 of 1)

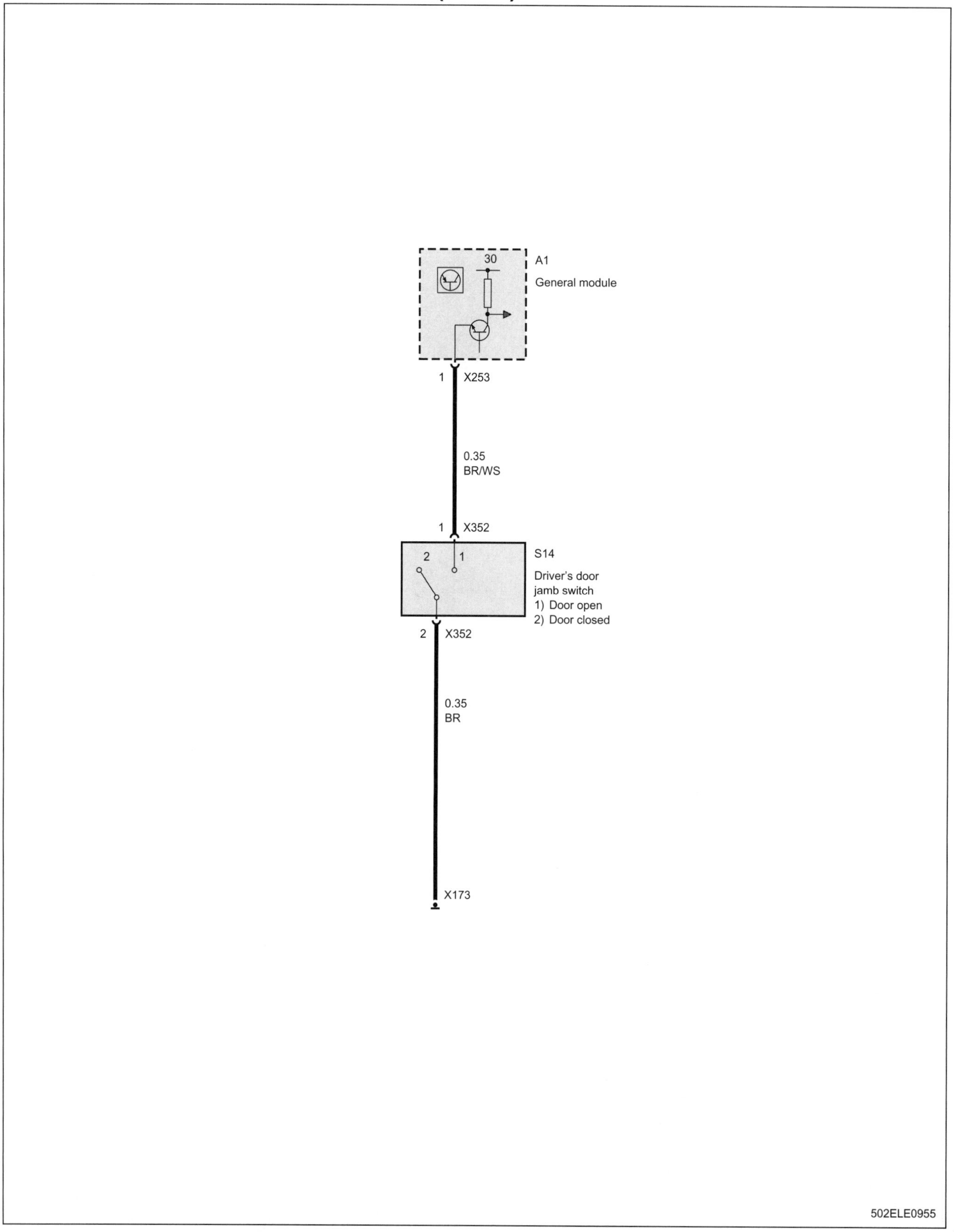

Interior Lights/Illumination
Front dome light/map reading assembly
(1 of 1)

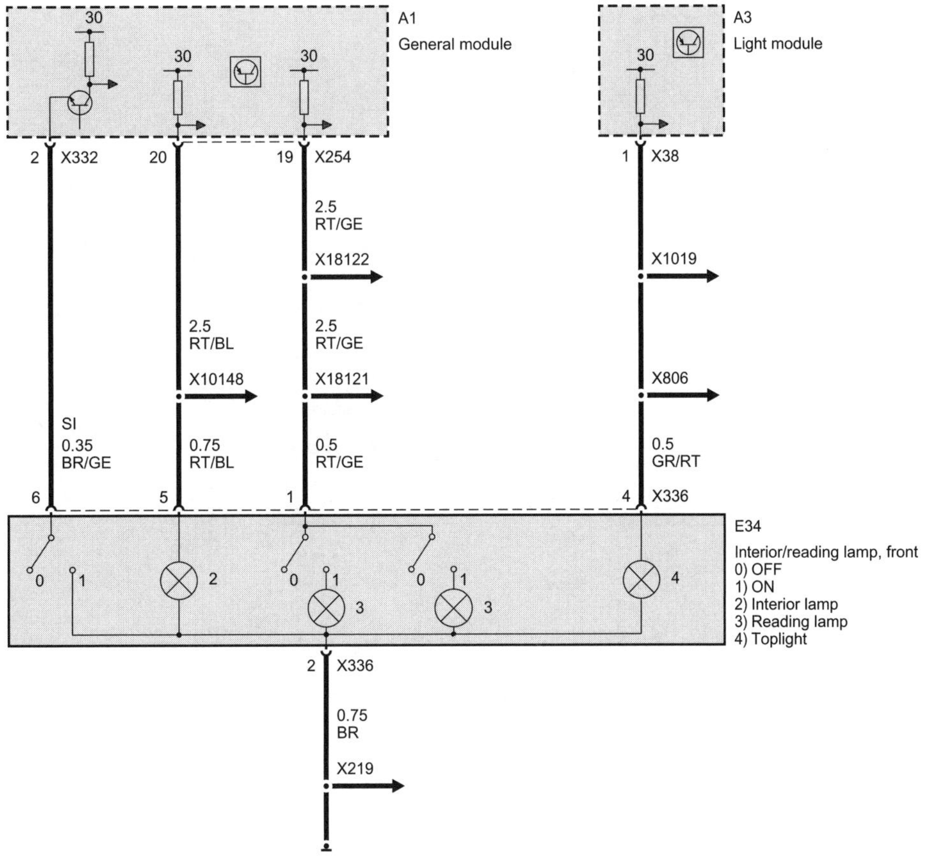

502ELE0054

Interior Lights/Illumination
Front door lighting

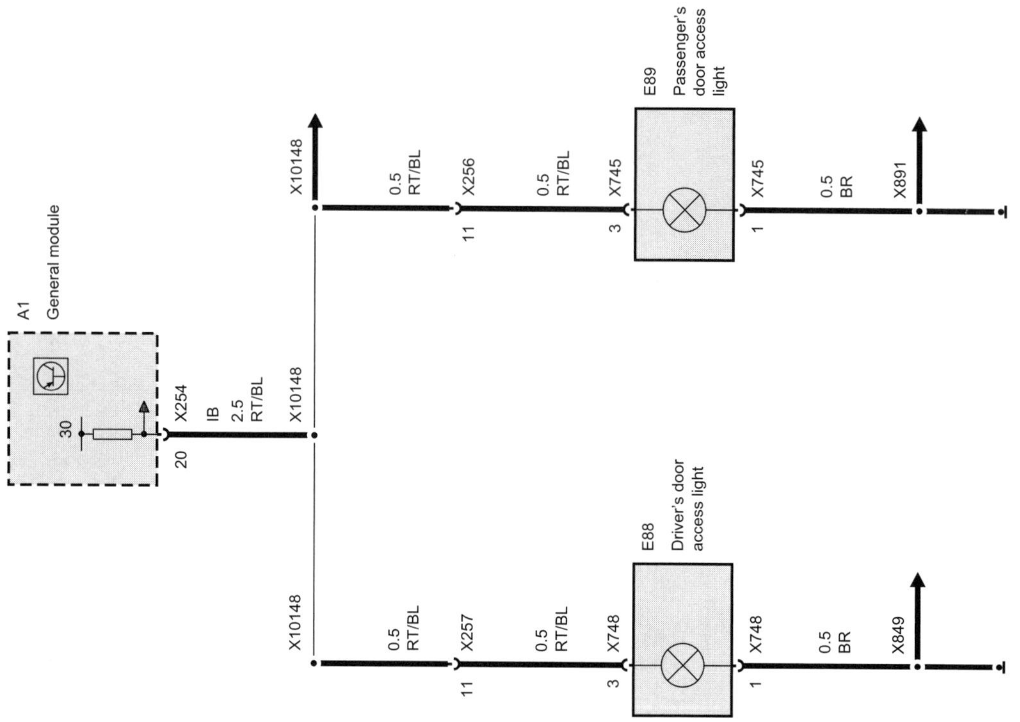

502ELE0053a

Interior Lights/Illumination
Front lighter

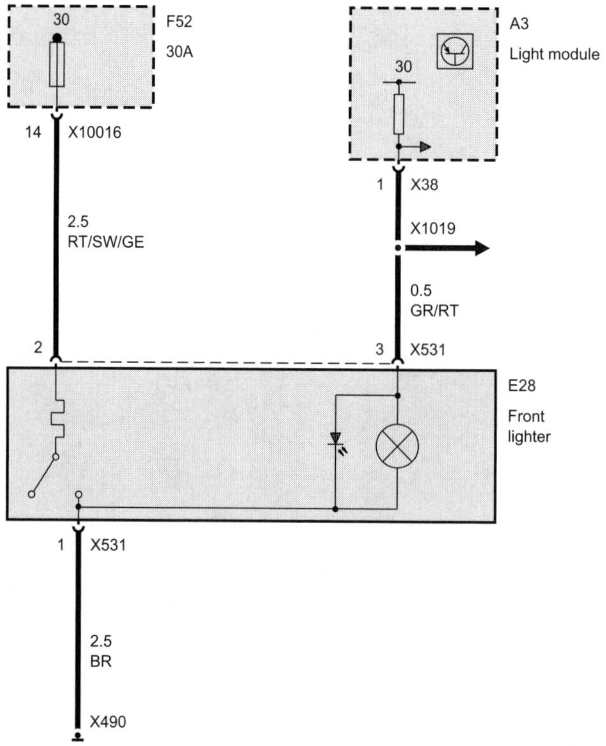

502ELE0053b

Interior Lights/Illumination
Glove box light
(1 of 1)

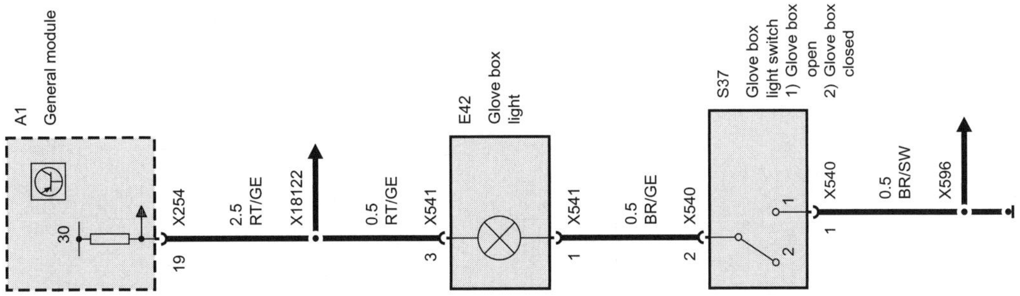

502ELE0066

Interior Lights/Illumination
Interior light, left rear
(1 of 1)

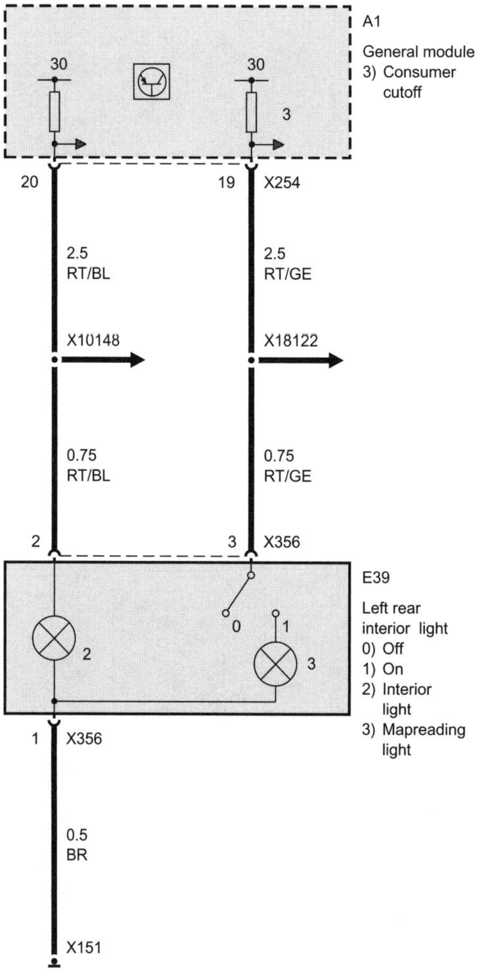

Interior Lights/Illumination
Makeup mirror lights
(1 of 1)

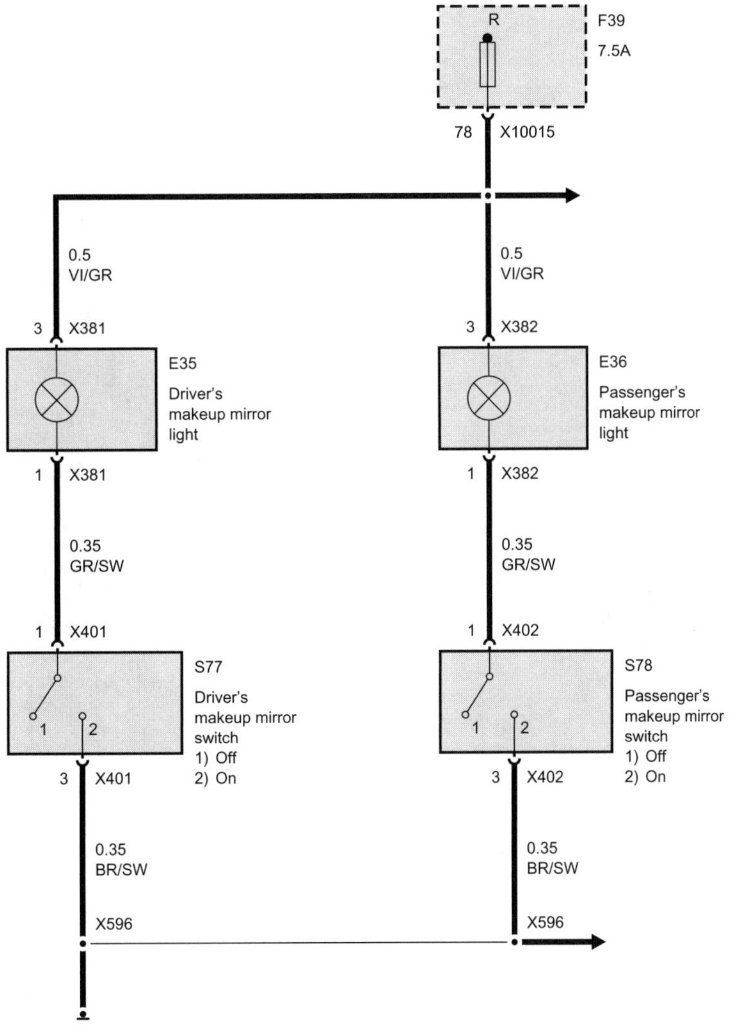

502ELE0111

Interior Lights/Illumination
Memory switch lighting, driver's side
(1 of 1)

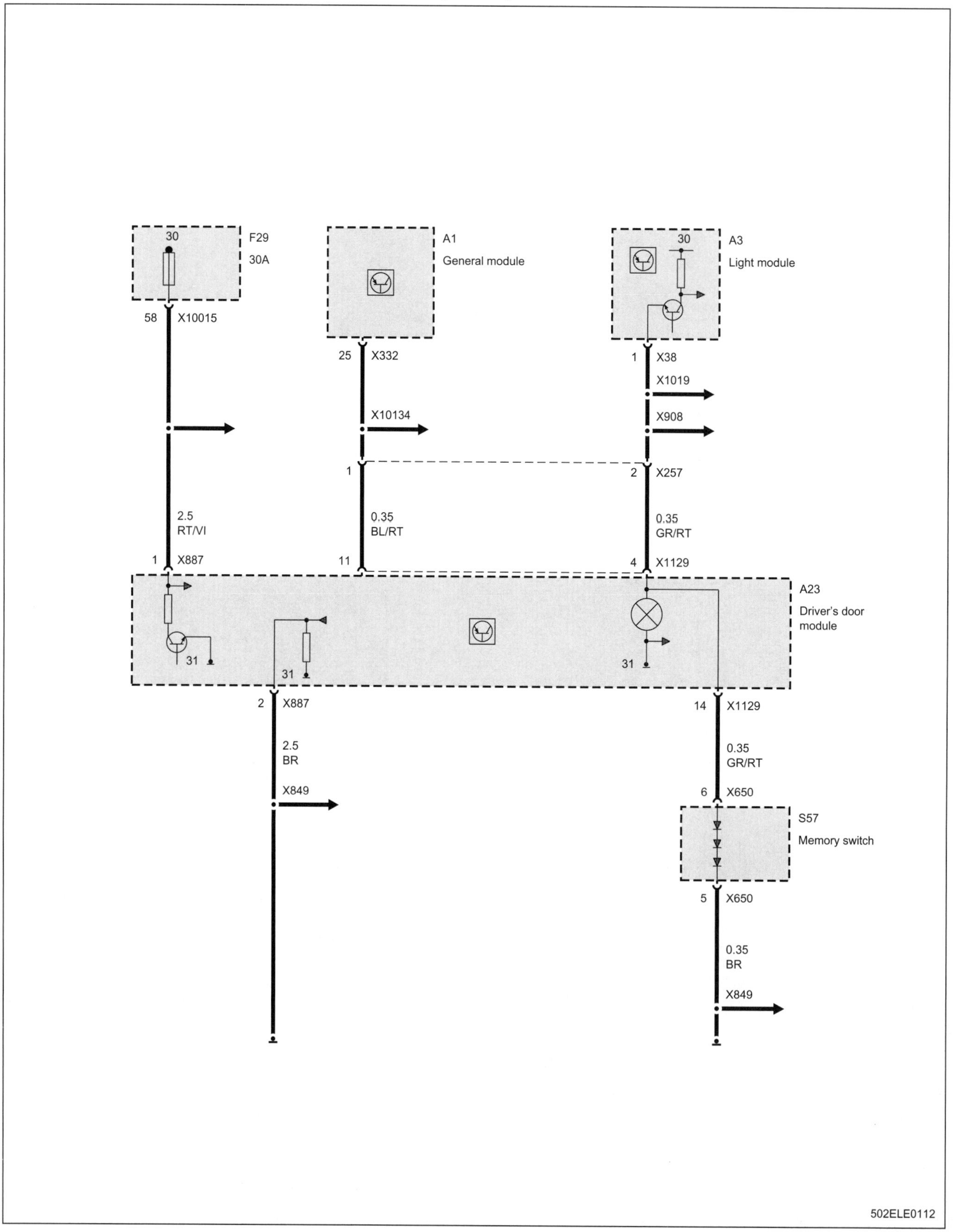

Interior Lights/Illumination
Rear access lights

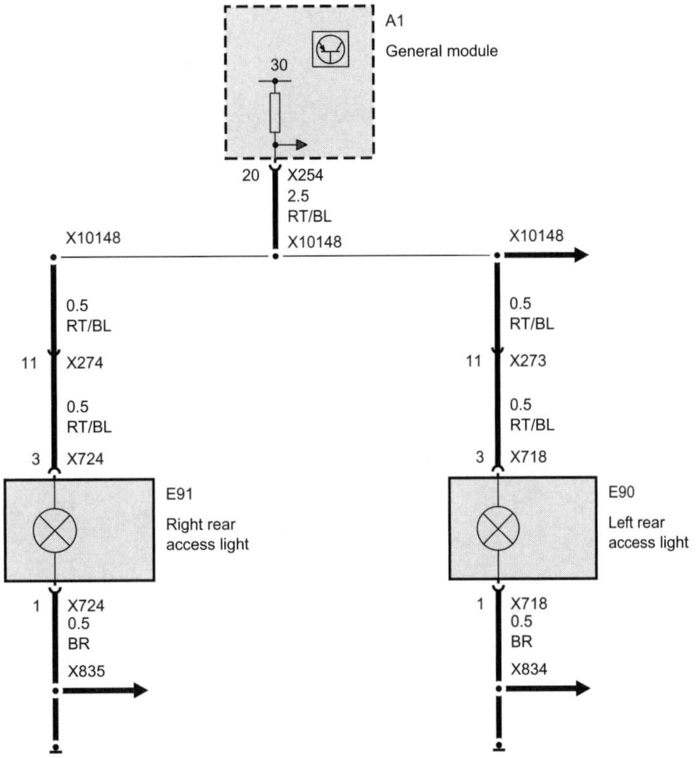

502ELE0150a

Interior Lights/Illumination
Rear ashtray light

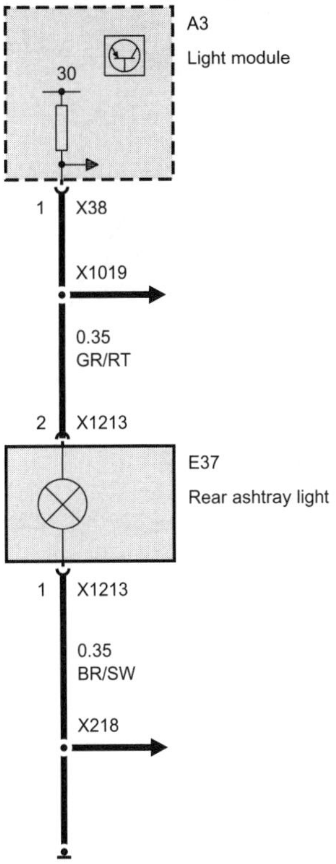

502ELE0150b

Interior Lights/Illumination
Rear cigarette lighter
(1 of 1)

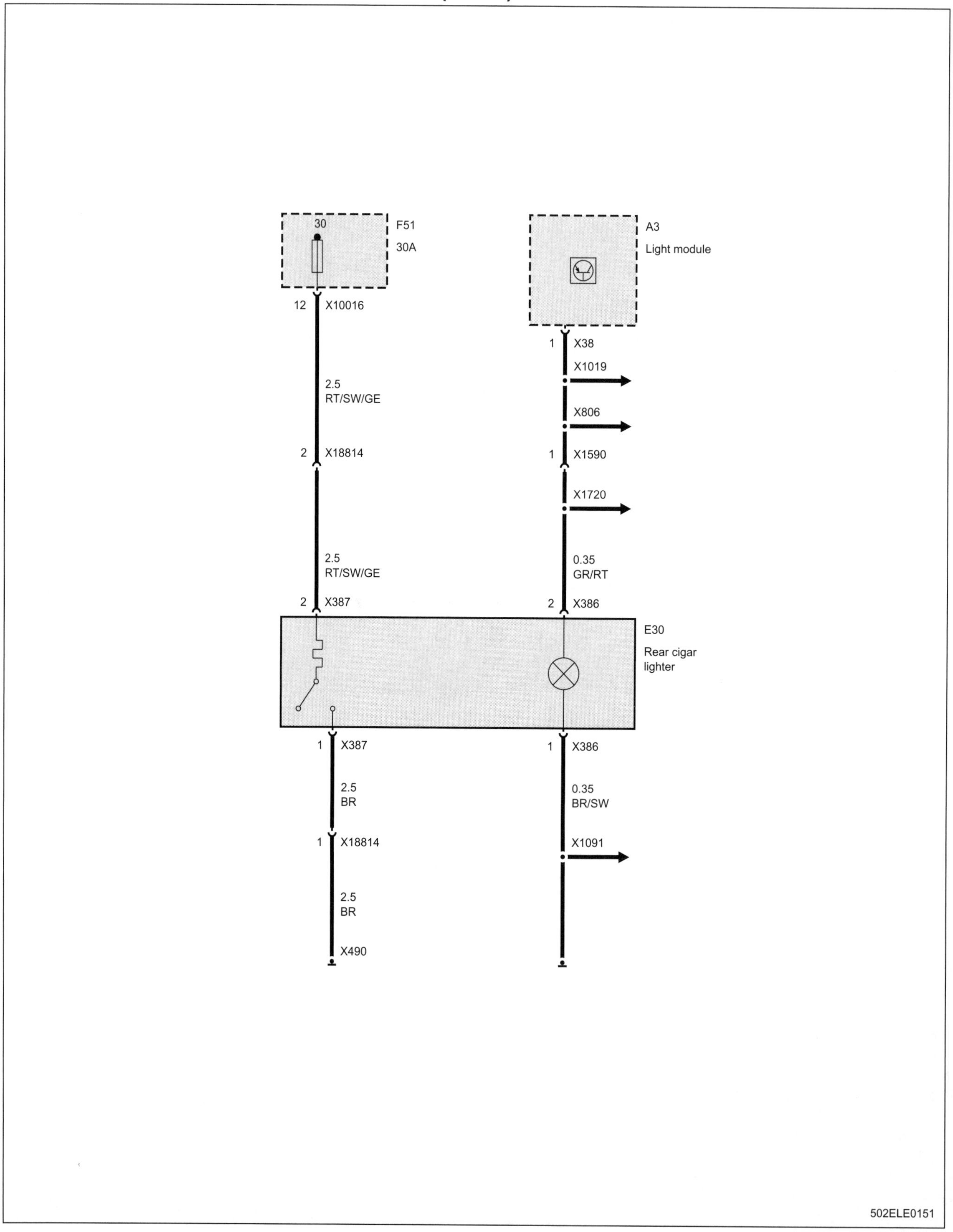

Interior Lights/Illumination
Interior light, right rear
(1 of 1)

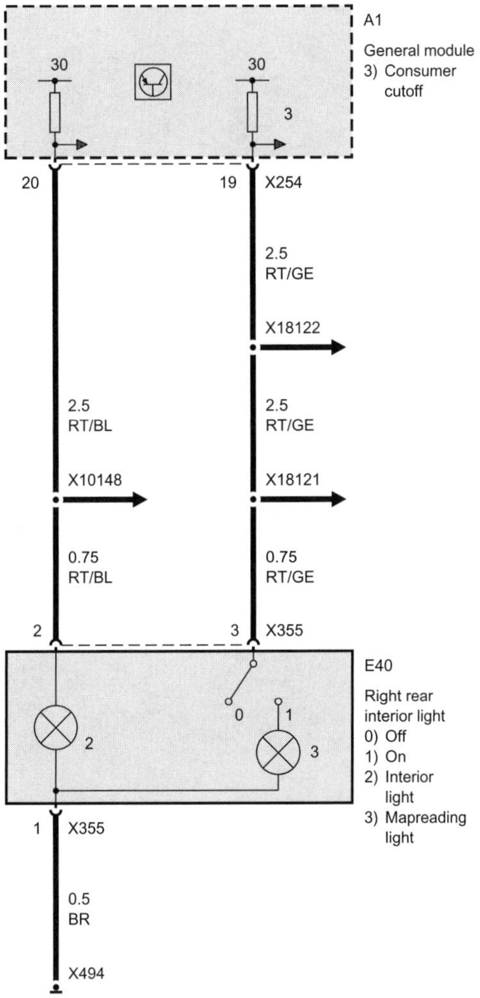

502ELE0174

Interior Lights/Illumination
Trunk compartment lights
(1 of 1)

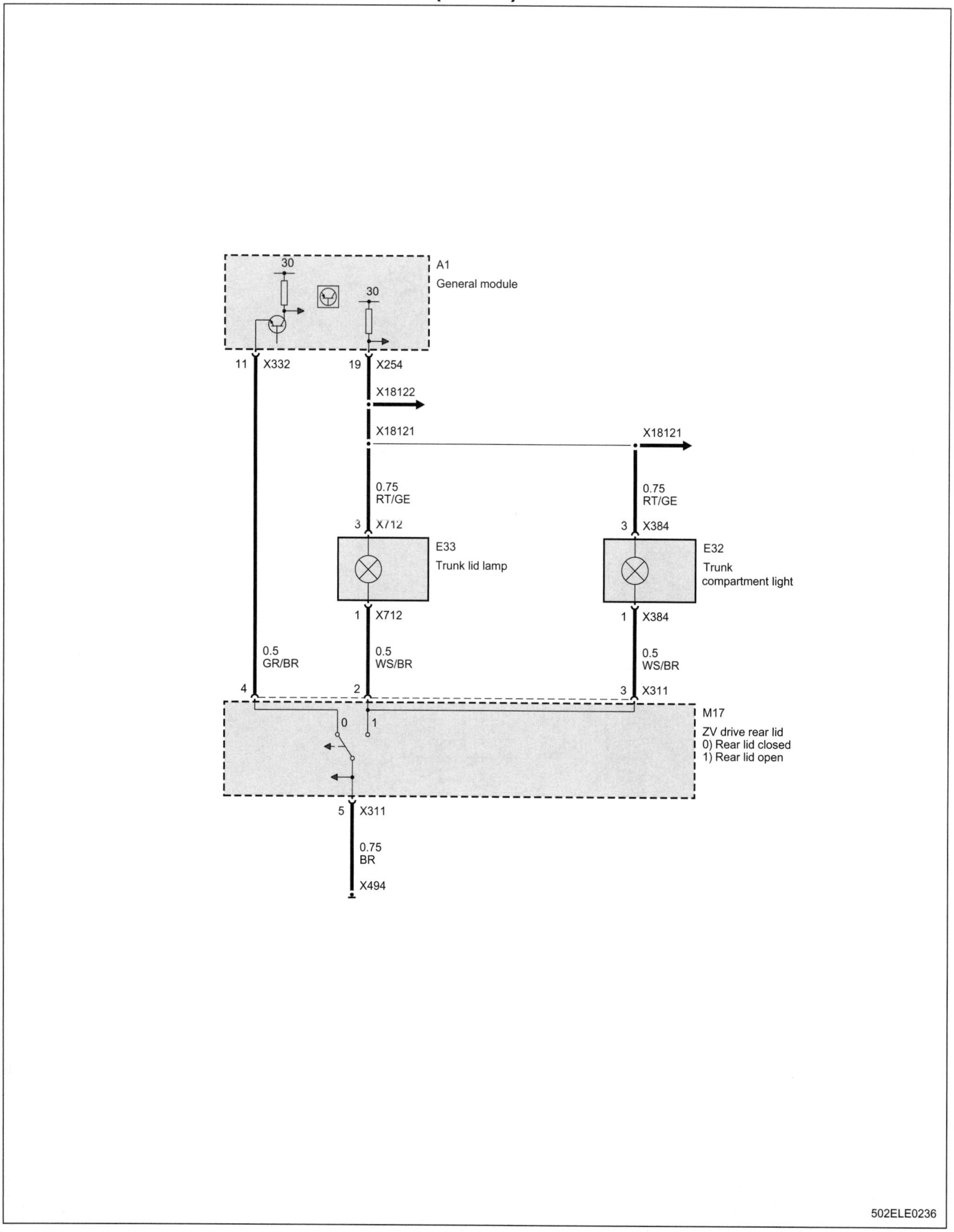

On-board Computer
On-board monitor (A196)
(1 of 2)

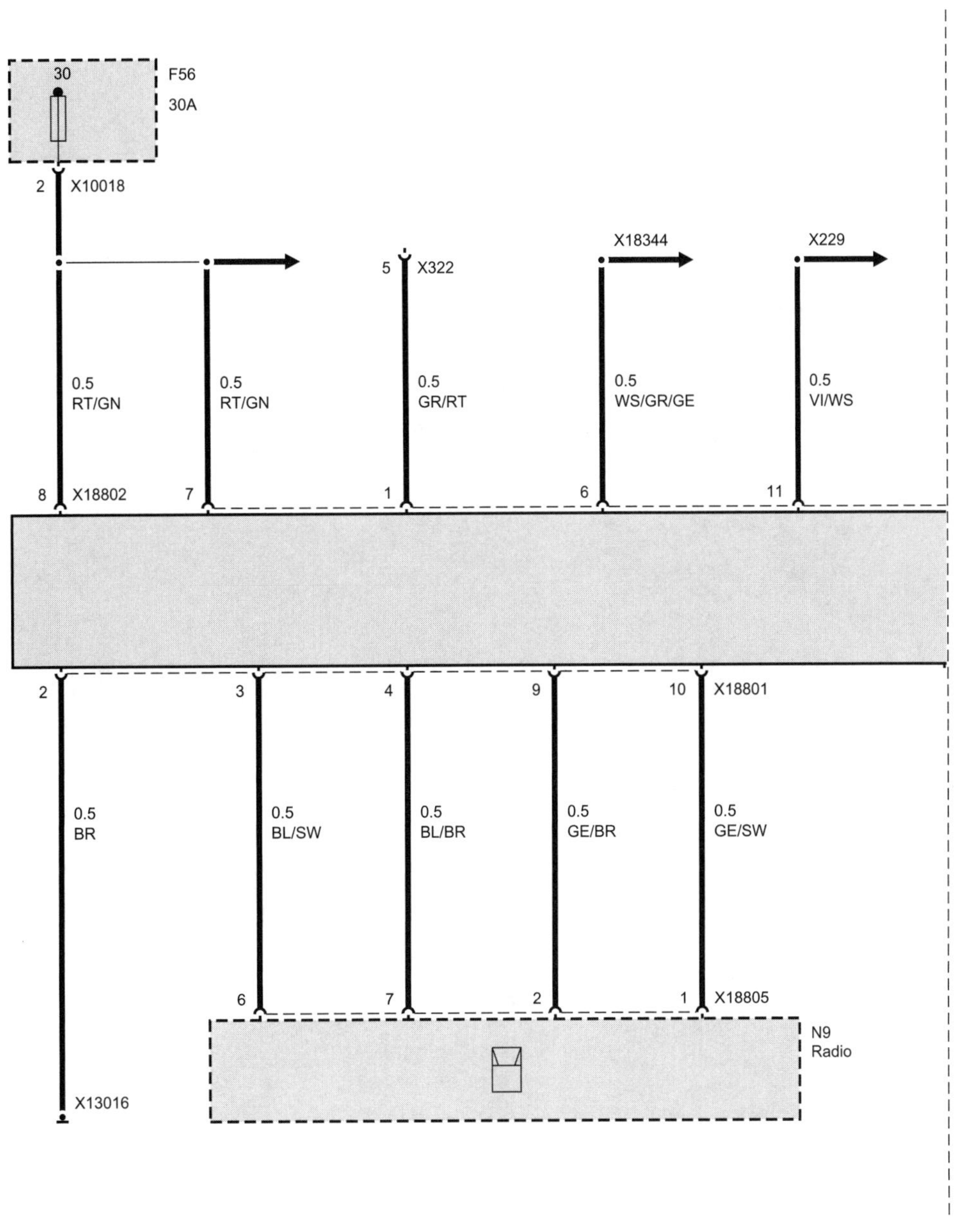

502ELE0366

On-board Computer
On-board monitor (A196)
(2 of 2)

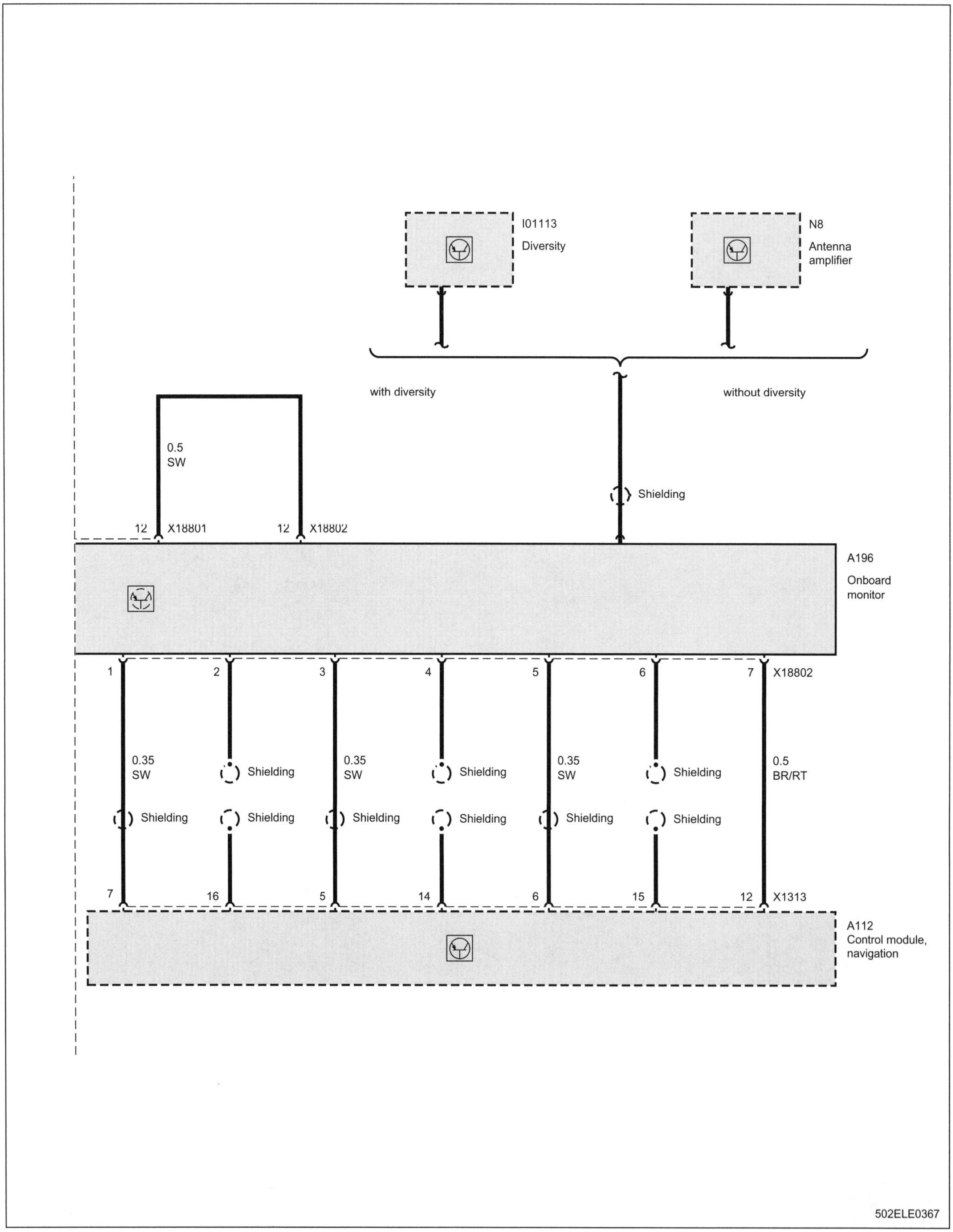
I01113
Diversity
N8
Antenna
amplifier
with diversity
without diversity
0.5
SW
Shielding
12
X18801
12
X18802
A196
Onboard
monitor
1
2
3
4
5
6
7
X18802
0.35
SW
Shielding
Shielding
0.35
SW
Shielding
0.35
SW
Shielding
0.5
BR/RT
Shielding
Shielding
Shielding
Shielding
Shielding
Shielding
7
16
5
14
6
15
12
X1313
A112
Control module,
navigation
502ELE0367

On-board Computer
On-board monitor interface

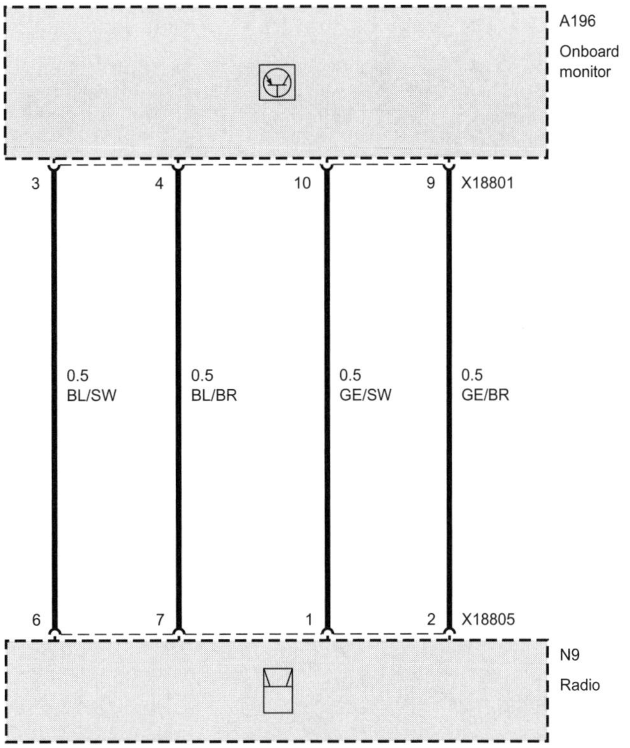

On-board Computer
Outside temperature display

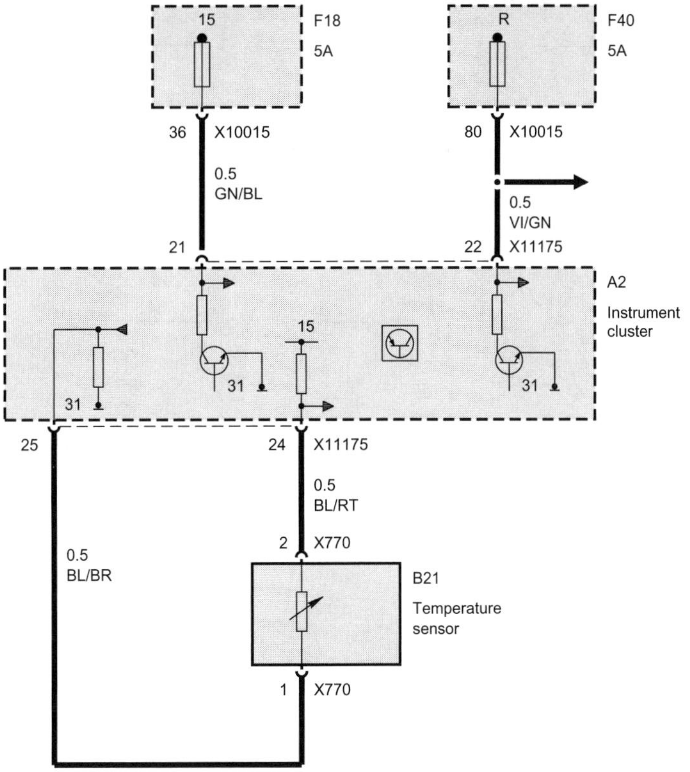

On-board Computer
Power, on-board monitor operating unit
(1 of 1)

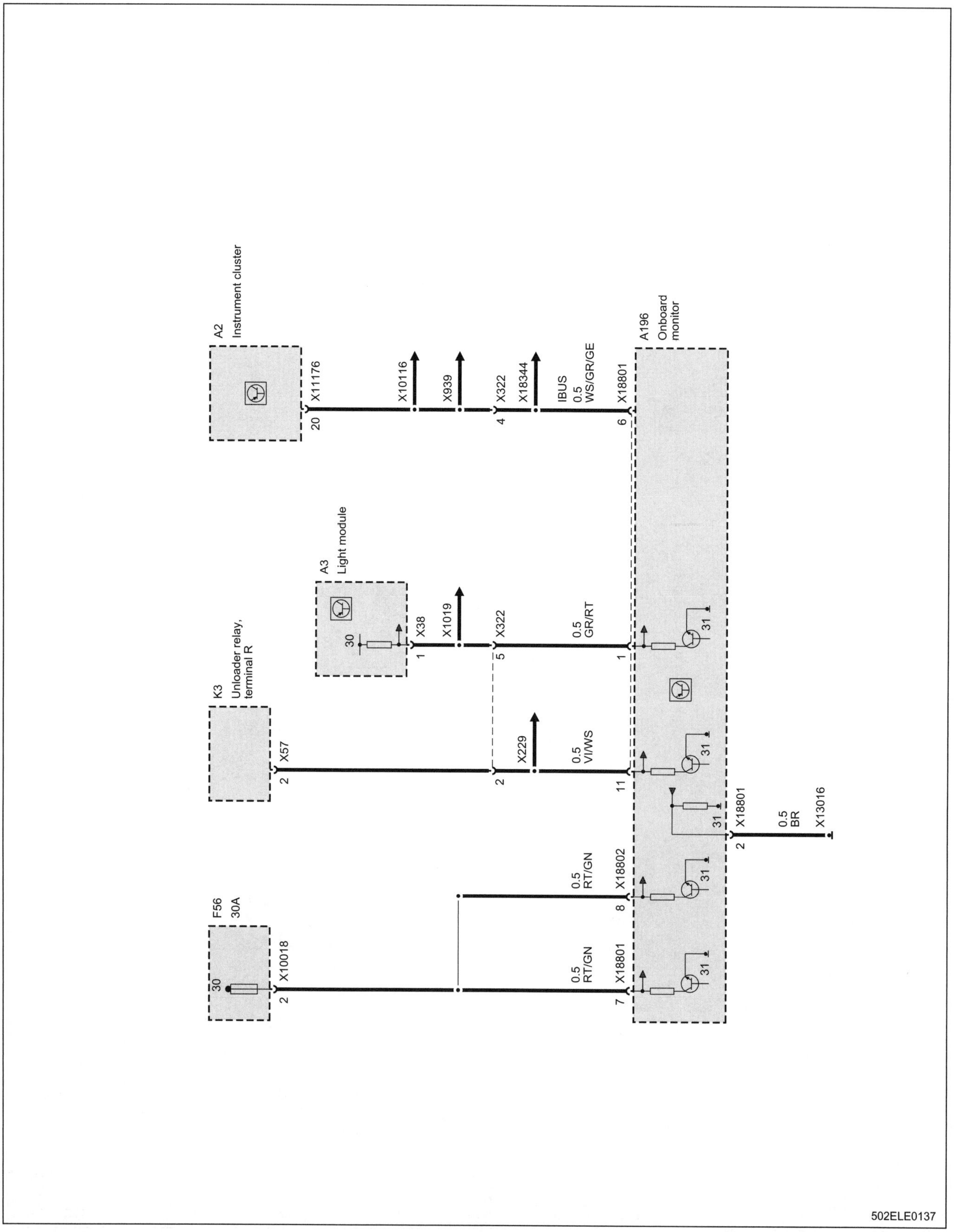

On-board Computer
Signal wire, on-board monitor operating unit
(1 of 1)

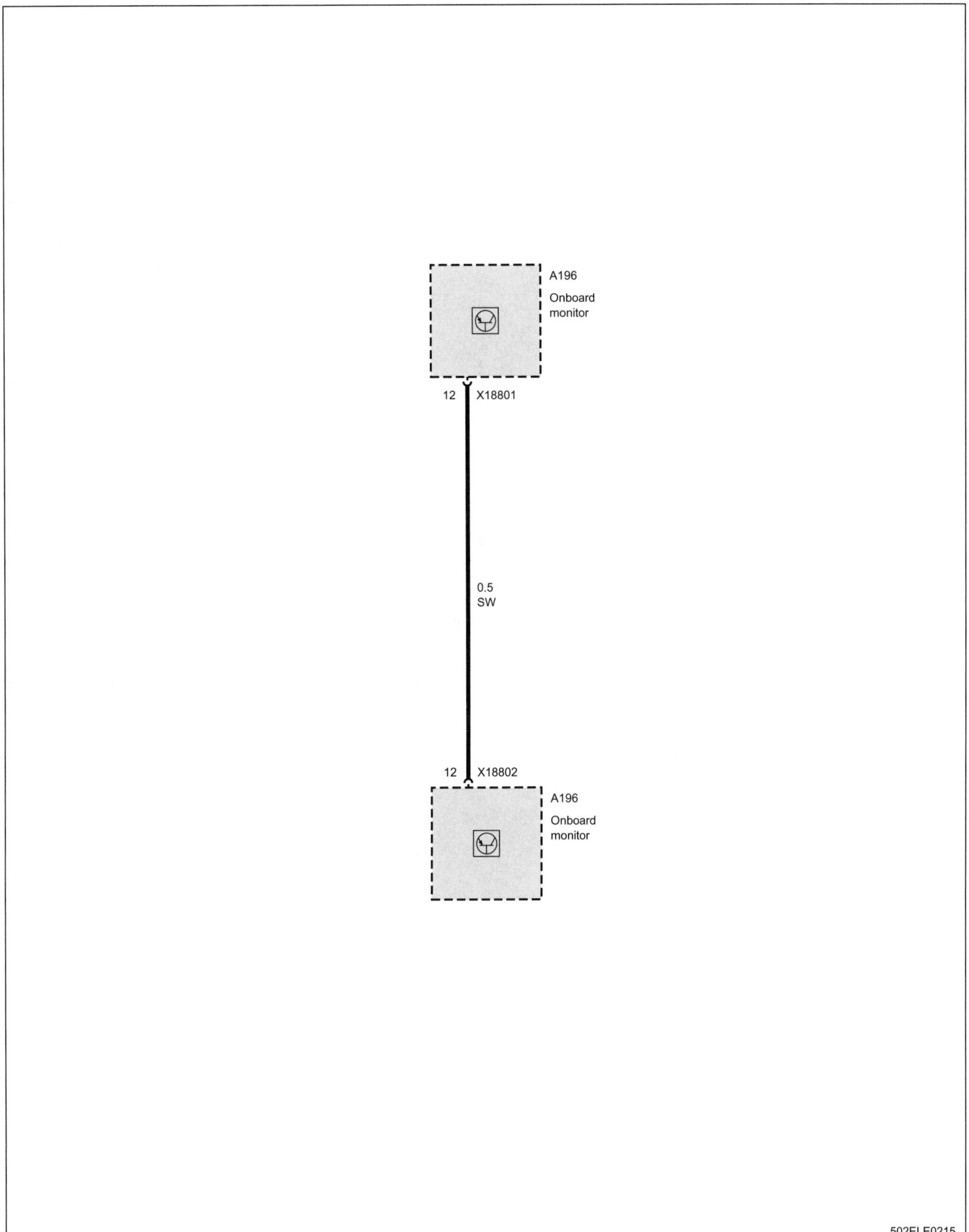

Park Distance Control
Park distance warning (overview)
(1 of 3)

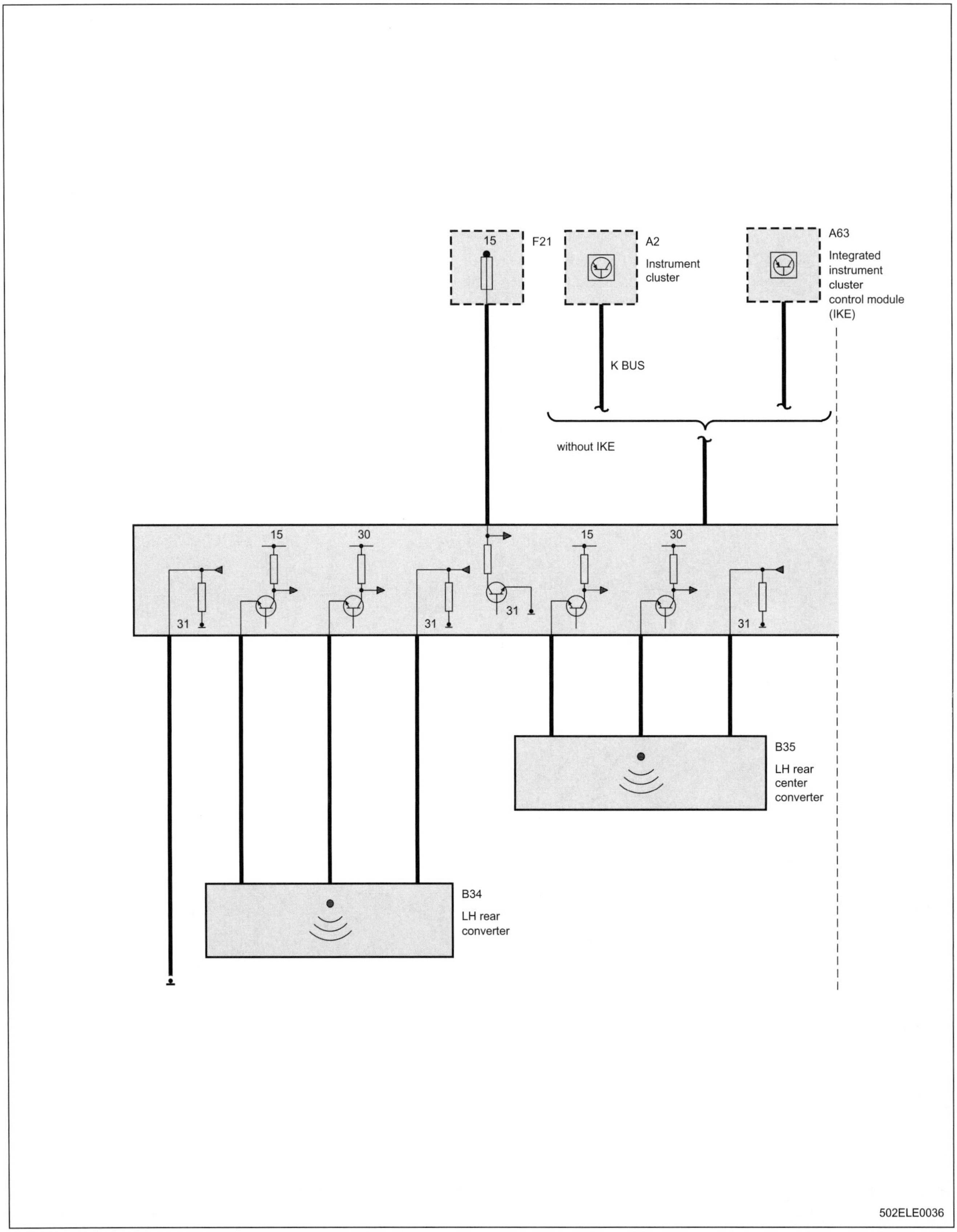

Park Distance Control
Park distance warning (overview)
(2 of 3)

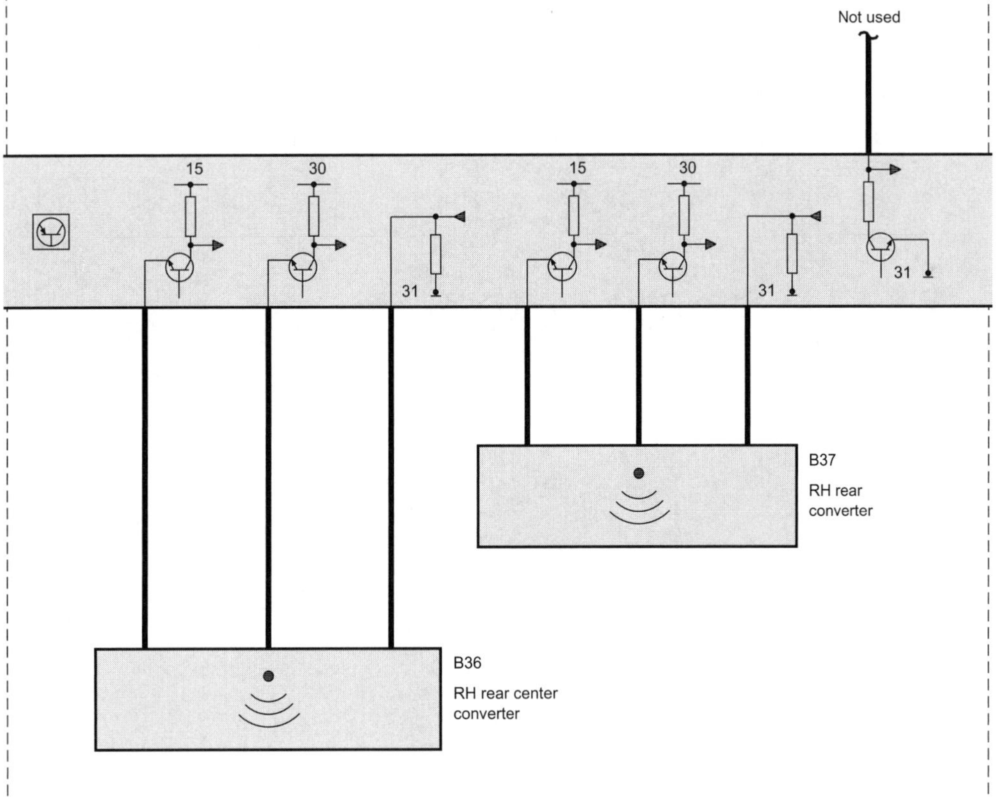

Park Distance Control
Park distance warning (overview)
(3 of 3)

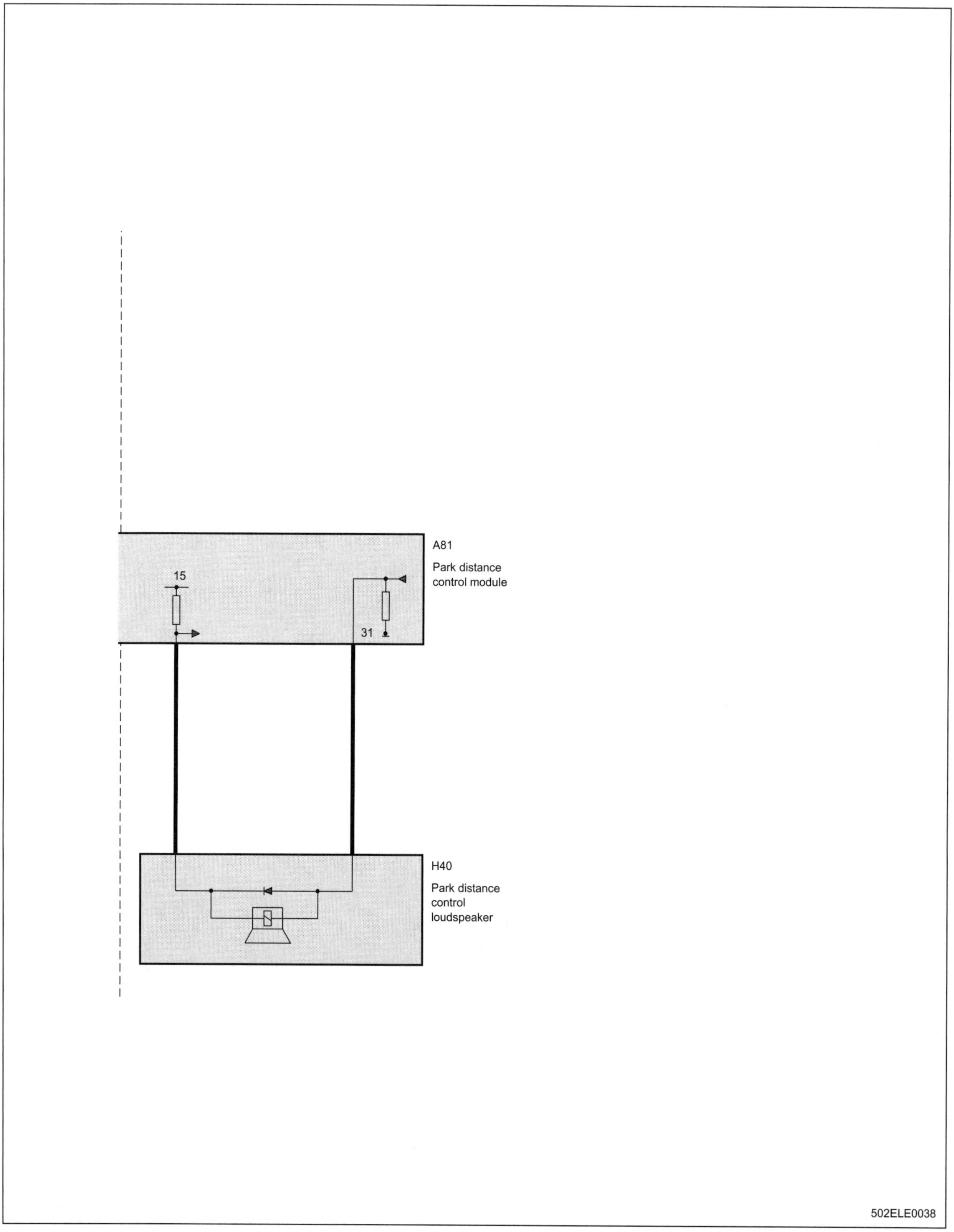

Park Distance Control
Park distance control module (A81)
(1 of 3)

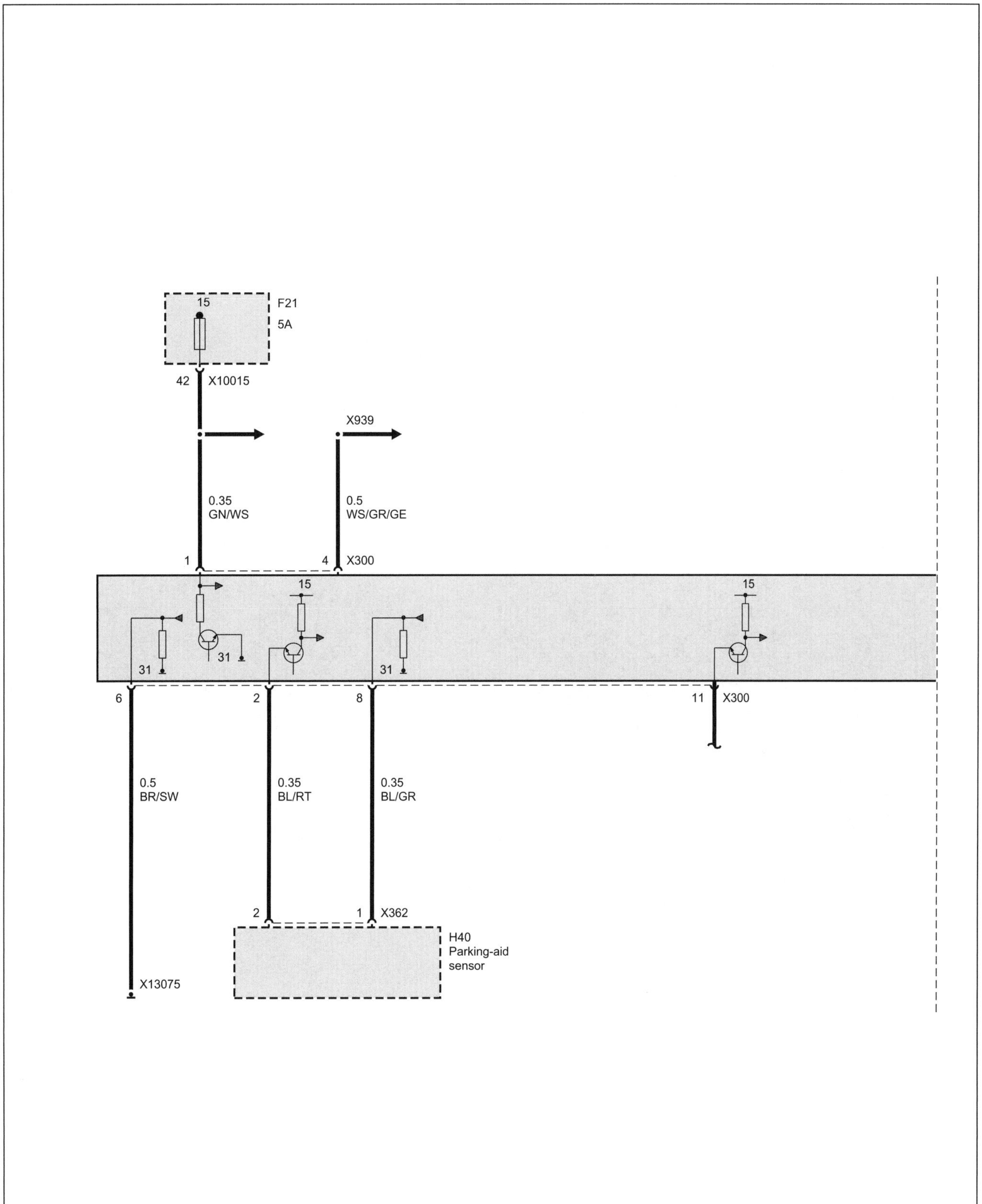

Park Distance Control
Park distance control module (A81)
(2 of 3)

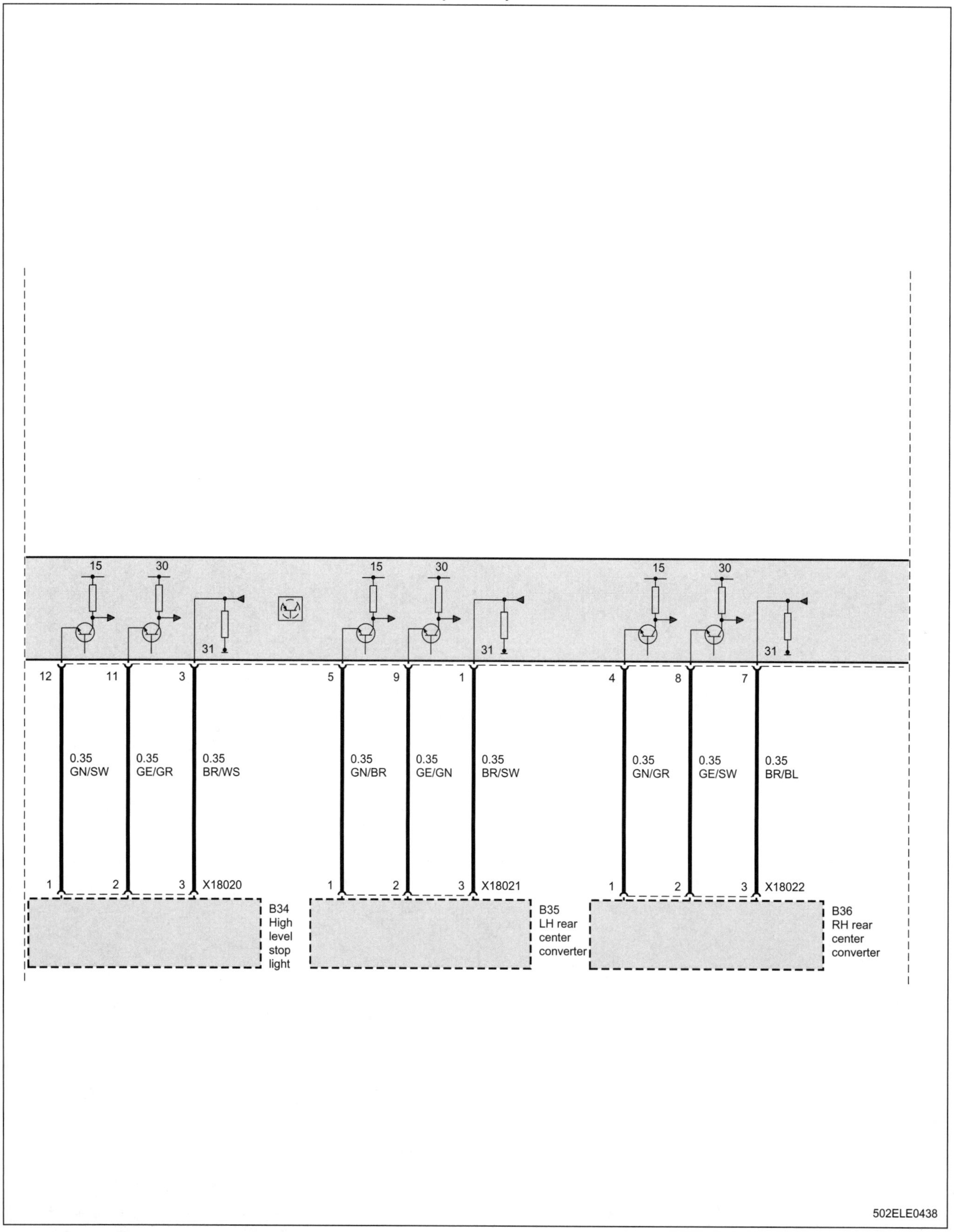

Park Distance Control
Park distance control module (A81)
(3 of 3)

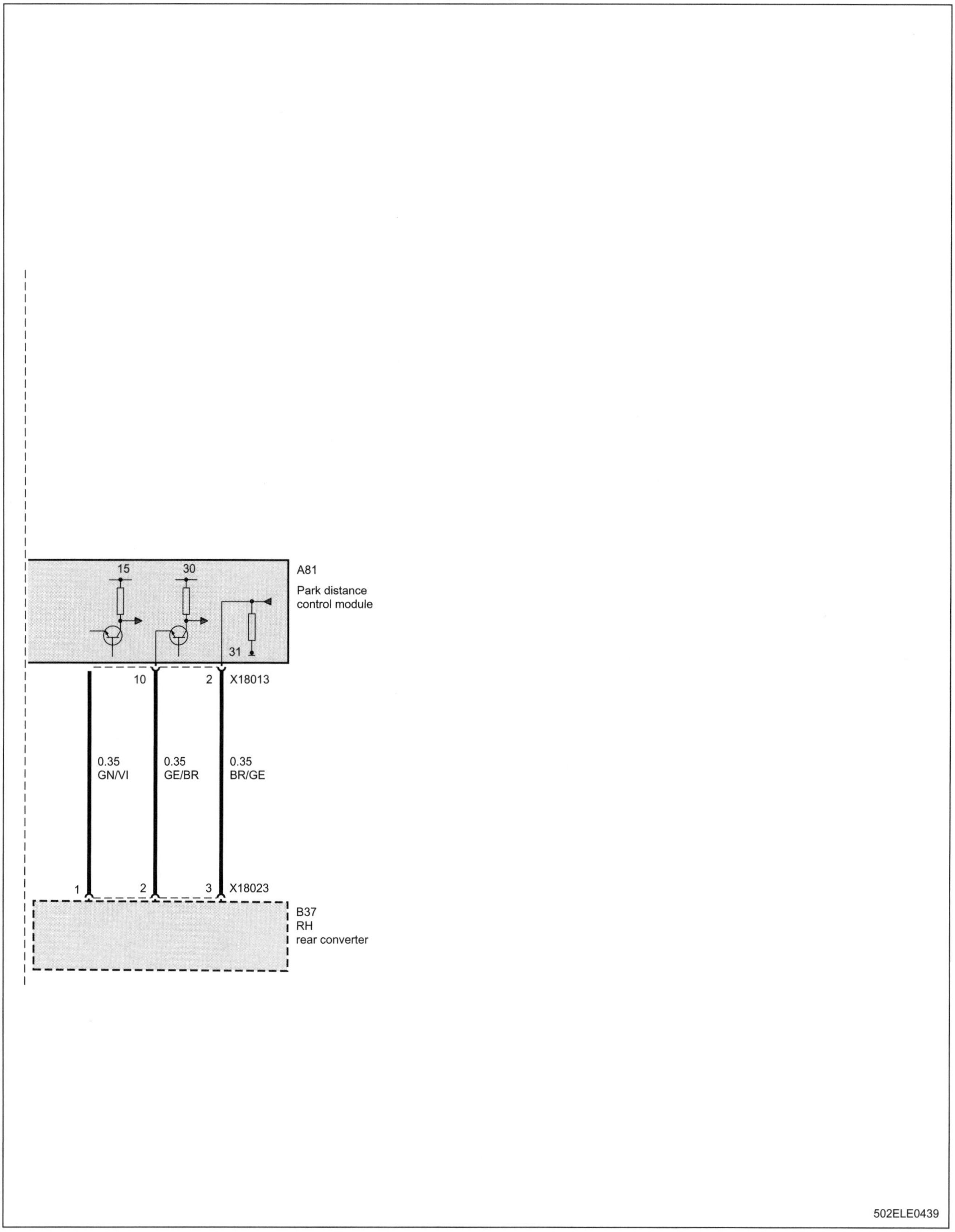

Park Distance Control
Park distance control module, power (A81)
(1 of 1)

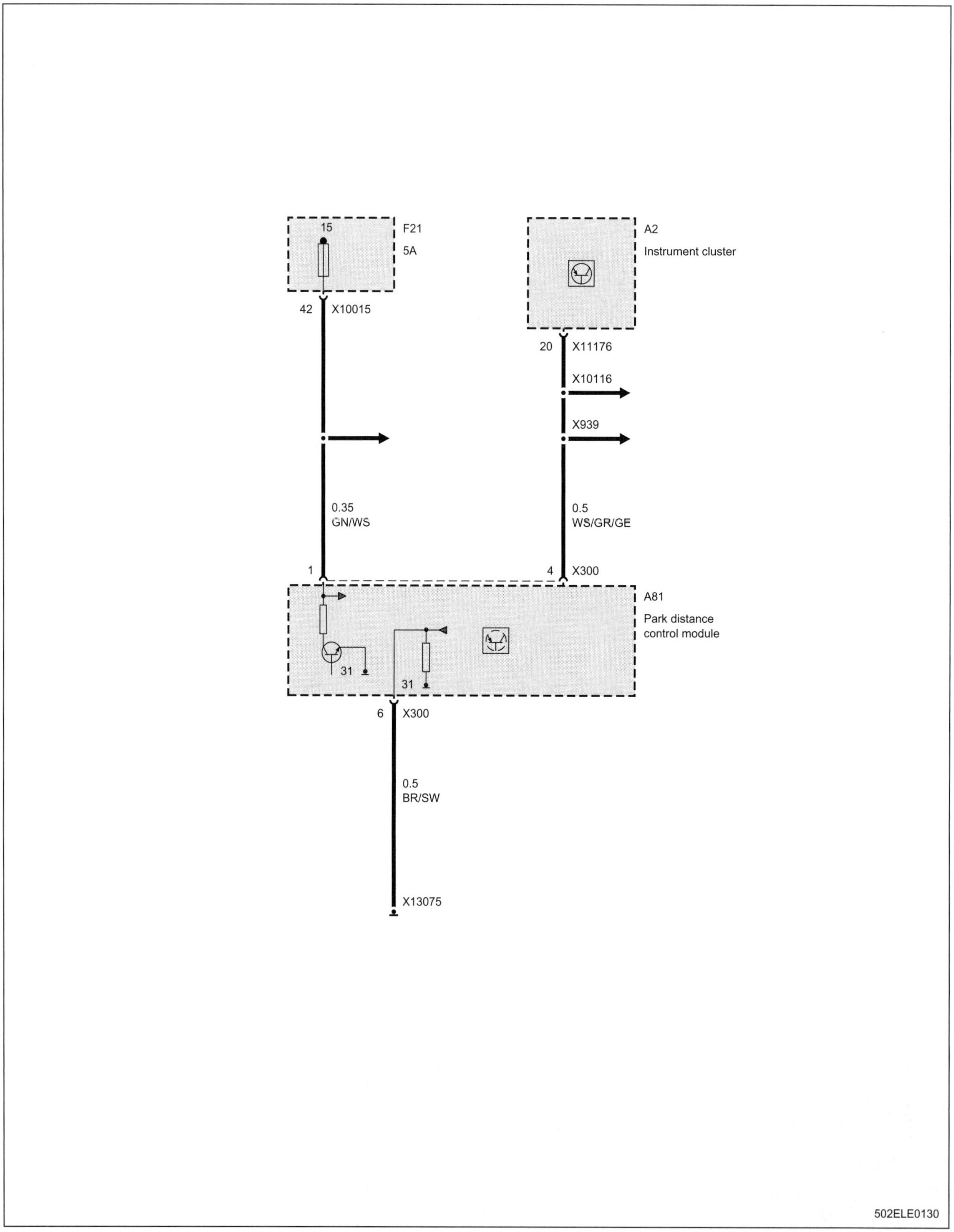

Park Distance Control
Back up signal
(1 of 1)

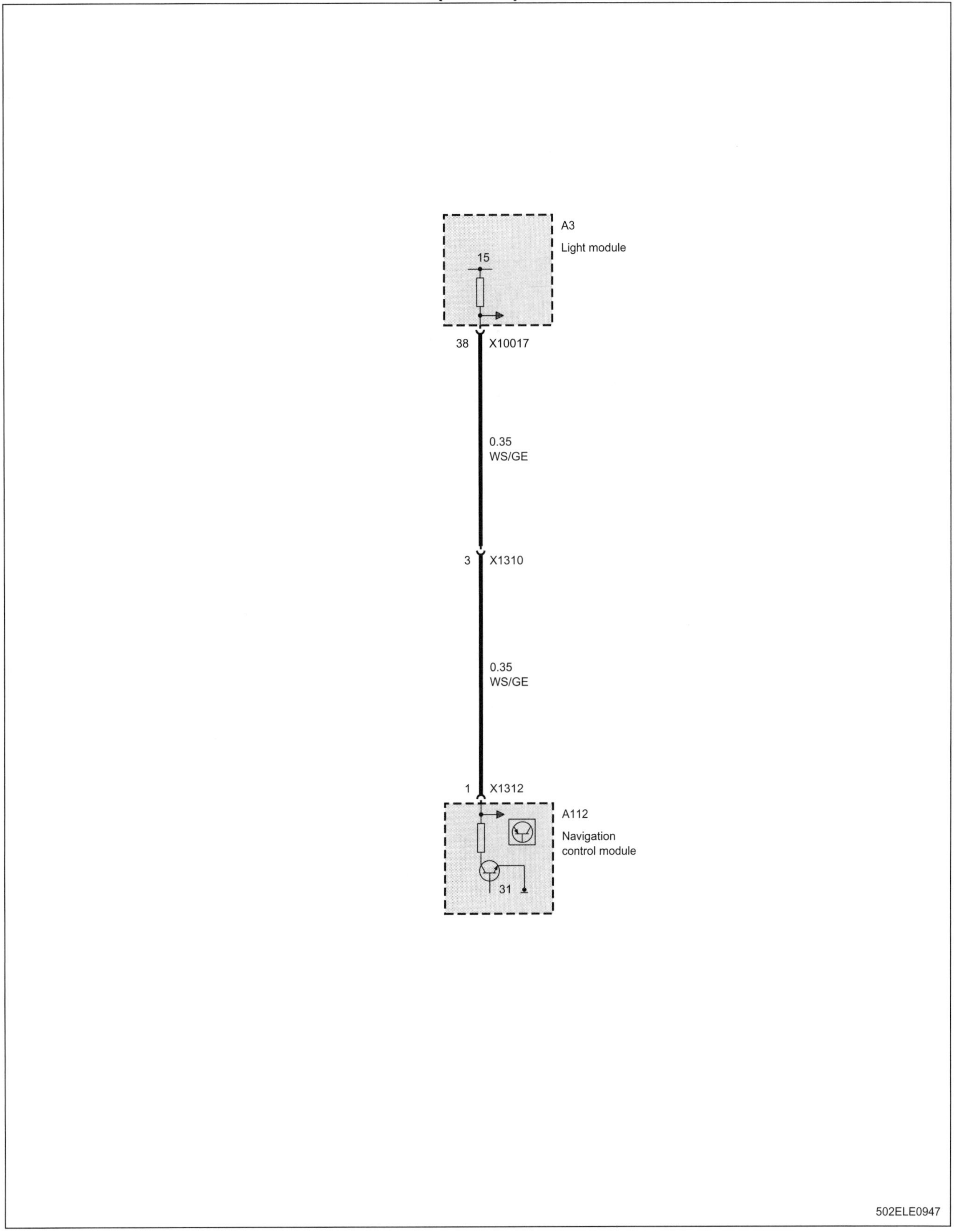

Park Distance Control Loudspeaker (H40)
(1 of 1)

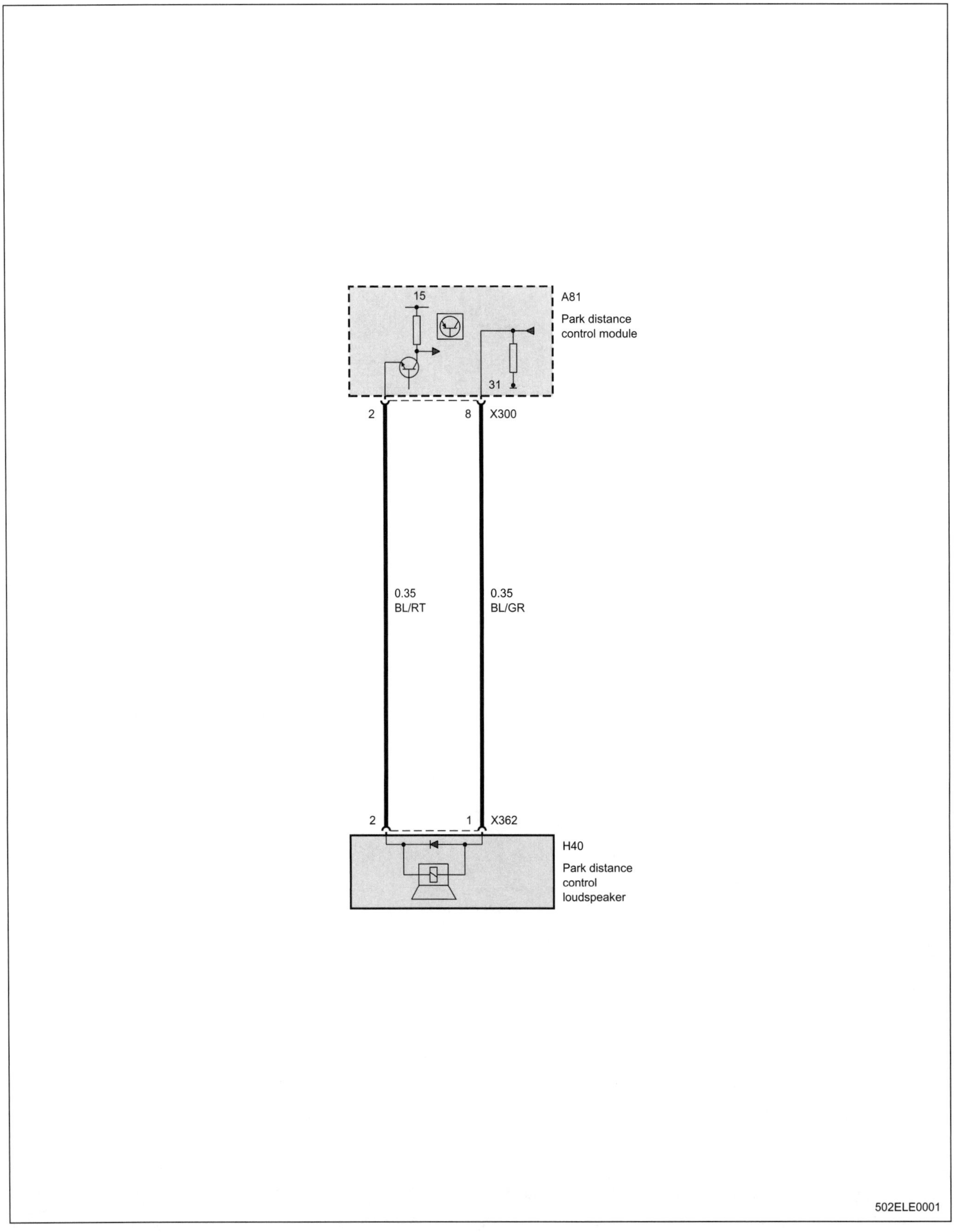
15
A81
Park distance
control module
31
2
8
X300
0.35
BL/RT
0.35
BL/GR
2
1
X362
H40
Park distance
control
loudspeaker
502ELE0001

Park Distance Control
PDC switch
(1 of 1)

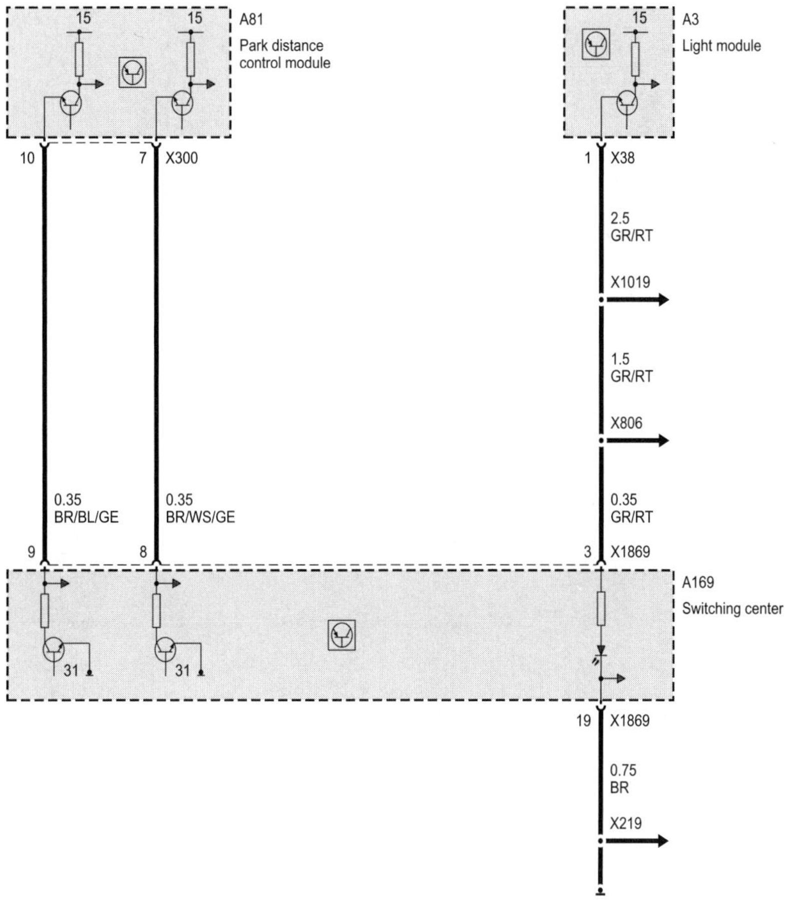

502ELE0129

Park Distance Control
Rear ultrasonic converter
(1 of 1)

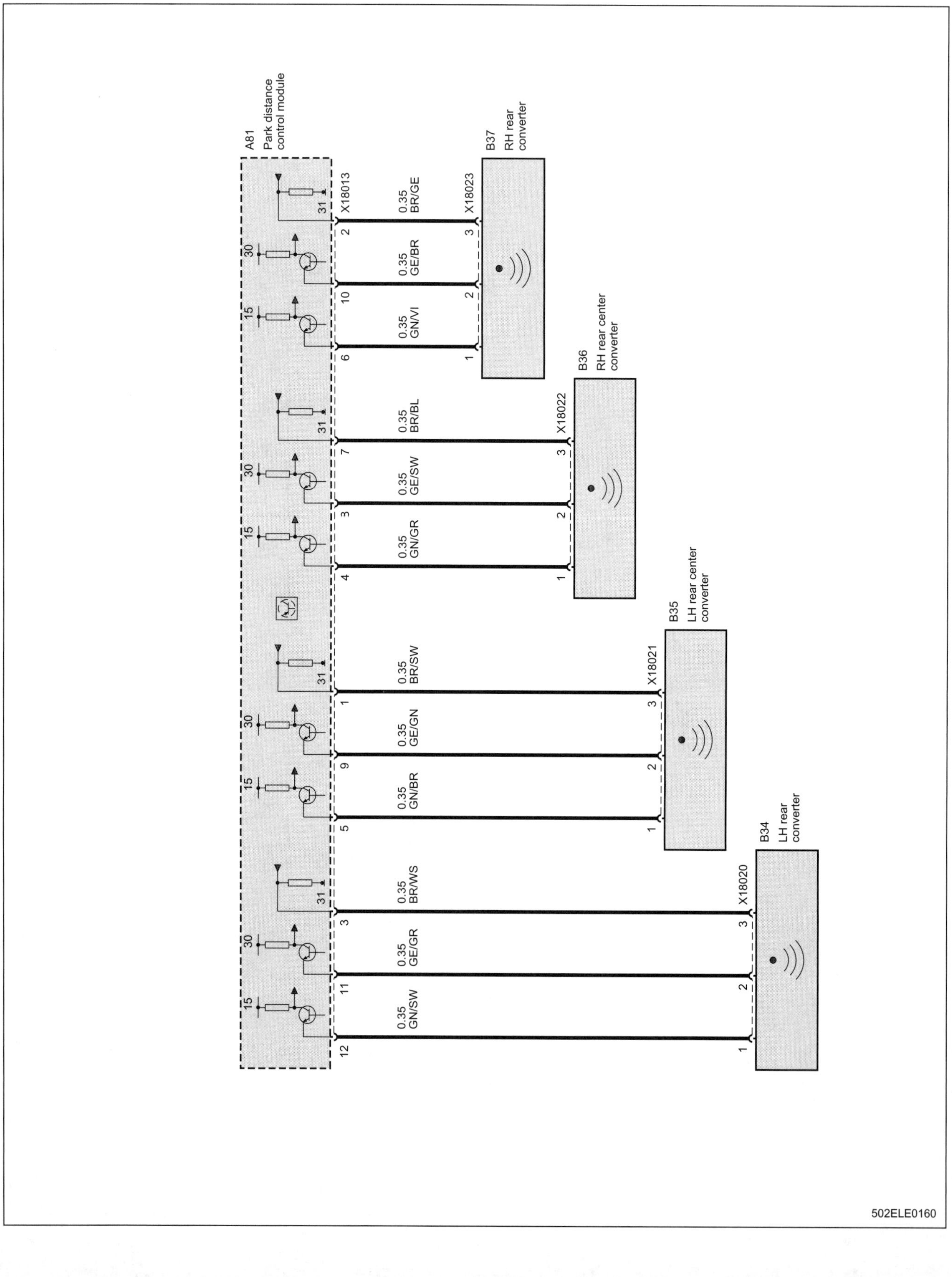

502ELE0160

Power Distribution
Voltage and power control (overview)
(1 of 1)

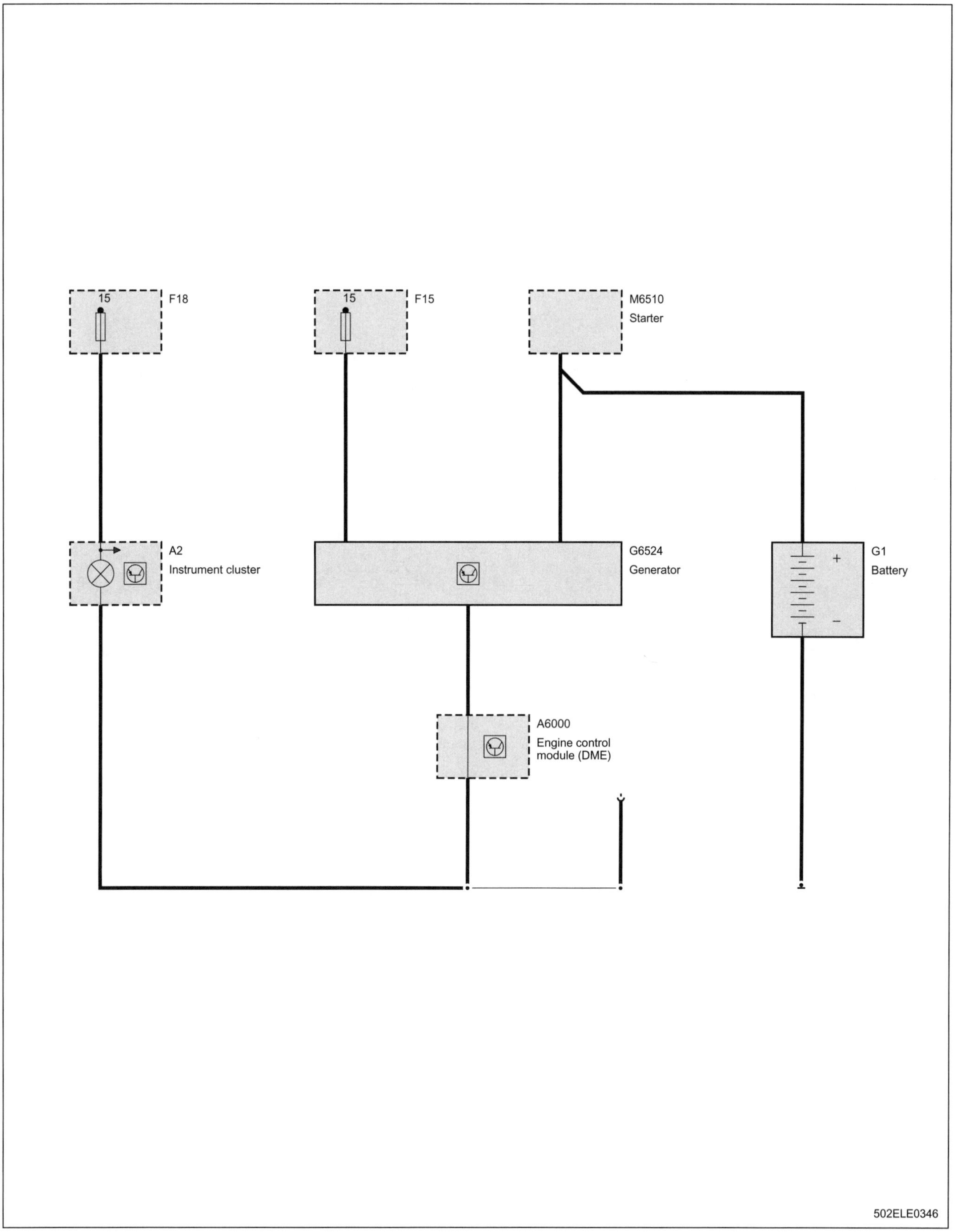

Power Distribution
Unloader relay, terminal 15 (K93)
(1 of 1)

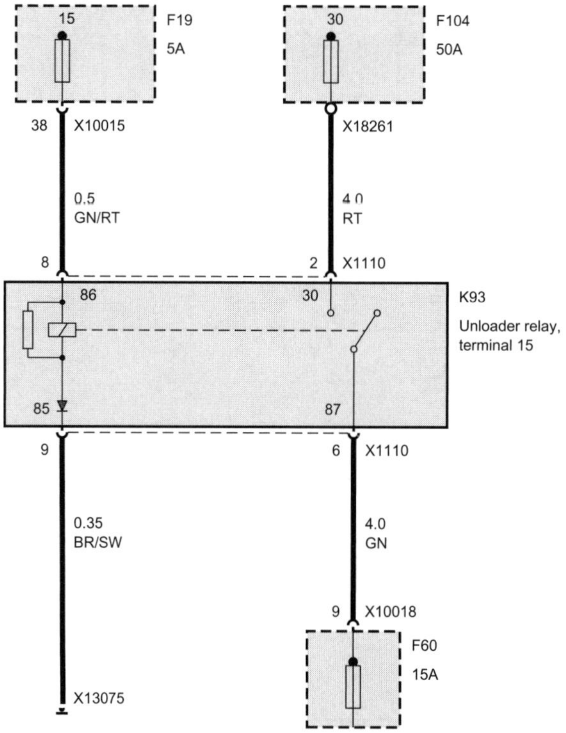

502ELE0561

Power Distribution
Battery (G1)
(1 of 1)

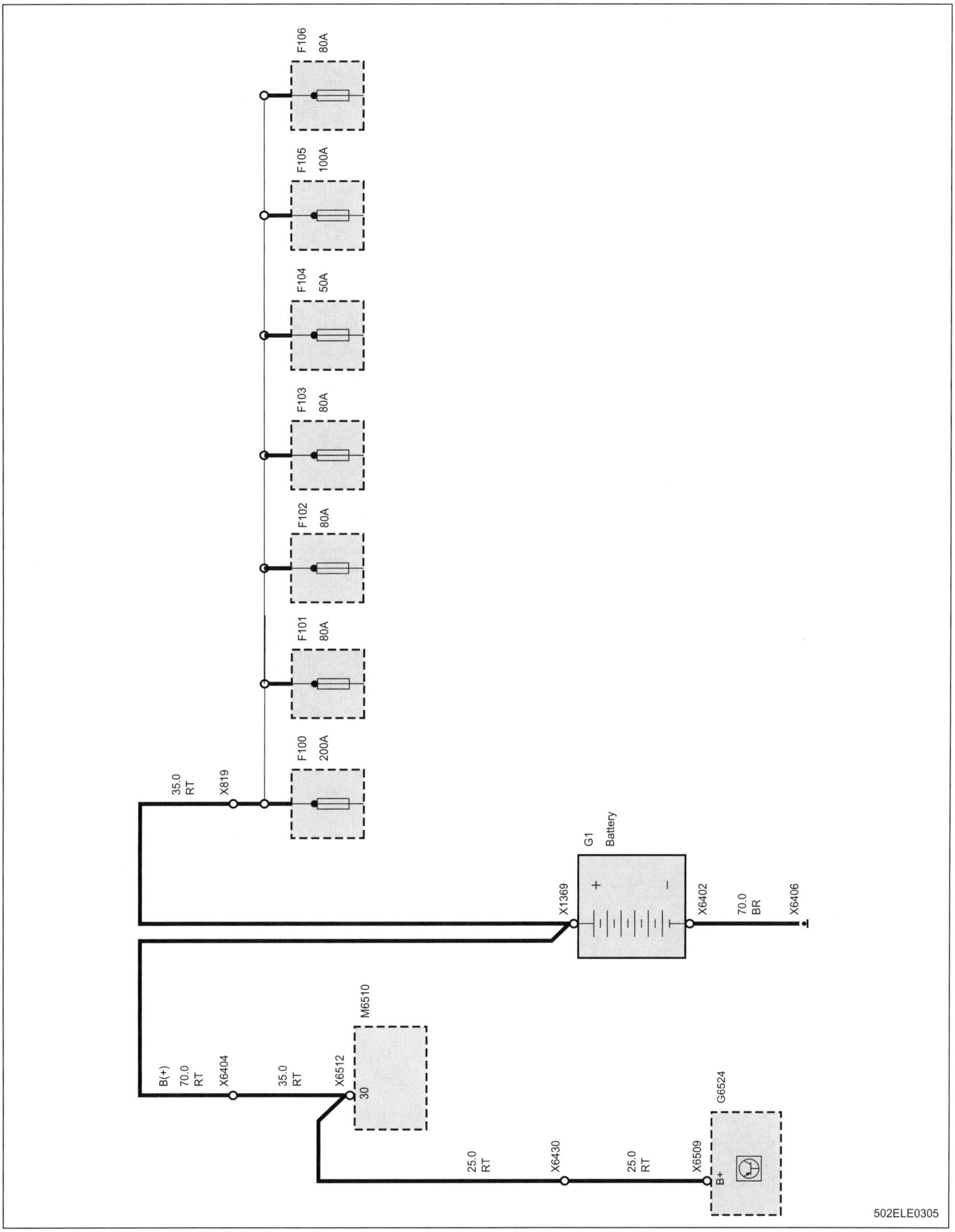
F106
80A
F105
100A
F104
50A
F103
80A
F102
80A
F101
80A
F100
200A
35.0
RT
X819
G1
Battery
X1369
X6402
70.0
BR
X6406
M6510
B(+)
70.0
RT
X6404
35.0
RT
X6512
30
G6524
25.0
RT
X6430
25.0
RT
X6509
B+
502ELE0305

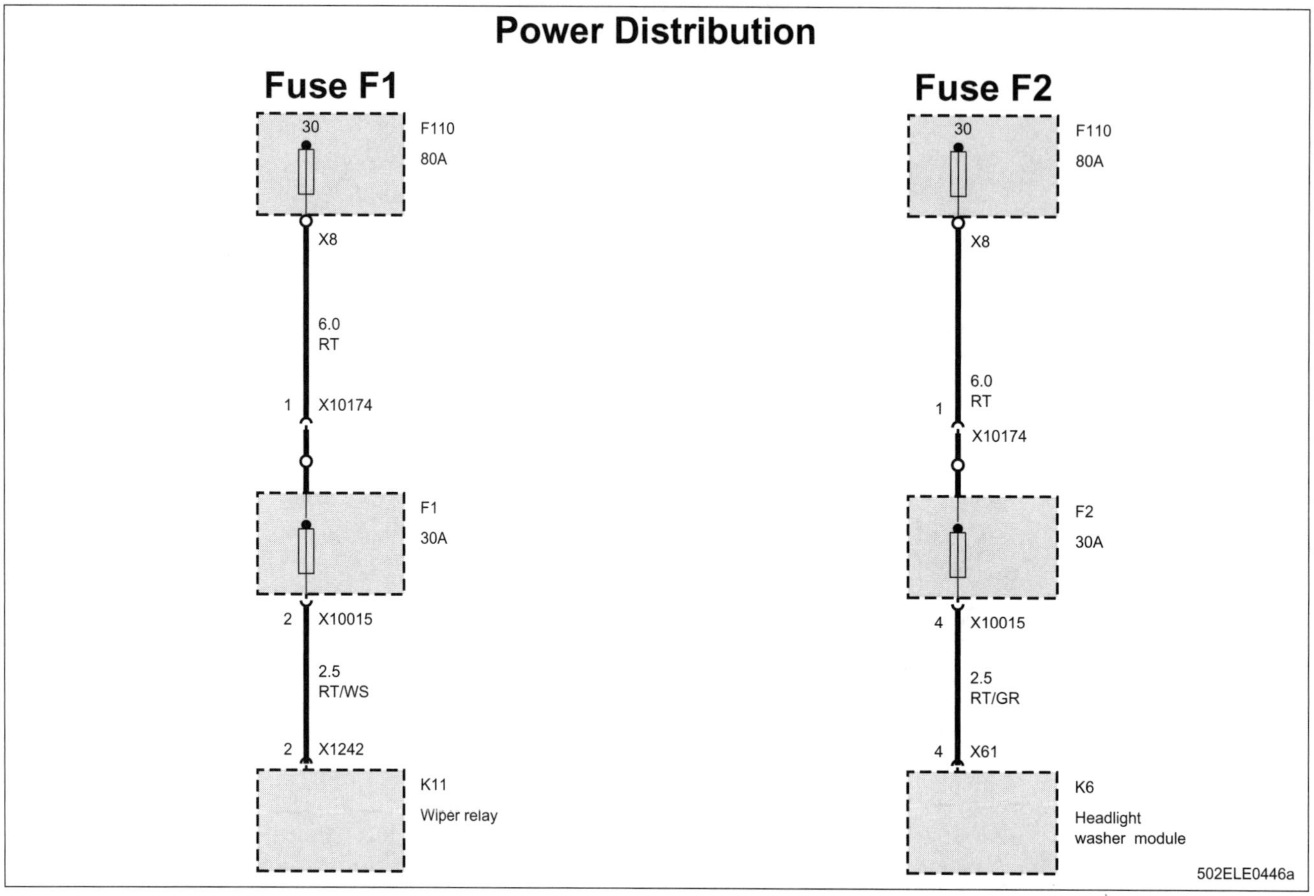
Power Distribution
Fuse F1
30
F110
80A
X8
6.0
RT
1
X10174
F1
30A
2
X10015
2.5
RT/WS
2
X1242
K11
Wiper relay
Fuse F2
30
F110
80A
X8
6.0
RT
1
X10174
F2
30A
4
X10015
2.5
RT/GR
4
X61
K6
Headlight
washer module
502ELE0446a

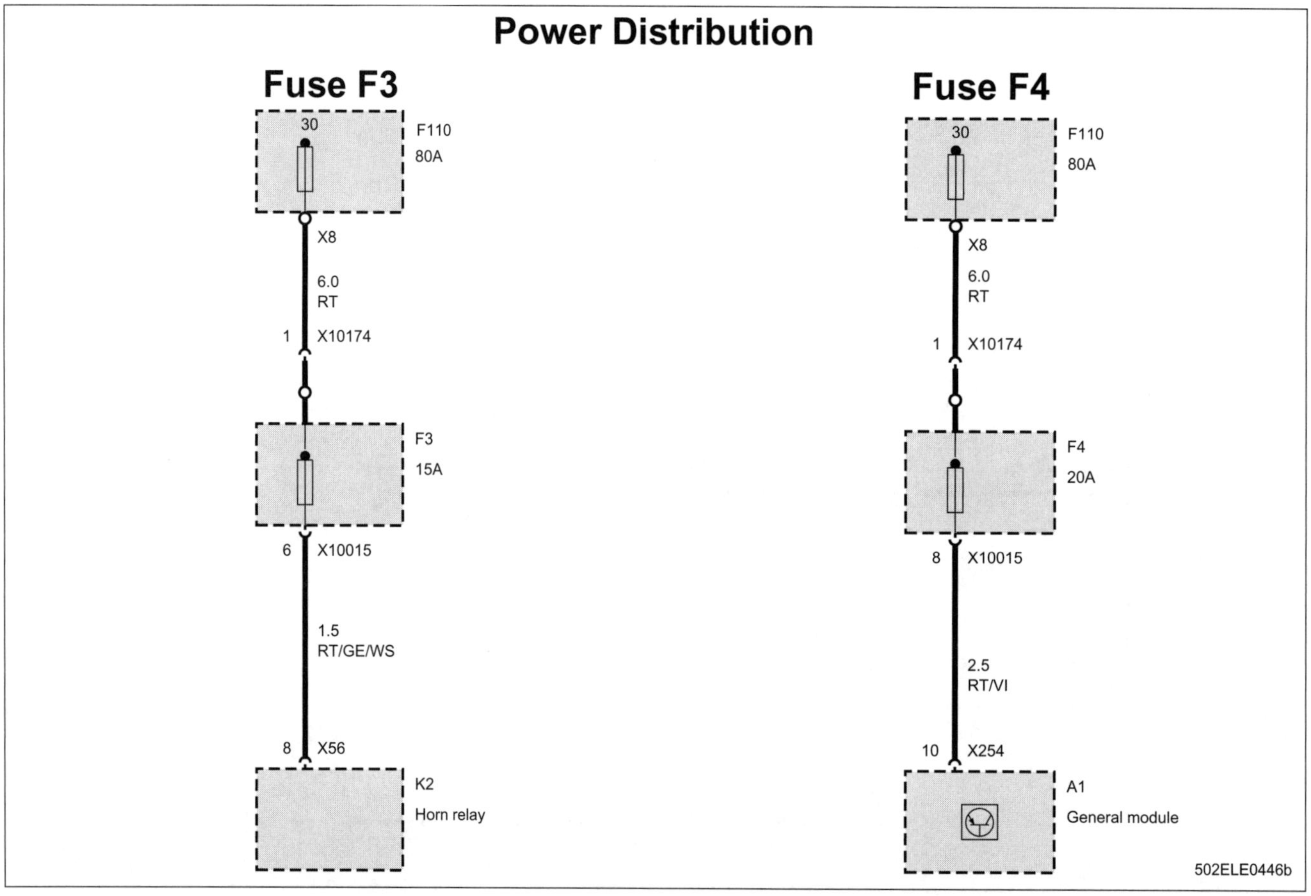
Power Distribution
Fuse F3
30
F110
80A
X8
6.0
RT
1
X10174
F3
15A
6
X10015
1.5
RT/GE/WS
8
X56
K2
Horn relay
Fuse F4
30
F110
80A
X8
6.0
RT
1
X10174
F4
20A
8
X10015
2.5
RT/VI
10
X254
A1
General module
502ELE0446b

Power Distribution

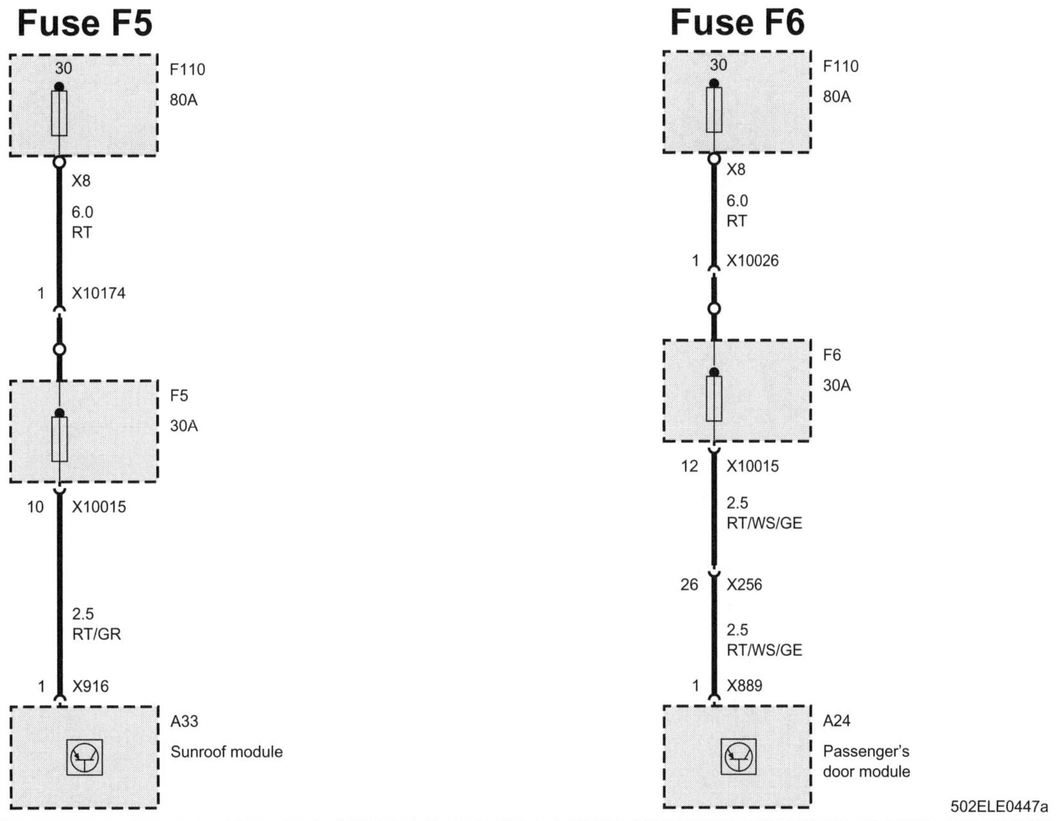

Power Distribution

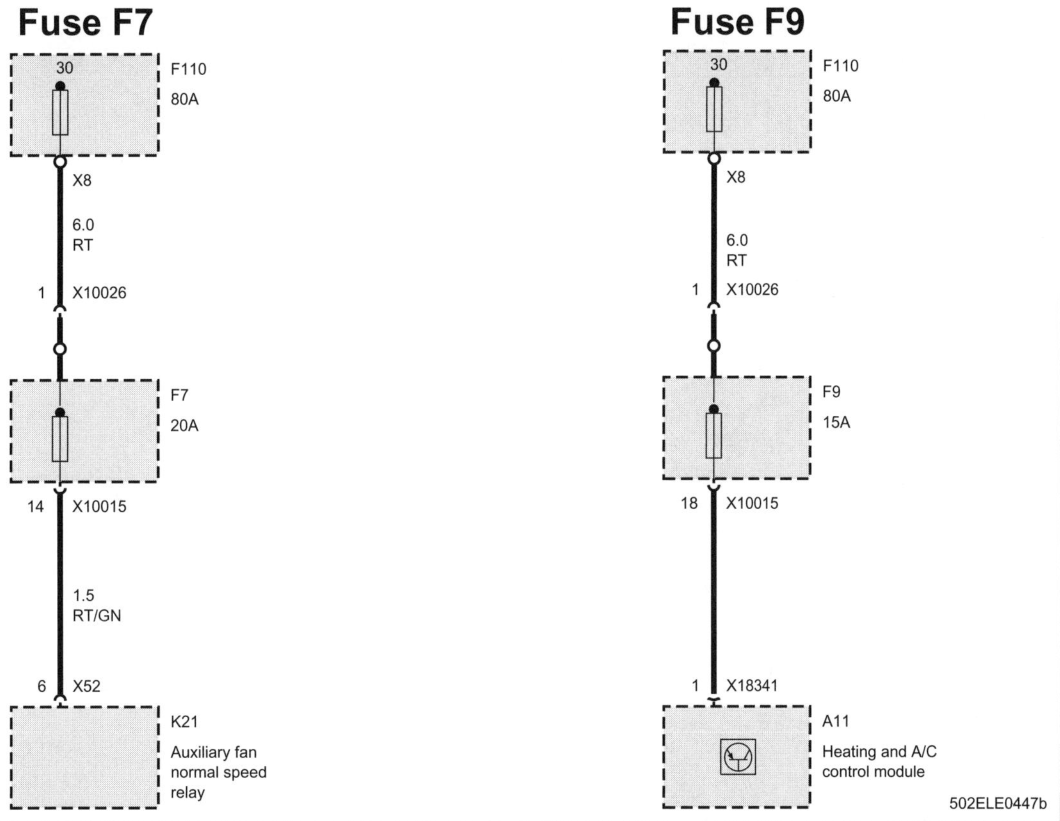

Power Distribution
Fuse F10

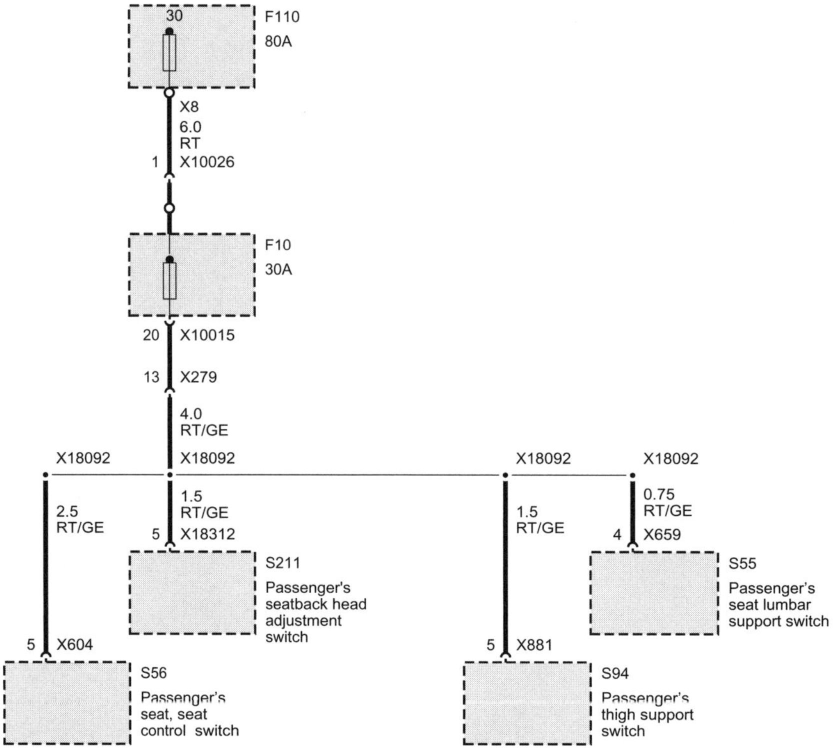

502ELE0448a

Power Distribution

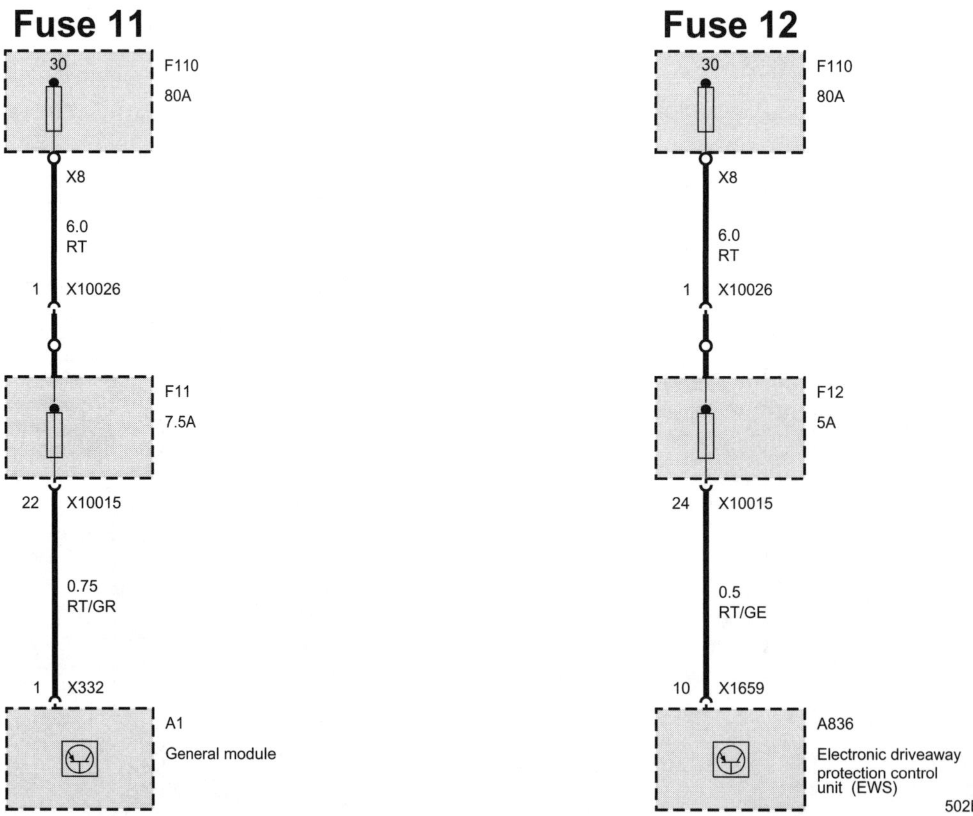

502ELE0448b

Power Distribution
Fuse F13
(1 of 3)

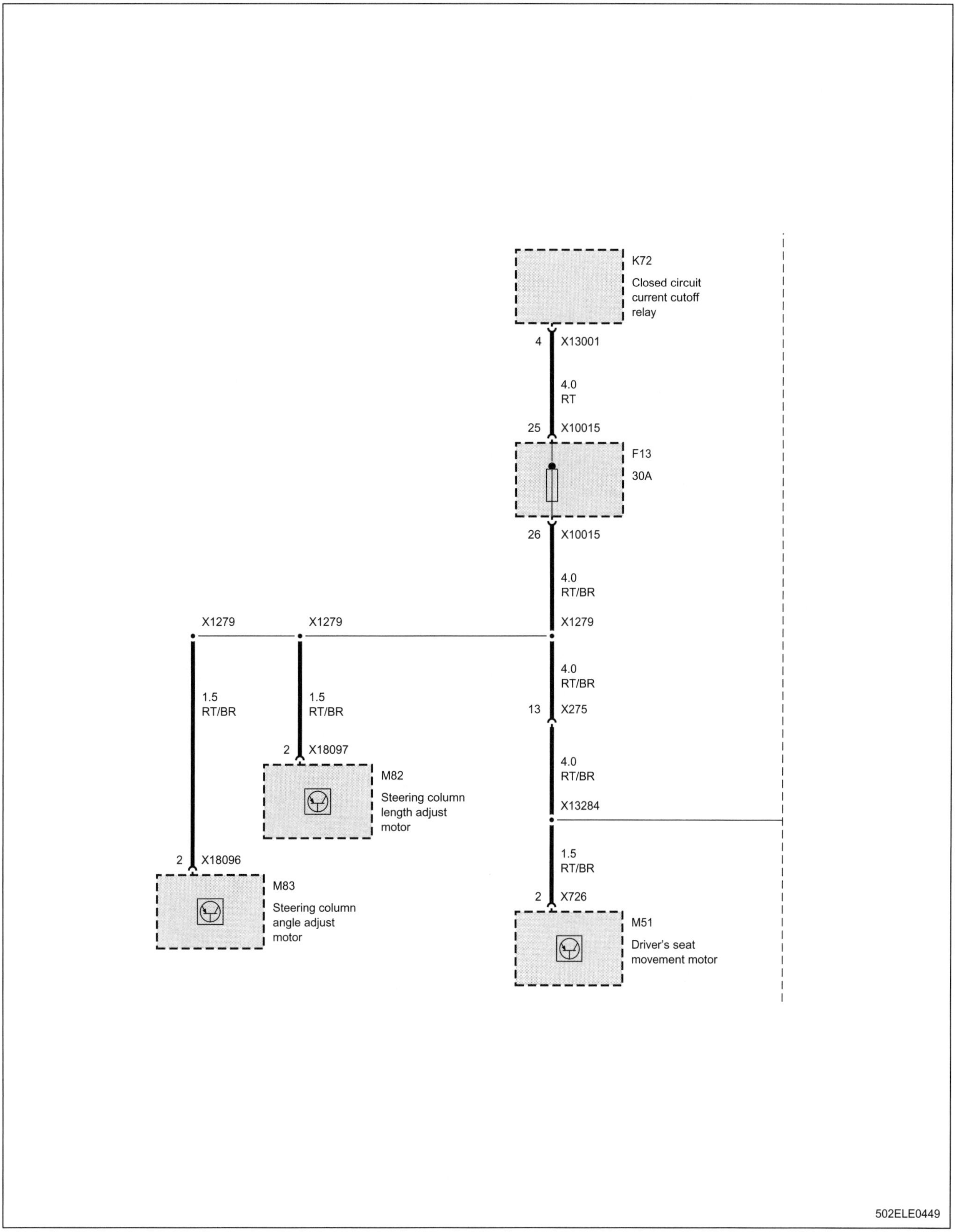
K72
Closed circuit current cutoff relay
4
X13001
4.0
RT
25
X10015
F13
30A
26
X10015
4.0
RT/BR
X1279
X1279
X1279
1.5
RT/BR
1.5
RT/BR
4.0
RT/BR
13
X275
2
X18097
M82
Steering column length adjust motor
4.0
RT/BR
X13284
2
X18096
M83
Steering column angle adjust motor
1.5
RT/BR
2
X726
M51
Driver's seat movement motor
502ELE0449

Power Distribution
Fuse F13
(2 of 3)

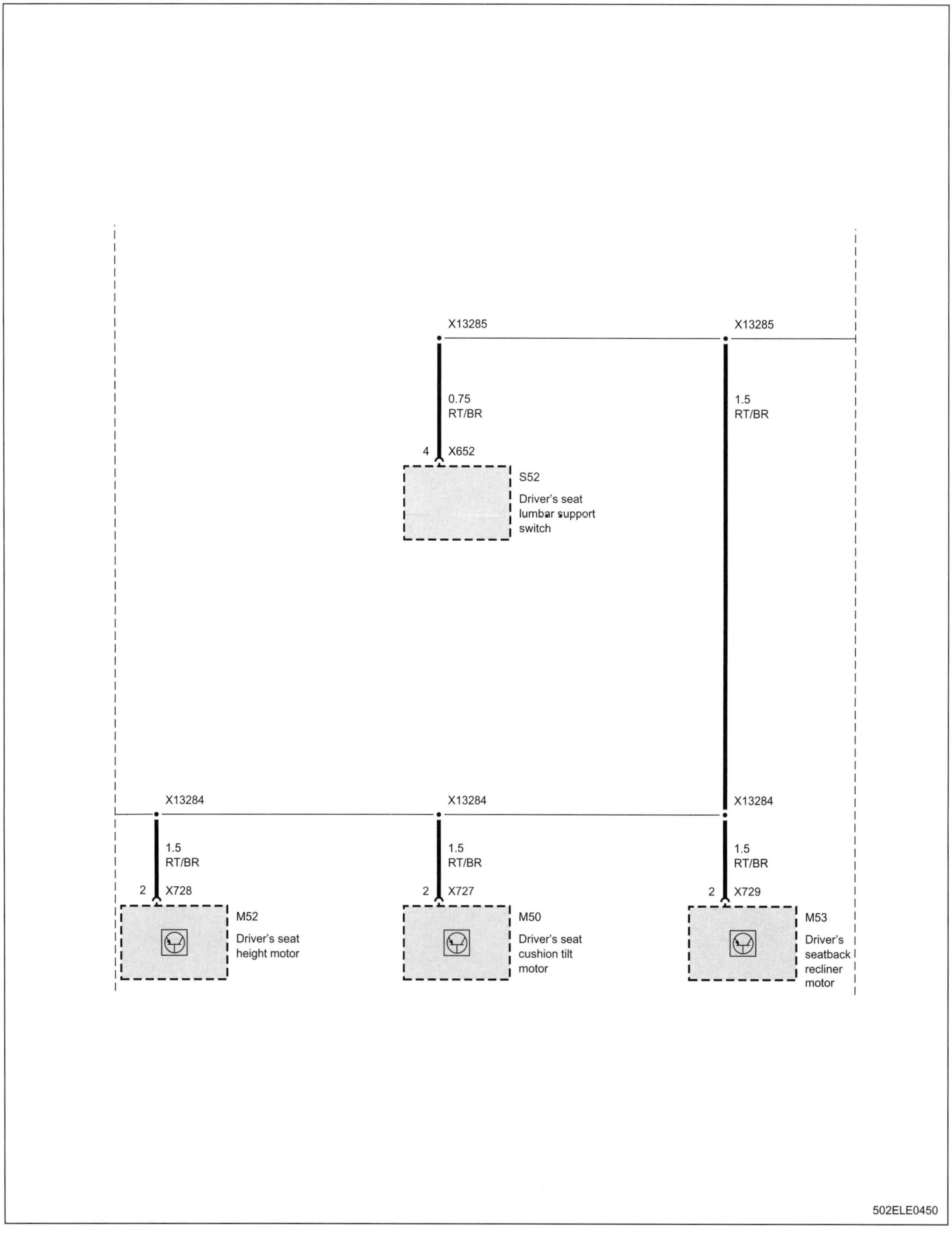
X13285
X13285
0.75
RT/BR
1.5
RT/BR
4
X652
S52
Driver's seat lumbar support switch
X13284
X13284
X13284
1.5
RT/BR
1.5
RT/BR
1.5
RT/BR
2
X728
2
X727
2
X729
M52
Driver's seat height motor
M50
Driver's seat cushion tilt motor
M53
Driver's seatback recliner motor
502ELE0450

Power Distribution
Fuse F13
(3 of 3)

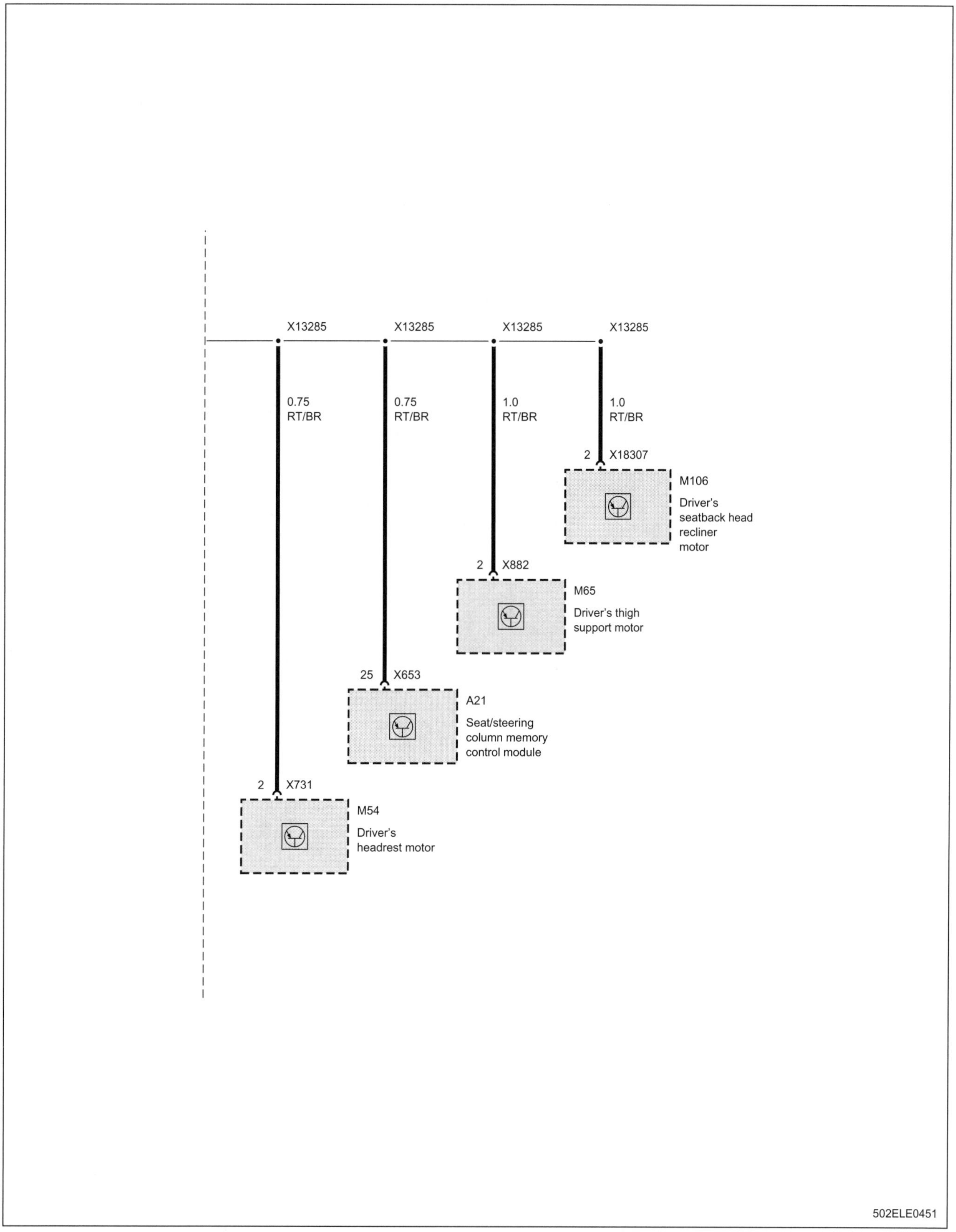
X13285
X13285
X13285
X13285
0.75
RT/BR
0.75
RT/BR
1.0
RT/BR
1.0
RT/BR
2
X18307
M106
Driver's seatback head recliner motor
2
X882
M65
Driver's thigh support motor
25
X653
A21
Seat/steering column memory control module
2
X731
M54
Driver's headrest motor
502ELE0451

Power Distribution
Fuse F14
(1 of 1)

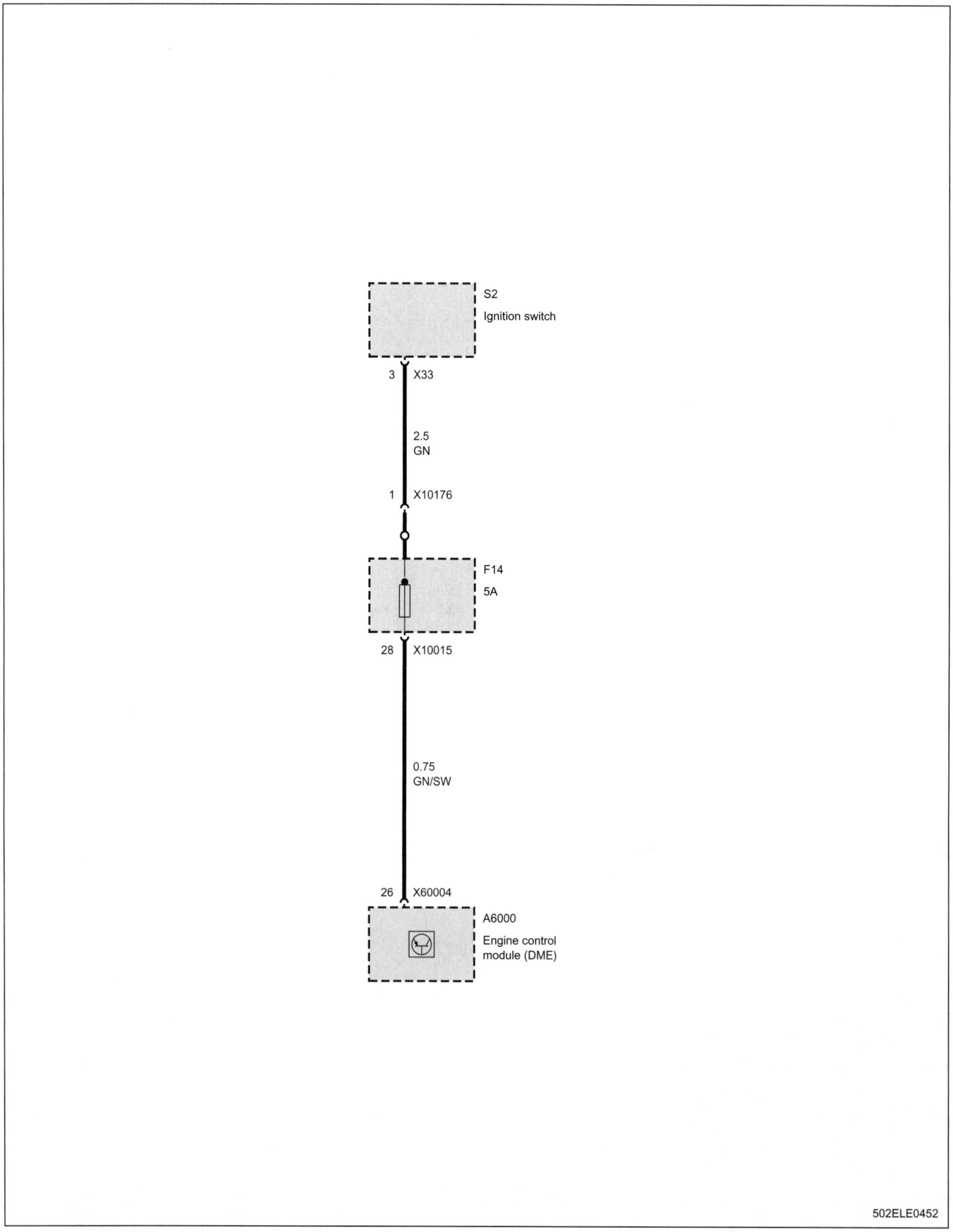
S2
Ignition switch
3
X33
2.5
GN
1
X10176
F14
5A
28
X10015
0.75
GN/SW
26
X60004
A6000
Engine control
module (DME)
502ELE0452

Power Distribution
Fuse F15
(1 of 1)

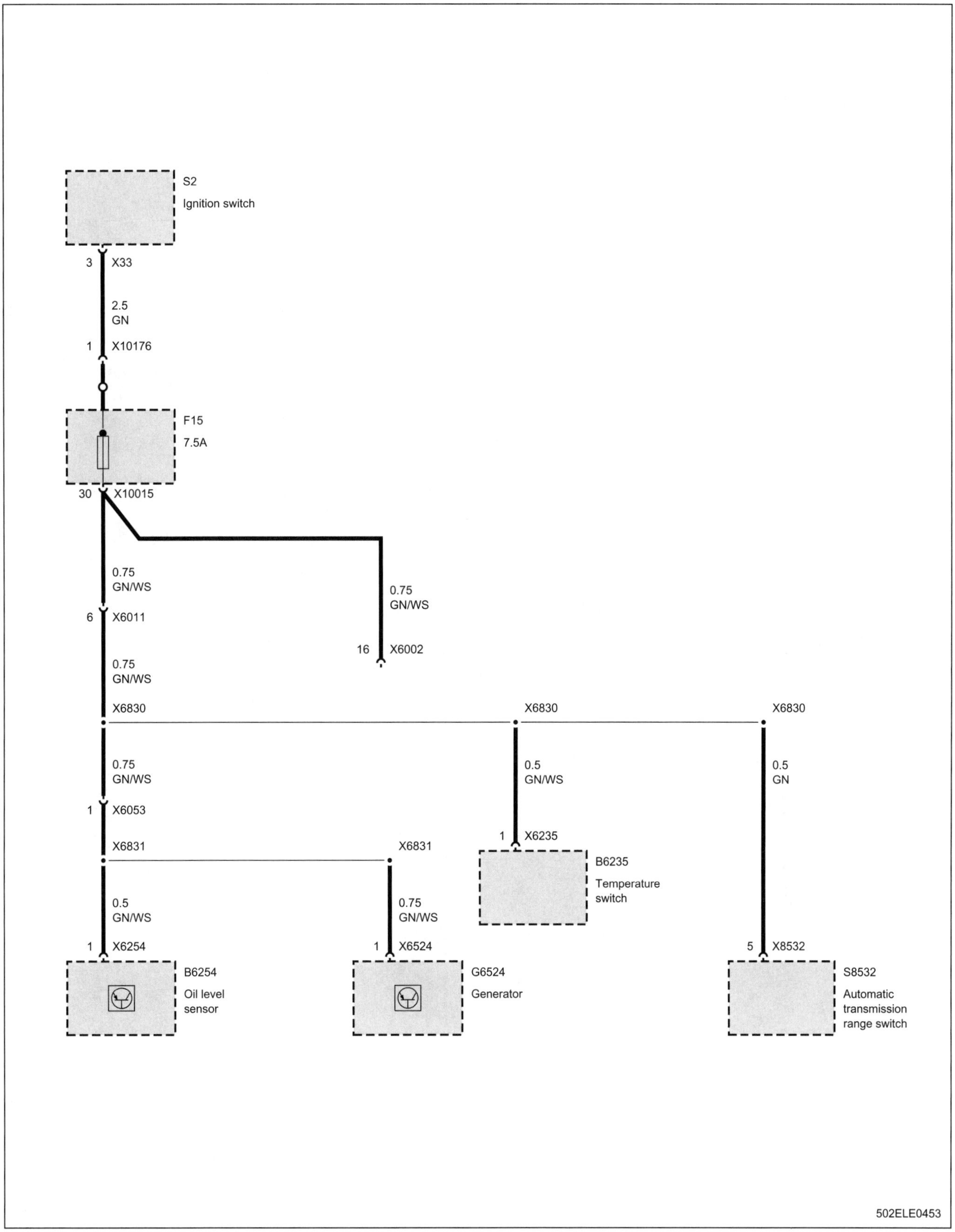
S2
Ignition switch
3 X33
2.5
GN
1 X10176
F15
7.5A
30 X10015
0.75
GN/WS
6 X6011
0.75
GN/WS
16 X6002
0.75
GN/WS
X6830
X6830
X6830
0.75
GN/WS
0.5
GN/WS
0.5
GN
1 X6053
X6831
X6831
1 X6235
B6235
Temperature
switch
0.5
GN/WS
0.75
GN/WS
1 X6254
1 X6524
5 X8532
B6254
Oil level
sensor
G6524
Generator
S8532
Automatic
transmission
range switch
502ELE0453

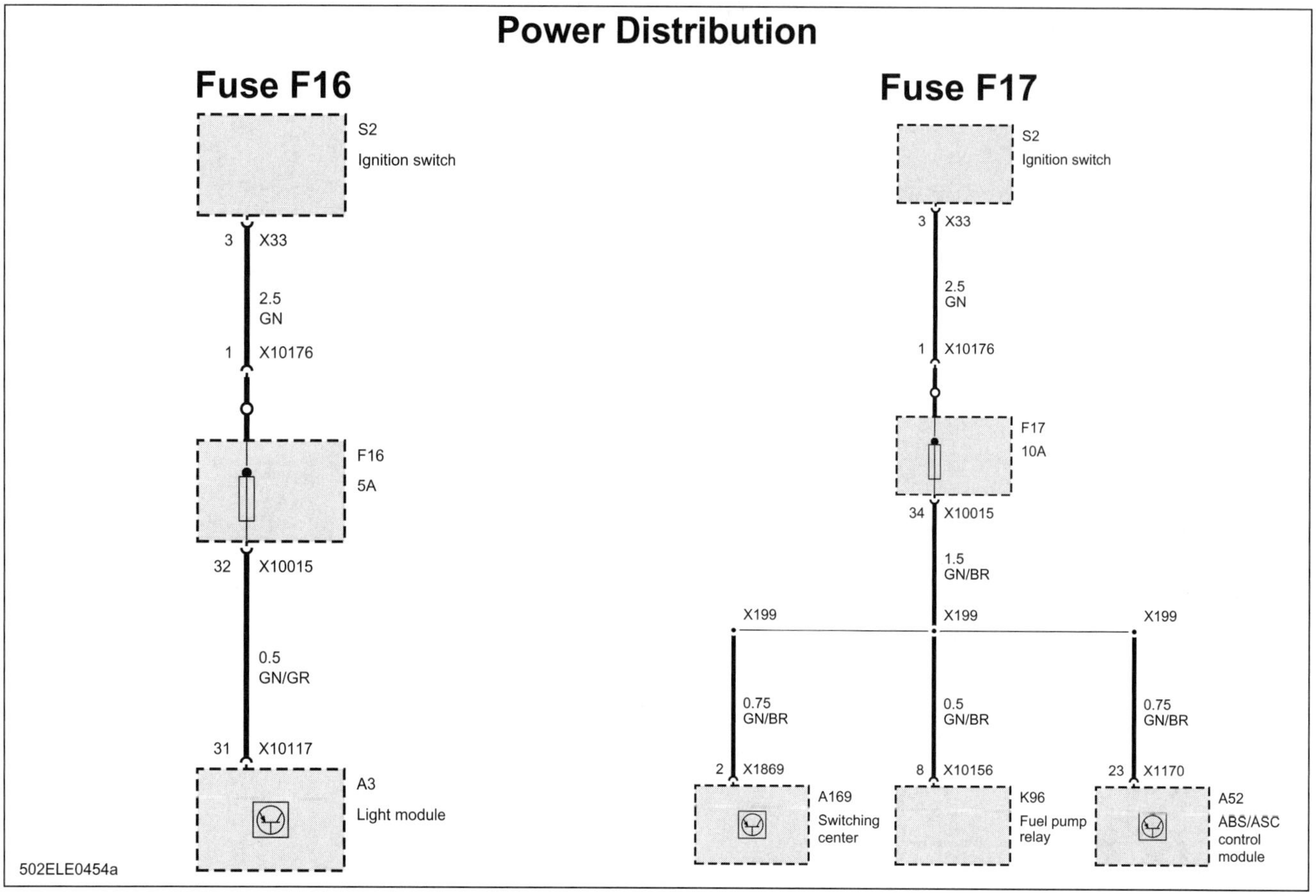
Power Distribution
Fuse F16
S2
Ignition switch
3 X33
2.5
GN
1 X10176
F16
5A
32 X10015
0.5
GN/GR
31 X10117
A3
Light module
Fuse F17
S2
Ignition switch
3 X33
2.5
GN
1 X10176
F17
10A
34 X10015
1.5
GN/BR
X199
X199
X199
0.75
GN/BR
0.5
GN/BR
0.75
GN/BR
2 X1869
8 X10156
23 X1170
A169
Switching center
K96
Fuel pump relay
A52
ABS/ASC control module
502ELE0454a

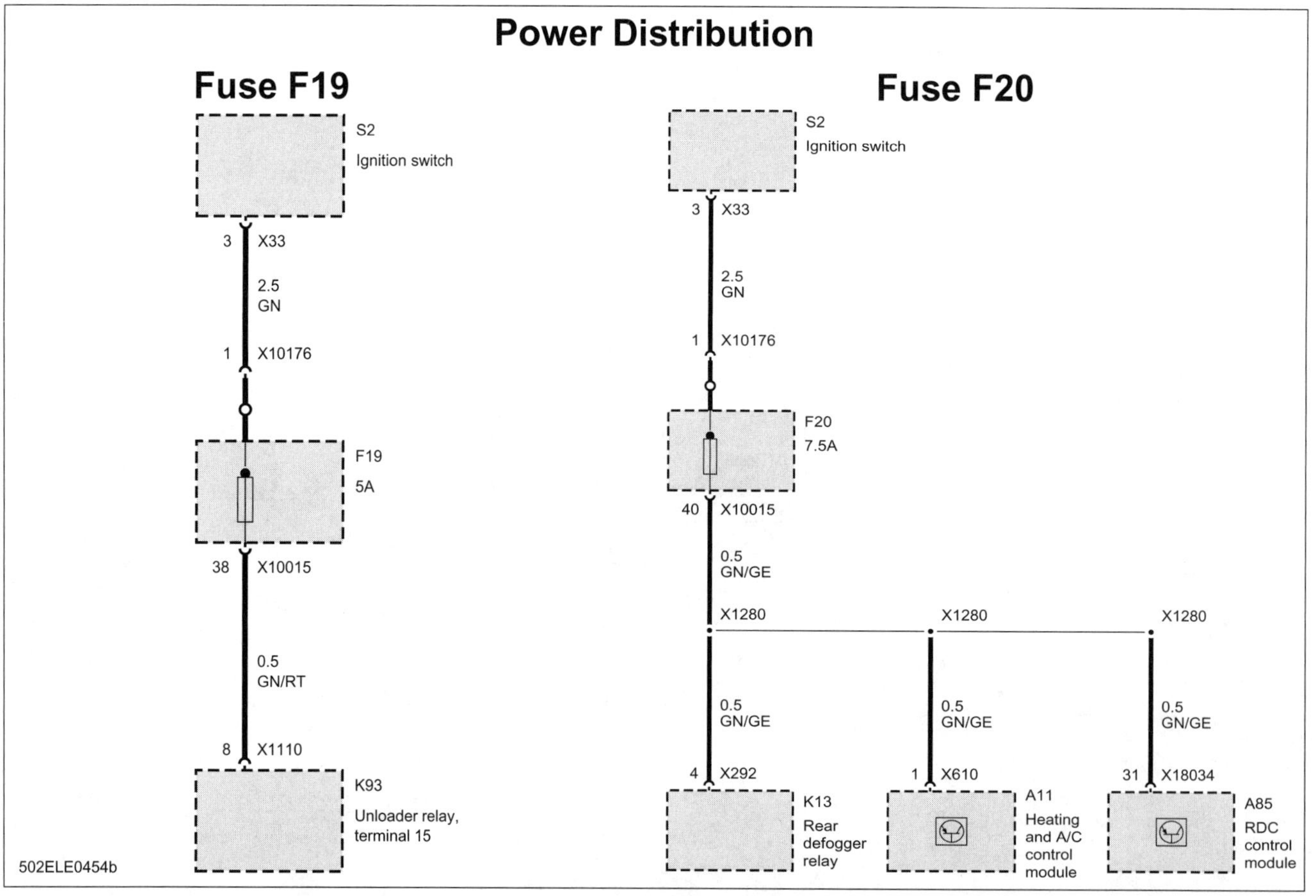
Power Distribution
Fuse F19
S2
Ignition switch
3 X33
2.5
GN
1 X10176
F19
5A
38 X10015
0.5
GN/RT
8 X1110
K93
Unloader relay, terminal 15
Fuse F20
S2
Ignition switch
3 X33
2.5
GN
1 X10176
F20
7.5A
40 X10015
0.5
GN/GE
X1280
X1280
X1280
0.5
GN/GE
0.5
GN/GE
0.5
GN/GE
4 X292
1 X610
31 X18034
K13
Rear defogger relay
A11
Heating and A/C control module
A85
RDC control module
502ELE0454b

Power Distribution
Fuse F21

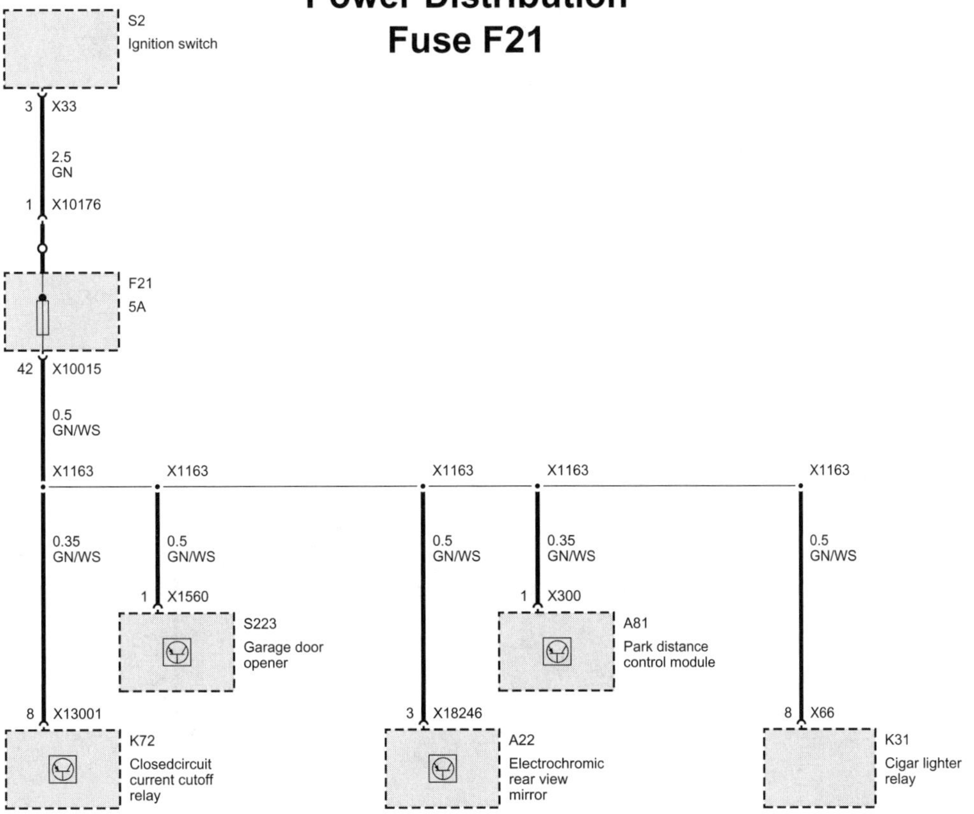

502ELE0455a

Power Distribution
Fuse F22
Fuse F23

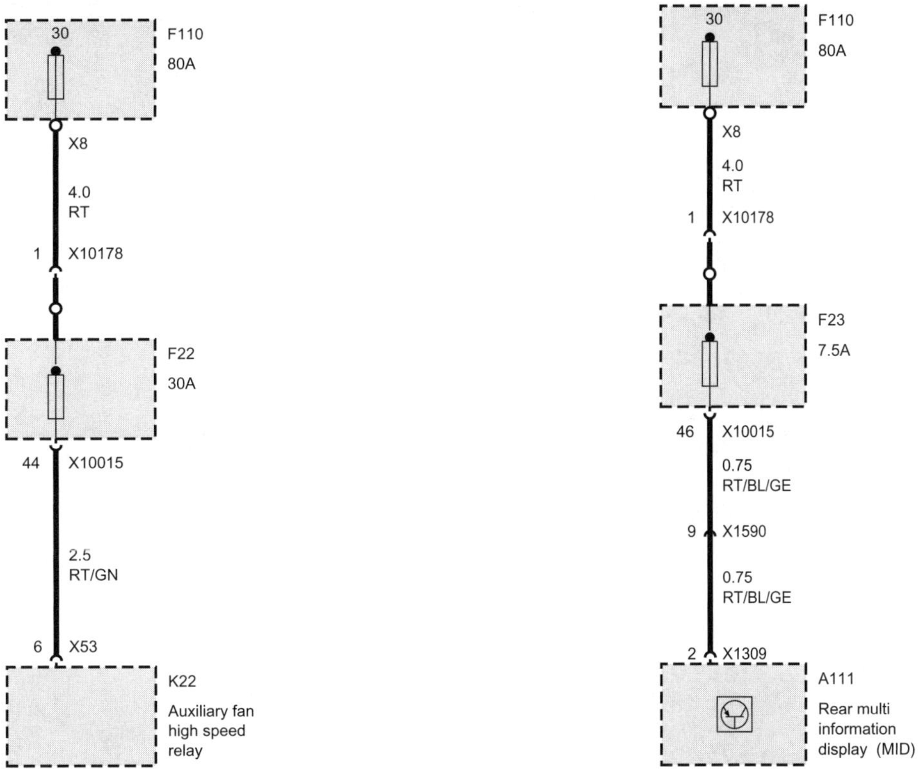

502ELE0455b

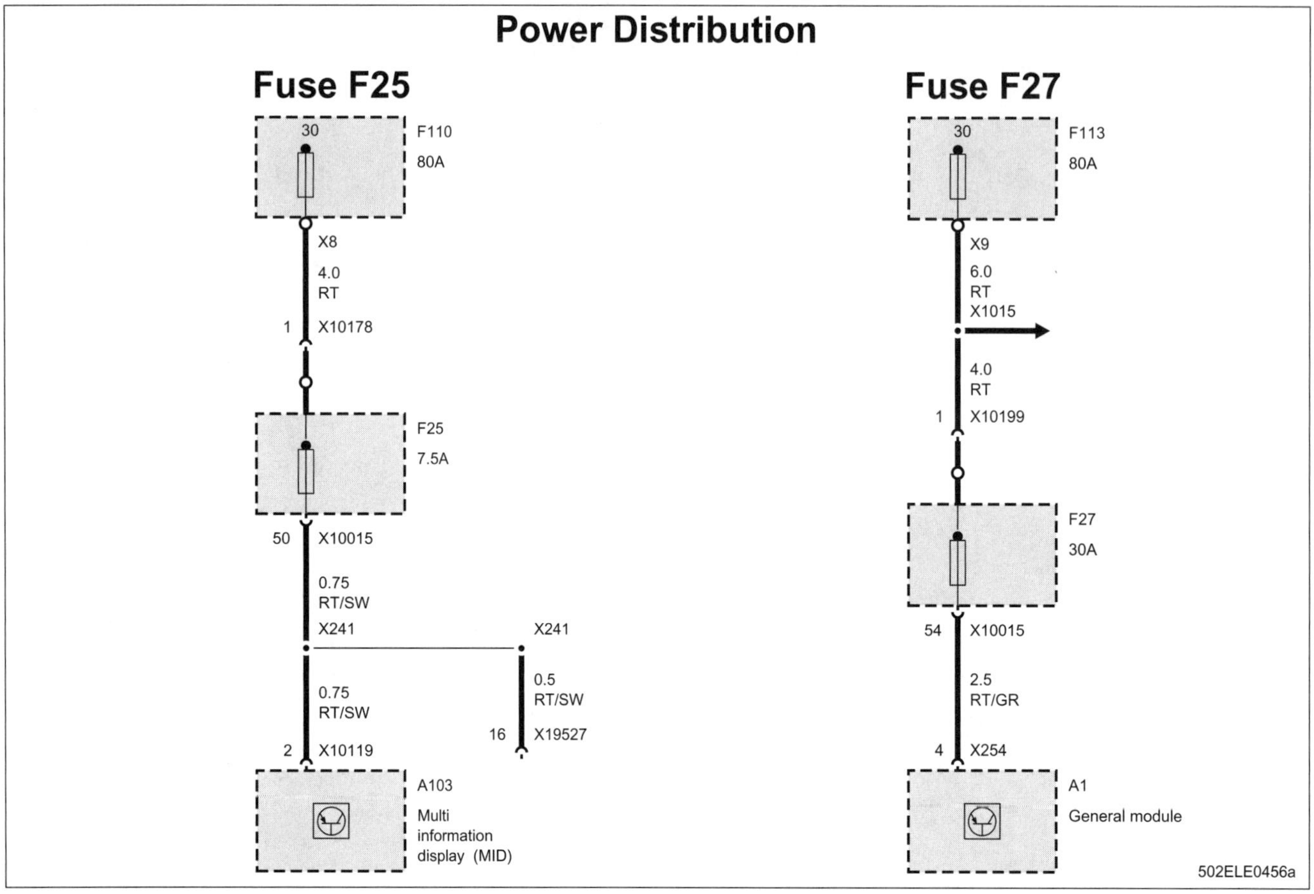
Power Distribution
Fuse F25
30
F110
80A
X8
4.0
RT
1
X10178
F25
7.5A
50
X10015
0.75
RT/SW
X241
X241
0.75
RT/SW
0.5
RT/SW
16
X19527
2
X10119
A103
Multi information display (MID)
Fuse F27
30
F113
80A
X9
6.0
RT
X1015
4.0
RT
1
X10199
F27
30A
54
X10015
2.5
RT/GR
4
X254
A1
General module
502ELE0456a

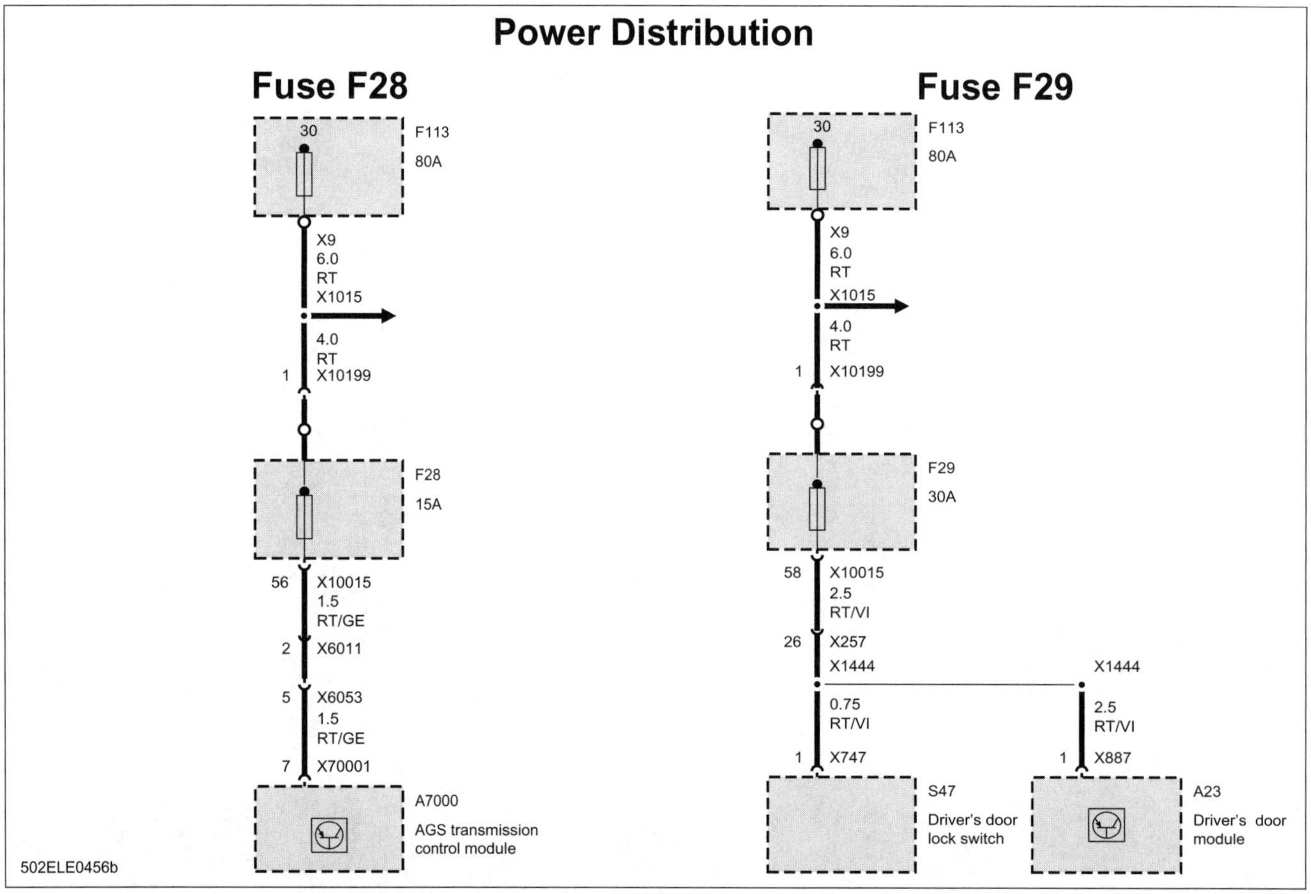
Power Distribution
Fuse F28
30
F113
80A
X9
6.0
RT
X1015
4.0
RT
1
X10199
F28
15A
56
X10015
1.5
RT/GE
2
X6011
5
X6053
1.5
RT/GE
7
X70001
A7000
AGS transmission control module
502ELE0456b
Fuse F29
30
F113
80A
X9
6.0
RT
X1015
4.0
RT
1
X10199
F29
30A
58
X10015
2.5
RT/VI
26
X257
X1444
X1444
0.75
RT/VI
2.5
RT/VI
1
X747
1
X887
S47
Driver's door lock switch
A23
Driver's door module

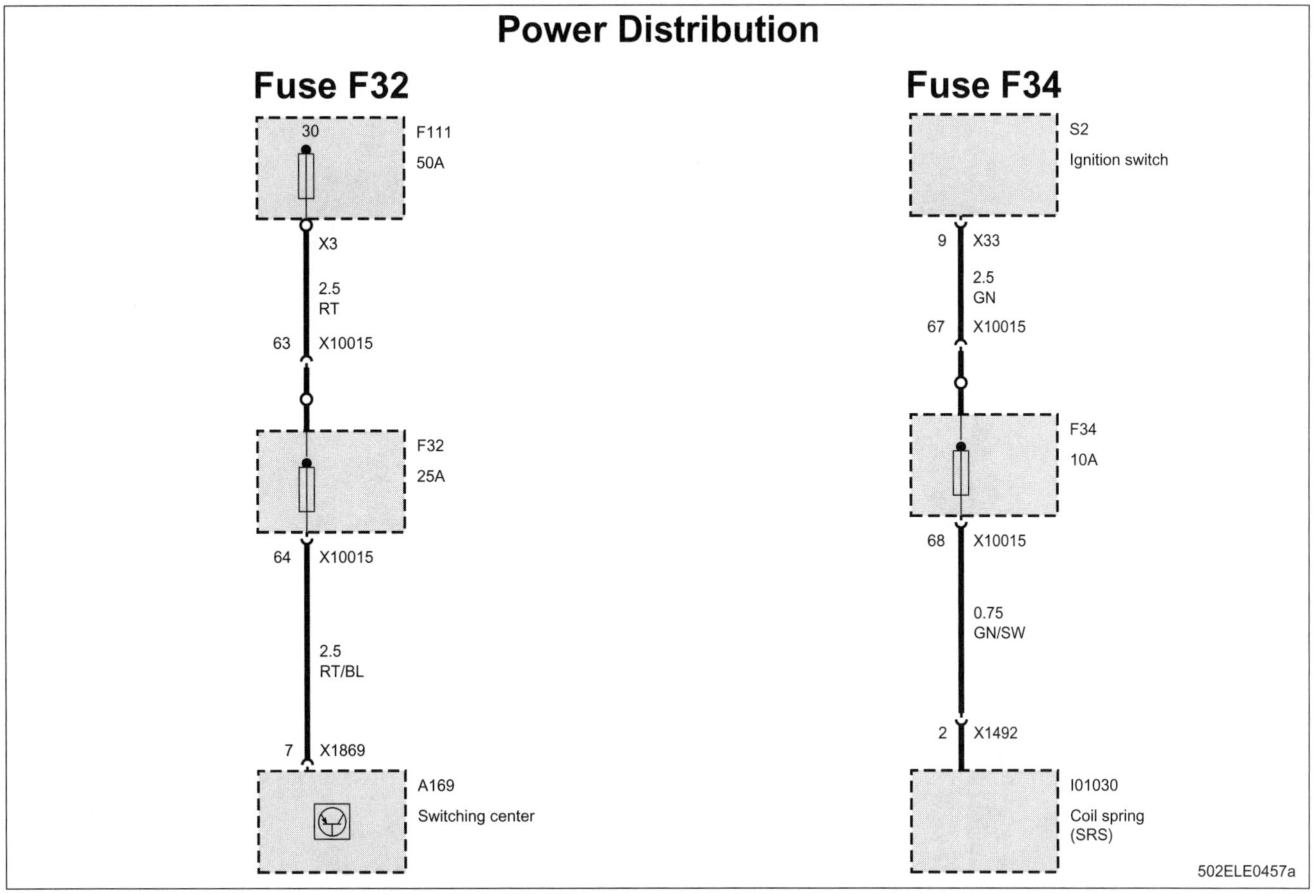
Power Distribution
Fuse F32
30
F111
50A
X3
2.5
RT
63
X10015
F32
25A
64
X10015
2.5
RT/BL
7
X1869
A169
Switching center
Fuse F34
S2
Ignition switch
9
X33
2.5
GN
67
X10015
F34
10A
68
X10015
0.75
GN/SW
2
X1492
I01030
Coil spring
(SRS)
502ELE0457a

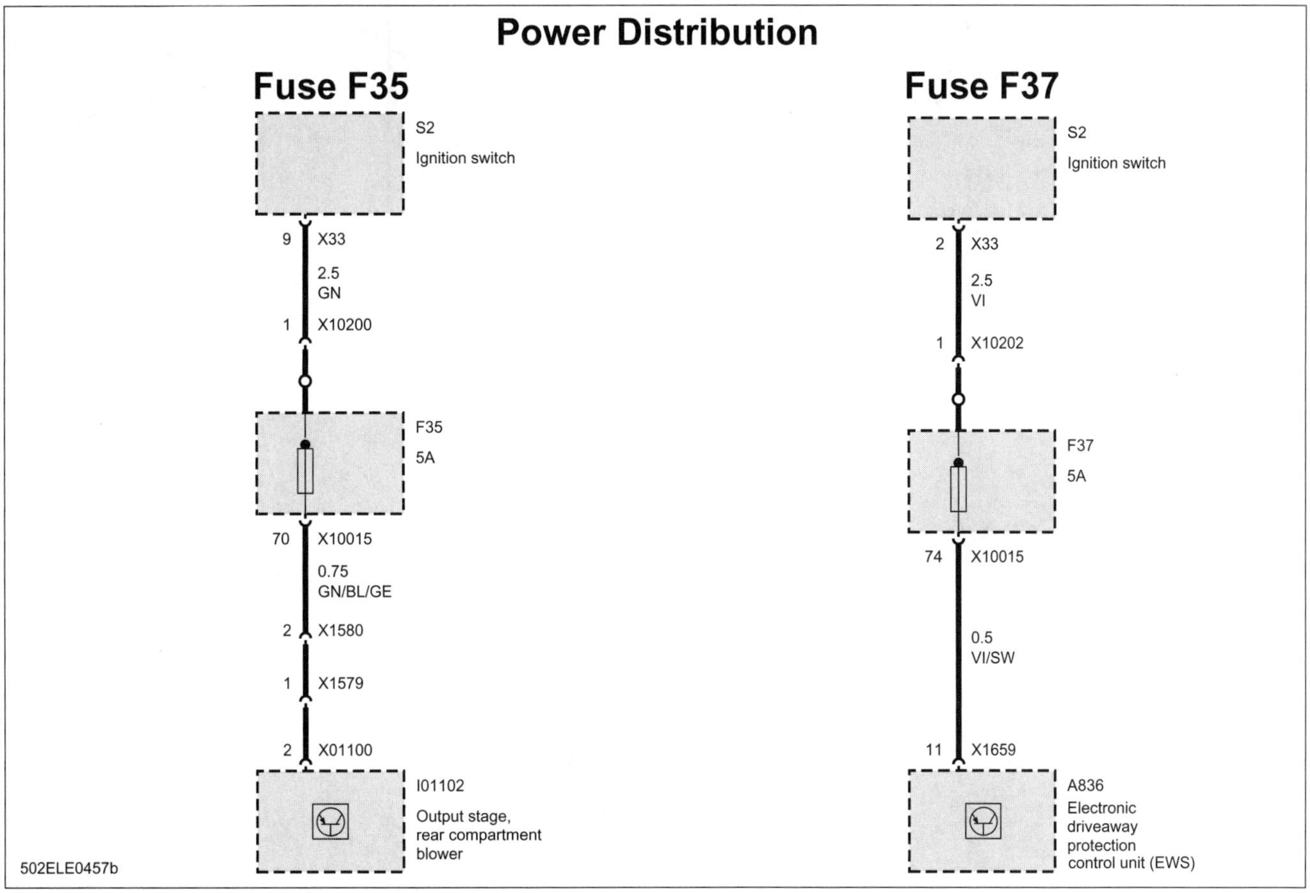
Power Distribution
Fuse F35
S2
Ignition switch
9
X33
2.5
GN
1
X10200
F35
5A
70
X10015
0.75
GN/BL/GE
2
X1580
1
X1579
2
X01100
I01102
Output stage,
rear compartment
blower
Fuse F37
S2
Ignition switch
2
X33
2.5
VI
1
X10202
F37
5A
74
X10015
0.5
VI/SW
11
X1659
A836
Electronic
driveaway
protection
control unit (EWS)
502ELE0457b

Power Distribution
Fuse F38
(1 of 1)

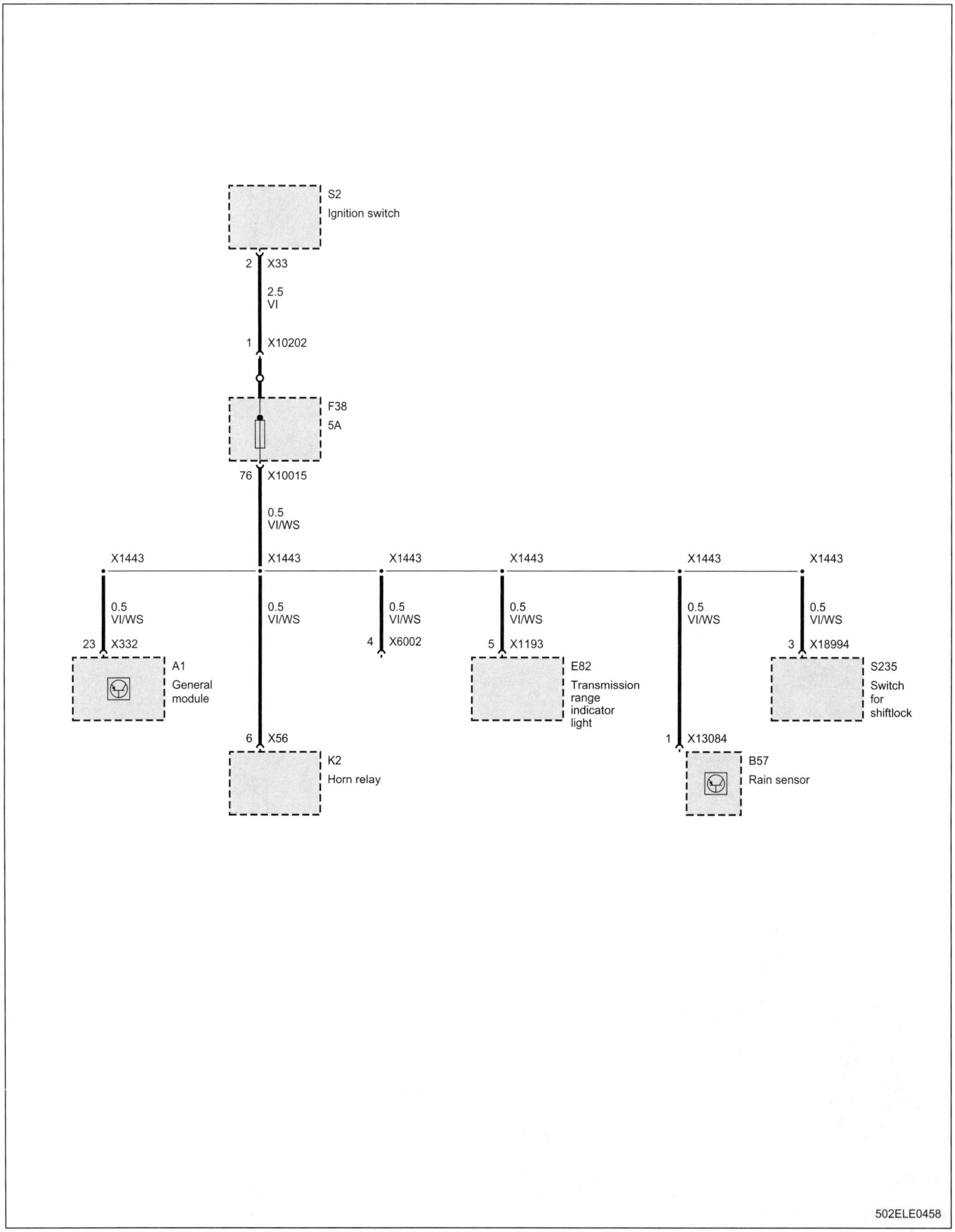
S2
Ignition switch
2 X33
2.5
VI
1 X10202
F38
5A
76 X10015
0.5
VI/WS
X1443
X1443
X1443
X1443
X1443
X1443
0.5
VI/WS
0.5
VI/WS
0.5
VI/WS
0.5
VI/WS
0.5
VI/WS
0.5
VI/WS
23 X332
4 X6002
5 X1193
3 X18994
A1
General module
E82
Transmission range indicator light
S235
Switch for shiftlock
6 X56
1 X13084
K2
Horn relay
B57
Rain sensor
502ELE0458

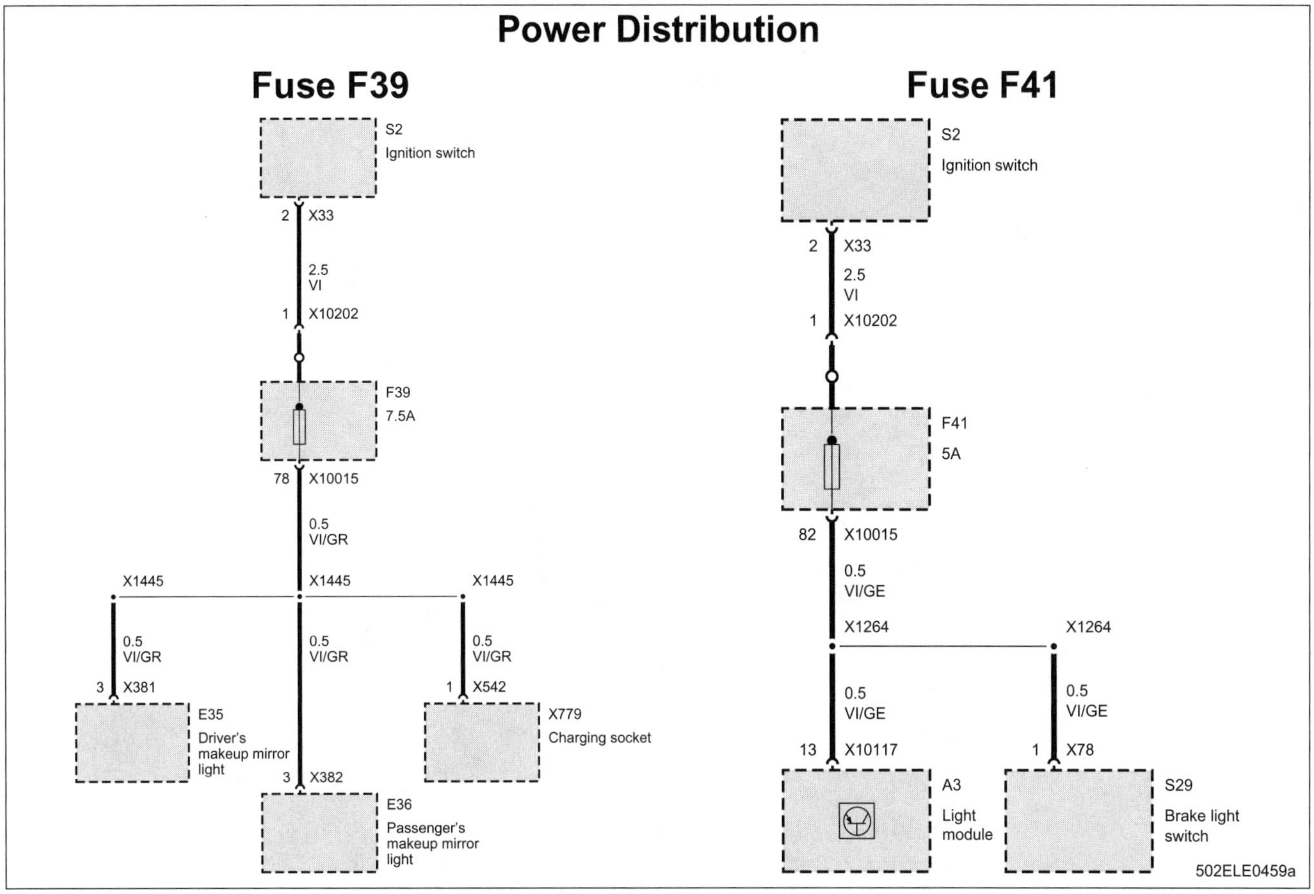
Power Distribution
Fuse F39
S2
Ignition switch
2 X33
2.5
VI
1 X10202
F39
7.5A
78 X10015
0.5
VI/GR
X1445
X1445
X1445
0.5
VI/GR
0.5
VI/GR
0.5
VI/GR
3 X381
E35
Driver's makeup mirror light
3 X382
E36
Passenger's makeup mirror light
1 X542
X779
Charging socket
Fuse F41
S2
Ignition switch
2 X33
2.5
VI
1 X10202
F41
5A
82 X10015
0.5
VI/GE
X1264
X1264
0.5
VI/GE
0.5
VI/GE
13 X10117
A3
Light module
1 X78
S29
Brake light switch
502ELE0459a

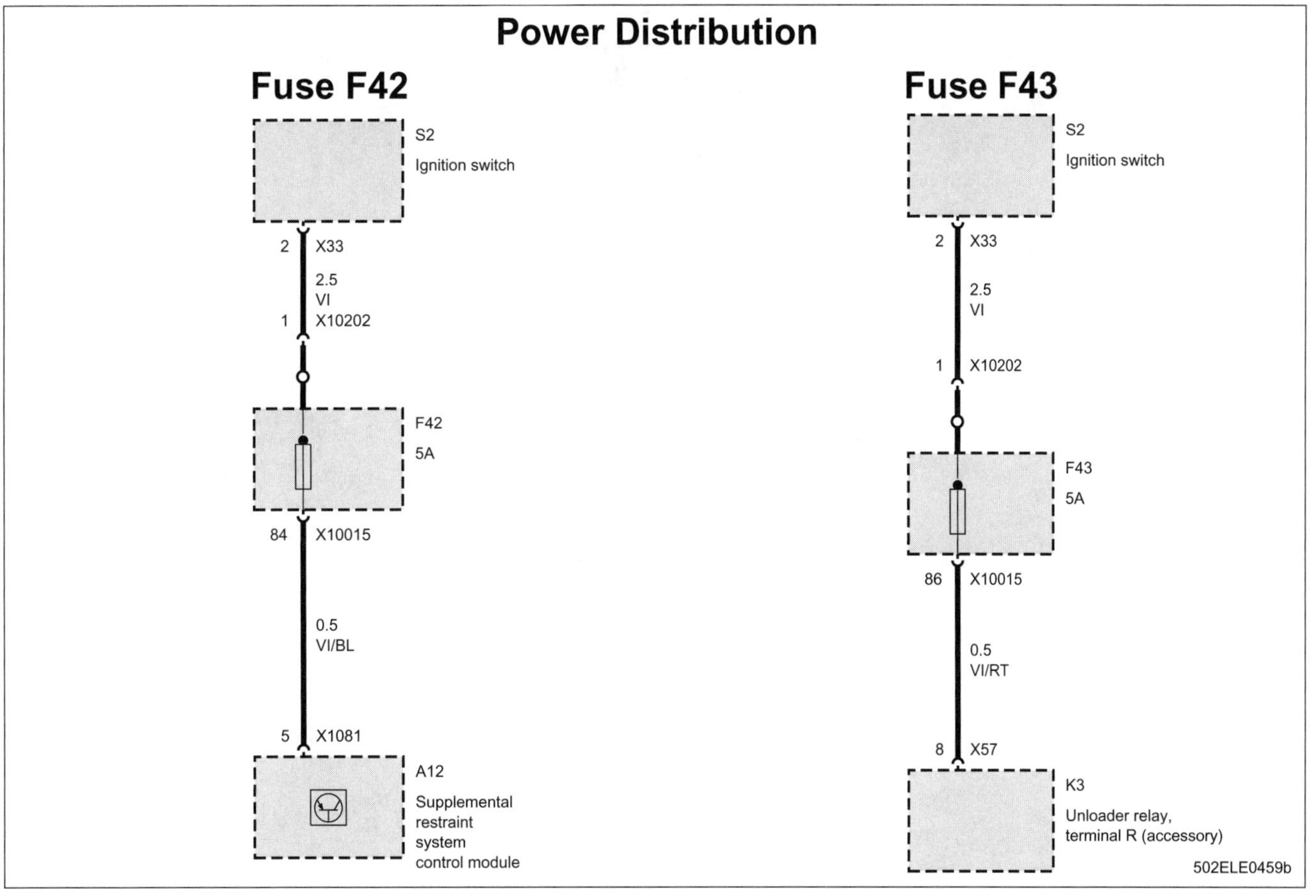
Power Distribution
Fuse F42
S2
Ignition switch
2 X33
2.5
VI
1 X10202
F42
5A
84 X10015
0.5
VI/BL
5 X1081
A12
Supplemental restraint system control module
Fuse F43
S2
Ignition switch
2 X33
2.5
VI
1 X10202
F43
5A
86 X10015
0.5
VI/RT
8 X57
K3
Unloader relay, terminal R (accessory)
502ELE0459b

Power Distribution Fuse F44

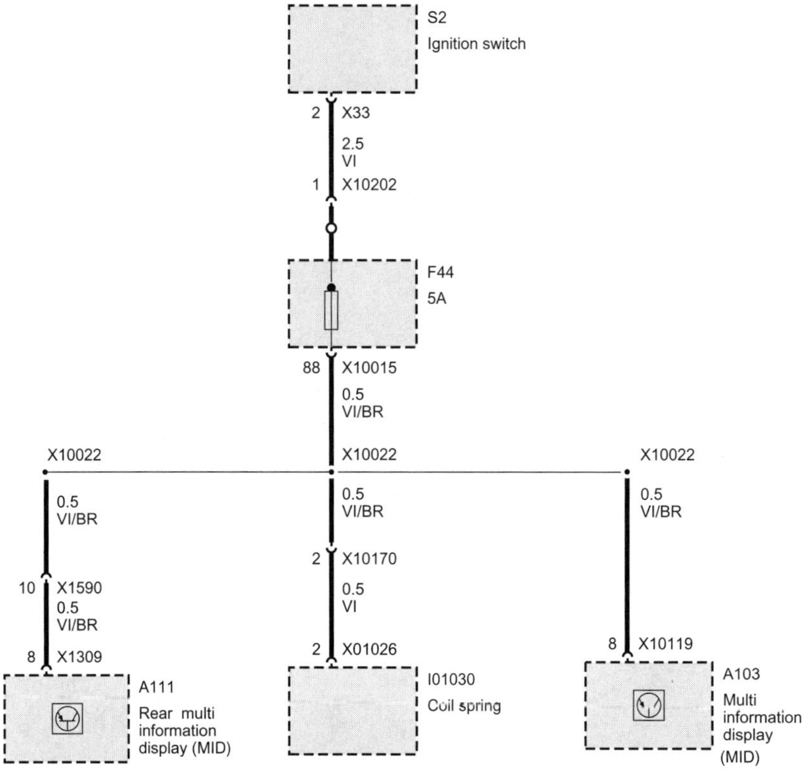

502ELE0460a

Power Distribution Fuse F45

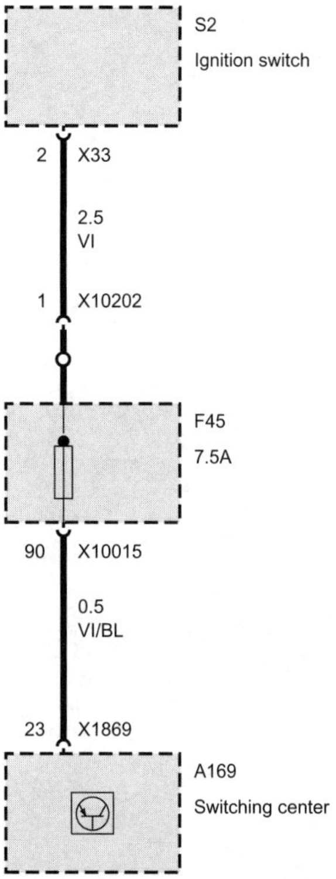

502ELE0460b

Power Distribution Fuse F47

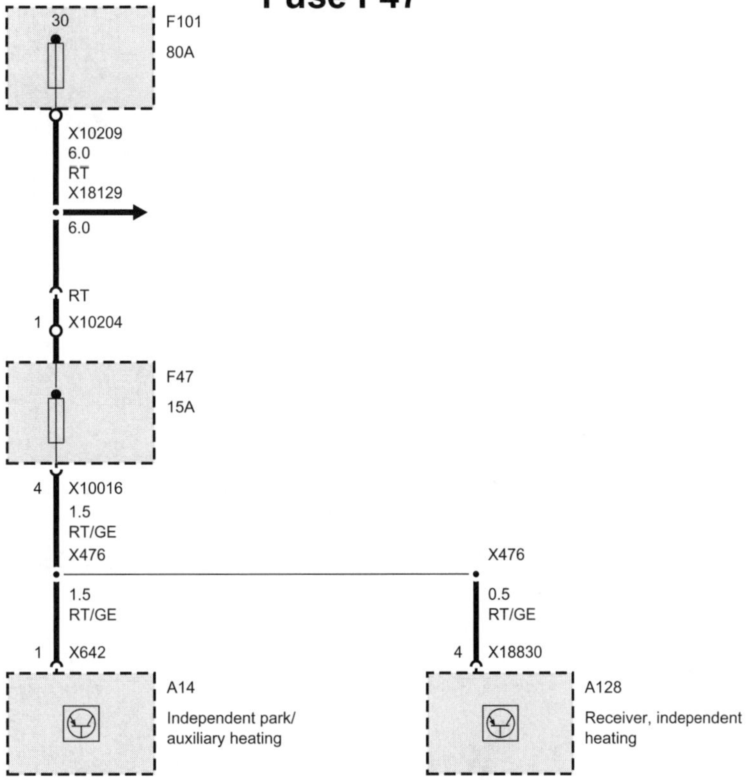

502ELE0461a

Power Distribution Fuse F48

502ELE0461b

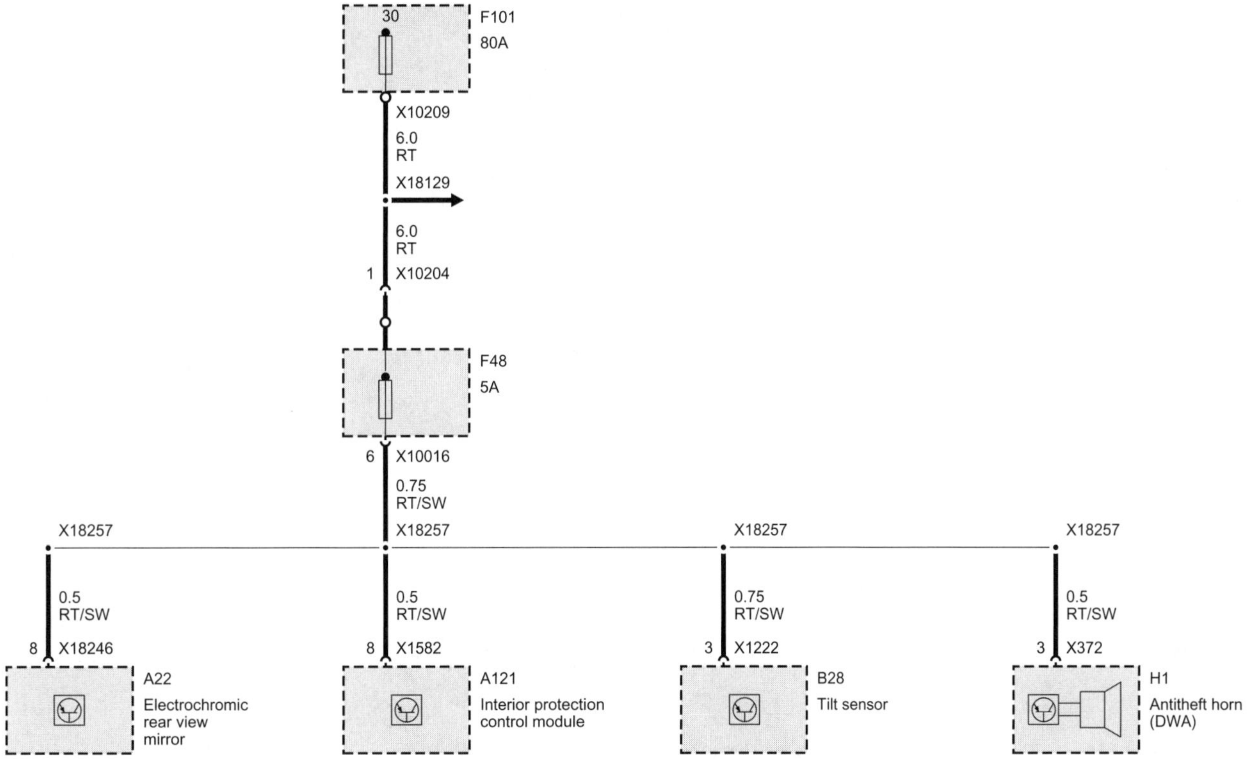

Power Distribution

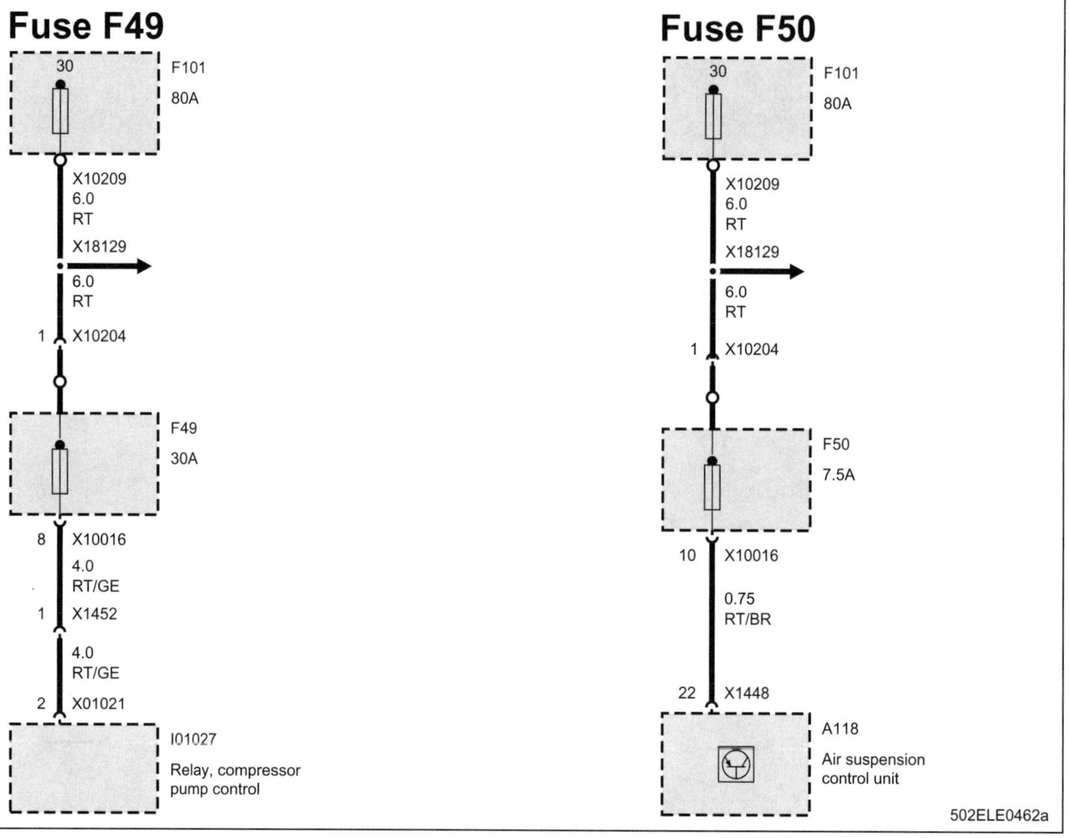
Fuse F49
30
F101
80A
X10209
6.0
RT
X18129
6.0
RT
1 X10204
F49
30A
8 X10016
4.0
RT/GE
1 X1452
4.0
RT/GE
2 X01021
I01027
Relay, compressor
pump control
Fuse F50
30
F101
80A
X10209
6.0
RT
X18129
6.0
RT
1 X10204
F50
7.5A
10 X10016
0.75
RT/BR
22 X1448
A118
Air suspension
control unit
502ELE0462a

Power Distribution

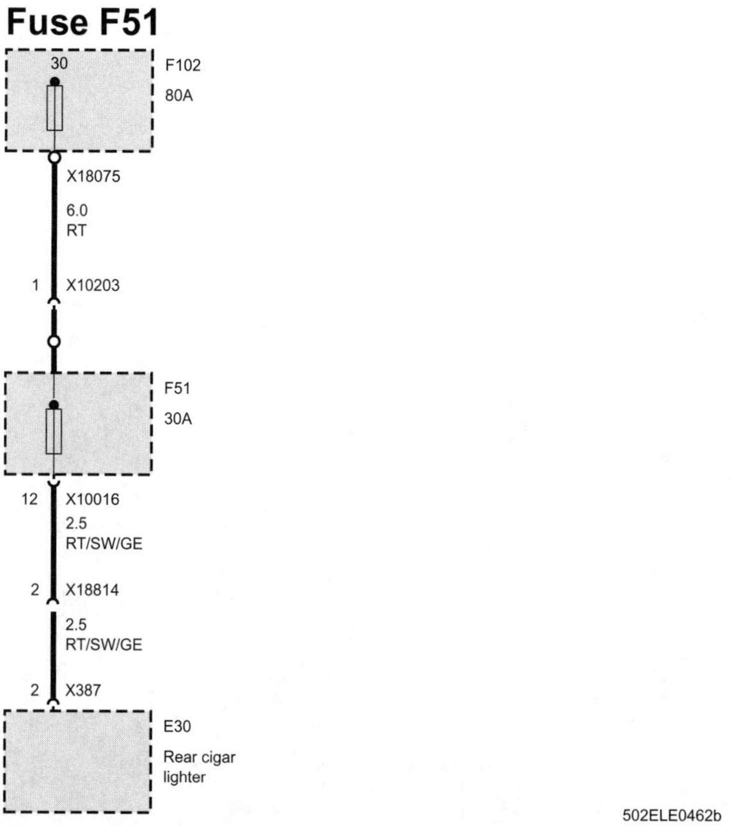
Fuse F51
30
F102
80A
X18075
6.0
RT
1 X10203
F51
30A
12 X10016
2.5
RT/SW/GE
2 X18814
2.5
RT/SW/GE
2 X387
E30
Rear cigar
lighter
502ELE0462b

Power Distribution
Fuse F53
(1 of 1)

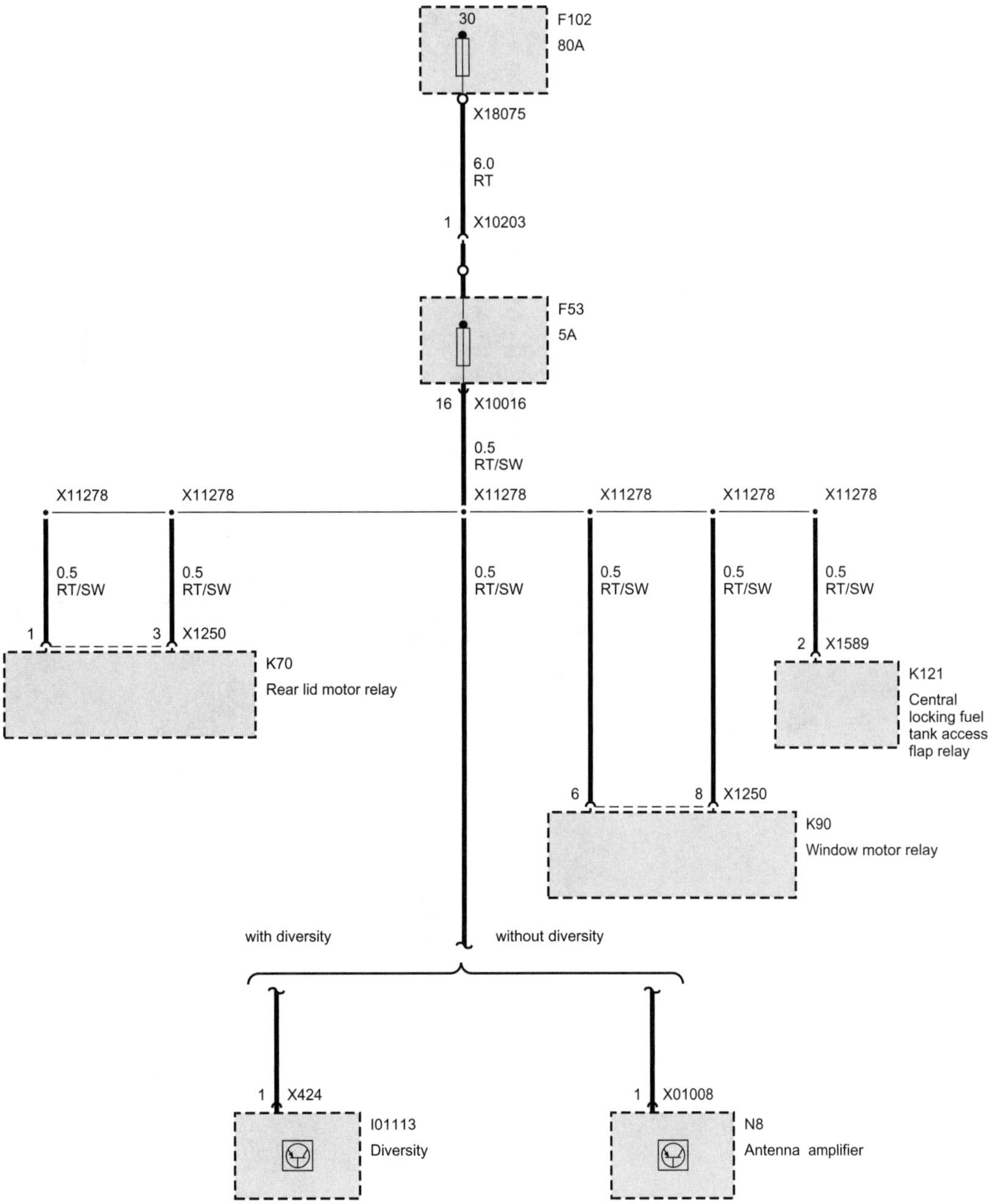
30
F102
80A
X18075
6.0
RT
1
X10203
F53
5A
16
X10016
0.5
RT/SW
X11278
X11278
X11278
X11278
X11278
X11278
0.5
RT/SW
0.5
RT/SW
0.5
RT/SW
0.5
RT/SW
0.5
RT/SW
0.5
RT/SW
1
3
X1250
K70
Rear lid motor relay
2
X1589
K121
Central locking fuel tank access flap relay
6
8
X1250
K90
Window motor relay
with diversity
without diversity
1
X424
I01113
Diversity
1
X01008
N8
Antenna amplifier
502ELE0463

Power Distribution Fuse F54

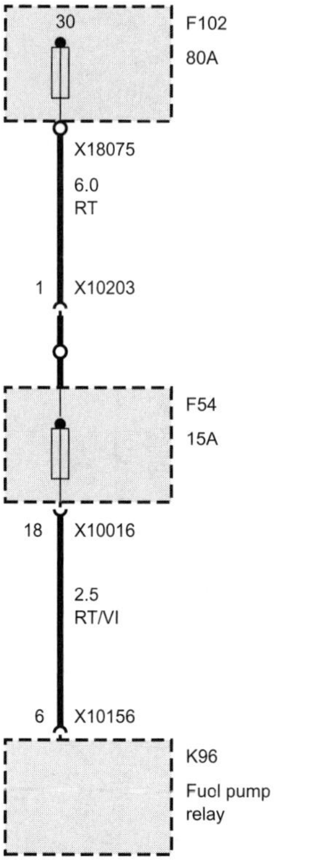

Power Distribution Fuse F55

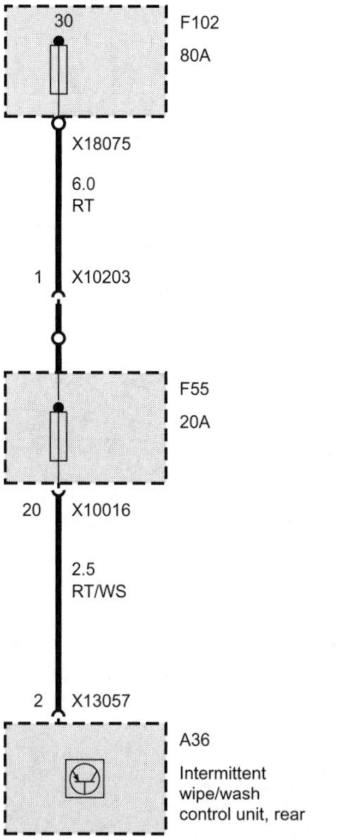

Power Distribution
Fuse 56
(1 of 2)

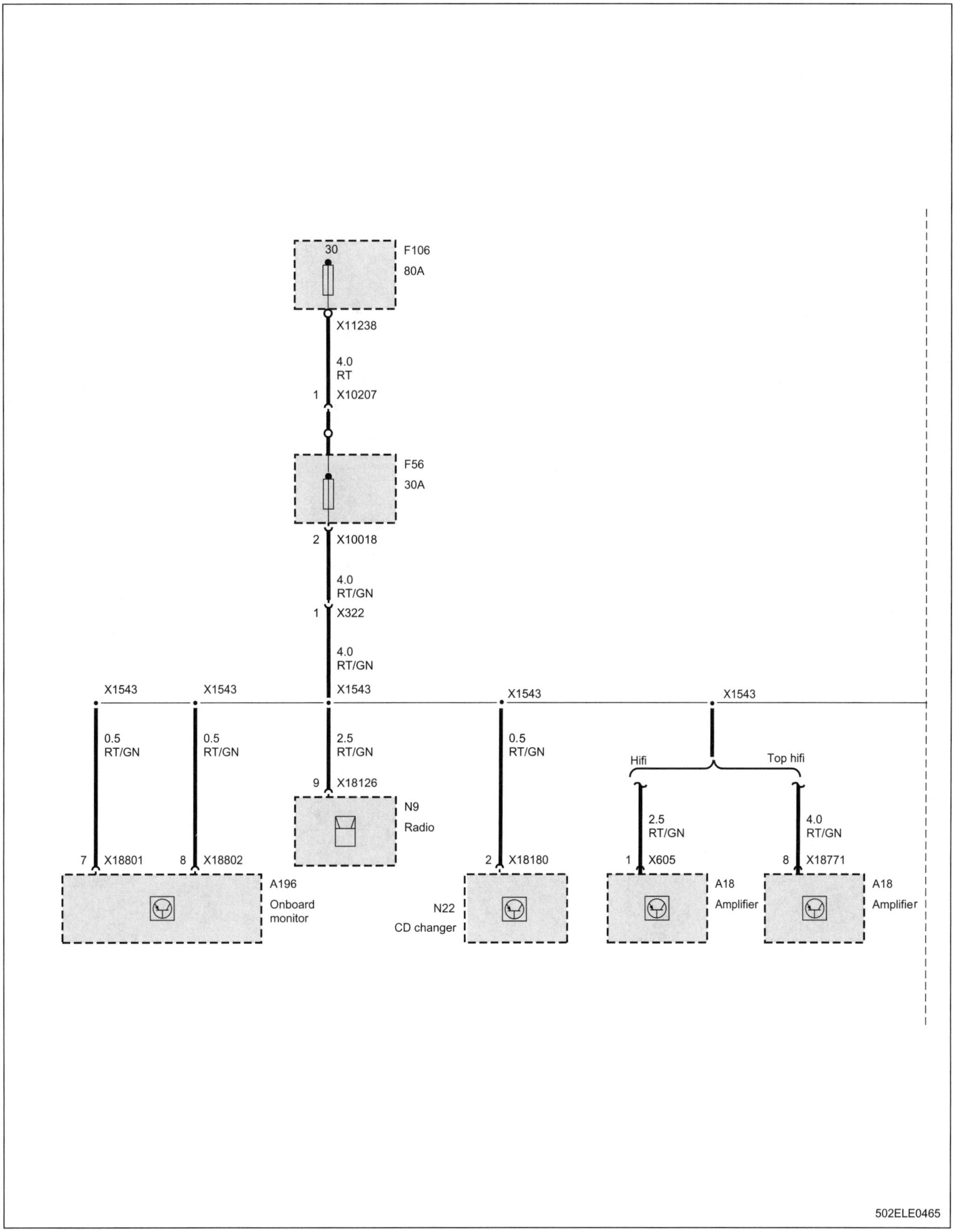
30
F106
80A
X11238
4.0
RT
1
X10207
F56
30A
2
X10018
4.0
RT/GN
1
X322
4.0
RT/GN
X1543
X1543
X1543
X1543
X1543
0.5
RT/GN
0.5
RT/GN
2.5
RT/GN
0.5
RT/GN
Hifi
Top hifi
9
X18126
N9
Radio
2.5
RT/GN
4.0
RT/GN
7
X18801
8
X18802
2
X18180
1
X605
8
X18771
A196
Onboard
monitor
N22
CD changer
A18
Amplifier
A18
Amplifier
502ELE0465

Power Distribution
Fuse F56
(2 of 2)

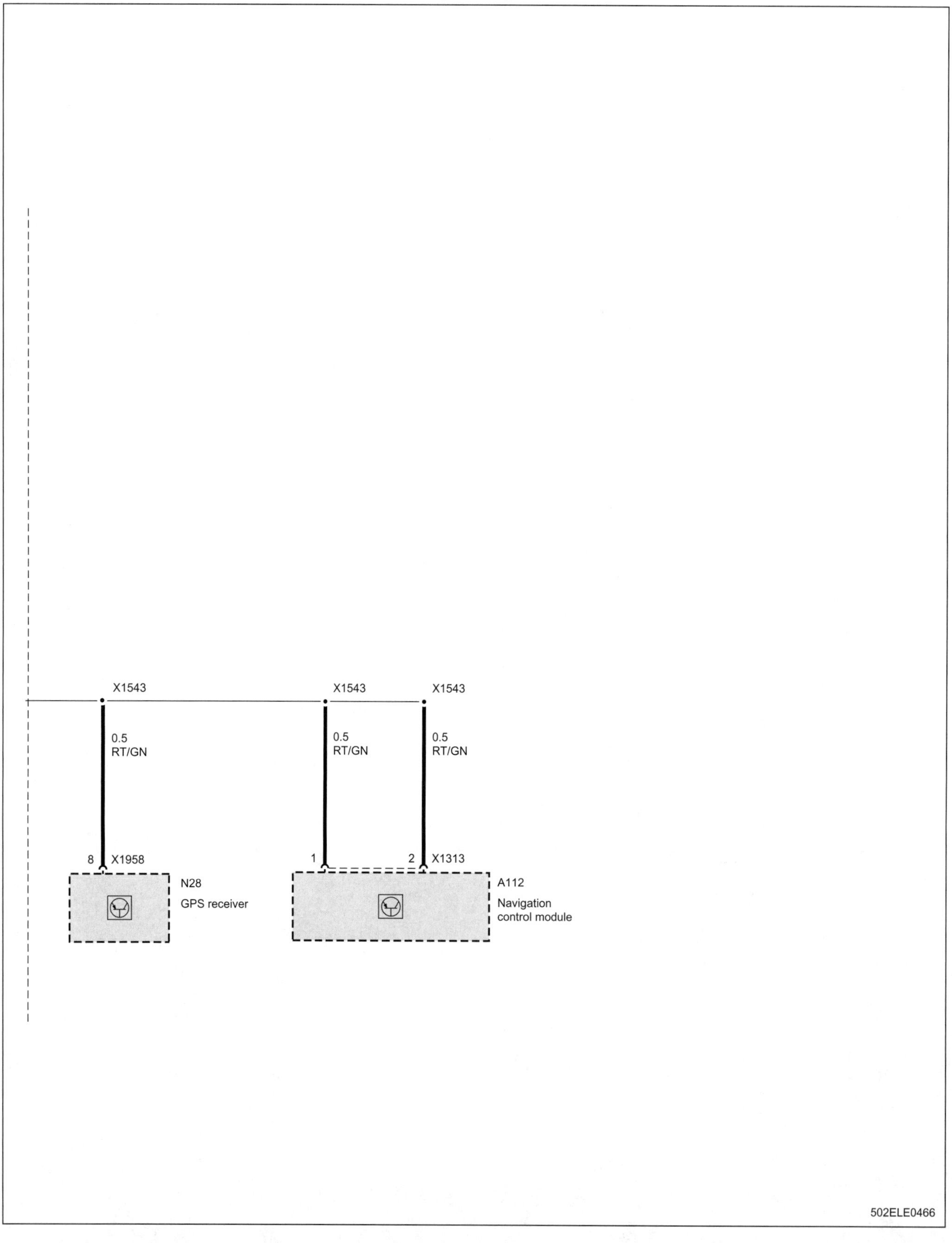
X1543
0.5
RT/GN
8
X1958
N28
GPS receiver
X1543
0.5
RT/GN
X1543
0.5
RT/GN
1
2
X1313
A112
Navigation
control module
502ELE0466

Power Distribution Fuse F57

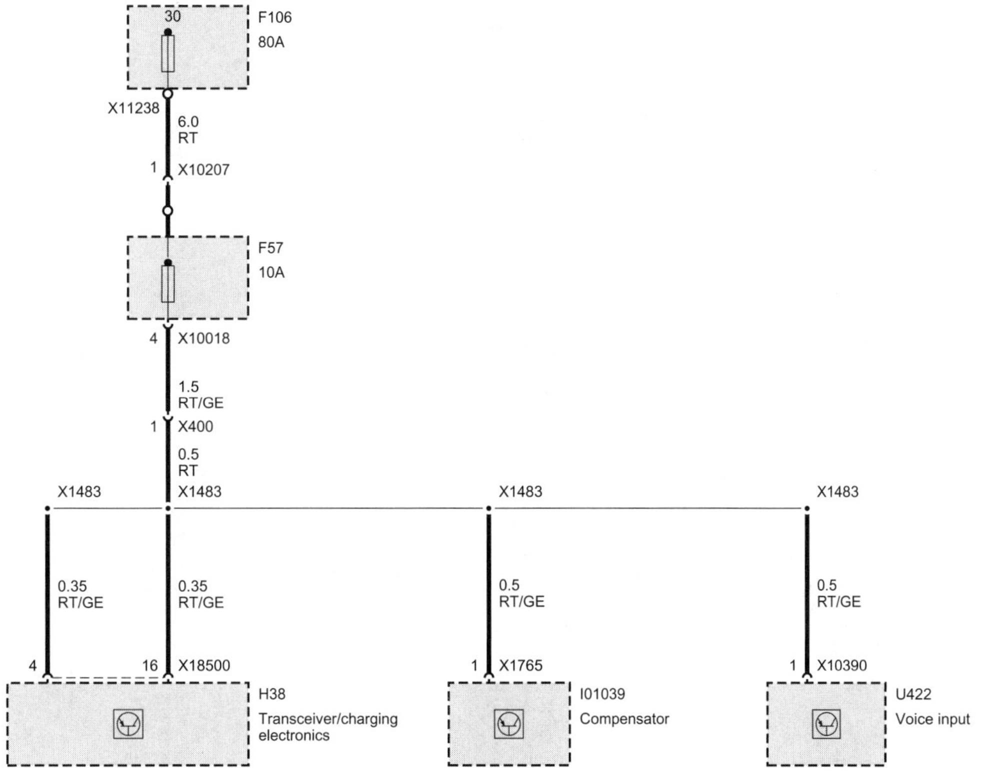

502ELE0467a

Power Distribution Fuse F58

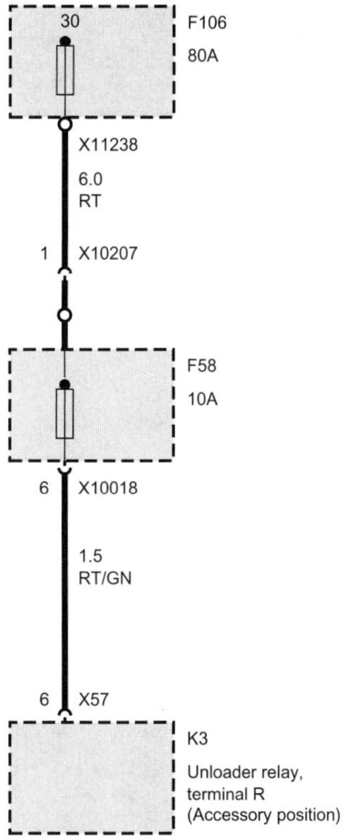

502ELE0467b

Power Distribution Fuse F59

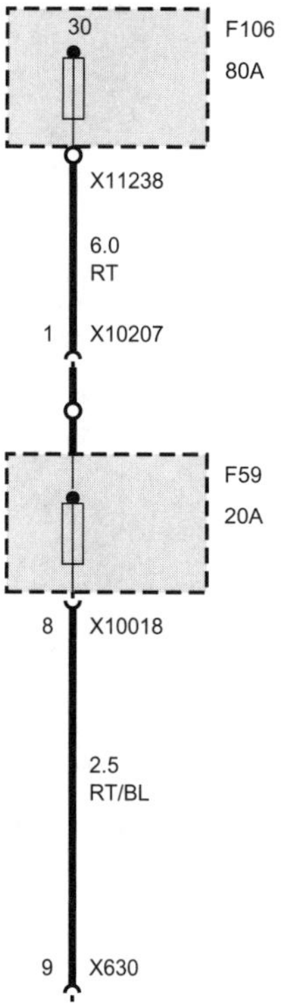

502ELE0468a

Power Distribution Fuse F60

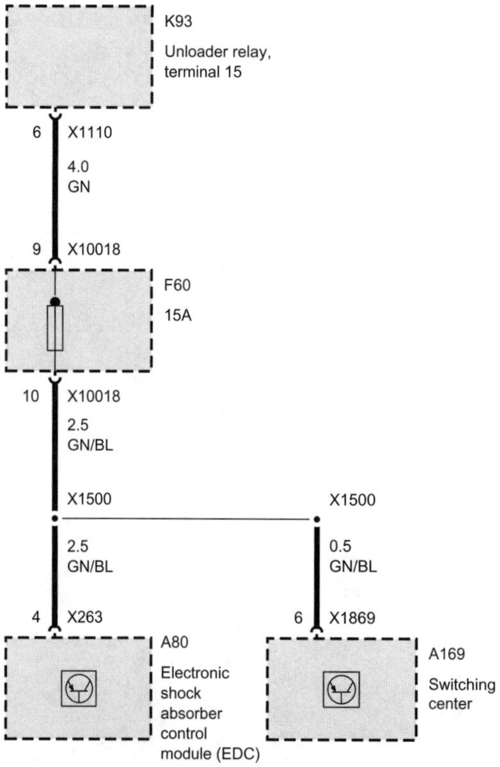

502ELE0468b

Power Distribution
Fuse F61
(1 of 1)

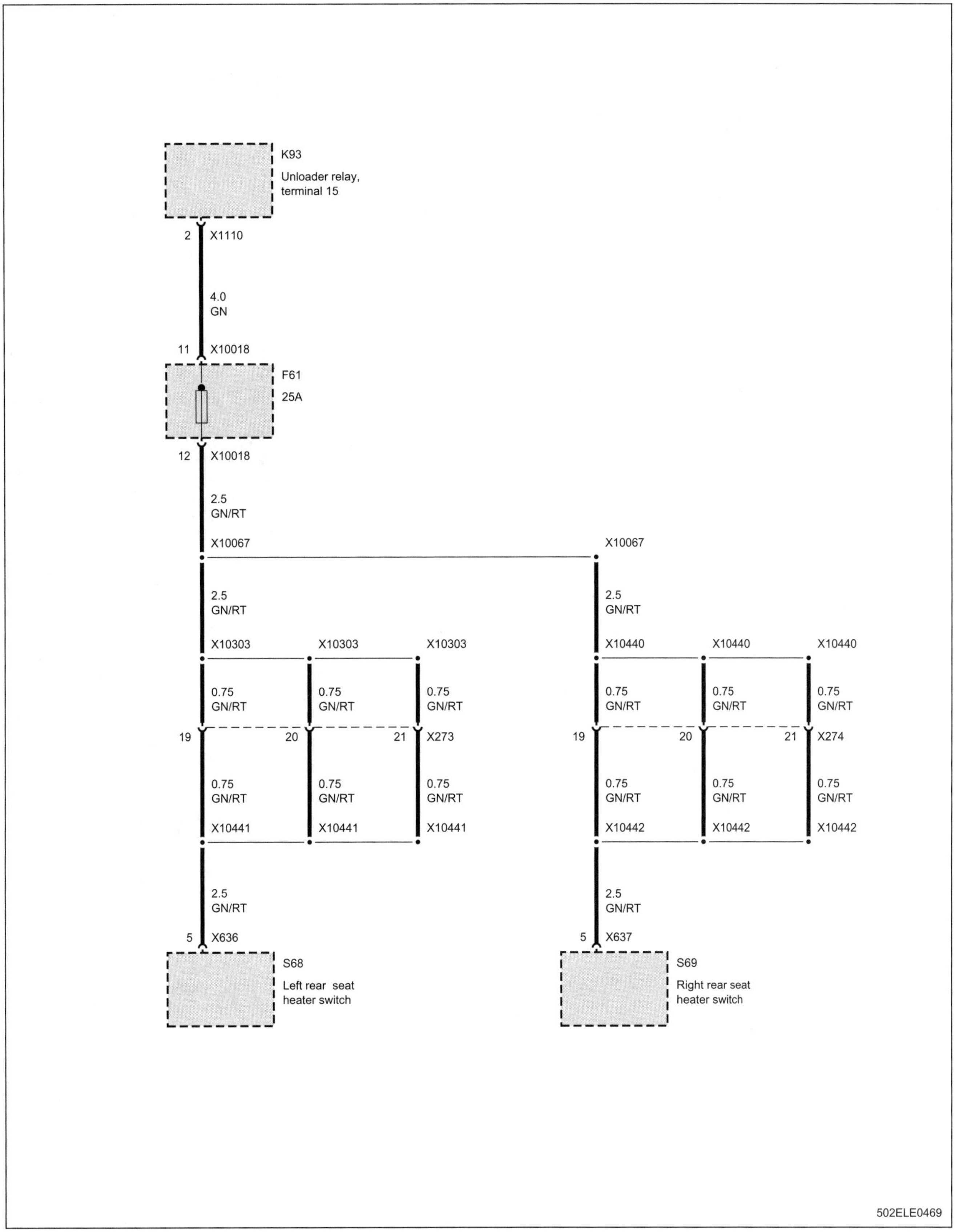
K93
Unloader relay, terminal 15
2 X1110
4.0 GN
11 X10018
F61
25A
12 X10018
2.5 GN/RT
X10067
X10067
2.5 GN/RT
2.5 GN/RT
X10303
X10303
X10303
X10440
X10440
X10440
0.75 GN/RT
19
20
21
X273
19
20
21
X274
X10441
X10441
X10441
X10442
X10442
X10442
2.5 GN/RT
5 X636
5 X637
S68
Left rear seat heater switch
S69
Right rear seat heater switch
502ELE0469

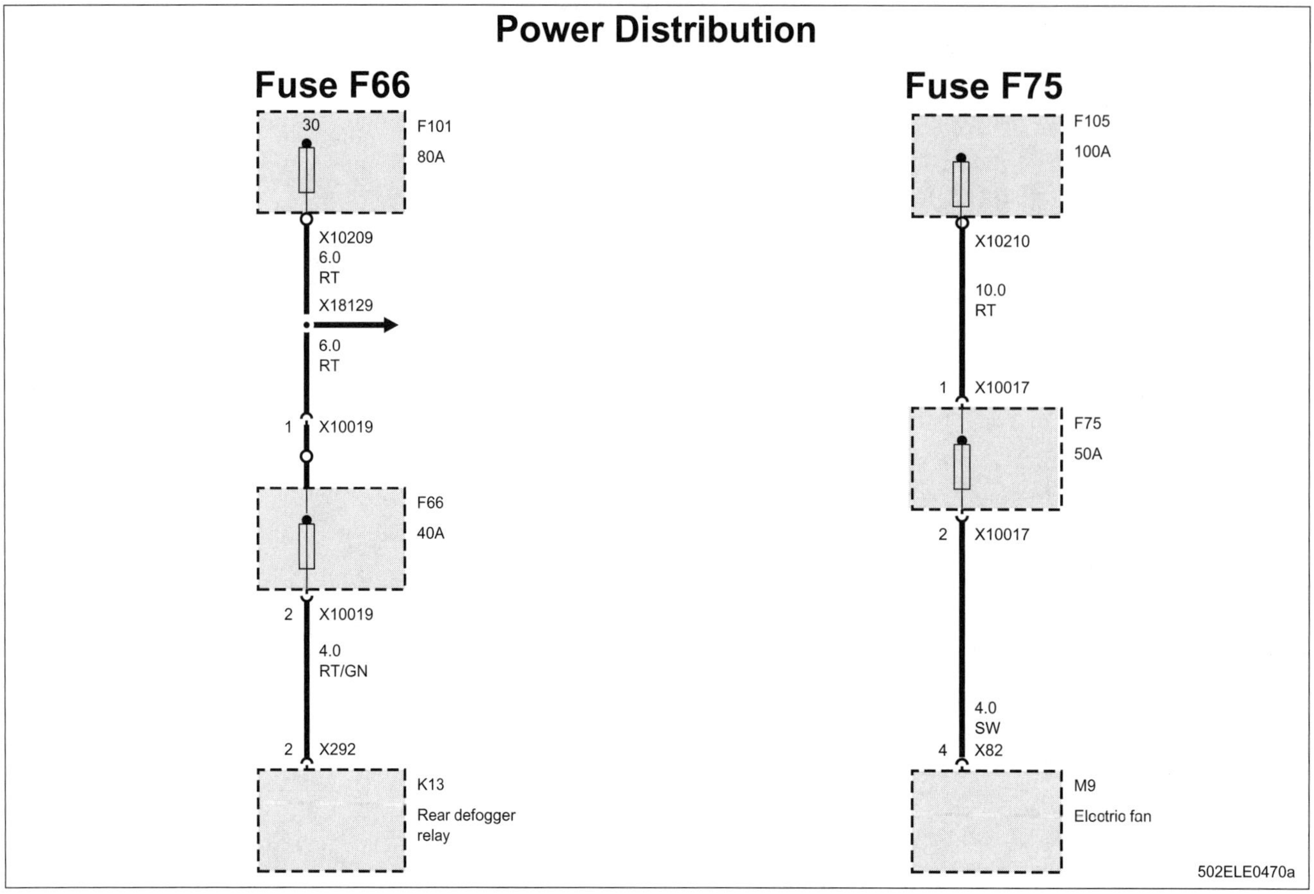
Power Distribution
Fuse F66
30
F101
80A
X10209
6.0
RT
X18129
6.0
RT
1 X10019
F66
40A
2 X10019
4.0
RT/GN
2 X292
K13
Rear defogger relay
Fuse F75
F105
100A
X10210
10.0
RT
1 X10017
F75
50A
2 X10017
4.0
SW
4 X82
M9
Electric fan
502ELE0470a

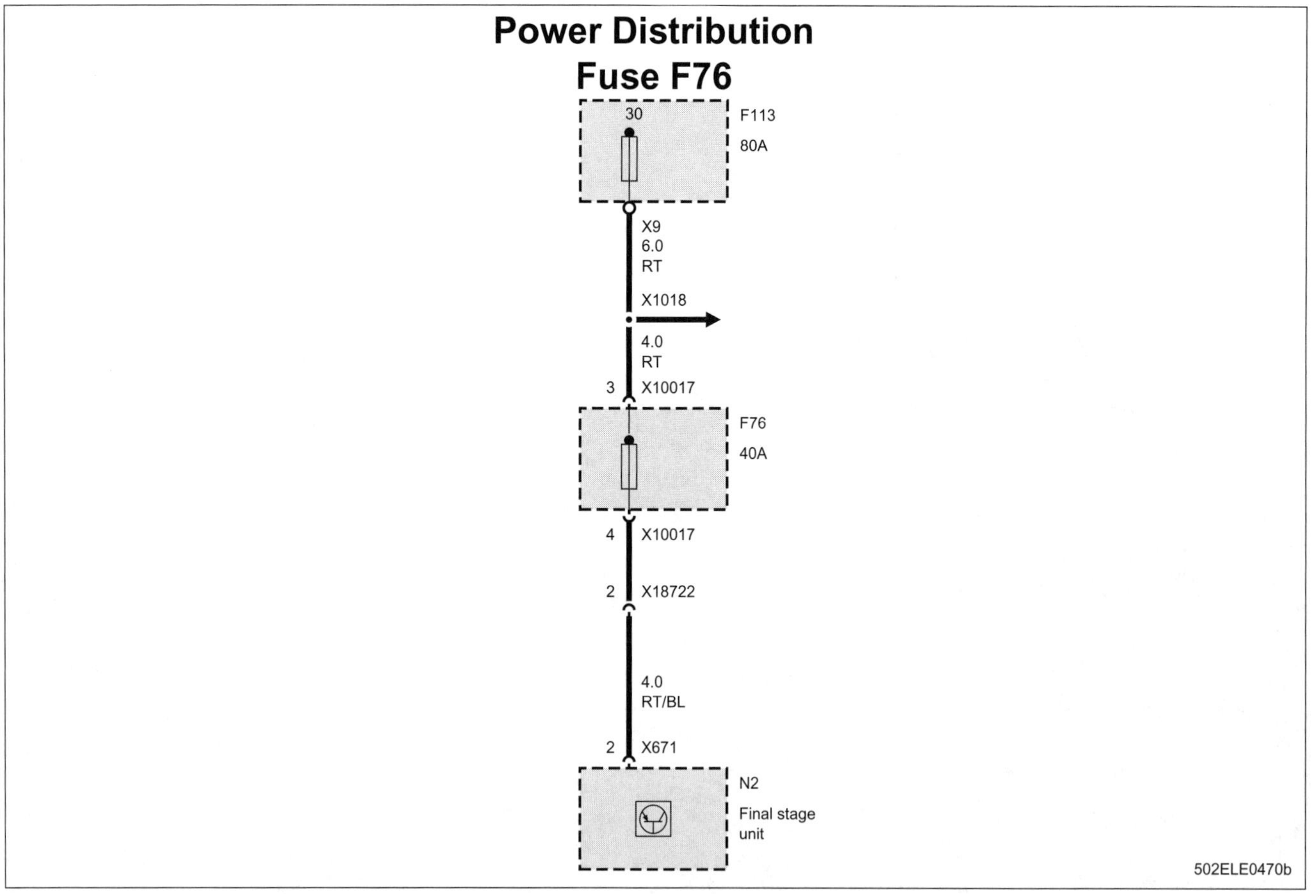
Power Distribution
Fuse F76
30
F113
80A
X9
6.0
RT
X1018
4.0
RT
3 X10017
F76
40A
4 X10017
2 X18722
4.0
RT/BL
2 X671
N2
Final stage unit
502ELE0470b

Power Distribution
Fuse F100
(1 of 1)

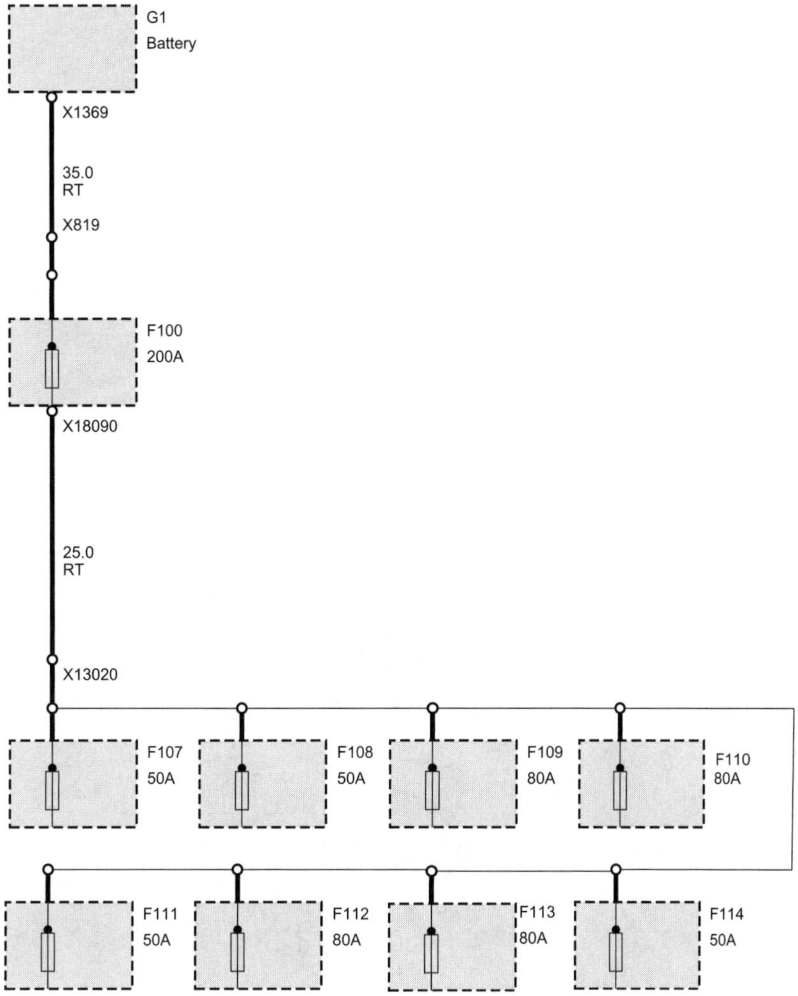
G1
Battery
X1369
35.0
RT
X819
F100
200A
X18090
25.0
RT
X13020
F107
50A
F108
50A
F109
80A
F110
80A
F111
50A
F112
80A
F113
80A
F114
50A
502ELE0471

Power Distribution
Fuse F101
(1 of 1)

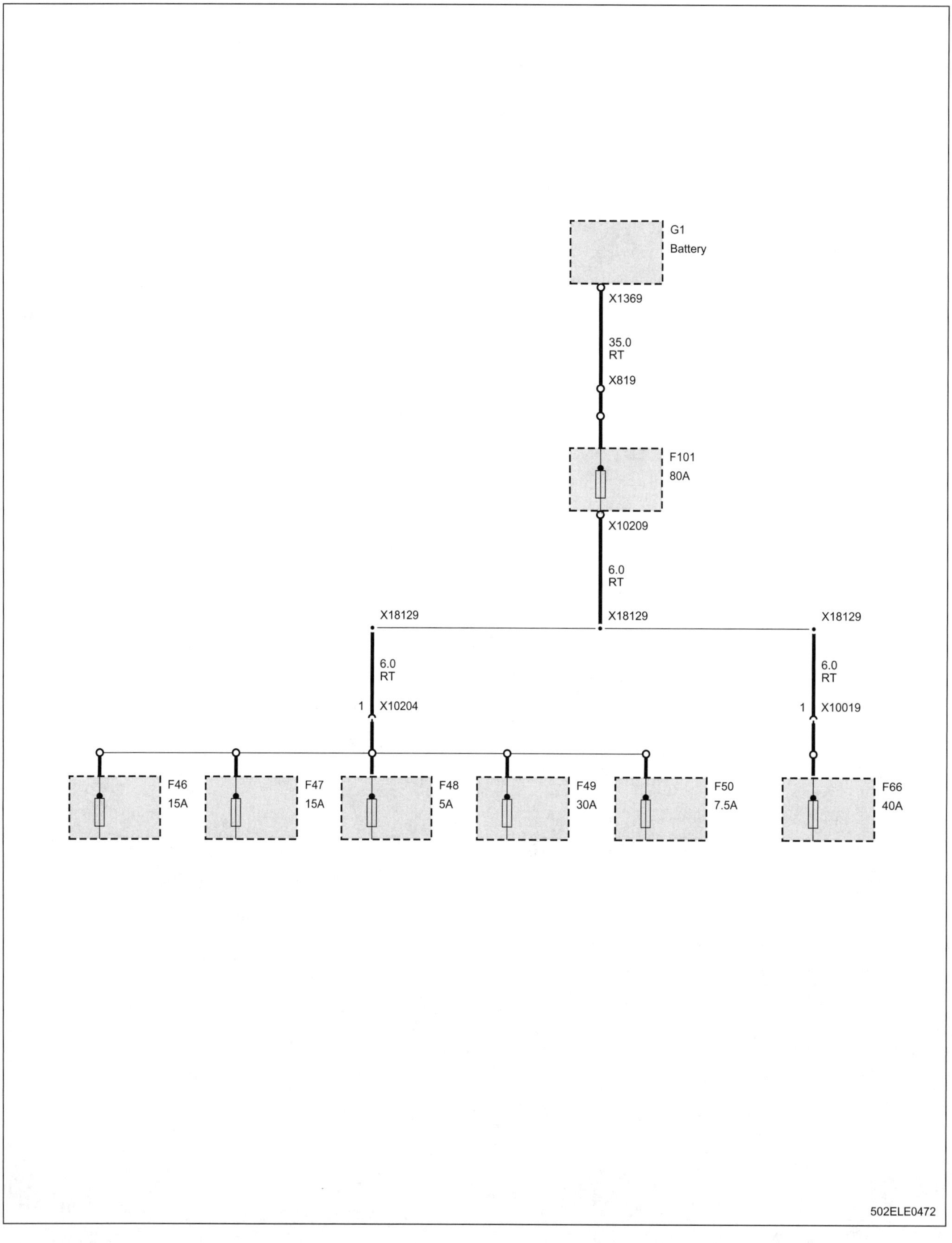
G1
Battery
X1369
35.0
RT
X819
F101
80A
X10209
6.0
RT
X18129
X18129
X18129
6.0
RT
1
X10204
6.0
RT
1
X10019
F46
15A
F47
15A
F48
5A
F49
30A
F50
7.5A
F66
40A
502ELE0472

Power Distribution Fuse F102

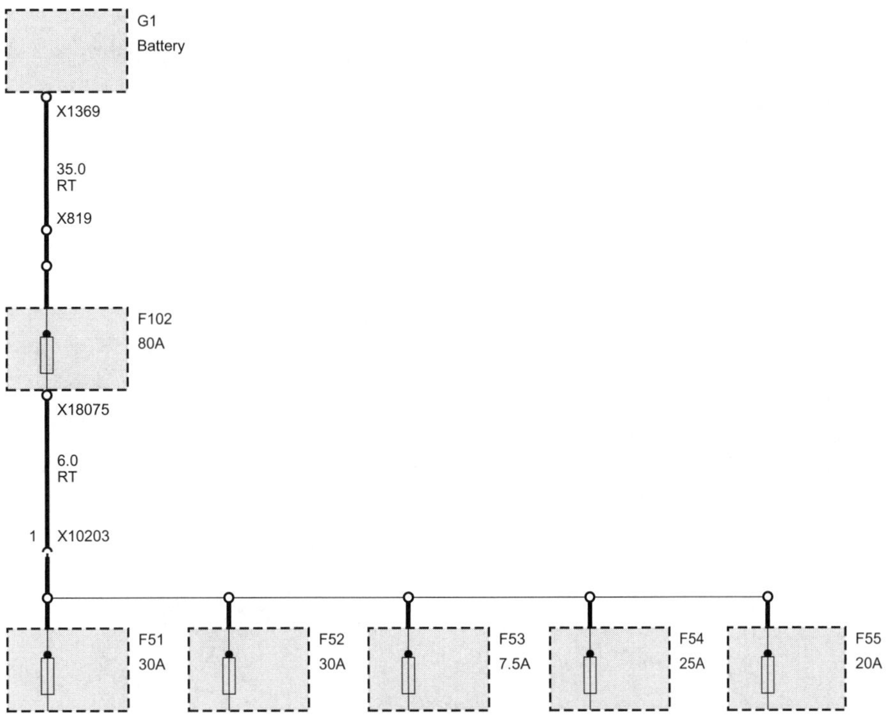

502ELE0473a

Power Distribution Fuse F103

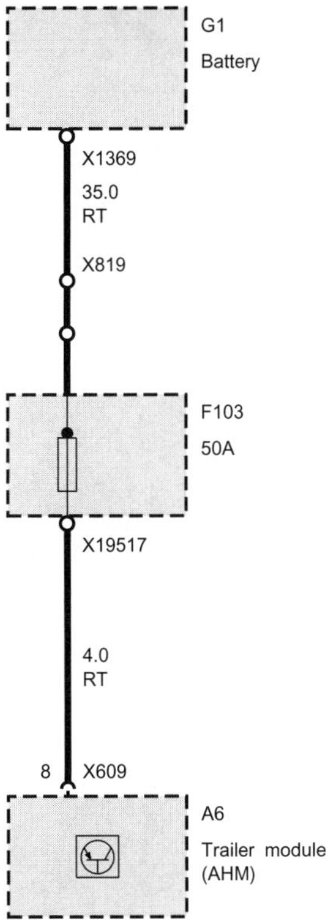

502ELE0473b

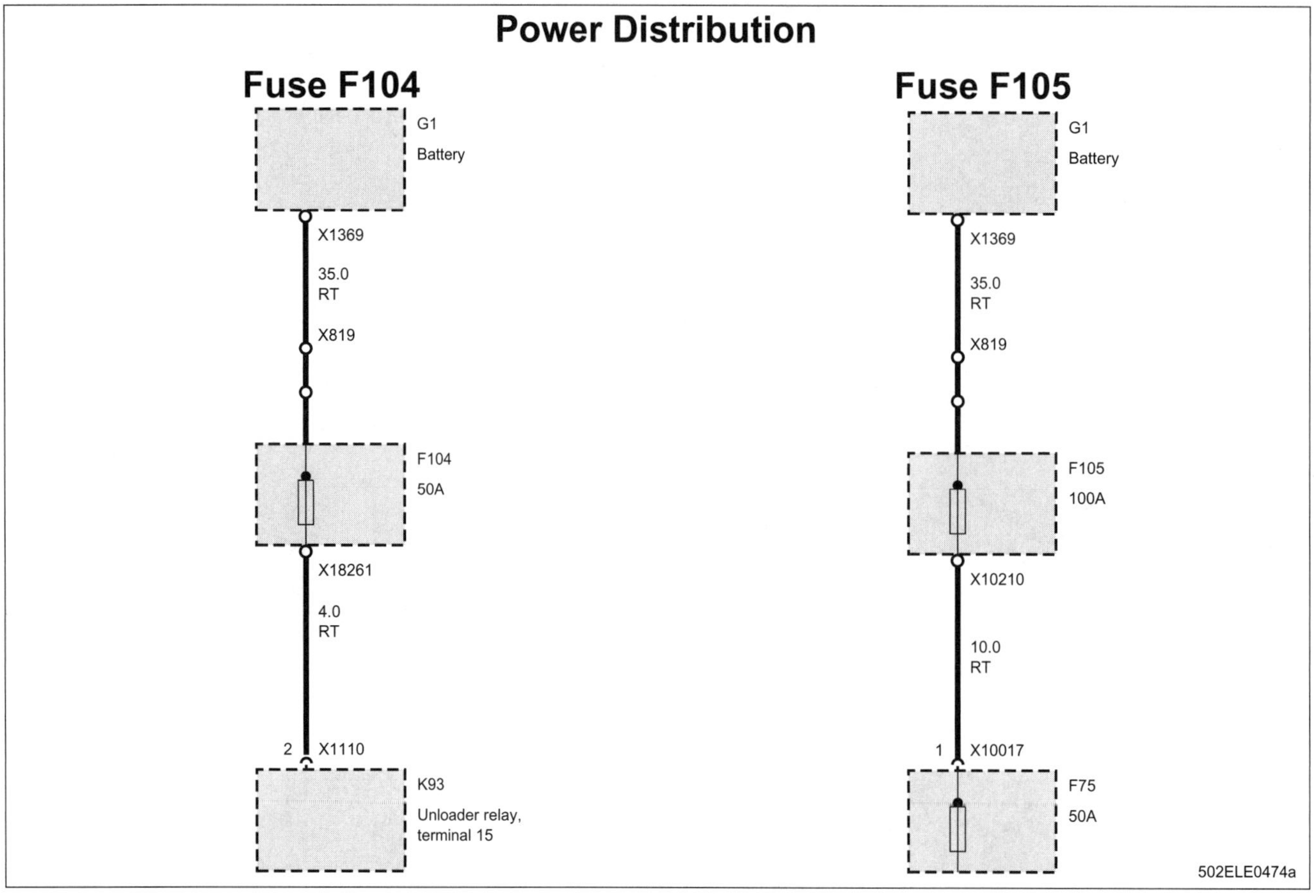
Power Distribution
Fuse F104
G1
Battery
X1369
35.0
RT
X819
F104
50A
X18261
4.0
RT
2
X1110
K93
Unloader relay, terminal 15
Fuse F105
G1
Battery
X1369
35.0
RT
X819
F105
100A
X10210
10.0
RT
1
X10017
F75
50A
502ELE0474a

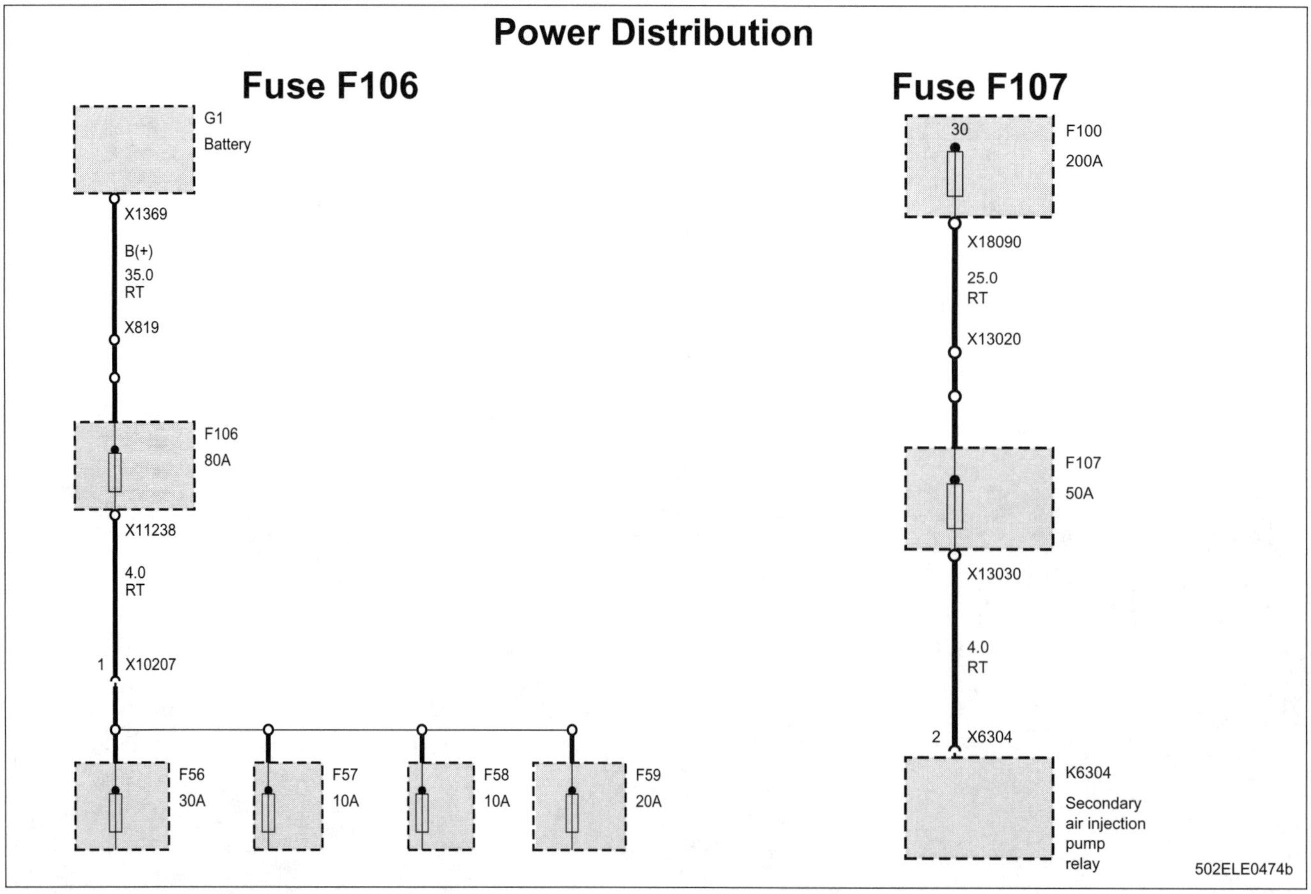
Power Distribution
Fuse F106
G1
Battery
X1369
B(+)
35.0
RT
X819
F106
80A
X11238
4.0
RT
1
X10207
F56
30A
F57
10A
F58
10A
F59
20A
Fuse F107
30
F100
200A
X18090
25.0
RT
X13020
F107
50A
X13030
4.0
RT
2
X6304
K6304
Secondary air injection pump relay
502ELE0474b

Power Distribution
Fuse F113
(1 of 2)

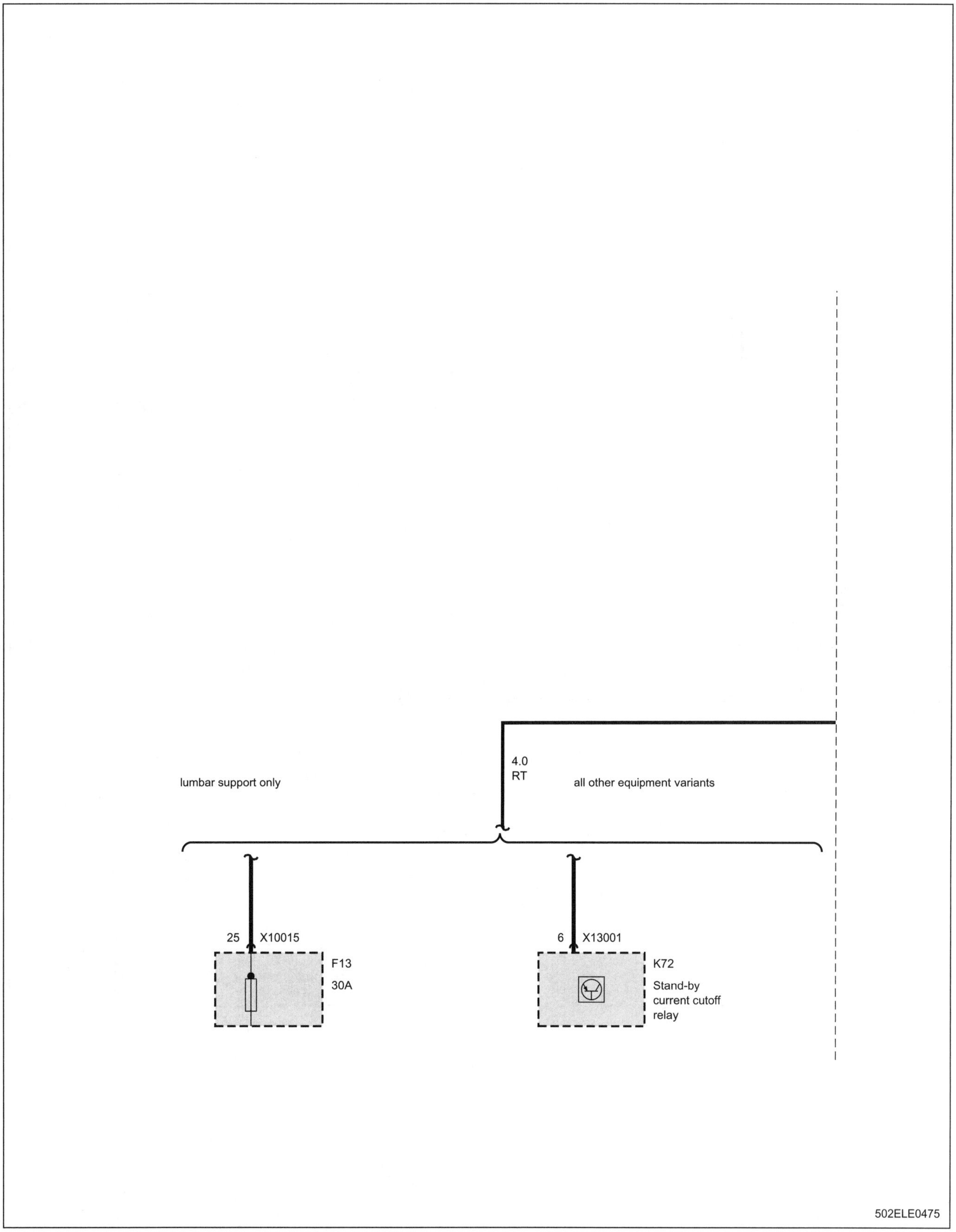
4.0
RT
lumbar support only
all other equipment variants
25
X10015
F13
30A
6
X13001
K72
Stand-by
current cutoff
relay
502ELE0475

Power Distribution
Fuse F113
(2 of 2)

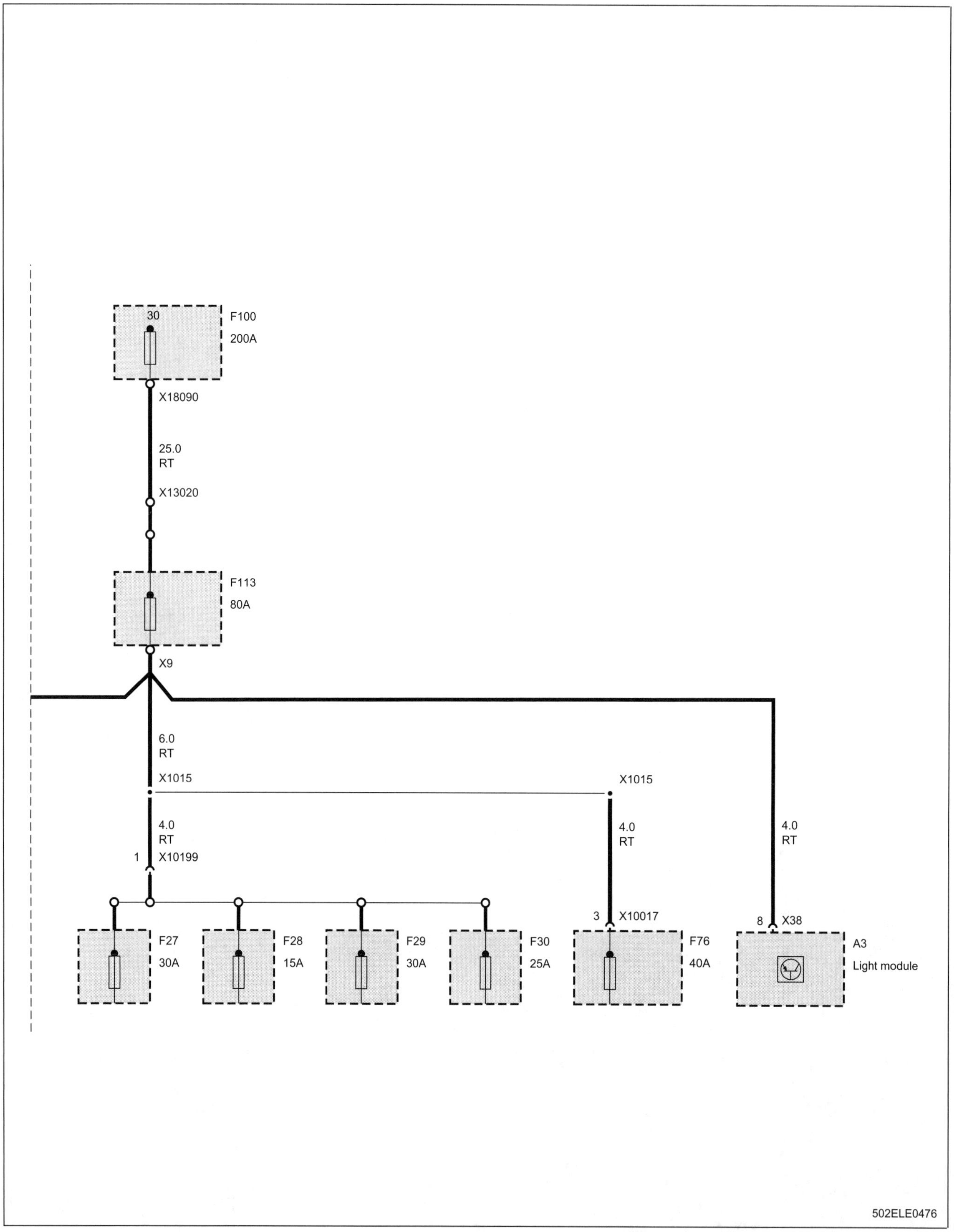
30
F100
200A
X18090
25.0
RT
X13020
F113
80A
X9
6.0
RT
X1015
X1015
4.0
RT
1
X10199
4.0
RT
4.0
RT
F27
30A
F28
15A
F29
30A
F30
25A
3
X10017
F76
40A
8
X38
A3
Light module
502ELE0476

Power Mirrors

Power mirror adjustment without memory (overview)

(1 of 2)

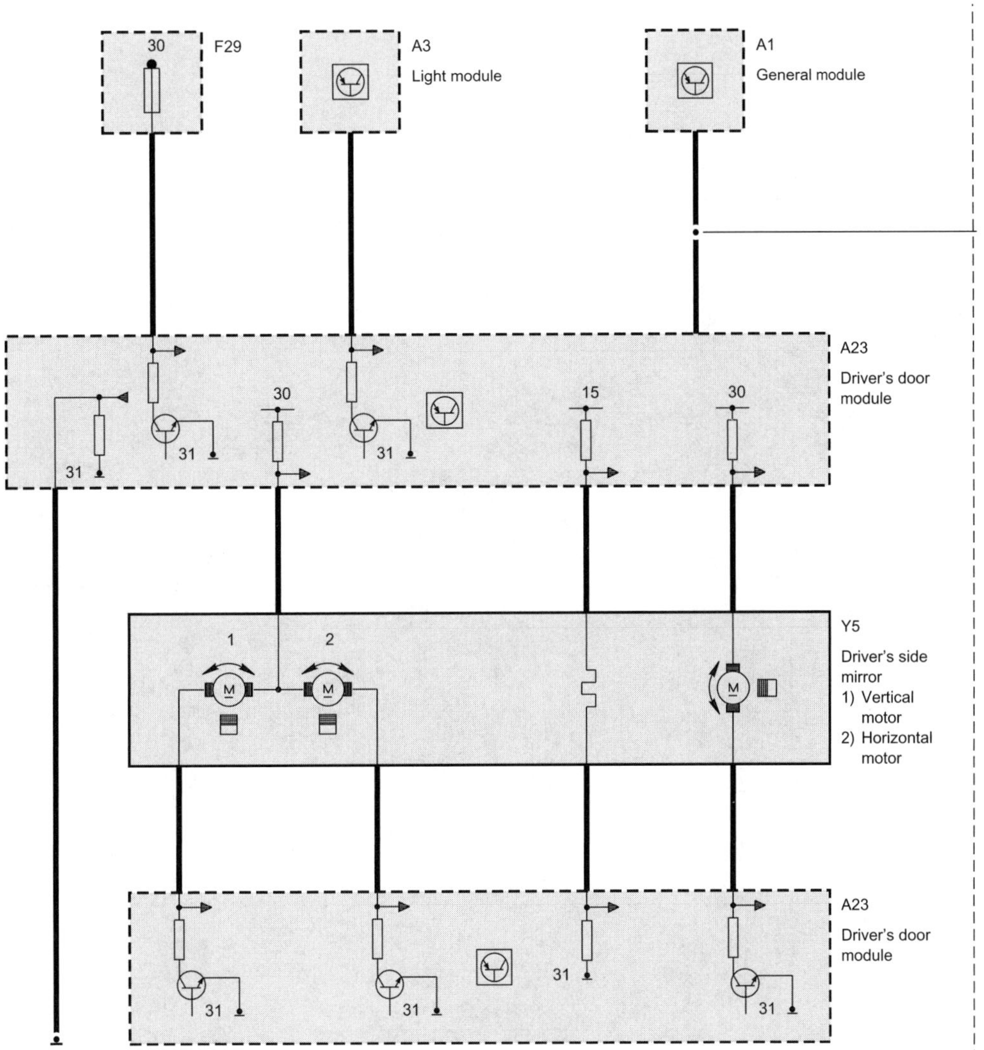

502ELE0134

Power Mirrors

Power mirror adjustment without memory (overview)

(2 of 2)

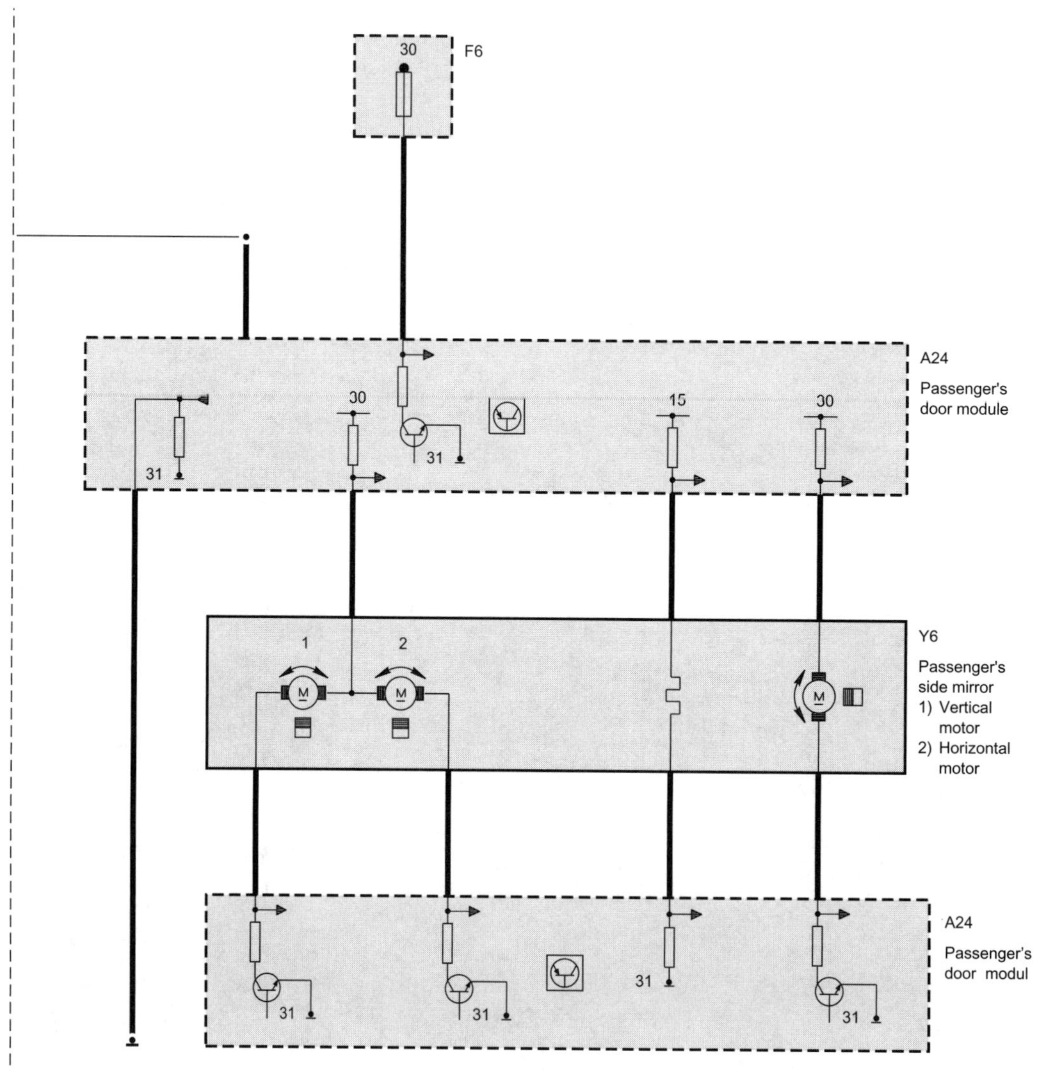

Power Mirrors
Driver's mirror with memory
(1 of 1)

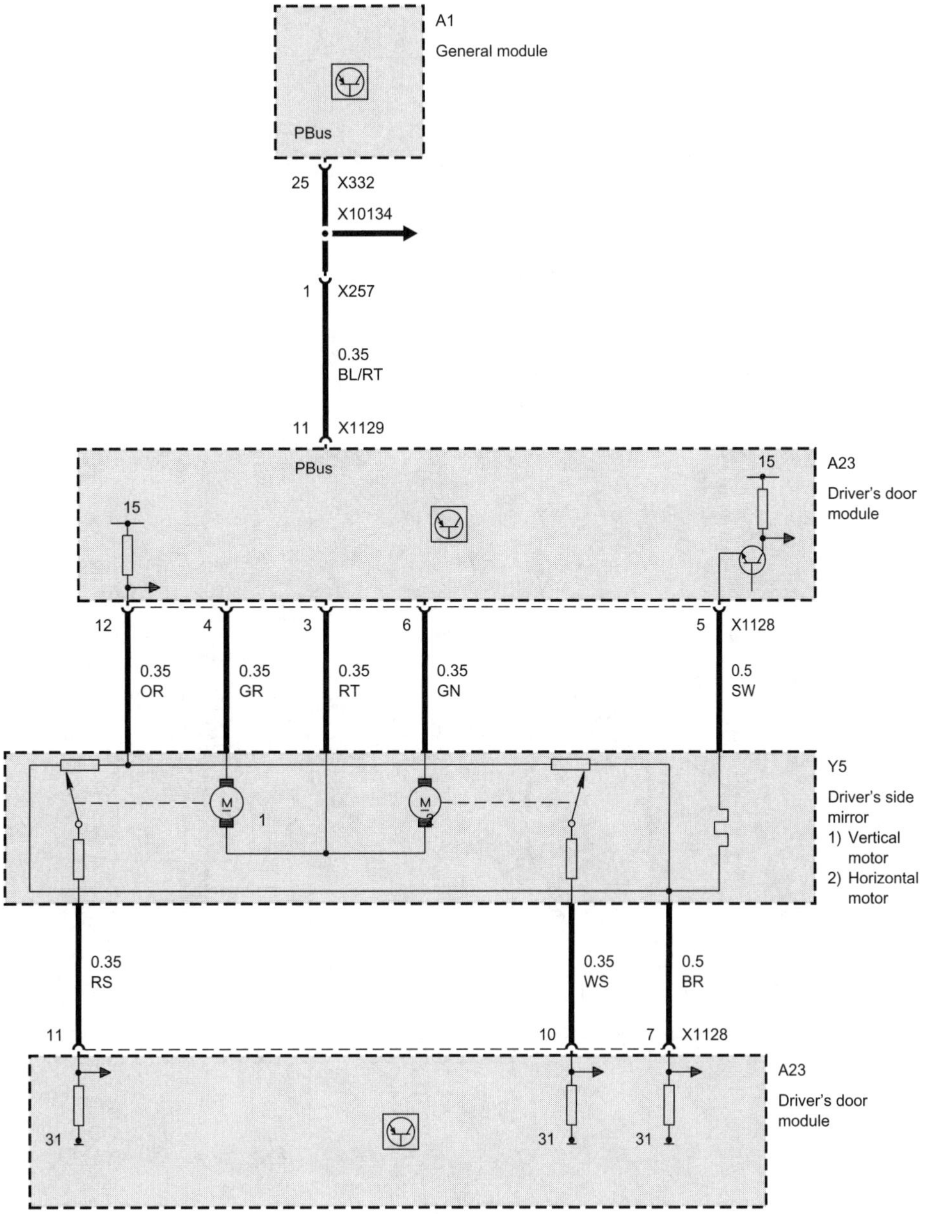

502ELE0042

Power Mirrors
Driver's side power mirror
(1 of 1)

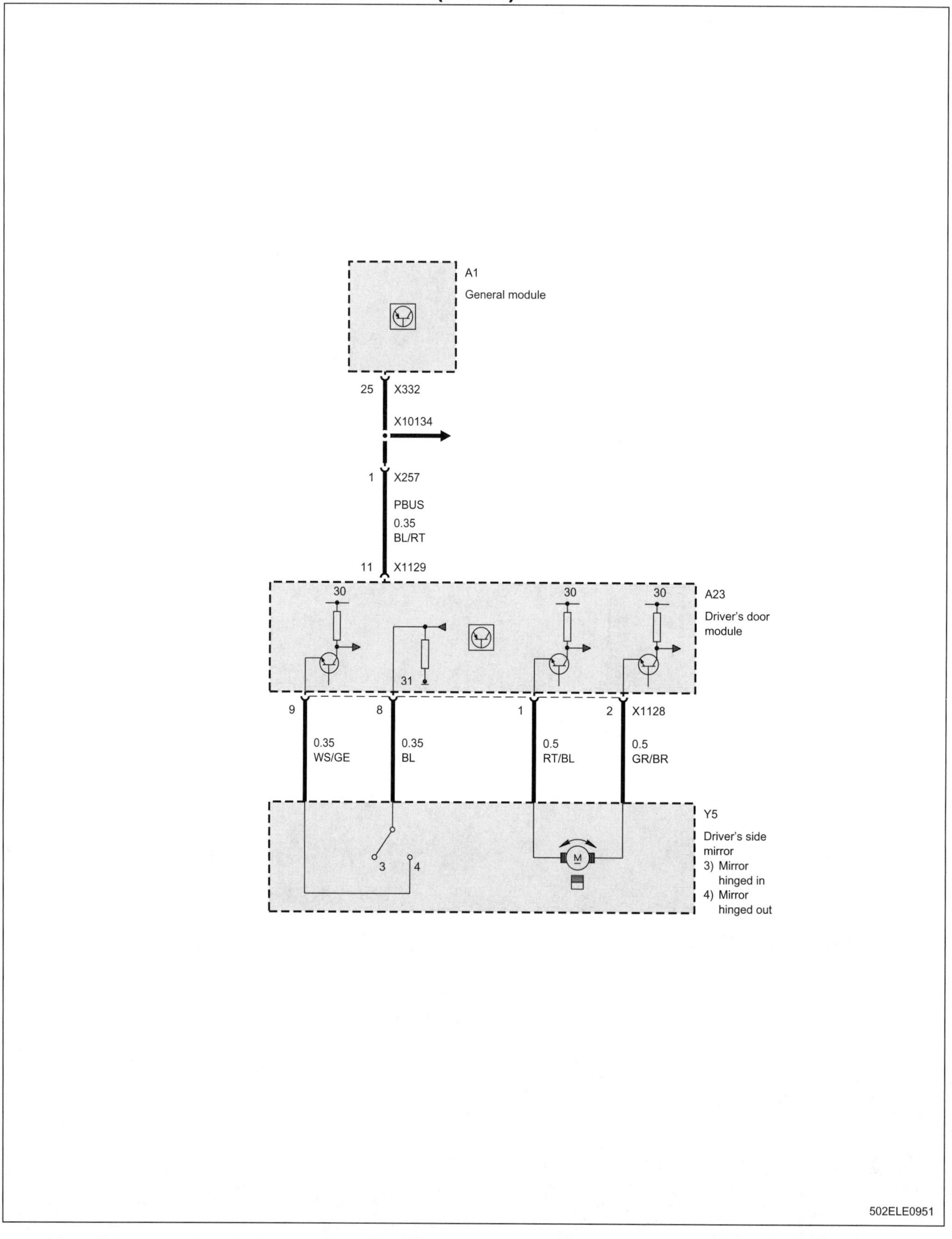
A1
General module
25
X332
X10134
1
X257
PBUS
0.35
BL/RT
11
X1129
30
30
30
31
A23
Driver's door
module
9
8
1
2
X1128
0.35
WS/GE
0.35
BL
0.5
RT/BL
0.5
GR/BR
3
4
M
Y5
Driver's side
mirror
3) Mirror
hinged in
4) Mirror
hinged out
502ELE0951

Power Mirrors
Electrochromic mirror
(1 of 1)

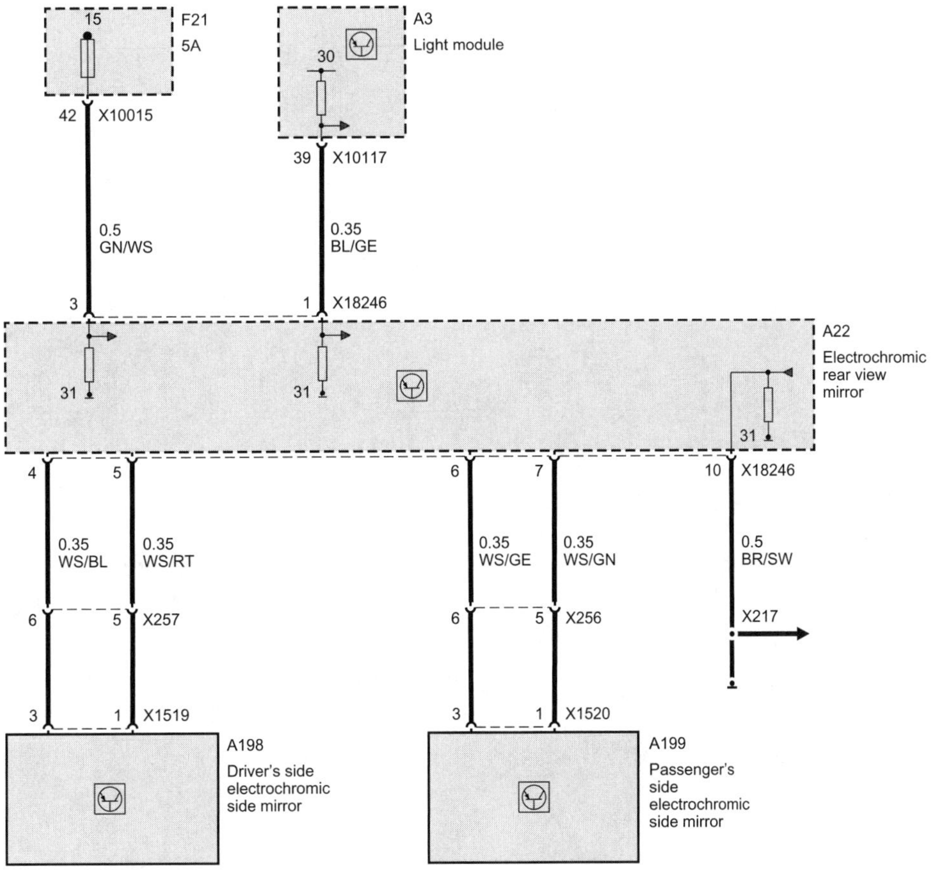
15
F21
5A
A3
Light module
30
42
X10015
39
X10117
0.5
GN/WS
0.35
BL/GE
3
1
X18246
A22
Electrochromic
rear view
mirror
31
31
31
4
5
6
7
10
X18246
0.35
WS/BL
0.35
WS/RT
0.35
WS/GE
0.35
WS/GN
0.5
BR/SW
6
5
X257
6
5
X256
X217
3
1
X1519
3
1
X1520
A198
Driver's side
electrochromic
side mirror
A199
Passenger's
side
electrochromic
side mirror
502ELE0050

Power Mirrors
Passenger's mirror with memory
(1 of 1)

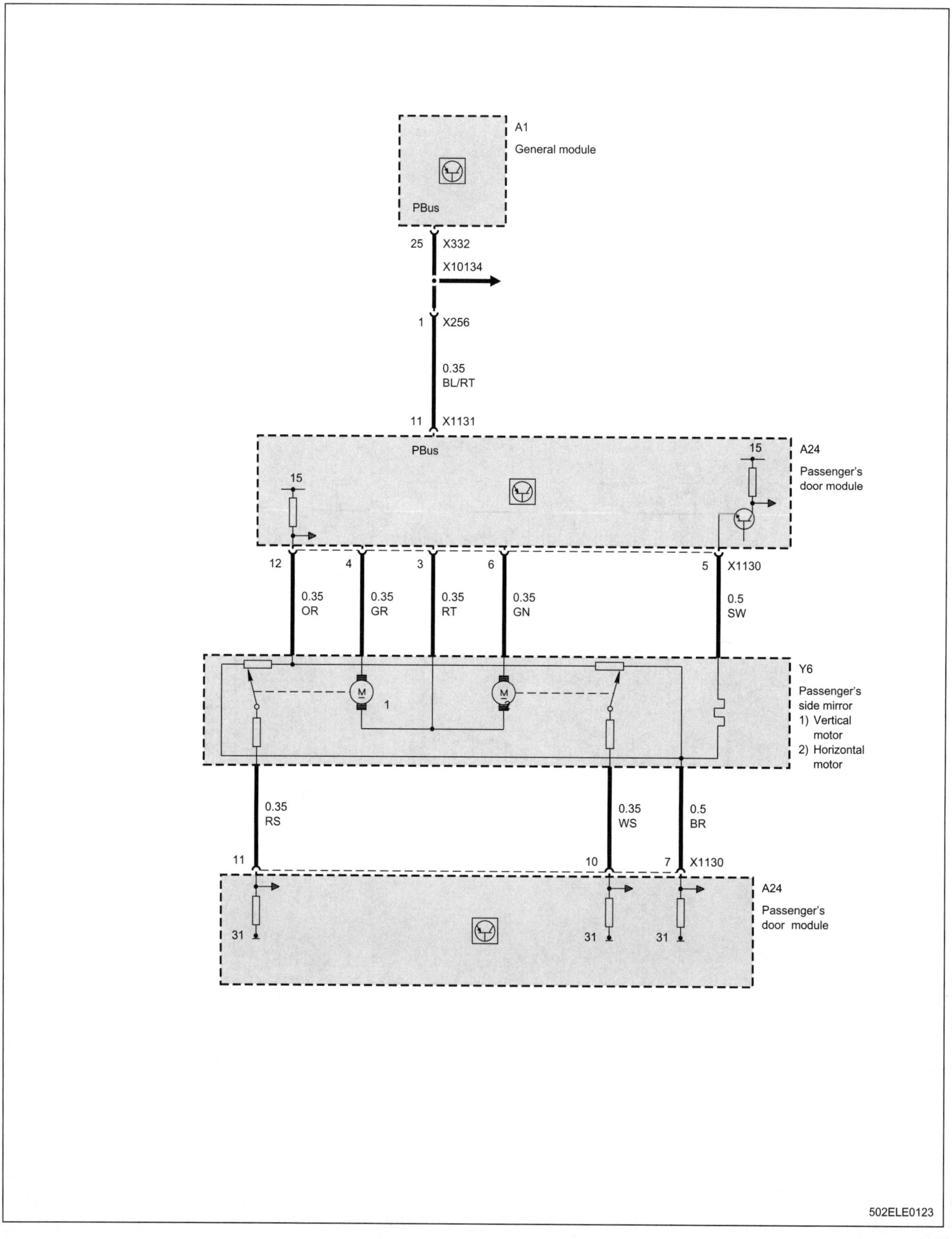

Power Mirrors
Passenger's hinged-window drive
(1 of 1)

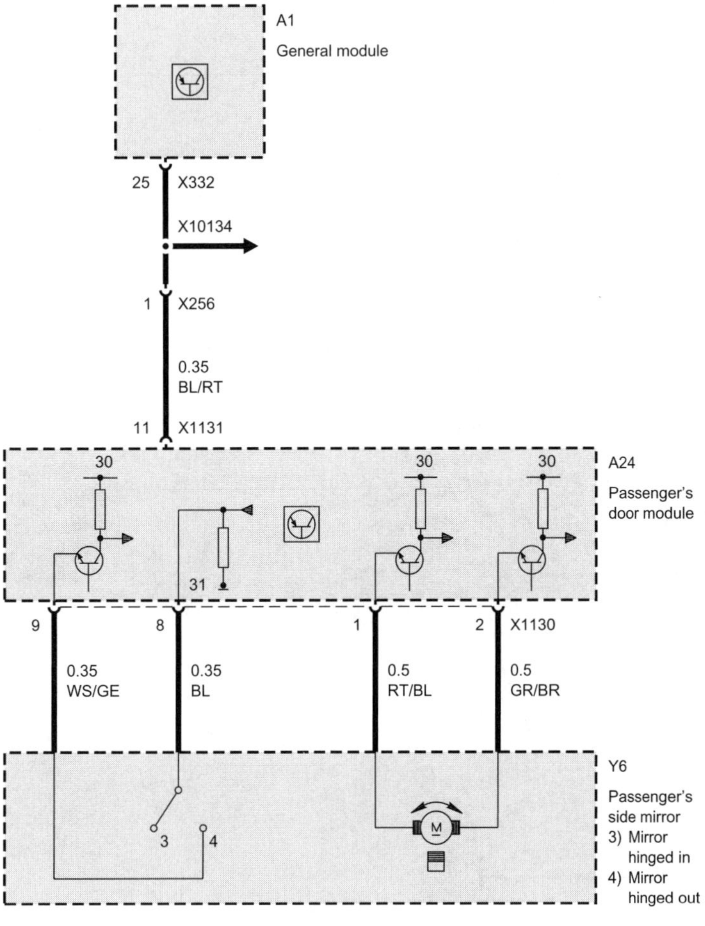

502ELE0121

Power Seats
Heated seats (overview)
(1 of 1)

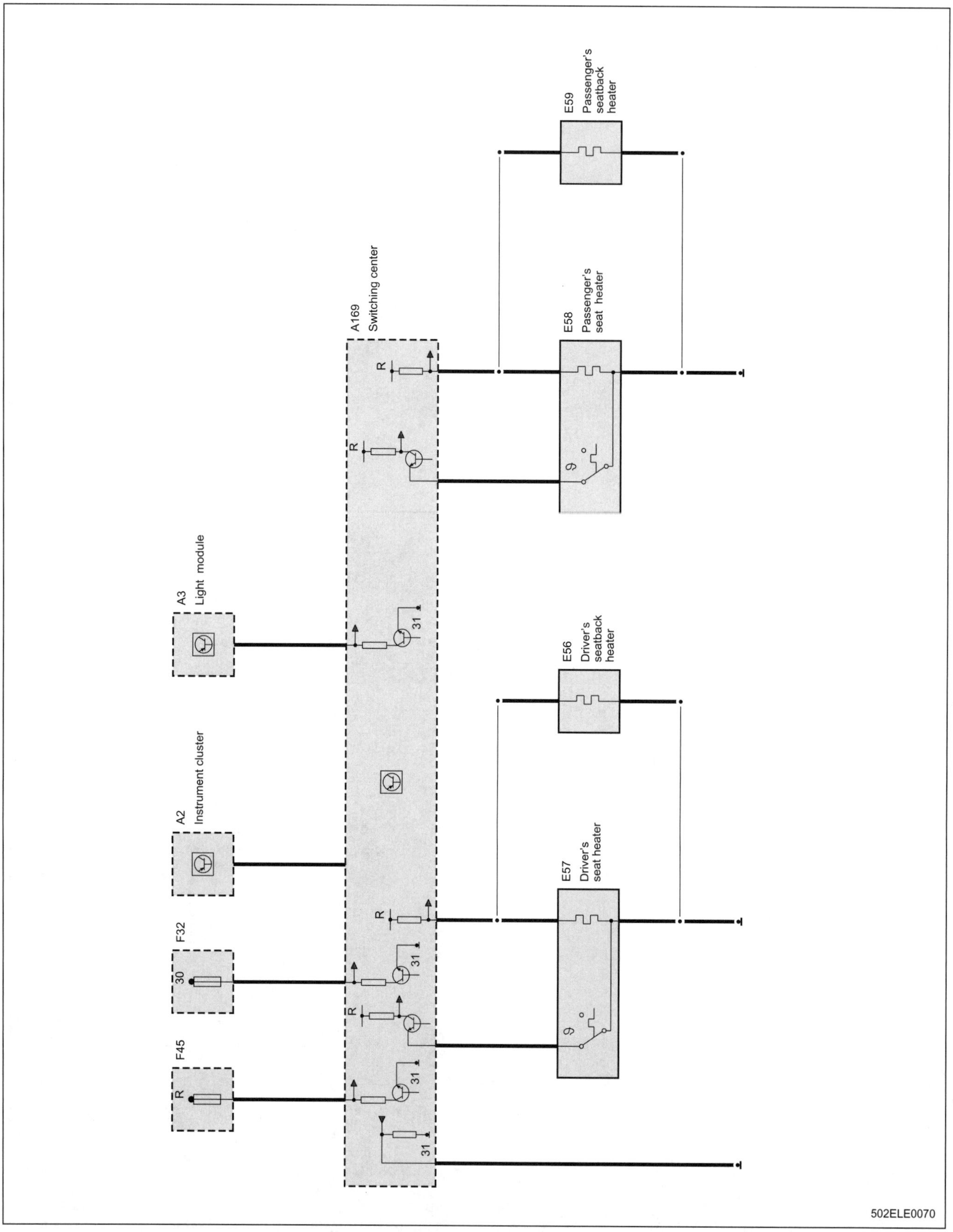
E59
Passenger's seatback heater
E58
Passenger's seat heater
A169
Switching center
A3
Light module
E56
Driver's seatback heater
A2
Instrument cluster
E57
Driver's seat heater
F32
F45
R
30
31
502ELE0070

Power Seats
Seat adjustment without memory (overview)
(1 of 3)

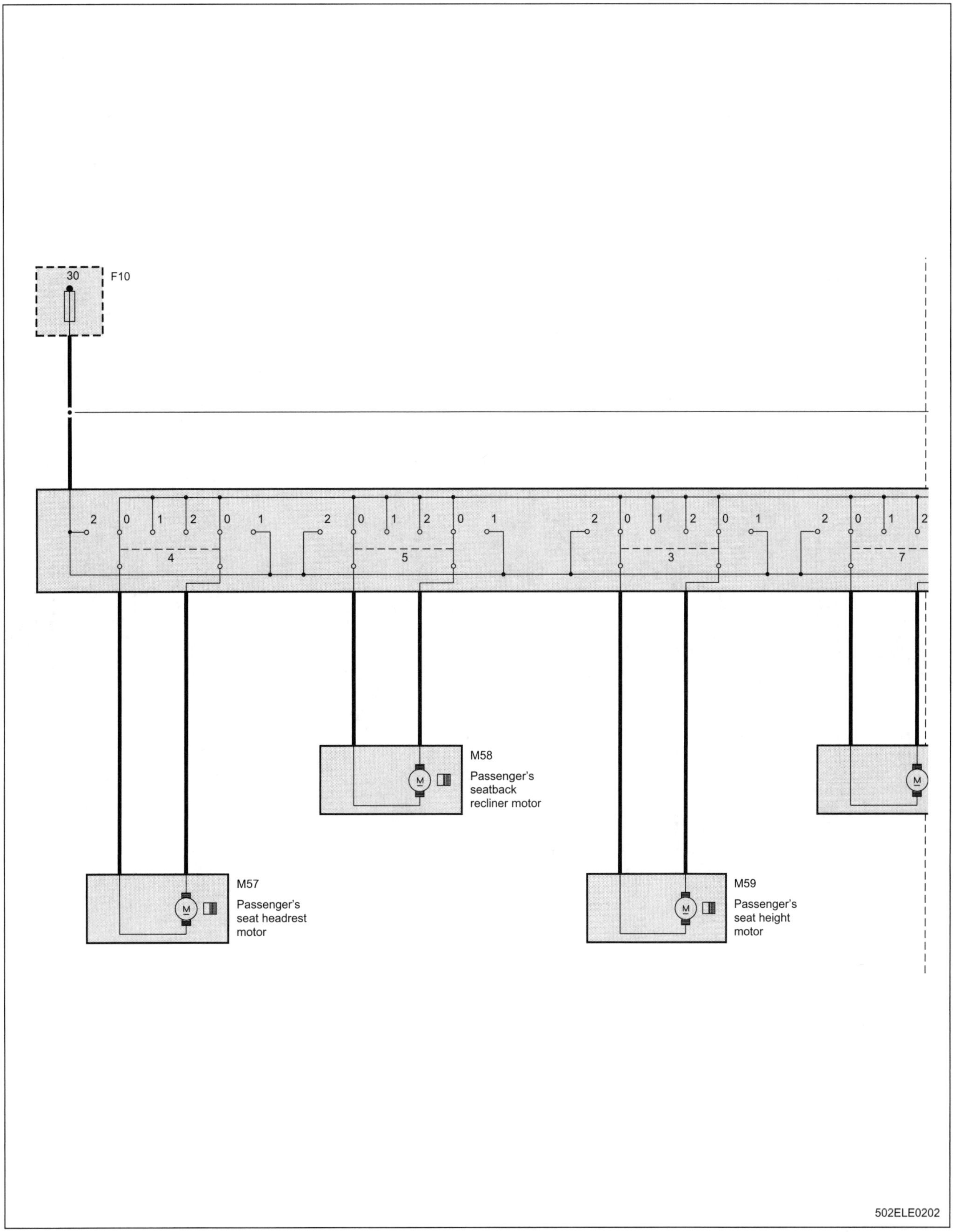

Power Seats
Seat adjustment without memory (overview)
(2 of 3)

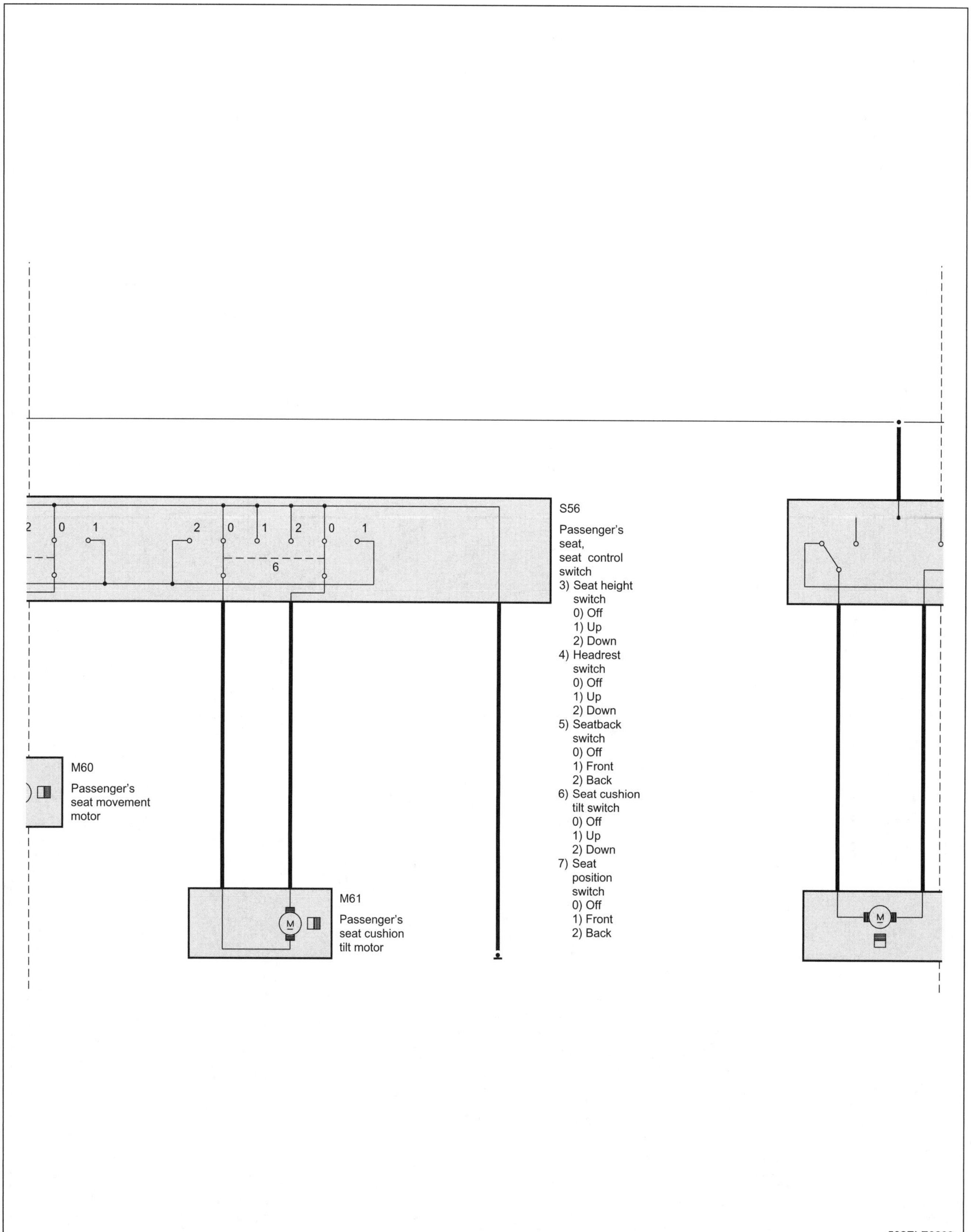

502ELE0203

Power Seats
Seat adjustment without memory (overview)
(3 of 3)

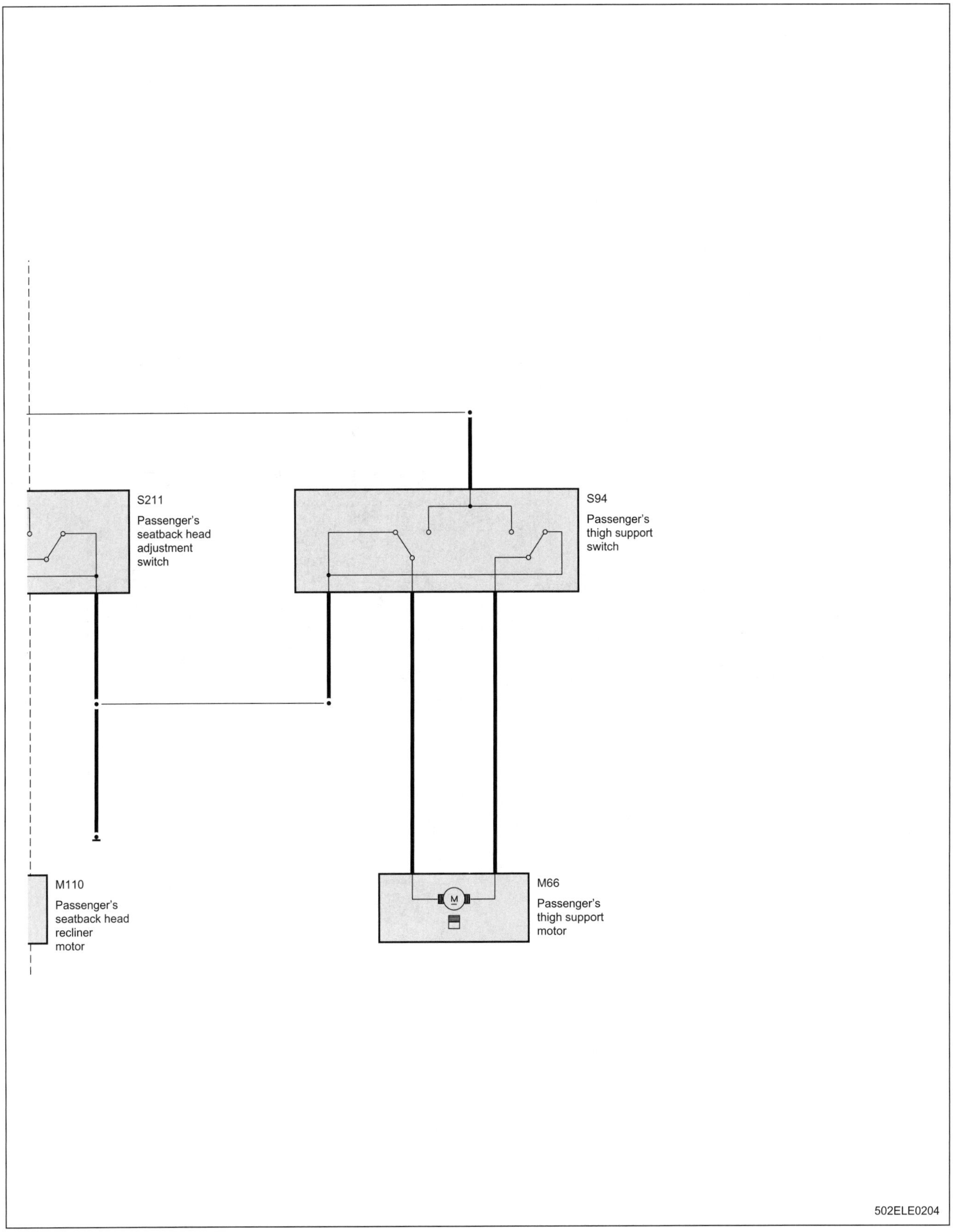

Power Seats
Seat/steering column memory control module (A21)
(1 of 4)

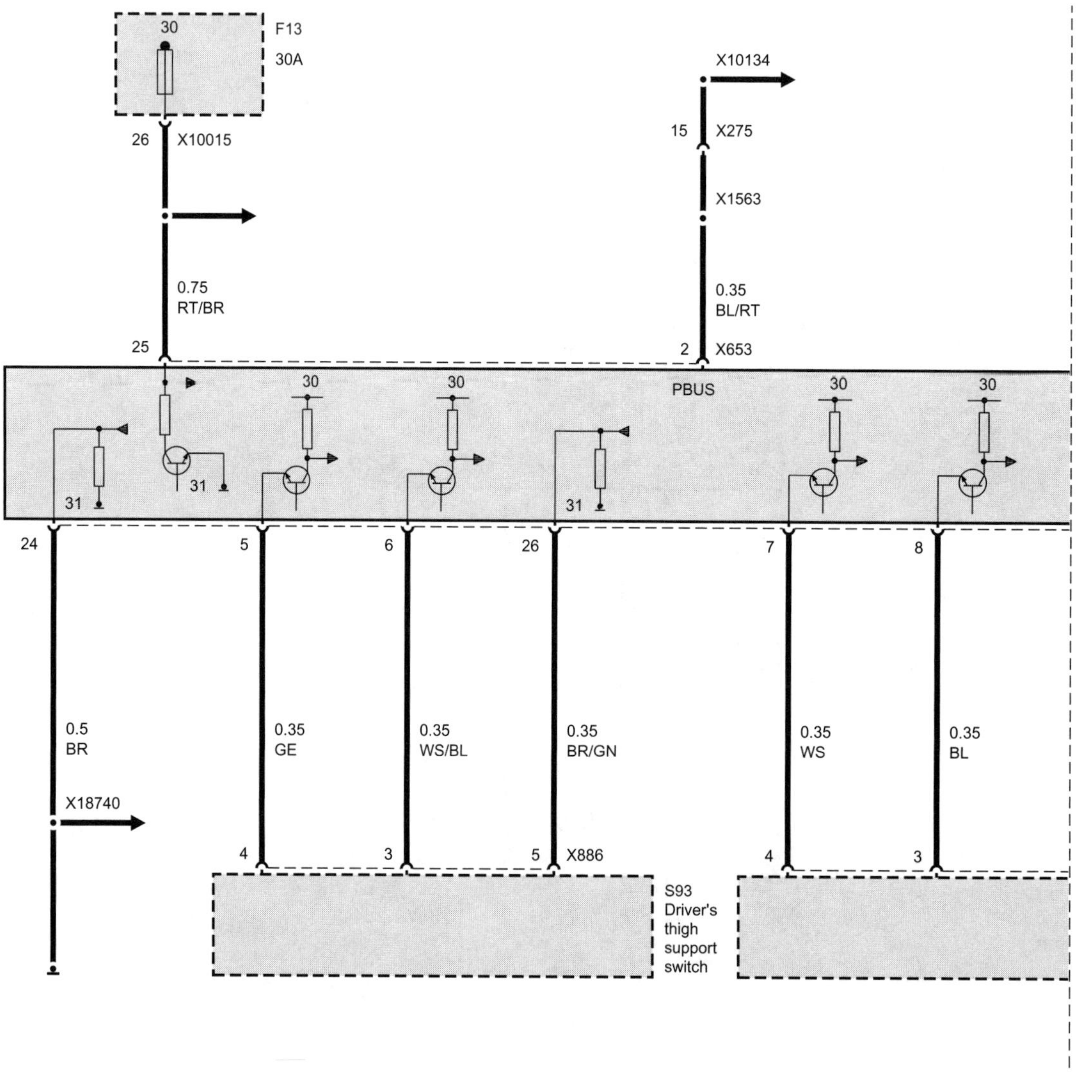

502ELE0403

Power Seats
Seat/steering column memory control module (A21)
(2 of 4)

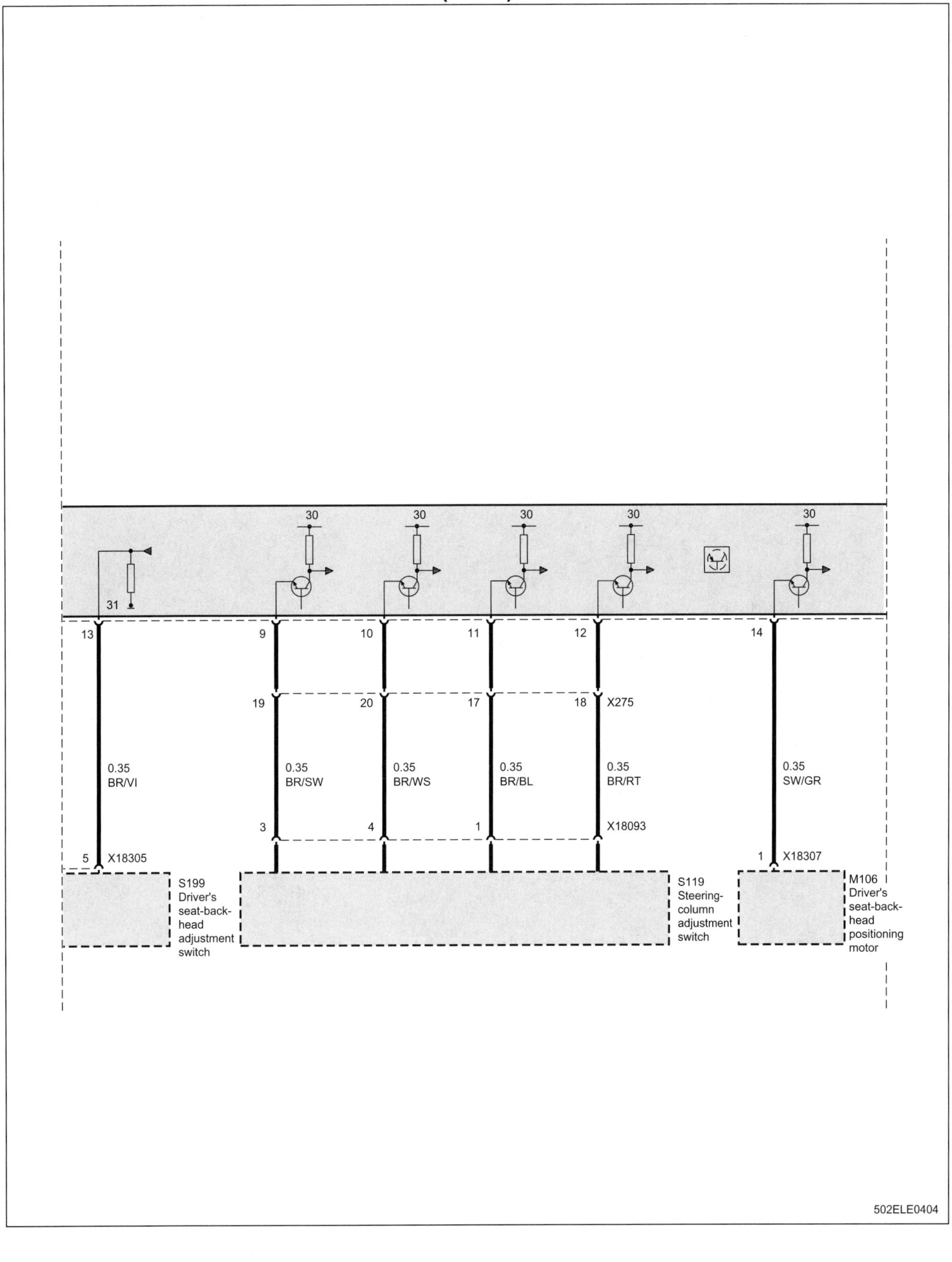

Power Seats
Seat/steering column memory control module (A21)
(3 of 4)

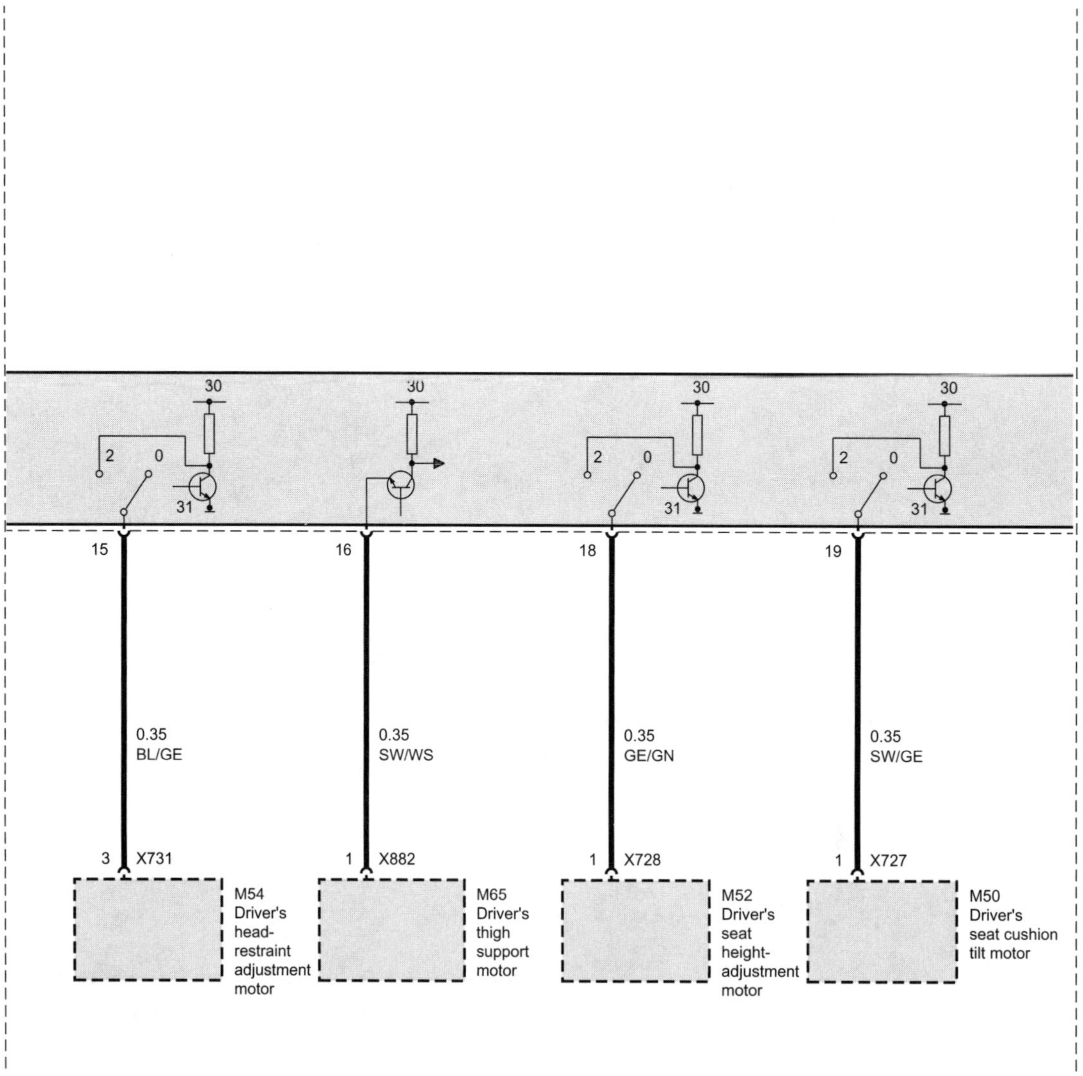

502ELE0405

Power Seats
Seat/steering column memory control module (A21)
(4 of 4)

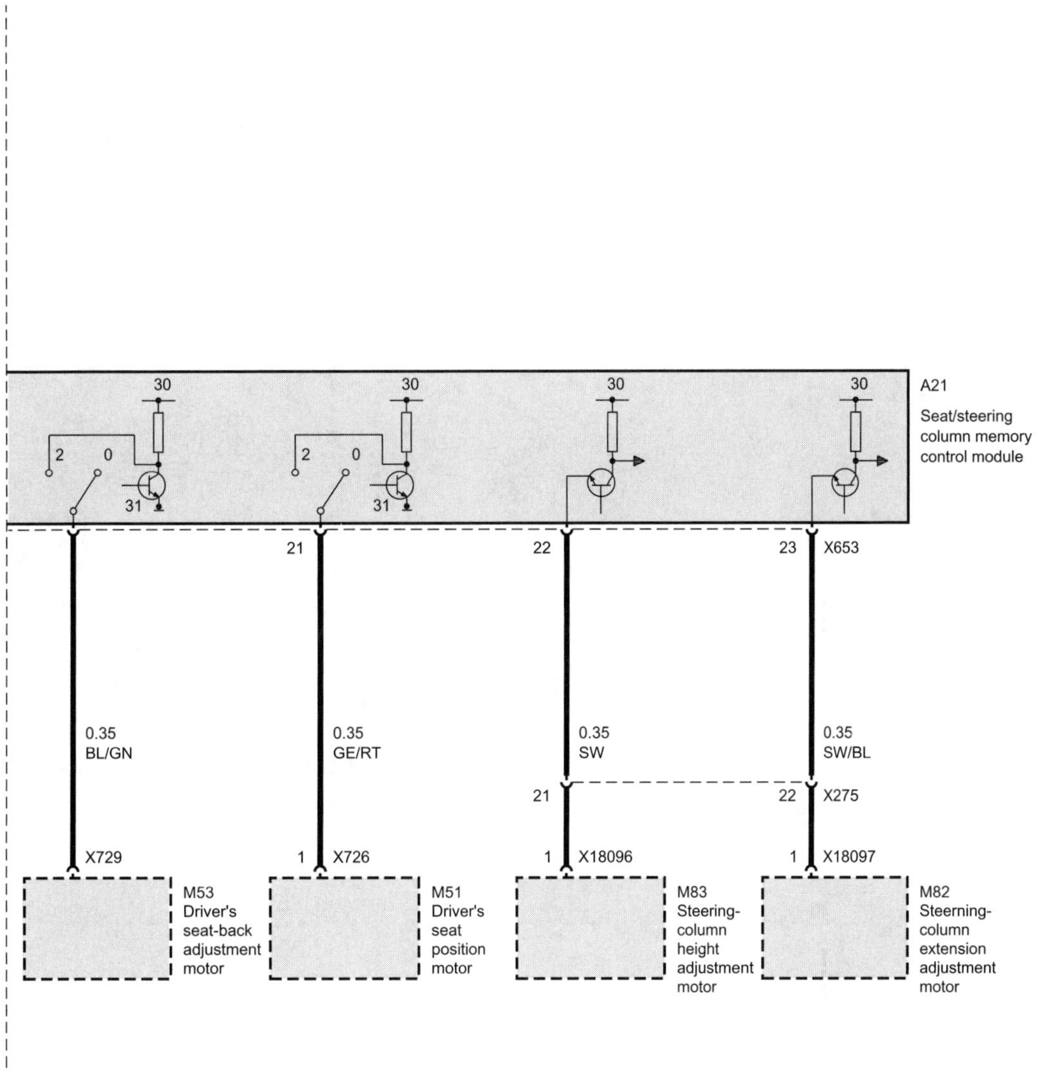

502ELE0406

Power Seats
Driver memory switch
(1 of 1)

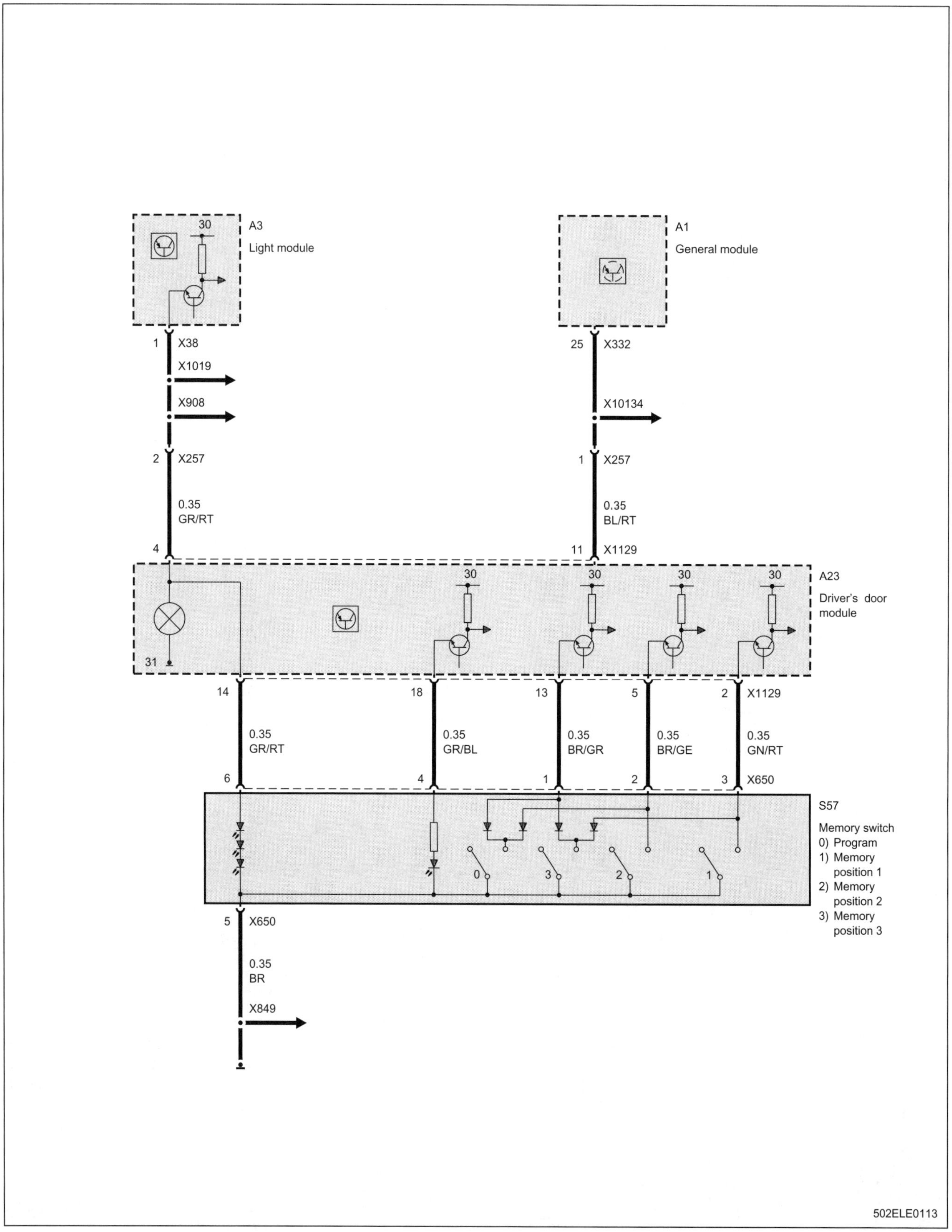
30
A3
Light module
A1
General module
1
X38
X1019
X908
2
X257
0.35
GR/RT
4
25
X332
X10134
1
X257
0.35
BL/RT
11
X1129
30
30
30
30
A23
Driver's door
module
31
14
18
13
5
2
X1129
0.35
GR/RT
0.35
GR/BL
0.35
BR/GR
0.35
BR/GE
0.35
GN/RT
6
4
1
2
3
X650
S57
Memory switch
0) Program
1) Memory position 1
2) Memory position 2
3) Memory position 3
0
3
2
1
5
X650
0.35
BR
X849
502ELE0113

Power Seats
Driver's seat adjustment with memory
(1 of 3)

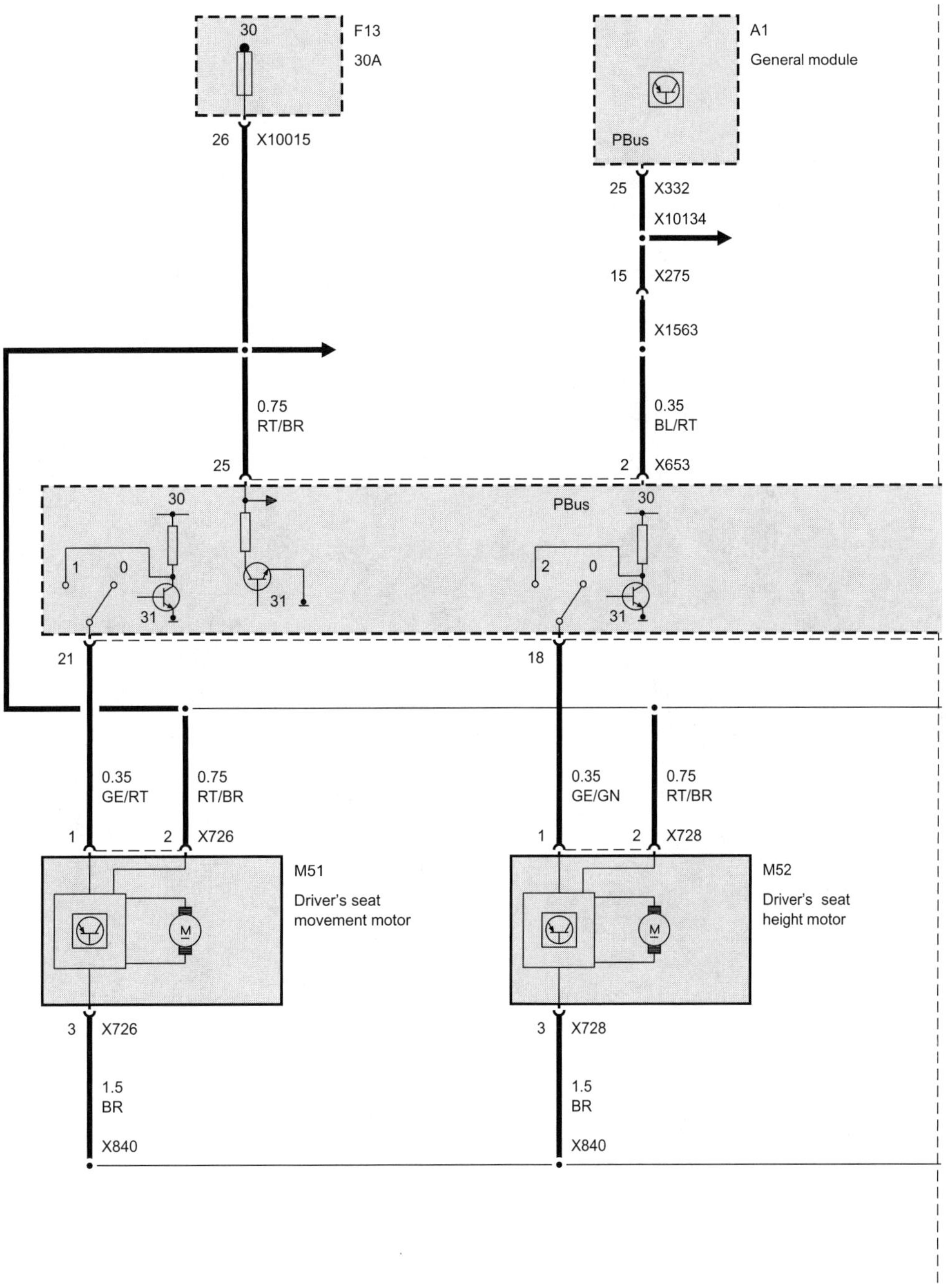

502ELE0043

Power Seats
Driver's seat adjustment with memory
(2 of 3)

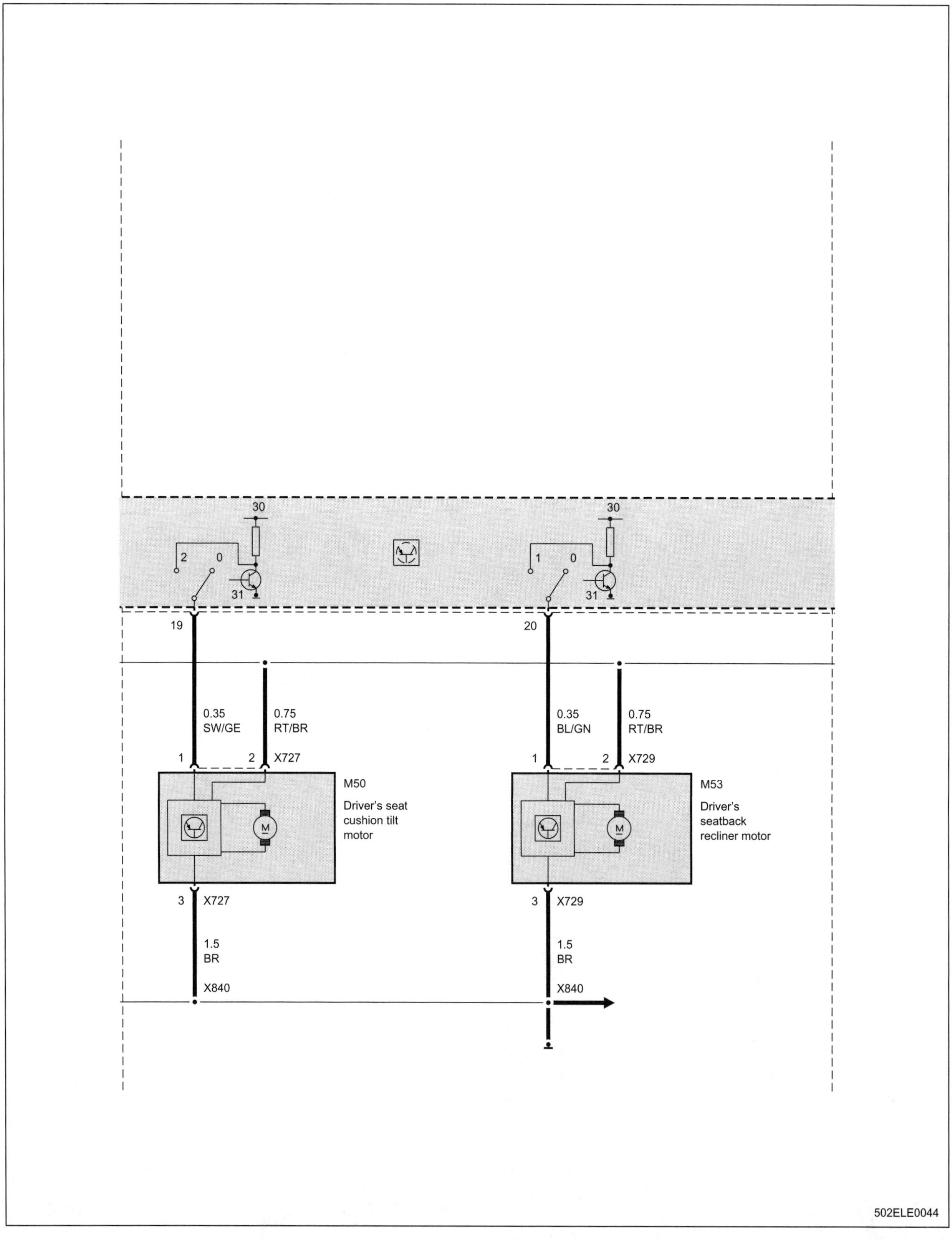

Power Seats
Driver's seat adjustment with memory
(3 of 3)

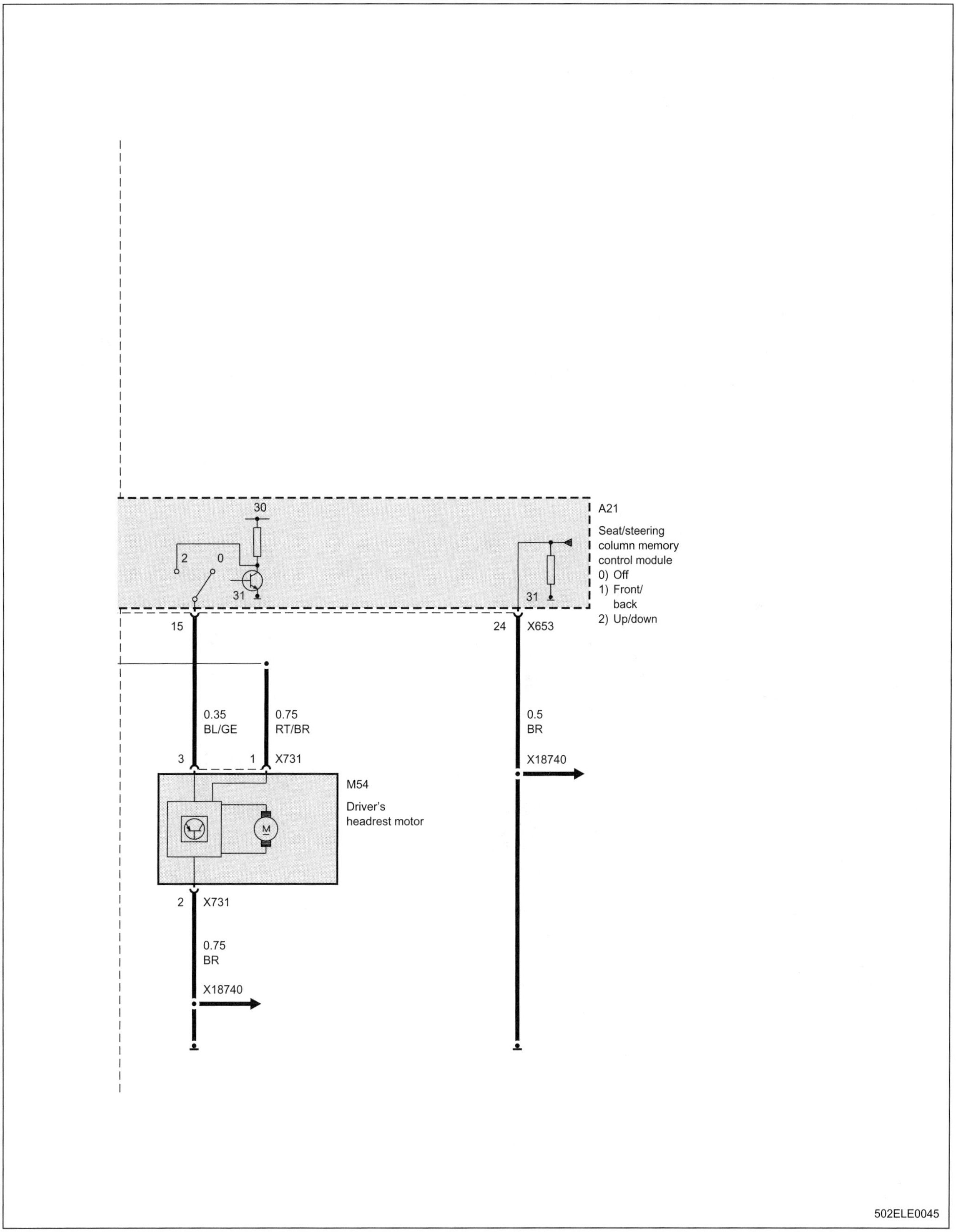

Power Seats
Driver's seat heating
(1 of 1)

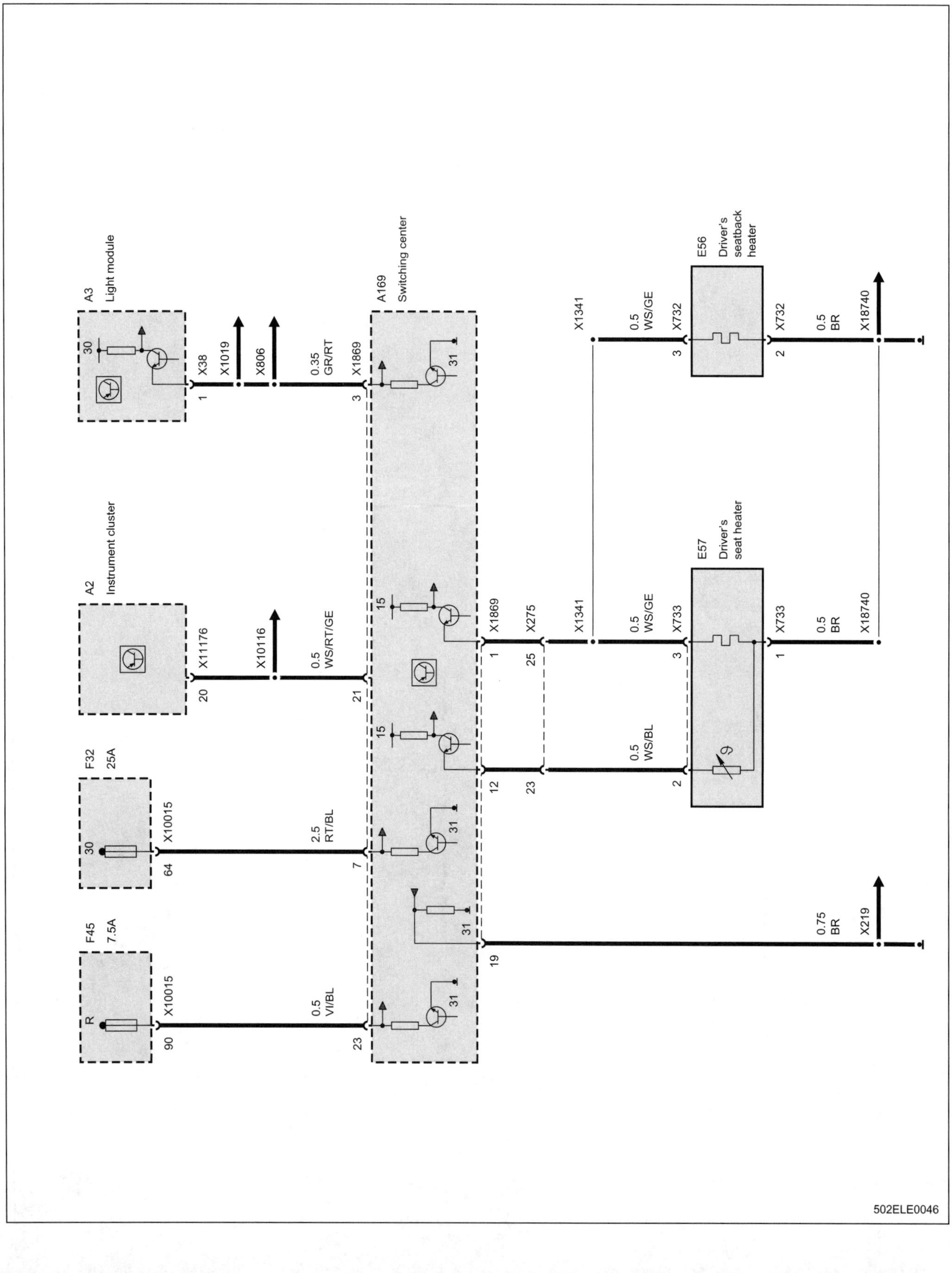
A3 Light module
A2 Instrument cluster
F32 25A
F45 7.5A
A169 Switching center
E56 Driver's seatback heater
E57 Driver's seat heater
X38
X1019
X806
0.35 GR/RT
X1869
X11176
X10116
0.5 WS/RT/GE
X10015
2.5 RT/BL
0.5 VI/BL
X275
X1341
0.5 WS/GE
0.5 WS/BL
X732
X733
0.5 BR
X18740
0.75 BR
X219
502ELE0046

Power Seats
Driver's seat lumbar support
(1 of 1)

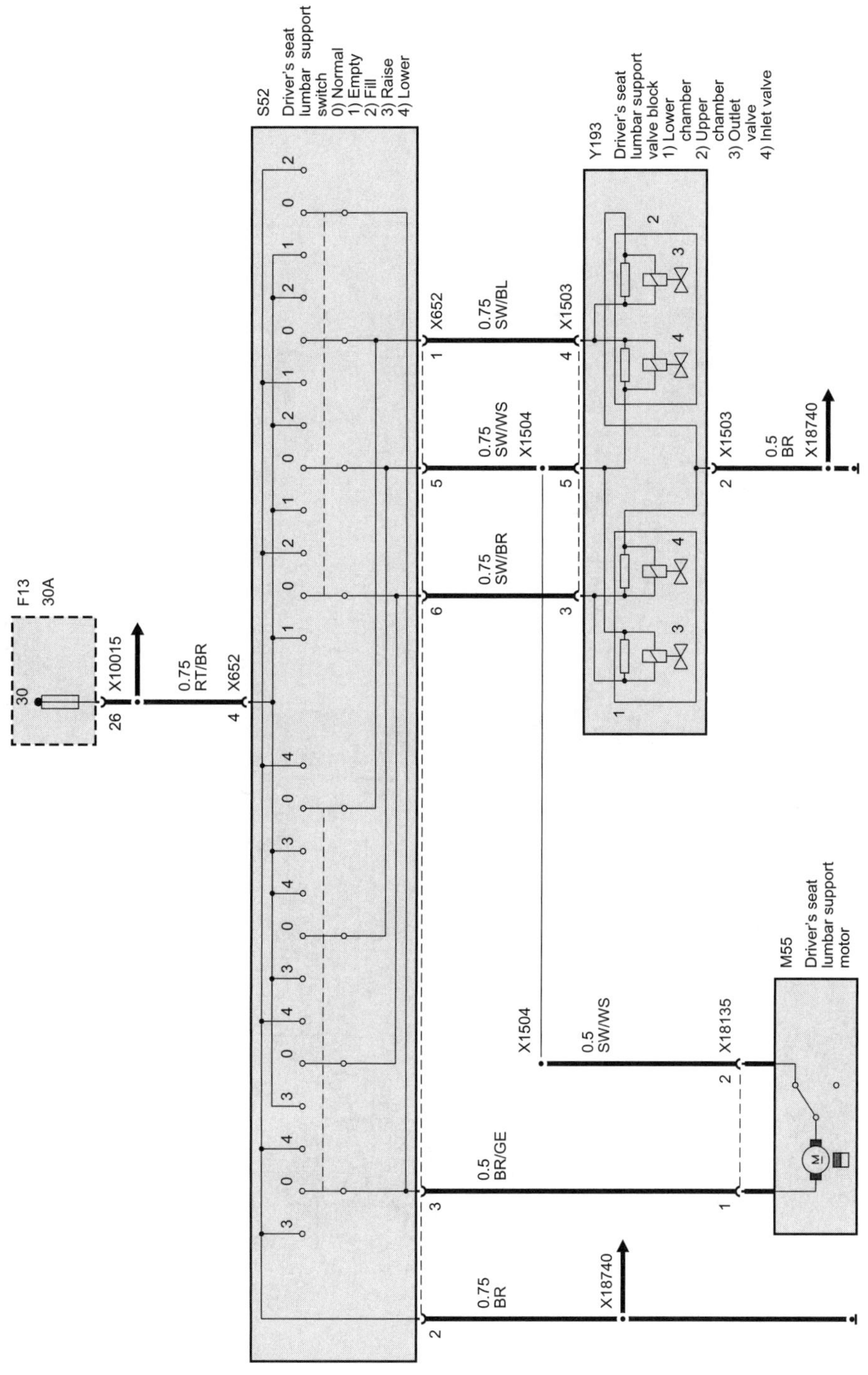

502ELE0041

Power Seats
Driver's seatback head adjust. with memory
(1 of 1)

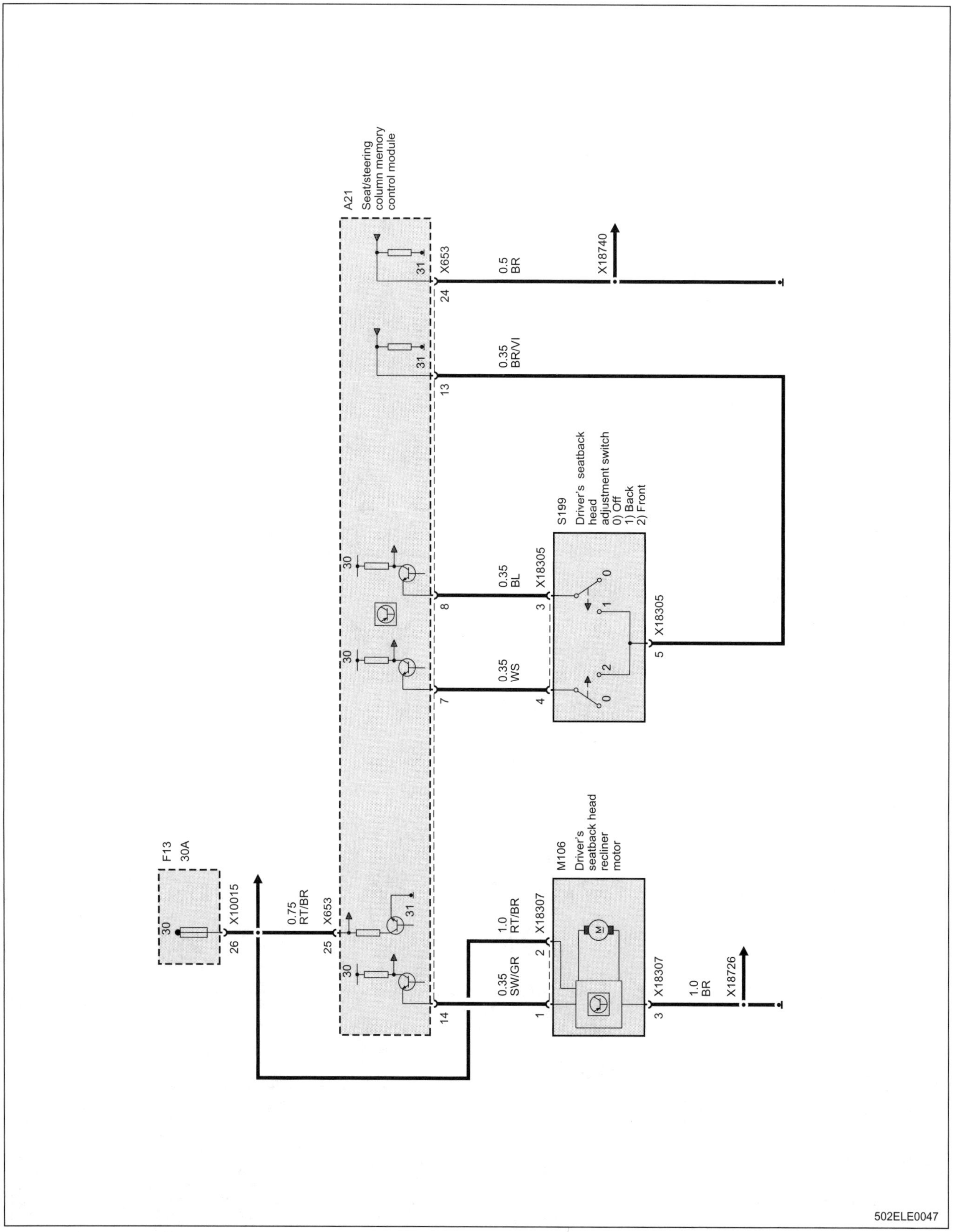

Power Seats
Driver's thigh support with memory
(1 of 1)

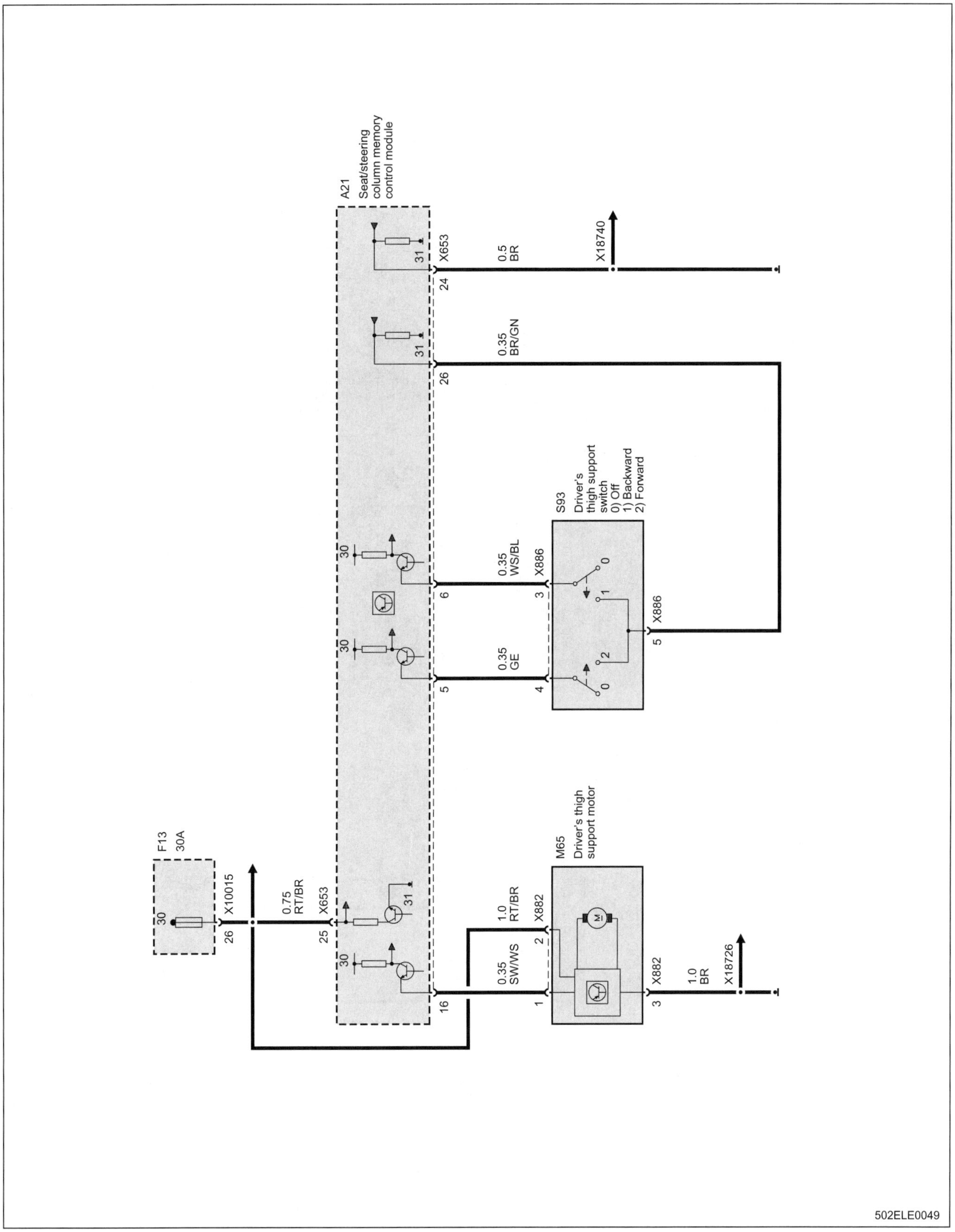

Power Seats
Passenger's lumbar support
(1 of 1)

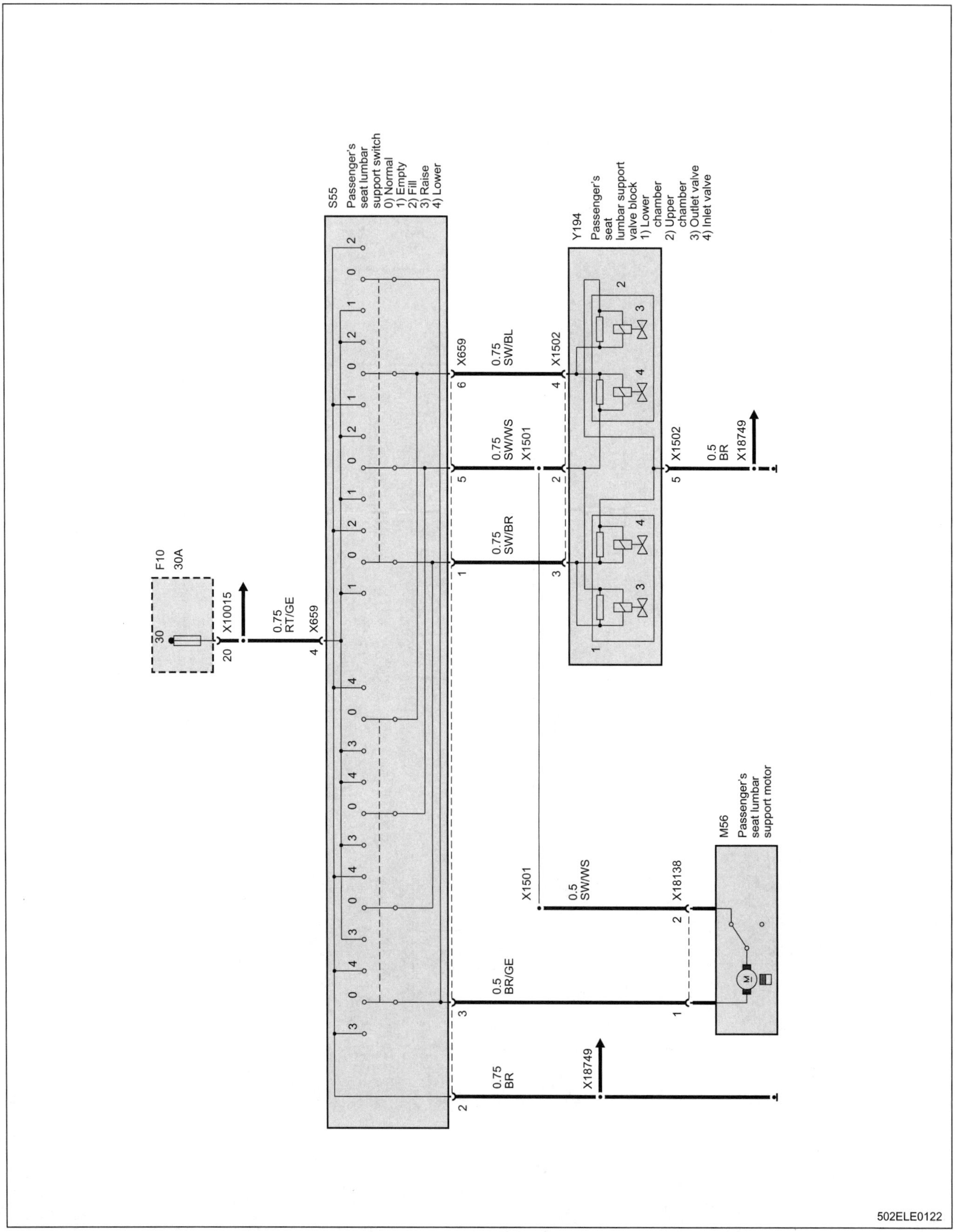
S55
Passenger's seat lumbar support switch
0) Normal
1) Empty
2) Fill
3) Raise
4) Lower
Y194
Passenger's seat lumbar support valve block
1) Lower chamber
2) Upper chamber
3) Outlet valve
4) Inlet valve
F10
30A
X10015
0.75 RT/GE
X659
X659
0.75 SW/BL
X1502
0.75 SW/WS
X1501
0.75 SW/BR
X1502
0.5 BR
X18749
M56
Passenger's seat lumbar support motor
X1501
0.5 SW/WS
X18138
0.5 BR/GE
0.75 BR
X18749
502ELE0122

Power Seats
Passenger's seat adjustment without memory
(1 of 2)

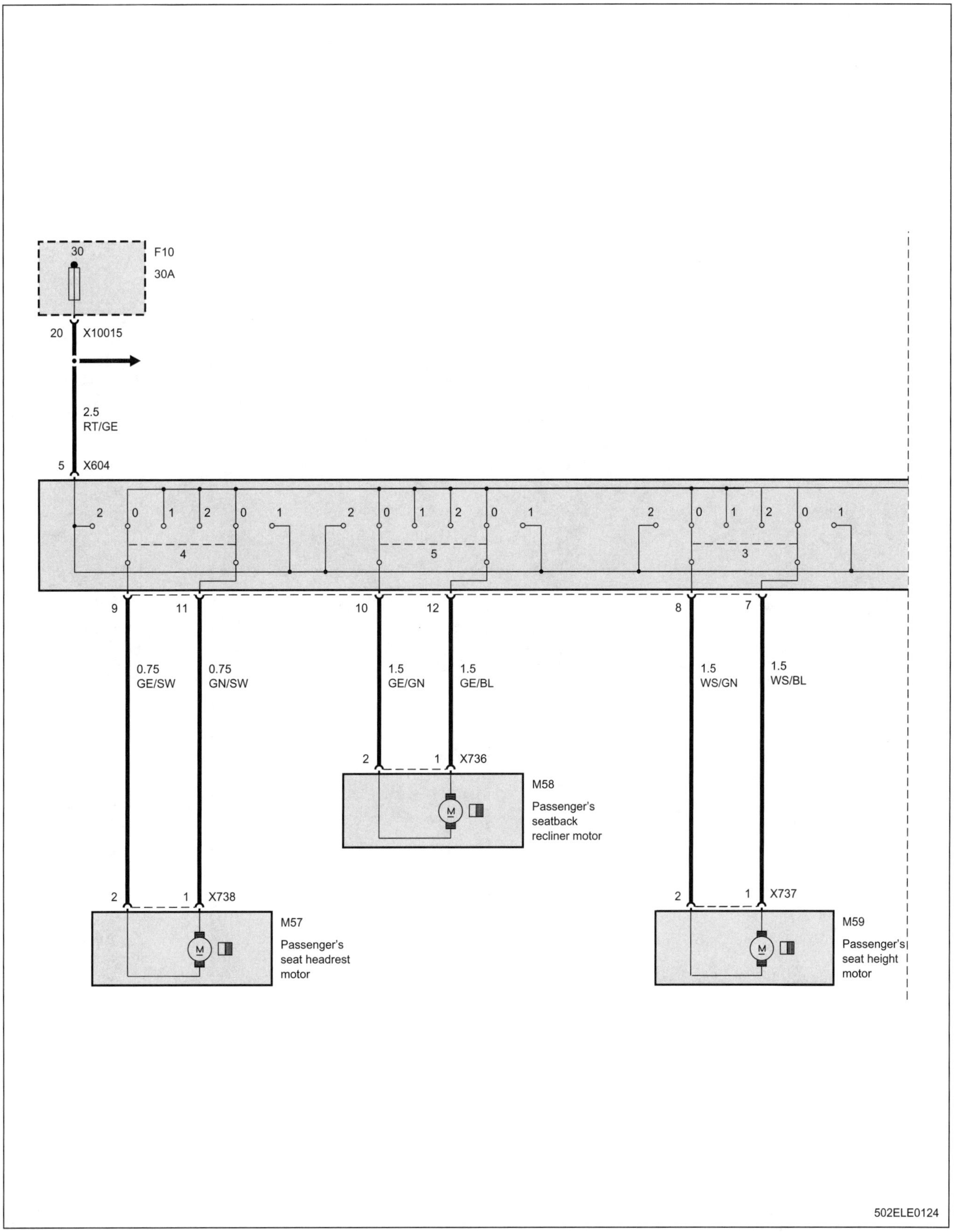

Power Seats
Passenger's seat adjustment without memory
(2 of 2)

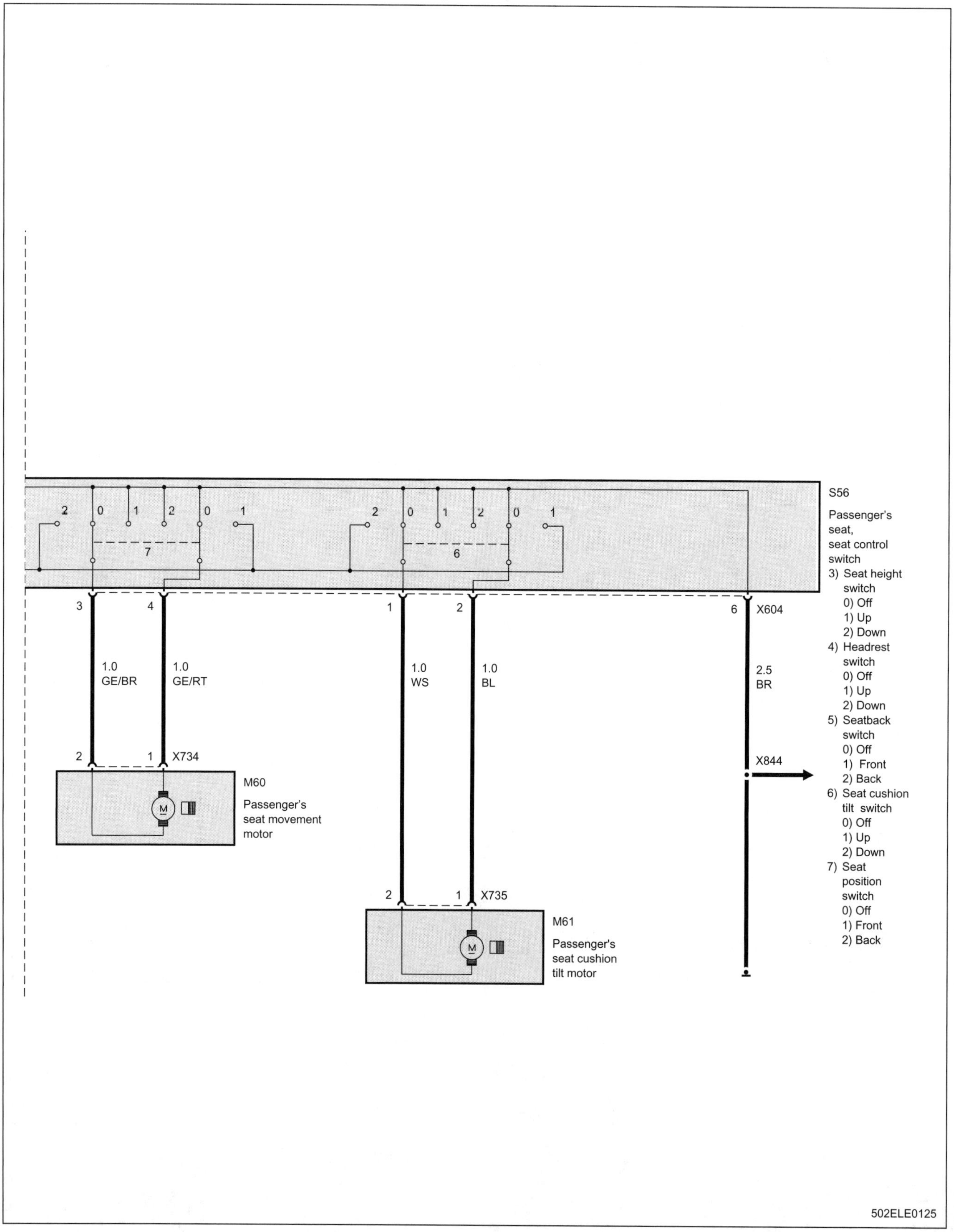

Power Seats
Passenger's seat heating
(1 of 1)

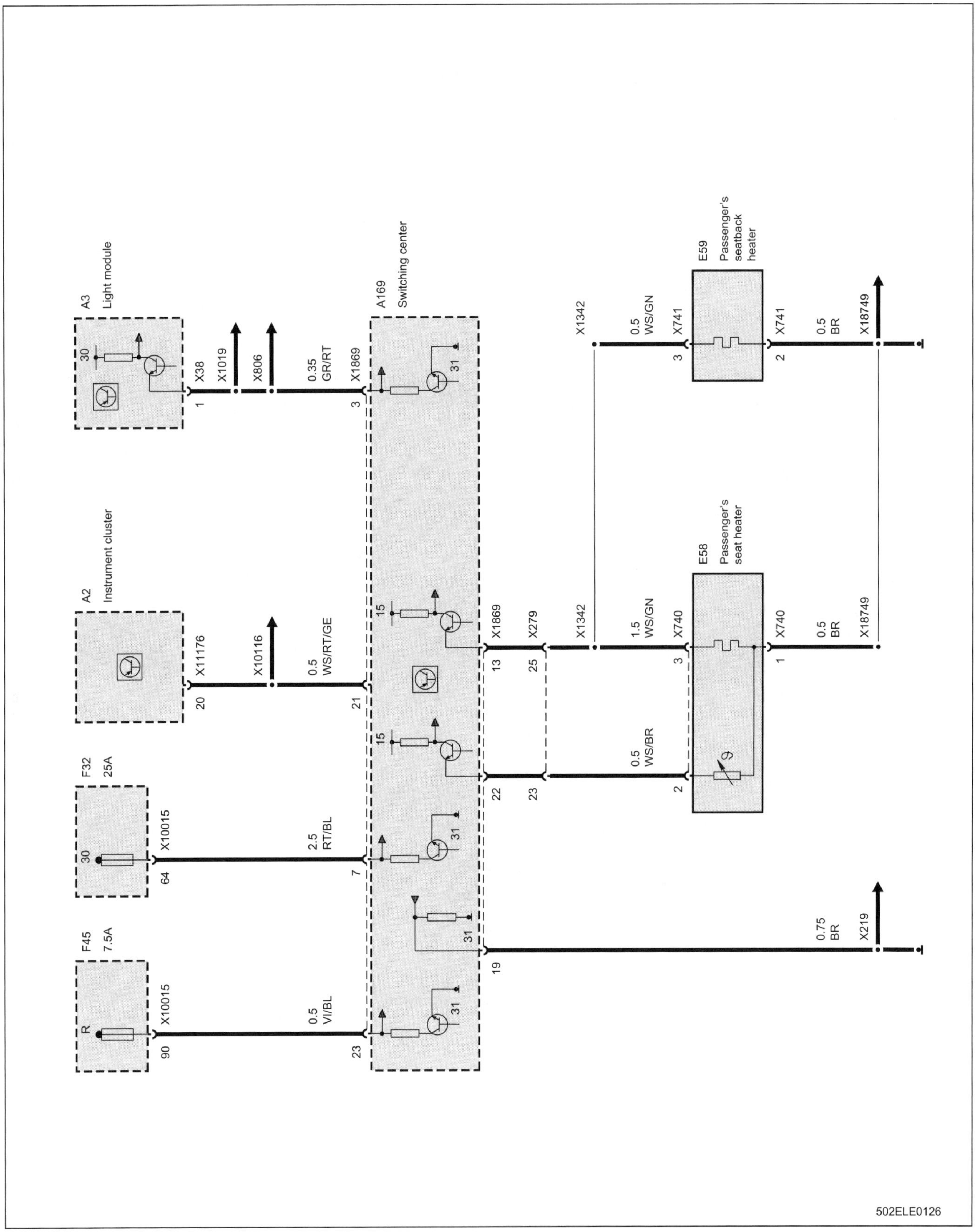
A3
Light module
A2
Instrument cluster
F32
25A
F45
7.5A
A169
Switching center
E59
Passenger's seatback heater
E58
Passenger's seat heater
X38
X1019
X806
0.35
GR/RT
X1869
X11176
X10116
0.5
WS/RT/GE
X10015
2.5
RT/BL
0.5
VI/BL
X279
X1342
0.5
WS/GN
X741
1.5
WS/GN
X740
0.5
WS/BR
0.5
BR
X18749
0.75
BR
X219
502ELE0126

Power Seats
Passenger's seatback adjust. without memory
(1 of 1)

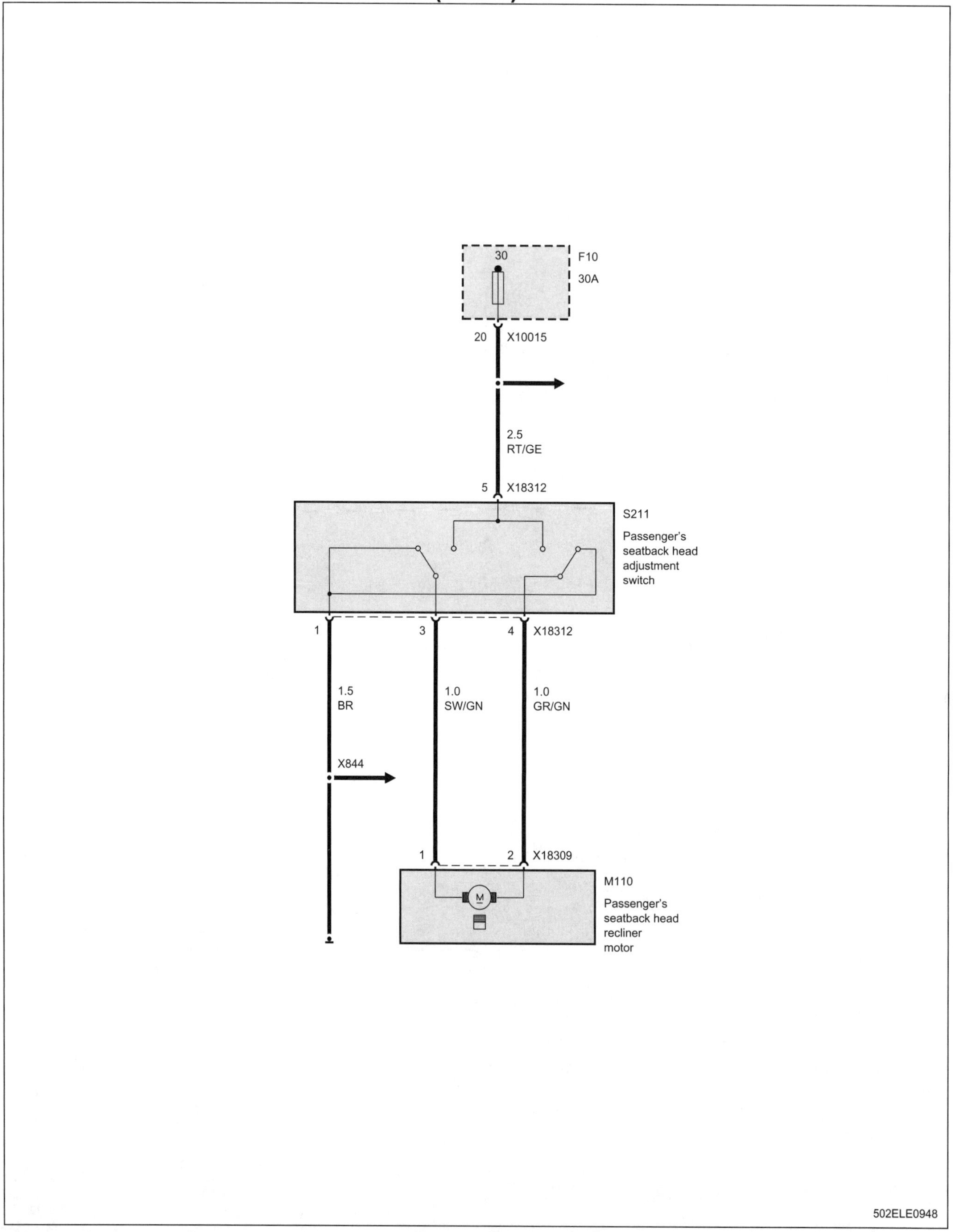

Power Seats
Passenger's thigh support without memory
(1 of 1)

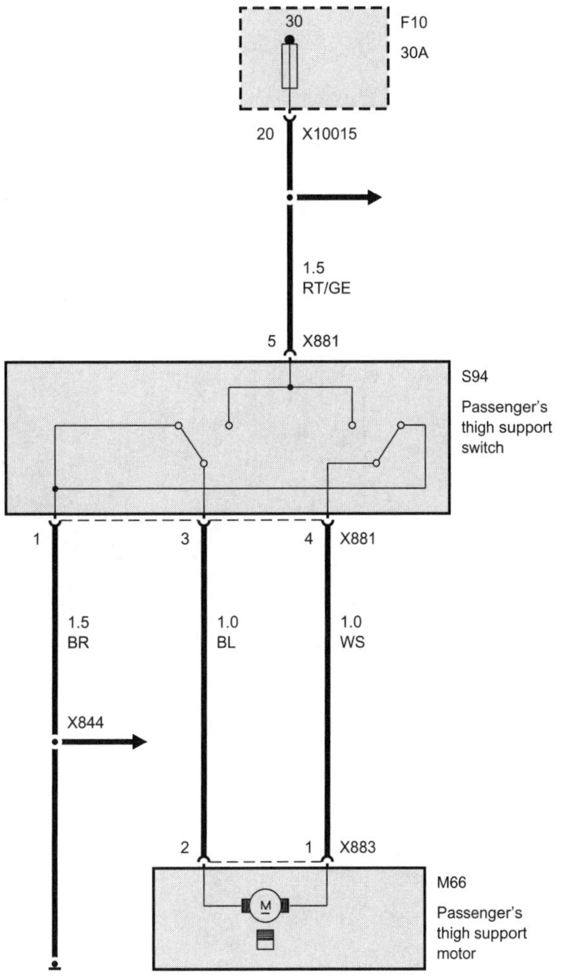

Power Sunroof/Sun Blind
Sun blind
(1 of 1)

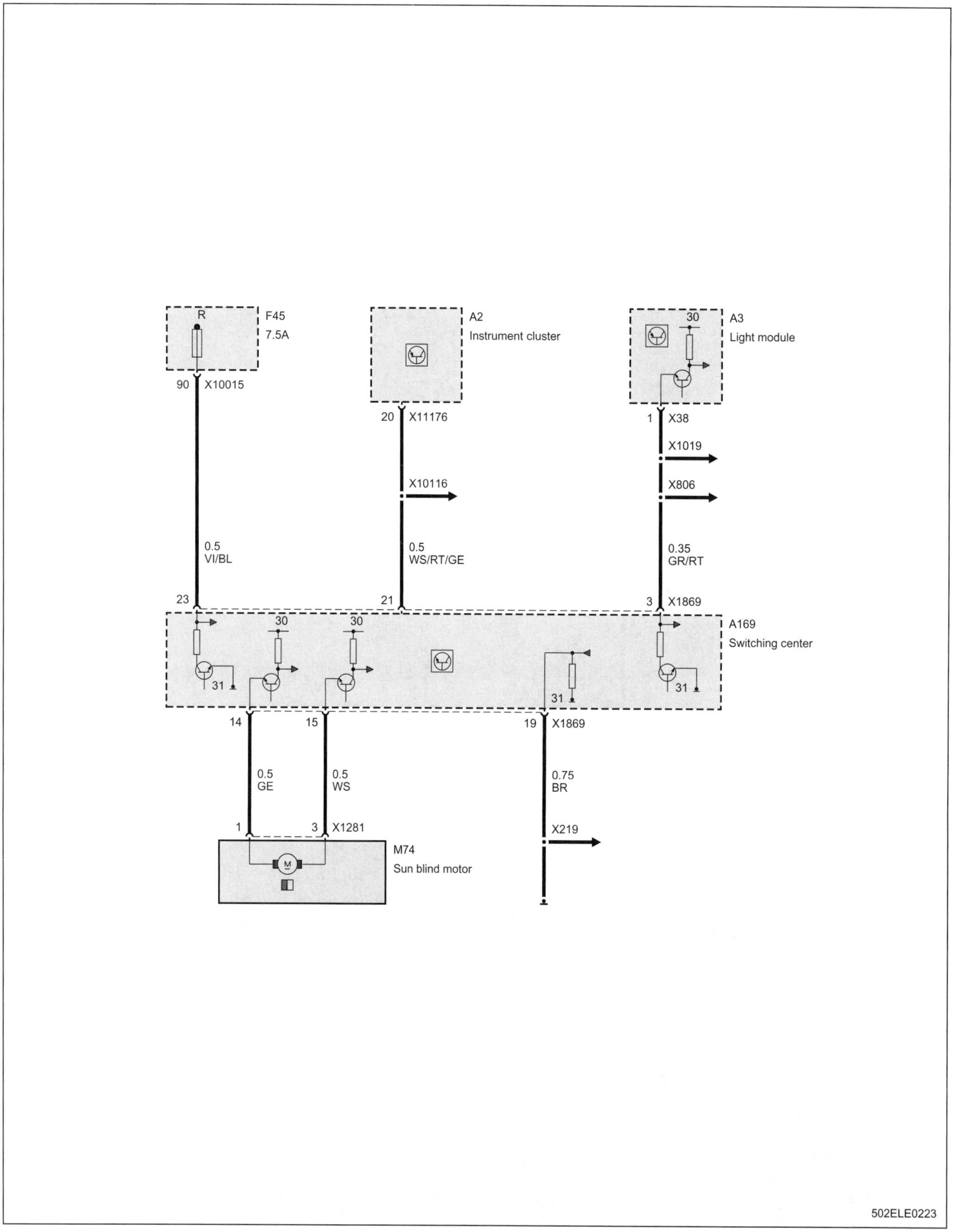
R
F45
7.5A
90
X10015
A2
Instrument cluster
20
X11176
X10116
30
A3
Light module
1
X38
X1019
X806
0.5
VI/BL
0.5
WS/RT/GE
0.35
GR/RT
23
21
3
X1869
30
30
A169
Switching center
31
31
31
14
15
19
X1869
0.5
GE
0.5
WS
0.75
BR
1
3
X1281
X219
M74
Sun blind motor
M
502ELE0223

Power Sunroof/Sun Blind
Sun blind with remote control
(1 of 1)

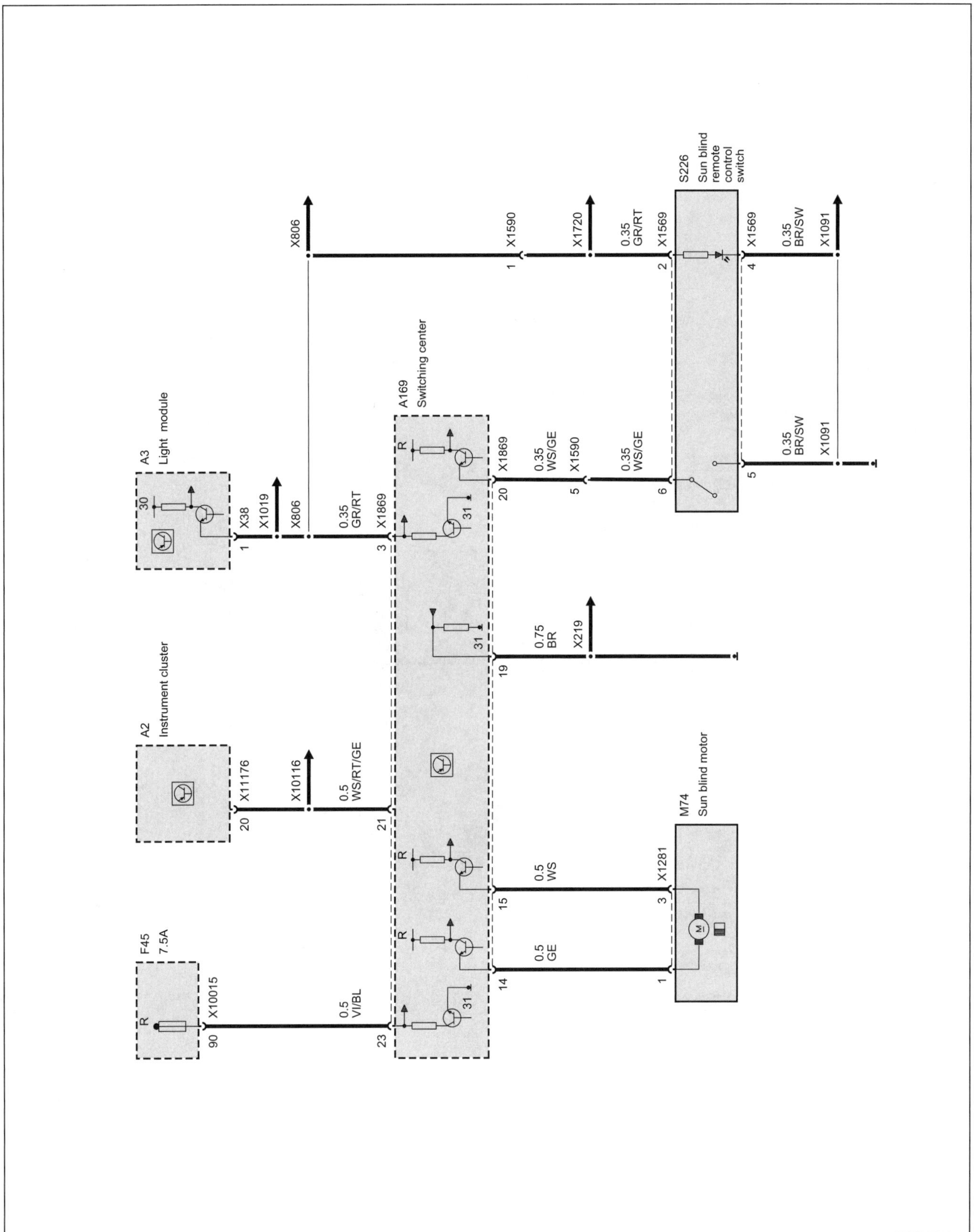

502ELE0224

Power Sunroof/Sun Blind
Sun blind
(1 of 1)

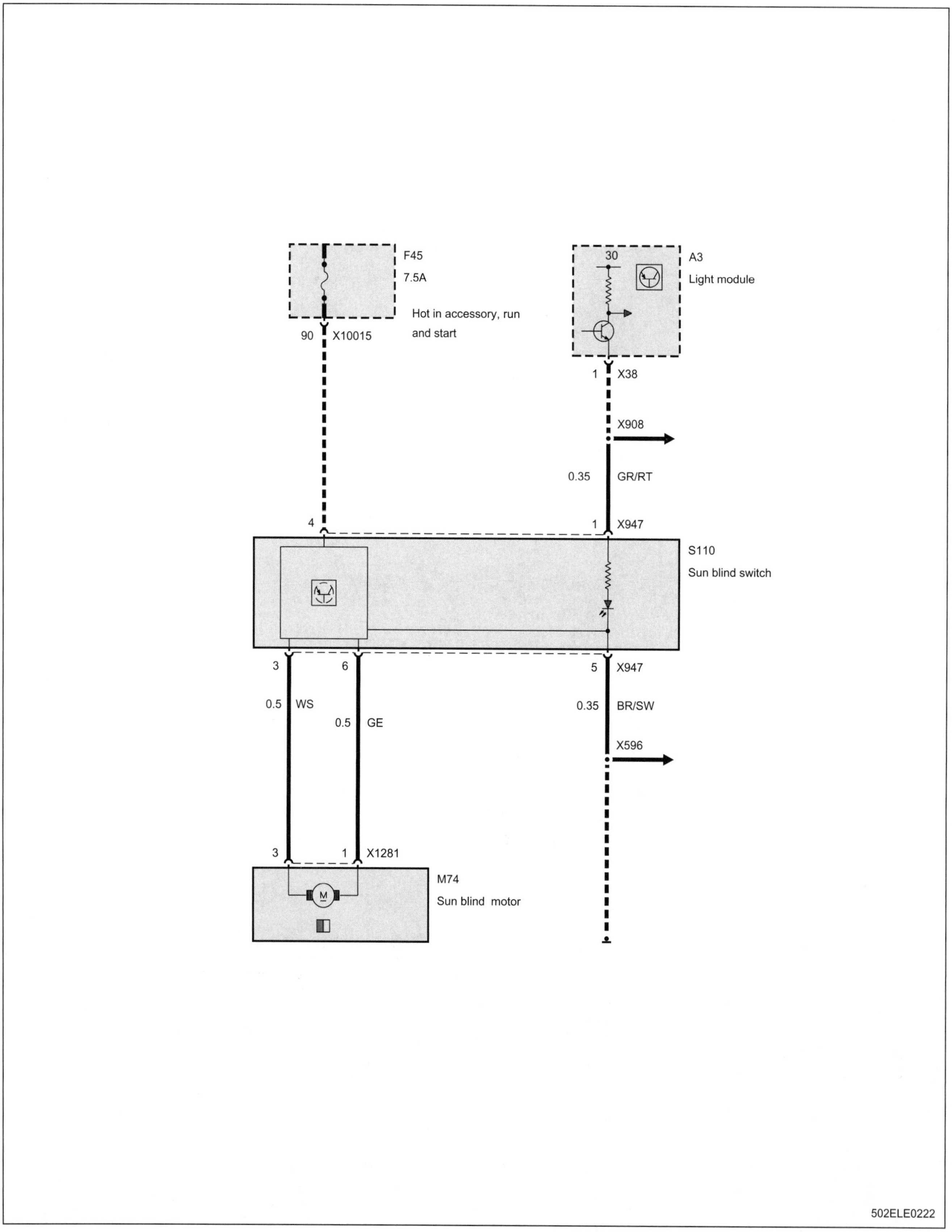
F45
7.5A
Hot in accessory, run and start
90
X10015
30
A3
Light module
1
X38
X908
0.35
GR/RT
4
1
X947
S110
Sun blind switch
3
6
X947
5
0.5
WS
0.5
GE
0.35
BR/SW
X596
3
1
X1281
M74
Sun blind motor
M
502ELE0222

Power Sunroof/Sun Blind
Sunroof
(1 of 1)

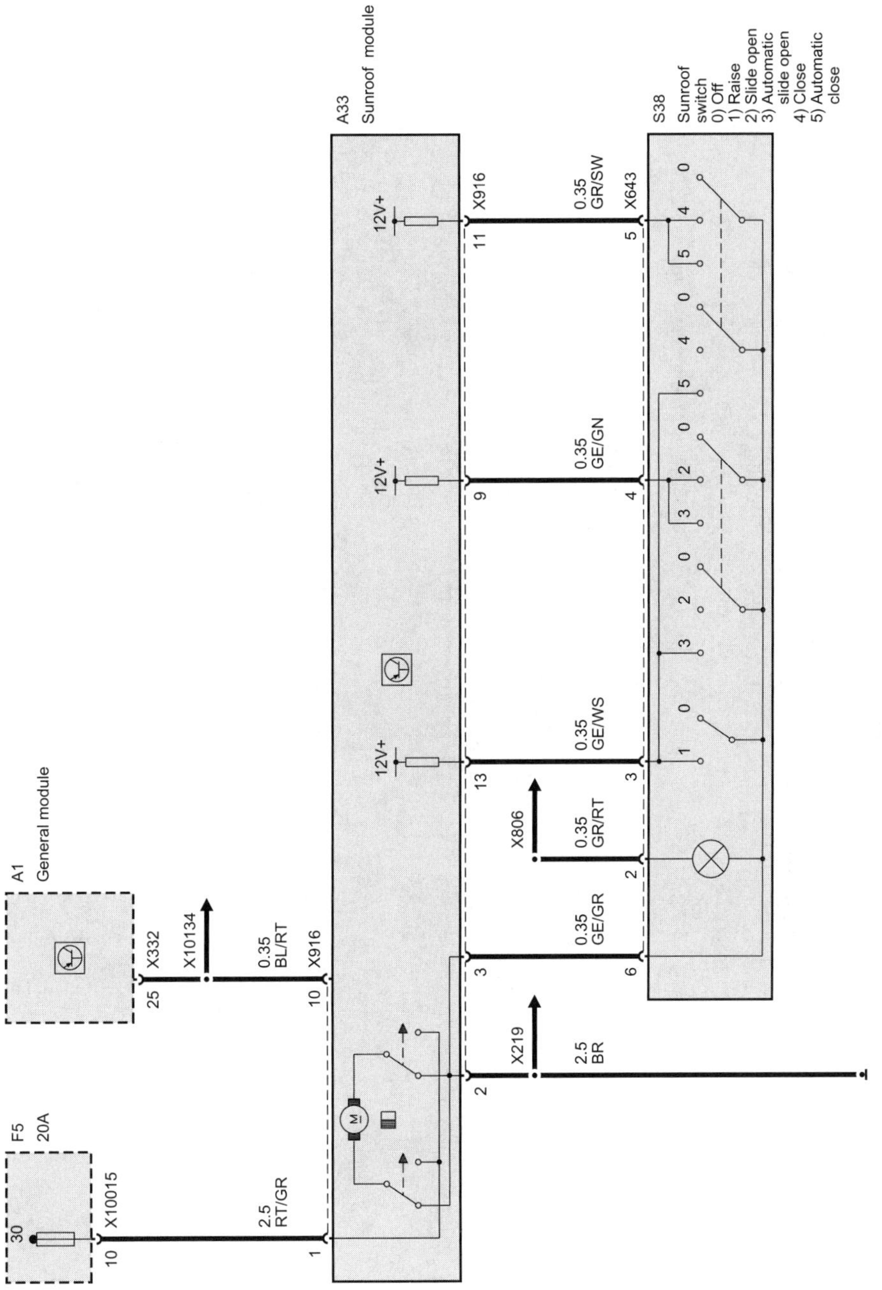

502ELE0225

Power Windows
Front window (overview)
(1 of 2)

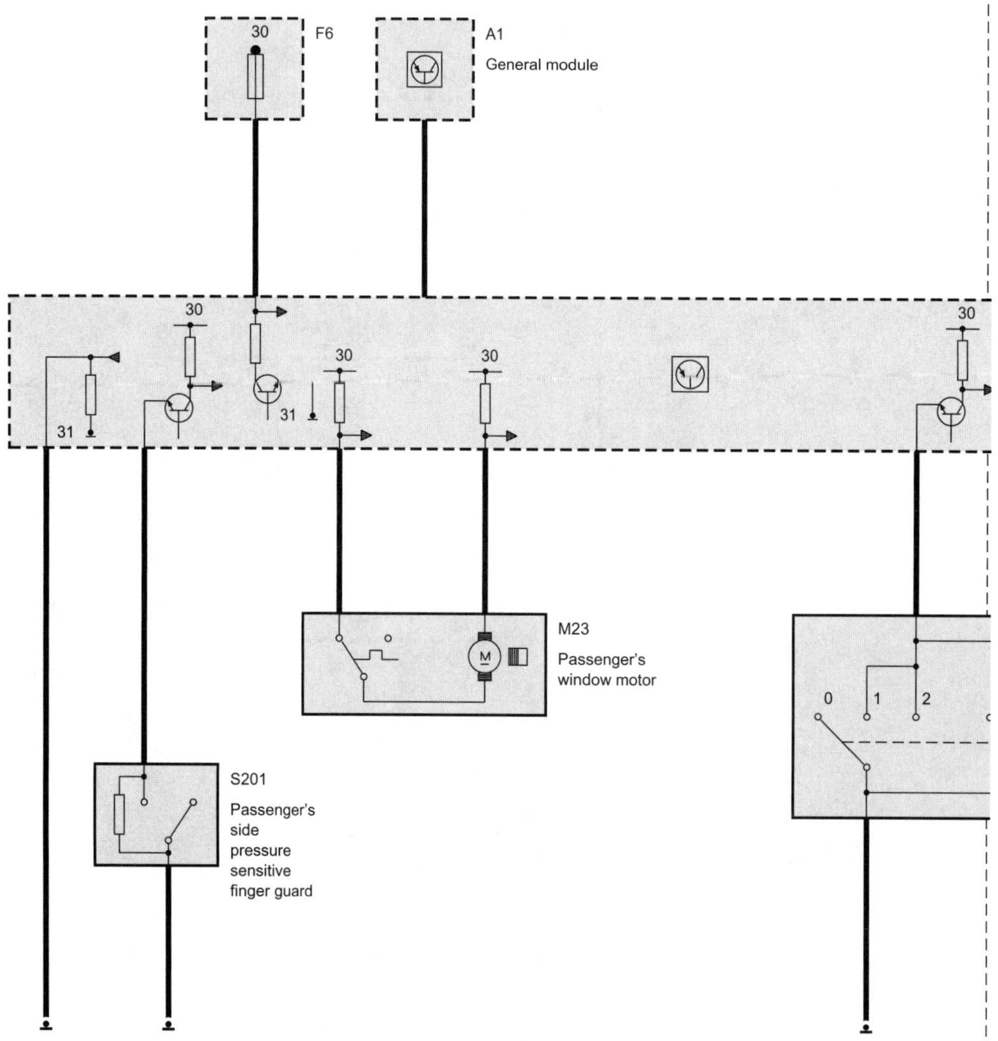

502ELE0061

Power Windows
Front window (overview)
(2 of 2)

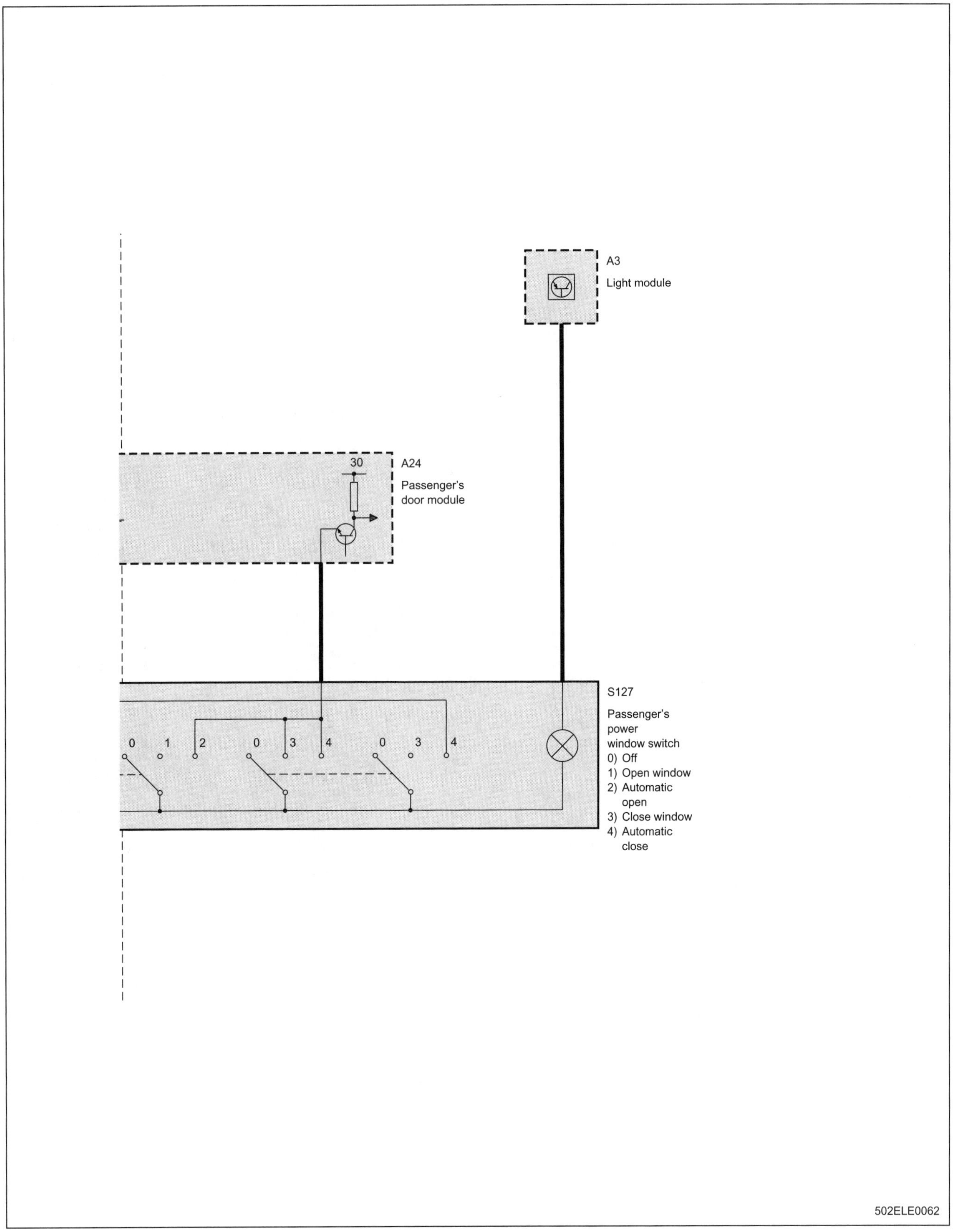
A3
Light module
30
A24
Passenger's
door module
0
1
2
0
3
4
0
3
4
S127
Passenger's
power
window switch
0) Off
1) Open window
2) Automatic
open
3) Close window
4) Automatic
close
502ELE0062

Power Windows
Rear window (overview)
(1 of 3)

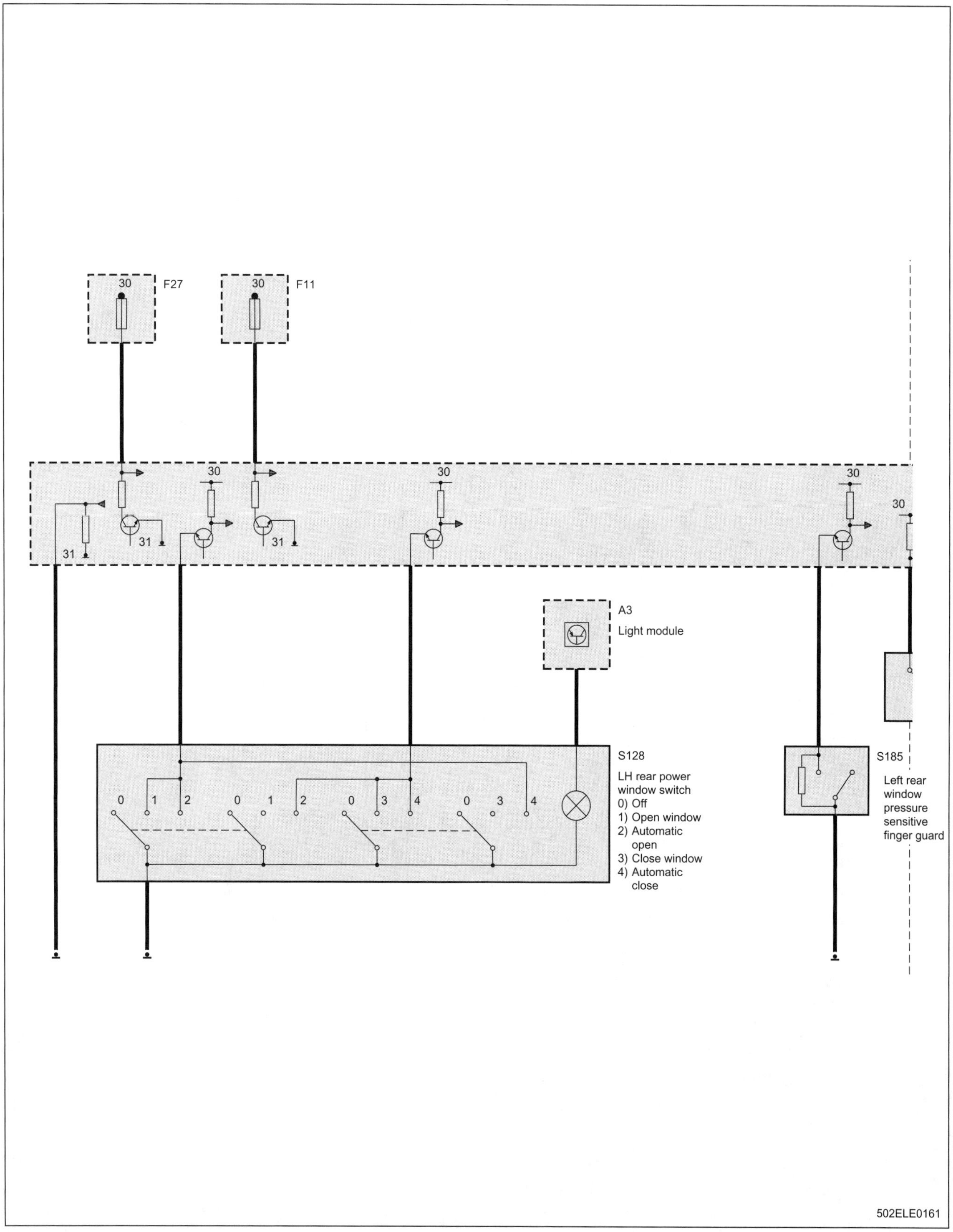
30
F27
30
F11
30
30
30
30
31
31
31
A3
Light module
S128
LH rear power window switch
0) Off
1) Open window
2) Automatic open
3) Close window
4) Automatic close
0 1 2 0 1 2 0 3 4 0 3 4
S185
Left rear window pressure sensitive finger guard
502ELE0161

Power Windows
Rear window (overview)
(2 of 3)

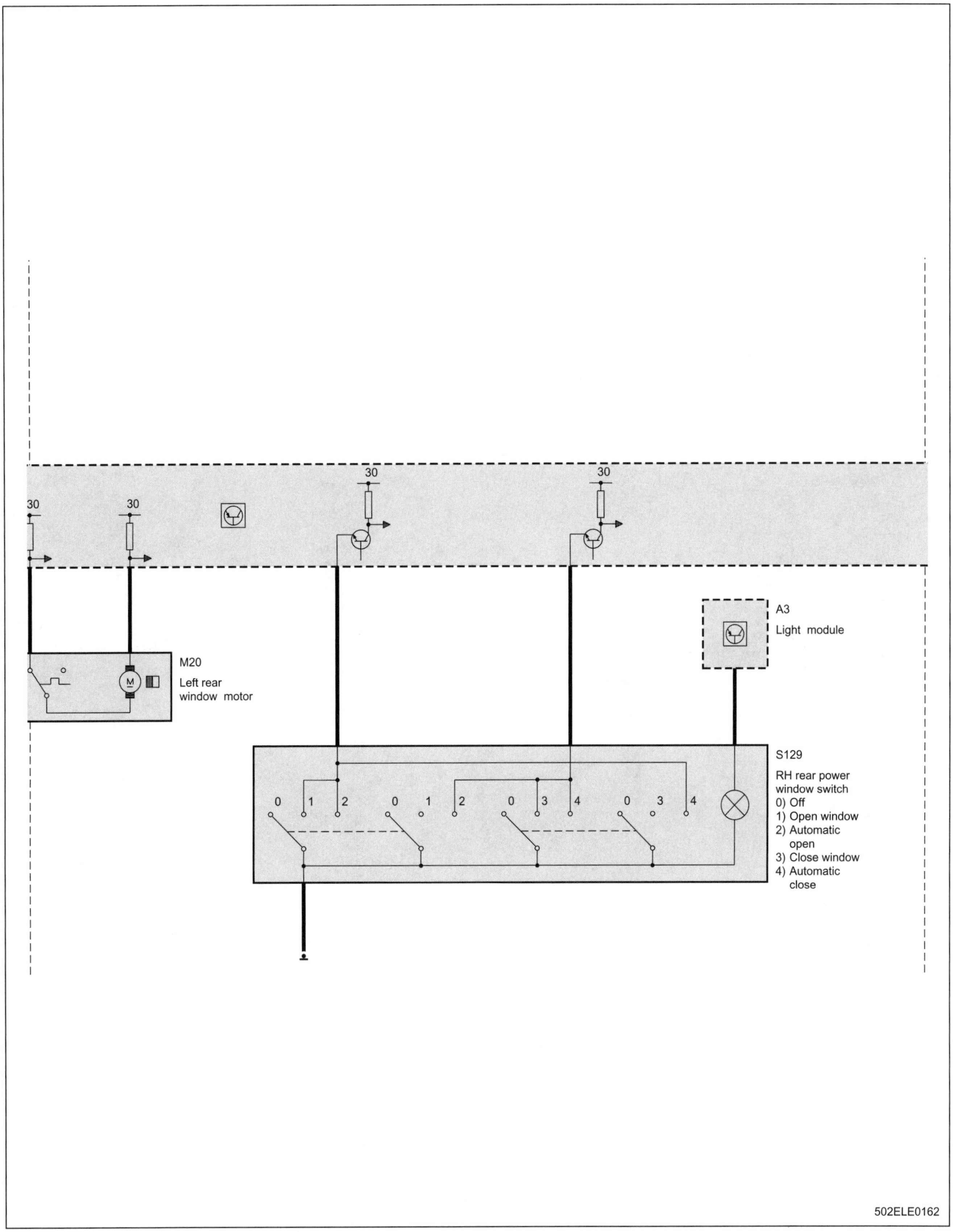
30
30
30
30
A3
Light module
M20
Left rear
window motor
S129
RH rear power
window switch
0) Off
1) Open window
2) Automatic
open
3) Close window
4) Automatic
close
0
1
2
0
1
2
0
3
4
0
3
4
502ELE0162

Power Windows
Rear window (overview)
(3 of 3)

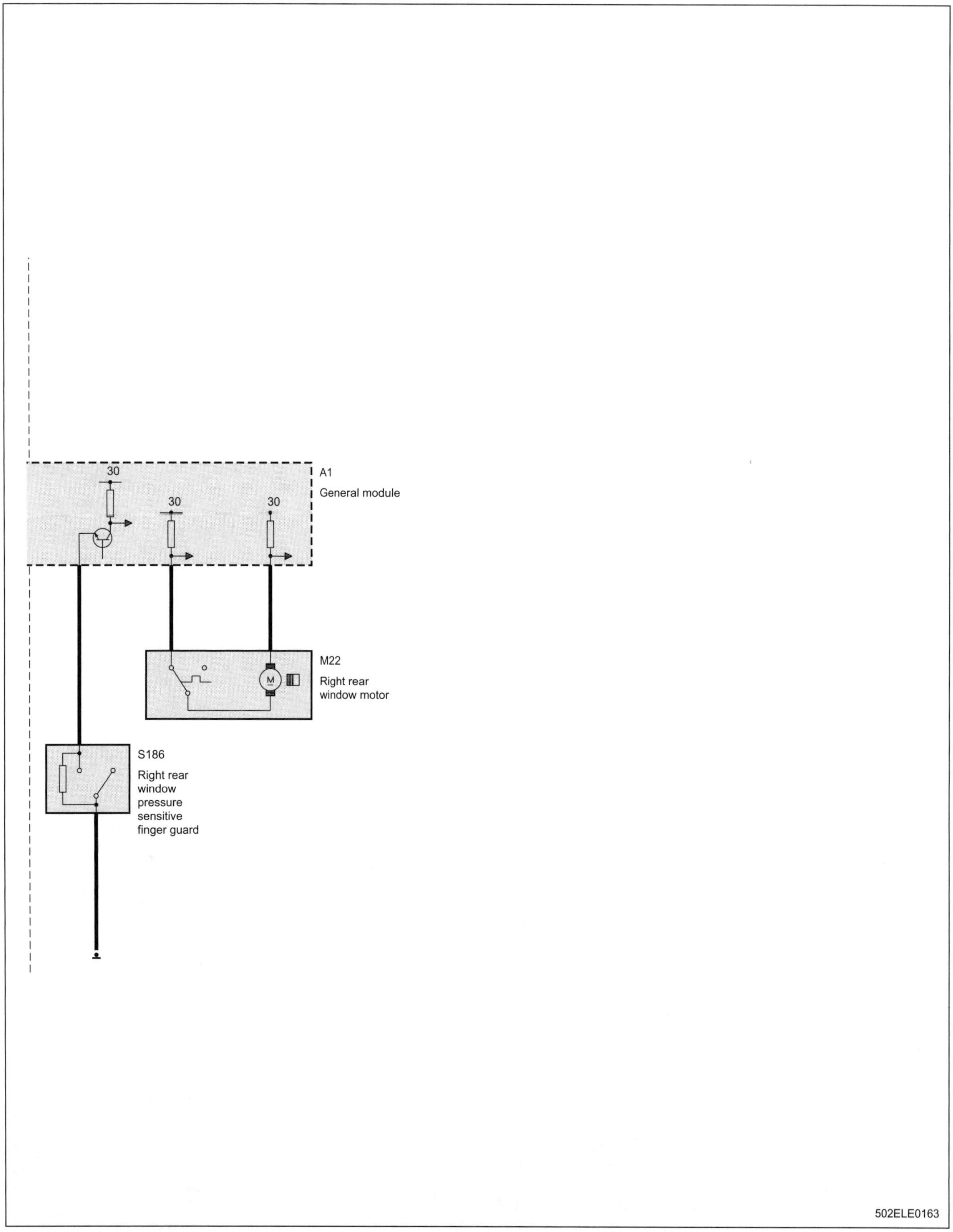

Power Windows
Driver's door module (A23)
(1 of 3)

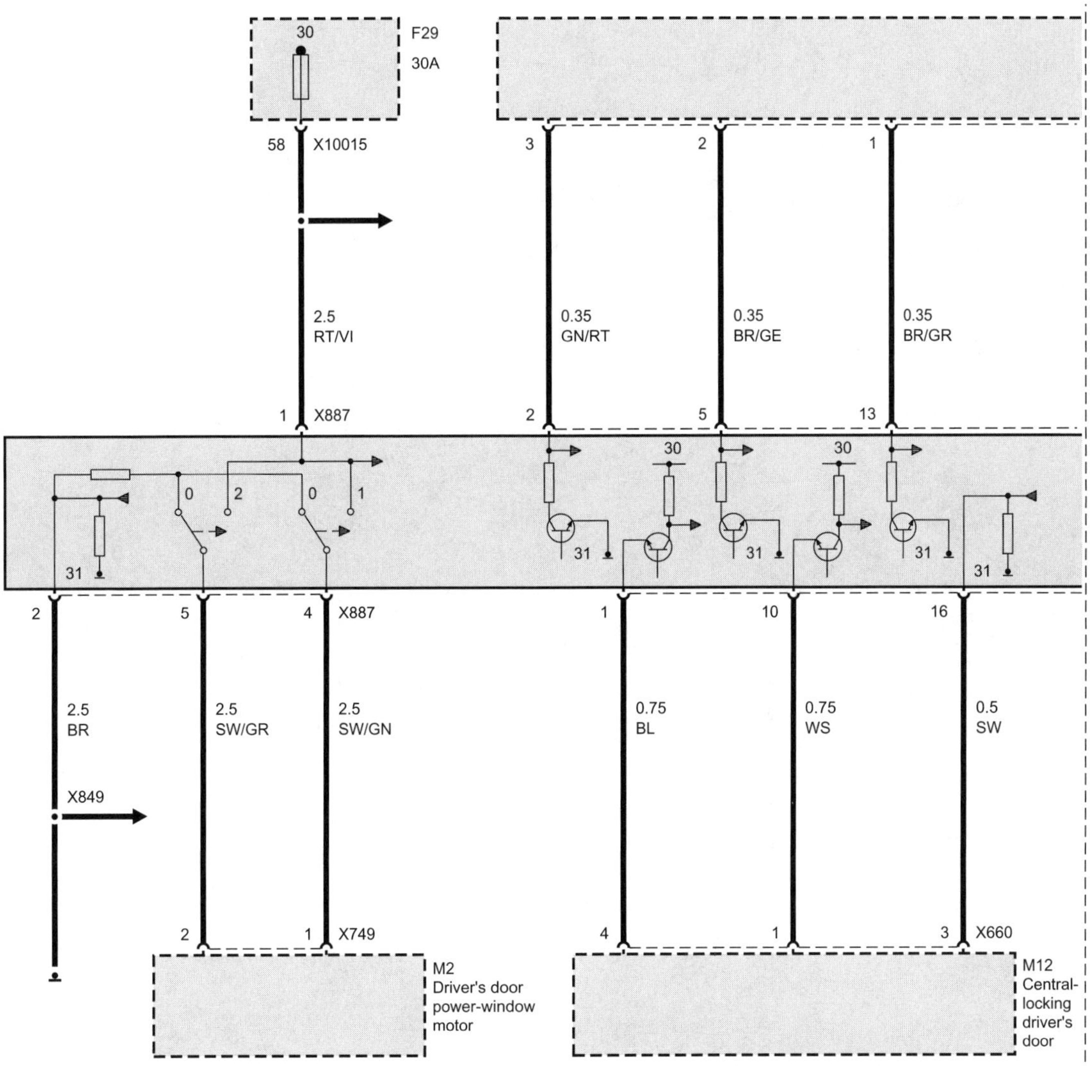

502ELE0407

Power Windows
Driver's door module (A23)
(2 of 3)

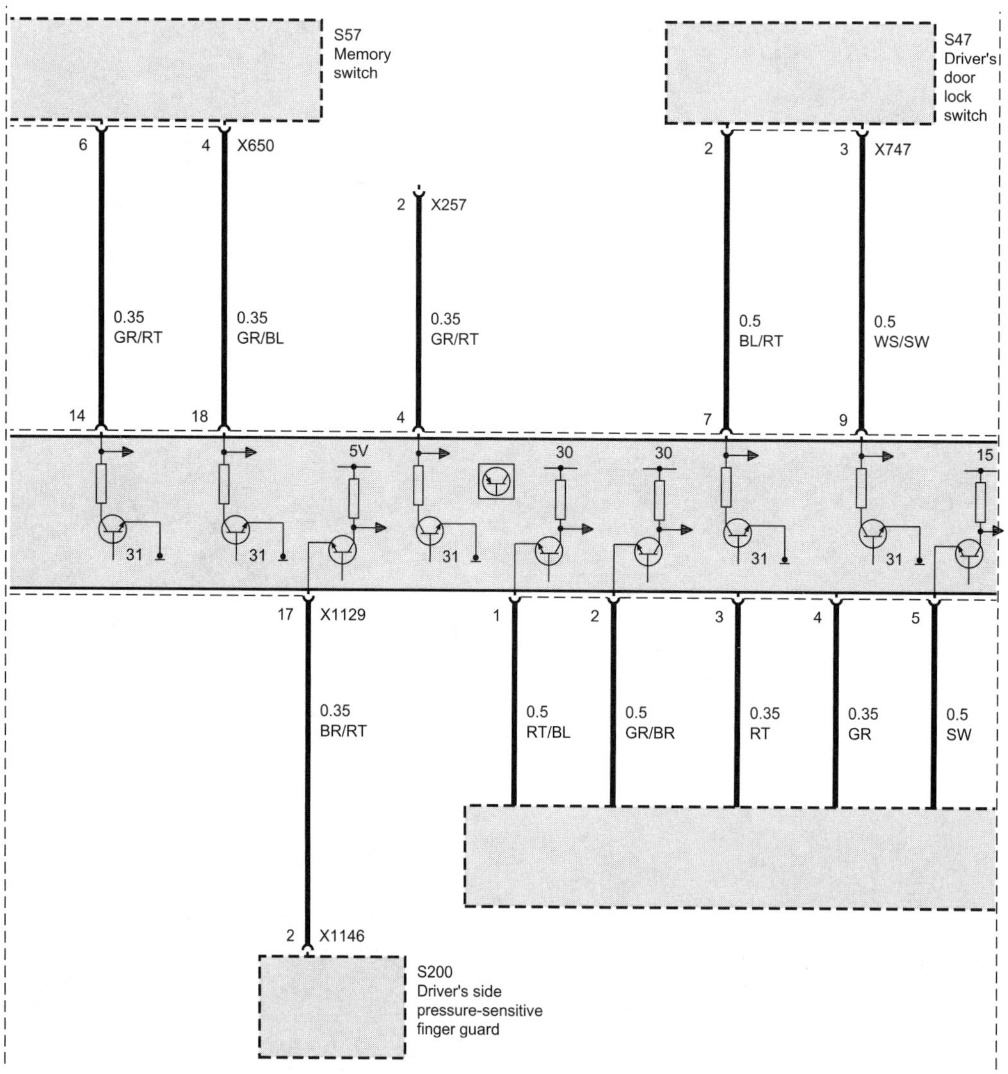

502ELE0408

Power Windows
Driver's door module (A23)
(3 of 3)

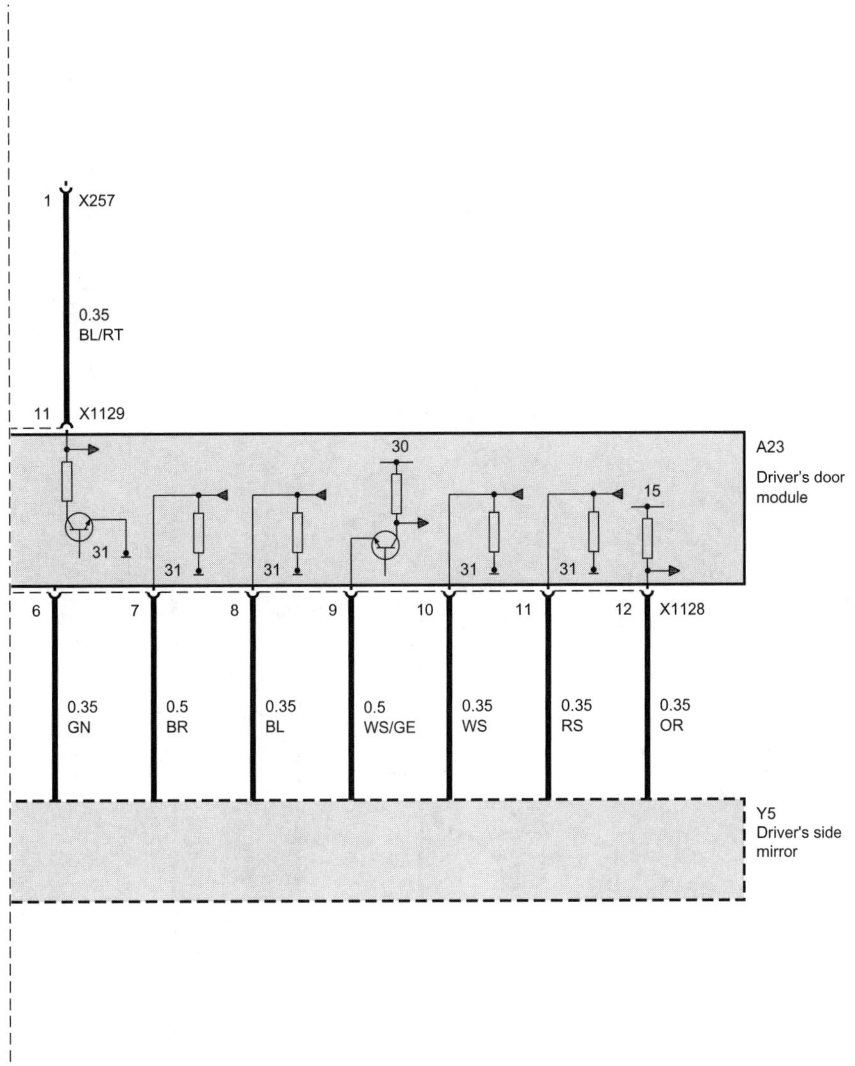

502ELE0409

Power Windows
Passenger's door module (A24)
(1 of 3)

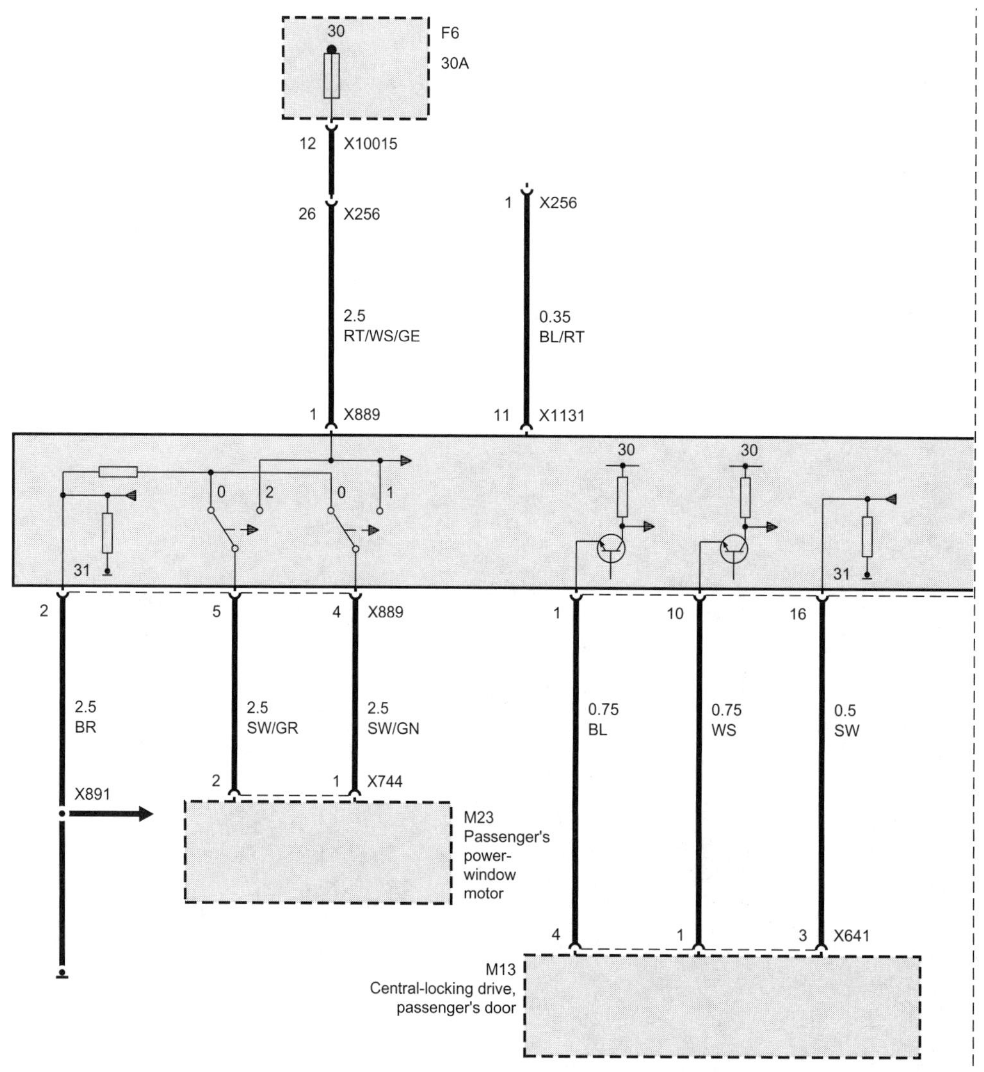

502ELE0410

Power Windows
Passenger's door module (A24)
(2 of 3)

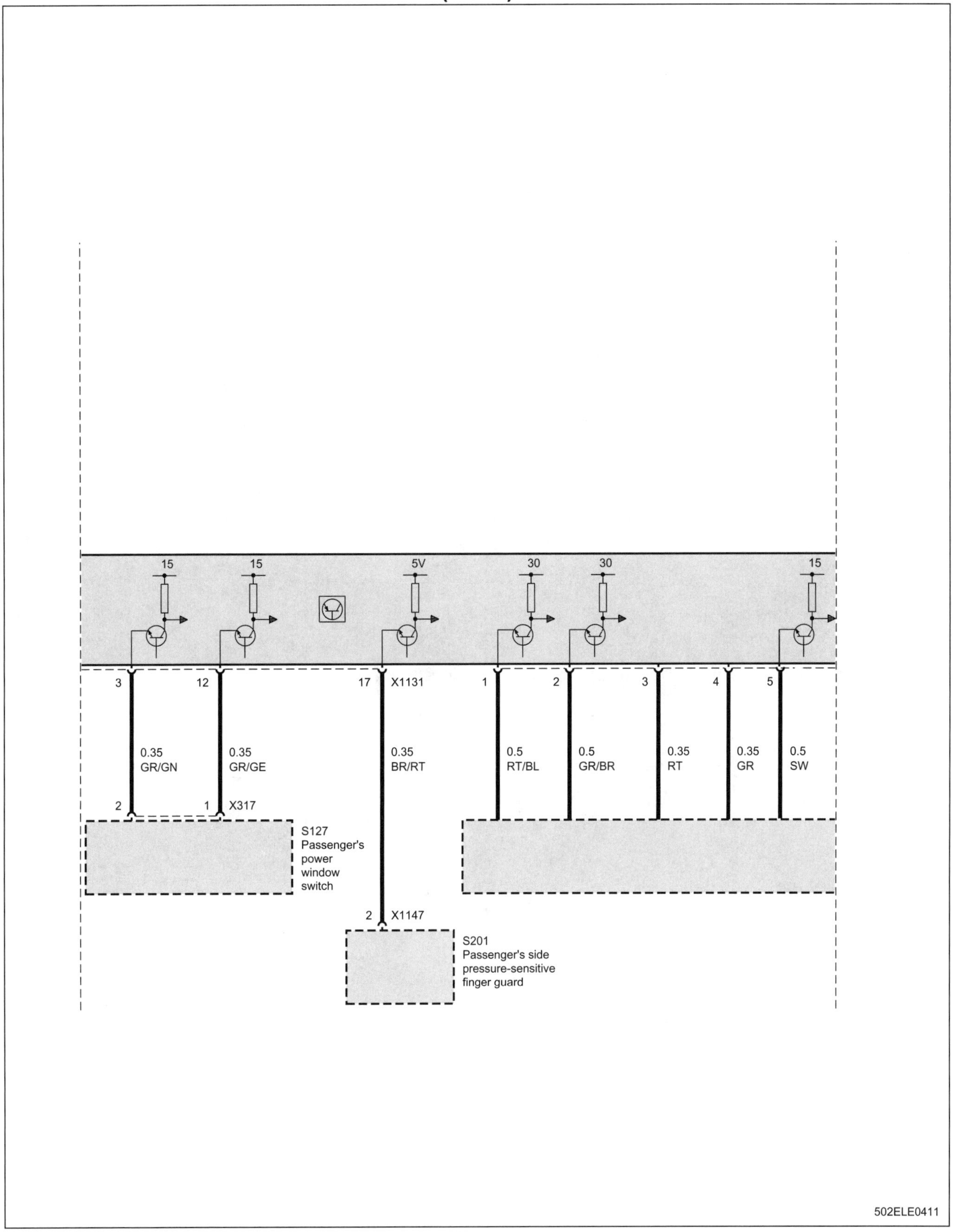
15
15
5V
30
30
15
3
12
17
X1131
1
2
3
4
5
0.35
GR/GN
0.35
GR/GE
0.35
BR/RT
0.5
RT/BL
0.5
GR/BR
0.35
RT
0.35
GR
0.5
SW
2
1
X317
S127
Passenger's
power
window
switch
2
X1147
S201
Passenger's side
pressure-sensitive
finger guard
502ELE0411

Power Windows
Passenger's door module (A24)
(3 of 3)

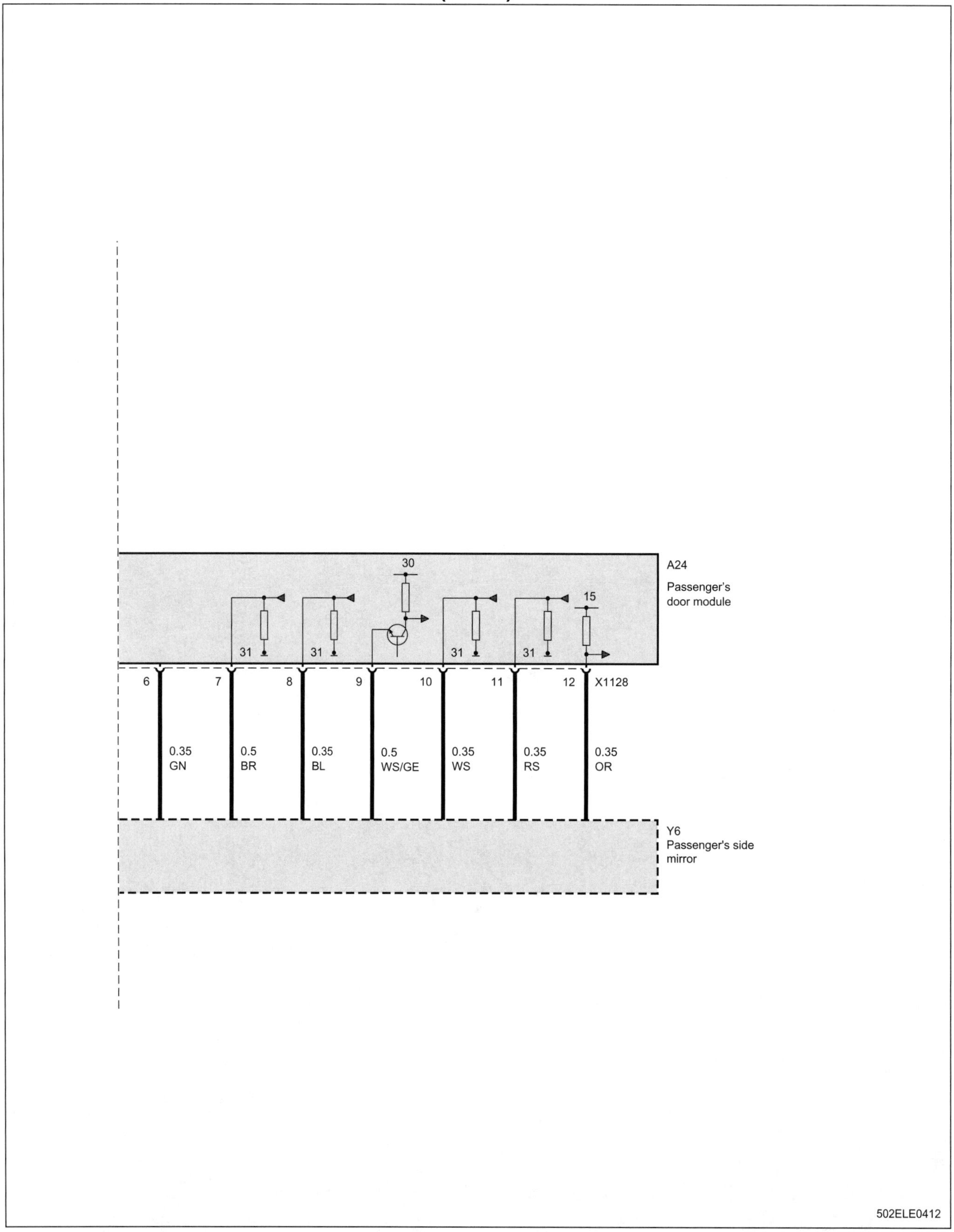
30
15
31
31
31
31
A24
Passenger's
door module
6
7
8
9
10
11
12
X1128
0.35
GN
0.5
BR
0.35
BL
0.5
WS/GE
0.35
WS
0.35
RS
0.35
OR
Y6
Passenger's side
mirror
502ELE0412

Power Windows
Driver's side power window motor
(1 of 1)

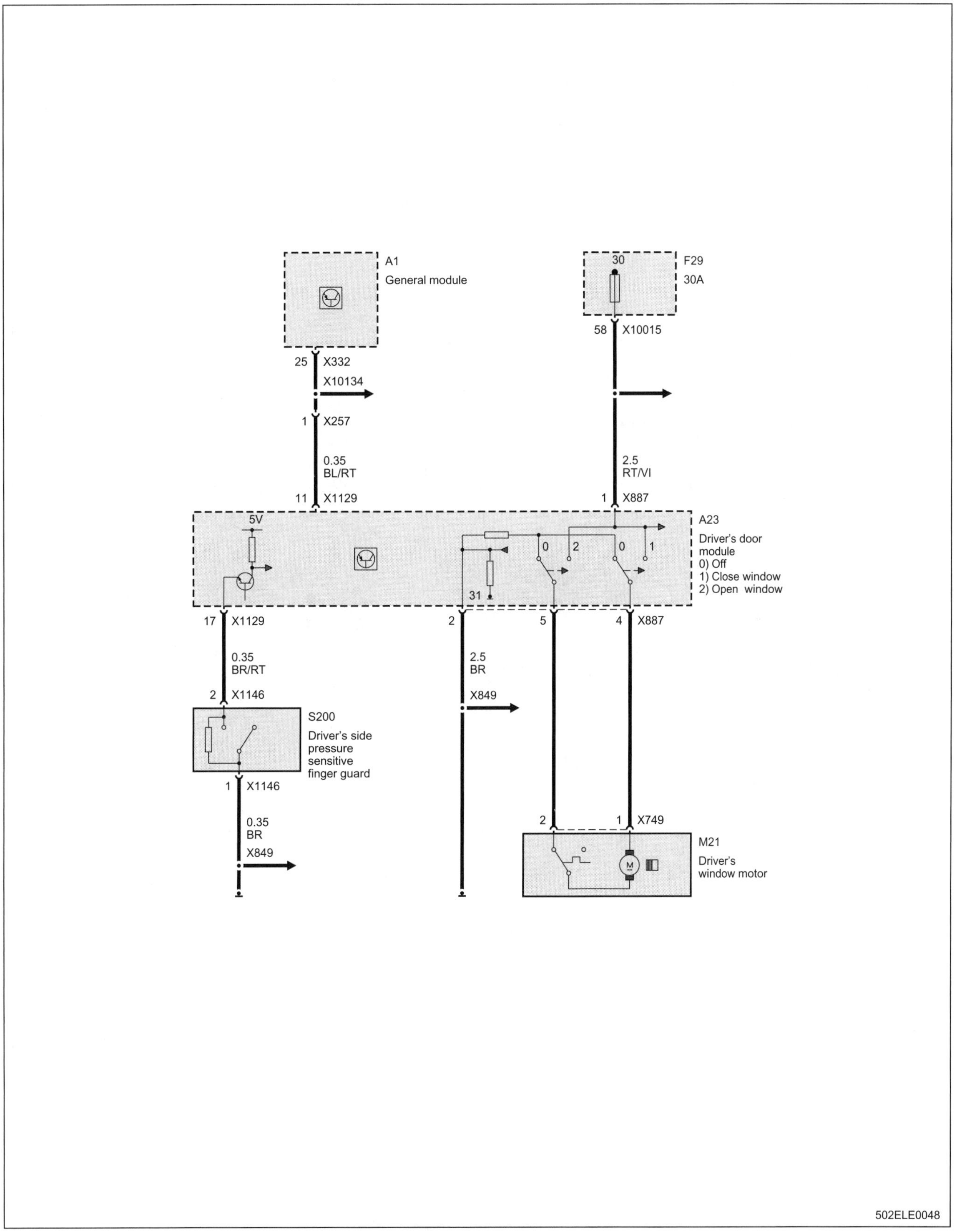

Power Windows
Passenger's side power window
(1 of 1)

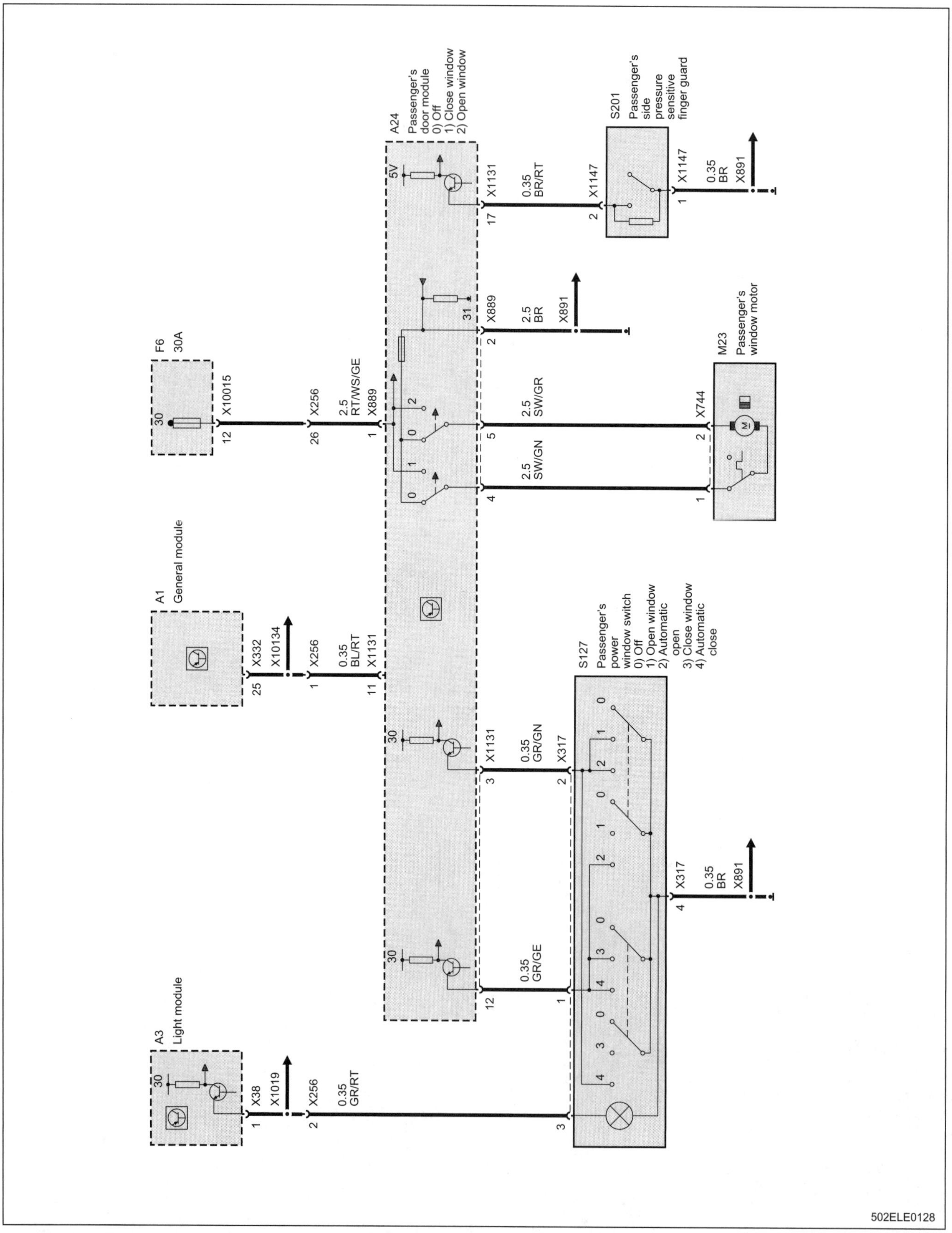
A24
Passenger's door module
0) Off
1) Close window
2) Open window
S201
Passenger's side pressure sensitive finger guard
F6
30A
M23
Passenger's window motor
A1
General module
S127
Passenger's power window switch
0) Off
1) Open window
2) Automatic open
3) Close window
4) Automatic close
A3
Light module
0.35 BR/RT
0.35 BR
2.5 BR
2.5 RT/WS/GE
2.5 SW/GR
2.5 SW/GN
0.35 BL/RT
0.35 GR/GN
0.35 GR/GE
0.35 GR/RT
X1131
X1147
X891
X889
X10015
X256
X744
X332
X10134
X317
X38
X1019
5V
30
31
502ELE0128

Power Windows
LH rear power window
(1 of 1)

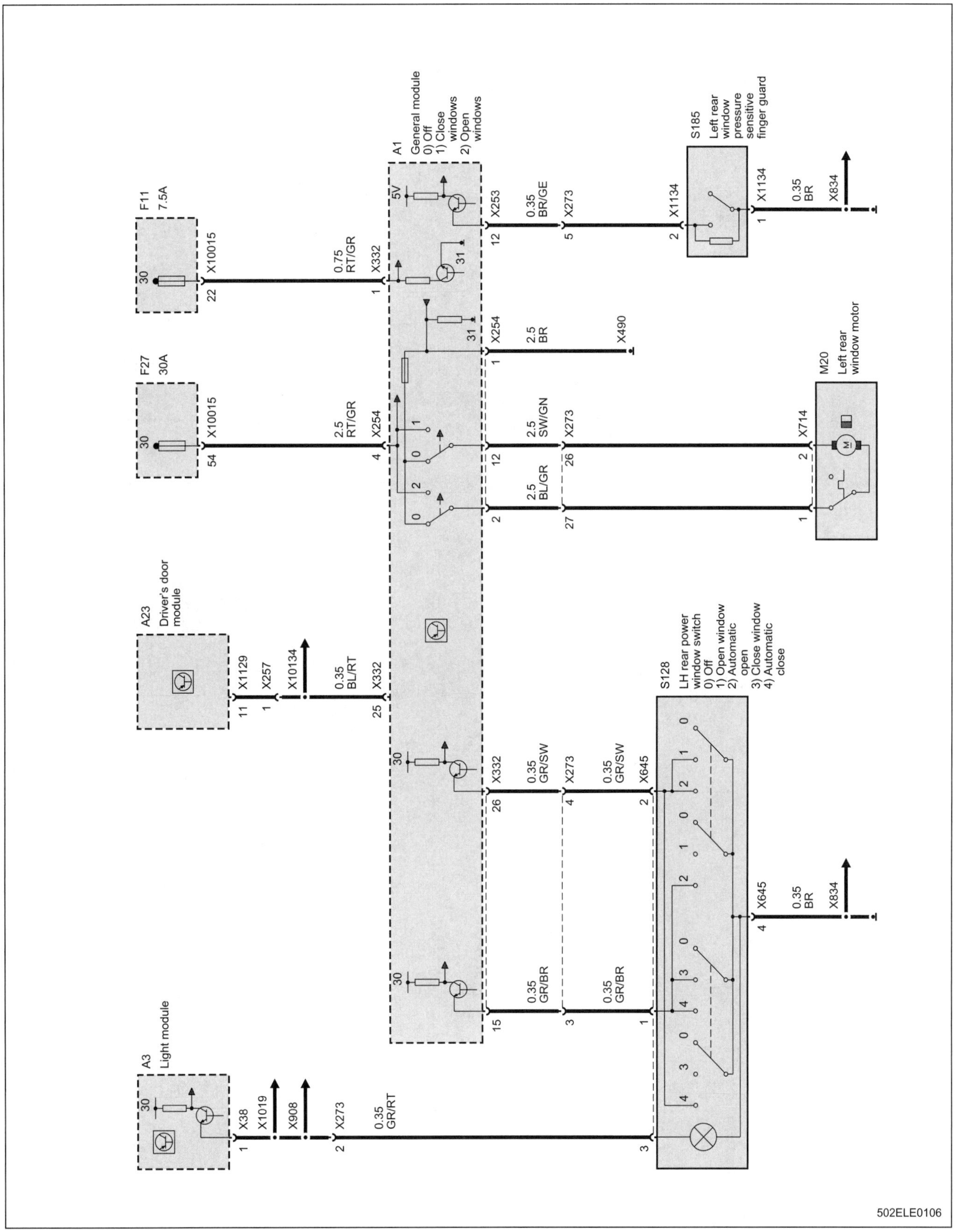
F11
7.5A
30
X10015
22
0.75
RT/GR
X332
1
F27
30A
X10015
54
2.5
RT/GR
X254
4
A23
Driver's door module
X1129
11
X257
1
X10134
0.35
BL/RT
X332
25
A3
Light module
X38
1
X1019
X908
X273
2
0.35
GR/RT
3
A1
General module
0) Off
1) Close windows
2) Open windows
5V
31
X253
12
0.35
BR/GE
X273
5
X254
1
2.5
BR
X490
2.5
SW/GN
X273
12
26
2.5
BL/GR
2
27
X332
26
0.35
GR/SW
X273
4
0.35
GR/SW
X645
2
15
0.35
GR/BR
3
0.35
GR/BR
1
S185
Left rear window pressure sensitive finger guard
X1134
2
X1134
1
0.35
BR
X834
M20
Left rear window motor
X714
2
1
S128
LH rear power window switch
0) Off
1) Open window
2) Automatic open
3) Close window
4) Automatic close
X645
4
0.35
BR
X834
502ELE0106

Power Windows
RH rear power window
(1 of 1)

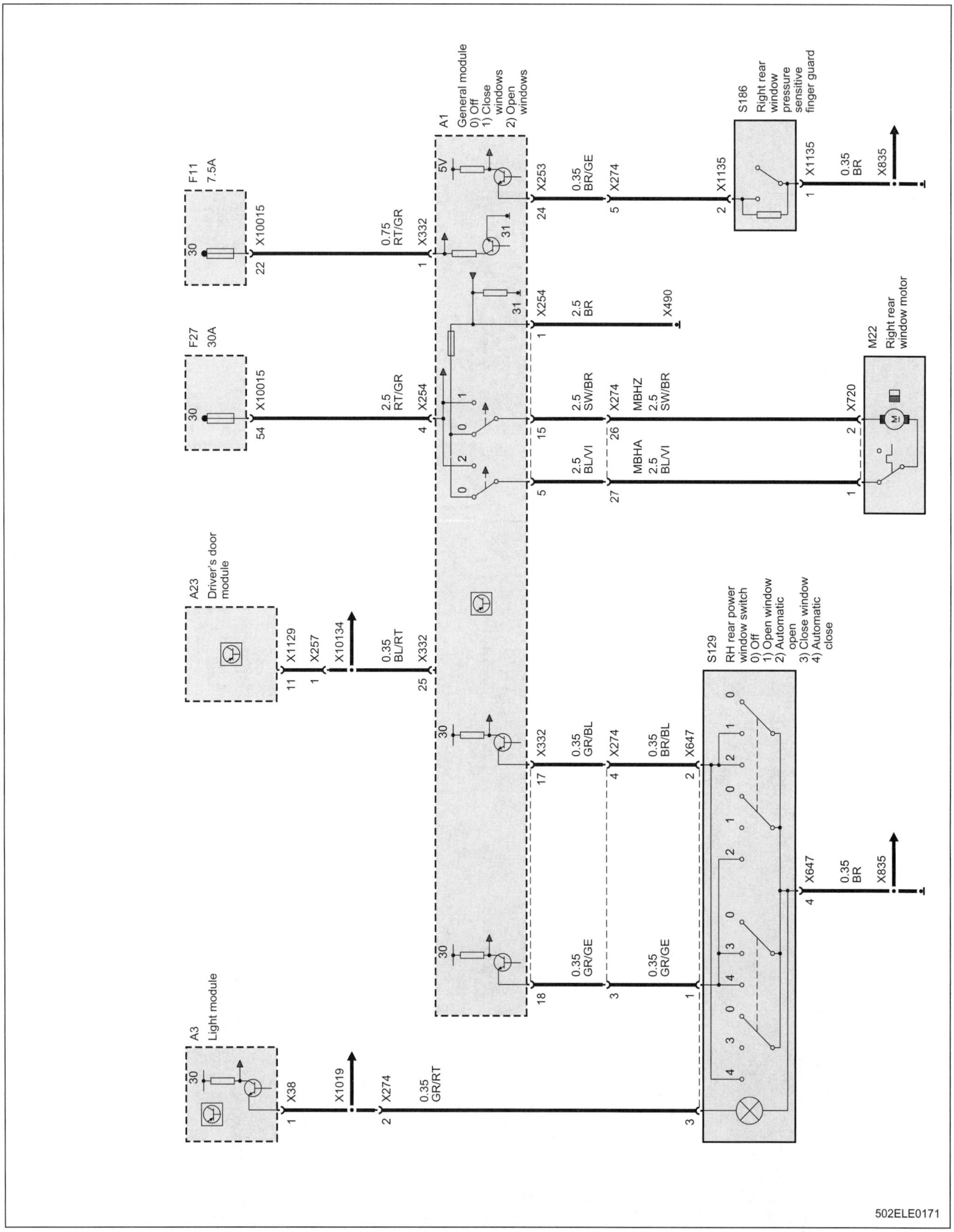

Radio/Telephone/GPS Navigation (overview)
(1 of 3)

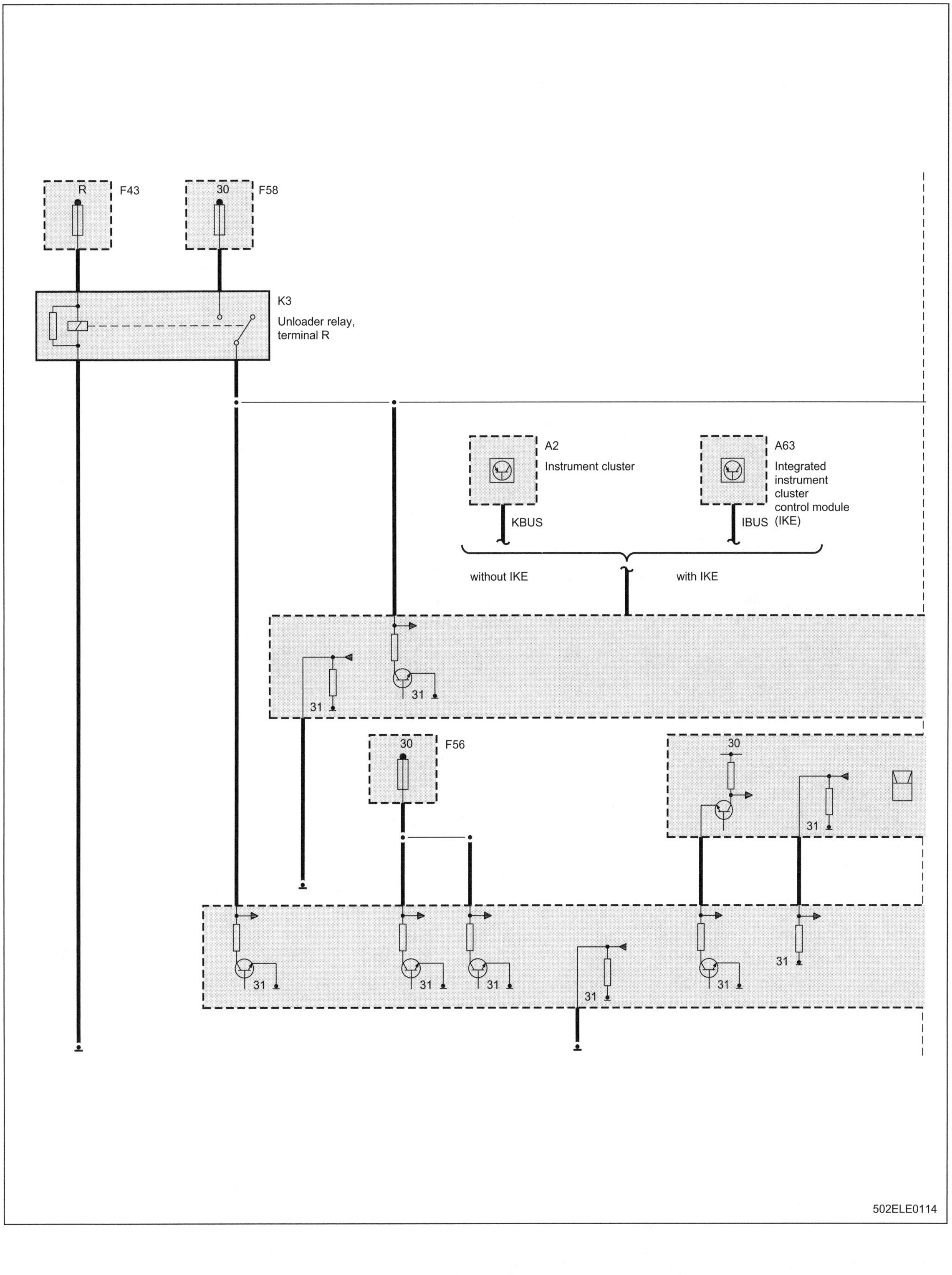
R
F43
30
F58
K3
Unloader relay,
terminal R
A2
Instrument cluster
A63
Integrated
instrument
cluster
control module
(IKE)
KBUS
IBUS
without IKE
with IKE
31
30
F56
30
31
31
31
31
31
31
31
31
502ELE0114

Radio/Telephone/GPS Navigation (overview)
(2 of 3)

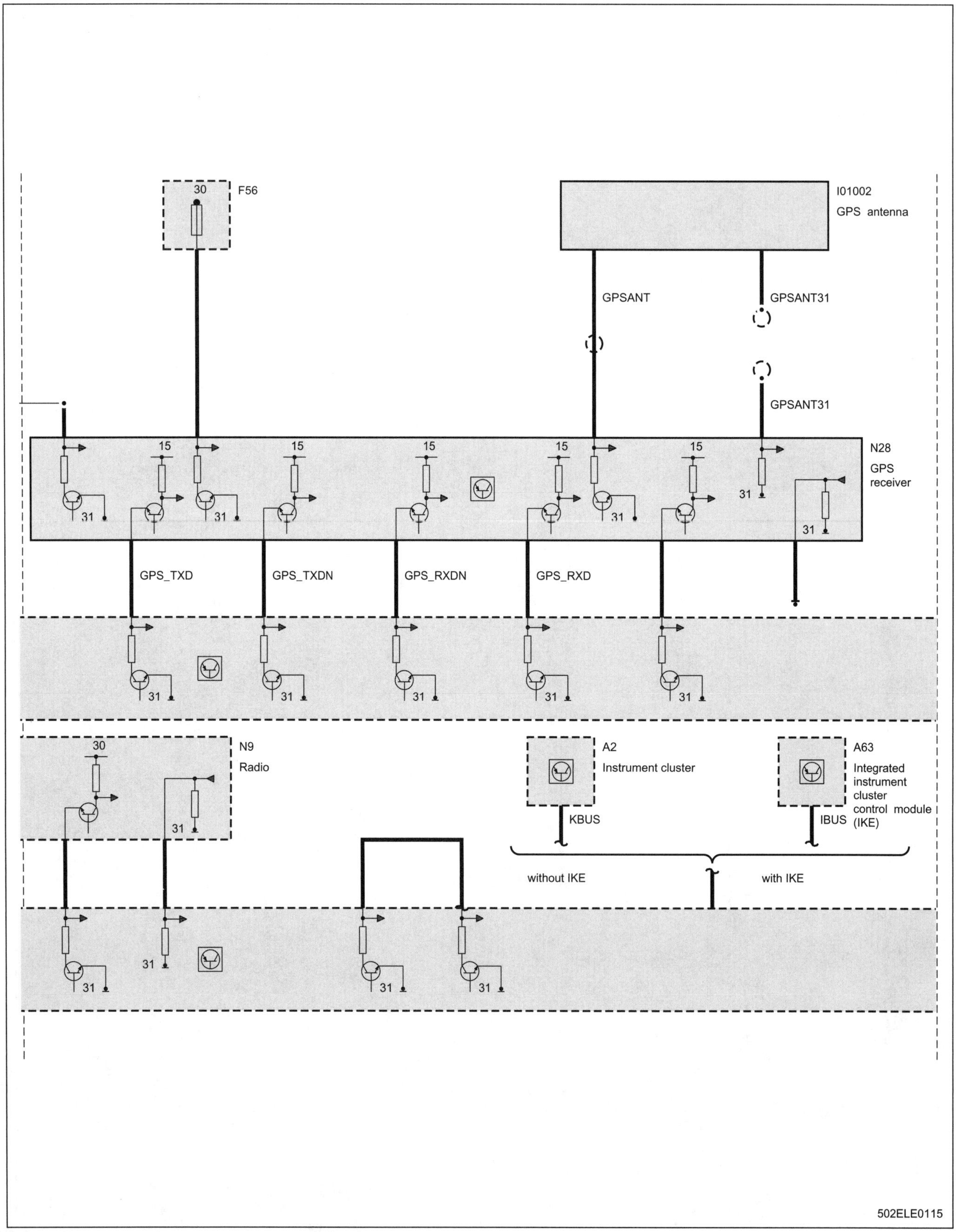
30
F56
I01002
GPS antenna
GPSANT
GPSANT31
GPSANT31
15
15
15
15
15
N28
GPS receiver
31
GPS_TXD
GPS_TXDN
GPS_RXDN
GPS_RXD
30
N9
Radio
A2
Instrument cluster
A63
Integrated instrument cluster control module (IKE)
KBUS
IBUS
without IKE
with IKE
502ELE0115

Radio/Telephone/GPS Navigation (overview)
(3 of 3)

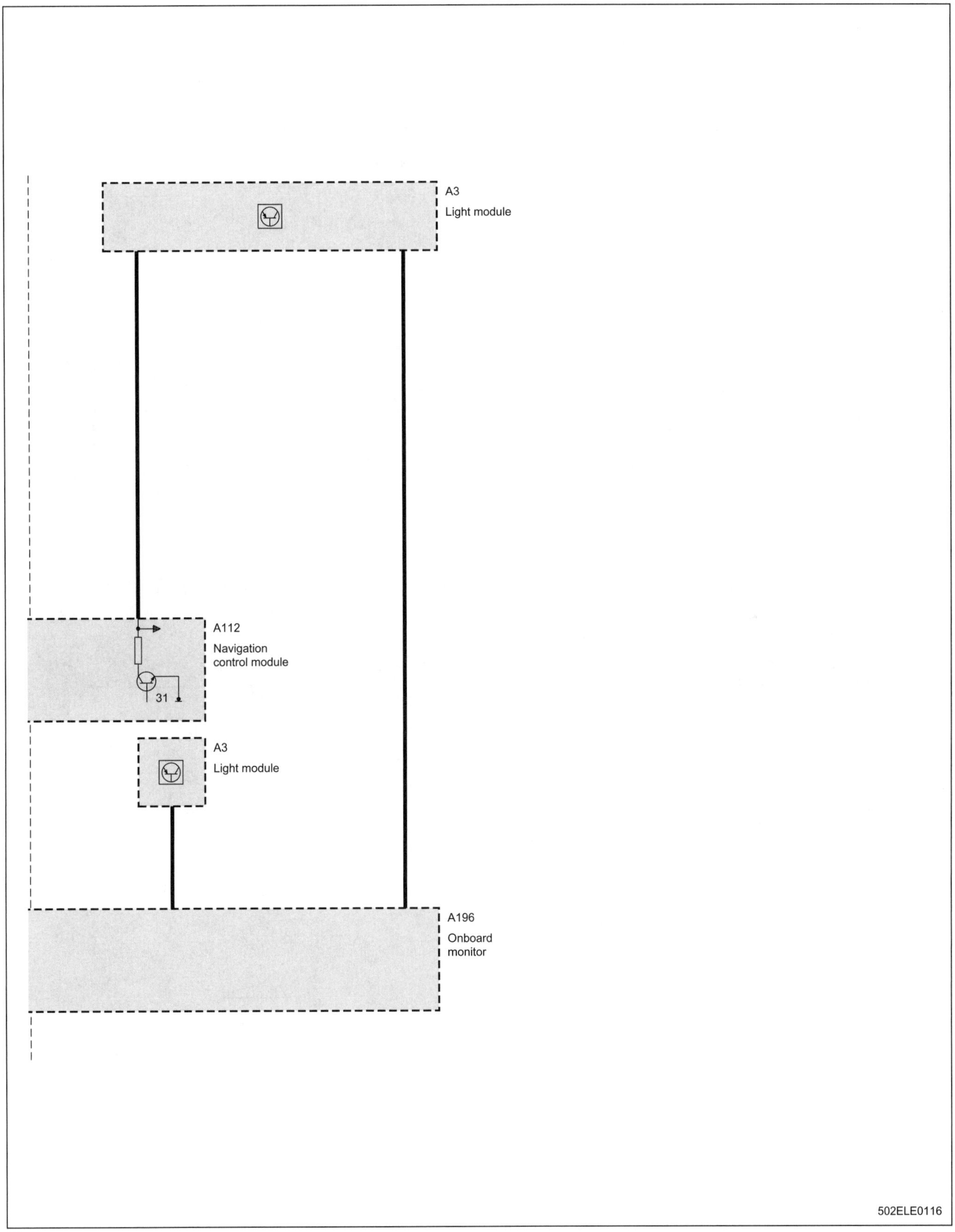
A3
Light module
A112
Navigation control module
31
A3
Light module
A196
Onboard monitor
502ELE0116

Radio/Telephone/GPS
Navigation control module (A112)
(1 of 2)

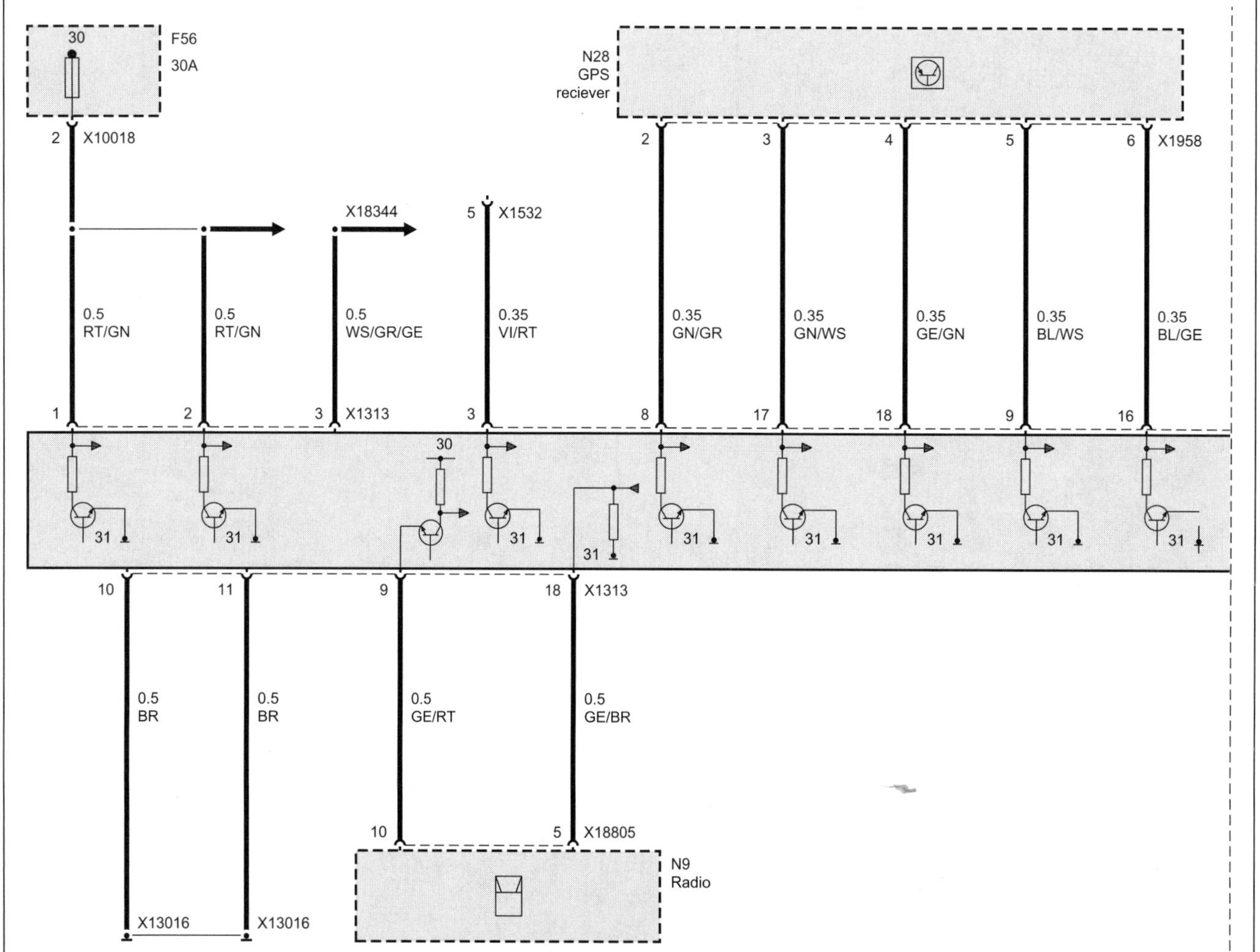

502ELE0356

Radio/Telephone/GPS
Navigation control module (A112)
(2 of 2)

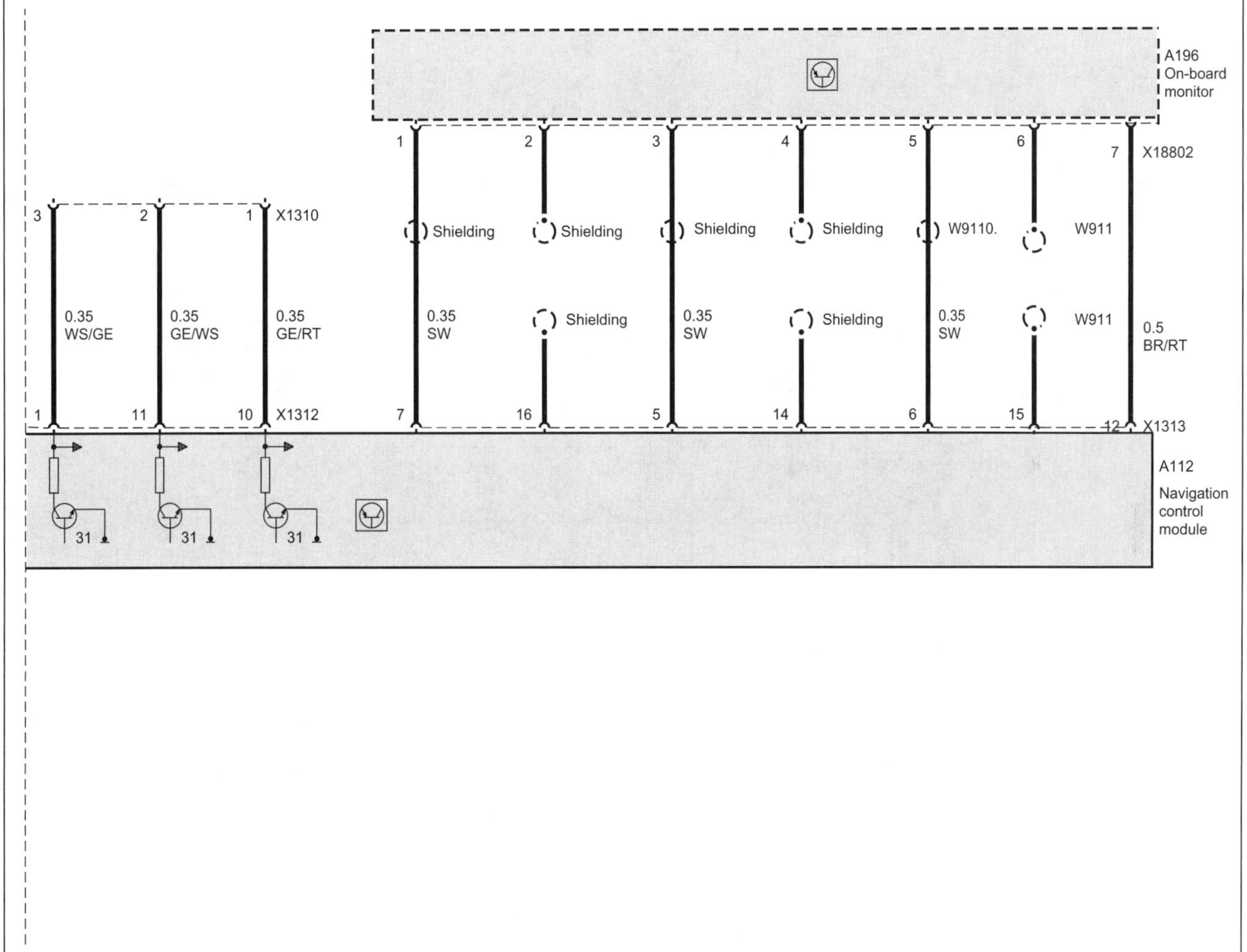

502ELE0357

Radio/Telephone/GPS
Radio (overview)
(1 of 3)

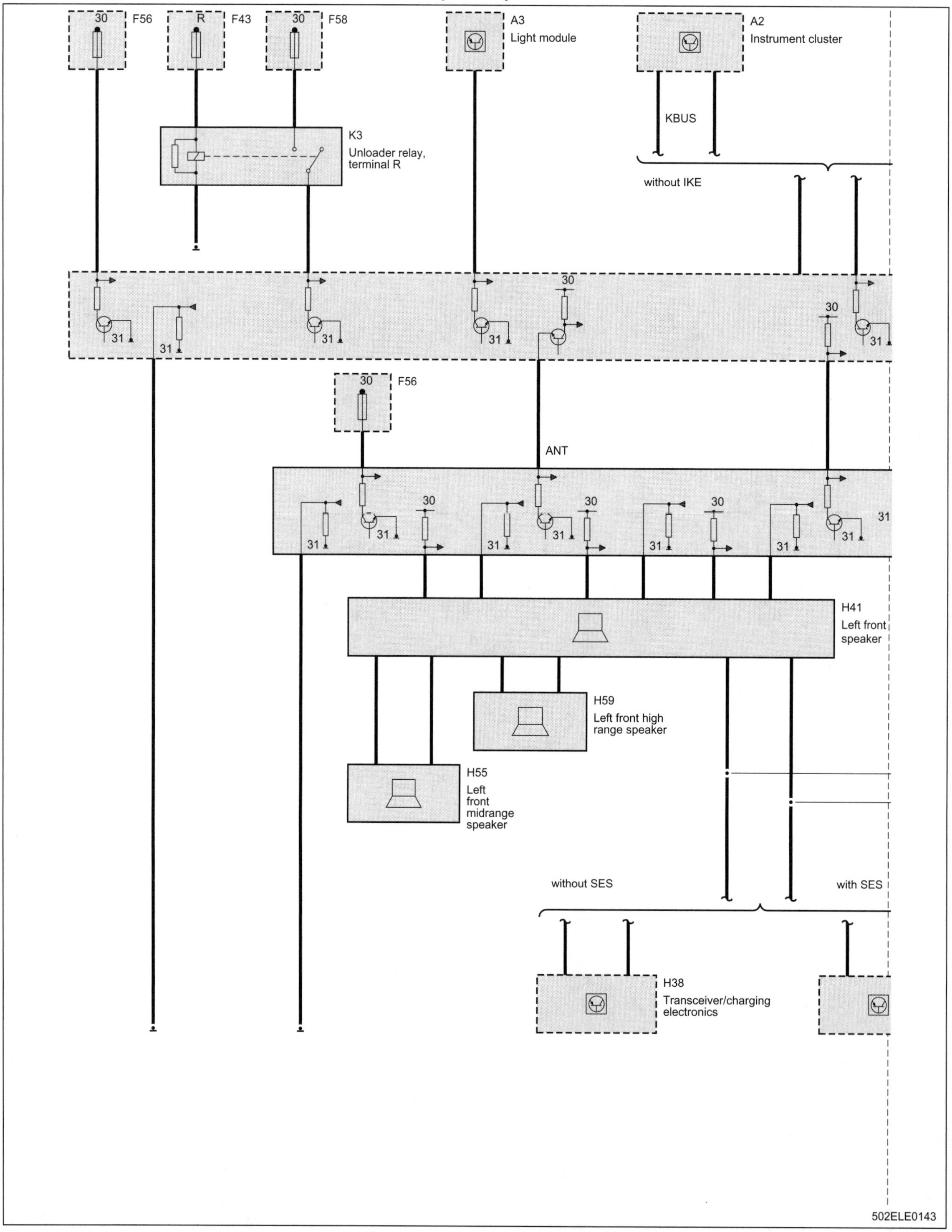
30
F56
R
F43
30
F58
A3
Light module
A2
Instrument cluster
KBUS
K3
Unloader relay, terminal R
without IKE
30
31
31
31
31
30
31
31
F56
30
ANT
30
30
30
31
31
31
31
31
31
31
31
H41
Left front speaker
H59
Left front high range speaker
H55
Left front midrange speaker
without SES
with SES
H38
Transceiver/charging electronics
502ELE0143

Radio/Telephone/GPS
Radio (overview)
(2 of 3)

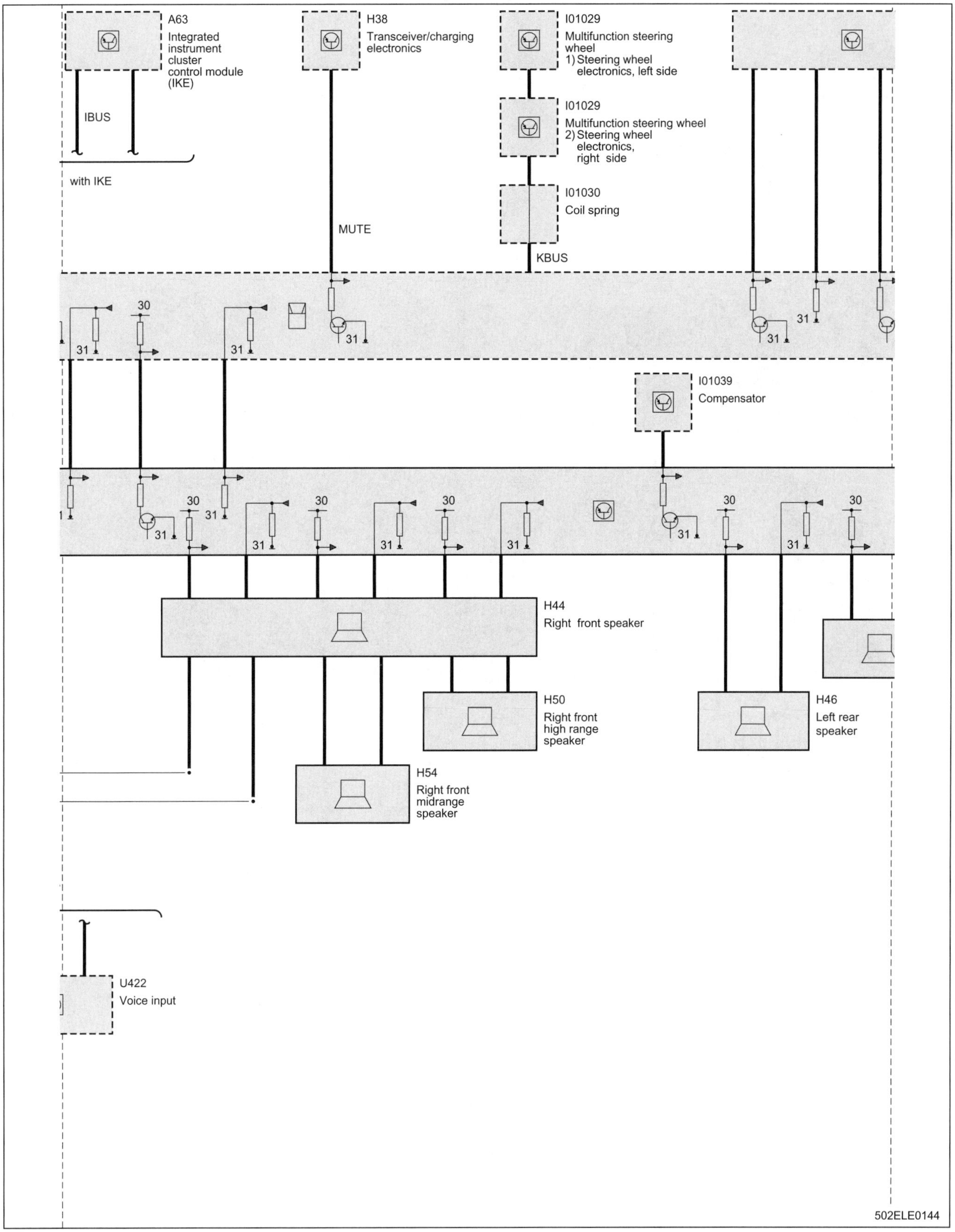
A63
Integrated instrument cluster control module (IKE)
IBUS
with IKE
H38
Transceiver/charging electronics
MUTE
I01029
Multifunction steering wheel
1) Steering wheel electronics, left side
I01029
Multifunction steering wheel
2) Steering wheel electronics, right side
I01030
Coil spring
KBUS
30
31
I01039
Compensator
H44
Right front speaker
H50
Right front high range speaker
H54
Right front midrange speaker
H46
Left rear speaker
U422
Voice input
502ELE0144

Radio/Telephone/GPS
Radio (overview)
(3 of 3)

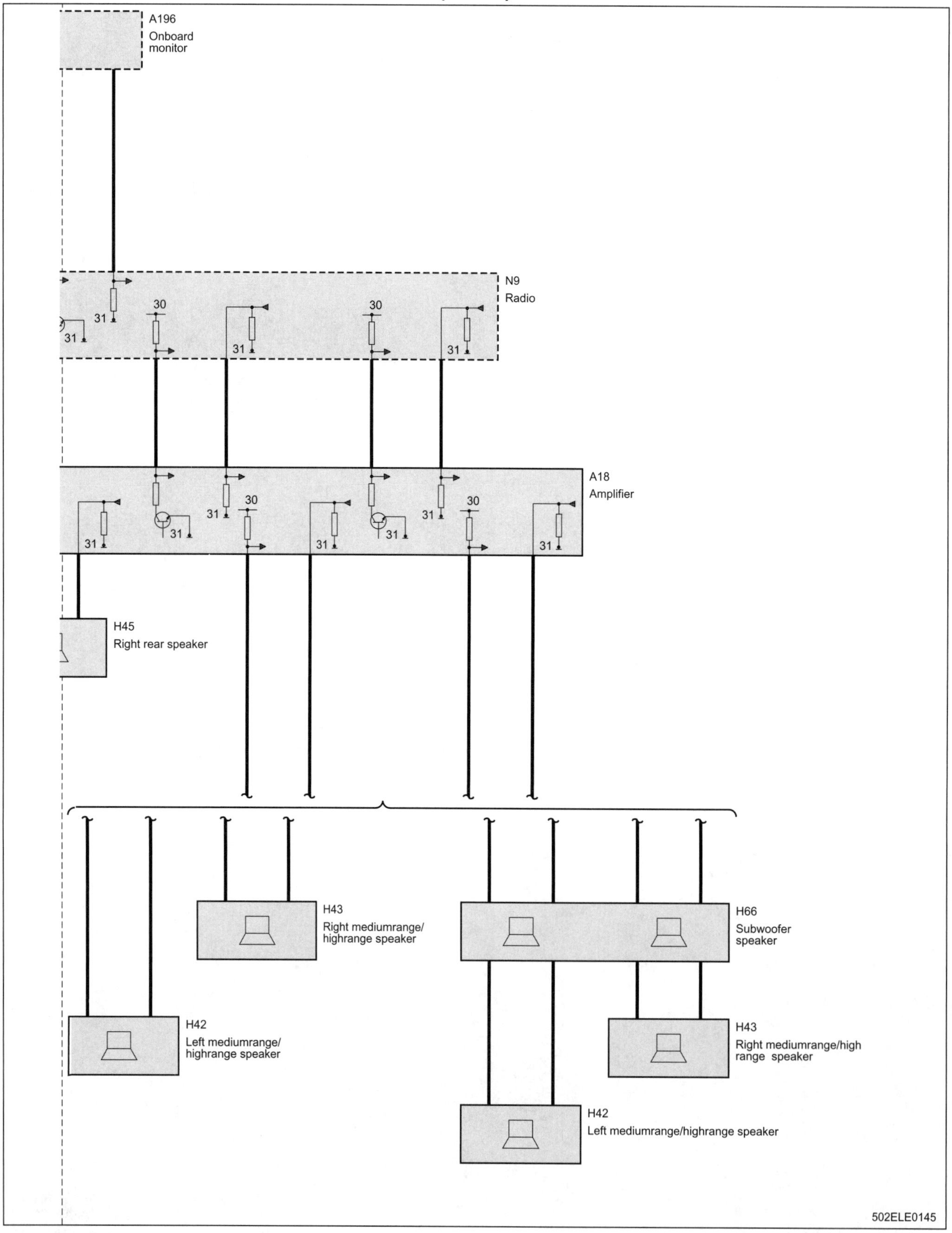
A196
Onboard monitor
N9
Radio
30
31
A18
Amplifier
H45
Right rear speaker
H43
Right mediumrange/ highrange speaker
H66
Subwoofer speaker
H42
Left mediumrange/ highrange speaker
H43
Right mediumrange/high range speaker
H42
Left mediumrange/highrange speaker
502ELE0145

Radio/Telephone/GPS
Radio/CD player antenna (overview)
(1 of 2)

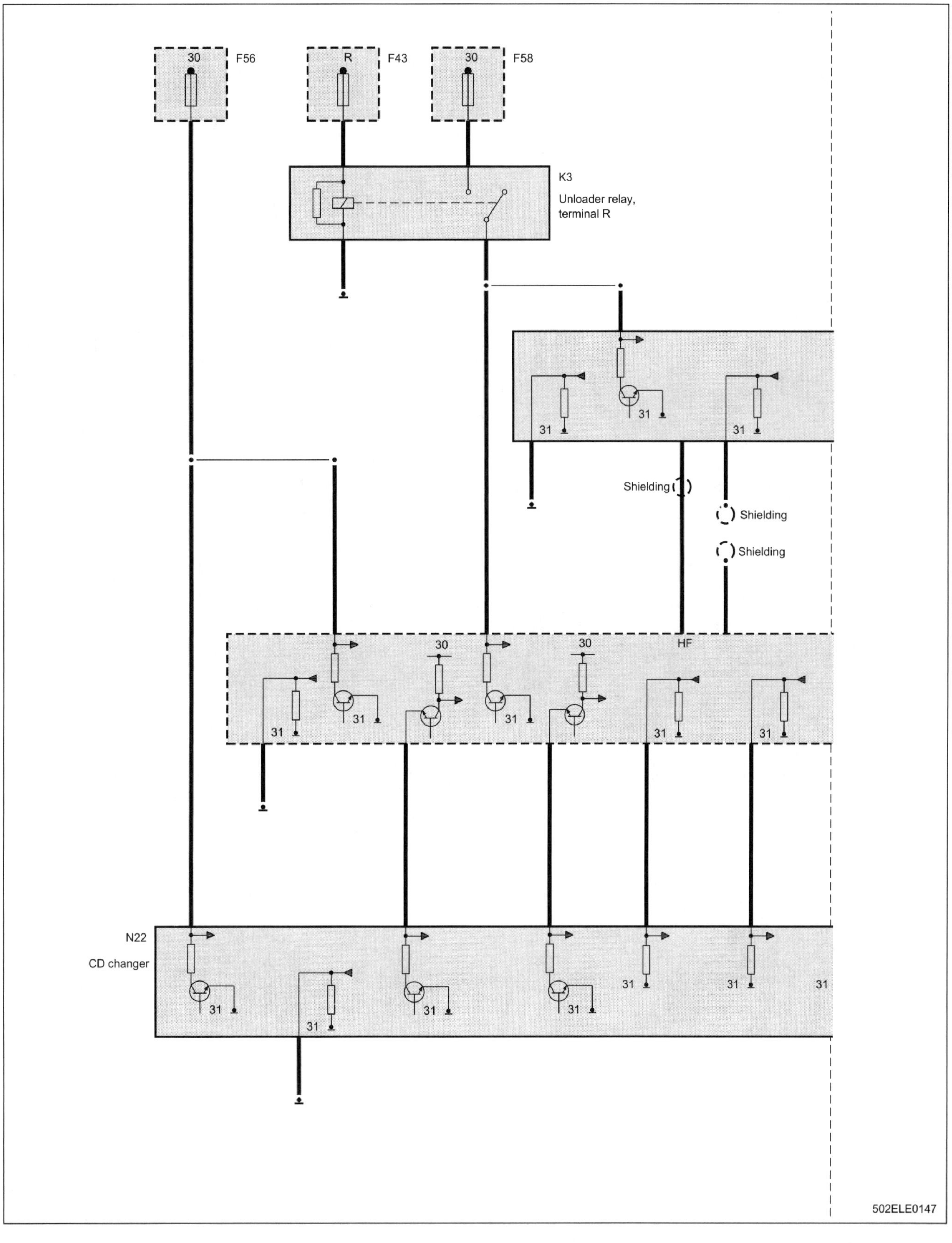

Radio/Telephone/GPS
Radio/CD player antenna (overview)
(2 of 2)

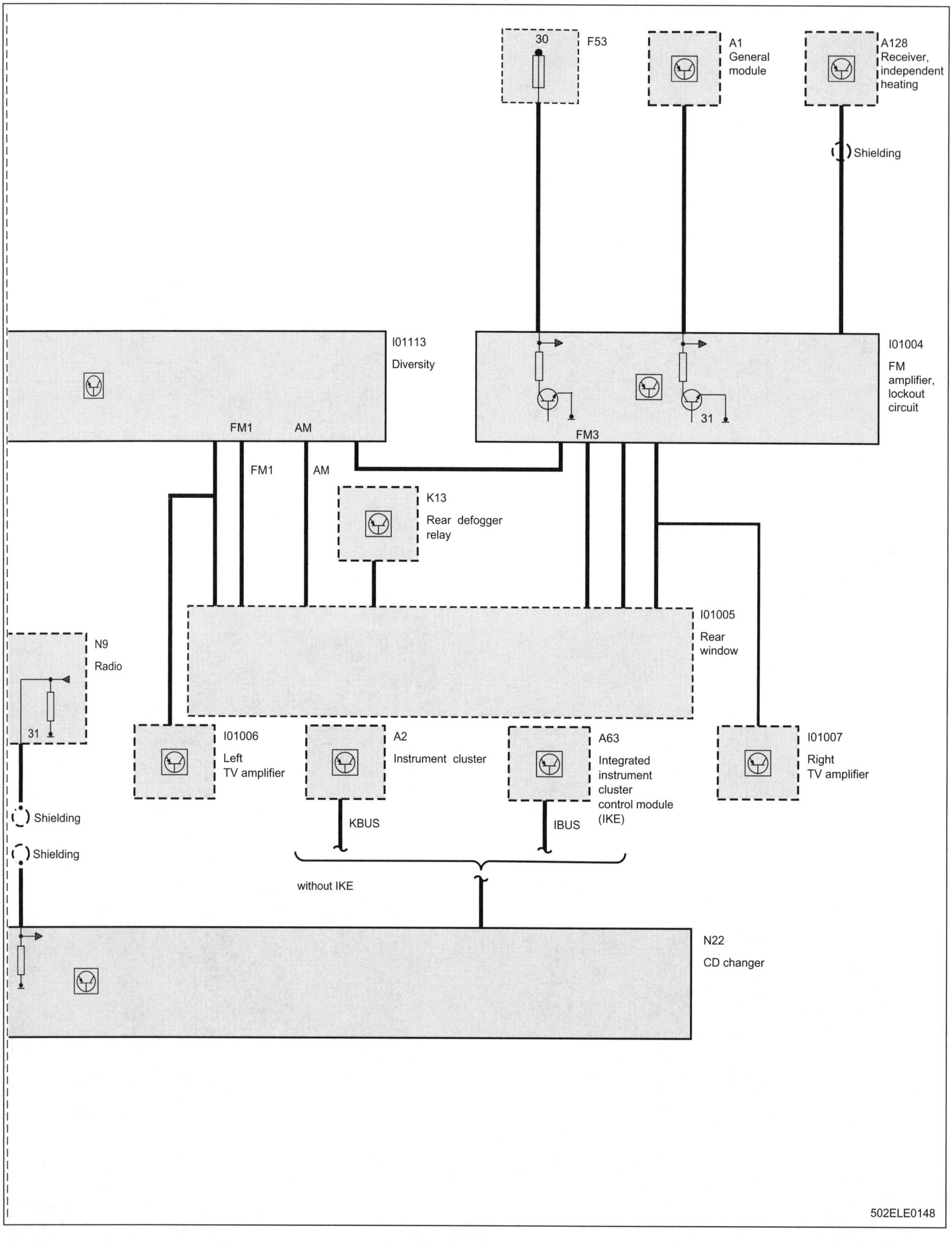

Radio/Telephone/GPS
Telephone transceiver I (overview)
(1 of 3)

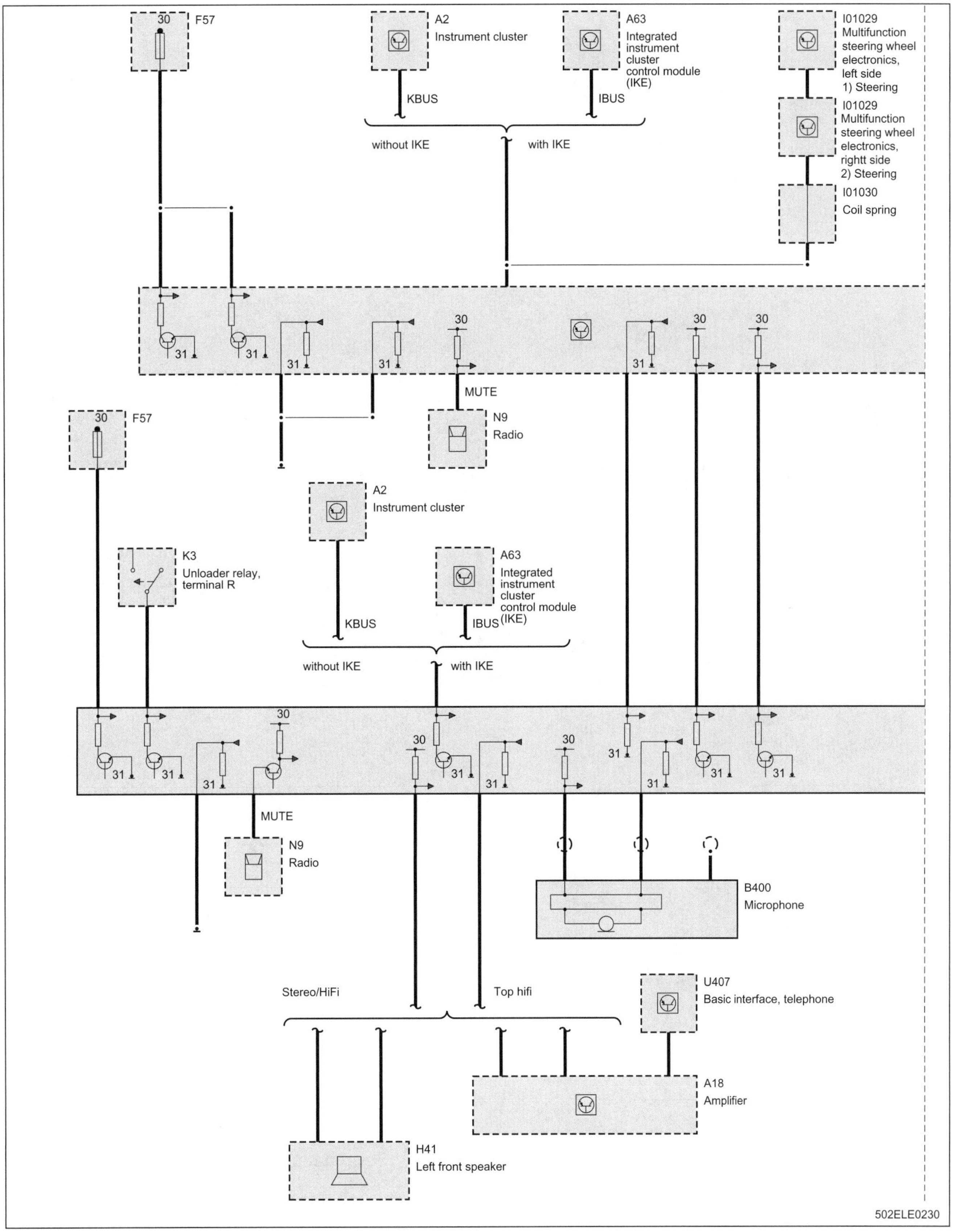

Radio/Telephone/GPS
Telephone transceiver I (overview)
(2 of 3)

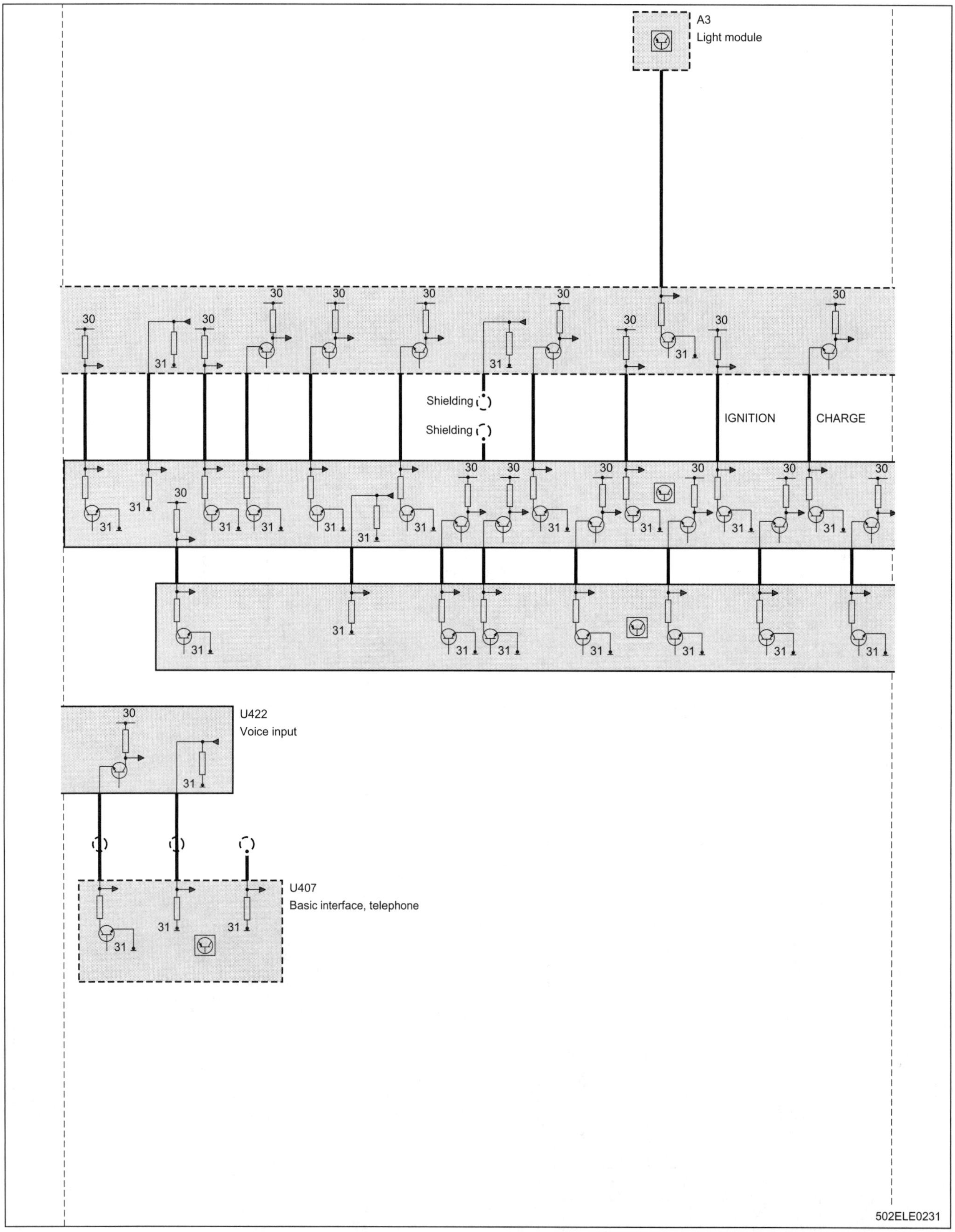

Radio/Telephone/GPS
Telephone transceiver I (overview)
(3 of 3)

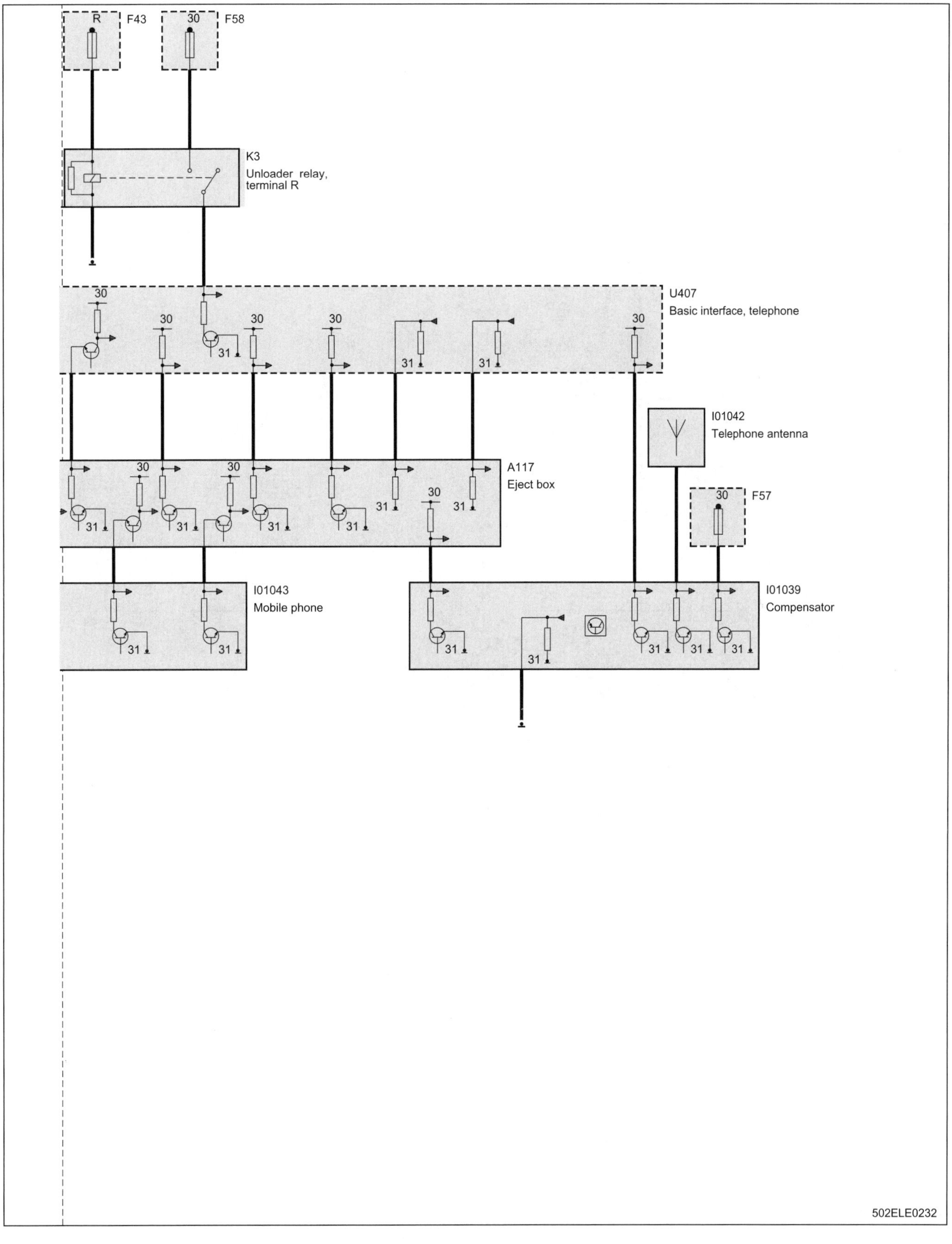

Radio/Telephone/GPS
Telephone transceiver II (overview)
(1 of 3)

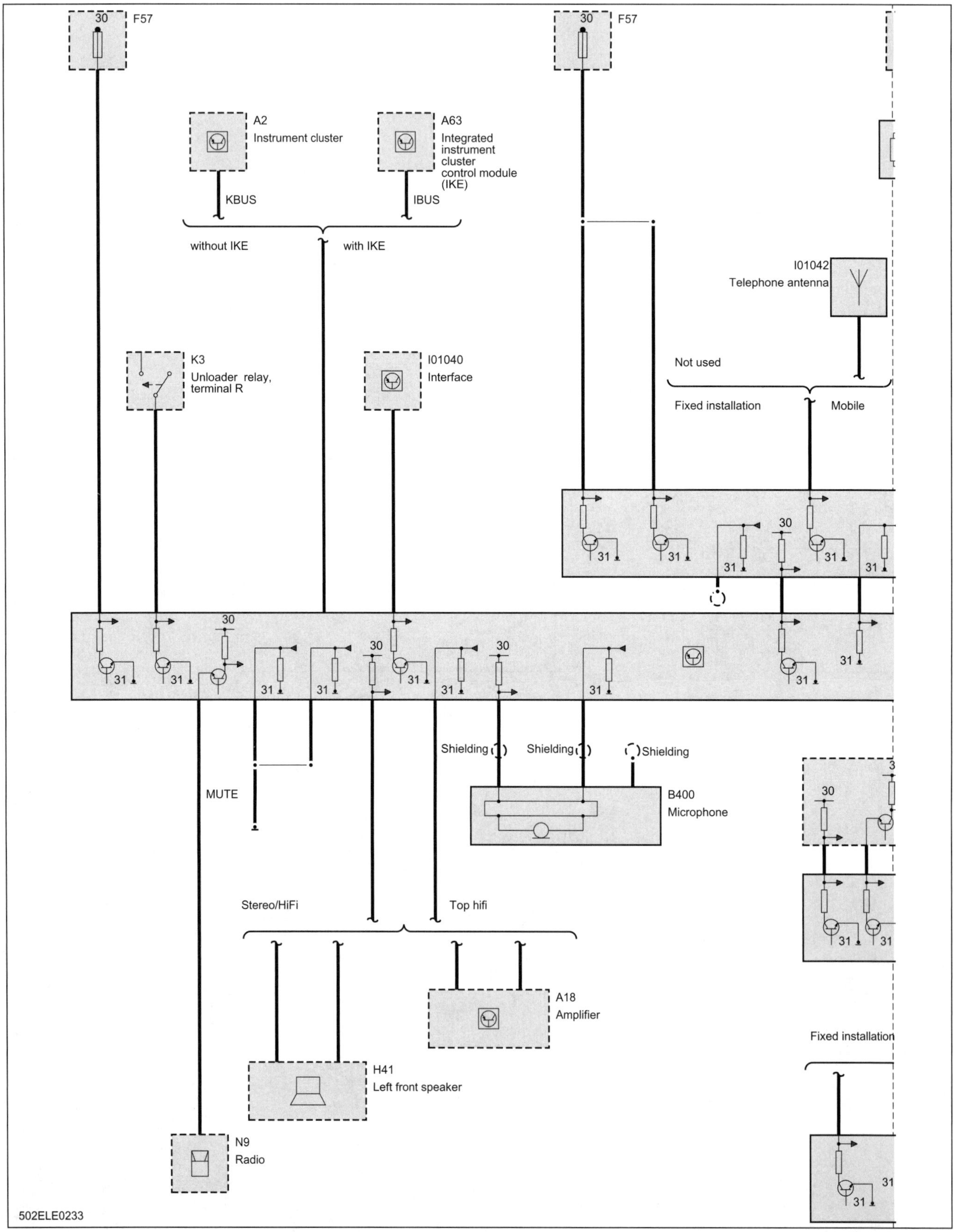

Radio/Telepone/GPS
Telephone transceiver II (overview)
(2 of 3)

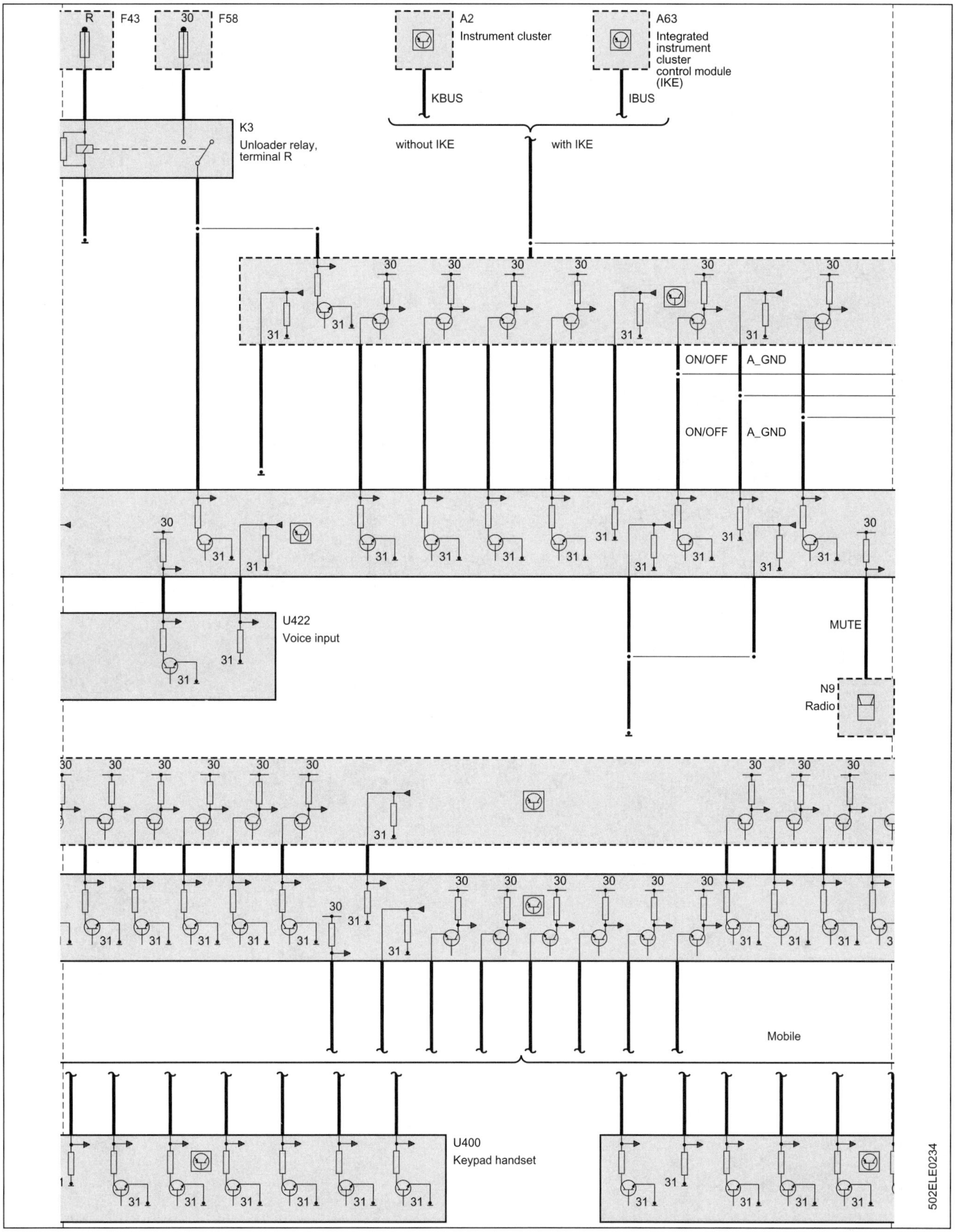

Radio/Telephone/GPS
Telephone transceiver II (overview)
(3 of 3)

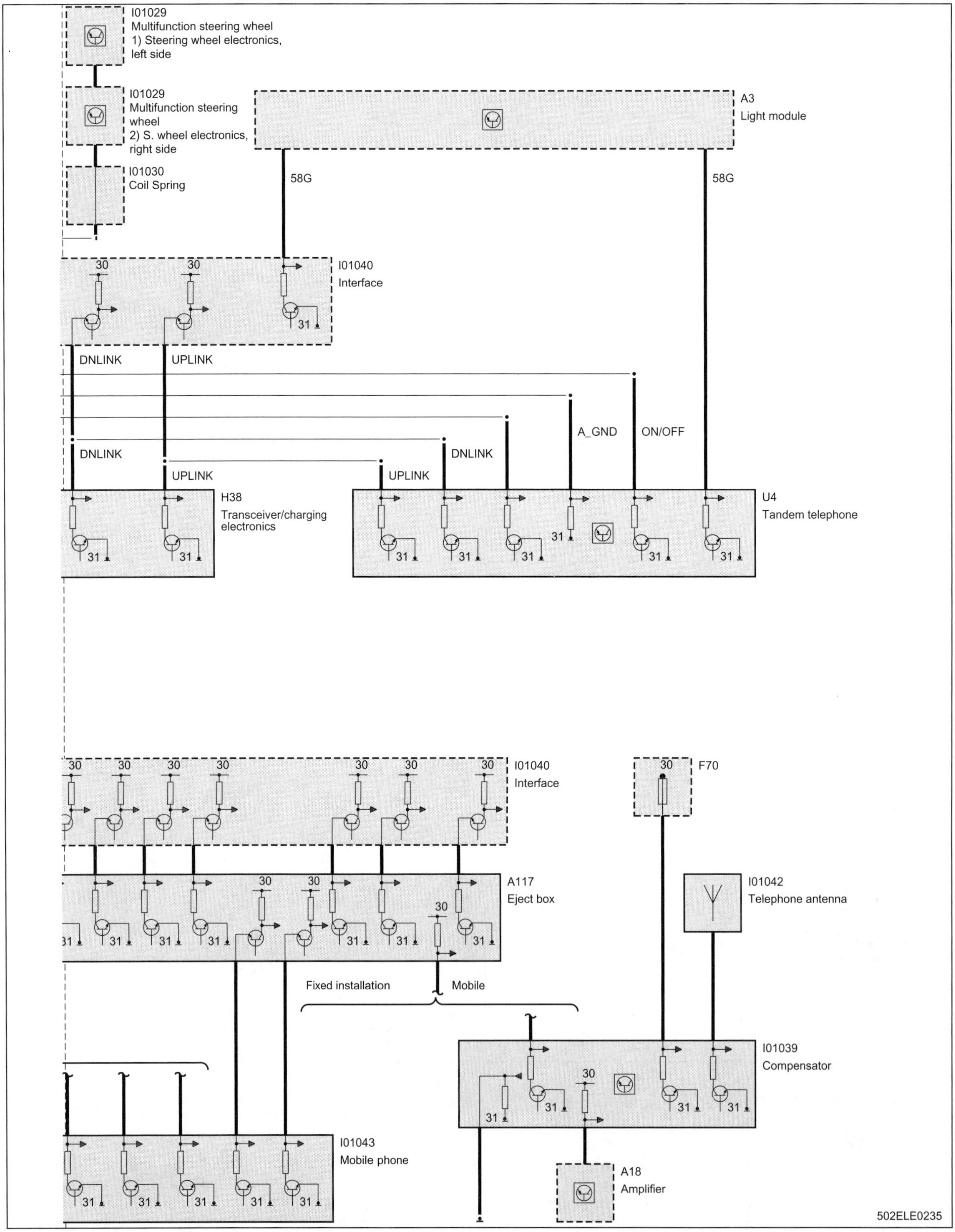

Radio/Telephone/GPS
Amplifier, top hifi (A18)
(1 of 4)

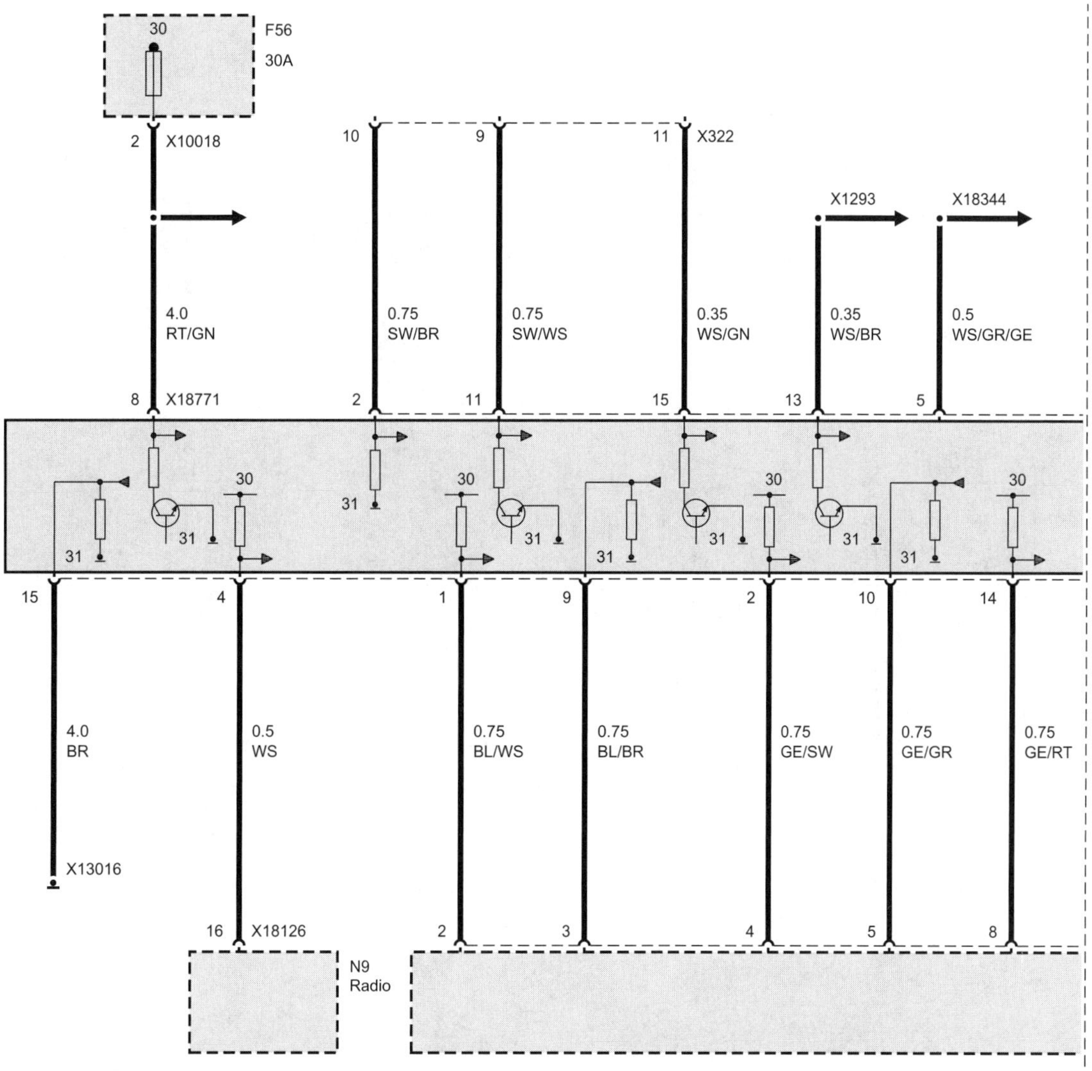

502ELE0362

Radio/Telephone/GPS
Amplifier, top hifi (A18)
(2 of 4)

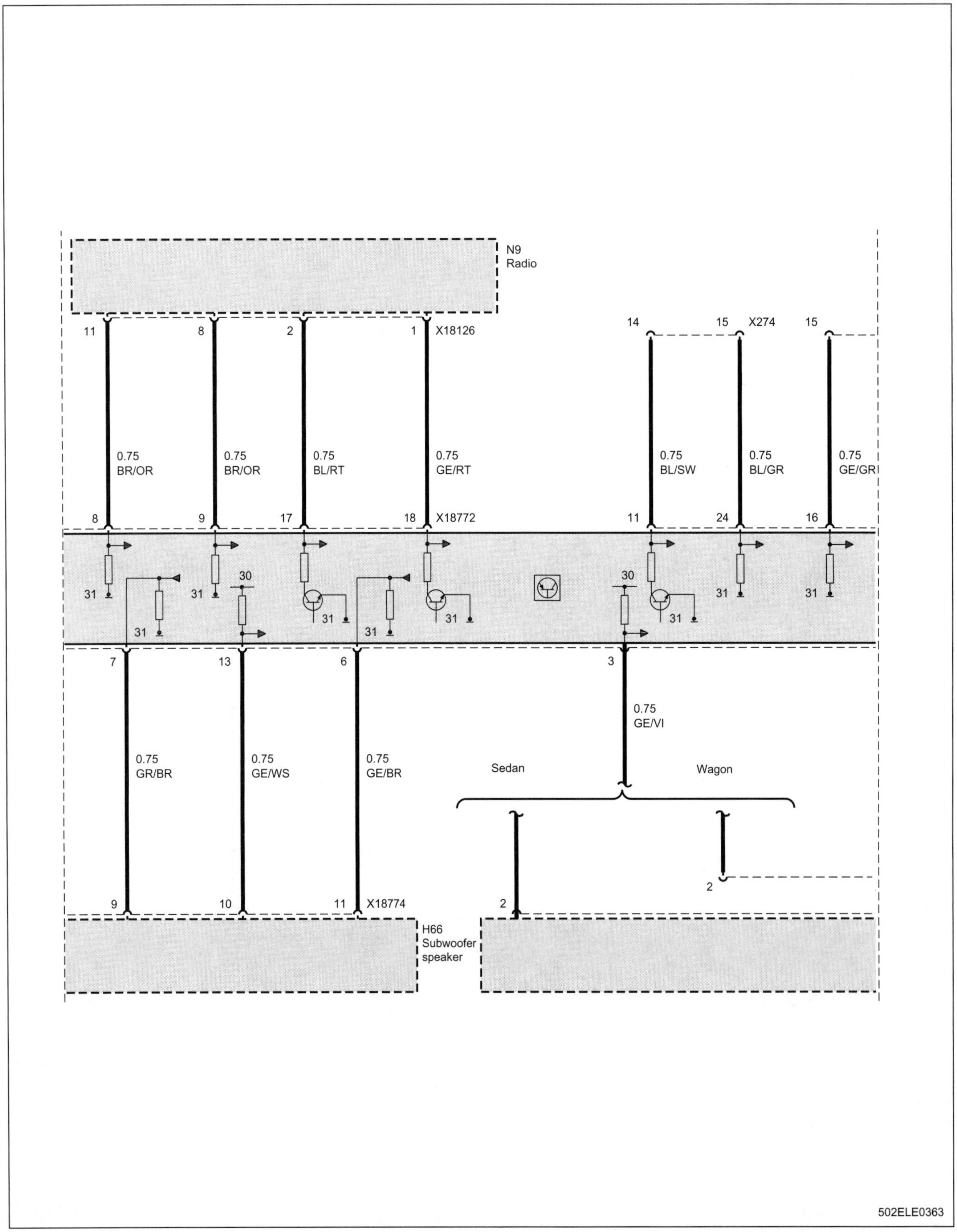
N9
Radio
11
8
2
1
X18126
14
15
X274
15
0.75
BR/OR
0.75
BR/OR
0.75
BL/RT
0.75
GE/RT
0.75
BL/SW
0.75
BL/GR
0.75
GE/GR
8
9
17
18
X18772
11
24
16
31
31
30
31
31
31
31
30
31
31
31
31
31
7
13
6
3
0.75
GE/VI
0.75
GR/BR
0.75
GE/WS
0.75
GE/BR
Sedan
Wagon
2
9
10
11
X18774
2
H66
Subwoofer
speaker
502ELE0363

Radio/Telephone/GPS
Amplifier, top hifi (A18)
(3 of 4)

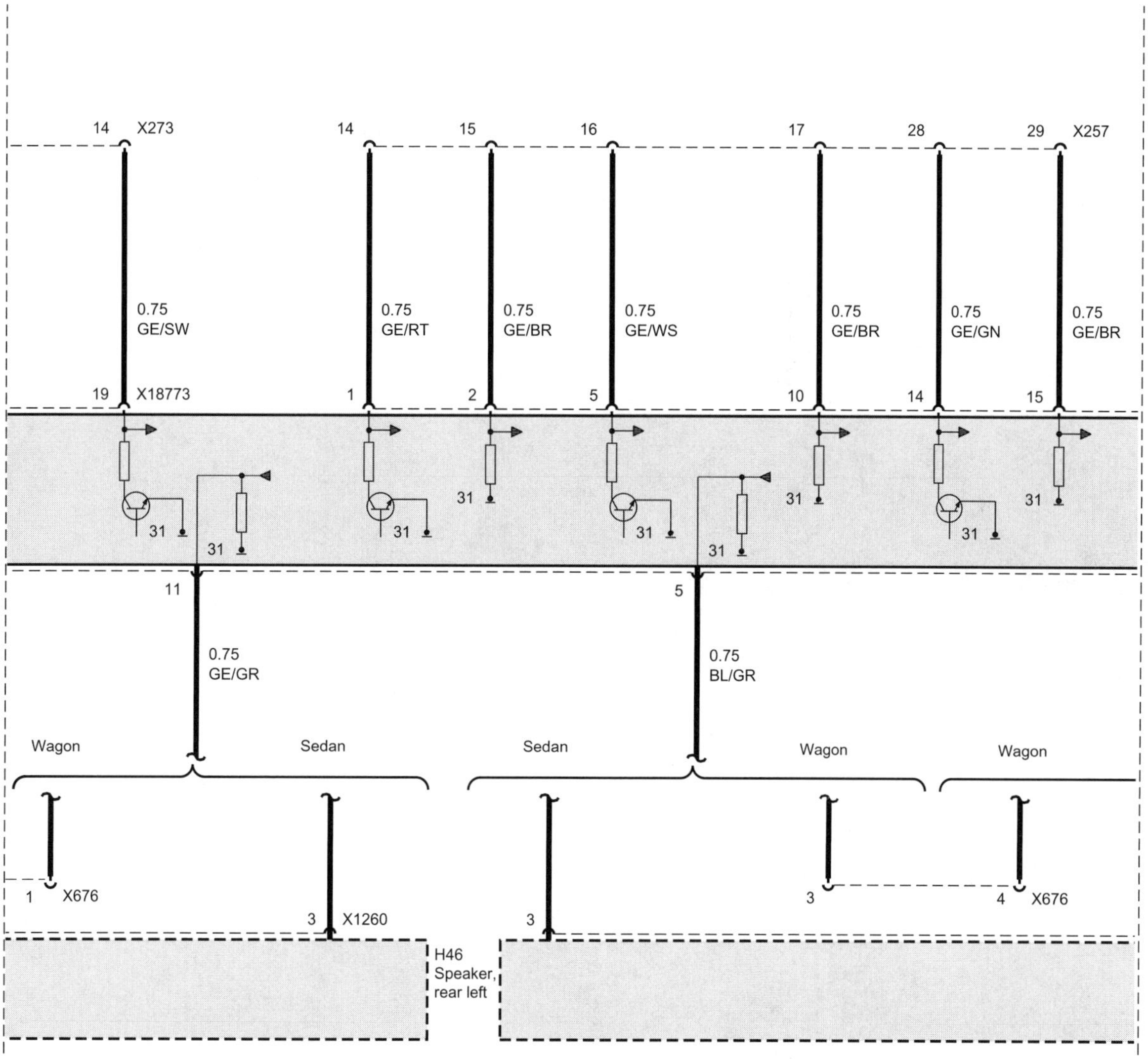

502ELE0364

Radio/Telephone/GPS Amplifier, top hifi (A18) (4 of 4)

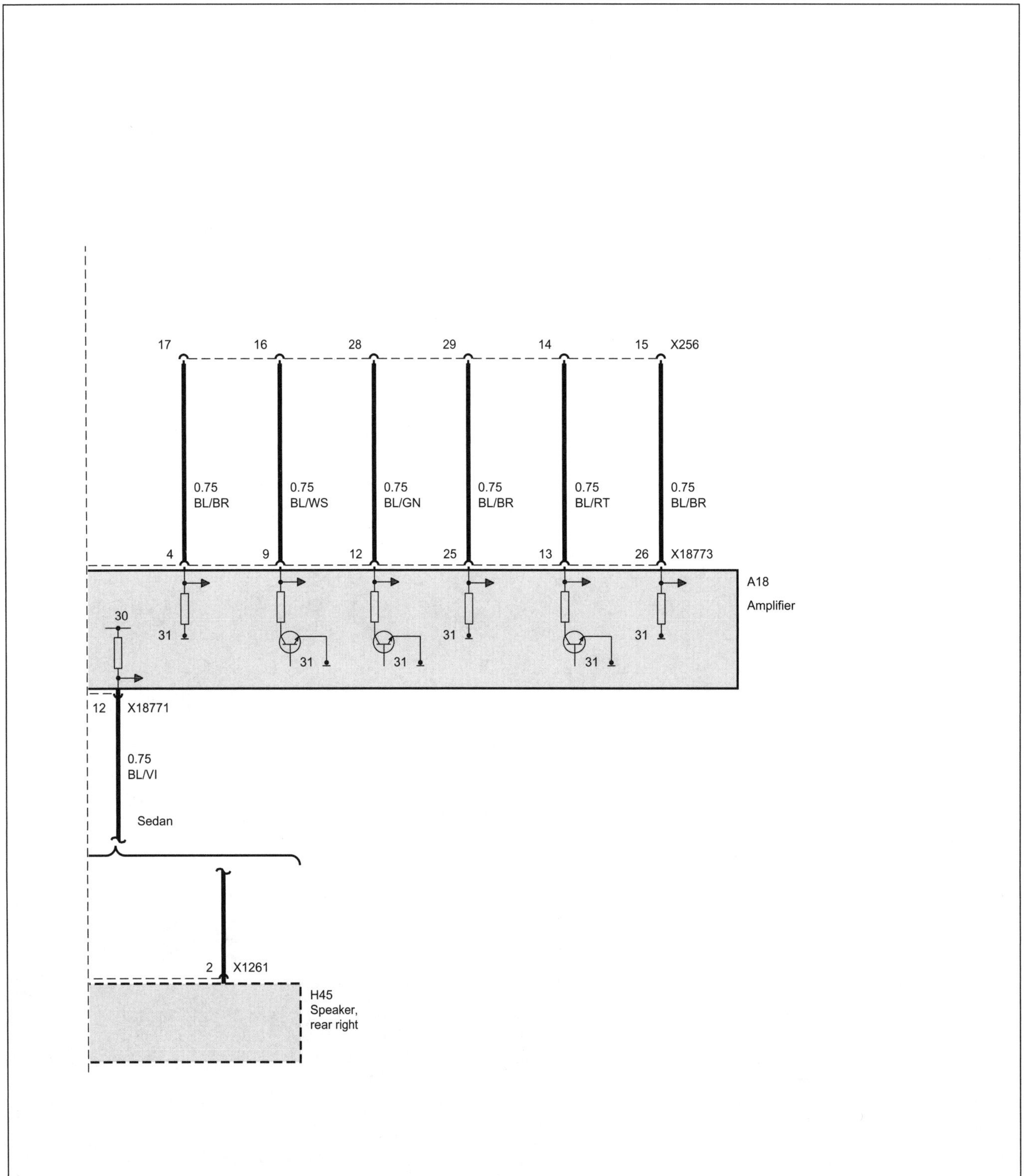
17
16
28
29
14
15
X256
0.75
BL/BR
0.75
BL/WS
0.75
BL/GN
0.75
BL/BR
0.75
BL/RT
0.75
BL/BR
4
9
12
25
13
26
X18773
A18
Amplifier
30
31
31
31
31
31
31
31
31
31
12
X18771
0.75
BL/VI
Sedan
2
X1261
H45
Speaker,
rear right
502ELE0365

Radio/Telephone/GPS
Eject box (A117)
(1 of 3)

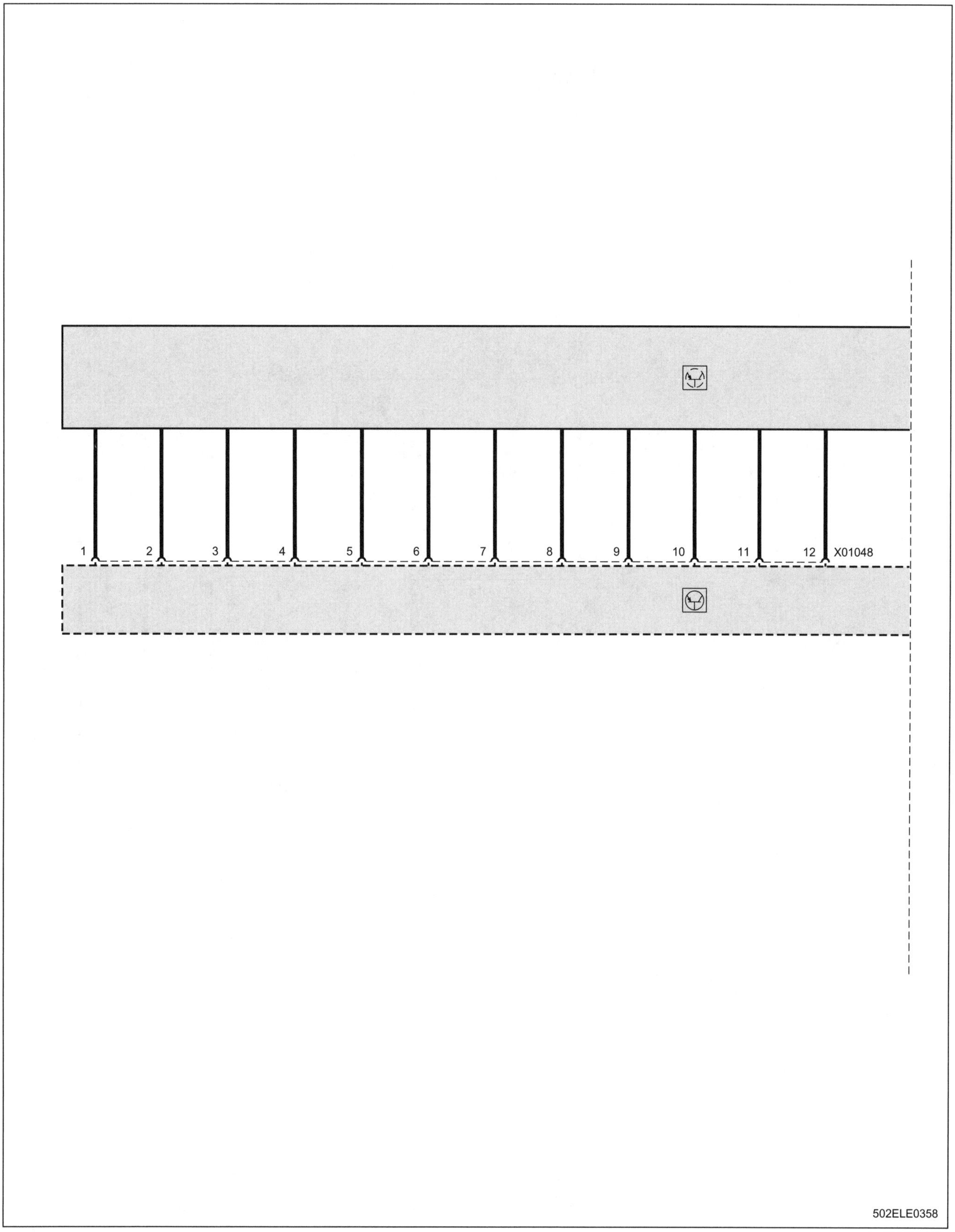

Radio/Telephone/GPS
Eject box (A117)
(2 of 3)

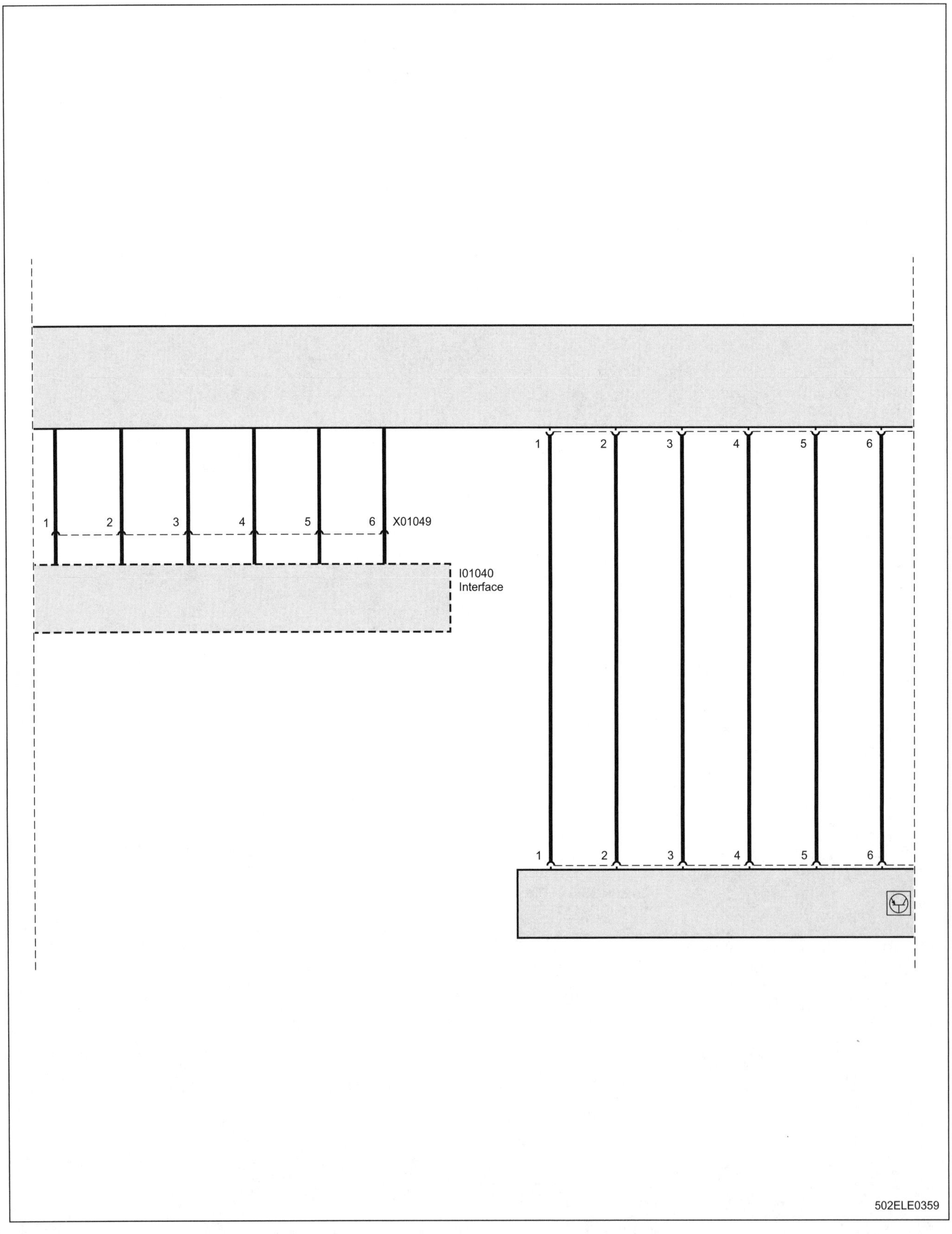
1
2
3
4
5
6
X01049
I01040
Interface
1
2
3
4
5
6
1
2
3
4
5
6
502ELE0359

Radio/Telephone/GPS
Eject box (A117)
(3 of 3)

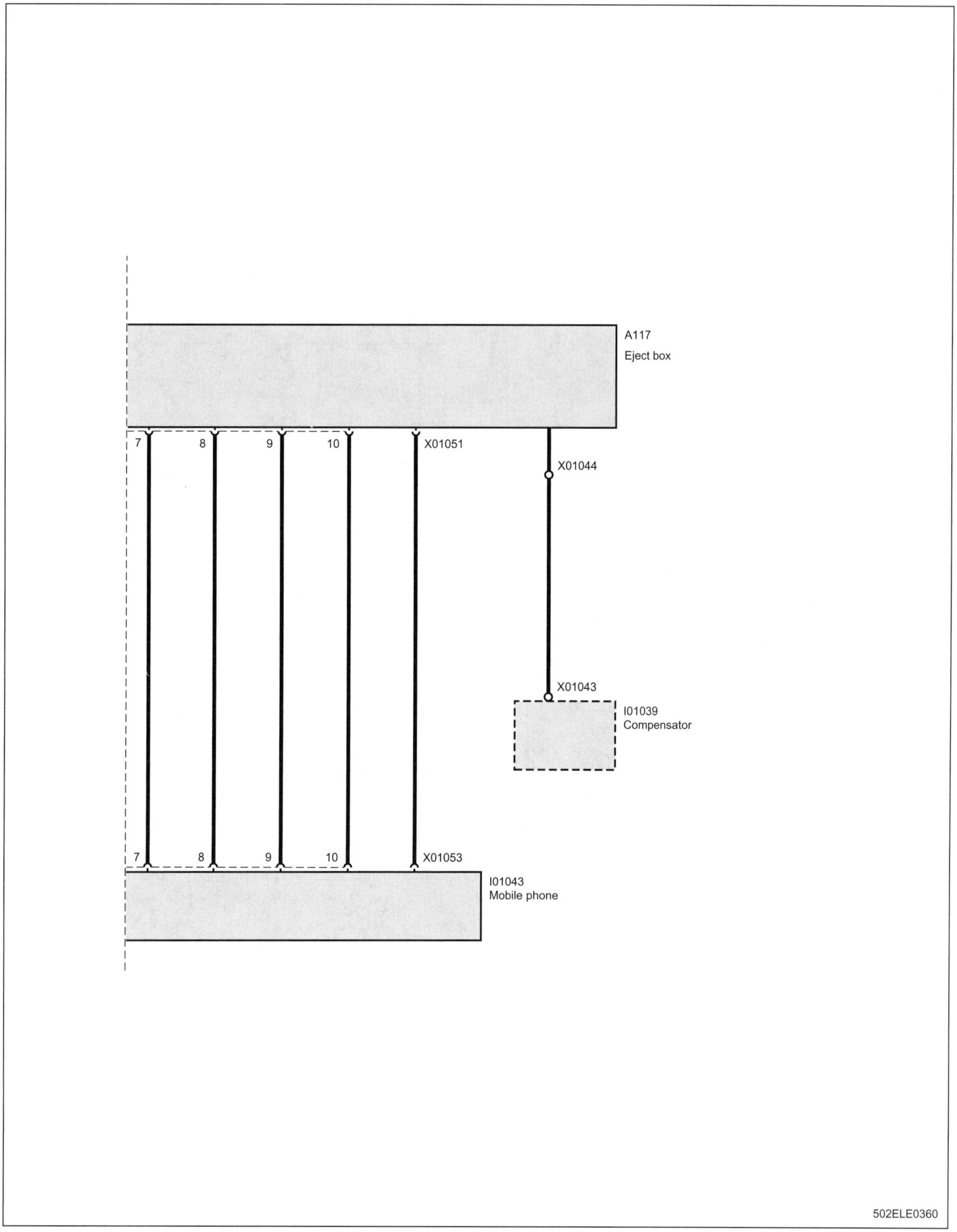
A117
Eject box
7
8
9
10
X01051
X01044
X01043
I01039
Compensator
7
8
9
10
X01053
I01043
Mobile phone
502ELE0360

Radio/Telephone/GPS
A197 Video module
(1 of 2)

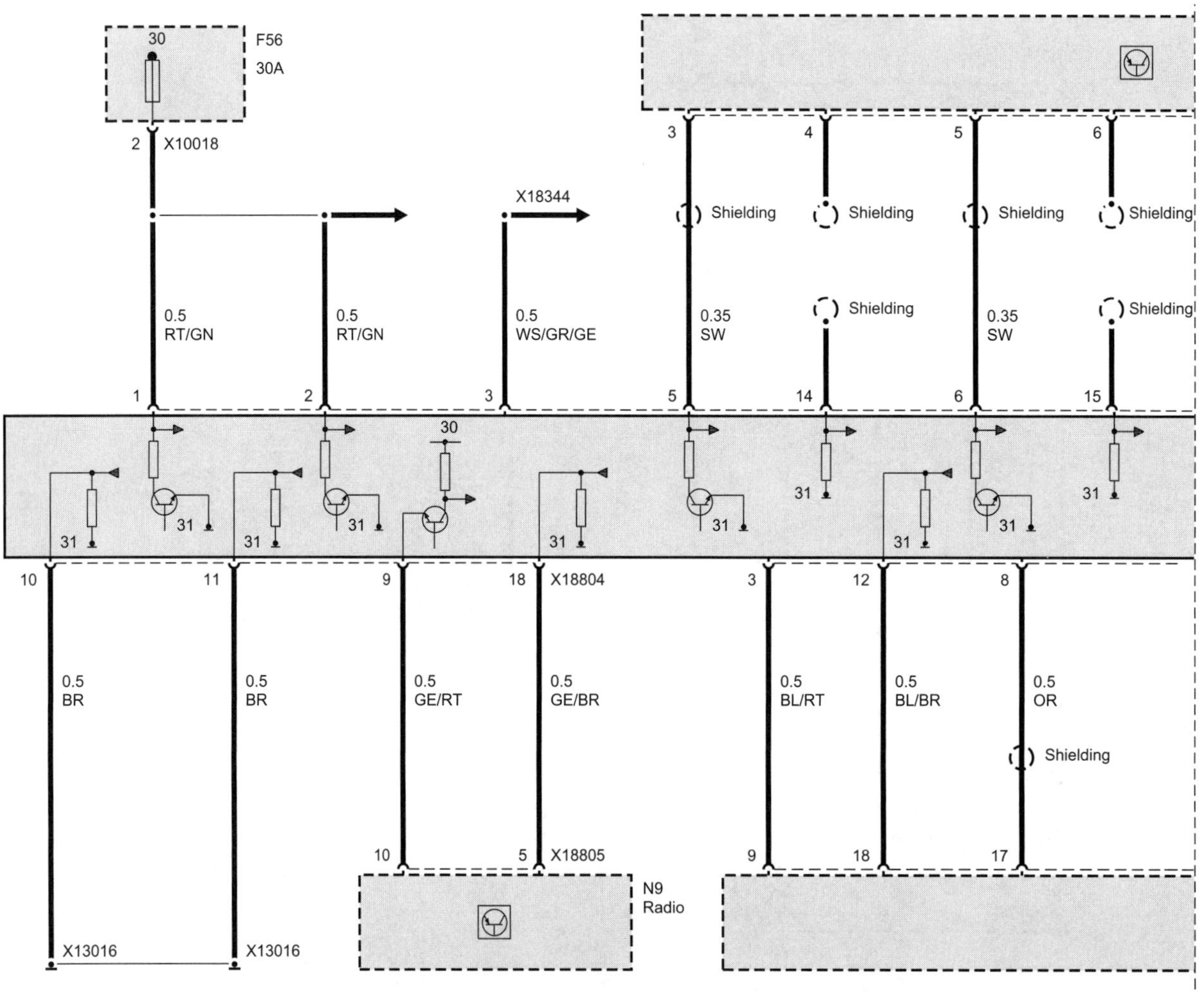
30
F56
30A
2
X10018
X18344
3
4
5
6
Shielding
Shielding
Shielding
Shielding
Shielding
Shielding
0.5
RT/GN
0.5
RT/GN
0.5
WS/GR/GE
0.35
SW
0.35
SW
1
2
3
5
14
6
15
30
31
10
11
9
18
X18804
3
12
8
0.5
BR
0.5
BR
0.5
GE/RT
0.5
GE/BR
0.5
BL/RT
0.5
BL/BR
0.5
OR
Shielding
10
5
X18805
9
18
17
N9
Radio
X13016
X13016
502ELE0401

Radio/Telephone/GPS
A197 Video module
(2 of 2)

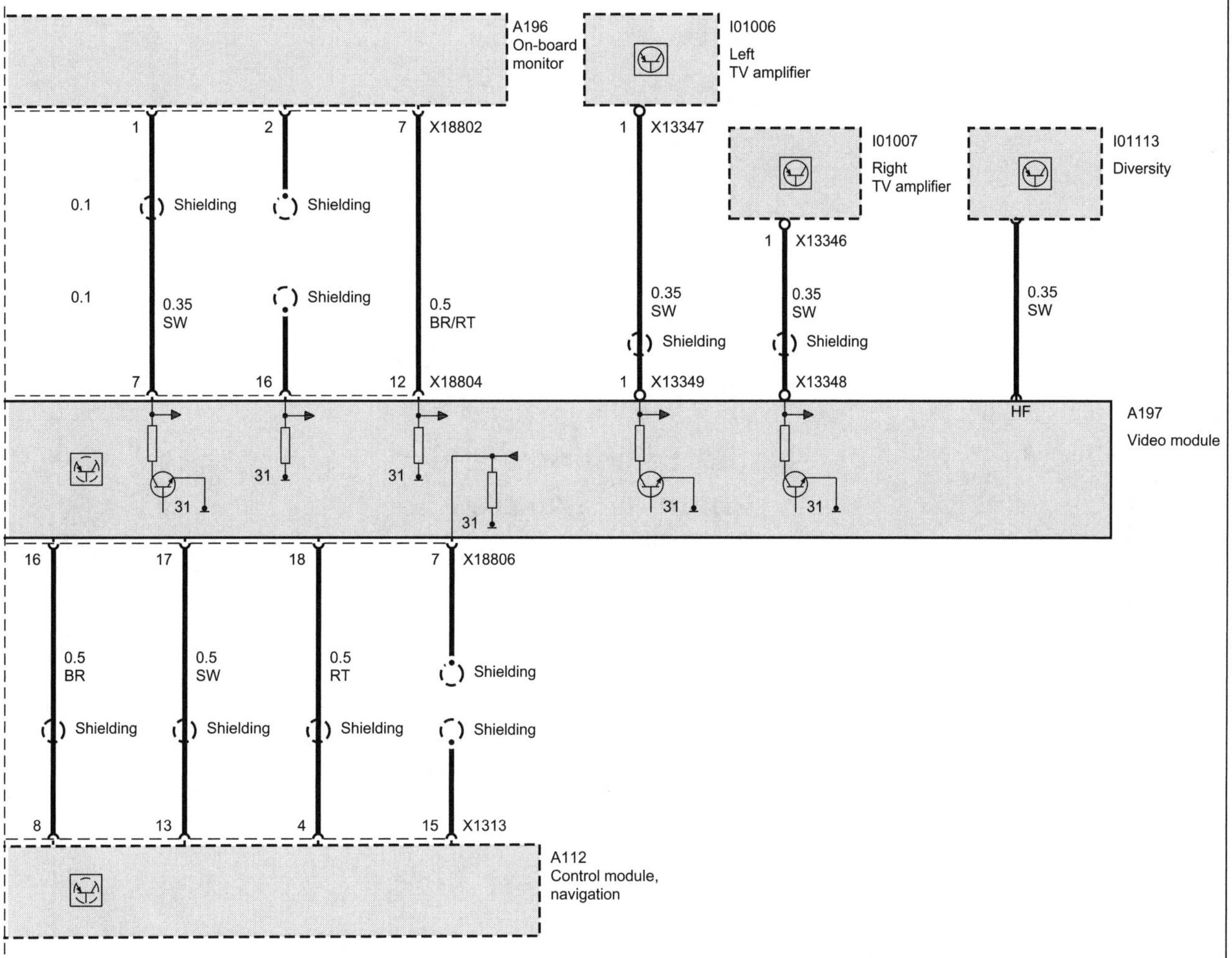
A196
On-board
monitor
I01006
Left
TV amplifier
I01007
Right
TV amplifier
I01113
Diversity
1
2
7
X18802
1
X13347
1
X13346
0.1
Shielding
Shielding
0.1
0.35
SW
Shielding
0.5
BR/RT
0.35
SW
Shielding
0.35
SW
Shielding
0.35
SW
7
16
12
X18804
1
X13349
X13348
HF
A197
Video module
31
31
31
31
31
31
16
17
18
7
X18806
0.5
BR
0.5
SW
0.5
RT
Shielding
Shielding
Shielding
Shielding
Shielding
8
13
4
15
X1313
A112
Control module,
navigation
502ELE0402

Radio/Telephone/GPS
Antenna amplifier

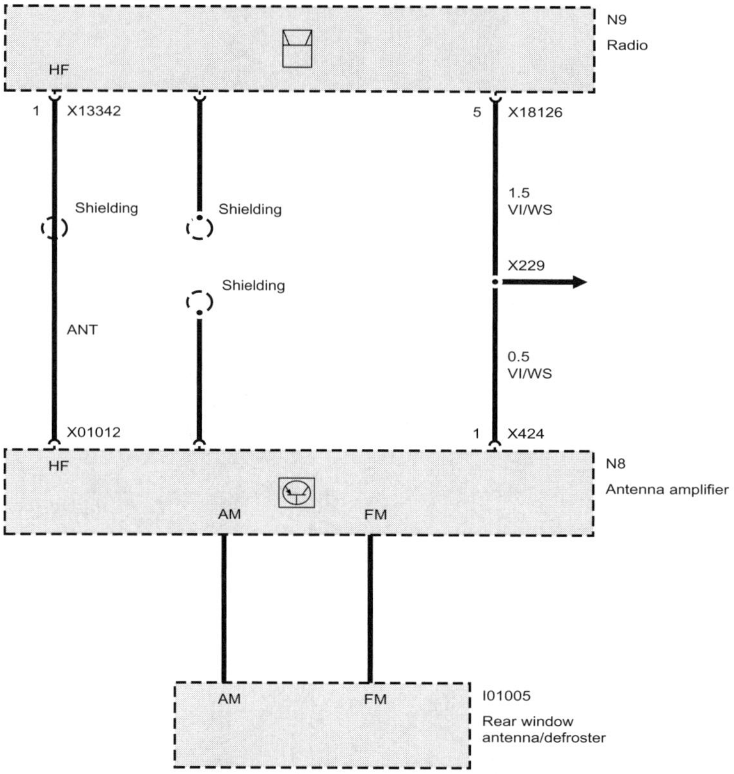

502ELE0004a

Radio/Telephone/GPS
Antenna diversity

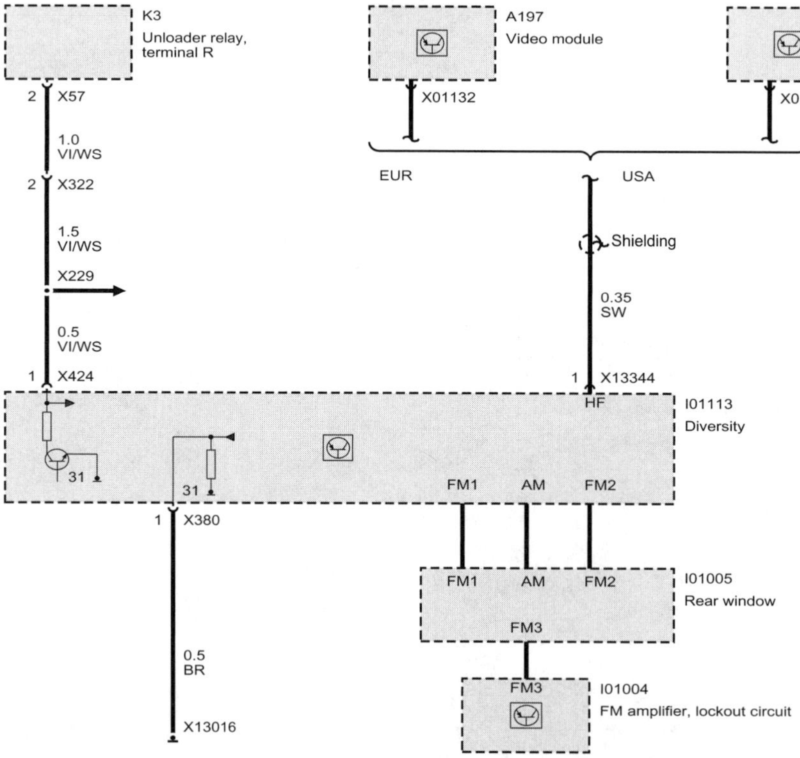

502ELE0004b

Radio/Telephone/GPS
CD changer
(1 of 1)

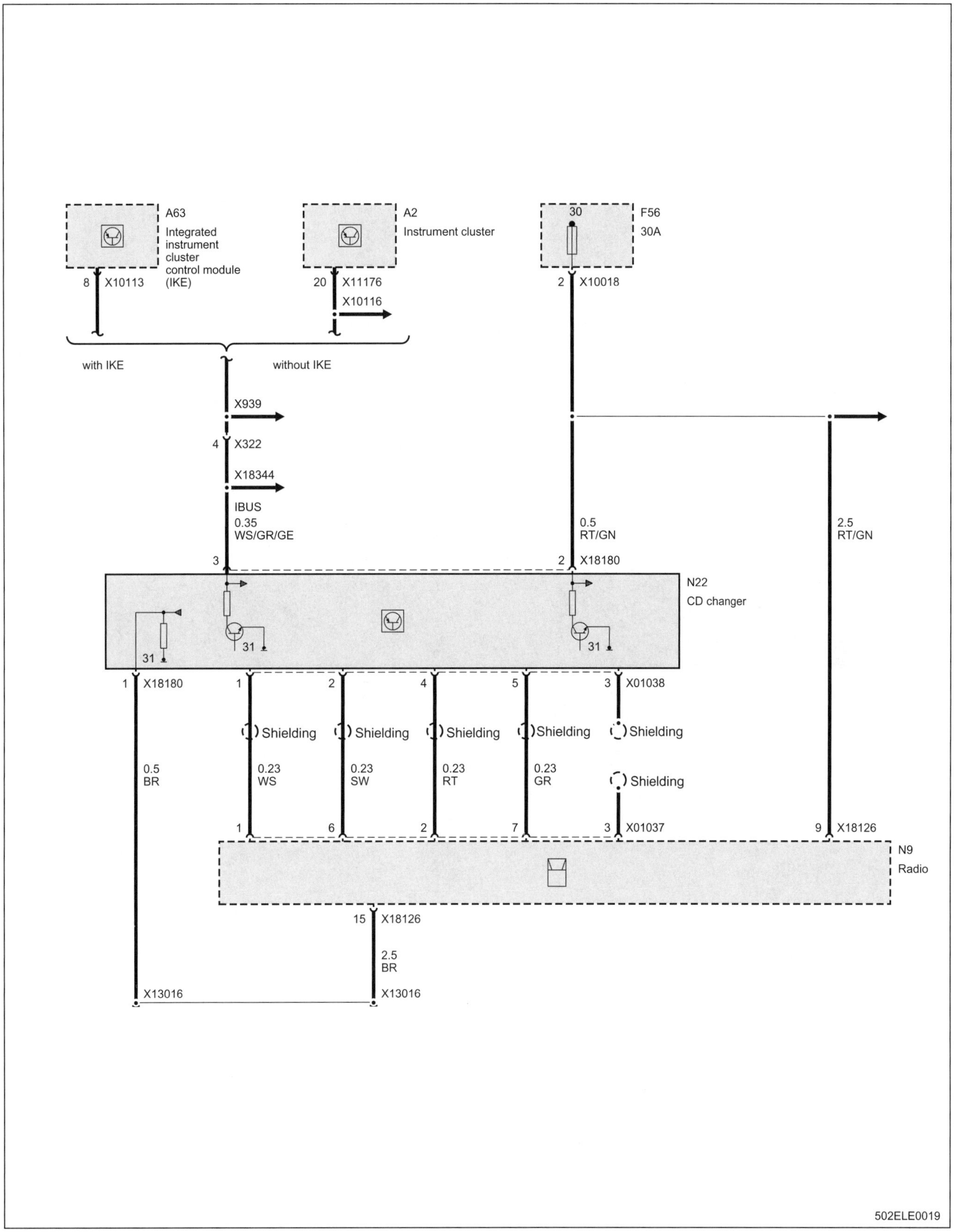
A63
Integrated instrument cluster control module (IKE)
8 X10113
A2
Instrument cluster
20 X11176
X10116
30
F56
30A
2 X10018
with IKE
without IKE
X939
4 X322
X18344
IBUS
0.35
WS/GR/GE
0.5
RT/GN
2.5
RT/GN
3
2 X18180
N22
CD changer
31
31
31
1 X18180
1
2
4
5
3 X01038
Shielding
Shielding
Shielding
Shielding
Shielding
Shielding
0.5
BR
0.23
WS
0.23
SW
0.23
RT
0.23
GR
1
6
2
7
3 X01037
9 X18126
N9
Radio
15 X18126
2.5
BR
X13016
X13016
502ELE0019

Radio/Telephone/GPS
Diversity (I01113)
(1 of 1)

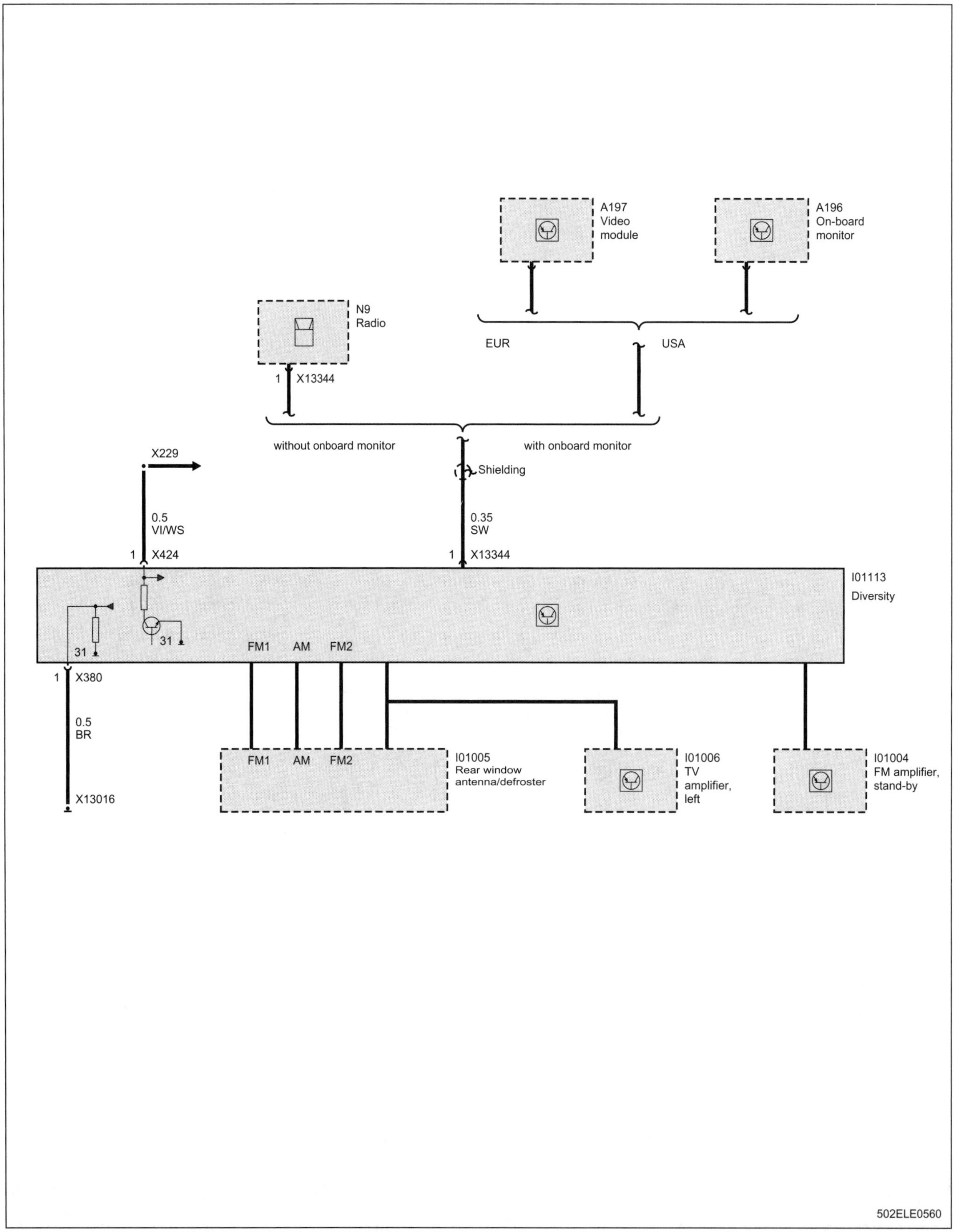

502ELE0560

Radio/Telephone/GPS
FM amplifier, lockout circuit (I01004)
(1 of 1)

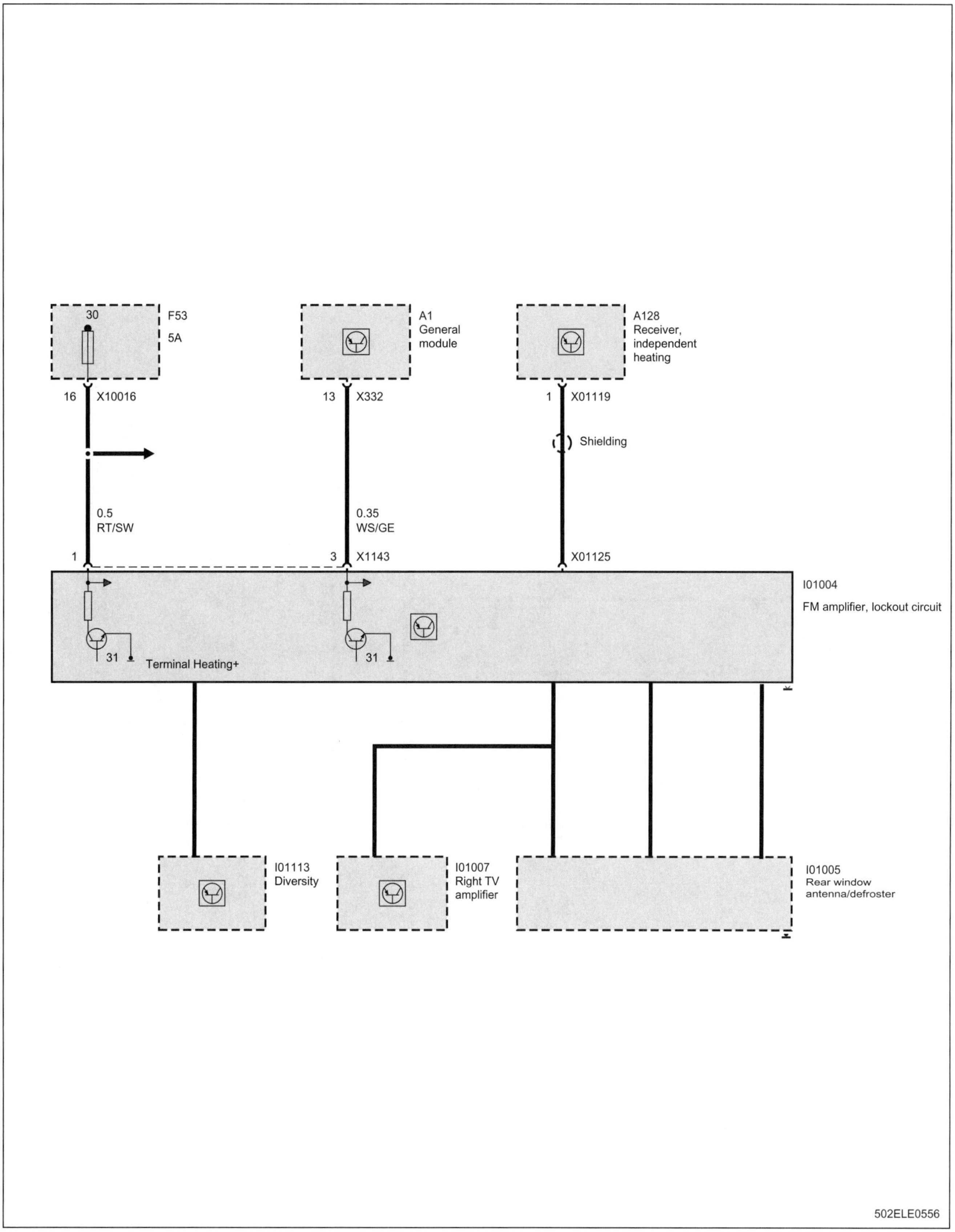

Radio/Telephone/GPS
Front loudspeaker with telephone
(1 of 3)

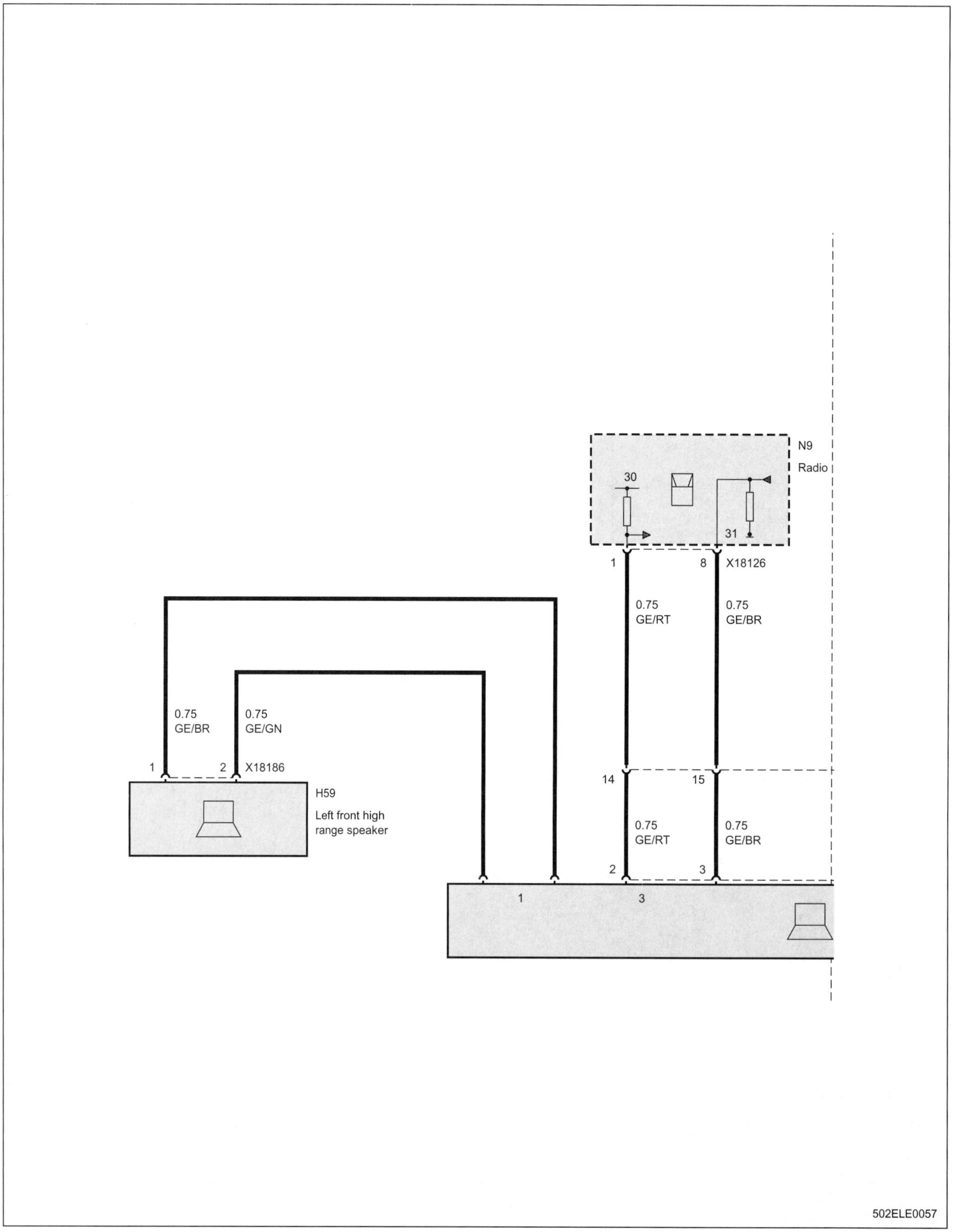

Radio/Telephone/GPS
Front loudspeaker with telephone
(2 of 3)

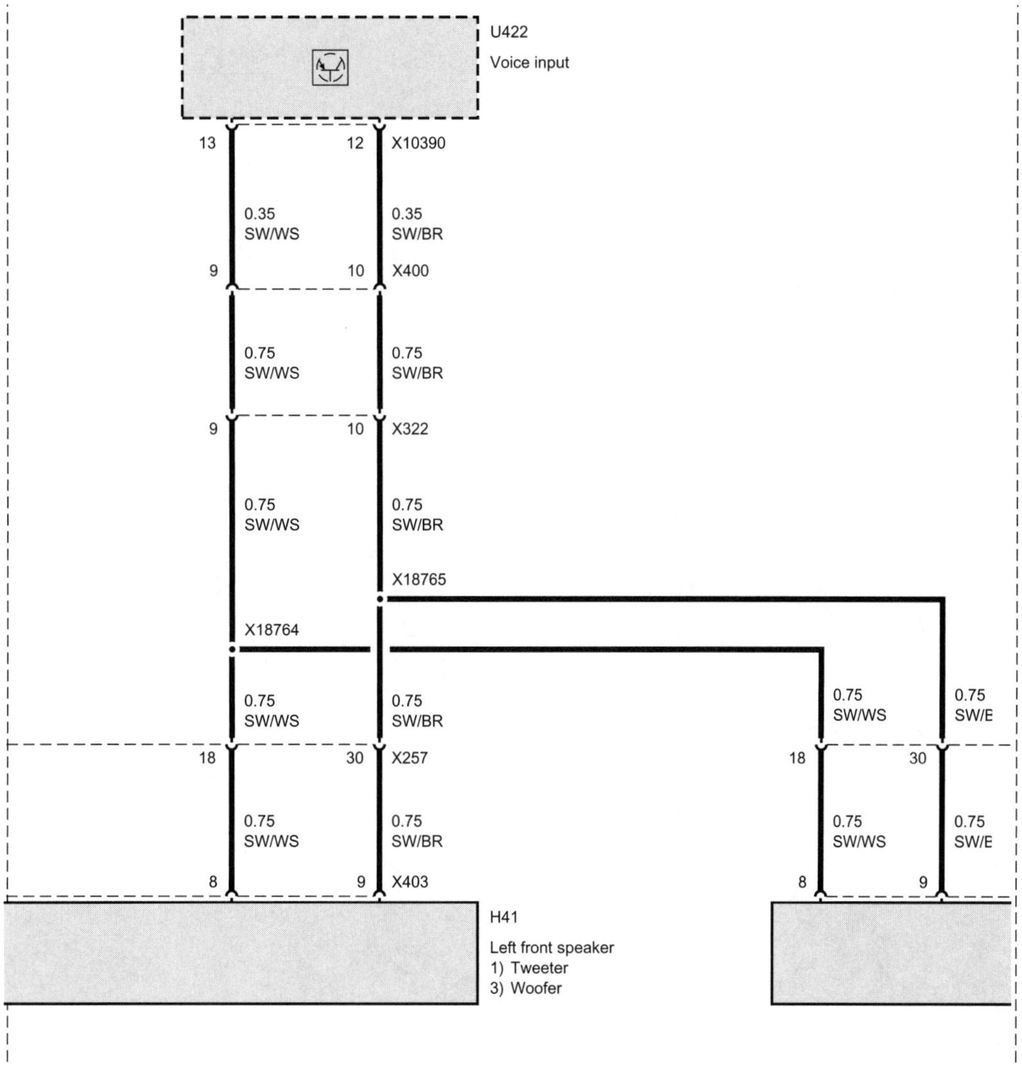

Radio/Telephone/GPS
Front loudspeaker with telephone
(3 of 3)

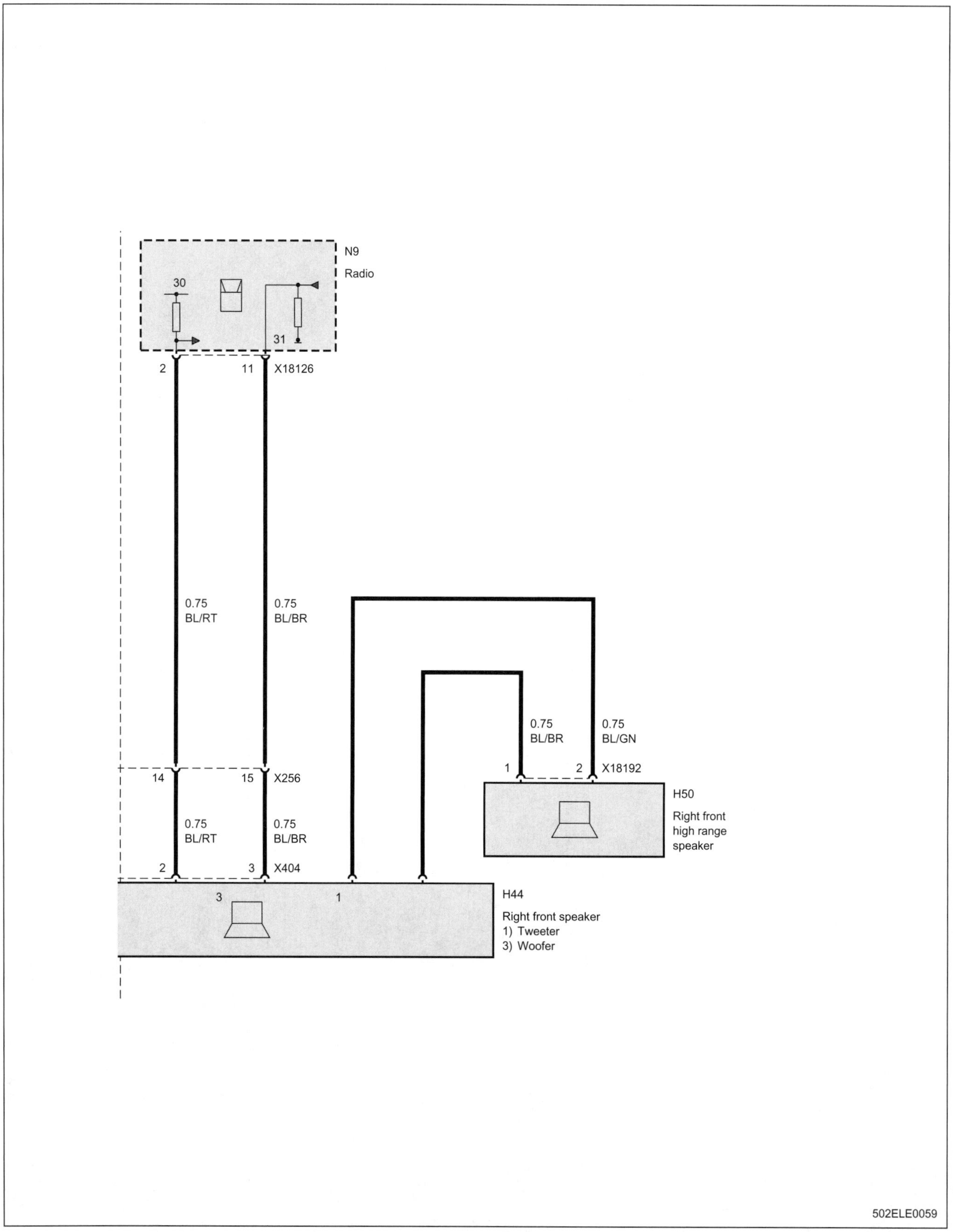

Radio/Telephone/GPS
GPS antenna

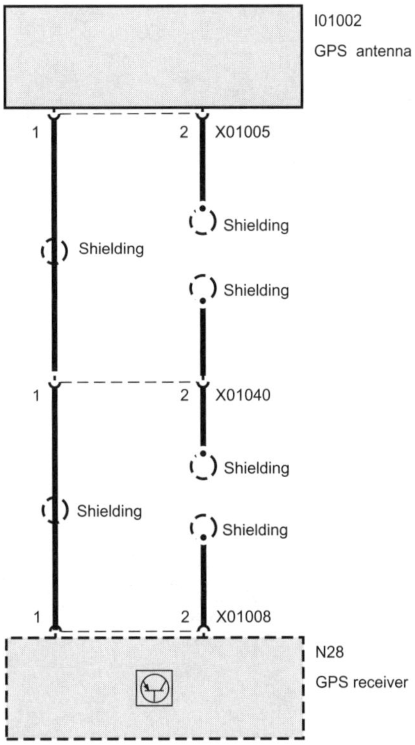

502ELE0067a

Radio/Telephone/GPS
GPS receiver power

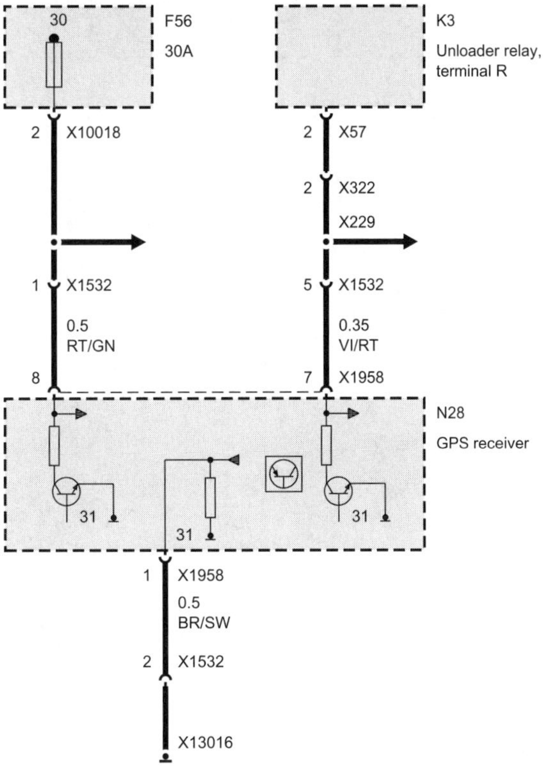

502ELE0067b

Radio/Telephone/GPS Interface (I01040)
(1 of 3)

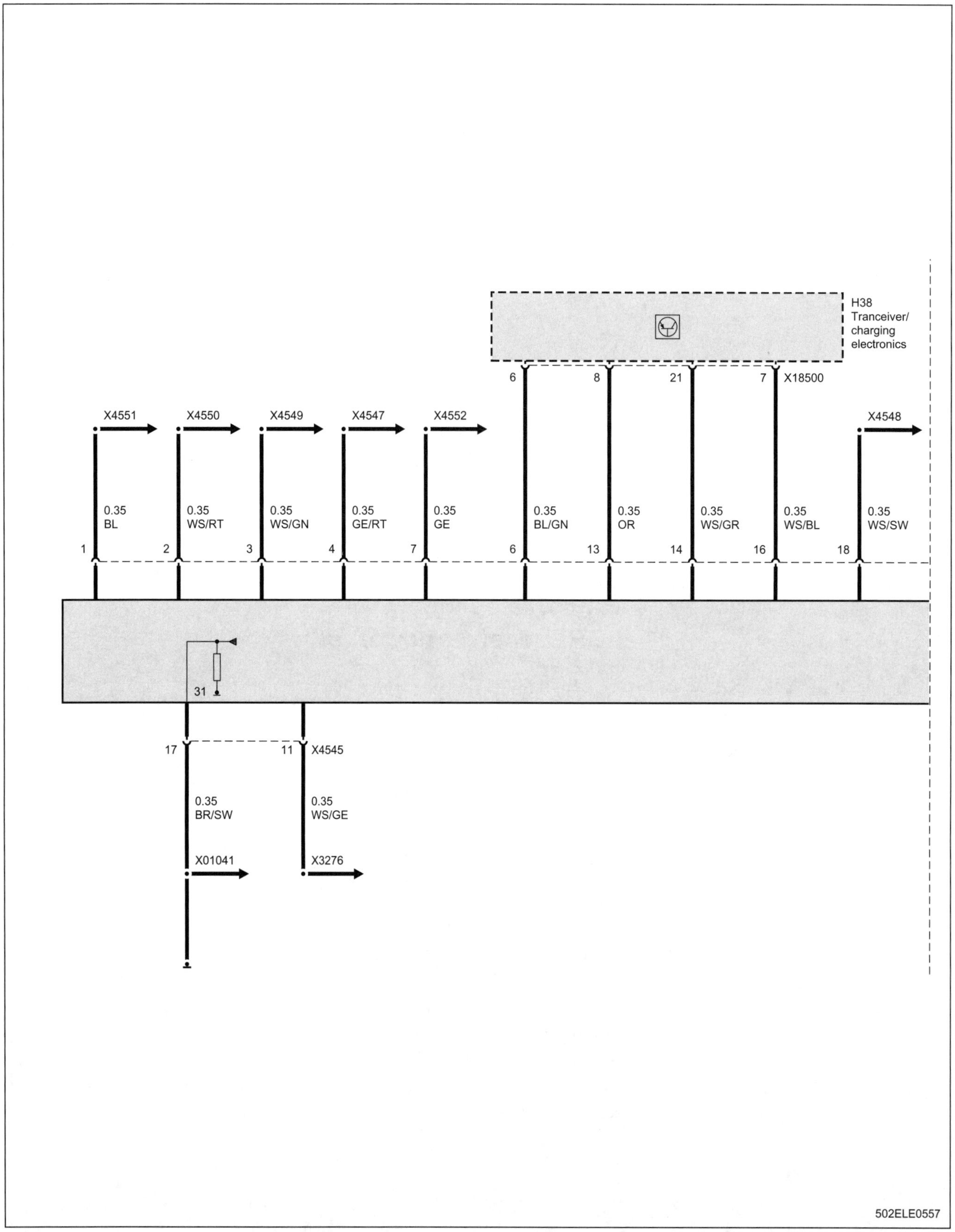
H38
Tranceiver/
charging
electronics
X18500
6
8
21
7
X4551
X4550
X4549
X4547
X4552
X4548
0.35
BL
0.35
WS/RT
0.35
WS/GN
0.35
GE/RT
0.35
GE
0.35
BL/GN
0.35
OR
0.35
WS/GR
0.35
WS/BL
0.35
WS/SW
1
2
3
4
7
6
13
14
16
18
31
17
11
X4545
0.35
BR/SW
0.35
WS/GE
X01041
X3276
502ELE0557

Radio/Telephone/GPS Interface (I01040)
(2 of 3)

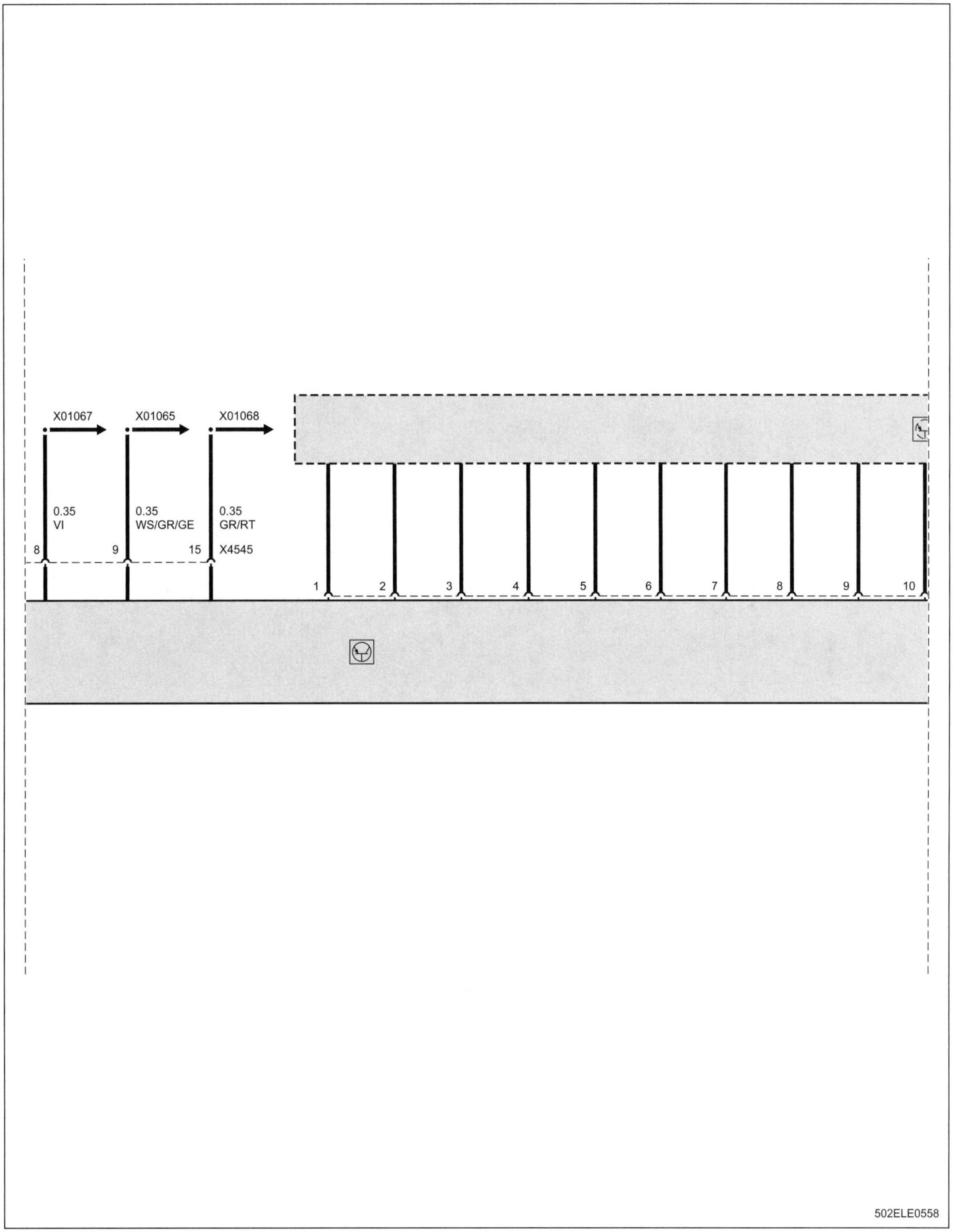
X01067
X01065
X01068
0.35
VI
0.35
WS/GR/GE
0.35
GR/RT
8
9
15
X4545
1
2
3
4
5
6
7
8
9
10
502ELE0558

Radio/Telephone/GPS Interface (I01040) (3 of 3)

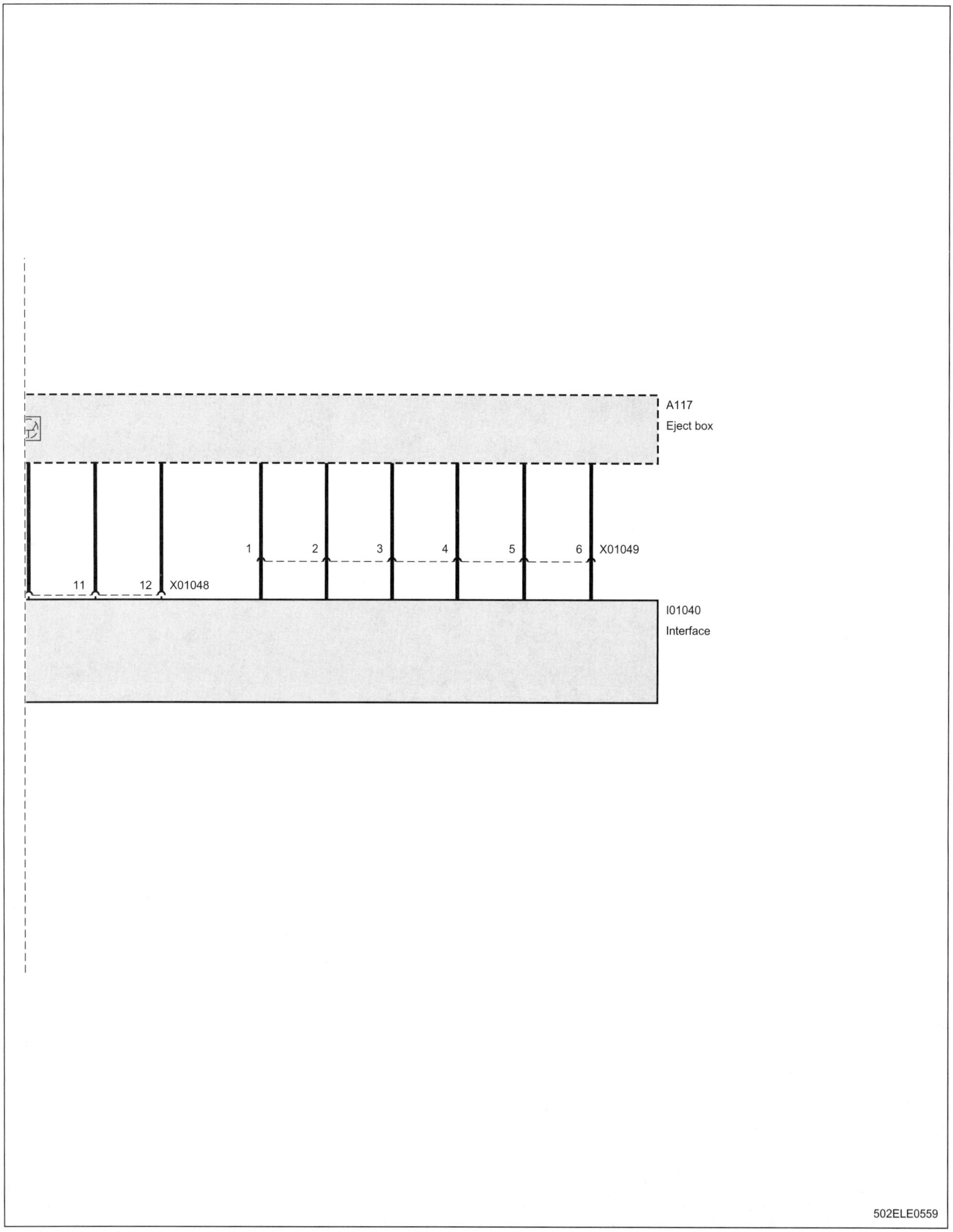
A117
Eject box
1
2
3
4
5
6
X01049
11
12
X01048
I01040
Interface
502ELE0559

Radio/Telephone/GPS
Interface on-board monitor/video module/radio
(1 of 1)

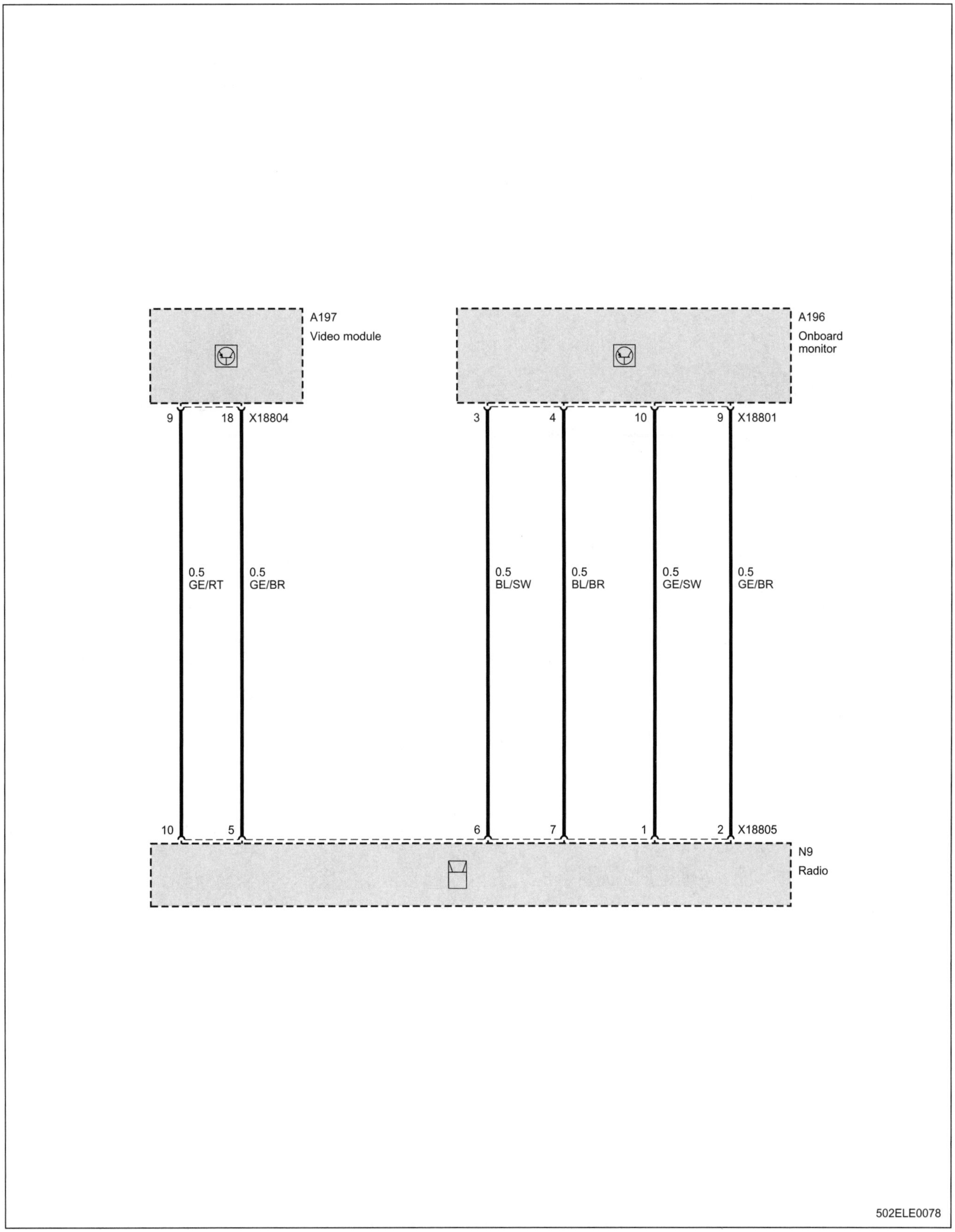

Radio/Telephone/GPS
Interface telephone/top hifi
(1 of 1)

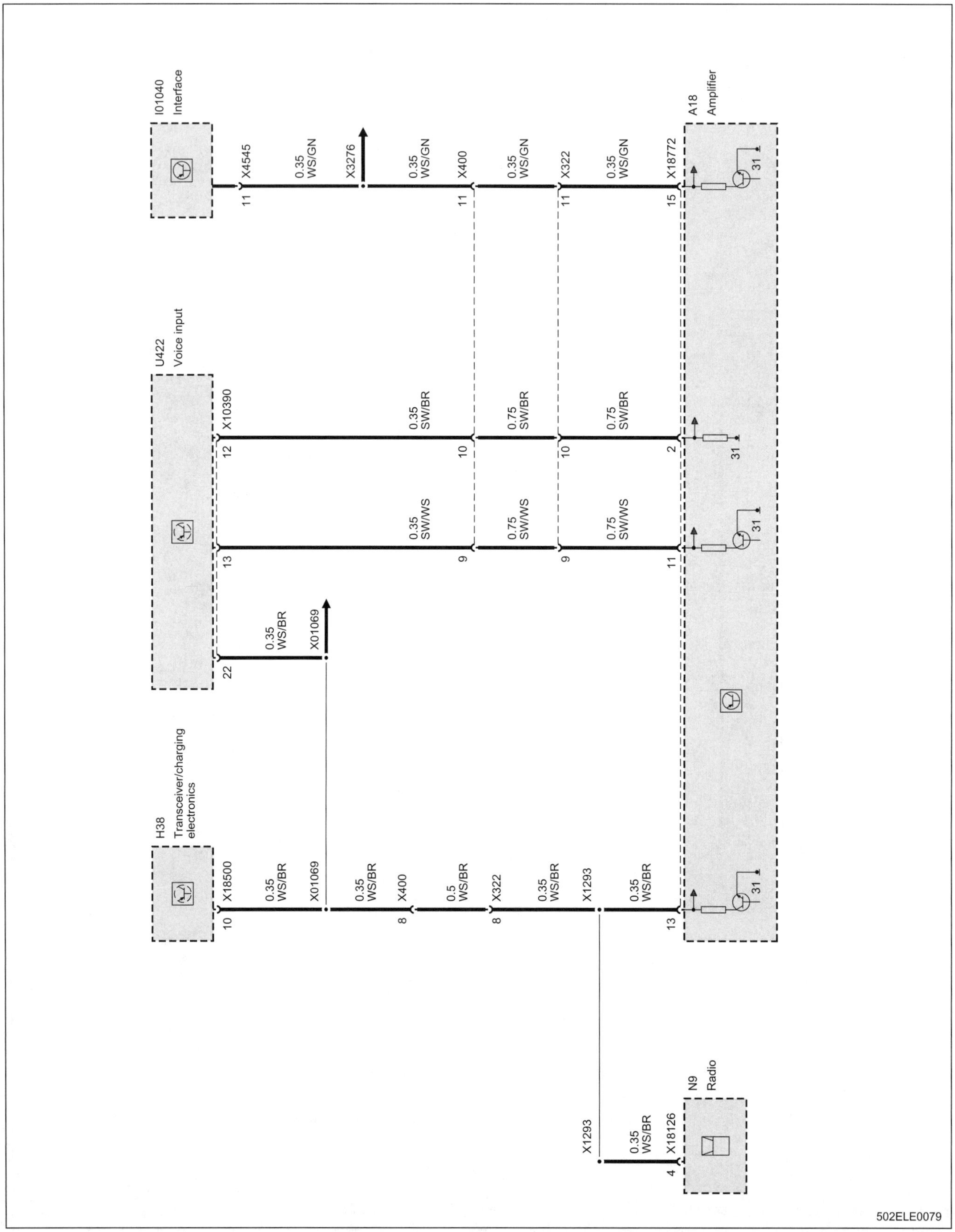

Radio/Telephone/GPS
Interface, navigation/on-board monitor
(1 of 1)

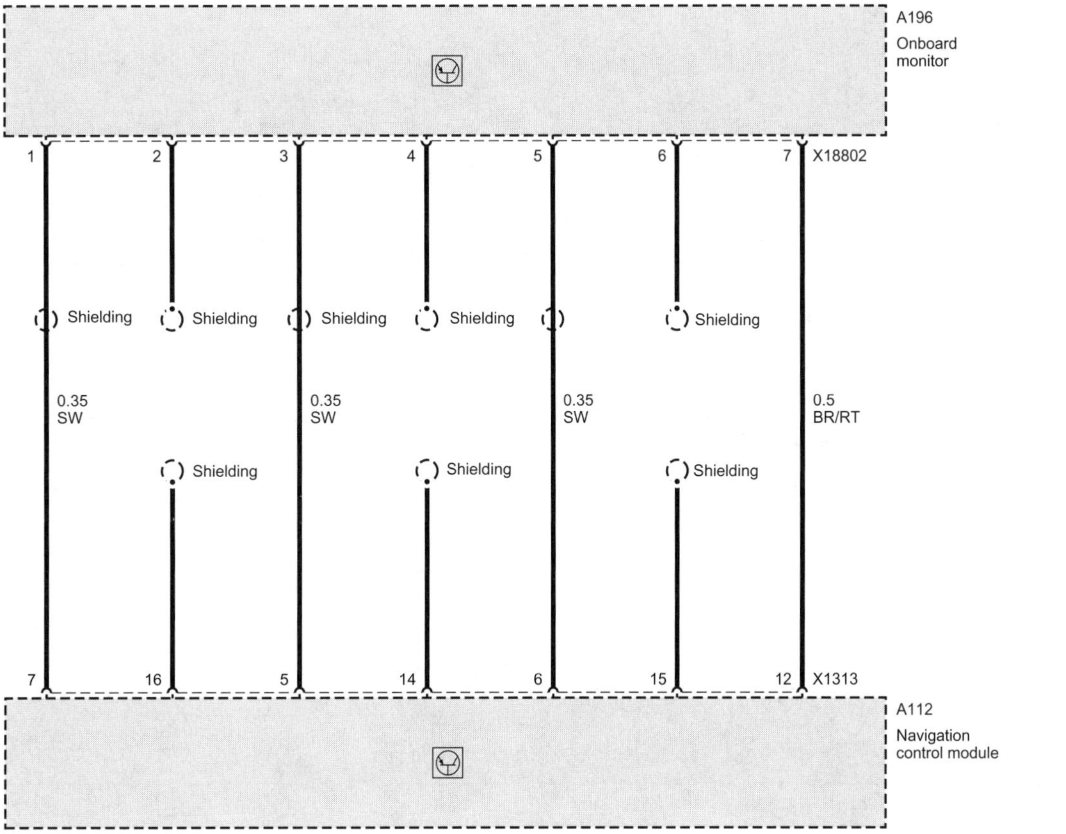

Radio/Telephone/GPS
Left front speaker with telephone
(1 of 2)

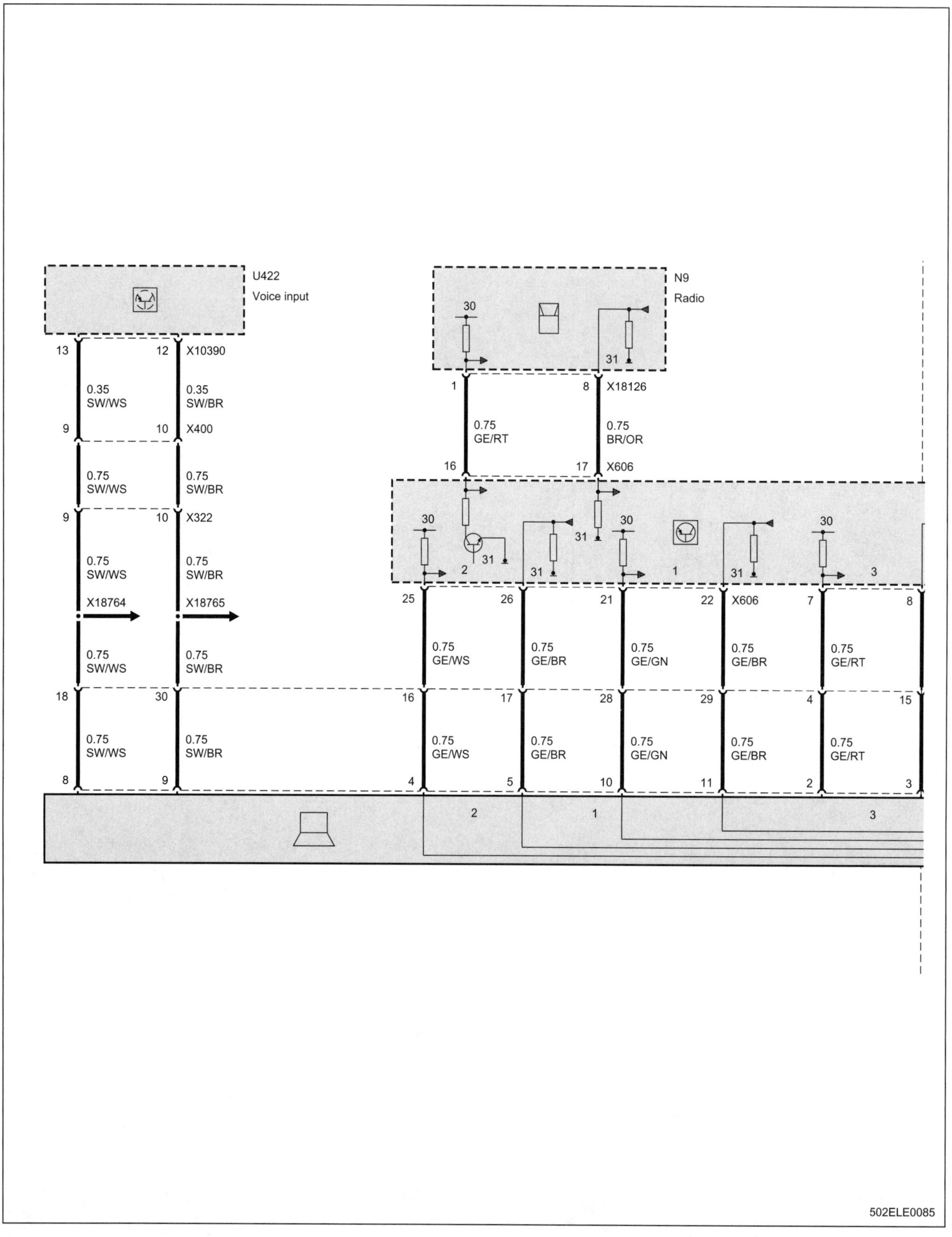

Radio/Telephone/GPS
Left front speaker with telephone
(2 of 2)

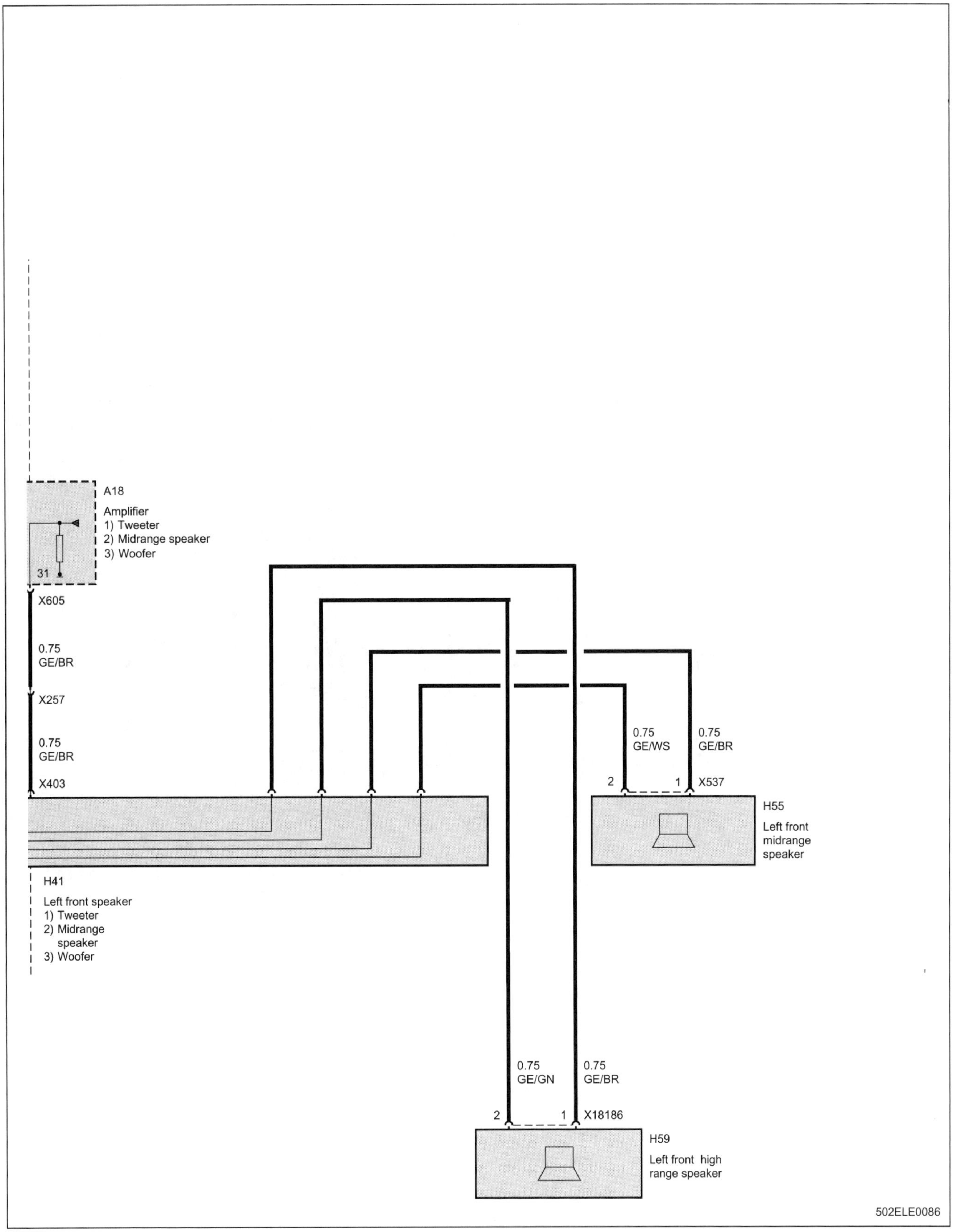

Radio/Telephone/GPS
Loudspeaker, LH front
(1 of 3)

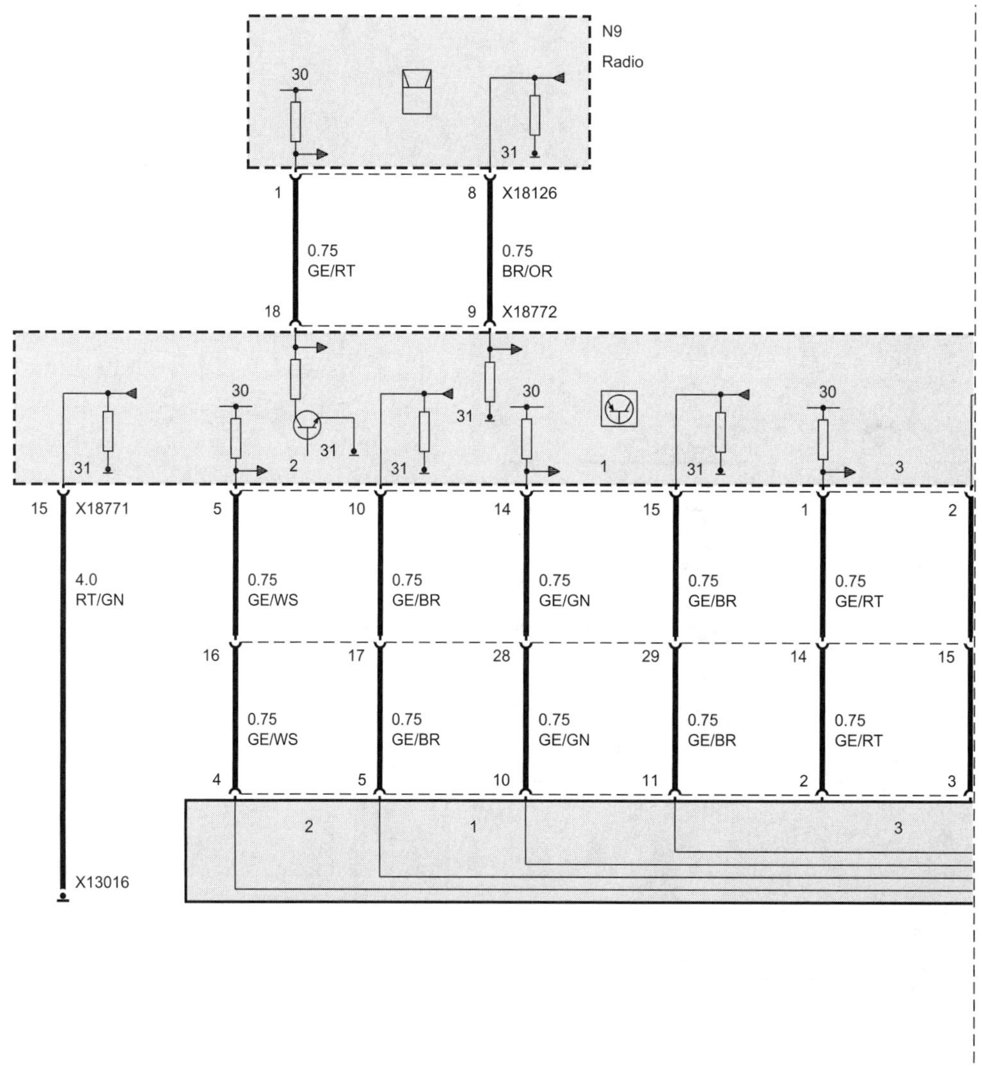

502ELE0103

Radio/Telephone/GPS
Loudspeaker, LH front
(2 of 3)

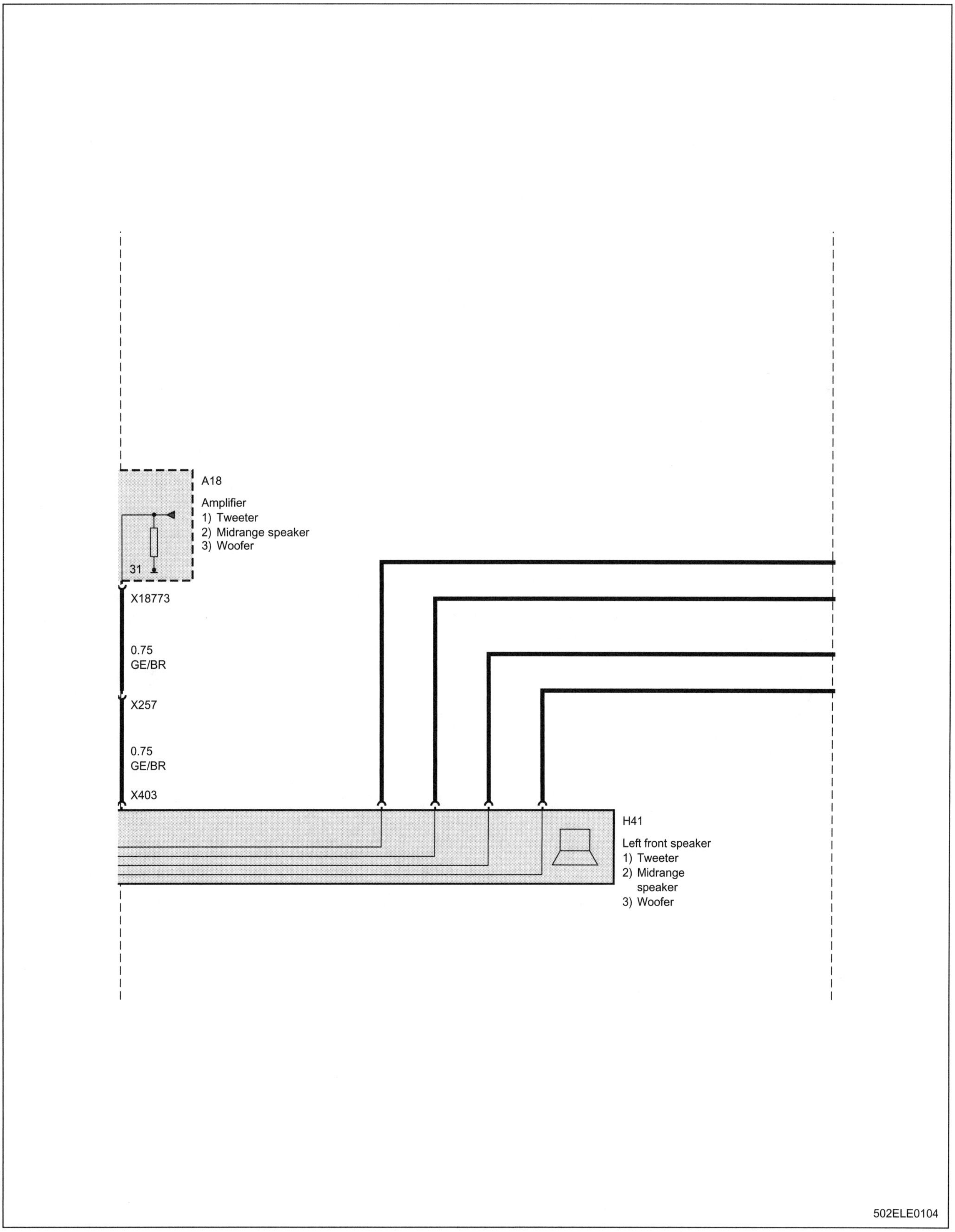
A18
Amplifier
1) Tweeter
2) Midrange speaker
3) Woofer
31
X18773
0.75
GE/BR
X257
0.75
GE/BR
X403
H41
Left front speaker
1) Tweeter
2) Midrange
speaker
3) Woofer
502ELE0104

Radio/Telephone/GPS
Loudspeaker, LH front
(3 of 3)

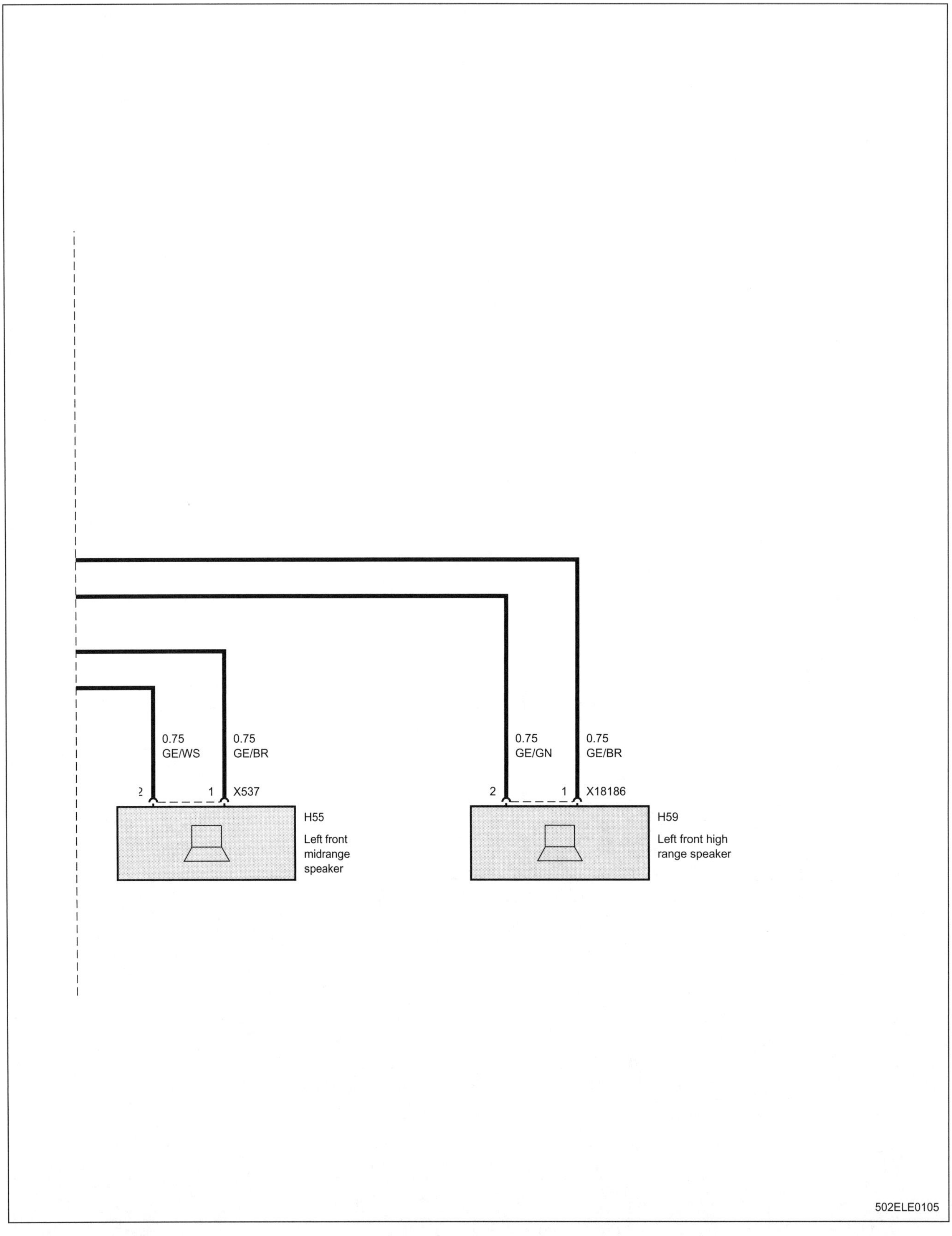
0.75
GE/WS
0.75
GE/BR
0.75
GE/GN
0.75
GE/BR
2
1
X537
2
1
X18186
H55
Left front
midrange
speaker
H59
Left front high
range speaker
502ELE0105

Radio/Telephone/GPS
Loudspeaker, RH front
(1 of 3)

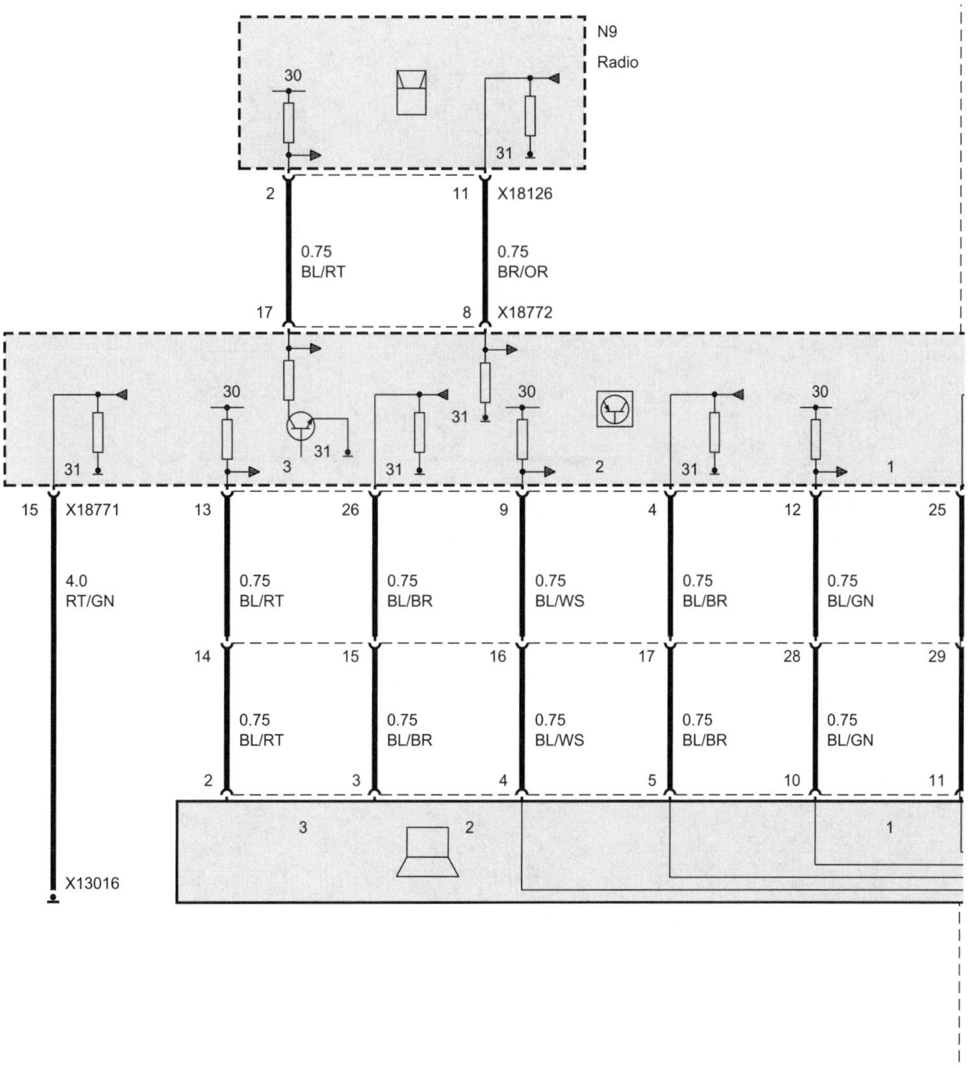

502ELE0167

Radio/Telephone/GPS
Loudspeaker, RH front
(2 of 3)

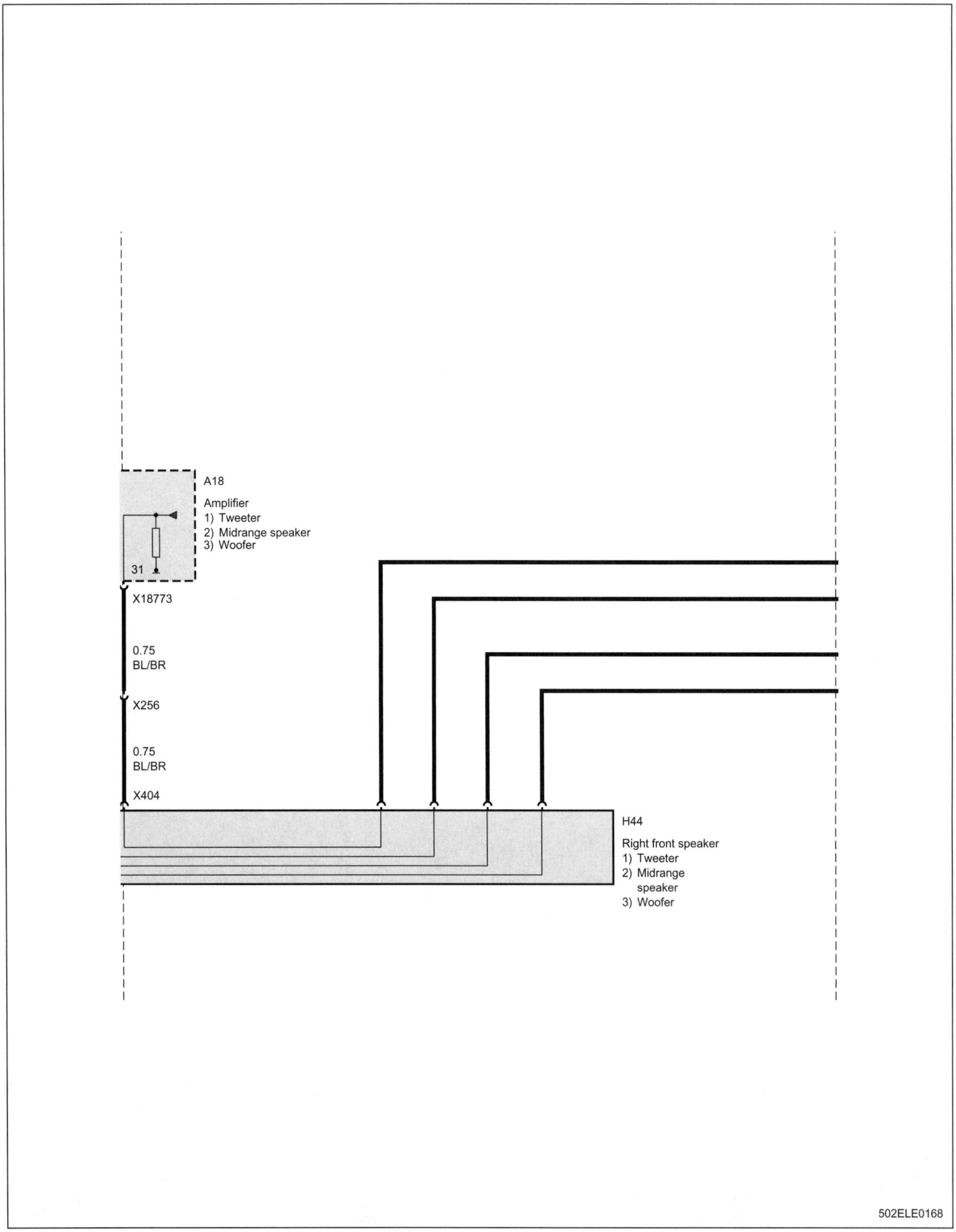
A18
Amplifier
1) Tweeter
2) Midrange speaker
3) Woofer
31
X18773
0.75
BL/BR
X256
0.75
BL/BR
X404
H44
Right front speaker
1) Tweeter
2) Midrange
speaker
3) Woofer
502ELE0168

Radio/Telephone/GPS
Loudspeaker, RH front
(3 of 3)

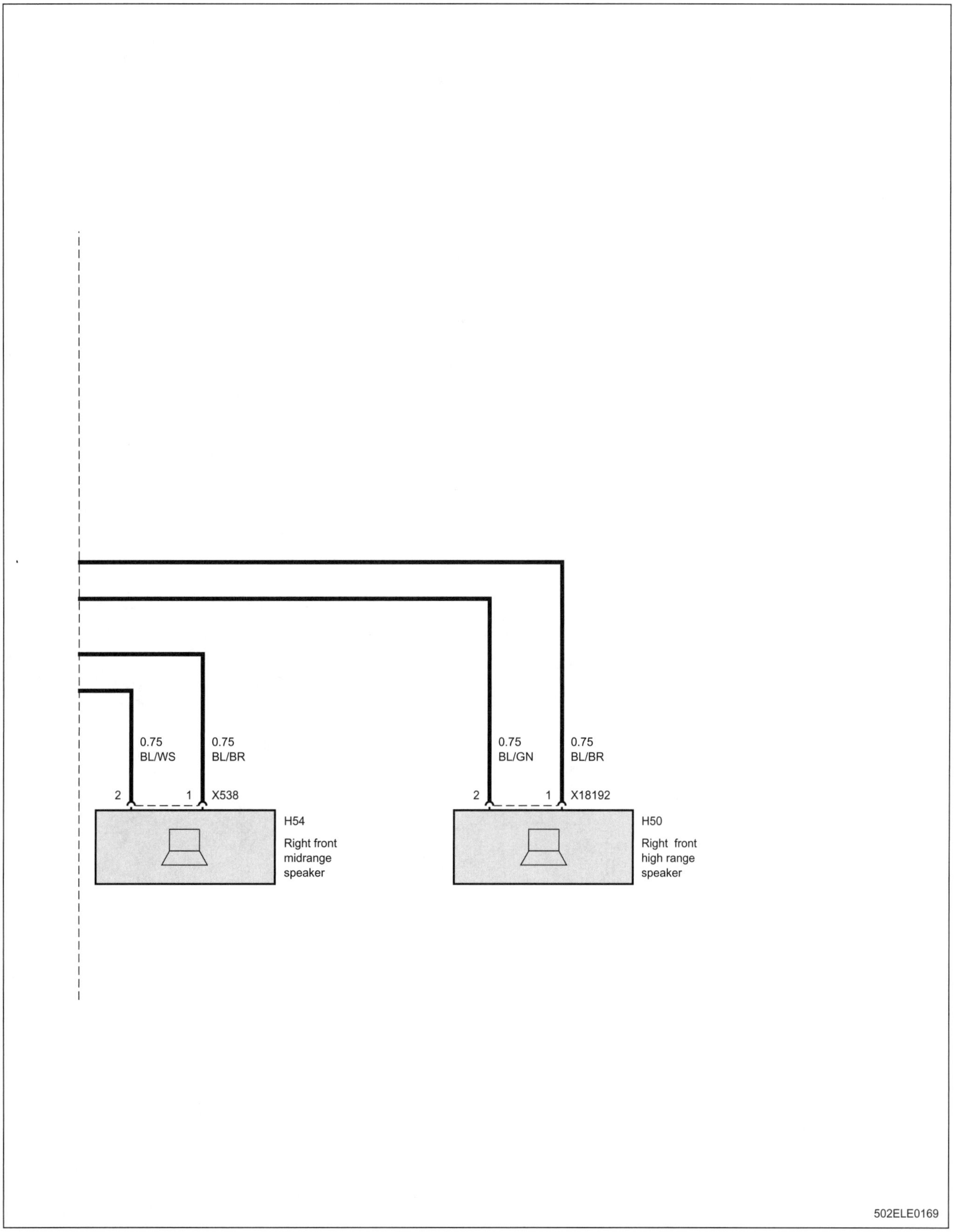
0.75
BL/WS
0.75
BL/BR
2
1
X538
H54
Right front midrange speaker
0.75
BL/GN
0.75
BL/BR
2
1
X18192
H50
Right front high range speaker
502ELE0169

Radio/Telephone/GPS
Antenna amplifier (N8)
(1 of 1)

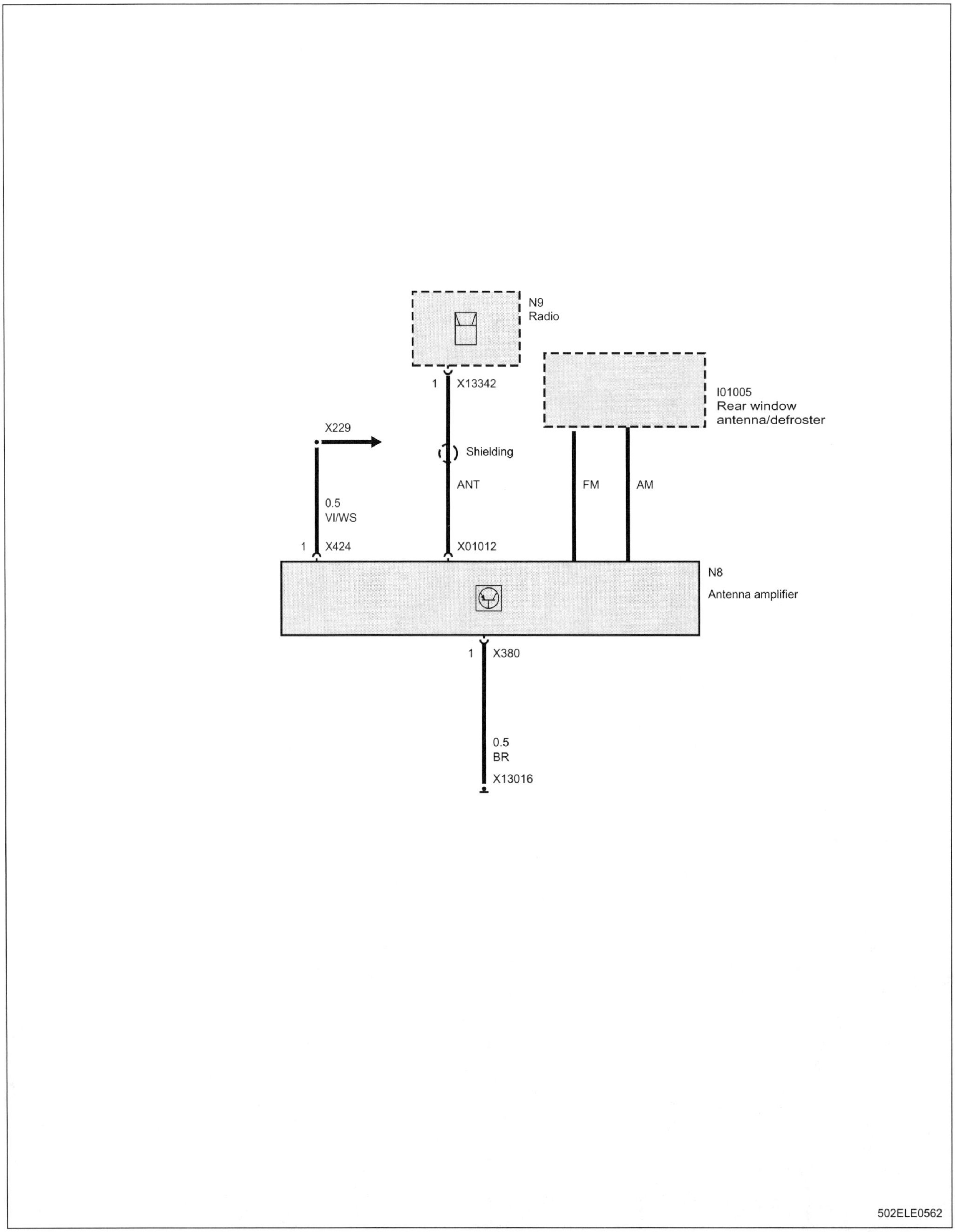
N9
Radio
1
X13342
I01005
Rear window
antenna/defroster
X229
Shielding
ANT
FM
AM
0.5
VI/WS
1
X424
X01012
N8
Antenna amplifier
1
X380
0.5
BR
X13016
502ELE0562

Radio/Telephone/GPS
Radio/Top hifi (N9)
(1 of 3)

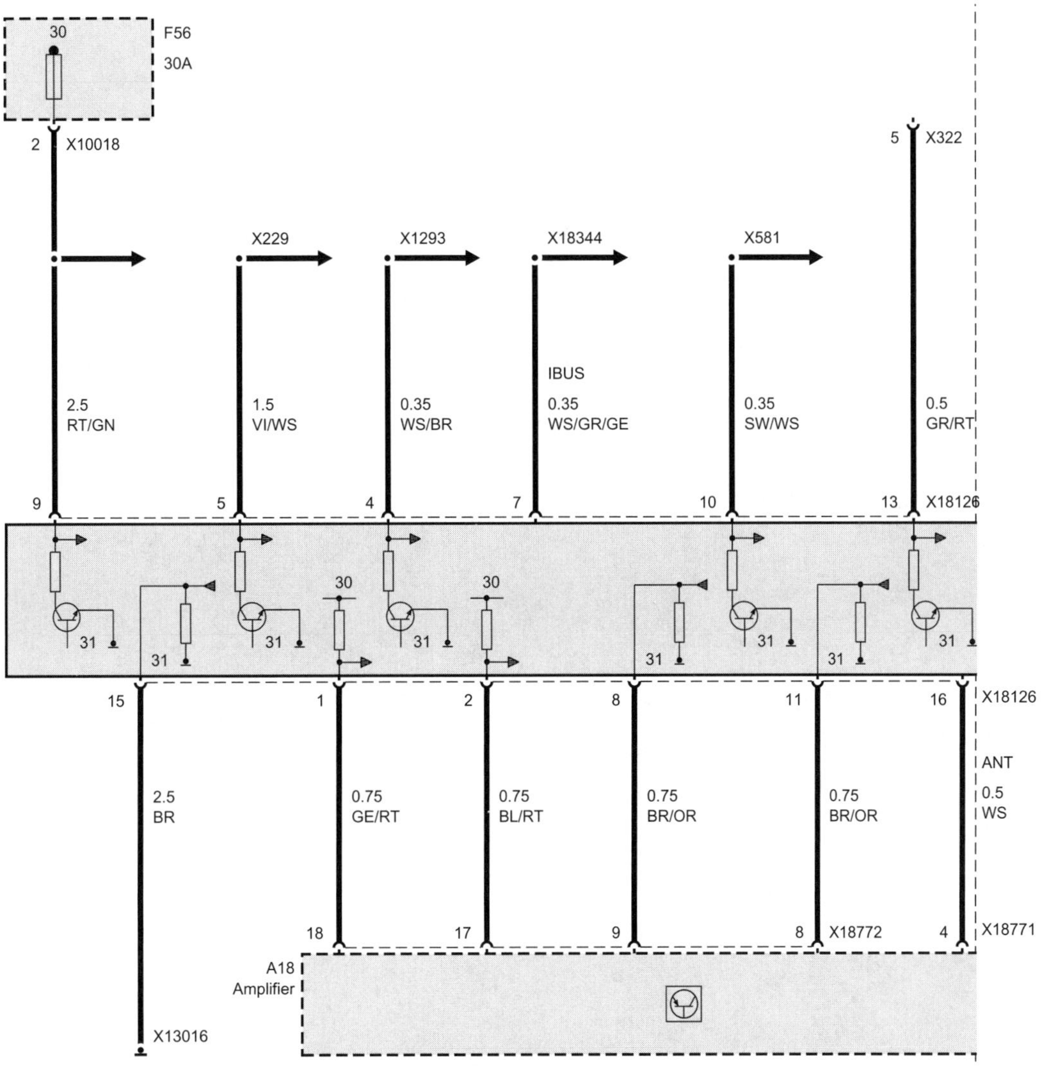

502ELE0563

Radio/Telephone/GPS
Radio/Top hifi (N9)
(2 of 3)

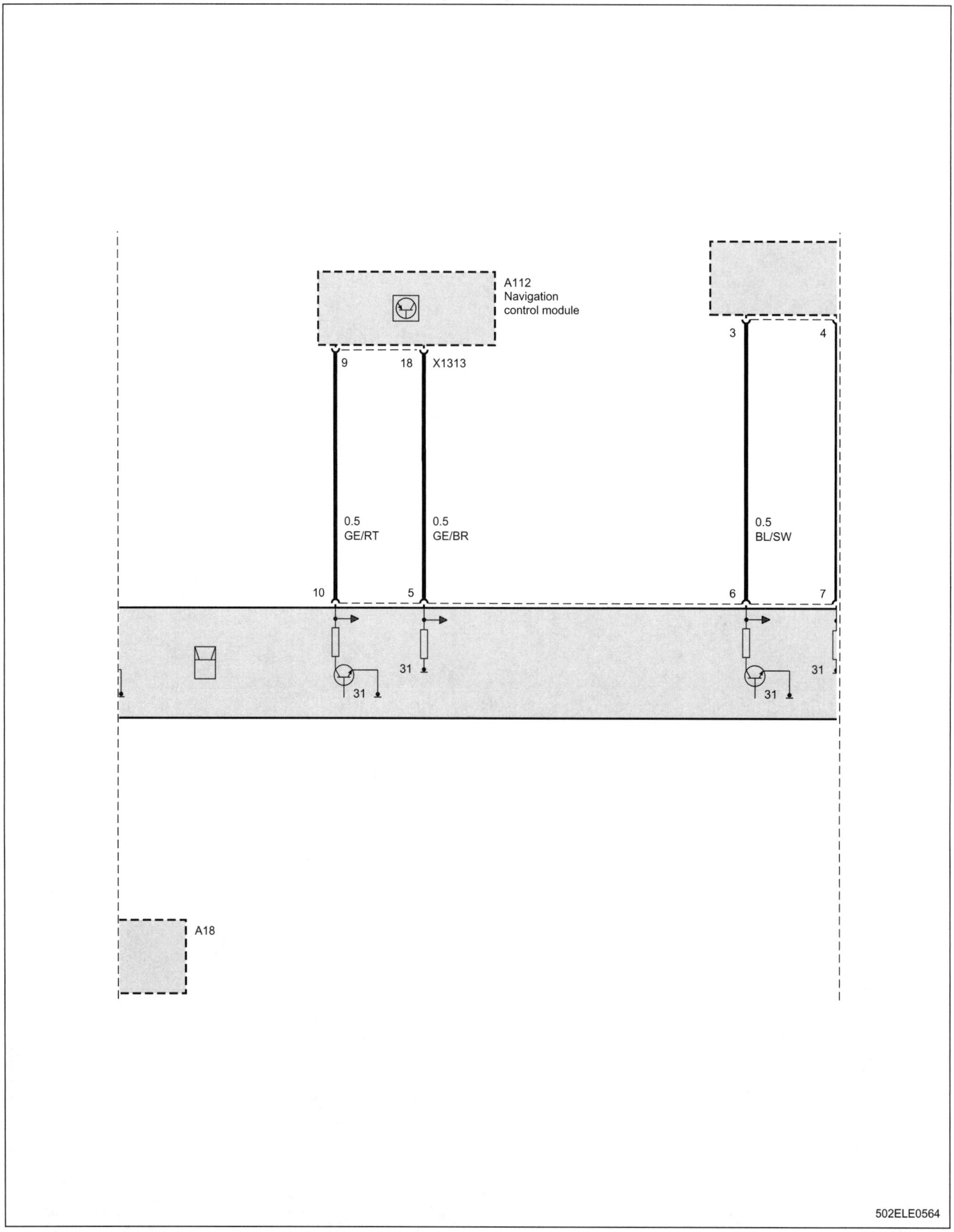
A112
Navigation
control module
9
18
X1313
3
4
0.5
GE/RT
0.5
GE/BR
0.5
BL/SW
10
5
6
7
31
31
31
31
31
A18
502ELE0564

Radio/Telephone/GPS
Radio/Top hifi (N9)
(3 of 3)

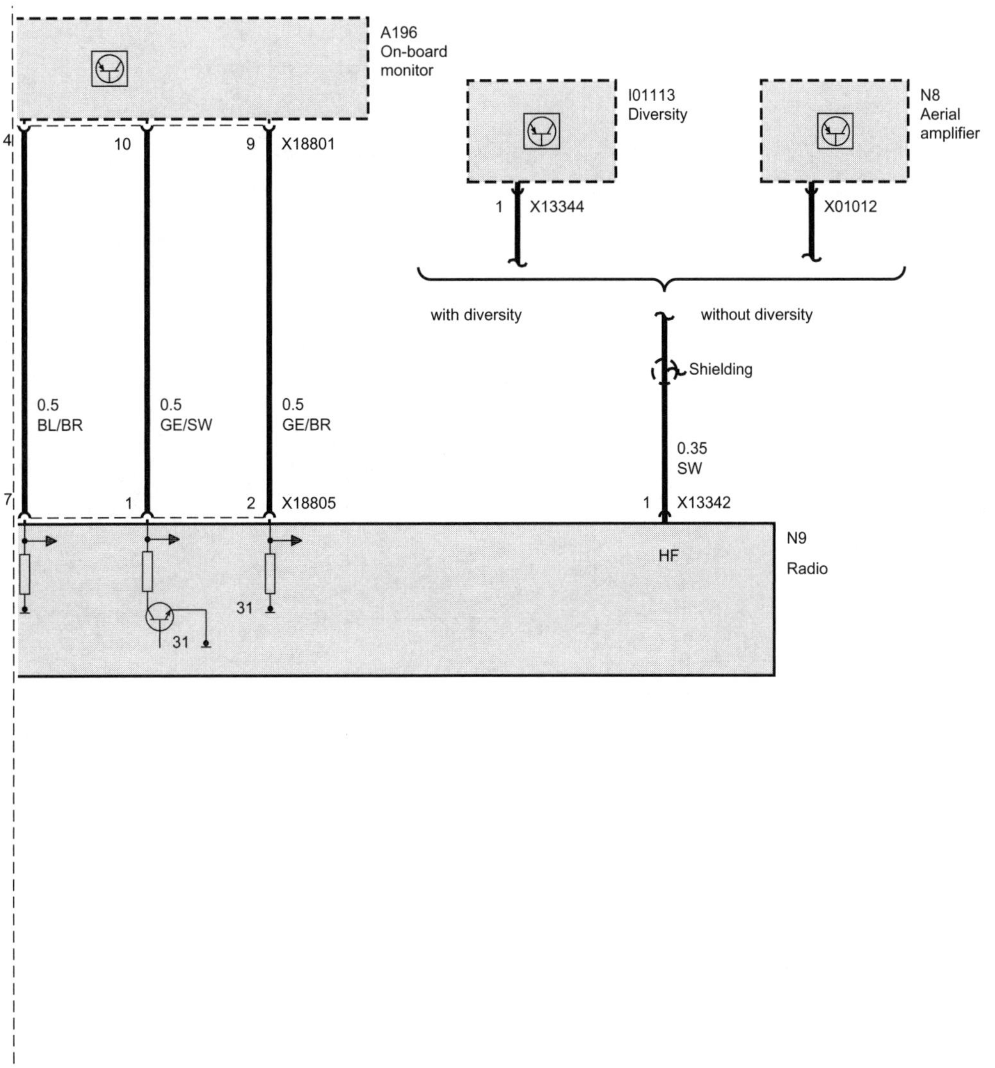

502ELE0565

Radio/Telephone/GPS
Navigation/GPS receiver (interface)
(1 of 1)

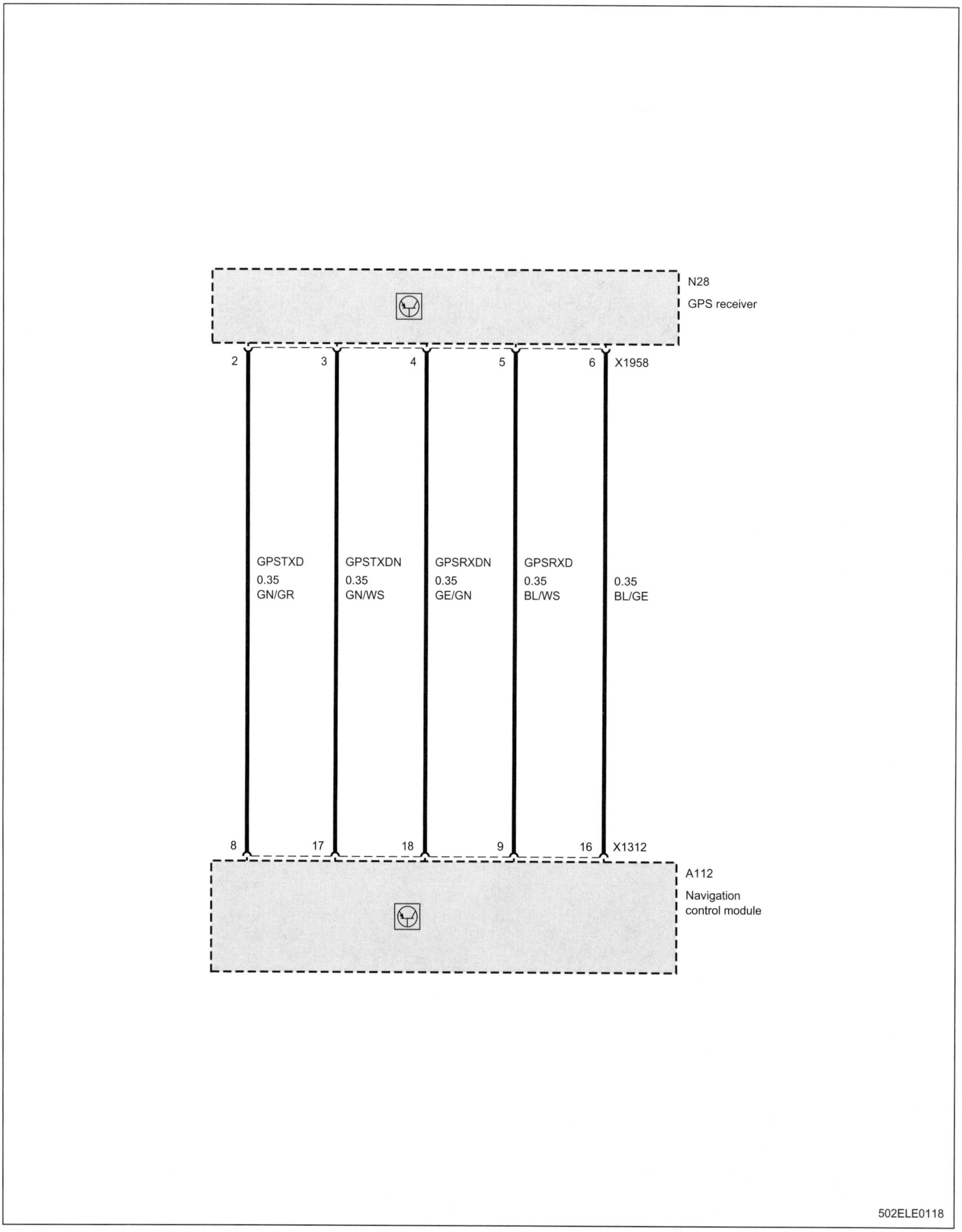

Radio/Telephone/GPS
Power supply, voice input system
(1 of 2)

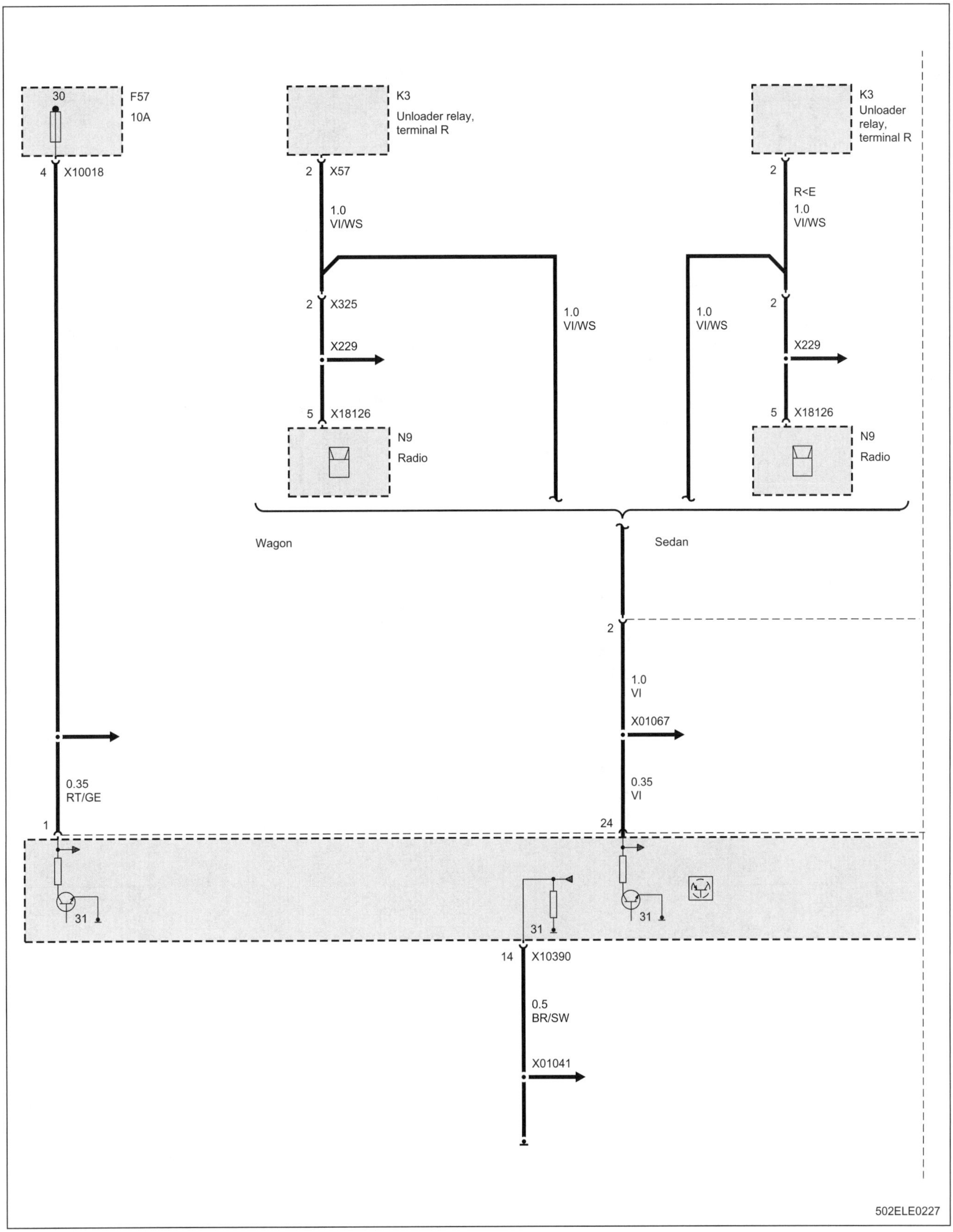

Radio/Telephone/GPS
Power supply, voice input system
(2 of 2)

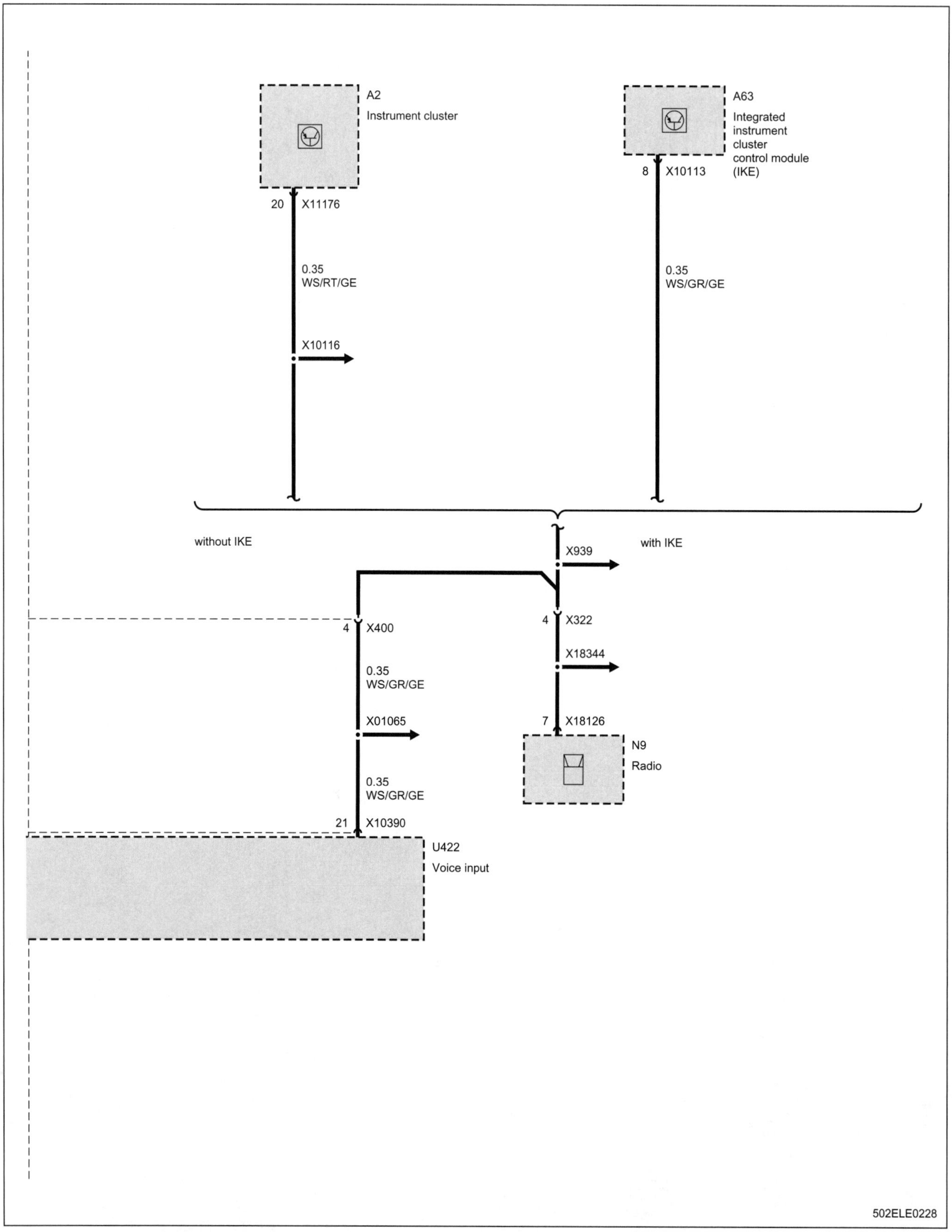

Radio/Telephone/GPS
Power, navigation
(1 of 1)

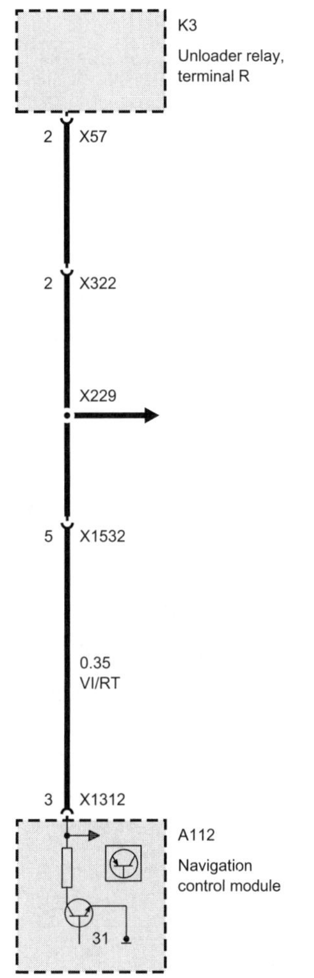

Radio/Telephone/GPS
Power, radio/hifi
(1 of 1)

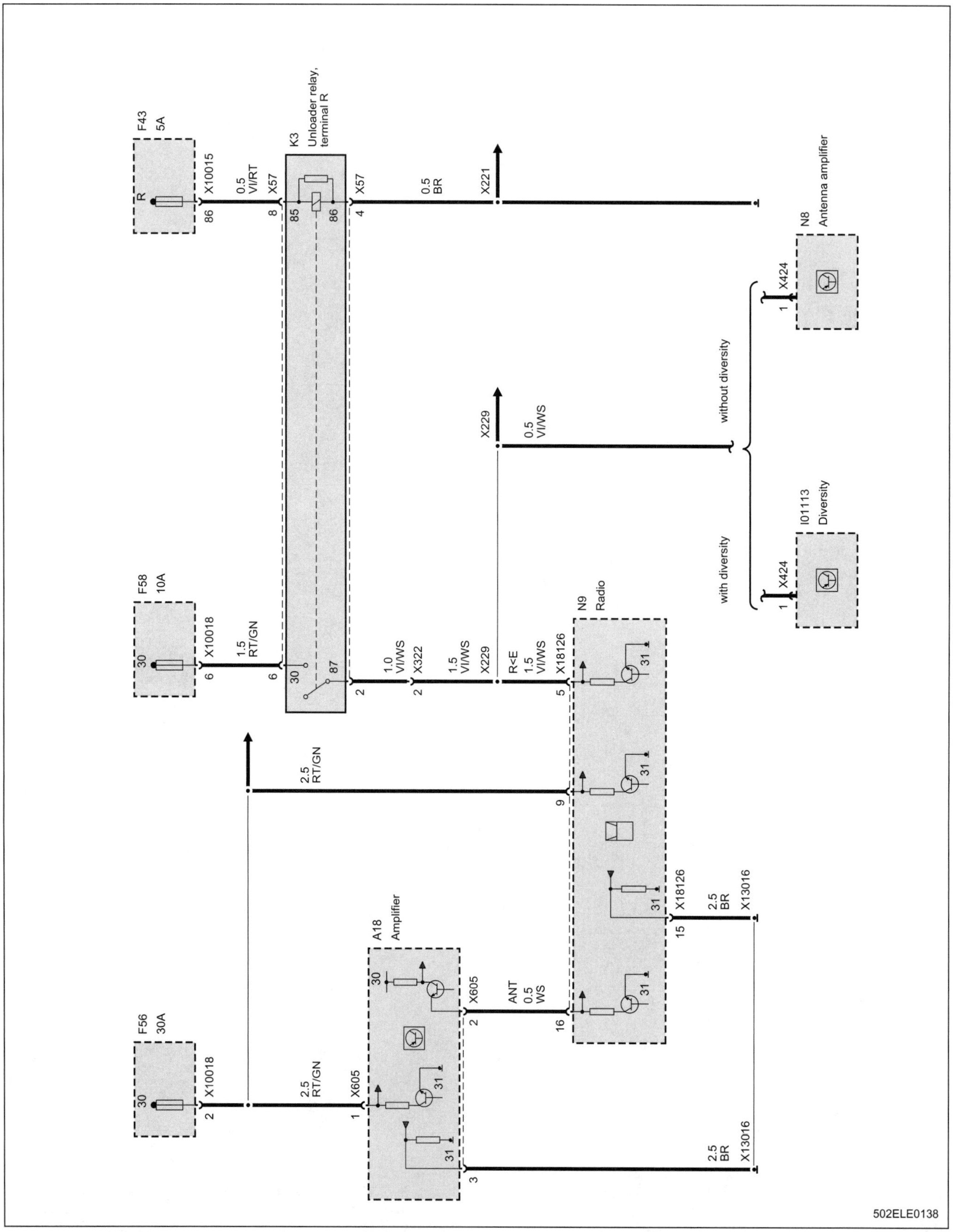
F43
5A
R
86
X10015
0.5
VI/RT
X57
8
K3
Unloader relay,
terminal R
85
86
X57
4
0.5
BR
X221
N8
Antenna amplifier
X424
1
without diversity
X229
0.5
VI/WS
with diversity
I01113
Diversity
X424
1
F58
10A
30
X10018
6
1.5
RT/GN
6
30
87
2
1.0
VI/WS
X322
2
1.5
VI/WS
X229
R<E
1.5
VI/WS
X18126
5
N9
Radio
31
2.5
RT/GN
9
X18126
31
15
2.5
BR
X13016
A18
Amplifier
30
X605
2
ANT
0.5
WS
16
F56
30A
30
X10018
2
2.5
RT/GN
X605
1
31
3
2.5
BR
X13016
502ELE0138

Radio/Telephone/GPS
Power, radio/stereo
(1 of 1)

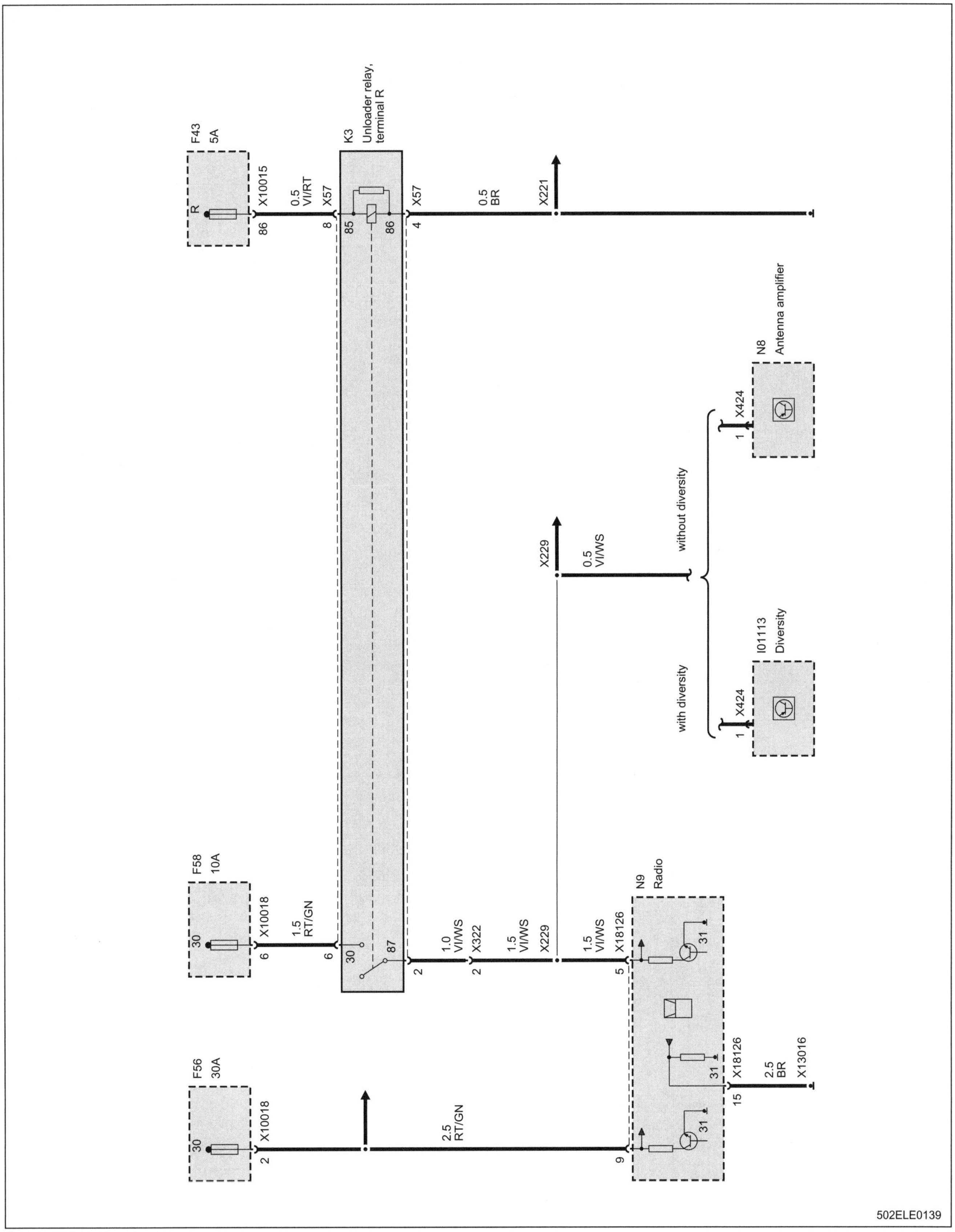
F43
5A
R
86
X10015
0.5
VI/RT
8
X57
K3
Unloader relay,
terminal R
85
86
4
X57
0.5
BR
X221
N8
Antenna amplifier
1
X424
without diversity
X229
0.5
VI/WS
with diversity
I01113
Diversity
1
X424
F58
10A
30
6
X10018
1.5
RT/GN
6
30
87
2
1.0
VI/WS
X322
2
1.5
VI/WS
X229
1.5
VI/WS
X18126
5
N9
Radio
31
31
X18126
15
2.5
BR
X13016
F56
30A
30
2
X10018
2.5
RT/GN
9
31
502ELE0139

Radio/Telephone/GPS
Power, radio/top hifi
(1 of 1)

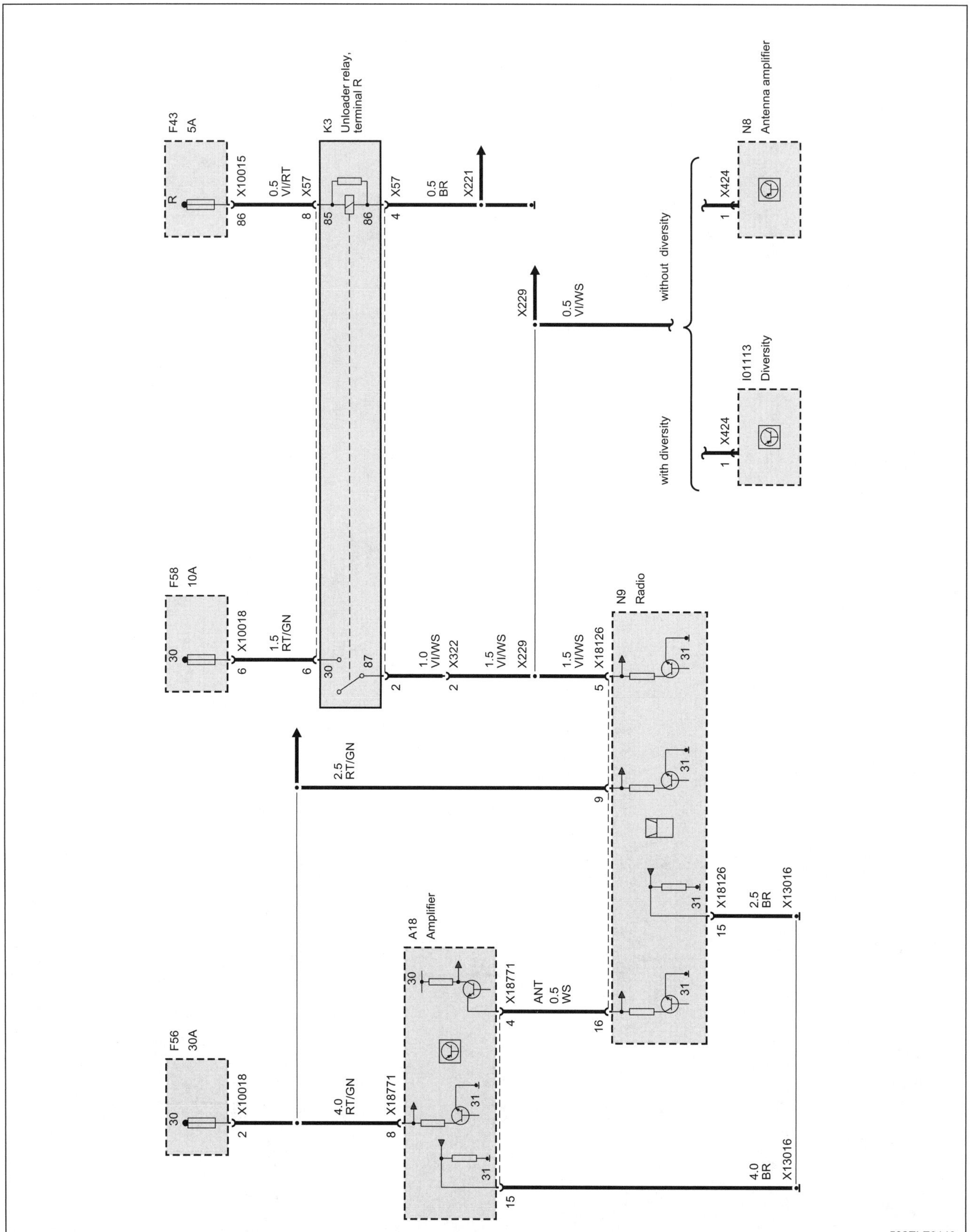

502ELE0140

Radio/Telephone/GPS
Power, video module
(1 of 1)

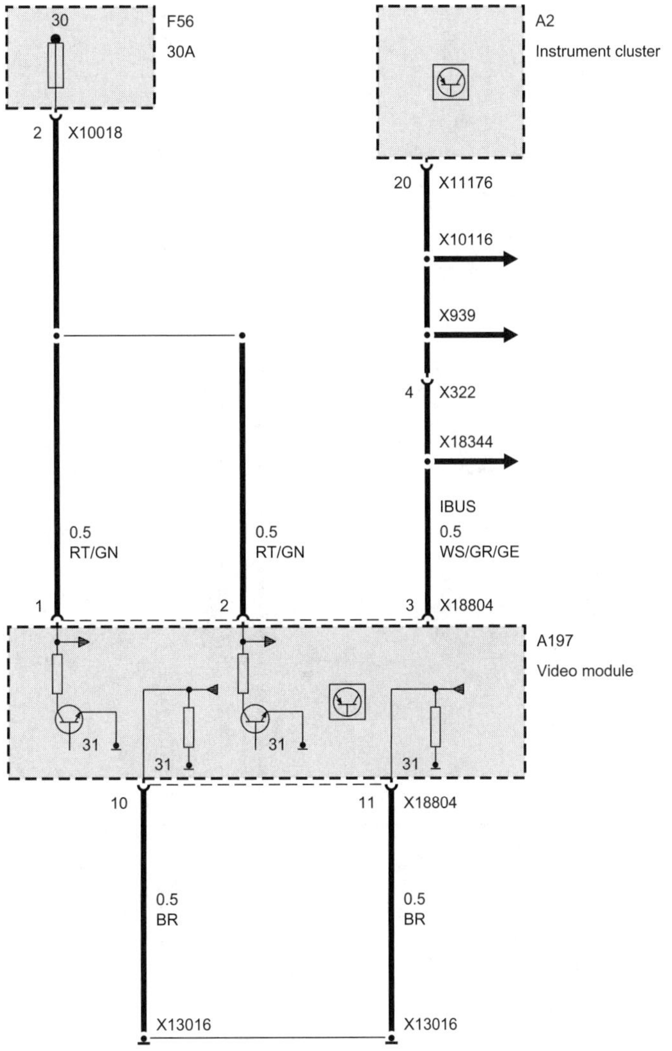

502ELE0142

Radio/Telephone/GPS
Radio remote control
(1 of 1)

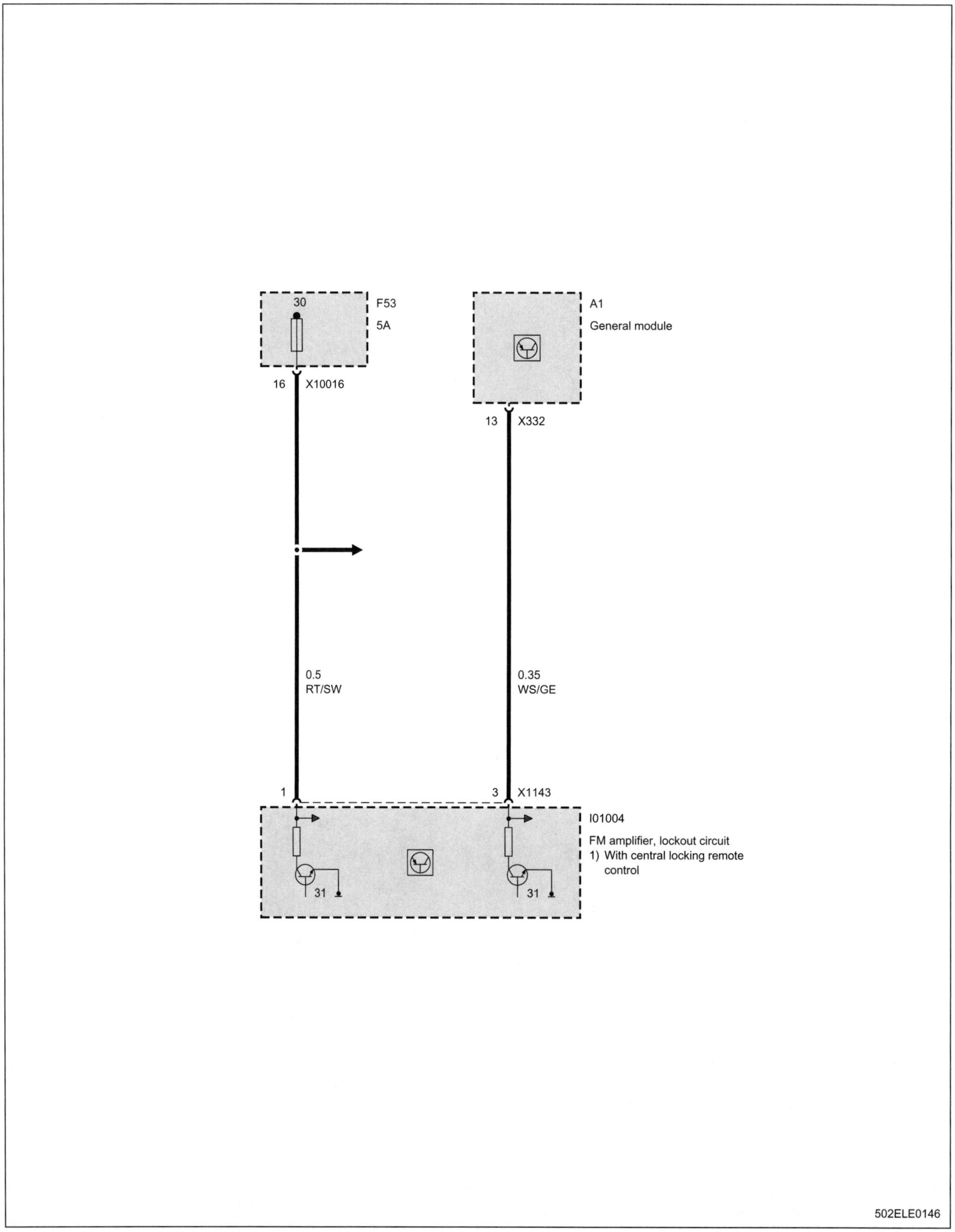
30
F53
5A
A1
General module
16
X10016
13
X332
0.5
RT/SW
0.35
WS/GE
1
3
X1143
I01004
FM amplifier, lockout circuit
1) With central locking remote control
31
31
502ELE0146

Radio/Telephone/GPS
Radio signal inputs
(1 of 1)

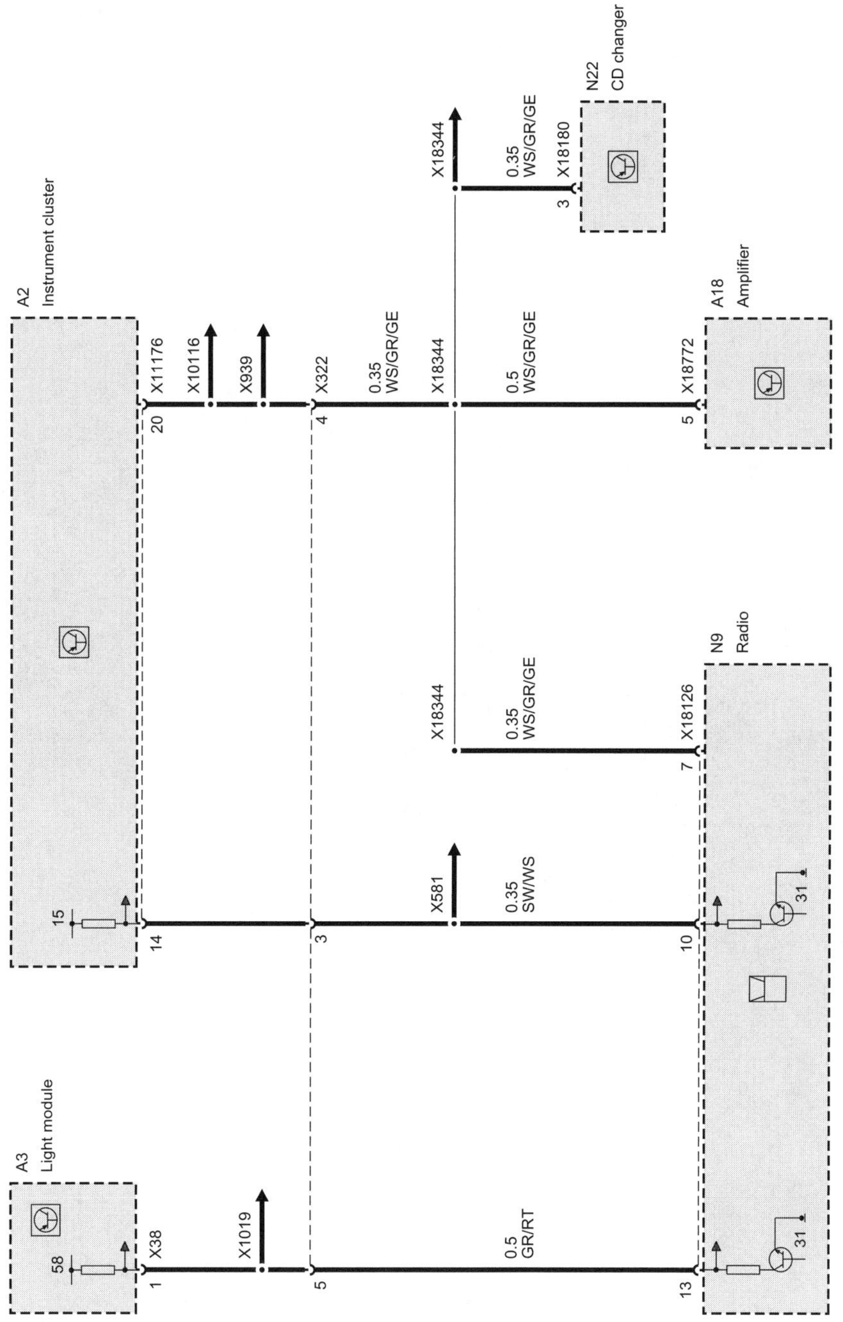

502ELE0214

Radio/Telephone/GPS
Rear loudspeaker I
(1 of 1)

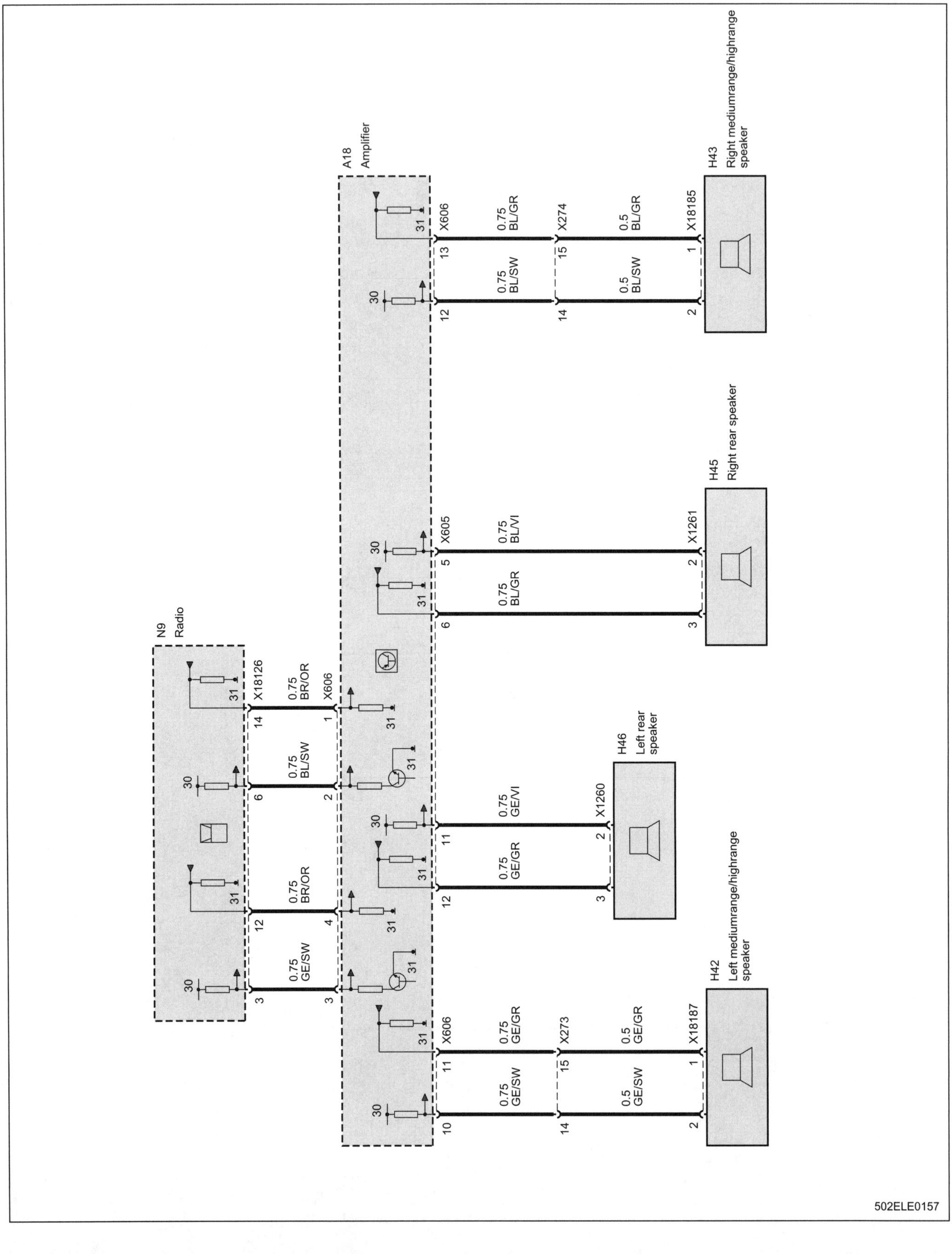
A18
Amplifier
N9
Radio
H43
Right mediumrange/highrange speaker
H45
Right rear speaker
H46
Left rear speaker
H42
Left mediumrange/highrange speaker
X606
X605
X274
X273
X18185
X18187
X18126
X1261
X1260
0.75 BL/GR
0.75 BL/SW
0.5 BL/GR
0.5 BL/SW
0.75 BL/VI
0.75 BR/OR
0.75 GE/VI
0.75 GE/GR
0.75 GE/SW
0.5 GE/GR
0.5 GE/SW
502ELE0157

Radio/Telephone/GPS
Rear loudspeaker II
(1 of 1)

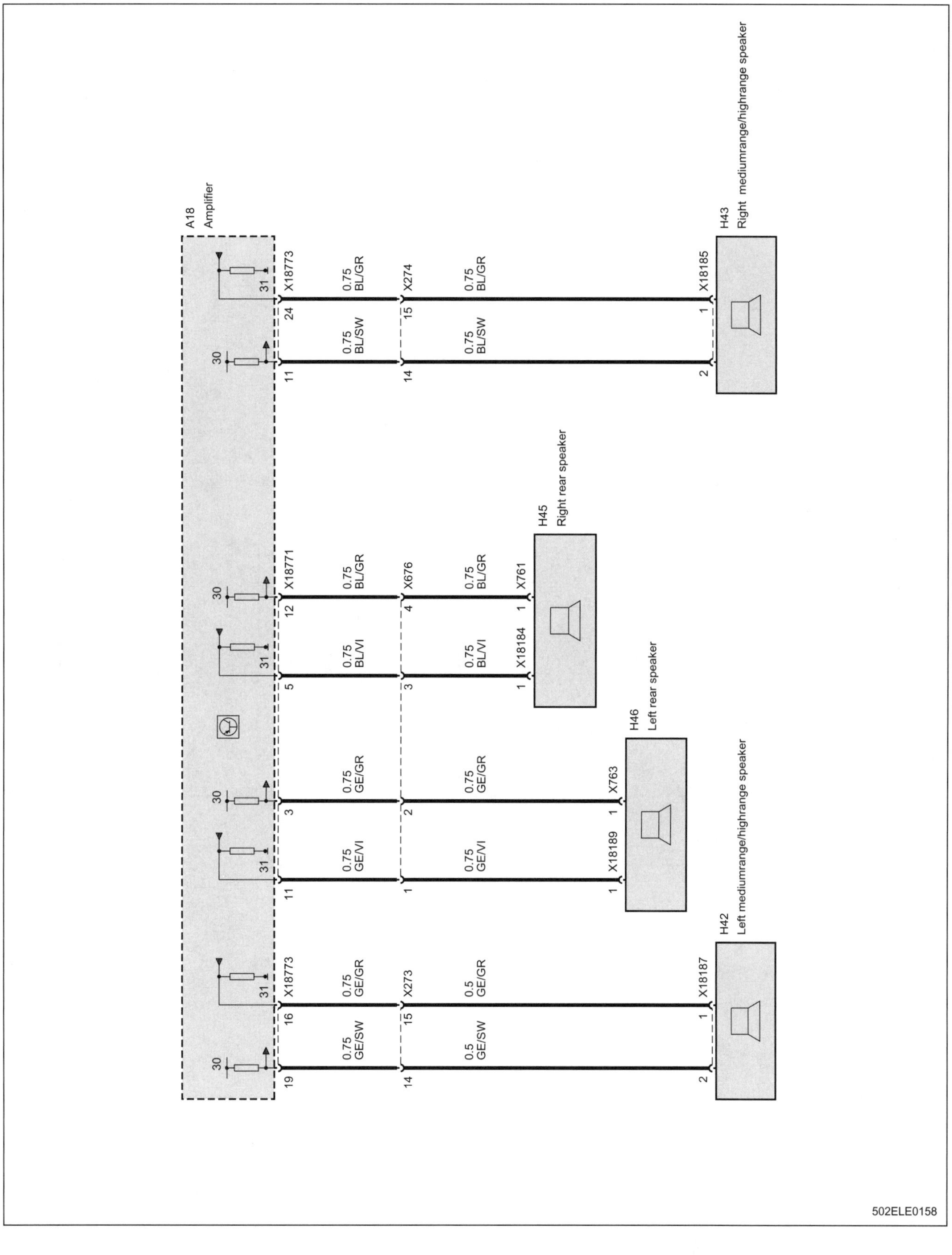
A18
Amplifier
30
31
X18773
24
11
0.75 BL/GR
0.75 BL/SW
X274
15
14
X18185
1
2
H43
Right mediumrange/highrange speaker
X18771
12
5
0.75 BL/GR
0.75 BL/VI
X676
4
3
X761
X18184
H45
Right rear speaker
3
11
0.75 GE/GR
0.75 GE/VI
2
1
X763
X18189
H46
Left rear speaker
X18773
16
19
0.75 GE/GR
0.75 GE/SW
X273
15
14
0.5 GE/GR
0.5 GE/SW
X18187
H42
Left mediumrange/highrange speaker
502ELE0158

Radio/Telephone/GPS
Right front speaker with telephone
(1 of 2)

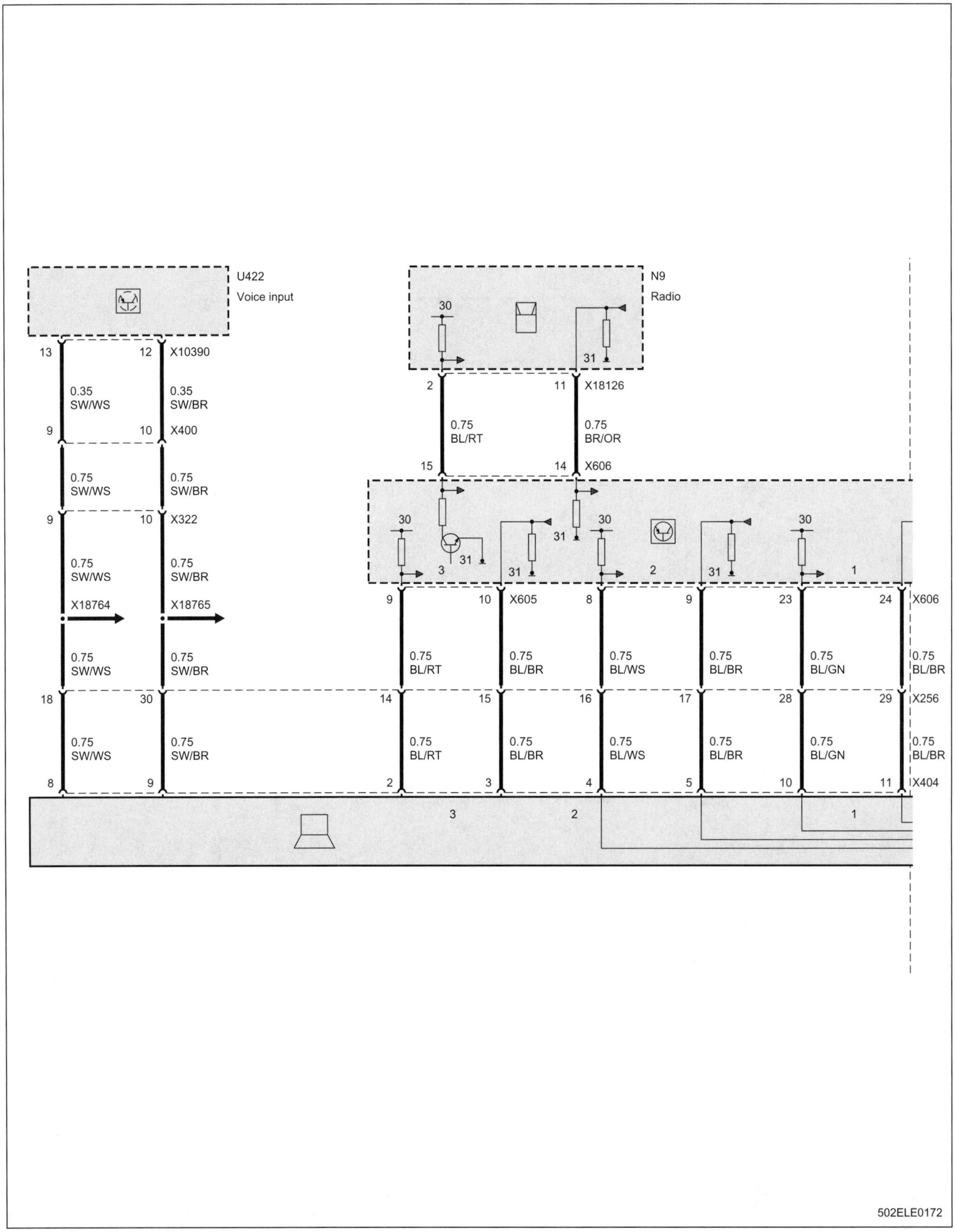

Radio/Telephone/GPS
Right front speaker with telephone
(2 of 2)

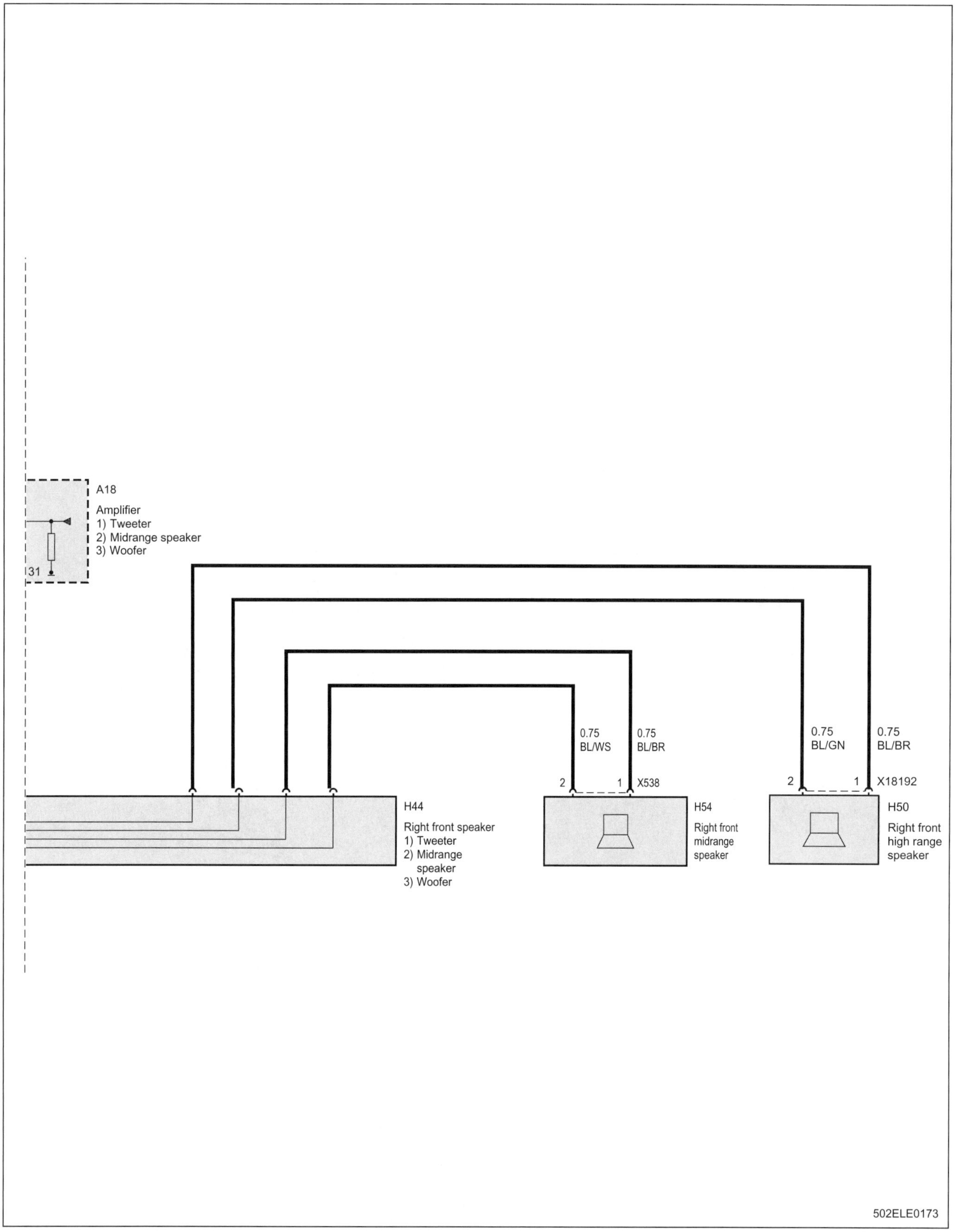

Radio/Telephone/GPS
Signal input, telephone
(1 of 1)

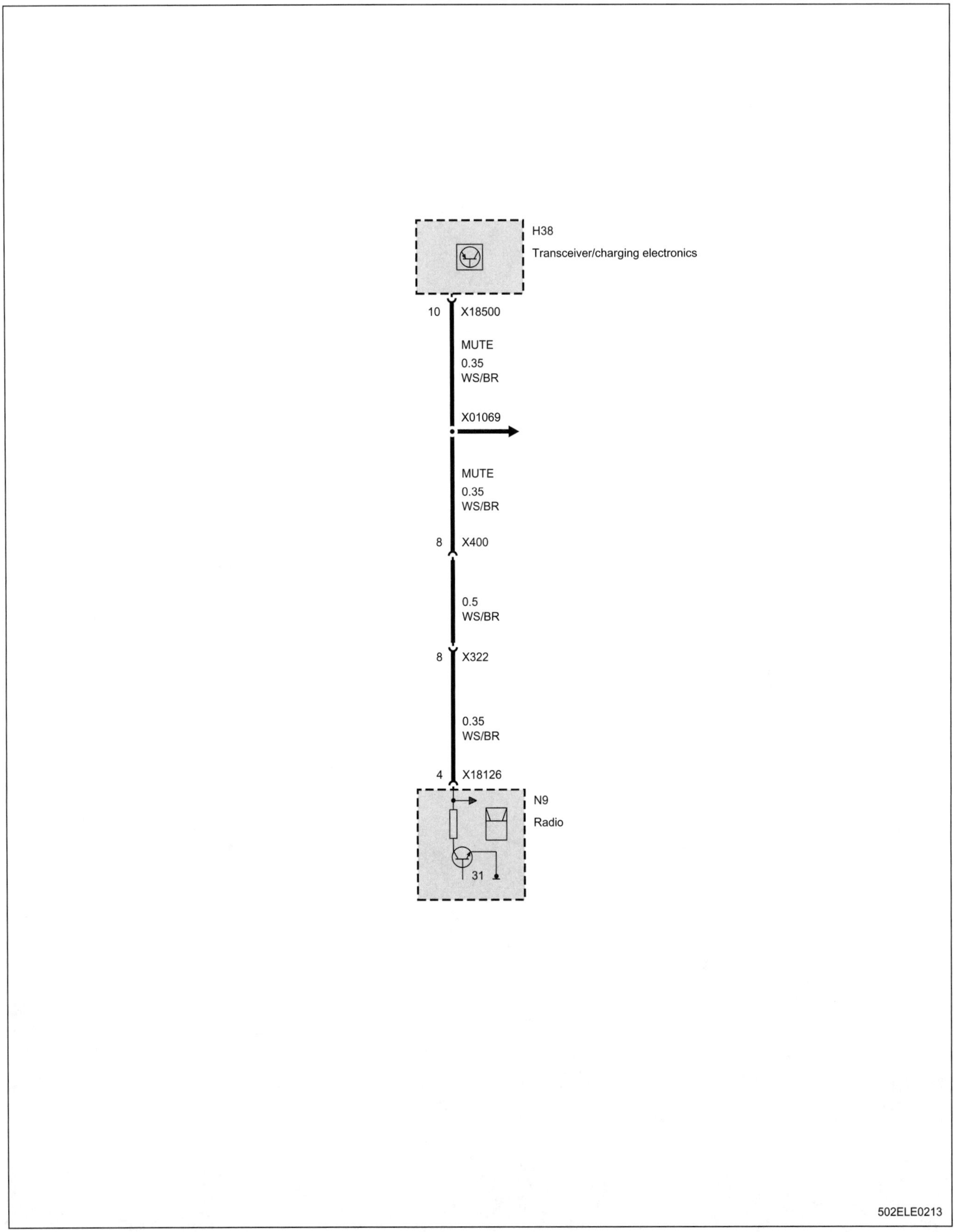

Radio/Telephone/GPS
Subwoofer speaker
(1 of 1)

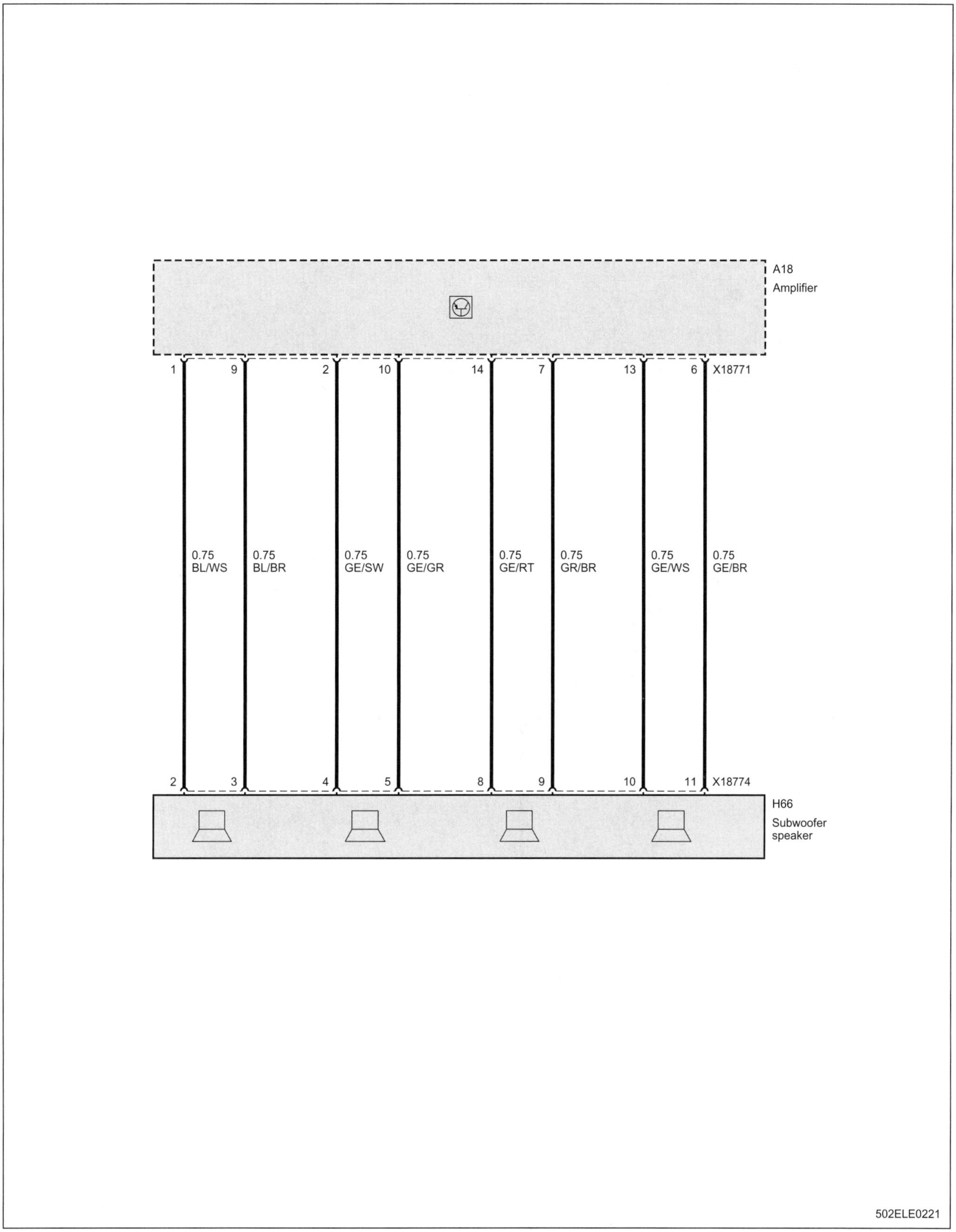
A18
Amplifier
1
9
2
10
14
7
13
6
X18771
0.75
BL/WS
0.75
BL/BR
0.75
GE/SW
0.75
GE/GR
0.75
GE/RT
0.75
GR/BR
0.75
GE/WS
0.75
GE/BR
2
3
4
5
8
9
10
11
X18774
H66
Subwoofer
speaker
502ELE0221

Radio/Telephone/GPS
Transceiver/charging electronics (H38)
(1 of 3)

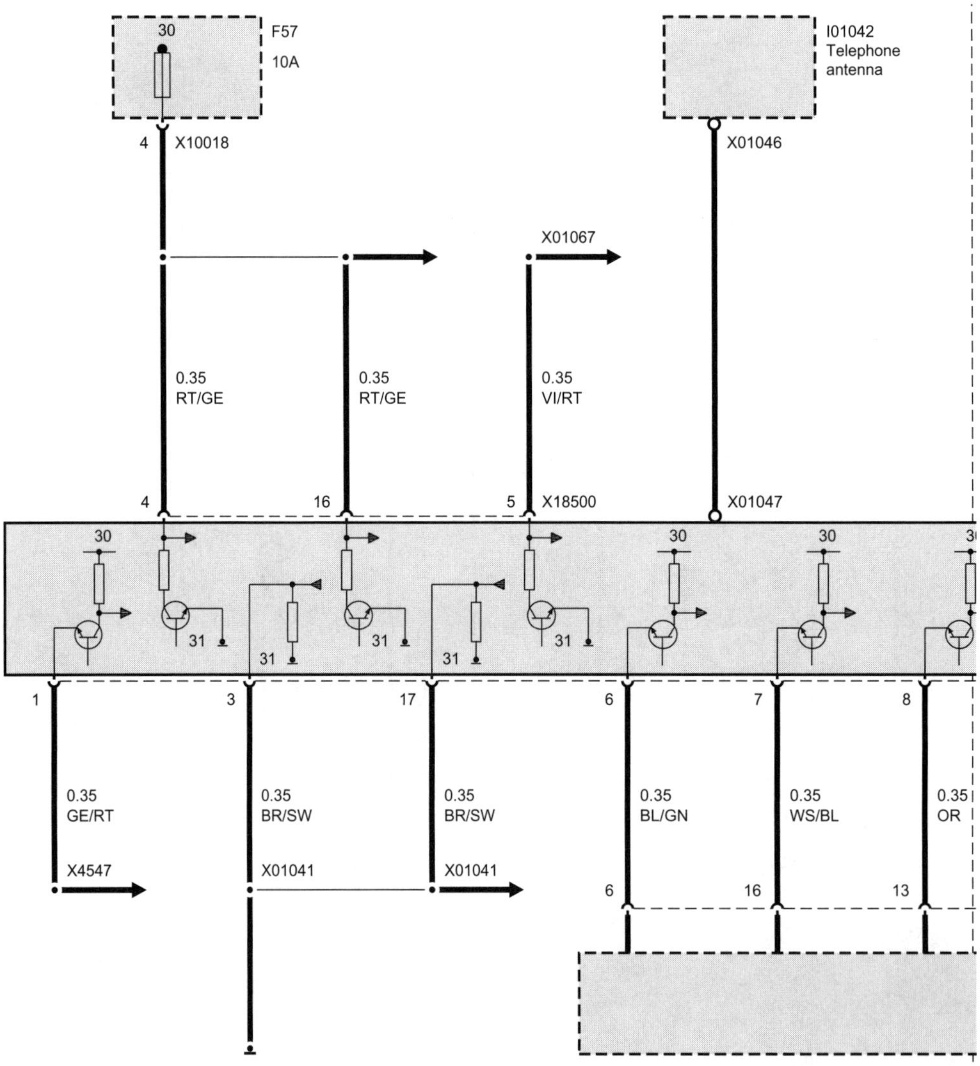

502ELE0553

Radio/Telephone/GPS
Transceiver/charging electronics (H38)
(2 of 3)

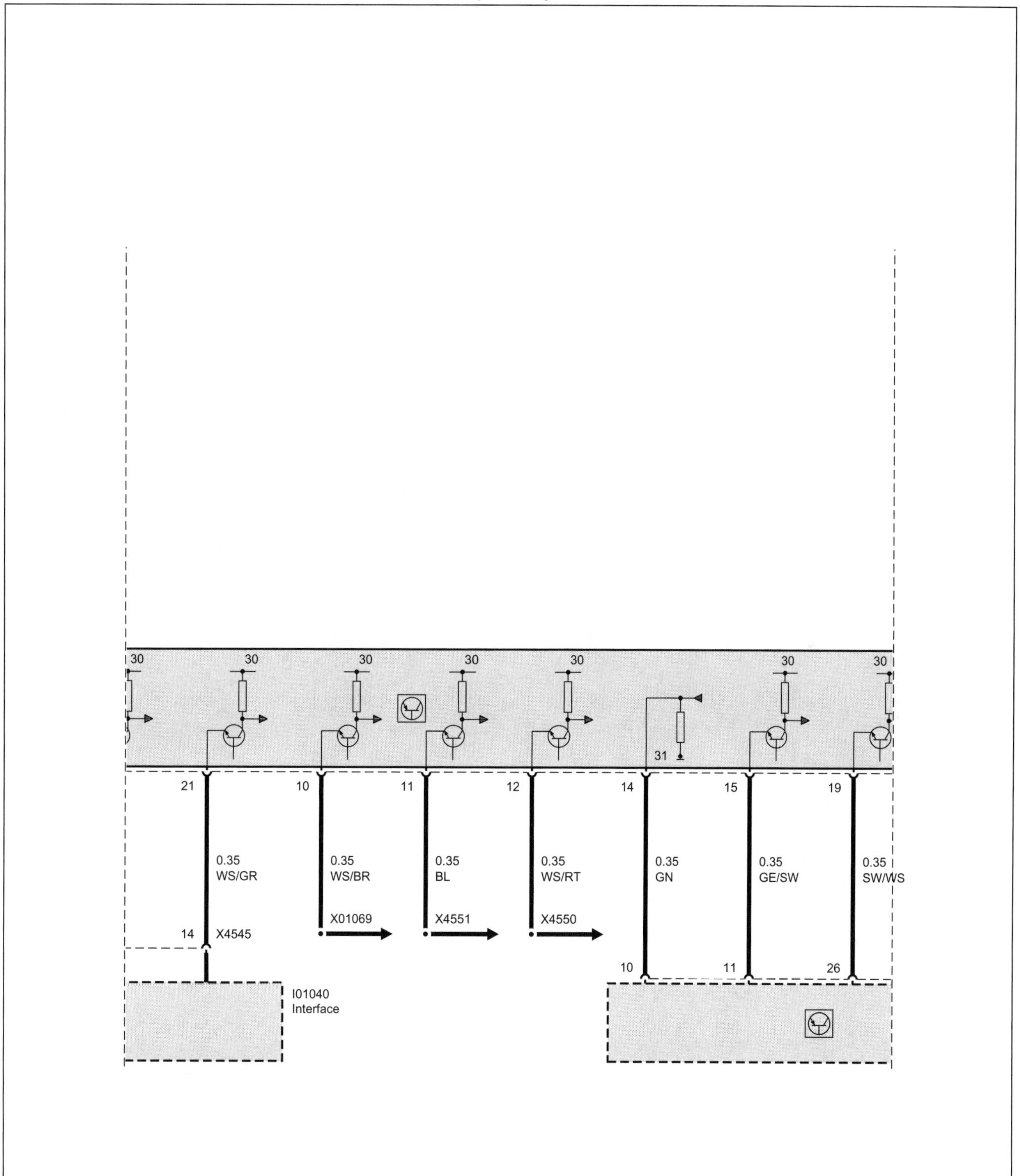

Radio/Telephone/GPS
Transceiver/charging electronics (H38)
(3 of 3)

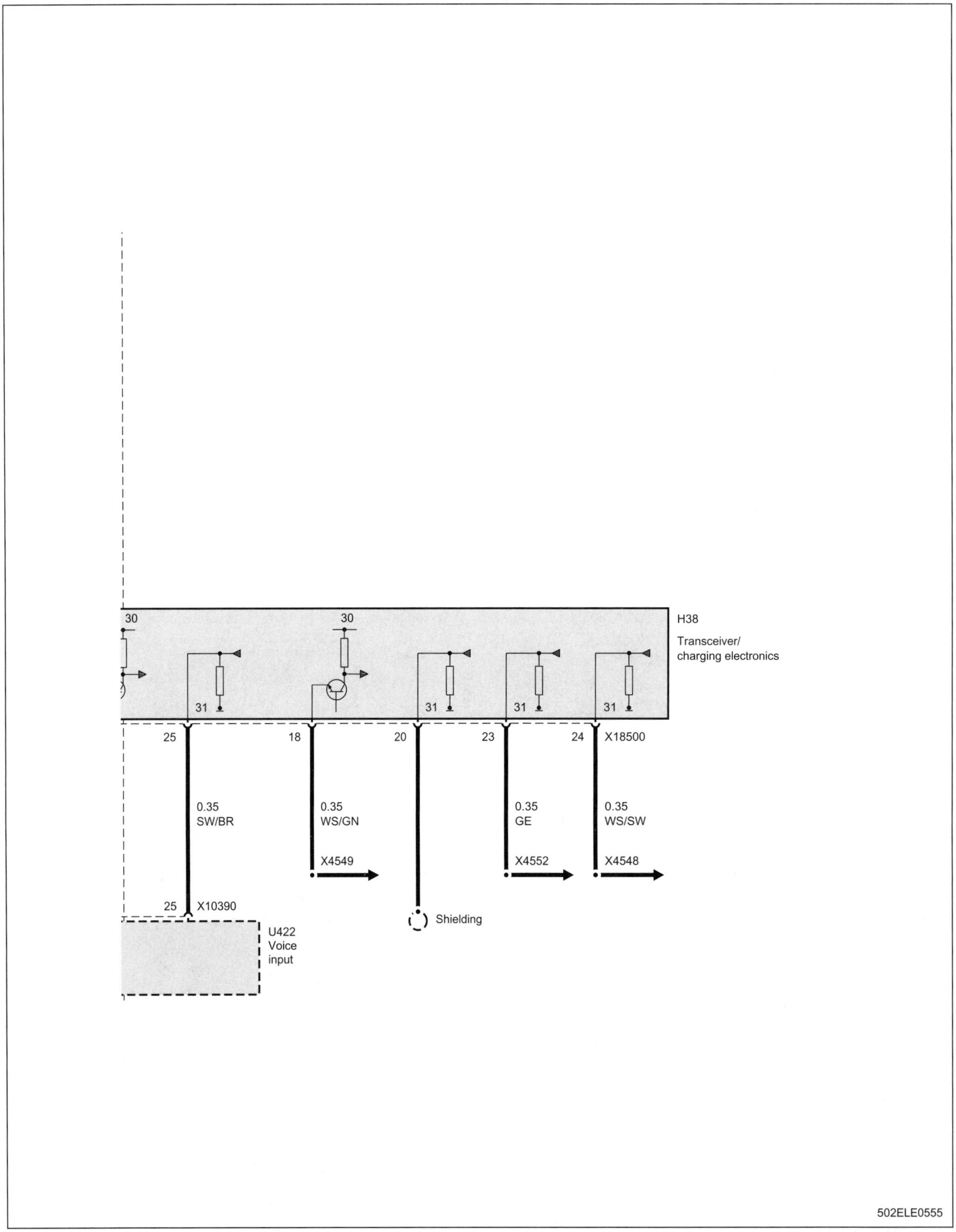

Radio/Telephone/GPS
Voice input
(1 of 1)

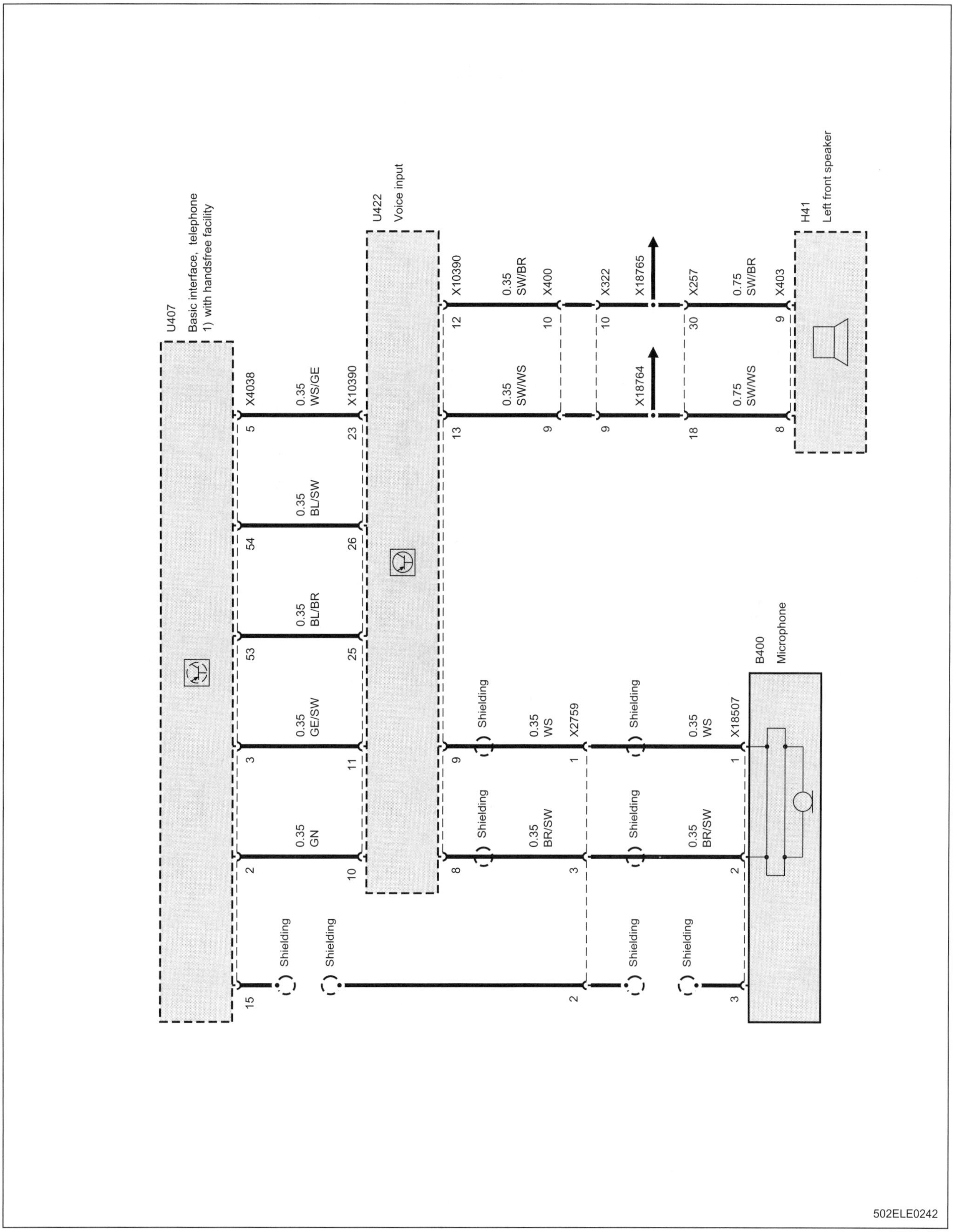
U407
Basic interface, telephone
1) with handsfree facility
U422
Voice input
H41
Left front speaker
B400
Microphone
X4038
X10390
X400
X322
X18765
X18764
X257
X403
X2759
X18507
0.35 WS/GE
0.35 BL/SW
0.35 BL/BR
0.35 GE/SW
0.35 GN
0.35 SW/BR
0.35 SW/WS
0.75 SW/BR
0.75 SW/WS
0.35 WS
0.35 BR/SW
Shielding
502ELE0242

Starting
Starter
(1 of 1)

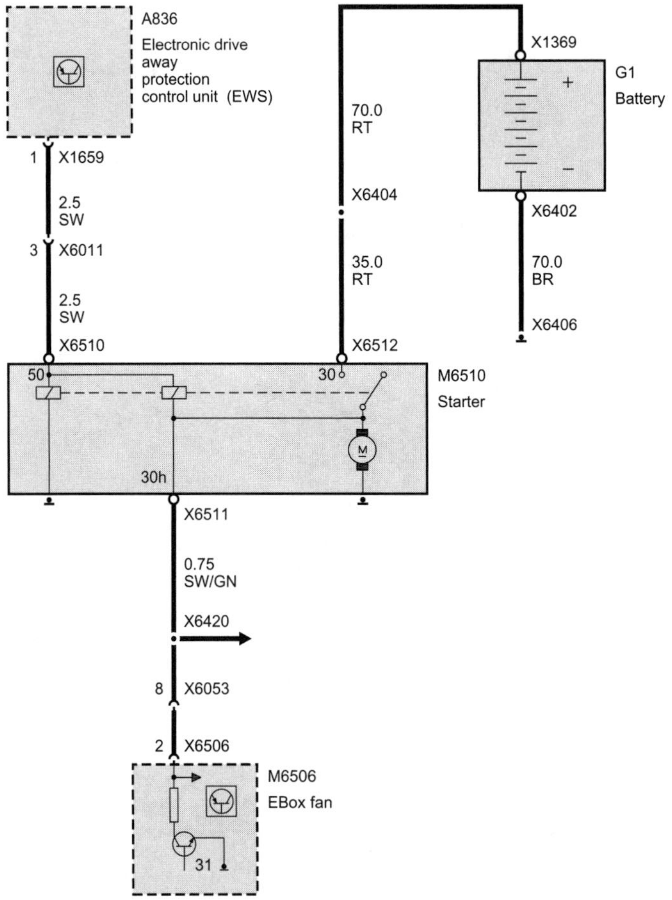
A836
Electronic drive away protection control unit (EWS)
1
X1659
2.5
SW
3
X6011
2.5
SW
X6510
70.0
RT
X6404
35.0
RT
X6512
X1369
G1
Battery
+
–
X6402
70.0
BR
X6406
50
30
M6510
Starter
M
30h
X6511
0.75
SW/GN
X6420
8
X6053
2
X6506
M6506
EBox fan
31

502ELE0333

Starting
Starter control (EWS)
(1 of 1)

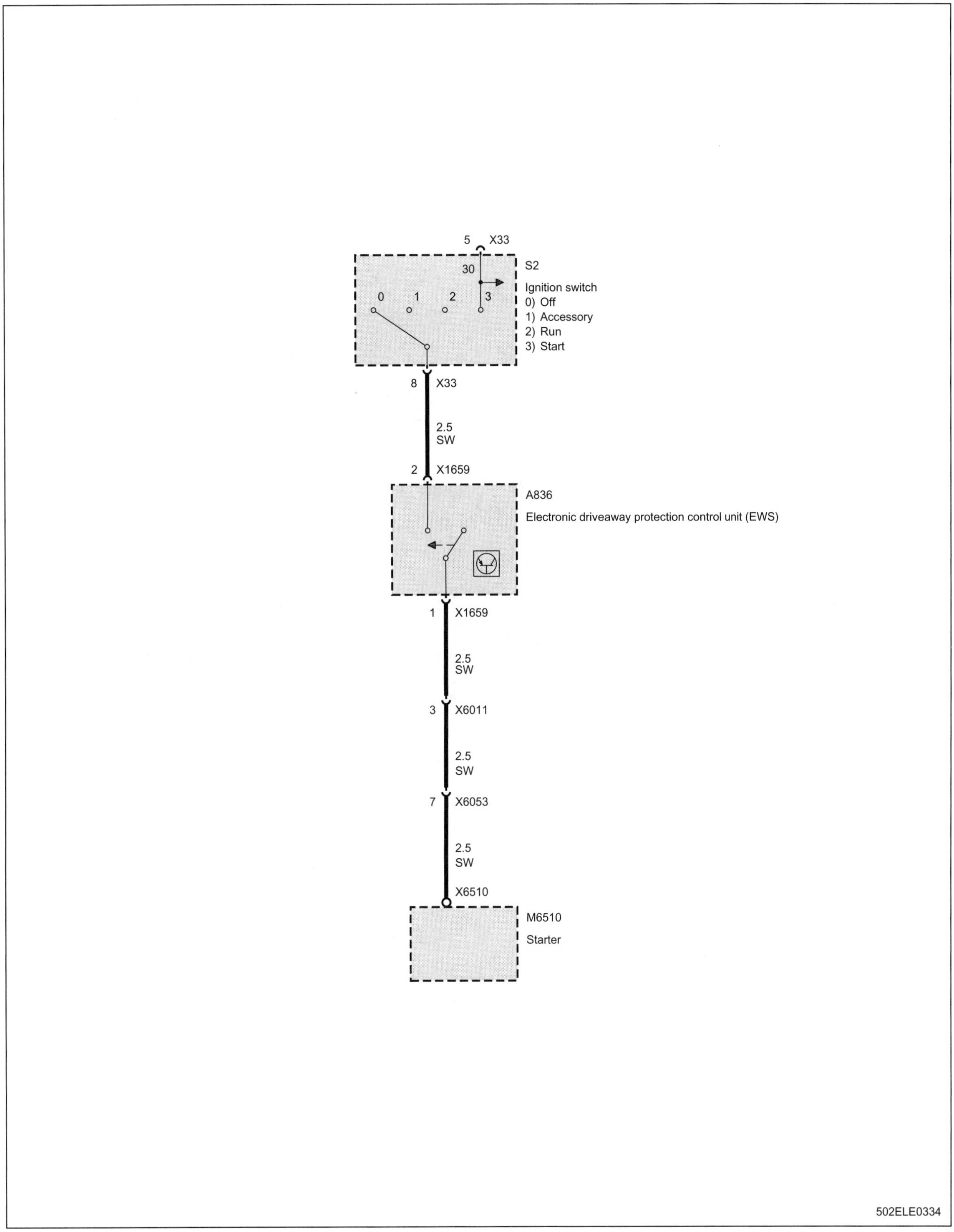
5 X33
30
S2
Ignition switch
0) Off
1) Accessory
2) Run
3) Start
0 1 2 3
8 X33
2.5
SW
2 X1659
A836
Electronic driveaway protection control unit (EWS)
1 X1659
2.5
SW
3 X6011
2.5
SW
7 X6053
2.5
SW
X6510
M6510
Starter
502ELE0334

Steering Column Power Adjustment
Seat/steering column/mirror memory (overview)
(1 of 5)

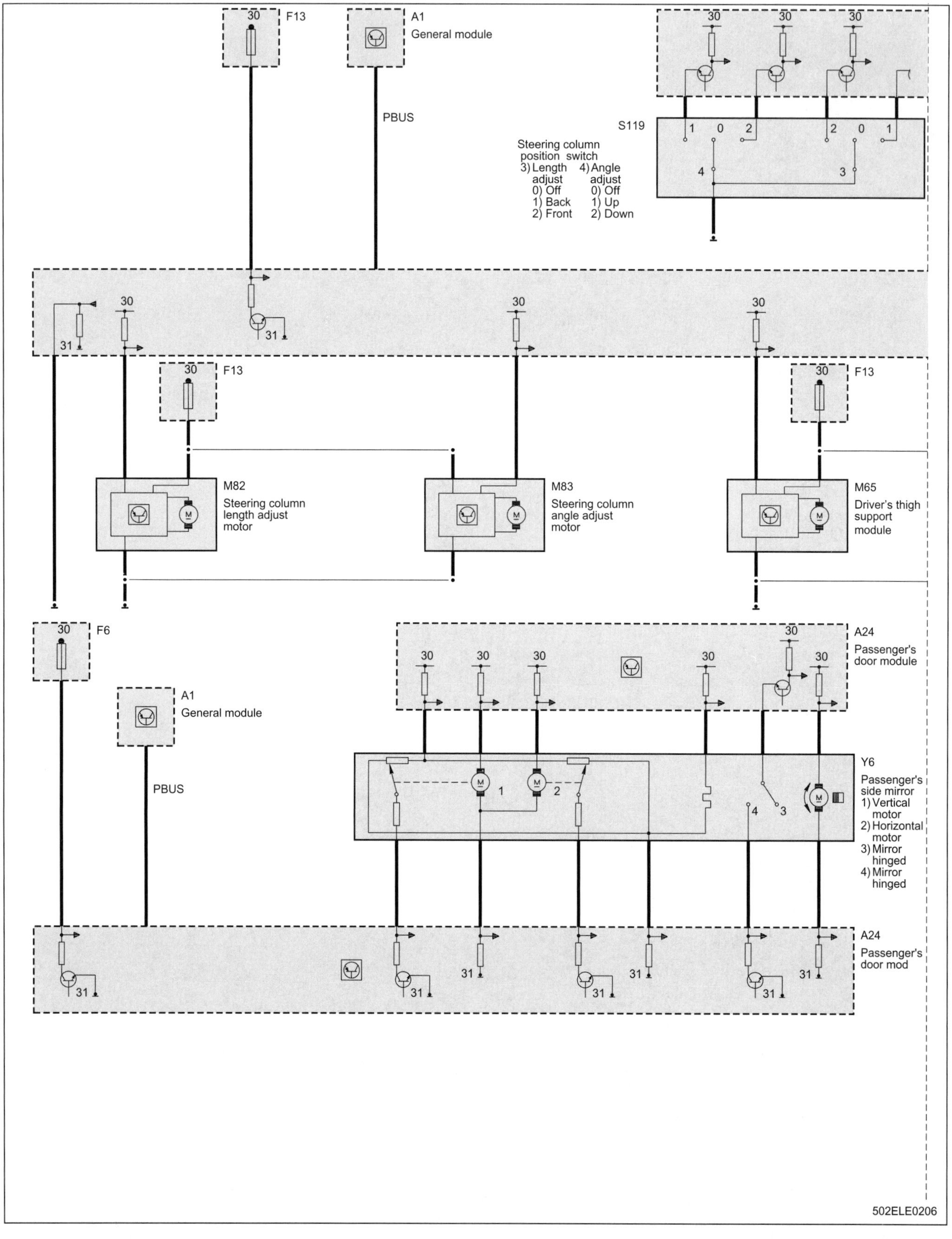

502ELE0206

Steering Column Power Adjustment
Seat/steering column/mirror memory (overview)
(2 of 5)

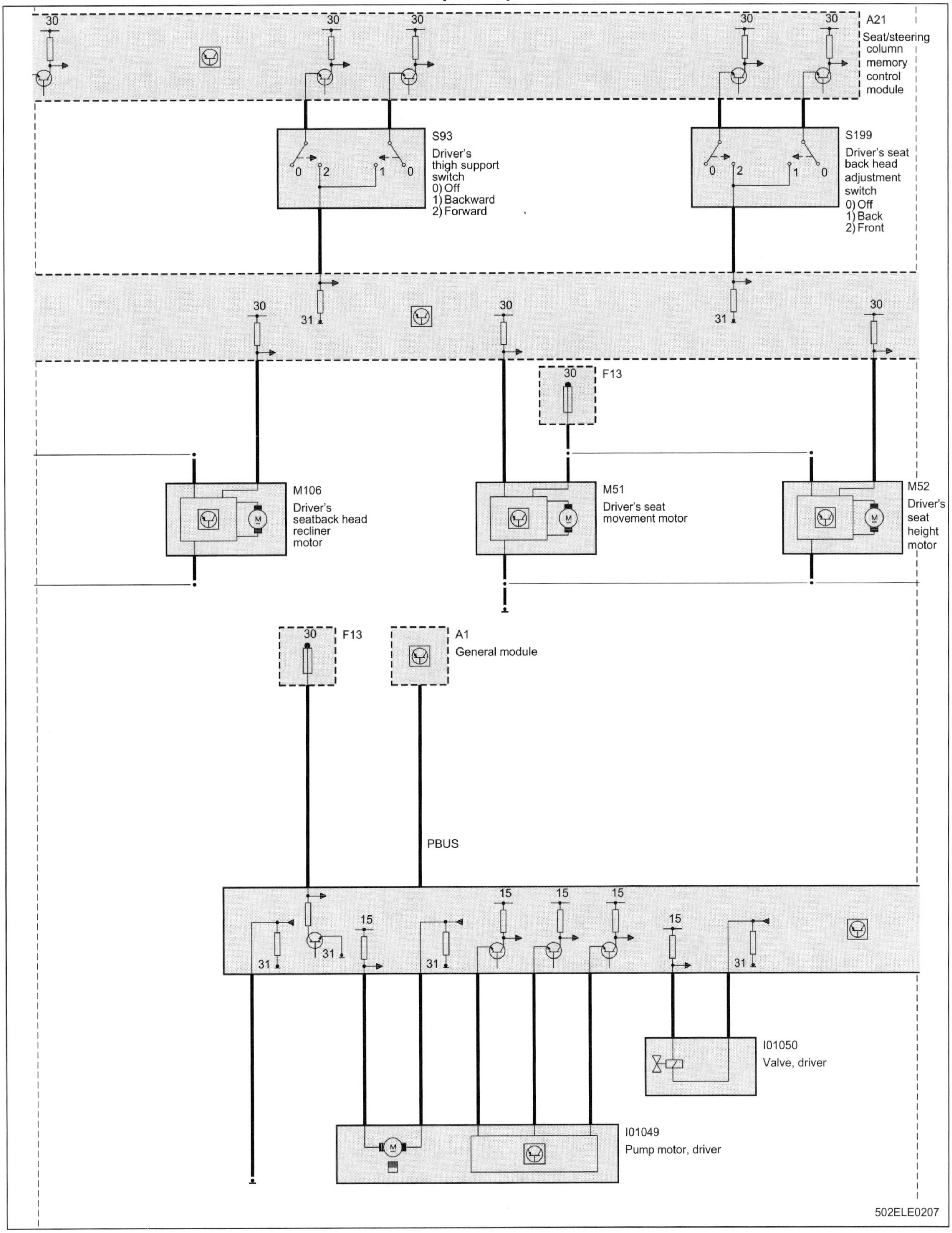

Steering Column Power Adjustment
Seat/steering column/mirror memory (overview)
(3 of 5)

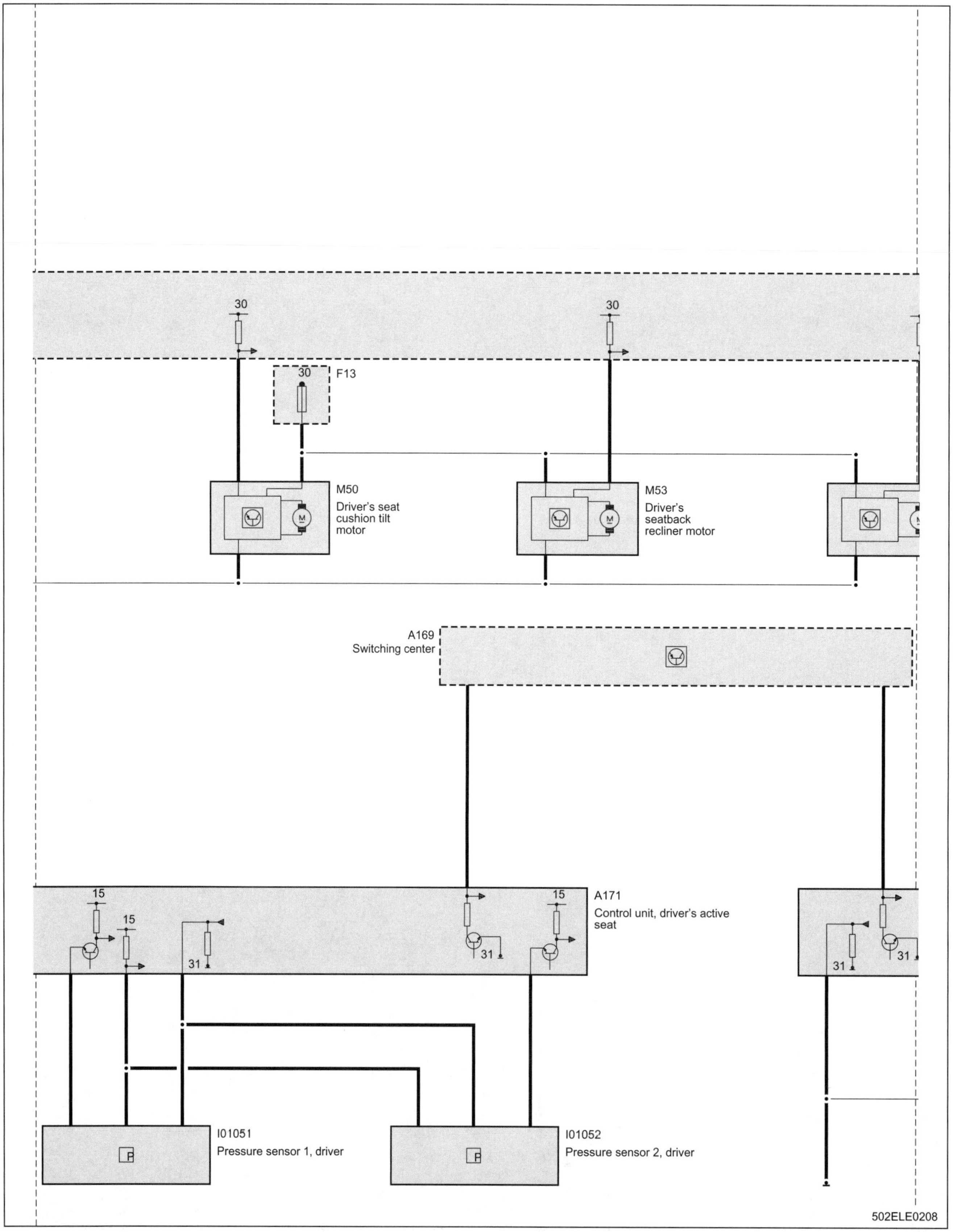

Steering Column Power Adjustment
Seat/steering column/mirror memory (overview)
(4 of 5)

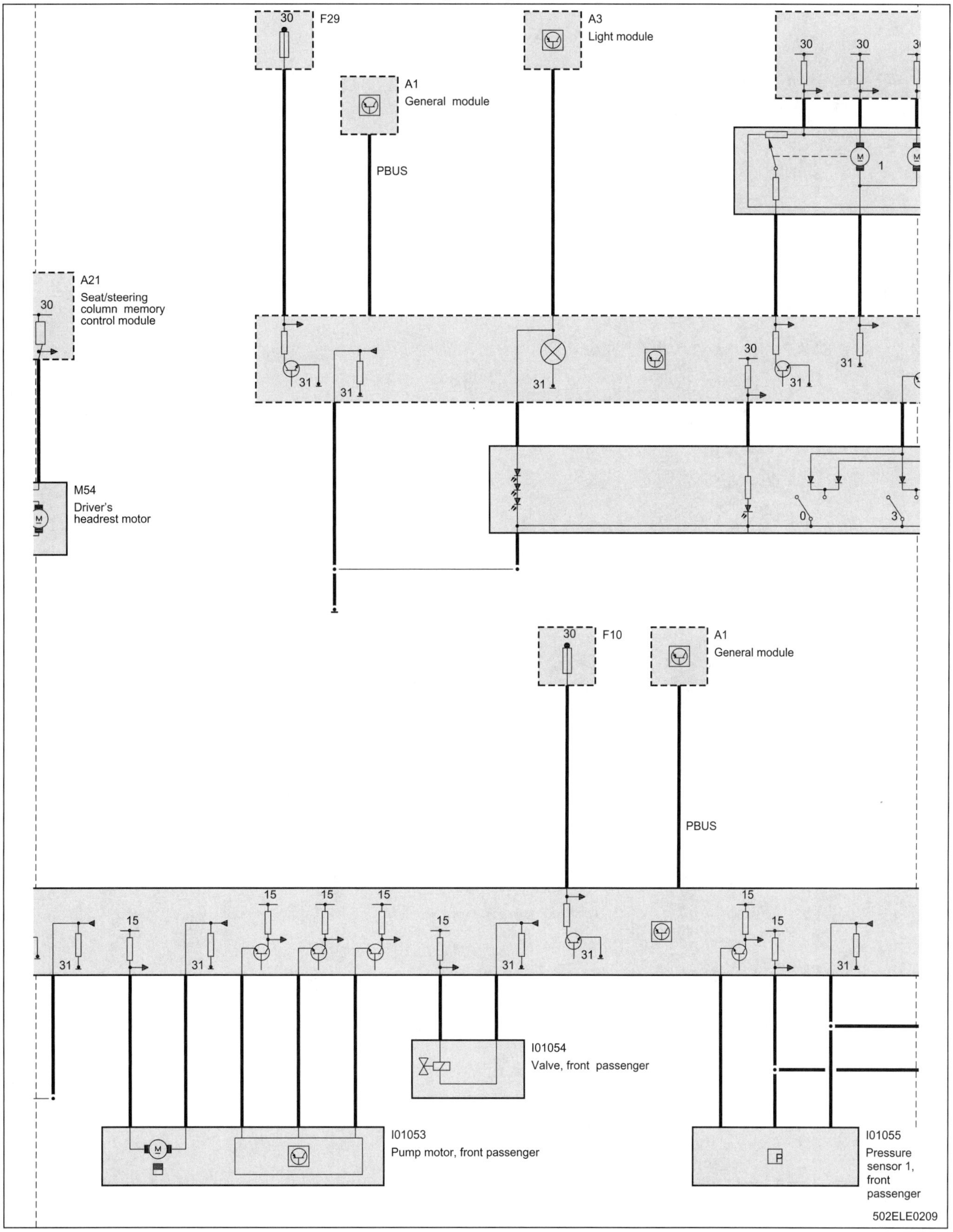

502ELE0209

Steering Column Power Adjustment
Seat/steering column/mirror memory (overview)
(5 of 5)

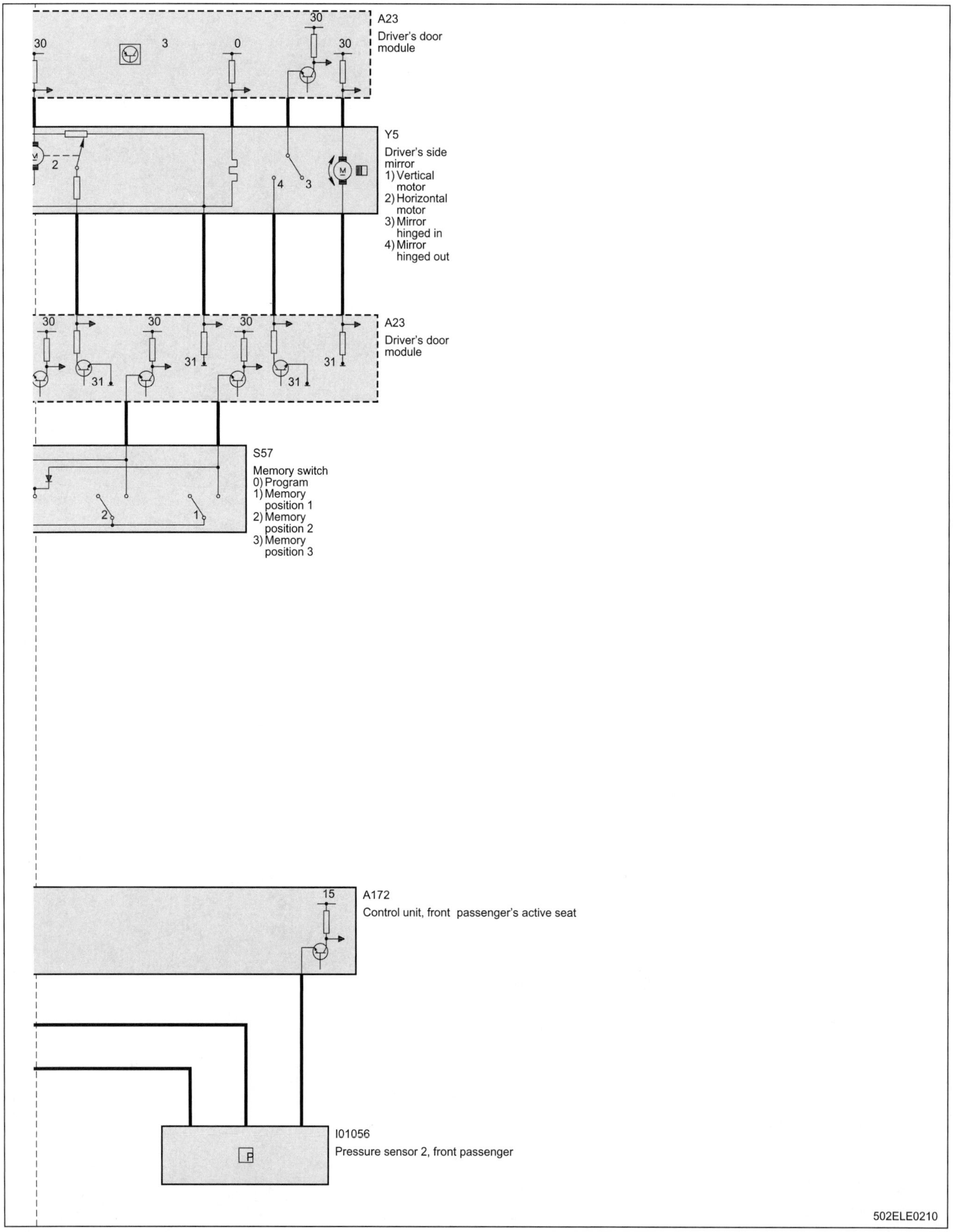

Steering Column Power Adjustment
Steering column adjustment with memory
(1 of 1)

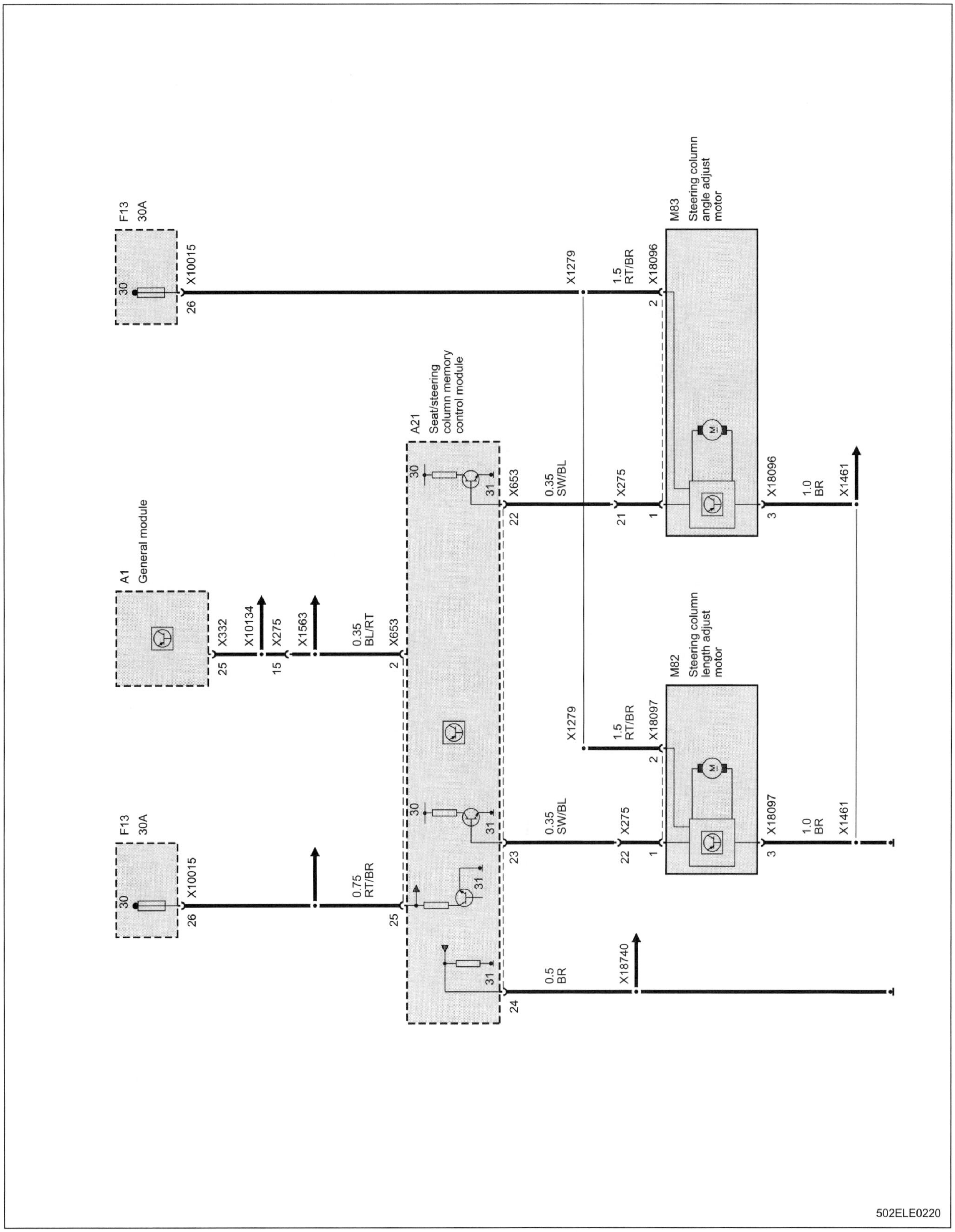

Steering Column Power Adjustment
Steering column adjustment switch (LSM)
(1 of 1)

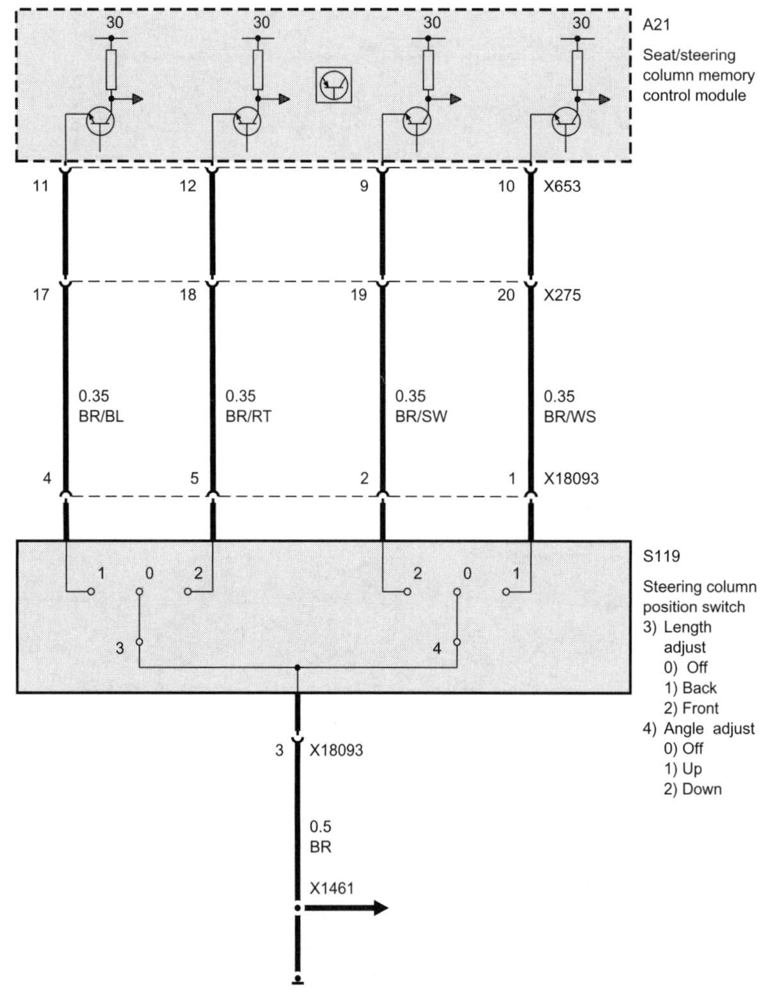

Transmission Electronics
Transmission control (overview)
(1 of 4)

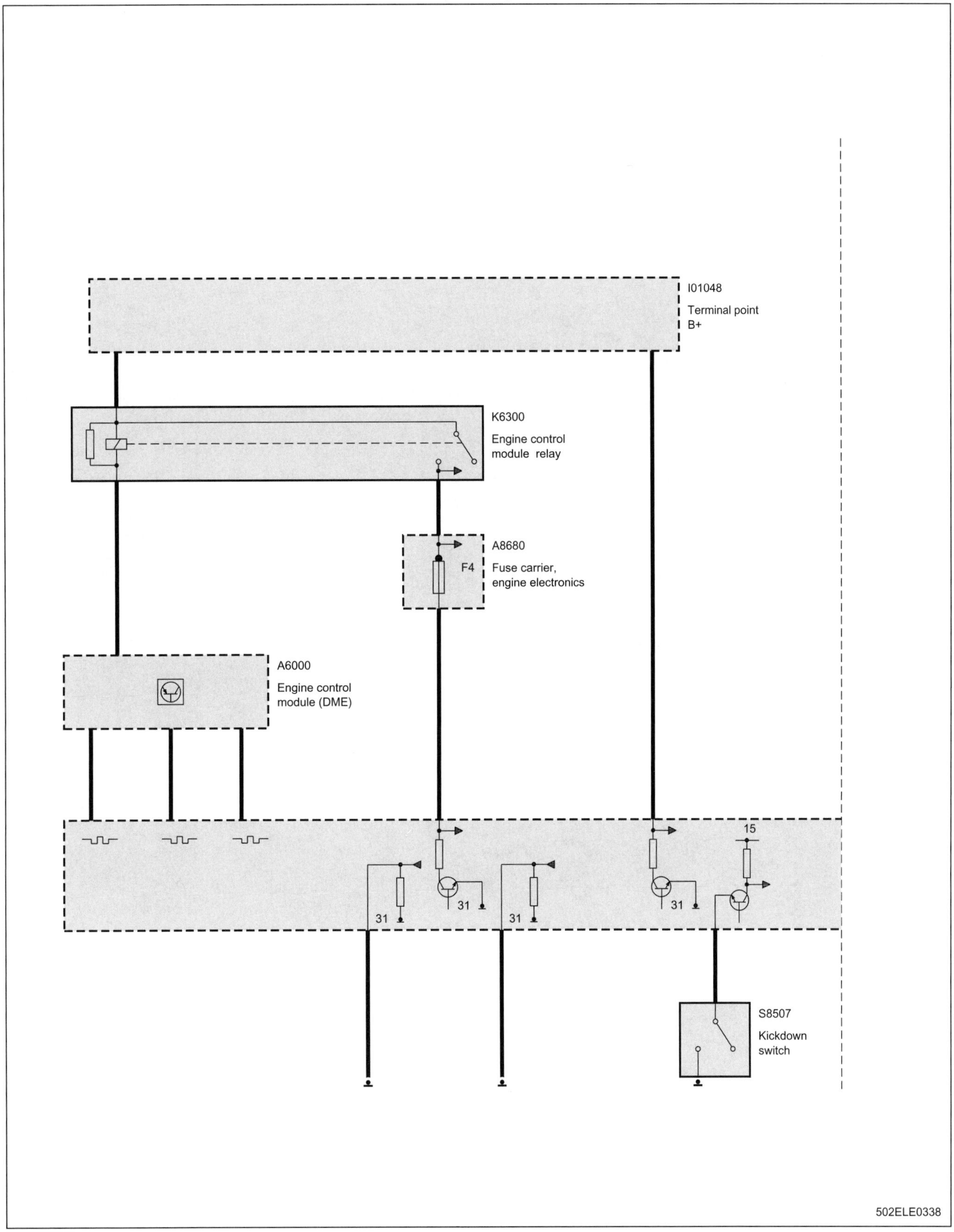

Transmission Electronics
Transmission control (overview)
(2 of 4)

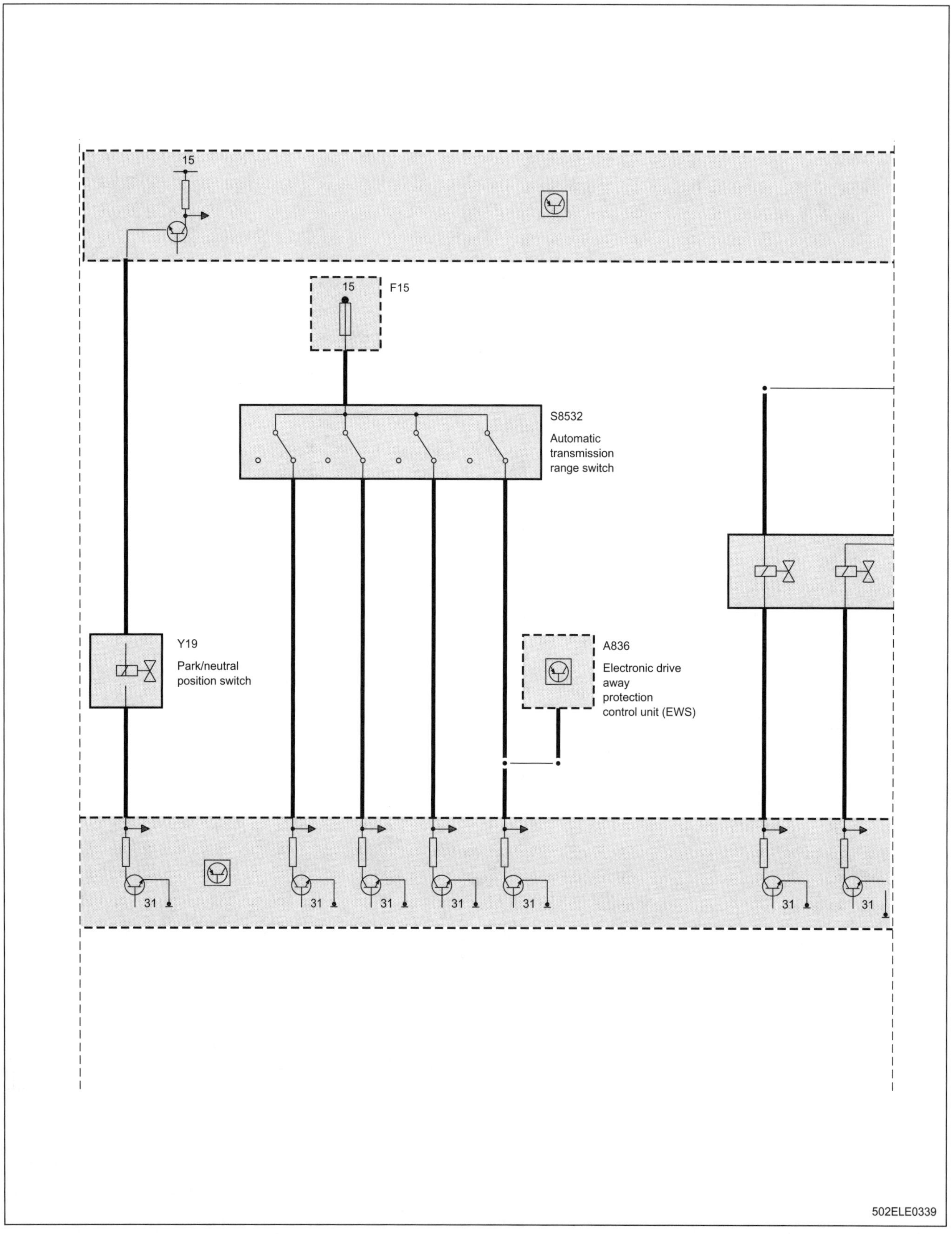

Transmission Electronics
Transmission control (overview)
(3 of 4)

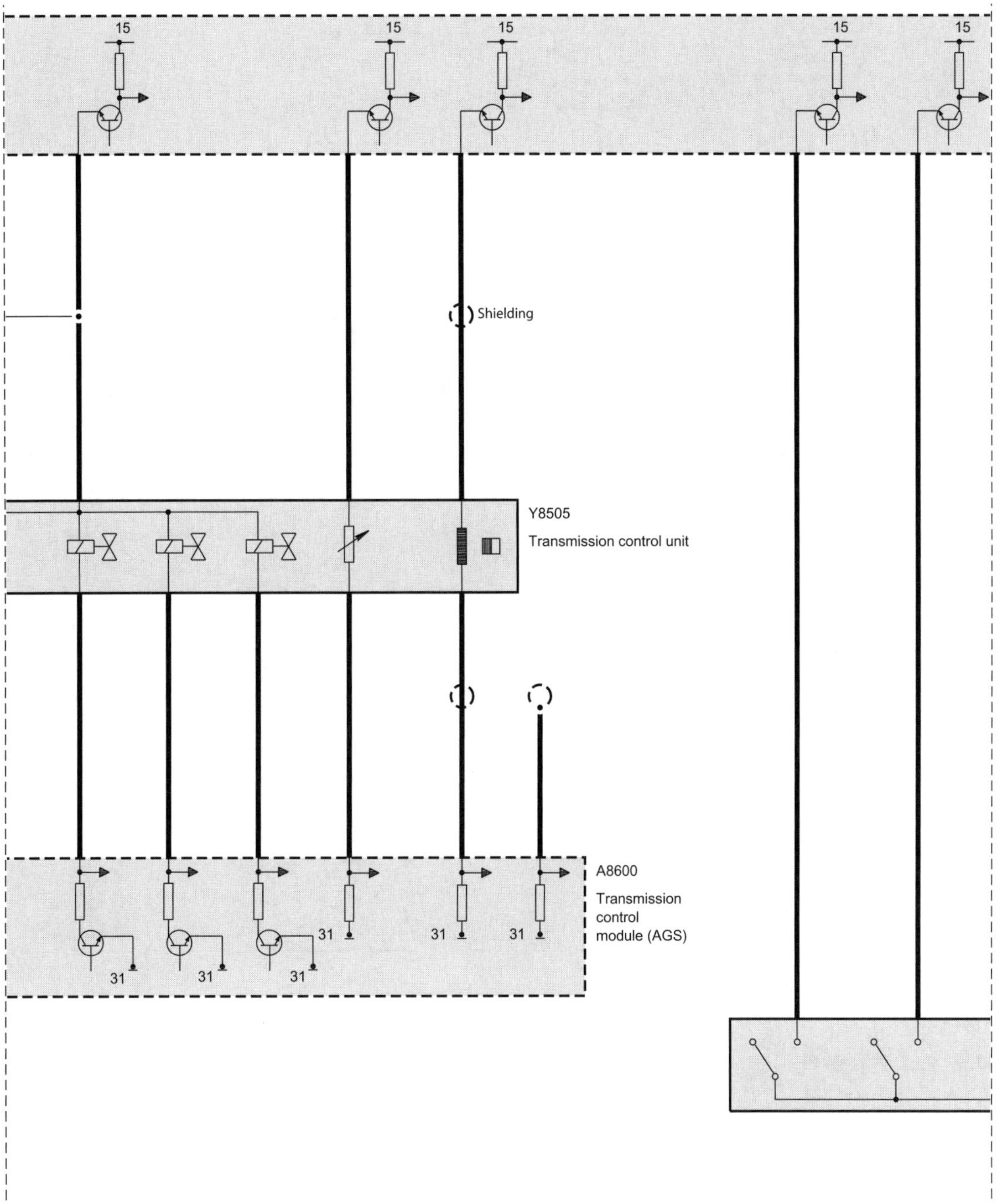

502ELE0340

Transmission Electronics
Transmission control (overview)
(4 of 4)

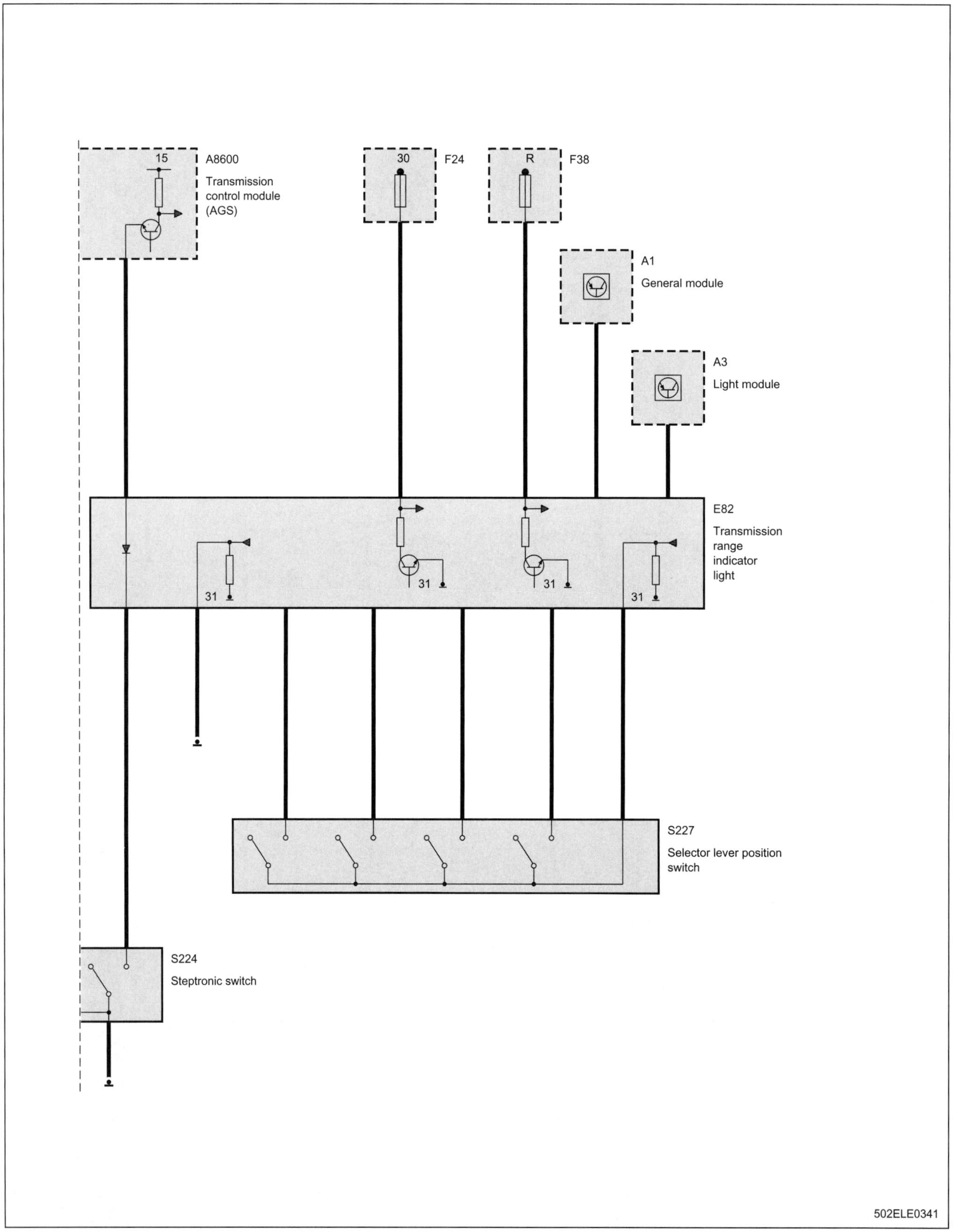

Electronic Suspension
Electronic shock absorber control module, EDC (A80)
(1 of 3)

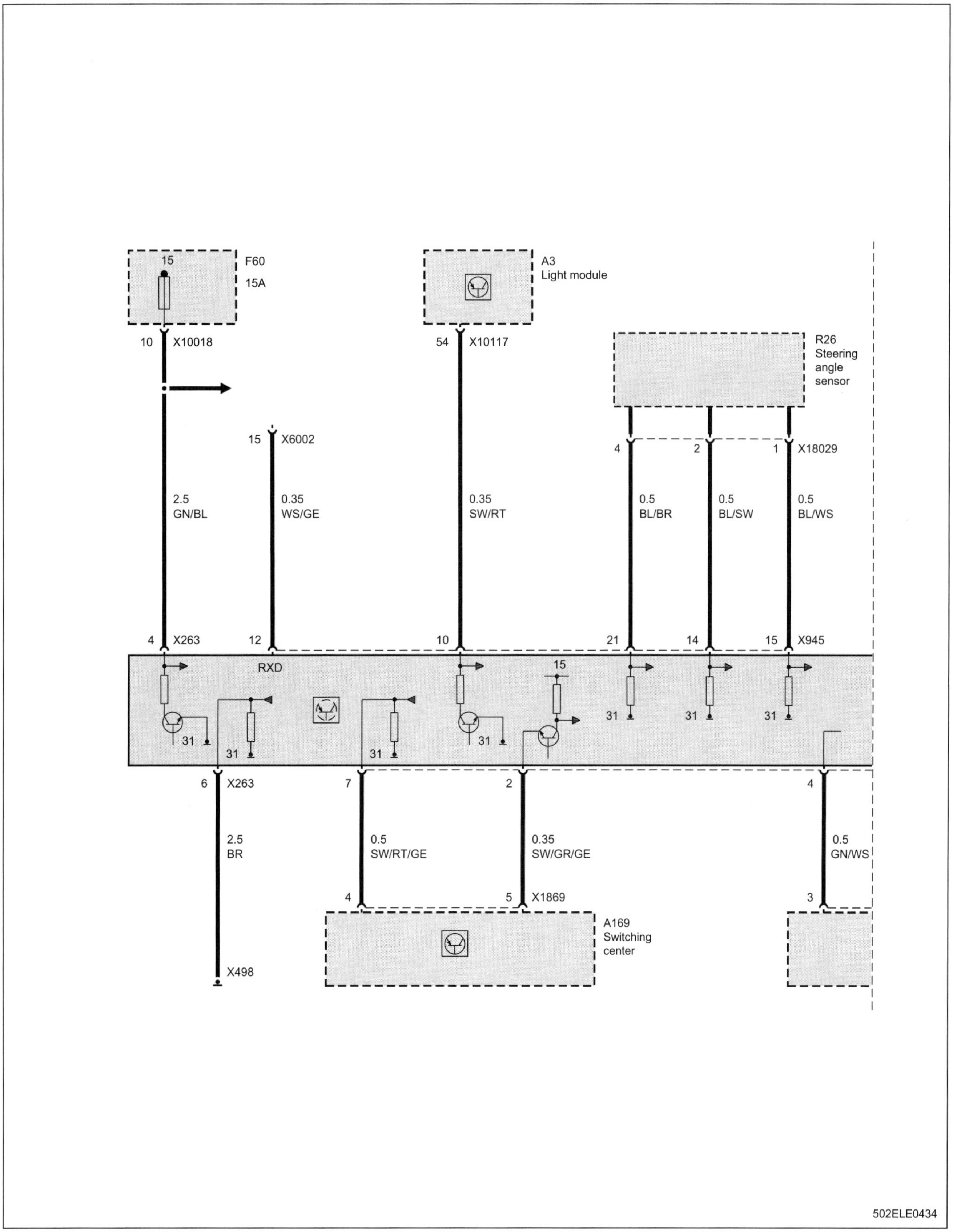

Electronic Suspension
Electronic shock absorber control module, EDC (A80)
(2 of 3)

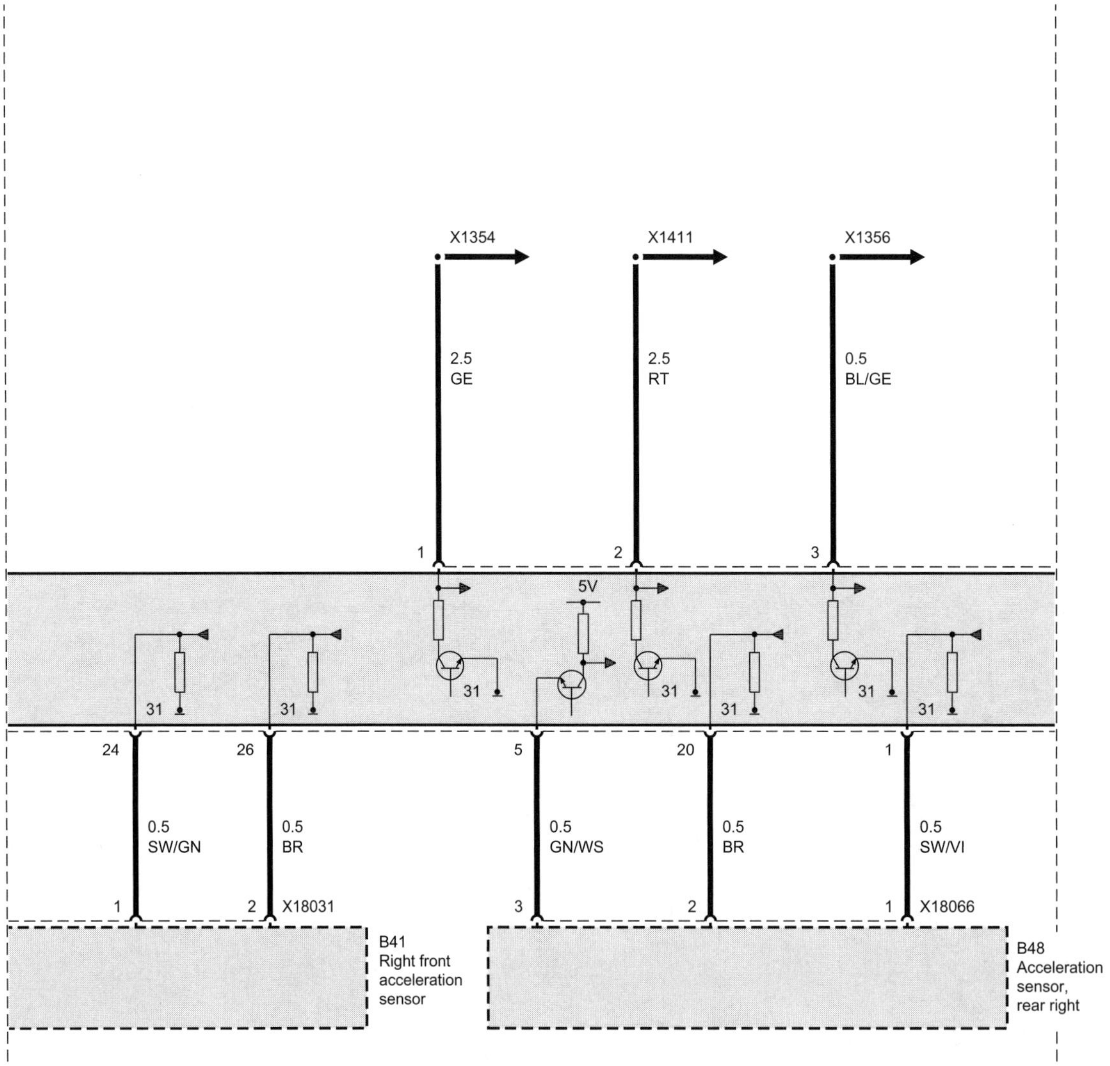

502ELE0435

Electronic Suspension
Electronic shock absorber control module, EDC (A80)
(3 of 3)

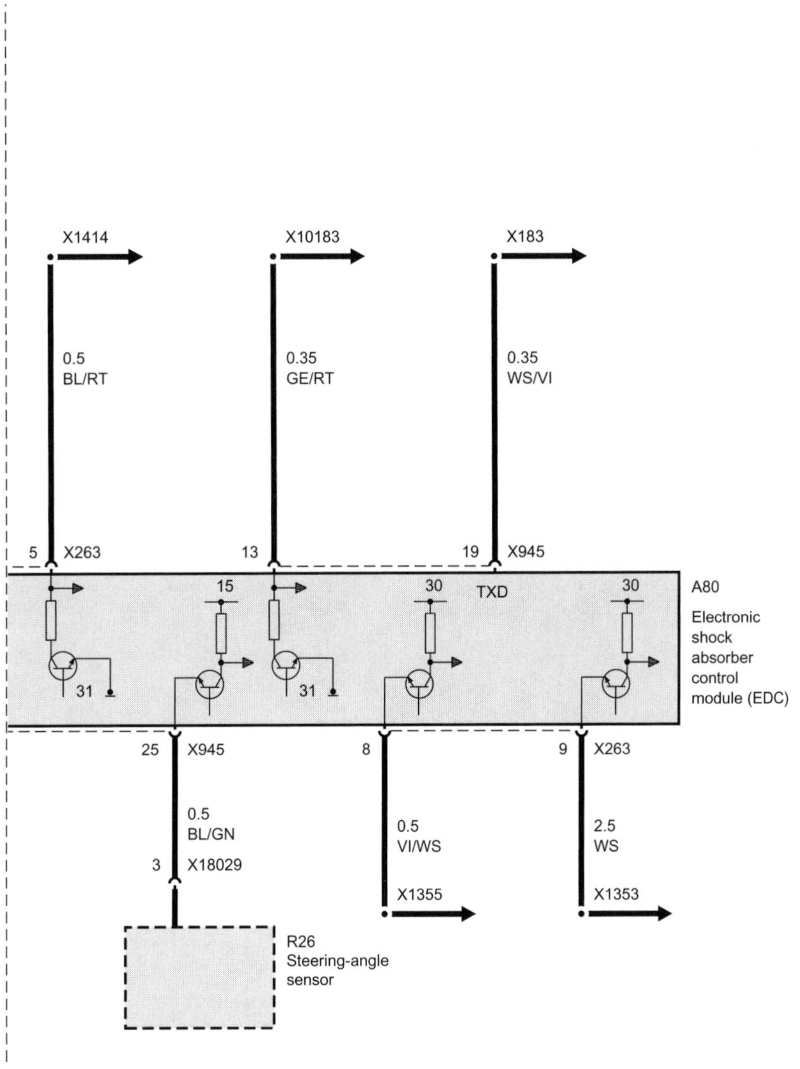

502ELE0436

Transmission Electronics
ATF oil temperature sensor, output shaft speed sensor
(1 of 1)

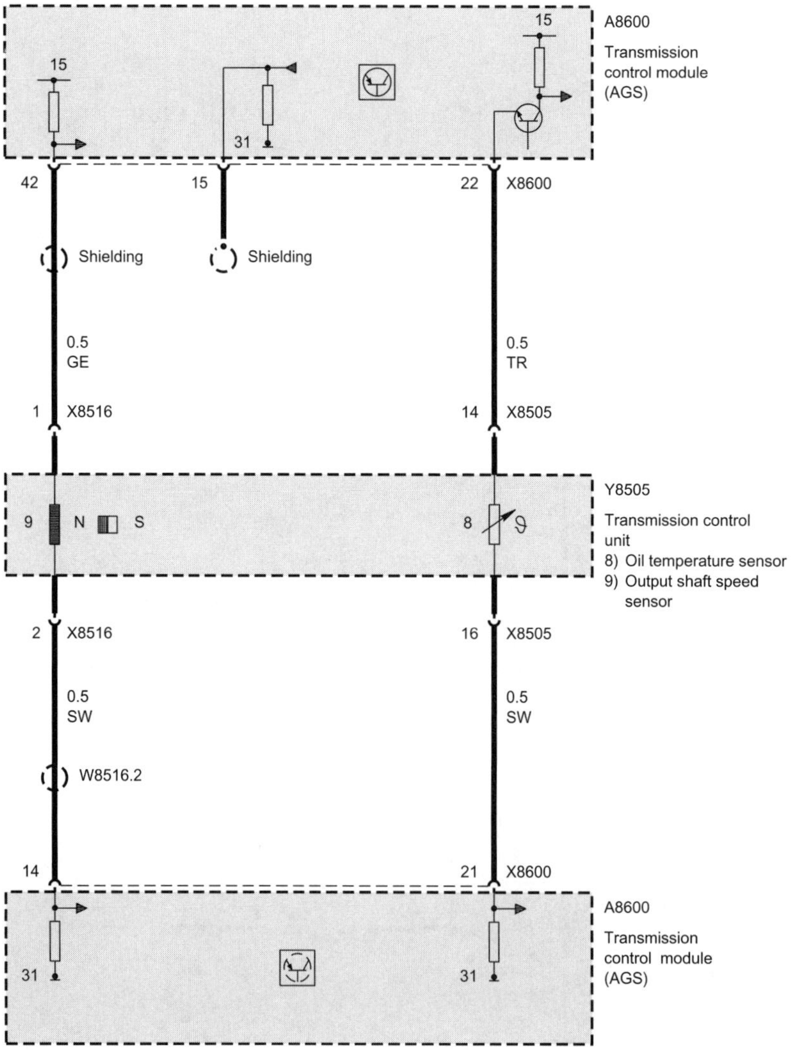

502ELE0306

Transmission Electronics
Solenoid valves, shift-lock
(1 of 1)

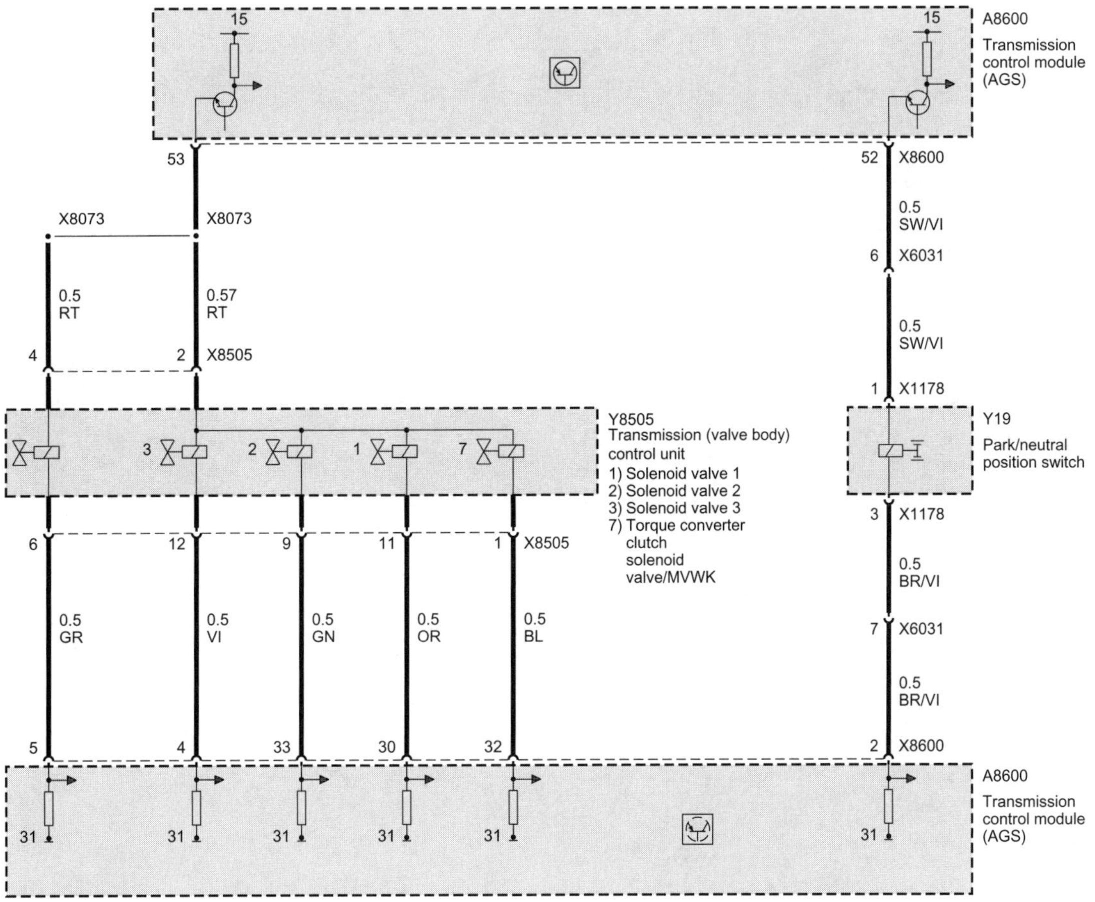

502ELE0307

Transmission Electronics
Kick-down switch

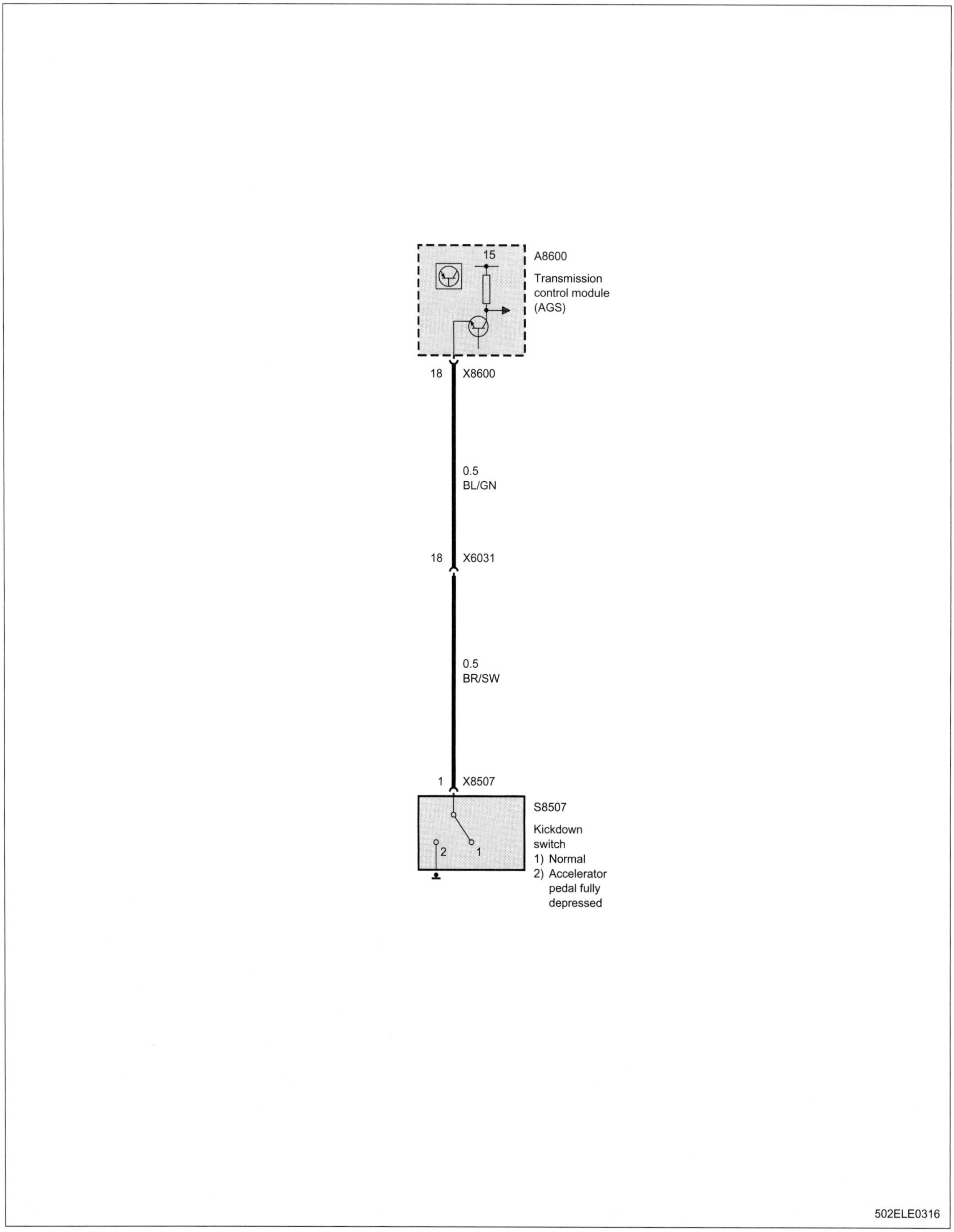
15
A8600
Transmission control module (AGS)
18
X8600
0.5
BL/GN
18
X6031
0.5
BR/SW
1
X8507
S8507
Kickdown switch
1) Normal
2) Accelerator pedal fully depressed
2
1
502ELE0316

Transmission Electronics
Selector-lever switch
(1 of 1)

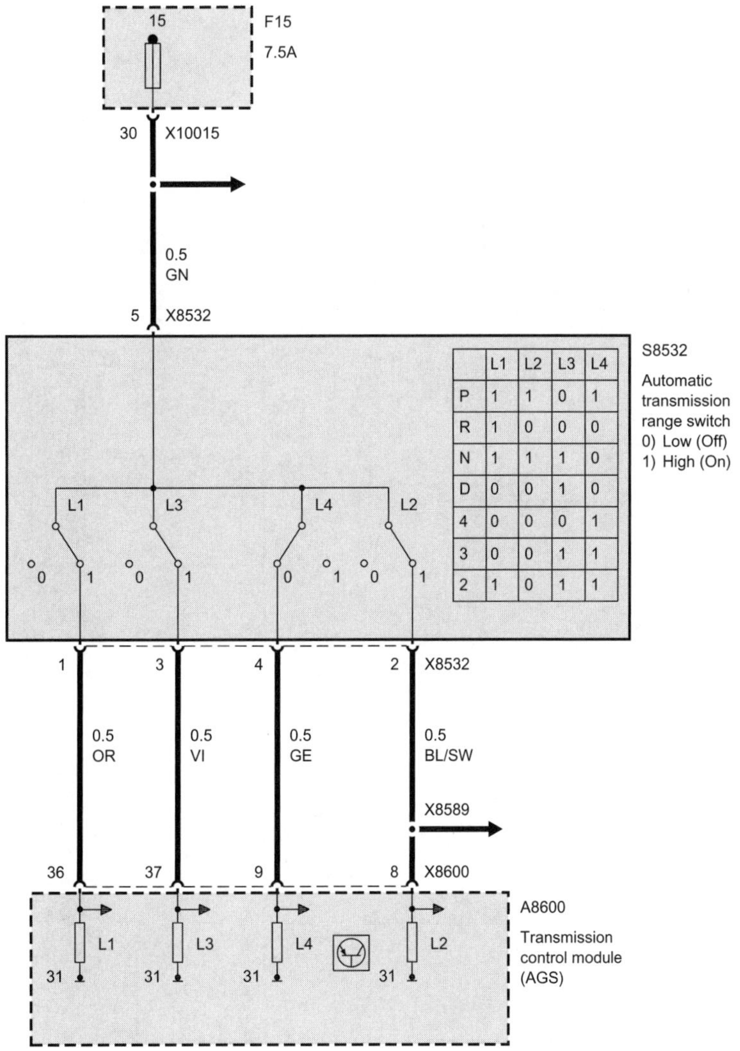

	L1	L2	L3	L4
P	1	1	0	1
R	1	0	0	0
N	1	1	1	0
D	0	0	1	0
4	0	0	0	1
3	0	0	1	1
2	1	0	1	1

502ELE0961

Transmission Electronics
Steptronic
(1 of 1)

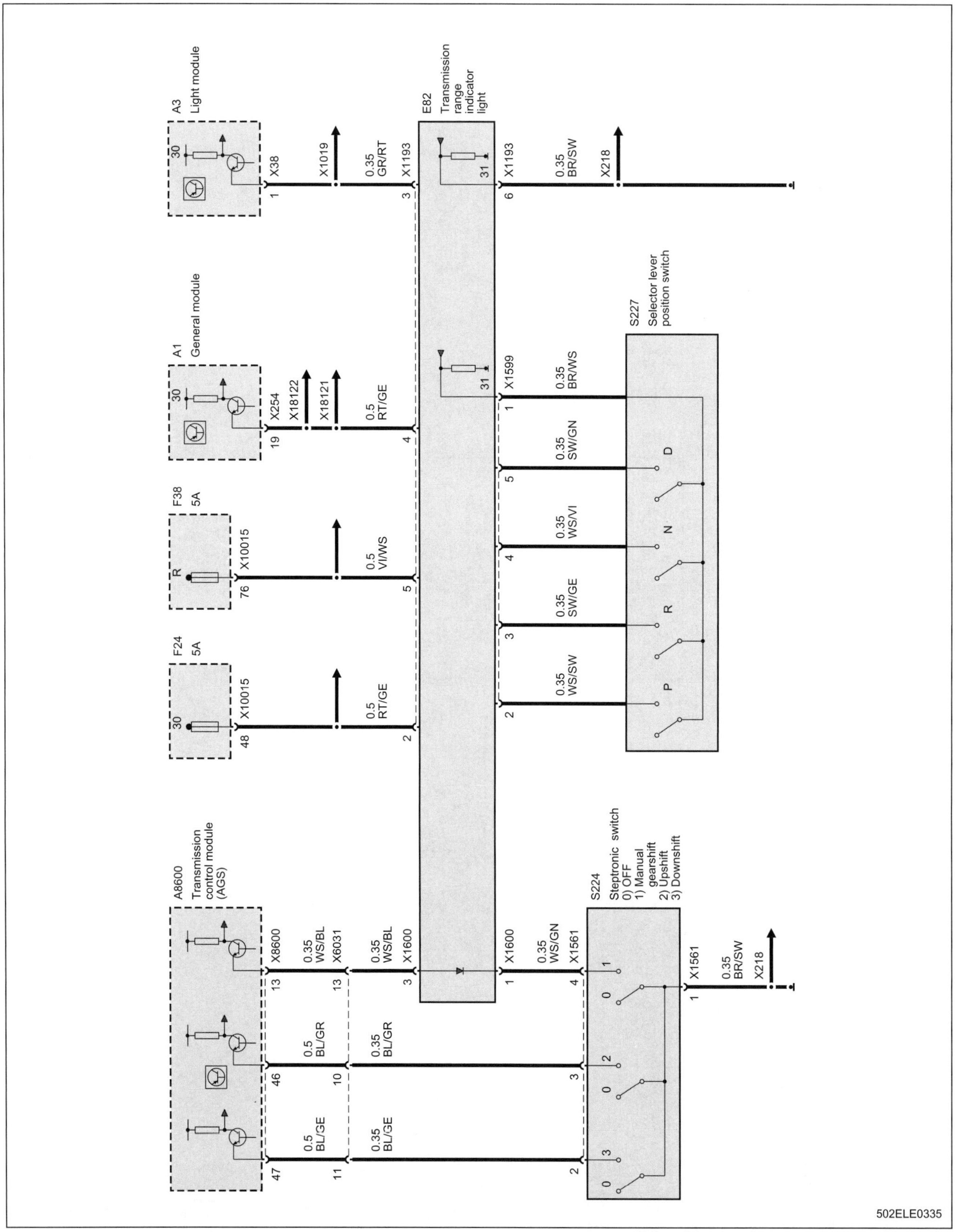
A3
Light module
A1
General module
F38
5A
F24
5A
A8600
Transmission control module (AGS)
E82
Transmission range indicator light
S227
Selector lever position switch
S224
Steptronic switch
0) OFF
1) Manual gearshift
2) Upshift
3) Downshift
X38
X1019
0.35 GR/RT
X1193
0.35 BR/SW
X218
X254
X18122
X18121
0.5 RT/GE
X1599
0.35 BR/WS
0.35 SW/GN
X10015
0.5 VI/WS
0.35 WS/VI
0.35 SW/GE
0.35 WS/SW
X8600
0.35 WS/BL
X6031
X1600
0.35 WS/GN
X1561
0.5 BL/GR
0.35 BL/GR
0.5 BL/GE
0.35 BL/GE
P
R
N
D
502ELE0335

Transmission Electronics
Transmission Control Module, Power
(1 of 1)

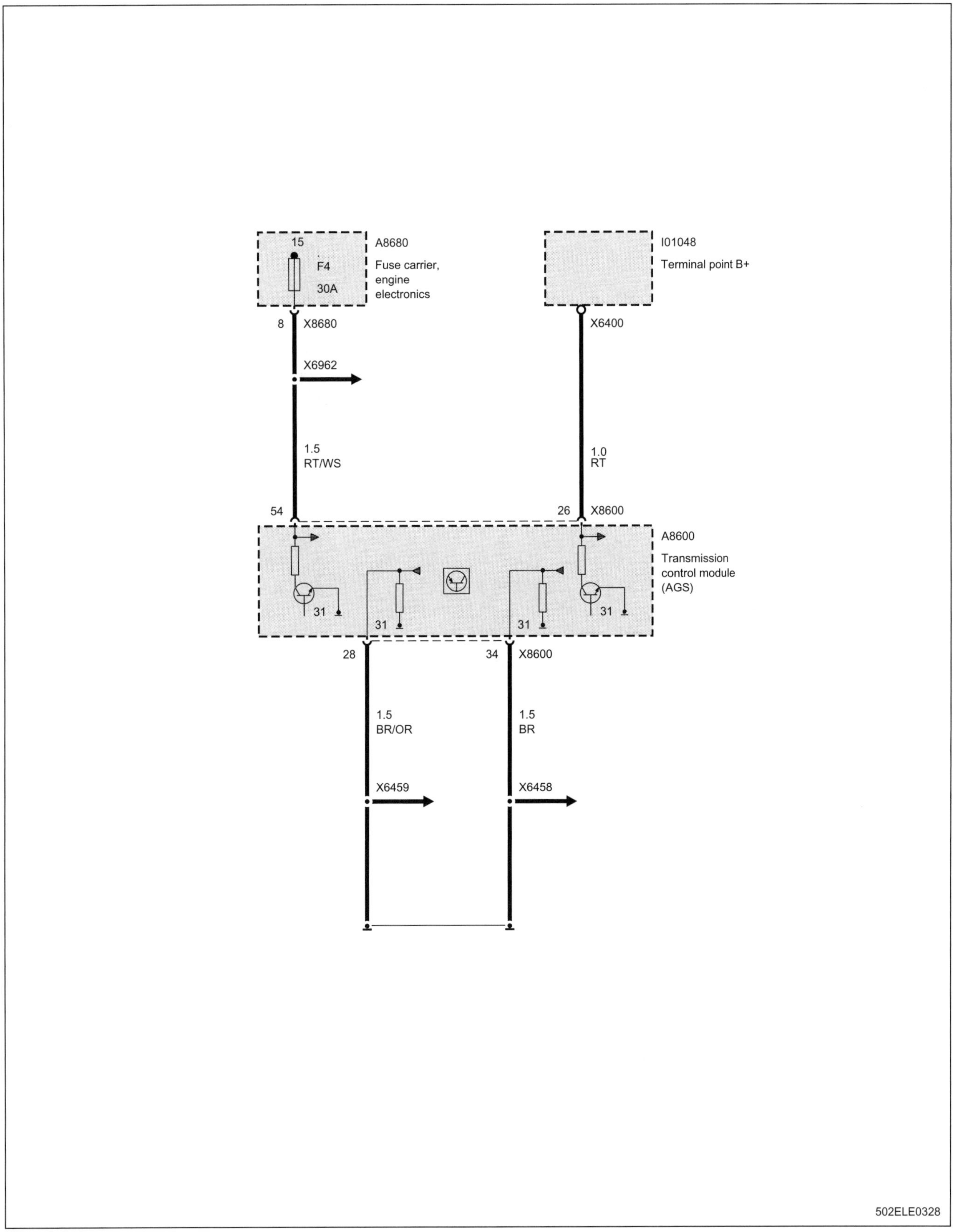

Warning Systems: Chimes
RDC (tire pressure control) (overview)
(1 of 2)

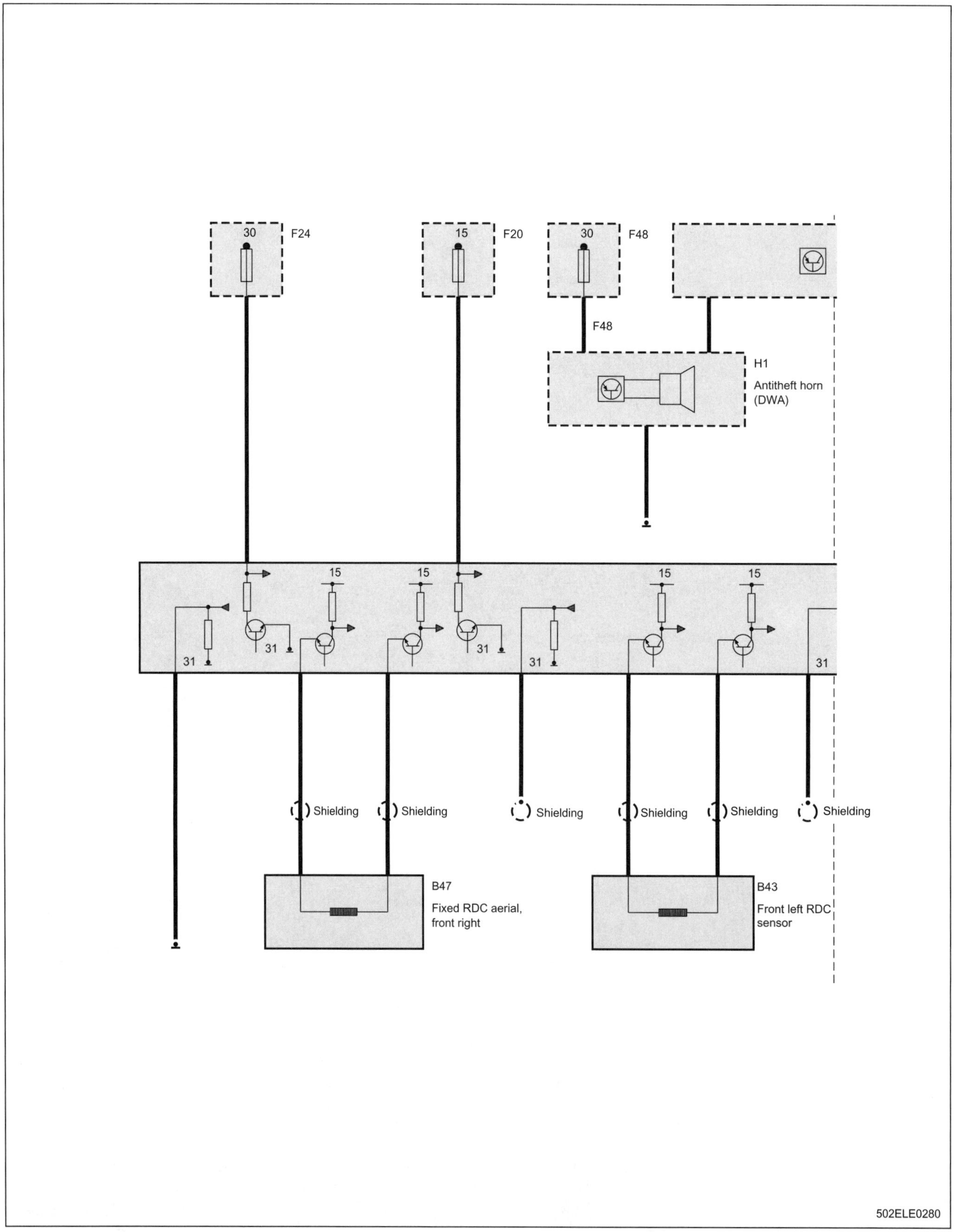

Warning Systems: Chimes
RDC (tire pressure control) (overview)
(2 of 2)

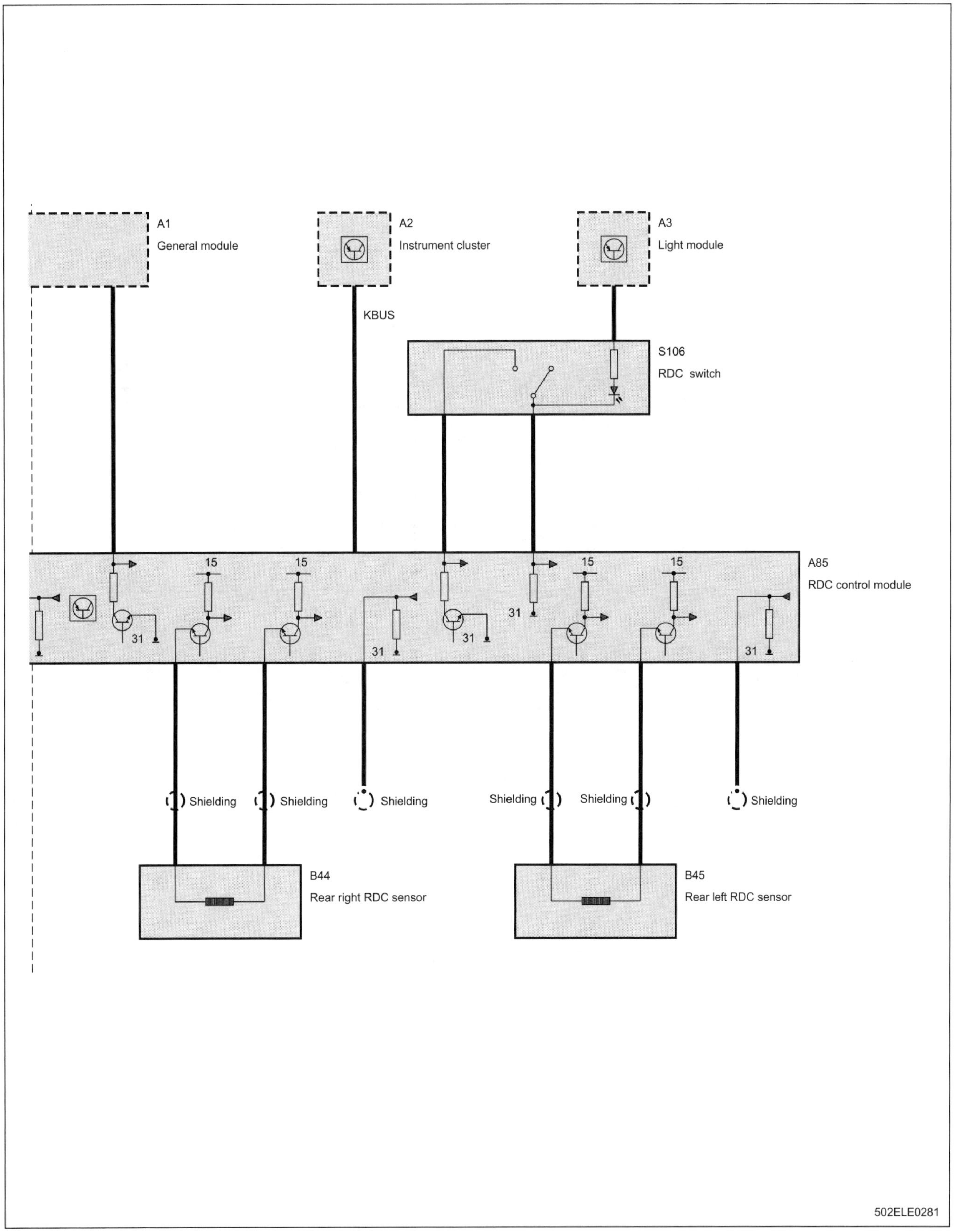

Warning Systems: Chimes
RDC (tire pressure control) control module (A85)
(1 of 3)

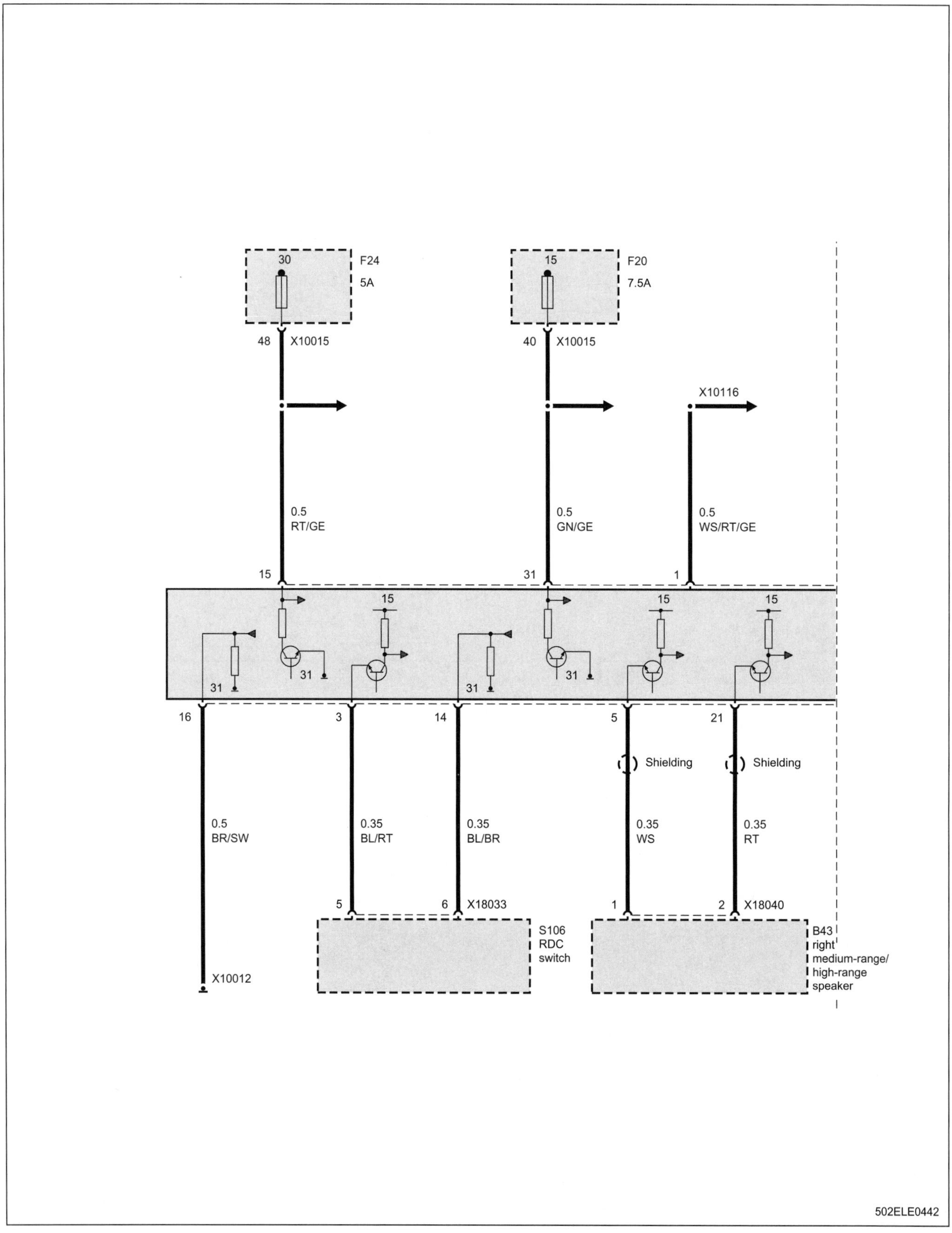

Warning Systems: Chimes
RDC (tire pressure control) control module (A85)
(2 of 3)

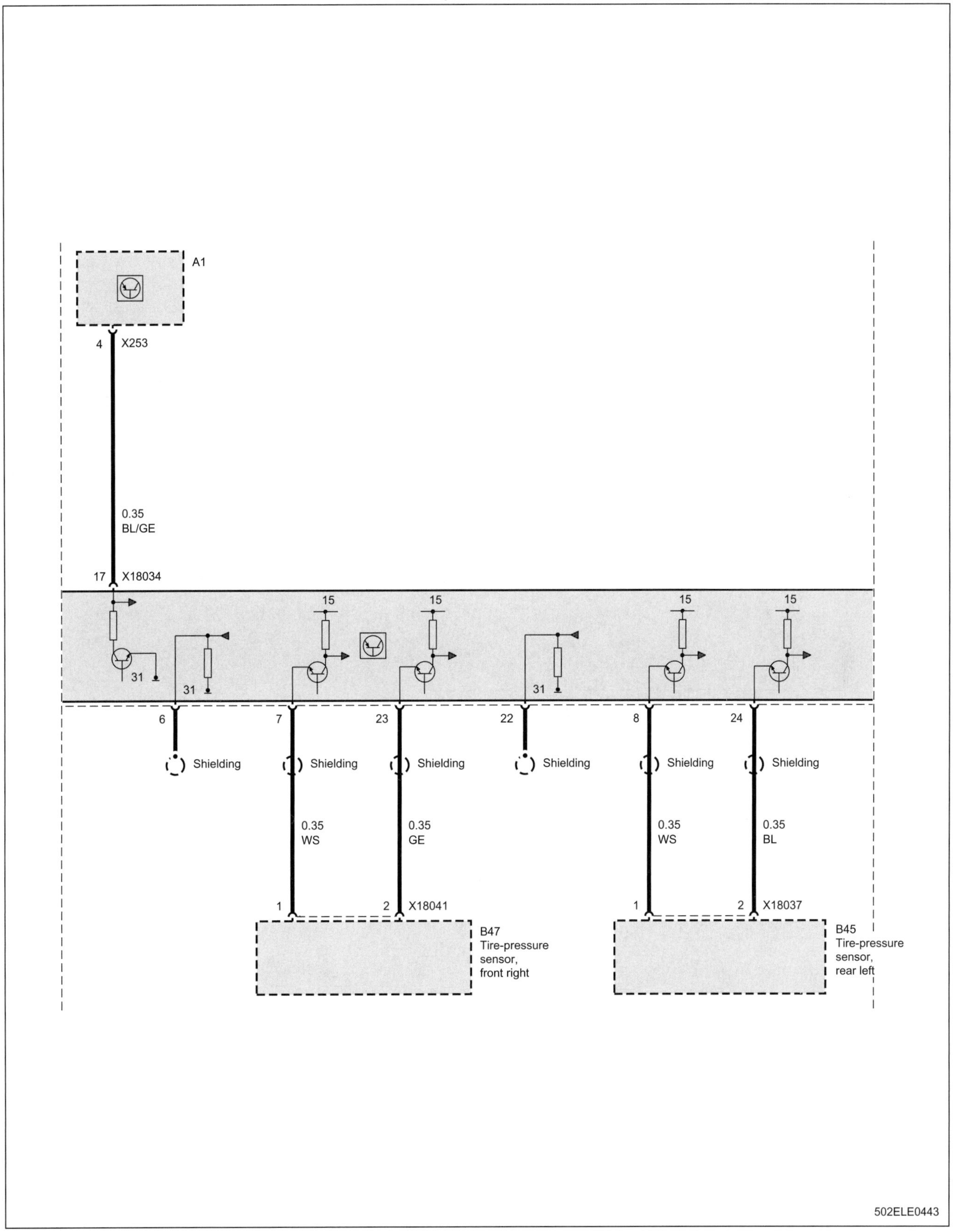

Warning Systems: Chimes

RDC (tire pressure control) control module (A85)

(3 of 3)

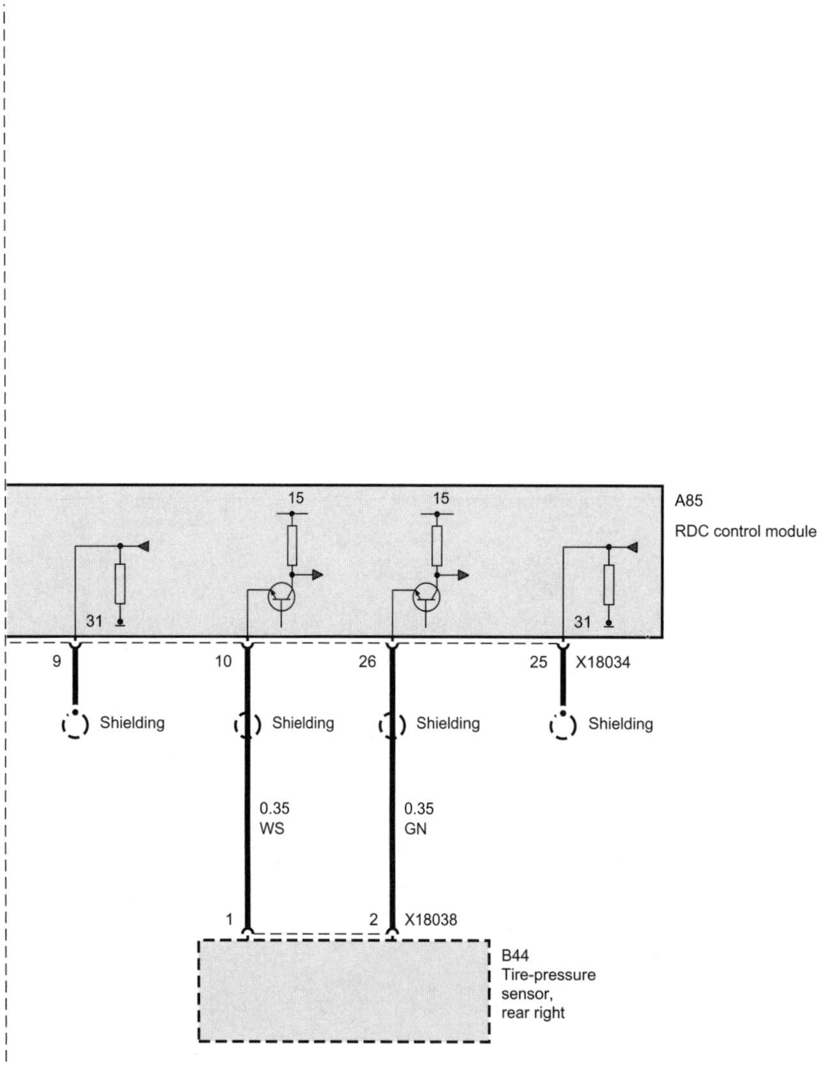

Warning Systems: Chimes
Chime module
(1 of 1)

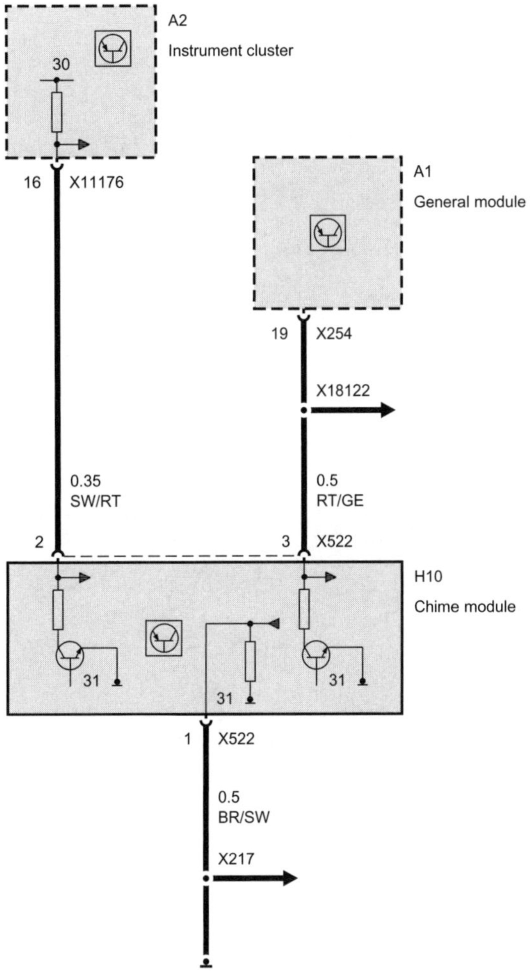

502ELE0027

Warning Systems: Chimes
RDC (tire pressure control) power
(1 of 1)

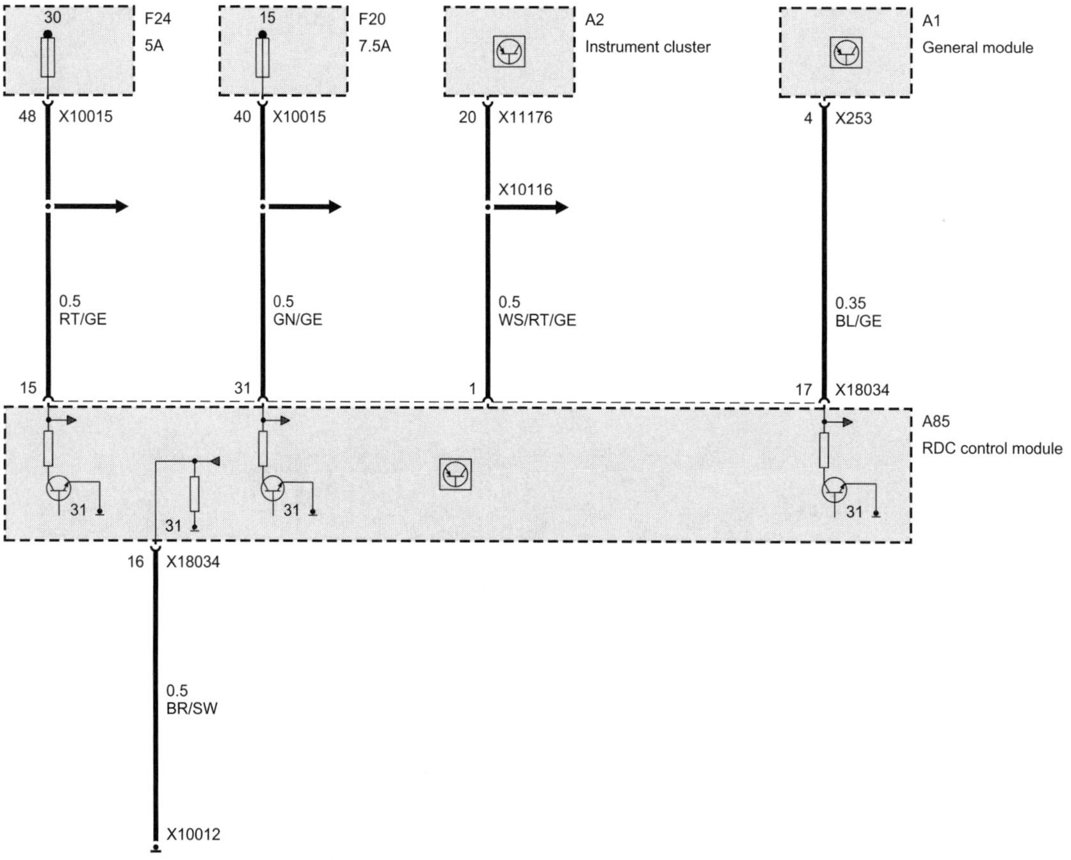

Warning Systems: Chimes
RDC (tire pressure control) sensor
(1 of 2)

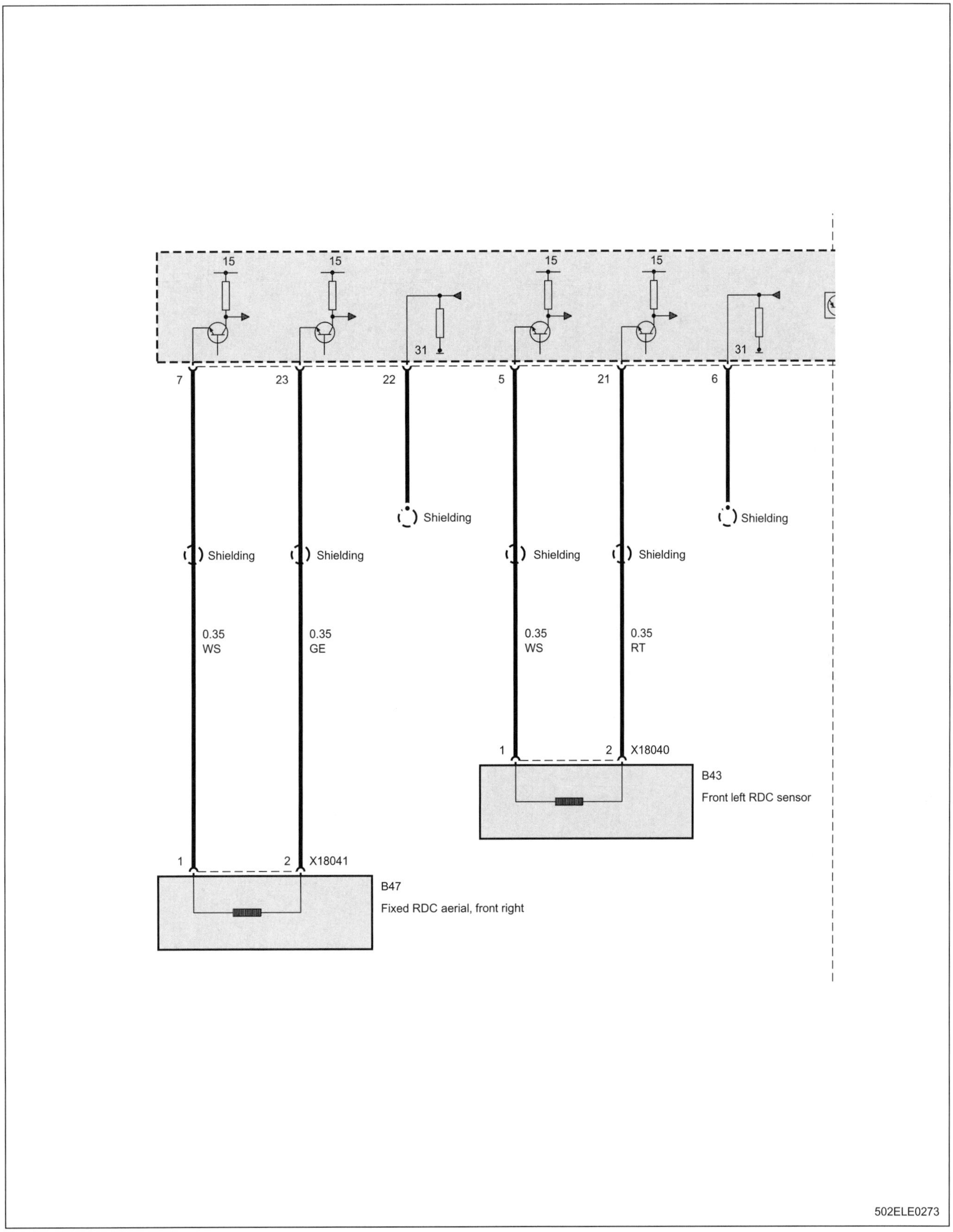

Warning Systems: Chimes
RDC (tire pressure control) sensor
(2 of 2)

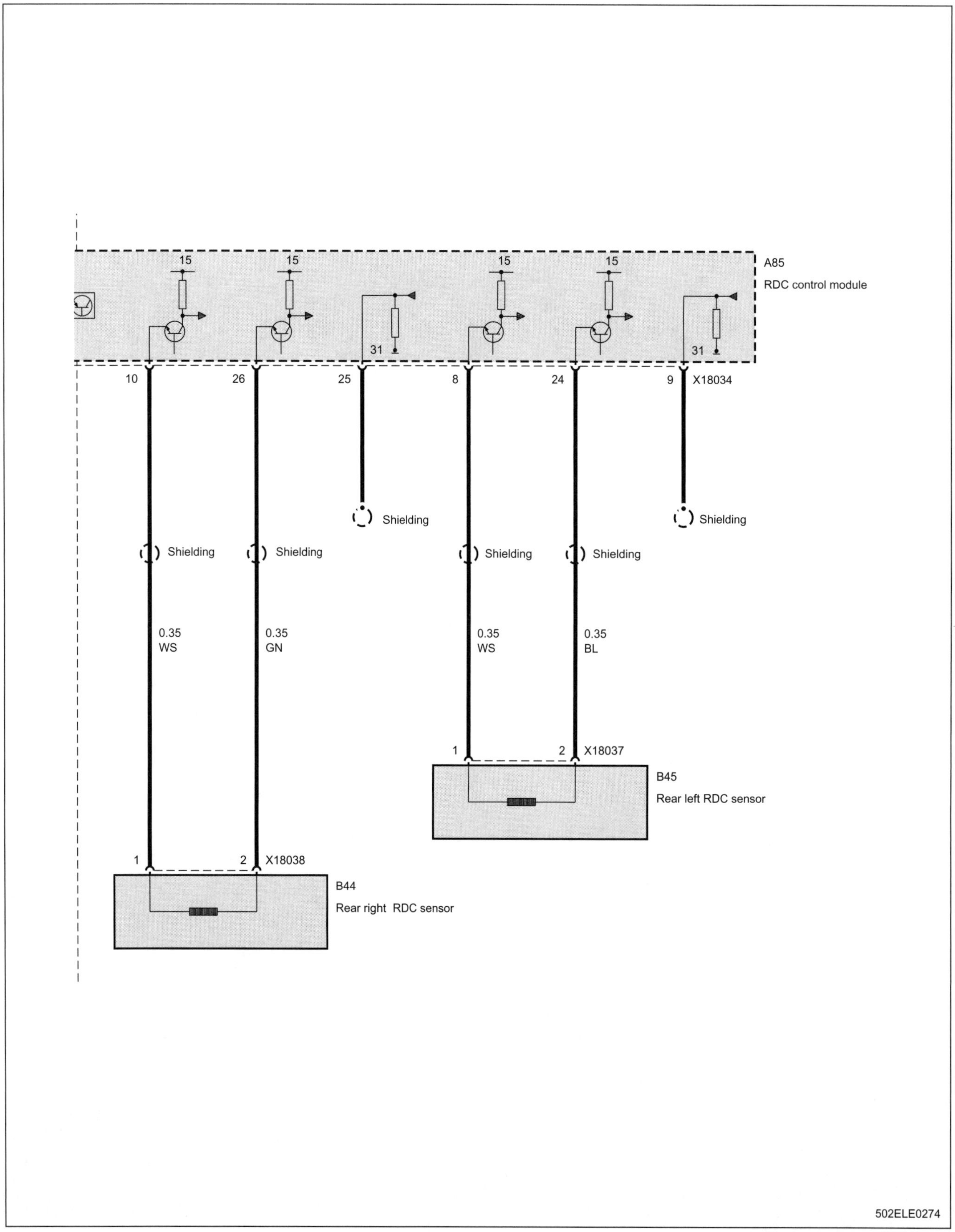

Warning Systems: Chimes
RDC (tire pressure control) switch
(1 of 1)

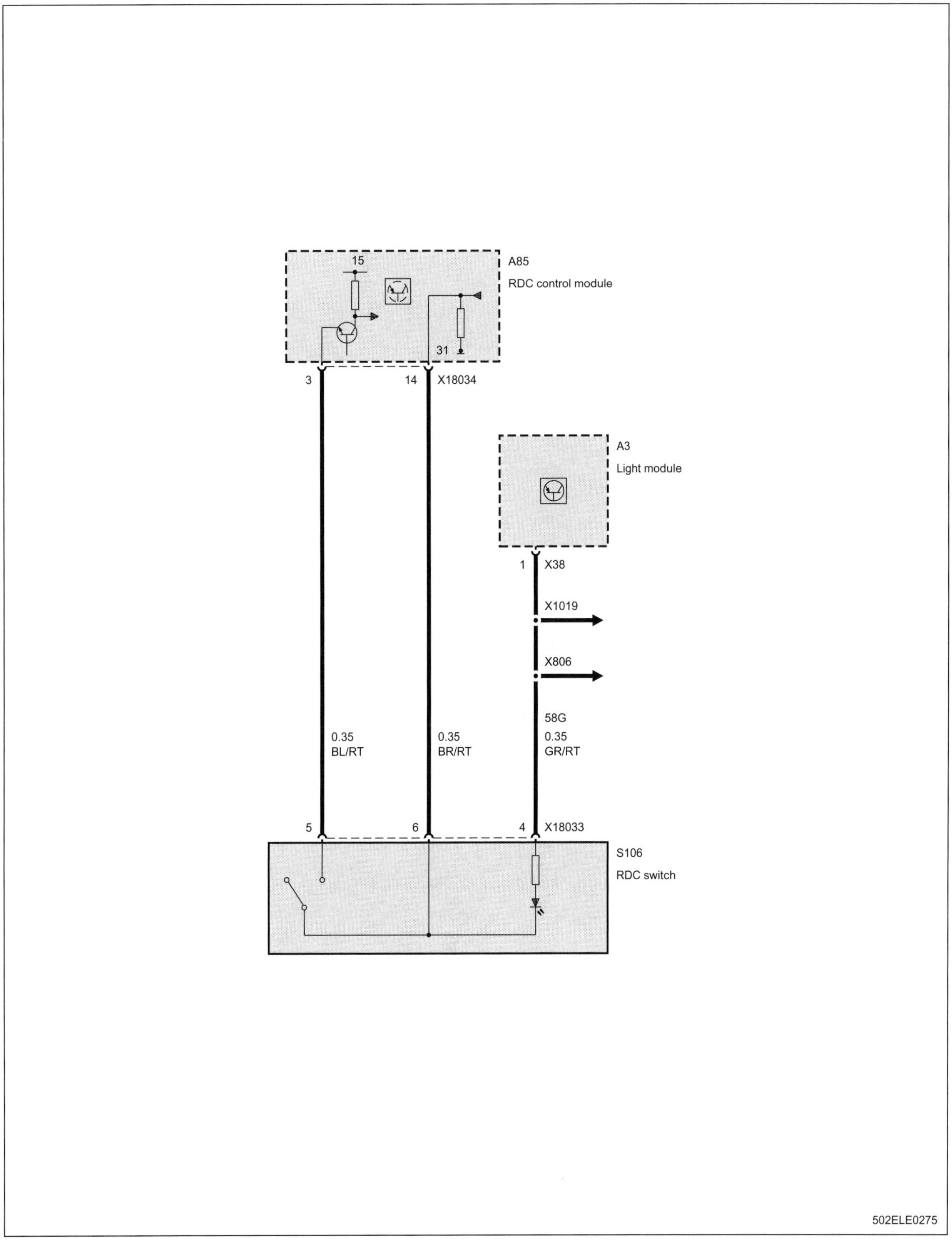

Wiper/Washer
Wipe and wash functions (overview)
(1 of 4)

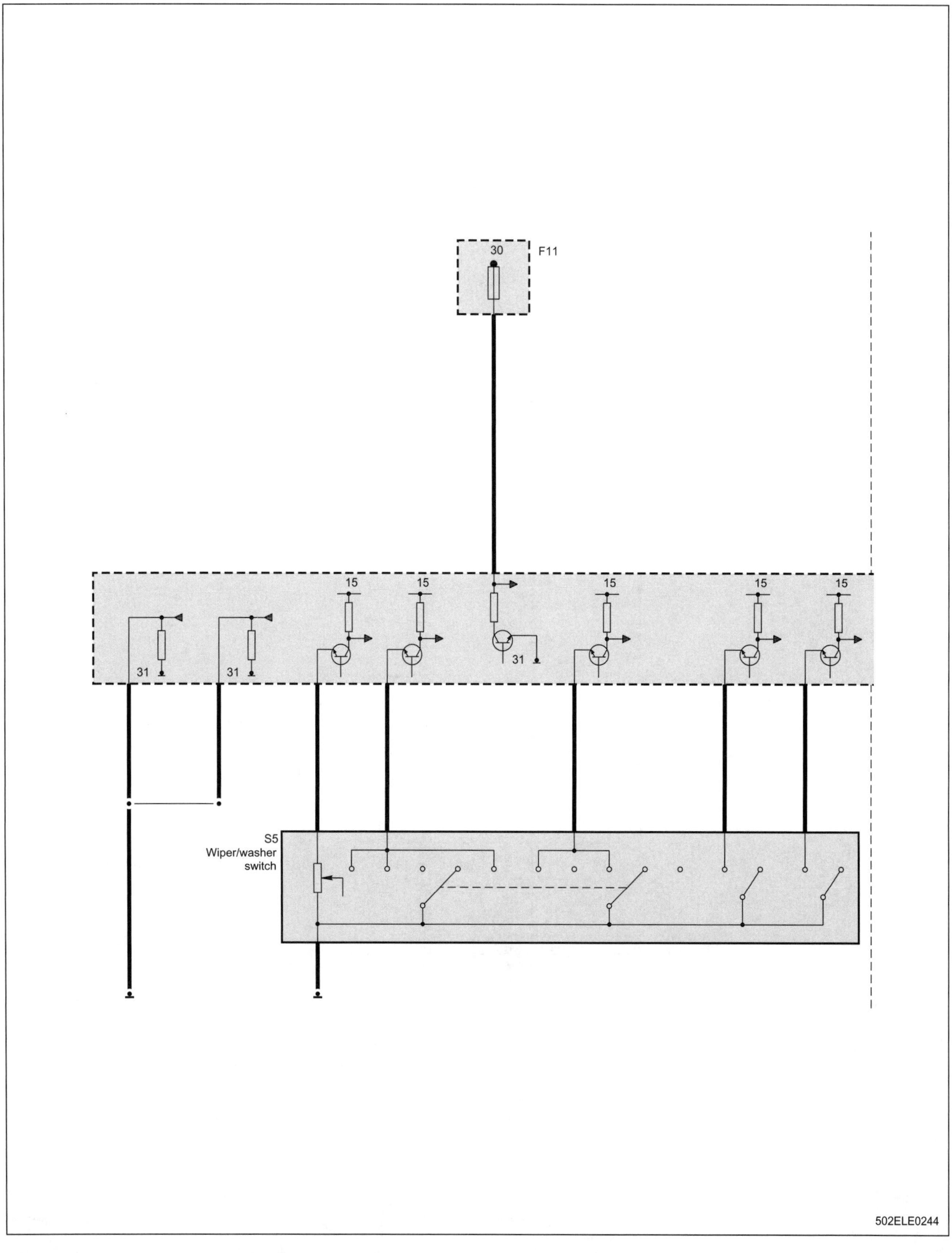

Wiper/Washer
Wipe and wash functions (overview)
(2 of 4)

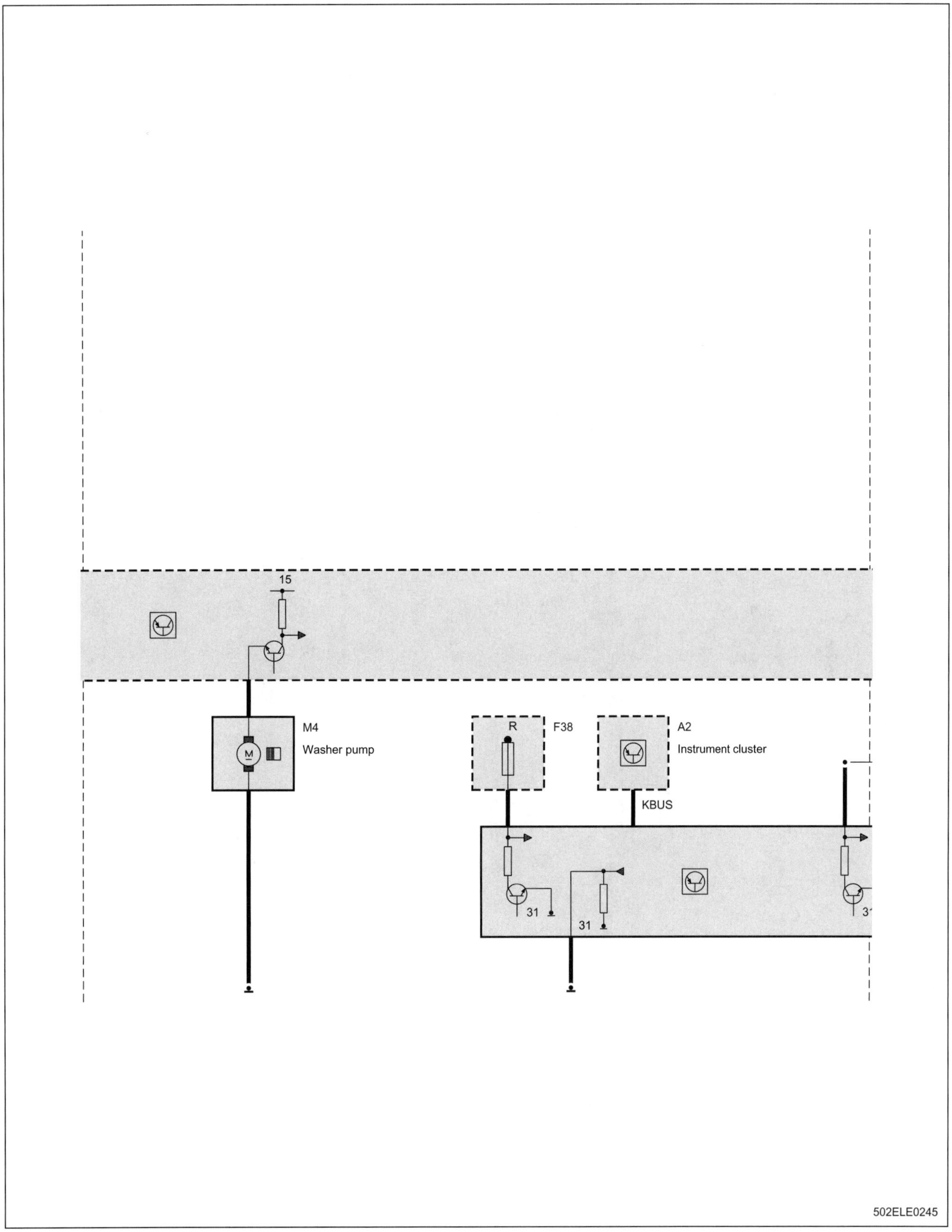

Wiper/Washer
Wipe and wash functions (overview)
(3 of 4)

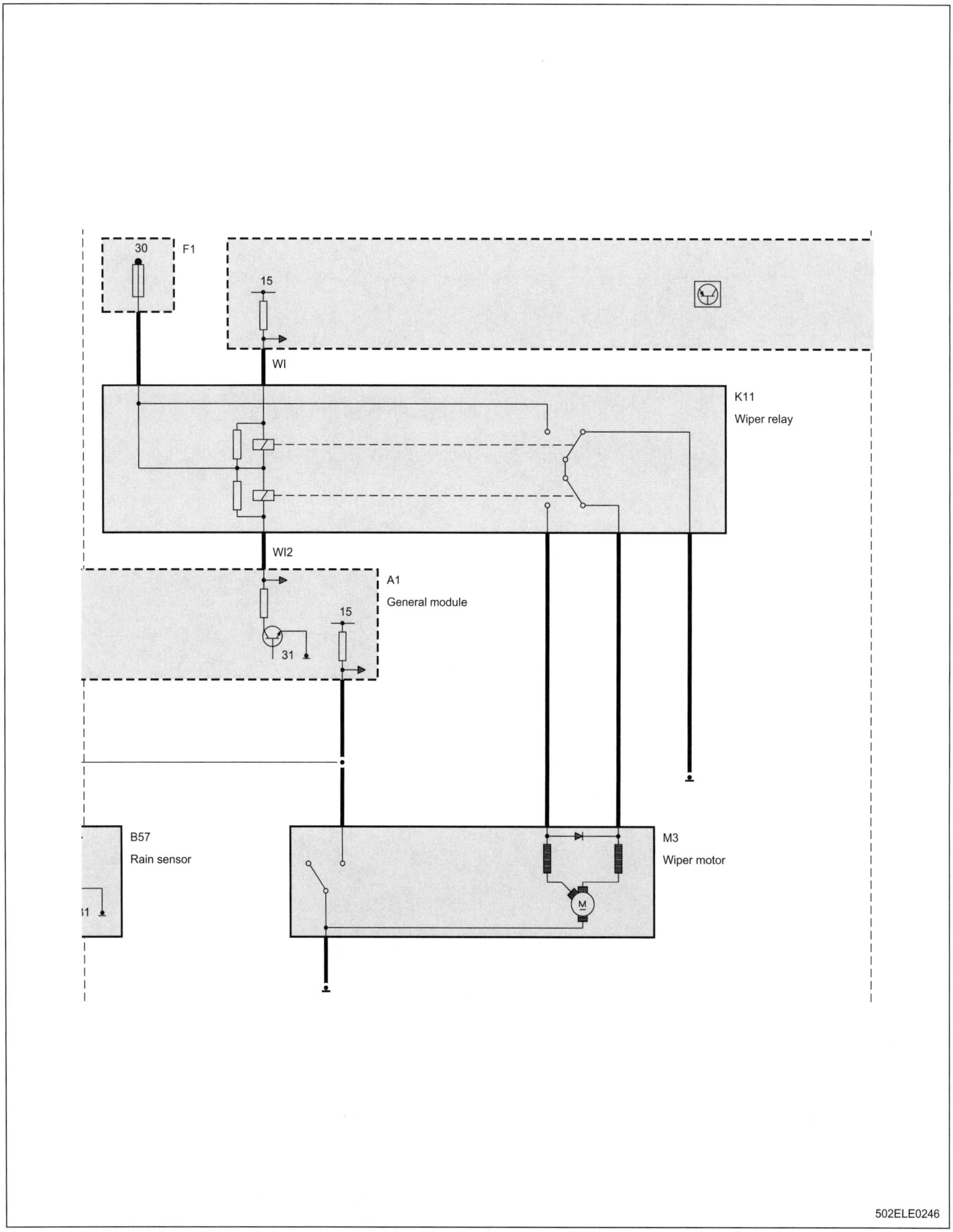

Wiper/Washer
Wipe and wash functions (overview)
(4 of 4)

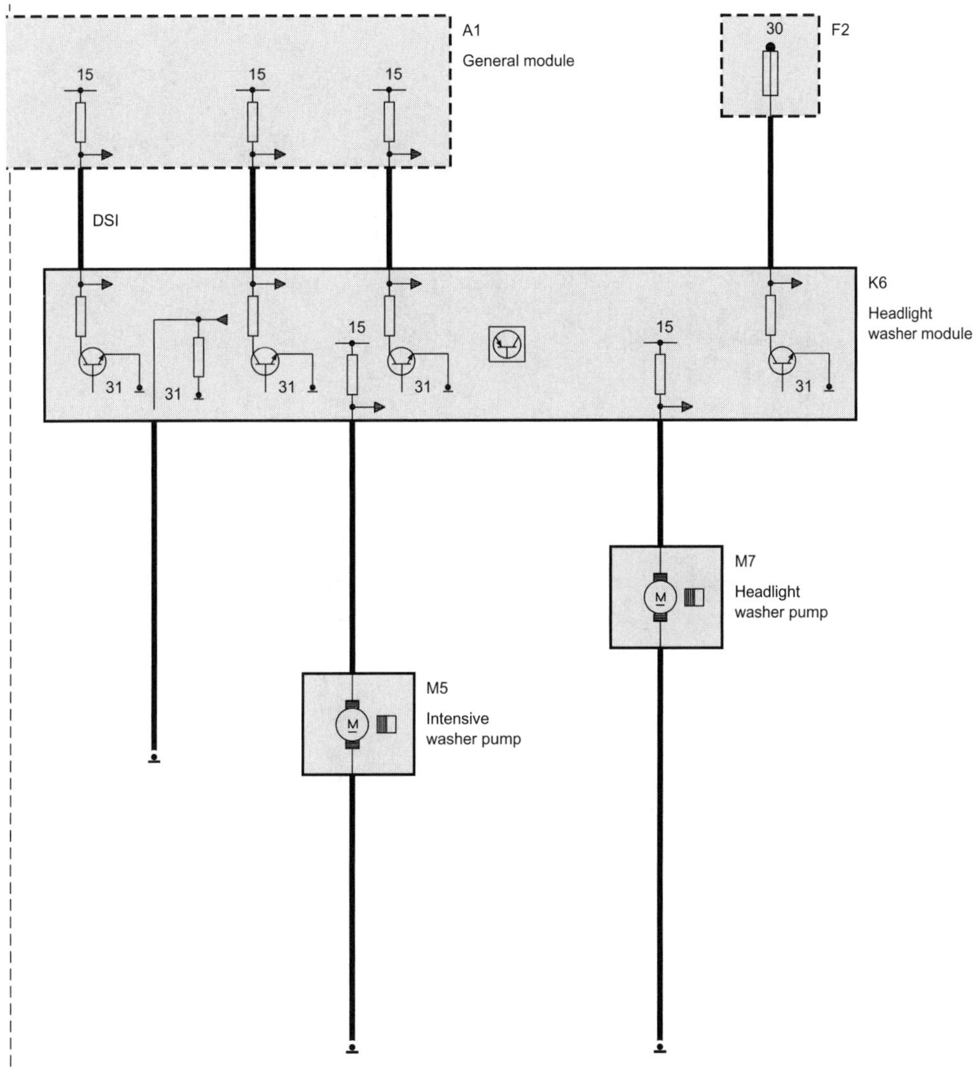

502ELE0247

Wiper/Washer
Headlight washer module (K6)
(1 of 1)

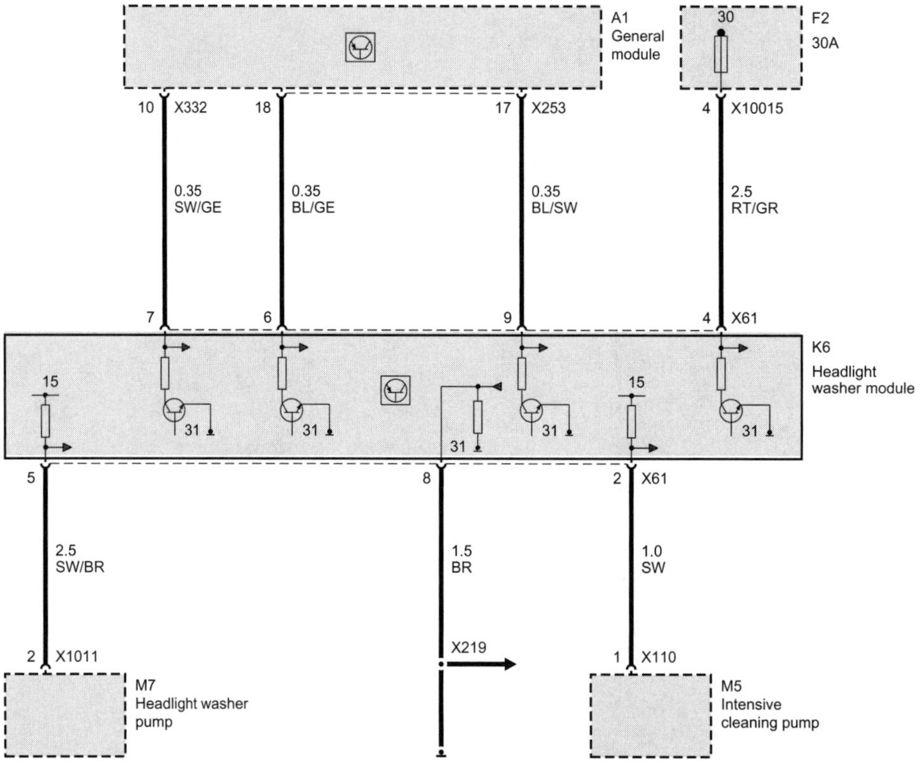

502ELE0960

Wiper/Washer
Rain sensor
(1 of 1)

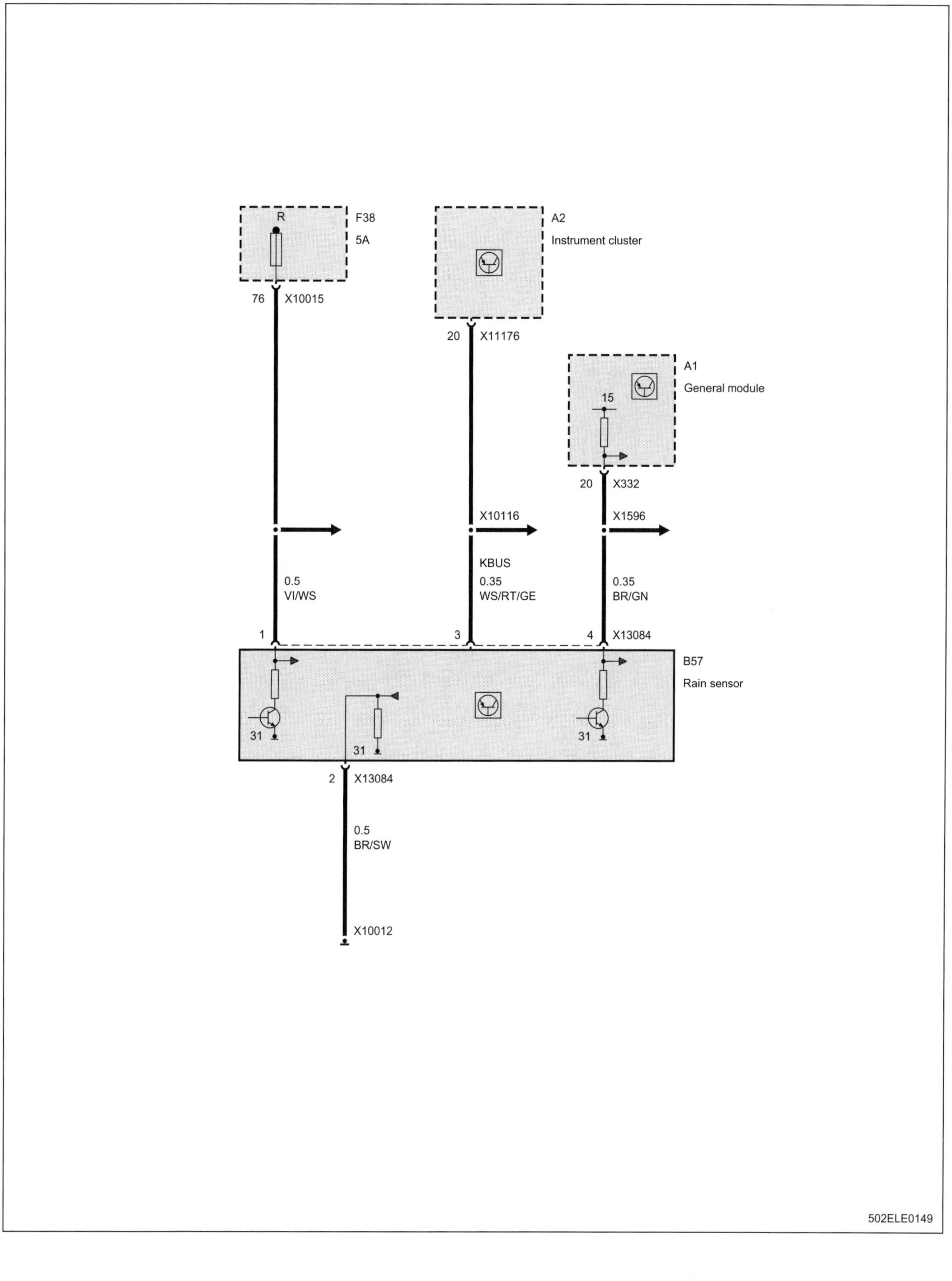
R
F38
5A
76
X10015
A2
Instrument cluster
20
X11176
A1
General module
15
20
X332
X10116
X1596
KBUS
0.5
VI/WS
0.35
WS/RT/GE
0.35
BR/GN
1
3
4
X13084
B57
Rain sensor
31
31
31
2
X13084
0.5
BR/SW
X10012
502ELE0149

Wiper/Washer
Headlight intensive wash
(1 of 1)

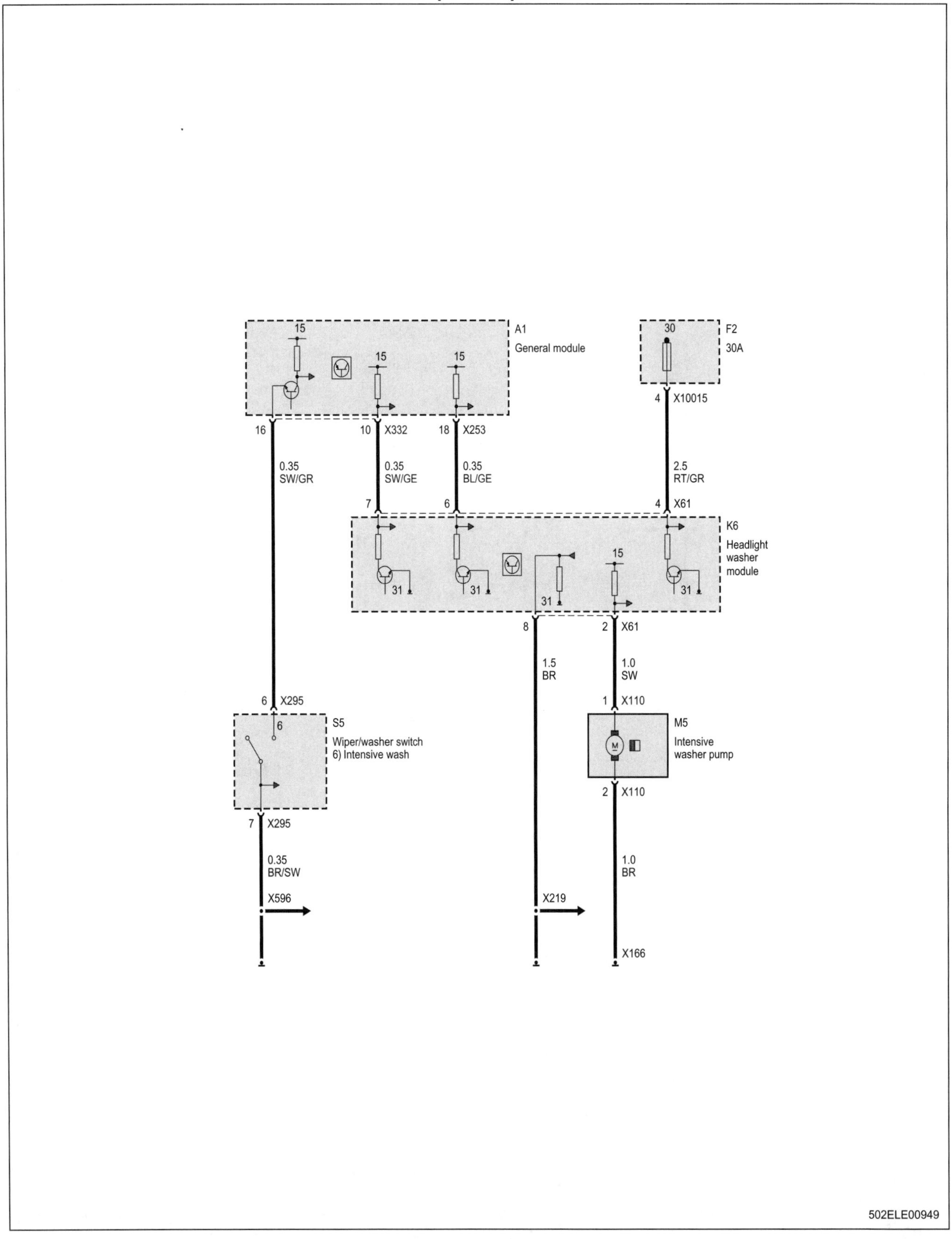
A1
General module
15
15
15
16
10 X332
18 X253
0.35
SW/GR
0.35
SW/GE
0.35
BL/GE
F2
30A
30
4 X10015
2.5
RT/GR
7
6
4 X61
K6
Headlight
washer
module
31
31
31
15
31
8
2 X61
1.5
BR
1.0
SW
6 X295
S5
Wiper/washer switch
6) Intensive wash
6
7 X295
0.35
BR/SW
X596
1 X110
M5
Intensive
washer pump
M
2 X110
1.0
BR
X219
X166
502ELE00949

Wiper/Washer
Headlight washer system
(1 of 1)

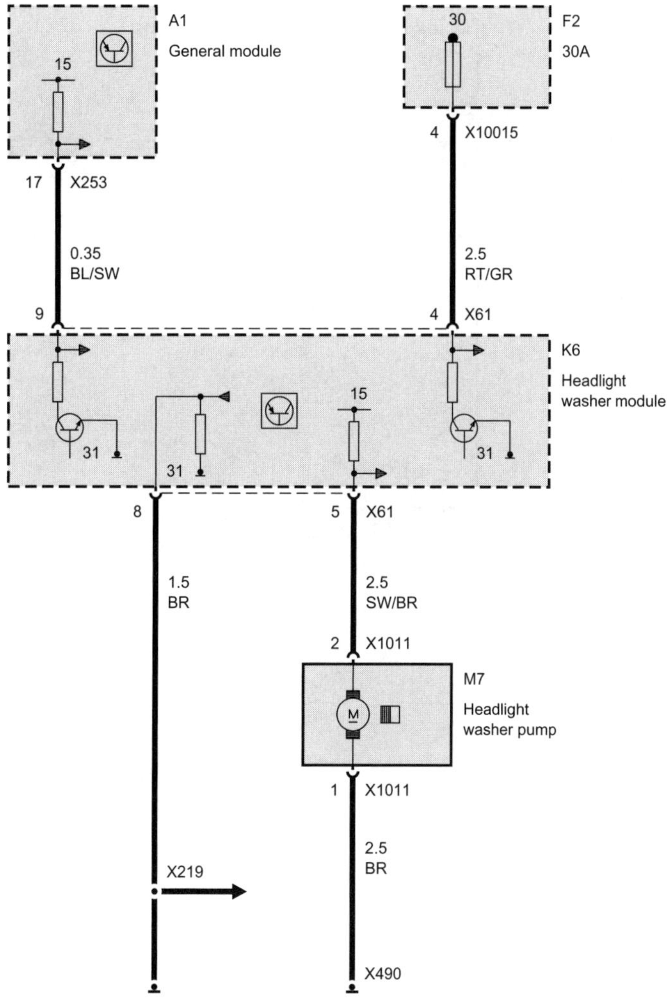

502ELE0952

Wiper/Washer
Wiper-washer control
(1 of 1)

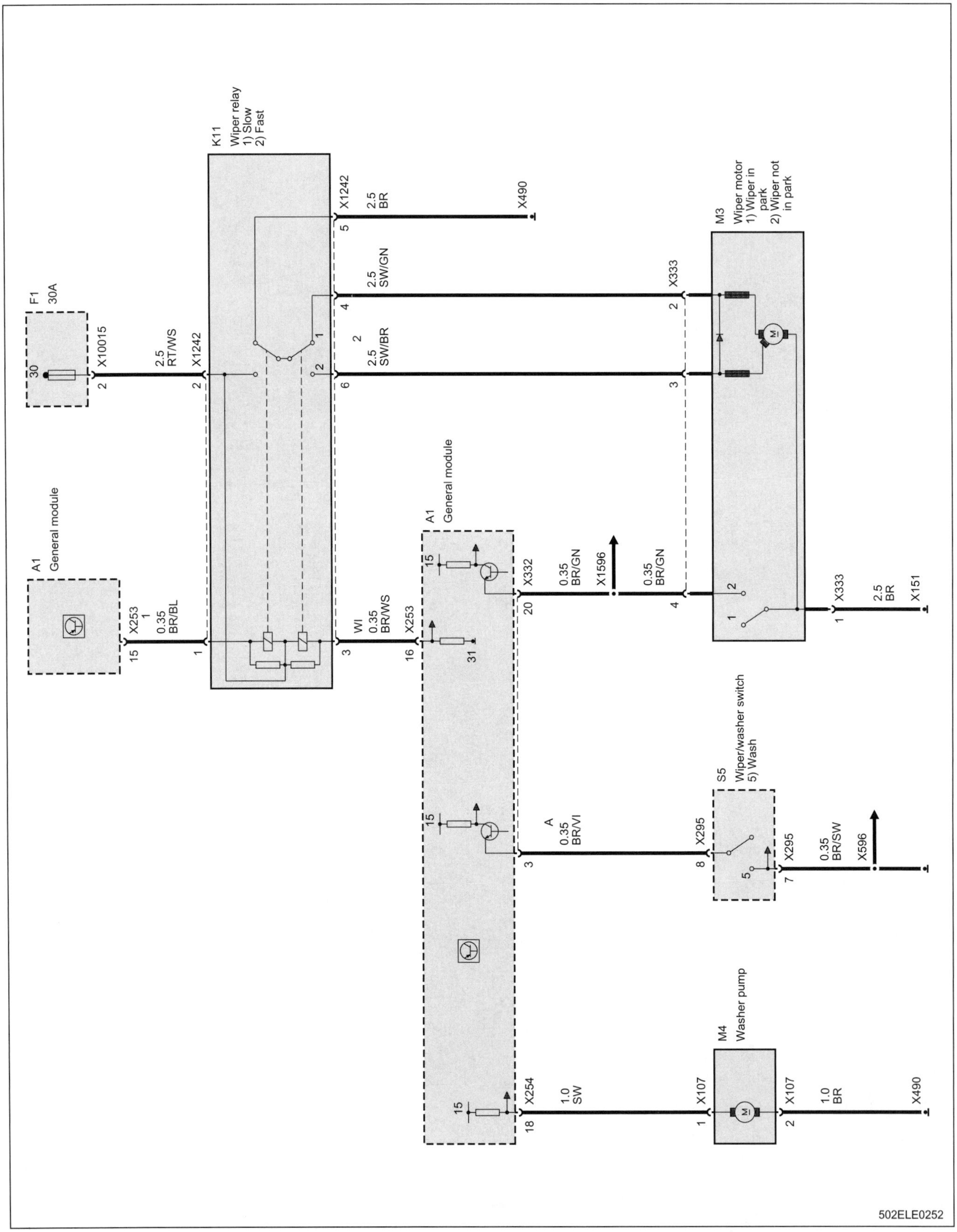
F1
30A
30
X10015
2.5
RT/WS
X1242
K11
Wiper relay
1) Slow
2) Fast
X1242
2.5
BR
X490
2.5
SW/GN
2.5
SW/BR
X333
M3
Wiper motor
1) Wiper in park
2) Wiper not in park
A1
General module
X253
0.35
BR/BL
WI
0.35
BR/WS
X253
A1
General module
X332
0.35
BR/GN
X1596
0.35
BR/GN
X333
2.5
BR
X151
A
0.35
BR/VI
X295
S5
Wiper/washer switch
5) Wash
X295
0.35
BR/SW
X596
M4
Washer pump
X254
1.0
SW
X107
X107
1.0
BR
X490
502ELE0252

Wiper/Washer
Wiper switch
(1 of 1)

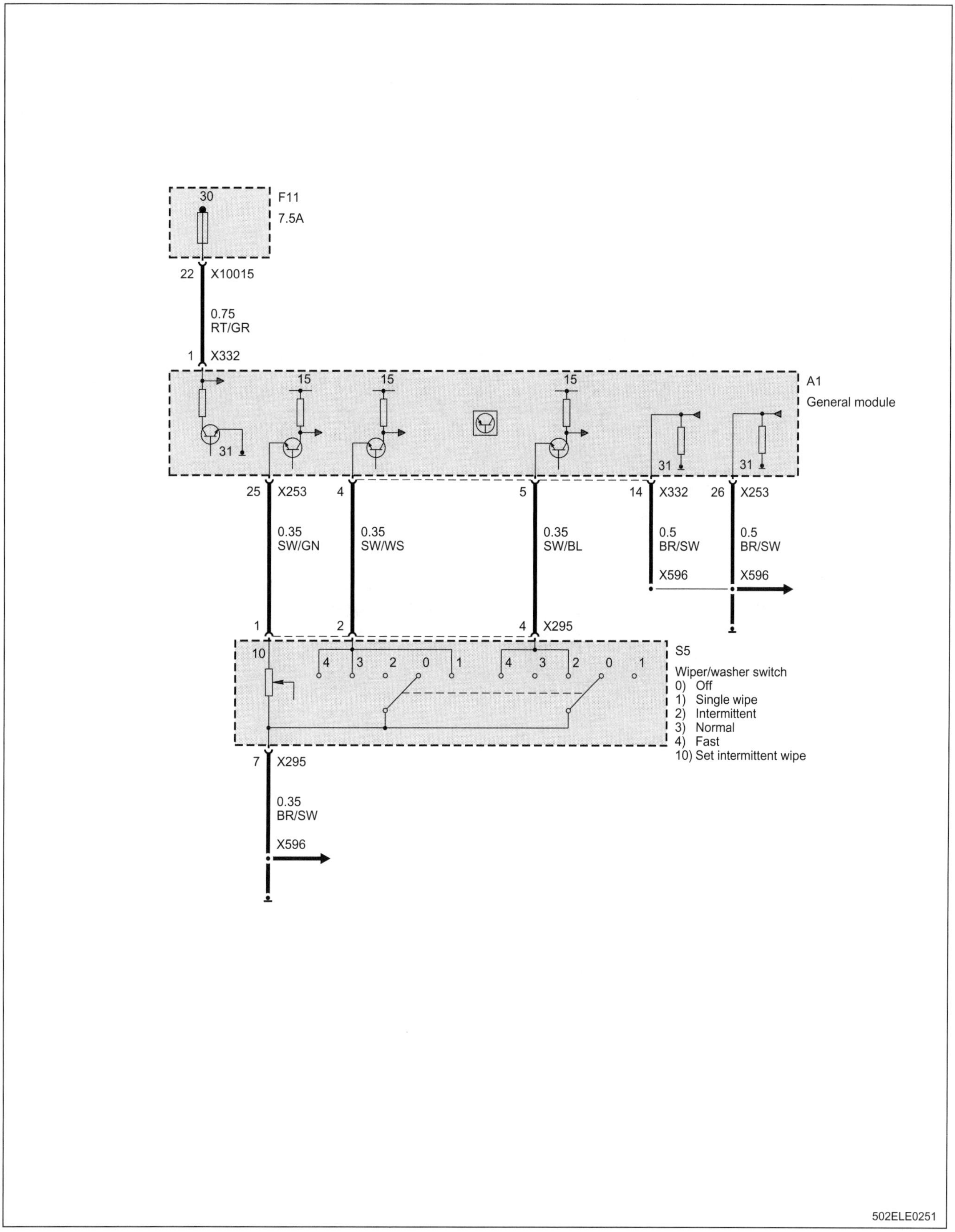
30
F11
7.5A
22
X10015
0.75
RT/GR
1
X332
15
15
15
A1
General module
31
31
31
25
X253
4
5
14
X332
26
X253
0.35
SW/GN
0.35
SW/WS
0.35
SW/BL
0.5
BR/SW
0.5
BR/SW
X596
X596
1
2
4
X295
10
4 3 2 0 1
4 3 2 0 1
S5
Wiper/washer switch
0) Off
1) Single wipe
2) Intermittent
3) Normal
4) Fast
10) Set intermittent wipe
7
X295
0.35
BR/SW
X596
502ELE0251

Wiper/Washer
Washer-nozzle heating

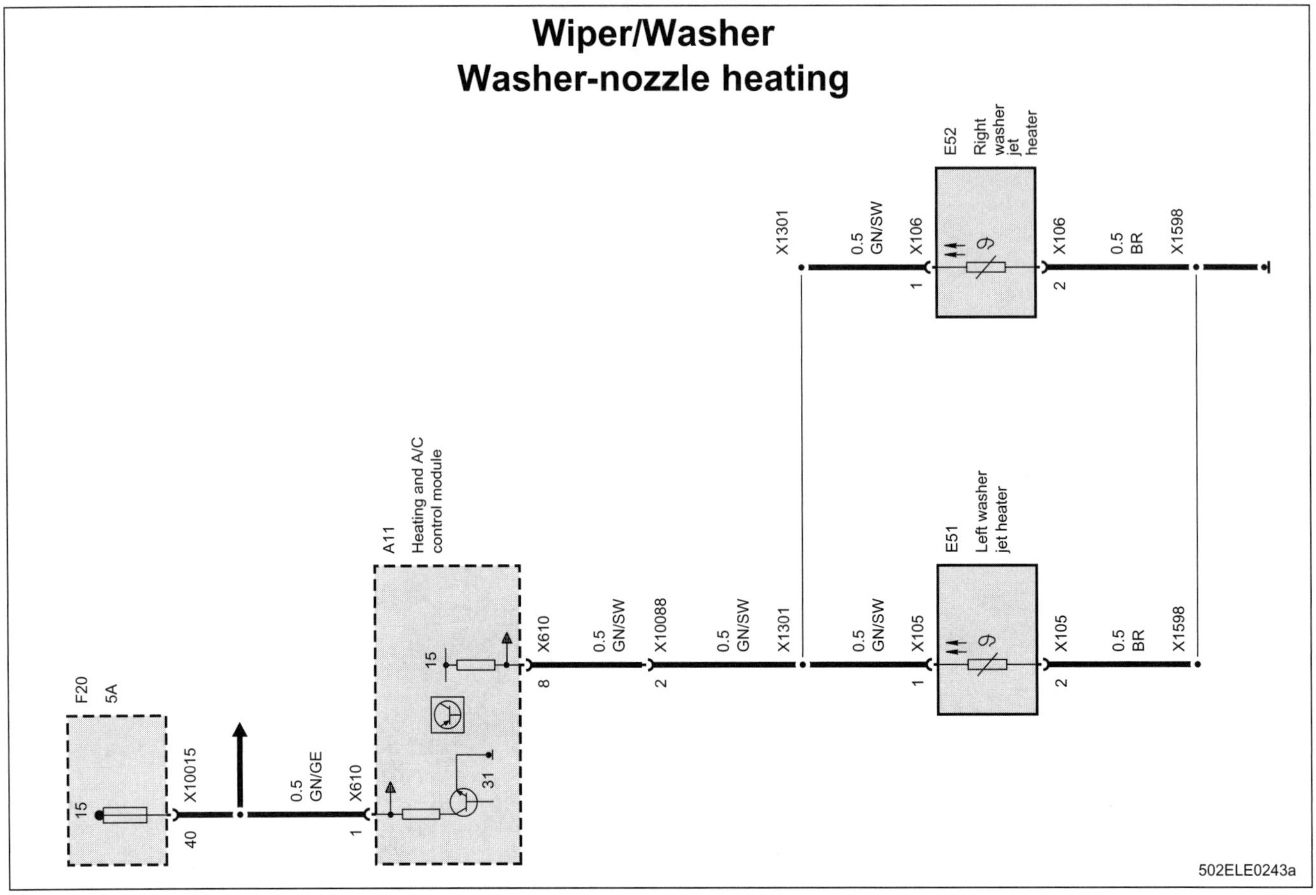

Air Conditioning and Heating
Water valve assembly

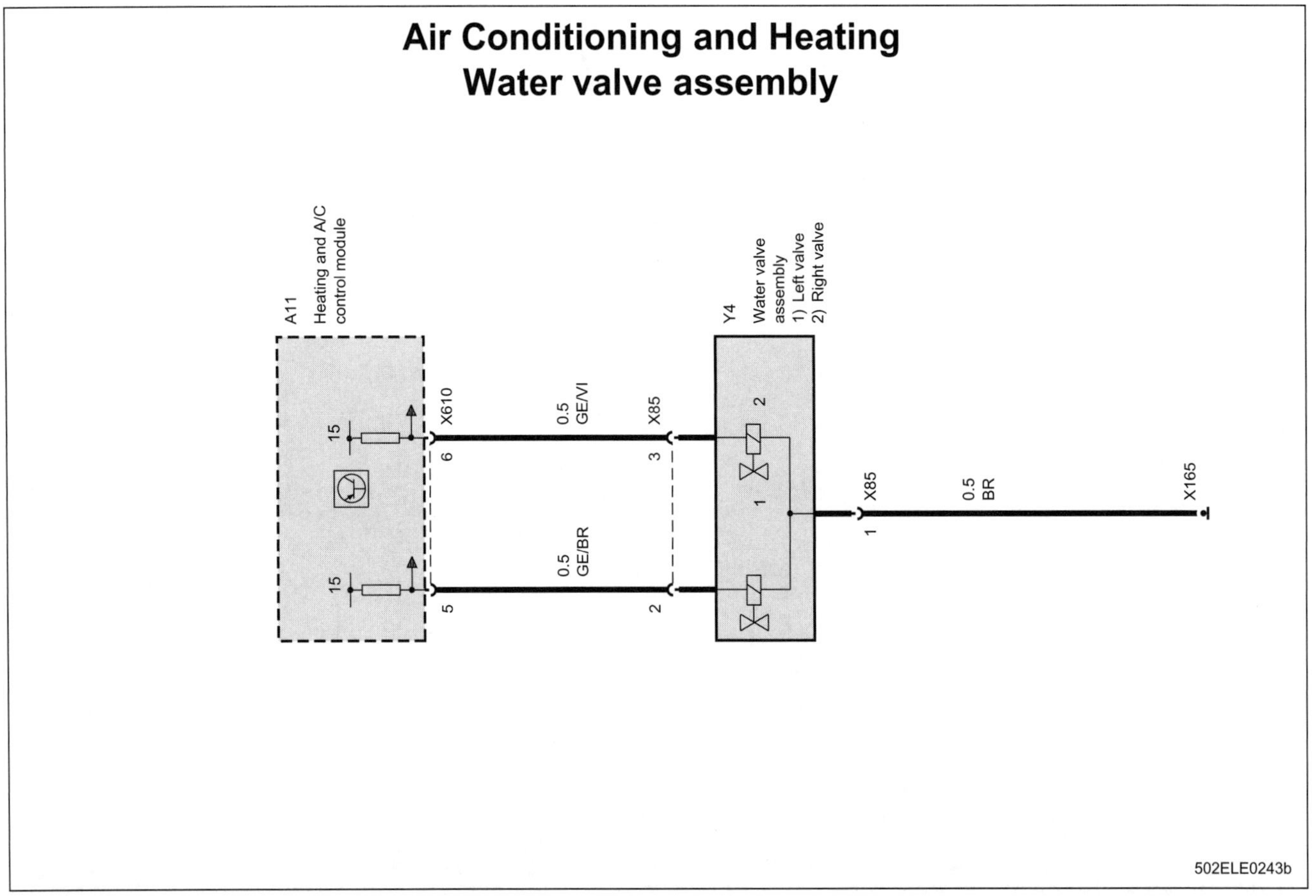

Ground Distribution
X46 Ground
(1 of 1)

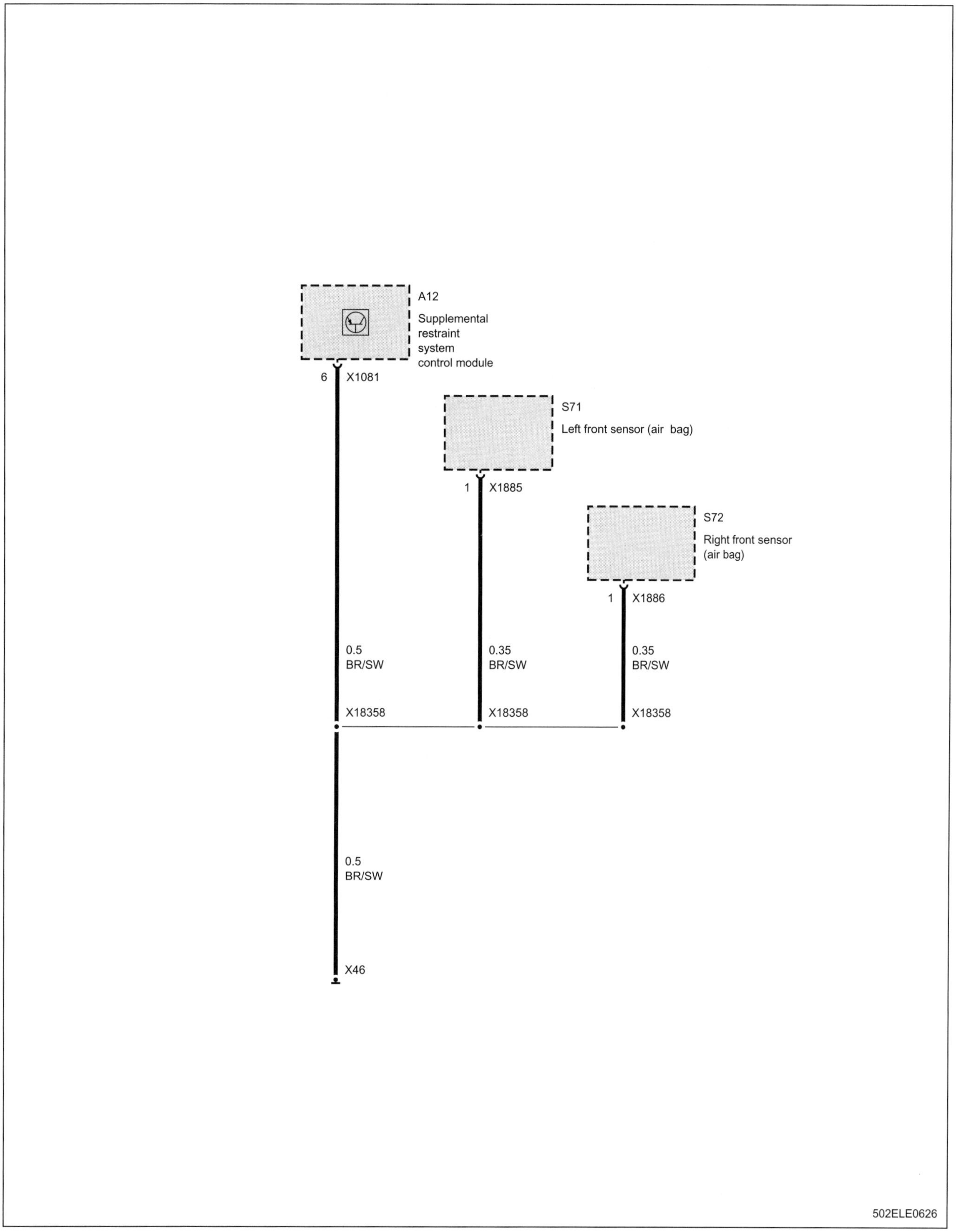
A12
Supplemental restraint system control module
6
X1081
S71
Left front sensor (air bag)
1
X1885
S72
Right front sensor (air bag)
1
X1886
0.5
BR/SW
0.35
BR/SW
0.35
BR/SW
X18358
X18358
X18358
0.5
BR/SW
X46
502ELE0626

Ground Distribution
X151 Ground
(1 of 1)

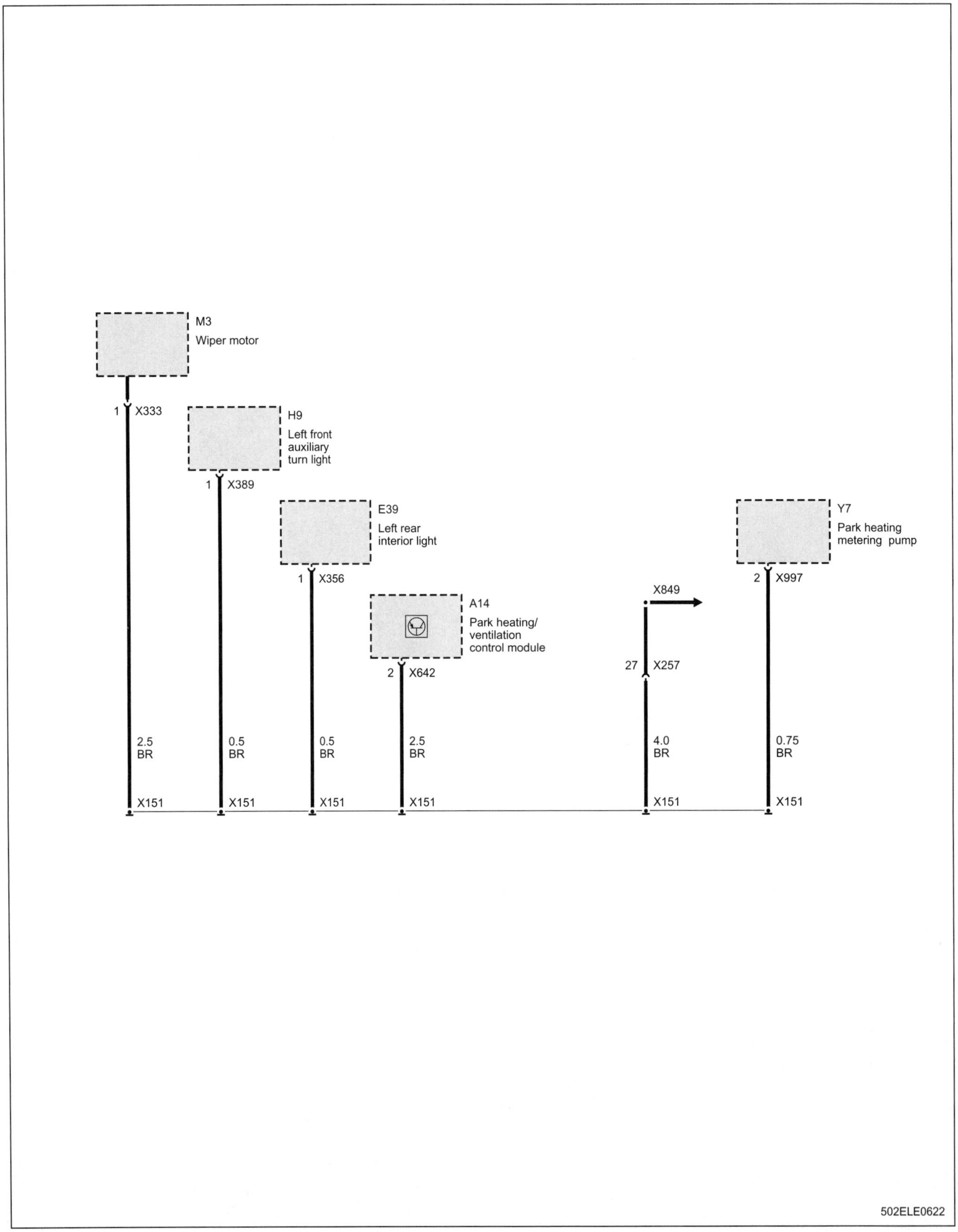
M3
Wiper motor
1 X333
2.5
BR
X151
H9
Left front
auxiliary
turn light
1 X389
0.5
BR
X151
E39
Left rear
interior light
1 X356
0.5
BR
X151
A14
Park heating/
ventilation
control module
2 X642
2.5
BR
X151
X849
27 X257
4.0
BR
X151
Y7
Park heating
metering pump
2 X997
0.75
BR
X151
502ELE0622

Ground Distribution
X166 Ground
(1 of 1)

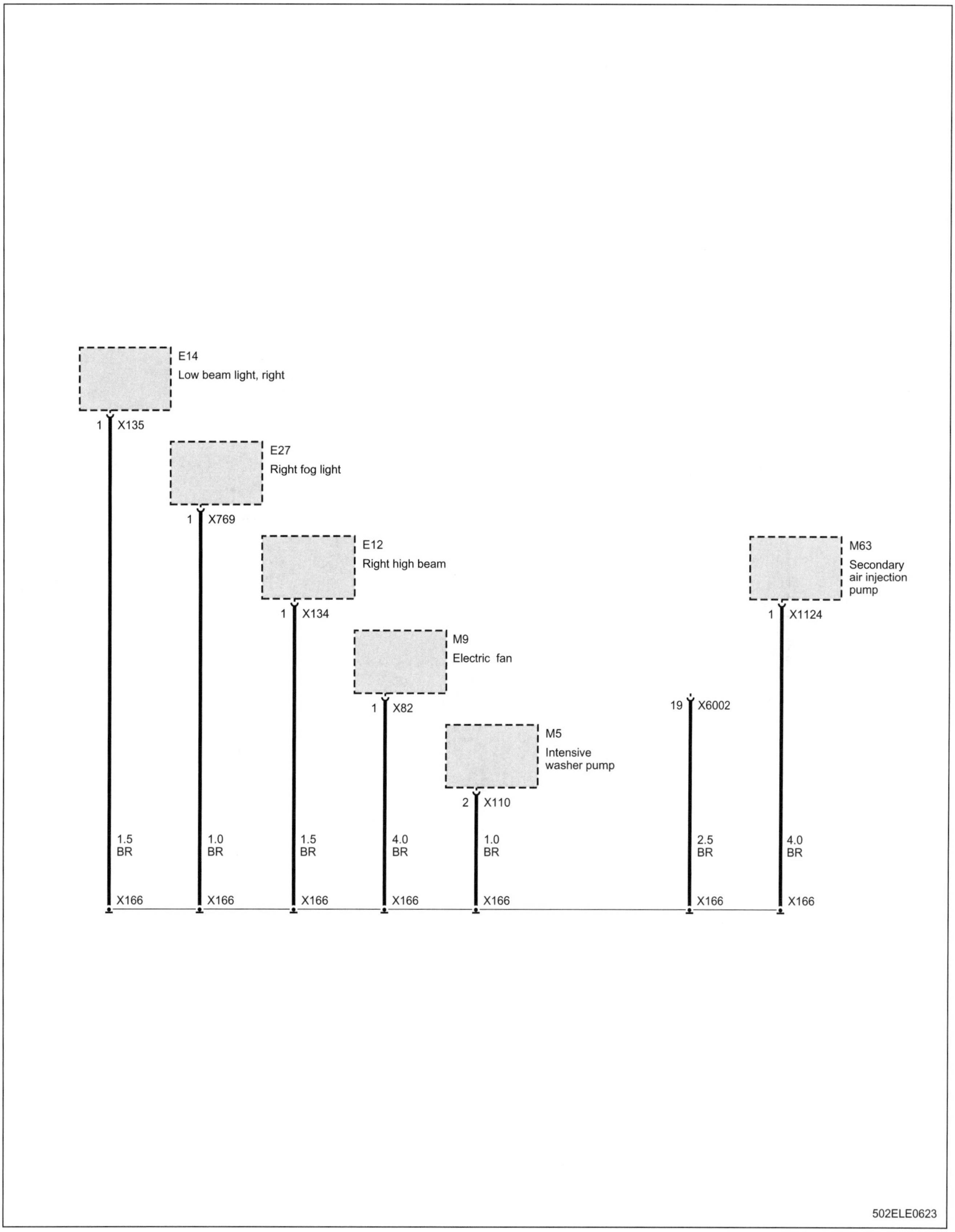

Ground Distribution
X173 Ground - Seats with memory
(1 of 1)

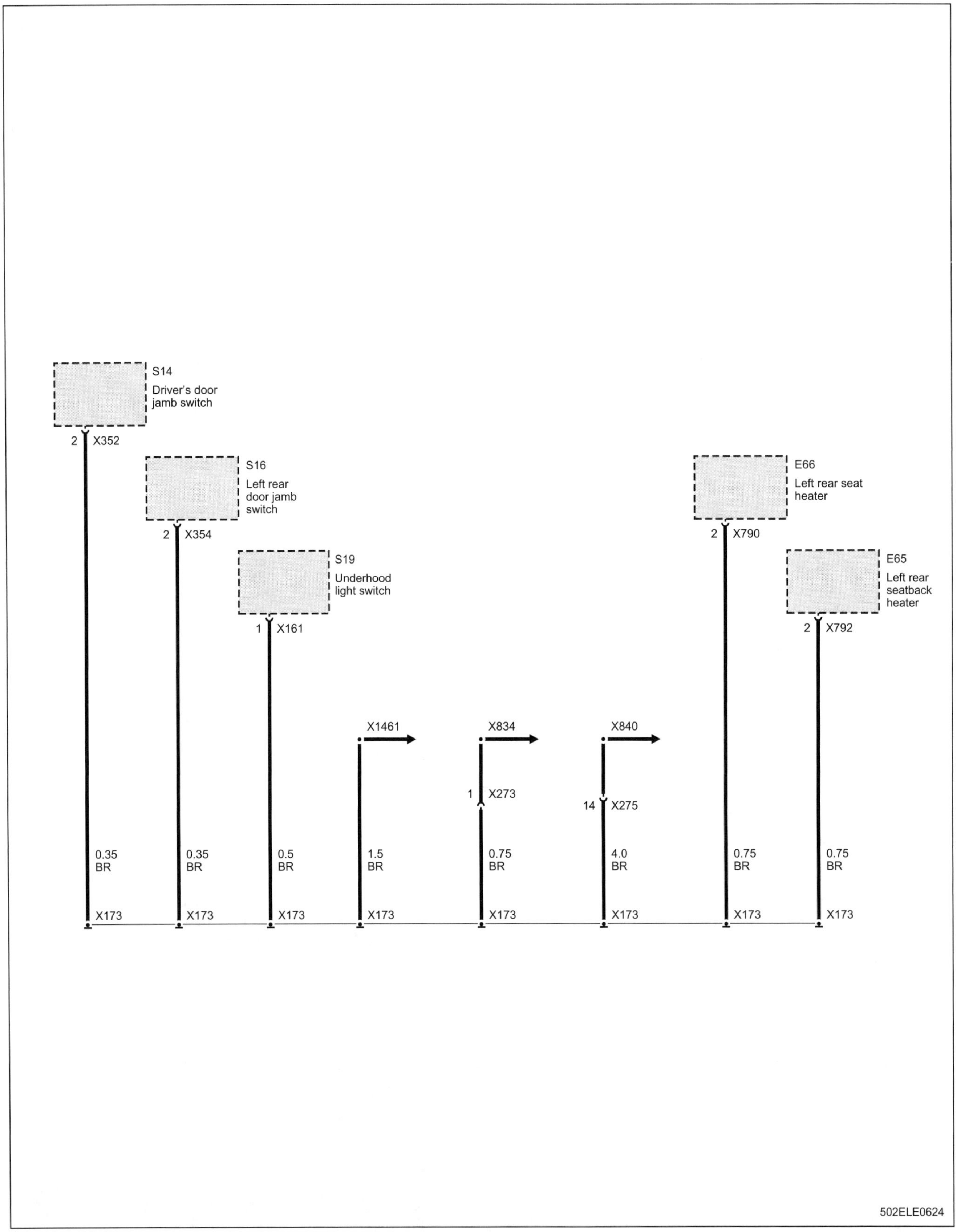

Ground Distribution
X173 Ground - Seats without memory
(1 of 1)

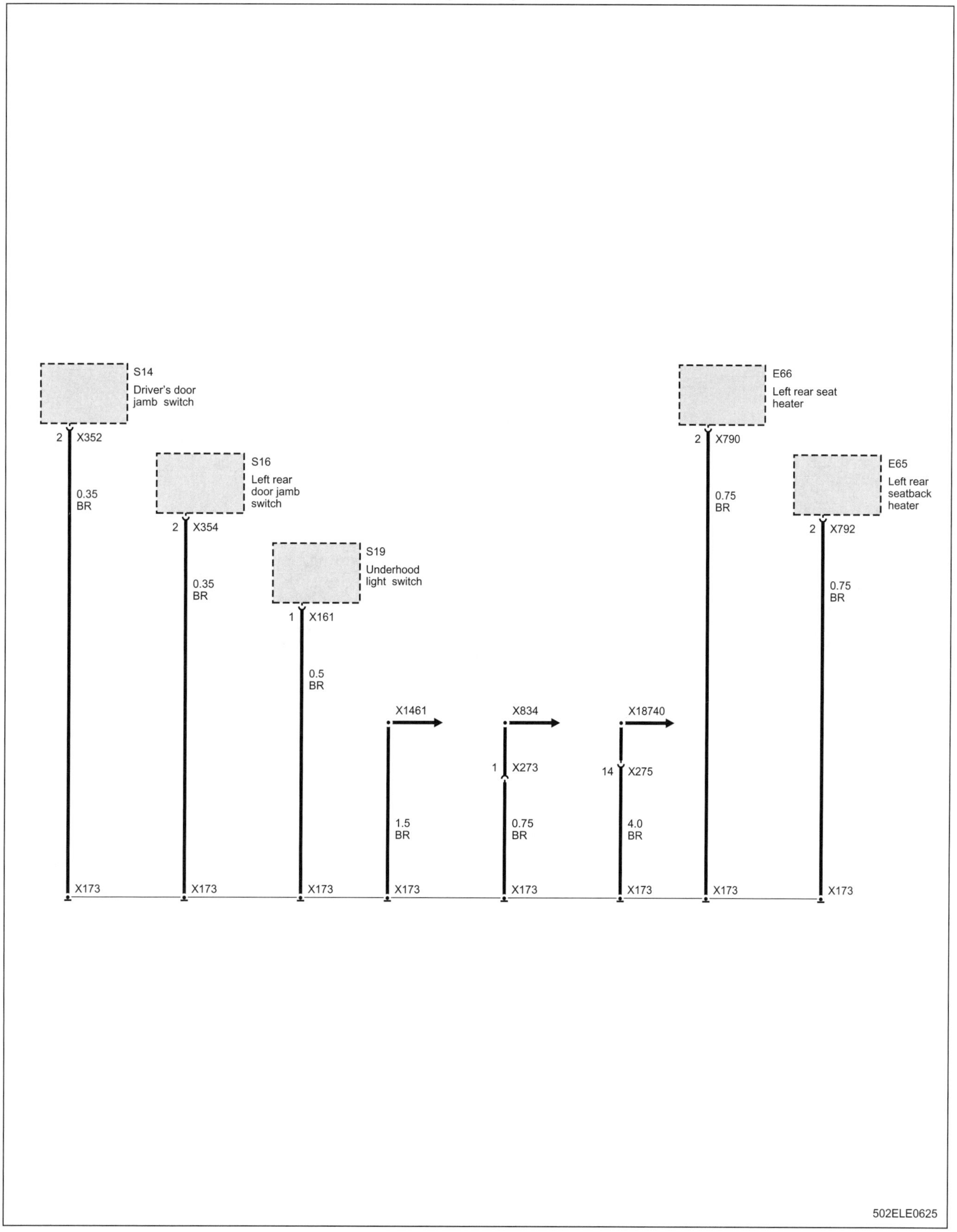

X-Connectors and Splices
X181 Splice - Brake light signal
(1 of 1)

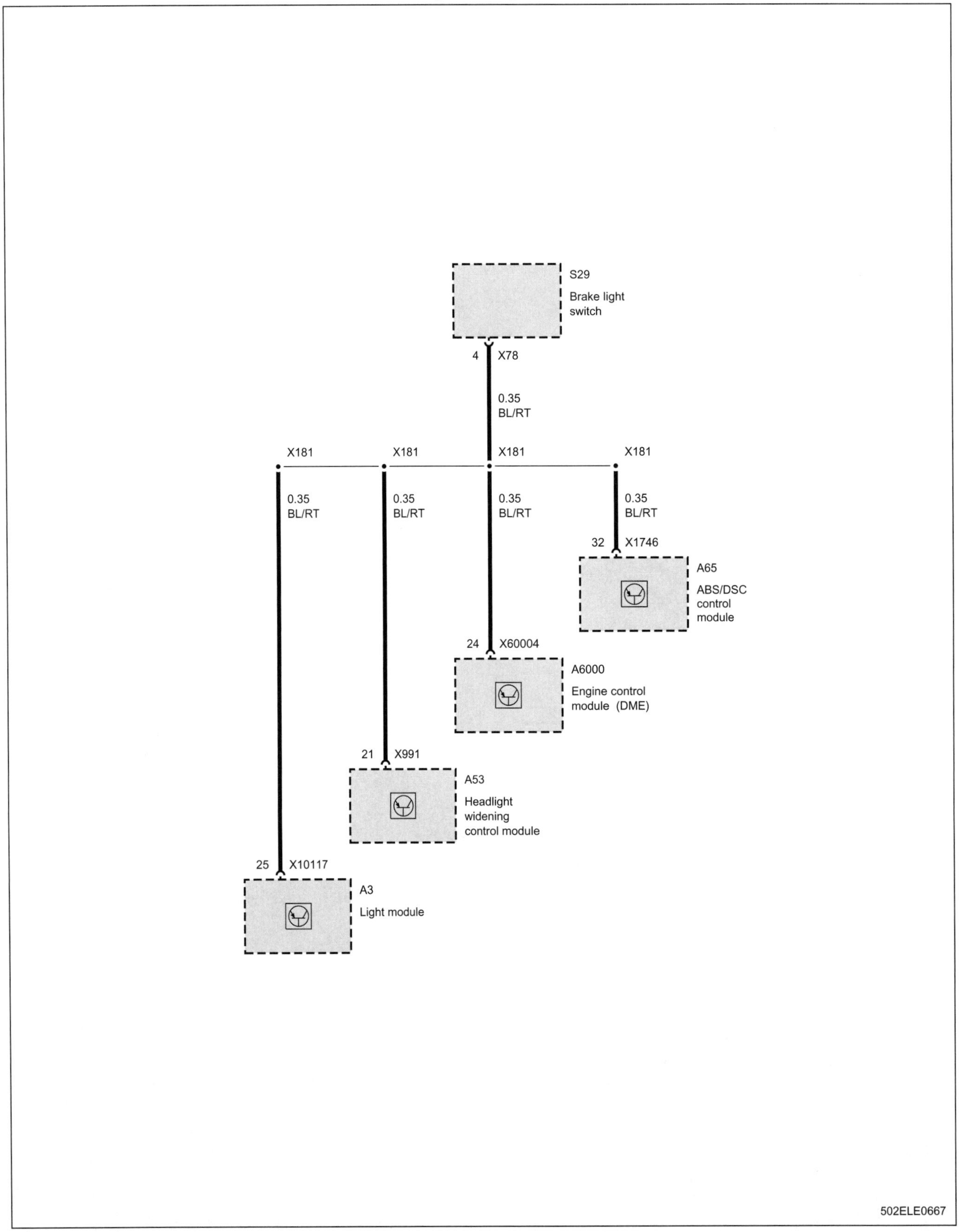

Ground Distribution
X217 Ground splice
(1 of 2)

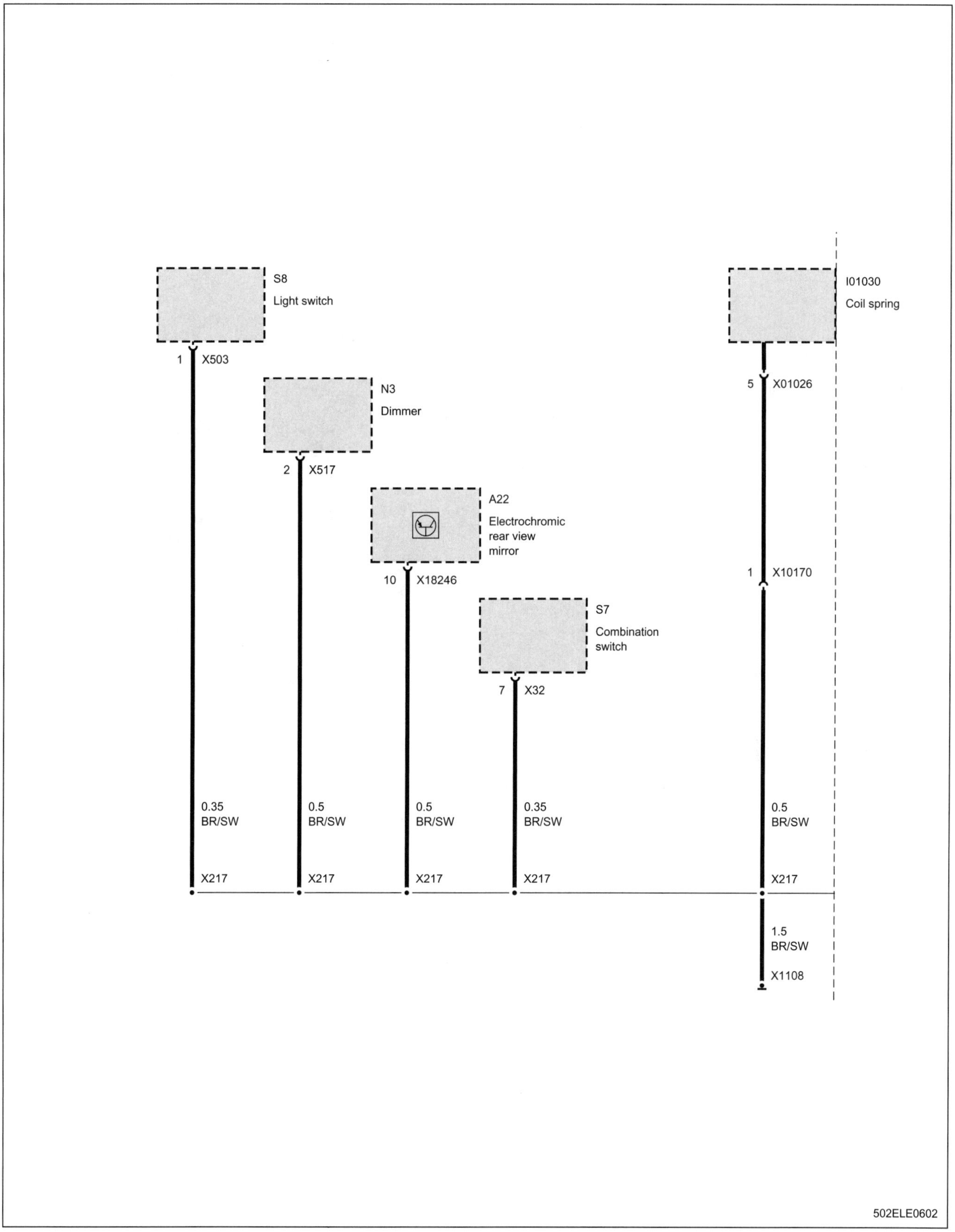
S8
Light switch
1 X503
N3
Dimmer
2 X517
A22
Electrochromic
rear view
mirror
10 X18246
S7
Combination
switch
7 X32
I01030
Coil spring
5 X01026
1 X10170
0.35
BR/SW
0.5
BR/SW
0.5
BR/SW
0.35
BR/SW
0.5
BR/SW
X217
X217
X217
X217
X217
1.5
BR/SW
X1108
502ELE0602

Ground Distribution
X217 Ground splice
(2 of 2)

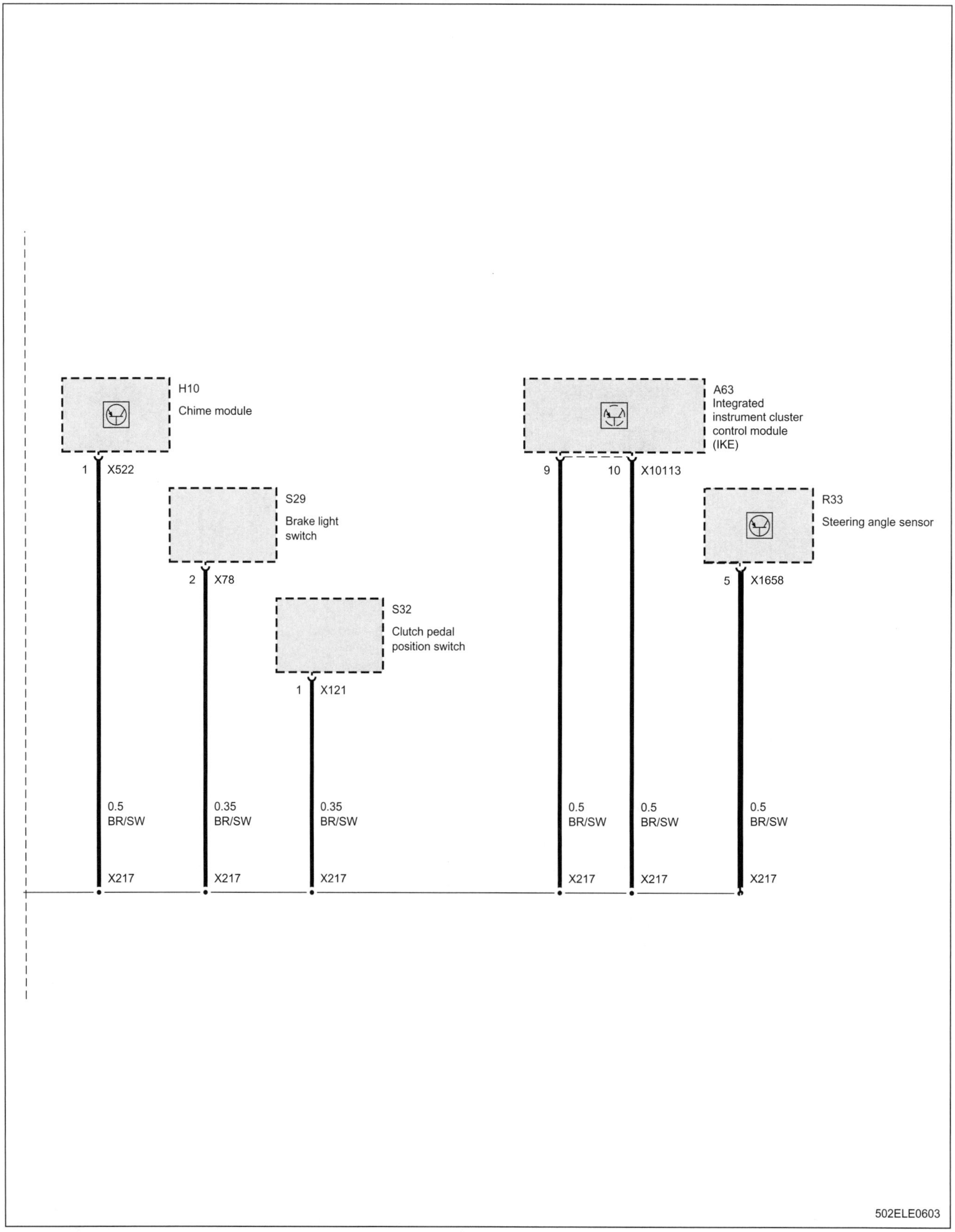
H10
Chime module
1 X522
S29
Brake light switch
2 X78
S32
Clutch pedal position switch
1 X121
A63
Integrated instrument cluster control module (IKE)
9
10 X10113
R33
Steering angle sensor
5 X1658
0.5 BR/SW
0.35 BR/SW
0.35 BR/SW
0.5 BR/SW
0.5 BR/SW
0.5 BR/SW
X217
X217
X217
X217
X217
X217
502ELE0603

Ground Distribution
X218 Ground splice
(1 of 1)

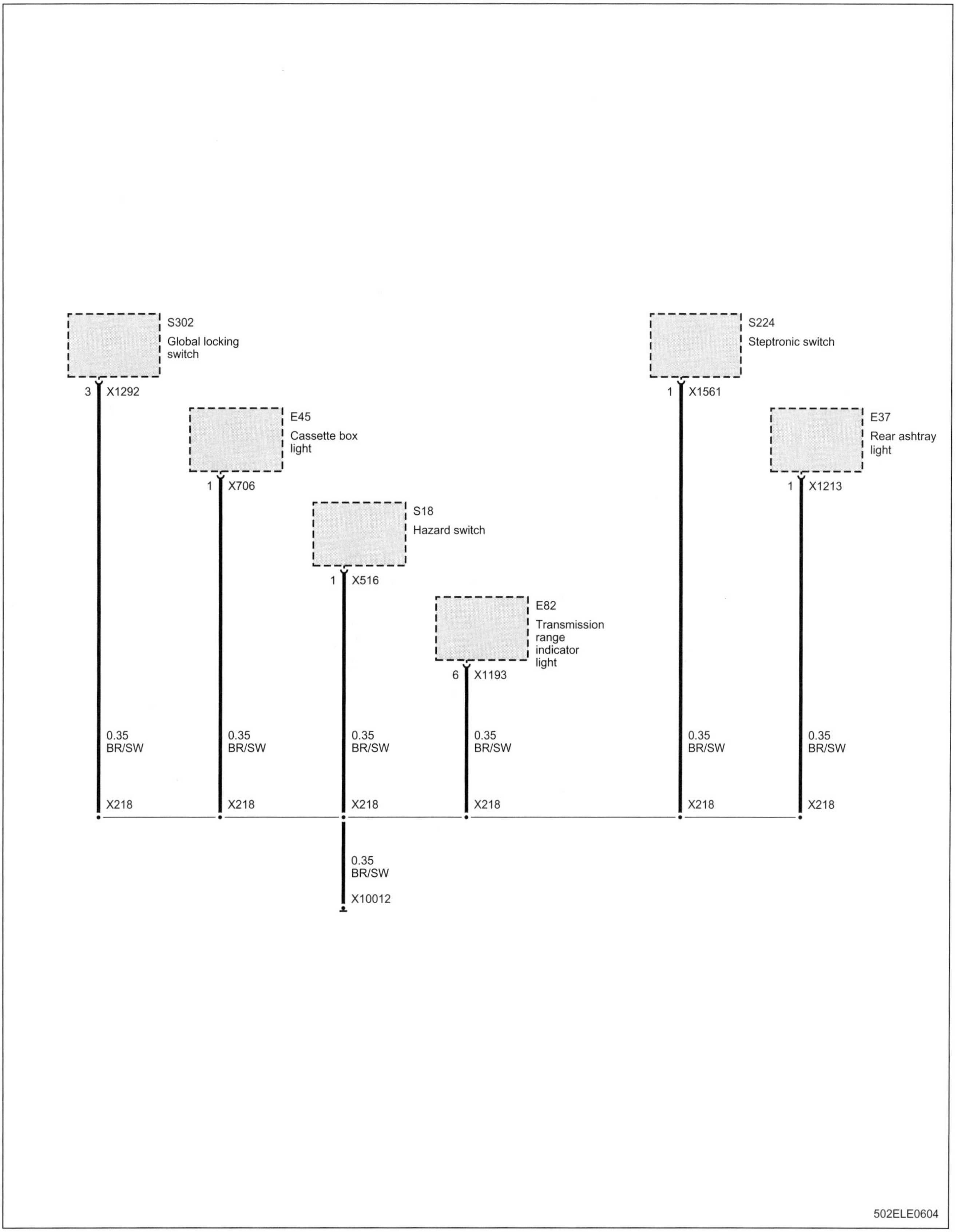
S302
Global locking switch
3 X1292
E45
Cassette box light
1 X706
S18
Hazard switch
1 X516
E82
Transmission range indicator light
6 X1193
S224
Steptronic switch
1 X1561
E37
Rear ashtray light
1 X1213
0.35 BR/SW
0.35 BR/SW
0.35 BR/SW
0.35 BR/SW
0.35 BR/SW
0.35 BR/SW
X218
X218
X218
X218
X218
X218
0.35 BR/SW
X10012
502ELE0604

Ground Distribution
X219 Ground splice
(1 of 1)

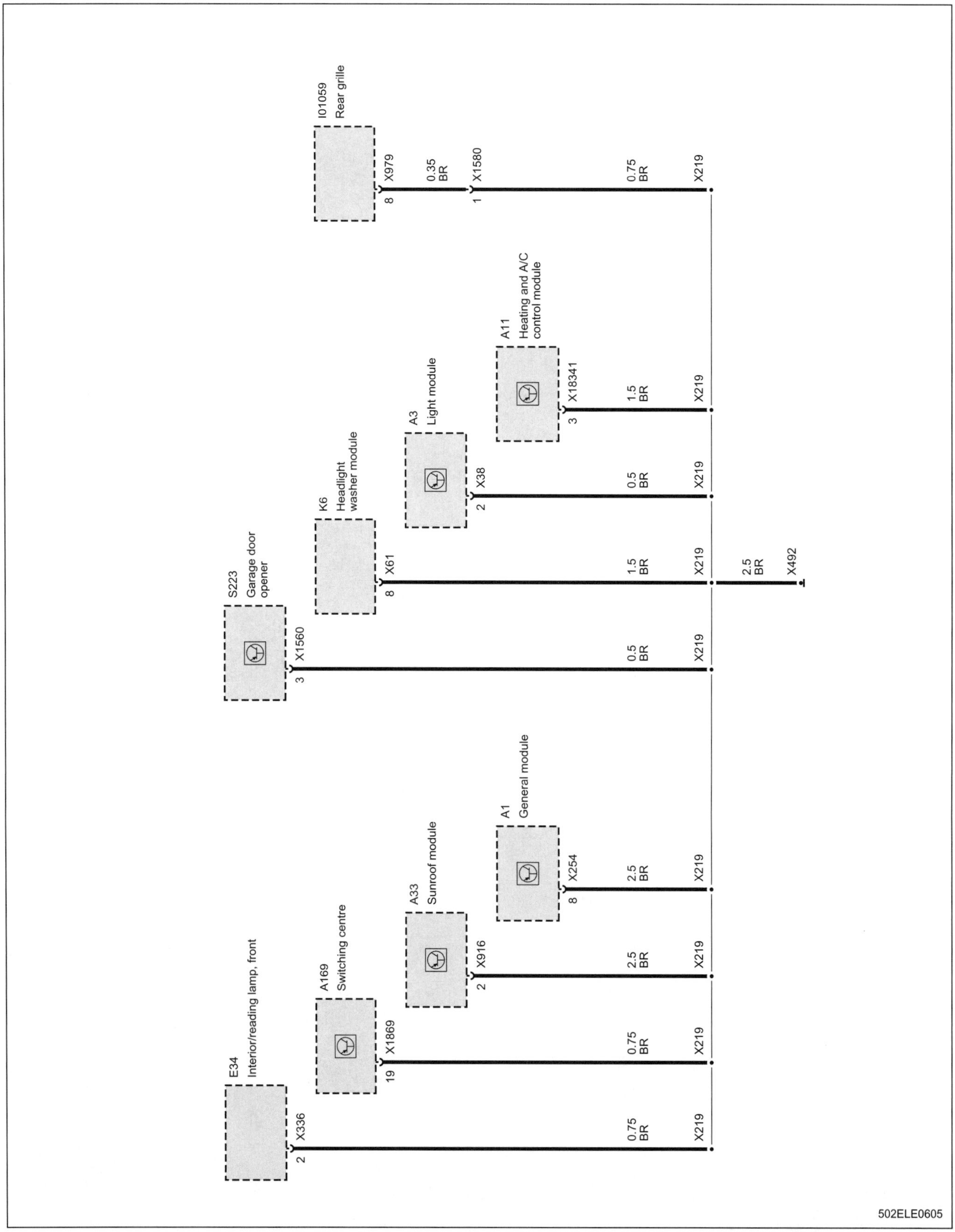
I01059
Rear grille
X979
8
0.35
BR
X1580
1
0.75
BR
X219
A11
Heating and A/C
control module
X18341
3
1.5
BR
X219
A3
Light module
X38
2
0.5
BR
X219
K6
Headlight
washer module
X61
8
1.5
BR
X219
2.5
BR
X492
S223
Garage door
opener
X1560
3
0.5
BR
X219
A1
General module
X254
8
2.5
BR
X219
A33
Sunroof module
X916
2
2.5
BR
X219
A169
Switching centre
X1869
19
0.75
BR
X219
E34
Interior/reading lamp, front
X336
2
0.75
BR
X219
502ELE0605

X-Connectors and Splices
X229 Splice
(1 of 1)

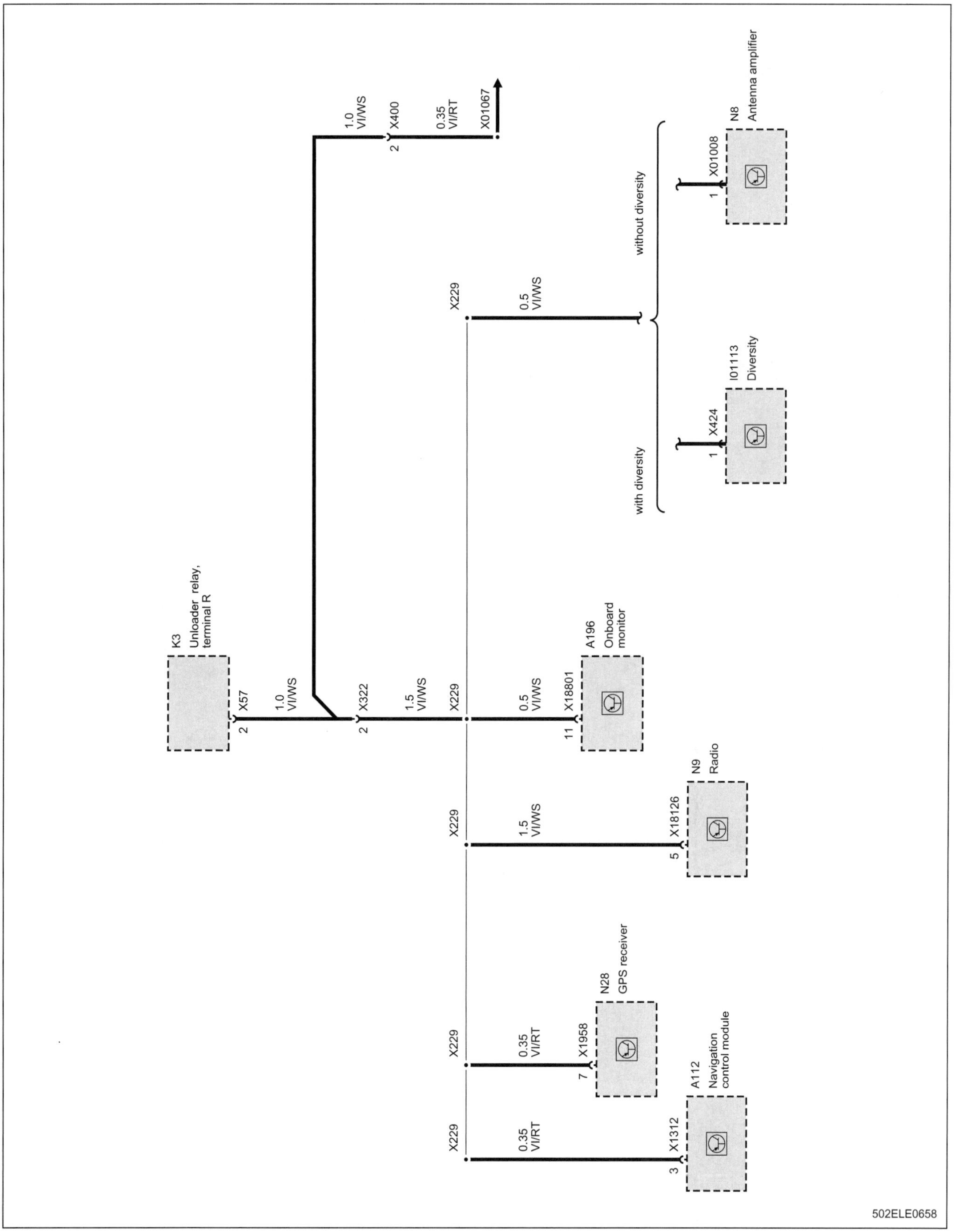
K3
Unloader relay, terminal R
2 X57
1.0 VI/WS
2 X322
1.5 VI/WS
X229
0.5 VI/WS
11 X18801
A196
Onboard monitor
1.0 VI/WS
2 X400
0.35 VI/RT
X01067
X229
0.5 VI/WS
without diversity
with diversity
1 X01008
N8
Antenna amplifier
1 X424
I01113
Diversity
X229
1.5 VI/WS
5 X18126
N9
Radio
X229
0.35 VI/RT
7 X1958
N28
GPS receiver
X229
0.35 VI/RT
3 X1312
A112
Navigation control module
502ELE0658

X-Connectors and Splices
X256 Connector - Passenger's door
(1 of 3)

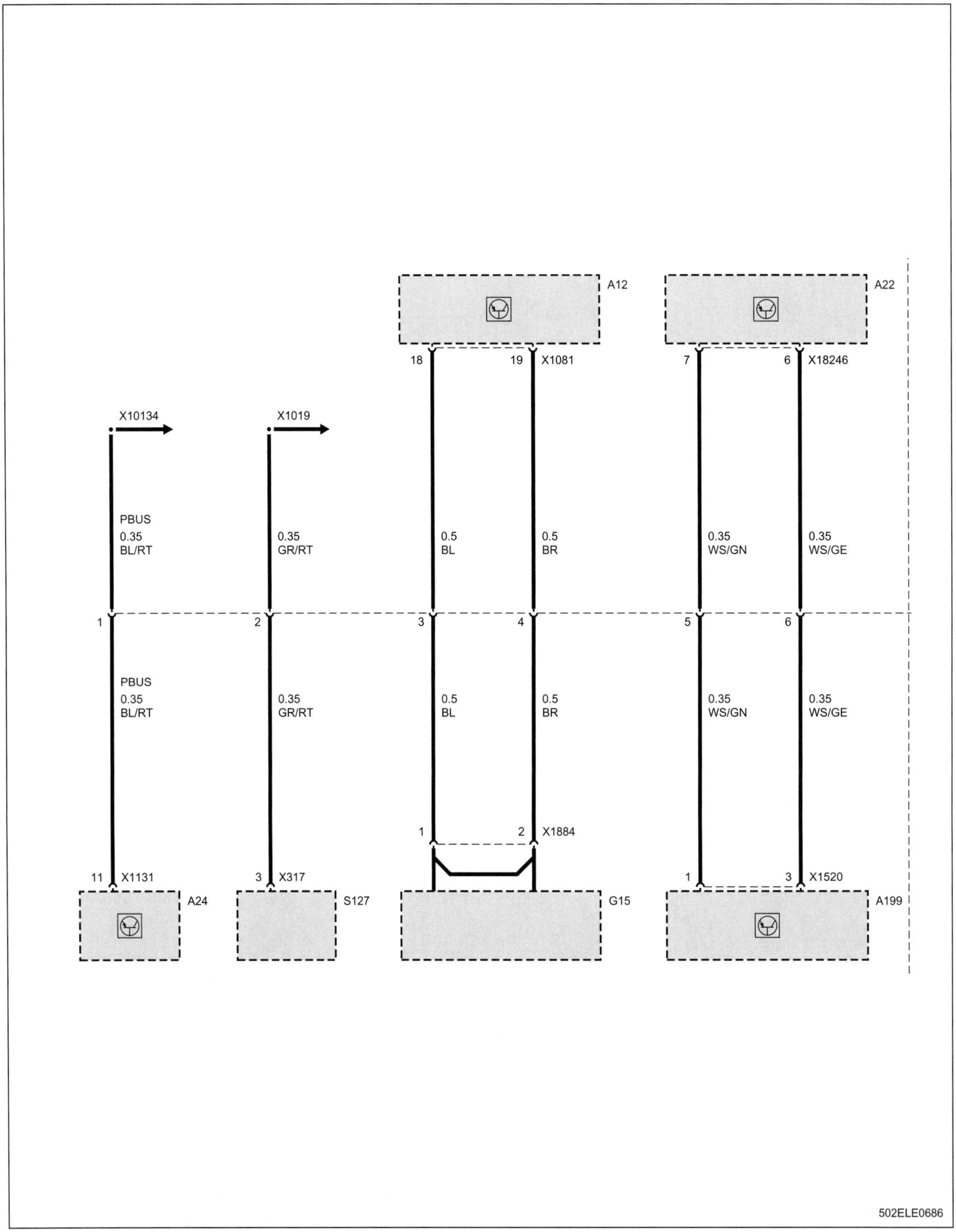

X-Connectors and Splices
X256 Connector - Passenger's door
(2 of 3)

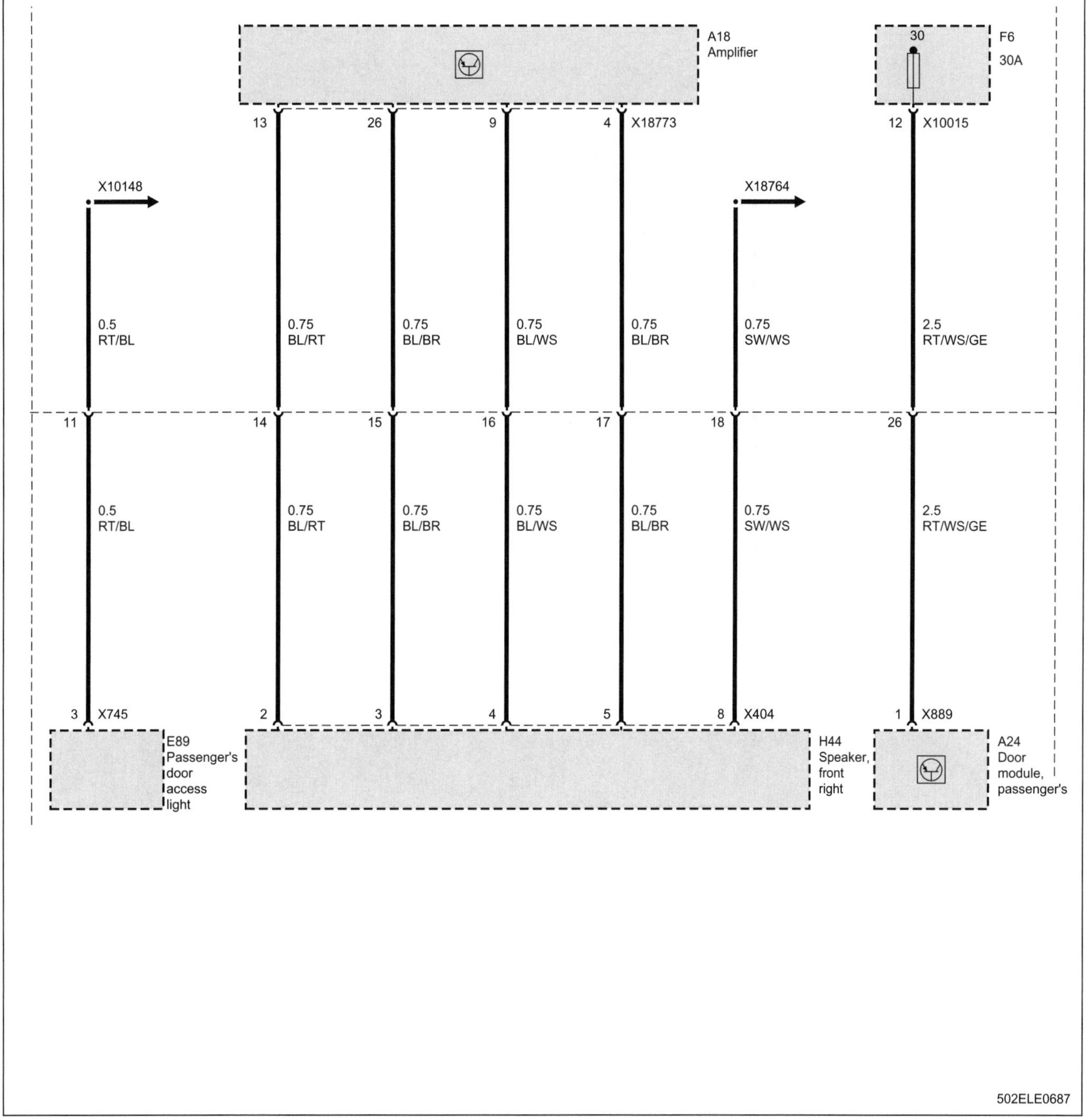

X-Connectors and Splices
X256 Connector - Passenger's door
(3 of 3)

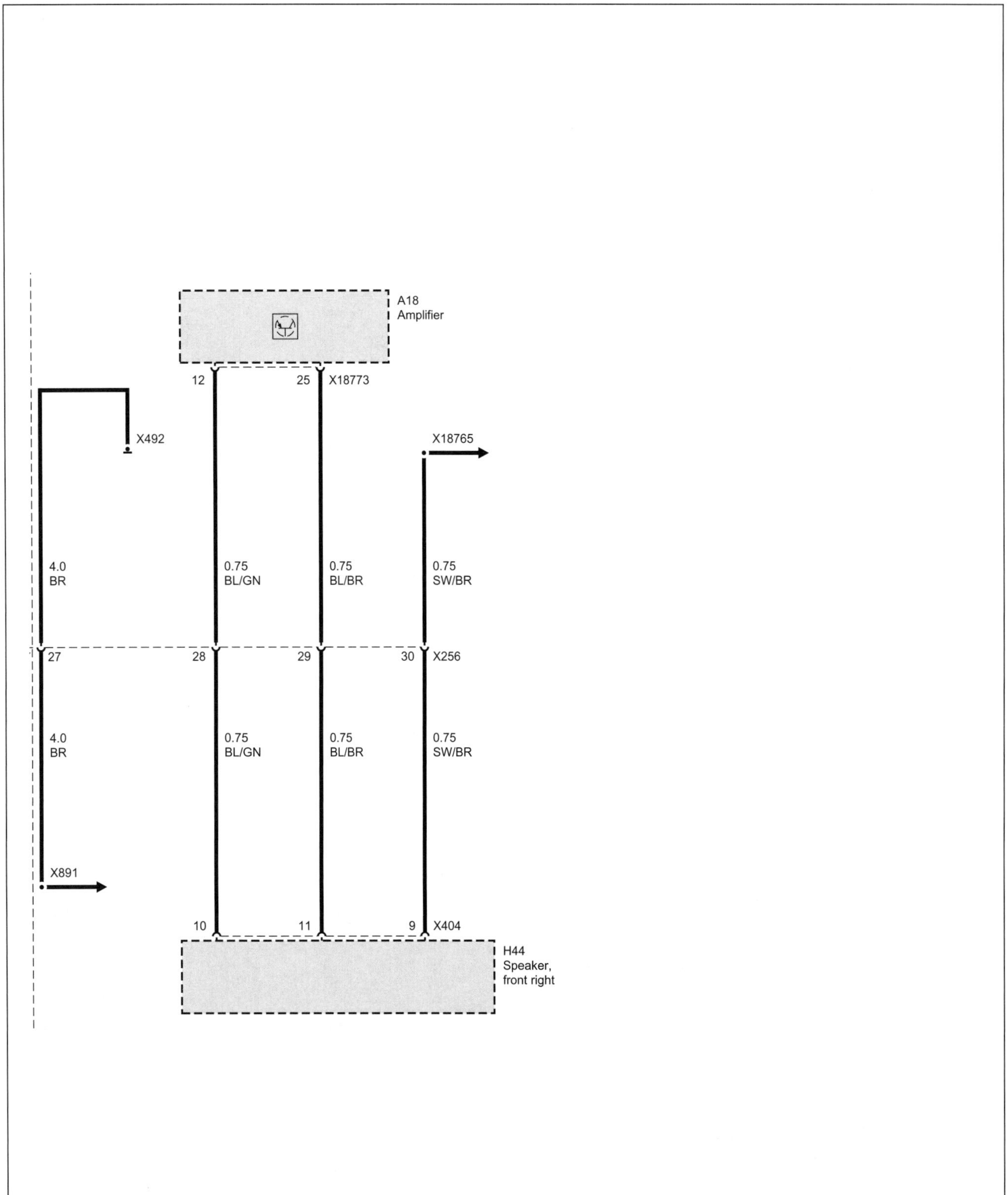

X-Connectors and Splices
X257 Connector - Driver's door
(1 of 3)

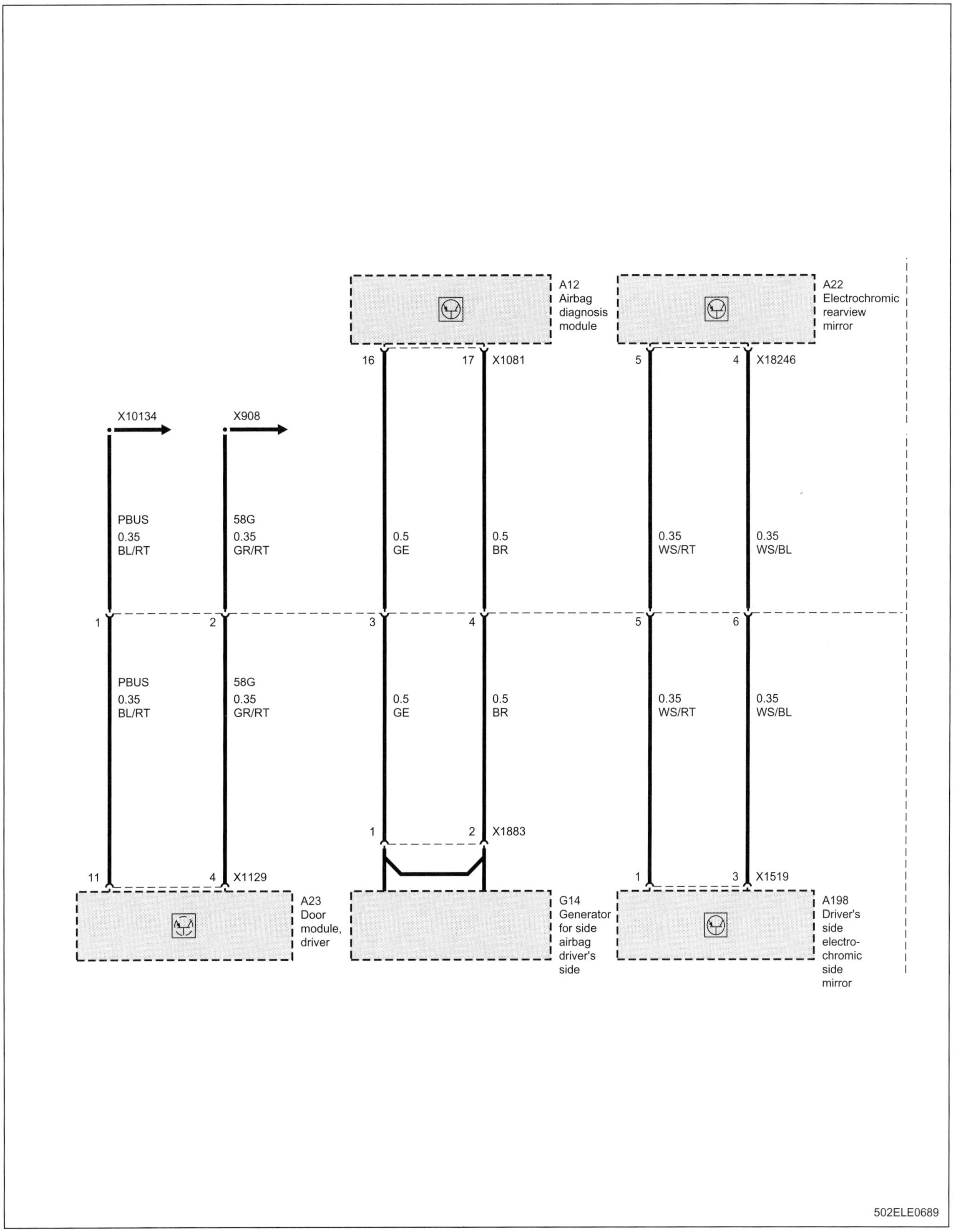

X-Connectors and Splices
X257 Connector - Driver's door
(2 of 3)

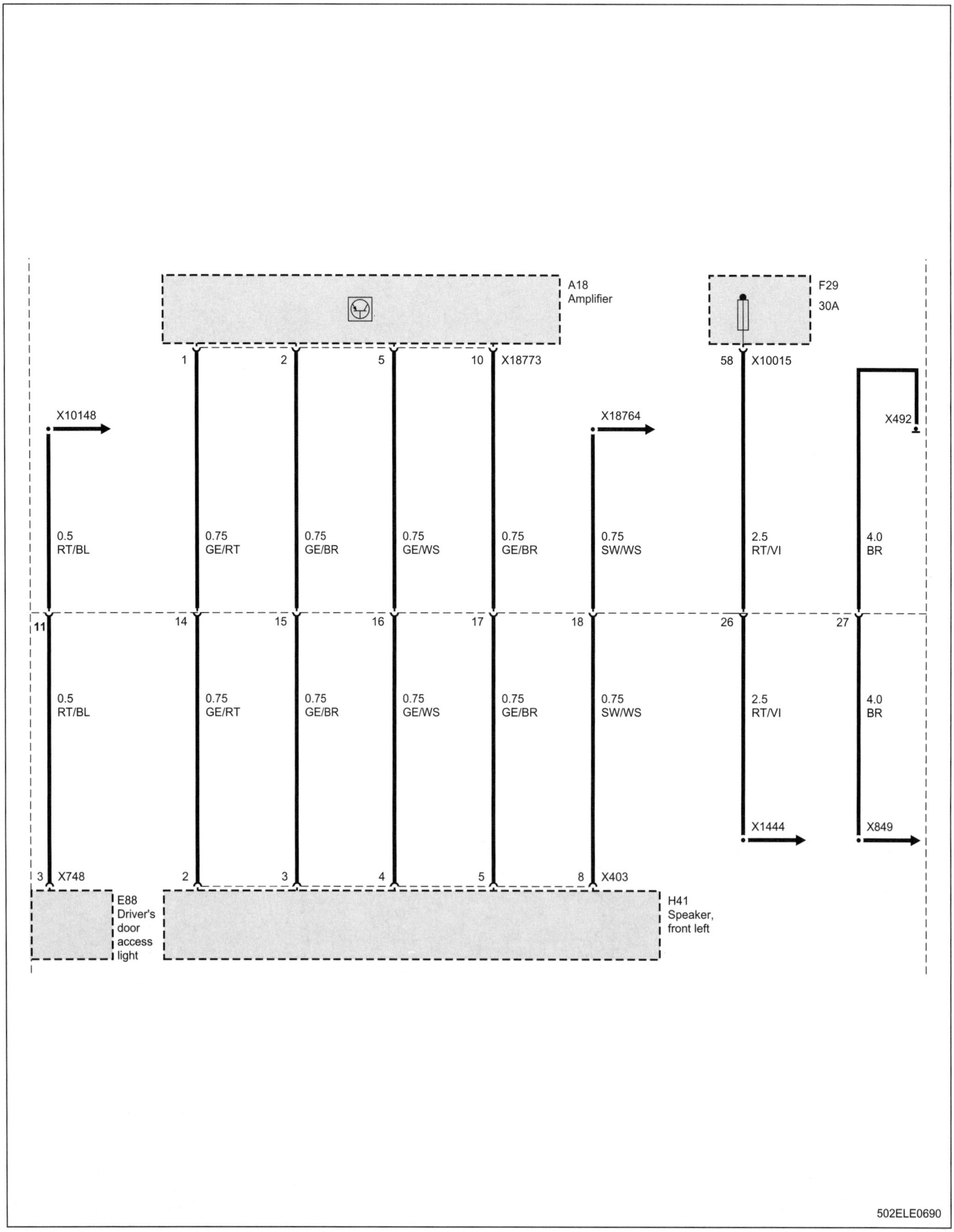

X-Connectors and Splices
X257 Connector - Driver's door
(3 of 3)

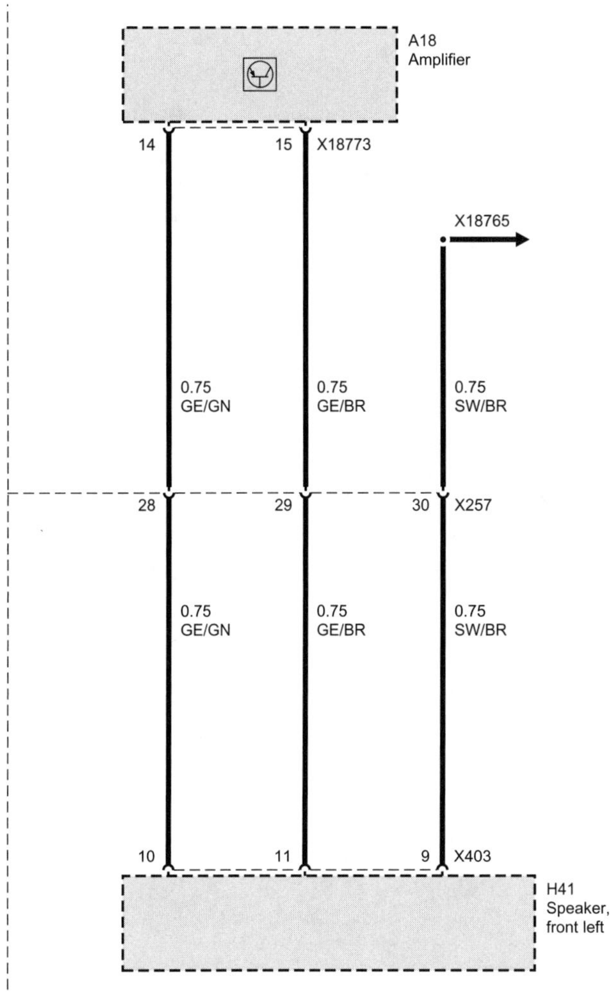

502ELE0691

X-Connectors and Splices
X273 Connector - Rear left door
(1 of 4)

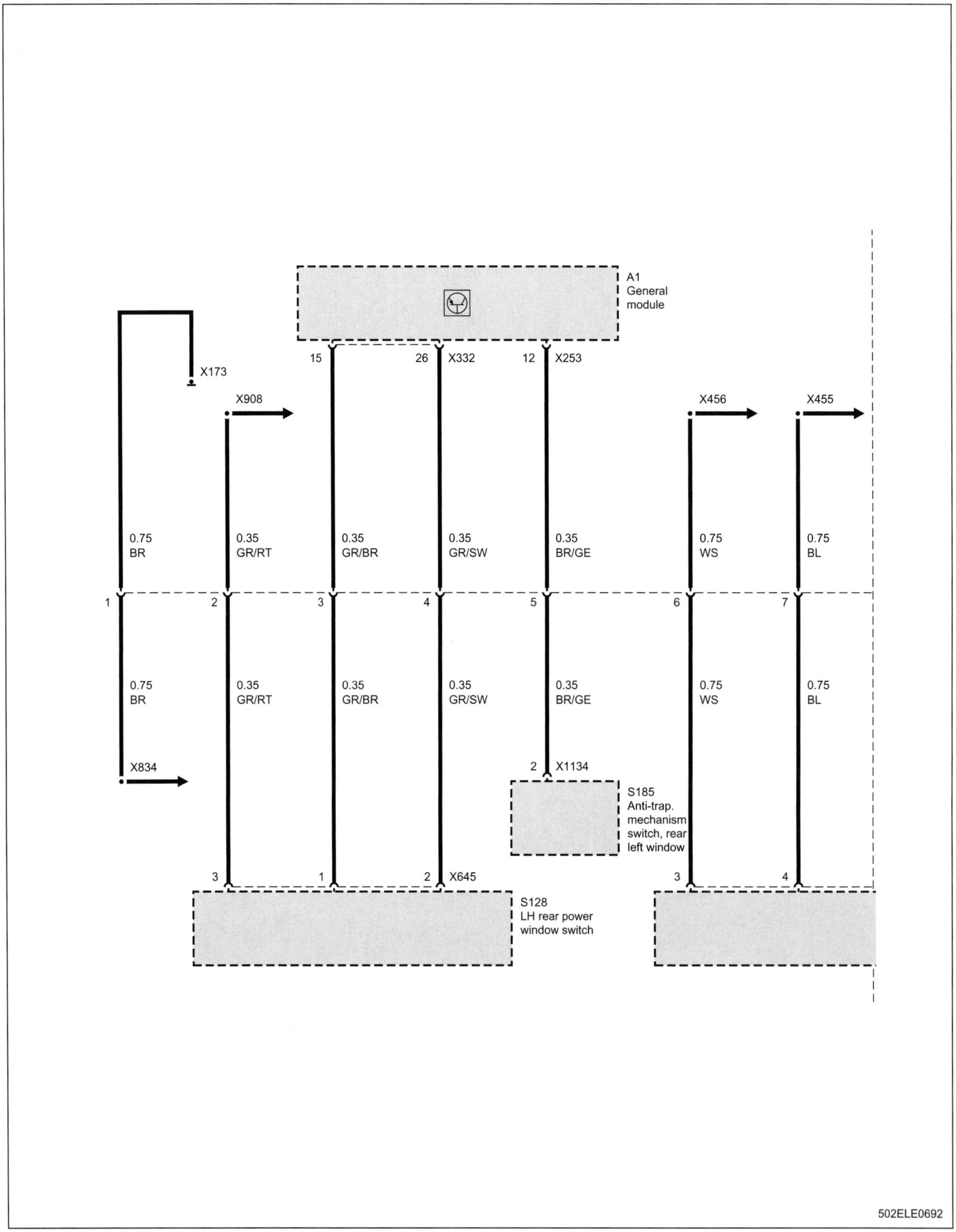

X-Connectors and Splices
X273 Connector - Rear left door
(2 of 4)

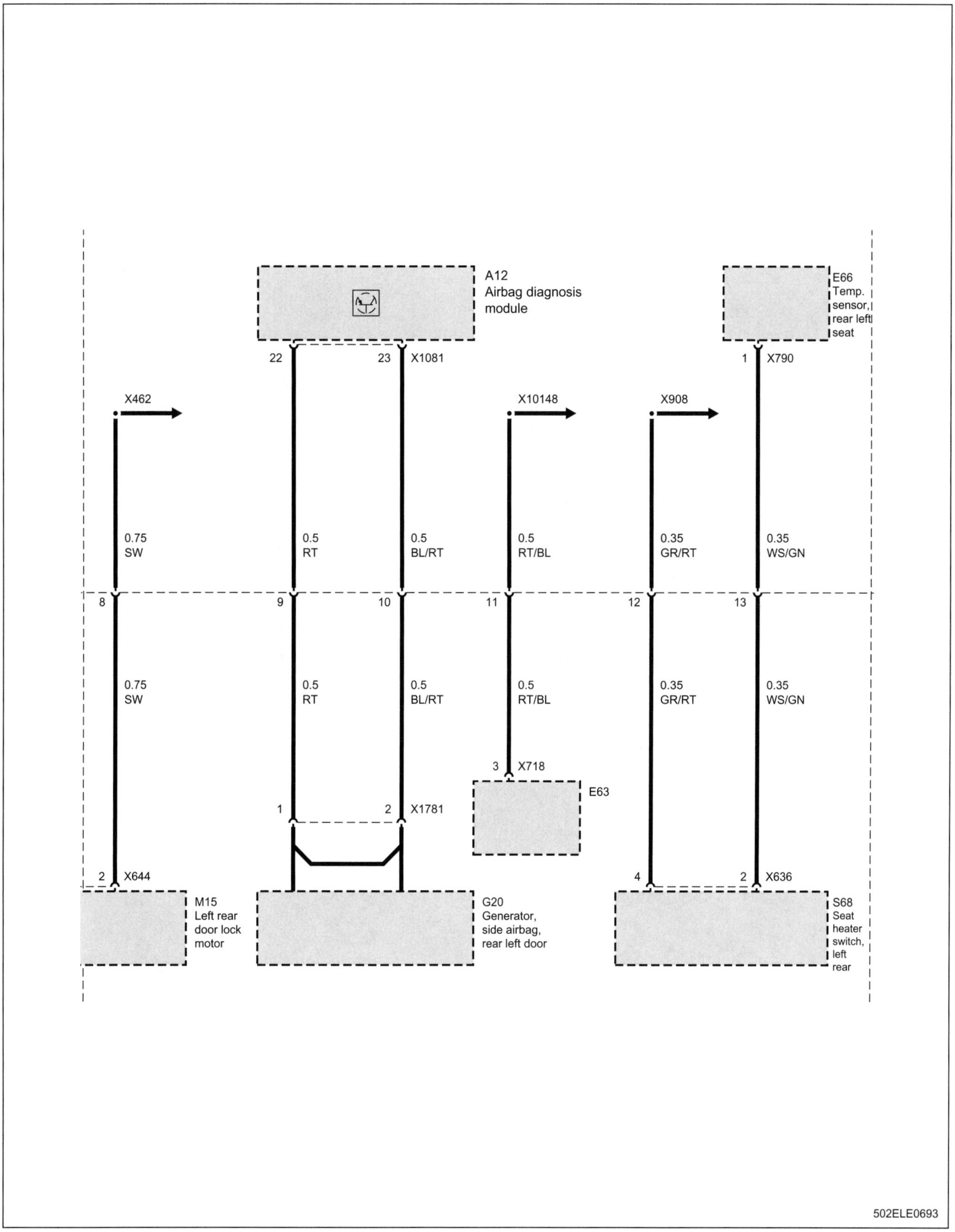

X-Connectors and Splices
X273 Connector - Rear left door
(3 of 4)

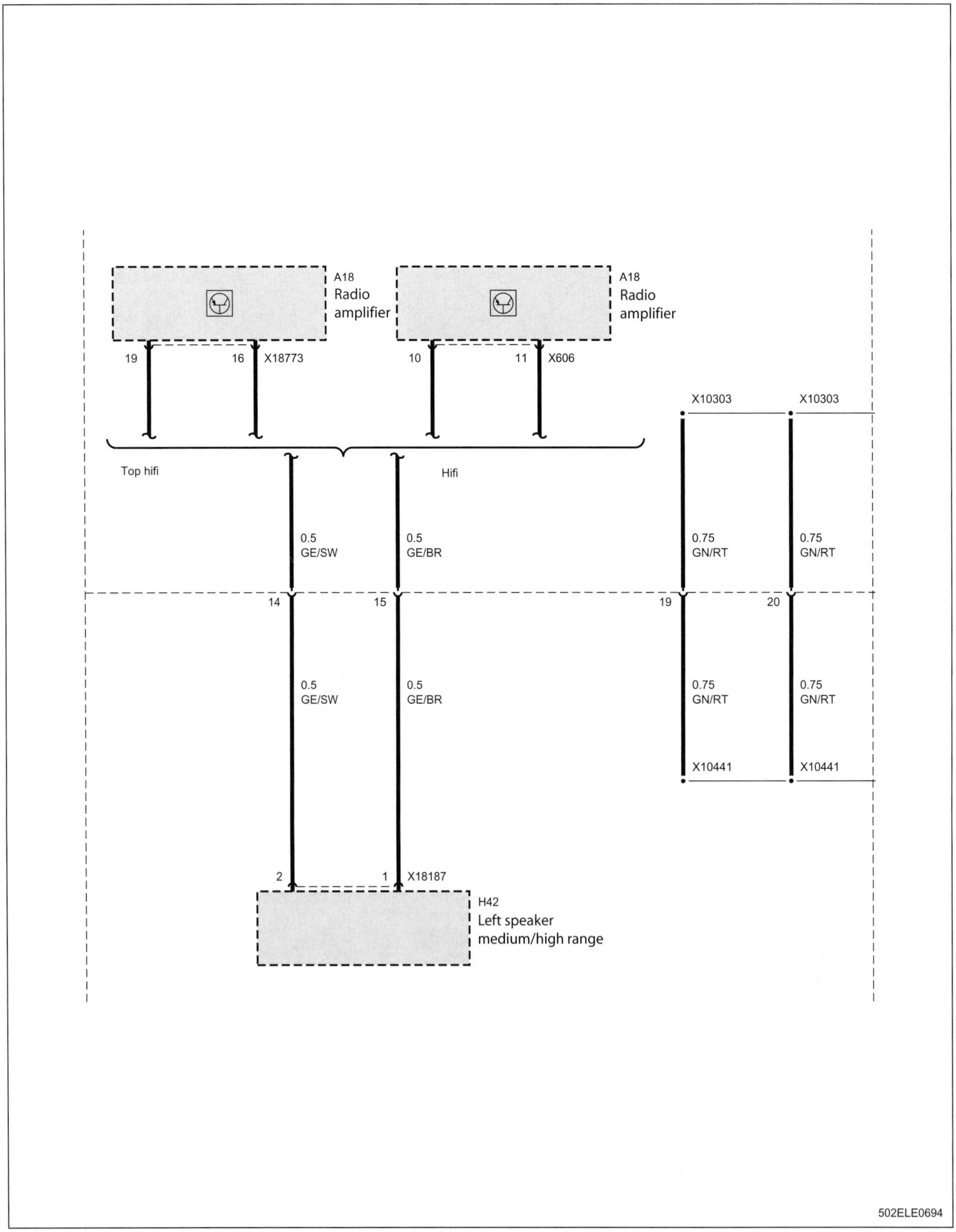

X-Connectors and Splices
X273 Connector - Rear left door
(4 of 4)

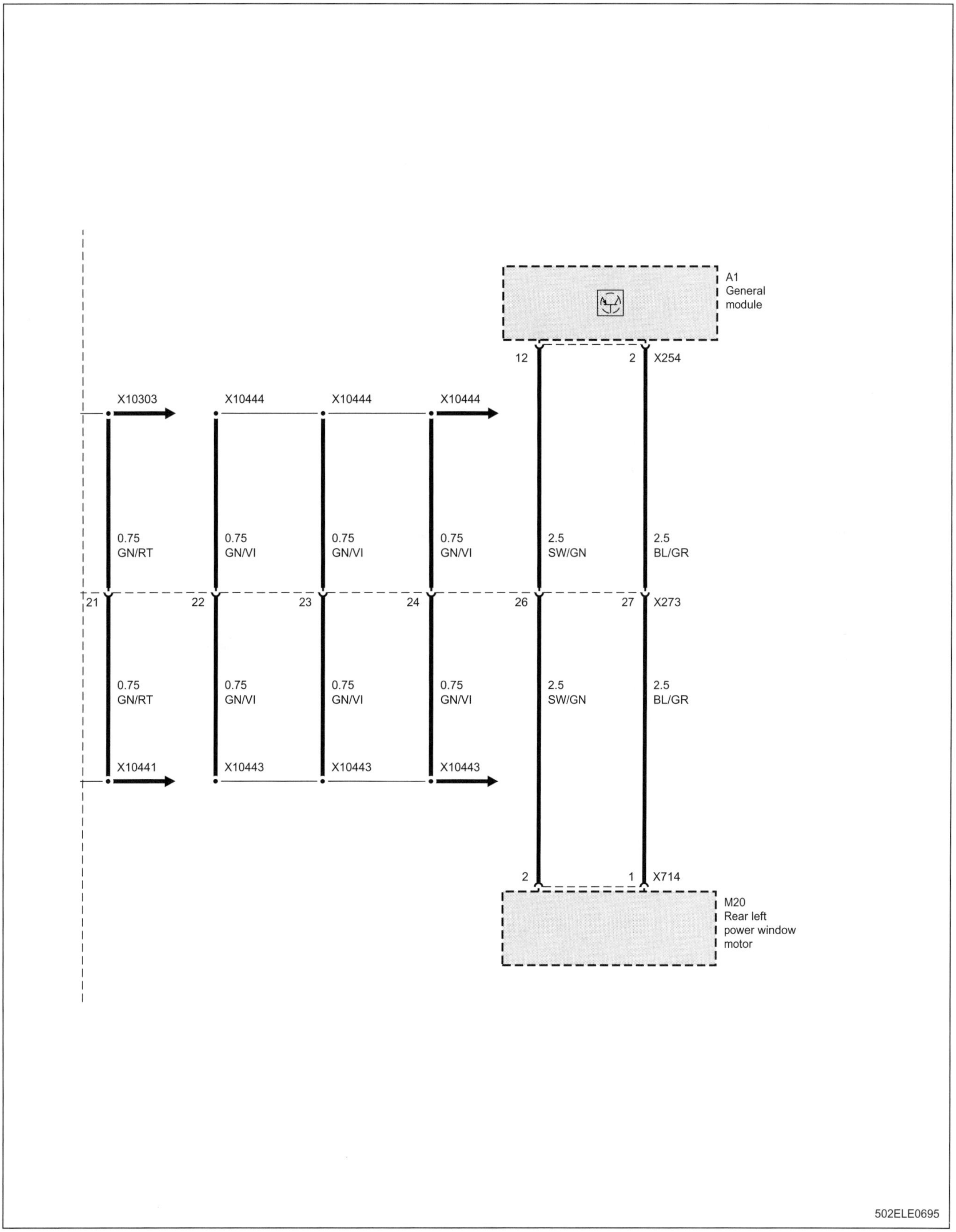

X-Connectors and Splices

X274 Connector - Rear right door

(1 of 4)

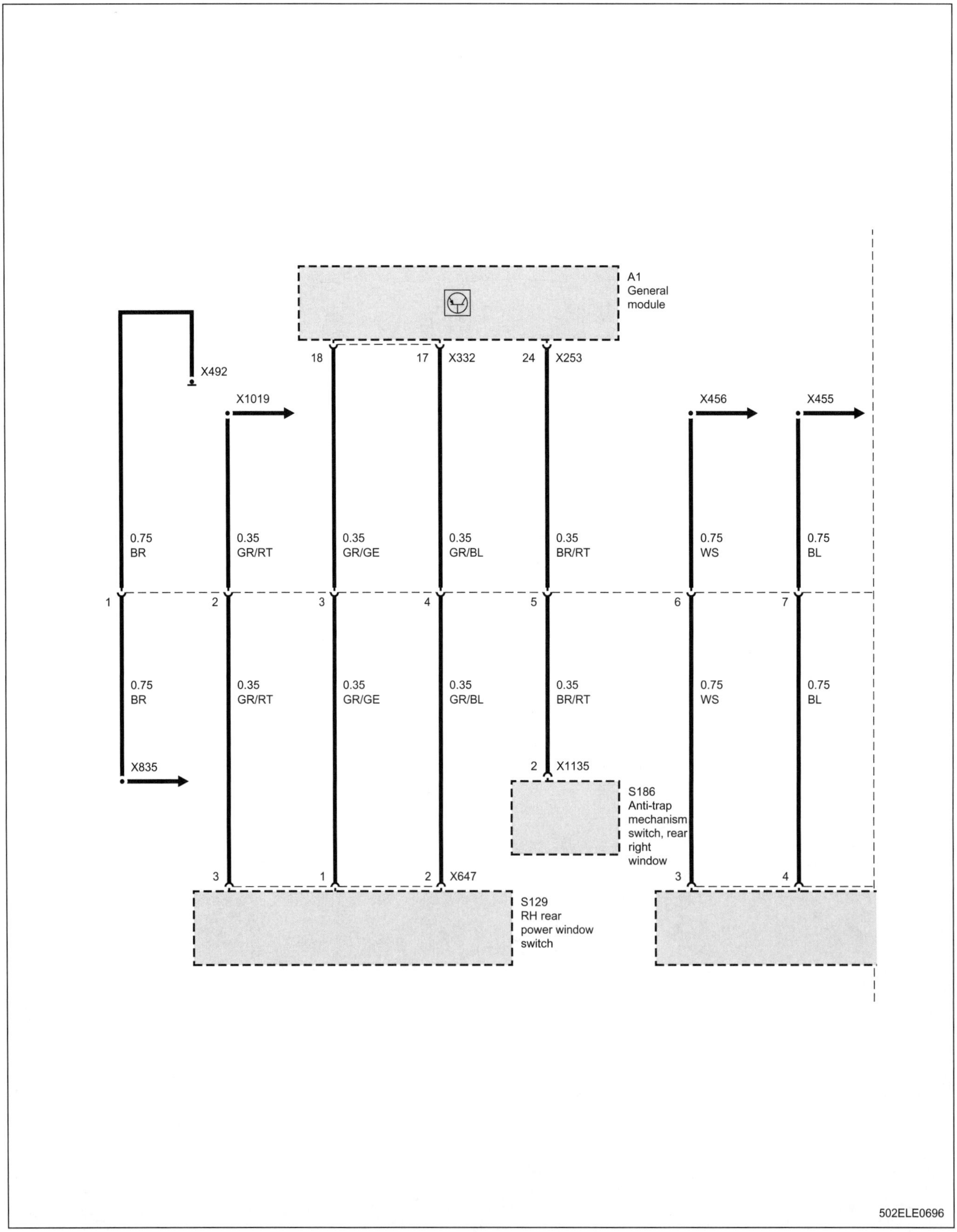

X-Connectors and Splices
X274 Connector - Rear right door
(2 of 4)

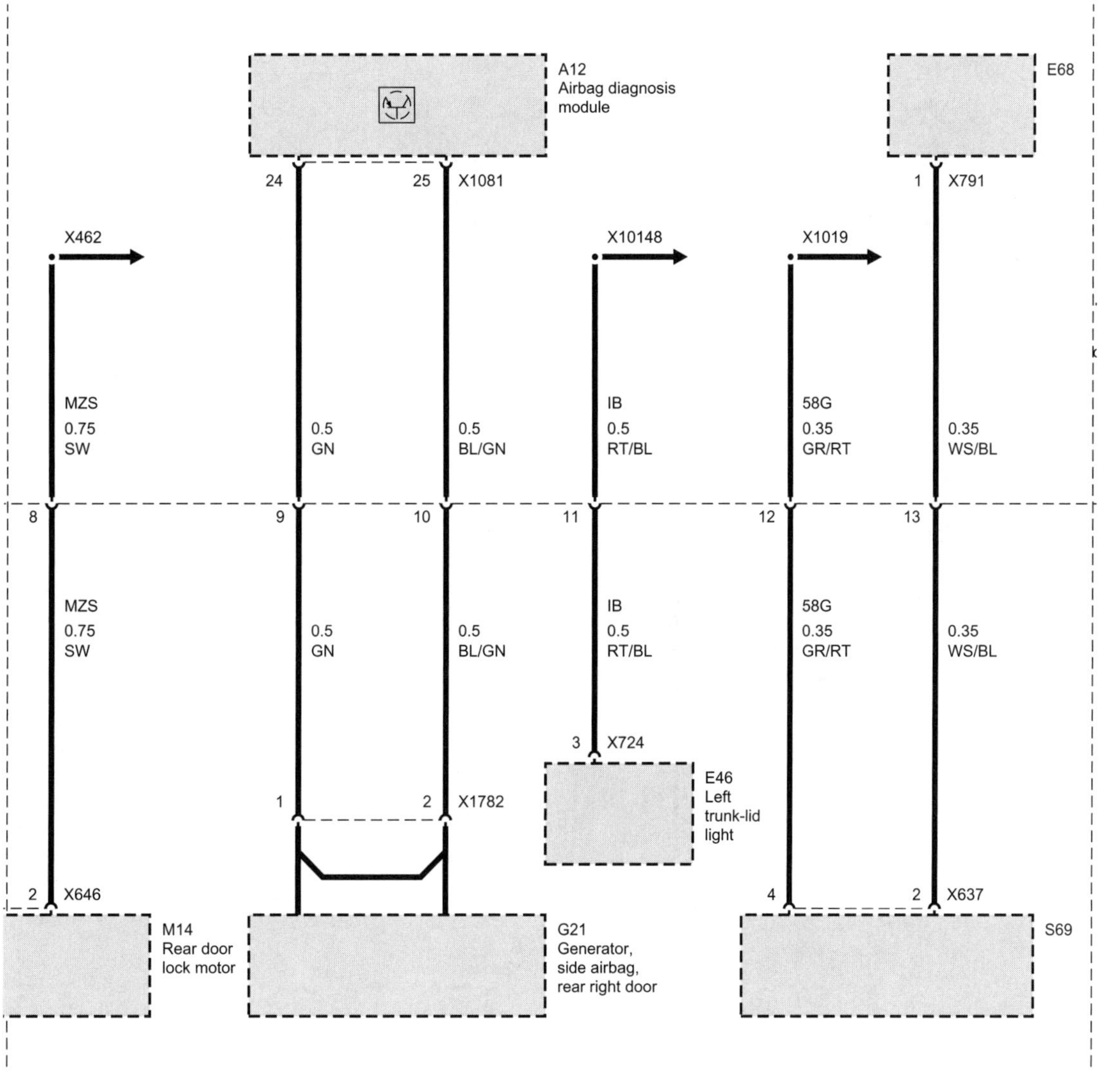

502ELE0697

X-Connectors and Splices
X274 Connector - Rear right door
(3 of 4)

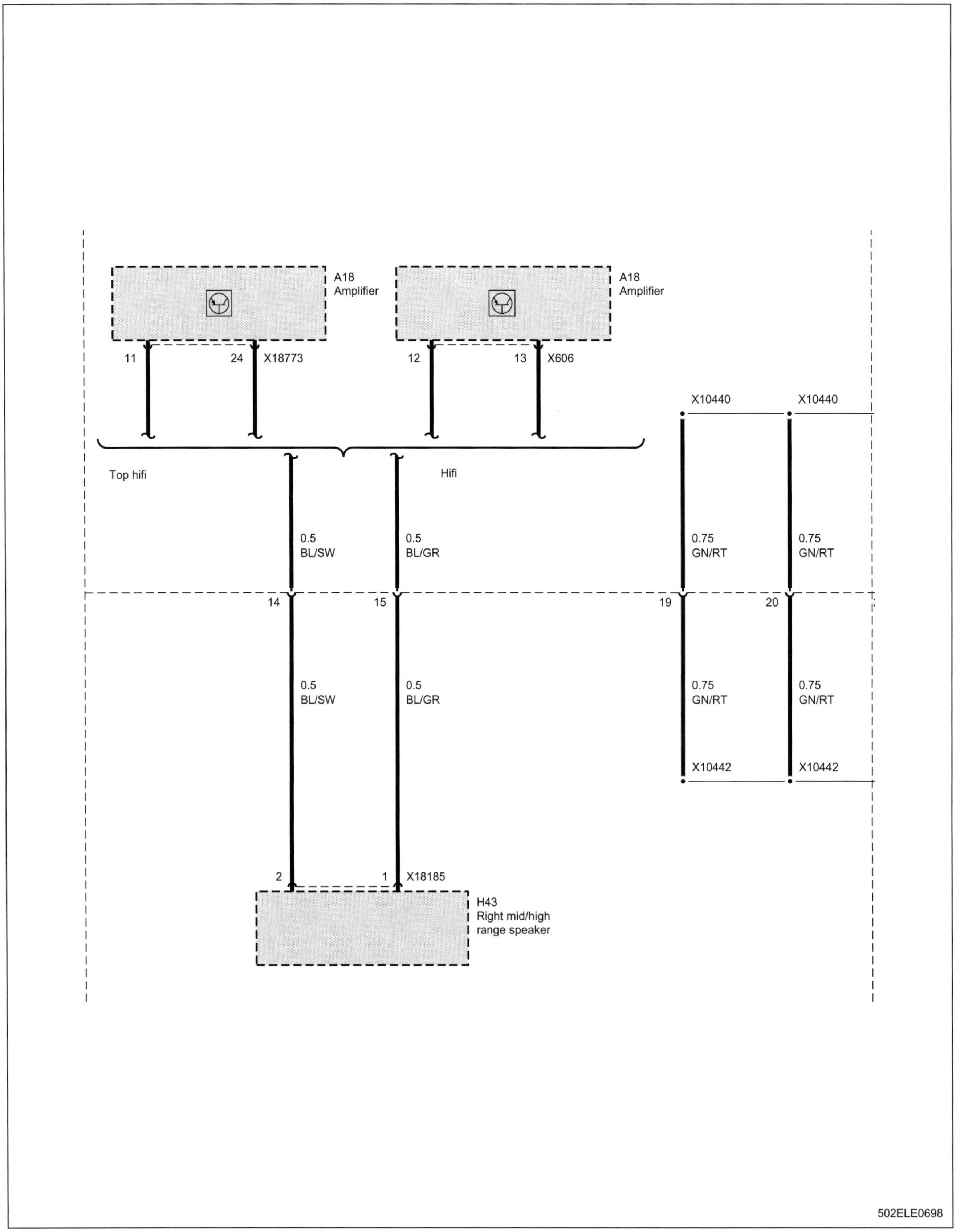

X-Connectors and Splices
X274 Connector - Rear right door
(4 of 4)

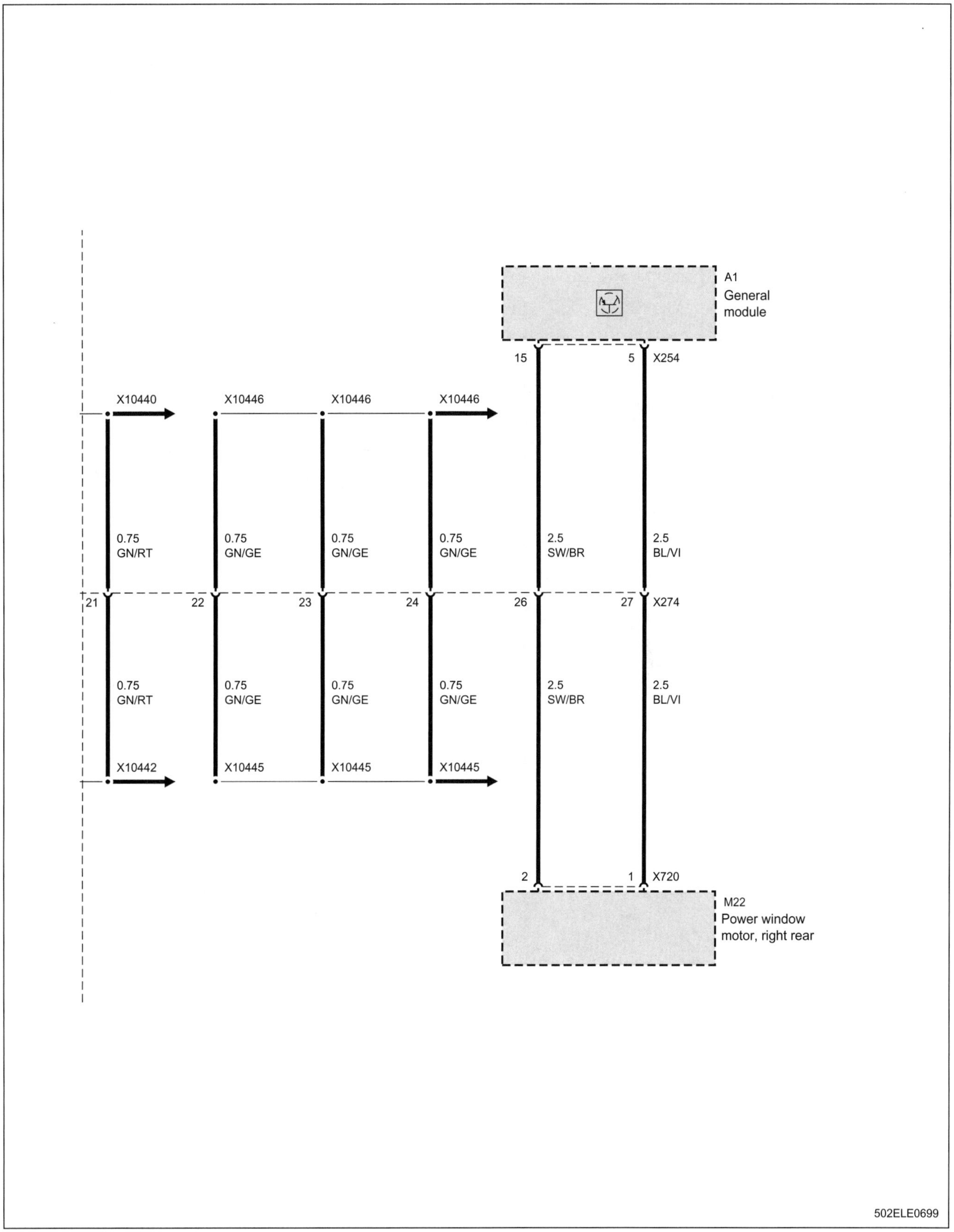

X-Connectors and Splices
X275 Connector - Driver's seat
(1 of 4)

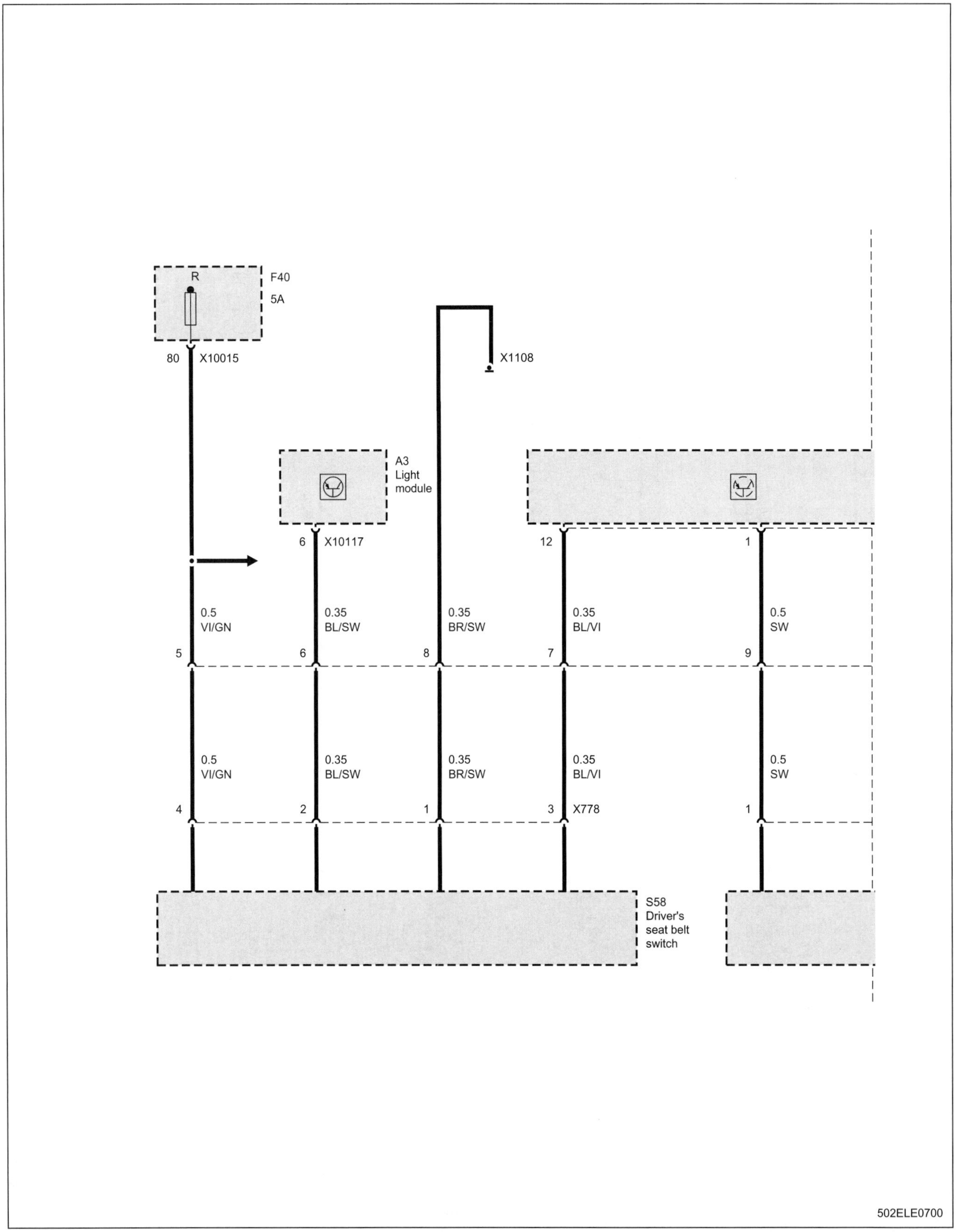

X-Connectors and Splices
X275 Connector - Driver's seat
(2 of 4)

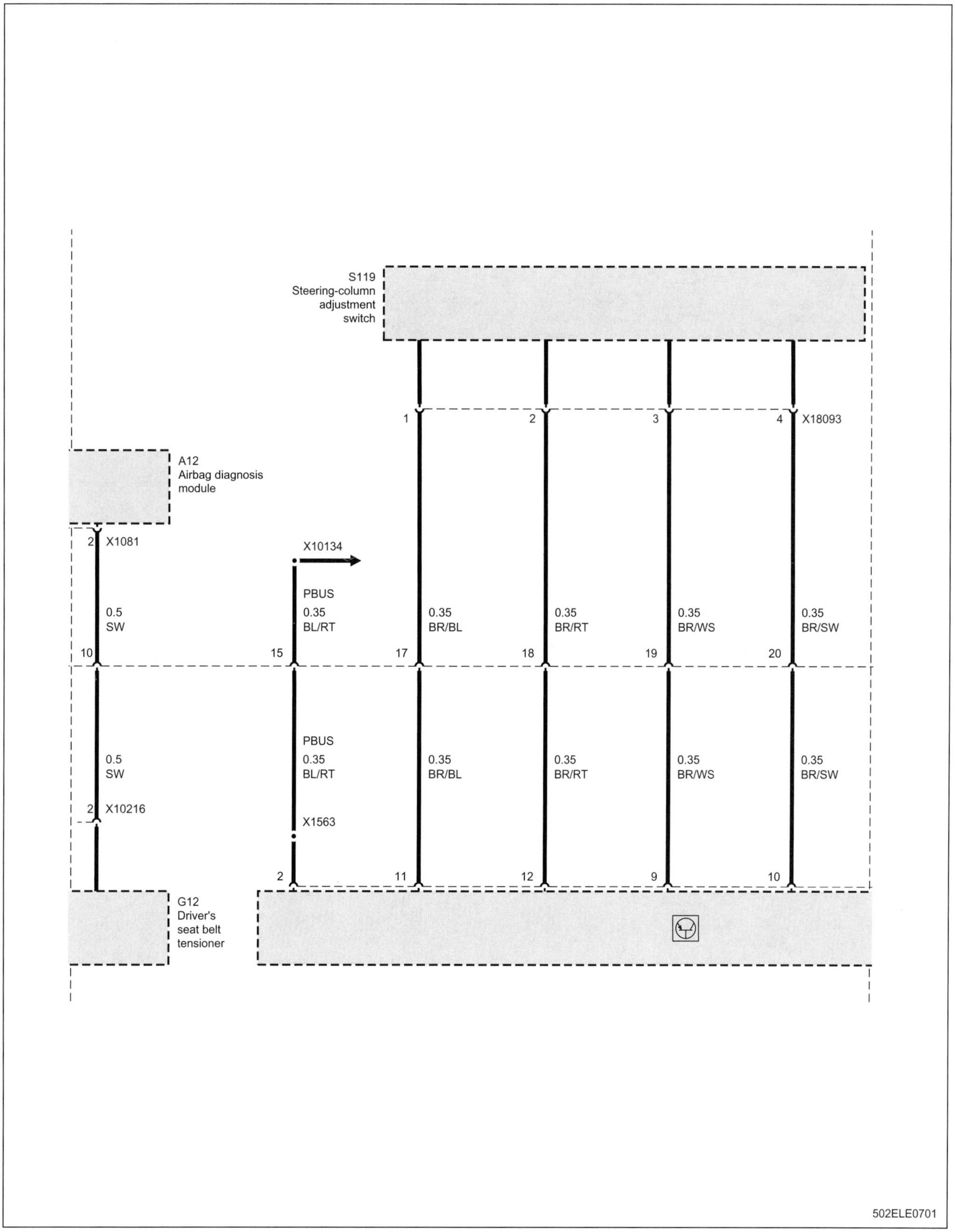

X-Connectors and Splices
X275 Connector - Driver's seat
(3 of 4)

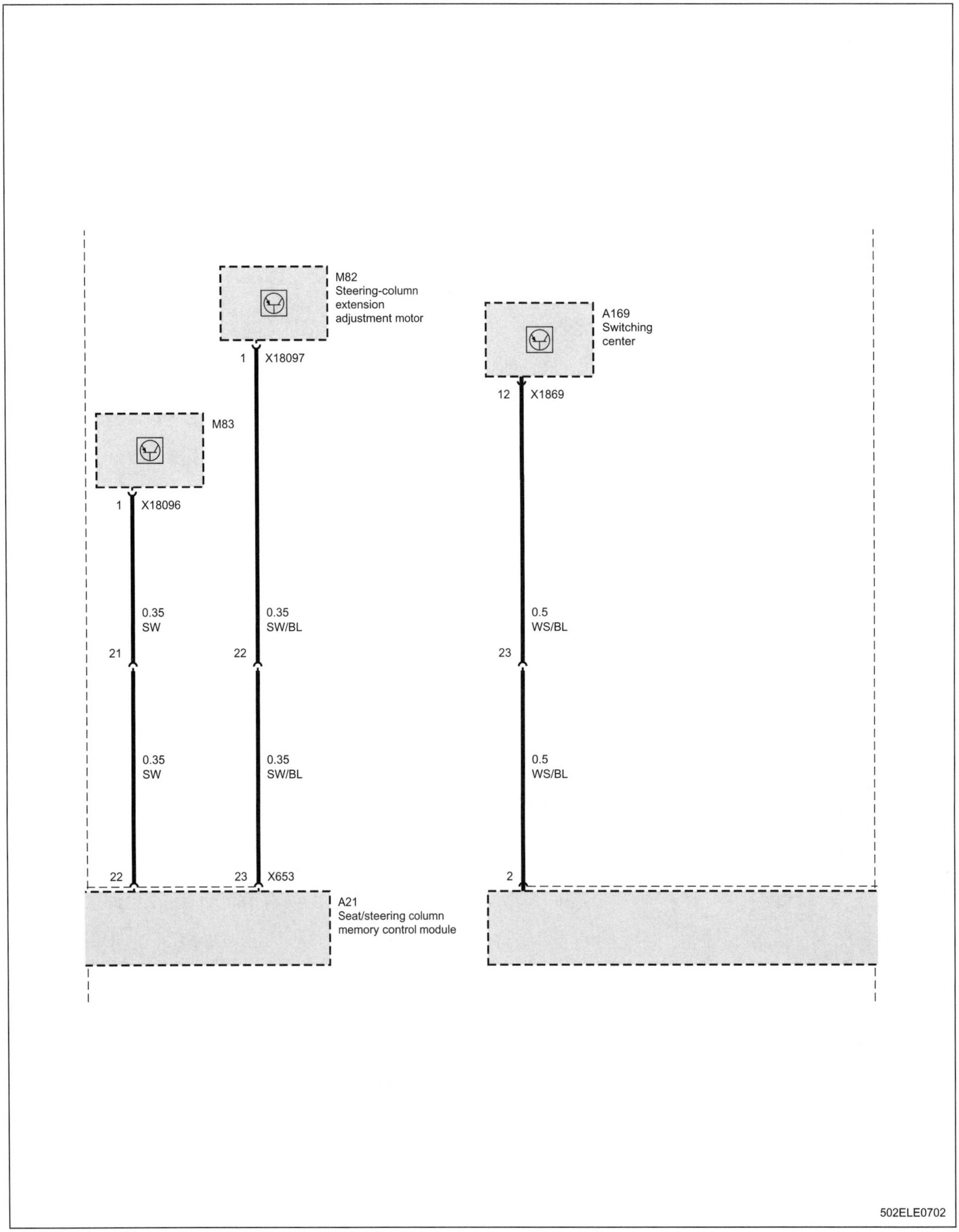

X-Connectors and Splices
X275 Connector - Driver's seat
(4 of 4)

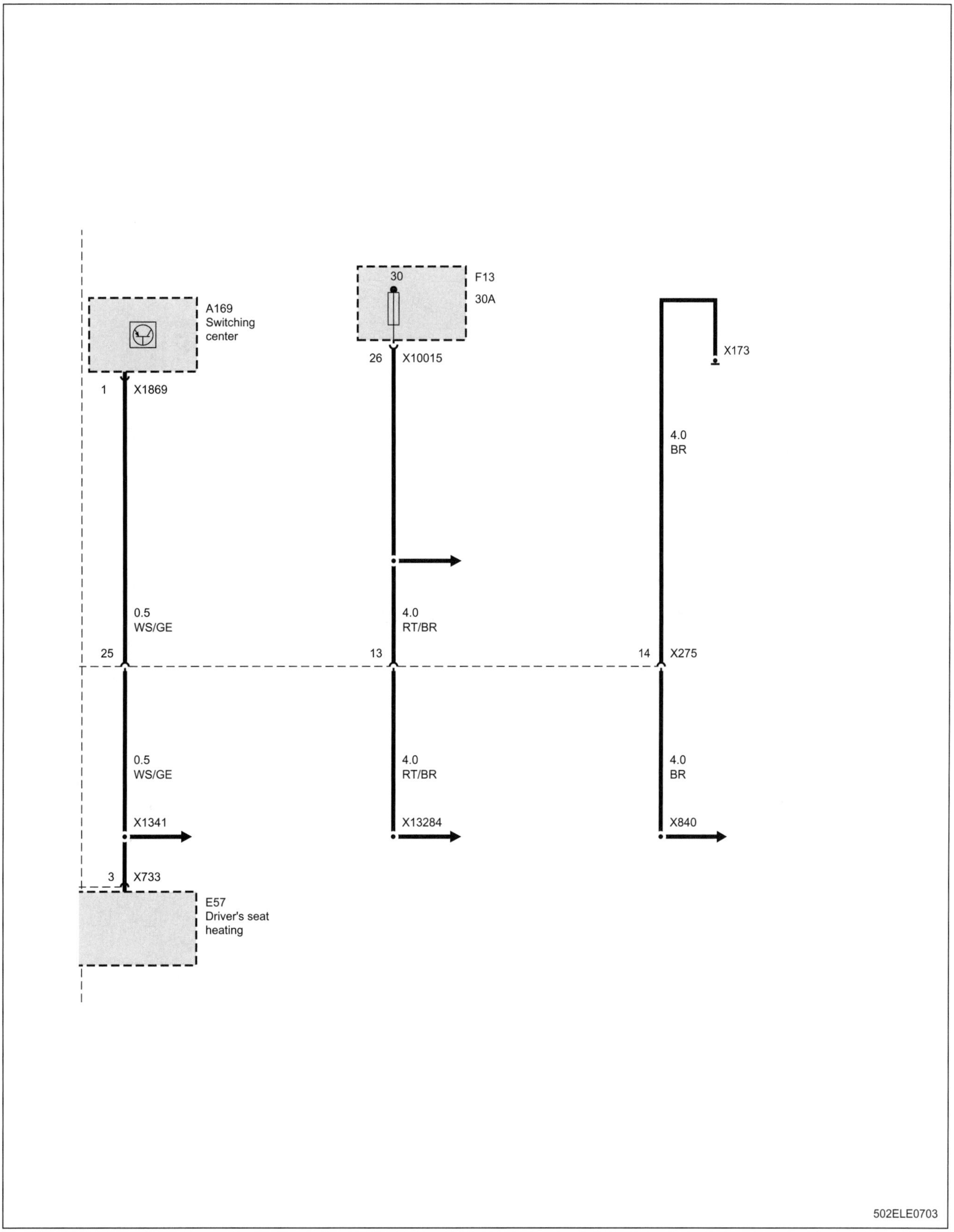

X-Connectors
X279 Connector - Passenger's seat
(1 of 2)

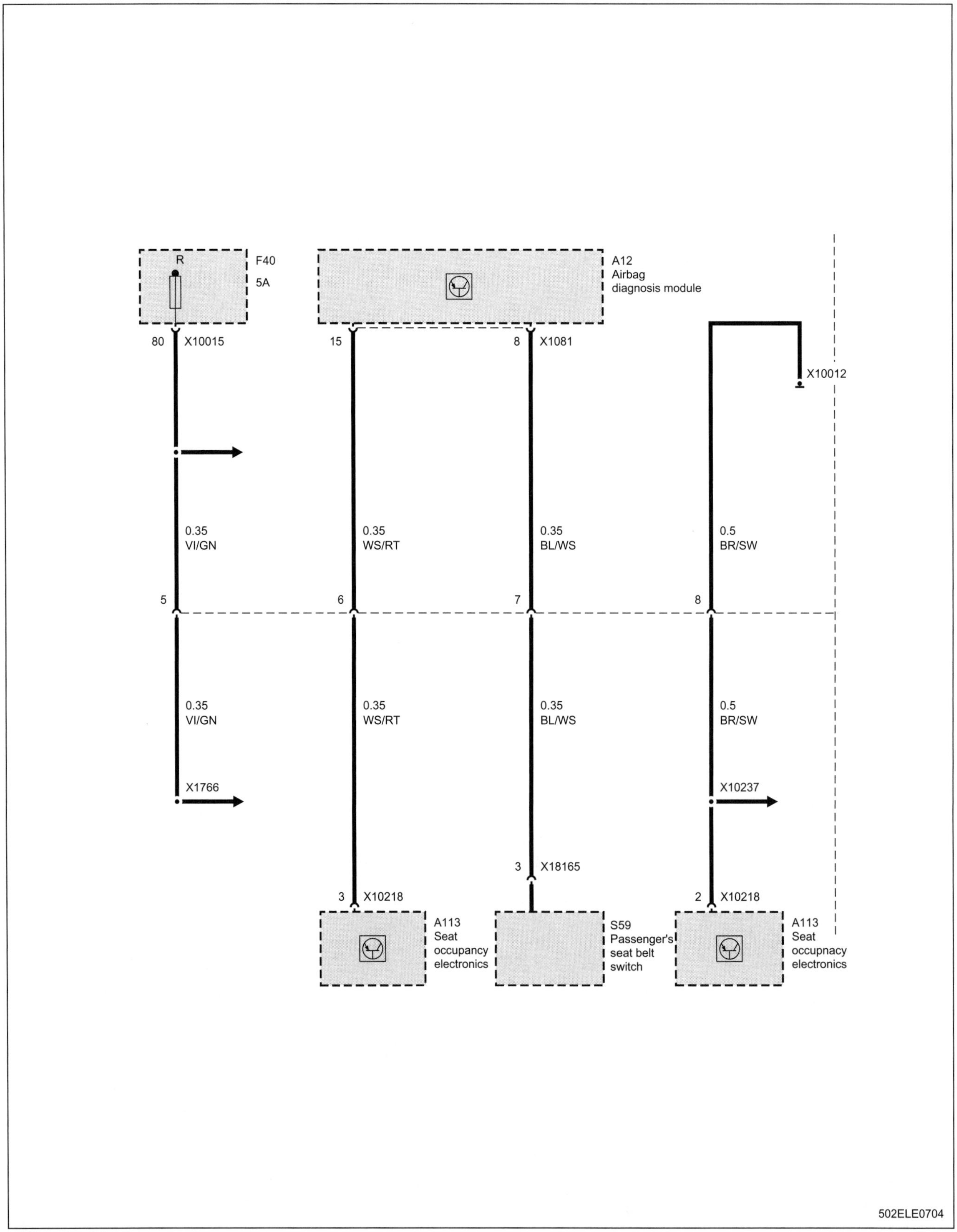

X-Connectors
X279 Connector - Passenger's seat
(2 of 2)

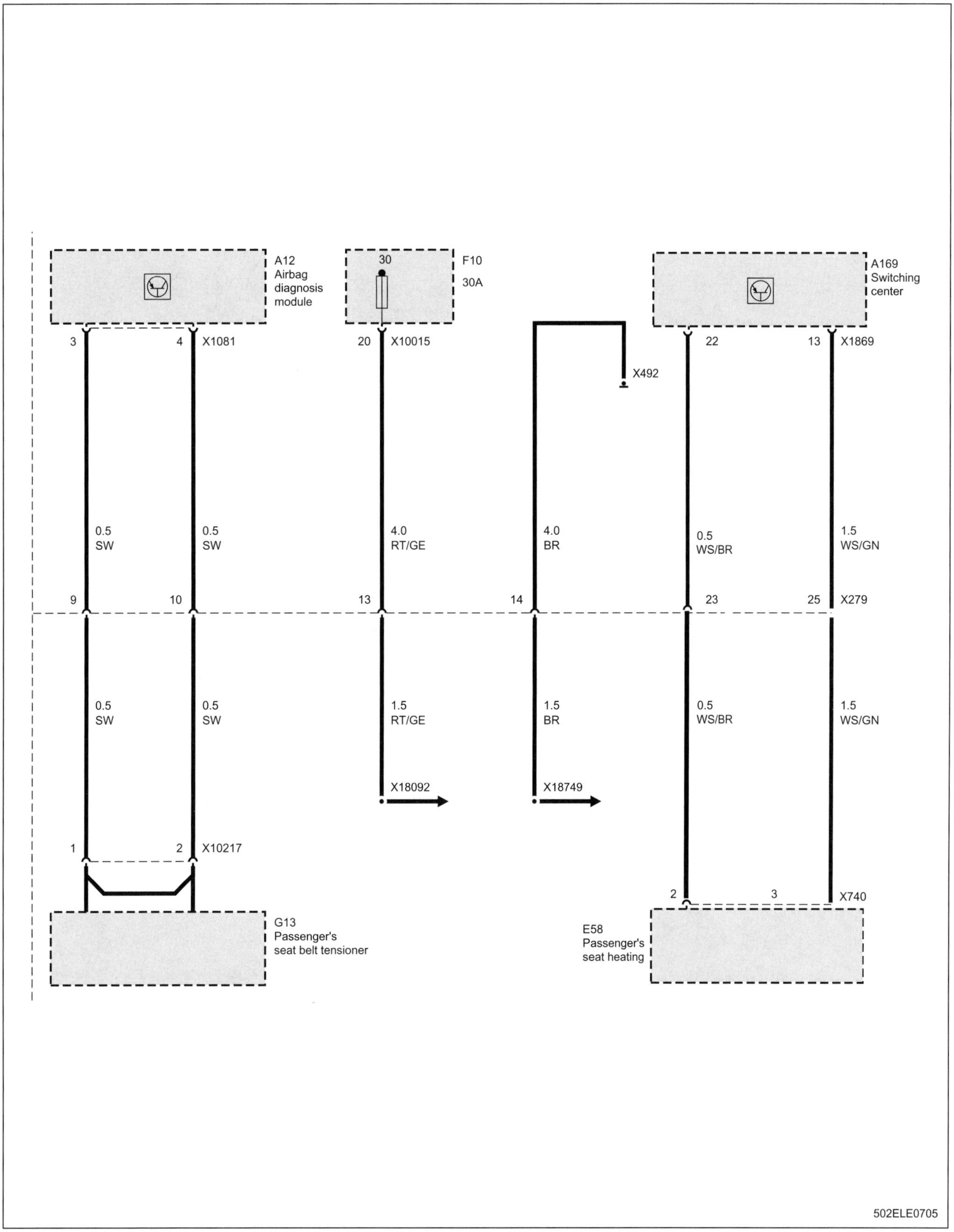

X-Connectors and Splices
X322 Connector
(1 of 3)

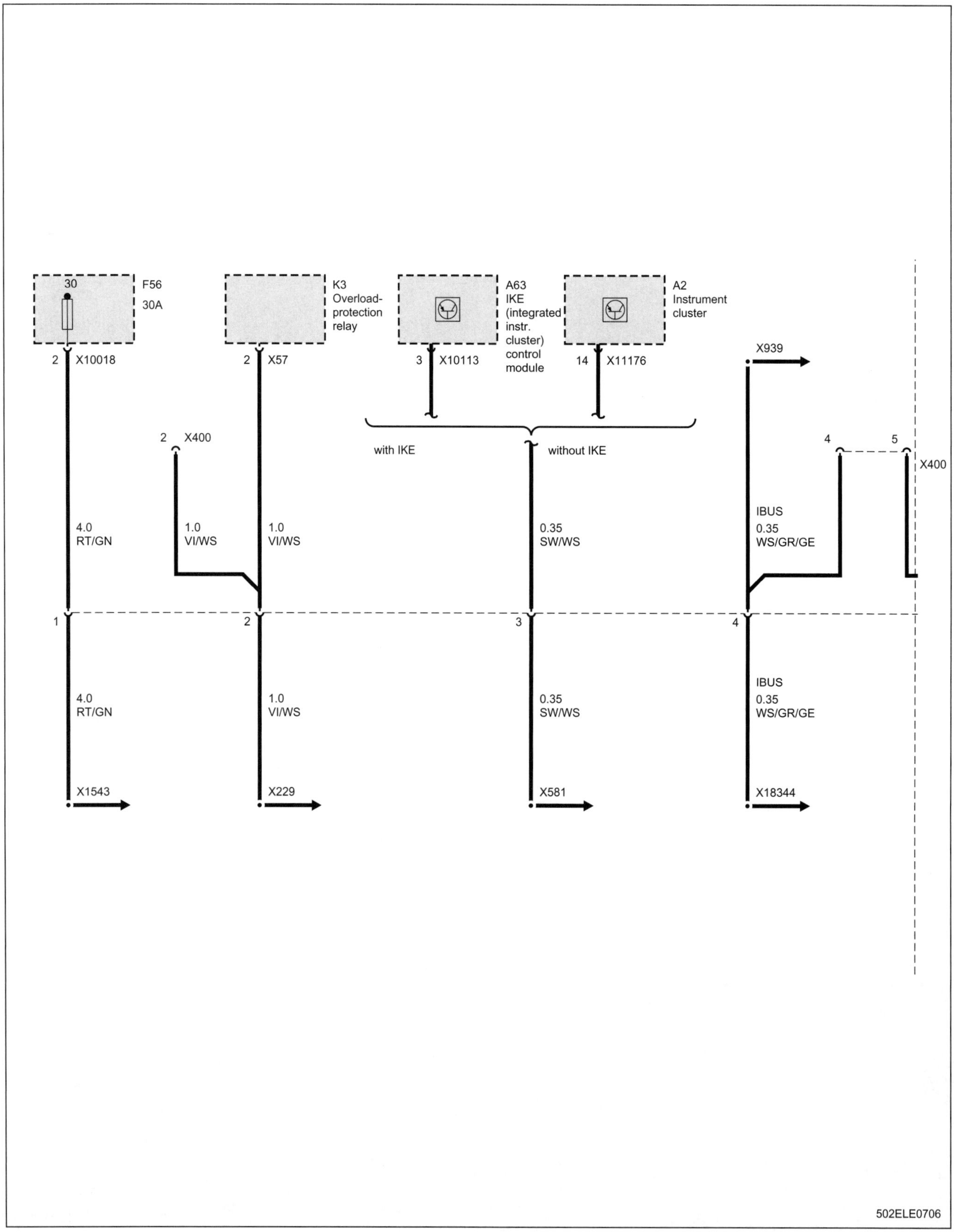
30
F56
30A
2 X10018
K3
Overload-
protection
relay
2 X57
A63
IKE
(integrated
instr.
cluster)
control
module
3 X10113
A2
Instrument
cluster
14 X11176
X939
2 X400
with IKE
without IKE
4
5
X400
4.0
RT/GN
1.0
VI/WS
1.0
VI/WS
0.35
SW/WS
IBUS
0.35
WS/GR/GE
1
2
3
4
4.0
RT/GN
1.0
VI/WS
0.35
SW/WS
IBUS
0.35
WS/GR/GE
X1543
X229
X581
X18344
502ELE0706

X-Connectors and Splices
X322 Connector
(2 of 3)

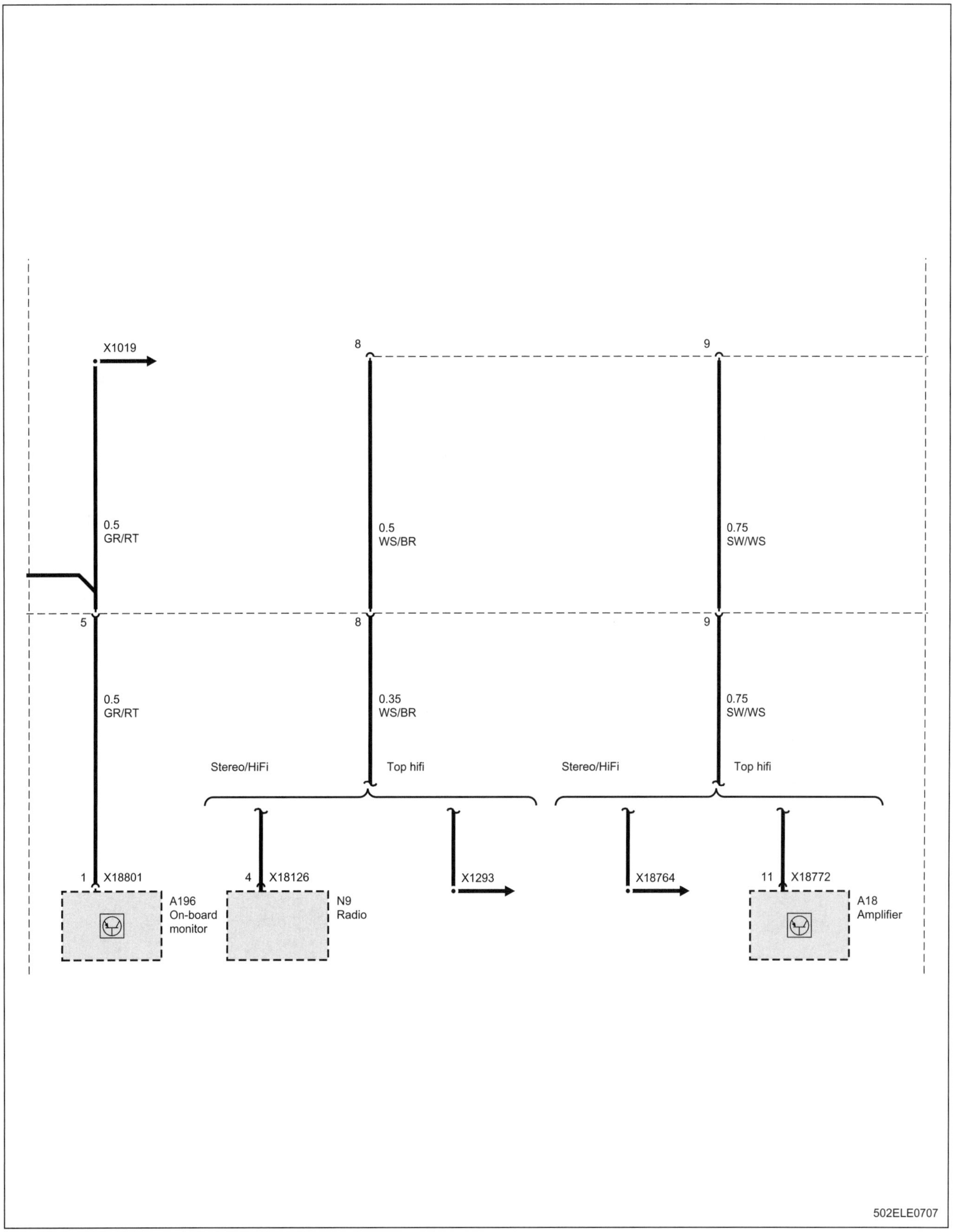
X1019
8
9
0.5
GR/RT
0.5
WS/BR
0.75
SW/WS
5
8
9
0.5
GR/RT
0.35
WS/BR
0.75
SW/WS
Stereo/HiFi
Top hifi
Stereo/HiFi
Top hifi
1
X18801
4
X18126
X1293
X18764
11
X18772
A196
On-board
monitor
N9
Radio
A18
Amplifier
502ELE0707

X-Connectors and Splices
X322 Connector
(3 of 3)

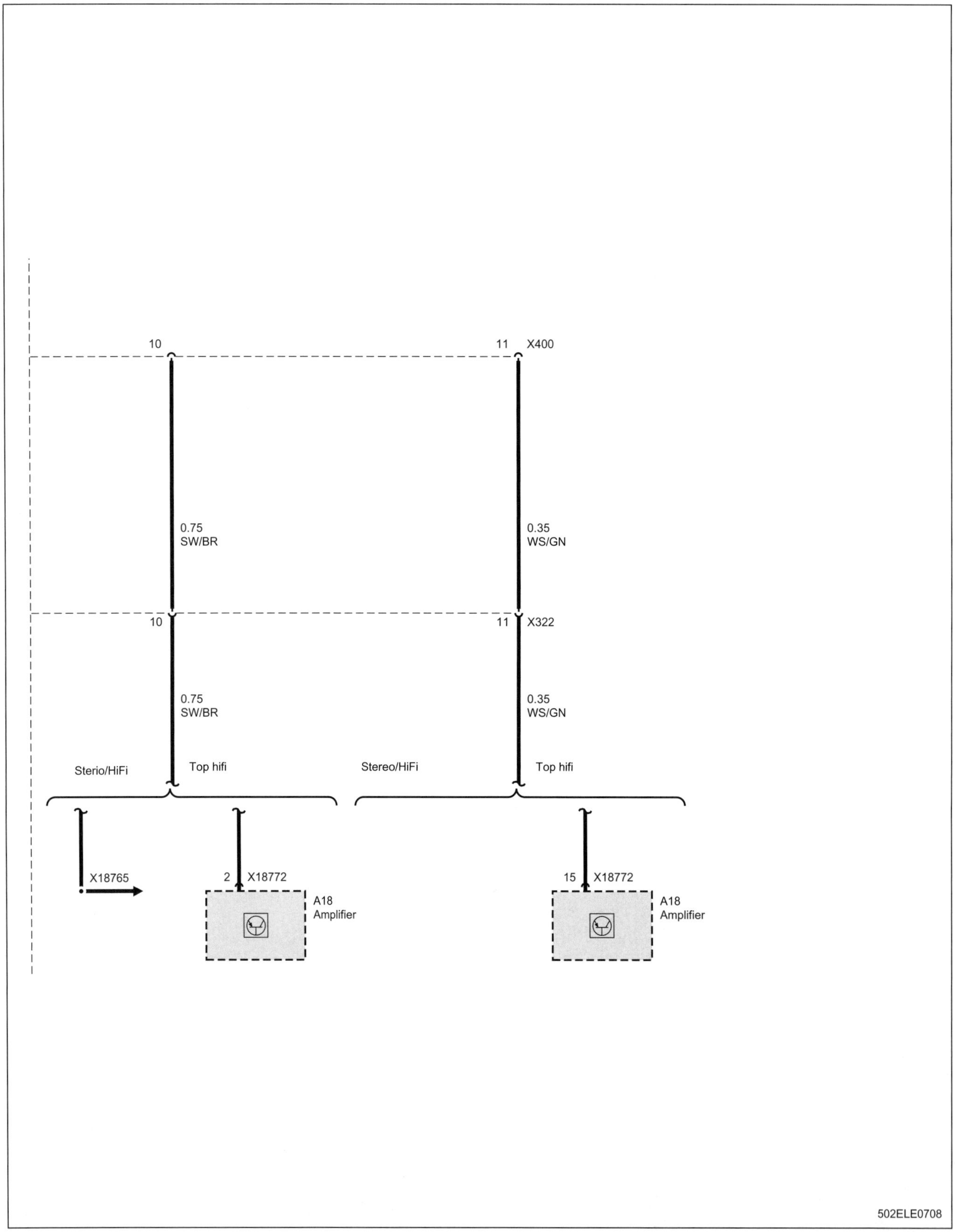
10
11
X400
0.75
SW/BR
0.35
WS/GN
10
11
X322
0.75
SW/BR
0.35
WS/GN
Sterio/HiFi
Top hifi
Stereo/HiFi
Top hifi
X18765
2
X18772
A18
Amplifier
15
X18772
A18
Amplifier
502ELE0708

X-Connectors and Splices
X325 Connector - Radio/Hifi II
(1 of 1)

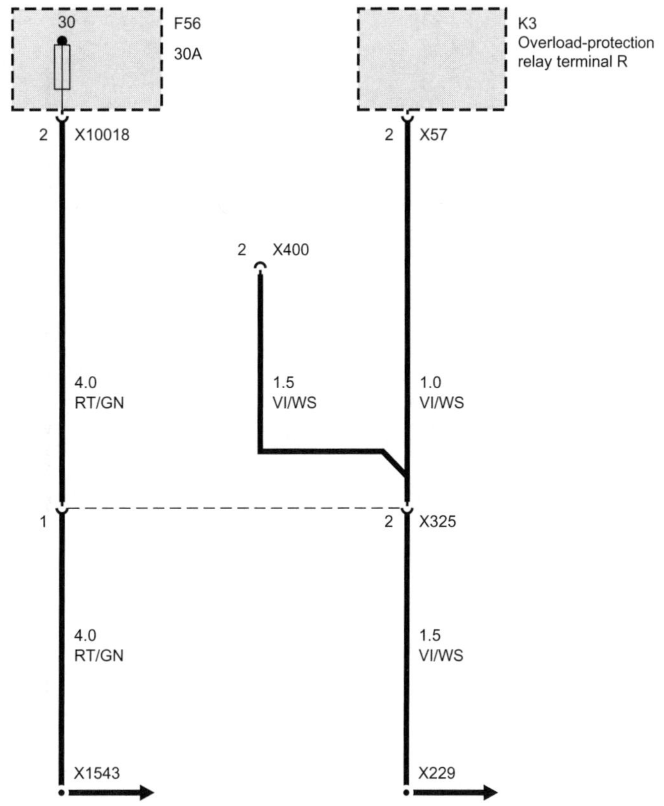

X-Connectors and Splices
X400 Connector - Telephone
(1 of 3)

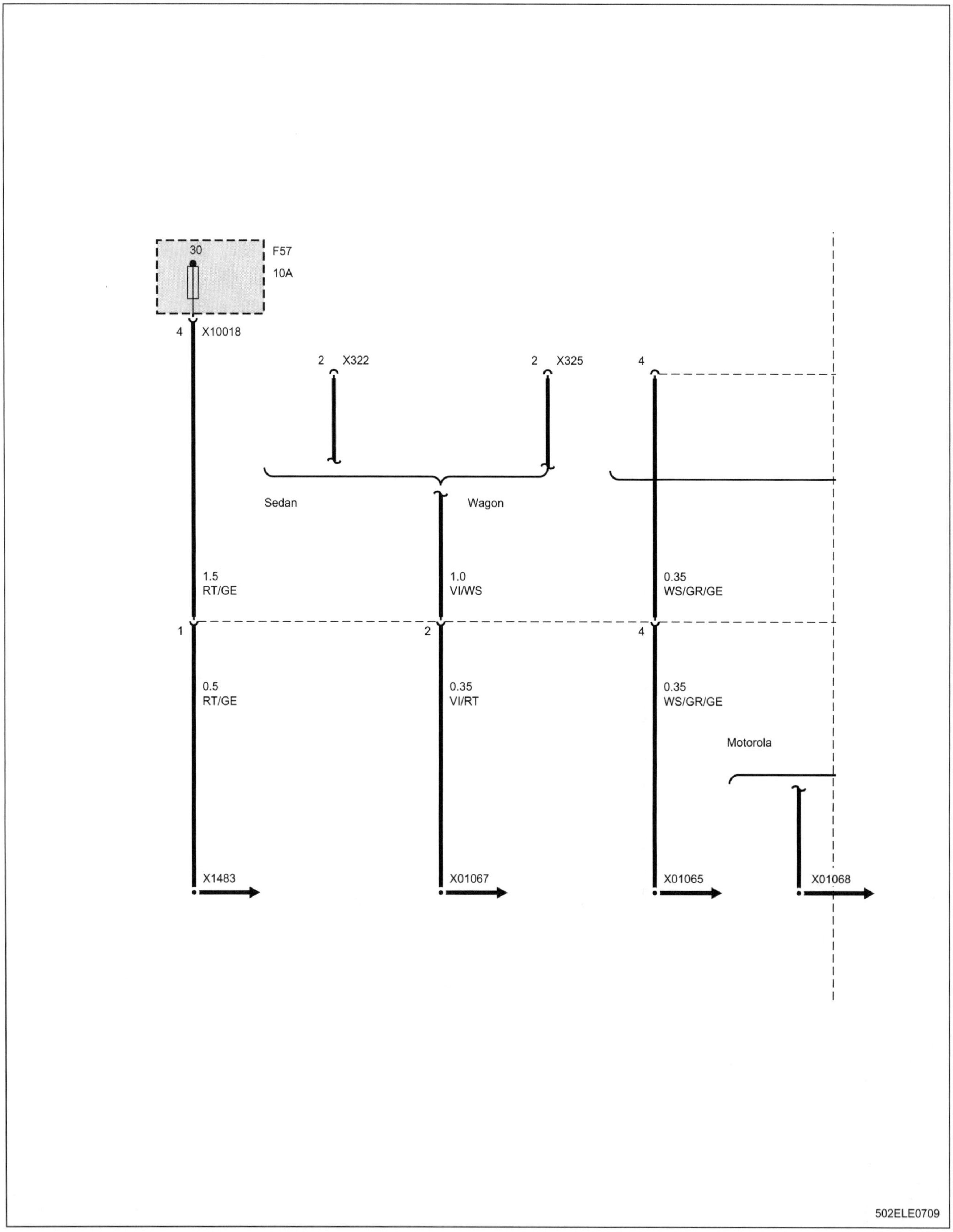

X-Connectors and Splices
X400 Connector - Telephone
(2 of 3)

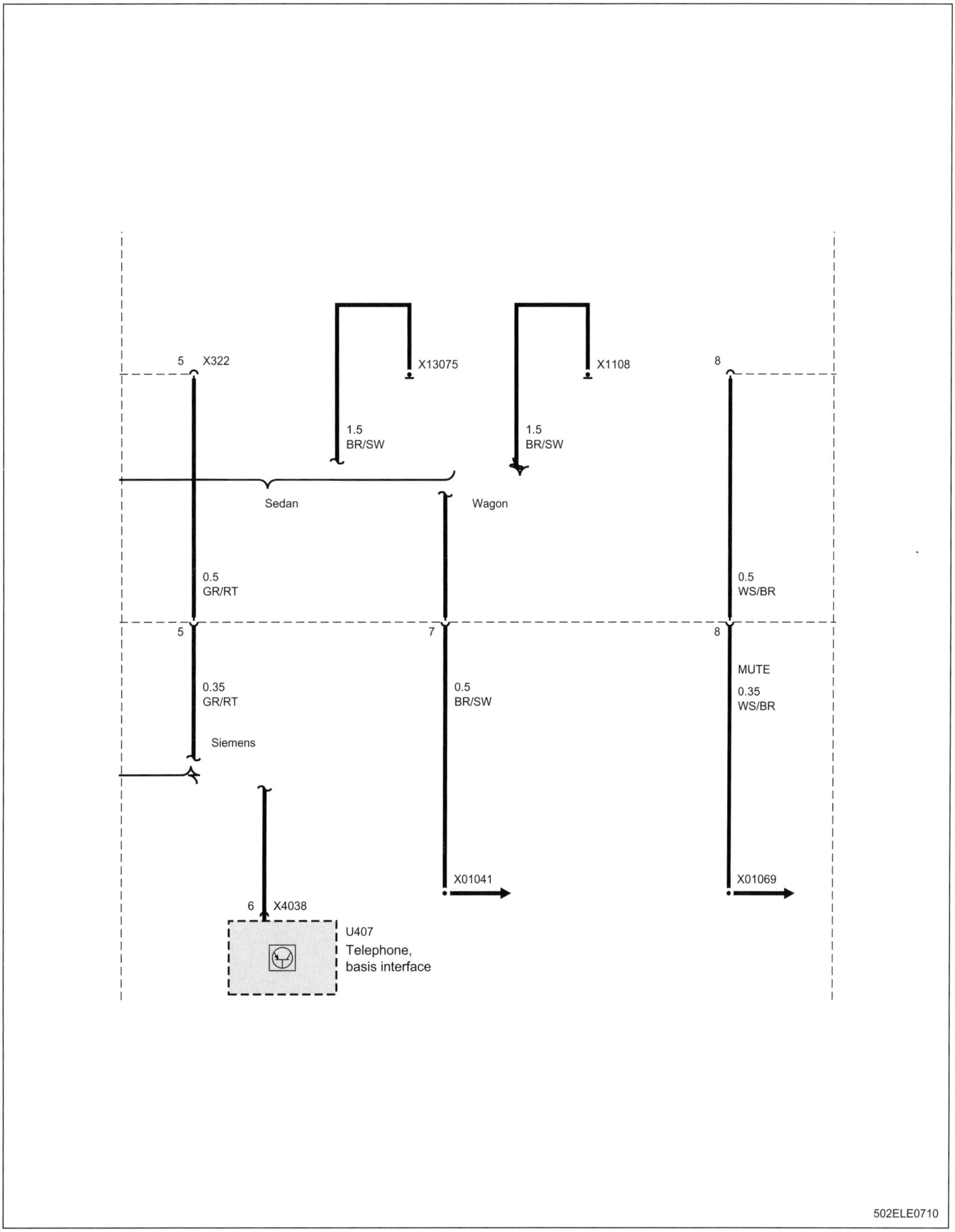

X-Connectors and Splices
X400 Connector - Telephone
(3 of 3)

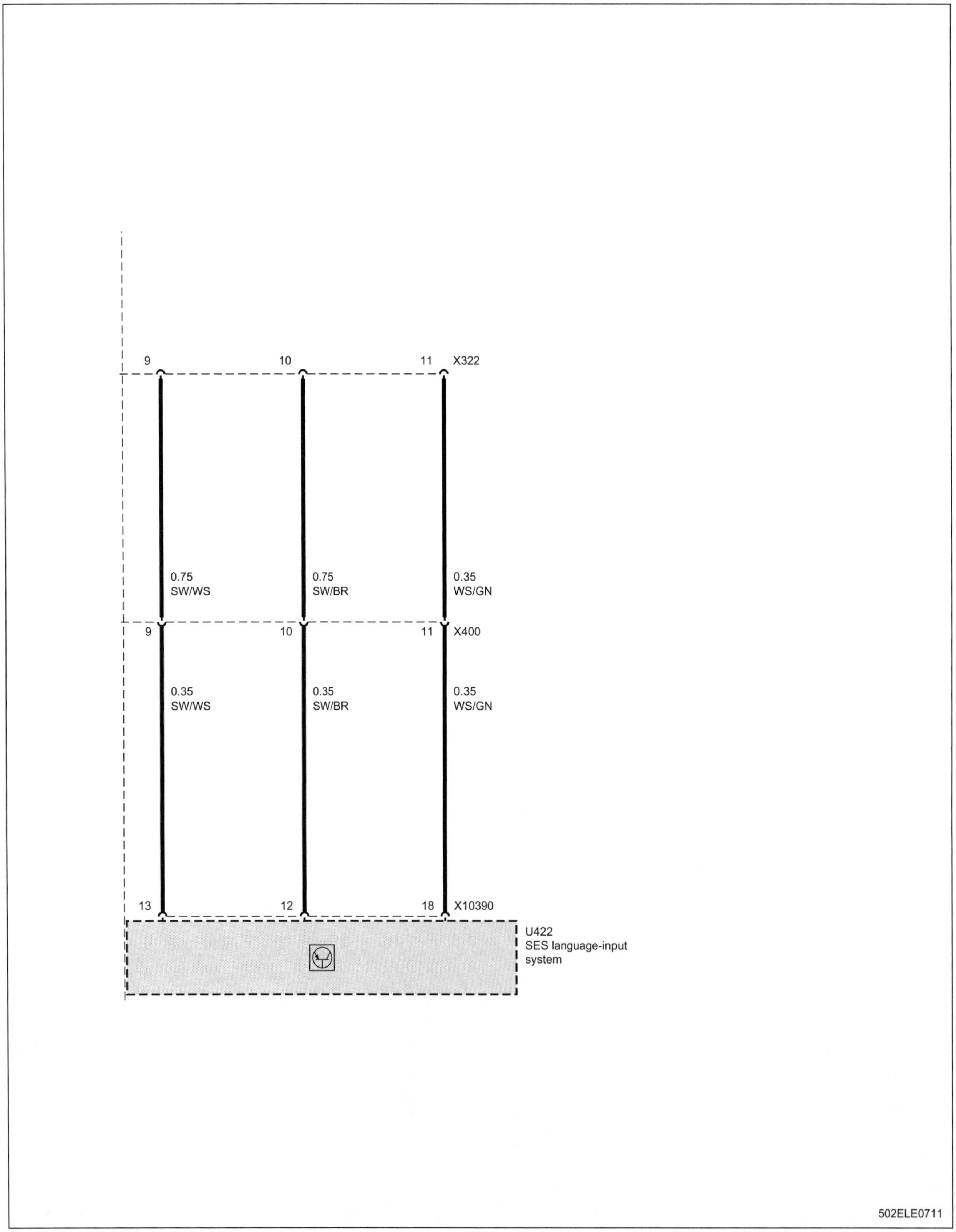

X-Connectors and Splices
X442 Connector - TXD
(1 of 1)

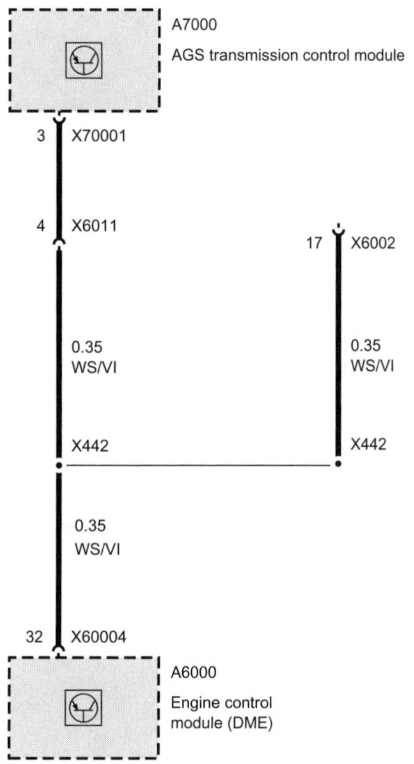

X-Connectors and Splices
X455 Splice - Central locking system
(1 of 1)

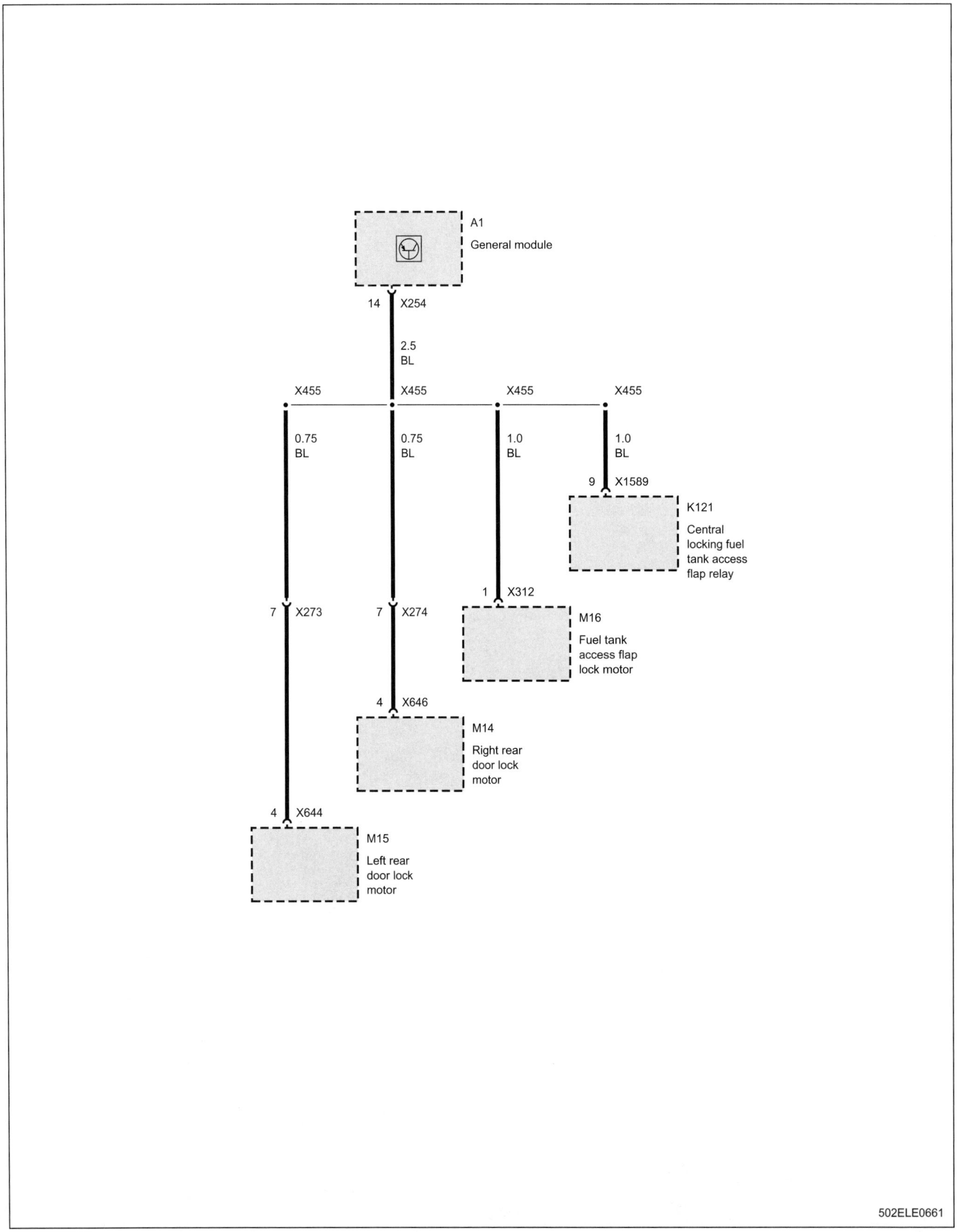

X-Connectors and Splices
X456 Splice - Central locking system

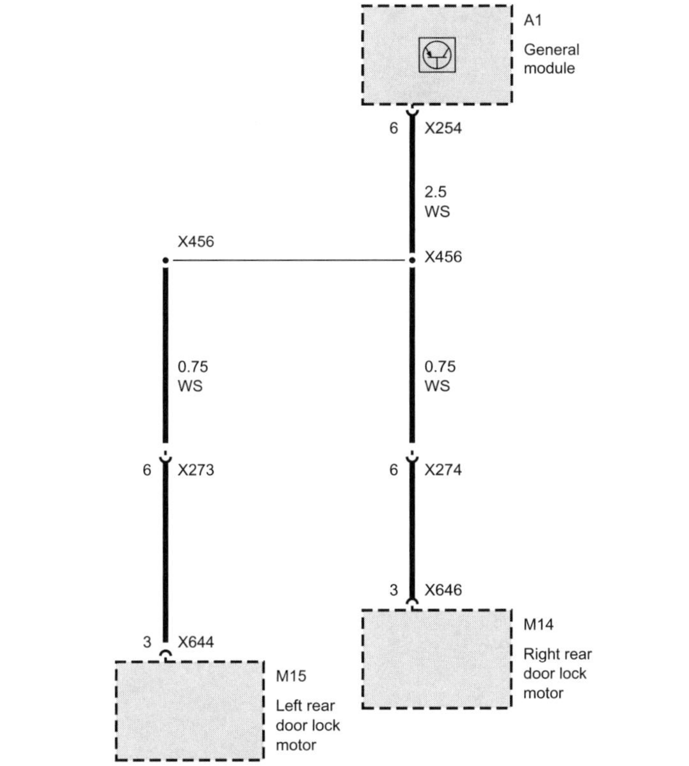

502ELE0663a

X-Connectors and Splices
X462 Splice - Central locking system

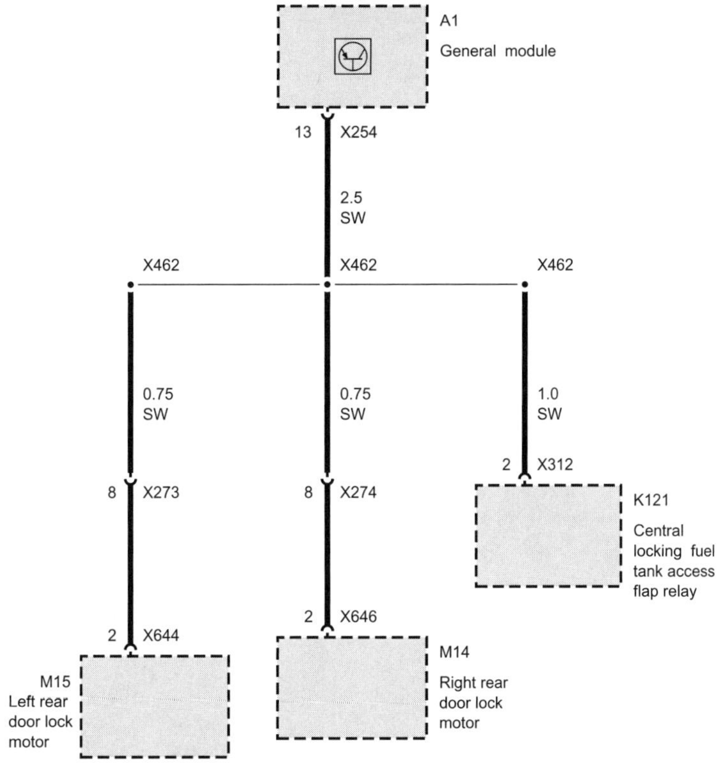

502ELE0663b

X-Connectors and Splices
X473 Connector - Interior lights
(1 of 1)

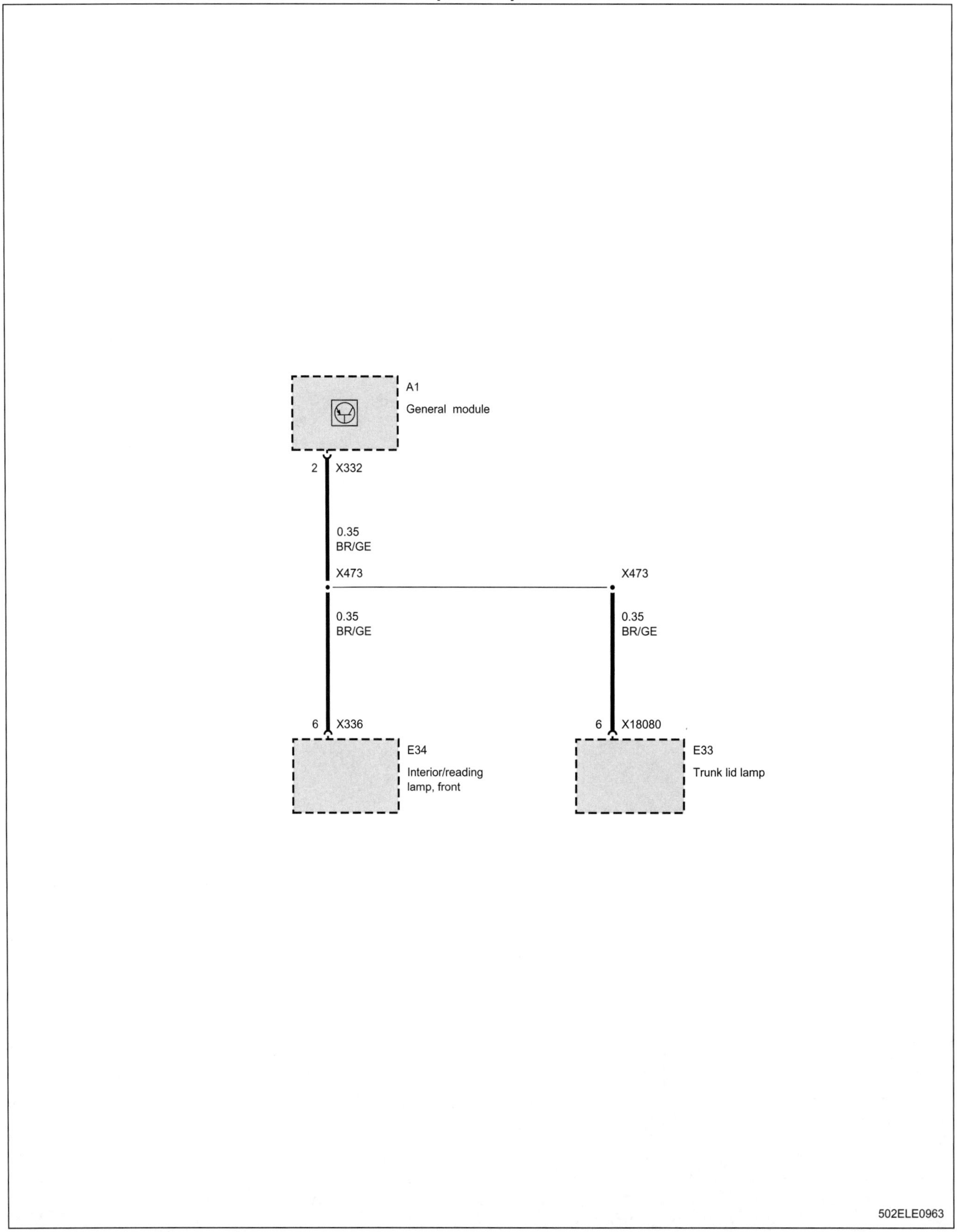

Ground Distribution X490 Ground (1 of 2)

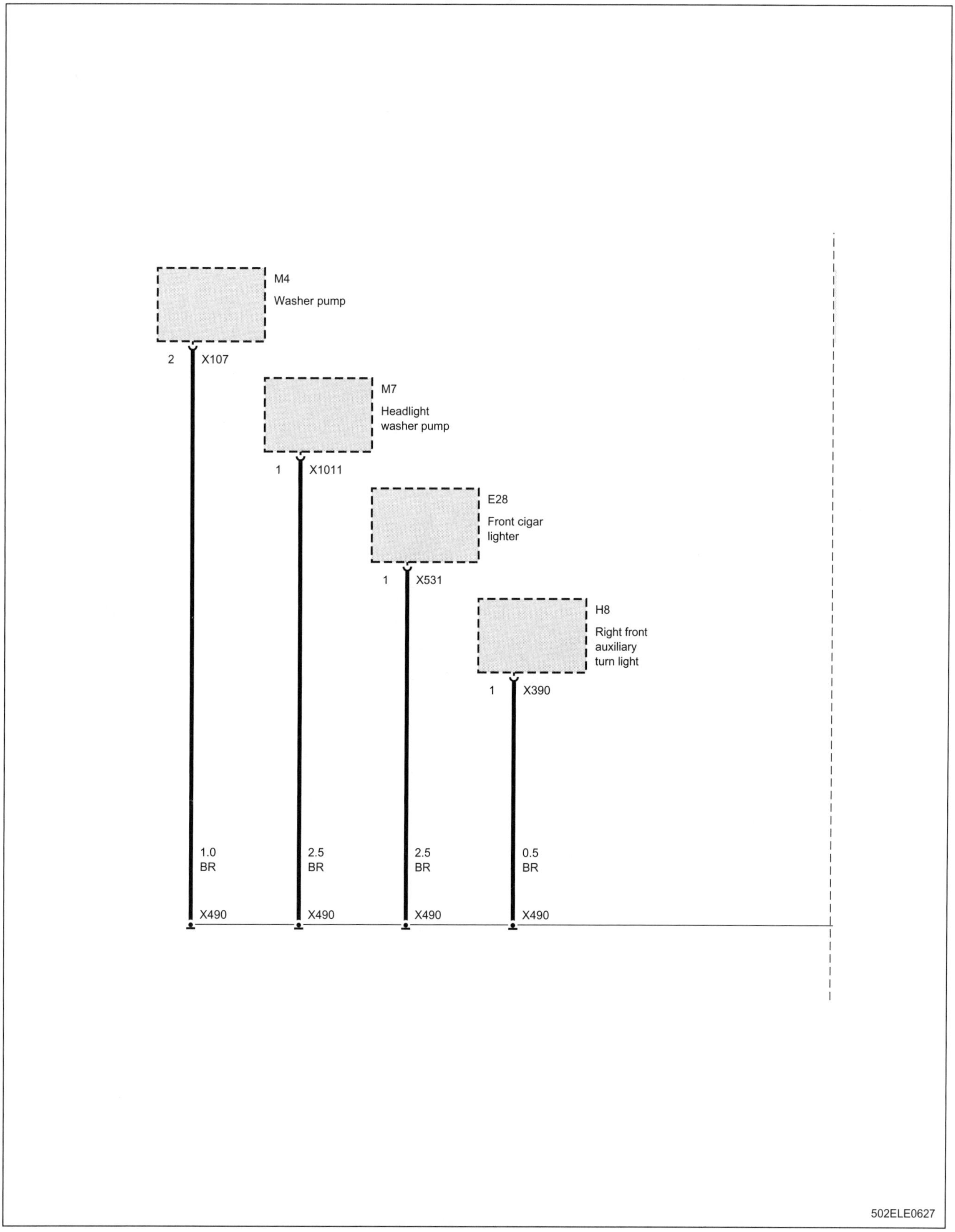
M4
Washer pump
2
X107
M7
Headlight
washer pump
1
X1011
E28
Front cigar
lighter
1
X531
H8
Right front
auxiliary
turn light
1
X390
1.0
BR
2.5
BR
2.5
BR
0.5
BR
X490
X490
X490
X490
502ELE0627

Ground Distribution
X490 Ground
(2 of 2)

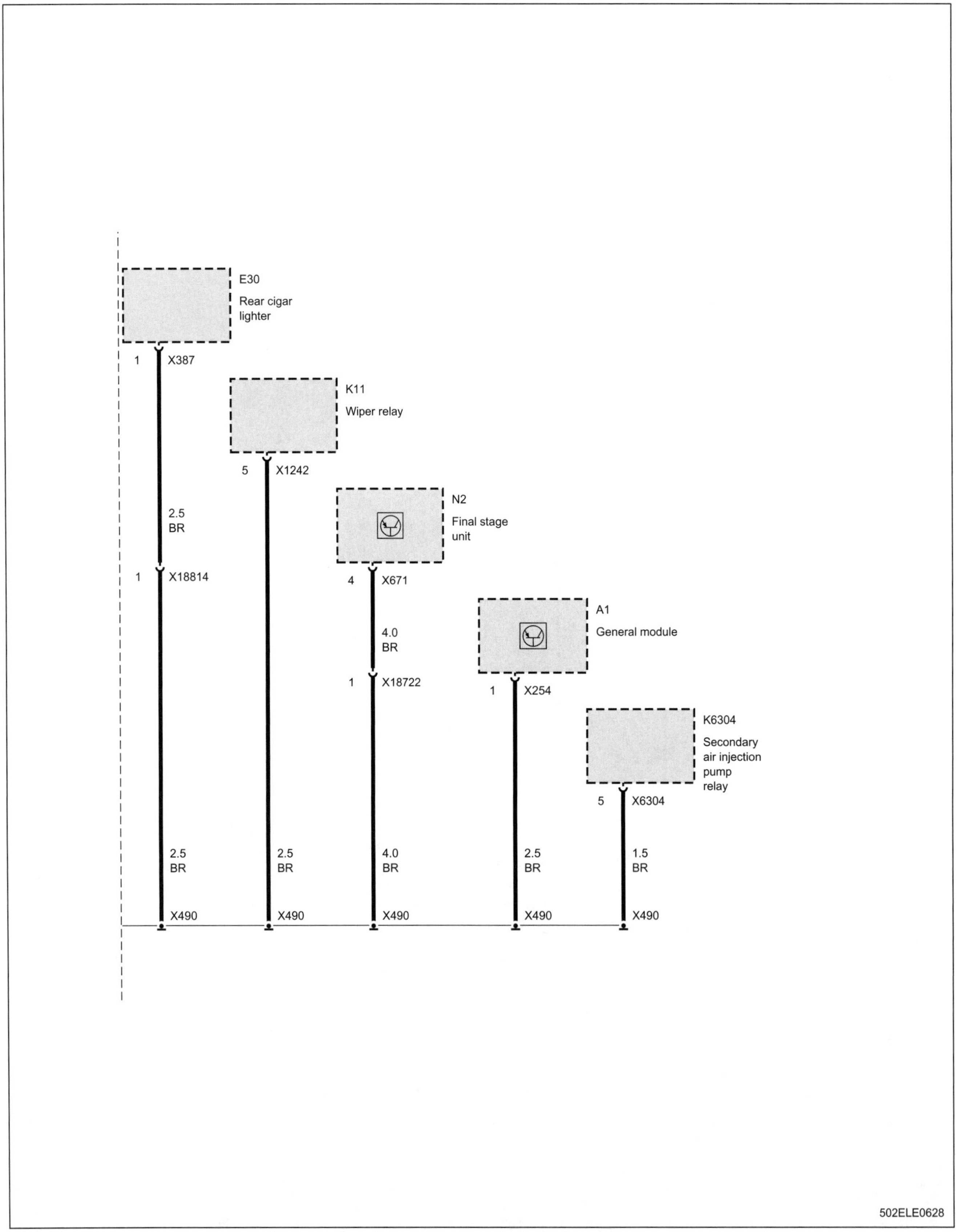
E30
Rear cigar lighter
1
X387
2.5
BR
1
X18814
2.5
BR
X490
K11
Wiper relay
5
X1242
2.5
BR
X490
N2
Final stage unit
4
X671
4.0
BR
1
X18722
4.0
BR
X490
A1
General module
1
X254
2.5
BR
X490
K6304
Secondary air injection pump relay
5
X6304
1.5
BR
X490
502ELE0628

Ground Distribution
X492 Ground I

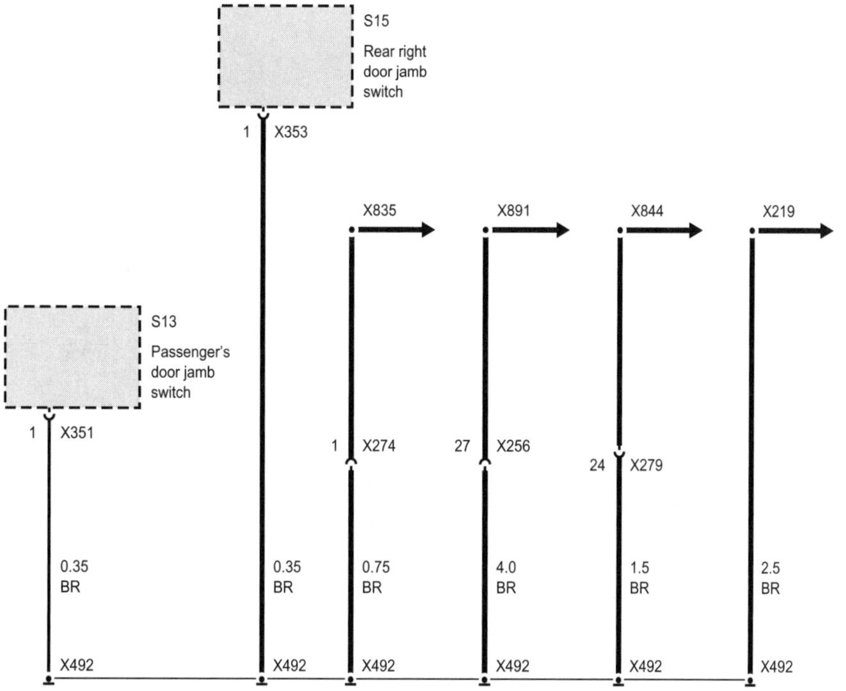

502ELE0629a

Ground Distribution
X492 Ground II

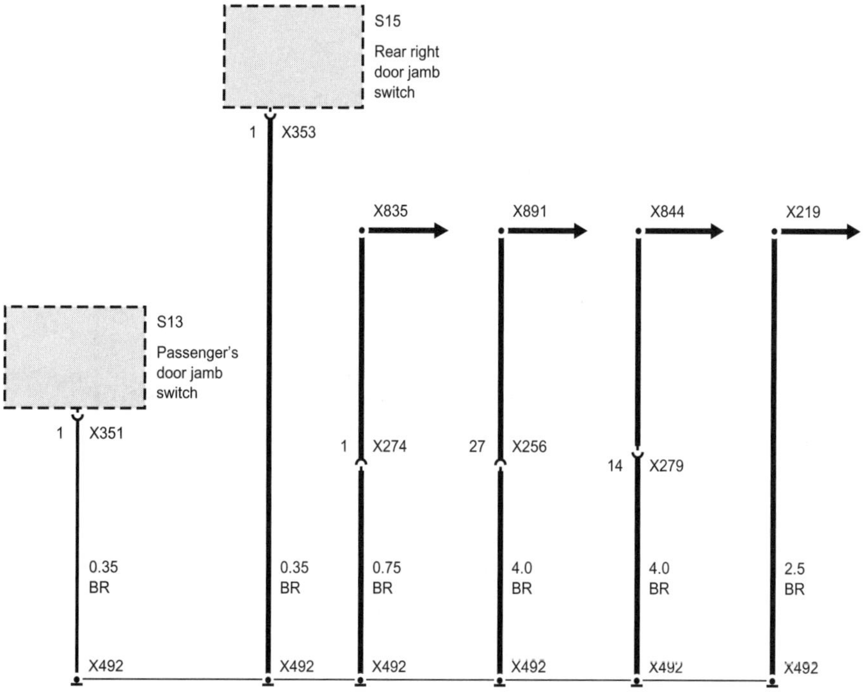

502ELE0629b

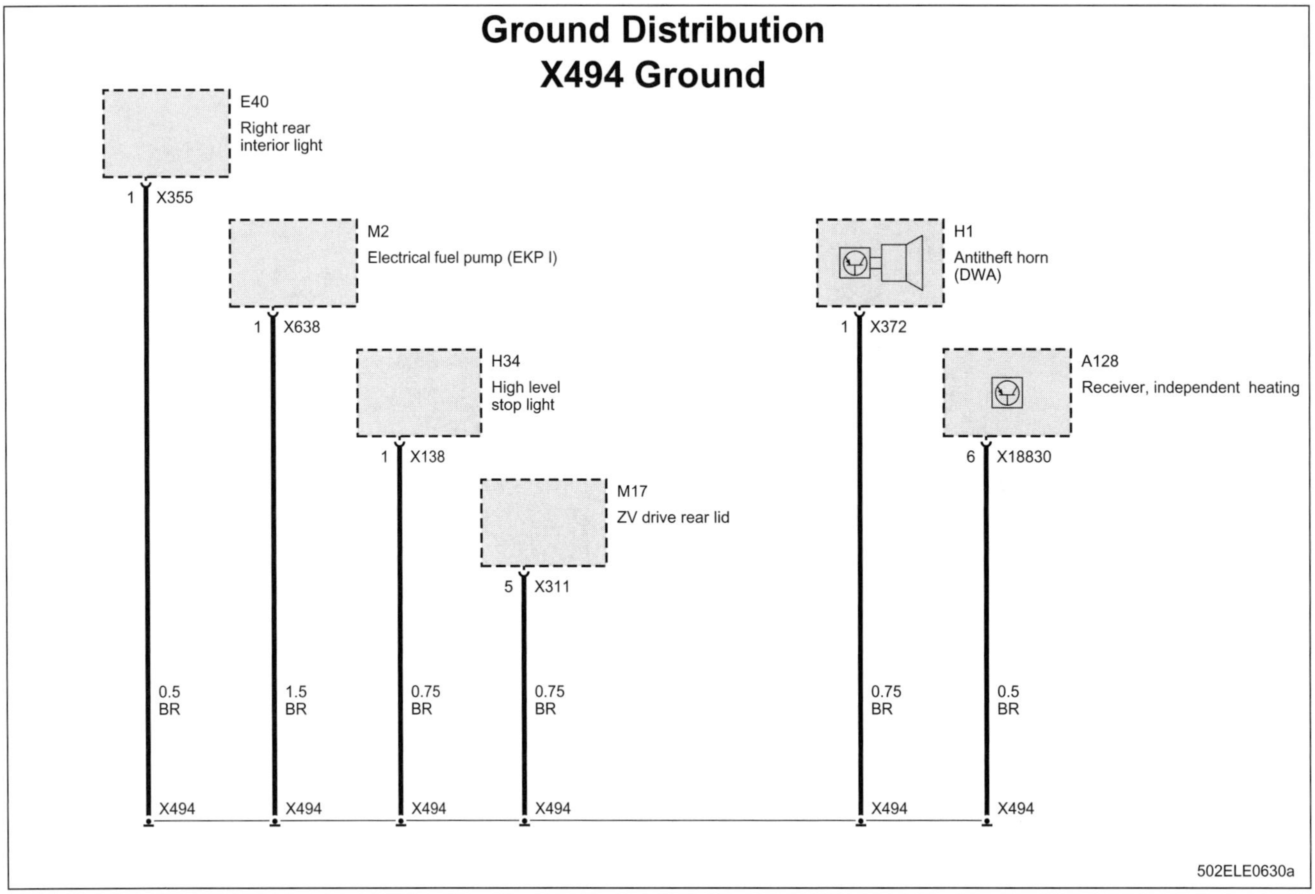
Ground Distribution
X494 Ground
E40
Right rear interior light
1 X355
M2
Electrical fuel pump (EKP I)
1 X638
H34
High level stop light
1 X138
M17
ZV drive rear lid
5 X311
H1
Antitheft horn (DWA)
1 X372
A128
Receiver, independent heating
6 X18830
0.5 BR
1.5 BR
0.75 BR
0.75 BR
0.75 BR
0.5 BR
X494
X494
X494
X494
X494
X494
502ELE0630a

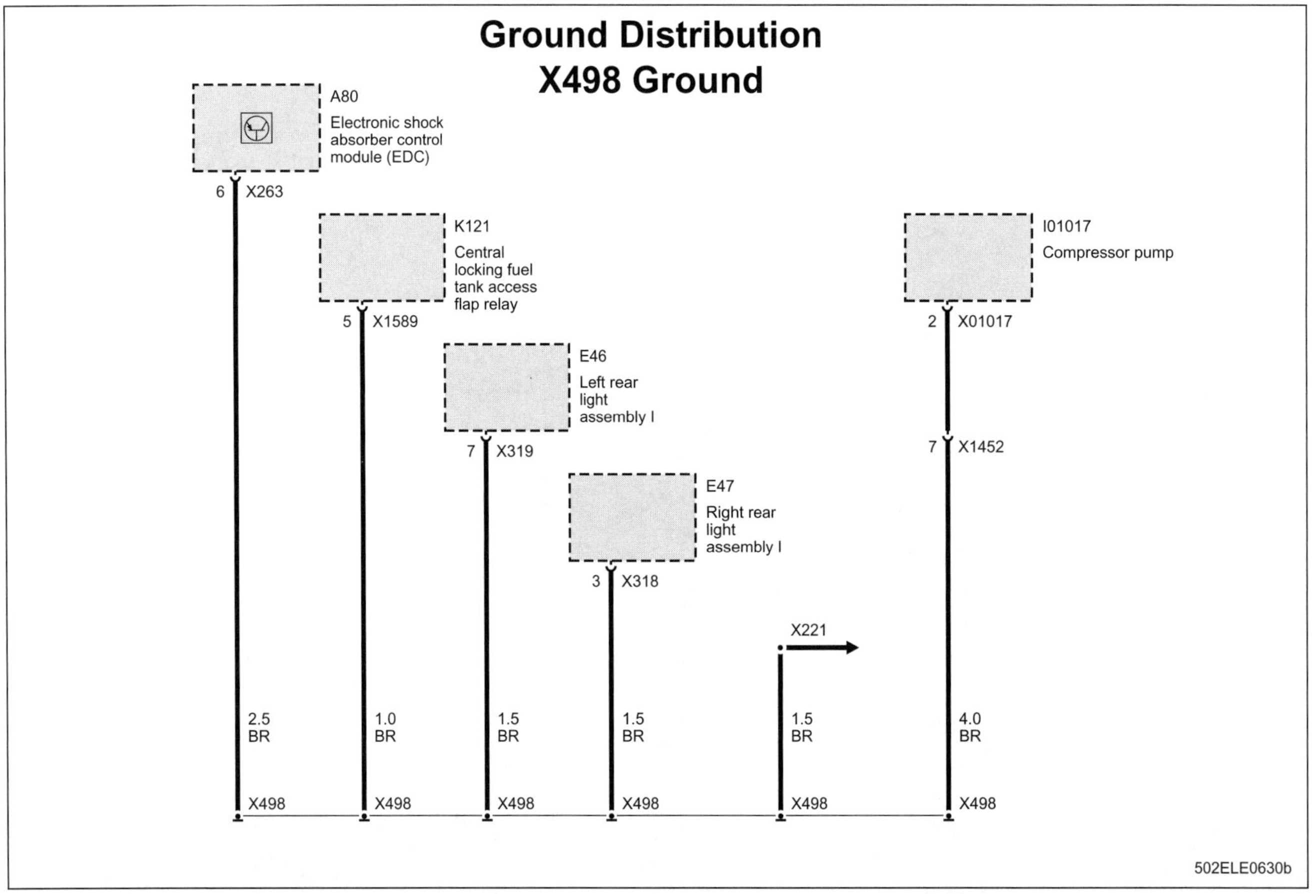
Ground Distribution
X498 Ground
A80
Electronic shock absorber control module (EDC)
6 X263
K121
Central locking fuel tank access flap relay
5 X1589
E46
Left rear light assembly I
7 X319
E47
Right rear light assembly I
3 X318
I01017
Compressor pump
2 X01017
7 X1452
X221
2.5 BR
1.0 BR
1.5 BR
1.5 BR
1.5 BR
4.0 BR
X498
X498
X498
X498
X498
X498
502ELE0630b

X-Connectors and Splices
X581 Connector - Speedometer output signal
(1 of 1)

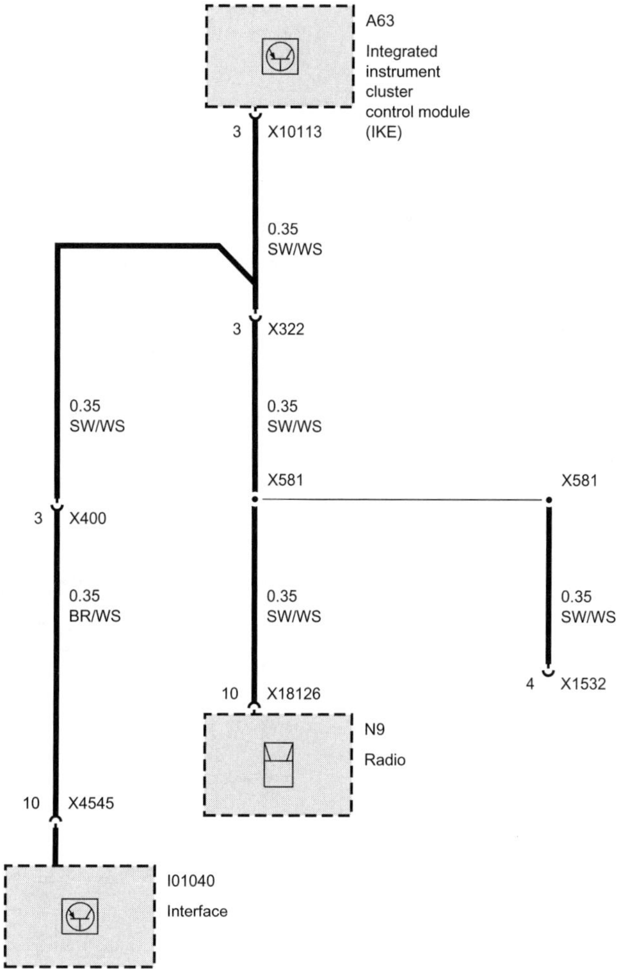

502ELE0638

Ground Distribution
X596 Ground splice
(1 of 3)

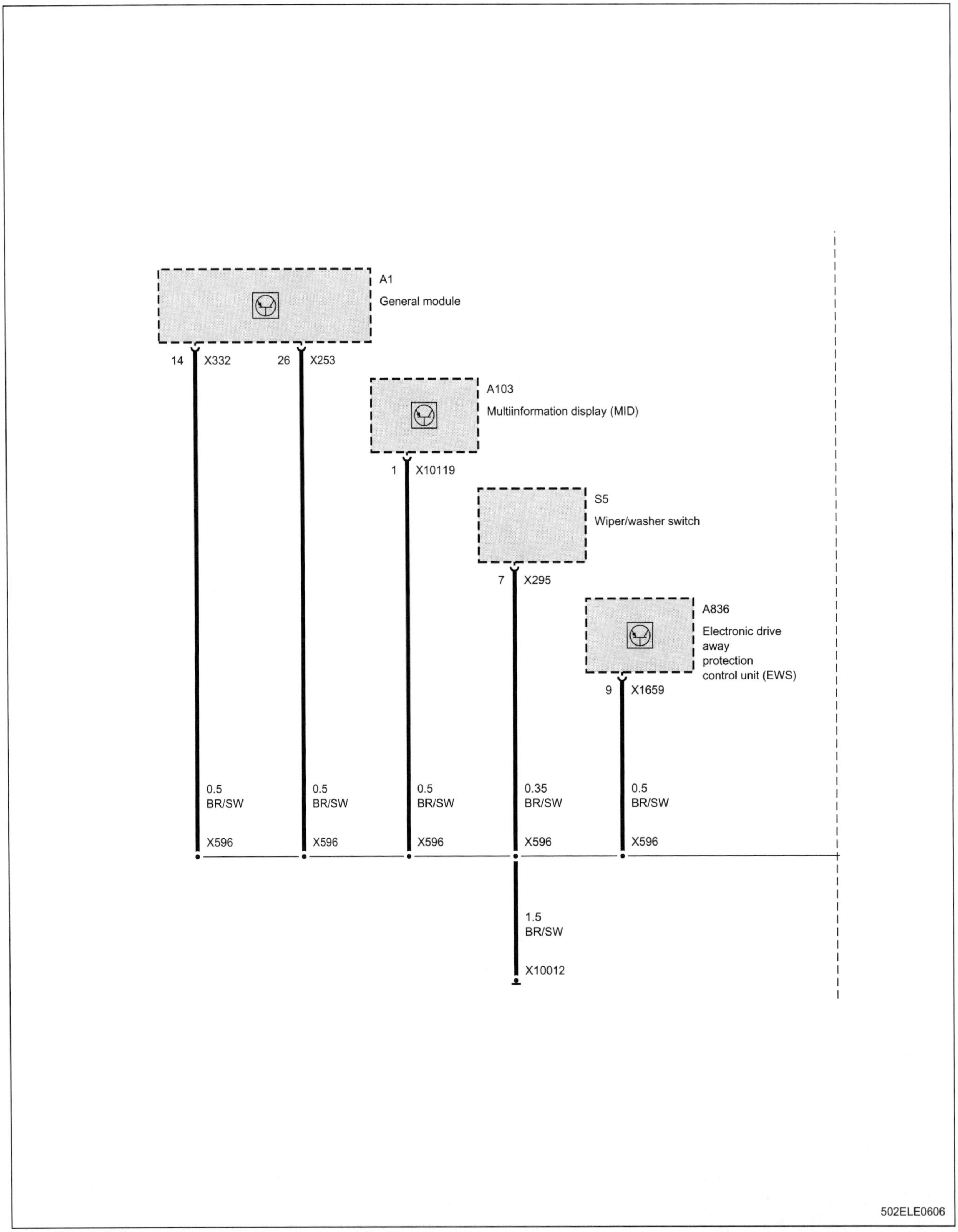
A1
General module
14
X332
26
X253
A103
Multiinformation display (MID)
1
X10119
S5
Wiper/washer switch
7
X295
A836
Electronic drive
away
protection
control unit (EWS)
9
X1659
0.5
BR/SW
X596
0.5
BR/SW
X596
0.5
BR/SW
X596
0.35
BR/SW
X596
0.5
BR/SW
X596
1.5
BR/SW
X10012
502ELE0606

Ground Distribution
X596 Ground splice
(2 of 3)

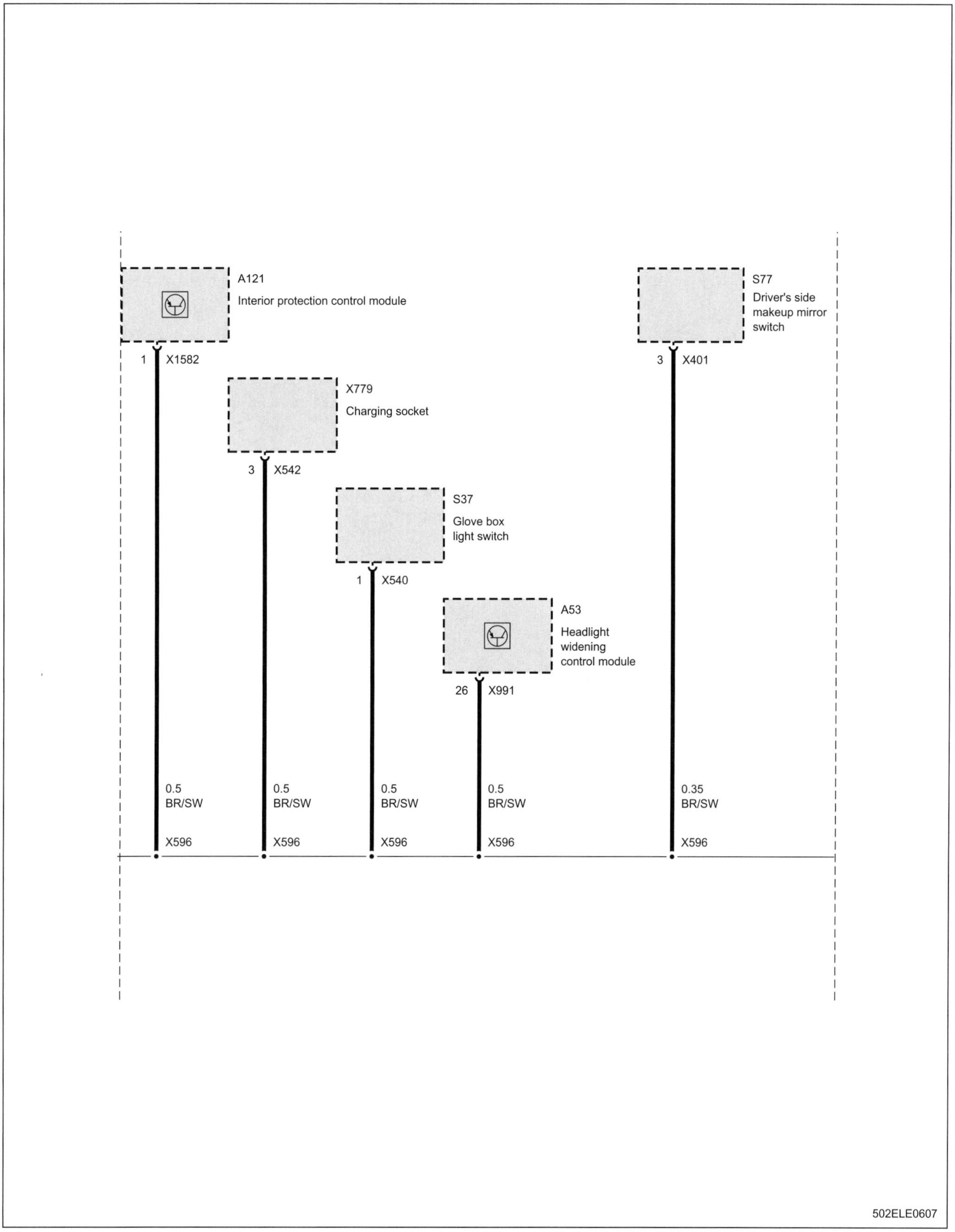
A121
Interior protection control module
1 X1582
X779
Charging socket
3 X542
S37
Glove box
light switch
1 X540
A53
Headlight
widening
control module
26 X991
S77
Driver's side
makeup mirror
switch
3 X401
0.5
BR/SW
X596
0.5
BR/SW
X596
0.5
BR/SW
X596
0.5
BR/SW
X596
0.35
BR/SW
X596
502ELE0607

Ground Distribution
X596 Ground splice
(3 of 3)

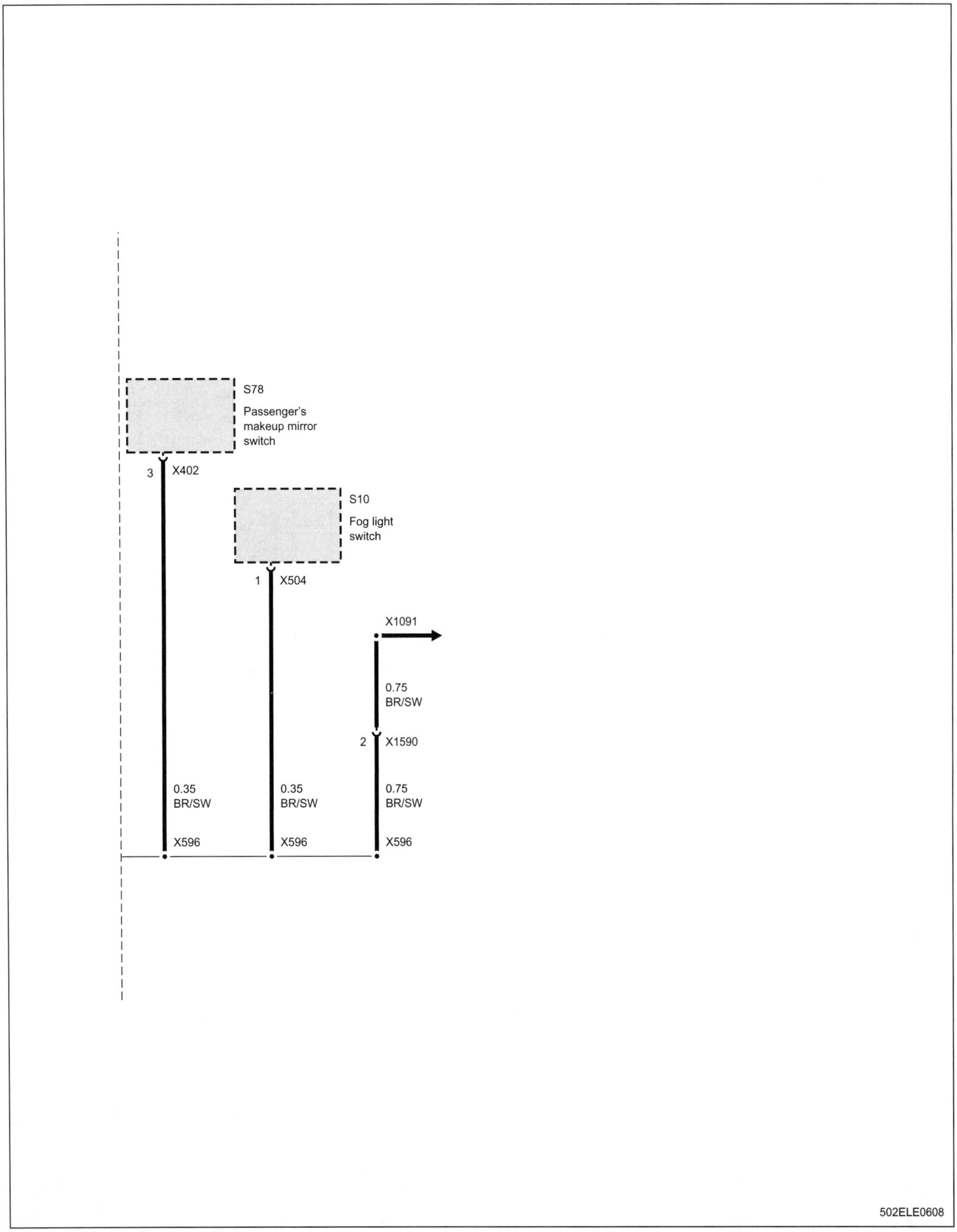
S78
Passenger's makeup mirror switch
3
X402
S10
Fog light switch
1
X504
X1091
0.75
BR/SW
2
X1590
0.35
BR/SW
0.35
BR/SW
0.75
BR/SW
X596
X596
X596
502ELE0608

X-connectors
X806 - Terminal 58g
(1 of 3)

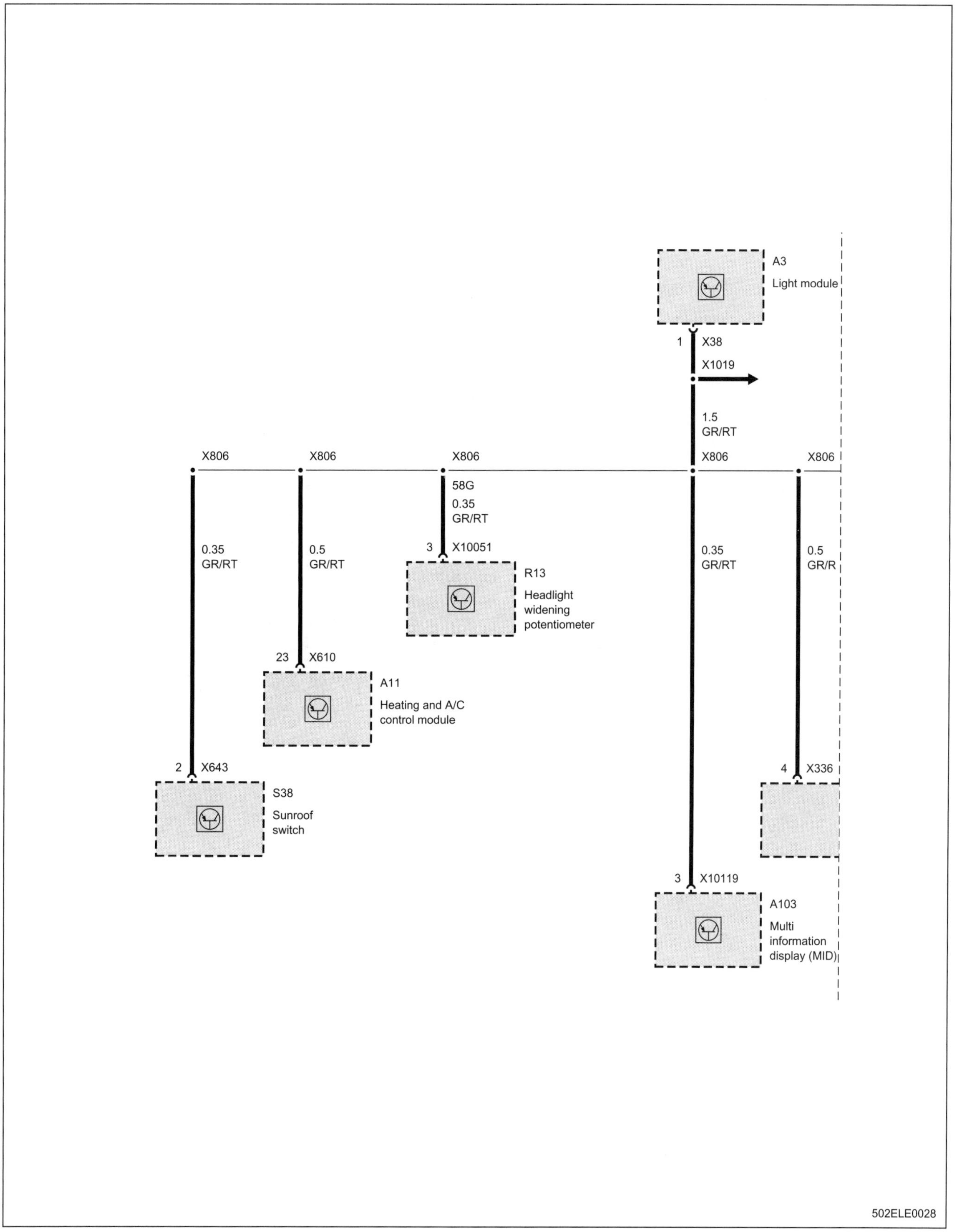
A3
Light module
1 X38
X1019
1.5
GR/RT
X806
X806
X806
X806
X806
58G
0.35
GR/RT
3 X10051
R13
Headlight
widening
potentiometer
0.35
GR/RT
0.5
GR/RT
0.35
GR/RT
0.5
GR/R
23 X610
A11
Heating and A/C
control module
2 X643
S38
Sunroof
switch
4 X336
3 X10119
A103
Multi
information
display (MID)
502ELE0028

X-connectors
X806 - Terminal 58g
(2 of 3)

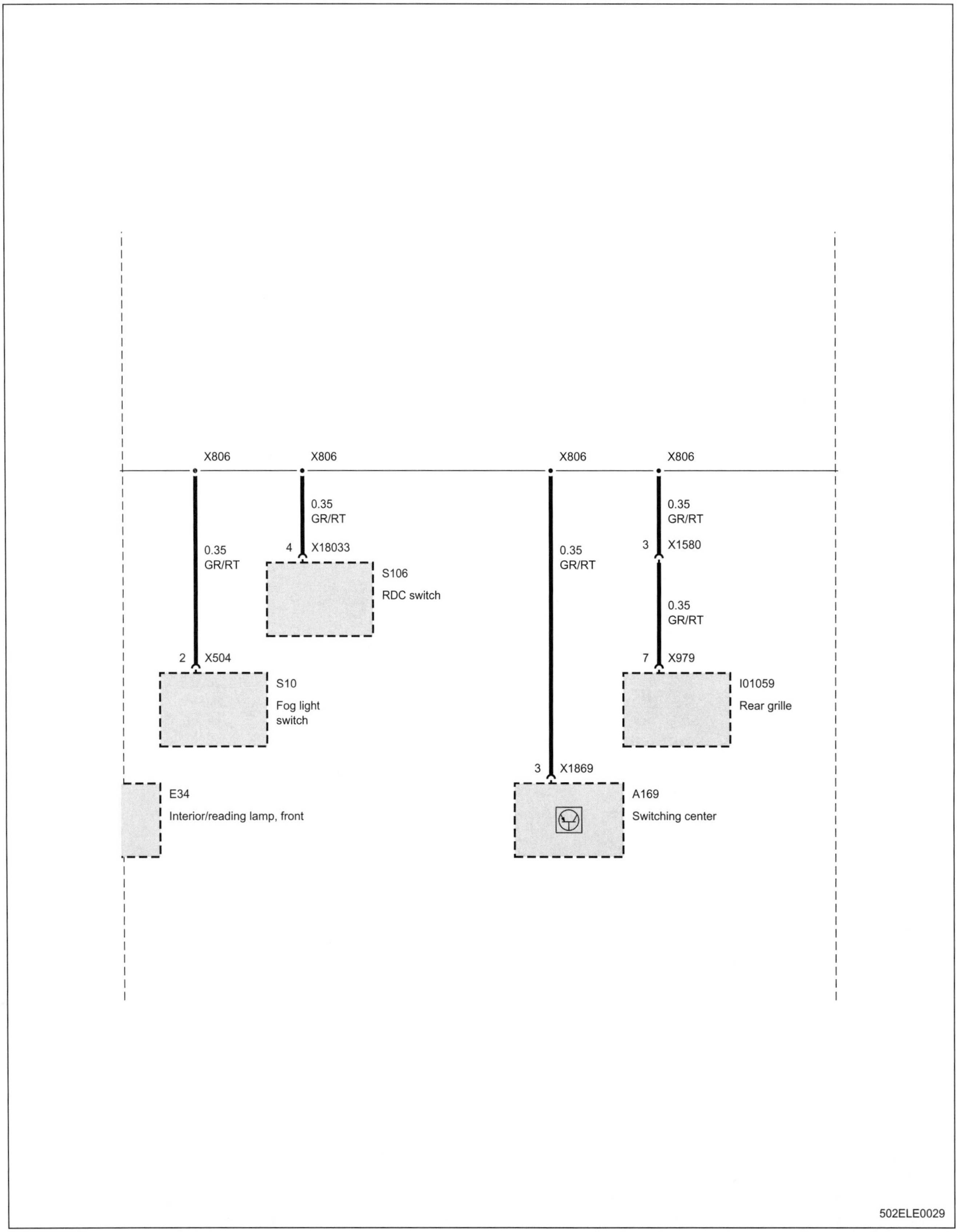
X806
X806
X806
X806
0.35
GR/RT
0.35
GR/RT
4 X18033
S106
RDC switch
0.35
GR/RT
0.35
GR/RT
3 X1580
0.35
GR/RT
2 X504
S10
Fog light
switch
7 X979
I01059
Rear grille
3 X1869
E34
Interior/reading lamp, front
A169
Switching center
502ELE0029

X-connectors
X806 - Terminal 58g
(3 of 3)

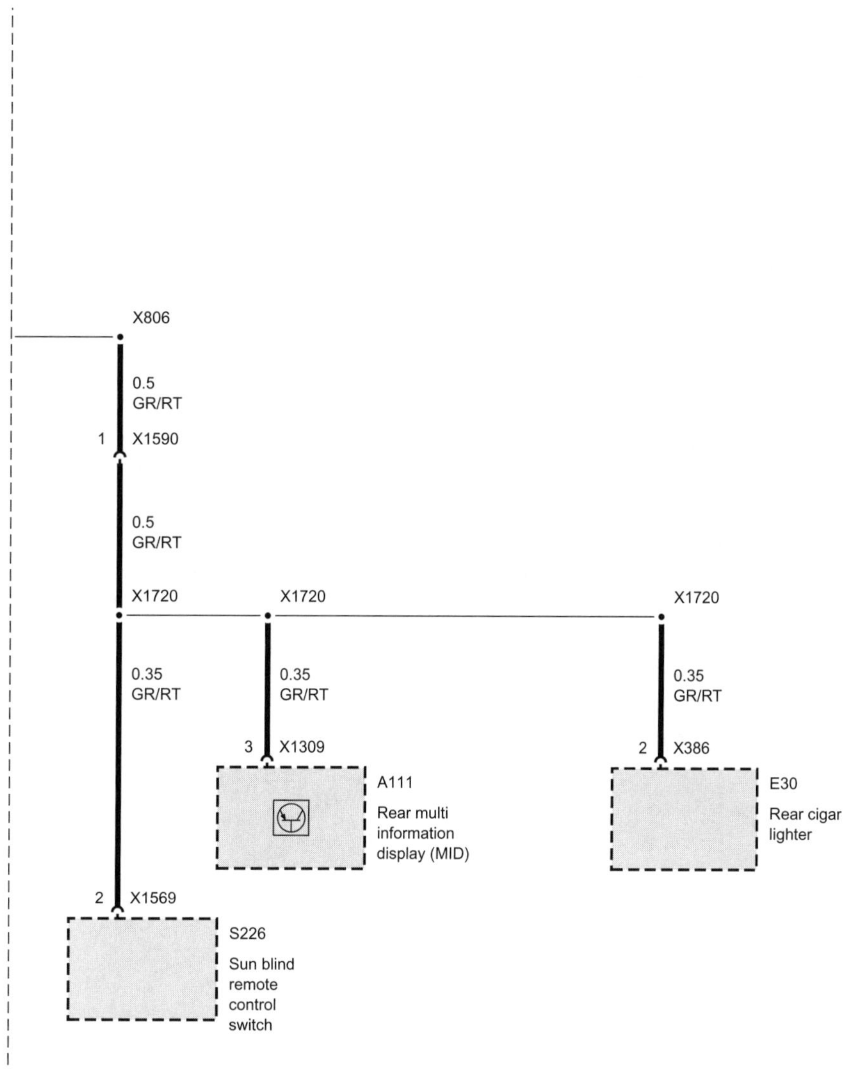
X806
0.5
GR/RT
1
X1590
0.5
GR/RT
X1720
X1720
X1720
0.35
GR/RT
0.35
GR/RT
0.35
GR/RT
3
X1309
A111
Rear multi
information
display (MID)
2
X386
E30
Rear cigar
lighter
2
X1569
S226
Sun blind
remote
control
switch
502ELE0030

Ground Distribution
X834 Ground splice
(1 of 1)

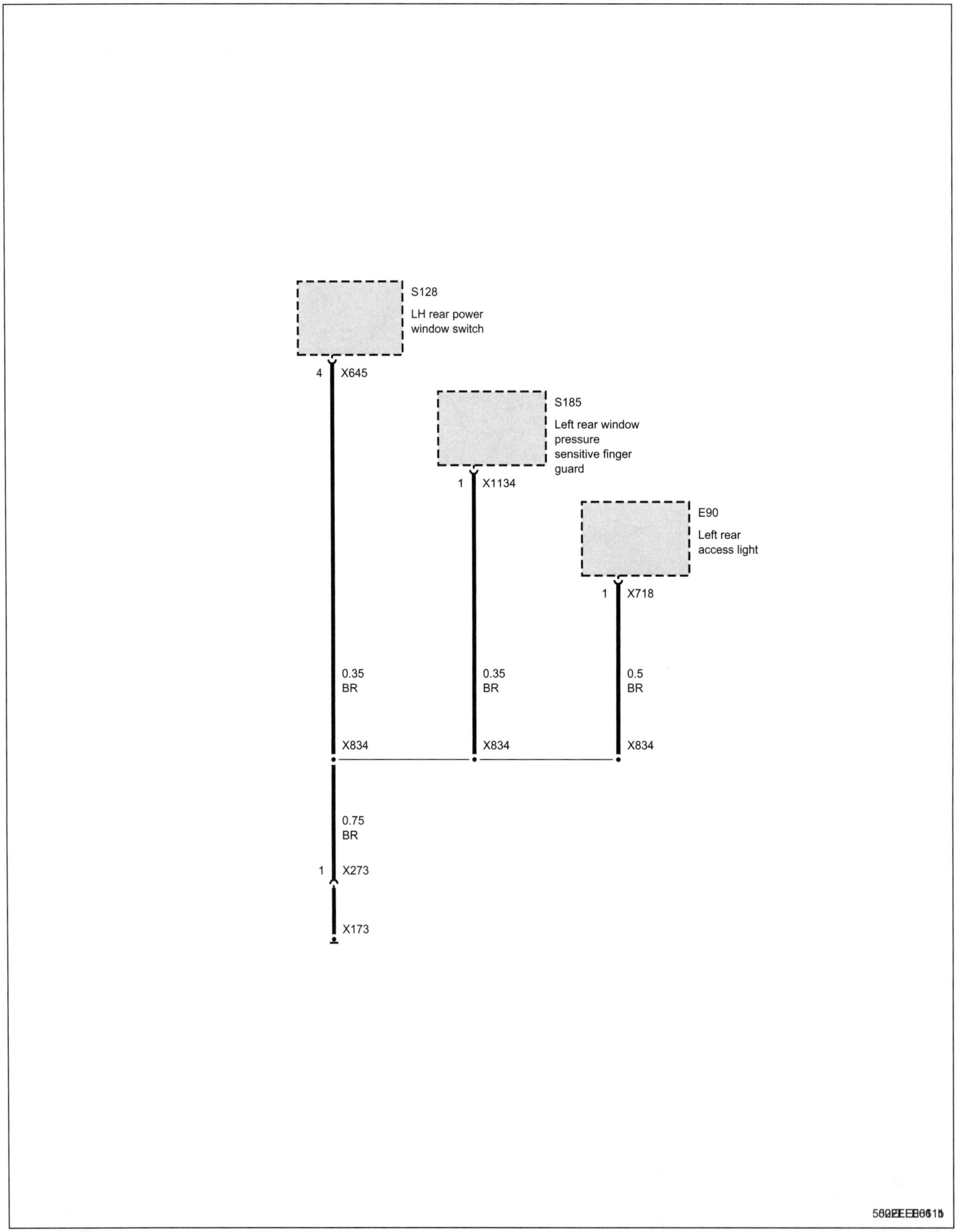
S128
LH rear power window switch
4
X645
S185
Left rear window pressure sensitive finger guard
1
X1134
E90
Left rear access light
1
X718
0.35
BR
0.35
BR
0.5
BR
X834
X834
X834
0.75
BR
1
X273
X173
5602EEB0615

Ground Distribution
X835 Ground splice

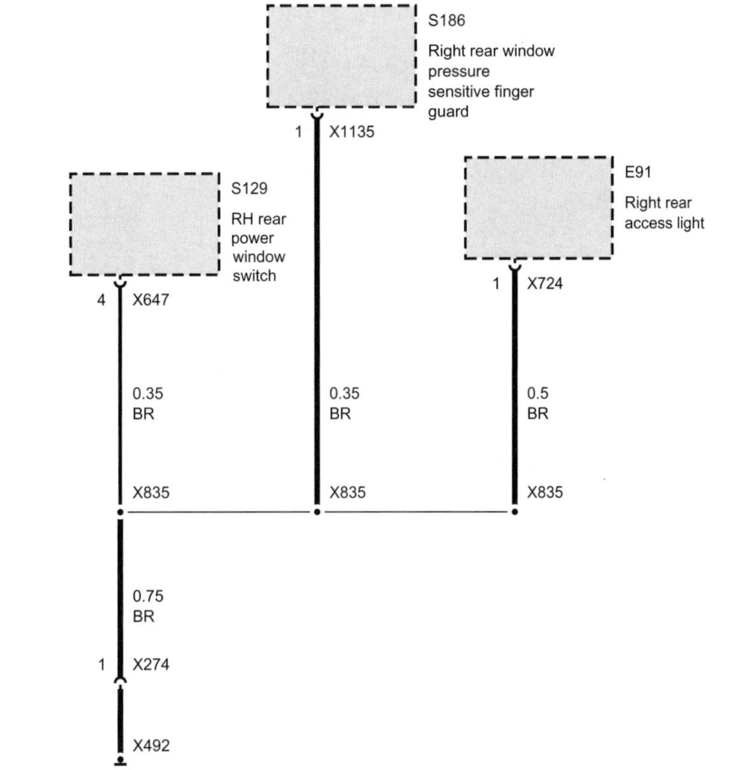

502ELE0612a

Ground Distribution
X840 Ground splice - Seats with memory

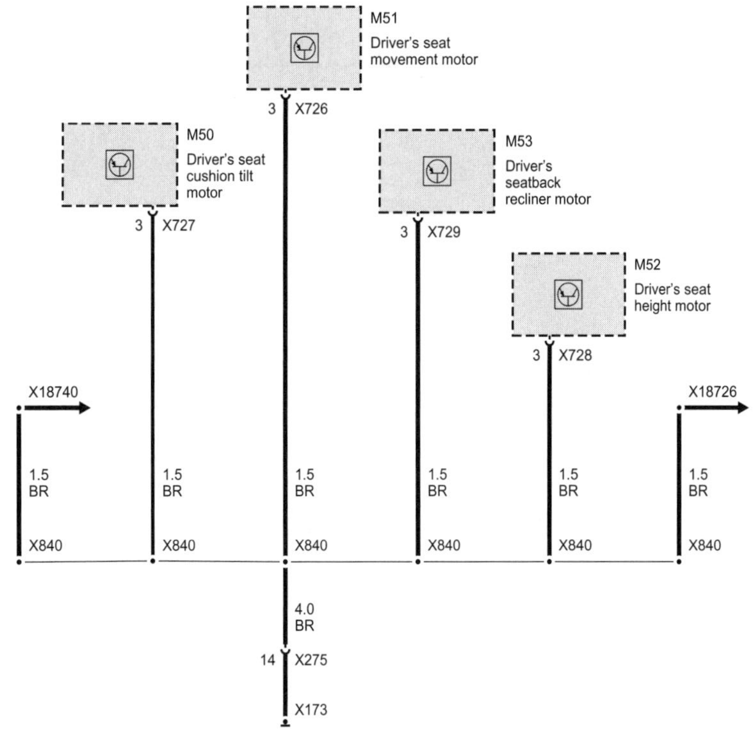

502ELE0612b

Ground Distribution
X844, X18749 Ground splice - Seats without memory
(1 of 1)

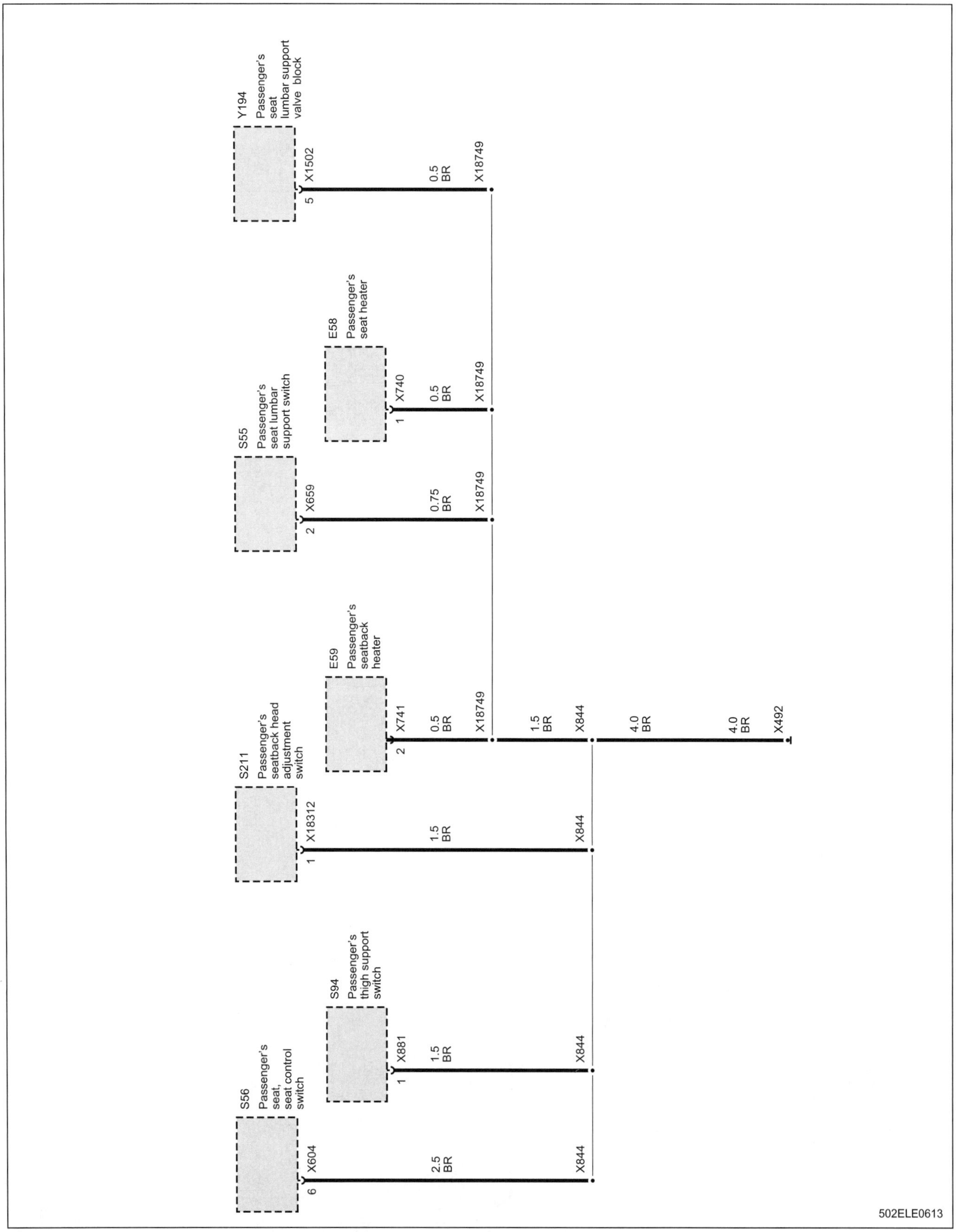

Ground Distribution
Ground splice X849
(1 of 1)

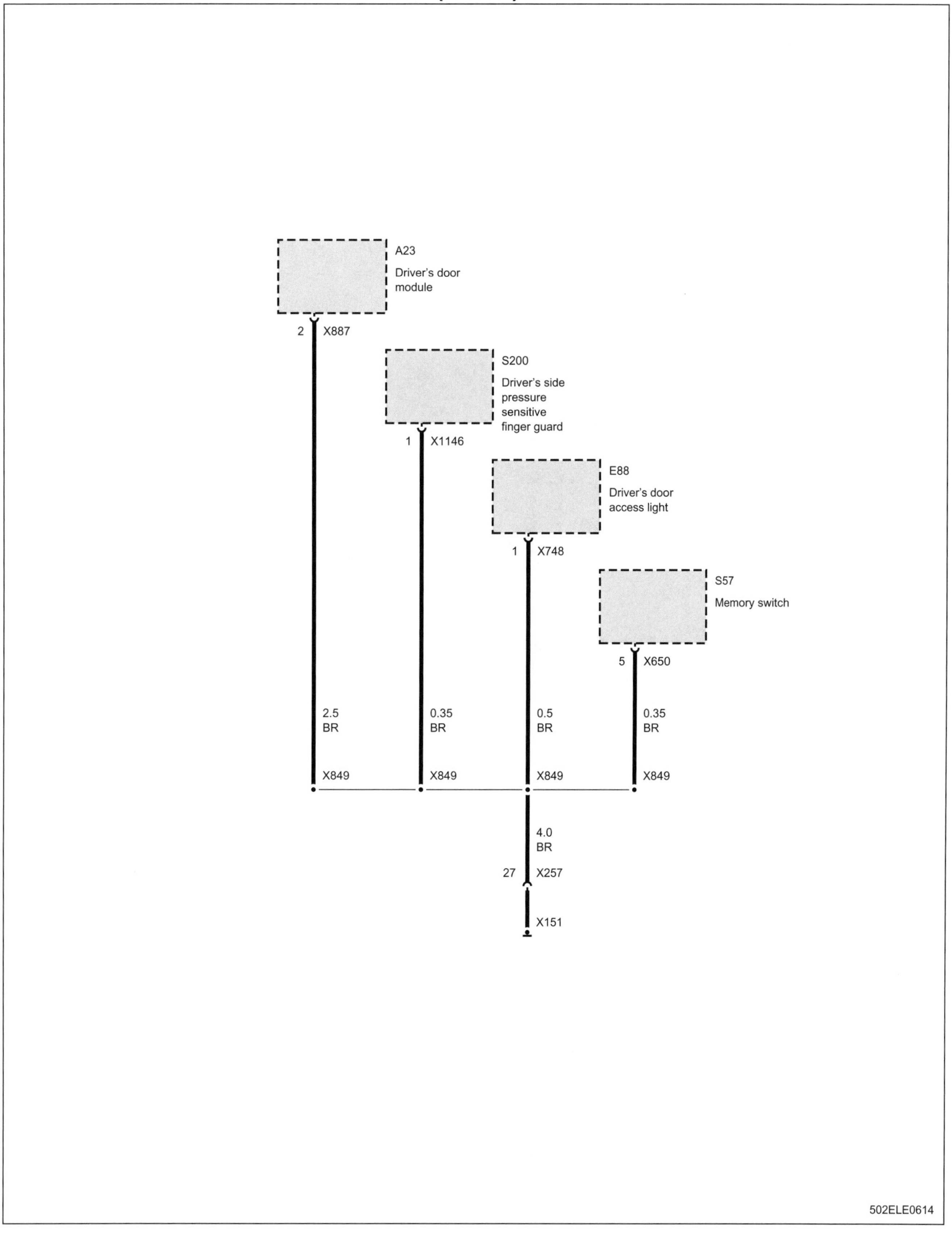

X-Connectors and Splices
X854 Splice - IHKA
(1 of 1)

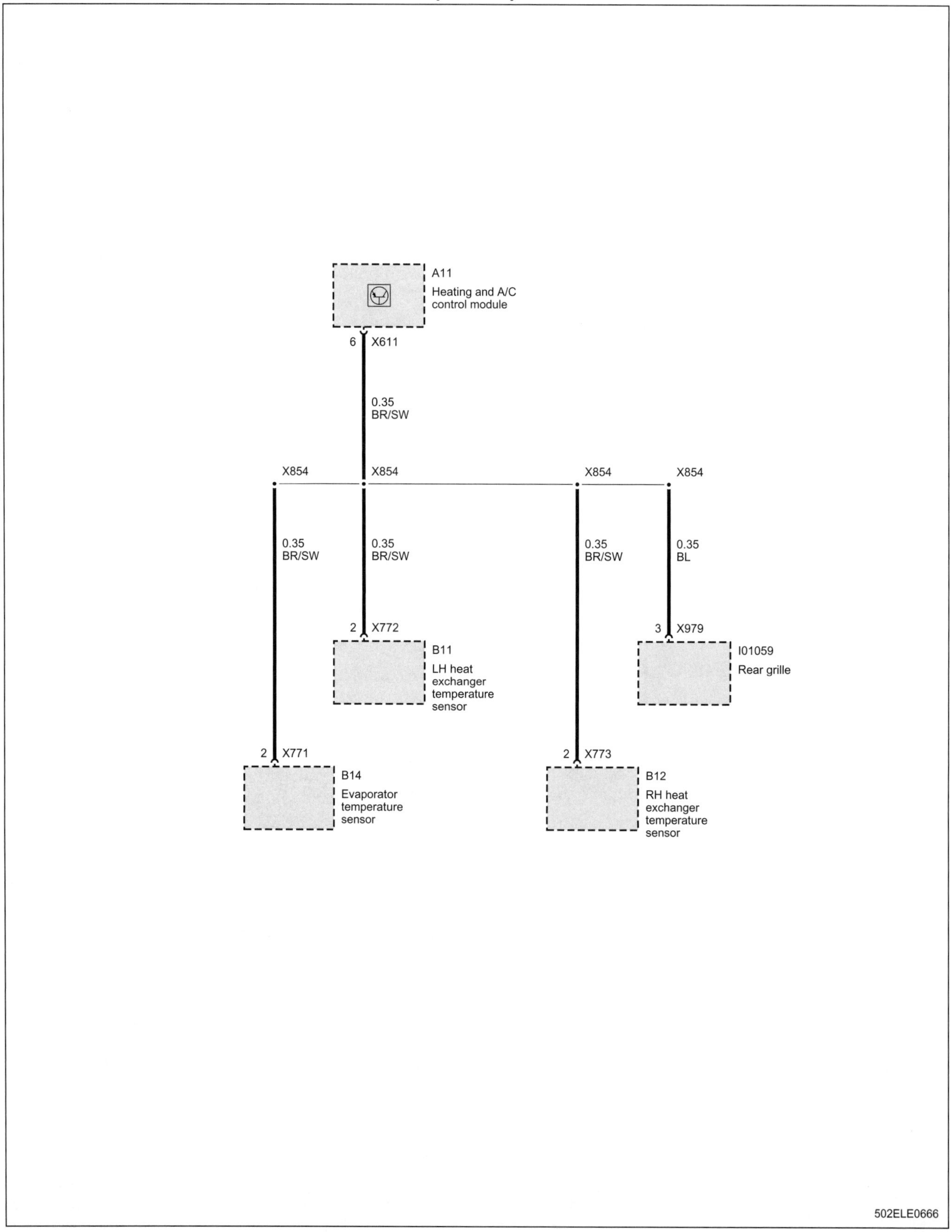
A11
Heating and A/C control module
6 X611
0.35 BR/SW
X854
X854
X854
X854
0.35 BR/SW
0.35 BR/SW
0.35 BR/SW
0.35 BL
2 X772
B11
LH heat exchanger temperature sensor
3 X979
I01059
Rear grille
2 X771
B14
Evaporator temperature sensor
2 X773
B12
RH heat exchanger temperature sensor
502ELE0666

X-Connectors and Splices
X880 Connector
(1 of 1)

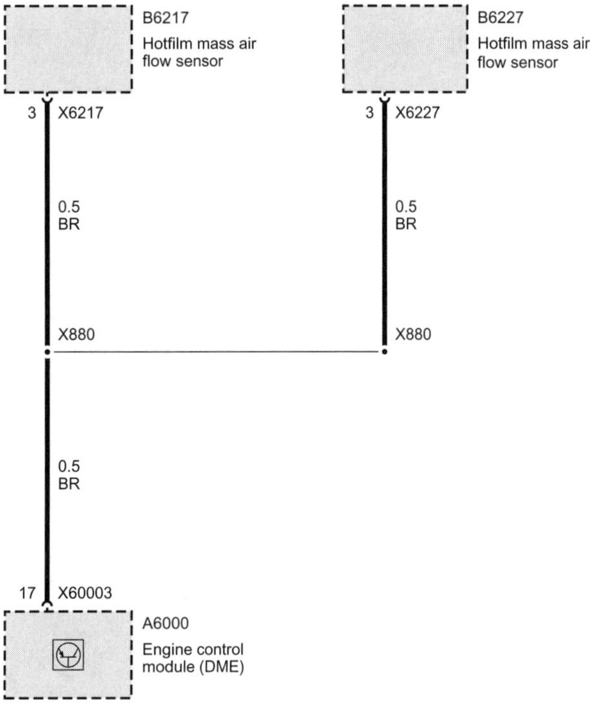
B6217
Hotfilm mass air flow sensor
3
X6217
0.5
BR
X880
B6227
Hotfilm mass air flow sensor
3
X6227
0.5
BR
X880
0.5
BR
17
X60003
A6000
Engine control module (DME)
502ELE0585

Ground Distribution
Ground splice X891
(1 of 1)

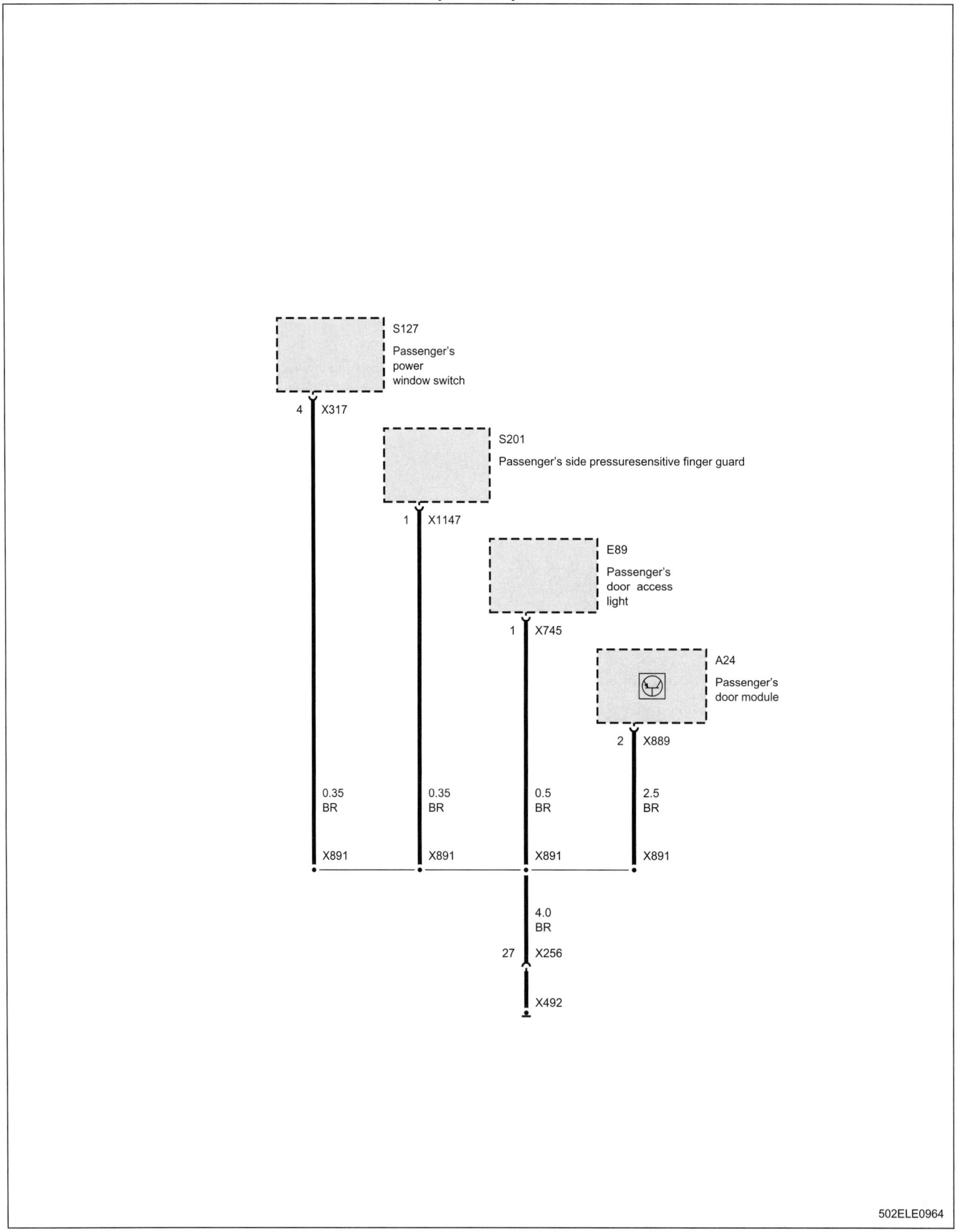
S127
Passenger's power window switch
4 X317
S201
Passenger's side pressuresensitive finger guard
1 X1147
E89
Passenger's door access light
1 X745
A24
Passenger's door module
2 X889
0.35 BR
0.35 BR
0.5 BR
2.5 BR
X891
X891
X891
X891
4.0 BR
27 X256
X492
502ELE0964

X-Connectors and Splices
X908 terminal 58g
(1 of 1)

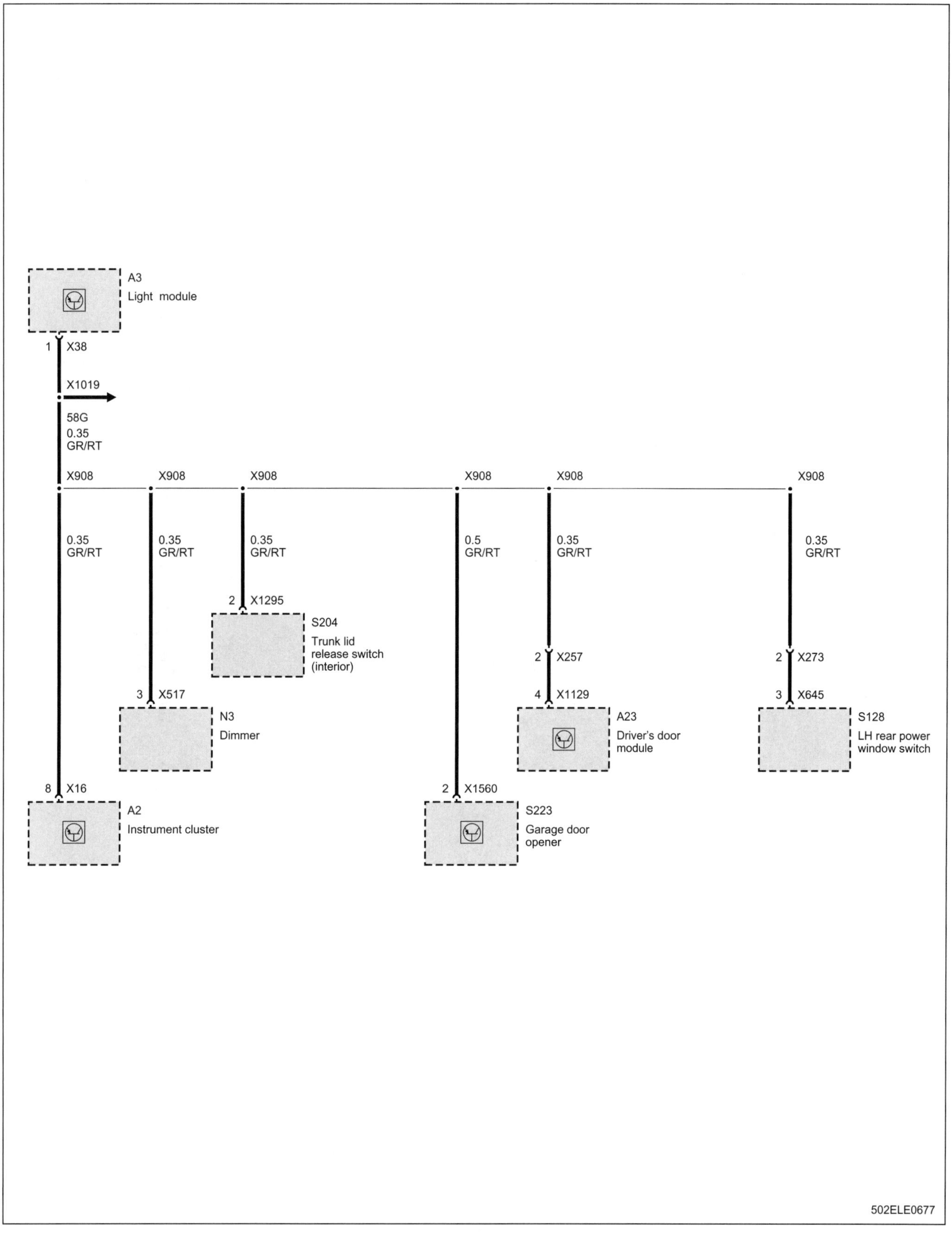
A3
Light module
1 X38
X1019
58G
0.35
GR/RT
X908
X908
X908
X908
X908
X908
0.35
GR/RT
0.35
GR/RT
0.35
GR/RT
0.5
GR/RT
0.35
GR/RT
0.35
GR/RT
2 X1295
S204
Trunk lid
release switch
(interior)
2 X257
2 X273
3 X517
N3
Dimmer
4 X1129
A23
Driver's door
module
3 X645
S128
LH rear power
window switch
8 X16
A2
Instrument cluster
2 X1560
S223
Garage door
opener
502ELE0677

BUS System
X939 K-bus connector
(1 of 1)

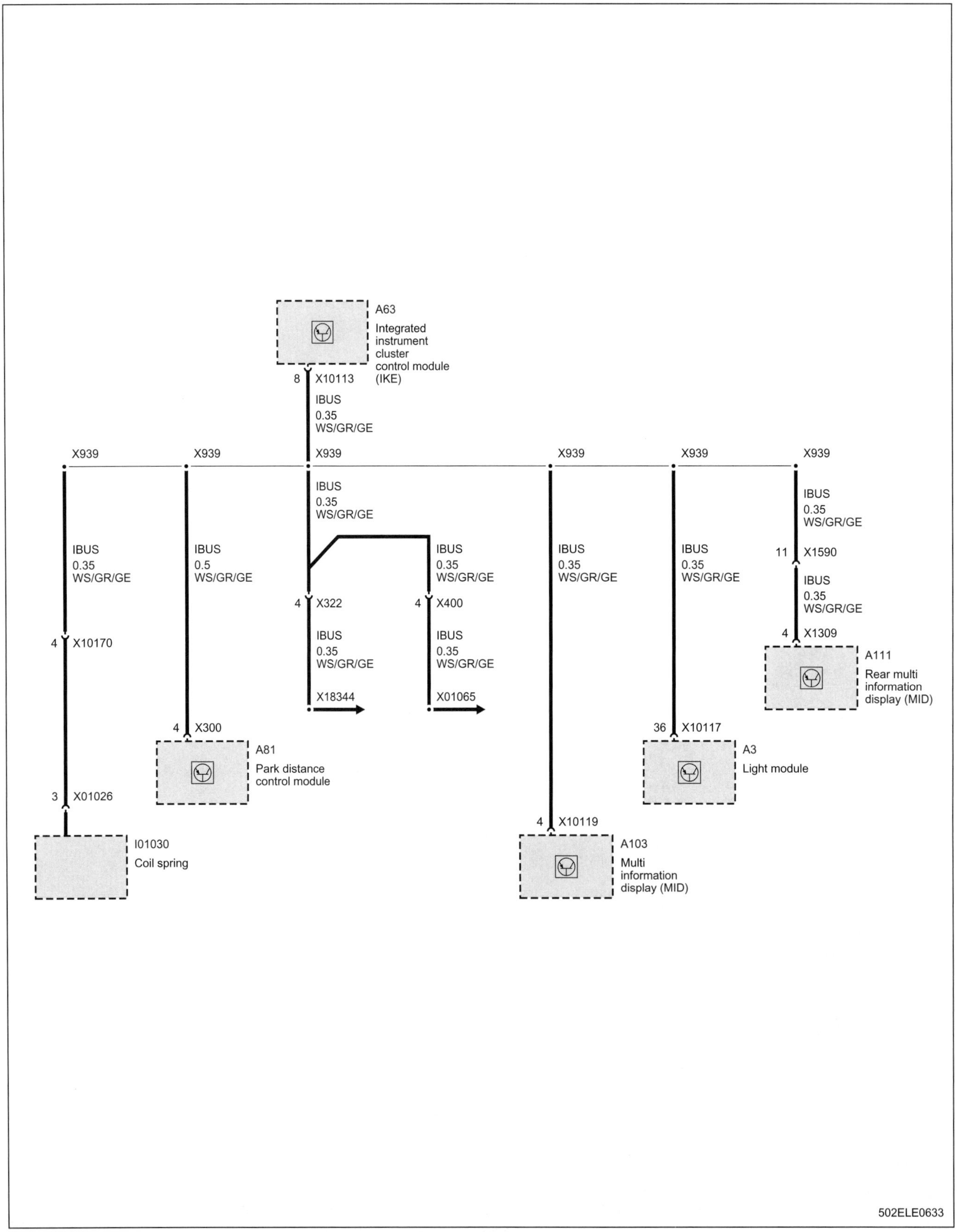
A63
Integrated instrument cluster control module (IKE)
8 X10113
IBUS 0.35 WS/GR/GE
X939
X939
X939
X939
X939
X939
IBUS 0.35 WS/GR/GE
IBUS 0.35 WS/GR/GE
IBUS 0.5 WS/GR/GE
IBUS 0.35 WS/GR/GE
IBUS 0.35 WS/GR/GE
IBUS 0.35 WS/GR/GE
IBUS 0.35 WS/GR/GE
11 X1590
IBUS 0.35 WS/GR/GE
4 X322
4 X400
IBUS 0.35 WS/GR/GE
IBUS 0.35 WS/GR/GE
X18344
X01065
4 X10170
4 X1309
A111
Rear multi information display (MID)
4 X300
A81
Park distance control module
36 X10117
A3
Light module
3 X01026
4 X10119
I01030
Coil spring
A103
Multi information display (MID)
502ELE0633

X-Connectors and Splices
X943 Connector
(1 of 1)

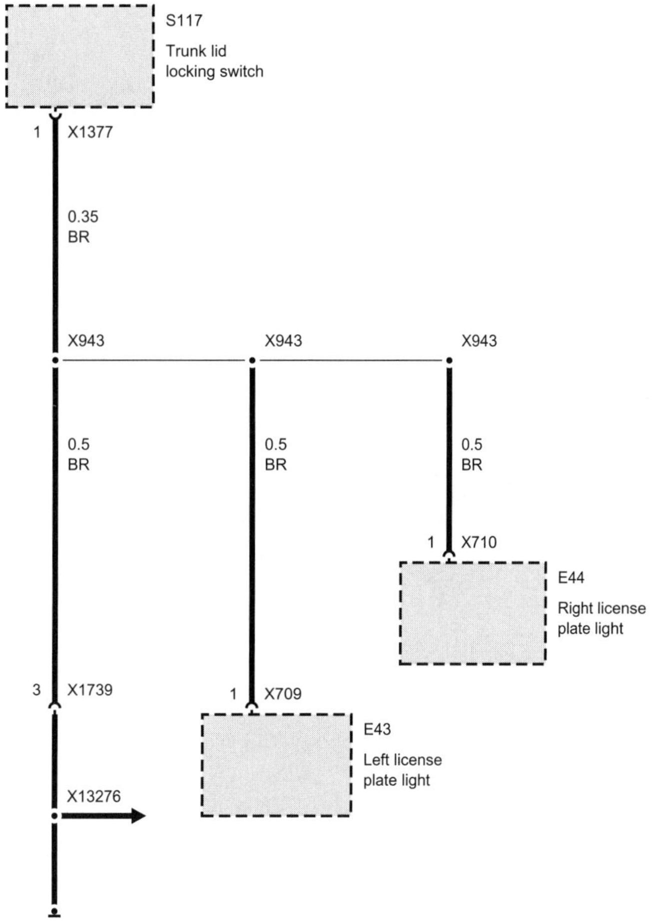
S117
Trunk lid
locking switch
1
X1377
0.35
BR
X943
X943
X943
0.5
BR
0.5
BR
0.5
BR
1
X710
E44
Right license
plate light
3
X1739
1
X709
E43
Left license
plate light
X13276
502ELE0586

Ground Distribution
X943 Ground connector
(1 of 1)

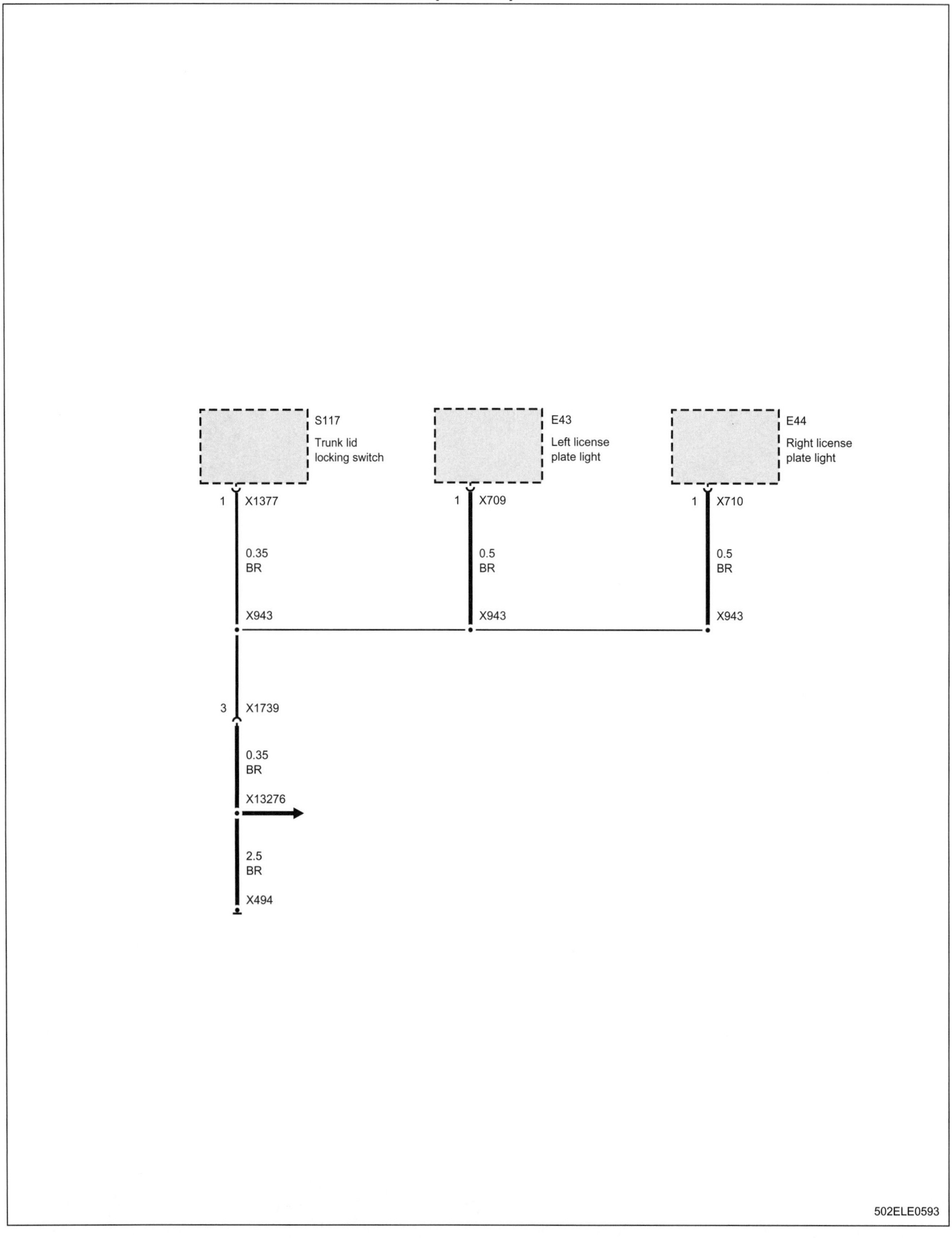

X-Connectors and Splices
X1019 Splice - Terminal 58g
(1 of 3)

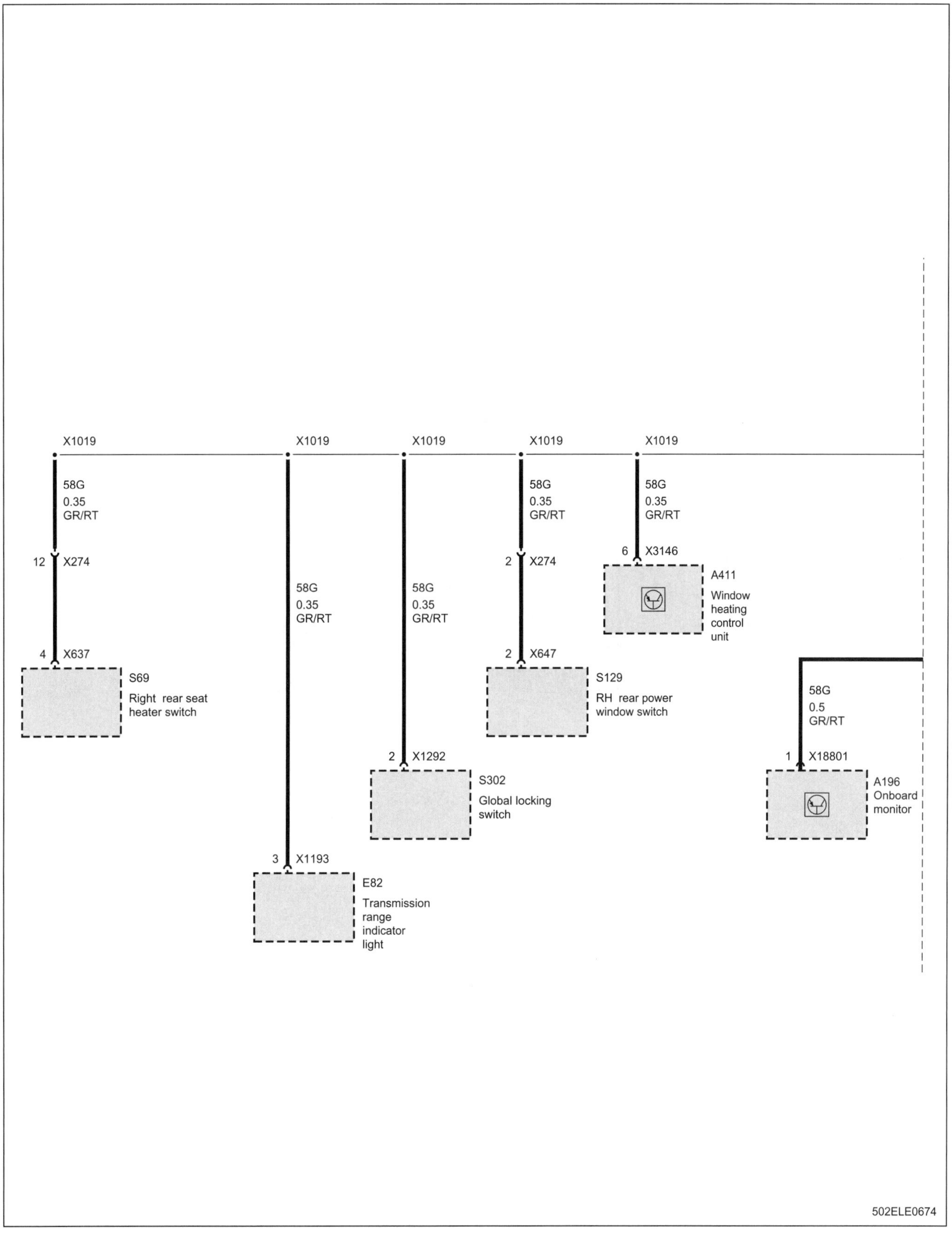

X-Connectors and Splices
X1019 Splice - Terminal 58g
(2 of 3)

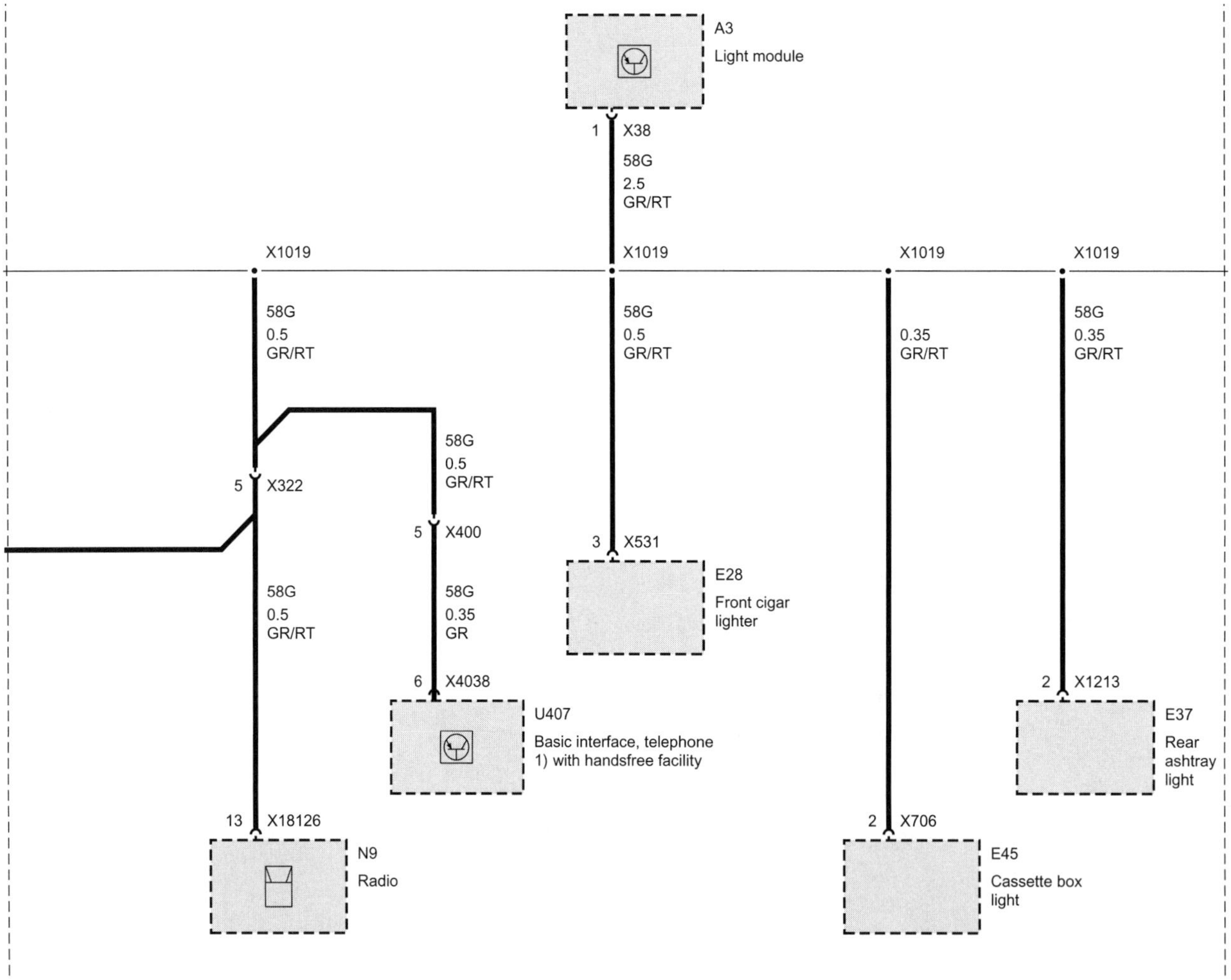

X-Connectors and Splices
X1019 Splice - Terminal 58g
(3 of 3)

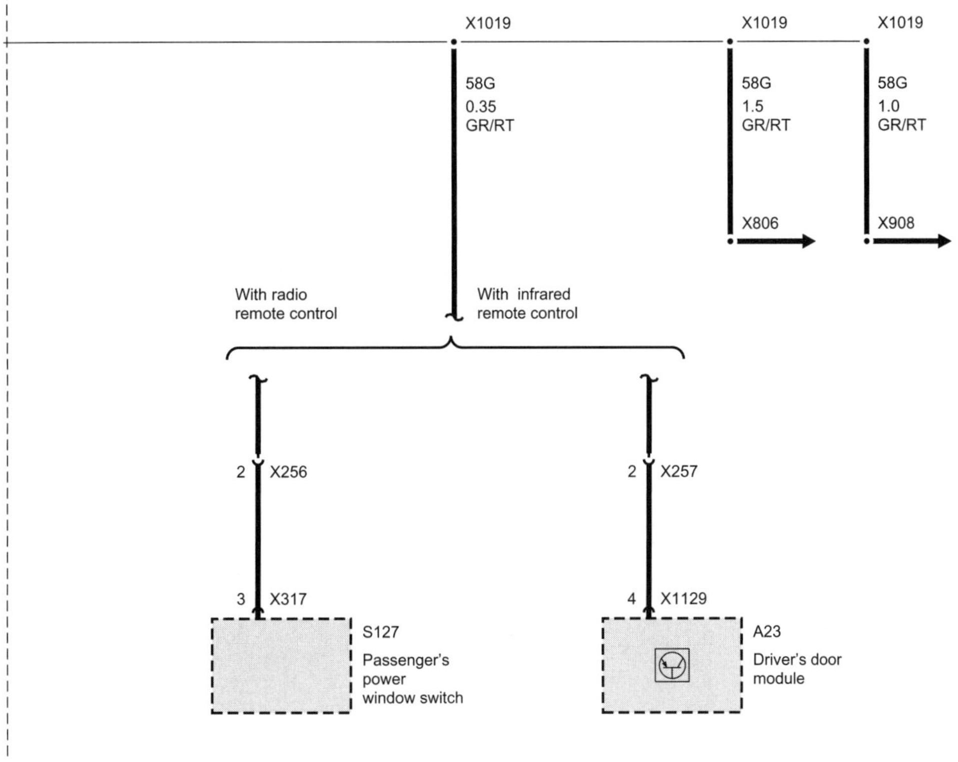

502ELE0676

X-Connectors and Splices
X1022 Splice
(1 of 1)

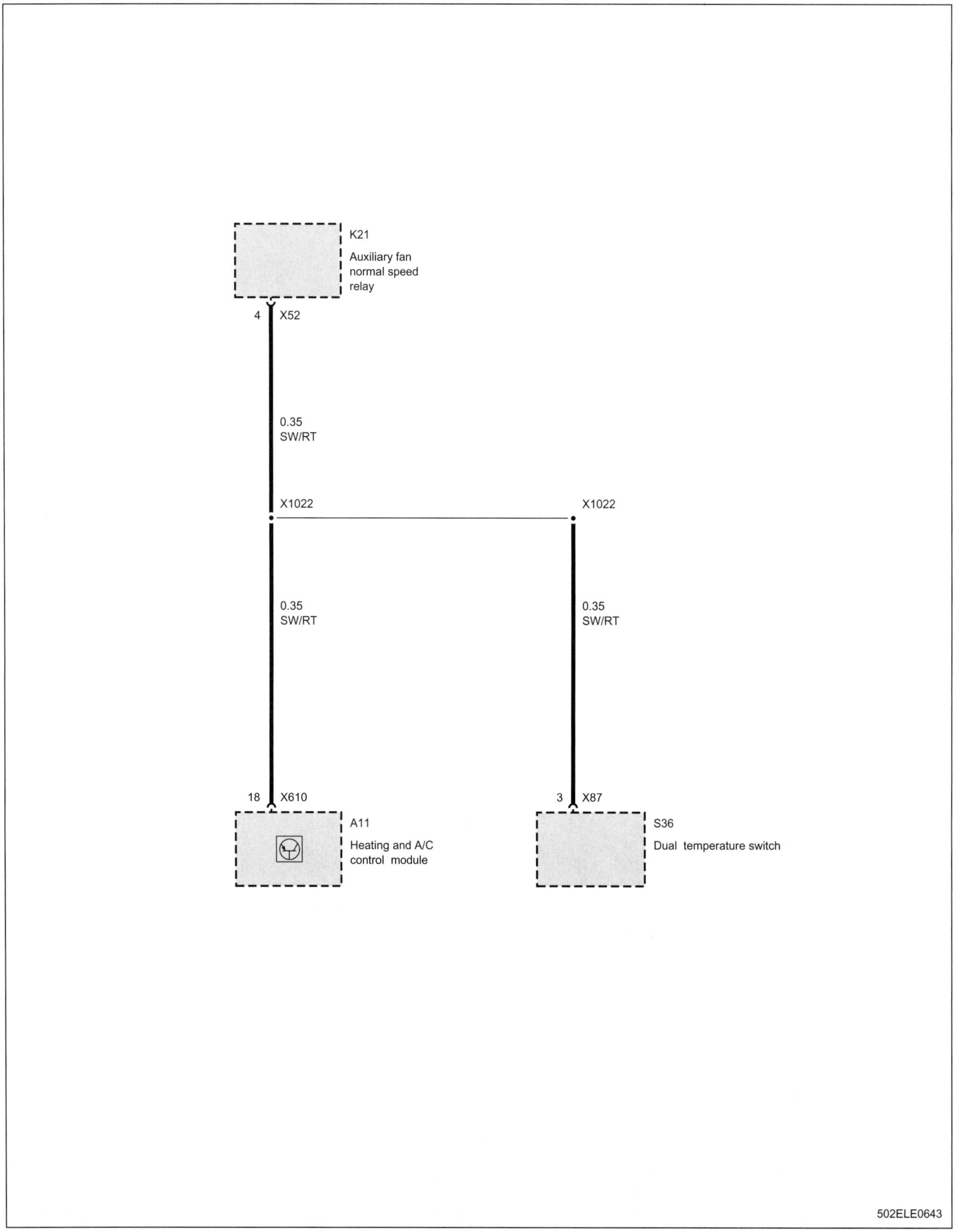
K21
Auxiliary fan normal speed relay
4
X52
0.35
SW/RT
X1022
X1022
0.35
SW/RT
0.35
SW/RT
18
X610
3
X87
A11
Heating and A/C control module
S36
Dual temperature switch
502ELE0643

Ground Distribution
X01025 Ground splice
(1 of 1)

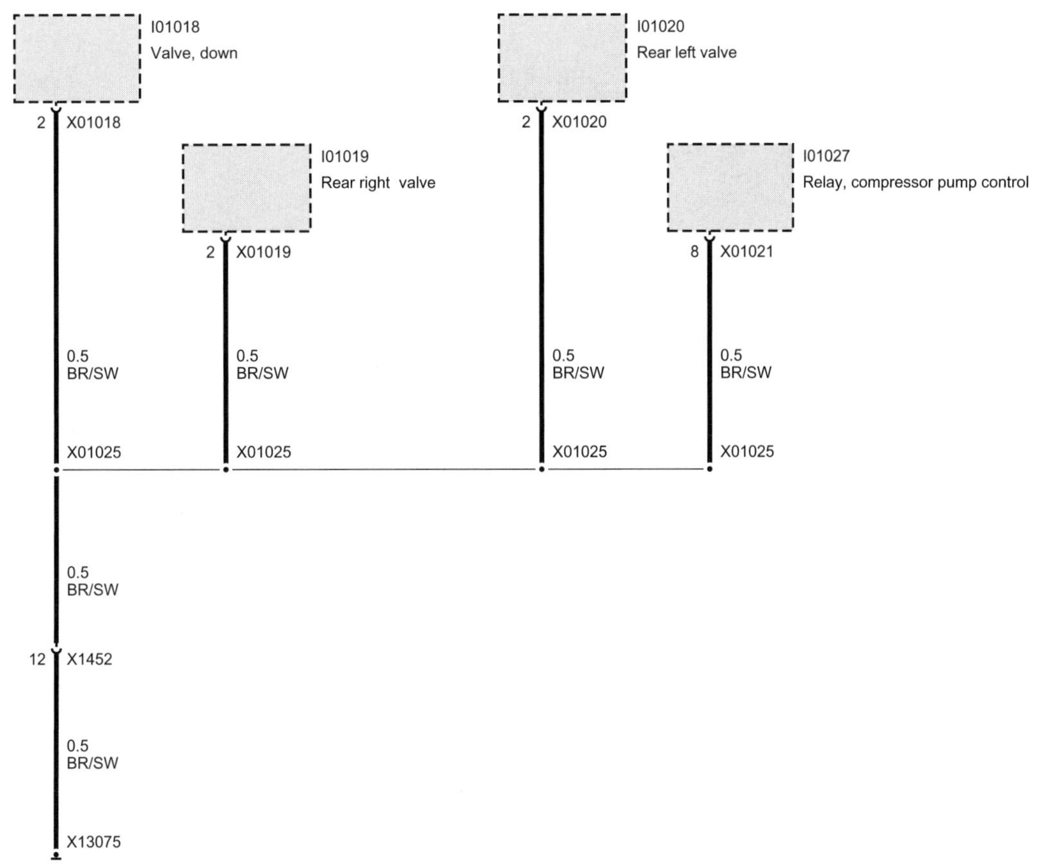
I01018
Valve, down
2 X01018
I01019
Rear right valve
2 X01019
I01020
Rear left valve
2 X01020
I01027
Relay, compressor pump control
8 X01021
0.5
BR/SW
X01025
12 X1452
X13075
502ELE0597

X-Connectors and Splices
X01040 Intermediate connector, GPS antenna
(1 of 1)

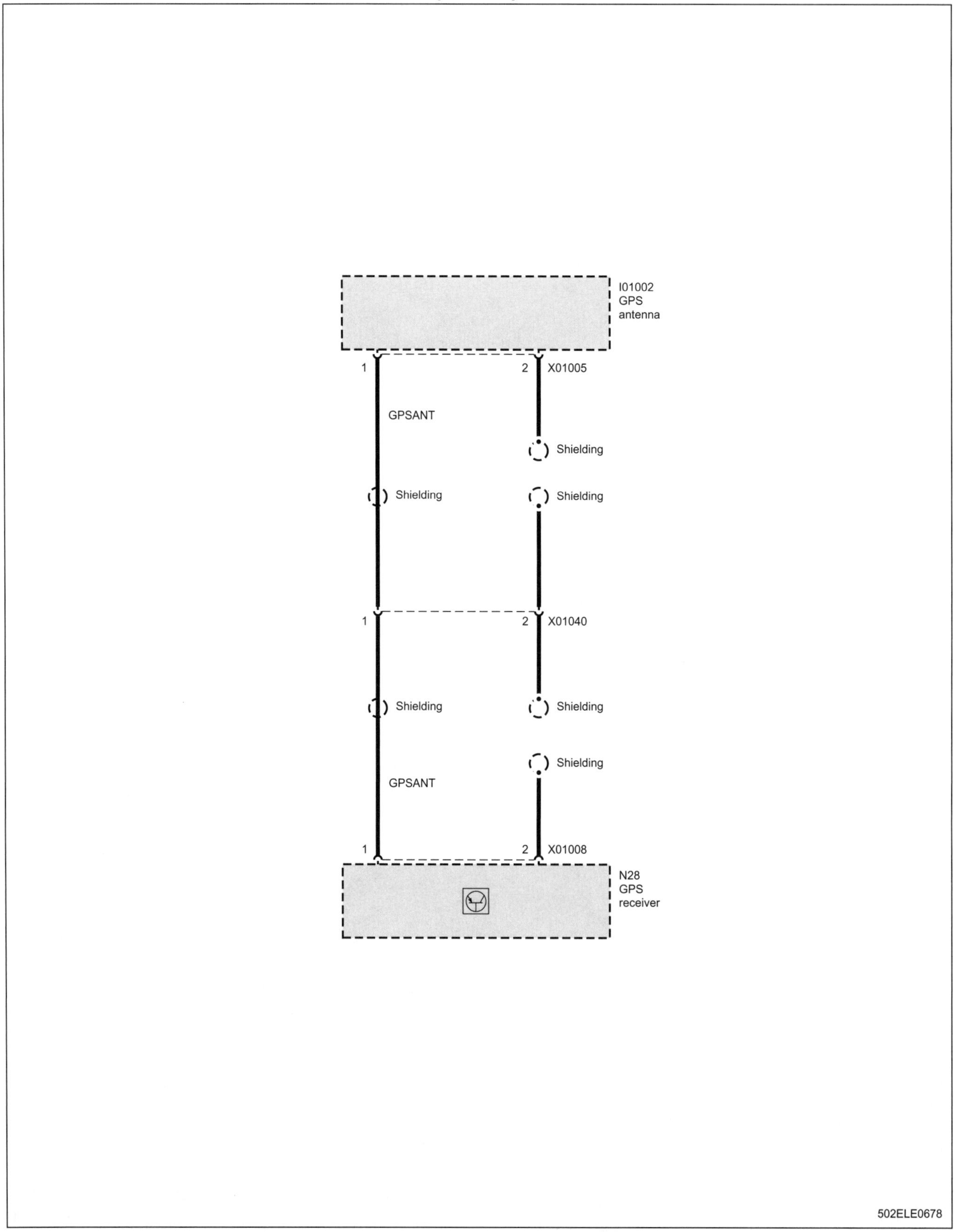

Ground Distribution
X01041 Ground connector
(1 of 1)

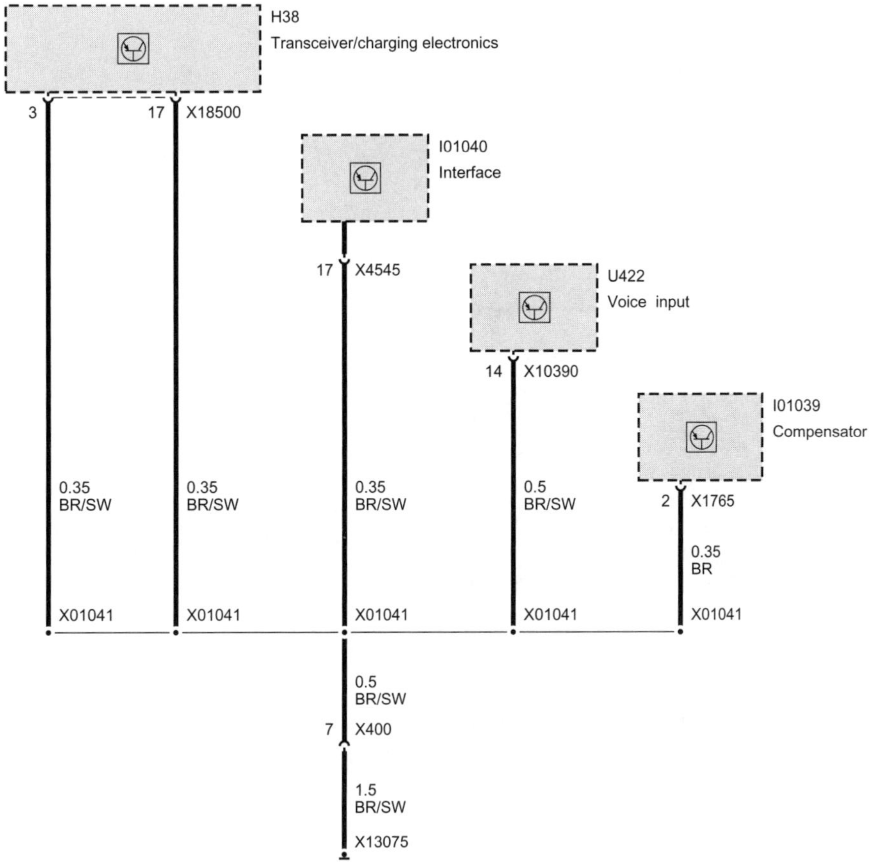

502ELE0637

BUS System
X01065 K-bus connector
(1 of 1)

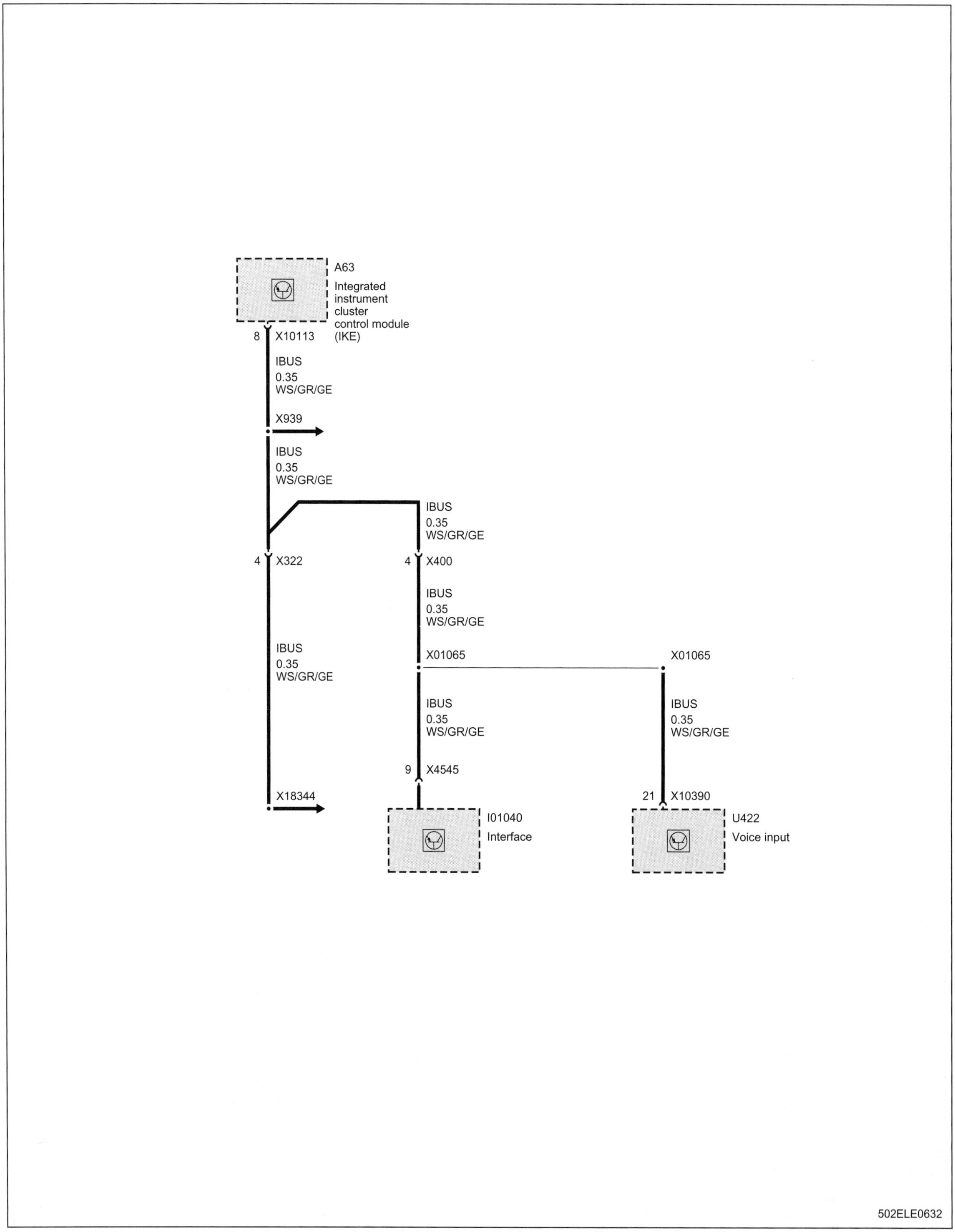
A63
Integrated instrument cluster control module (IKE)
8
X10113
IBUS
0.35
WS/GR/GE
X939
IBUS
0.35
WS/GR/GE
IBUS
0.35
WS/GR/GE
4
X322
4
X400
IBUS
0.35
WS/GR/GE
IBUS
0.35
WS/GR/GE
X01065
X01065
IBUS
0.35
WS/GR/GE
IBUS
0.35
WS/GR/GE
9
X4545
X18344
21
X10390
I01040
Interface
U422
Voice input
502ELE0632

X-Connectors and Splices
X01067 Connector
(1 of 1)

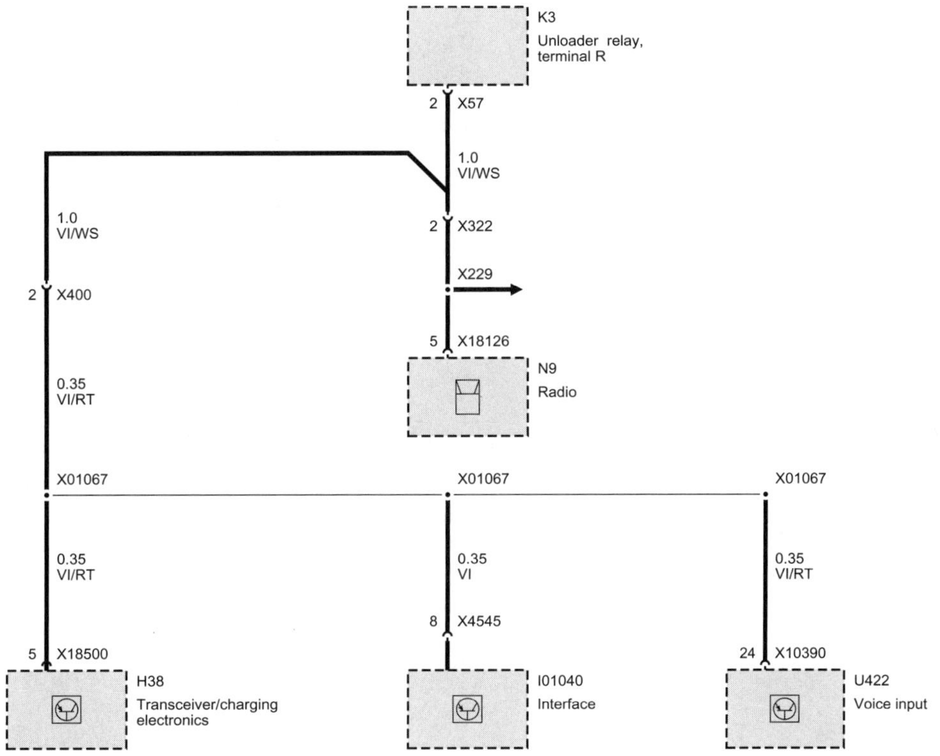

502ELE0569

X-Connectors and Splices
X01069 MUTE connector
(1 of 1)

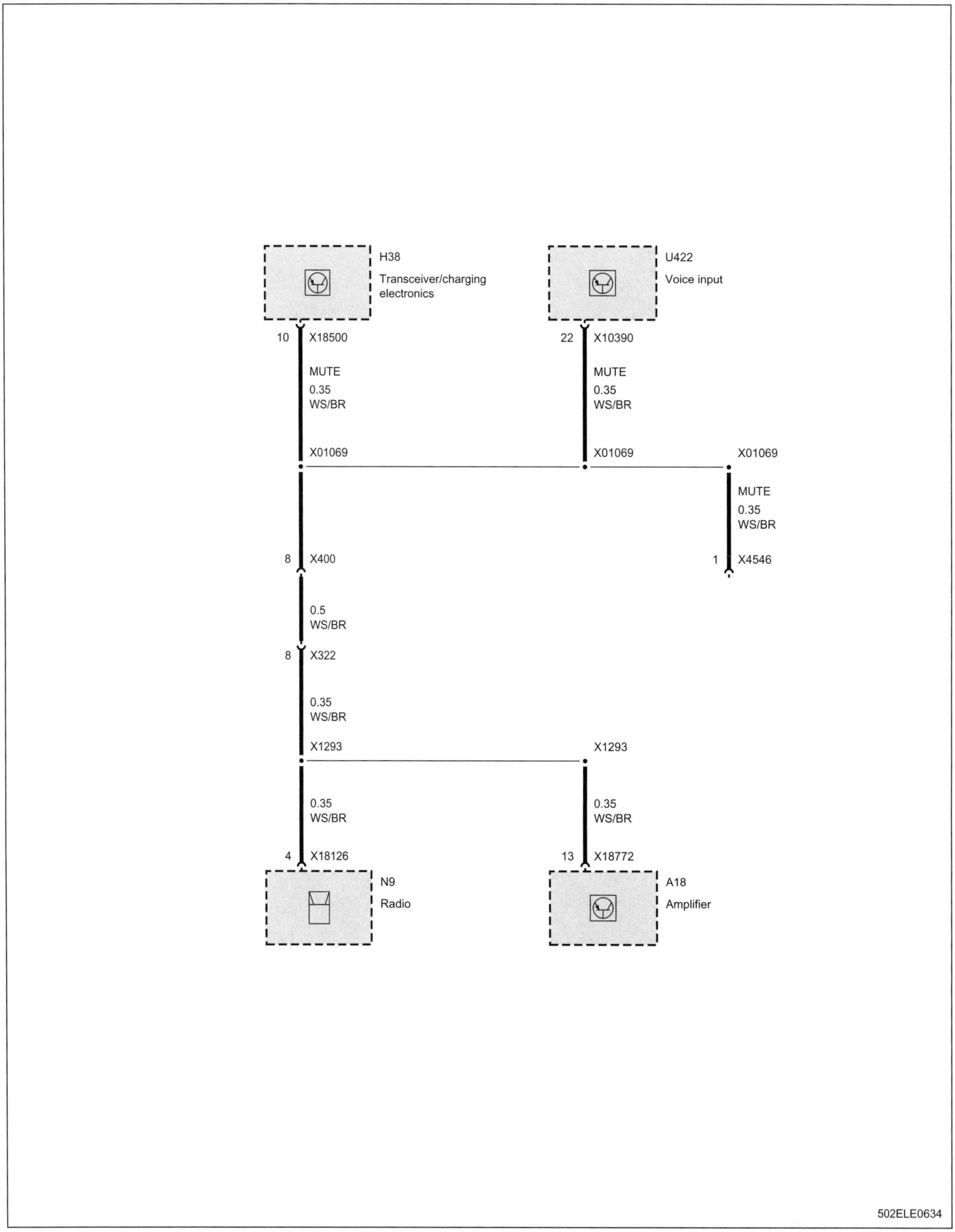

X-Connectors and Splices
X01070, X01071 Connector - Telephone
(1 of 1)

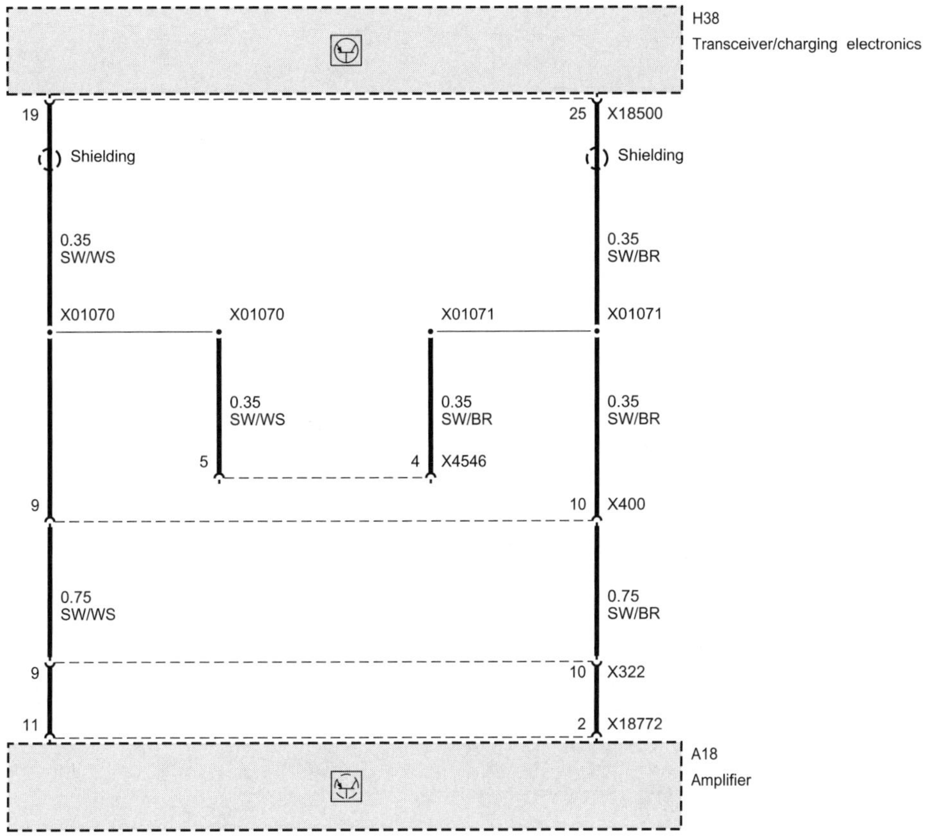

502ELE0639

X-Connectors and Splices
X01086 Connector - Intermediate trailer
(1 of 1)

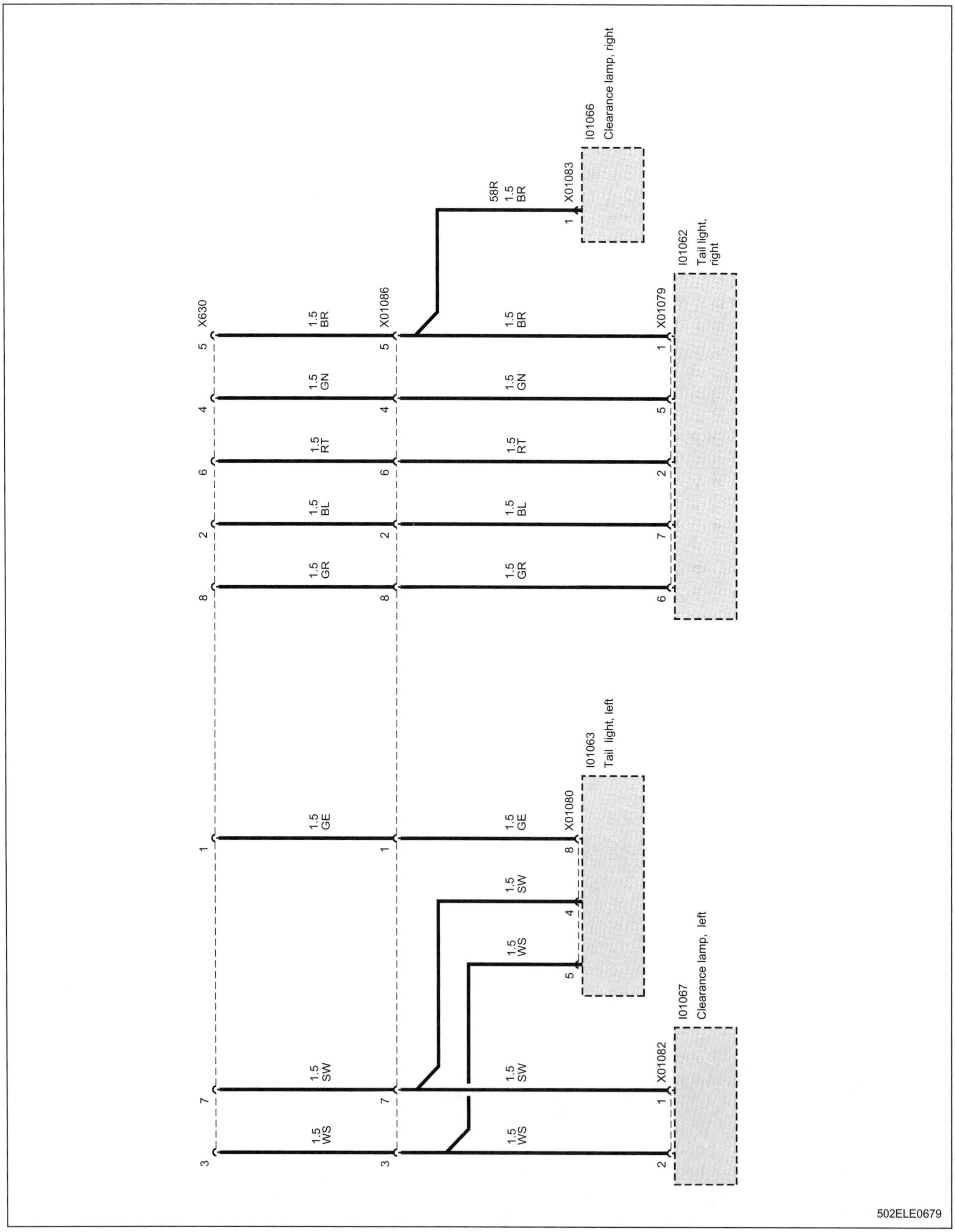

Ground Distribution
X1091 Ground connector
(1 of 1)

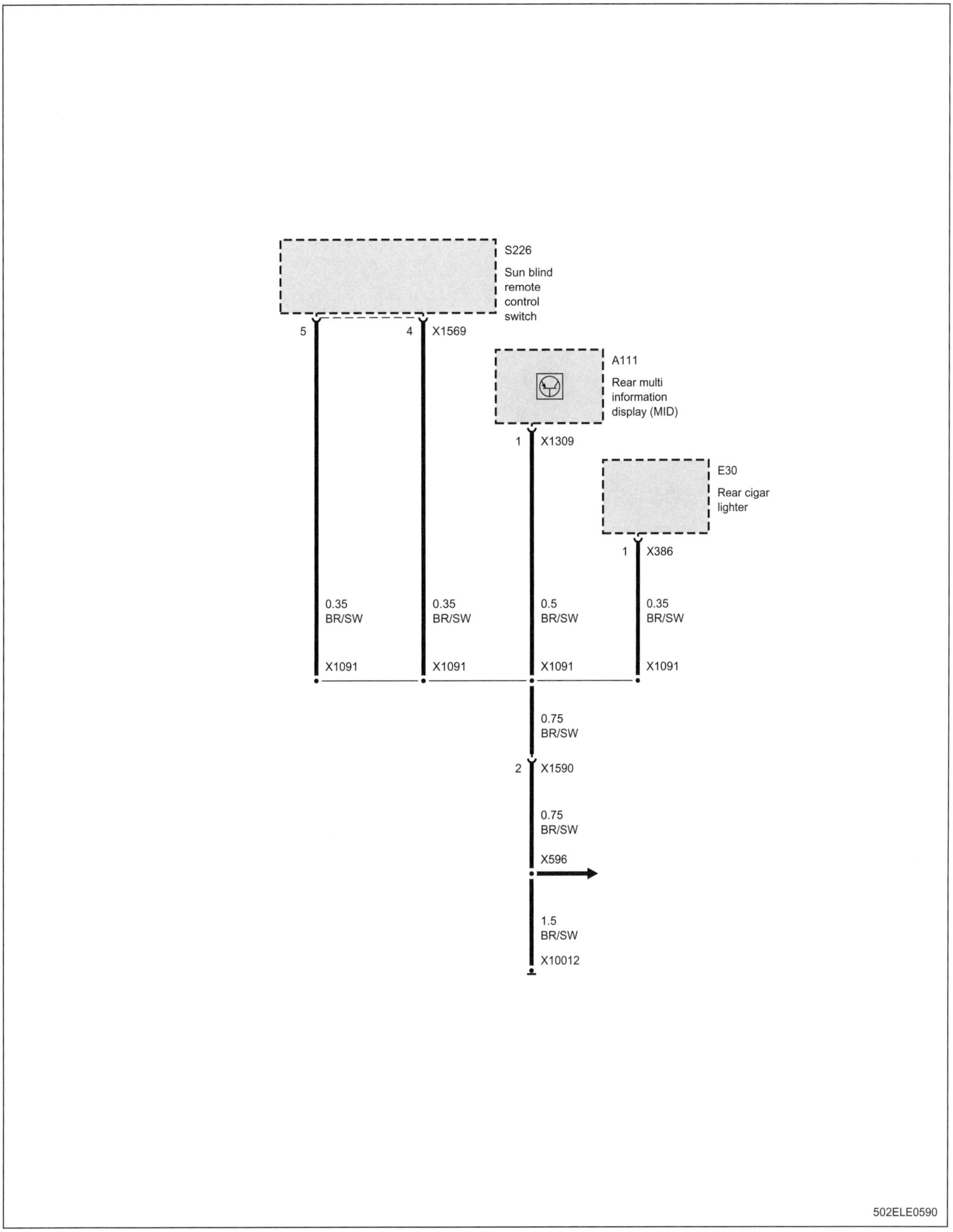

X-Connectors and Splices
X01098 Connector
(1 of 1)

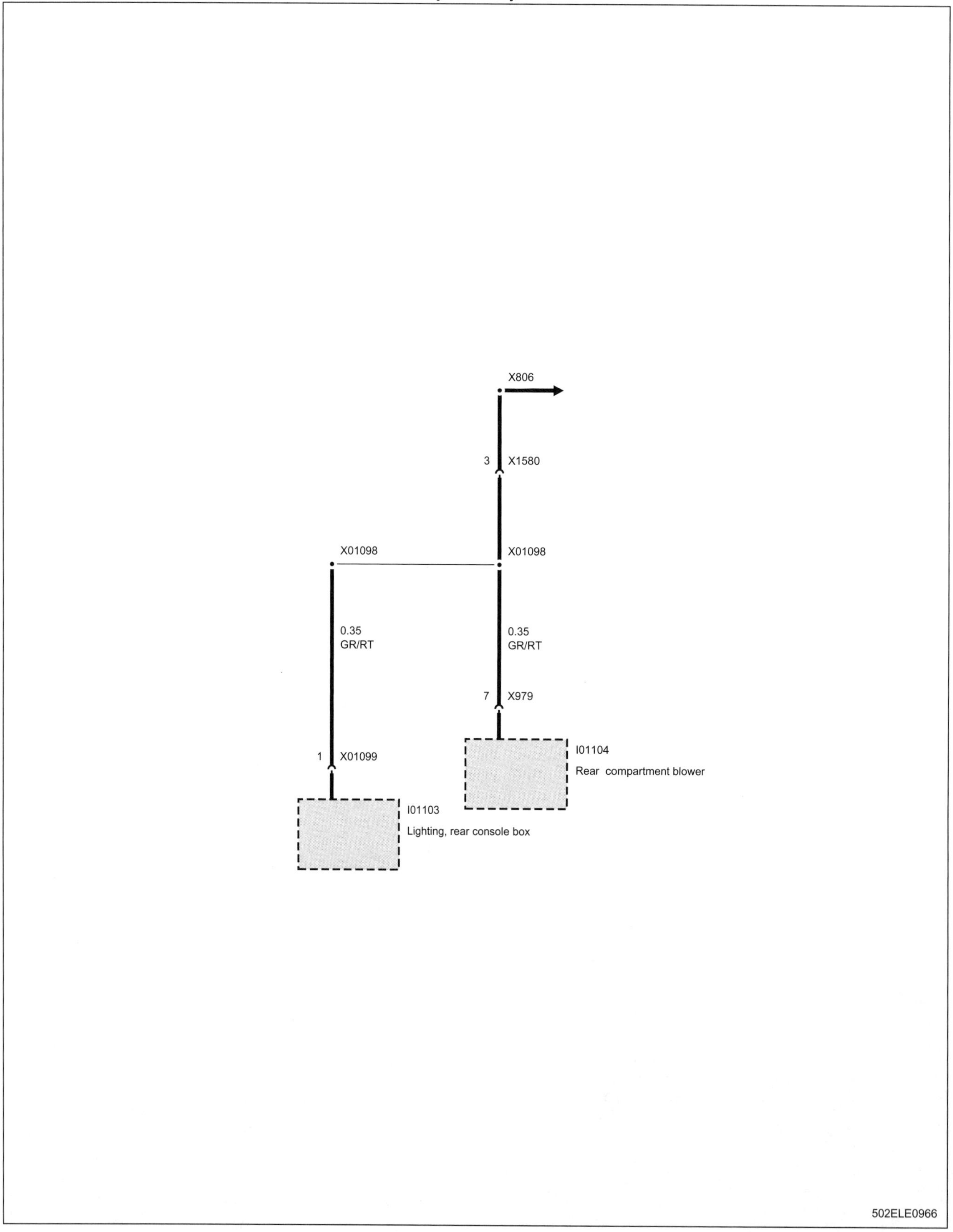
X806
3 X1580
X01098
X01098
0.35
GR/RT
0.35
GR/RT
7 X979
1 X01099
I01104
Rear compartment blower
I01103
Lighting, rear console box
502ELE0966

X-Connectors and Splices
X1101 Splice
(1 of 1)

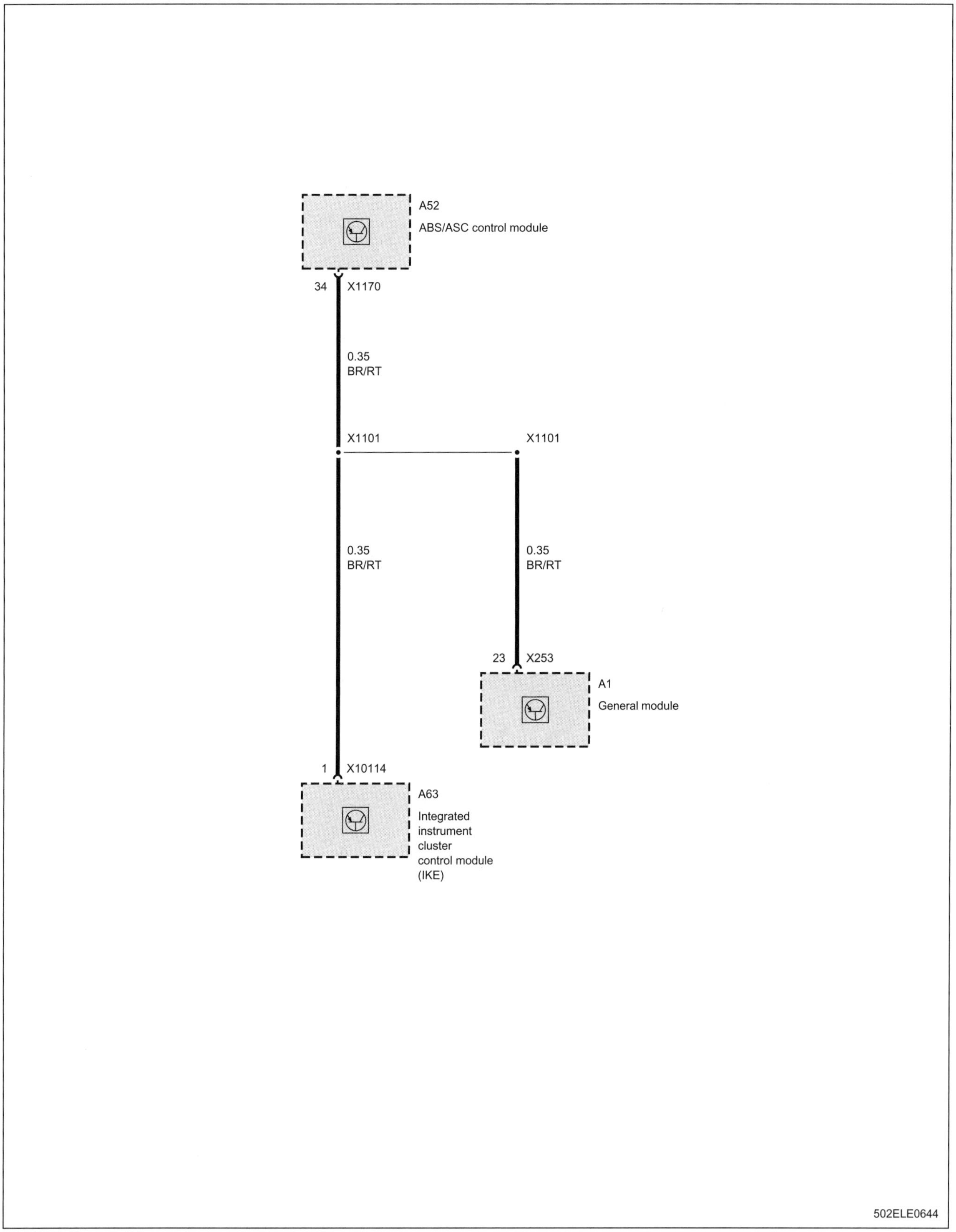
A52
ABS/ASC control module
34
X1170
0.35
BR/RT
X1101
X1101
0.35
BR/RT
0.35
BR/RT
23
X253
A1
General module
1
X10114
A63
Integrated
instrument
cluster
control module
(IKE)
502ELE0644

X-Connectors and Splices
X1101, X2230 Splices
(1 of 1)

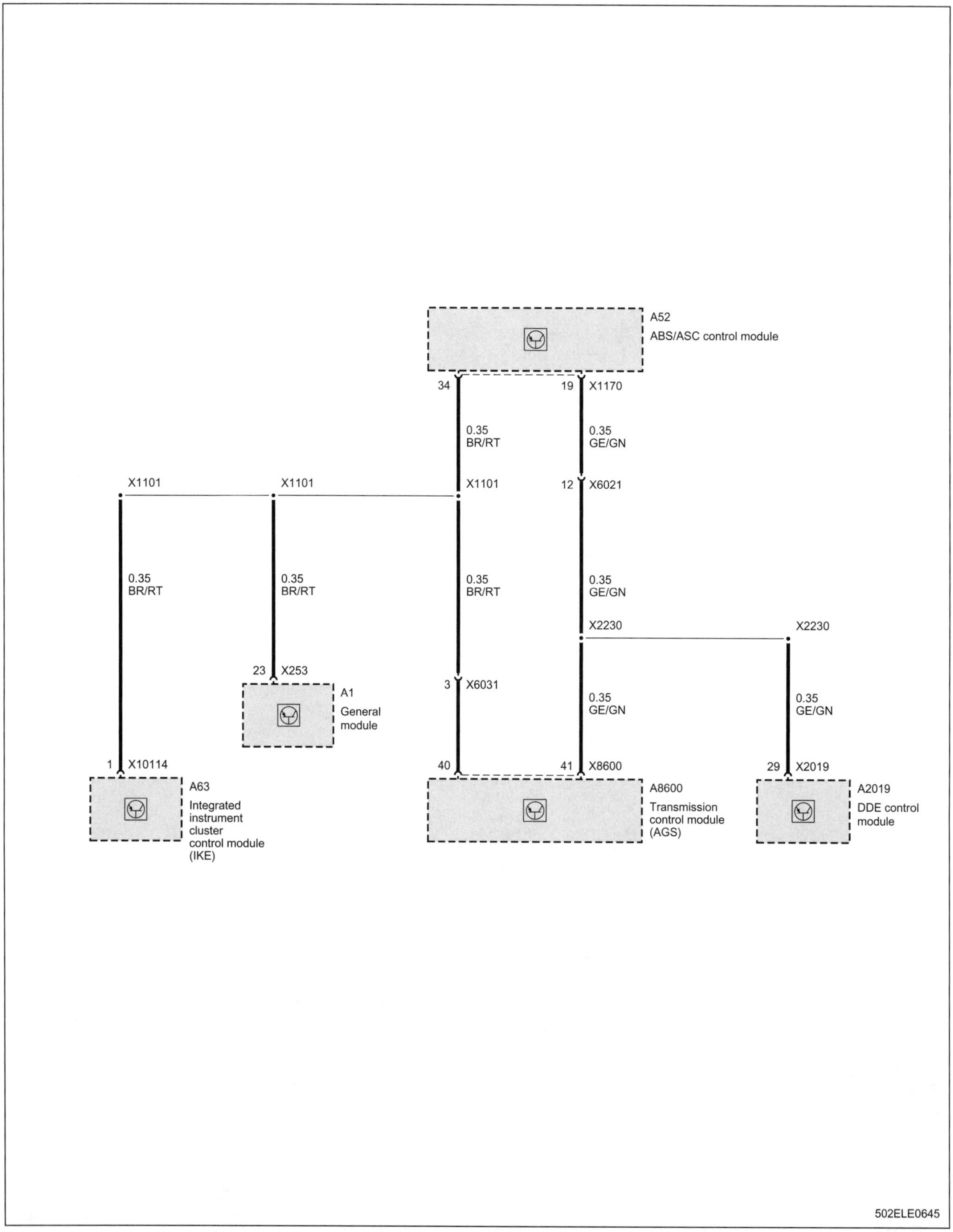

Ground Distribution
X1106 Ground
(1 of 1)

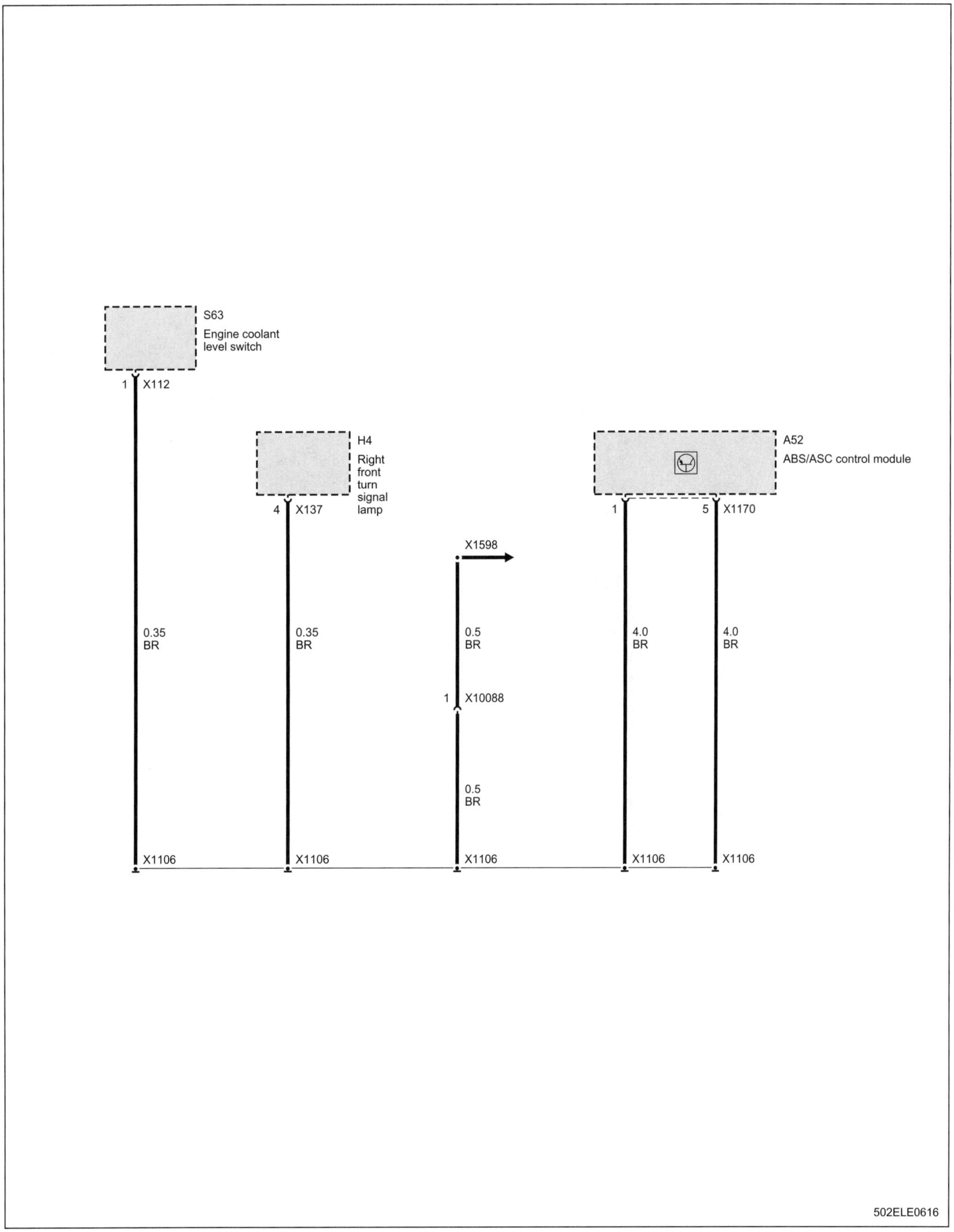
S63
Engine coolant level switch
1 X112
0.35 BR
X1106
H4
Right front turn signal lamp
4 X137
0.35 BR
X1106
X1598
0.5 BR
1 X10088
0.5 BR
X1106
A52
ABS/ASC control module
1
5 X1170
4.0 BR
4.0 BR
X1106
X1106
502ELE0616

Ground Distribution
Ground X1108
(1 of 1)

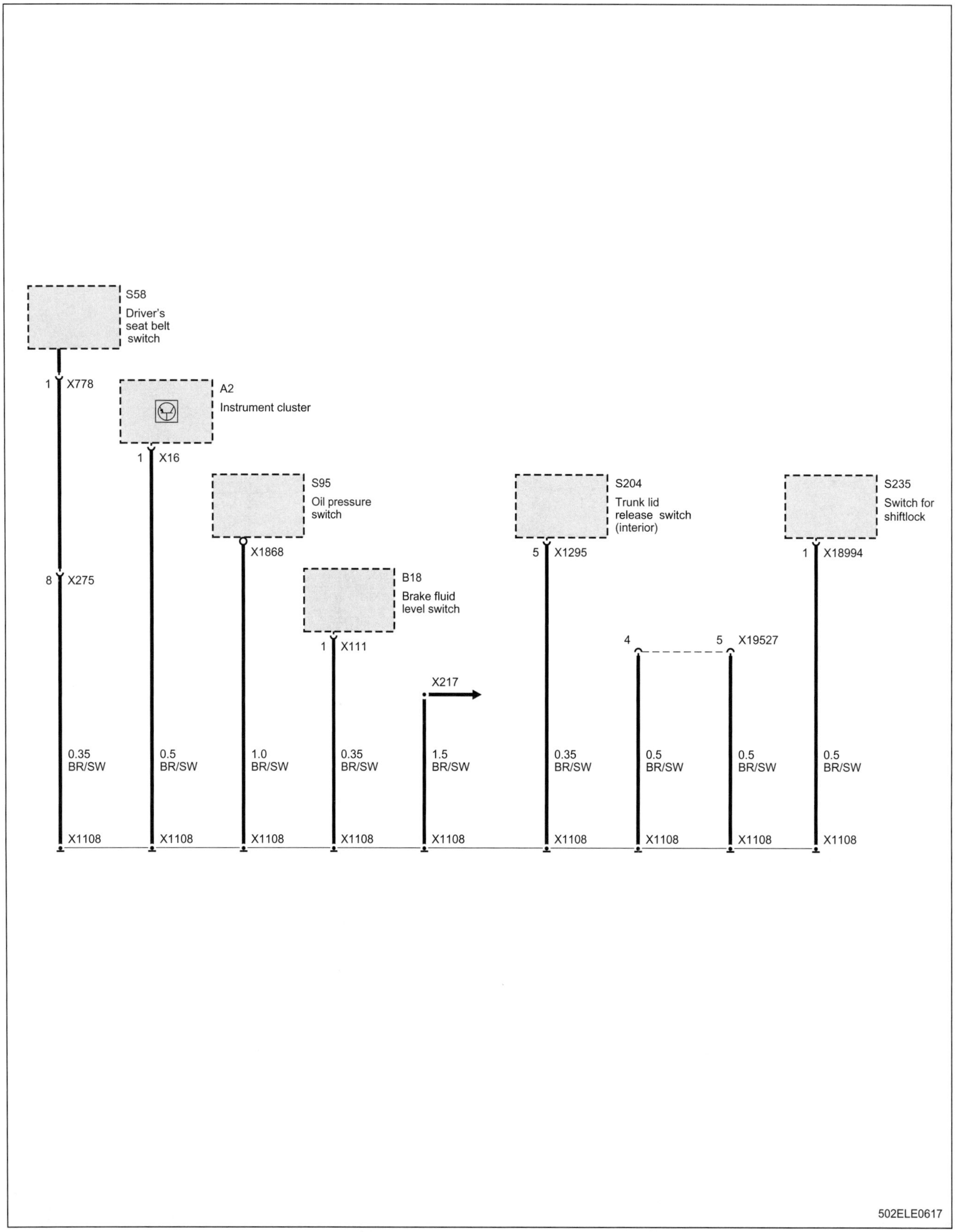
S58
Driver's seat belt switch
1 X778
8 X275
A2
Instrument cluster
1 X16
S95
Oil pressure switch
X1868
B18
Brake fluid level switch
1 X111
X217
S204
Trunk lid release switch (interior)
5 X1295
4
5 X19527
S235
Switch for shiftlock
1 X18994
0.35 BR/SW
0.5 BR/SW
1.0 BR/SW
0.35 BR/SW
1.5 BR/SW
0.35 BR/SW
0.5 BR/SW
0.5 BR/SW
0.5 BR/SW
X1108
502ELE0617

X-Connectors and Splices
X1123 Connector - Brake fluid level
(1 of 1)

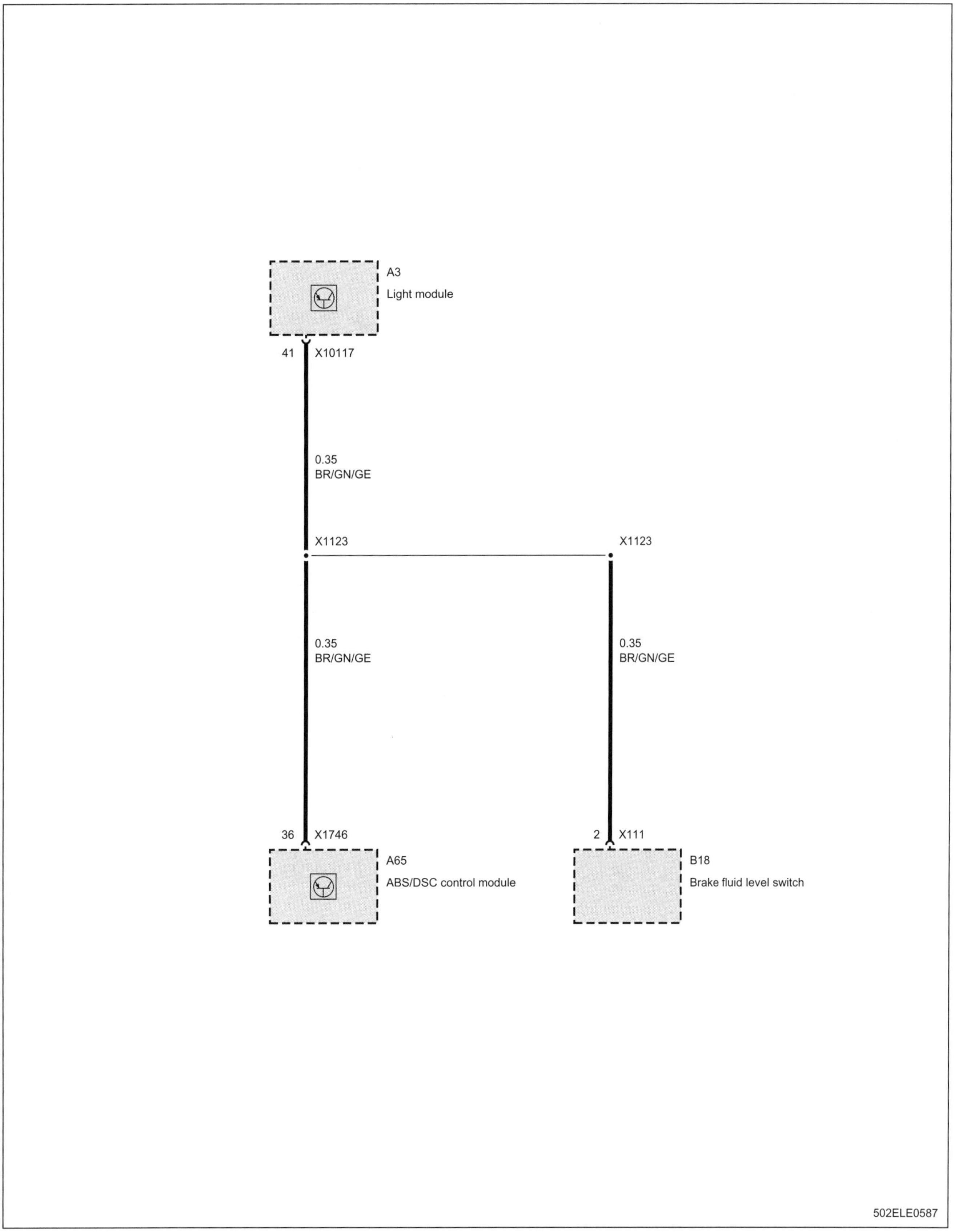

X-Connectors and Splices
X1218 Splice
(1 of 1)

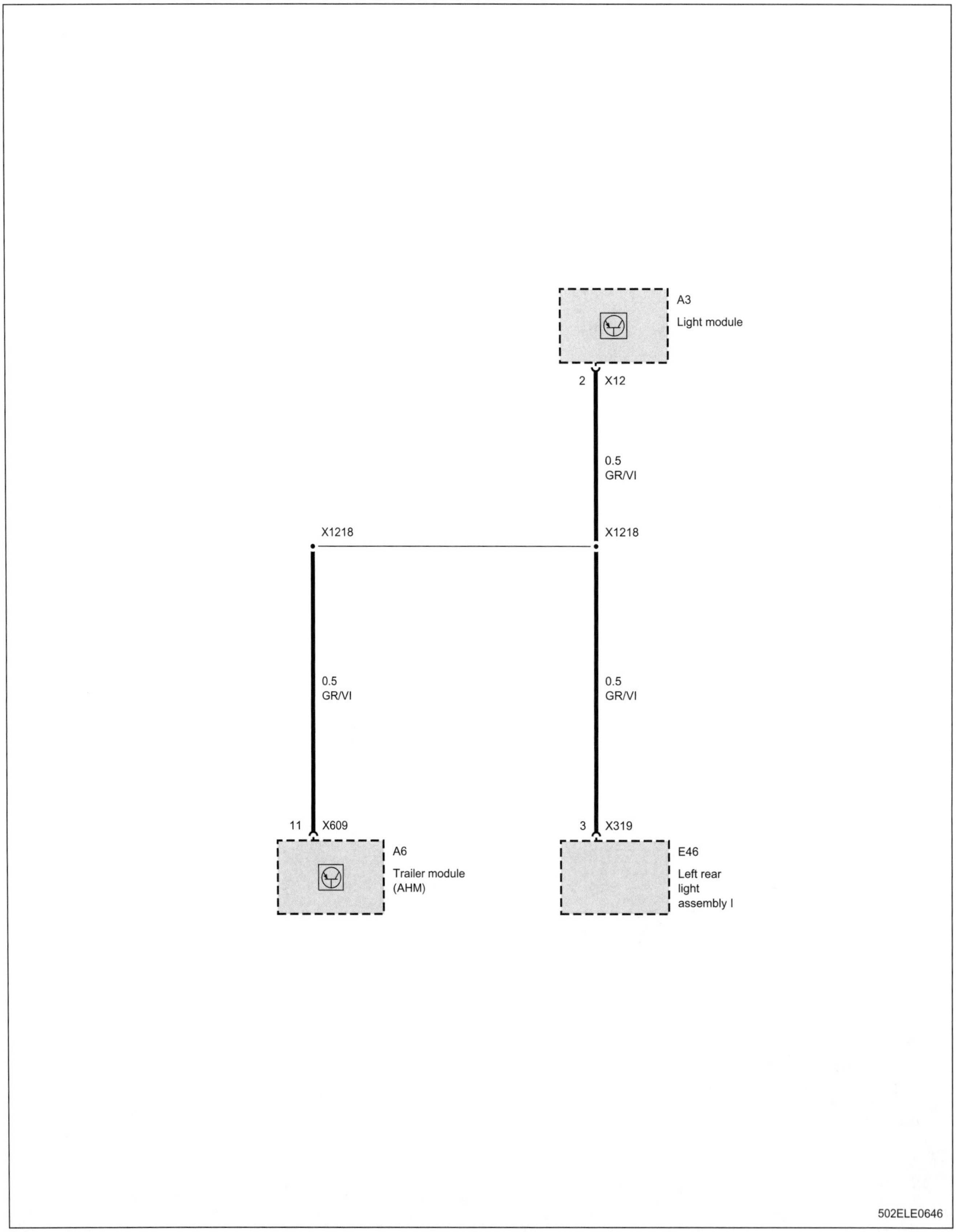
A3
Light module
2 X12
0.5
GR/VI
X1218
X1218
0.5
GR/VI
0.5
GR/VI
11 X609
A6
Trailer module
(AHM)
3 X319
E46
Left rear
light
assembly l
502ELE0646

X-Connectors and Splices
X1232 Connector
(1 of 1)

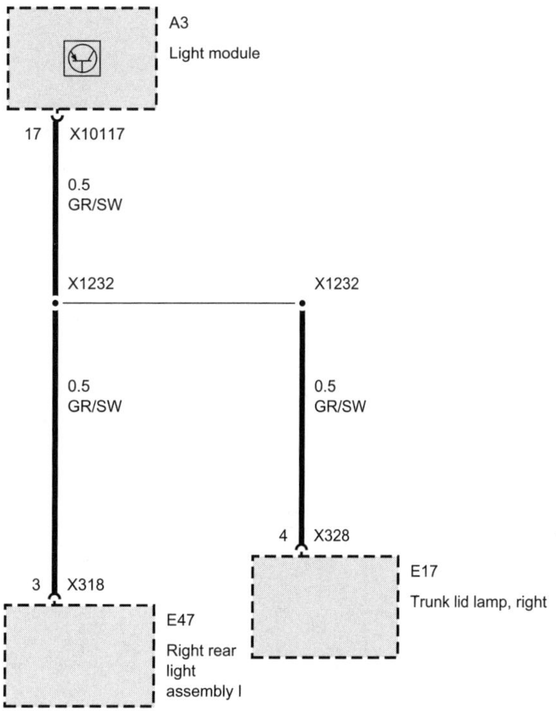

502ELE0570

X-Connectors and Splices
Splice X1293
(1 of 1)

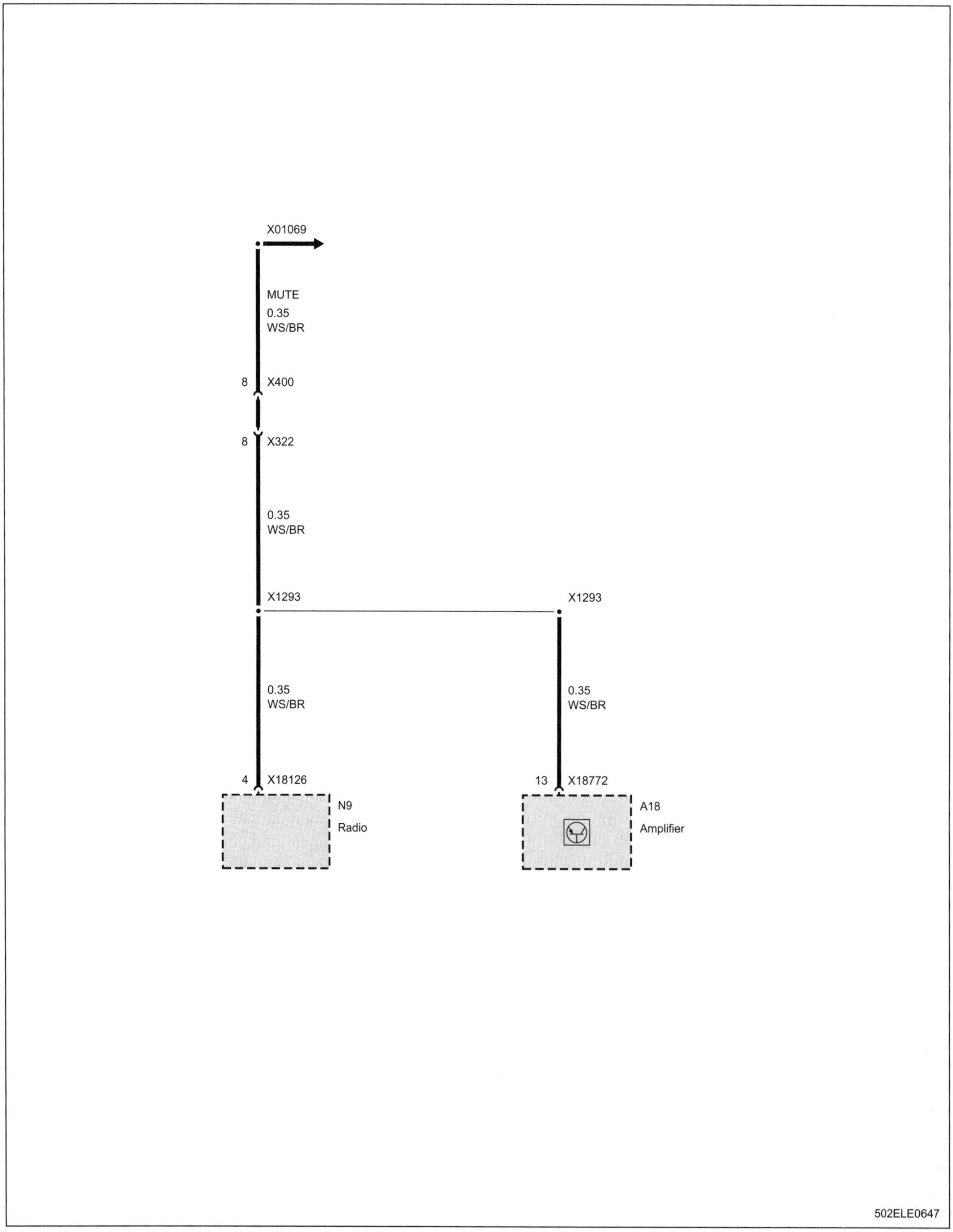
X01069
MUTE
0.35
WS/BR
8 X400
8 X322
0.35
WS/BR
X1293
X1293
0.35
WS/BR
0.35
WS/BR
4 X18126
13 X18772
N9
Radio
A18
Amplifier
502ELE0647

X-Connectors and Splices
X1310 Navigation connector
(1 of 1)

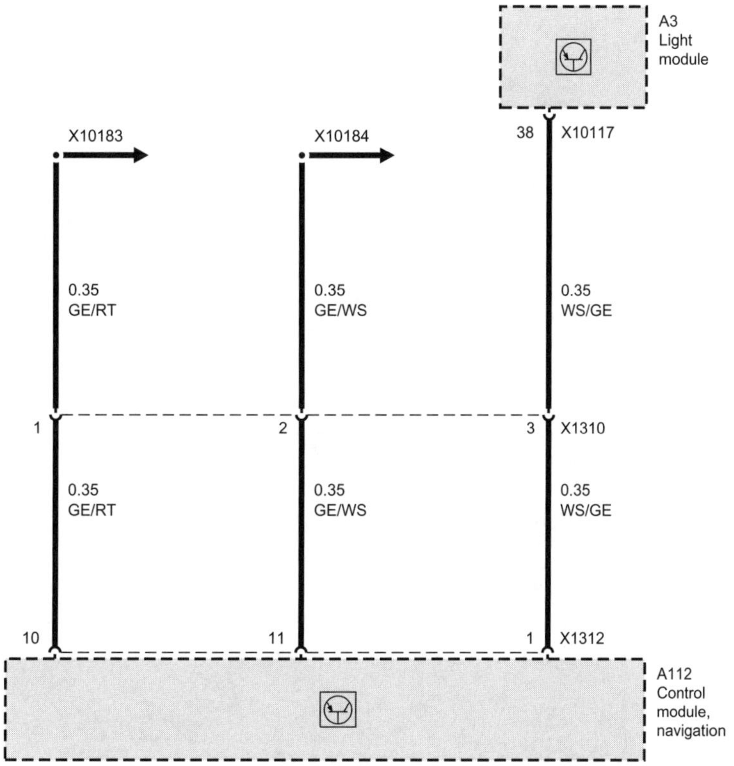

502ELE0680

X-Connectors and Splices
X1353 Splice
(1 of 1)

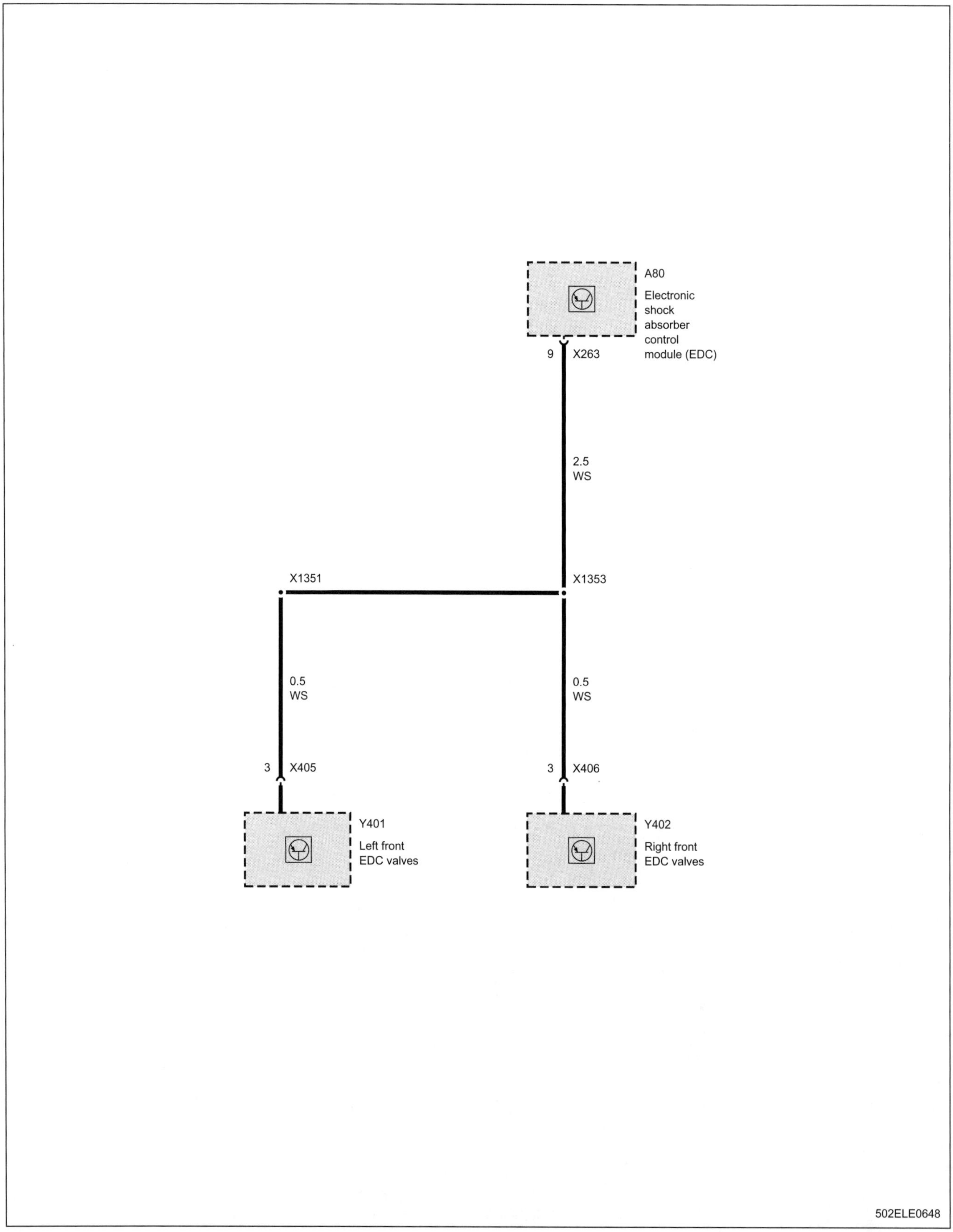
A80
Electronic shock absorber control module (EDC)
9
X263
2.5
WS
X1351
X1353
0.5
WS
0.5
WS
3
X405
3
X406
Y401
Left front EDC valves
Y402
Right front EDC valves
502ELE0648

X-Connectors and Splices
X1354 Splice
(1 of 1)

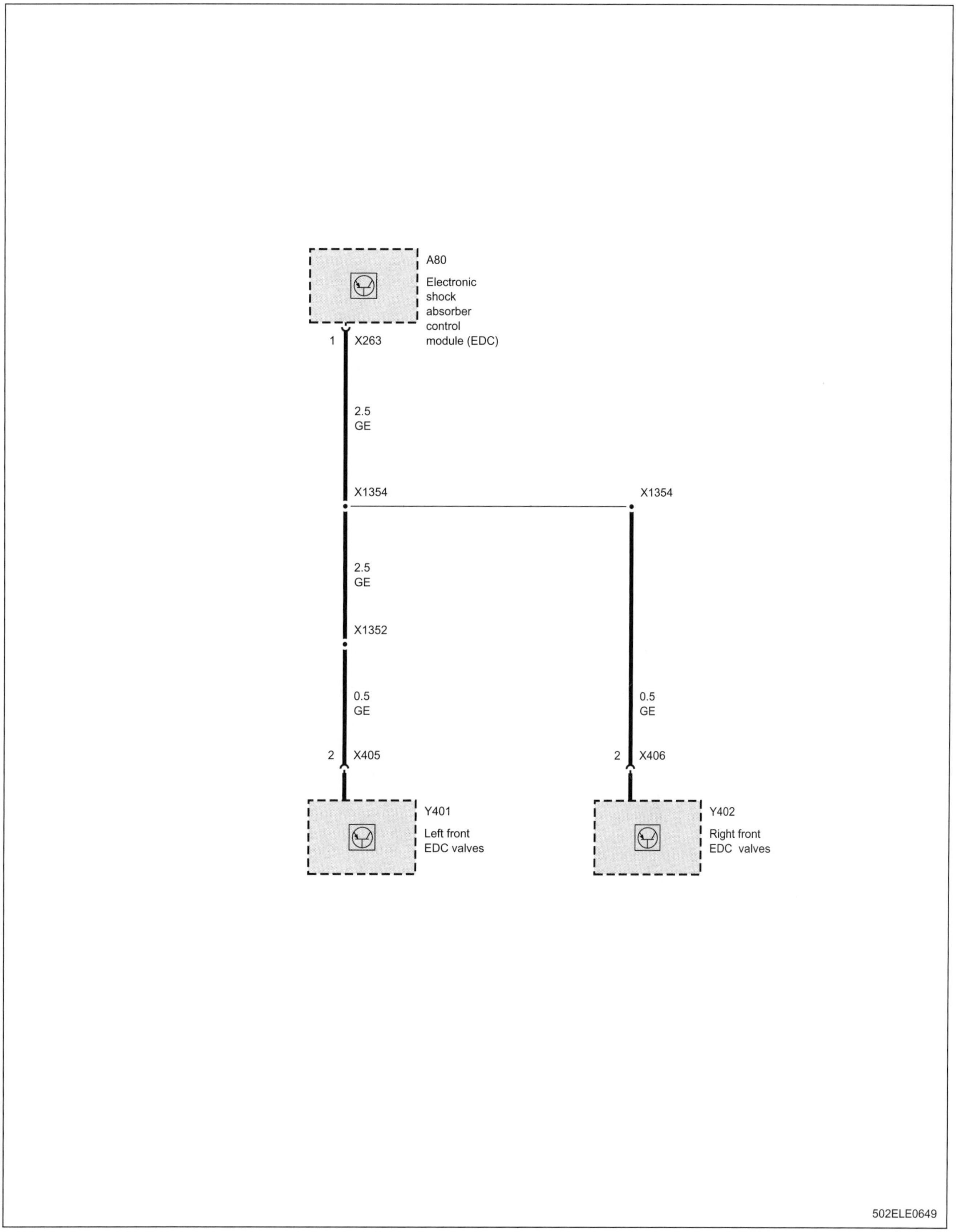

X-Connectors and Splices
X1355 Splice
(1 of 1)

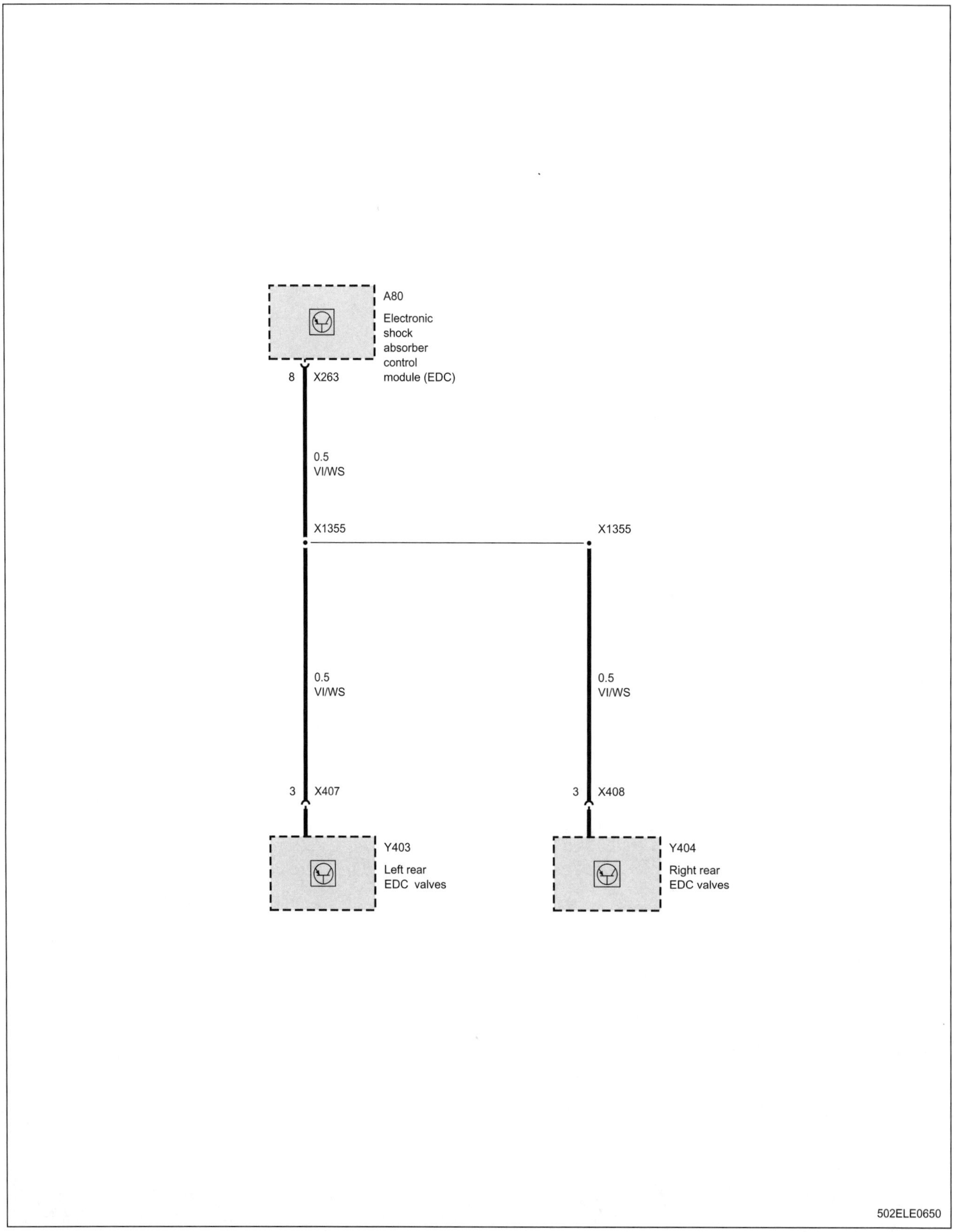
A80
Electronic shock absorber control module (EDC)
8
X263
0.5
VI/WS
X1355
X1355
0.5
VI/WS
0.5
VI/WS
3
X407
3
X408
Y403
Left rear EDC valves
Y404
Right rear EDC valves
502ELE0650

X-Connectors and Splices
X1356 Splice
(1 of 1)

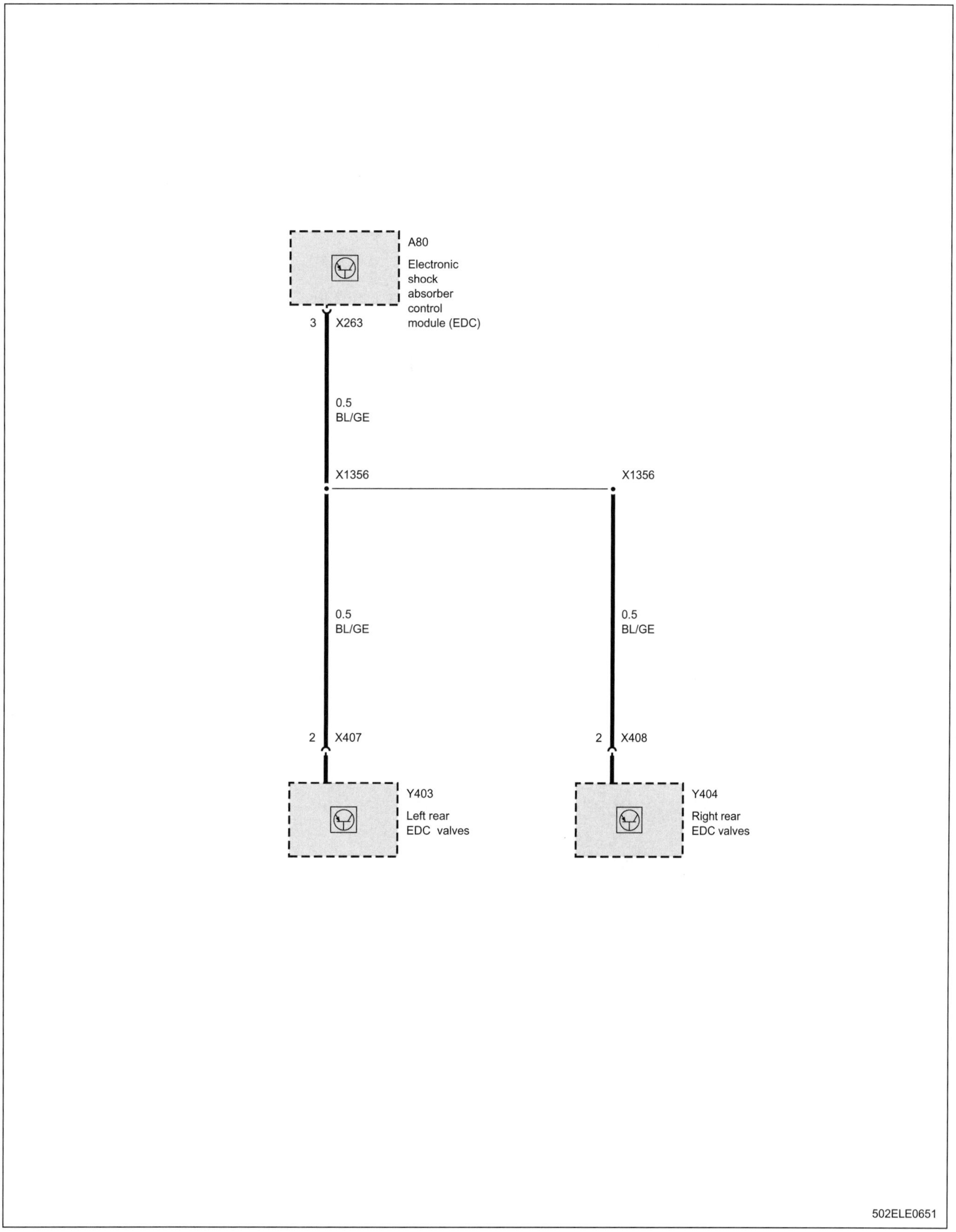
A80
Electronic shock absorber control module (EDC)
3
X263
0.5
BL/GE
X1356
X1356
0.5
BL/GE
0.5
BL/GE
2
X407
2
X408
Y403
Left rear EDC valves
Y404
Right rear EDC valves
502ELE0651

X-Connectors and Splices
X1411 Splice
(1 of 1)

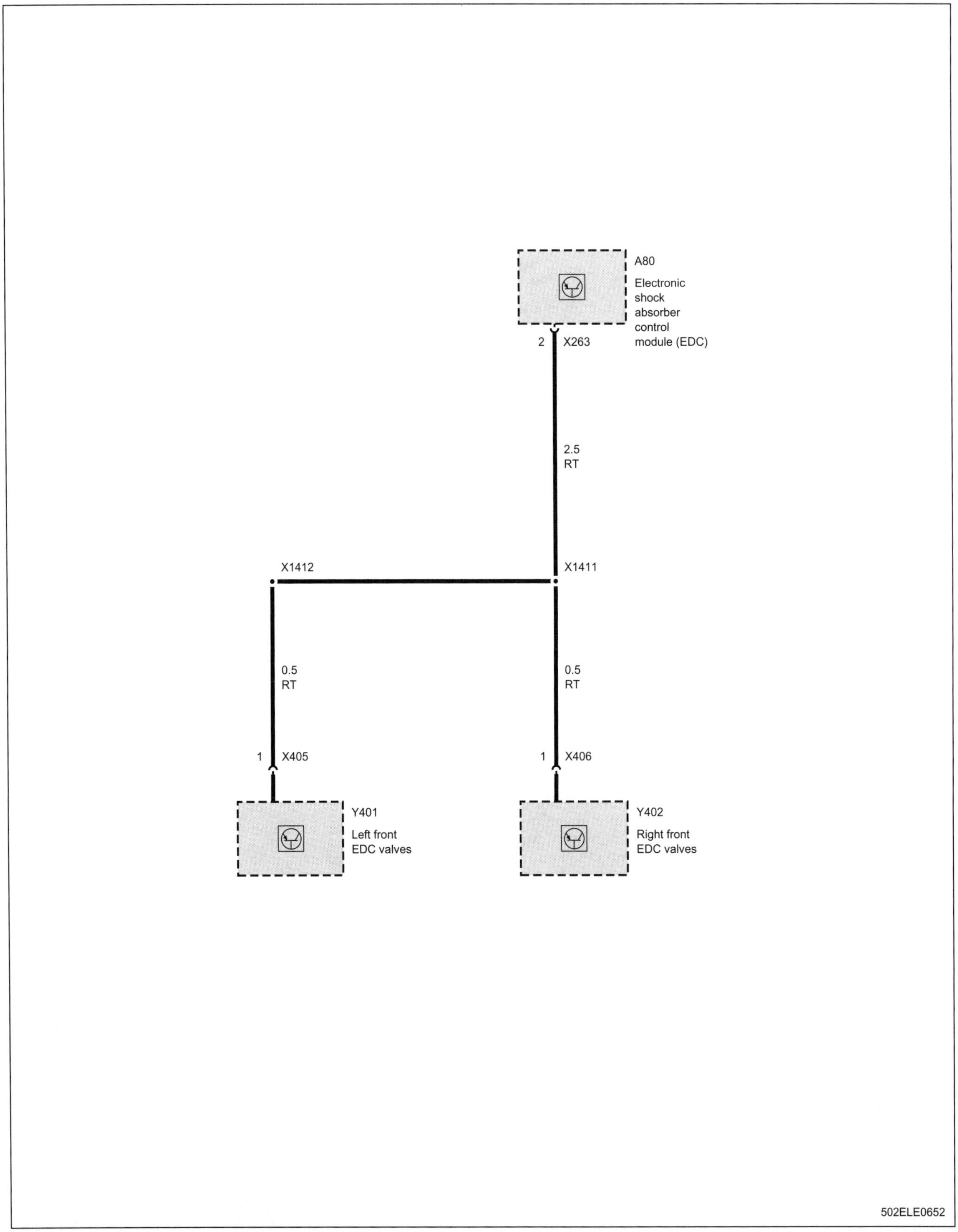
A80
Electronic shock absorber control module (EDC)
2
X263
2.5
RT
X1412
X1411
0.5
RT
0.5
RT
1
X405
1
X406
Y401
Left front EDC valves
Y402
Right front EDC valves
502ELE0652

X-Connectors and Splices
X1452 Plug connector
(1 of 1)

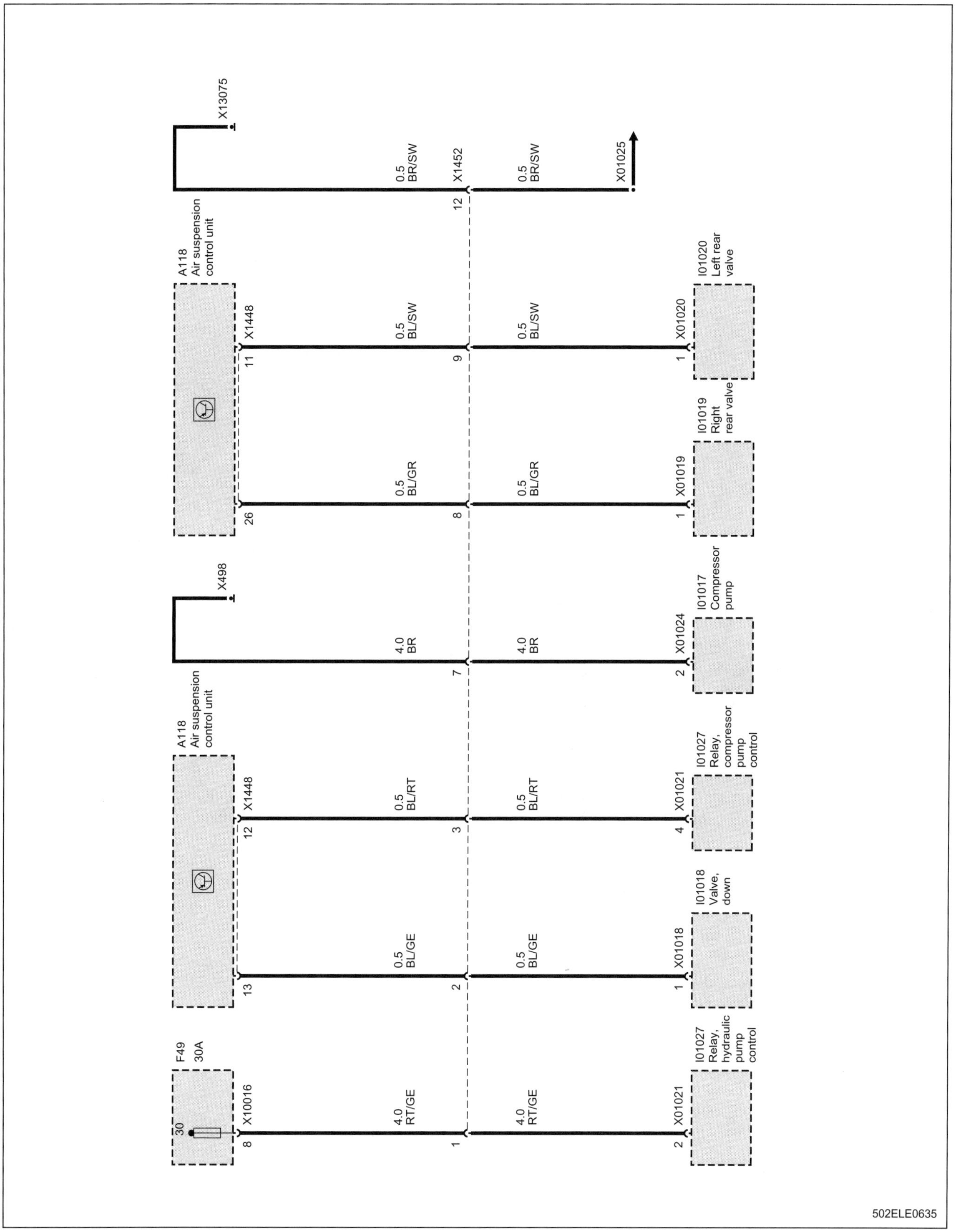

Ground Distribution
X1461 Ground splice
(1 of 1)

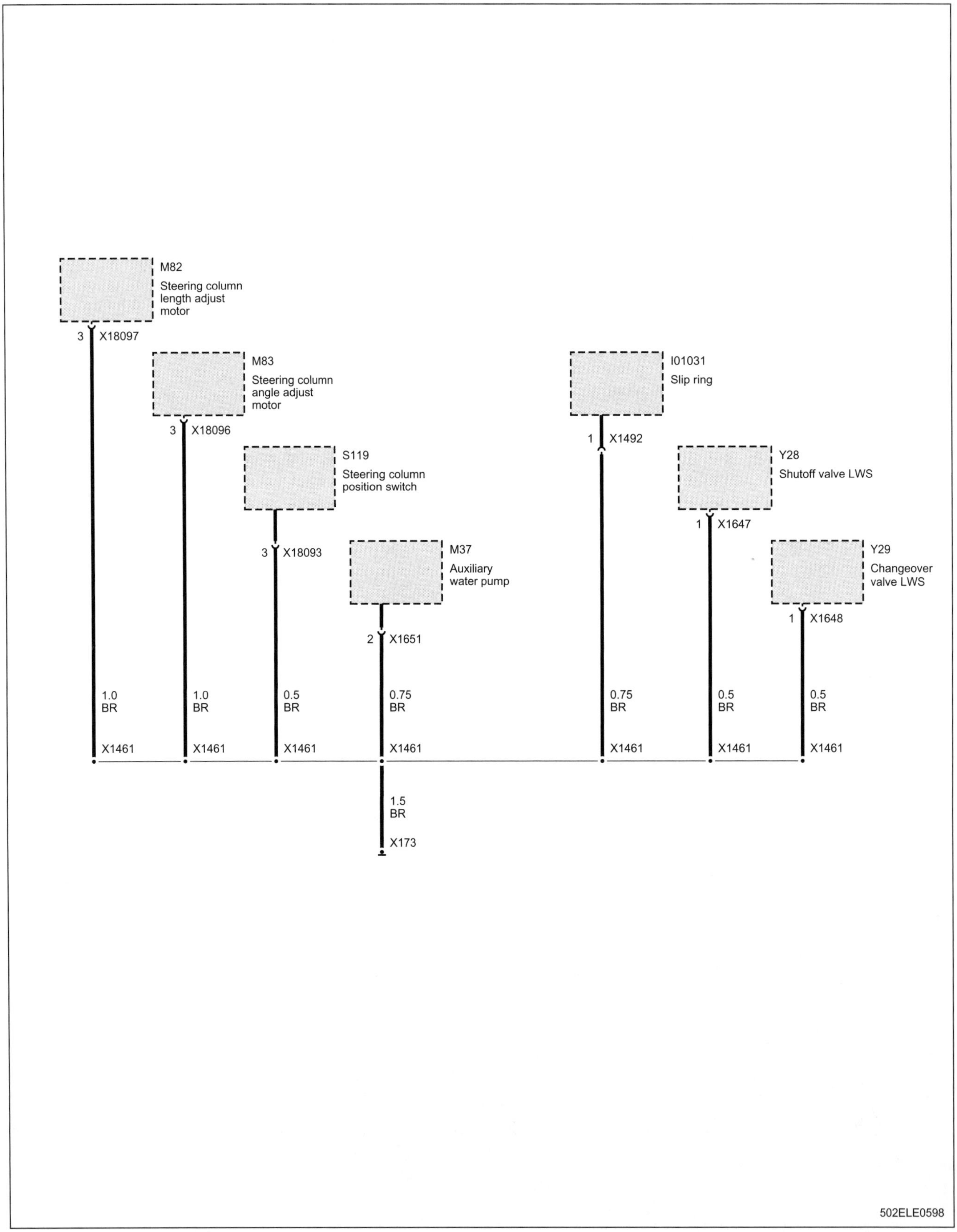
M82
Steering column length adjust motor
3 X18097
M83
Steering column angle adjust motor
3 X18096
S119
Steering column position switch
3 X18093
M37
Auxiliary water pump
2 X1651
I01031
Slip ring
1 X1492
Y28
Shutoff valve LWS
1 X1647
Y29
Changeover valve LWS
1 X1648
1.0 BR
1.0 BR
0.5 BR
0.75 BR
0.75 BR
0.5 BR
0.5 BR
X1461
X1461
X1461
X1461
X1461
X1461
X1461
1.5 BR
X173
502ELE0598

X-Connectors and Splices
X1532 Connector - Navigation
(1 of 2)

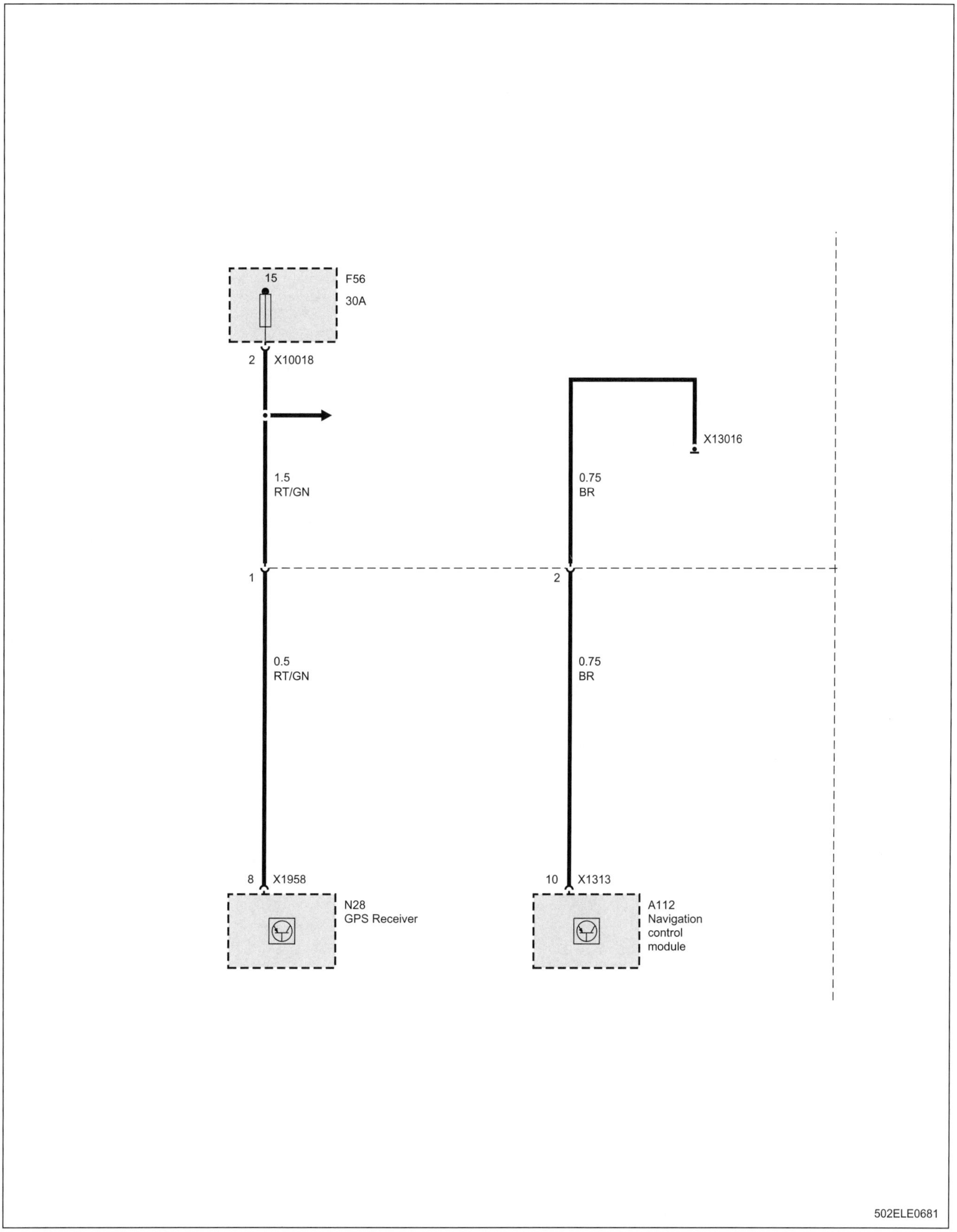

X-Connectors and Splices
X1532 Connector - Navigation
(2 of 2)

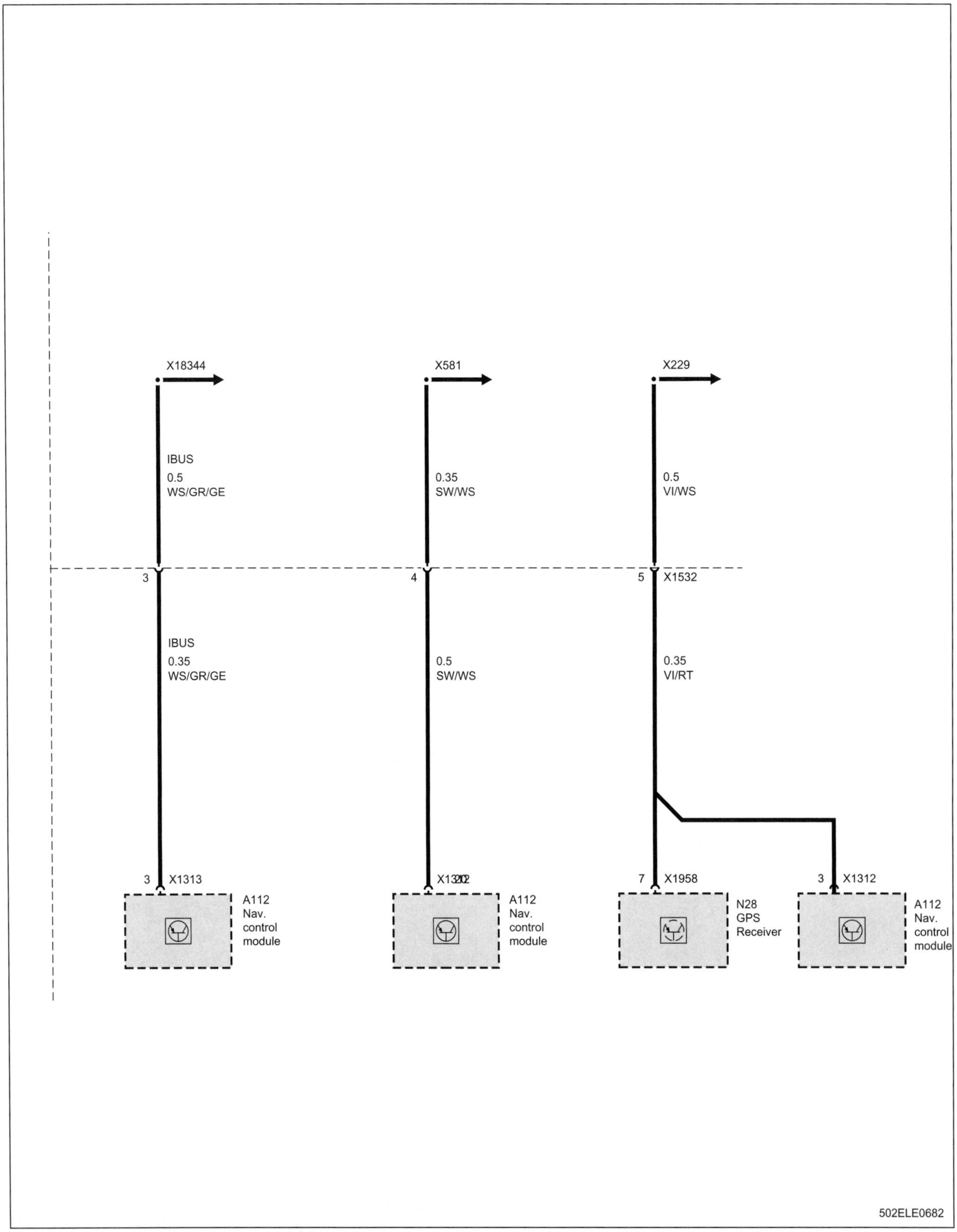

X-Connectors and Splices
X1563 Connector
(1 of 1)

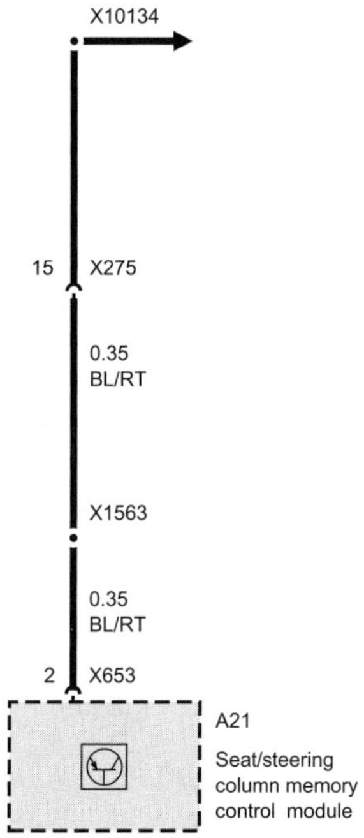

X-Connectors and Splices
X1590 Connector - Center armrest plug
(1 of 1)

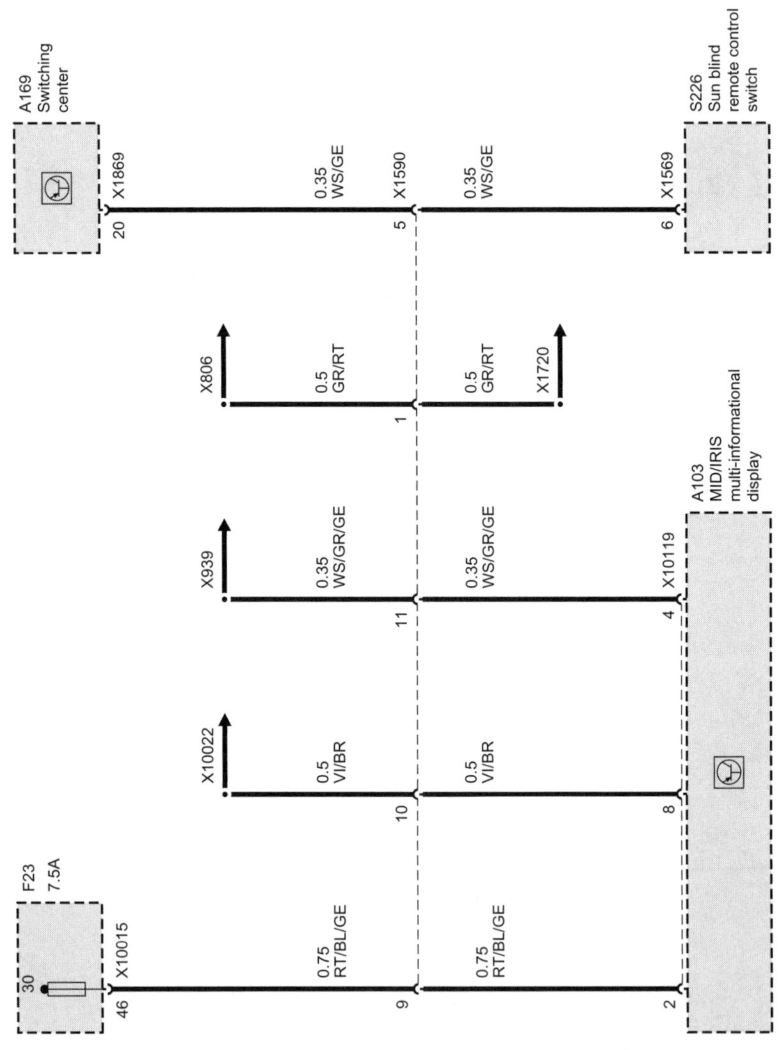

502ELE0683

X-Connectors and Splices
X1596 Splice
(1 of 1)

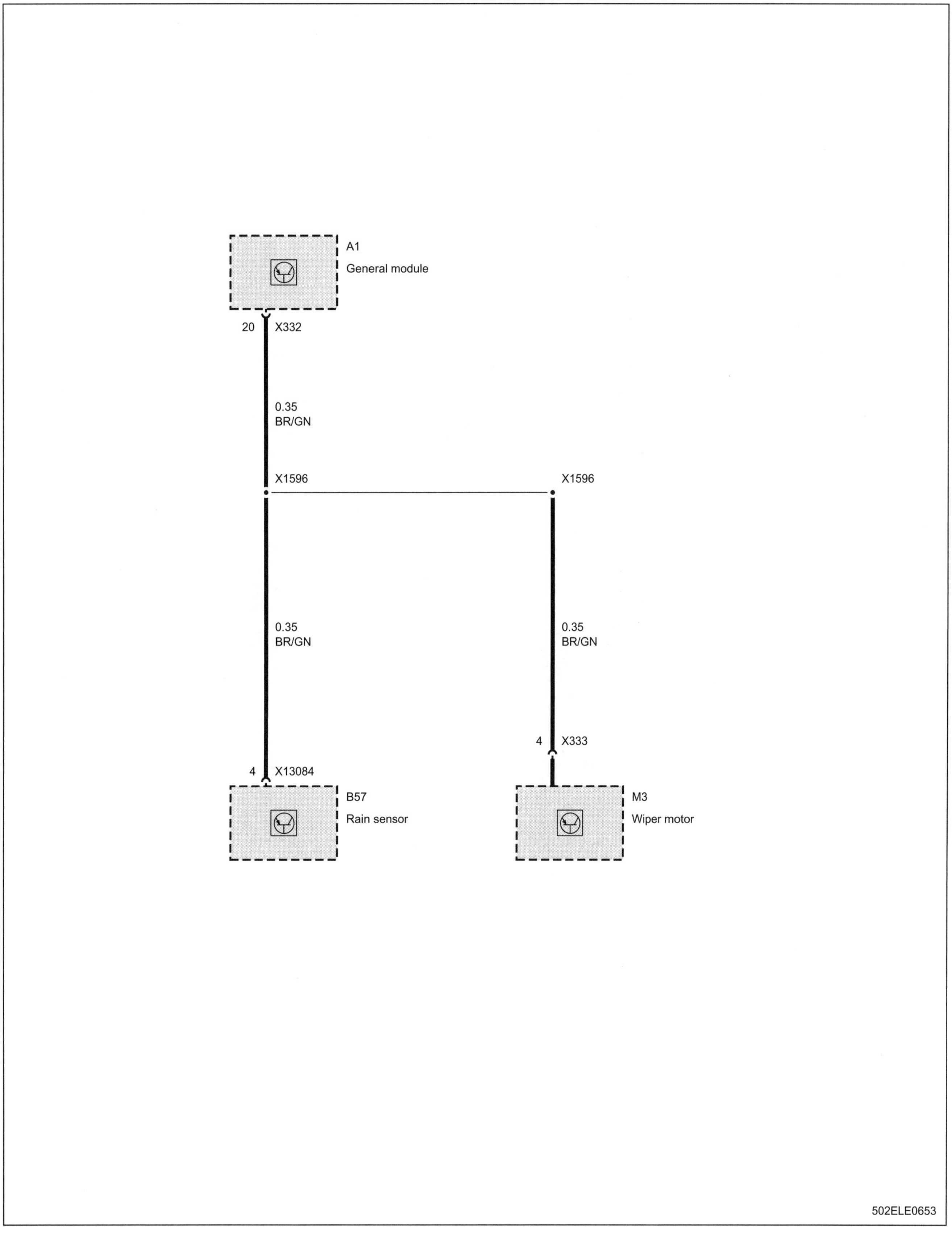
A1
General module
20
X332
0.35
BR/GN
X1596
X1596
0.35
BR/GN
0.35
BR/GN
4
X333
4
X13084
B57
Rain sensor
M3
Wiper motor
502ELE0653

Ground Distribution
X1598 Ground splice
(1 of 1)

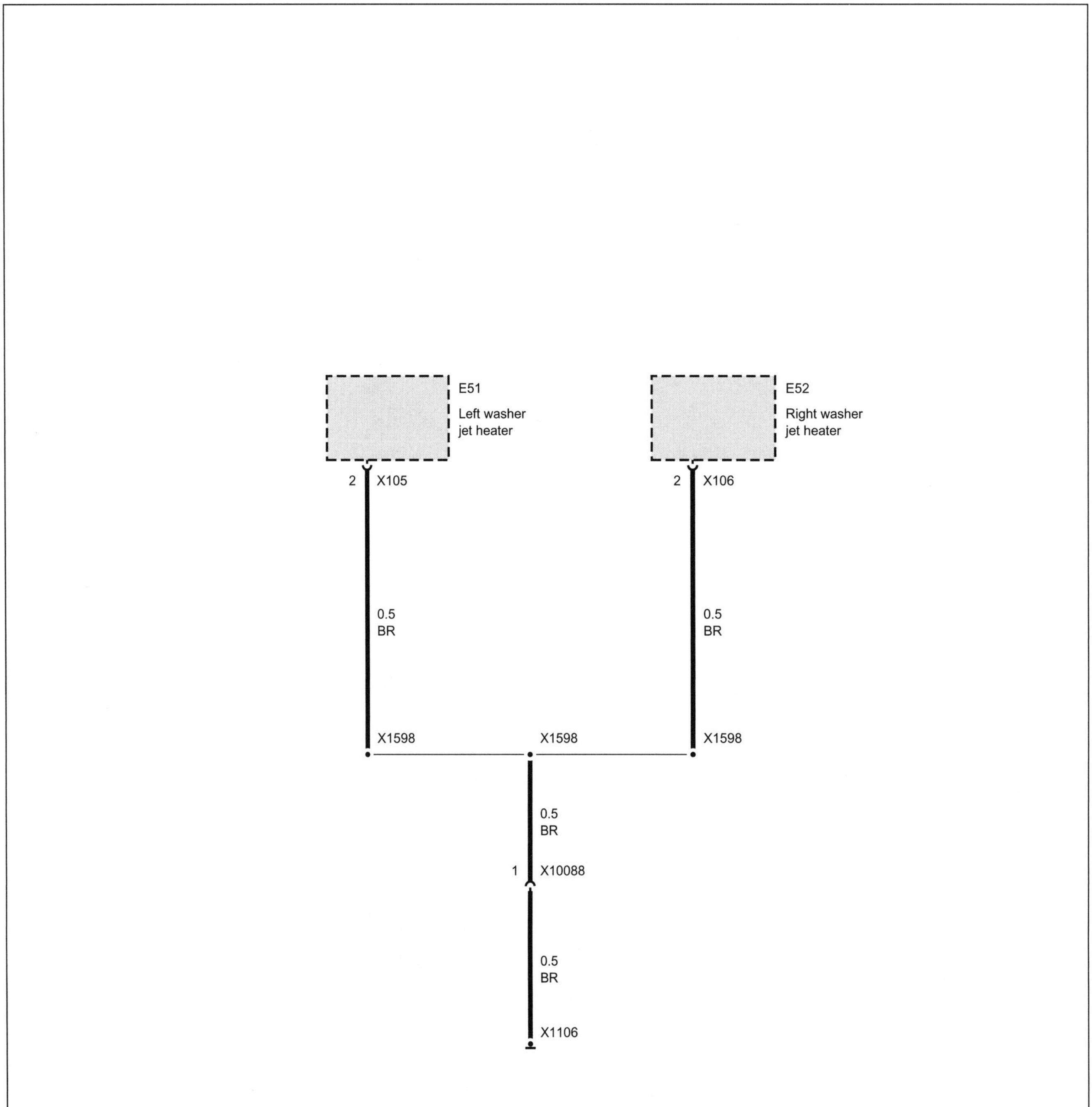
E51
Left washer
jet heater
E52
Right washer
jet heater
2
X105
2
X106
0.5
BR
0.5
BR
X1598
X1598
X1598
0.5
BR
1
X10088
0.5
BR
X1106
502ELE0599

X-Connectors and Splices
X1650 Splice
(1 of 1)

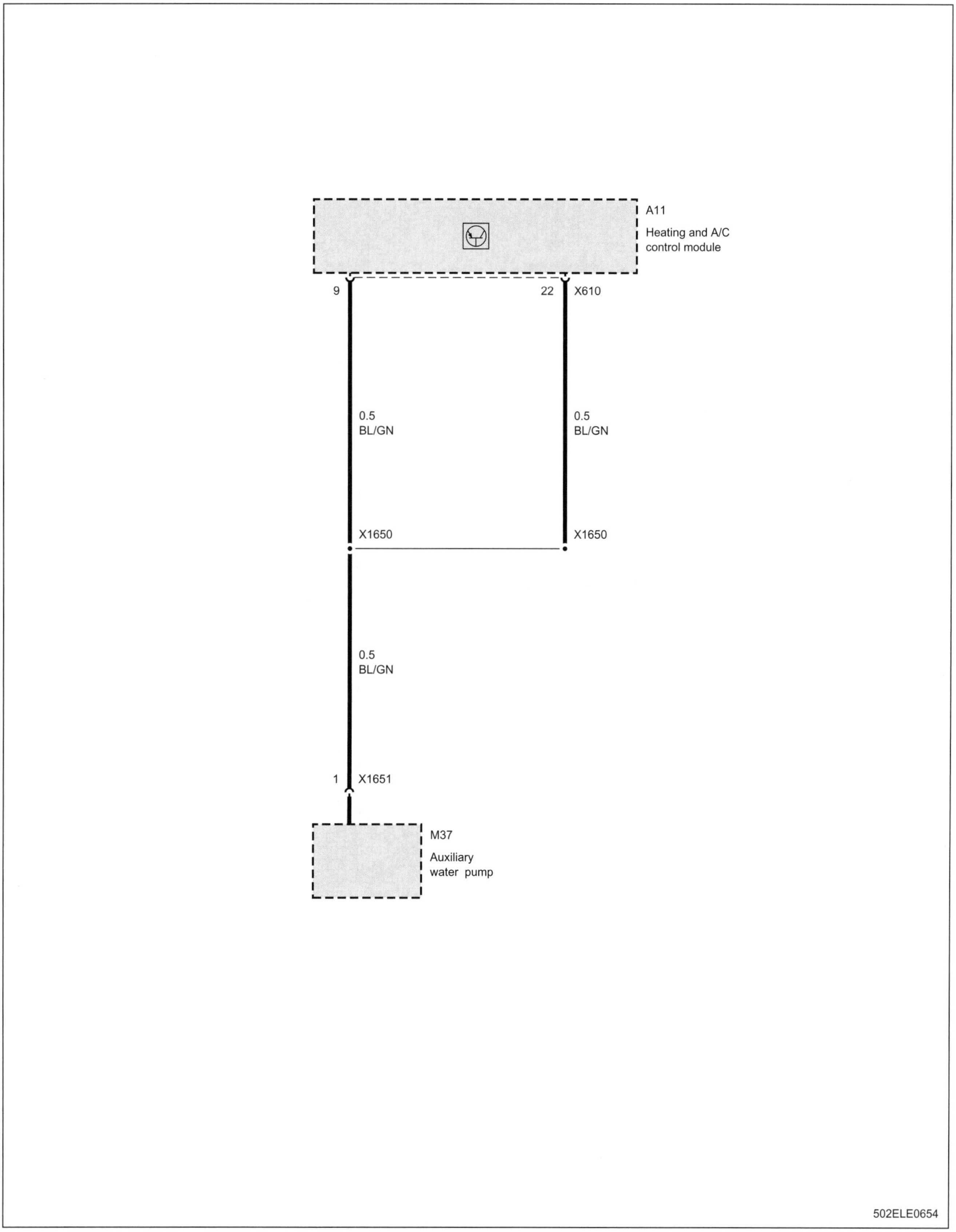

X-Connectors and Splices
X1744, X1745 Splices
(1 of 1)

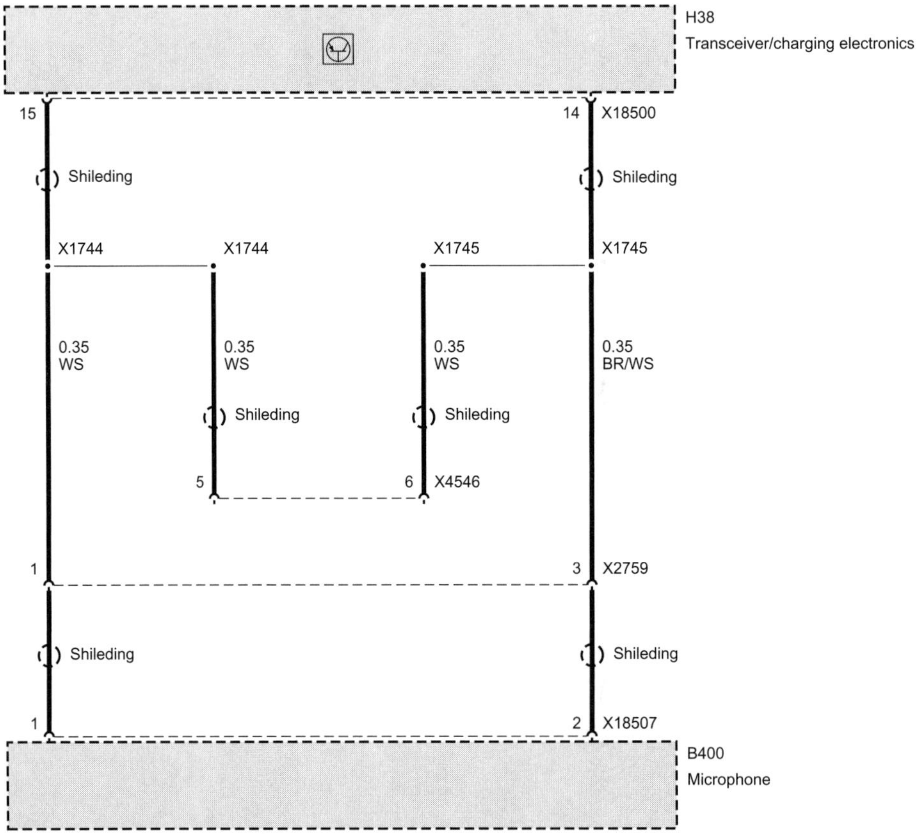

X-Connectors and Splices
X1766 Splice
(1 of 1)

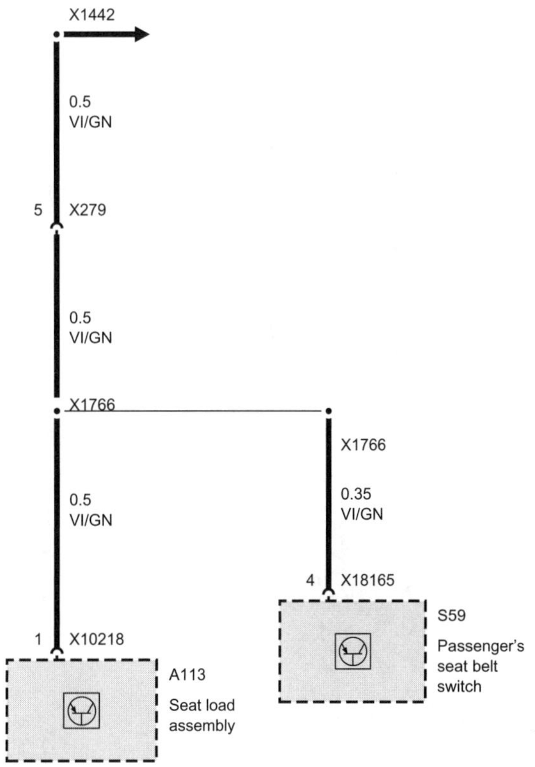

502ELE0656

X-Connectors and Splices
X2039, X183 Connectors - TXD
(1 of 1)

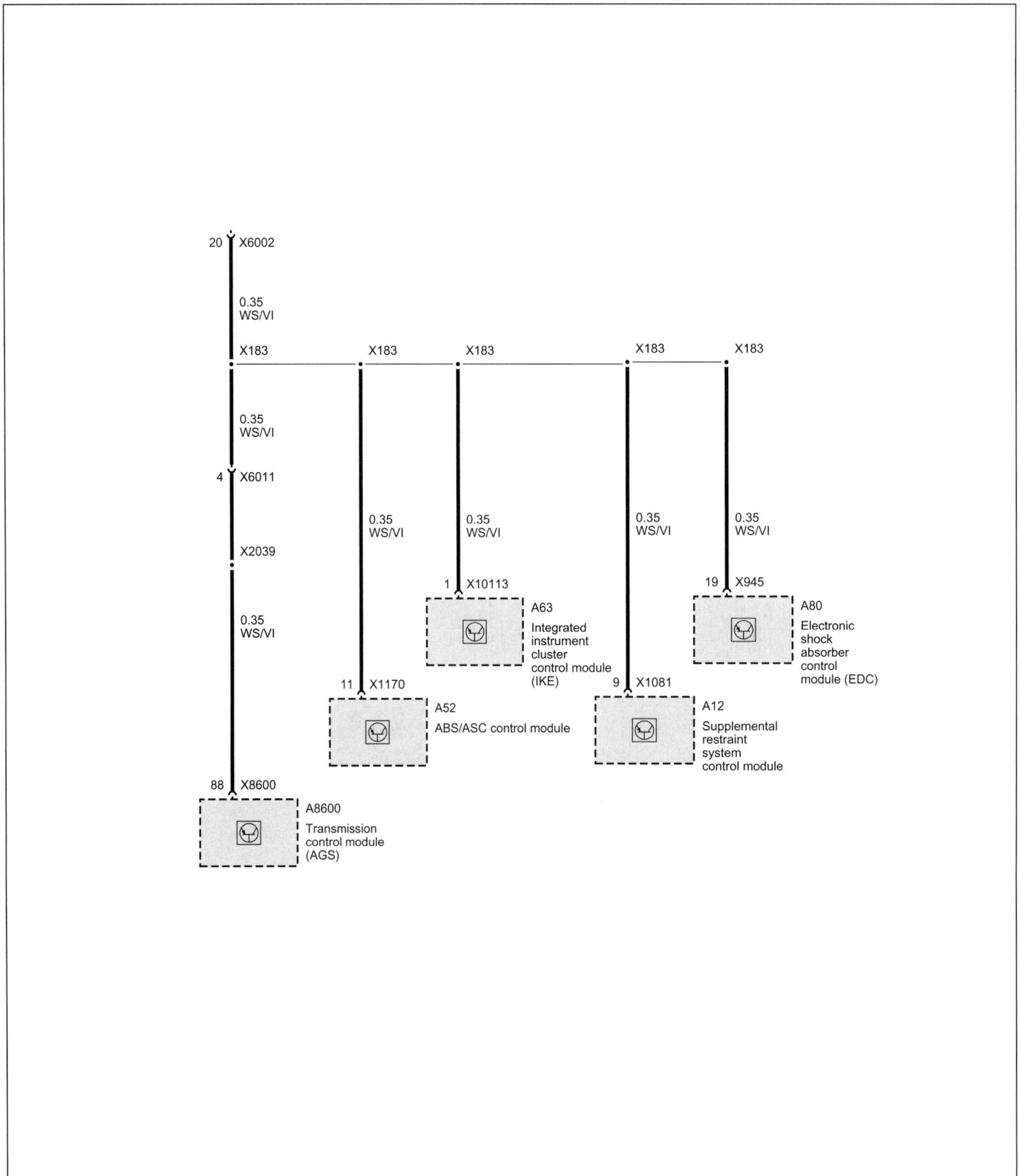

Ground Distribution
X2042, X2151 Ground splice
(1 of 1)

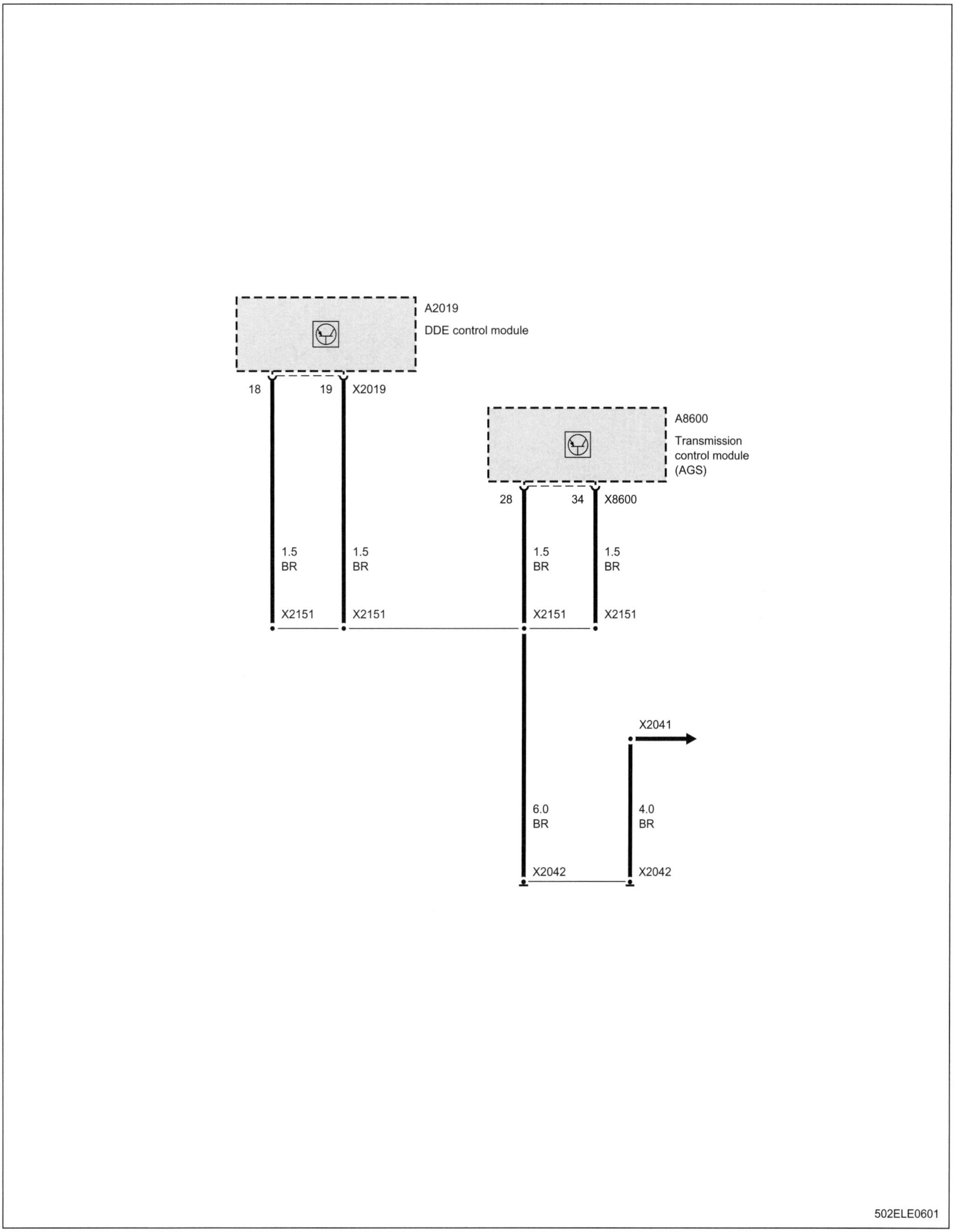

X-Connectors and Splices
X2053 Connector - Sensor ground
(1 of 1)

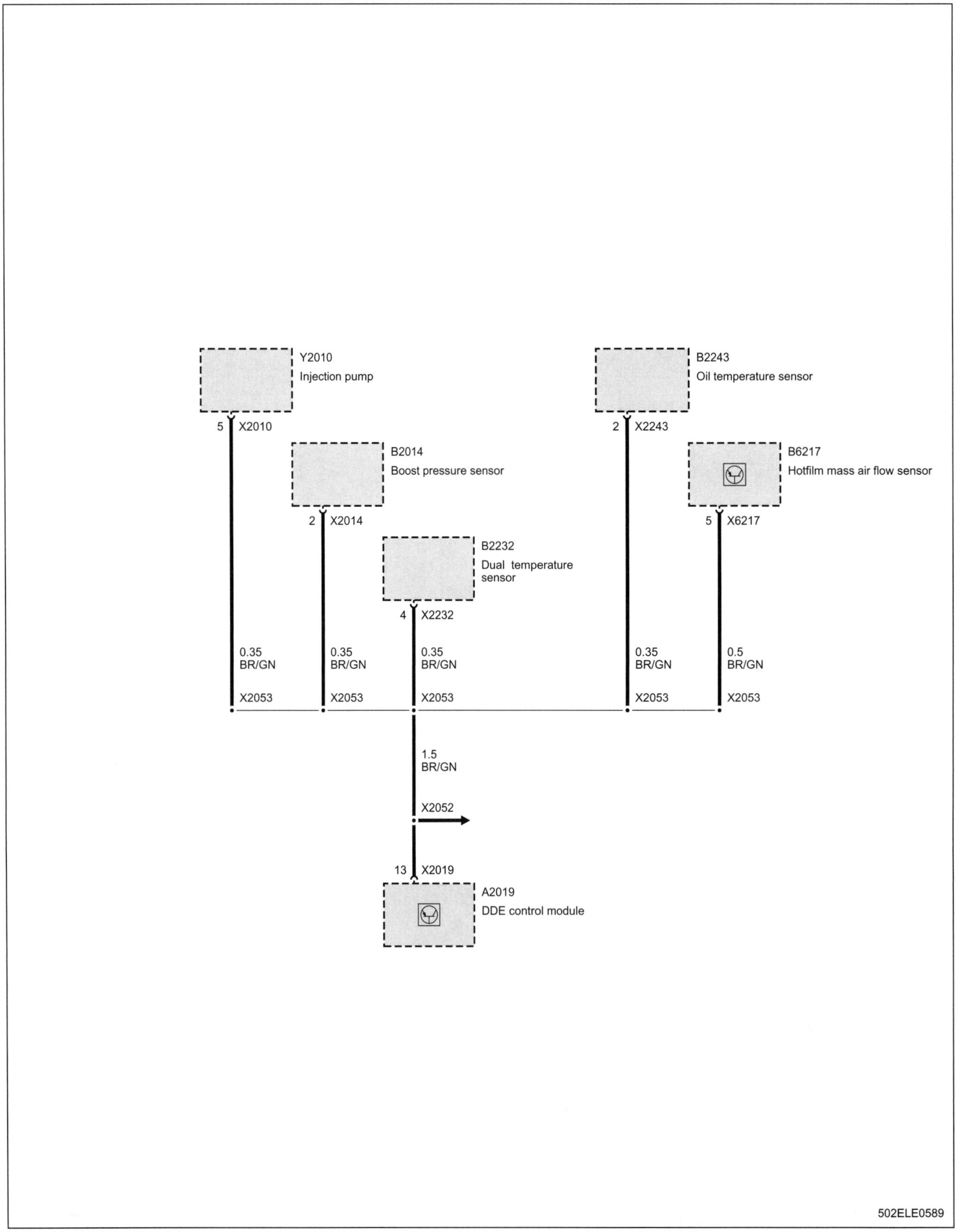

X-Connectors and Splices
X2131 Splice
(1 of 1)

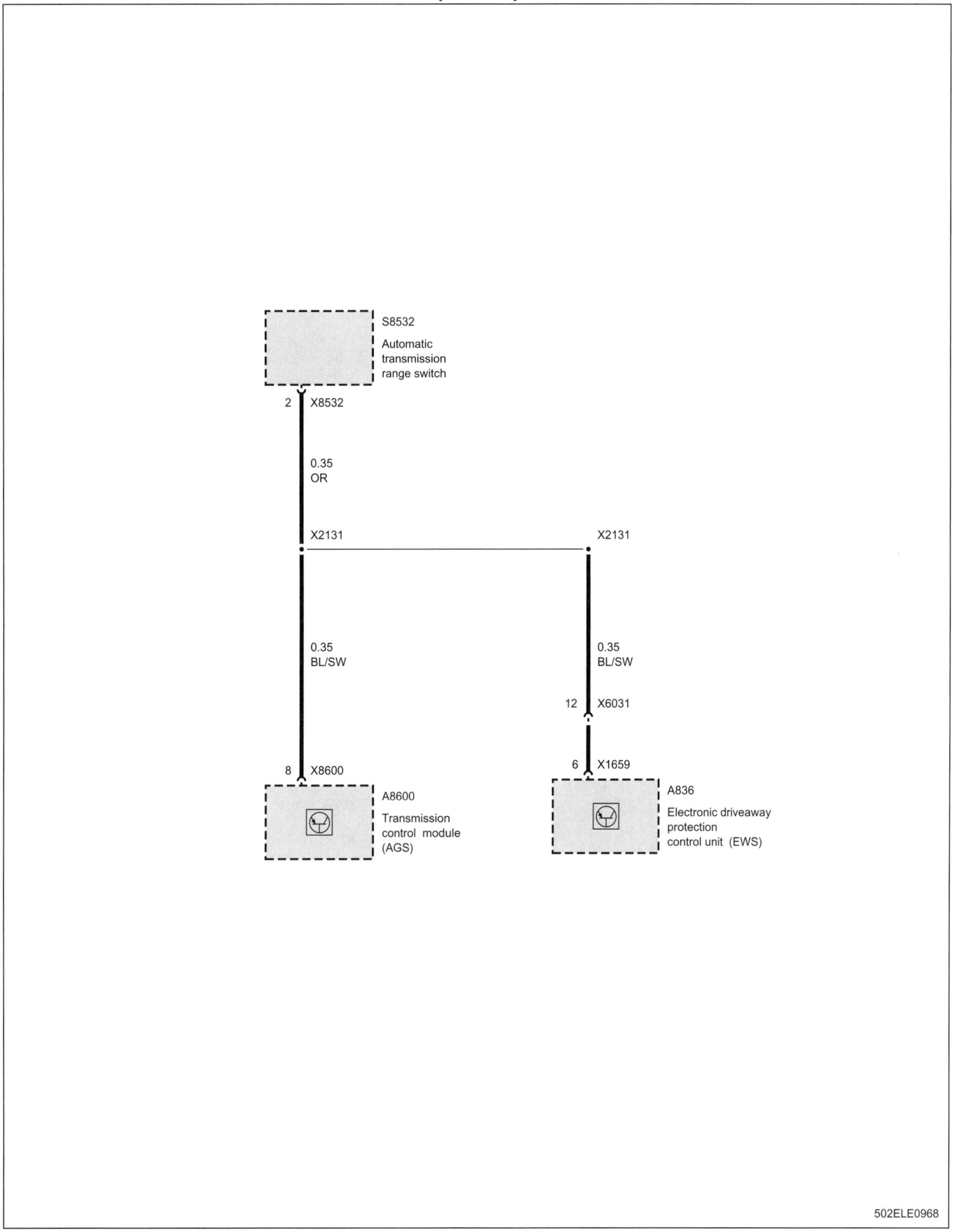

X-Connectors and Splices
X2233 Splice
(1 of 1)

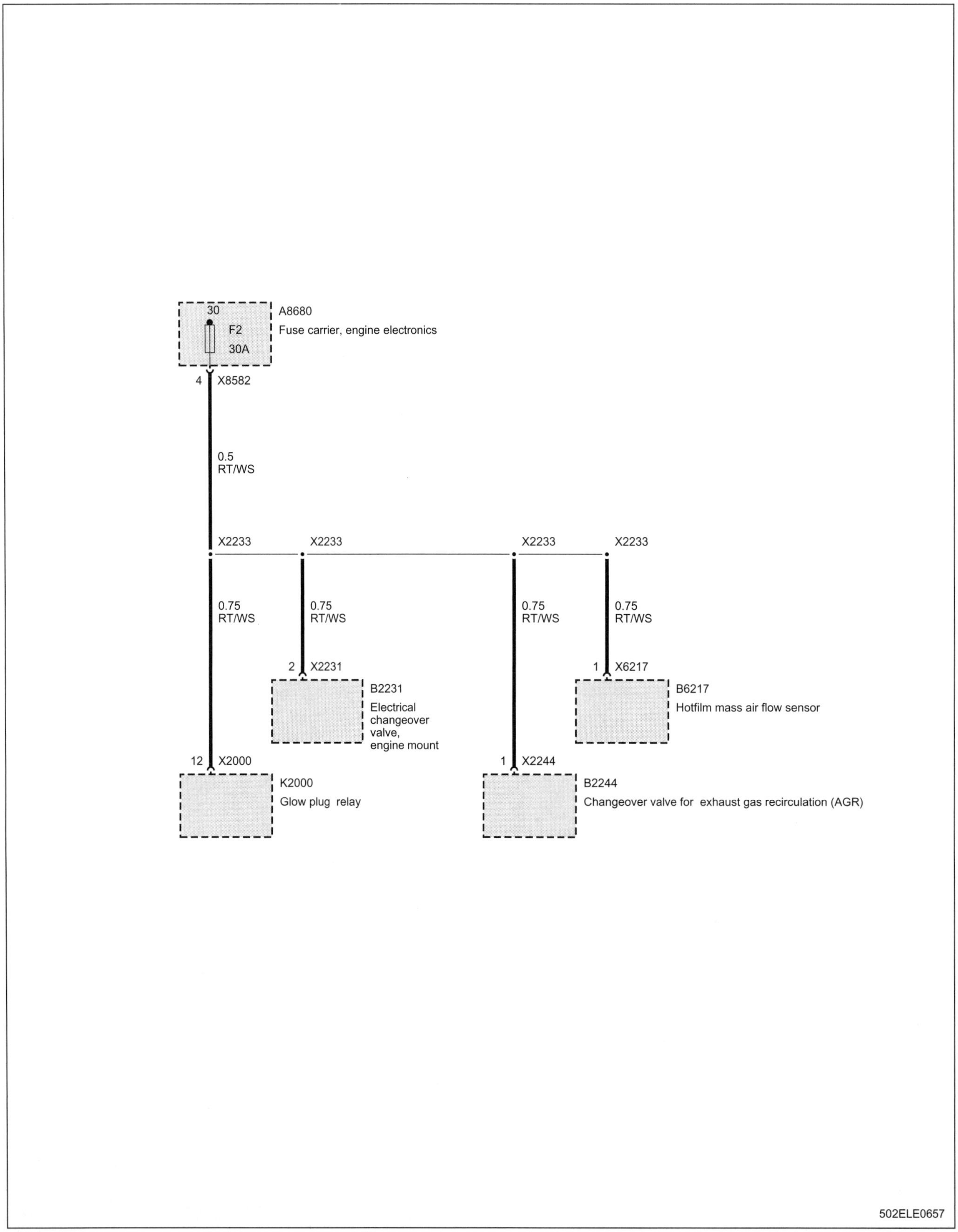
30
F2
30A
A8680
Fuse carrier, engine electronics
4
X8582
0.5
RT/WS
X2233
X2233
X2233
X2233
0.75
RT/WS
0.75
RT/WS
0.75
RT/WS
0.75
RT/WS
2
X2231
B2231
Electrical changeover valve, engine mount
1
X6217
B6217
Hotfilm mass air flow sensor
12
X2000
K2000
Glow plug relay
1
X2244
B2244
Changeover valve for exhaust gas recirculation (AGR)
502ELE0657

X-Connectors and Splices
X2759 Plug connector - Microphone
(1 of 1)

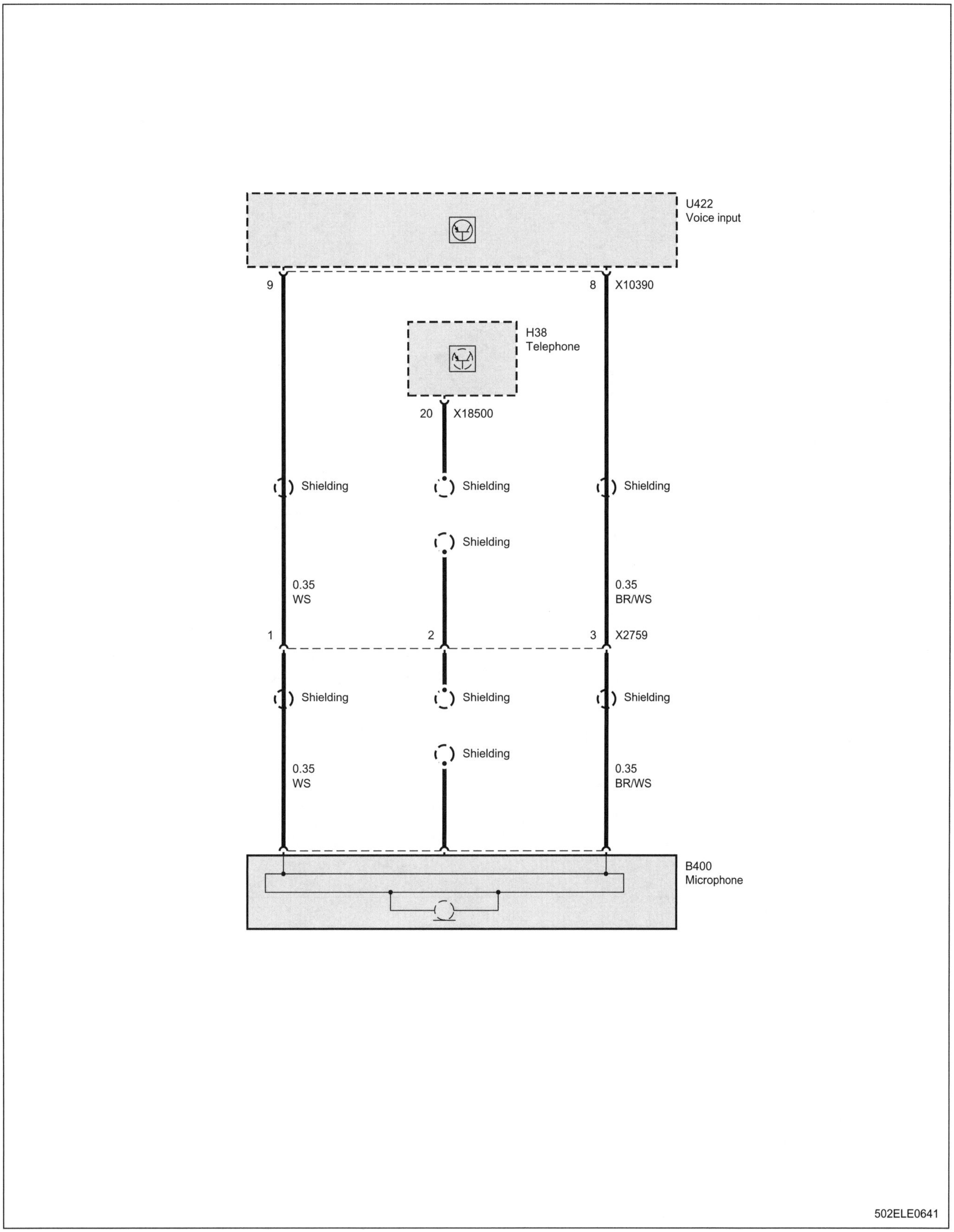

X-Connectors and Splices
X3250 Connector
(1 of 1)

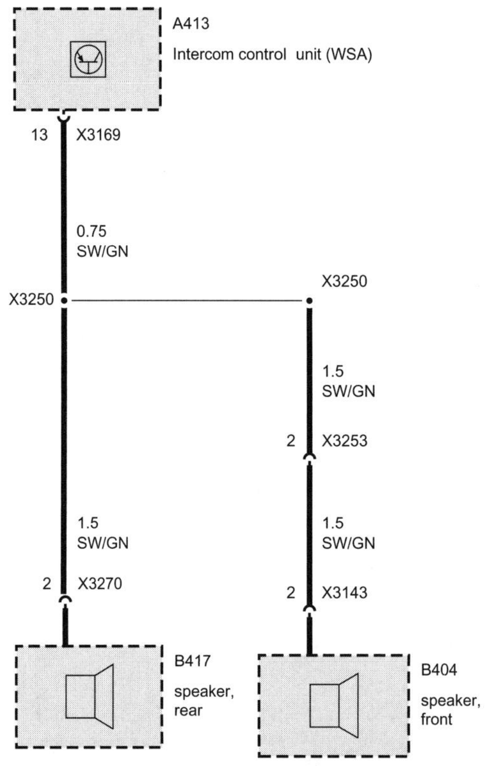

X-Connectors and Splices
Connector X3251

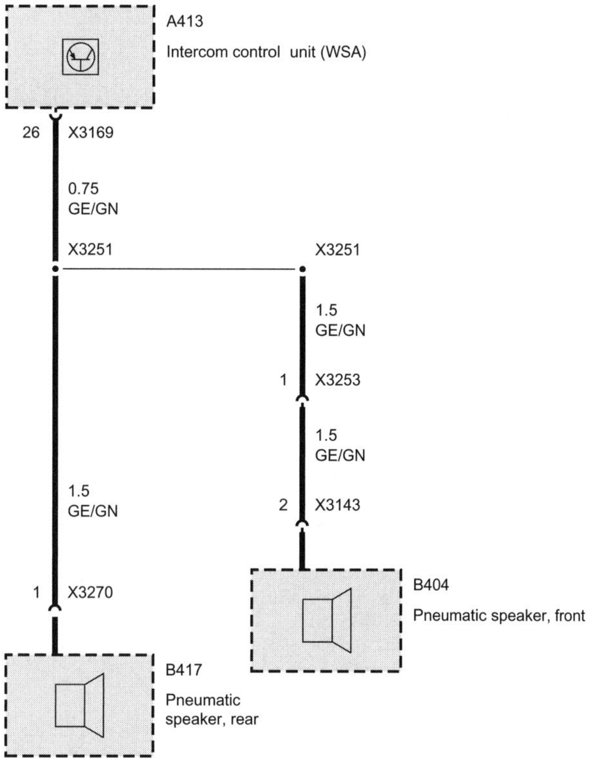

502ELE0573a

X-Connectors and Splices
Connector X3276

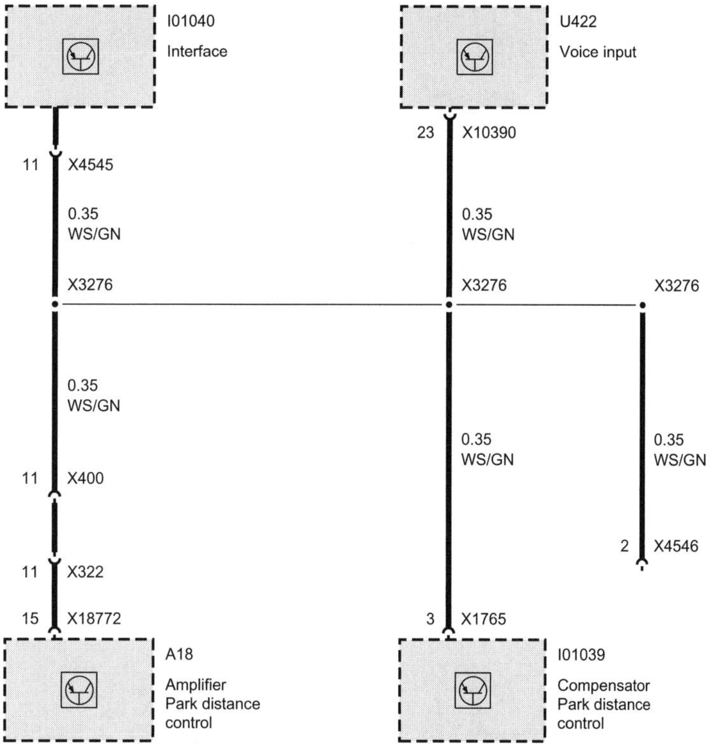

502ELE0573b

X-Connectors and Splices
X3359 Connector
(1 of 1)

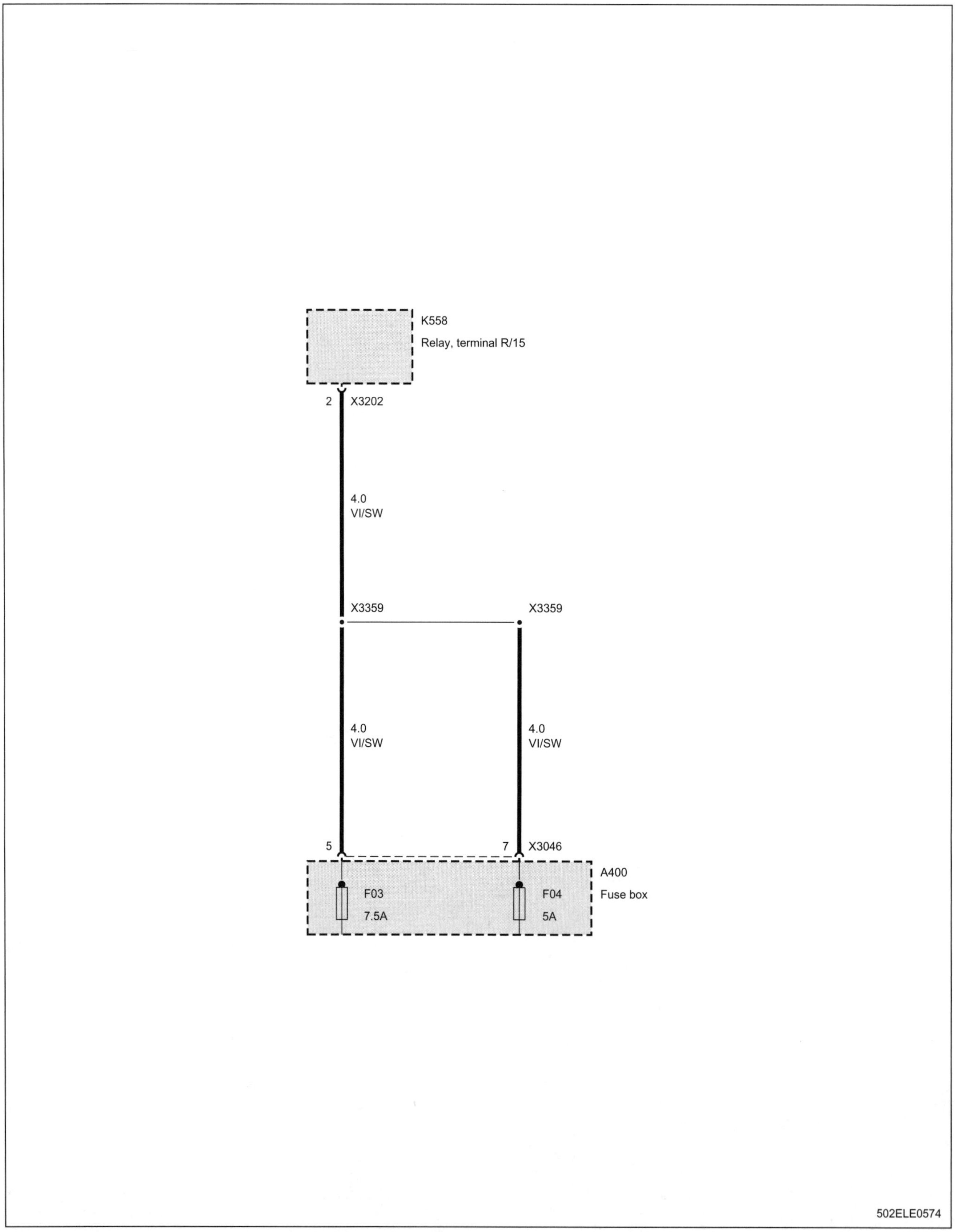
K558
Relay, terminal R/15
2
X3202
4.0
VI/SW
X3359
X3359
4.0
VI/SW
4.0
VI/SW
5
7
X3046
A400
Fuse box
F03
7.5A
F04
5A
502ELE0574

X-Connectors and Splices
X3471 Connector
(1 of 1)

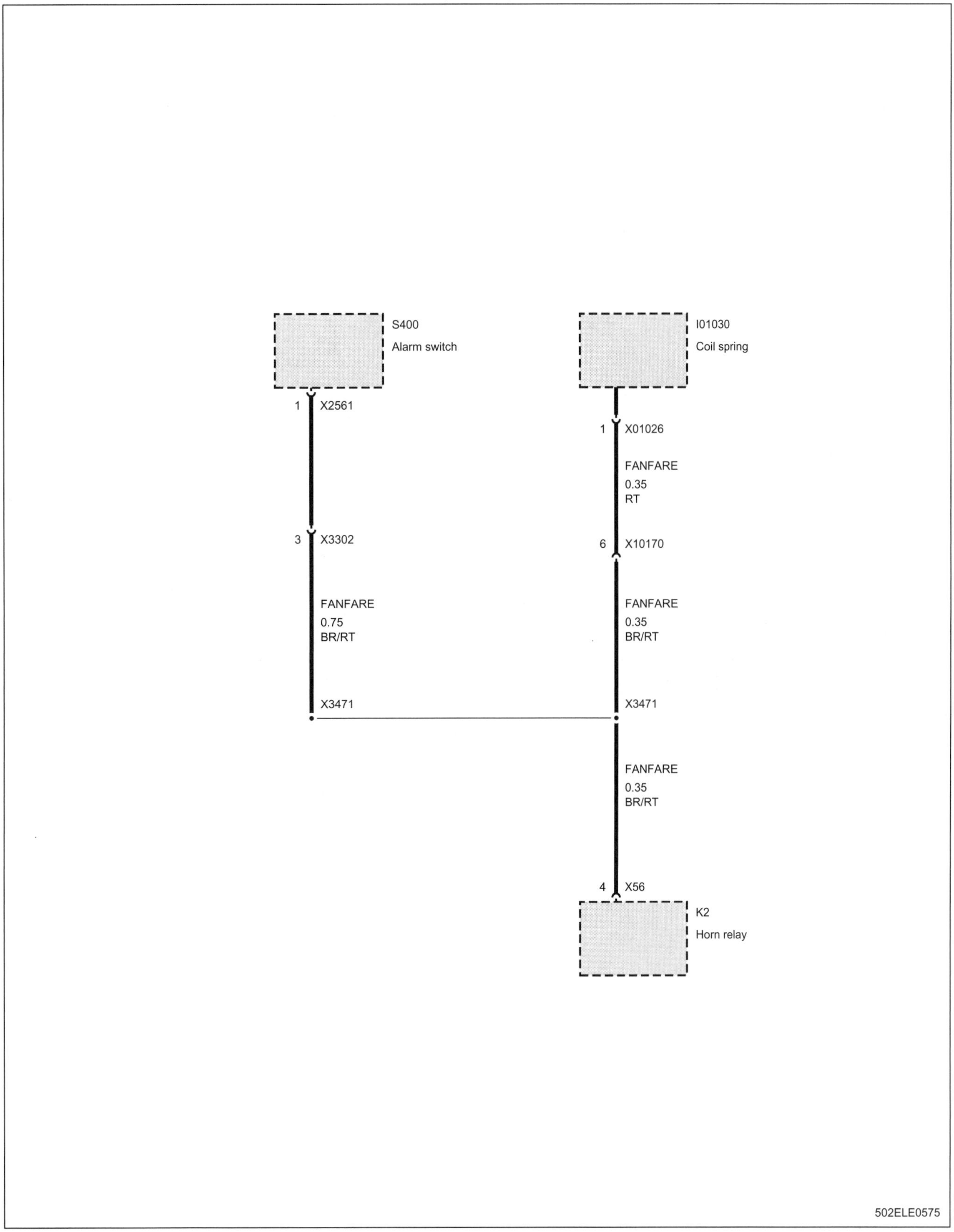
S400
Alarm switch
I01030
Coil spring
1
X2561
1
X01026
FANFARE
0.35
RT
3
X3302
6
X10170
FANFARE
0.75
BR/RT
FANFARE
0.35
BR/RT
X3471
X3471
FANFARE
0.35
BR/RT
4
X56
K2
Horn relay
502ELE0575

X-Connectors and Splices
X3477 Connector

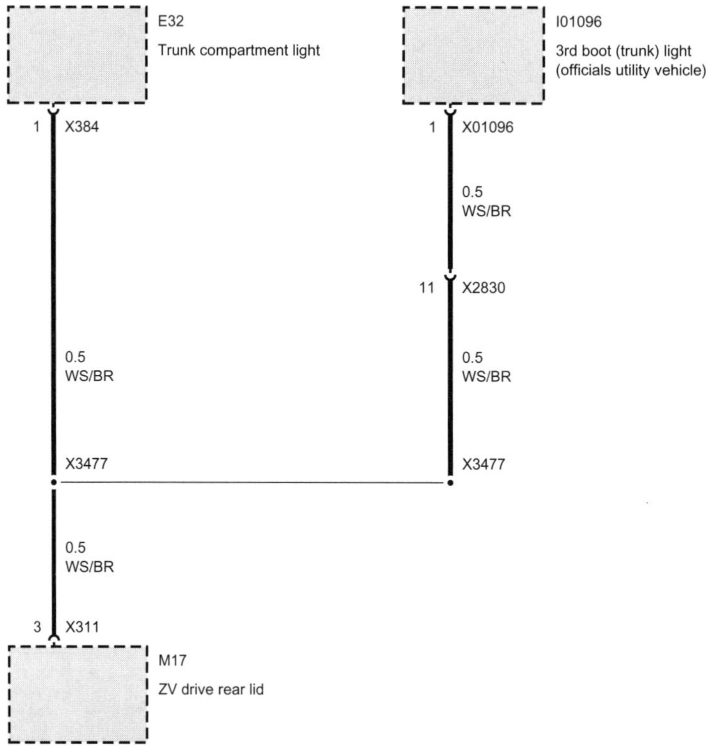

502ELE0576a

X-Connectors and Splices
X3479 Connector

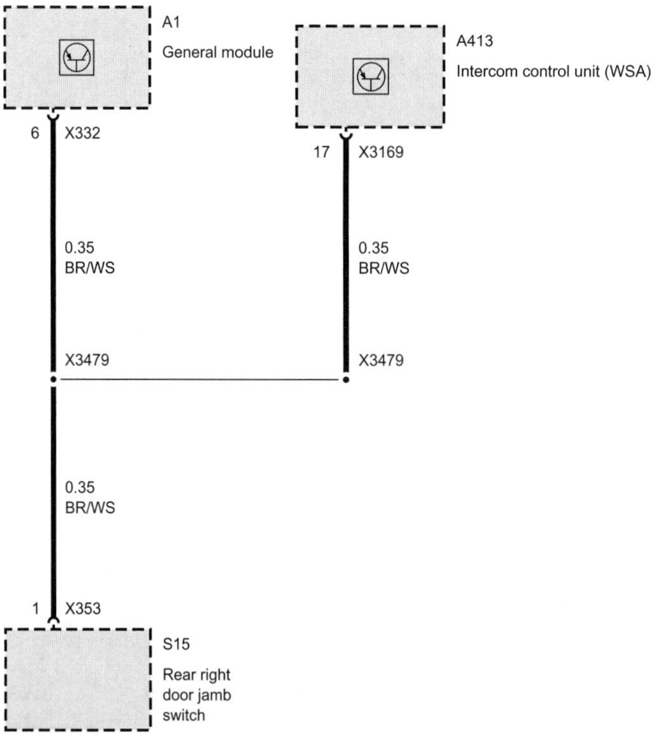

502ELE0576b

X-Connectors and Splices
X3481 Connector

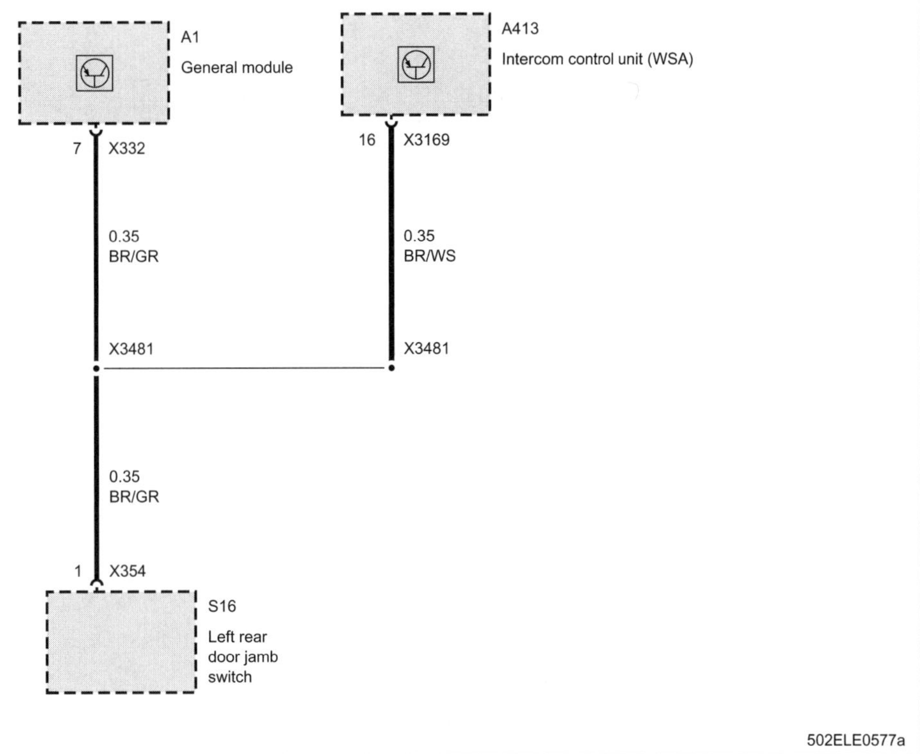

X-Connectors and Splices
X3482 Connector

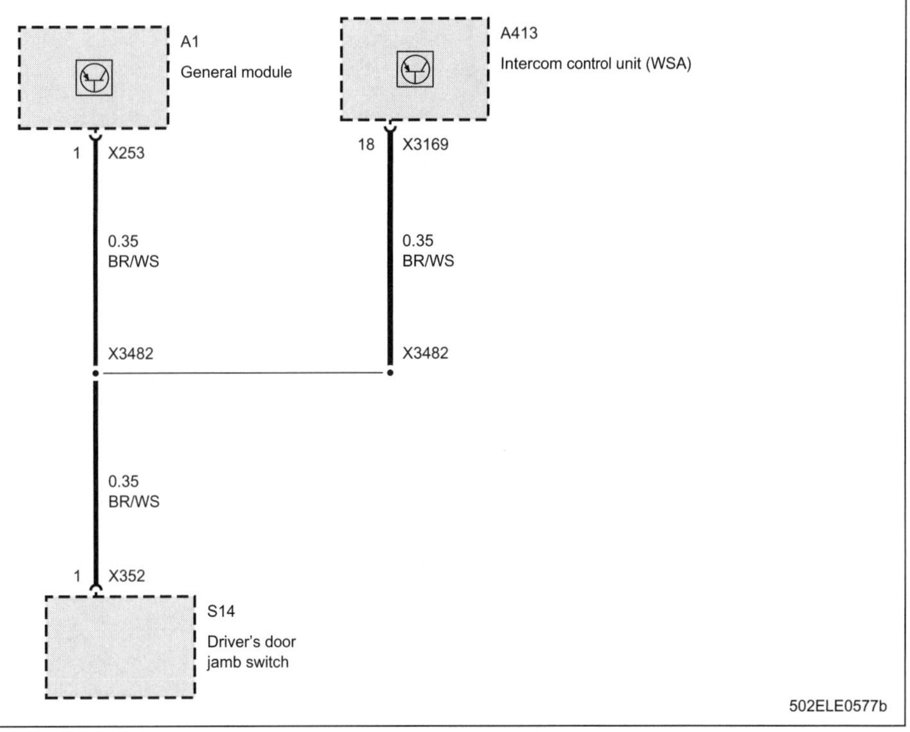

X-Connectors and Splices
X3483 Connector

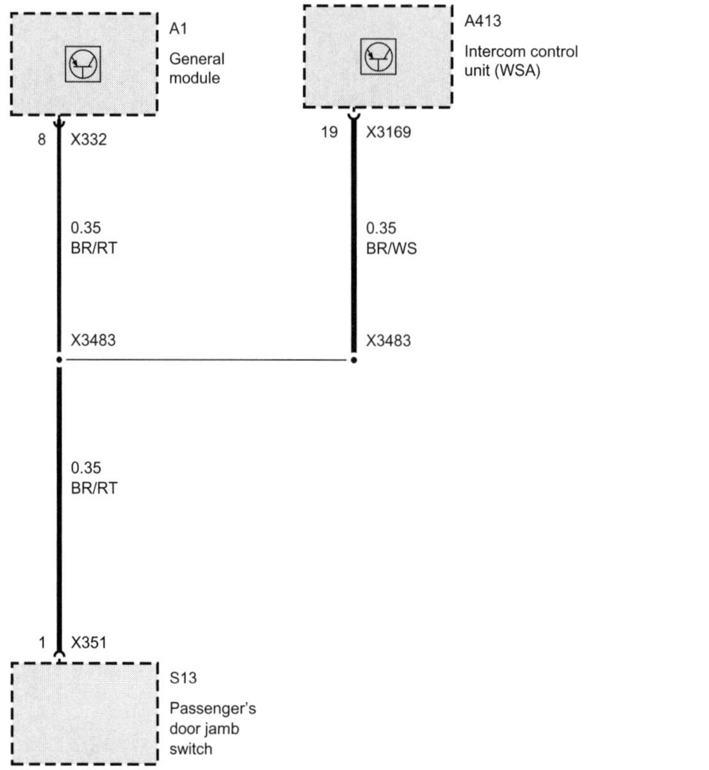

502ELE0578a

X-Connectors and Splices
X3484 Connector

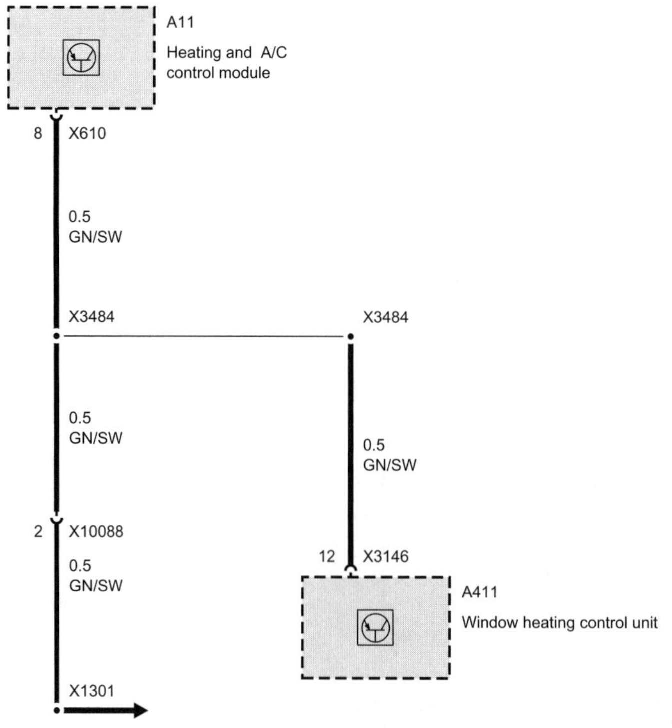

502ELE0578b

X-Connectors and Splices
Splice X4547
(1 of 1)

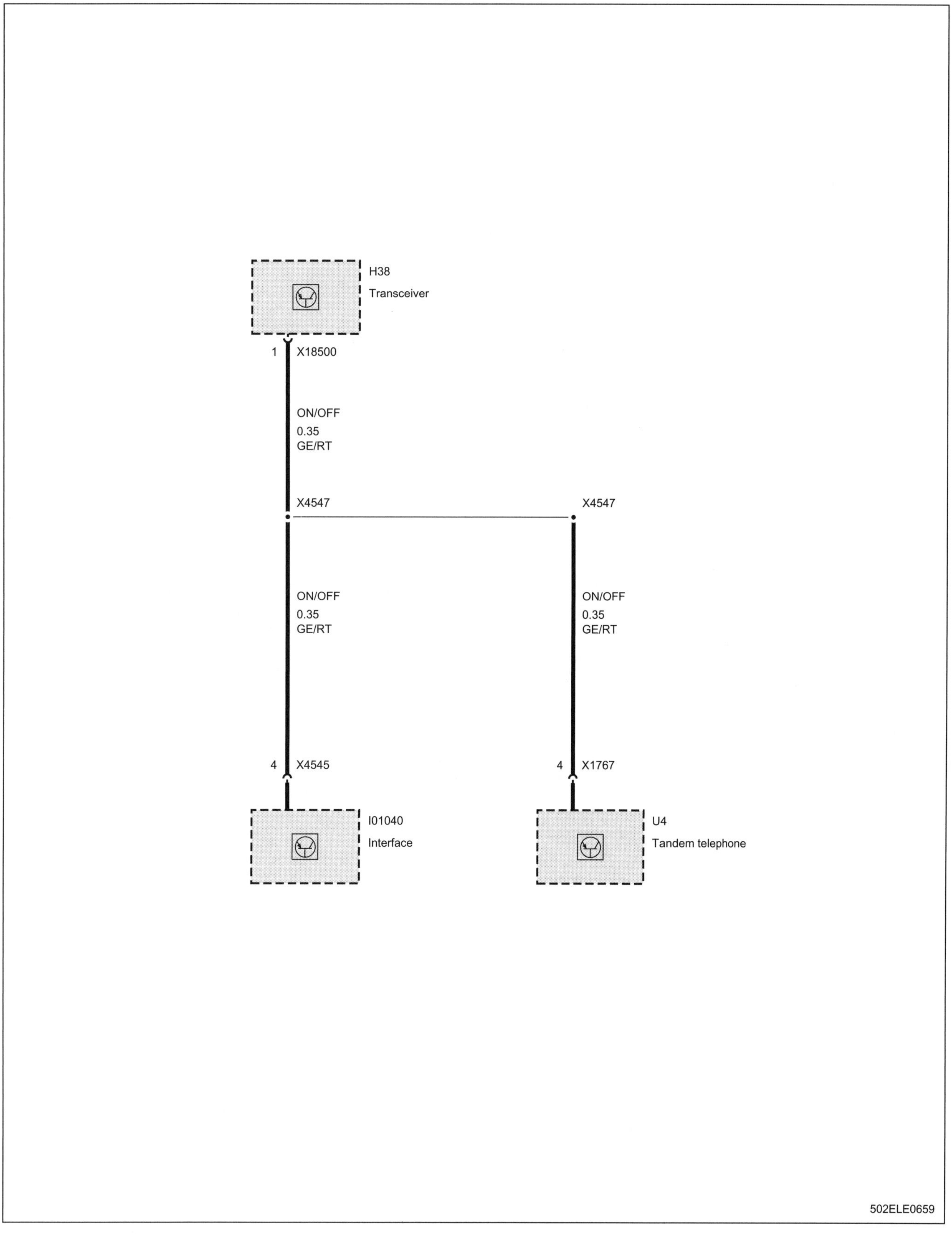
H38
Transceiver
1
X18500
ON/OFF
0.35
GE/RT
X4547
X4547
ON/OFF
0.35
GE/RT
ON/OFF
0.35
GE/RT
4
X4545
4
X1767
I01040
Interface
U4
Tandem telephone
502ELE0659

X-Connectors and Splices
X4549 Splice
(1 of 1)

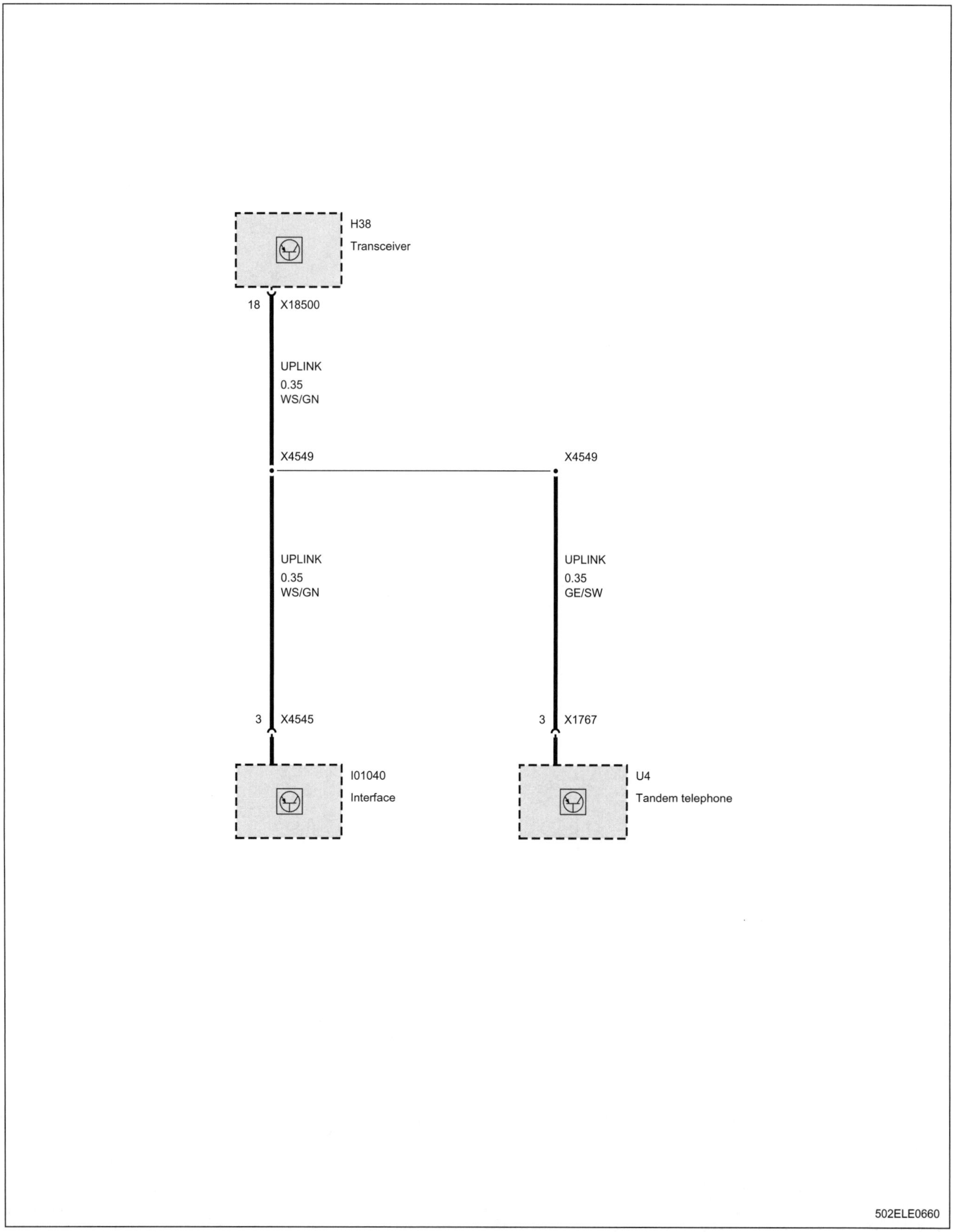
H38
Transceiver
18
X18500
UPLINK
0.35
WS/GN
X4549
X4549
UPLINK
0.35
WS/GN
UPLINK
0.35
GE/SW
3
X4545
3
X1767
I01040
Interface
U4
Tandem telephone
502ELE0660

X-Connectors and Splices
X4550 Splice

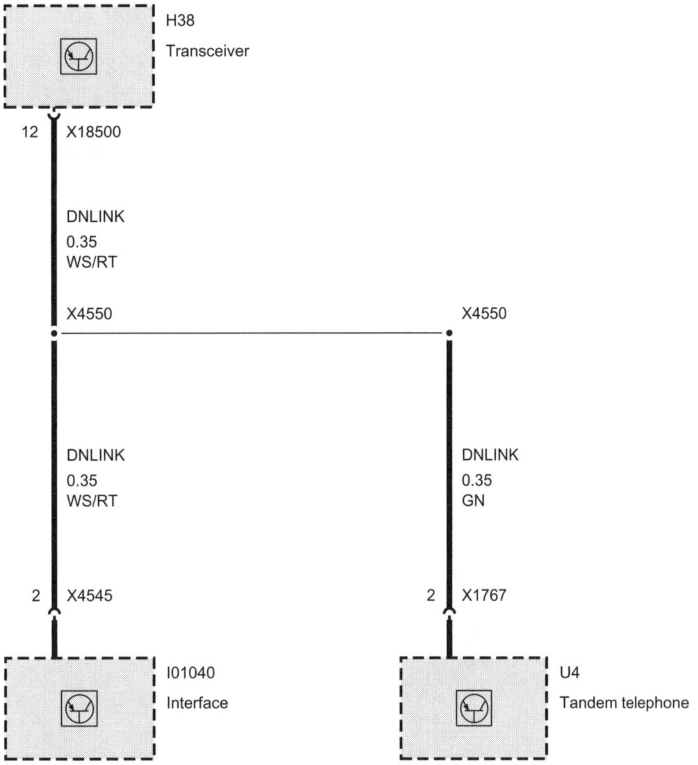

502ELE0662a

X-Connectors and Splices
X4551 Splice

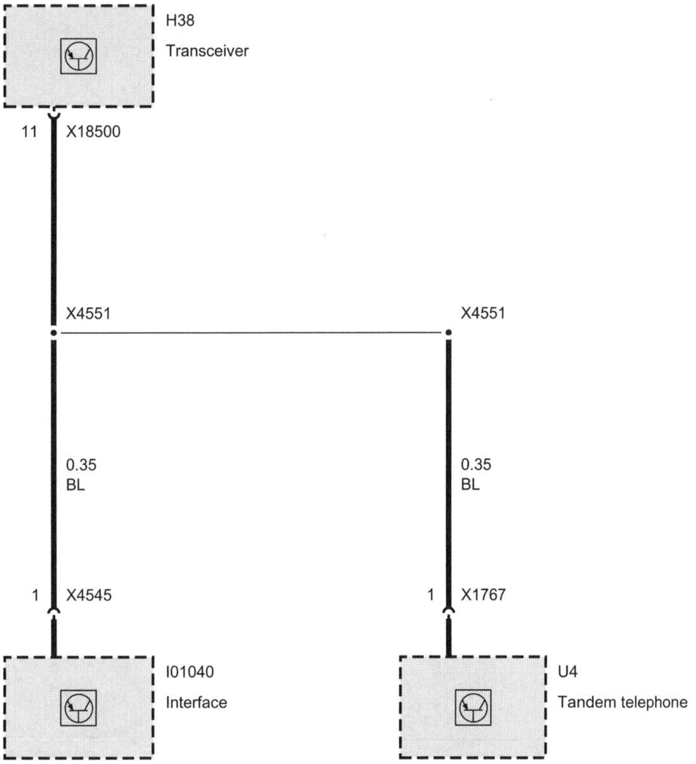

502ELE0662b

X-Connectors and Splices
X6002 Connector - Diagnostic
(1 of 2)

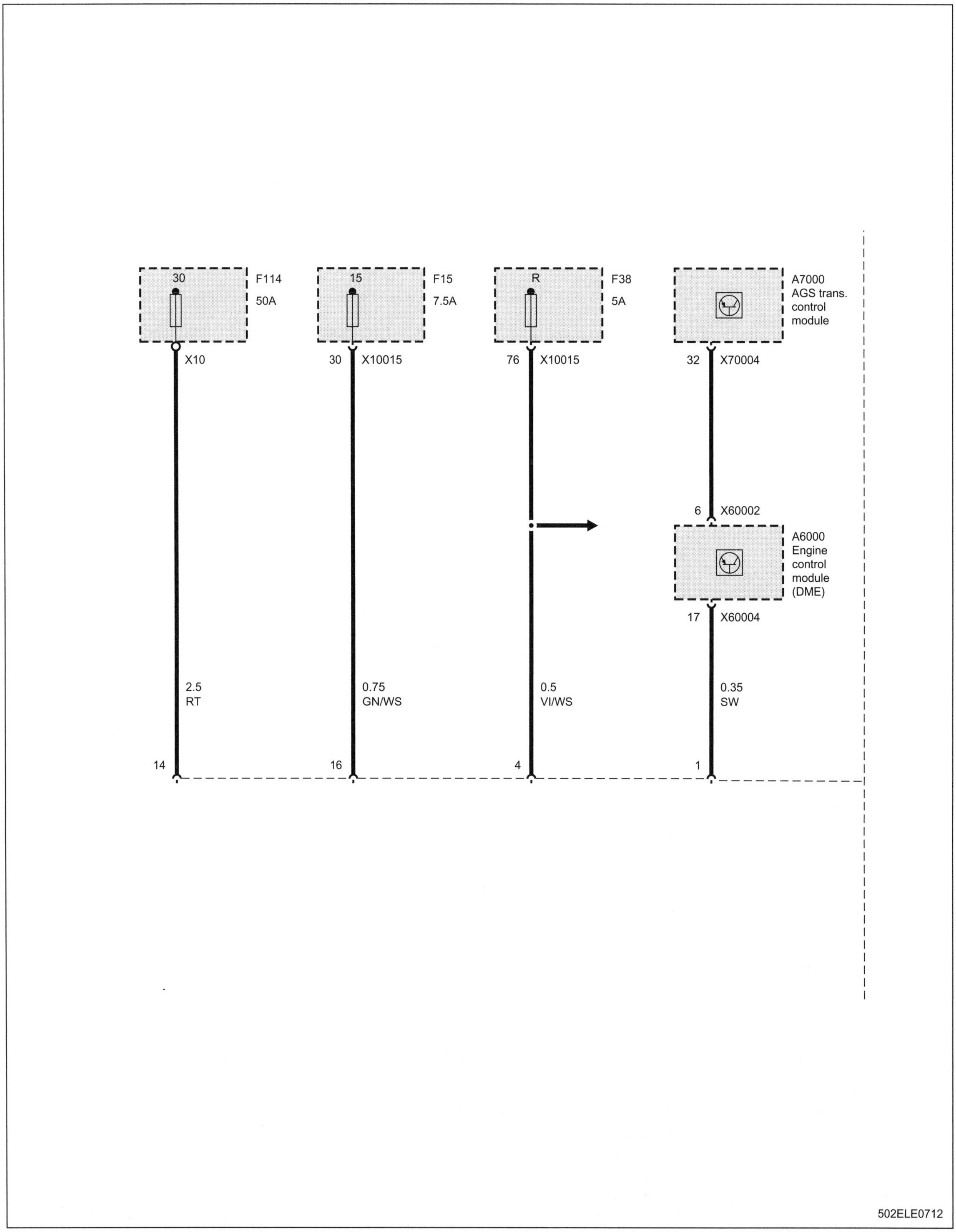

X-Connectors and Splices
X6002 Connector - Diagnostic
(2 of 2)

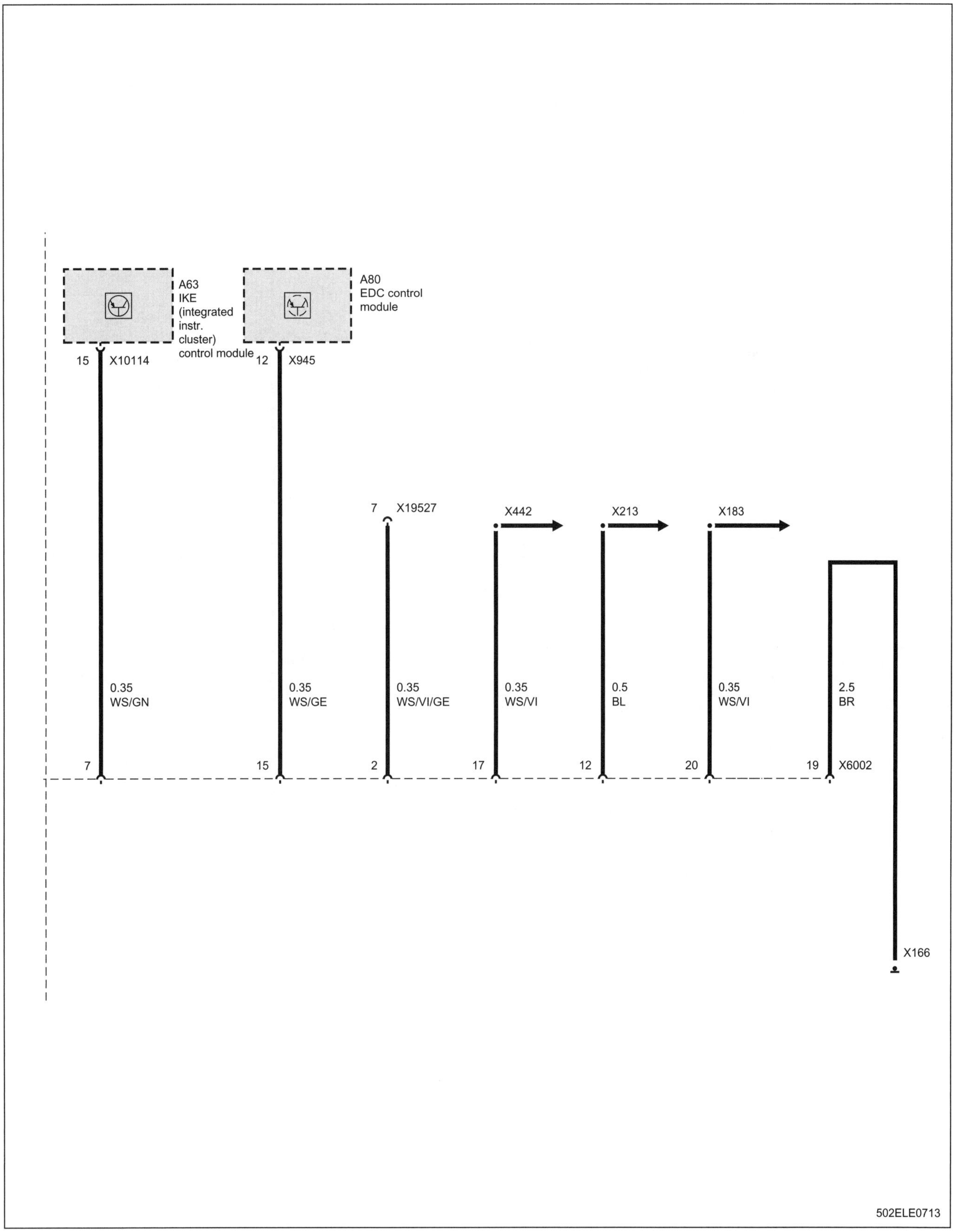

X-Connectors and Splices
X6011 Engine plug connector I
(1 of 3)

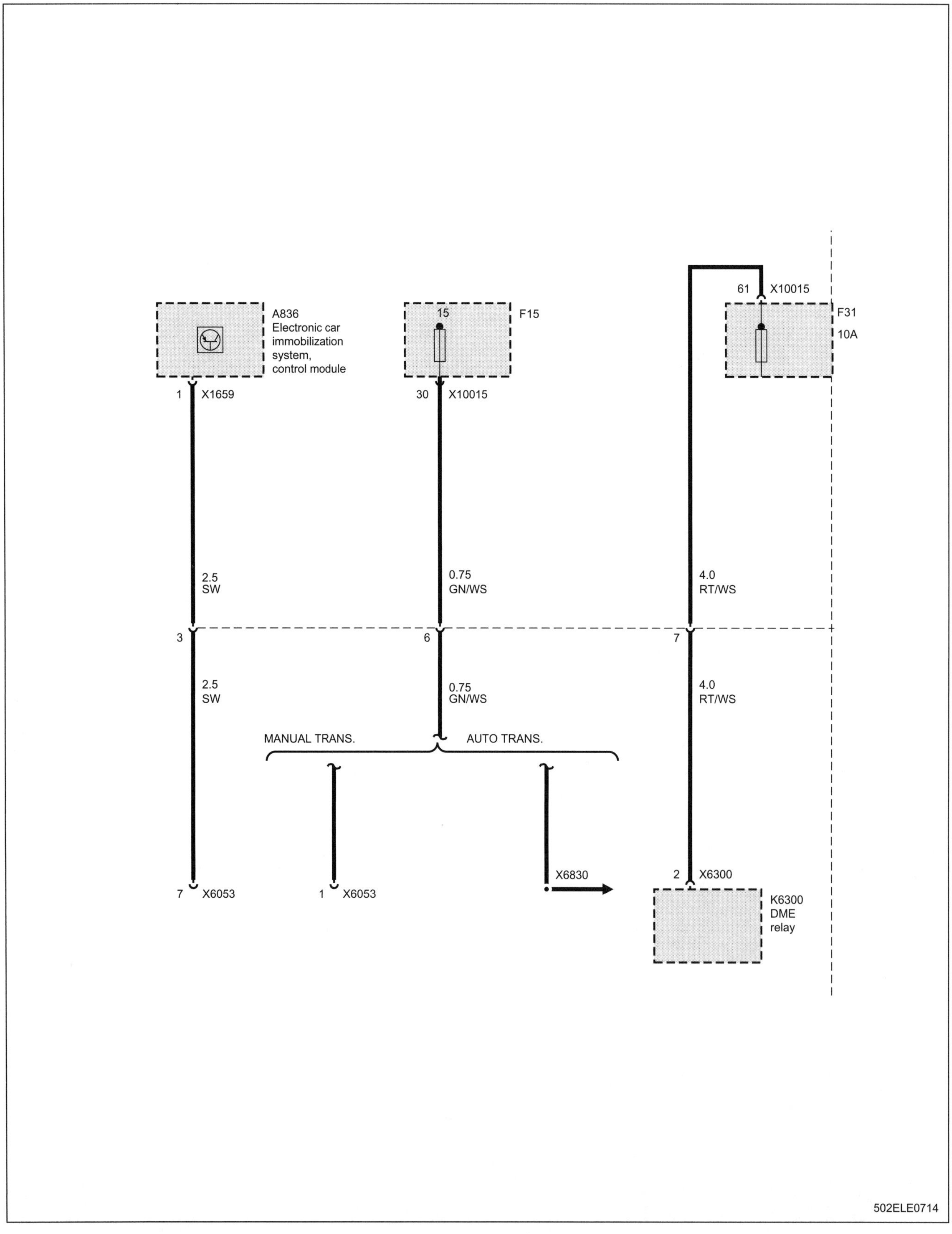

X-Connectors and Splices
X6011 Engine plug connector I
(2 of 3)

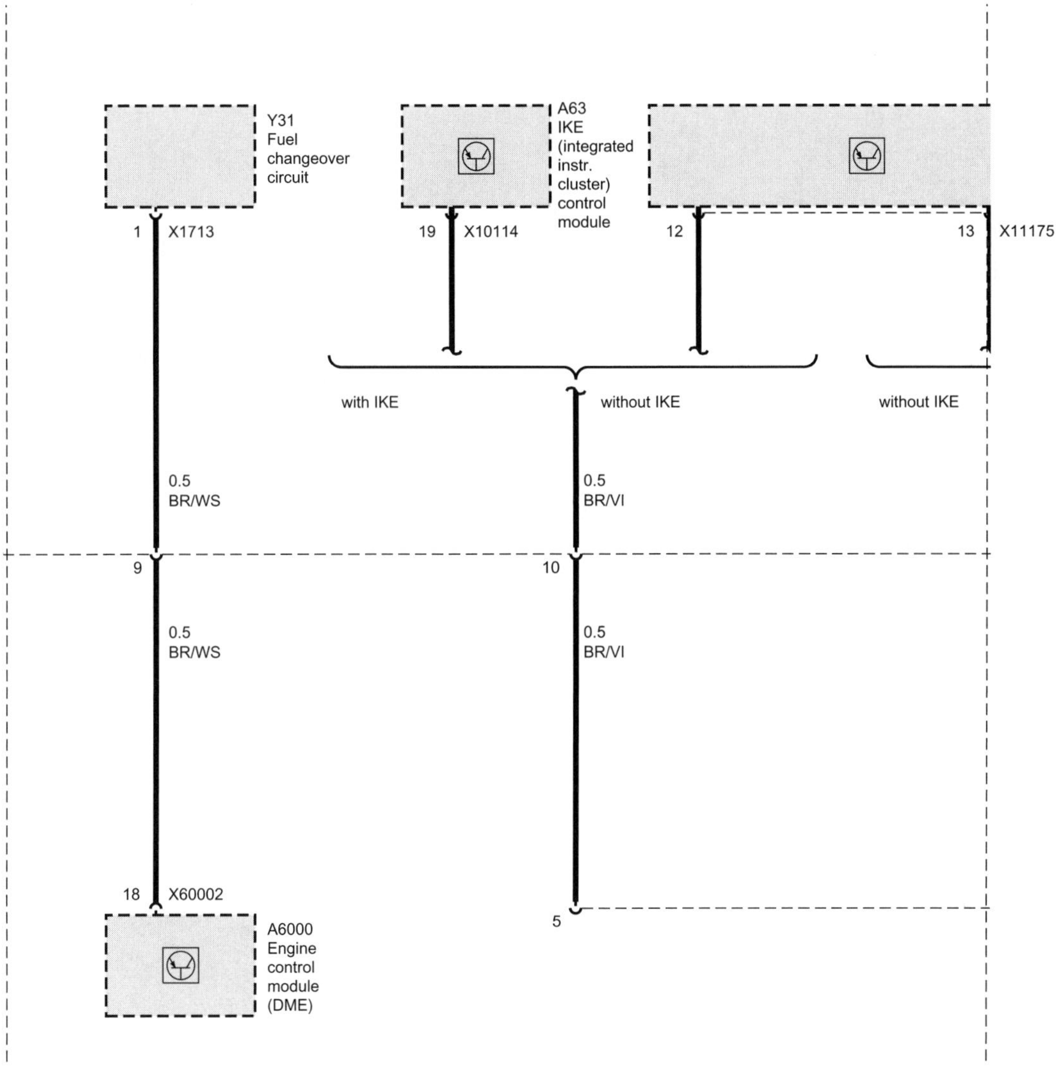

502ELE0715

X-Connectors and Splices
X6011 Engine plug connector I
(3 of 3)

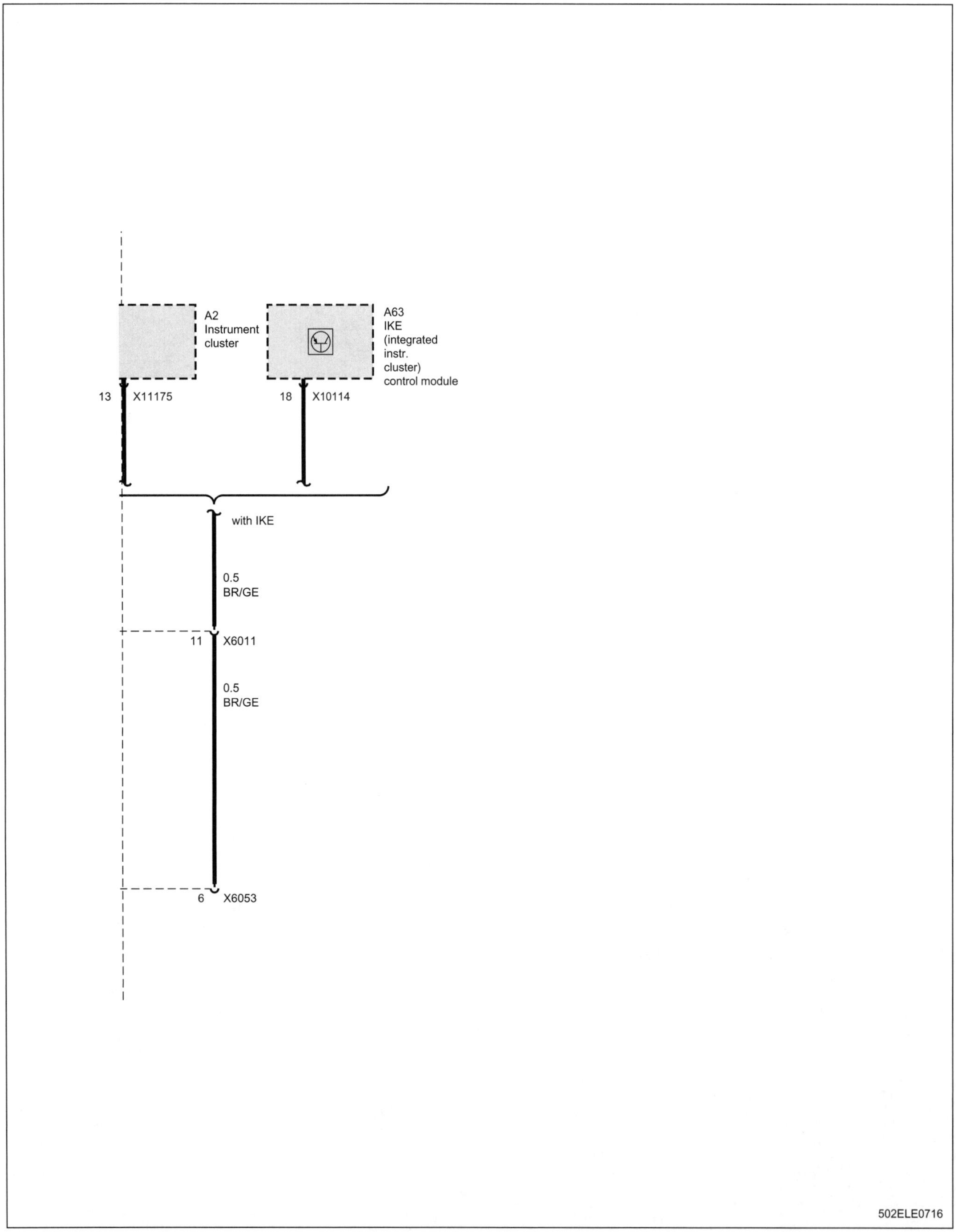

X-Connectors and Splices
X6031 Engine plug connector III
(1 of 1)

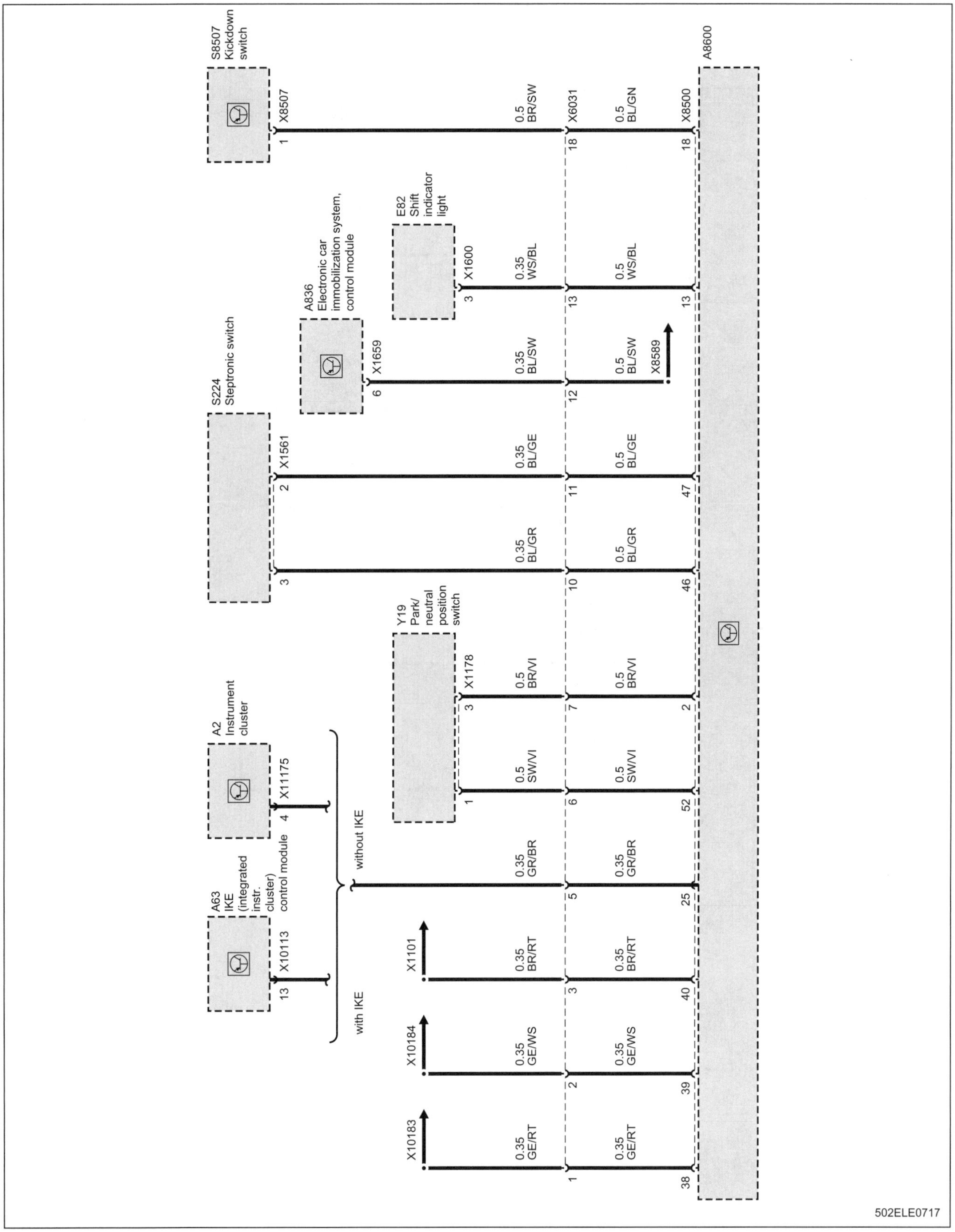

X-Connectors and Splices
X6053 Plug connection - Engine wiring harness
(1 of 1)

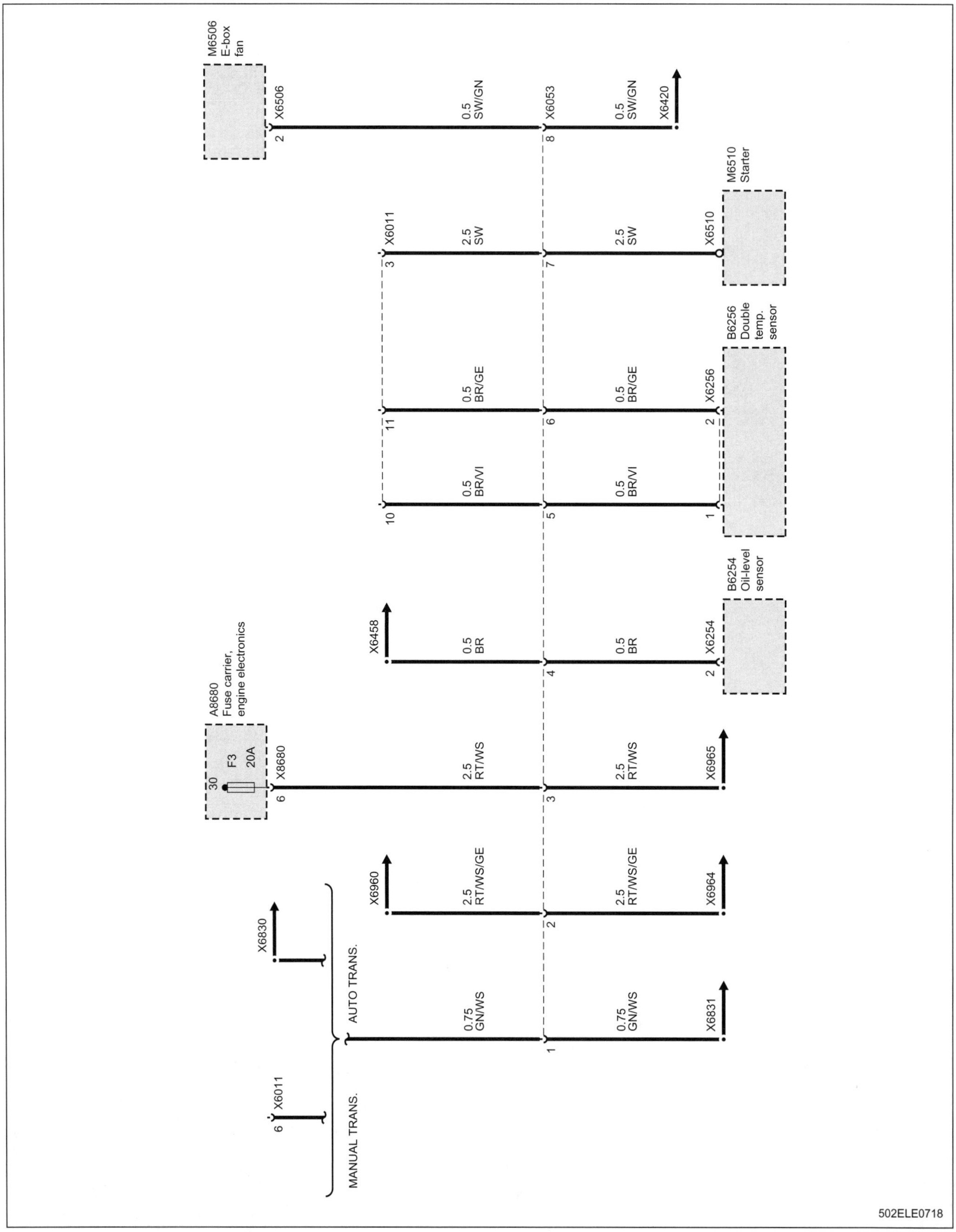

X-Connectors and Splices
X6054 Plug connection - Engine wiring harness II
(1 of 1)

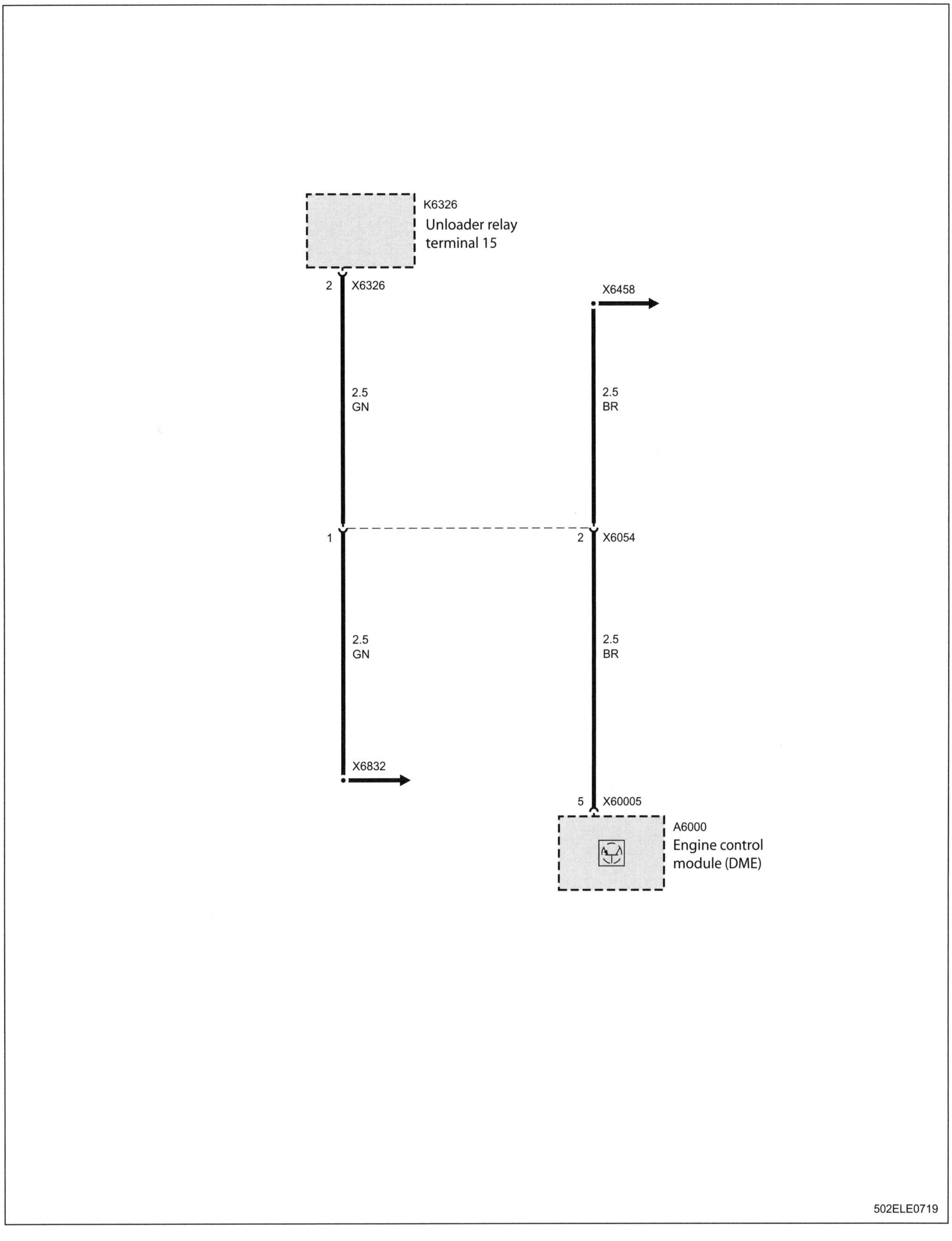

X-Connectors and Splices
X6420 Splice
(1 of 1)

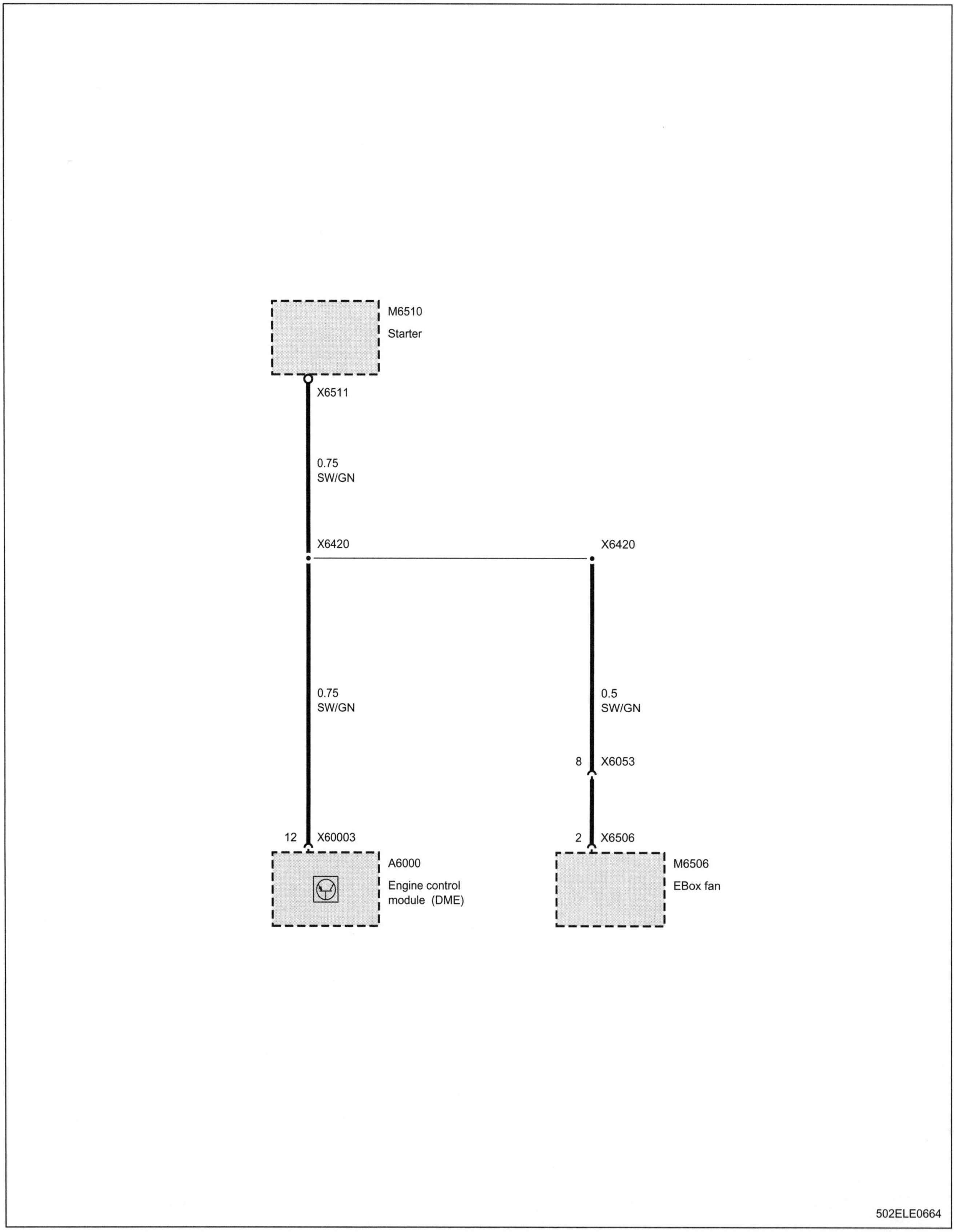
M6510
Starter
X6511
0.75
SW/GN
X6420
X6420
0.75
SW/GN
0.5
SW/GN
8
X6053
12
X60003
2
X6506
A6000
Engine control
module (DME)
M6506
EBox fan
502ELE0664

Ground Distribution
X6452 Ground
(1 of 1)

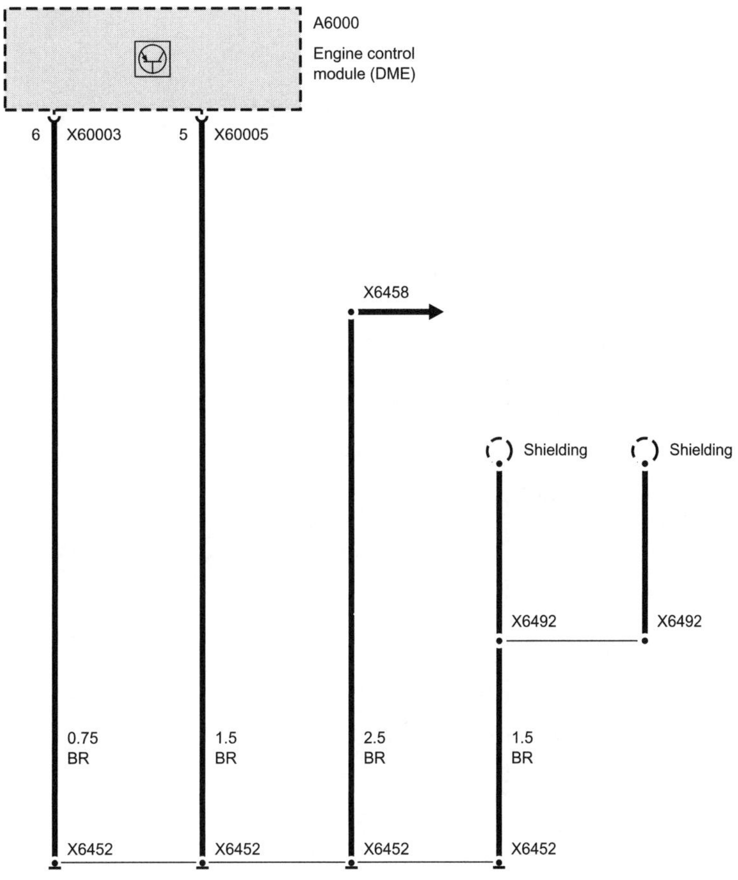

502ELE0631

Ground Distribution
X6453 Ground, engine
(1 of 1)

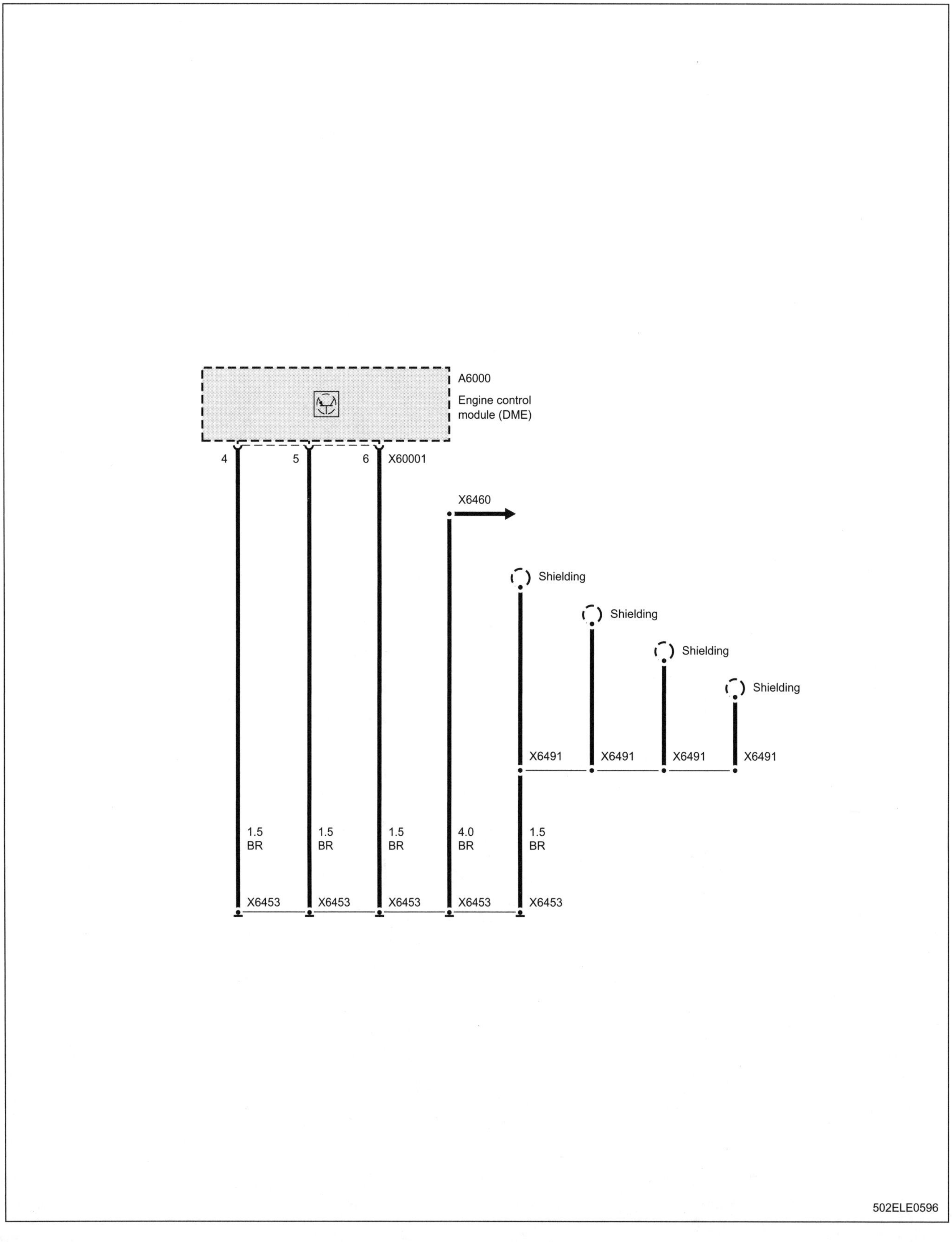
A6000
Engine control
module (DME)
4
5
6
X60001
X6460
Shielding
Shielding
Shielding
Shielding
X6491
X6491
X6491
X6491
1.5
BR
1.5
BR
1.5
BR
4.0
BR
1.5
BR
X6453
X6453
X6453
X6453
X6453
502ELE0596

Ground Distribution
X6454 Ground splice
(1 of 1)

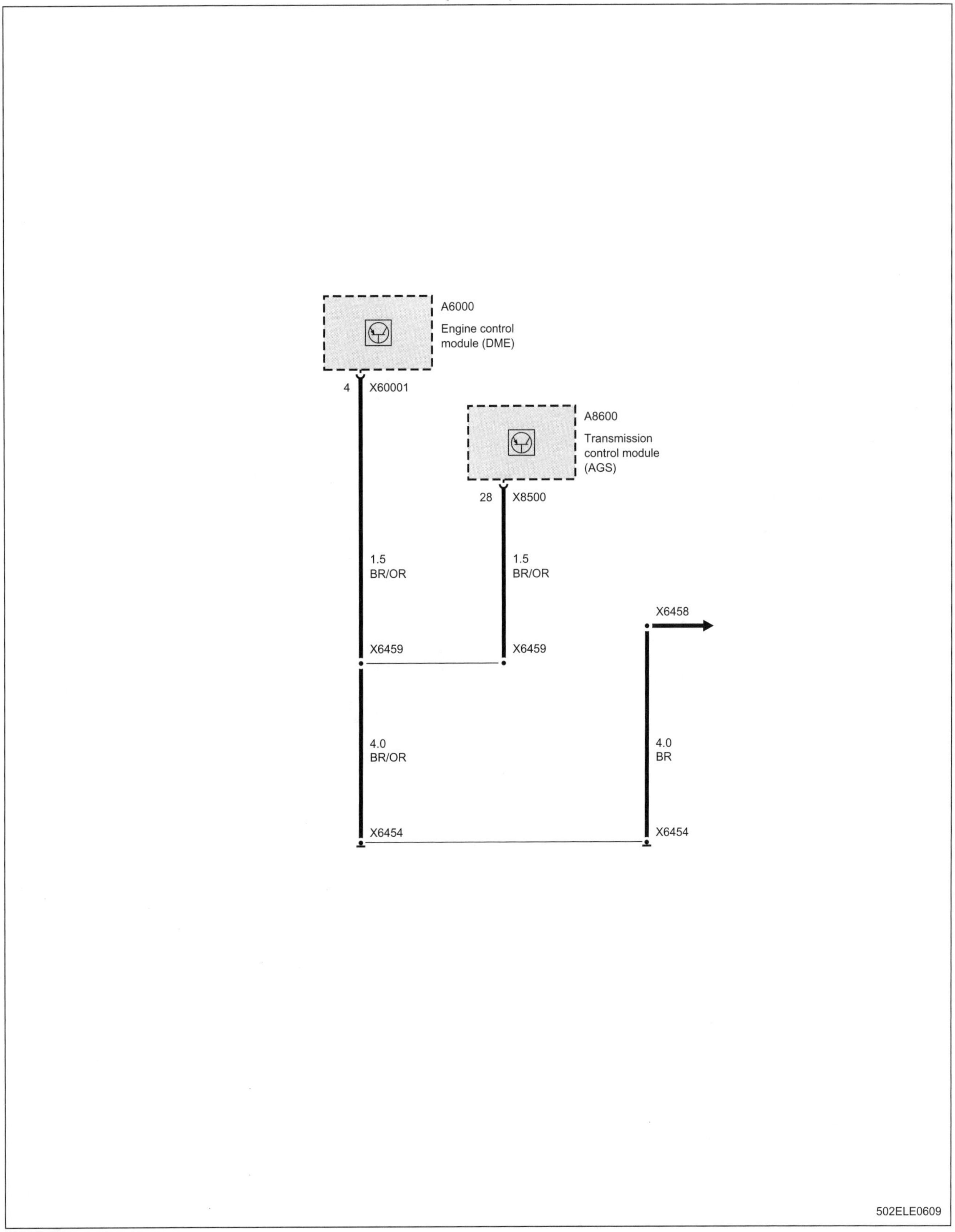

Ground Distribution
X6456 Ground connection
(1 of 1)

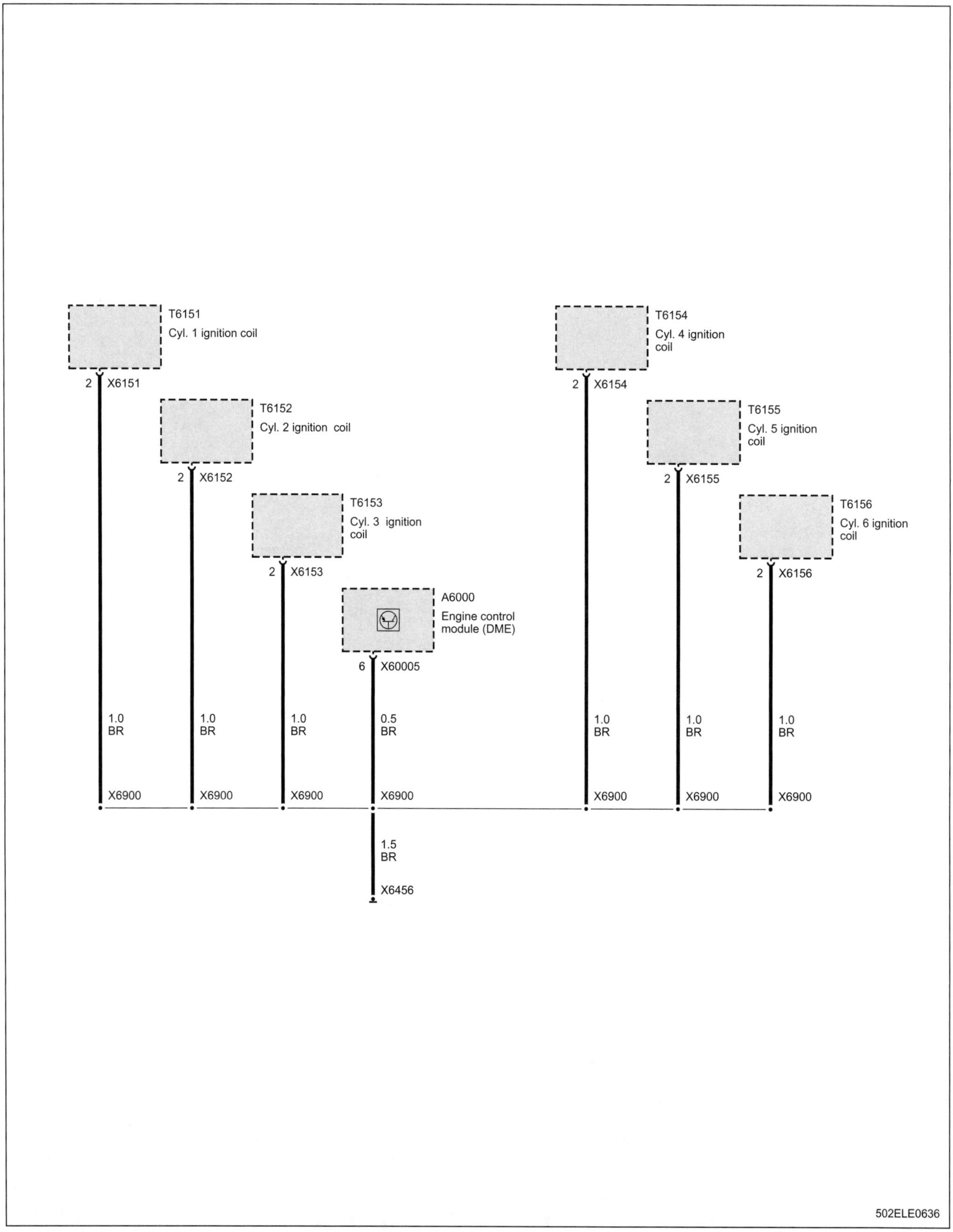

Ground Distribution
X6458 Ground splice
(1 of 1)

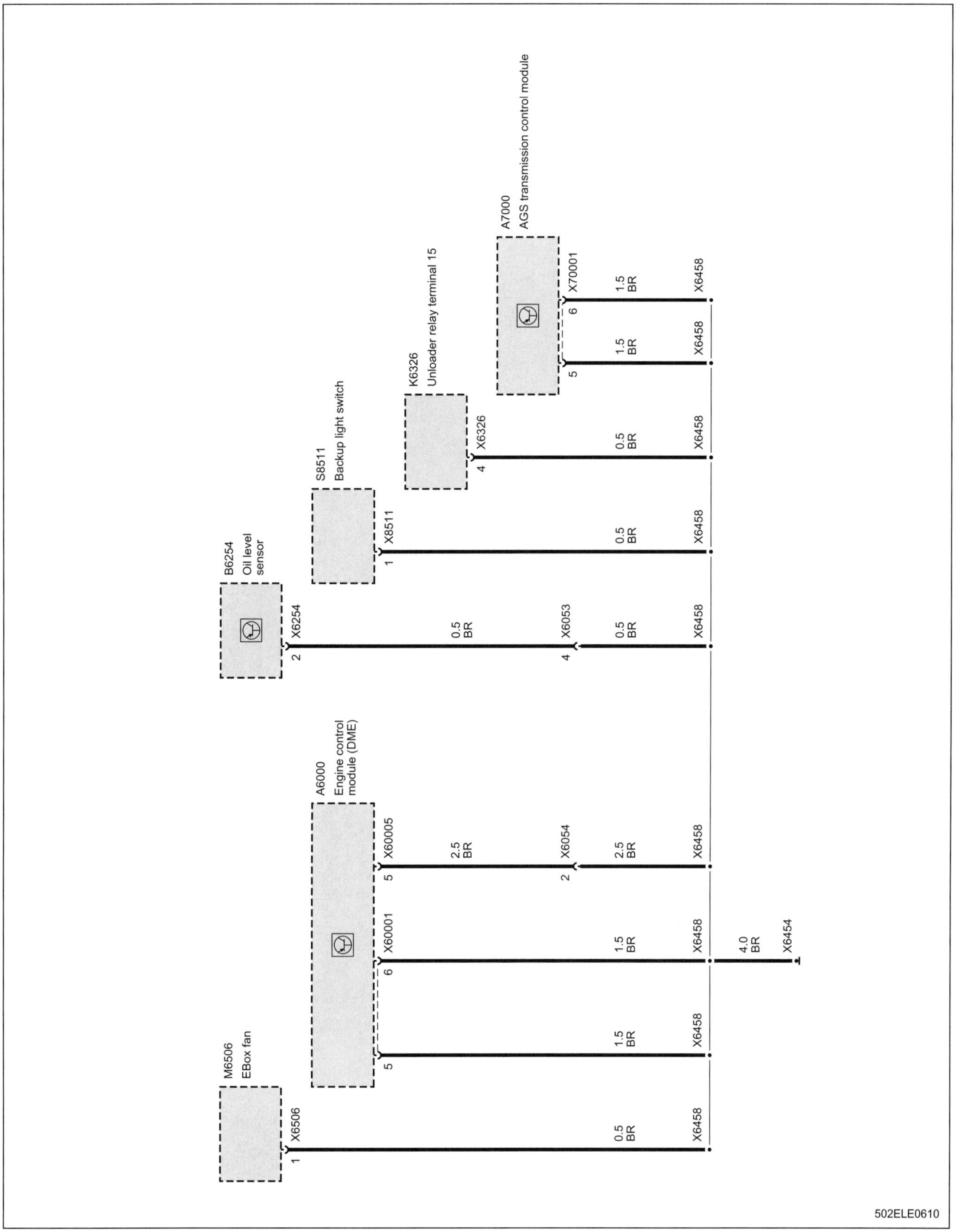
A7000
AGS transmission control module
X70001
6
5
1.5
BR
X6458
K6326
Unloader relay terminal 15
X6326
4
0.5
BR
S8511
Backup light switch
X8511
1
B6254
Oil level sensor
X6254
2
X6053
4
A6000
Engine control module (DME)
X60005
5
2.5
BR
X6054
2
X60001
6
4.0
BR
X6454
M6506
EBox fan
X6506
1
502ELE0610

X-Connectors and Splices
X6832 Connector
(1 of 1)

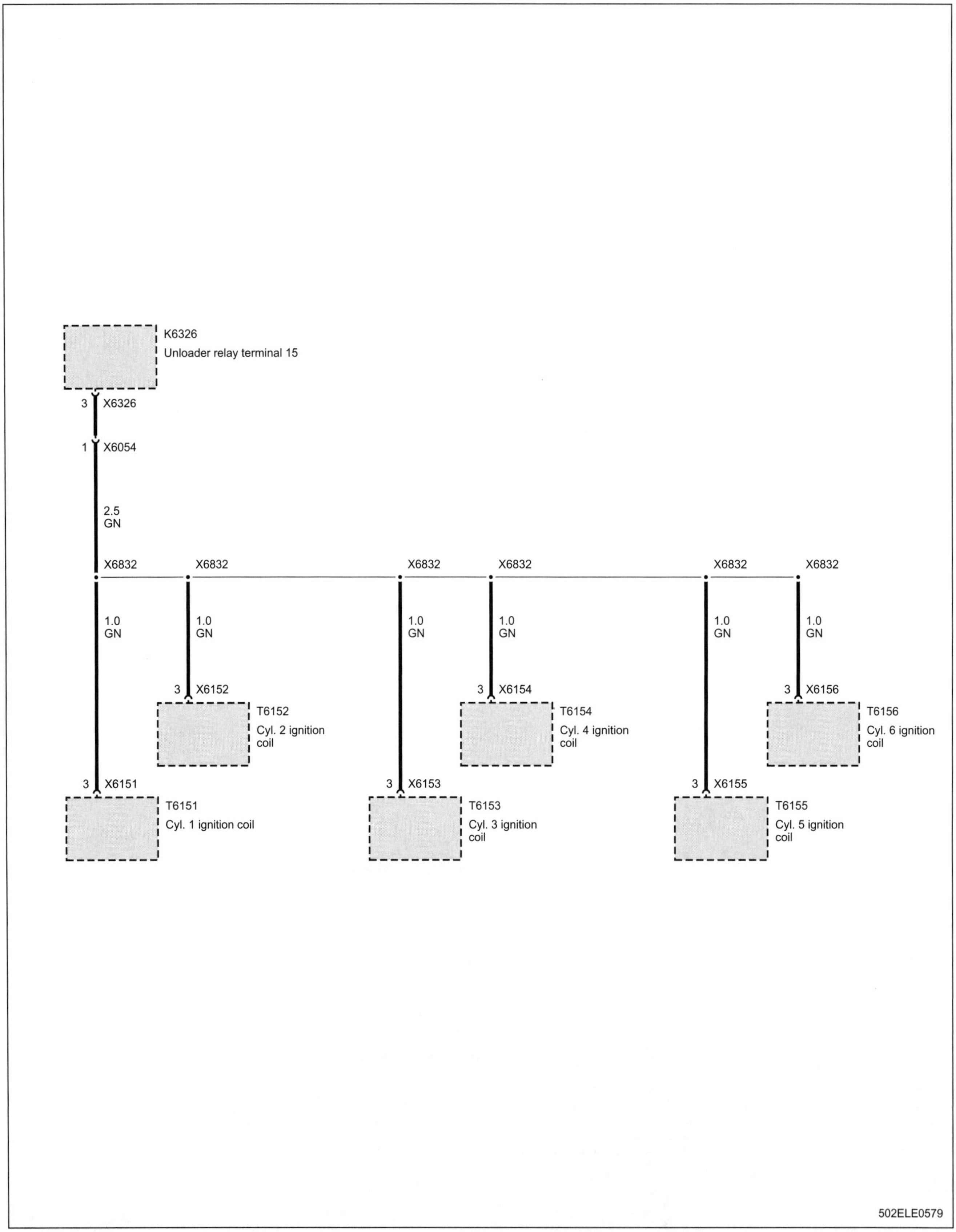
K6326
Unloader relay terminal 15
3 X6326
1 X6054
2.5
GN
X6832
X6832
X6832
X6832
X6832
X6832
1.0
GN
3 X6152
T6152
Cyl. 2 ignition coil
3 X6154
T6154
Cyl. 4 ignition coil
3 X6156
T6156
Cyl. 6 ignition coil
3 X6151
T6151
Cyl. 1 ignition coil
3 X6153
T6153
Cyl. 3 ignition coil
3 X6155
T6155
Cyl. 5 ignition coil
502ELE0579

Ground Distribution
X6841 Ground connector
(1 of 1)

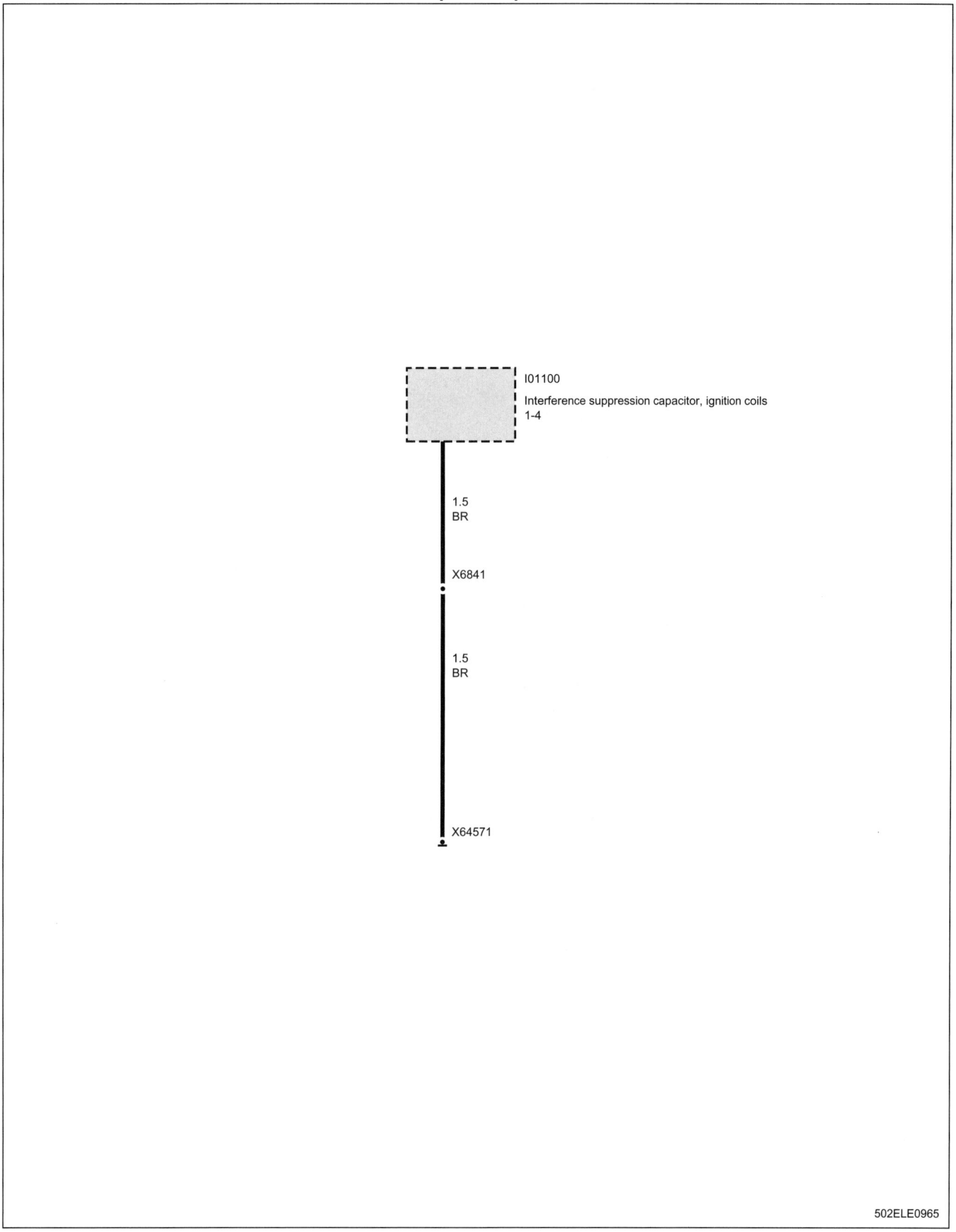

X-Connectors and Splices
X6960 Connector
(1 of 1)

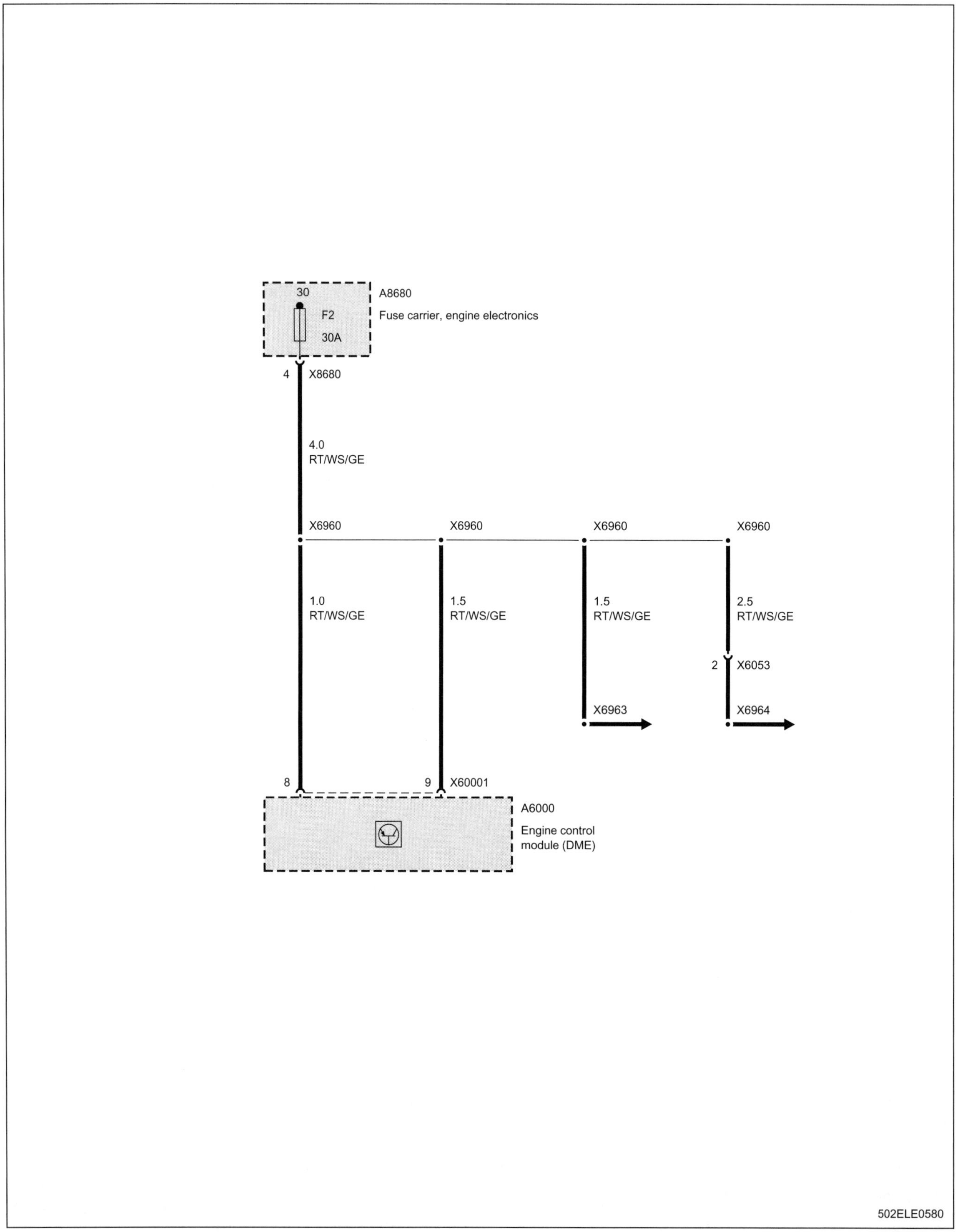
30
F2
30A
A8680
Fuse carrier, engine electronics
4
X8680
4.0
RT/WS/GE
X6960
X6960
X6960
X6960
1.0
RT/WS/GE
1.5
RT/WS/GE
1.5
RT/WS/GE
2.5
RT/WS/GE
2
X6053
X6963
X6964
8
9
X60001
A6000
Engine control
module (DME)
502ELE0580

X-Connectors and Splices
X6962 Connector
(1 of 1)

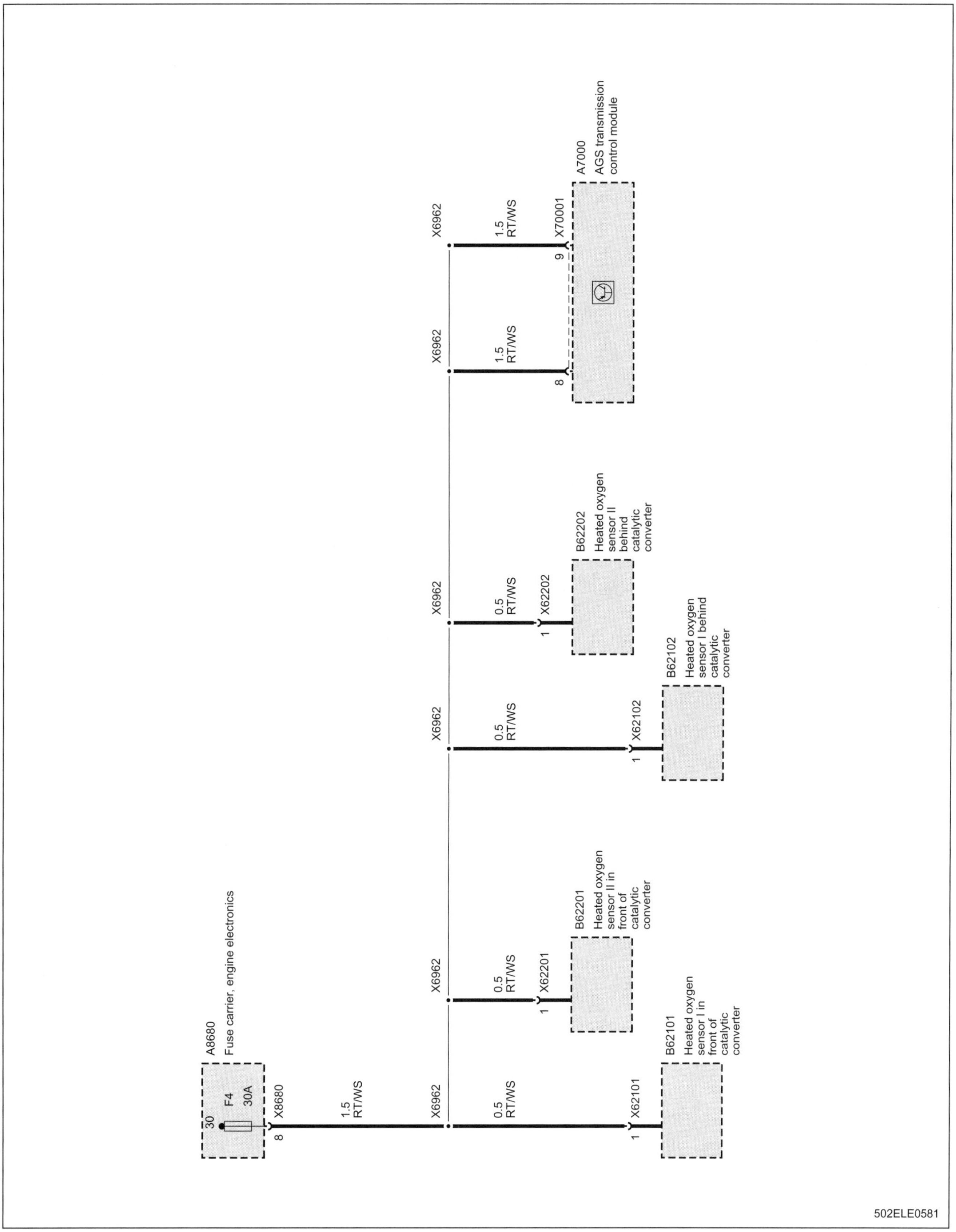

X-Connectors and Splices
X6963 Connector
(1 of 1)

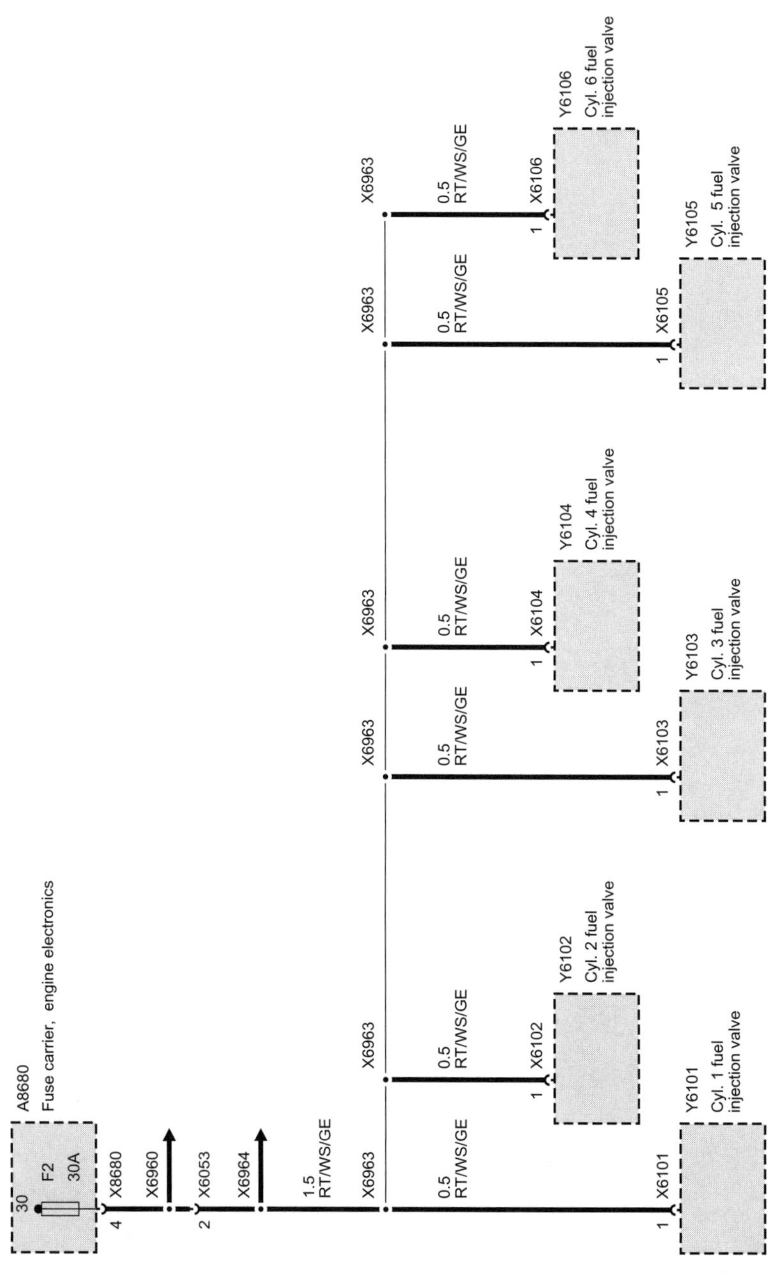
A8680
Fuse carrier, engine electronics
30
F2
30A
4
X8680
X6960
2
X6053
X6964
1.5
RT/WS/GE
X6963
0.5
RT/WS/GE
1
X6101
Y6101
Cyl. 1 fuel
injection valve
X6963
0.5
RT/WS/GE
1
X6102
Y6102
Cyl. 2 fuel
injection valve
X6963
0.5
RT/WS/GE
1
X6103
Y6103
Cyl. 3 fuel
injection valve
X6963
0.5
RT/WS/GE
1
X6104
Y6104
Cyl. 4 fuel
injection valve
X6963
0.5
RT/WS/GE
1
X6105
Y6105
Cyl. 5 fuel
injection valve
X6963
0.5
RT/WS/GE
1
X6106
Y6106
Cyl. 6 fuel
injection valve
502ELE0582

X-Connectors and Splices
X6964 Connector
(1 of 1)

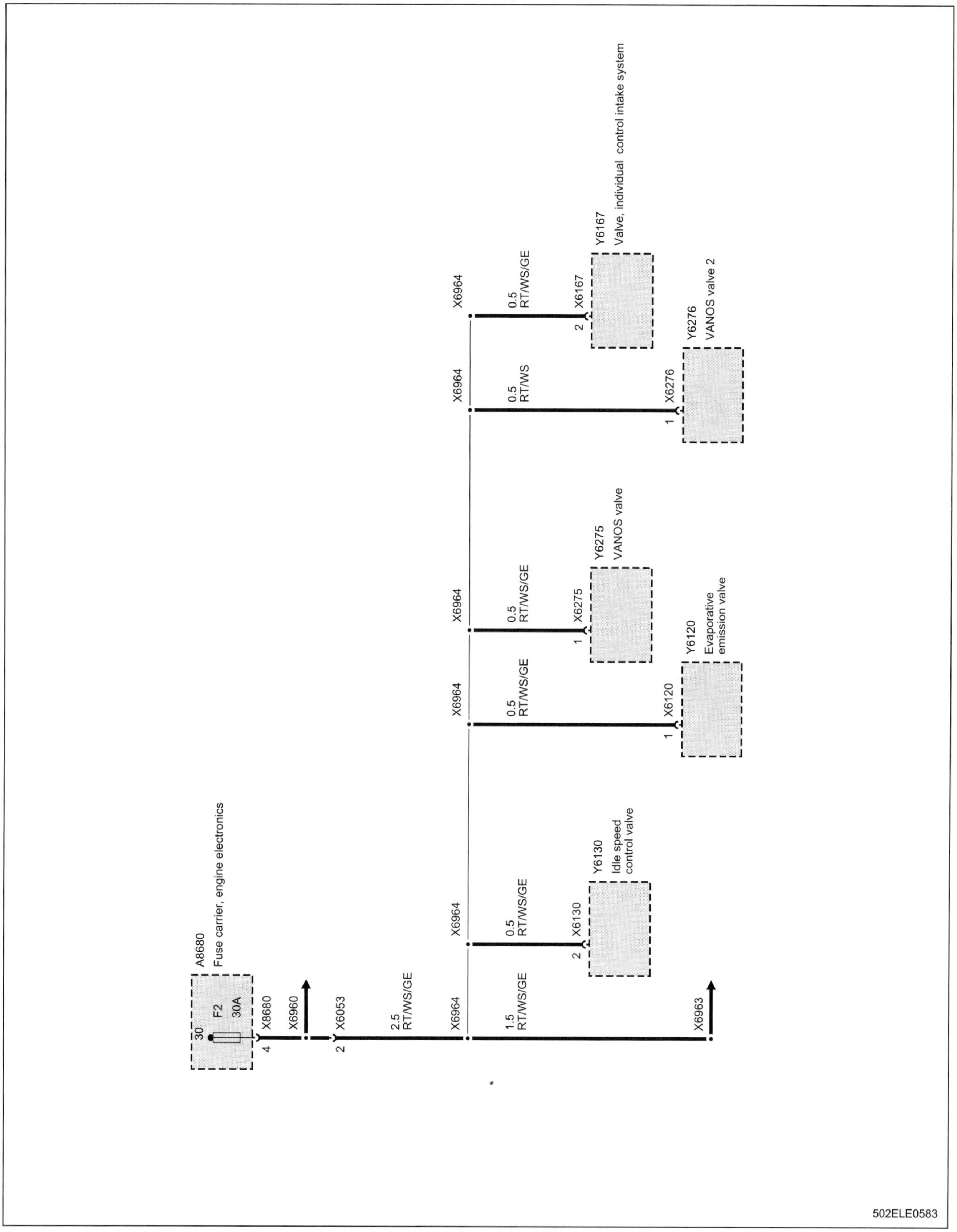
A8680
Fuse carrier, engine electronics
30
F2
30A
4
X8680
X6960
2
X6053
2.5
RT/WS/GE
X6964
1.5
RT/WS/GE
X6963
X6964
0.5
RT/WS/GE
2
X6130
Y6130
Idle speed
control valve
X6964
0.5
RT/WS/GE
1
X6120
Y6120
Evaporative
emission valve
X6964
0.5
RT/WS/GE
1
X6275
Y6275
VANOS valve
X6964
0.5
RT/WS
1
X6276
Y6276
VANOS valve 2
X6964
0.5
RT/WS/GE
2
X6167
Y6167
Valve, individual control intake system
502ELE0583

X-Connectors and Splices
X6965 Connector
(1 of 1)

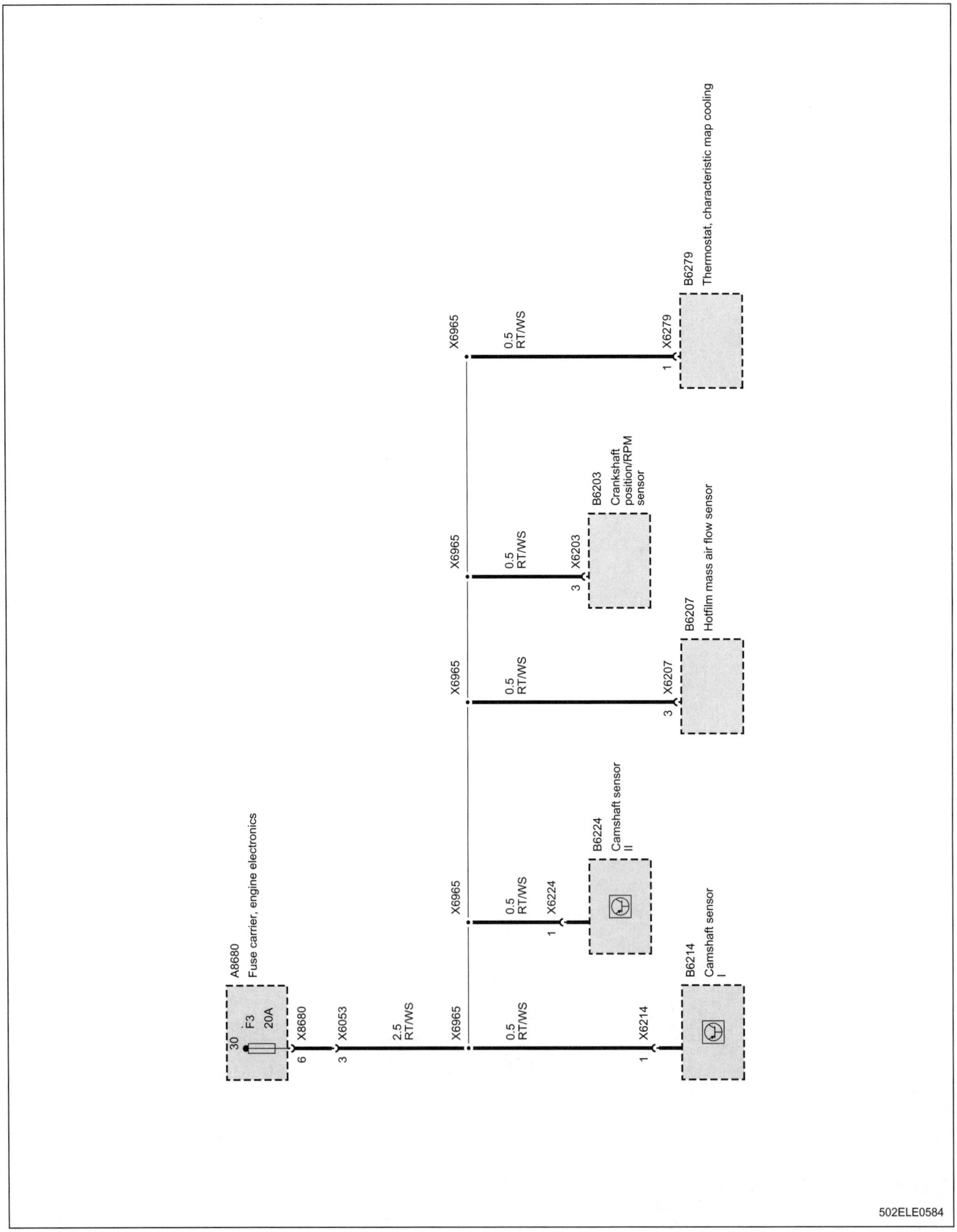
B6279
Thermostat, characteristic map cooling
X6965
0.5
RT/WS
X6279
1
B6203
Crankshaft
position/RPM
sensor
X6965
0.5
RT/WS
X6203
3
B6207
Hotfilm mass air flow sensor
X6965
0.5
RT/WS
X6207
3
B6224
Camshaft sensor
II
X6965
0.5
RT/WS
X6224
1
A8680
Fuse carrier, engine electronics
30
F3
20A
X8680
6
X6053
3
2.5
RT/WS
X6965
0.5
RT/WS
X6214
1
B6214
Camshaft sensor
I
502ELE0584

X-Connectors and Splices
X8073 Splice
(1 of 1)

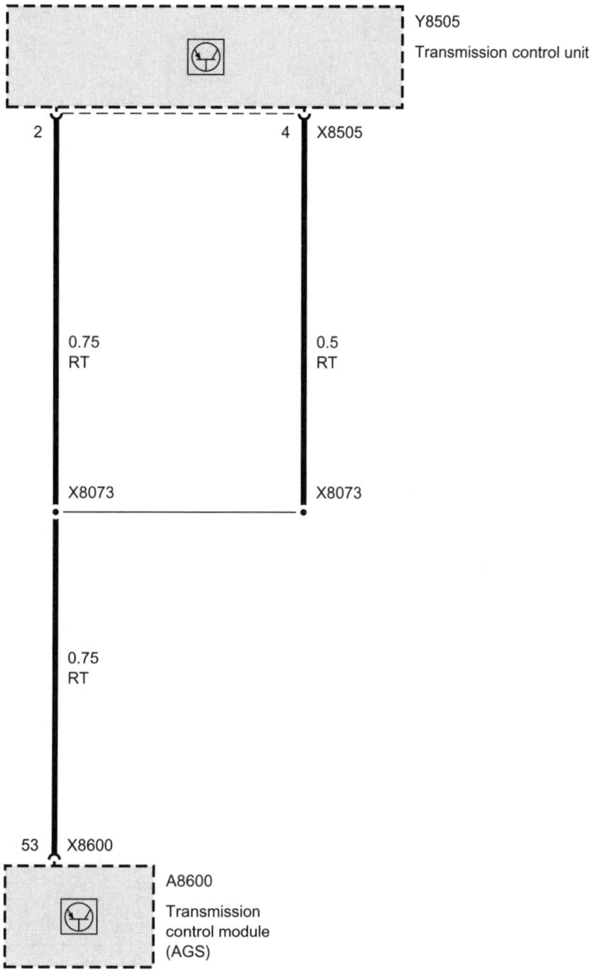

502ELE0665

X-Connectors and Splices
X8589 Splice - Park/Neutral signal
(1 of 1)

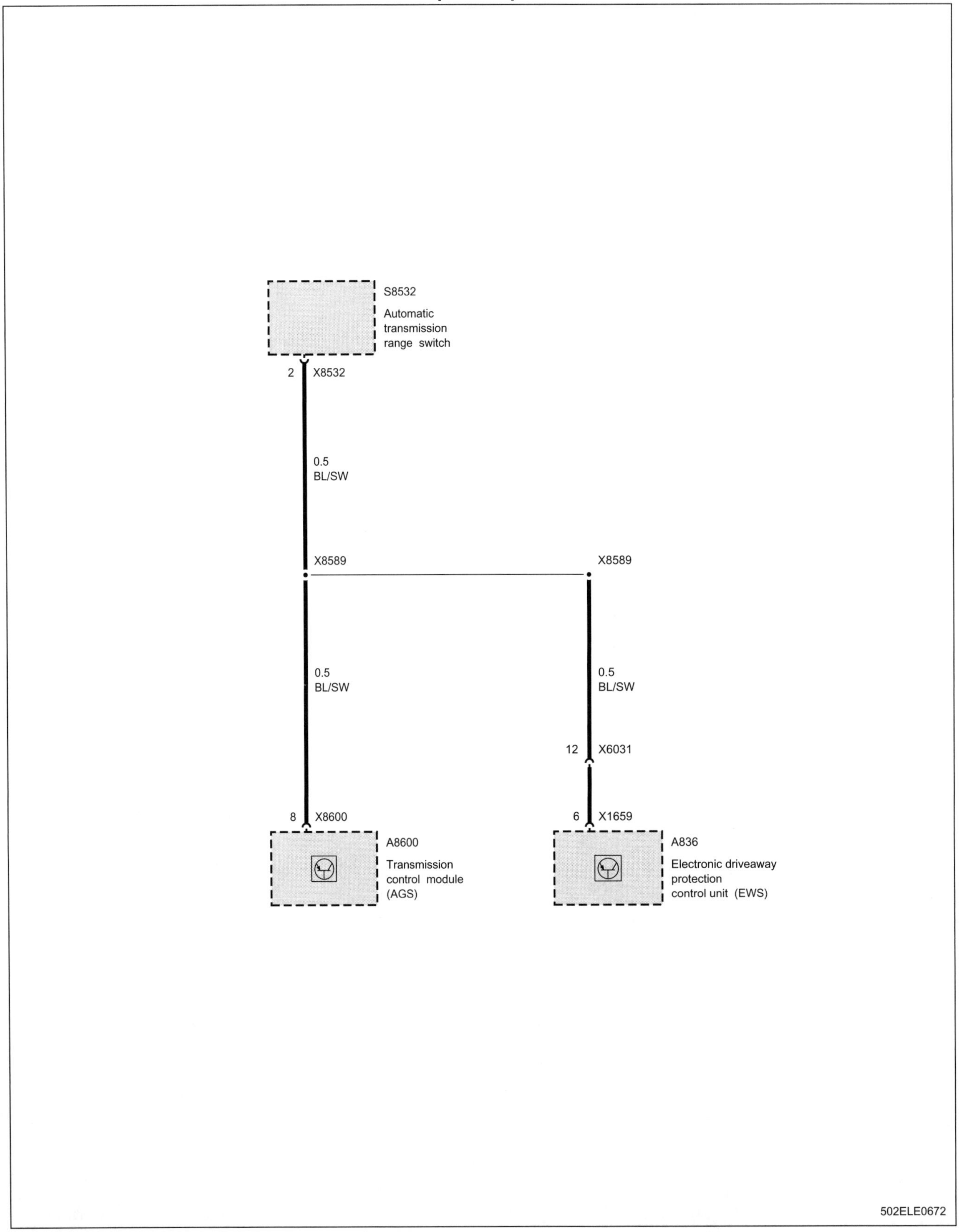

Ground Distribution
Ground X10012
(1 of 1)

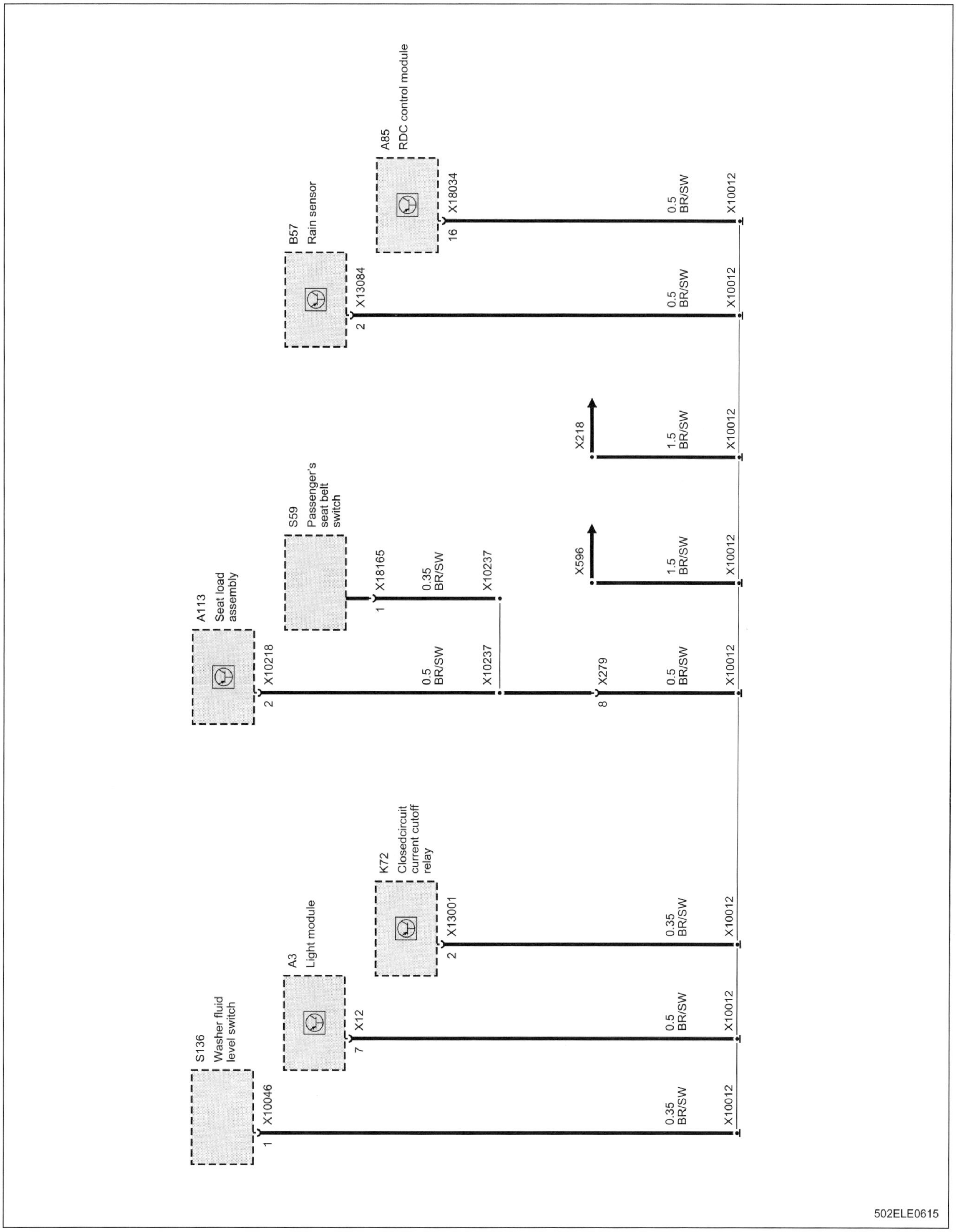
A85
RDC control module
X18034
16
0.5
BR/SW
X10012
B57
Rain sensor
X13084
2
0.5
BR/SW
X10012
X218
1.5
BR/SW
X10012
S59
Passenger's
seat belt
switch
X18165
1
0.35
BR/SW
X10237
X596
1.5
BR/SW
X10012
A113
Seat load
assembly
X10218
2
0.5
BR/SW
X10237
X279
8
0.5
BR/SW
X10012
K72
Closedcircuit
current cutoff
relay
X13001
2
0.35
BR/SW
X10012
A3
Light module
X12
7
0.5
BR/SW
X10012
S136
Washer fluid
level switch
X10046
1
0.35
BR/SW
X10012
502ELE0615

X-Connectors and Splices
X10088 Spray jet connector
(1 of 1)

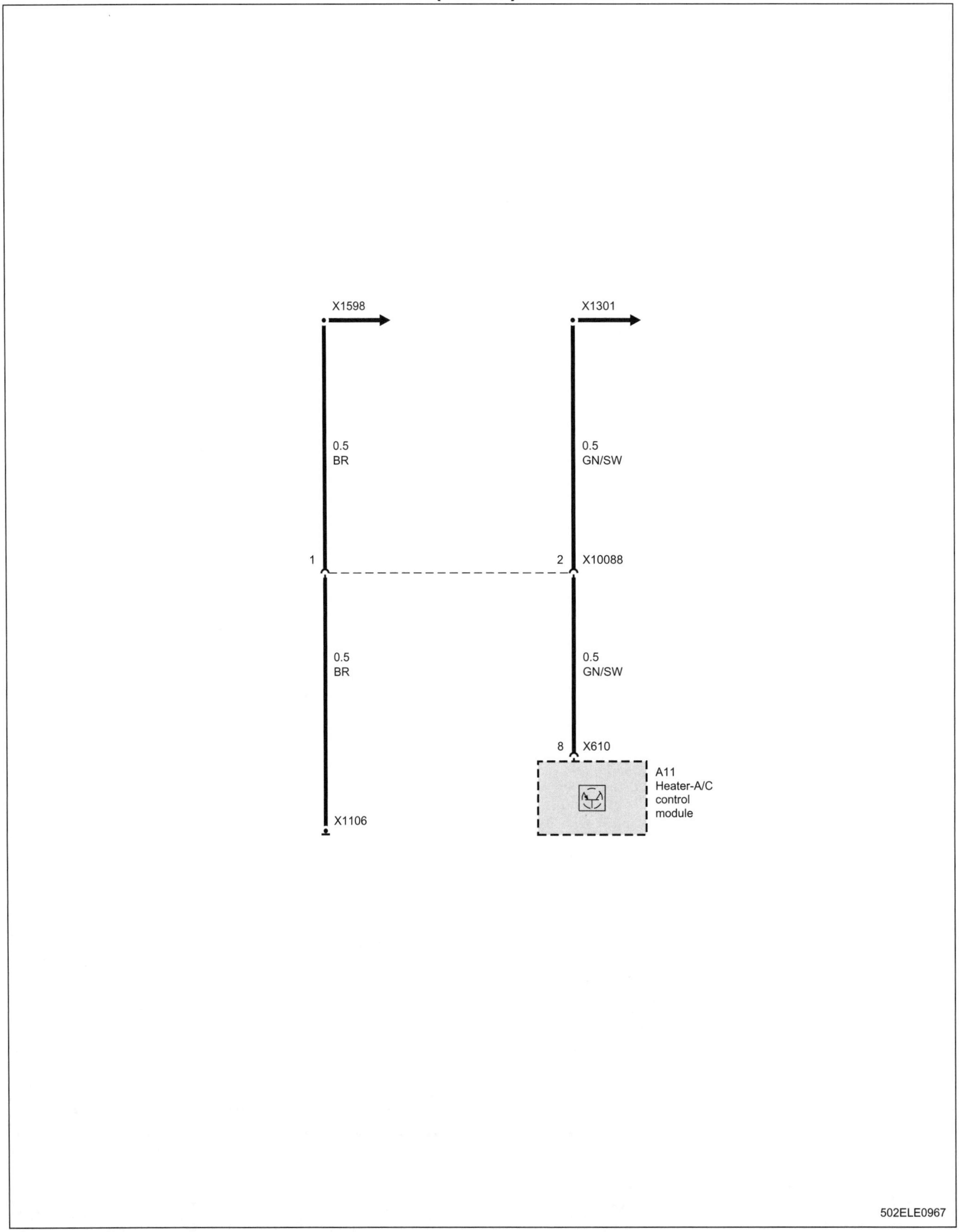

X-Connectors and Splices
X10116 Splice - K-bus
(1 of 2)

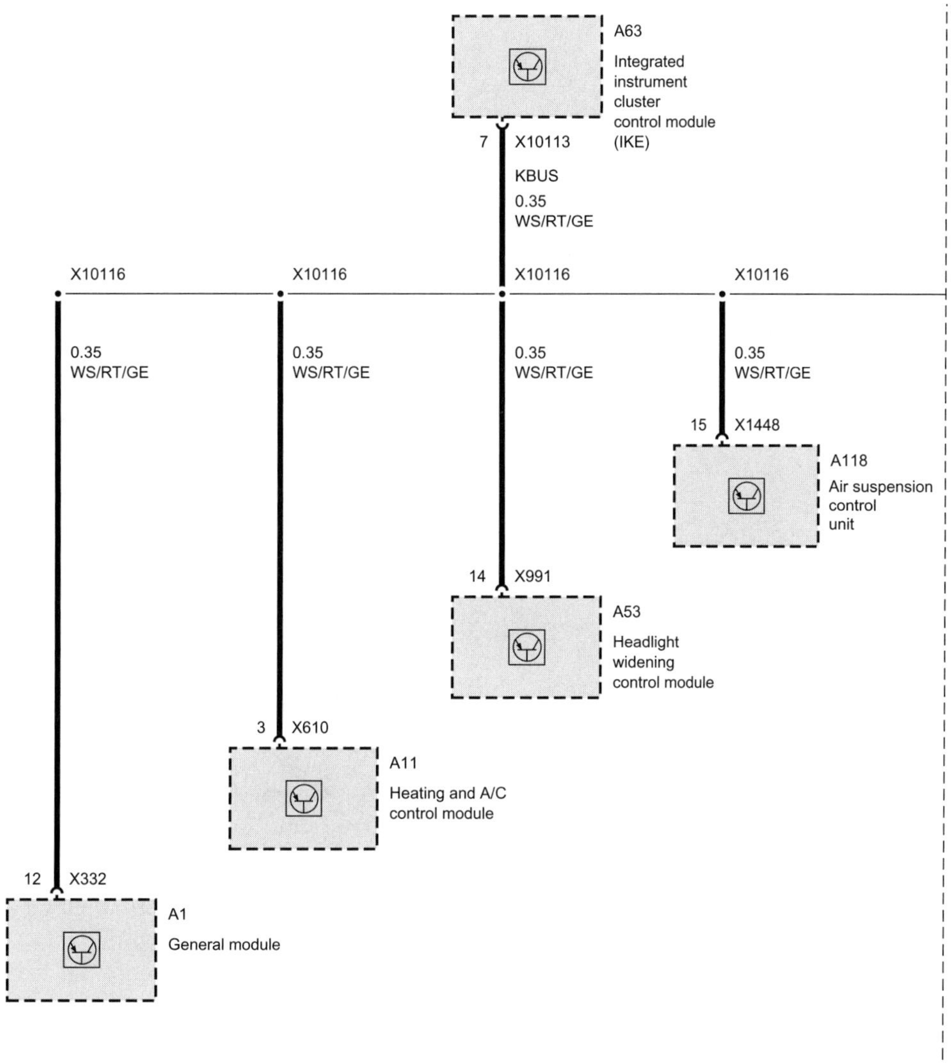

502ELE0670

X-Connectors and Splices
X10116 Splice - K-bus
(2 of 2)

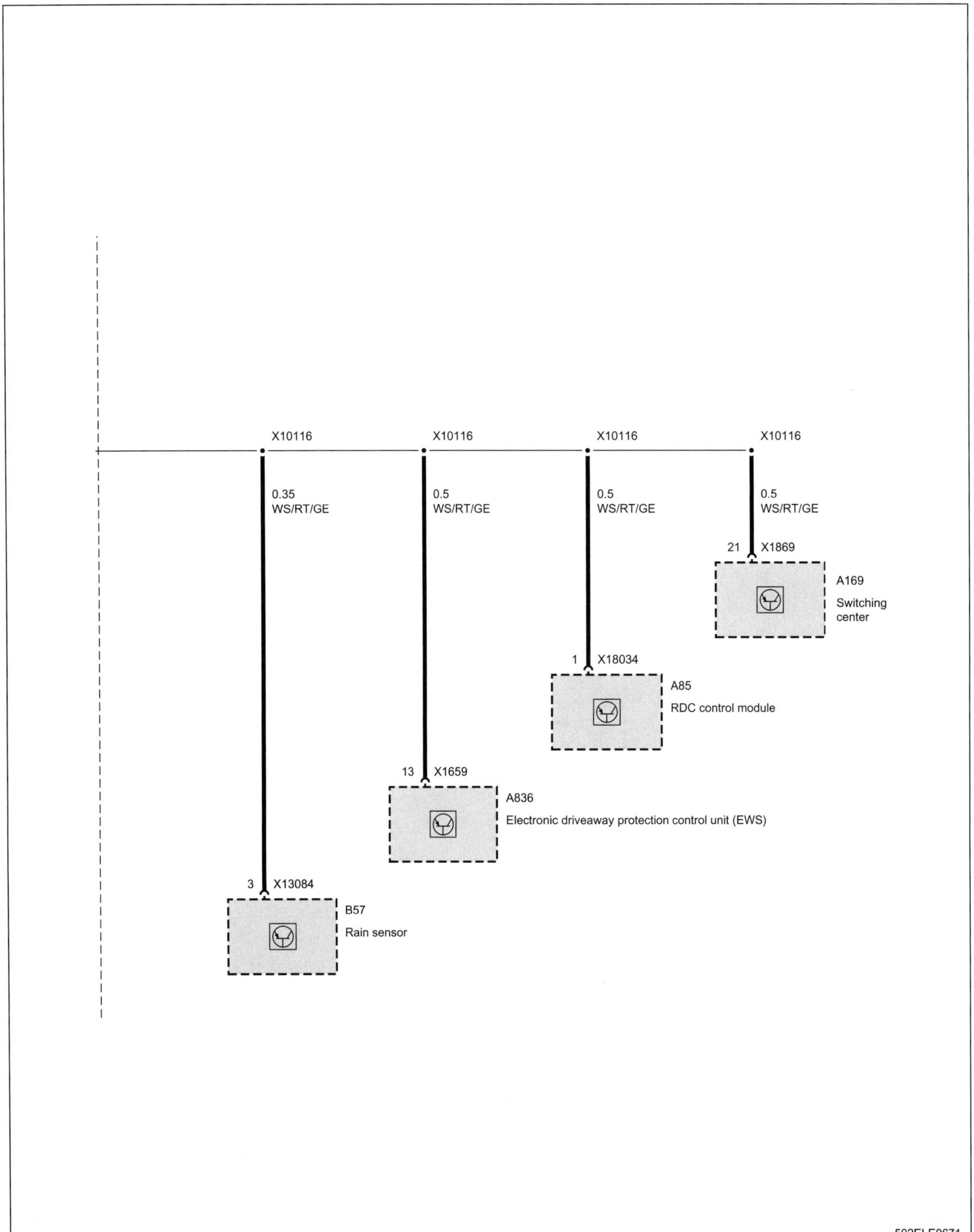

X-Connectors and Splices
X10148 Connector - Interior lights
(1 of 1)

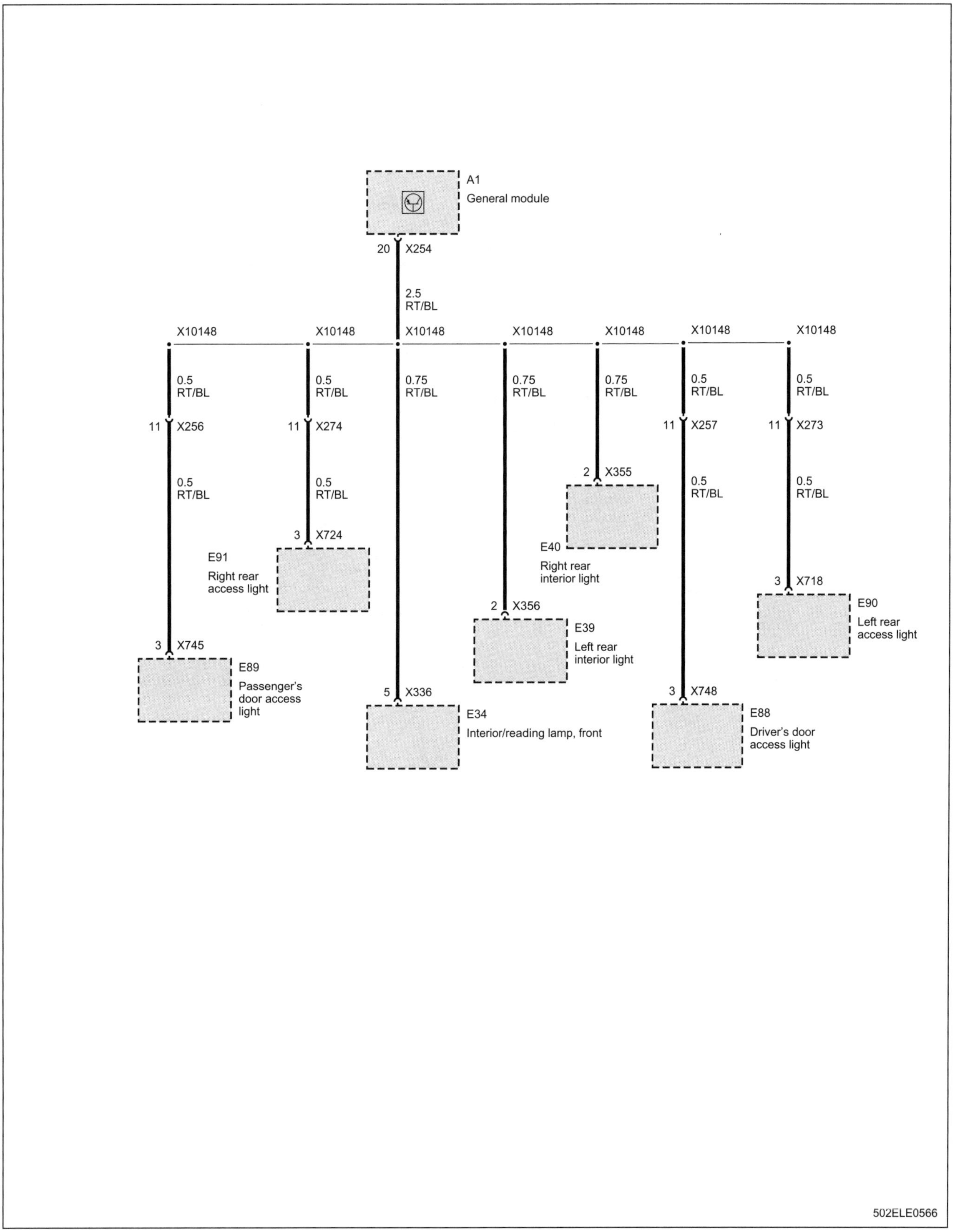

Ground Distribution
X13016 Ground, Radio/hifi
(1 of 1)

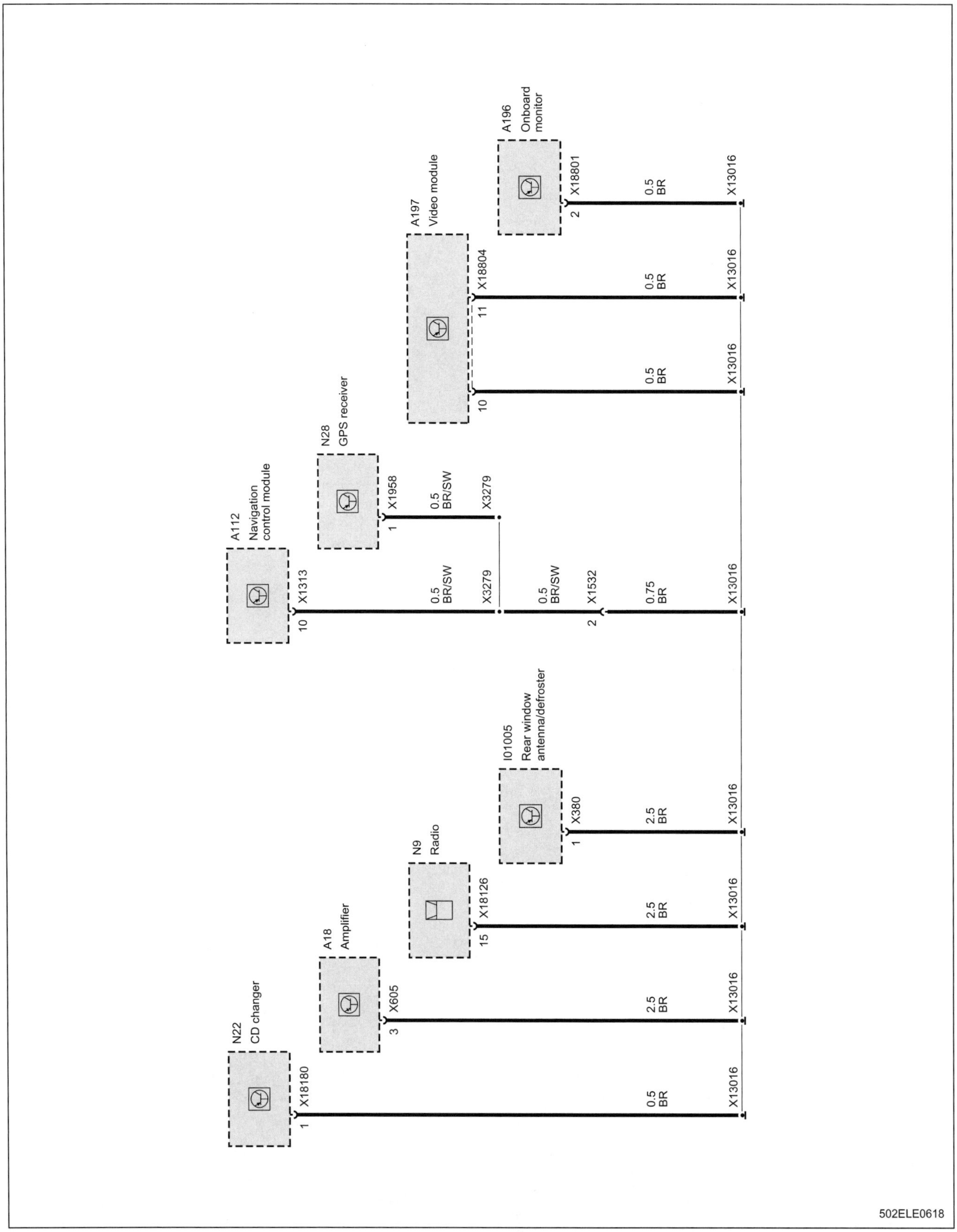

Ground Distribution
X13016 Ground - Radio/Stereo
(1 of 1)

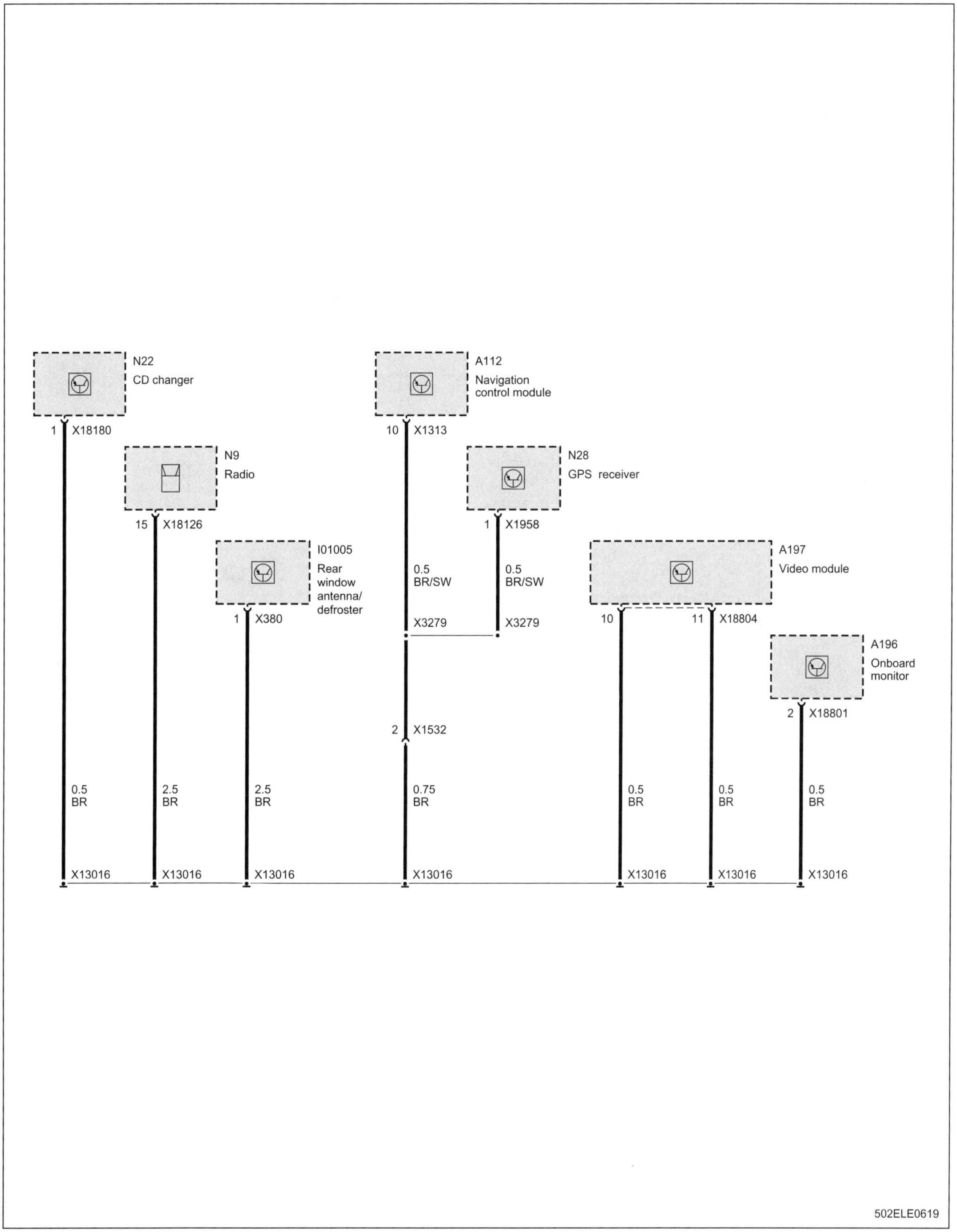

Ground Distribution
X13016 Ground - Top hifi
(1 of 1)

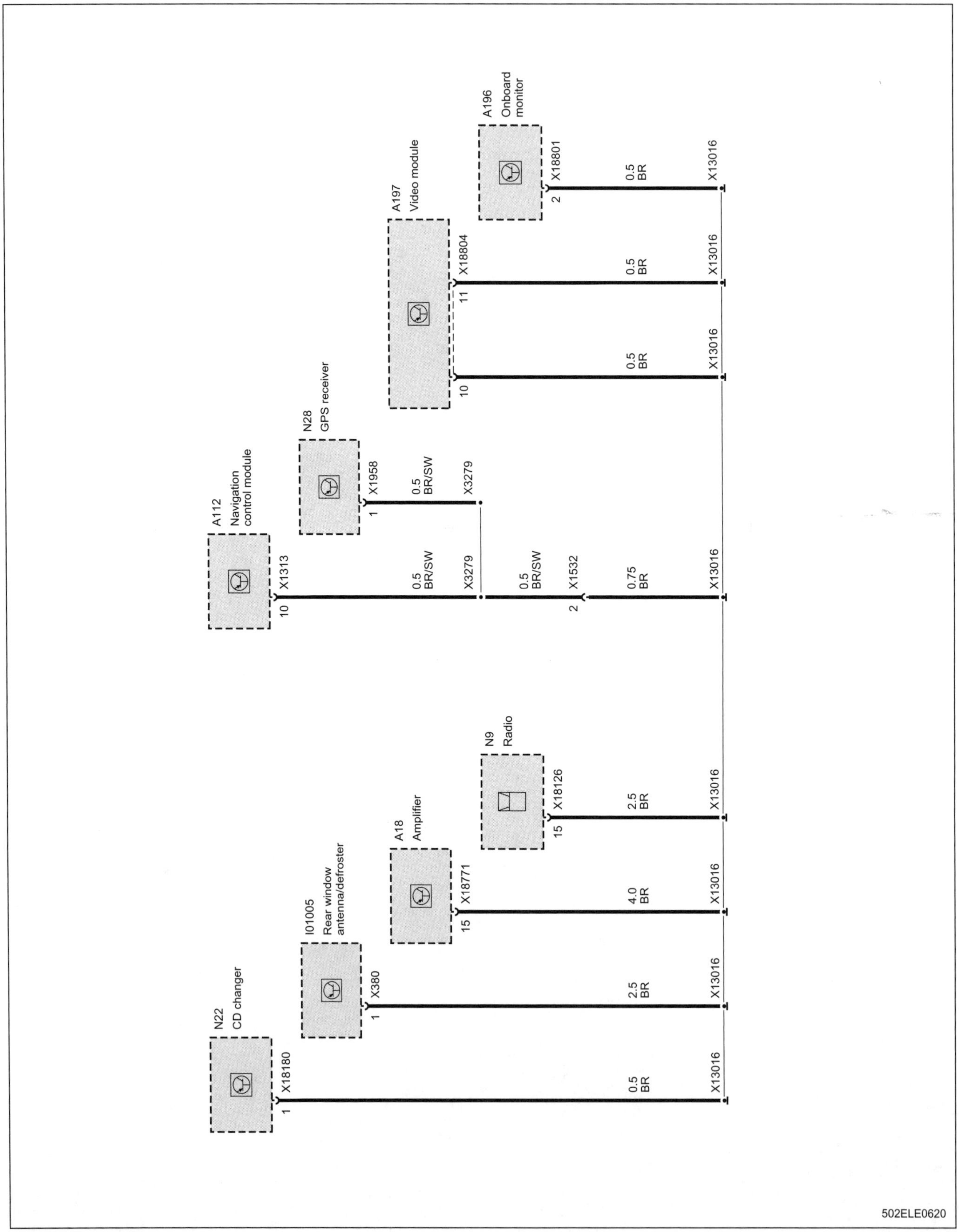

X-Connectors and Splices
X18121 Splice - Consumer cutoff
(1 of 1)

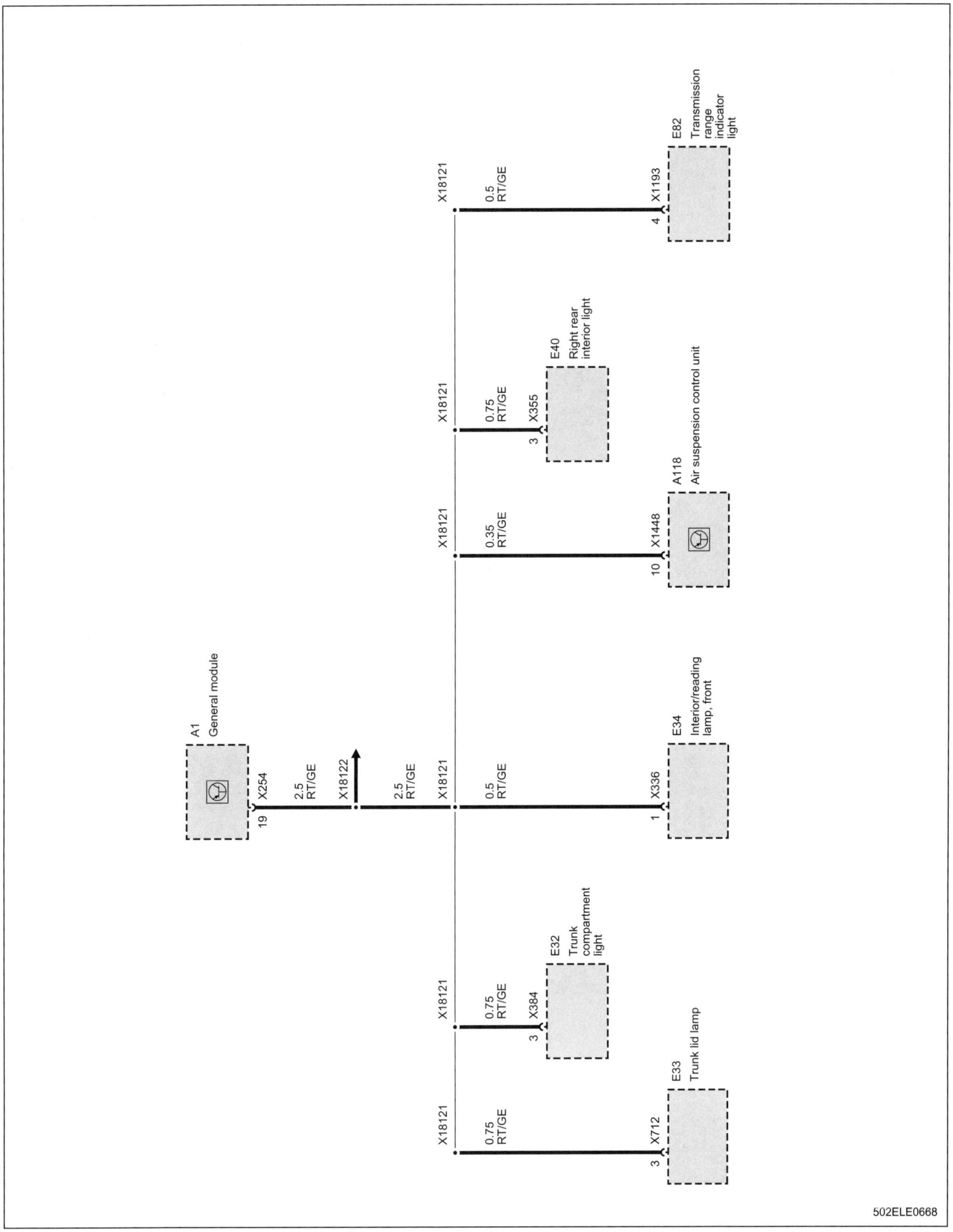

X-Connectors and Splices
X18122 Splice - Consumer cutoff
(1 of 1)

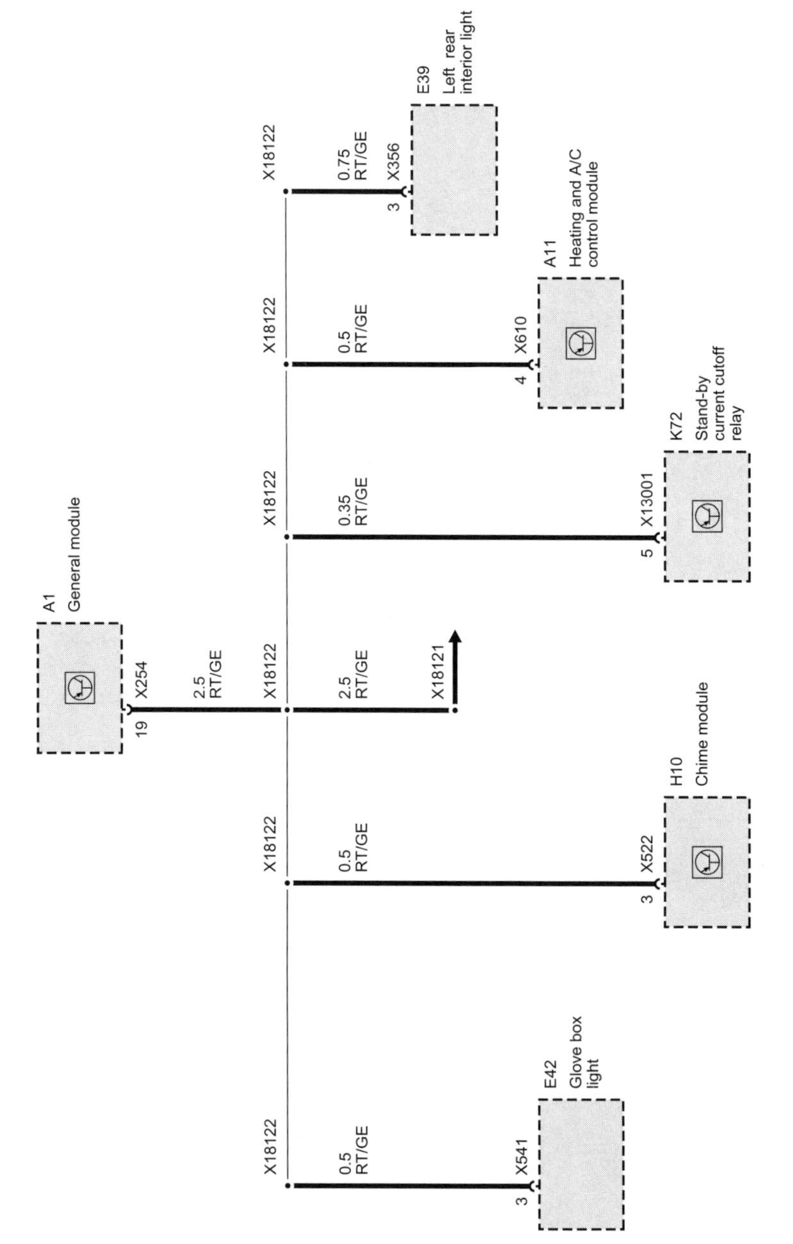

502ELE0669

X-Connectors and Splices
X18145 Plug connector - Brake pad sensor

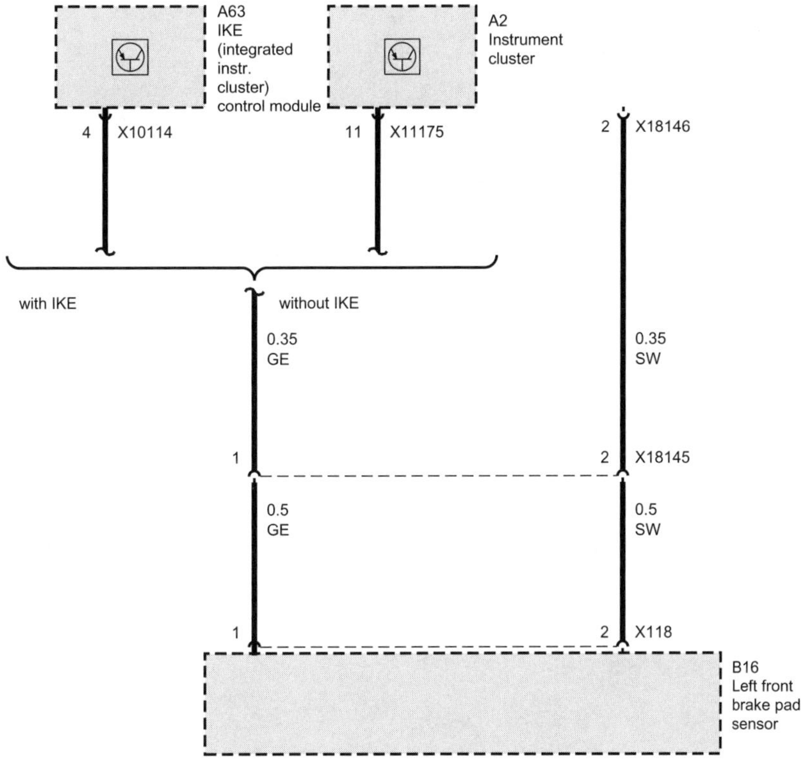

502ELE0684a

X-Connectors and Splices
X18146 Plug connector - Brake pad sensor

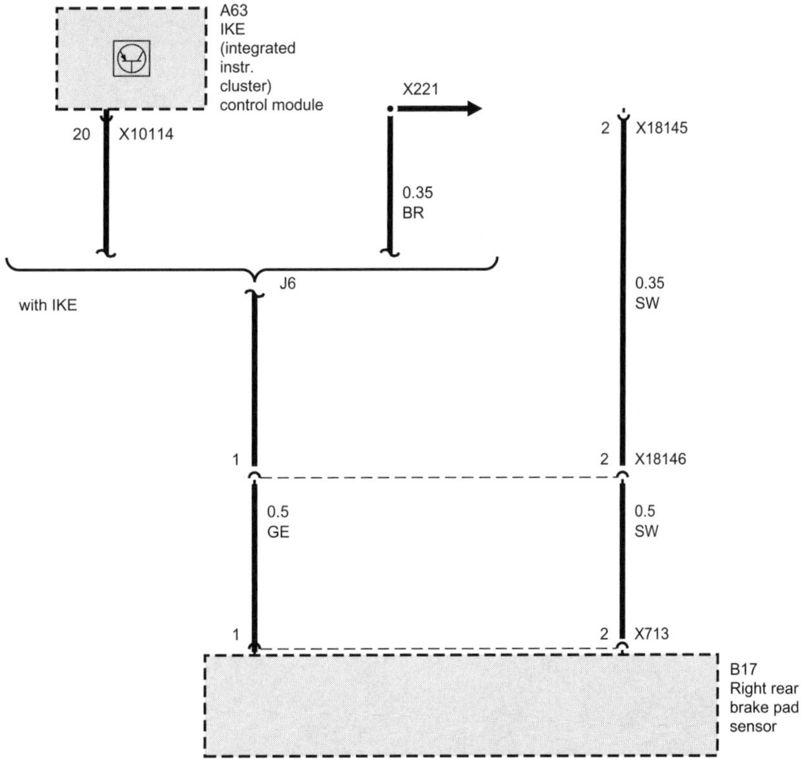

502ELE0684b

X-Connectors and Splices
X18344 Splice I/K-bus - Top hifi
(1 of 1)

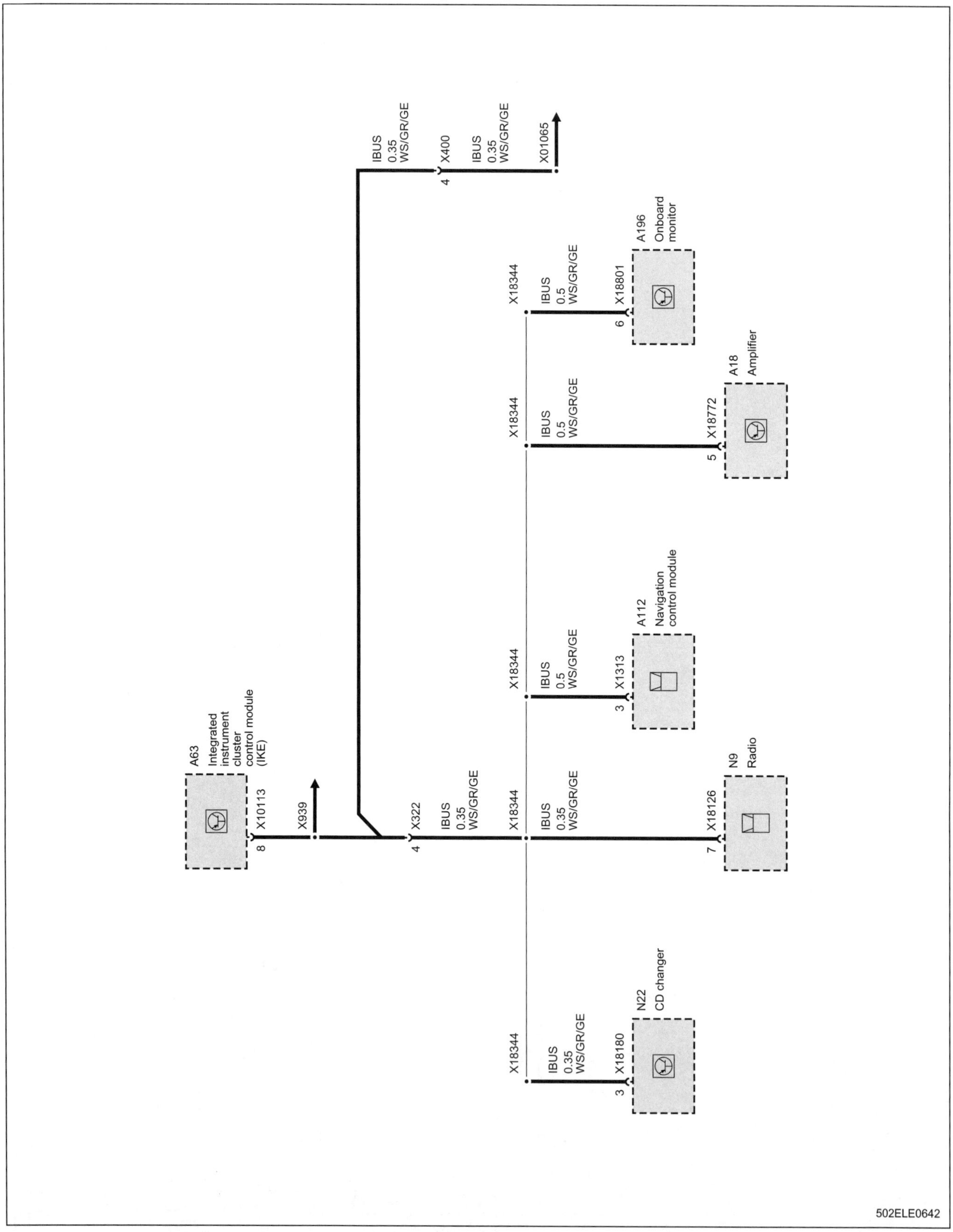

Ground Distribution
X18726 Ground connector
(1 of 1)

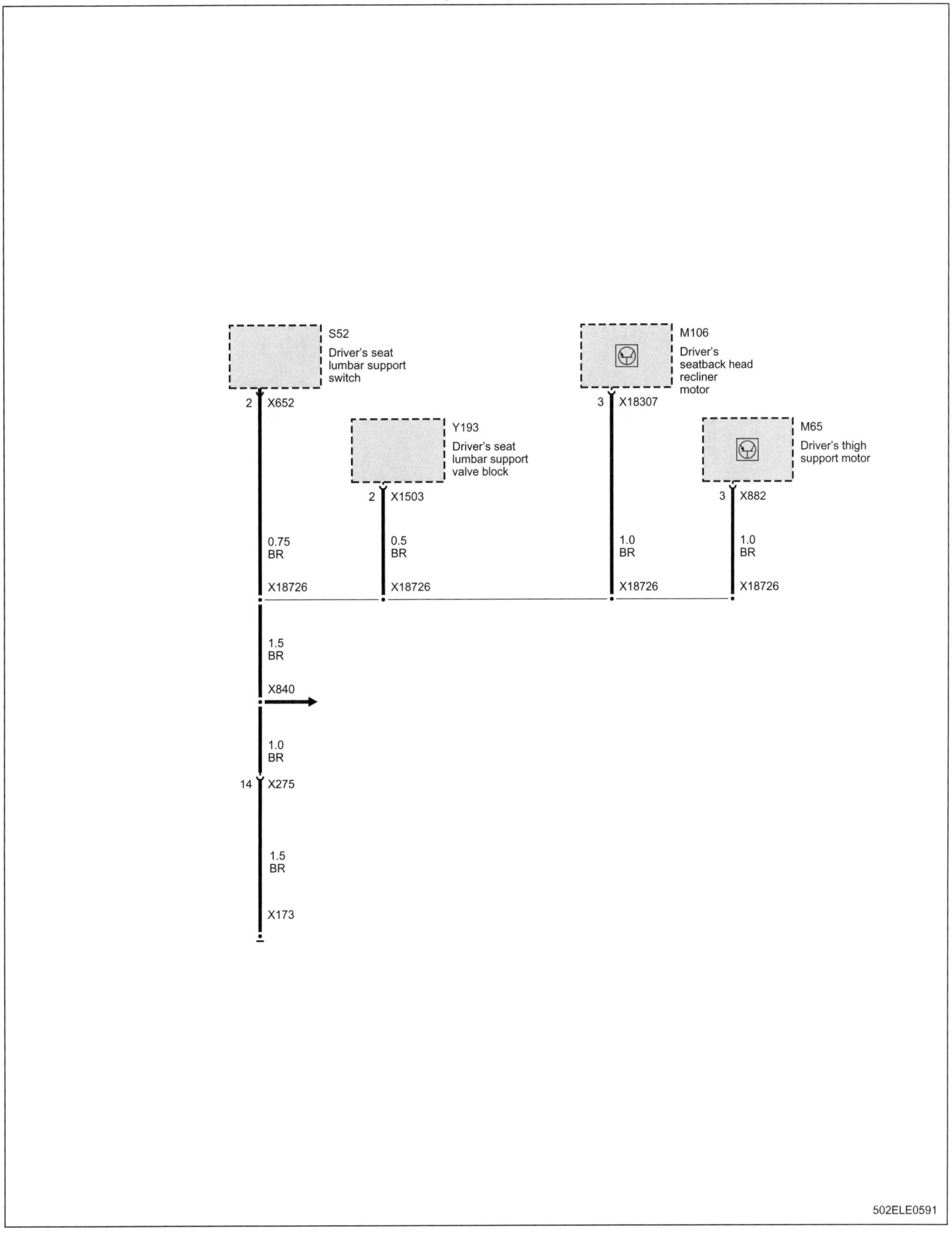

Ground Distribution
X18740 Ground splice - Seats with memory
(1 of 1)

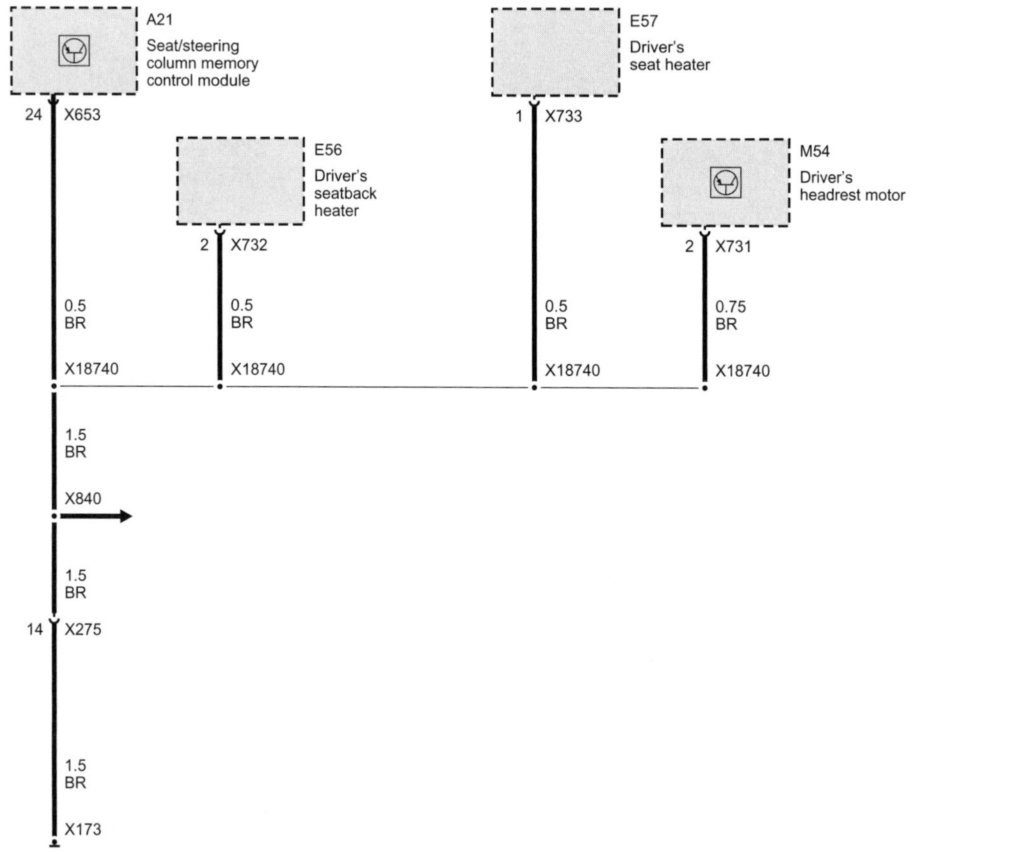

Ground Distribution
X18749 Ground connector - Seats without memory
(1 of 1)

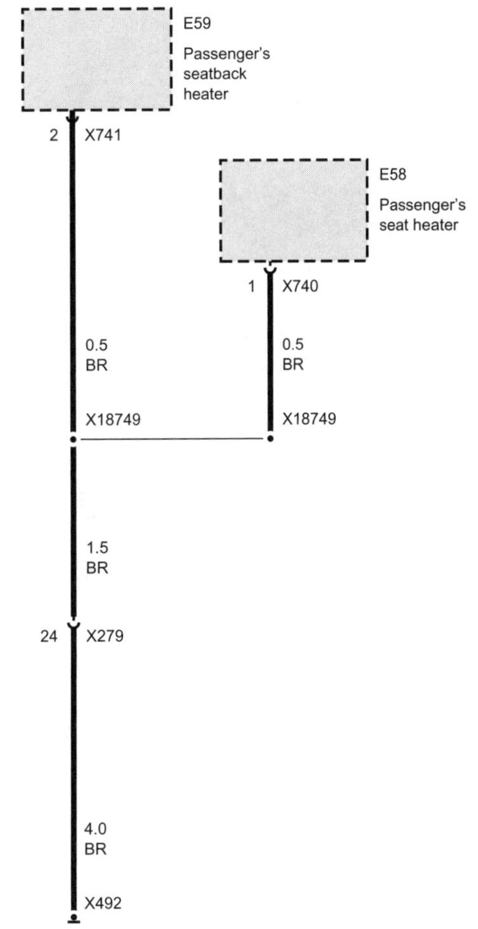

X-Connectors and Splices
X18764 Splice - Telephone

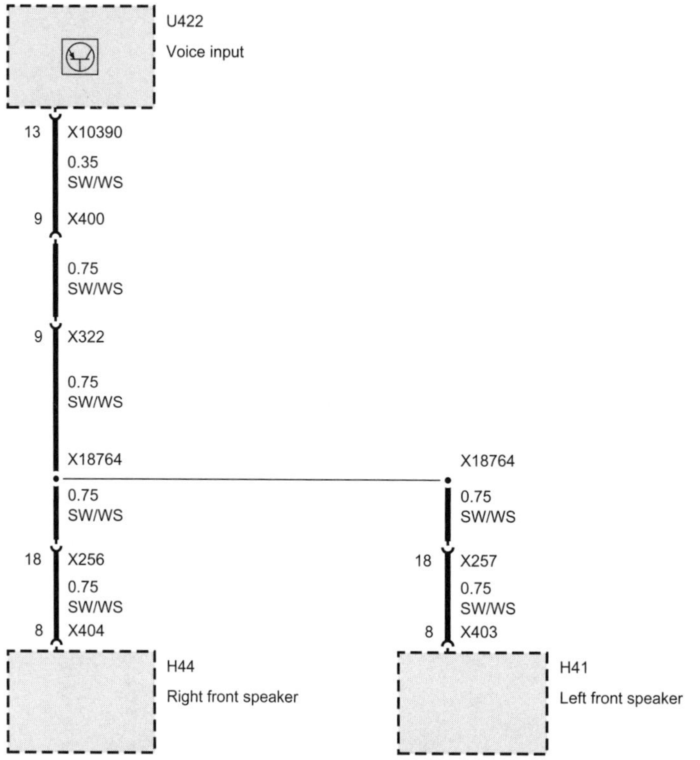

502ELE0673a

X-Connectors and Splices
X18765 Splice - Telephone

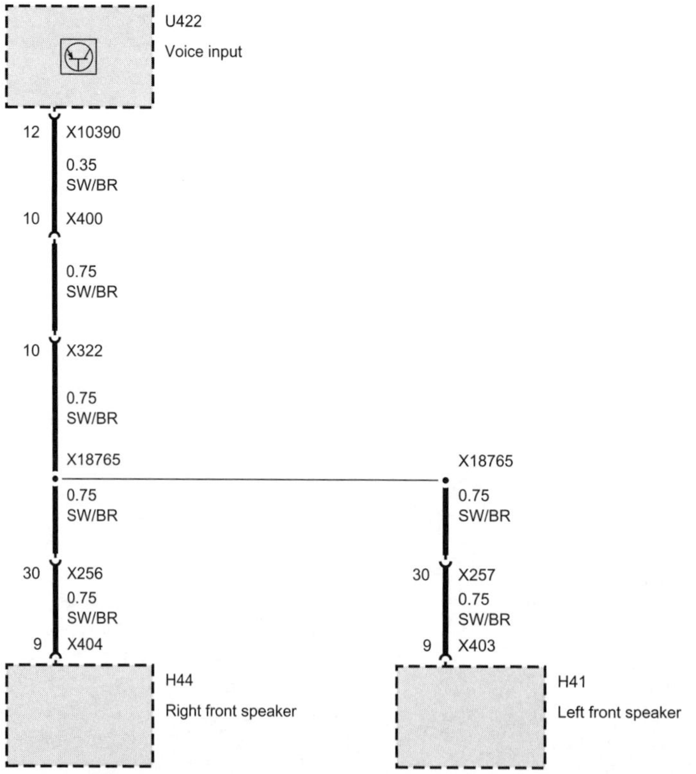

502ELE0673b

X-Connectors and Splices
X19527 OBDII socket
(1 of 1)

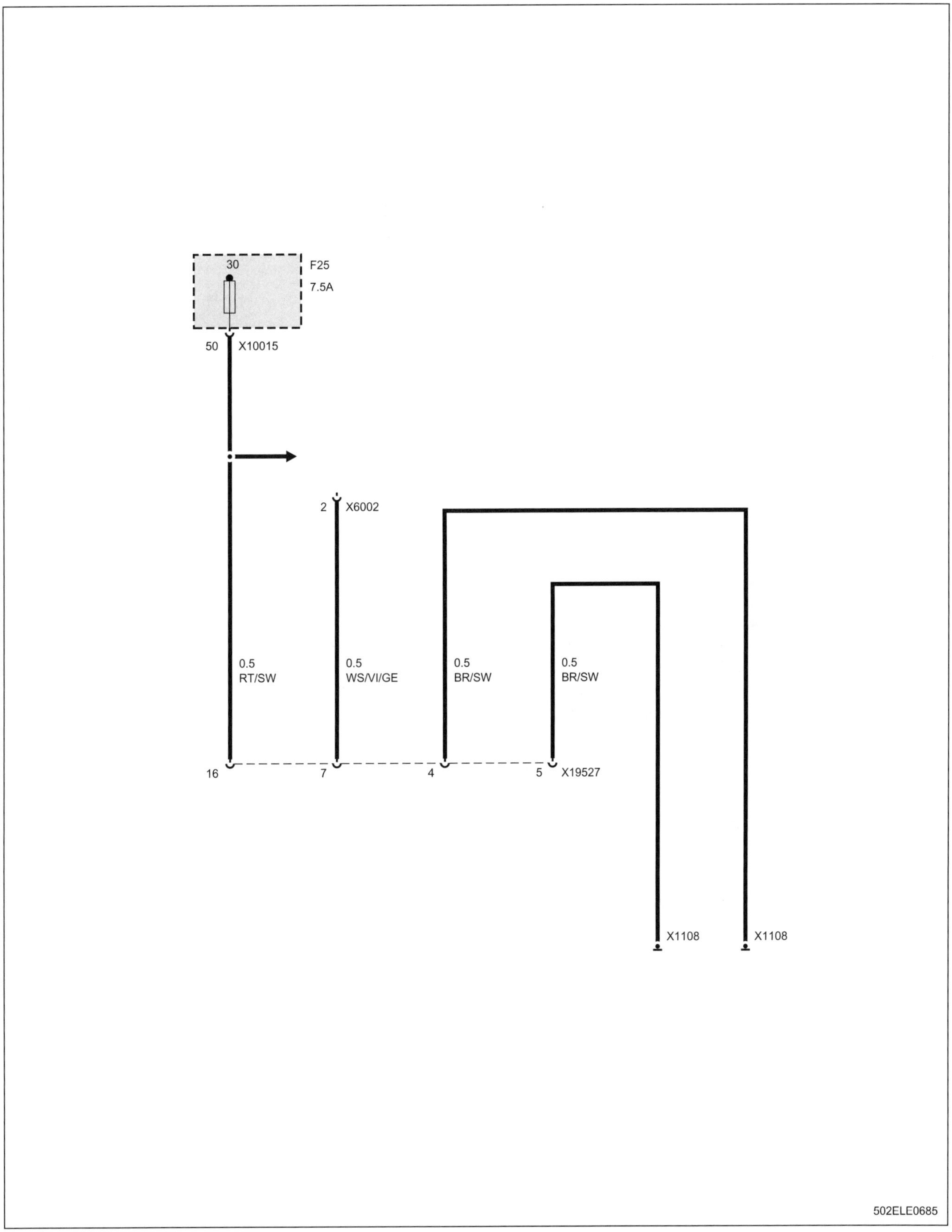

Ground Distribution
X64561 Ground distribution

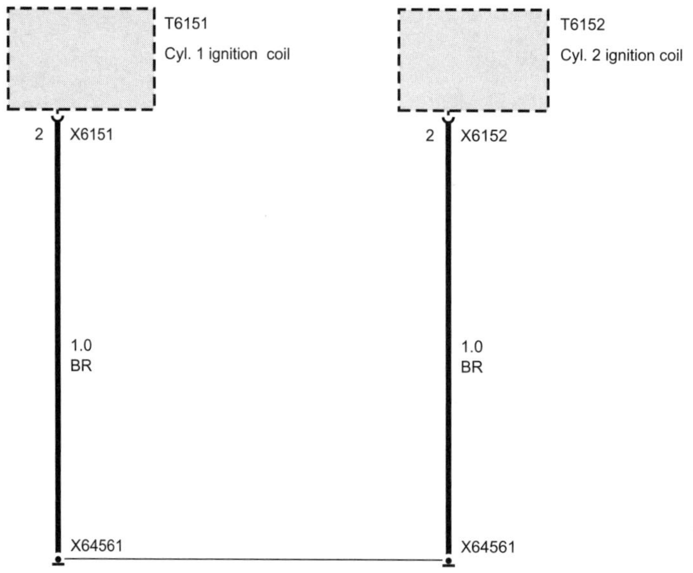

502ELE0594a

Ground Distribution
X64563 Ground distribution

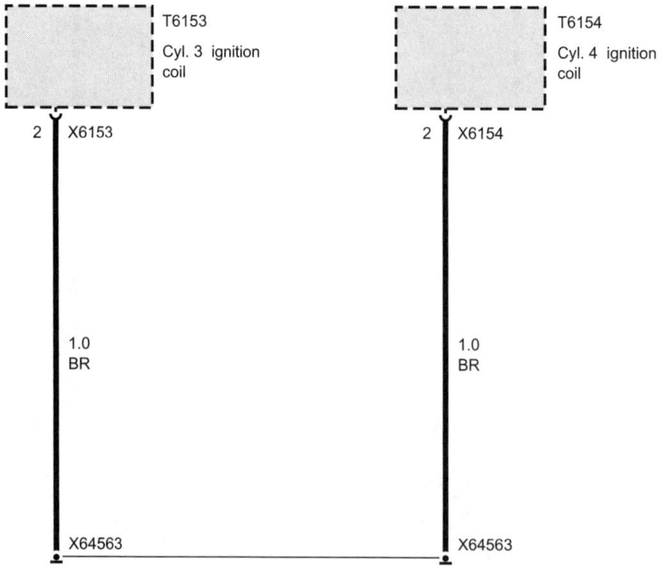

502ELE0594b

Ground Distribution
X64565 Ground distribution

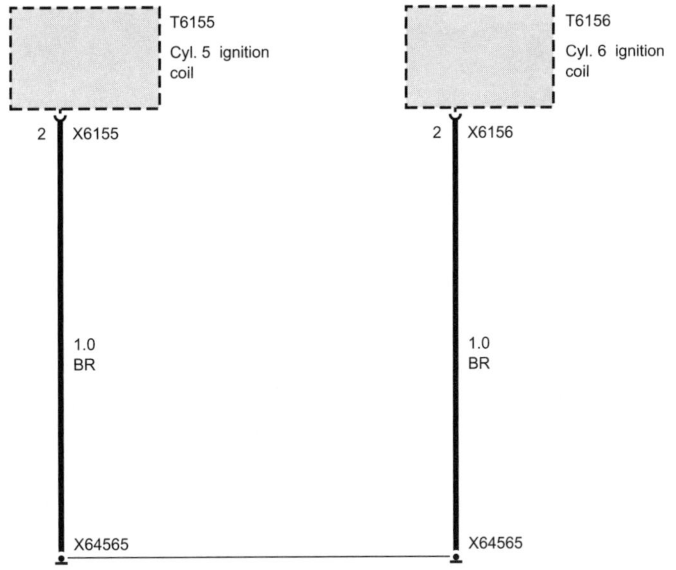

502ELE0595a

Ground Distribution
X64567 Ground distribution

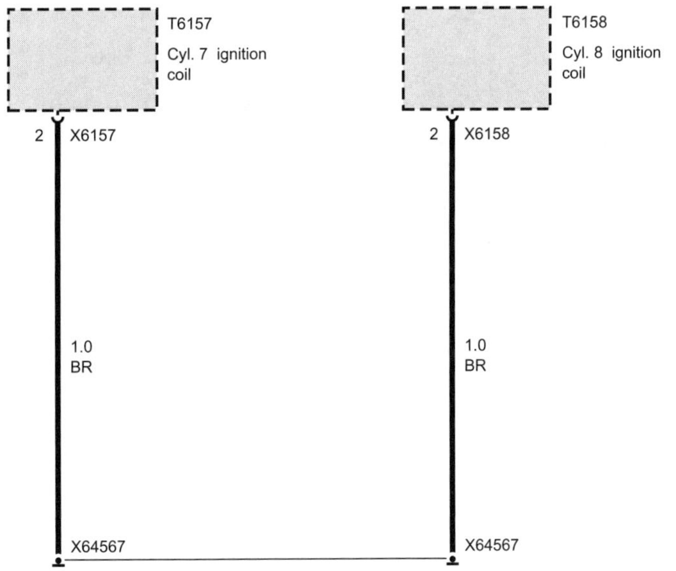

502ELE0595b

BUS System
CAN interface I
(1 of 1)

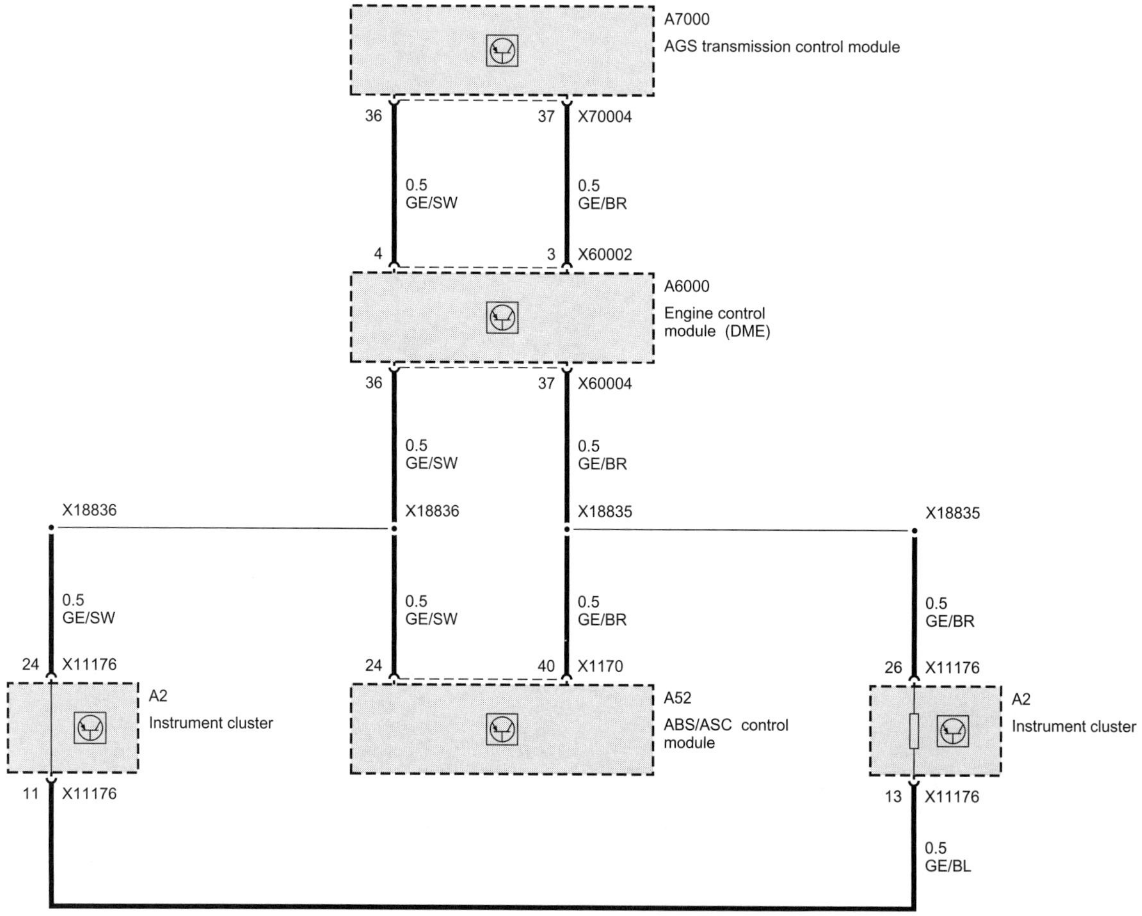

502ELE0260

BUS System
CAN interface II
(1 of 1)

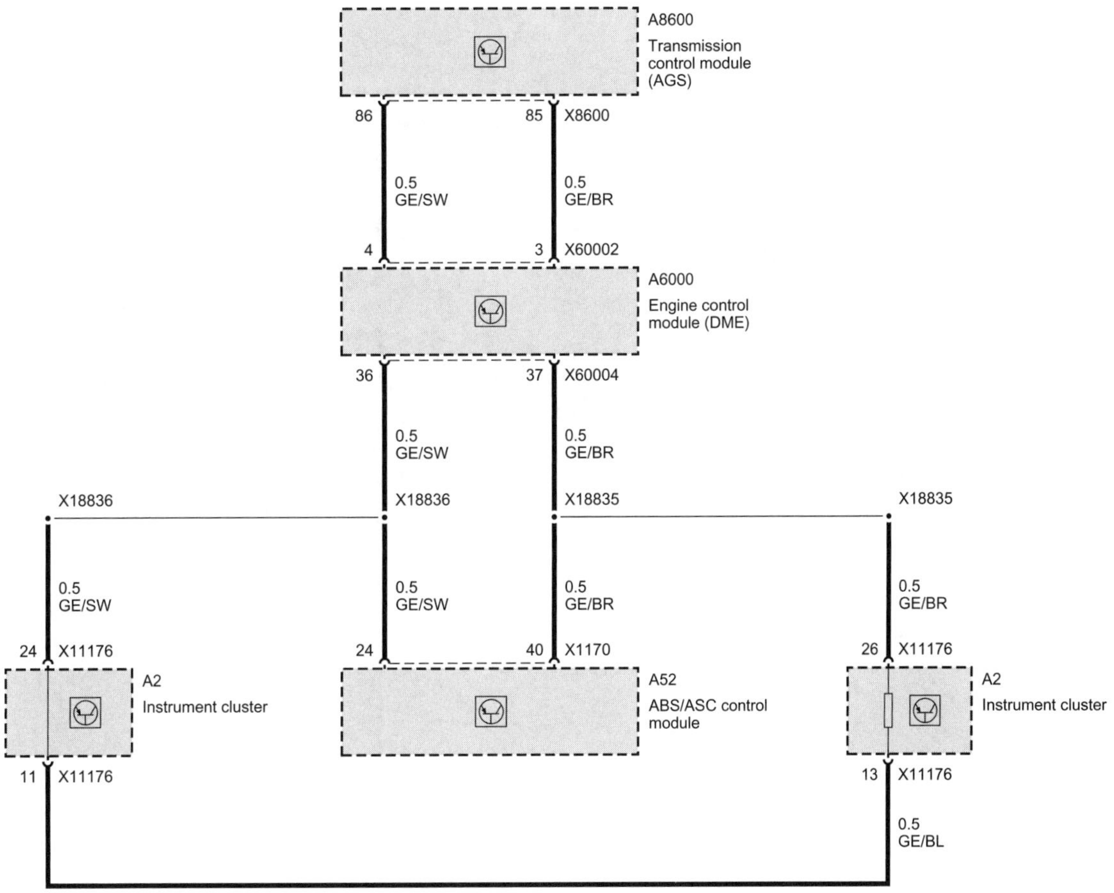

502ELE0284

BUS System
K-bus, light signal
(1 of 1)

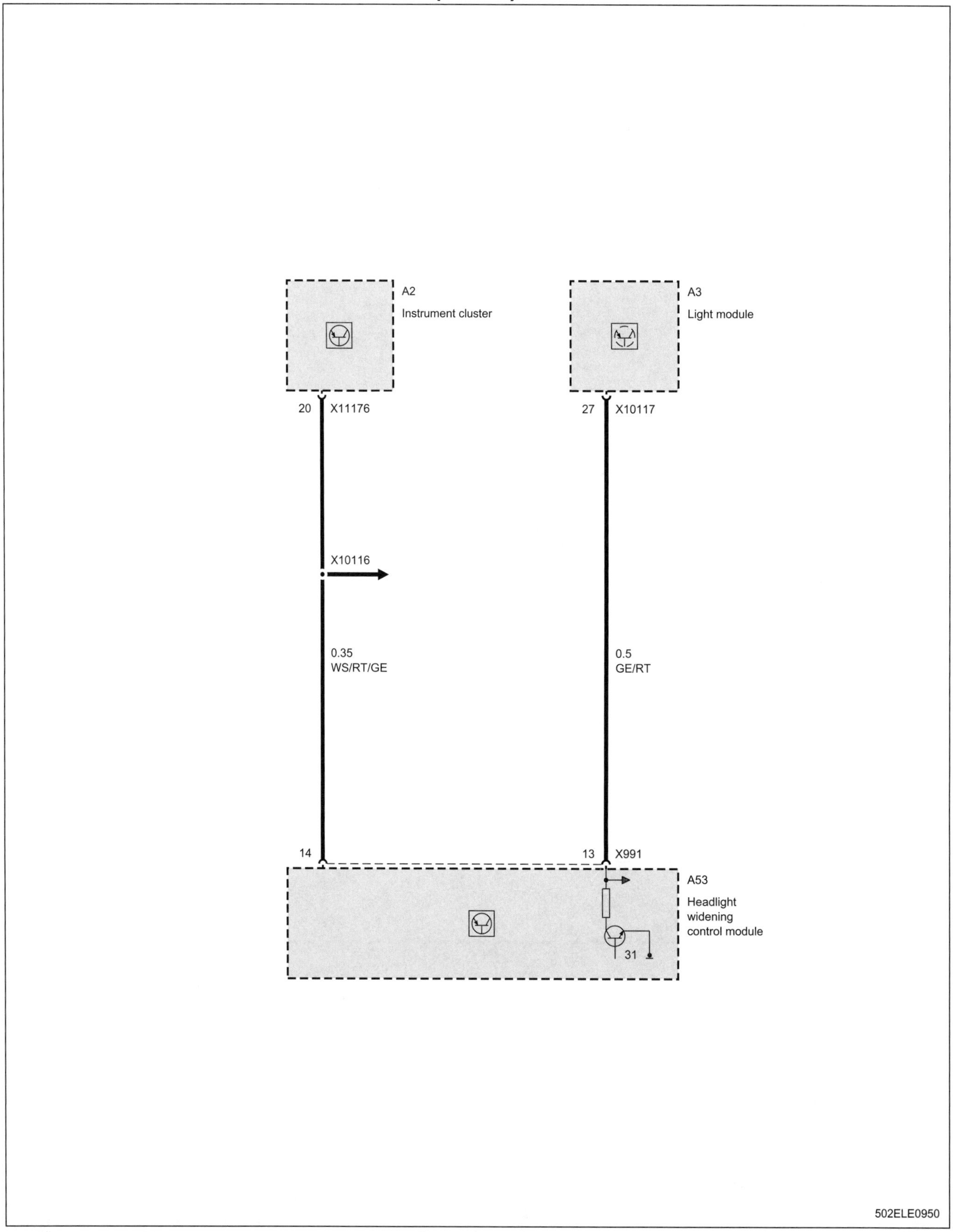
A2
Instrument cluster
A3
Light module
20
X11176
27
X10117
X10116
0.35
WS/RT/GE
0.5
GE/RT
14
13
X991
A53
Headlight
widening
control module
31
502ELE0950

BUS System
K-bus, power
(1 of 1)

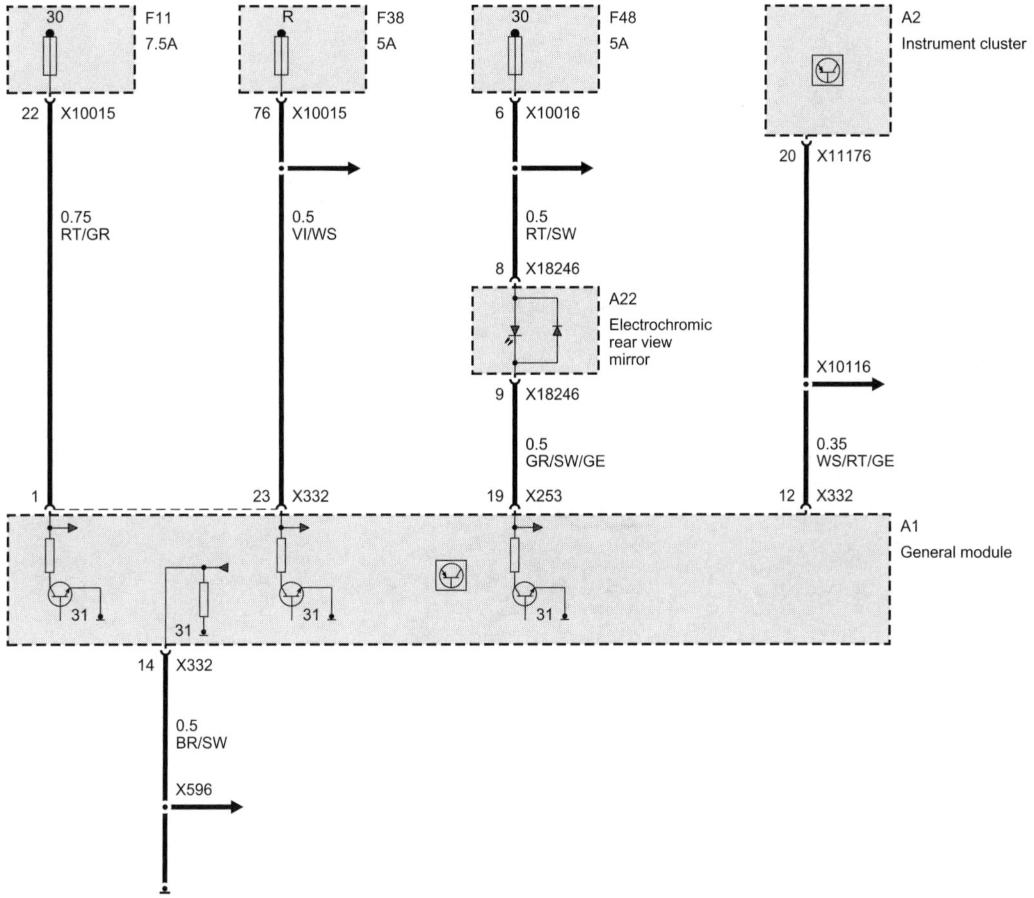
30
F11
7.5A
R
F38
5A
30
F48
5A
A2
Instrument cluster
22 X10015
76 X10015
6 X10016
20 X11176
0.75
RT/GR
0.5
VI/WS
0.5
RT/SW
8 X18246
A22
Electrochromic
rear view
mirror
9 X18246
X10116
0.5
GR/SW/GE
0.35
WS/RT/GE
1
23 X332
19 X253
12 X332
A1
General module
31
31
31
31
14 X332
0.5
BR/SW
X596
502ELE0136

BUS System
X10116 Splice - K-bus
(1 of 1)

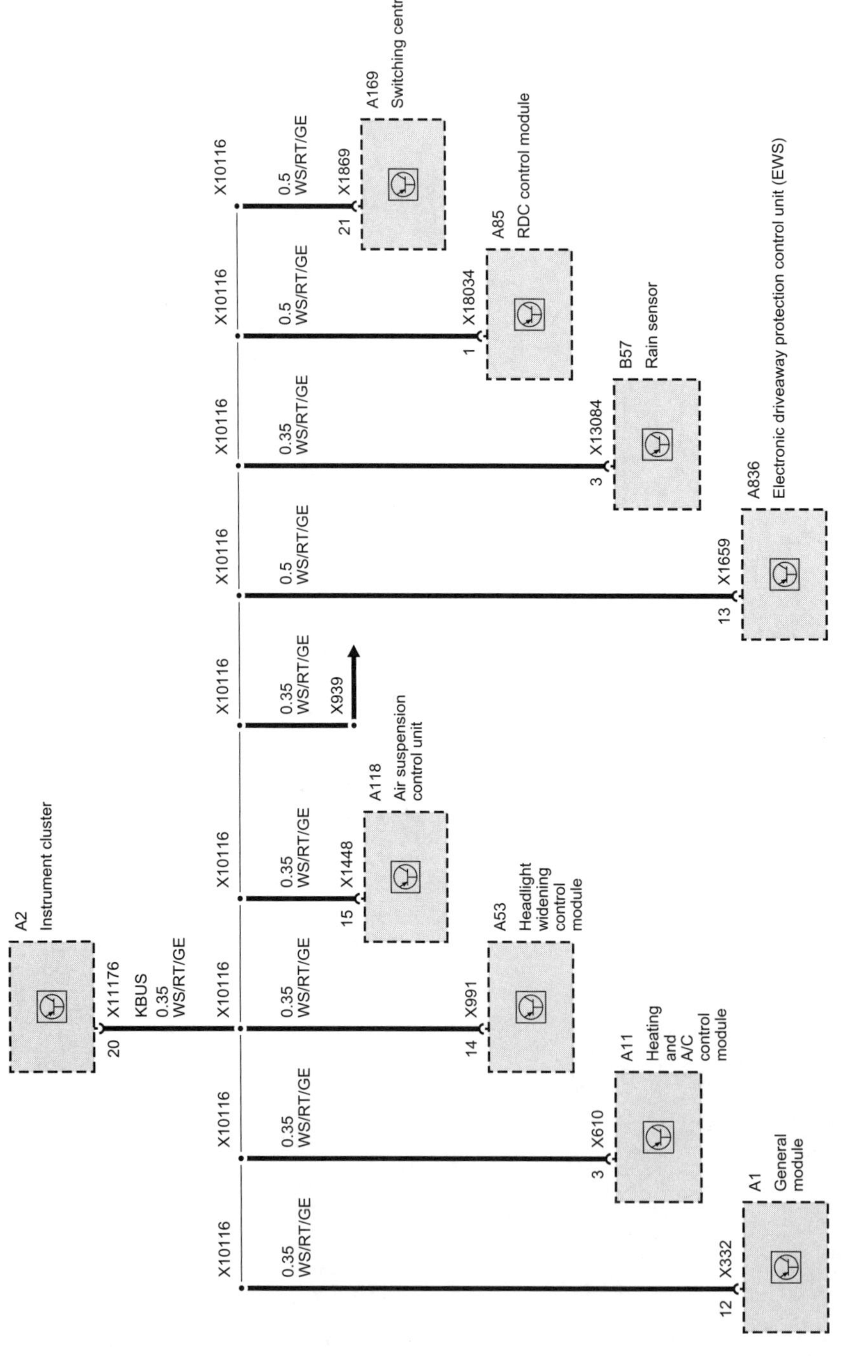
A2
Instrument cluster
20
X11176
KBUS
0.35
WS/RT/GE
X10116
0.5
WS/RT/GE
21
X1869
A169
Switching centre
1
X18034
A85
RDC control module
0.35
3
X13084
B57
Rain sensor
13
X1659
A836
Electronic driveaway protection control unit (EWS)
X939
15
X1448
A118
Air suspension control unit
14
X991
A53
Headlight widening control module
3
X610
A11
Heating and A/C control module
12
X332
A1
General module
502ELE0217

BUS System
X10134 Splice - P-bus
(1 of 1)

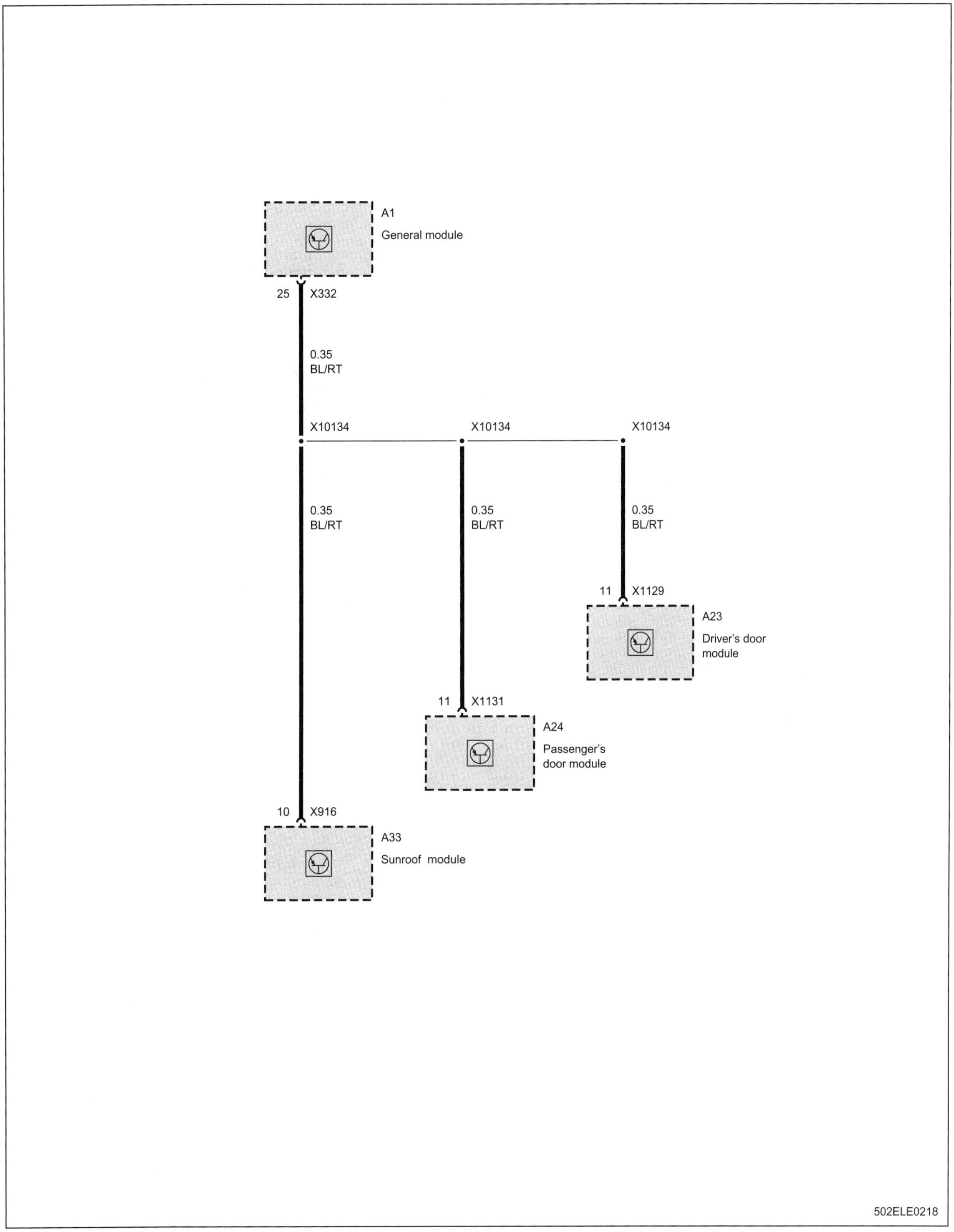
A1
General module
25
X332
0.35
BL/RT
X10134
X10134
X10134
0.35
BL/RT
0.35
BL/RT
0.35
BL/RT
11
X1129
A23
Driver's door module
11
X1131
A24
Passenger's door module
10
X916
A33
Sunroof module
502ELE0218

General Module (Central Body Electronics)
General module (A1)
(1 of 3)

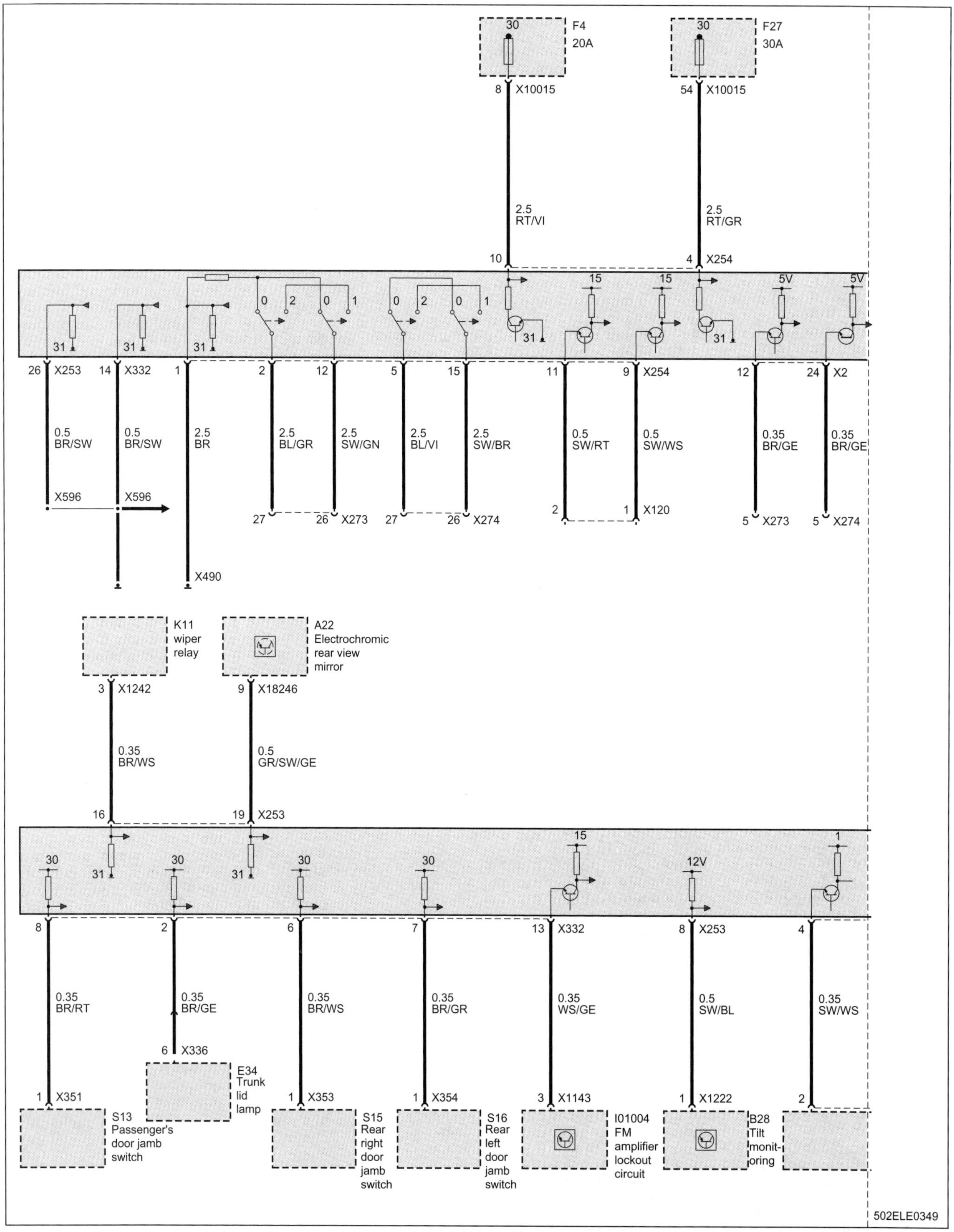

General Module (Central Body Electronics)
General module (A1)
(2 of 3)

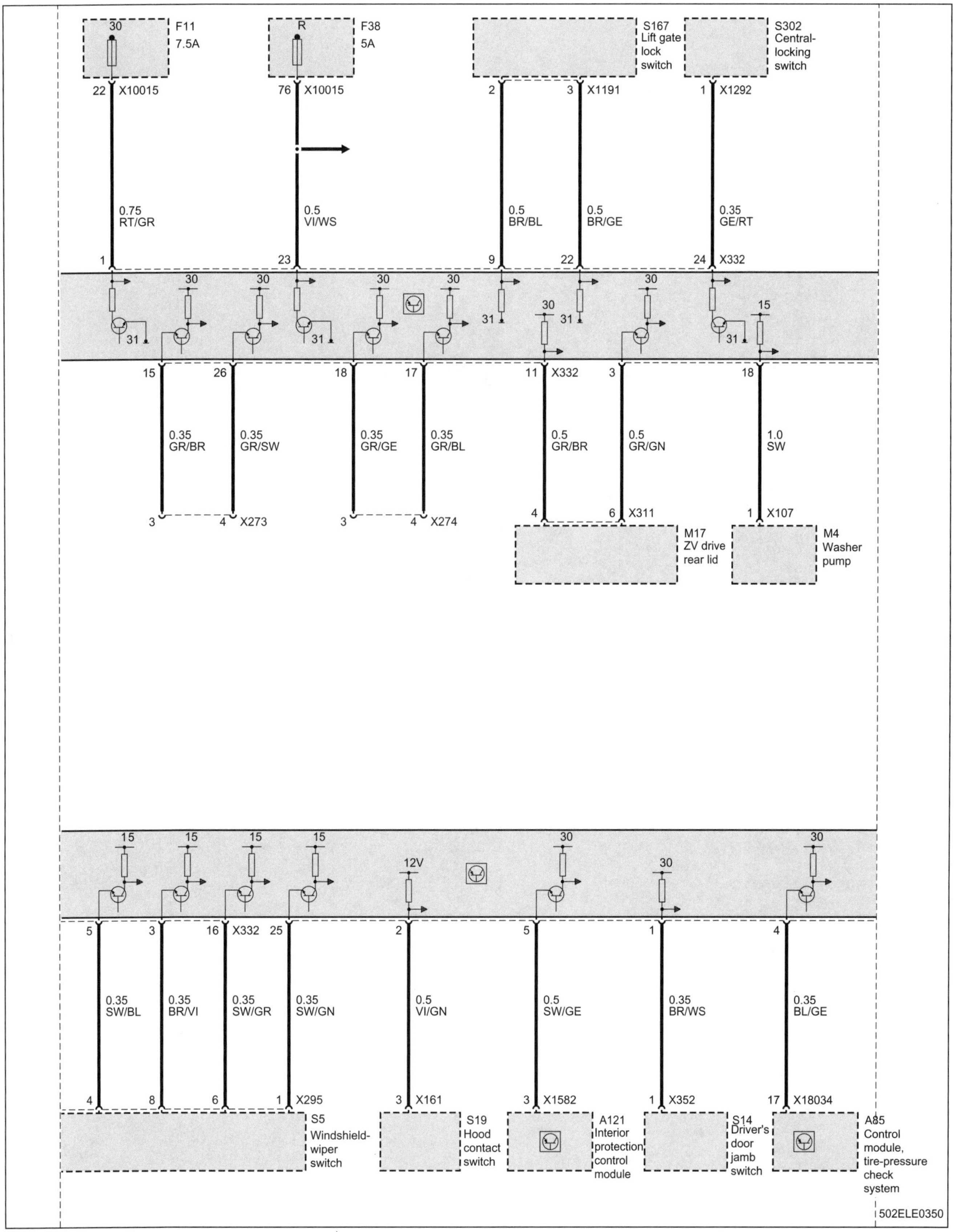

General Module (Central Body Electronics)
General module (A1)
(3 of 3)

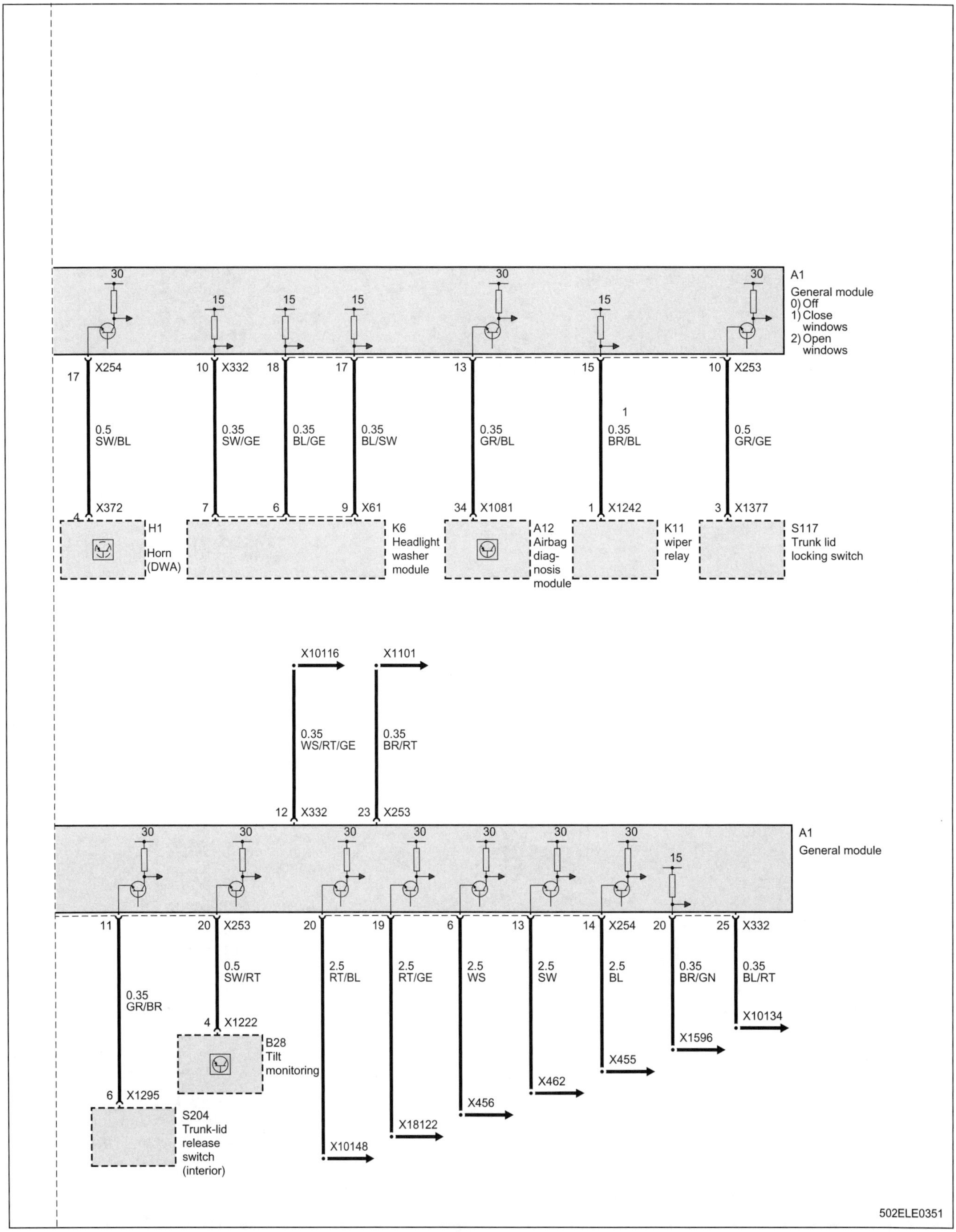

General Module (Central Body Electronics)
General module (A1), power
(1 of 1)

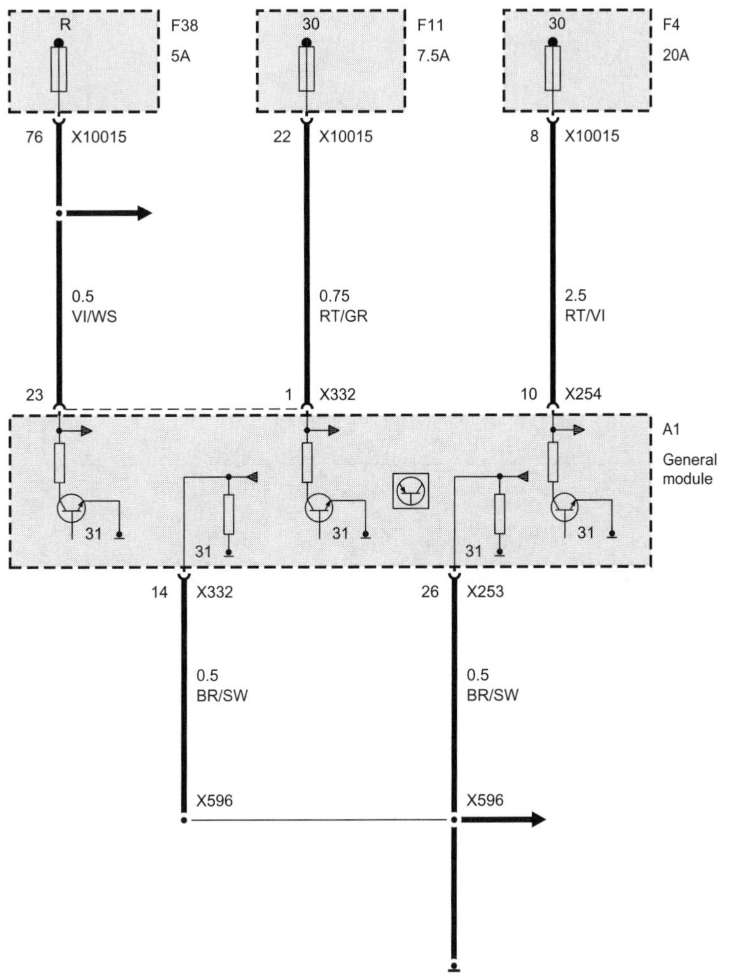

General Module (Central Body Electronics)
Closed circuit current cut-off relay (K72)
(1 of 1)

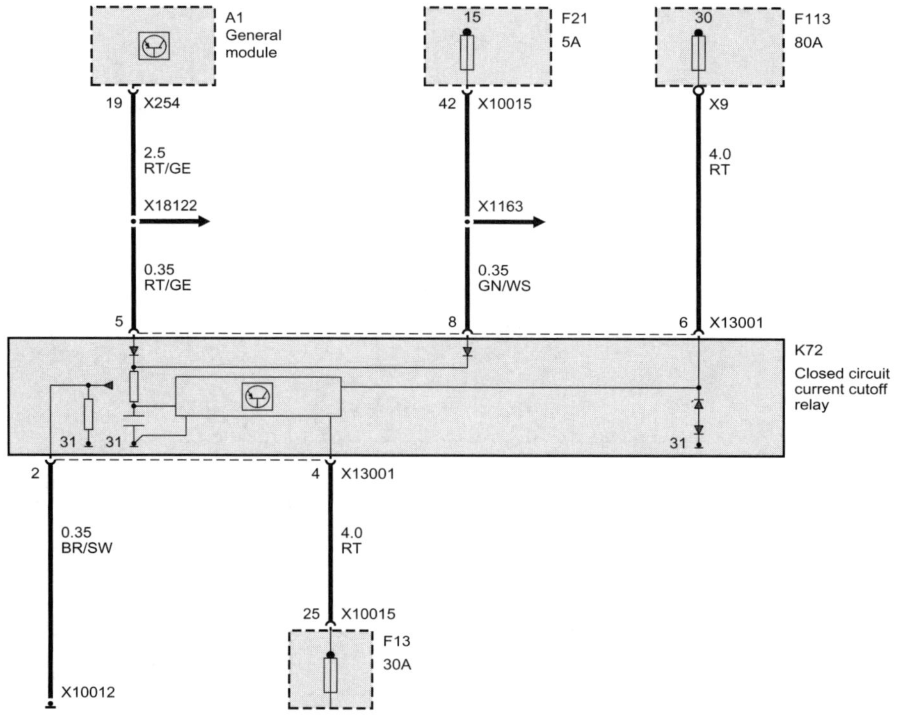

General Module (Central Body Electronics)
Door contact, rear left
(1 of 1)

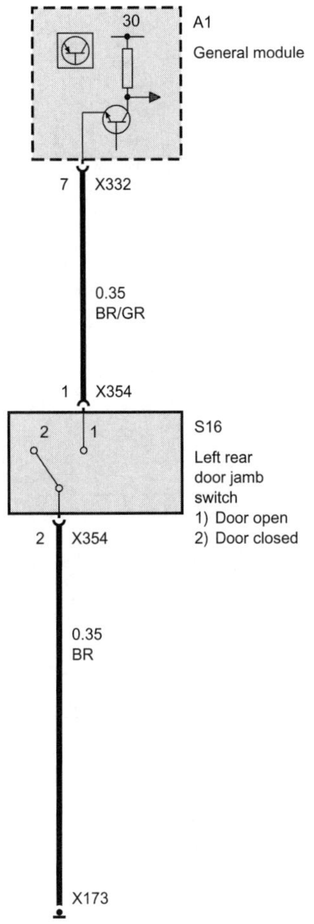

502ELE0942

General Module (Central Body Electronics)
Door contact, rear right
(1 of 1)

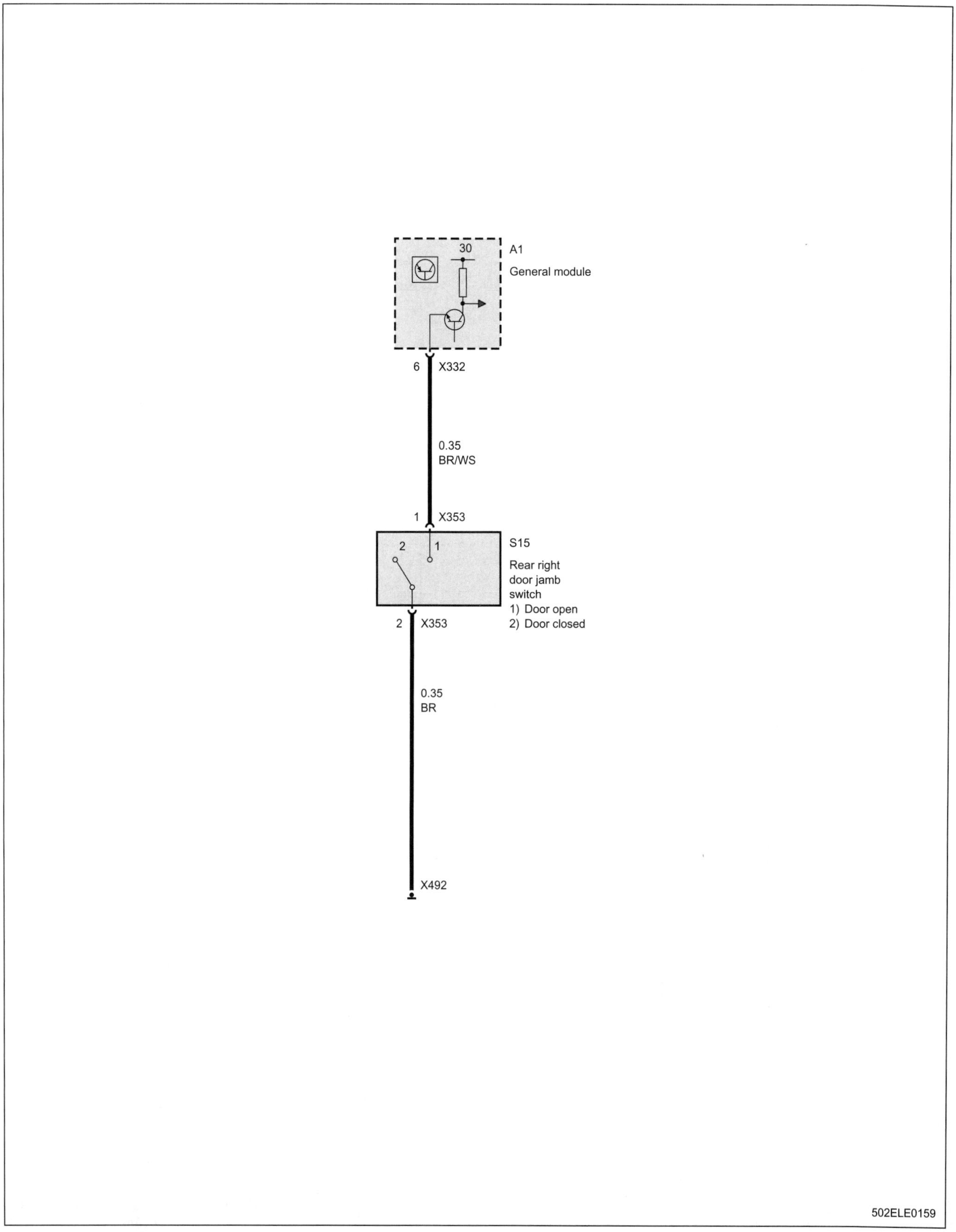

General Module (Central Body Electronics)
Trunk lid actuation (ex. wagon)
(1 of 1)

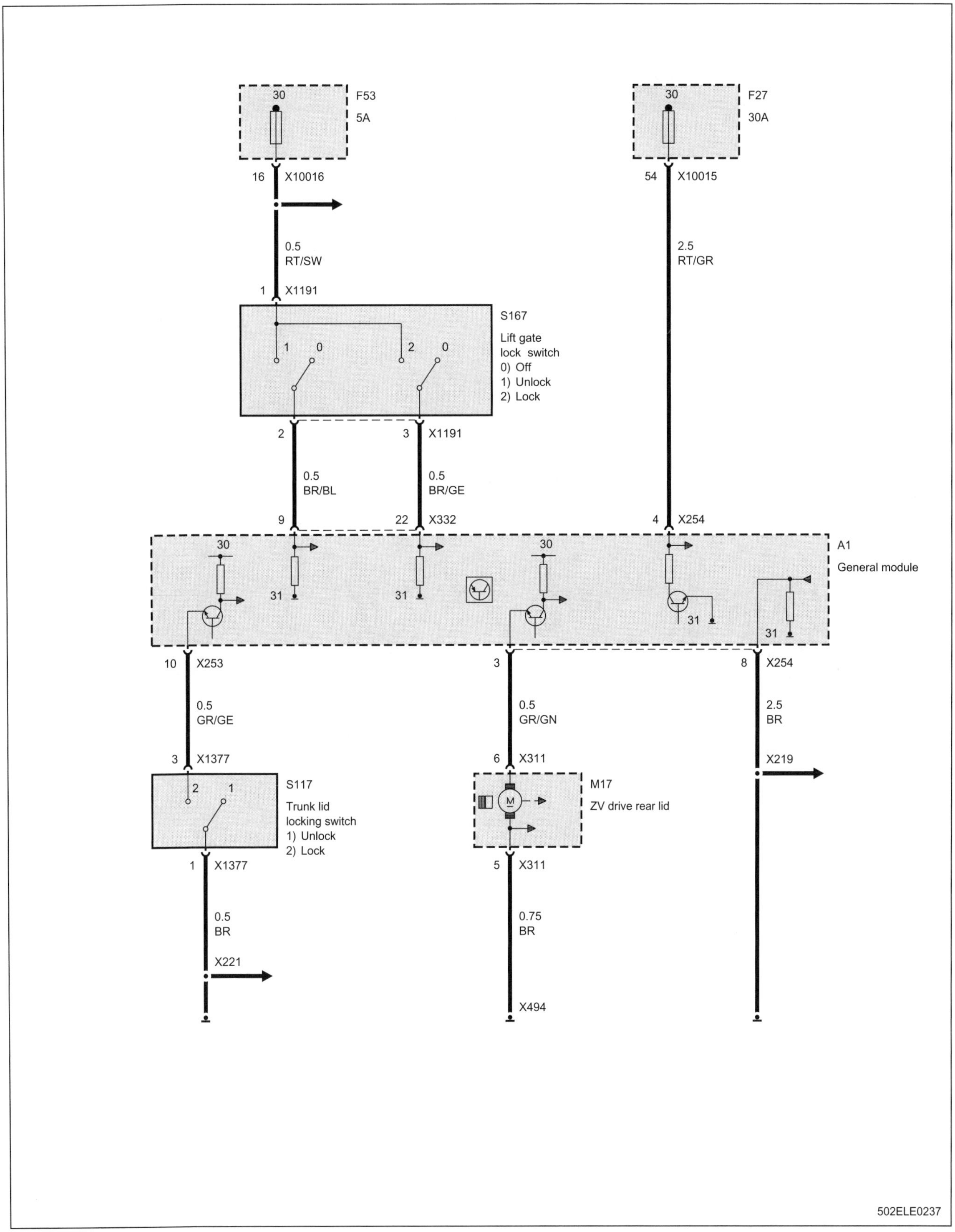

General Module (Central Body Electronics)
Lift gate actuation (wagon)
(1 of 3)

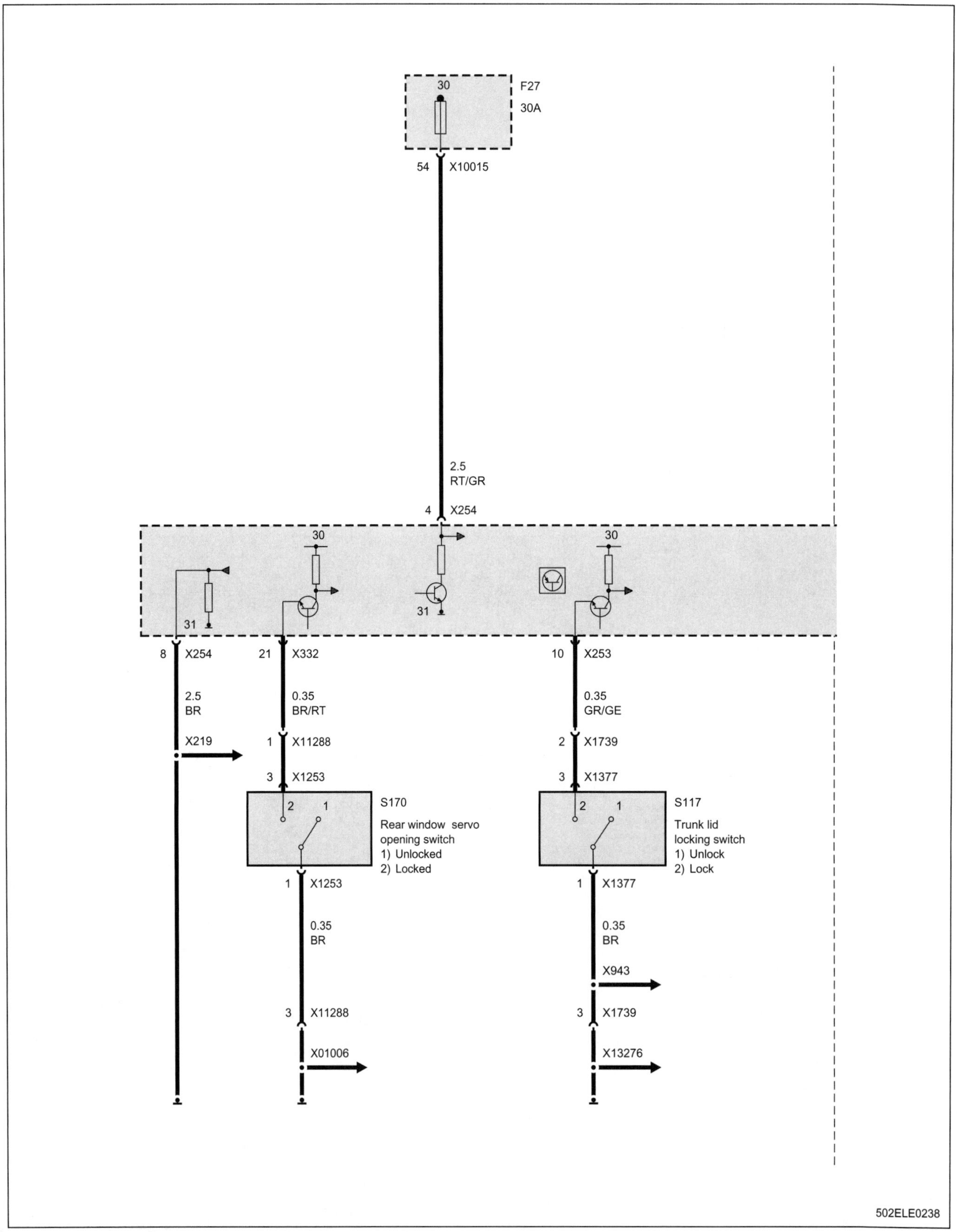

General Module (Central Body Electronics)
Lift gate actuation (wagon)
(2 of 3)

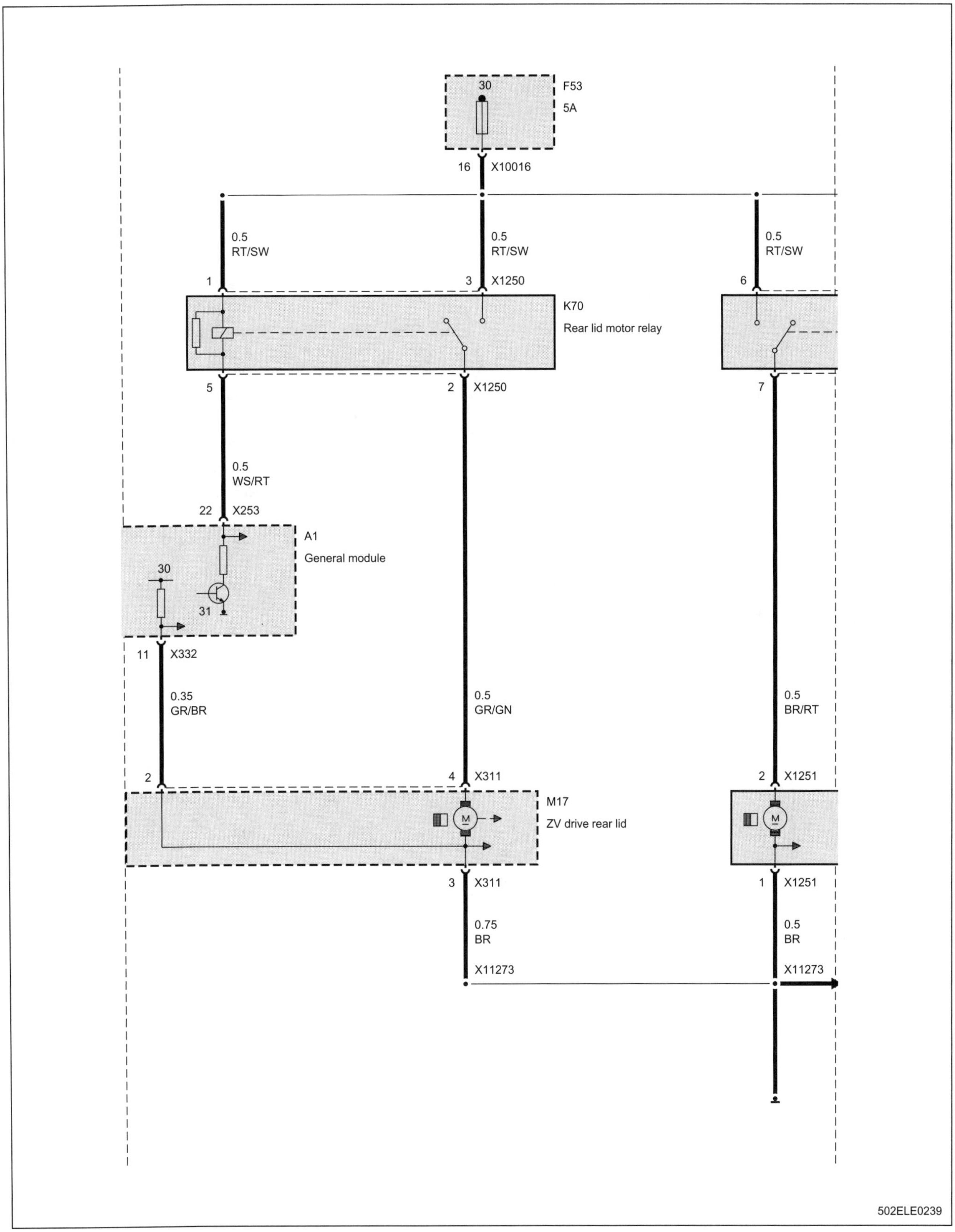

General Module (Central Body Electronics)
Lift gate actuation (wagon)
(3 of 3)

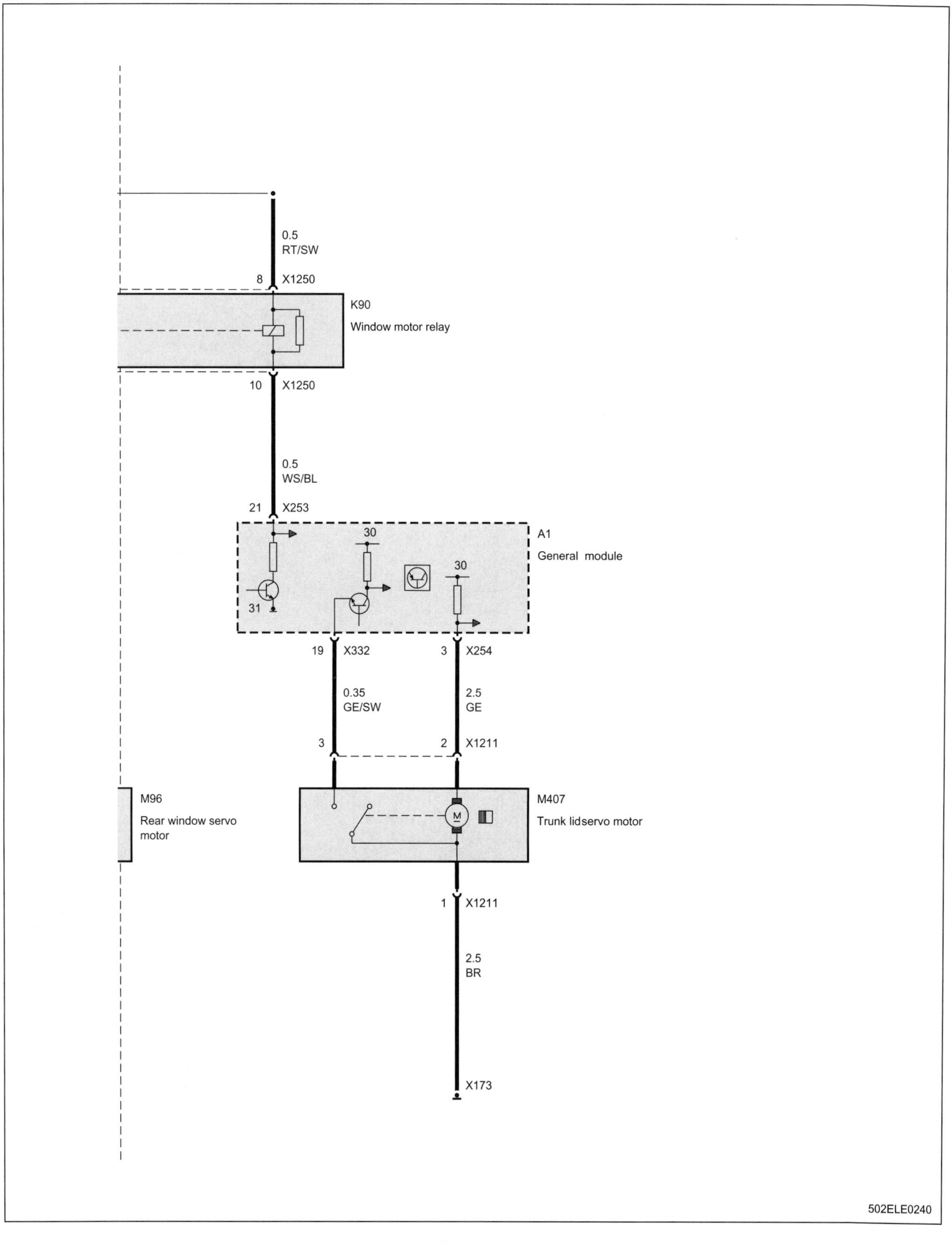

Fuses
Fuse carrier, engine electronics (A8680)
(1 of 1)

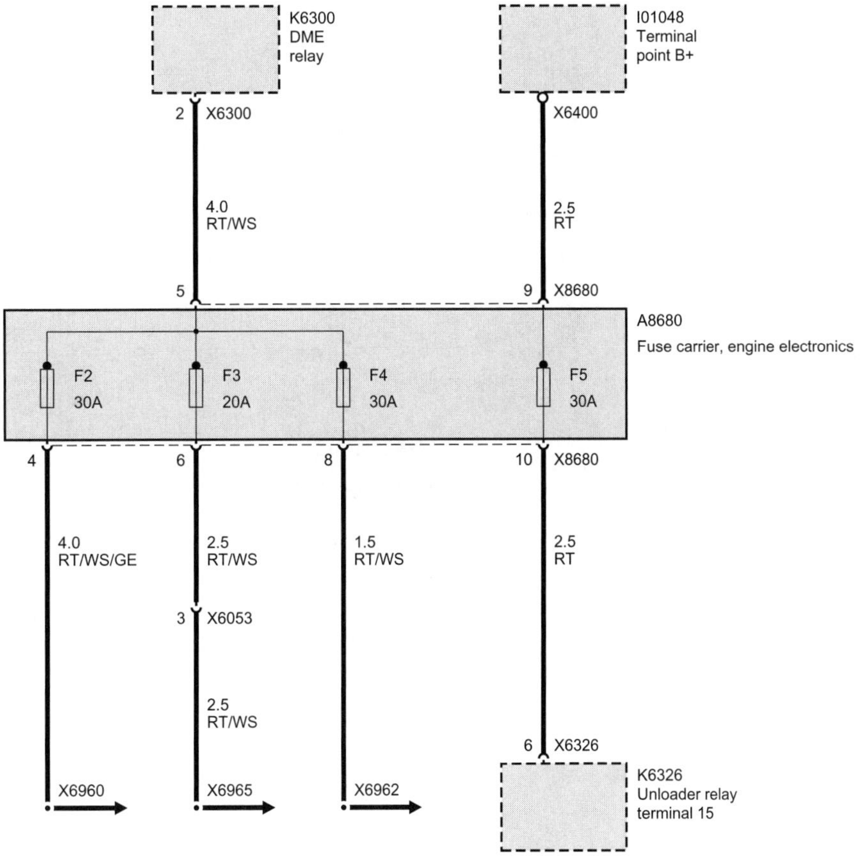

502ELE0445

Multifunction Steering Wheel
Steering wheel with IKE
(1 of 3)

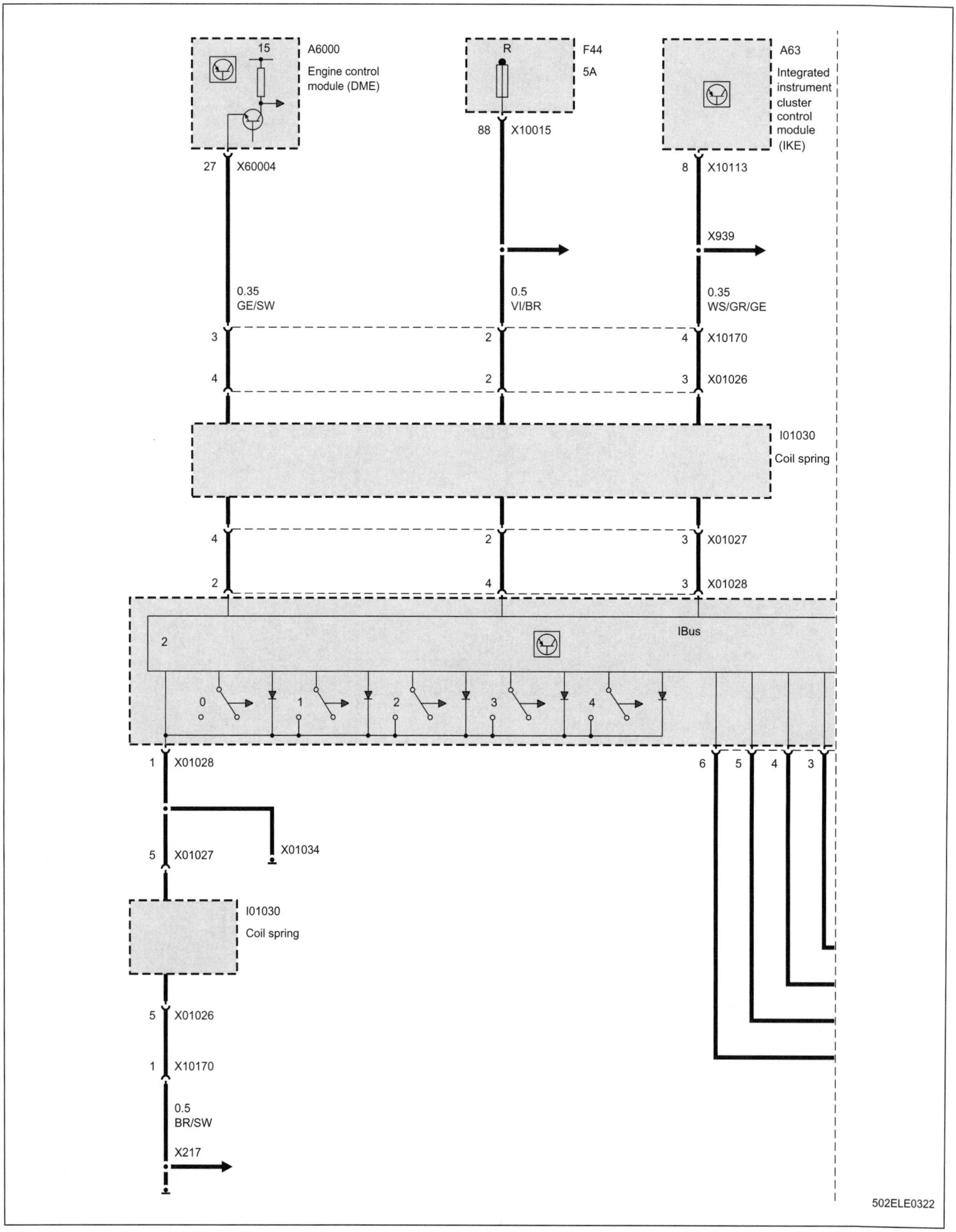

Multifunction Steering Wheel
Steering wheel with IKE
(2 of 3)

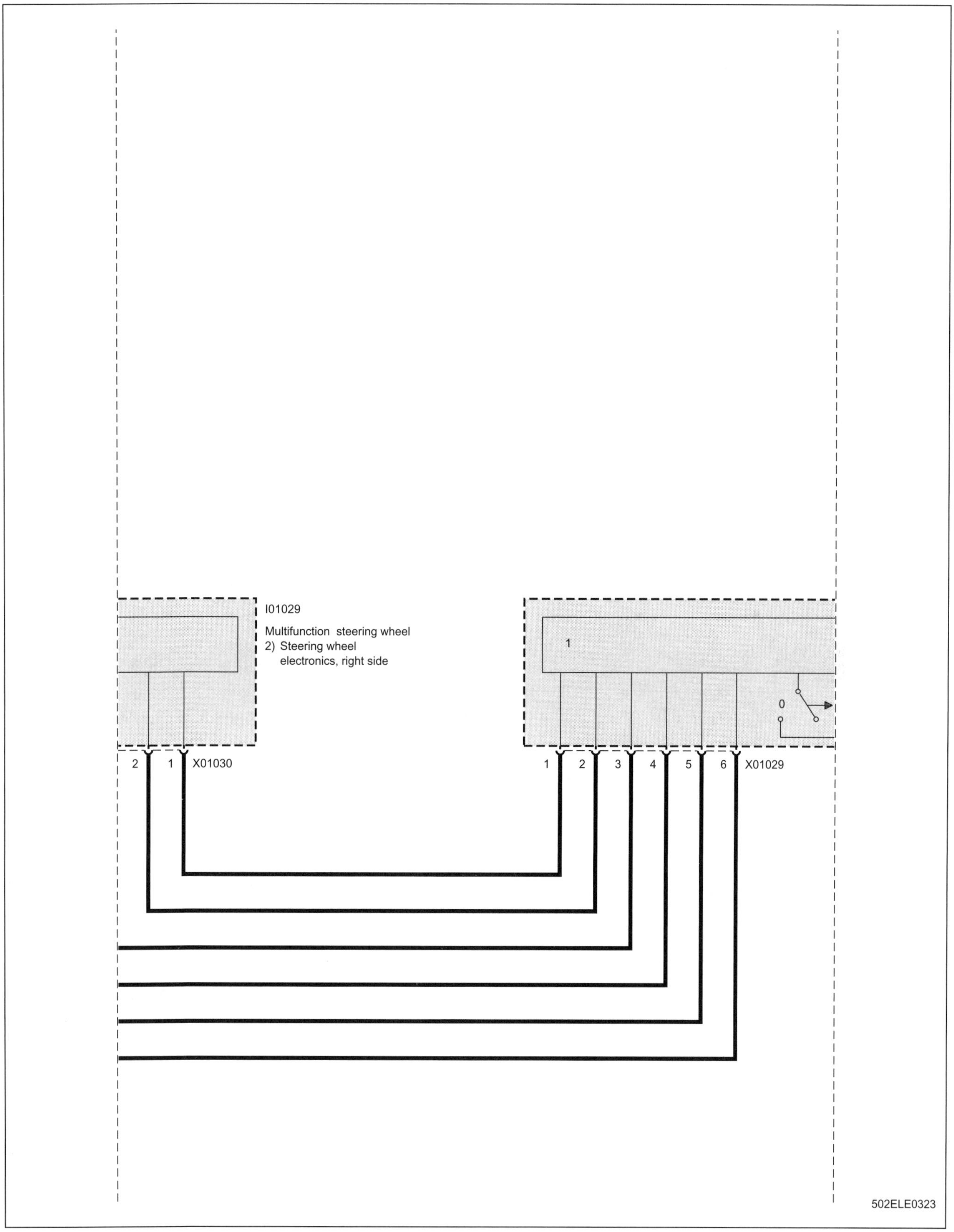

Multifunction Steering Wheel
Steering wheel with IKE
(3 of 3)

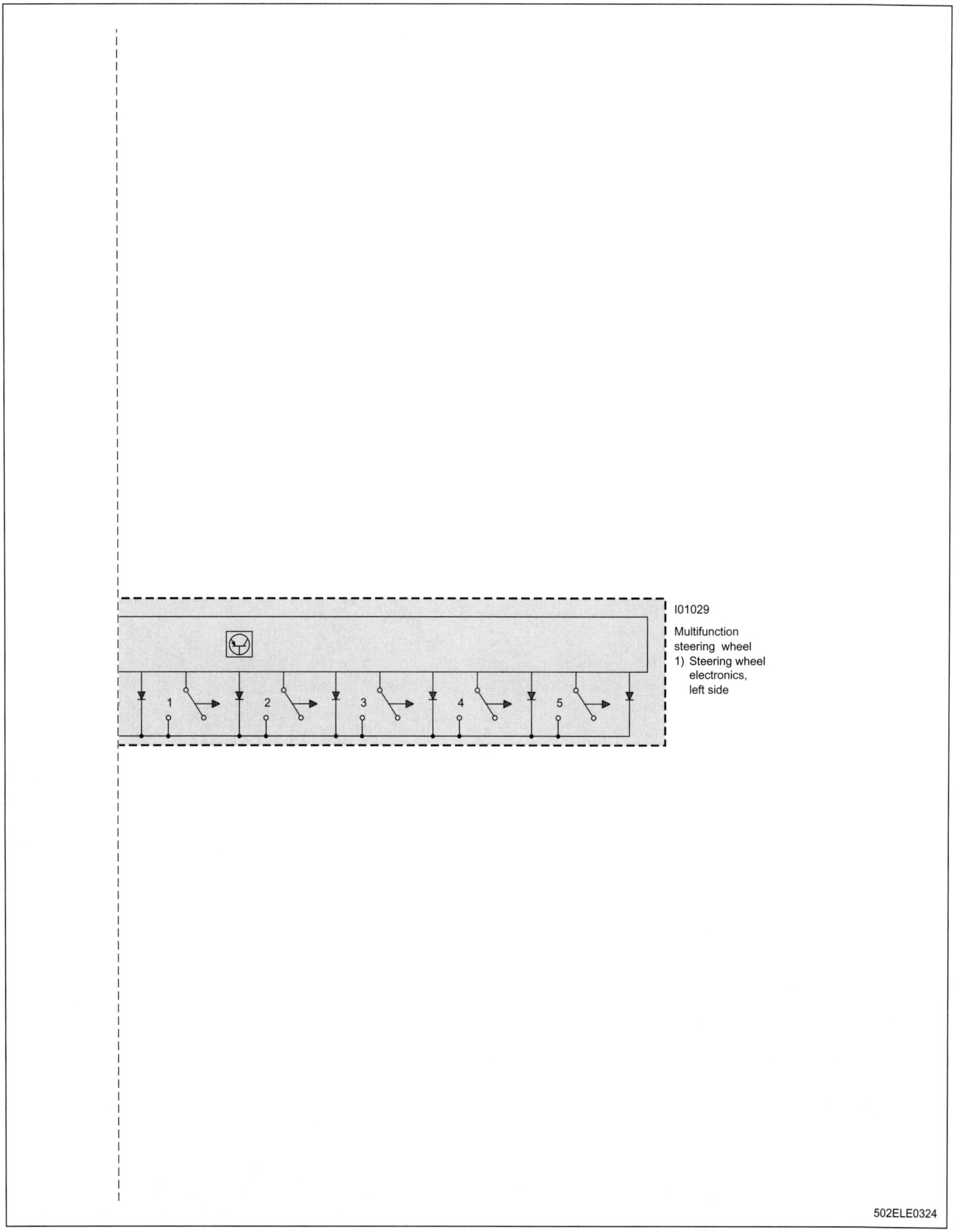

Multifunction Steering Wheel
Steering wheel without IKE
(1 of 3)

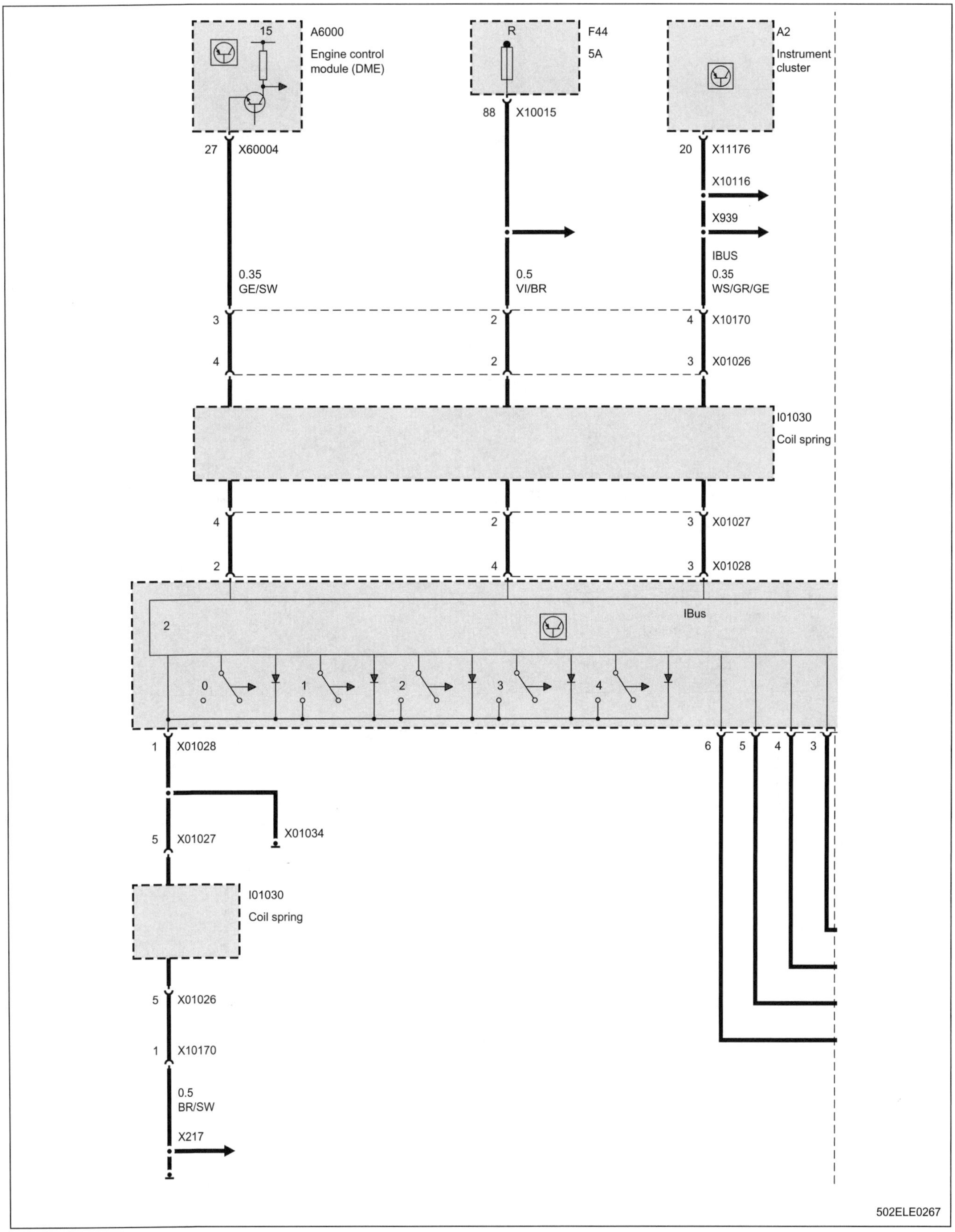

502ELE0267

Multifunction Steering Wheel
Steering wheel without IKE
(2 of 3)

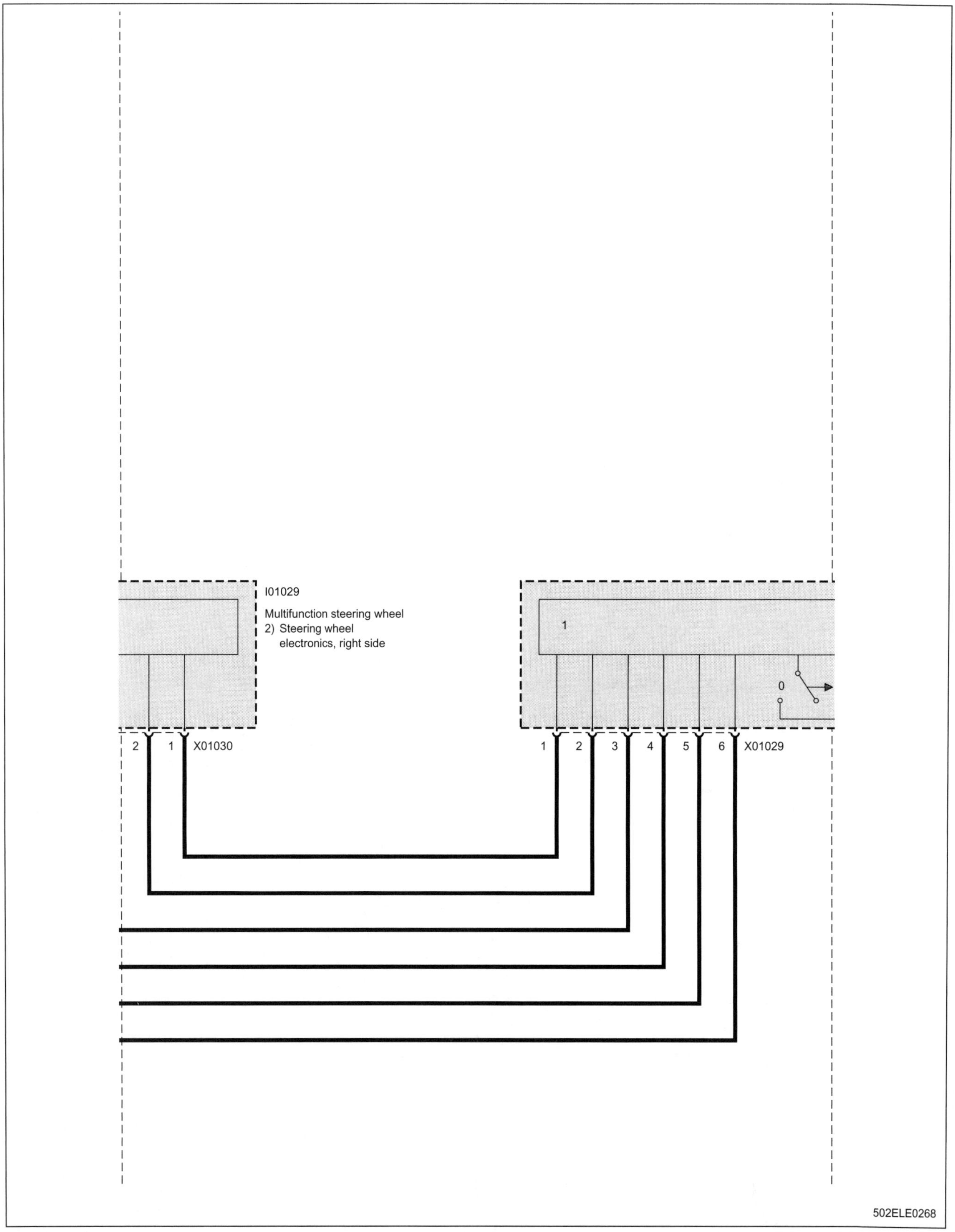

Multifunction Steering Wheel
Steering wheel without IKE
(3 of 3)

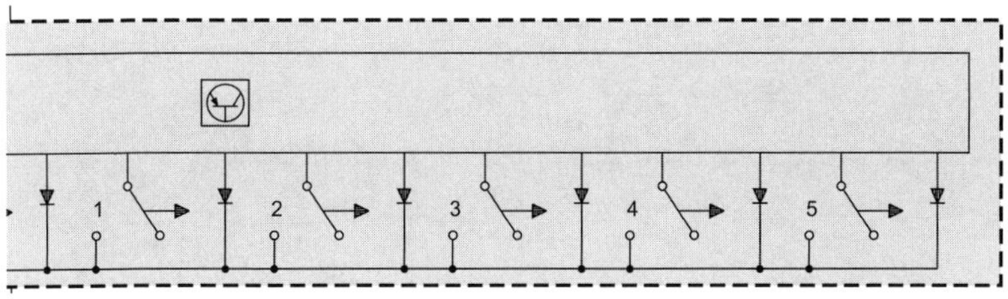

I01029

Multifunction steering wheel
1) Steering wheel electronics, left side

502ELE0269

Multifunction Steering Wheel
Steering wheel heater
(1 of 1)

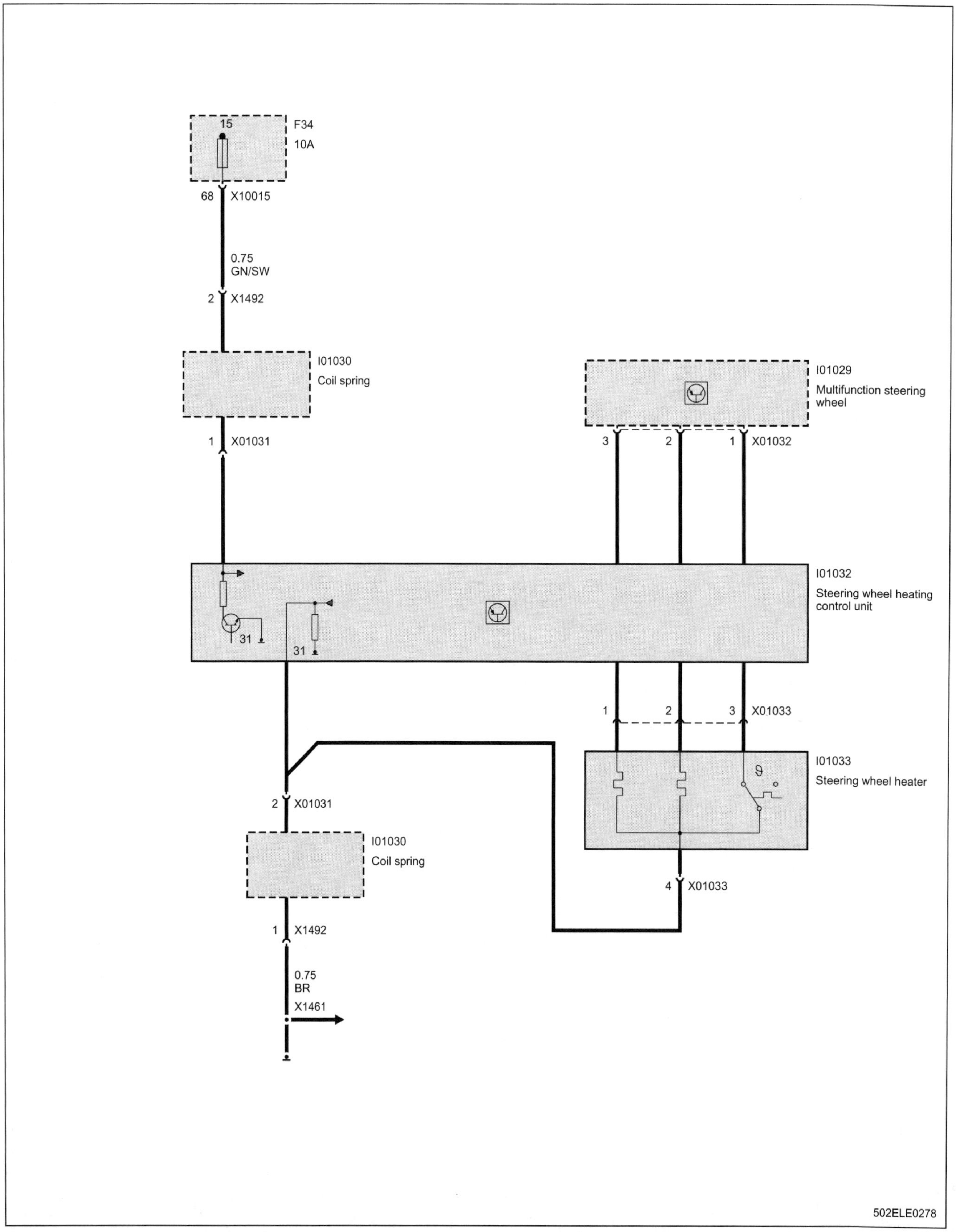

> ***WARNING***
>
> *Your common sense, good judgement, and general alertness are crucial to safe and successful service work. Before attempting any work on your BMW, be sure to read* **001 General Warnings and Cautions** *and the copyright page at the front of the manual. Review these warnings and cautions each time you prepare to work on your BMW. Please also read any warnings and cautions that accompany the procedures in the manual.*

> **WARNING**
>
> *Your common sense, good judgement, and general alertness are crucial to safe and successful service work. Before attempting any work on your BMW, be sure to read* **001 General Warnings and Cautions** *and the copyright page at the front of the manual. Review these warnings and cautions each time you prepare to work on your BMW. Please also read any warnings and cautions that accompany the procedures in the manual.*

> ***WARNING***
>
> *Your common sense, good judgement, and general alertness are crucial to safe and successful service work. Before attempting any work on your BMW, be sure to read* **001 General Warnings and Cautions** *and the copyright page at the front of the manual. Review these warnings and cautions each time you prepare to work on your BMW. Please also read any warnings and cautions that accompany the procedures in the manual.*

WARNING

Your common sense, good judgement, and general alertness are crucial to safe and successful service work. Before attempting any work on your BMW, be sure to read **001 General Warnings and Cautions** *and the copyright page at the front of the manual. Review these warnings and cautions each time you prepare to work on your BMW. Please also read any warnings and cautions that accompany the procedures in the manual.*

J

K

L

M